Professional
ASP.NET 2.0 Server Control and Component Development

Professional
ASP.NET 2.0 Server Control and Component Development

Dr. Shahram Khosravi

WILEY

Wiley Publishing, Inc.

Professional ASP.NET 2.0 Server Control and Component Development

Published by
Wiley Publishing, Inc.
10475 Crosspoint Boulevard
Indianapolis, IN 46256
www.wiley.com

Copyright © 2006 by Wiley Publishing, Inc., Indianapolis, Indiana

Published simultaneously in Canada

ISBN-13: 978-0-471-79350-2
ISBN-10: 0-471-79350-7

Manufactured in the United States of America

10 9 8 7 6 5 4 3 2

1MA/RZ/QX/QW/IN

Library of Congress Cataloging-in-Publication Data is available from the Publisher.

For general information on our other products and services please contact our Customer Care Department within the United States at (800) 762-2974, outside the United States at (317) 572-3993 or fax (317) 572-4002.

About the Author

Shahram Khosravi

Shahram Khosravi started working as a software engineer while still in college. After completing his Ph.D., he continued working on cutting-edge software development projects. Shahram is a senior software engineer, consultant, author, and instructor specializing in ASP.NET, Web services, .NET technologies, XML technologies, ADO.NET, C#, 3D computer graphics, Human Interface (HI) usability, and design patterns. He has more than 10 years of experience in object-oriented analysis, design, and programming. Shahram has written articles on the .NET Framework, ADO.NET, ASP.NET, and XML technologies for industry leading magazines such as *Dr. Dobb's Journal*, *asp.netPRO* magazine, and Microsoft MSDN Online. He is a great enthusiast for using, teaching, and writing about the latest Microsoft technologies, and provides consulting and training services to help others use them in their own software products.

Credits

Senior Acquisitions Editor
Jim Minatel

Development Editor
Brian MacDonald

Technical Editor
Scott Spradlin

Production Editor
Felicia Robinson

Copy Editor
Kim Cofer

Editorial Manager
Mary Beth Wakefield

Production Manager
Tim Tate

Vice President and Executive Group Publisher
Richard Swadley

Vice President and Executive Publisher
Joseph B. Wikert

Graphics and Production Specialists
Jennifer Click
Brooke Graczyk
Denny Hager
Barbara Moore
Barry Offringa
Lynsey Osborn
Alicia B. South
Julie Trippetti

Quality Control Technicians
John Greenough
Leeann Harney
Jessica Kramer
Christy Pingleton
Rob Springer
Brian H. Walls

Proofreading and Indexing
Techbooks

Acknowledgments

I would first like to thank Jim Minatel, the senior acquisitions editor on the book or giving me the opportunity to write this exciting book. Huge thanks go to Brian MacDonald, the book's development editor. Thanks for all your valuable input, comments, and suggestions. I've really enjoyed working with you on this wonderful project. I'd also like to thank Scott Spradlin, the book's technical editor, for his work. Thanks for your valuable input. Thanks also go to Felicia Robinson, the book's production editor. Additional thanks go to (Kim Cofer, the copy editor and Techbooks, the proofreader). I would also like to thank my friends for understanding my absence.

Contents

Contents

Contents

Contents

Contents

Contents

Contents

Contents

Contents

Contents

Contents

Contents

Introduction

Welcome to *Professional ASP.NET 2.0 Server Control and Component Development*. The ASP.NET 2.0 Framework consists of two groups of components. The first group contains server controls, that is, those components that directly or indirectly derive from the ASP.NET `Control` base class. This group includes security controls, tabular and hierarchical data source controls such as `SqlDataSource` and `XmlDataSource`, Web Parts controls set, data-bound controls, and so on.

The second group contains the rest of the ASP.NET 2.0 components including HTTP modules, HTTP handlers, HTTP handler factories, security components such as `RolePrincipal`, `RoleManagerModule`, role providers, `MembershipUser` and membership providers, data control fields such as `BoundField`, data source control parameters such as `ControlParameter`, `ISerializable`, schema importer extensions, and so on.

This book covers both groups of ASP.NET 2.0 components. In other words, this book shows you how to develop not only server controls, which belong to the first group, but also components that belong to the second group.

Who This Book Is For

This book is aimed at the ASP.NET developer who wants to learn how to build custom server controls and components for the first time. No knowledge of authoring custom server controls and components is assumed.

What This Book Covers

This book provides you with detailed step-by-step recipes and real-world server controls and components developed using these recipes to help you gain the skills, knowledge, and experience that you need to develop:

❑ **Ajax-enabled controls and components:** This book has four chapters dedicated to this topic where you'll learn how to develop Ajax-enabled controls and components. These controls are characterized by the following characteristics and features, which enables them to break free from the traditional "click-and-wait" user unfriendly user interaction pattern:

   ❑ **Their rich client-side functionality:** This book shows you how to use client-side technologies such as XHTML/HTML, CSS, DOM, XML, and JavaScript to implement Ajax-enabled controls and components with rich client-side functionality.

   ❑ **Their asynchronous communication with the server:** You'll learn how to use the ASP.NET 2.0 client-callback mechanism to implement complex Ajax-enabled controls and components that make asynchronous client callbacks to the server without having to perform full page postbacks.

❑ **Exchanging XML data with the server:** You'll see how to use client-side and server-side XML technologies to develop Ajax-enabled controls and components that exchange data with the server in XML format and use DHTML to dynamically generate HTML from the XML data that they receive from the server to display the data.

❑ **Ajax patterns:** You'll also discover how to use Ajax patterns such as Predictive Fetch, Periodic Refresh, Submission Throttling, and Explicit Submission to develop Ajax-enabled controls and components that contain the logic that determines the best time to exchange data with the server to enable end users to interact with the application without interruptions and irritating waiting periods.

❑ **ASP.NET 2.0 Web Parts controls:** Four chapters cover the Web Parts controls set, where you'll learn how to implement the following:

  ❑ Custom `WebPart`, `EditorPart`, `CatalogPart`, `WebPartZoneBase`, `WebPartChrome`, `WebPartVerb`, and `WebPartManager` controls

  ❑ The `IWebPart`, `IWebActionable`, `IWebEditable`, and `IPersonalizable` interfaces

  ❑ Static, dynamic, and programmatic Web Parts connections

  ❑ Custom data-bound `WebPart` controls with minimal effort. This book implements a set of base data-bound controls named `BaseDataBoundWebPart`, `DataBoundWebPart`, and `CompositeDataBoundWebPart` that you can derive from to implement custom data-bound `WebPart` controls that can access any type of data store and can automate all of its data operations such as delete, update, insert, sorting, and paging so the page developer can use them declaratively without writing a single line of code.

❑ **ASP.NET 2.0 security, role management, and membership components:** You'll find five chapters dedicated to these topics where you'll learn how to develop role providers, membership providers, custom role manager modules, custom role principals, and custom `MembershipUser`.

❑ **ASP.NET 2.0 tabular and hierarchical data source controls:** This book has five chapters that teach you how to develop custom tabular and hierarchical data source controls to expose tabular and hierarchical data from your own favorite data store, whether the data store itself is tabular or hierarchical.

❑ **ASP.NET 2.0 tabular data-bound controls:** The four chapters that cover this topic show you how to develop tabular data-bound controls as complex as `GridView` that can access any type of data store and can automate all of their data operations such as delete, update, insert, sorting, and paging so the page developer can use them declaratively without writing any code.

❑ **Custom schema importer extensions and ISerializable:** You'll discover how to implement custom schema importer extensions and the `ISerializable` interface to customize the proxy class code generation and to customize the serialization and deserialization of your custom components. This book also shows you how to use these techniques to improve the performance of XML Web services that send huge amounts of data.

❑ **Provider-Based Services:** You'll also learn how to enable the services that your Web applications provide to their clients to access any type of data store without code changes. For example, RSS feeds are one of the services that most Web applications provide to their clients. You'll learn how to implement a RSS service provider that can feed RSS from any type of data store such as SQL Server, XML documents, Oracle, flat files, XML Web services, and so on.

How This Book Is Structured

As the list of controls and components presented in the previous section shows, there are different types of ASP.NET custom controls and components. You have to extend a particular extensible part of the ASP.NET 2.0 Framework to implement each type of custom control or component. For example, you have to extend the ASP.NET 2.0 `BaseDataBoundControl`, `DataBoundControl`, or `CompositeData BoundControl` to implement custom tabular data-bound controls. Or you have to extend the ASP.NET 2.0 tabular data source control model to implement custom data source controls. Therefore, having a solid understanding of the extensible parts of the ASP.NET 2.0 Framework will put you in a much better position to extend them to write custom server controls and components.

This book takes the following approach to teach you how to implement each type of custom control or component:

1. First, it drills down to the details of the extensible part of the ASP.NET 2.0 Framework that you need to extend to write the specified type of custom control or component. It doesn't present the extensible part as a black box. Instead it uses a detailed step-by-step approach to implement a functional replica of the extensible part, discusses the replica's code in detail, and provides an in-depth coverage of the techniques, tools, and technologies used in the code. Such a practical hands-on approach allows you to learn about the extensible part by actually implementing it. This allows you to play with the code and to tweak the code here and there to see for yourself how the extensible parts work from the inside out and how you can extend them.

2. Then, it provides you with a detailed practical step-by-step recipe for developing the specified type of custom control or component.

3. It then uses the recipe to implement one or more practical real-world custom controls or components of the specified type that you can use in your own Web applications. It also discusses the important parts of these custom components' code in detail and provide an in-depth coverage of the techniques, tools, and technologies used in the code. Such in-depth code discussions and technical coverage will provide you with the practical skills, knowledge, and experience you need to develop custom components such as the ones listed in the previous section.

The contents of each chapter break down like this:

❑ Chapter 1, "The ASP.NET 2.0 Framework," follows a request from the time it arrives in IIS all the way through the ASP.NET request processing architecture to give you the big picture of the ASP.NET 2.0 Framework. It then discusses why you need to develop custom controls and components.

❑ Chapter 2, "Developing Simple Custom Controls and User Controls," develops a simple custom control, annotates it with design-time attributes, deploys it, adds it to the Visual Studio Toolbox, and uses it in a Web page. Then, it implements a simple user control, adds properties and methods to it, and uses it in a Web page.

❑ Chapter 3, "Developing Custom-Styled Controls," discusses the methods and properties of the `WebControl` base class in detail and derives from this base class to implement a custom control. Next, it implements a custom `Style` class and a custom control that uses it.

❑ Chapter 4, "Developing Custom Controls That Raise Events," defines what an event is, discusses the .NET event design pattern in detail, and uses the pattern to implement an event. It then shows you how to use the `EventHandler` class to optimize your control's events. Next, it develops a custom control that implements the `IPostBackEventHandler` and `IPostBackDataHandler` interfaces. Finally, it discusses the page life cycle in detail.

❑ Chapter 5, "Developing Custom Composite Controls," defines what a composite control is, provides you with a detailed step-by-step recipe for developing custom composite controls, and uses the recipe to implement a custom composite control.

❑ Chapter 6, "Developing Custom Templated Controls," defines what a templated control is, implements a custom templated control, shows you how to write a templated control that supports data-binding expressions, and finally looks under the hood of templates where you learn how to create templates programmatically.

❑ Chapter 7, "Developing Custom Controls with Complex Properties," implements a custom composite control that exposes complex properties such as style properties, and presents two different approaches to managing the state of complex properties across page postbacks: implementing the IStateManager and implementing a custom type converter. The chapter teaches you how to implement the IStateManager interface and how to implement your own custom type converter.

❑ Chapter 8, "ASP.NET Request Processing Architecture," first discusses the ASP.NET requesting processing architecture in detail. It provides you with step-by-step recipes to develop custom HTTP modules, HTTP handler factories, HTTP handlers, and control builders. It then uses these recipes to develop a custom HTTP module and a custom HTTP handler factory that perform URL rewriting, a custom HTTP handler that generates RSS feeds, and a custom control builder.

❑ Chapter 9, "Data Binding," discusses the basic concepts and principles of ASP.NET data binding and implements a custom data-bound control.

❑ Chapter 10, "XML Web Services," begins by showing you how to develop and consume an ASP.NET XML Web service. Then, it takes you under the hood of the ASP.NET XML Web service infrastructure and develops a custom component that enables your components to programmatically download the WSDL document, generate the code for proxy class, and compile the code to an assembly. It then uses this custom component to develop a custom XmlResolver that retrieves XML data from an XML Web service.

❑ Chapter 11, "Implementing Schema Importer Extensions and ISerializable Interface," shows you how to implement ISerializable and a custom schema importer extension to customize the code for the proxy class. It then shows you how to use these techniques to dramatically improve the performance of XML Web services that send huge amounts of data. This chapter also discusses CodeDom in detail

❑ Chapter 12, "Understanding the ASP.NET 2.0 Tabular Data Source Control Model," looks under the hood of the main components of the ASP.NET 2.0 tabular data source control model, that is, IDataSource, DataSourceControl, and DataSourceView, and implements a fully functional replica of the ASP.NET 2.0 SqlDataSource control to make the discussions of the chapter more concrete.

❑ Chapter 13, "The ASP.NET 2.0 Data Source Control Parameter Model," discusses *parameters*, components that enable tabular data source controls such as SqlDataSource to get the value of the parameters such as those used in a SQL statement or stored procedure from any type of source. This chapter implements replicas of the main components of the ASP.NET 2.0 data source control parameter model, that is, Parameter and its subclasses, ParameterCollection, and the built-in support of tabular data source controls for parameters to help you understand these components better. This chapter then implements three custom parameters.

❑ Chapter 14, "Developing ASP.NET 2.0 Custom Tabular Data Source Controls," implements a custom tabular data source control named XmlWebServiceDataSource to show you how to implement your own custom tabular data source controls to access your favorite data store. The XmlWebServiceDataSource control allows its clients to access an XML Web service.

❑ Chapter 15, "Understanding the ASP.NET 2.0 Hierarchical Data Source Control Model," implements replicas of the main components of the ASP.NET 2.0 hierarchical data source control model, that is, `IHierarchicalDataSource`, `HierarchicalDataSourceControl`, `IHierarchyData`, `IHierarchicalEnumerable`, and `HierarchicalDataSourceView` to help you understand the model from the inside out. It also implements a fully functional replica of the `XmlDataSource` control to make the discussions of the chapter more concrete.

❑ Chapter 16, "Developing ASP.NET 2.0 Custom Hierarchical Data Source Controls," implements a custom hierarchical data source control named `CustomSqlDataSource` that extends the functionality of the `SqlDataSource` control to provide hierarchical data-bound controls such as `TreeView` with hierarchical views of the underlying database table. This chapter shows you how to implement `HierarchicalDataSourceControl`, `IHierarchyData`, `IHierarchicalEnumerable`, and `HierarchicalDataSourceView`.

❑ Chapter 17, "Understanding the ASP.NET 2.0 Tabular Data-Bound Control Model," implements fully functional replicas of the main components of the ASP.NET 2.0 tabular data-bound control model, that is, the `BaseDataBoundControl`, `DataBoundControl`, and `CompositeDataBoundControl` base classes to help you understand them better. The chapter develops three custom tabular data-bound controls that derive from these three base classes. Finally, it develops a master/detail data-bound control that can access any type of data store and automates all its data operations such as delete, update, insert, and sorting so the page developers can use it declaratively without writing a single line of code.

❑ Chapter 18, "The ASP.NET 2.0 Data Control Field Model," covers data control fields, which are components that enable tabular data-bound controls such as `GridView` to provide end users with the appropriate user interface for viewing and editing any type of database field. This chapter looks under the hood of the main components of the data control field model, that is, `DataControlField`, `DataControlFieldCollection`, and built-in support of tabular data-bound controls for the `DataControlField` API. This chapter also implements two custom data control fields.

❑ Chapter 19, "Developing ASP.NET 2.0 Custom Tabular Data-Bound Controls," discusses the ASP.NET 2.0 `GridView` control, which is the most complex ASP.NET 2.0 tabular data-bound control. This chapter implements a fully functional replica of the `GridView` control to help you gain the skills, knowledge, and experience you need to implement a custom tabular data-bound control as complex as `GridView`.

❑ Chapter 20, "Why You Need the ASP.NET 2.0 Membership/Role Model," reviews the ASP.NET 1.x security model and its shortcomings to prepare you for the next chapters where the ASP.NET 2.0 security model is discussed in detail.

❑ Chapter 21, "Understanding the ASP.NET 2.0 Membership Model," implements functional replicas of the main components of the ASP.NET 2.0 membership model, such as `Membership` and `MembershipUser`, to help you understand this model from the inside out. This chapter also shows you how to develop your own custom security controls.

❑ Chapter 22 is entitled "Developing Custom MembershipProvider and MembershipUser Components." Most Web application store their user membership information in SQL Server databases with different schemas than `aspnetdb`. Therefore they can't use the standard `SqlMembershipProvider` provider. This chapter implements a fully functional replica of `SqlMembershipProvider` to help you gain the skills, knowledge, and experience you need to develop a custom membership provider that will be able to access a SQL Server database with a different schema than `aspnetdb`. This chapter also shows you how to implement custom `MembershipProvider` and custom `MembershipUser` components to extend the Membership API to add support for new methods and properties.

❏ Chapter 23, "Understanding the ASP.NET Role Management Model," looks under the hood of the main components of the ASP.NET 2.0 role management model, that is, `Roles`, `RoleProvider`, `RolePrinicipal`, and `RoleManagerModule`, to help you gain a solid understanding of the model. The chapter also discusses the `IPrincipal` and `IIdentity` interfaces in detail.

❏ Chapter 24, "Developing Custom Role Providers, Modules, and Principals," implements a custom role provider named `XmlRoleProvider` to store role information in and retrieve role information from an XML document. This chapter discusses `XmlReader` streaming, `XmlWriter` streaming, `XPathNavigator` random-access cursor-style, and DOM random access XML APIs and their pros and cons in detail. This chapter then implements a custom `RolePrincipal` and a custom `RoleManagerModule` that cache role information in the ASP.NET `Cache` object.

❏ Chapter 25 discusses "Developing Custom Provider-Based Services." The services that most Web applications offer their clients involve storing data in and retrieving data from a data store. This chapter provides you with a step-by-step recipe for implementing provider-based services that can store the required data in and retrieve the required data from any type of data store. The chapter then uses the recipe to implement a provider-based RSS reader that can generate RSS data from any type of data store such as SQL Server, Oracle, and others.

❏ Chapter 26, "Developing Ajax-Enabled Controls and Components: Client-Side Functionality," provides you with a step-by-step detailed recipe for using XHTML/HTML, CSS, DOM, XML, and JavaScript client-side technologies to implement the client-side functionality of Ajax-enabled controls and components. It then uses the recipe to implement two Ajax-enabled controls. This chapter also provides an in-depth coverage of topics such as embedded resources and substitution, and deploying script files.

❏ Chapter 27, "Developing Ajax-Enabled Controls and Components: Asynchronous Client Callback," shows you how to use the ASP.NET 2.0 client-callback mechanism to implement Ajax-enabled controls and components that make asynchronous client callbacks to the server. This chapter implements replicas of the main components of the client-callback mechanism to help you understand this mechanism from the inside out. It then implements four Ajax-enabled controls and components that make asynchronous client callbacks to the server.

❏ Chapter 28, "Developing Ajax-Enabled Controls and Components: Ajax Patterns," first provides you with in-depth coverage of the Google XML Web service API. It then discusses a popular Ajax pattern known as Predictive Fetch and uses the pattern to develop an Ajax-enabled control named `AjaxGoogleSearch` that makes asynchronous client callbacks to the Google XML Web service to perform a Google search.

❏ Chapter 29, "Developing Ajax-Enabled Controls and Components: More Ajax Patterns," discusses three popular Ajax patterns known as Periodic Refresh, Submission Throttling, and Explicit Submission in detail. It then uses the Periodic Refresh pattern to implement an Ajax-enabled control named `AjaxNotifier` that periodically polls the server and sends automatic notifications. Next, it uses the Submission Throttling pattern to implement a WYSIWYG HTML editor named `AjaxHtmlEditor` that asynchronously sends the text the user is typing to the server as the user is typing without interrupting the user. Finally, the chapter uses both Submission Throttling and Explicit Submission patterns to implement a spell-checker named `AjaxSpellChecker` that uses the Google XML Web service API to spell-check the text as the user is typing without interrupting the user.

❏ Chapter 30, "Understanding the ASP.NET 2.0 Web Parts Framework," begins by reviewing the main controls in the Web Parts control set to give you the big picture. It then uses examples to show you how to declaratively turn any standard ASP.NET server control, custom control, and user control to a `WebPart`, how to use tool parts such as `AppearanceEditorPart`, `LayoutEditorPart`, `BehaviorEditorPart`, `PropertyGridEditorPart`, `Declarative CatalogPart`, and `PageCatalogPart`, and how to export and import `WebPart` controls.

❑ Chapter 31, "Developing Custom WebPart, EditorPart, and CatalogPart Controls," first looks under the hood of `WebPart`, `EditorPart`, `CatalogPart`, and `WebPartVerb` base classes, and then implements custom `WebPart`, `EditorPart`, `CatalogPart`, and `WebPartVerb` components that derive from these base classes. The chapter then shows you how to implement the `IWebPart`, `IWebActionable`, `IWebEditable`, and `IPersonalizable` interfaces. The chapter also discusses the structure of `WebPart` description XML file and the `WebPartDescription` class in detail.

❑ Chapter 32, "Developing Custom WebPartZoneBase Controls," looks under the hood of the ASP.NET 2.0 `WebZone`, `WebPartZoneBase`, `WebPartZone`, and `WebPartChrome` base classes to help you gain a solid understanding of these base classes and implements three custom `WebPartZone` controls and one custom `WebPartChrome` chrome.

❑ Chapter 33, "WebPartManager, Web Parts Connections, and Data-Bound WebPart Controls," implements a custom `WebPartManager` that uses the ASP.NET 2.0 role management model. The chapter then looks under the hood of the `ProviderConnectionPoint`, `ConsumerConnectionPoint`, and `WebPartConnection` base classes, discusses static, dynamic, and programmatic connections in detail, and develops several provider and consumer `WebPart` controls that support these three types of connections. This chapter then implements three base classes named `BaseDataBoundWebPart`, `DataBoundWebPart`, and `CompositeDataBoundWebPart` that you can derive from to implement custom data-bound `WebPart` controls that can access any type of data store and can automate all their data operations such as delete, update, insert, sorting, and paging so the page developer can use them declaratively without writing a single line of code. This chapter then implements two data-bound `WebPart` controls name `GridViewWebPart` and `MasterDetailGridViewWebPart`.

What You Need to Use This Book

You can use any edition of Visual Studio 2005 and SQL Server 2005 to run the code samples and to use the databases of this book. If you don't have access to the full versions of Visual Studio 2005 or SQL Server 2005, you can download free copies of Visual Web Developer 2005 Express Edition from `http://msdn.microsoft.com/vstudio/express/vwd/` and SQL Server 2005 Express Edition from `http://msdn.microsoft.com/sql/express/`. These free editions are all you need to run the code samples and to use the databases of this book.

Conventions

To help you get the most from the text and keep track of what's happening, we've used a number of conventions throughout the book.

> **Boxes like this one hold important, not-to-be forgotten information that is directly relevant to the surrounding text.**

Tips, hints, tricks, and asides to the current discussion are offset and placed in italics like this.

As for styles in the text:

- ❑ We *highlight* new terms and important words when we introduce them.
- ❑ We show keyboard strokes like this: Ctrl+A.
- ❑ We show filenames, URLs, and code within the text like so: `persistence.properties`.
- ❑ We present code in two different ways:

```
In code examples we highlight new and important code with a gray background.
```

```
The gray highlighting is not used for code that's less important in the present
context, or has been shown before.
```

Source Code

As you work through the examples in this book, you may choose either to type in all the code manually or to use the source code files that accompany the book. All of the source code used in this book is available for download at `http://www.wrox.com`. Once at the site, simply locate the book's title (either by using the Search box or by using one of the title lists) and click the Download Code link on the book's detail page to obtain all the source code for the book.

Because many books have similar titles, you may find it easiest to search by ISBN; this book's ISBN is 0-471-79350-7 (changing to 978-0-471-79350-2 as the new industry-wide 13-digit ISBN numbering system is phased in by January 2007).

Once you download the code, just decompress it with your favorite compression tool. Alternatively, you can go to the main Wrox code download page at `http://www.wrox.com/dynamic/books/download.aspx` to see the code available for this book and all other Wrox books.

Errata

We make every effort to ensure that there are no errors in the text or in the code. However, no one is perfect, and mistakes do occur. If you find an error in one of our books, like a spelling mistake or faulty piece of code, we would be very grateful for your feedback. By sending in errata you may save another reader hours of frustration and at the same time you will be helping us provide even higher quality information.

To find the errata page for this book, go to `http://www.wrox.com` and locate the title using the Search box or one of the title lists. Then, on the book details page, click the Book Errata link. On this page you can view all errata that has been submitted for this book and posted by Wrox editors. A complete book list including links to each book's errata is also available at `www.wrox.com/misc-pages/booklist.shtml`.

If you don't spot "your" error on the Book Errata page, go to www.wrox.com/contact/techsupport.shtml and complete the form there to send us the error you have found. We'll check the information and, if appropriate, post a message to the book's errata page and fix the problem in subsequent editions of the book.

p2p.wrox.com

For author and peer discussion, join the P2P forums at p2p.wrox.com. The forums are a Web-based system for you to post messages relating to Wrox books and related technologies and interact with other readers and technology users. The forums offer a subscription feature to e-mail you topics of interest of your choosing when new posts are made to the forums. Wrox authors, editors, other industry experts, and your fellow readers are present on these forums.

At http://p2p.wrox.com you will find a number of different forums that will help you not only as you read this book, but also as you develop your own applications. To join the forums, just follow these steps:

1. Go to p2p.wrox.com and click the Register link.

2. Read the terms of use and click Agree.

3. Complete the required information to join as well as any optional information you wish to provide and click Submit.

4. You will receive an e-mail with information describing how to verify your account and complete the joining process.

> *You can read messages in the forums without joining P2P but in order to post your own messages, you must join.*

Once you join, you can post new messages and respond to messages other users post. You can read messages at any time on the Web. If you would like to have new messages from a particular forum e-mailed to you, click the Subscribe to this Forum icon by the forum name in the forum listing.

For more information about how to use the Wrox P2P, be sure to read the P2P FAQs for answers to questions about how the forum software works as well as many common questions specific to P2P and Wrox books. To read the FAQs, click the FAQ link on any P2P page.

The ASP.NET 2.0 Framework

This chapter begins with the following definition of the ASP.NET Framework:

ASP.NET is a Framework that processes requests for Web resources.

In other words, ASP.NET is a request processing architecture or framework. This description of the Framework prompts you to think, "If ASP.NET is a request processing architecture or framework, every component of the framework must exist for one reason and one reason only; that is, to contribute one way or another to the process of handling requests for Web resources."

Think of the components of the ASP.NET Framework in terms of their roles in the overall request handling process. Instead of asking, "What does this component do?" you should ask, "What does this component do to *help process the request?*"

Therefore, this chapter follows a request for a resource from the time it arrives in the Web server (IIS) all the way through the ASP.NET request processing architecture to identify components of the framework that participate or contribute directly or indirectly to the request handling process. However, to keep the discussions simple and focused, the details of these components are left to the following chapters. In short, the main goal of this chapter is to help you understand the big picture.

Following the Request

To make the discussion more concrete, consider the request for a simple Web page named `Default.aspx`, shown in Listing 1-1. This page consists of a textbox and a button. The user enters a name and clicks the button to post the page back to the server where the name is processed.

Listing 1-1: The Default.aspx page

```
<%@ Page Language="C#" AutoEventWireup="true" CodeFile="Default.aspx.cs"
Inherits="_Default" %>
<html xmlns="http://www.w3.org/1999/xhtml">
<body>
  <form id="form1" runat="server">
    <strong>Name: </strong>
    <asp:TextBox runat="server" ID="NameTextBox" />
    <br /> <br />
    <asp:Button runat="server" OnClick="SubmitCallback" Text="Submit" />
  </form>
</body>
</html>
```

Figure 1-1 follows the request all the way through the request processing architecture. The block arrows represent the request as it passes through different components. Everything starts when the user attempts to download the Default.aspx page; that is, the user makes a request for this page.

As Figure 1-1 shows, Internet Information Services (IIS) picks up the request and passes it to an ISAPI extension named aspnet_isapi.dll. After passing through some intermediary components, the request finally arrives in a .NET component named HttpRuntime. This component creates an instance of a .NET class named HttpContext that contains the complete information about the request, and exposes this information in the form of well-known, convenient managed objects such as Request, Response, Server, and so on. The cylinders in Figure 1-1 represent the HttpContext object as it's passed from one component to another.

The request finally arrives in a .NET component named HttpApplication. This component creates a pipeline of .NET components known as HTTP modules to perform preprocessing operations such as authentication and authorization. The results of these operations are stored in the HttpContext object.

After HTTP modules preprocess the request, HttpApplication passes the preprocessed request to a component known as an HTTP handler. The main responsibility of an HTTP handler is to generate the markup text that is sent back to the requester as part of the response. Different types of HTTP handlers generate different types of markup texts. For example, the HTTP handler that handles the requests for the .aspx extension, such as the Default.aspx page shown in Listing 1-1, generates HTML markup text similar to Listing 1-2. The HTTP handler that handles the requests for the .asmx extension, on the other hand, generates XML markup text.

Listing 1-2: The markup text that the HTTP handler generates in response to a request for the Default.aspx page

```
<html xmlns="http://www.w3.org/1999/xhtml">
<body>
  <form name="form1" method="post" action="Default.aspx" id="form2">
    <strong>Name: </strong>
    <input name="NameTextBox" type="text" id="Text1" />
    <br /><br />
    <input type="submit" name="Button1" value="Submit" id="Submit1" />
  </form>
</body>
</html>
```

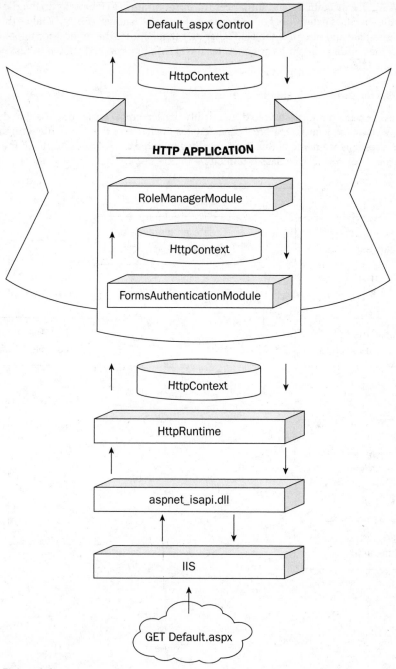

Figure 1-1

Therefore, ASP.NET instantiates and initializes the appropriate HTTP handler to handle or process the request for the specified extension. For example, as Figure 1-2 shows, ASP.NET takes the following actions to instantiate and initialize the HTTP handler that handles the request for the Default.aspx page; that is, the handler that emits or generates the HTML markup text shown in Listing 1-2 out of the Default.aspx file:

1. Parses the Default.aspx file.

2. Uses the parsed information to dynamically implement a control or class that derives from the Page class. By default, ASP.NET concatenates the name of the .aspx file with the string aspx and uses it as the name of this dynamically generated class. For example, in the case of the Default.aspx file, this class is named Default_aspx.

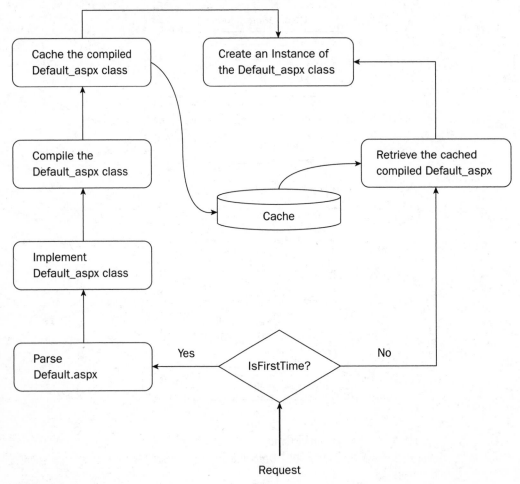

Figure 1-2

If you're curious as to what the code for this class looks like, here is what you need to do to view the code. Introduce a syntax error in the `Default.aspx.cs` *and set the* `Debug` *attribute on the* `Page` *directive to true to run the application in debug mode. Now if you access the* `Default.aspx` *page, you'll get a page with a link named "Show Complete Compilation Source." Click this link to view the code for the dynamically generated class. Notice that the class is named* `Default_aspx`.

3. Dynamically compiles the control or class.

4. Caches the compiled class.

5. Dynamically creates an instance of the compiled control.

6. Assigns the task of handling the request for the `Default.aspx` file to this instance.

The HTTP handler that processes the request for the `Default.aspx` file is a control or class named `Default_aspx` that ASP.NET dynamically implements from the contents of the `Default.aspx` file. As Figure 1-2 shows, the first four actions are taken only the very first time `Default.aspx` is being accessed. To handle the subsequent requests, ASP.NET simply retrieves the cached compiled `Default_aspx` class from the ASP.NET `Cache` object, creates an instance of the class, and assigns the task of handling the request to this instance.

Why Develop Custom Components?

As the previous section shows the request for a resource goes through different components of the ASP.NET request processing architecture, where each component contributes toward the final markup text that is sent back to the requester as part of the response message. As discussed, the content or type of the final markup text depends on the type of the requested resource, which normally depends on its extension. For example, the final markup text contains HTML if the request was made for an `.aspx` extension, and XML if the request was made for an `.asmx` extension.

The ASP.NET request processing architecture contains two groups of components:

❑ Components that directly contribute to the generation of the final markup text. This group includes server controls such as `TextBox`, `LiteralControl`, `Xml`, and so on.

❑ Components that indirectly contribute to the generation of the final markup text.

As an example of a component that contributes indirectly, consider the `RoleManagerModule` HTTP module shown in Figure 1-1. As you'll see later in this book, at the end of each request, this module retrieves the roles the current user is in from an object known as `principal`, and stores them in a cookie that is sent back to the requesting browser as part of the response.

At the beginning each request, on the other hand, the module retrieves the roles from the cookie and caches them in the `principal` object that represents the current user. Storing roles in a cookie improves the overall performance of a Web application because it's much more efficient to retrieve roles from a cookie than a database.

These roles affect the final markup text that is sent back to the user. For example, the application may only allow users in certain roles to access the `Default.aspx` page. Users who are not in one of those roles will receive a different HTML markup text that contains an error message.

You might be wondering why you would want to develop custom components. Why customize when you can use the existing standard ASP.NET controls and components?

This chapter invites you to change the way you think about the ASP.NET controls and components. This new perspective allows you to think of ASP.NET components in terms of their direct or indirect contributions to the final markup text that is sent back to the requester as part of the response message.

In light of this new perspective, you can easily address the preceding question. You need to develop custom components because there are many situations in which the contributions of the existing standard ASP.NET components do not add up to the markup text that would adequately service the request. The following sections provide a few examples of such situations to give you a flavor of what you can achieve with the skills, knowledge, and experience that this book provides you. Keep in mind that the examples and situations here make up only a very small portion of the situations and examples covered in this book.

Data Source Controls

Developing data-driven Web applications is a huge challenge because data comes from many different types of data stores, such as relational databases, XML documents, flat files, and Web services, to name a few. It's a challenge because different types of data stores use different types of data access APIs.

As you'll see in Chapters 12, 13, 14, and 15, a data source control is a component that acts as an adapter between the data store and your application. Your application can talk to any type of data store as long as there is an adapter for that type of data store. You can't use the same adapter to talk to two different types of data stores, however — each type of data store has its own adapter.

The ASP.NET Framework comes with standard data source controls for a handful of data stores, such as SQL Server and XML documents. This leaves out numerous data stores that your application cannot talk to. This is where you as the developer come into play. If you know how to develop a data source control, you can easily develop a data source control for your favorite data store to allow your application to talk to the data store without changing a single line of code in your application! Chapters 12–15 will help you gain the skills, knowledge, and experience that you need to develop data source controls.

Role Manager Modules and Principals

As discussed previously, the standard ASP.NET `RoleManagerModule` stores the current user's role information in a cookie to improve the performance of your application. This leaves out those clients that don't support cookies or where cookies are disabled.

Chapters 20 and 24 help you learn to develop a role manager module that can store the current user's role information in other sources, such as the `Session` object. Those chapters also teach you how to implement the `IPrincipal` interface to develop your own custom principals.

Role Providers

If you're using the ASP.NET 2.0 Framework to develop a brand new Web application, and if your clients don't have any requirements as to where and in what format or schema you should store your application's role information, you can store the role information in the standard SQL Server database named aspnetdb. However, if you have to move your existing applications to the new Framework, you can't afford to dump the database where your application has been storing role information for the last few years and start using the aspnetdb database. Or if you're using the ASP.NET 2.0 Framework to develop a brand new Web application but you're required to store your application's role information in a non-SQL Server data store such as XML documents or a SQL Server database with a different schema than the aspnetdb database, you can't use the aspnetdb database.

Chapters 20, 23, and 24 teach you everything you need to develop a role provider that will allow you to integrate your desired role data store (both relational such as SQL Server and Oracle, and non-relational such as XML documents) with the role management features of the ASP.NET 2.0 Framework.

Membership Providers

Much like the role provider, if you have applications that you need to move from ASP.NET 1.x to 2.0, you can't afford to dump the databases where you have been storing you user membership information for the last few years and jump to the new aspnetdb database. Or if you're developing a brand new ASP.NET 2.0 Web application but you're required to store your application's user membership information in a non-SQL Server data store such as XML documents or a SQL Server database with a different schema than the aspnetdb database, you can't use the aspnetdb database. Chapters 20, 21, and 22 teach you everything you need to develop a membership provider that will allow you to integrate your desired membership data store (both relational and non-relational) with the new ASP.NET 2.0 user membership feature.

Customizing XML Web Services and Their Clients

The ASP.NET 2.0 XML Web service infrastructure comes with two new exciting features that work together to provide you with amazing customization power. First, it allows you to implement the IXmlSerializable interface to take complete control over the serialization and deserialization of your custom components. Second, it allows you to implement your own custom schema importer extension to customize the code for the proxy class. These two features work hand-in-hand to empower you to resolve problems that you couldn't handle otherwise. One of these common problems is the significant degradation of the performance and responsiveness of XML Web services that expose huge amounts of data. Chapter 11 builds on Chapter 10 to teach you how to implement your own custom schema importer extensions to customize the proxy code generation and how to implement the IXmlSerializable interface to customize the serialization and deserialization of your custom components.

Developing Ajax-Enabled Controls and Components

Asynchronous JavaScript And Xml (Ajax) is a popular Web application development approach that allows a Web application to break free from the traditional click-and-wait user interaction pattern characterized by irritating waiting periods. An Ajax-enabled control or component exhibits the following four important characteristics:

❑ It has rich client-side functionality that uses client-side resources to handle user interactions. Chapter 26 provides you with a detailed step-by-step recipe for using XHTML/HTML, CSS, DOM, and JavaScript client-side technologies to implement the client-side functionality of an Ajax-enabled control or component. Chapter 26 then uses the recipe to develop two Ajax-enabled controls.

❑ It uses an asynchronous client callback to communicate with the server without having to perform a full-page postback. Chapter 27 shows you how to use the ASP.NET 2.0 client-callback mechanism to develop Ajax-enabled controls that make asynchronous client-callback requests to the server. Chapter 27 then uses the ASP.NET 2.0 client-callback mechanism to implement several Ajax-enabled controls and components.

❑ It exchanges data with the server in XML format. Chapter 27, 28, and 29 show you how to develop Ajax-enabled controls and components that use XML, DOM, and JavaScript client-side technologies to read the XML data that they receive from the server and to generate the HTML that displays the XML data. These three chapters also implement several Ajax-enabled controls and components that exchange data with the server in XML format.

❑ Its communication with the server is governed by Ajax patterns. Chapters 28 and 29 discuss the Predictive Fetch, Periodic Refresh, Submission Throttling, and Explicit Submission Ajax patterns in detail and use these patterns to implement several Ajax-enabled controls and components.

Developing Web Parts Controls

One of the most exciting and anticipated new features of the ASP.NET 2.0 Framework is its rich support for Web Parts. Chapters 28, 29, 30, and 31 build on earlier chapters to provide you with a comprehensive and in-depth coverage of the ASP.NET Web Parts Framework, where you'll learn how to develop your own custom `WebPart`, `EditorPart`, `CatalogPart`, `WebPartZone`, `WebPartManager`, `WebPartVerb`, and `WebPartChrome` components. This book also implements a set of base data-bound Web Parts controls that you can use to develop custom data-bound Web Parts controls that support the following features:

❑ They can access any type of data store. This is very important in data-driven Web applications where data come from many different types of data stores such as Microsoft SQL Server, Oracle, XML documents, flat files, Web services, and so on.

❑ Page developers can use them declaratively on an ASP.NET page without writing a single line of code.

❑ You can develop them with minimal coding effort.

❑ They automate all data operations such as `Select`, `Delete`, `Update`, and `Insert` without a single line of code from page developers.

Developing Custom Data Control Fields

Displaying and editing database records are two of the most common operations in data-driven Web applications. These applications use the appropriate user interface to display database records and to allow end users to edit these records. The type of the user interface depends on the type of the data being displayed or edited.

For example, it makes more sense to provide end users with a CheckBox control to edit a Boolean field than a TextBox control where the user must enter error-prone text such as "true" or "false." As you'll see in Chapter 18, the ASP.NET Framework comes with components known as *data control fields*, where each component is designed to present the end user with the specific type of user interface to display and edit a data field.

However, the existing data control fields leave out lot of common situations that you as the developer have to deal with. For example, one of the common scenarios in most Web applications is to allow users to edit foreign key fields. None of the existing data control fields provides support for foreign key editing. Chapter 18 teaches you everything you need to know to develop your own custom data control fields to deal with these common situations.

Developing Custom HTTP Handlers and Modules

As discussed, every HTTP handler is specifically designed to handle requests for a specific extension. The ASP.NET Framework comes with standard handlers that handle common extensions such as .aspx and .asmx. However, there are situations in which you would want to write your own custom HTTP handlers to handle custom extensions.

For example, many Web applications nowadays provide RSS feeds. It makes lot of sense to implement a custom HTTP handler that handles requests for .rss extensions. Such a dedicated HTTP handler will allow you to bypass the normal page life cycle and feed RSS right from this dedicated HTTP handler. Chapter 8 shows you how to develop your own custom HTTP handlers and modules.

Developing Custom Provider-Based Services

ASP.NET 2.0 uses the Provider Pattern to implement most of its new features and services such as membership, role management, profiles, and so on. This exciting pattern allows these features and services to support any type of data store. Chapter 27 shows you how to develop your own provider-based services that can use any type of data store, and you develop a provider-based RSS service that can emit RSS feeds from any type of data store such as Microsoft SQL Server, Oracle, XML documents, file system, and so on.

Summary

The main goals of this chapter were twofold: to provide you with a brief overview of different components of the ASP.NET Framework, and to make a case as to why you need to extend these components to implement your own custom server controls and components.

Although ASP.NET 2.0 does provide a variety of useful server controls and components, there are numerous situations in which it can't provide enough functionality to fit your needs. This book provides you with the experience, knowledge, and skills you need to develop custom controls and components that tackle these situations. This chapter outlined just a few of the situations where custom controls and components are your best option, and you'll see all of them by the end of the book. The next chapter starts with the most basic custom controls.

2

Developing Simple Custom Controls and User Controls

The previous chapter discussed in detail why you need to develop custom controls and components. There are two basic types of ASP.NET server controls: custom controls and user controls. To implement a custom control, you have to implement a class in a procedural language such as C# or VB.NET that derives from a base class such as `Control`. You implement a user control the same way you implement a regular ASP.NET page; you can use the same drag-and-drop WYSIWYG approach to develop the user control.

This chapter begins with the discussion of custom controls and walks you through the details of the implementation of a simple custom control to show you how to do the following:

❑ Implement a custom control that derives from the `Control` base class and overrides its `Render` method

❑ Deploy your custom controls

❑ Use your custom controls in an ASP.NET page

❑ Add properties to your custom controls to allow the page developer to customize them

❑ Add design-time attributes to your custom controls to allow them act like other standard ASP.NET server controls in the Visual Studio environment

❑ Add your custom controls to the Visual Studio Toolbox so they can be dragged and dropped onto the Visual Studio designer surface

The chapter then walks you through the details of the implementation of a simple user control, where you'll see how to add custom properties and methods to your user controls, and use your user controls in a Web page.

Information Hiding

Consider the Web page shown in Figure 2-1, which collects the user's credit card information and posts the page back to the server. This Web page consists of four labels, three drop-down lists, two text boxes, and one pushbutton. You can easily implement the HTML markup text for this Web page as shown in Listing 2-1.

Figure 2-1

Listing 2-1: The HTML markup text for the Web page shown in Figure 2-1

```html
<html xmlns="http://www.w3.org/1999/xhtml">
<head><title>Untitled Page </title></head>
<body>
  <form method="post" action="Default.aspx" id="form1">
    <table id="ccf" style="font-weight: bold;">
      <tr>
        <td><strong>Payment Method</strong></td>
        <td>
          <select style="width:100%;">
            <option value="Visa">Visa</option>
            <option value="MasterCard">MasterCard</option>
          </select>
        </td>
      </tr>
      <tr>
        <td><strong>Credit Card No.</strong></td><td><input type="text" /></td>
      </tr>
      <tr>
        <td><strong>Cardholder's Name</strong></td><td><input type="text" /></td>
      </tr>
```

```
     <tr>
       <td><strong>Expiration Date</strong></td>
       <td>
         <select>
           <option value="1">01</option>
           ...
         </select> 
         <select>
           <option value="2005">2005</option>
           ...
         </select>
       </td>
     </tr>
     <tr>
       <td colspan="2" align="center"><input type="submit" value="Submit" /></td>
     </tr>
   </table>
  </form>
 </body>
</html>
```

In this chapter you learn how to transform the nested HTML markup text within the form element's opening and closing tags into a server control named `CreditCardForm1` that hides this HTML markup text from page developers. This allows them to implement the same Web page shown in Figure 2-1 with only one line of markup text, shown highlighted in Listing 2-2.

Listing 2-2: The CreditCardForm1 custom control hides its implementation from page developers

```
<html xmlns="http://www.w3.org/1999/xhtml" >
<head><title>Untitled Page</title></head>
<body>
    <form id="form1" runat="server">
      <custom:CreditCardForm1 runat="server" ID="ccf" />
    </form>
</body>
</html>
```

Think of the `CreditCardForm1` control as a container that encapsulates the HTML shown in Listing 2-1. The `CreditCardForm1` custom control derives from a standard ASP.NET base class named `Control`. Every server control directly or indirectly derives from the `Control` base class. In fact, deriving from this base class is what makes a server control a server control.

This base class provides server controls with the infrastructure they need to operate as a server control in the ASP.NET Framework. One of these infrastructural methods is a method named `Render`. This method is where a server control generates or renders its HTML markup text.

The word "render" has a special meaning in the context of server control development, which is different from the common meaning of the word where rendering refers to the Web browser's task of displaying or rendering the HTML markup that the browser receives from the server. Rendering in the context of server control development means generating the HTML markup text that the server sends to the browser. In other words, server controls render (generate) the HTML markup text that browsers render (display).

At runtime, the containing page creates an instance of a class named `HtmlTextWriter` and passes the instance into the `Render` methods of the server controls that the page contains. The `HtmlTextWriter` class exposes a method named `Write` that these server controls can use to write out their HTML markup text. Listing 2-3 contains the code for the `CreditCardForm1` control's implementation of the `Render` method. What this method does is really simple. It scans through the HTML shown in Listing 2-1 line by line and passes each line into the `Write` method of `HtmlTextWriter` object.

For example, the first line of this HTML is the opening tag of the table HTML element and its attributes:

```
<table style='width:287px;height:124px;border-width:0;'>
```

This HTML line is simply passed into the `Write` method of the `HtmlTextWriter` instance:

```
writer.Write("<table style='width:287px;height:124px;border-width:0;'>");
```

The same thing is repeated for every line of HTML shown in Listing 2-1. As you can see, there's really no magic to implementing a simple custom control. It's as easy as 1-2-3:

1. Write down the HTML that you want to generate (such as the HTML shown in Listing 2-1).

2. Write a class that derives from the `Control` class.

3. Override the `Render` method to pass your HTML line by line into the `Write` method of the `HtmlTextWriter`.

Listing 2-3: The CreditCardForm1 custom control

```
namespace CustomComponents
{
  public class CreditCardForm1 : Control
  {
    protected override void Render(HtmlTextWriter writer)
    {
      writer.Write("<table style='width:287px;height:124px;border-width:0;'>");
      writer.Write("<tr>");
      writer.Write("<td>Payment Method</td>");
      writer.Write("<td>");
      writer.Write("<select name='PaymentMethod' id='PaymentMethod'
                  style='width:100%;'>");
      writer.Write("<option value='0'>Visa</option>");
      writer.Write("<option value='1'>MasterCard</option>");
      writer.Write("</select>");
      writer.Write("</td>");
      writer.Write("</tr>");
      writer.Write("<tr>");
      writer.Write("<td>Credit Card No.</td>");
      writer.Write("<td><input name='CreditCardNo' id='CreditCardNo'
                  type='text' /></td>");
      writer.Write("</tr>");
      writer.Write("<tr>");
      writer.Write("<td>Cardholder's Name</td>");
      writer.Write("<td><input name='CardholderName' id='CardholderName'
                  type='text' /></td>");
```

```
writer.Write("</tr>");
writer.Write("<tr>");
writer.Write("<td>Expiration Date</td>");
writer.Write("<td>");
writer.Write("<select name='Month' id='Month'>");
for (int day = 1; day < 13; day++)
{
  if (day < 10)
    writer.Write("<option value='" + day.ToString() + "'>" + "0" +
                 day.ToString() + "</option>");
  else
    writer.Write("<option value='" + day.ToString() + "'>" +
                 day.ToString() + "</option>");
}
writer.Write("</select>");
writer.Write(" ");
writer.Write("<select name='Year' id='Year'>");
for (int year = 2005; year < 2015; year++)
{
  writer.Write("<option value='" + year.ToString() + "'>" +
               year.ToString() + "</option>");
}
writer.Write("</select>");
writer.Write("</td>");
writer.Write("</tr>");
writer.Write("<tr>");
writer.Write("<td align='center' colspan='2'>");
writer.Write("<input type='submit' value='Submit' />");
writer.Write("</td>");
writer.Write("</tr>");
writer.Write("</table>");

    base.Render(writer);
  }
 }
}
```

The `HtmlTextWriter` class derives from the `TextWriter` abstract base class. Each subclass of the `TextWriter` base class is specifically designed to write a stream of text characters into a specific storage. For example, the `StringWriter` and `StreamWriter` subclasses write a stream of text characters into a string and stream (such as a `FileStream`), respectively. The `HtmlTextWriter` subclass of the `TextWriter` base class, on the other hand, is specifically designed to write a stream of HTML markup text characters into a server control's output stream.

Encapsulating HTML markup text in a single server control provides the following important benefits:

❑   You can keep optimizing the encapsulated HTML markup text without breaking existing applications. For example, you can modify the `Render` method shown in Listing 2-3 to pass a different type of HTML into the `Write` method that uses this control because this listing has no knowledge of what HTML you're passing into the `Write` method. This will not affect Listing 2-2 in any way.

This is an example of object-oriented information hiding principle where a component (`CreditCardForm1`) hides the details of its implementation (the HTML markup text) from its clients. This provides you with the well-known benefits of information hiding.

❑　　Others can write new custom controls that inherit the features of your control, and can extend your control to support new features without having to reimplement the features that your control already supports.

❑　　Page developers can use your control with minimal lines of markup text as shown in Listing 2-2.

❑　　Your control can be added to the Toolbox of Visual Studio to allow page developers to drag and drop your control on the designer surface.

Deploying Your Custom Controls

You have to compile your custom control to an assembly and deploy the assembly to the client side to allow clients to use your custom control in their Web applications. How you plan on deploying the assembly determines how you have to compile your custom control. You have two options when it comes to deploying a custom control. One option is to add the assembly that contains your custom control to the bin directory of the client's Web application that needs to use your custom control. This will only allow pages in that application to use your custom control. If this is the option you're considering and you're building from the command line, use the following command to compile the CreditCardForm1.cs file:

```
csc /t:library /out:CustomComponents.dll /r:System.dll /r:System.Web.dll
CreditCardForm1.cs
```

Another deployment option is to add the assembly that contains your custom control to the Global Assembly Cache (GAC) of the client's machine to allow all Web applications running on that machine to use your custom control. However, only strongly named assemblies can be added to the GAC. A strong assembly name consists of four parts: assembly name, version, culture, and public key token. If you're building from the command line, create a file named AssemblyInfo.cs (or any other desired name), add the following code to the file, and move the file to the directory where CreditCardForm1.cs file is located:

```
using System.Runtime.CompilerServices;
using System.Runtime.InteropServices;

[assembly: AssemblyCulture("")]
[assembly: AssemblyVersion("1.0.0.0")]
[assembly: AssemblyKeyFile("KeyFile.snk")]
```

If you're building in Visual Studio, add this code to the AssemblyInfo.cs.

KeyFile.snk is the signature file that you have to use to sign the assembly. You can use the following command to create the signature file:

```
sn -k KeyFile.snk
```

If you're building from the command line, use the following command to compile and sign the CreditCardForm1.cs file to a strongly named assembly, which will be named CustomComponents.dll:

```
csc /t:library /out:CustomComponents.dll /r:System.dll /r:System.Web.dll
AssemblyInfo.cs CreditCardForm1.cs
```

The next order of business is to add the strongly named assembly `CustomComponents.dll` to the GAC. You can use the Windows Explorer to access the GAC and to drag and drop the assembly.

Using Custom Controls in a Web Page

Clients of your custom control must use the `Register` directive to register your custom control before they can use it in their Web page:

```
<%@ Register TagPrefix="custom" Namespace="CustomComponents" %>
```

The `Register` directive exposes two important attributes named `TagPrefix` and `Namespace`. Clients must assign the namespace that contains your custom control to the `Namespace` attribute. Because the `CreditCardForm1` custom control belongs to the `CustomComponent` namespace, the `Namespace` attribute is set to the string value `"CustomComponents"`. This shows that your custom control must belong to a namespace to allow page developers to register it so they can use it declaratively on an ASP.NET Web page. The following code shows how clients use the `CreditCardForm1` custom control in a Web page:

```
<%@ Page Language="C#" AutoEventWireup="true" CodeFile="CreditCardForm1.aspx.cs"
Inherits="CreditCardForm1" %>

<%@ Register TagPrefix="custom" Namespace="CustomComponents" %>
<!DOCTYPE html PUBLIC "-//W3C//DTD XHTML 1.1//EN"
"http://www.w3.org/TR/xhtml11/DTD/xhtml11.dtd">
<html xmlns="http://www.w3.org/1999/xhtml">
<head><title>Untitled Page</title></head>
<body>
  <form id="form1" runat="server">
    <custom:CreditCardForm1 runat="server" ID="ccf" />
  </form>
</body>
</html>
```

There are two different ways for page developers to instantiate your custom control:

❑   They can use the new operator in their C# or VB.NET code to explicitly create an instance of your control:

```
CreditCardForm1 ccf = new CreditCardForm1();
```

❑   They can declare your control on an ASP.NET Web page:

```
<custom:CreditCardForm1 runat="server" ID="ccf" />
```

You control doesn't have to belong to a namespace for page developers to use it programmatically in their C# or VB.NET code. In other words, the namespace becomes a requirement if you want to enable page developers to use your control declaratively on an ASP.NET Web page. That said, you should always encapsulate your custom controls in a namespace because most page developers prefer declarative programming over programming in a procedural language such as C# or VB.NET.

Adding Properties to Your Custom Controls

Figure 2-1 shows that the `CreditCardForm1` custom control consists of four labels and one pushbutton. The `Render` method in Listing 2-3 hard-codes these four labels and the label of the button. Listing 2-4 illustrates a new version of this control named `CreditCardForm2` that exposes five public properties to allow page developers to customize these labels.

Listing 2-4: The CreditCardForm2 custom control exposes five properties

```
namespace CustomComponents
{
  public class CreditCardForm2 : Control
  {
    private string paymentMethodText = "Payment Method";
    private string creditCardNoText = "Credit Card No.";
    private string cardholderNameText = "Cardholder's Name";
    private string expirationDateText = "Expiration Date";
    private string submitButtonText = "Submit";

    public virtual string PaymentMethodText
    {
      get { return this.paymentMethodText; }
      set { this.paymentMethodText = value; }
    }

    public virtual string CreditCardNoText
    {
      get { return this.creditCardNoText; }
      set { this.creditCardNoText = value; }
    }

    public virtual string CardholderNameText
    {
      get { return this.cardholderNameText; }
      set { this.cardholderNameText = value; }
    }

    public virtual string ExpirationDateText
    {
      get { return this.expirationDateText; }
      set { this.expirationDateText = value; }
    }

    public virtual string SubmitButtonText
    {
      get { return this.submitButtonText; }
      set { this.submitButtonText = value; }
    }

    protected override void Render(HtmlTextWriter writer)
    {
      . . .
    }
  }
}
```

Notice that each property uses a private field as its backing store. Also notice that the previously hard-coded string values are assigned to these private fields. Listing 2-5 shows the new version of the Render method that replaces the hard-coded string values with these properties.

A property of a class consists of up to two parts that begin with the keywords get *and* set. *These two parts are known as the getter and setter of the property, respectively. The main responsibility of a getter is to get or retrieve the current value of the property from the specified storage. The main responsibility of a setter, on the other hand, is to set or store the value assigned to the property in the specified storage. This storage or backing store could be anything. For example, the properties shown in Listing 2-5 use private fields as their backing stores. The word "storage" is used here in its general sense. For example, the storage or backing store of a getter could be a piece of code that dynamically evaluates the current value of the property.*

Listing 2-5: The Render method of the CreditCardForm2 control

```
namespace CustomComponents
{
  public class CreditCardForm2 : Control
  {
    ...
    protected override void Render(HtmlTextWriter writer)
    {
      writer.Write("<table style='width:287px;height:124px;border-width:0;'>");
      writer.Write("<tr>");
      writer.Write("<td>" + PaymentMethodText + "</td>");
      writer.Write("<td>");
      ...
      writer.Write("<tr>");
      writer.Write("<td>" + CreditCardNoText + "</td>");
      writer.Write("<td><input name='CreditCardNo' id='CreditCardNo'
                   type='text' /></td>");
      writer.Write("</tr>");
      writer.Write("<tr>");
      writer.Write("<td>" + CardholderNameText + "</td>");
      writer.Write("<td><input name='CardholderName' id='CardholderName'
                   type='text' /></td>");
      writer.Write("</tr>");
      writer.Write("<tr>");
      writer.Write("<td>" + ExpirationDateText + "</td>");
      writer.Write("<td>");
      writer.Write("<select name='Month' id='Month'>");

      writer.Write("<select name='Month' id='Month'>");

      for (int day = 1; day < 13; day++)
      {
        if (day < 10)
          writer.Write("<option value='" + day.ToString() + "'>" + "0" +
                   day.ToString() + "</option>");
        else
          writer.Write("<option value='" + day.ToString() + "'>" + day.ToString() +
                   "</option>");
      }
```

(continued)

Listing 2-5: *(continued)*

```
        writer.Write("</select>");
        writer.Write(" ");
        writer.Write("<select name='Year' id='Year'>");
        for (int year = 2005; year < 2015; year++)
        {
            writer.Write("<option value='" + year.ToString() + "'>" + year.ToString() +
                        "</option>");
        }
        writer.Write("</select>");
        writer.Write("</td>");
        writer.Write("</tr>");
        writer.Write("<tr>");
        writer.Write("<td align='center' colspan='2'>");
        writer.Write("<input type='submit' value='" + SubmitButtonText + "' />");
        writer.Write("</td>");
        writer.Write("</tr>");
        writer.Write("</table>");

        base.Render(writer);
    }
  }
}
```

Adding Design-Time Attributes to Your Custom Controls

When you're writing your custom control, you must keep in mind that page developers will be using your custom control in Visual Studio environment, where they have come to expect certain standard behaviors and look and feel from server controls. For example, page developers expect to see a one-line description when they select a property from the property browser.

You must annotate your custom control with design-time attributes to allow your control to behave like standard ASP.NET server controls in the Visual Studio environment.

Property-Level Attributes

When page developers select the CreditCardForm2 control in Visual Studio, they expect the property browser to show the following information about the PaymentMethodText, CreditCardNoText, CardholderNameText, ExpirationDateText, and SubmitButtonText properties:

- ❑   Their names and values
- ❑   A one-line description for each property that describes what the property does
- ❑   The default value for each property
- ❑   A specific category for each property to allow page developers to group and organize properties in the property browser

You can annotate these five properties with the `BrowsableAttribute`, `DescriptionAttribute`, `DefaultValueAttribute`, and `CategoryAttribute` design-time attributes to specify the preceding information about these properties. For example, consider the following code:

```
[BrowsableAttribute(true)]
[DescriptionAttribute("Gets and sets the payment method")]
[DefaultValueAttribute("Payment Method")]
[CategoryAttribute("Appearance")]
public virtual string PaymentMethodText
{
  get { return this.paymentMethodText; }
  set { this.paymentMethodText = value; }
}
```

This code takes the following actions:

1. Annotates the `PaymentMethodText` property with the `BrowsableAttribute(true)` attribute to instruct the property browser to display the name and value of this property. By default, every public property is considered browsable. You should use this attribute on read-only properties to tell the property browser not to display them because there is no point in displaying a property if page developers can't change its value.

2. Annotates the property with the `DescriptionAttribute("Gets and sets the payment method")` attribute to instruct the property browser to display the text "Gets and sets the payment method" every time the page developer selects the property.

3. Annotates the property with the `DefaultValueAttribute("Payment Method")` attribute to instruct the property browser to display the text "Payment Method" as the default value of the property.

4. Annotates the property with the `CategoryAttribute("Appearance")` attribute to instruct the property browser to display this property under the Appearance category.

Class-Level Attributes

When page developers select a server control in Visual Studio, they expect to see a particular property of the control highlighted. This property is known as the default property of the server control. The following code annotates the `CreditCardForm2` custom control with the `DefaultPropertyAttribute` (`"CardholderNameText"`) to mark the `CardholderNameText` property as the default property:

```
[DefaultPropertyAttribute("CardholderNameText")]
public class CreditCardForm2 : Control
```

When page developers drag `CreditCardForm2` from the Toolbox onto the designer surface, the designer automatically adds the following line to the respective ASP.NET Web page:

```
<cc1:CreditCardForm2 ID="CreditCardForm2" runat="server"/>
```

The following code annotates the `CreditCardForm2` custom control with the class-level attribute `ToolboxDataAttribute` to specify default values for the properties of the `CreditCardForm2` control:

```
[ToolboxData("<{0}:CreditCardForm2 PaymentMethodText='Payment Options'
CreditCardNoText='Credit Card Number' CardholderNameText='Cardholder Full Name'
SubmitButtonText = 'Send'  runat='server'></{0}:CreditCardForm2>")]
public class CreditCardForm2 : Control
```

This attribute instructs the designer to add the following line to the `.aspx` page when the page developer drags `CreditCardForm2` from the Toolbox onto the designer surface:

```
<ccl:CreditCardForm2 runat='server' CardholderNameText='Cardholder Full Name'
CreditCardNoText='Credit Card Number'
PaymentMethodText='Payment Options' SubmitButtonText='Send'>
</ccl:CreditCardForm2>
```

Assembly-Level Attributes

As discussed, when page developers drag a `CreditCardForm2` control from the Toolbox onto the design surface, the designer adds the following two lines to the `.aspx` file:

```
<%@ Register Assembly="CustomComponents" Namespace="CustomComponents"
TagPrefix="cc1" %>
...
<cc1:CreditCardForm2 ID="CreditCardForm2" runat="server"/>
```

Notice that the designer uses the default `cc1` as the prefix. You can add the following assembly-level attribute to the `AssemblyInfo.cs` file to instruct the designer to use `"custom"` as the tag prefix:

```
using System.Web.UI;
[assembly: TagPrefix("CustomComponents","custom")]
```

With this addition, the designer will use the `custom` prefix instead of `cc1`:

```
<%@ Register Assembly="CustomComponents" Namespace="CustomComponents"
TagPrefix="custom" %>
...
<custom:CreditCardForm2 ID="CreditCardForm2" runat="server"/>
```

If you're building your assembly from the command line, you must create the `AssemblyInfo.cs` file, add the following code to the file, and move the file to the directory where the `CreditCardForm2.cs` file is located:

```
using System.Reflection;
using System.Runtime.CompilerServices;
using System.Web.UI;
[assembly: TagPrefix("CustomComponents","custom")]
```

You must then use the following command to compile both the `AssemblyInfo.cs` and `CreditCardForm2.cs` files:

```
csc /t:library /out:CustomComponents.dll /r:System.dll /r:System.Web.dll
AssemblyInfo.cs CreditCardForm2.cs
```

Adding Your Custom Control to the Visual Studio Toolbox

Create a new project in Visual Studio that contains a single page (such as `Default.aspx`). Follow these steps to add the `CreditCardForm2` custom control to the Visual Studio Toolbox:

1. Right-click the Toolbox area and select Choose Items from the pop-up menu to launch the Choose Toolbox Items dialog box.

2. Use the Browse button to navigate to the directory where the assembly that contains `CreditCardForm2` control is located and select the assembly (see Figure 2-2).

Now you can drag the `CreditCardForm2` control from the Toolbox onto the designer surface. Notice that the designer automatically adds the previously discussed lines to the `.aspx` file.

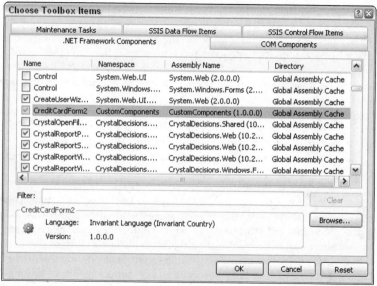

Figure 2-2

The HtmlTextWriter-Related Enumerations

The `Render` methods of `CreditCardForm1` and `CreditCardForm2` controls (see Listings 2-3 and 2-5) both pass string values to the `Write` method of the `HtmlTextWriter` class. Strings pose the following problems:

❑ String manipulation is always error-prone and compilers don't catch the errors. For example, the following typo is only caught in runtime:

```
Writer.Write("<spon/>");
```

❑ You lose the Visual Studio's IntelliSense support.

❑ You have to emit different HTML markup text for different browsers.

23

The HtmlTextWriterTag, HtmlTextWriterAttribute, and HtmlTextWriterStyle enumerations resolve all of these problems. The HtmlTextWriterTag enumeration exposes values with the same names as the HTML 4.0 tags. For example, HtmlTextWriterTag.Span corresponds to the <span> HTML tag. The HtmlTextWriterAttribute enumeration exposes values with the same names as the HTML 4.0 attributes. For example, HtmlTextWriterAttribute.Id corresponds to the id HTML attribute. Finally, the HtmlTextWriterStyle enumeration exposes values with the same names as the CSS style attributes. For example, HtmlTextWriterStyle.Width corresponds to the width CSS style attribute.

These three enumerations provide the following benefits:

- ❑ Because the values of these enumerations are typed, you can benefit from the compiler type-checking capability to avoid problems associated with string manipulations.

- ❑ Visual Studio provides IntelliSense support for these enumerations.

- ❑ The ASP.NET Framework comes with two versions of these enumerations. One version complies with the HTML 4.0 standard, and the other version complies with the HTML 3.2 standard. The ASP.NET Framework allows the clients of your custom control to configure their environment to have the ASP.NET Framework use the appropriate version of these enumerations. Your custom control doesn't have to do extra work to create different HTML markup texts for different browsers. As long as you're using these enumerations, the ASP.NET Framework will automatically use the right versions. You can't benefit from this feature if you are using strings.

To take advantage of these three benefits, you have to write a new custom control named CreditCardForm3 whose Render method uses the HtmlTextWriterTag, HtmlTextWriterAttribute, and HtmlTextWriterStyle enumerations instead of string values. This seems to suggest, because you're writing a new class, that you have to also rewrite all the properties and property- and class-level attributes that you wrote for CreditCardForm2.

That would indeed be the case if the Render method weren't declared as virtual. Therefore, you can derive CreditCardForm3 from CreditCardForm2 and override the Render method without having to reimplement the properties and attributes you implemented for CreditCardForm2 because CreditCardForm3 inherits all of them. You should always declare as virtual those methods of your custom control that you anticipate others may want to override to provide their own implementations. This is how others get to extend your custom control to add support for new features.

Listing 2-6 shows the CreditCardForm3 control's implementation of the Render method.

Listing 2-6: Using the HtmlTextWriterTag, HtmlTextWriterAttribute, and HtmlTextWriterStyle enumerations

```
public class CreditCardForm3 : CreditCardForm2
{
  protected override void Render(HtmlTextWriter writer)
  {
    writer.AddStyleAttribute(HtmlTextWriterStyle.Width, "287px");
    writer.AddStyleAttribute(HtmlTextWriterStyle.Height, "124px");
    writer.AddStyleAttribute(HtmlTextWriterStyle.BorderWidth, "0");
    writer.AddAttribute(HtmlTextWriterAttribute.Id, "mytable");
    writer.RenderBeginTag(HtmlTextWriterTag.Table);
```

```
writer.RenderBeginTag(HtmlTextWriterTag.Tr);
writer.RenderBeginTag(HtmlTextWriterTag.Td);
writer.Write(PaymentMethodText);
writer.RenderEndTag();
writer.RenderBeginTag(HtmlTextWriterTag.Td);
writer.AddAttribute(HtmlTextWriterAttribute.Name, "PaymentMethod");
writer.AddAttribute(HtmlTextWriterAttribute.Id, "PaymentMethod");
writer.AddStyleAttribute(HtmlTextWriterStyle.Width, "100%");
writer.RenderBeginTag(HtmlTextWriterTag.Select);

writer.AddAttribute(HtmlTextWriterAttribute.Value, "0");
writer.RenderBeginTag(HtmlTextWriterTag.Option);
writer.Write("Visa");
writer.RenderEndTag();

writer.AddAttribute(HtmlTextWriterAttribute.Value, "1");
writer.RenderBeginTag(HtmlTextWriterTag.Option);
writer.Write("MasterCard");
writer.RenderEndTag();

writer.RenderEndTag();
writer.RenderEndTag();
writer.RenderEndTag();

writer.RenderBeginTag(HtmlTextWriterTag.Tr);
writer.RenderBeginTag(HtmlTextWriterTag.Td);
writer.Write(CreditCardNoText);
writer.RenderEndTag();
writer.RenderBeginTag(HtmlTextWriterTag.Td);
writer.AddAttribute(HtmlTextWriterAttribute.Name, "CreditCardNo");
writer.AddAttribute(HtmlTextWriterAttribute.Id, "CreditCardNo");
writer.AddAttribute(HtmlTextWriterAttribute.Type, "text");
writer.RenderBeginTag(HtmlTextWriterTag.Input);
writer.RenderEndTag();
writer.RenderEndTag();
writer.RenderEndTag();

writer.RenderBeginTag(HtmlTextWriterTag.Tr);
writer.RenderBeginTag(HtmlTextWriterTag.Td);
writer.Write(CardholderNameText);
writer.RenderEndTag();
writer.RenderBeginTag(HtmlTextWriterTag.Td);
writer.AddAttribute(HtmlTextWriterAttribute.Name, "CardholderName");
writer.AddAttribute(HtmlTextWriterAttribute.Id, "CardholderName");
writer.AddAttribute(HtmlTextWriterAttribute.Type, "text");
writer.RenderBeginTag(HtmlTextWriterTag.Input);
writer.RenderEndTag();
writer.RenderEndTag();
writer.RenderEndTag();

writer.RenderBeginTag(HtmlTextWriterTag.Tr);
writer.RenderBeginTag(HtmlTextWriterTag.Td);
writer.Write(ExpirationDateText);
```

(continued)

Listing 2-6: *(continued)*

```
      writer.RenderEndTag();
      writer.RenderBeginTag(HtmlTextWriterTag.Td);
      writer.AddAttribute(HtmlTextWriterAttribute.Name, "Month");
      writer.AddAttribute(HtmlTextWriterAttribute.Id, "Month");
      writer.RenderBeginTag(HtmlTextWriterTag.Select);

      for (int day = 1; day < 13; day++)
      {
        writer.AddAttribute(HtmlTextWriterAttribute.Value, day.ToString());
        writer.RenderBeginTag(HtmlTextWriterTag.Option);

        if (day < 10)
          writer.Write("0" + day.ToString());
        else
          writer.Write(day);

        writer.RenderEndTag();
      }

      writer.RenderEndTag();
      writer.Write(" ");

      writer.AddAttribute(HtmlTextWriterAttribute.Name, "Year");
      writer.AddAttribute(HtmlTextWriterAttribute.Id, "Year");
      writer.RenderBeginTag(HtmlTextWriterTag.Select);

      for (int year = 2005; year < 2015; year++)
      {
        writer.AddAttribute(HtmlTextWriterAttribute.Value, year.ToString());
        writer.RenderBeginTag(HtmlTextWriterTag.Option);
        writer.Write(year);
        writer.RenderEndTag();
      }

      writer.RenderEndTag();

      writer.RenderEndTag();
      writer.RenderEndTag();

      writer.RenderBeginTag(HtmlTextWriterTag.Tr);
      writer.AddAttribute(HtmlTextWriterAttribute.Align, "center");
      writer.AddAttribute(HtmlTextWriterAttribute.Colspan, "2");
      writer.RenderBeginTag(HtmlTextWriterTag.Td);
      writer.AddAttribute(HtmlTextWriterAttribute.Type, "submit");
      writer.AddAttribute(HtmlTextWriterAttribute.Value, SubmitButtonText);
      writer.RenderBeginTag(HtmlTextWriterTag.Input);
      writer.RenderEndTag();
      writer.RenderEndTag();
      writer.RenderEndTag();
      writer.RenderEndTag();
    }
  }
```

Recall that the main goal of the `Render` method is to generate the HTML markup text that displays your control on the client browser. The HTML markup text consists of HTML elements such as `table`, `tr`, `td`, `th`, `select`, `option`, `input`, and so on. In general, every HTML element consists of up to five parts:

- Opening tag, such as `<table>`, `<tr>`, `<td>`, `<th>`, `<select>`, `<option>`, `<input>`, and so on.

- Attributes, such as `id`, `name`, `type`, `value`, and so on. Attributes of an element are rendered on its opening tag, like this: `<table id="mytable" name="mytable">`.

- Style attributes, such as `width`, `height`, and so on. Style attributes of an element are rendered on its opening tag as part of its style attribute, like this: `<table style="width:100px;height:200px">`.

- Content. The content of an element consists of text, other elements, or both.

- Closing tag, such as `</table>`, `</tr>`, and so on.

The `HtmlTextWriter` class exposes one method for rendering each of the preceding parts as follows:

- `RenderBeginTag`: Renders or generates the opening tag of an HTML element.

- `AddAttribute`: This method is called once for each attribute to generate or render the attribute on the opening tag of the HTML element. This method must be called before `RenderBeginTag`.

- `AddStyleAttribute`: This method is called once for each style attribute to generate or render the attribute as part of the style attribute of the HTML element. This method must also be called before `RenderBeginTag`. ASP.NET automatically generates a single attribute named `style` that contains all of the style attributes such as `width`, `height`, and so on. In other words, multiple calls of the `AddStyleAttribute` method are accumulated in a single `style` attribute on the opening tag of the element.

- `Write`: Recall that an HTML element can contain text, other elements, or both. Use the `Write` method to generate any type of textual content such as `string`, `int`, `float`, and so on. You should use the `RenderBeginTag`, `AddAttribute`, `AddStyleAttribute`, and `RenderEndTag` methods to generate non-textual content, that is, child elements of an element.

- `RenderEndTag`: Renders or generates the closing tag of an HTML element.

As an example, walk through the part of the Listing 2-6 that generates the table HTML element:

```
writer.AddStyleAttribute(HtmlTextWriterStyle.Width, "287px");
writer.AddStyleAttribute(HtmlTextWriterStyle.Height, "124px");
writer.AddStyleAttribute(HtmlTextWriterStyle.BorderWidth, "0");
writer.AddAttribute(HtmlTextWriterAttribute.Id, "mytable");
writer.RenderBeginTag(HtmlTextWriterTag.Table);
...
Writer.RenderEndTag();
```

This listing takes the following actions:

1. Calls `AddStyleAttribute` three times to generate the `width`, `height`, and `border-width` CSS style attributes. These methods use the `Width`, `Height`, and `BorderWidth` members of the `HtmlTextWriterStyle` enumeration instead of the string values `"width"`, `"height"`, and `"border-width"` to take advantage of the previously mentioned benefits of this enumeration.

2. Calls `AddAttribute` to generate the `id` attribute. This method uses the `Id` member of the `HtmlTextWriterAttribute` enumeration instead of the string value `"id"` to take advantage of the previously mentioned benefits of this enumeration.

3. Calls `RenderBeginTag` to generate the opening tag of the table HTML element (`<table>`). This method uses the `Table` member of the `HtmlTextWriterTag` enumeration.

4. Calls `RenderEndTag` to generate the closing tag of the table HTML element (`</table>`).

State Management

As Listing 2-4 shows, all five properties of the `CreditCardForm3` control use private fields as their backing store. This is not an issue in a desktop application where the same instance of a control is used in the same session. However, this is a major issue in a Web application, where different instances of a control are used in the same session. As an example, consider a Web page that uses the `CreditCardForm3` control as shown in Listing 2-7.

Notice that the very first time that this page is accessed, the `Page_Load` method sets the `CardholderNameText`, `PaymentMethodText`, and `SubmitButtonText` properties of the `CreditCardForm3` control to string values `"Full Name"`, `"Payment Options"`, and `"Send"`, which are different from their default values, `"Cardholder's Name"`, `"Payment Method"`, and `"Submit"`, respectively.

Listing 2-7: Web page that uses CreditCardForm3

```
<%@ Page Language="C#" %>
<%@ Register TagPrefix="custom" Namespace="CustomComponents" %>
<!DOCTYPE html PUBLIC "-//W3C//DTD XHTML 1.1//EN"
"http://www.w3.org/TR/xhtml11/DTD/xhtml11.dtd">
<script runat="server">
  void Page_Load(object sender, EventArgs e)
  {
    if (!IsPostBack)
    {
      creditcardform.CardholderNameText = "Full Name";
      creditcardform.PaymentMethodText = "Payment Options";
      creditcardform.SubmitButtonText = "Send";
    }
  }
</script>

<html xmlns="http://www.w3.org/1999/xhtml">
<head runat="server">
  <title>Untitled Page</title>
</head>
<body>
  <form id="form1" runat="server">
    <custom:CreditCardForm3 runat="server" ID="creditcardform" />
  </form>
</body>
</html>
```

Figure 2-3 shows the Web page after the first request where the three labels corresponding to these three properties display the string values `"Full Name"`, `"Payment Options"`, and `"Send"`, respectively.

Figure 2-3

If you click the Send button to post the page back to the server, you'll get back the page shown in Figure 2-4. The three labels corresponding to the `PaymentMethodText`, `CardholderNameText`, and `SubmitButtonText` properties display the default values of these properties. This shows that the values of these properties are reset to their default values.

Figure 2-4

When ASP.NET is done with processing the first request, it disposes the `CreditCardForm3` object used to process the request. When an object is disposed, its property values are lost forever. When the second request arrives, ASP.NET creates a new `CreditCardForm3` object and sets its properties to their default values.

This is the secret of the scalability of ASP.NET Web applications. If these applications were to maintain state across page requests, it would be impossible for them to support thousands of visitors a day. That said, if the properties of your custom control need to maintain their values across page postbacks, you have to take extra steps.

The Control class exposes a collection property named ViewState. The great thing about this collection is that it automatically saves and loads its content across page postbacks without any coding on your part. You should use this collection as the backing store for those properties of your custom control that need to maintain their values across page postbacks. In other words, the getters and setters of these properties must delegate to the ViewState collection instead of private fields.

Therefore, you now need to write a new custom control named CreditCardForm4, whose PaymentMethodText, CreditCardNoText, CardholderNameText, ExpirationDateText, and SubmitButtonText properties use ViewState as their backing store instead of private fields. This new control is shown in Listing 2-8.

As before, you can avoid having to reimplement the Render method and property- and class-level attributes by having CreditCardForm4 derive from CreditCardForm3. Because the properties of CreditCardForm3 are declared virtual, CreditCardForm4 can override them to provide its own implementation as shown in Listing 2-8.

Listing 2-8: Using ViewState as backing store for properties

```
public class CreditCardForm4 : CreditCardForm3
{
  public override string PaymentMethodText
  {
    get { return ViewState["PaymentMethodText"] != null ?
                     (string)ViewState["PaymentMethodText"] : "PaymentMethod"; }
    set { ViewState["PaymentMethodText"] = value; }
  }

  public override string CreditCardNoText
  {
    get { return ViewState["CreditCardNoText"] != null ?
                     (string)ViewState["CreditCardNoText"] : "CreditCardNo"; }
    set { ViewState["CreditCardNoText"] = value; }
  }

  public override string CardholderNameText
  {
    get { return ViewState["CardholderNameText"] != null ?
                  (string)ViewState["CardholderNameText"] : "CardholderName"; }
    set { ViewState["CardholderNameText"] = value; }
  }

  public override string ExpirationDateText
  {
```

```
        get { return ViewState["ExpirationDateText"] != null ?
                    (string)ViewState["ExpirationDateText"] : "Expiration Date"; }
        set { ViewState["ExpirationDateText"] = value; }
    }

    public override string SubmitButtonText
    {
        get { return ViewState["SubmitButtonText"] != null ?
                        (string)ViewState["SubmitButtonText"] : "Submit"; }
        set { ViewState["SubmitButtonText"] = value; }
    }
}
```

If you repeat the same exercise shown in Figures 2-3 and 2-4, you'll notice this time around the labels maintain their text values across page postbacks and are not reset to their default values. You can think of the ViewState collection as a bag of objects where you can put any type of object. In other words, this bag stores the values of the properties of your custom control as items of type System.Object regardless of their real types, and returns these values as items of type System.Object. That is why the getter of each property must convert (type cast) the item that it retrieves from the ViewState collection to the real type of the property before it returns the value.

At the end of each request, ASP.NET uses the type converter associated with each object contained in the ViewState to convert the object to its string representation. A type converter is a class that derives from the TypeConverter base class and knows how to convert its associated type to a given target type, such as System.String.

Basic .NET types such as Int32 and Boolean come with their own type converters such as Int32Converter and BooleanConverter. As you'll see in Chapter 7, you can write your own custom type converter that knows how to convert from your custom type to another type.

After converting each object to its string representation, ASP.NET stores these string values to a hidden field named __VIEWSTATE and sends them to the client. Therefore, the size of the string representations of the objects you store in ViewState matters.

When it comes to storing objects to ViewState you must keep the following two important things in mind:

❑   ViewState is optimized to convert certain types such as System.String, System.Int32, System.Boolean, System.Drawing.Color, System.Unit, and Hashtable, Array, and ArrayList of Int32, Boolean, Color, and Unit values. If your custom control needs to store other types to ViewState, you should write a custom type converter that is optimized to convert your custom type to its string representation.

❑   Because the string representations of the objects you add to ViewState are stored on the ASP.NET page, you must store only necessary information to ViewState to reduce the size of the ASP.NET page. For example, you shouldn't store values that you can easily evaluate for each request.

User Controls

In general there are two approaches to server control development. The previous sections discussed the first approach, also known as custom control development, where you derive from a base class such as `Control` to implement a server control.

This section discusses the second approach to server control development, known as *user control development*. Creating a user control is just like creating a regular ASP.NET Web page except for a few differences, as discussed shortly. Here are the main steps you must implement to create a user control:

1. Create a text file with the filename extension `.ascx`. This is the first difference between a user control and an ASP.NET Web page where the extension `.aspx` is used.

2. Add the `@Control` directive on the top of the text file and set its `Language` attribute to your language of choice, such as C#. This is the second difference between a user control and a Web page where the `@Page` directive is used instead of `@Control`.

3. Add HTML markup text and ASP.NET server controls to the text file. You can use any HTML tag except for `html`, `body`, and `form`. This is because user controls cannot be used alone and must be used as part of a hosting Web page. This is the third difference between a user control and a Web page. Because a Web page stands on its own, end users can directly access it. The same doesn't hold true for user controls.

As an example, develop the user control version of the `CreditCardForm4` custom control. This user control is named `CreditCardFormUserControl` as shown in Listing 2-9.

Listing 2-9: The CreditCardFormUserControl user control

```
<%@ Control Language="C#" %>

<table id="ccf" style="font-weight: bold;">
  <tr>
    <td>
      <asp:Label runat="server" ID="PaymentMethodLabel" Text="Payment Method"
      Font-Bold="true" />
    </td>
    <td>
      <asp:DropDownList runat="server" ID="PaymentMethodDropDownList" Width="100%">
        <asp:ListItem Text="Visa" Value="Visa" />
        <asp:ListItem Text="MasterCard" Value="MasterCard" />
      </asp:DropDownList>
    </td>
  </tr>
  <tr>
    <td>
      <asp:Label runat="server" ID="CreditCardNoLabel" Text="Credit Card No."
      Font-Bold="true" />
    </td>
    <td>
```

```
          <asp:TextBox runat="server" ID="CreditCardNoTextBox" />
        </td>
     </tr>
     <tr>
       <td>
         <asp:Label runat="server" ID="CardholderNameLabel"
         Text="Cardholder's Name" Font-Bold="true" />
       </td>
       <td>
         <asp:TextBox runat="server" ID="CardholderNameTextBox" />
       </td>
     </tr>
     <tr>
       <td>
         <asp:Label runat="server" ID="ExpirationDateLabel"
         Text="Expiration Date" Font-Bold="true" />
       </td>
       <td>
         <asp:DropDownList runat="server" ID="MonthDropDownList">
           <asp:ListItem Text="1" Value="1" />
           <asp:ListItem Text="2" Value="2" />
         </asp:DropDownList> 
         <asp:DropDownList runat="server" ID="YearDropDownList">
           <asp:ListItem Text="2005" Value="2005" />
           <asp:ListItem Text="2006" Value="2006" />
         </asp:DropDownList>
       </td>
     </tr>
     <tr>
       <td>
         <asp:Button runat="server" Text="Submit" ID="SubmitButton" />
       </td>
     </tr>
   </table>
```

Using a User Control

It's really easy to use a user control in a Web page:

1. Use the @Register directive to register the user control and respectively set the TagPrefix, TagName, and Src attributes of this directive to the tag prefix, tag name, and the path to the .ascx file that contains the user control. You can set the values of the tag prefix and tag name attributes to any valid string values as long as these two values together form a unique pair on the page.

2. Use the tag prefix and tag name to declare the tag that represents the user control. Because a user control is a server control, you must also set the value of the runat attribute.

Listing 2-10 contains a Web page that uses the CreditCardFormUserControl user control.

Listing 2-10: A Web page that uses the CreditCardFormUserControl user control

```
<%@ Page Language="C#" %>
<%@ Register TagPrefix="user" TagName="CreditCardForm"
Src="~/CreditCardFormUserControl.ascx" %>
<html xmlns="http://www.w3.org/1999/xhtml">
<body>
  <form id="form1" runat="server">
    <user:CreditCardForm runat="server" ID="CreditCardForm1" />
  </form>
</body>
</html>
```

Adding Properties to User Controls

You can add custom properties to user controls as you did for custom controls to allow the page developer to customize the control. Listing 2-11 shows a version of the CreditCardFormUserControl that exposes properties that the page developer can use to set the labels on the control. Notice that each property delegates to the Text property of its associated Label server control. This control, like all server controls, manages its state across page postbacks, which means that you don't need and shouldn't use the ViewState collection to store the values of these properties.

Listing 2-11: Adding properties to a user control

```
<%@ Control Language="C#" ClassName="CreditCardFormUserControl" %>

<script runat="server">
  public virtual string PaymentMethodText
  {
    get { return PaymentMethodLabel.Text; }
    set { PaymentMethodLabel.Text = value; }
  }

  public virtual string CreditCardNoText
  {
    get { return CreditCardNoLabel.Text; }
    set { CreditCardNoLabel.Text = value; }
  }

  public virtual string CardholderNameText
  {
    get { return CardholderNameLabel.Text; }
    set { CardholderNameLabel.Text = value; }
  }

  public virtual string ExpirationDateText
  {
    get { return ExpirationDateLabel.Text; }
    set { ExpirationDateLabel.Text = value; }
  }

  public virtual string SubmitButtonText
  {
    get { return SubmitButton.Text; }
```

```
      set { SubmitButton.Text = value; }
    }
</script>

<table id="ccf" style="font-weight: bold;">
  <tr>
    <td>
      <asp:Label runat="server" ID="PaymentMethodLabel" Text="Payment Method"
      Font-Bold="true" />
    </td>
    <td>
      <asp:DropDownList runat="server" ID="PaymentMethodDropDownList" Width="100%">
        <asp:ListItem Text="Visa" Value="Visa" />
        <asp:ListItem Text="MasterCard" Value="MasterCard" />
      </asp:DropDownList>
    </td>
  </tr>
  <tr>
    <td>
      <asp:Label runat="server" ID="CreditCardNoLabel" Text="Credit Card No."
      Font-Bold="true" />
    </td>
    <td>
      <asp:TextBox runat="server" ID="CreditCardNoTextBox" />
    </td>
  </tr>
  <tr>
    <td>
      <asp:Label runat="server" ID="CardholderNameLabel" Text="Cardholder's Name"
      Font-Bold="true" />
    </td>
    <td>
      <asp:TextBox runat="server" ID="CardholderNameTextBox" />
    </td>
  </tr>
  <tr>
    <td>
      <asp:Label runat="server" ID="ExpirationDateLabel" Text="Expiration Date"
      Font-Bold="true" />
    </td>
    <td>
      <asp:DropDownList runat="server" ID="MonthDropDownList">
        <asp:ListItem Text="1" Value="1" />
        <asp:ListItem Text="2" Value="2" />
      </asp:DropDownList> 
      <asp:DropDownList runat="server" ID="YearDropDownList">
        <asp:ListItem Text="2005" Value="2005" />
        <asp:ListItem Text="2006" Value="2006" />
      </asp:DropDownList>
    </td>
  </tr>
  <tr>
    <td>
      <asp:Button runat="server" Text="Submit" ID="SubmitButton" />
    </td>
  </tr>
</table>
```

Adding Methods to User Controls

You can add custom methods to your user control, which page developers can call from their code. For example, Listing 2-12 illustrates a version of the `CreditCardFormUserControl` user control that exposes a method named `SetExpirationDate` that page developers can call from their programs to programmatically set the expiration date.

Listing 2-12: Adding methods to a user control

```
<%@ Control Language="C#" ClassName="CreditCardFormUserControl" %>

<script runat="server">
  public void SetExpirationDate(DateTime expirationDate)
  {
    ListItem monthItem =
            MonthDropDownList.Items.FindByValue(expirationDate.Month.ToString());
    int monthIndex = MonthDropDownList.Items.IndexOf(monthItem);
    MonthDropDownList.SelectedIndex = monthIndex;

    ListItem yearItem =
             YearDropDownList.Items.FindByValue(expirationDate.Year.ToString());
    int yearIndex = YearDropDownList.Items.IndexOf(yearItem);
    YearDropDownList.SelectedIndex = yearIndex;
  }
</script>

<table id="ccf" style="font-weight: bold;">
  <tr>
    <td>
      <asp:Label runat="server" ID="PaymentMethodLabel" Text="Payment Method"
      Font-Bold="true" />
    </td>
    <td>
      <asp:DropDownList runat="server" ID="PaymentMethodDropDownList" Width="100%">
        <asp:ListItem Text="Visa" Value="Visa" />
        <asp:ListItem Text="MasterCard" Value="MasterCard" />
      </asp:DropDownList>
    </td>
  </tr>
  <tr>
    <td>
      <asp:Label runat="server" ID="CreditCardNoLabel" Text="Credit Card No."
      Font-Bold="true" />
    </td>
    <td>
      <asp:TextBox runat="server" ID="CreditCardNoTextBox" />
    </td>
  </tr>
  <tr>
    <td>
      <asp:Label runat="server" ID="CardholderNameLabel" Text="Cardholder's Name"
      Font-Bold="true" />
    </td>
</table>
```

```
        <td>
          <asp:TextBox runat="server" ID="CardholderNameTextBox" />
        </td>
      </tr>
      <tr>
        <td>
          <asp:Label runat="server" ID="ExpirationDateLabel" Text="Expiration Date"
          Font-Bold="true" />
        </td>
        <td>
          <asp:DropDownList runat="server" ID="MonthDropDownList">
            <asp:ListItem Text="1" Value="1" />
            <asp:ListItem Text="2" Value="2" />
          </asp:DropDownList> 
          <asp:DropDownList runat="server" ID="YearDropDownList">
            <asp:ListItem Text="2005" Value="2005" />
            <asp:ListItem Text="2006" Value="2006" />
          </asp:DropDownList>
        </td>
      </tr>
      <tr>
        <td>
          <asp:Button runat="server" Text="Submit" ID="SubmitButton" />
        </td>
      </tr>
    </table>
```

Listing 2-13 contains a Web page that calls the `SetExpirationDate` method of the
`CreditCardFormUserControl` control.

Listing 2-13: A Web page that uses SetExpirationDate

```
<%@ Page Language="C#" %>
<%@ Register TagPrefix="user" TagName="CreditCardForm"
Src="~/CreditCardFormUserControl.ascx" %>

<script runat="server">
  void Page_Load(object sender, EventArgs e)
  {
    CreditCardForm1.SetExpirationDate(DateTime.Now);
  }
</script>

<html xmlns="http://www.w3.org/1999/xhtml">
<body>
  <form id="form1" runat="server">
    <user:CreditCardForm runat="server" ID="CreditCardForm1" />
  </form>
</body>
</html>
```

You'll see more examples of user controls in Chapters 28, 29, 30, and 31, where user controls are placed
in `WebPartZoneBase` zones to act as Web Part controls.

Under the Hood

The page framework processes an `.ascx` file (a user control) the same way it processes an `.aspx` file, with few differences:

1. First it parses the `.ascx` file as it does the `.aspx` file.

2. It then dynamically generates a class that represents the content of the `.ascx` file. The big difference between this class and the dynamically generated class that represents an `.aspx` file is that the former derives from the `UserControl` base class, whereas the latter derives from the `Page` base class. The @`Control` directive exposes an attribute named `ClassName` that you can use to specify the name of this dynamically generated class. If you don't set this attribute, the page framework appends the `_ascx` string to the .ascx filename and uses that as the name of the class. For example, if you've saved the `UserControlCreditCardForm` user control in a file named `UserControlCreditCardForm.ascx`, the page framework will use the `UserControlCreditCardForm_ascx` string as the name of the dynamically generated class. Because there is no guarantee that the page framework will always follow this naming convention, you should always set this attribute.

   Recall that the page developer can set the `TagPrefix` and `TagName` attributes of the `Register` directive to any desired string value. As discussed, the page developer uses the combination of the `TagPrefix` and `TagName` to declare the associated user control on an ASP.NET page. This may seem to suggest that the actual name of the dynamically generated class shouldn't really matter to the page developer.

   This statement is true as long as the page developer uses the user control declaratively on an ASP.NET page. However, there are times when the page developer may have to use the `FindControl` method of the containing page to access the user control programmatically from within their C# or VB.NET code. The `FindControl` method returns the user control as an object of type `Control`. If you set the `ClassName` attribute, you'll make it possible for page developers to type cast the return value of this method to the actual type of the user control so they can access its properties and methods in programmatic fashion.

3. The framework dynamically compiles the class.

4. It caches the compiled class in the `Cache` object.

5. It dynamically creates an instance of the compiled class.

As this discussion shows, user controls use the same development pattern as regular ASP.NET pages. This development pattern is characterized by the following two important characteristics:

❑ You can use a drag-and-drop WYSIWYG approach to develop your user control in the Visual Studio environment with minimal efforts. You can't do the same with custom controls.

❑ Programmers who feel more comfortable with declarative programming languages such as HTML and XML should feel at home with user controls where they can use HTML-like tags to declaratively develop the control without writing a lot of code in a procedural language such as C# or VB.NET. As discussed in the previous section, the page framework parses this declarative code into .NET managed code. In other words, user controls make life easy on declarative programmers by putting the burden of generating the code on the page framework. Custom controls, on the other hand, put the burden of writing the code entirely on the programmer. Custom controls are on the other extreme of the programming spectrum where nothing can be implemented in an HTML-like language.

However, all this convenience comes with a price. You lose the flexibility and extensibility that custom controls provide. You'll see ample examples of this flexibility and extensibility in this book. That said, user controls play an important role in ASP.NET Web Parts Framework. This is discussed thoroughly in Chapters 28, 29, 30, and 31, where user controls are placed in `WebPartZoneBase` zones to act as runtime `WebPart` controls.

Summary

This chapter showed you how to develop a simple custom control that derives from the `Control` base class, deploy it, and use your custom control in an ASP.NET page. You also learned how to add simple properties to your custom control, annotate your custom controls with design-time attributes to smoothly integrate your control into the Visual Studio environment, and add your custom control to the Visual Studio Toolbox. It also discussed the issue of maintaining state in a Web application, and showed you how to use the `ViewState` object to manage the state of your controls across page postbacks.

After the discussion of custom controls, you learned how to develop user controls and how to add properties and methods to user controls.

Now that you have a handle on what simple custom controls are and what they do, you're ready to move on to the next chapter where you learn how to enable your custom controls to expose CSS style attributes as top-level, strongly typed style properties.

3

Developing Custom-Styled Controls

In the previous chapter you developed three different versions of the credit card form custom control named `CreditCardForm2`, `CreditCardForm3`, and `CreditCardForm4`. As discussed, each version derives from the previous version to inherit the desired features and to extend it to add support for new features. That is, `CreditCardForm4` derives from `CreditCardForm3`, which in turn derives from `CreditCardForm2`, which derives from the `Control` base class.

The `Control` class isn't the only available base class. Another important base class is the `WebControl` class. `WebControl` derives from `Control` and uses an instance of an ASP.NET class named `Style` to add support for strongly typed style properties. This chapter begins by discussing the `Style` class and shows you how this class manages to expose CSS style attributes as strongly typed style properties. You then examine `WebControl` and implement a new version of the credit card form custom control named `CreditCardForm5`, which derives from `WebControl`.

Style

As shown in Listing 2-6 in the preceding chapter, the `Render` method of the `CreditCardForm3` and `CreditCardForm4` controls calls the `AddStyleAttribute` method of the `HtmlTextWriter` class multiple times to render the CSS style attributes of the `table` HTML element. The portion of this code is repeated in Listing 3-1.

Listing 3-1: The portion of Listing 2-6 that generates the style attributes of the table HTML element

```
writer.AddStyleAttribute(HtmlTextWriterStyle.Width, "287px");
writer.AddStyleAttribute(HtmlTextWriterStyle.Height, "124px");
writer.AddStyleAttribute(HtmlTextWriterStyle.BorderWidth, "0");
writer.RenderBeginTag(HtmlTextWriterTag.Table);
...
Writer.RenderEndTag();
```

As Listing 3-1 shows, the second argument of the AddStyleAttribute method is a string that contains the value of the CSS style attribute specified in the first argument. In other words, AddStyleAttribute treats the CSS style attribute values as string values. The trouble with string values is that they aren't type-safe and are therefore error-prone. For example, the following typo in the string value of the border-width CSS style attribute will not be caught until runtime, when it's too late:

```
writer.AddStyleAttribute(HtmlTextWriterStyle.BorderWidth, ")");
```

The Style class provides a solution that consists of the following steps:

1.   Exposes the CSS style attributes as strongly typed properties. This provides you with the following benefits:

  a.   You can take advantage of the Visual Studio's IntelliSense support to catch the errors as you're writing the code.

  b.   You can take advantage of the type-checking capability of compilers to catch the errors as you're compiling the code.

  For example, the Style class exposes the border-width CSS style attribute as a property of type Unit named BorderWidth. Because the BorderWidth property is typed, both the Visual Studio's IntelliSense and compiler easily detect the typo, that is, ")".

2.   Automatically maps its strongly typed properties to their respective CSS style attributes and calls the AddStyleAttribute method of the HtmlTextWriter class as many times as necessary to render these CSS style attributes. All you have to do is set the properties of the Style class. The mapping and rendering is automatically taken care of.

The Style class exposes the following properties to represent common CSS style attributes:

❑   public Color BackColor { get; set; }

❑   public Color BorderColor { get; set; }

❑   public BorderStyle BorderStyle { get; set; }

❑   public Unit BorderWidth { get; set; }

❑   public string CssClass { get; set; }

❑   public FontInfo Font { get; }

❑   public Color ForeColor { get; set; }

❑   `public Unit Height { get; set; }`

❑   `public Unit Width { get; set; }`

As you can see, the `Style` class doesn't support all CSS style attributes. This is where its subclasses come into play. For example, the `TableStyle` class derives from the `Style` base class and extends its functionality to add support for table-related CSS style attributes.

As a matter of fact, as you'll see later in this chapter, you can implement your own style class that derives from the `Style` class or one of its subclasses and extends it to add support for CSS style attributes that none of the existing `Style` subclasses support.

WebControl

The `Render` method of a server control generates the HTML markup text that the client browser uses to display the control. For example, Listing 3-2 shows the HTML markup text generated by the `Render` method of the `CreditCardForm3` control.

Listing 3-2: The HTML markup text that the Render method of the CreditCardForm3 control generates

```
!-- This HTML block contains the opening tag of the containing HTML element -->
<table


<!-- This HTML block contains the HTML attributes of the containing HTML element -->
id="mytable"
style="width:287px; height:124px; border-width:0;">


<!-- This HTML block contains the nested HTML within the opening and closing
     tags of the containing HTML element -->
<tr>
  <td><strong>Payment Method</strong></td>
  <td>
    <select style="width:100%;">
      <option value="Visa">Visa</option>
      <option value="MasterCard">MasterCard</option>
    </select>
  </td>
</tr>
<tr>
  <td><strong>Credit Card No.</strong></td><td><input type="text" /></td>
</tr>
<tr>
  <td><strong>Cardholder'name</strong></td><td><input type="text" /></td>
</tr>
<tr>
  <td><strong>Expiration Date</strong></td>
```

(continued)

Listing 3-2: *(continued)*

```
      <td>
        <select>
          <option value="1">01</option>
          ...
        </select> 
        <select>
          <option value="2005">2005</option>
          ...
        </select>
      </td>
    </tr>
    <tr>
      <td><input type="submit" value="Submit" /></td>
    </tr>


    <!-- This HTML block contains the closing tag of the containing HTML element ‡
    </table>
```

As Listing 3-2 shows, the HTML markup text that the `Render` method of a control generates can be divided into four HTML blocks.

The first HTML block contains the opening tag of the outermost element, also known as the *containing* HTML element. As the name implies, this element contains all of the other elements in the HTML markup text that the `Render` method generates. Every control normally has a single outermost or containing HTML element. For example, the containing HTML element of `CreditCardForm3` is a `table` HTML element.

The second HTML block contains the attributes of the containing HTML element. For example, the second HTML block in Listing 3-2 contains the attributes of the containing `table` HTML element of `CreditCardForm3`:

```
id="mytable" style="width:287px; height:124px; border-width:0;"
```

The third HTML block contains the nested HTML content within the opening and closing tags of the containing HTML element. For example, the third HTML block in Listing 3-2 contains the nested HTML within the opening and closing tags of the containing `table` HTML element of `CreditCardForm3` as shown here:

```
    <tr>
      <td><strong>Payment Method</strong></td>
      <td>
        <select style="width:100%;">
          <option value="Visa">Visa</option>
          <option value="MasterCard">MasterCard</option>
        </select>
      </td>
    </tr>
    <tr>
```

```
    <td><strong>Credit Card No.</strong></td><td><input type="text" /></td>
  </tr>
  <tr>
    <td><strong>Cardholder'name</strong></td><td><input type="text" /></td>
  </tr>
  <tr>
    <td><strong>Expiration Date</strong></td>
    <td>
      <select>
        <option value="1">01</option>
        ...
      </select> 
      <select>
        <option value="2005">2005</option>
        ...
      </select>
    </td>
  </tr>
  <tr>
    <td><input type="submit" value="Submit" /></td>
  </tr>
```

Finally, the fourth HTML block contains the closing tag of the containing HTML element. For example, the fourth HTML block in Listing 3-2 contains the closing tag of the containing `table` HTML element of `CreditCardForm3` control.

Listing 3-3 shows a portion of Listing 2-6. Recall that this listing contains the code for the `Render` method of the `CreditCardForm3` control. As Listing 3-3 shows, the `Render` method of a control can be divided into four code blocks, where each code block is responsible for rendering one of the four HTML blocks just discussed.

The first code block renders the second HTML block, that is, the HTML attributes of the containing HTML element. For example, the first code block in Listing 3-3 renders the second HTML block in Listing 3-2, the id and `style` HTML attributes of the containing `table` HTML element of the `CreditCardForm3` control:

```
w.AddAttribute(HtmlTextWriterAttribute.Id,"mytable");
w.AddStyleAttribute(HtmlTextWriterStyle.Width,"287px");
w.AddStyleAttribute(HtmlTextWriterStyle.Height,"124px");
w.AddStyleAttribute(HtmlTextWriterStyle.BorderWidth,"0");
```

The second code block renders the first HTML block, that is, the opening tag of the containing HTML element. For example, the second code block in Listing 3-3 renders the first HTML block in Listing 3-2, the opening tag of the containing `table` HTML element of the `CreditCardForm3` control:

```
w.RenderBeginTag(HtmlTextWriterTag.Table);
```

The third code block renders the third HTML block, that is, the nested HTML within the opening and closing tags of the containing HTML element. For example, the third code block in Listing 3-3 renders the third HTML block in Listing 3-2, the nested HTML within the opening and closing tags of the containing `table` HTML element:

```
    w.RenderBeginTag(HtmlTextWriterTag.Tr);
    w.RenderBeginTag(HtmlTextWriterTag.Td);
    w.Write(PaymentMethodText);
    w.RenderEndTag();
    ...
```

The fourth code block renders the fourth HTML block, that is, the closing tag of the containing HTML element. For example, the fourth code block in Listing 3-3 renders the fourth HTML block in Listing 3-2, the closing tag of the containing `table` HTML element of the `CreditCardForm3` control:

```
    w.RenderEndTag();
```

Listing 3-3: The Render method of the CreditCardForm3 control

```
protected override void Render(HtmlTextWriter w)
{
    // This code block renders the second HTML block in Listing 3-2, i.e. the id and
    // style HTML attributes of the containing table HTML element
    w.AddAttribute(HtmlTextWriterAttribute.Id,"mytable");
    w.AddStyleAttribute(HtmlTextWriterStyle.Width,"287px");
    w.AddStyleAttribute(HtmlTextWriterStyle.Height,"124px");
    w.AddStyleAttribute(HtmlTextWriterStyle.BorderWidth,"0");


    // This code block renders the first HTML block in Listing 3-2, i.e. the opening
    // tag of the containing table HTML element
    w.RenderBeginTag(HtmlTextWriterTag.Table);


    // This code block renders the third HTML block in Listing 3-2, i.e. the nested
    //    HTML within the opening and closing tags of the containing table HTML element
    w.RenderBeginTag(HtmlTextWriterTag.Tr);
    w.RenderBeginTag(HtmlTextWriterTag.Td);
    w.Write(PaymentMethodText);
    w.RenderEndTag();
    ...


    // This code block renders the fourth HTML block in Listing 3-2, i.e. the closing
    // tag of the containing table HTML element
    w.RenderEndTag();
}
```

As you can see, the `Render` method of a control such as `CreditCardForm3` contains four different code blocks, and each block renders a completely different type of HTML markup text. This is not a good method design because a method must be specifically designed to perform a single task. If your method is doing too many things, every time you make a little code change, you may end up breaking something else because everything is so tangled together.

Imagine that someone wants to render a new attribute on the containing `table` HTML element. The page developer has no choice but to override the entire `Render` method, including those parts that have absolutely nothing to do with the new attribute. Why should this person reimplement the nested HTML within the opening and closing tags of the containing `table` element, if all the developer wants to do is to render a simple attribute on the containing element itself? Enter `WebControl`.

The WebControl class takes a completely different approach. Instead of sticking all of the previously mentioned four code blocks in one method (Render), WebControl delegates the responsibility of rendering each of the four HTML blocks to a separate method as shown in the following table:

Method	Description
protected virtual void AddAttributesToRender(HtmlTextWriter writer)	The subclasses of the WebControl should override this method to contain the code block that renders the HTML attributes of the containing HTML element.
public virtual void RenderBeginTag(HtmlTextWriter writer)	The subclasses of the WebControl should override this method to contain the code block that renders the opening tag of the containing HTML element.
protected virtual void RenderContents(HtmlTextWriter writer)	The subclasses of the WebControl should override this method to contain the code block that renders the nested HTML within the opening and closing tags of the containing HTML element.
public virtual void RenderEndTag(HtmlTextWriter writer)	The subclasses of the WebControl should override this method to contain the code block that renders the closing tag of the containing HTML element.

Overriding the Render Method

WebControl derives from the Control class, and overrides its Render method to delegate the responsibility of rendering the previously mentioned four HTML blocks to their associated methods, as shown in Listing 3-4.

Listing 3-4: The WebControl class's implementation of the Render method

```
protected internal override void Render(HtmlTextWriter writer)
{
  RenderBeginTag(writer);
  RenderContents(writer);
  RenderEndTag(writer);
}
```

You may be wondering what ever happened to RenderAttributes method. As you'll see shortly, this method is called from within the RenderBeginTag.

TagKey

The containing element, by default, is a span HTML element. In other words, the RenderBeginTag and RenderEndTag methods generate the opening and closing tags of the span HTML element (<span> and </span>). However, the WebControl class doesn't hard-code the span HTML element as the containing element. Instead, it exposes a read-only property named TagKey that specifies the HTML element that will be used as the containing HTML element.

47

As you'll see later, you can override the TagKey property to specify an HTML element of your choice as the containing HTML element of your custom control. The TagKey property is of type HtmlTextWriterTag enumeration. Because this enumeration doesn't support all possible HTML tags, WebControl exposes another property of type string named TagName that you can override to use an HTML element that this enumeration doesn't support. Listing 3-5 shows how the TagKey property is implemented.

Listing 3-5: The WebControl class's implementation of the TagKey property

```
protected virtual HtmlTextWriterTag TagKey
{
  get {return HtmlTextWriterTag.Span;}
}
```

RenderBeginTag

Listing 3-6 shows how the RenderBeginTag method uses the TagKey and TagName properties to render the opening tag of the containing HTML element.

Listing 3-6: The WebControl class's implementation of the RenderBeginTag method

```
public virtual void RenderBeginTag(HtmlTextWriter writer)
{
  AddAttributesToRender(writer);
  if (TagKey != HtmlTextWriterTag.Unknown)
    writer.RenderBeginTag(TagKey);
  else
    writer.RenderBeginTag(this.TagName);
}
```

As Listing 3-6 shows, RenderBeginTag takes the following steps:

1. Calls the AddAttributesToRender method to generate the HTML attributes of the containing HTML element.

2. Calls the RenderBeginTag method of the HtmlTextWriter object and passes the value of the TagKey or TagName property into it to render the opening tag of the containing element.

AddAttributesToRender

Listing 3-7 shows the WebControl class's implementation of the AddAttributesToRender method.

Listing 3-7: The WebControl class's implementation of the AddAttributesToRender method

```
protected virtual void AddAttributesToRender(HtmlTextWriter writer)
{
  writer.AddAttribute(HtmlTextWriterAttribute.Id, ClientID);
  writer.AddAttribute(HtmlTextWriterAttribute.Accesskey, AccessKey);

  if (!this.Enabled)
```

```
        writer.AddAttribute(HtmlTextWriterAttribute.Disabled, "disabled");

    writer.AddAttribute(HtmlTextWriterAttribute.Tabindex, TabIndex.ToString());
    writer.AddAttribute(HtmlTextWriterAttribute.Title, ToolTip);

    ControlStyle.AddAttributesToRender(writer, this);

    AttributeCollection collection1 = this.Attributes;
    IEnumerator iter = Attributes.Keys.GetEnumerator();
    while (iter.MoveNext())
    {
      string key = (string)iter.Current;
      writer.AddAttribute(key, Attributes[key]);
    }
}
```

Recall that the main responsibility of the `AddAttributesToRender` method is to render the HTML attributes of the containing HTML element. These HTML attributes can be divided into two groups as follows:

❑ CSS style attributes such as `width`, `height`, and `border-width`

❑ Non-CSS style attributes such as `id`, `title`, `tabindex`, `accesskey`, and `disabled`

Non-CSS Style Attributes

`WebControl` exposes five properties named `ClientID`, `AccessKey`, `Enabled`, `Tabindex`, and `ToolTip` to represent the `id`, `accesskey`, `disabled`, `tabindex`, and `title` HTML attributes of the containing HTML element. As the highlighted code in Listing 3-8 shows, the `AddAttributesToRender` method calls the `AddAttribute` method of the `HtmlTextWriter` object once for each of these five HTML attributes and passes the value of the respective property into it.

Listing 3-8: AddAttributesToRender renders non-CSS style attributes of the containing element

---

```
protected virtual void AddAttributesToRender(HtmlTextWriter writer)
{
  writer.AddAttribute(HtmlTextWriterAttribute.Id, ClientID);
  writer.AddAttribute(HtmlTextWriterAttribute.Accesskey, AccessKey);

  if (!this.Enabled)
    writer.AddAttribute(HtmlTextWriterAttribute.Disabled, "disabled");

  writer.AddAttribute(HtmlTextWriterAttribute.Tabindex, TabIndex.ToString());
  writer.AddAttribute(HtmlTextWriterAttribute.Title, ToolTip);

  ControlStyle.AddAttributesToRender(writer, this);

  AttributeCollection collection1 = this.Attributes;
  IEnumerator iter = Attributes.Keys.GetEnumerator();
  while (iter.MoveNext())
  {
```

(continued)

Listing 3-8: *(continued)*

```
        string key = (string)iter.Current;
        writer.AddAttribute(key, Attributes[key]);
    }
}
```

The possible HTML non-CSS style attributes of the containing HTML element aren't limited to the `id`, `accesskey`, `disabled`, `tabindex`, and `title` HTML attributes. In other words, `WebControl` doesn't expose strongly typed properties for all HTML non-CSS style attributes. If you need to set an HTML attribute that has no associated strongly typed property, you can add the attribute and its value to the `Attributes` collection property of the `WebControl` class.

As the highlighted code in Listing 3-9 shows, the `AddAttributesToRender` method iterates through the HTML attributes contained in the `Attributes` collection and calls the `AddAttribute` method of the `HtmlTextWriter` object once for each enumerated attribute.

Listing 3-9: AddAttributesToRender renders the contents of the Attributes collection

```
protected virtual void AddAttributesToRender(HtmlTextWriter writer)
{
    writer.AddAttribute(HtmlTextWriterAttribute.Id, ClientID);
    writer.AddAttribute(HtmlTextWriterAttribute.Accesskey, AccessKey);

    if (!this.Enabled)
        writer.AddAttribute(HtmlTextWriterAttribute.Disabled, "disabled");

    writer.AddAttribute(HtmlTextWriterAttribute.Tabindex, TabIndex.ToString());
    writer.AddAttribute(HtmlTextWriterAttribute.Title, ToolTip);

    ControlStyle.AddAttributesToRender(writer, this);

    AttributeCollection collection1 = this.Attributes;
    IEnumerator iter = Attributes.Keys.GetEnumerator();
    while (iter.MoveNext())
    {
        string key = (string)iter.Current;
        writer.AddAttribute(key, Attributes[key]);
    }
}
```

CSS Style Attributes

The `AddAttributesToRender` method of `WebControl` doesn't directly call the `AddStyleAttribute` method of the `HtmlTextWriter` object to render the CSS style attributes as it did to render non-CSS style attributes. As the highlighted code in Listing 3-10 shows, the `AddAttributesToRender` method calls the `AddAttributesToRender` method of the `ControlStyle` property of the `WebControl` class and passes the `HtmlTextWriter` object into it.

Listing 3-10: AddAttributesToRender delegates the rendering of the CSS style attributes to ControlStyle

```
protected virtual void AddAttributesToRender(HtmlTextWriter writer)
{
  writer.AddAttribute(HtmlTextWriterAttribute.Id, ClientID);
  writer.AddAttribute(HtmlTextWriterAttribute.Accesskey, AccessKey);

  if (!this.Enabled)
    writer.AddAttribute(HtmlTextWriterAttribute.Disabled, "disabled");

  writer.AddAttribute(HtmlTextWriterAttribute.Tabindex, TabIndex.ToString());
  writer.AddAttribute(HtmlTextWriterAttribute.Title, ToolTip);

  ControlStyle.AddAttributesToRender(writer, this);

  AttributeCollection collection1 = this.Attributes;
  IEnumerator iter = Attributes.Keys.GetEnumerator();
  while (iter.MoveNext())
  {
    string key = (string)iter.Current;
    writer.AddAttribute(key, Attributes[key]);
  }
}
```

The `AddAttributesToRender` method of the `WebControl` class delegates the responsibility of calling the `HtmlTextWriter` object to render the CSS style attributes to the `AddAttributesToRender` method of the `ControlStyle` property of the `WebControl` class.

Listing 3-11 contains the definition of the `ControlStyle` property.

Listing 3-11: The ControlStyle property of the WebControl class

```
private Style controlStyle;
public Style ControlStyle
{
  get
  {
    if (controlStyle == null)
    {
      controlStyle = CreateControlStyle();
      ...
    }
    return this.controlStyle;
  }
}
```

The `WebControl` class's implementation of the `ControlStyle` property doesn't directly contain the code that creates the `style` object. Instead, it delegates the responsibility of creating the style object to the `CreateControlStyle` method of the `WebControl` class.

As Listing 3-12 shows, the WebControl class's implementation of the CreateControlStyle method creates an instance of the Style class.

Listing 3-12: The WebControl class's implementation of the CreateControlStyle method

```
protected virtual Style CreateControlStyle()
{
  return new Style(ViewState);
}
```

You can override this method to create an instance of an appropriate Style subclass. For example, as you'll see later in this chapter, because CreditCardForm5 displays its contents in a table, it makes more sense to use an instance of the TableStyle class than the generic Style class. One thing to keep in mind is that you have to pass the ViewState collection of your control to the constructor of the Style subclass. In other words, your control must share its ViewState with its ControlStyle.

RenderContents

RenderContents renders the contents within the opening and closing tags of the containing HTML element. Listing 3-13 shows the WebControl class's implementation of the RenderContent method.

Listing 3-13: The WebControl class's implementation of RenderContents

```
protected internal virtual void RenderContents(HtmlTextWriter writer)
{
  base.Render(writer);
}
```

Notice that RenderContents doesn't render HTML markup text on its own, and simply calls the Render method of its base class, that is, the Control class. It's the responsibility of the subclasses of the WebControl class to override the RenderContents method to generate the desired HTML markup text. As you'll see later in this chapter, the CreditCardForm5 custom control overrides this method to generate the HTML markup text that displays the credit card form control on the client browser.

RenderEndTag

RenderEndTag generates the closing tag of the containing HTML element, which is </span> by default. As Listing 3-14 shows, the WebControl class's implementation of the RenderEndTag method simply calls the RenderEndTag method of the HtmlTextWriter object to render the closing tag.

Listing 3-14: The WebControl class's implementation of RenderEndTag

```
public virtual void RenderEndTag(HtmlTextWriter writer)
{
  writer.RenderEndTag();
}
```

In summary, when you implement a custom control that derives from WebControl you can override the following methods and properties of the WebControl class:

- ❑ `TagKey`: Override this property if your custom control needs to use a different containing HTML element than the default `span` HTML element.

- ❑ `TagName`: Override this property if your custom control needs to use an HTML element as the containing HTML element that the `HtmlTextWriterTag` enumeration doesn't support.

- ❑ `AddAttributesToRender`: As mentioned, `WebControl` doesn't expose properties for all possible HTML attributes of the containing HTML element. When you write a custom control that exposes one or more properties to represent the HTML attributes that `WebControl` doesn't support, you have to override the `AddAttributesToRender` method to use these new properties to render the respective HTML attributes.

- ❑ `RenderBeginTag`: Override this property if your custom control needs to use multiple opening tags. This happens very rarely, but you can do it if you need to.

- ❑ `RenderContents`: Override this method to render the HTML contents of your custom control.

- ❑ `RenderEndTag`: Override this method if your custom control needs to use multiple closing tags associated with the multiple opening tags mentioned before.

Deriving from the WebControl Class

In this section you implement a custom control named `CreditCardForm5` that derives from `WebControl` and overrides its methods and properties.

Because `CreditCardForm5` displays its contents in a table, you first need to override the `TagKey` property of `WebControl` to specify the `table` HTML element as the containing element:

```
protected override HtmlTextWriterTag TagKey
{
   get { return HtmlTextWriterTag.Table; }
}
```

Next, because the `table` HTML element is used as the containing element, override the `CreateControlStyle` method of `WebControl` to specify a `TableStyle` object as the `ControlStyle` as shown in Listing 3-15.

Listing 3-15: The CreateControlStyle method

```
protected override Style CreateControlStyle()
{
   return new TableStyle(ViewState);
}
```

As mentioned earlier, you must pass the `ViewState` collection of the `CreditCardForm5` control to the constructor of the `TableStyle` class because the control must share its `ViewState` with its `ControlStyle`.

Because the `TableStyle` class derives from the `Style` class, it inherits all of the properties that the `Style` class exposes, such as `BackColor`, `BorderColor`, `BorderStyle`, `BorderWidth`, `CssClass`, `Font`, `Height`, `Width`, and `ForeColor`. The `TableStyle` class also exposes properties of its own, including `GridLines`, `CellSpacing`, `CellPadding`, `HorizontalAlign`, and `BackImageUrl`.

CreditCardForm5 must expose one property for each new property of the TableStyle class, where the getter and setter of the property must delegate to the respective property of the TableStyle class as shown in the following code:

```
public virtual GridLines GridLines
{
  get { return ((TableStyle)ControlStyle).GridLines; }
  set { ((TableStyle)ControlStyle).GridLines = value; }
}

public virtual int CellSpacing
{
  get { return ((TableStyle)ControlStyle).CellSpacing; }
  set { ((TableStyle)ControlStyle).CellSpacing = value; }
}

public virtual int CellPadding
{
  get { return ((TableStyle)ControlStyle).CellPadding; }
  set { ((TableStyle)ControlStyle).CellPadding = value; }
}

public virtual HorizontalAlign HorizontalAlign
{
  get { return ((TableStyle)ControlStyle).HorizontalAlign; }
  set { ((TableStyle)ControlStyle).HorizontalAlign = value; }
}

public virtual string BackImageUrl
{
  get { return ((TableStyle)ControlStyle).BackImageUrl; }
  set { ((TableStyle)ControlStyle).BackImageUrl = value; }
}
```

As this code shows, you must declare these properties as virtual to allow others to override them to provide their own implementations. You may be wondering about the properties that the TableStyle class inherits from the Style class. WebControl has already taken care of these properties for you. In other words, following the same approach as yours, WebControl exposes properties whose getters and setters delegate to the respective properties of the Style class. Because CreditCardForm5 derives from WebControl, it automatically inherits these properties.

Finally, you must override the RenderContents method of WebControl as shown in Listing 3-16.

Listing 3-16: The overridden RenderContents method

```
protected override void RenderContents(HtmlTextWriter writer)
{
  writer.RenderBeginTag(HtmlTextWriterTag.Tr);
  writer.RenderBeginTag(HtmlTextWriterTag.Td);
  writer.Write(PaymentMethodText);
  writer.RenderEndTag();
  writer.RenderBeginTag(HtmlTextWriterTag.Td);
  writer.AddAttribute(HtmlTextWriterAttribute.Name, PaymentMethodSelectName);
```

```
writer.AddAttribute(HtmlTextWriterAttribute.Id, PaymentMethodSelectId);
writer.AddStyleAttribute(HtmlTextWriterStyle.Width, "100%");
writer.RenderBeginTag(HtmlTextWriterTag.Select);

writer.AddAttribute(HtmlTextWriterAttribute.Value, "0");
writer.RenderBeginTag(HtmlTextWriterTag.Option);
writer.Write("Visa");
writer.RenderEndTag();

writer.AddAttribute(HtmlTextWriterAttribute.Value, "1");
writer.RenderBeginTag(HtmlTextWriterTag.Option);
writer.Write("MasterCard");
writer.RenderEndTag();

writer.RenderEndTag();
writer.RenderEndTag();
writer.RenderEndTag();
writer.RenderBeginTag(HtmlTextWriterTag.Tr);
writer.RenderBeginTag(HtmlTextWriterTag.Td);
writer.Write(CreditCardNoText);
writer.RenderEndTag();
writer.RenderBeginTag(HtmlTextWriterTag.Td);
writer.AddAttribute(HtmlTextWriterAttribute.Name, CreditCardNoTextInputName);
writer.AddAttribute(HtmlTextWriterAttribute.Id, CreditCardNoTextInputId);
writer.AddAttribute(HtmlTextWriterAttribute.Type, "text");
writer.RenderBeginTag(HtmlTextWriterTag.Input);
writer.RenderEndTag();
writer.RenderEndTag();
writer.RenderEndTag();
writer.RenderBeginTag(HtmlTextWriterTag.Tr);
writer.RenderBeginTag(HtmlTextWriterTag.Td);
writer.Write(CardholderNameText);
writer.RenderEndTag();
writer.RenderBeginTag(HtmlTextWriterTag.Td);
writer.AddAttribute(HtmlTextWriterAttribute.Name, CardholderNameTextInputName);
writer.AddAttribute(HtmlTextWriterAttribute.Id, CardholderNameTextInputId);
writer.AddAttribute(HtmlTextWriterAttribute.Type, "text");
writer.RenderBeginTag(HtmlTextWriterTag.Input);
writer.RenderEndTag();
writer.RenderEndTag();
writer.RenderEndTag();

writer.RenderBeginTag(HtmlTextWriterTag.Tr);
writer.RenderBeginTag(HtmlTextWriterTag.Td);
writer.Write(ExpirationDateText);
writer.RenderEndTag();
writer.RenderBeginTag(HtmlTextWriterTag.Td);
writer.AddAttribute(HtmlTextWriterAttribute.Name, MonthSelectName);
writer.AddAttribute(HtmlTextWriterAttribute.Id, MonthSelectId);
writer.RenderBeginTag(HtmlTextWriterTag.Select);

for (int day = 1; day < 13; day++)
{
  writer.AddAttribute(HtmlTextWriterAttribute.Value, day.ToString());
```

(continued)

Listing 3-16: *(continued)*

```
     writer.RenderBeginTag(HtmlTextWriterTag.Option);

     if (day < 10)
       writer.Write("0" + day.ToString());
     else
       writer.Write(day);

     writer.RenderEndTag();
   }

   writer.RenderEndTag();
   writer.Write(" ");

   writer.AddAttribute(HtmlTextWriterAttribute.Name, YearSelectName);
   writer.AddAttribute(HtmlTextWriterAttribute.Id, YearSelectId);
   writer.RenderBeginTag(HtmlTextWriterTag.Select);

   for (int year = 2005; year < 2015; year++)
   {
     writer.AddAttribute(HtmlTextWriterAttribute.Value, year.ToString());
     writer.RenderBeginTag(HtmlTextWriterTag.Option);
     writer.Write(year);
     writer.RenderEndTag();
   }

   writer.RenderEndTag();

   writer.RenderEndTag();
   writer.RenderEndTag();

   writer.RenderBeginTag(HtmlTextWriterTag.Tr);
   writer.AddAttribute(HtmlTextWriterAttribute.Align, "center");
   writer.AddAttribute(HtmlTextWriterAttribute.Colspan, "2");
   writer.RenderBeginTag(HtmlTextWriterTag.Td);
   writer.AddAttribute(HtmlTextWriterAttribute.Type, "submit");
   writer.AddAttribute(HtmlTextWriterAttribute.Value, "Submit");
   writer.AddAttribute(HtmlTextWriterAttribute.Name, SubmitInputName);
   writer.AddAttribute(HtmlTextWriterAttribute.Id, SubmitInputId);
   writer.RenderBeginTag(HtmlTextWriterTag.Input);
   writer.RenderEndTag();
   writer.RenderEndTag();
   writer.RenderEndTag();
 }
```

The main difference between the `RenderContents` method in Listing 3-16 and the `Render` method in Listing 2-6 is that `RenderContents` doesn't render the containing table HTML element and its associated HTML attributes. `RenderContents` does just what its name says it does: it renders the contents within the containing HTML element's opening and closing tags.

Another difference between these two listings is that `CreditCardForm5` doesn't hard-code the values of the `name` and `id` HTML attributes of the three select HTML elements and two input HTML elements whose type HTML attributes are set to the string value `"text"`. Instead `CreditCardForm5` exposes five protected virtual read-only properties that return the values of the name and id HTML attributes. Because these properties are declared as virtual, the subclasses of the CreditCardForm5 control can override them to provide their own implementations, as you'll see later in this chapter.

Listing 3-17 and Figure 3-1 show an ASP.NET Web page that uses the CreditCardForm5 control. As this listing shows, page developers use the GridLines, CellSpacing, CellPadding, HorizontalAlign, and BackImageUrl style properties of the CreditCardForm5 control to set the values of the CSS style attributes of the containing table HTML element. The CreditCardForm5 control hides the underlying table HTML element and its style attributes from page developers and provides them with a convenient set of properties to set these style attributes.

Listing 3-17: A Web page that uses the CreditCardForm5 custom control

```
<%@ Page Language="C#" AutoEventWireup="true" CodeFile="Default5.aspx.cs"
Inherits="Default4" %>

<%@ Register TagPrefix="custom" Namespace="CustomComponents" %>
<!DOCTYPE html PUBLIC "-//W3C//DTD XHTML 1.1//EN"
"http://www.w3.org/TR/xhtml11/DTD/xhtml11.dtd">
<html xmlns="http://www.w3.org/1999/xhtml">
<head runat="server">
  <title>Untitled Page</title>
</head>
<body>
  <form id="form1" runat="server">
    <custom:CreditCardForm5 BackColor="Black" ForeColor="White" runat="server"
    ID="ccf" Font-Bold="true" Font-Italic="true" GridLines="None" CellSpacing="5"
    BackImageUrl="images4.bmp" Font-Size="Larger"
    BorderColor="Yellow" BorderWidth="20px" BorderStyle="Ridge" />
  </form>
</body>
</html>
```

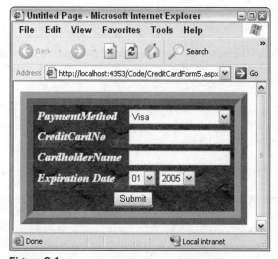

Figure 3-1

Developing a Custom Style Class

The Style class and its subclasses, such as TableStyle and TableItemStyle, support a handful of CSS style attributes. You must write your own style class that derives from the Style class or one of its subclasses to add support for other CSS style attributes.

In this section you implement a new custom style named CustomTableStyle that derives from TableStyle and extends its functionality to add support for the CSS style attribute background-repeat. This style attribute allows page developers to specify in which direction the specified background image should be repeated. The possible values of the CSS style attribute background-repeat are repeat, repeat-x, repeat-y, no-repeat, and inherit.

First, you need to define a new enumeration named BackImageRepeat whose values map to the values of the CSS style attribute background-repeat:

```
public enum BackImageRepeat
{
    Repeat, RepeatX, RepeatY, NoRepeat, Inherit
}
```

Next, choose the appropriate base class for your custom style class. This base class must be either the Style class or one of its subclasses. If you choose TableStyle as the base class for CustomTableStyle, you'll save yourself from having to add support for CSS style attributes that TableStyle already supports.

Then you need to derive your custom style from the chosen base class:

```
public class CustomTableStyle : TableStyle
```

You need to expose a default public constructor for your custom style class. The public default constructor of a custom style class normally doesn't contain any code. The following code shows the default constructor of CustomTableStyle class:

```
public CustomTableStyle() { }
```

The clients of your custom style class that use the default constructor to instantiate your class expect the class to use its own ViewState collection to manage the states of its properties across page postbacks. You'll see an example of this in Chapter 7.

Your custom style class must also expose a constructor that takes a single argument of type StateBag. This constructor must pass this argument to its base constructor as shown here. Notice that this constructor doesn't contain any code either:

```
public CustomTableStyle(StateBag viewState) : base(viewState) { }
```

The clients of your custom style class that use this constructor to instantiate your class pass their own StateBag collection to your class and expect your class to use their StateBag collection to manage its properties across page postbacks. Listing 3-15 shows an example of this case where the CreditCardForm5 control passes its own ViewState collection as an argument to the constructor of the TableStyle class.

Your custom style class must expose one strongly typed style property for each new CSS style attribute that it supports. Each property must use the `ViewState` collection of the `Style` class as its backing store. `CustomStyleTable` exposes a style property of the type `BackImageRepeat` enumeration that maps to the `background-repeat` CSS style attribute:

```
public BackImageRepeat BackImageRepeat
{
  get
  {
    return ViewState["BackImageRepeat"] != null ?
           (BackImageRepeat)ViewState["BackImageRepeat"] : BackImageRepeat.NoRepeat;
  }
  set { ViewState["BackImageRepeat"] = value; }
}
```

Because each strongly typed style property of your custom style class must use the `ViewState` collection as its backing store, when the page developer sets the value of a property, the setter of the property automatically adds a new item with a specified key to the `ViewState` collection. Therefore, the existence of an item with the specified key is the indication that the value of its associated property has been set.

Your custom style class should implement a method named `IsSet` that takes a single argument of type `string` and returns a Boolean value. This method must use its argument value as the key to the `ViewState` collection to check whether the collection contains an item with the specified key. `IsSet` returns true if the item exists in the collection, and false otherwise:

```
internal bool IsSet(string key)
{
  return ViewState[key] != null;
}
```

Your custom style class must override the `IsEmpty` property of its base class, as shown here where `CustomTableStyle` overrides the `IsEmpty` property of the `TableStyle` class:

```
protected override bool IsEmpty
{
  get { return base.IsEmpty && !IsSet("BackImageRepeat"); }
}
```

The getter of the `IsEmpty` property of your custom style class must contain a single logical-AND expression that consists of the following operands:

❑   `base.IsEmpty`

❑   One or more `!IsSet(key)` statements, where `key` is used to locate the associated item in the `ViewState` collection as discussed before

The `IsEmpty` property of your custom style class in effect specifies whether any of the style properties of your custom style class is set.

Because the setter of each property of your custom style class adds a new item to the `ViewState` collection, the `Style` class exposes a method named `Reset` that your custom style class must override to remove the items that its properties have added to the `ViewState` collection.

CustomTableStyle overrides the Reset method of the TableStyle class like this:

```
public override void Reset()
{
  base.Reset();
  if (IsEmpty)
    return;

  if (IsSet("BackImageRepeat"))
    ViewState.Remove("BackImageRepeat");
}
```

Follow these steps to implement the Reset method of your custom style class:

1. Call the Reset method of your custom style class's base class:

```
base.Reset();
```

2. Call the IsEmpty property of your custom style class to check whether any of its properties are set. If not, return because there is nothing to clean up.

3. Call the IsSet method once for each style property of your custom style class to check whether the property has been set. If so, call the Remove method of the ViewState collection to remove the item from the collection.

The Style class exposes a method named FillStyleAttributes that takes a collection object as its argument. Your custom style class must override this method to add the CSS style attributes that it supports to this collection. The Style class includes the logic that automatically iterates through the attributes in this collection and calls the AddStyleAttribute method of the respective HtmlTextWriter object to render each enumerated style attribute.

Here's the CustomTableStyle class's implementation of the FillStyleAttributes method:

```
protected override void FillStyleAttributes(CssStyleCollection attributes,
                                            IUrlResolutionService urlResolver)
{
  base.FillStyleAttributes(attributes, urlResolver);

  if (IsSet("BackImageRepeat"))
    attributes.Add("background-repeat", GetBackImageRepeat(this.BackImageRepeat));
}
```

Follow these steps to implement the FillStyleAttributes method of your custom style class:

1. Call the FillStyleAttributes method of the base class:

```
base.FillStyleAttributes(attributes, urlResolver);
```

2. Call the IsSet method once for each style property of your custom style class to check whether the property has been set. If so, add the CSS style attribute associated with the property to the collection passed in as argument to the FillStyleAttributes method.

The `Style` class exposes a method named `CopyFrom` that takes an argument of type `Style`. Your custom style class must override the `CopyFrom` method of its base class to copy the property values of the style object passed in as argument to its associated style properties:

```
public override void CopyFrom(Style s)
{
  if (s == null)
    return;

  base.CopyFrom(s);
  CustomTableStyle cs = s as CustomTableStyle;
  if (cs == null || cs.IsEmpty)
    return;

  if (cs.IsSet("BackImageRepeat"))
    this.BackImageRepeat = cs.BackImageRepeat;
}
```

Follow these steps to implement the `CopyFrom` method of your custom style class:

1. Check whether the style object passed in as argument is null. If so, return because there is nothing to copy:

```
if (s == null)
  return;
```

2. Call the `CopyFrom` method of the base class of your custom style class:

```
base.CopyFrom(s);
```

3. Return, if either of the following two conditions is met:

   ❑ The style object passed in as argument is not an instance of your custom style class.

   ❑ The style object is an instance of your custom style class but none of its style properties are set; that is, it is empty.

4. Call the `IsSet` method once for each style property of the style object passed in as argument to check whether the property has been set. If so, assign the value of the style property to the respective property of your custom style class.

Your custom style class must also override the `MergeWith` method of its base class to merge the style property values of the style object passed in as argument with its own respective style properties:

```
public override void MergeWith(Style s)
{
  if (s == null)
    return;

  if (IsEmpty)
  {
    CopyFrom(s);
    return;
```

```
  }

    CustomTableStyle cs = s as CustomTableStyle;
    if (cs == null || cs.IsEmpty)
      return;

    if (cs.IsSet("BackImageRepeat") && !IsSet("BackImageRepeat"))
      this.BackImageRepeat = cs.BackImageRepeat;
}
```

Follow these steps to implement the `MergeWith` method of your custom style class:

1. Check whether the style object passed in as argument is null. If so, do nothing and return.

2. Check whether any of the properties of your custom style class are set. If not, call the `CopyFrom` method because you're not really merging the property values of the style object, you're copying them.

3. Return, if either of the following two conditions is met:

   ❑ The style object passed in as argument is not an instance of your custom style class.

   ❑ The style object is an instance of your custom style class but none of its style properties are set; that is, it is empty.

4. Assign the values of each style property of the style object passed in as argument to the respective property of your custom style class if both of the following conditions are met:

   ❑ The style property of the style object is set.

   ❑ The respective style property of your custom style class is not set.

Using Your Custom Style Class

In the previous section you implemented a custom style class named `CustomTableStyle`. Here, you implement a custom control named `CustomStyledCreditCardForm5` that derives from the `CreditCardForm5` control and extends its functionality to add support for the `CustomTableStyle` class.

Follow these steps to implement a custom control that uses your custom style class:

1. Override the `CreateControlStyle` method to create and to return an instance of your custom style class. As the following code shows, the `CustomStyledCreditCardForm5` control overrides the `CreateControlStyle` method to create and to return an instance of the `CustomTableStyle` class:

```
protected override Style CreateControlStyle()
{
  return new CustomTableStyle(ViewState);
}
```

Your custom control's implementation of the `CreateControlStyle` method must use the constructor of your custom style class that takes the `ViewState` collection of the custom control as its argument. In other words, your custom control must share the same `ViewState` collection with your custom style class.

2. Expose one style property for each style property of your custom style class. Each style property of your custom control must use the respective style property of your custom style class as its backing store. The `CustomStyledCreditCardForm5` control exposes a style property named `BackImageRepeat` that uses the `BackImageRepeat` property of the `CustomTableStyle` class as its backing store:

```
public virtual BackImageRepeat BackImageRepeat
{
  get { return ((CustomTableStyle)ControlStyle).BackImageRepeat; }
  set { ((CustomTableStyle)ControlStyle).BackImageRepeat = value; }
}
```

The following code shows an ASP.NET page that uses the `CustomStyledCreditCardForm5` control and sets its `BackImageRepeat` property to `RepeatY` to repeat the specified image along the y axis only. Figure 3-2 shows the result.

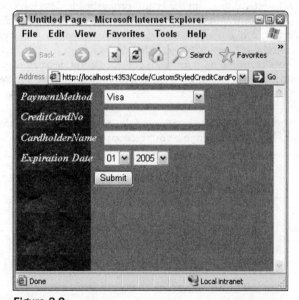

Figure 3-2

```
<%@ Page Language="C#" AutoEventWireup="true" CodeFile="Default7.aspx.cs"
Inherits="Default7" %>

<%@ Register TagPrefix="custom" Namespace="CustomComponents" %>
<!DOCTYPE html PUBLIC "-//W3C//DTD XHTML 1.1//EN"
"http://www.w3.org/TR/xhtml11/DTD/xhtml11.dtd">
<html xmlns="http://www.w3.org/1999/xhtml">
```

```
<head runat="server">
  <title>Untitled Page</title>
</head>
<body style="background-image: url(sky.bmp); background-repeat: repeat-y;
background-color: #f9f2f4;">
  <form id="form1" runat="server">
    <custom:CustomStyledCreditCardForm5 runat="server" ID="ccf"
    BackImageRepeat="RepeatY" BackImageUrl="images4.bmp" BackColor="Yellow"
    ForeColor="White" Font-Bold="true" Font-Italic="true" GridLines="None"
    CellSpacing="5" Style="left: 0px; position: absolute; top: 0px;
                          background-color: gray;" Height="88px"
    Width="231px" />
  </form>
</body>
</html>
```

Summary

This chapter provided in-depth coverage of the main methods and properties of the WebControl base class. You learned how to extend these methods and properties to develop your own custom controls. You implemented a custom control that derives from the WebControl base class to take advantage of its support for style properties. You also saw how to develop your own custom style class. You implemented a custom style class named CustomTableStyle that derives from the TableStyle class and extends its functionality to add support for the background-repeat CSS style attribute. Finally, you saw how to develop a custom control that uses your own custom style class, and you developed a custom control that uses the CustomTableStyle class.

Now that you've seen how to customize and extend the WebControl base class, you can move on to the next chapter, where you learn how to enable your custom controls to raise events.

Developing Custom Controls that Raise Events

In the previous chapter you implemented a custom control named CreditCardForm5 that derives from WebControl and overrides its methods and properties. This chapter shows you how to develop custom controls that raise events. It begins by explaining what an event is and what role it plays in standard and custom controls.

You'll see the .NET event implementation pattern that you should use to implement the events of your custom controls, and you'll implement a custom control that uses the pattern to implement an event named ValidatingCreditCard.

Then, you learn how to use EventHandlerList class to optimize the events of your custom controls and develop a custom control that uses this class. You learn how to implement the IPostBackEventHandler and IPostBackDataHandler interfaces to map postback events to the events of your custom control.

Finally, this chapter presents the page life cycle and describes different phases that the page goes through from the time it springs into life to the time when the response is sent to the requesting browser.

About Events

An *event* is a notification that a component, such as your custom control, sends its clients to notify them that something has occurred. For example, the CreditCardForm5 control developed in the previous chapter must send a notification to its clients every time the user clicks the Submit button to allow them to take the appropriate action.

In the case of the `CreditCardForm5` control, the notification must also include the credit card information, because the clients need to send the information to another site to validate. The information that clients need to process the event that your custom control raises is known as *event data* or *notification data*.

Sending events and notification data is only half the story. The other half is the client registration for these events and their associated data. In other words, the clients must *register* to receive these events.

Because your custom control will be used by different clients with different architectures, the mechanism through which your control sends its events and their associated data and through which the clients of your control register for receiving them must not tie your control to any specific client. This mechanism must isolate your control from its clients, where your control has no way of knowing what type of clients it's sending its events to, or what type of clients are registering to receive these events. Enter .NET *delegates*.

Delegates do just what their names say they do, that is, they act as delegates for your custom controls. Instead of sending its events directly to its clients—which would tie your control to specific clients— your control sends them via .NET delegates. Instead of registering directly with your control—which would tie your control to specific clients—the clients register via .NET delegates. In other words, your control uses delegates to send its events, and the clients use delegates to register.

.NET Event Design Pattern

One of the problems with the `CreditCardForm5` custom control is that when the user clicks the Submit button, the control doesn't raise an event to allow its clients to validate the credit card information. Therefore you need to implement a new custom control named `CreditCardForm6` that derives from `CreditCardForm5` and extends its functionality to add support for this event.

First, you need to choose an appropriate name for the event. The event that `CreditCardForm6` raises will be called `ValidatingCreditCard` because this event is raised to allow the clients to validate credit card information. Next, you need to perform the following tasks:

- ❏ Implement or choose the appropriate event data class
- ❏ Declare or choose the appropriate event delegate class
- ❏ Enable your custom control to raise the event

The following sections discuss these three steps in detail.

Event Data and Event Delegate Class

Here are the steps you must follow to implement or choose the appropriate event data class. First you need to identify the event data associated with the event you're trying to implement. Recall that the event data is the information that the clients of your custom control need in order to process the event. Skip this step if your custom control is raising an event that doesn't require any data. The event that `CreditCardForm6` raises must provide its clients with the following information:

- ❏ Payment method
- ❏ Credit card number
- ❏ Cardholder's name
- ❏ Expiration date

Now you need to check whether there is already a class that derives from the EventArgs class or one of its subclasses that exposes properties that correspond to the identified event data. Classes that directly or indirectly derive from the EventArgs base class and hold event data are known as *event data classes*. If you can find an existing event data class that supports your event, your custom control must use that class. If you search through the existing .NET event data classes, you won't find a class that exposes properties such as CreditCardNumber, CardholderName, and so on. In other words, none of the existing classes can hold the event data you identified for the CreditCardForm6 control.

If you don't find an existing event data class that can hold your event data, you'll need to implement your own custom event data class that derives from EventArgs or one of its subclasses and exposes properties that correspond to your event data. By convention, the name of the event data class consists of the name of the event and the keyword EventArgs. Following this convention, the event data class of CreditCardForm6 will be called ValidatingCreditCardEventArgs. Listing 4-1 shows the implementation of the ValidatingCreditCardEventArgs event data class. Notice that this class exposes one property for each identified event datum.

Listing 4-1: The ValidatingCreditCardEventArgs class

```
namespace CustomComponents
{
  using System;

  public enum PaymentMethod
  {
    Visa = 0, MasterCard = 1
  }

  public class ValidatingCreditCardEventArgs : EventArgs
  {
    private PaymentMethod paymentMethod;
    public PaymentMethod PaymentMethod
    {
      get { return paymentMethod; }
    }

    private string creditCardNo;
    public string CreditCardNo
    {
      get { return creditCardNo; }
    }

    private string cardholderName;
```

(continued)

Listing 4-1: *(continued)*

```
    public string CardholderName
    {
      get { return cardholderName; }
    }

    private DateTime expirationDate;
    public DateTime ExpirationDate
    {
      get { return expirationDate; }
    }

    public ValidatingCreditCardEventArgs(PaymentMethod paymentMethod,
                                         string creditCardNo,
                                         string cardholderName,
                                         DateTime expirationDate)

    {
      this.paymentMethod = paymentMethod;
      this.creditCardNo = creditCardNo;
      this.cardholderName = cardholderName;
      this.expirationDate = expirationDate;
    }
  }
}
```

Because you had to write your own custom event data class, you must also declare your own custom delegate. By convention, this delegate should expose two arguments. The first argument should be of type `System.Object`, and should refer to the instance of your custom control that raises the event. The second argument should be an instance of your custom event data class.

By convention, the name of your custom delegate should consist of the name of the event and the keyword `EventHandler`. Following this convention, the delegate for the `ValidatingCreditCard` event will be called `ValidatingCreditCardEventHandler`.

The following code shows the declaration of the `ValidatingCreditCardEventHandler` delegate class. Notice that the second argument of this delegate is an instance of the respective event data class, `ValidatingCreditCardEventArgs`:

```
namespace CustomComponents
{
  public delegate void ValidatingCreditCardEventHandler(object sender,
                                           ValidatingCreditCardEventArgs

e);
}
```

As you can see, declaring a delegate is very similar to declaring a method. The only difference is that the declaration of a delegate contains the keyword `delegate`. This similarity is not a coincidence. A delegate is a class that encapsulates a callback method with the same signature as the delegate itself. The clients of your custom control wrap their callback methods for your events in delegates and add these delegates to the list of existing delegates, as discussed shortly. Keep in mind that a delegate is a class, not a method. It encapsulates a method, but it's not a method itself. However, delegates are different from regular classes in that you don't implement a delegate class. You just declare it as you did for the `ValidatingCreditCardEventHandler` delegate. You may be wondering who in the world then implements the delegate that you declare. The answer is "the compiler and CLR." The keyword "delegate" signals the compiler that it needs to implement the content of the delegate class.

Enabling Your Custom Control to Raise the Event

Listing 4-2 contains the code for the portion of the `CreditCardForm6` control that enables the control to raise the `ValidatingCreditCard` event.

Listing 4-2: The CreditCardForm6 control

```
namespace CustomComponents
{
  public class CreditCardForm6 : CreditCardForm5, . . .
  {
    public event ValidatingCreditCardEventHandler ValidatingCreditCard;

    protected virtual void OnValidatingCreditCard(ValidatingCreditCardEventArgs e)
    {
      if (ValidatingCreditCard != null)
        ValidatingCreditCard(this, e);
    }
  }
}
```

Here are the steps you must follow to enable your control to raise a specified event. First, your custom control must use an instance of your delegate and the keyword `event` to define the event. For example, the `CreditCardForm6` control uses an instance of the `ValidatingCreditCardEventHandler` delegate and the keyword `event` to define the `ValidatingCreditCard` event:

```
public event ValidatingCreditCardEventHandler ValidatingCreditCard;
```

If a client wants to register for the `ValidatingCreditCard` event of the `CreditCardForm6` control, it must take the following actions:

1. Implement a method with the same signature as the `ValidatingCreditCardEventHandler` delegate. In other words, the method must take two arguments of type `System.Object` and `ValidatingCreditCardEventArgs`, respectively, and return `void`. For example:

```
void ClientCallback (object sender, ValidatingCreditCardEventArgs e);
```

2. Create an instance of the `ValidatingCreditCardEventHandler` delegate to encapsulate the method:

```
ValidatingCreditCardEventHandler mydelegate =
                    new ValidatingCreditCardEventHandler(ClientCallback);
```

Event delegates, such as the preceding `ValidatingCreditCard` event delegate, are a subset of delegates known as *multicast delegates*. Like any other multicast delegate, an event delegate contains an internal linked list known as an *invocation list*.

The client of your control must use the notation += to add the delegate that encapsulates the client call-back method (in this case, the mydelegate delegate) to the invocation list of a given event delegate of your custom control. For example, the client of the CreditCardForm6 control must use the notation += to add the mydelegate delegate that contains the ClientCallback method to the invocation list of the ValidatingCreditCard event delegate:

```
CreditCardForm6 form;
...
ValidatingCreditCardEventHandler mydelegate =
                        new ValidatingCreditCardEventHandler(ClientCallback);
form.ValidatingCreditCard += mydelegate;
...
void ClientCallback (object sender, ValidatingCreditCardEventArgs e)
{
    ...
}
```

Your custom control must implement a protected virtual method that calls the event delegate to send notifications to its clients. By convention, the name of this method consists of the keyword on and the name of the event. Following this convention, the CreditCardForm6 control implements a method named OnValidatingCreditCard as follows:

```
protected virtual void OnValidatingCreditCard(ValidatingCreditCardEventArgs e)
{
    if (ValidatingCreditCard != null)
      ValidatingCreditCard(this, e);
}
```

This method first checks whether any delegates are added to the invocation list of the ValidatingCreditCard event delegate. If so, the method calls the ValidatingCreditCard event delegate and passes the ValidatingCreditCardEventArgs object that contains the event data into it. The ValidatingCreditCard event delegate, in turn, calls the delegates in its invocation list and passes the ValidatingCreditCardEventArgs object into them.

Each delegate in the invocation list, in turn, calls the client callback method that it encapsulates and passes the ValidatingCreditCardEventArgs object into it.

Event Optimization

The previous section defined the ValidatingCreditCard event as a public field. Defining the event delegates of your custom control as fields introduces two problems:

❑   The compiler generates one private delegate field for each event delegate field of your custom control, regardless of whether the clients have actually added any delegates to the invocation list of these event delegates. This wastes a lot of server memory, especially when your custom control exposes a lot of events.

❑ The compiler generates one Add and one Remove method for each event delegate field of your custom control. These methods are called behind the scenes when clients use the += and -= notations to add and remove their delegates from the invocation lists of the event delegates of your custom control. These compiler-generated methods are thread-safe, that is, they include extra code to synchronize threads that are accessing these methods. What this means is that every time clients add a delegate to or remove a delegate from an event delegate of your custom control, they have to first get the lock. This introduces an unnecessary overhead because most page developers don't use multiple threads and therefore there is no need for thread synchronization.

The .NET Framework comes with a class named EventHandlerList to address these two performance issues. EventHandlerList is a linked list of delegates, which is optimized for adding and removing delegates. Listing 4-3 presents the new version of the CreditCardForm6 control that uses the EventHandlerList.

Listing 4-3: The CreditCardForm6 control

```
namespace CustomComponents
{
  public class CreditCardForm6 : CreditCardForm5, . . .
  {
    private static readonly object ValidatingCreditCardEventKey = new object();

    public event ValidatingCreditCardEventHandler ValidatingCreditCard
    {
      add { Events.AddHandler(ValidatingCreditCardEventKey, value); }
      remove { Events.RemoveHandler(ValidatingCreditCardEventKey, value); }
    }

    protected virtual void OnValidatingCreditCard(ValidatingCreditCardEventArgs e)
    {
      ValidatingCreditCardEventHandler handler =
          Events[ValidatingCreditCardEventKey] as ValidatingCreditCardEventHandler;

      if (handler != null)
        handler(this, e);
    }
  }
}
```

To use EventHandlerList in your custom control, you first need to define a private static key for each event that your custom control exposes. The following code defines a key for the ValidatingCreditCard event:

```
private static readonly object ValidatingCreditCardEventKey = new object();
```

Because the key is static (it is shared among all instances of the CreditCardForm6 control), the memory is allocated only once.

Next, you need to define your events as properties, not fields. These event properties have a different syntax than regular properties. The following code defines the `ValidatingCreditCard` event property:

```
public event ValidatingCreditCardEventHandler ValidatingCreditCard
{
    add { Events.AddHandler(ValidatingCreditCardEventKey, value); }
    remove { Events.RemoveHandler(ValidatingCreditCardEventKey, value); }
}
```

Notice that event properties use `add` and `remove` instead of `get` and `set`. The `CreditCardForm6` custom control, like any other control, inherits a property of type `EventHandlerList` named `Events` from the `Control` class. When clients use the `+=` notation to add a delegate to the invocation list of the `ValidatingCreditCard` event delegate, the `add` method automatically calls the `AddHandler` method of the `EventHandlerList` class and passes the event key and the client delegate into it.

The `EventHandlerList` class maintains an internal linked list, which can have zero or one entry for each event delegate. The `AddHandler` method checks whether this internal list contains an entry for an event delegate with the given event key. If it does, the method calls the `Combine` method of the `Delegate` class to add the client delegate to the invocation list of the event delegate. If this internal list doesn't contain an entry for an event delegate with the given event key, the `AddHandler` method adds a new entry.

Finally, you need to use the `EventHandlerList` in your implementation of the method that raises the event. The following code shows the new version of the `OnValidatingCreditCard` method:

```
protected virtual void OnValidatingCreditCard(ValidatingCreditCardEventArgs e)
{
    ValidatingCreditCardEventHandler handler =
            Events[ValidatingCreditCardEventKey] as ValidatingCreditCardEventHandler;

    if (handler != null)
        handler(this, e);
}
```

This method uses the event key as an index to the `Events` list to access the `ValidatingCreditCard` event delegate. The `Events` list returns null if it doesn't contain an entry for the `ValidatingCreditCard` event delegate. This happens when no client has subscribed to the `ValidatingCreditCard` event.

Using the `EventHandlerList` class automatically resolves the two previously mentioned performance problems with the event fields:

❑ Because the events aren't declared as fields, the compiler doesn't generate private fields for these events. This avoids wasting server memory especially when your custom control raises a lot of events.

❑ The `AddHandler` and `RemoveHandler` methods of the `EventHandlerList` class aren't thread-safe. This means that there is no need for acquiring a lock every time an event is added to the list or removed from the list. This avoids unnecessary thread synchronization overhead because most page developers don't use multiple threads.

Postback

In the previous sections you implemented a custom control named `CreditCardForm6` that exposes an event named `ValidatingCreditCard`. Listing 4-4 shows a Web page that uses the `CreditCardForm6` custom control and registers a method named `ClientCallback` as a callback for the `ValidatingCreditCard` event. This method retrieves the credit card information from the `ValidatingCreditCardEventArgs` object (passed in as its second argument) and uses a `Label` control to display the information.

Listing 4-4: A Web page that uses the CreditCardForm6 control

```
<%@ Page Language="C#" %>
<%@ Register TagPrefix="custom" Namespace="CustomComponents" %>

<script runat="server">
  protected void ClientCallback(object sender, ValidatingCreditCardEventArgs e)
  {
  info.Text = "Payment Method: ";
  info.Text += (e.PaymentMethod == PaymentMethod.Visa ? "Visa" : "MasterCard");
  info.Text += "<br/>";
  info.Text += "Credit Card No.: ";
  info.Text += e.CreditCardNo;
  info.Text += "<br/>";
  info.Text += "Cardholder's Name: ";
  info.Text += e.CardholderName;
  info.Text += "<br/>";
  info.Text += "Expiration Date: ";
  info.Text += e.ExpirationDate.Month;
  info.Text += "/";
  info.Text += e.ExpirationDate.Year;
  }
</script>

<html xmlns="http://www.w3.org/1999/xhtml">
<head runat="server"><title>Untitled Page</title></head>
<body>
  <form id="form1" runat="server">
    <custom:CreditCardForm6 runat="server"
    OnValidatingCreditCard="ClientCallback" /><br /><br />
    <asp:Label runat="server" ID="info" />
  </form>
</body>
</html>
```

If you compile and run this page and click the Submit button, nothing will happen! The `ClientCallback` method isn't called, which means the `CreditCardForm6` control doesn't raise the `ValidatingCreditCard` event as expected. This means that the `OnValidatingCreditCard` method of the `CreditCardForm6` control isn't called because it's the responsibility of this method to raise the event. Therefore, clicking the Submit button and posting the page back to the server doesn't invoke the `OnValidatingCreditCard` method.

To put it differently, the CreditCardForm6 control has no clue that the page is posted back and that it's supposed to raise the ValidatingCreditCard event. This raises the question: Whose job is it to inform a server control such as CreditCardForm6 that a postback has occurred? The answer is "the containing page."

Take a look at how the page manages to inform a server control that a postback has occurred. Recall that every HTML element has an HTML attribute named name. When an HTML element such as the Submit button causes a postback to occur, the value of its name HTML attribute is posted back to the server so the server knows which HTML element caused the postback.

The containing page performs the following tasks:

1. It retrieves the value of the name attribute of the HTML element that caused the postback. In the case of CreditCardForm6 control, the page retrieves the value of the name attribute of the Submit button because the Submit button is the HTML element that causes the postback.

2. It searches through its control tree for a server control whose UniqueID has the same value as the name attribute of the HTML element that caused the postback. In the case of CreditCardForm6 control, the page searches for a server control whose UniqueID has the same value as the name attribute of the Submit button.

3. If the page finds a control with the specified UniqueID value, it checks whether the control implements the IPostBackEventHandler interface. This interface exposes a single method named RaisePostBackEvent. Therefore, implementing this interface is the indication that the control exposes a method named RaisePostBackEvent. If the control implements the interface, the page calls its RaisePostBackEvent method. What the control does inside this method is the control's business. In other words, after calling the RaisePostBackEvent method, the page is out of the picture as far as the postback event goes.

The trick is to ensure that the name attribute of the Submit button has the same value as the UniqueID property of the CreditCardForm6 control. Because CreditCardForm6 derives from CreditCardForm5, it inherits the CreditCardForm5 control's implementation of the RenderContents method. This implementation was presented in Listing 3-17. The following code contains the portion of Listing 3-17 that renders the Submit button:

```
protected override void RenderContents(HtmlTextWriter writer)
{
    . . .
    writer.RenderBeginTag(HtmlTextWriterTag.Tr);
    writer.AddAttribute(HtmlTextWriterAttribute.Align, "center");
    writer.AddAttribute(HtmlTextWriterAttribute.Colspan, "2");
    writer.RenderBeginTag(HtmlTextWriterTag.Td);
    writer.AddAttribute(HtmlTextWriterAttribute.Type, "submit");
    writer.AddAttribute(HtmlTextWriterAttribute.Value, "Submit");
    writer.AddAttribute(HtmlTextWriterAttribute.Name, SubmitInputName);
    writer.AddAttribute(HtmlTextWriterAttribute.Id, SubmitInputId);
    writer.RenderBeginTag(HtmlTextWriterTag.Input);
    writer.RenderEndTag();
    writer.RenderEndTag();
    writer.RenderEndTag();
}
```

As the highlighted portion of the code illustrates, the `RenderContents` method renders the value of the `SubmitInputName` property of the `CreditCardForm5` control as the value of the `name` HTML attribute of the `Submit` button. `CreditCardForm6` inherits the following implementation of the `SubmitInputName` property from `CreditCardForm5` control:

```
protected virtual string SubmitInputName
{
  get { return "Submit"; }
}
```

This means that the `RenderContents` method of the `CreditCardForm5` control assigns the `Submit` string value to the `name` attribute of the Submit button. As discussed, you have to ensure that the `name` attribute of the `Submit` button has the same value as the `UniqueID` property of the `CreditCardForm5` control. This raises the following question: Who sets the value of the `UniqueID` property of a control? The answer is "the containing page." Because the values of the `name` attribute of the Submit button and the `UniqueID` property of the `CreditCardForm5` control are set by two different entities, specifically `RenderContents` and the containing page, these values are bound to be different. This means that the page's search for the server control with the `UniqueID` value of `Submit` is bound to fail.

In conclusion, when the user clicks the Submit button, the `CreditCardForm6` control doesn't raise the `ValidatingCreditCard` event for two reasons. First, the `UniqueID` value of the `CreditCardForm6` control isn't the `Submit` string value. That is why the page's search for a server control with this `UniqueID` value failed. You can't manually change the value of the `UniqueID` property of the `CreditCardForm6` control to `Submit` because this property is marked read-only to ensure that only the containing page can set its value.

Therefore, the only alternative is to ensure that the `RenderContents` method assigns the value of the `UniqueID` property of the `CreditCardForm6` control to the `name` attribute of the Submit button. Because the `RenderContents` method assigns the value of the `SubmitInputName` property of the `CreditCardForm6` control to the `name` attribute of the Submit button, all you have to do is override the `SubmitInputName` property to return the value of the `UniqueID` property of the control:

```
protected override string SubmitInputName
{
  get { return this.UniqueID; }
}
```

The second reason is that the `CreditCardForm6` control doesn't implement the `IPostBackEventHandler` interface. The next section shows you how to implement this interface.

C# Interface Implementation Pattern

When you develop a custom component that implements an interface (such as `IPostBackEventHandler`), you first need to implement a protected virtual method for each method of the interface and a protected property for each property of the interface. The method must have the same signature as its respective interface method. Recall that the signature of a method consists of its name, argument types, and return type. The property must have the same return type as its associated interface property. This will allow the subclasses of your component to override these protected methods and properties to provide their own implementations.

Because the `CreditCardForm6` control must implement the `IPostBackEventHandler` interface, which exposes the `RaisePostBackEvent` method, the control exposes a protected virtual method with same signature as the `RaisePostBackEvent` method:

```
protected virtual void RaisePostBackEvent(string args)
{
   ...
}
```

The implementation of this method is discussed in next section.

You also need to explicitly implement each method of the interface, where you have to take the following actions:

- ❑ Qualify the name of each method and property with the name of the interface.

- ❑ Do not use any modifiers such as `private`, `public`, and so on.

- ❑ Call the respective protected virtual method (property) from each method (property).

Because the `CreditCardForm6` control must implement the `IPostBackEventHandler` interface, which exposes the `RaisePostBackEvent` method, the control explicitly implements this method to call the respective protected virtual method:

```
void IPostBackEventHandler.RaisePostBackEvent(string args)
{
   this.RaisePostBackEvent(args);
}
```

Postback Event

The `CreditCardForm6` control's implementation of the `RaisePostBackEvent` method calls the `OnValidatingCreditCard` method to raise the `ValidatingCreditCard` event, as shown in Listing 4-5.

Listing 4-5: The RaisePostBackEvent method calls the OnValidatingCreditCard method to raise the ValidatingCreditCard event

```
protected virtual void RaisePostBackEvent(string args)
{
   ValidatingCreditCardEventArgs ve =
          new ValidatingCreditCardEventArgs(PaymentMethod, CreditCardNo,
                                   CardholderName, ExpirationDate);
   OnValidatingCreditCard(ve);
}
```

As Listing 4-5 shows, the `OnValidatingCreditCard` method requires an input argument of type `ValidatingCreditCardEventArgs`. Recall that `ValidatingCreditCardEventArgs` is the event data class for the ValidatingCreditCard event. In other words, the RaisePostBackEvent method must create a ValidatingCreditCardEventArgs object and populate it with the event data or credit card information; specifically, the payment method, credit card number, cardholder's name, and expiration date. Where can the RaisePostBackEvent method get the credit card information? The next section provides the answer.

Postback Data

When the user clicks the Submit button of the CreditCardForm6 control, the form data, including the selected values of the three select HTML elements and the text values of the two input HTML elements, are posted back to the server. The CreditCardForm6 control must access the posted form data to retrieve the selected values of the payment method and expiration date select HTML elements and the text values of the credit card number and cardholder's name input HTML elements and use these values to populate the ValidatingCreditCardEventArgs object shown in Listing 4-3.

The CreditCardForm6 control must implement the IPostBackDataHandler interface to express interest in accessing the posted form data. This interface exposes two methods: LoadPostData and RaisePostDataChangedEvent. When the user clicks the Submit button and posts the form data back to the server, the page calls the LoadPostData method of the CreditCardForm6 control and passes a collection of type NameValueCollection that contains the posted form data into the method.

The CreditCardForm6 control follows the C# interface implementation pattern discussed earlier to implement the IPostBackDataHandler interface:

1. It implements a protected virtual method with the same signature as the LoadPostData method of the IPostBackDataHandler interface as shown in Listing 4-4.

2. It explicitly implements the LoadPostData method of the interface to call the protected virtual method:

```
bool IPostBackDataHandler.LoadPostData(string postDataKey,
                                       NameValueCollection values)
{
  return this.LoadPostData(postDataKey, values);
}
```

3. It implements a protected virtual method with the same signature as the RaisePostData EventChanged method of the IPostBackDataHandler interface, as discussed in the following sections.

4. It explicitly implements the RaisePostDataEventChanged method of the interface to call the protected virtual method:

```
protected virtual void RaisePostDataChangedEvent()
{
  this.RaisePostDataChangedEvent();
}
```

LoadPostData

Listing 4-6 contains the code for the LoadPostData method.

Listing 4-6: The LoadPostData method

```
protected virtual bool LoadPostData(string postDataKey, NameValueCollection values)
{
  PaymentMethod paymentMethod = values[PaymentMethodSelectName] == "0" ?
                                PaymentMethod.Visa : PaymentMethod.MasterCard;
  if (paymentMethod != PaymentMethod)
  {
    PaymentMethod = paymentMethod;
    hasPaymentMethodChanged = true;
  }

  string creditCardNo = values[CreditCardNoTextInputName];
  if (creditCardNo != CreditCardNo)
  {
    CreditCardNo = creditCardNo;
    hasCreditCardNoChanged = true;
  }

  string cardholderName = values[CardholderNameTextInputName];
  if (cardholderName != CardholderName)
  {
    CardholderName = cardholderName;
    hasCardholderNameChanged = true;
  }

  int month = int.Parse(values[MonthSelectName]);
  int year = int.Parse(values[YearSelectName]);
  DateTime expirationDate = new DateTime(year, month, 25);
  if (expirationDate != ExpirationDate)
  {
    ExpirationDate = expirationDate;
    hasExpirationDateChanged = true;
  }

  if (!string.IsNullOrEmpty(values[SubmitInputName]))
    Page.RegisterRequiresRaiseEvent(this);

  return hasPaymentMethodChanged ||
         hasCreditCardNoChanged ||
         hasCardholderNameChanged ||
         hasExpirationDateChanged;
}
```

As discussed, when the user clicks the Submit button and posts the page back to the server, the page calls the LoadPostData method of the CreditCardForm6 control and passes a NameValueCollection collection into it. This collection contains a name/value pair for each form HTML element where the name contains the value of the name attributes of the element and value contains the value that the element has posted back to the server. In other words, this collection contains five name/value pairs associated with the five form elements that the CreditCardForm6 contains, the payment method and expiration date select HTML elements, the credit card number, and cardholder name text fields.

Therefore the `LoadPostData` method must use the value of the `name` attribute of each `form` HTML element as an index to the `NameValueCollection` to access the value associated with the element. For example, the method must use the value of the `name` HTML attribute of the payment method `select` HTML element as an index to the `NameValueCollection` to access the selected value of the element. Recall that the selected value of this element represents the payment method that the user has selected.

The `CreditCardForm5` control exposes five properties named `PaymentMethodSelectName`, `CreditCardNoTextInputName`, `CardholderNameTextInputName`, `MonthSelectName`, and `YearSelectName` that specify the values of the `name` attributes of the payment method `select` HTML element, credit card number text field, cardholder name text field, month, and year `select` HTML elements. Therefore, as shown in Listing 4-4, the `LoadPostData` method uses the values of these five properties as index into the `NameValueCollection` to access their associated values.

This assumes that these five properties have unique values on the page. You can check whether this is indeed a right assumption. Listing 4-7 presents these five properties of the `CreditCardForm5` control.

Listing 4-7: The properties of the CreditCardForm5 control

```
protected virtual string PaymentMethodSelectName
{
  get { return "PaymentMethod"; }
}


protected virtual string CreditCardNoTextInputName
{
  get { return "CreditCardNo"; }
}


protected virtual string CardholderNameTextInputName
{
  get { return "CardholderName"; }
}


protected virtual string MonthSelectName
{
  get { return "Month"; }
}


protected virtual string YearSelectName
{
  get { return "Year"; }
}
```

As shown in Listing 4-7, the values of these properties are unique within the scope of the `CreditCardForm5` control itself, but not within the scope of the page, where more than one instance of the control can be present. If the `LoadPostData` method is to use the values of these properties to access their associated values in the `NameValueCollection`, these properties must have unique values on the page to avoid name conflicts when more than one instance of the `CreditCardForm6` control is used on the same page. This raises the question: How can you guarantee that these properties will have unique values regardless of how many instances of the `CreditCardForm6` are used on the page?

Recall that the page ensures that the `UniqueID` properties of all instances of the `CreditCardForm6` control have unique values on the page. Therefore, you can use the value of this property as a naming scope for the values of these five properties. Here is what you need to do to accomplish this:

1. Come up with a set of string identifiers for the payment method and expiration date `select` HTML elements and the credit card number and cardholder name text fields. These identifiers must be unique within the scope of the `CreditCardForm6` control. For this example, use these string identifiers: `PaymentMethod`, `CreditCardNo`, `CardholderName`, `Month`, and `Year`.

2. Prepend the value of the `UniqueID` property of the `CreditCardForm6` control to the unique identifiers using the colon character as the separator. Because the value of the `UniqueID` is unique on the page and the value of the associated identifier is unique within the scope of the `CreditCardForm6` control, the combination of these two values will be unique on the page.

As Listing 4-8 shows, `CreditCardForm6` overrides the `PaymentMethodSelectName`, `CreditCard NoTextInputName`, `CardholderNameTextInputName`, `MonthSelectName`, and `YearSelectName` properties of the `CreditCardForm5` class to use the two-step approach just described to return unique values for these properties. This is yet another example that shows how important it is to declare as virtual those properties or methods of your custom control that you expect others may want to override to provide different implementations. Because these properties of the `CreditCardForm5` were marked as virtual, `CreditCardForm6` can override them to return unique values.

Listing 4-8: CreditCardForm6 overrides the properties of CreditCardForm5

```
protected override string PaymentMethodSelectName
{
   get { return this.UniqueID + ":PaymentMethod"; }
}

protected override string CreditCardNoTextInputName
{
   get { return this.UniqueID + ":CreditCardNo"; }
}

protected override string CardholderNameTextInputName
{
   get { return this.UniqueID + ":CardholderName"; }
}

protected override string MonthSelectName
{
   get { return this.UniqueID + ":Month"; }
}

protected override string YearSelectName
{
   get { return this.UniqueID + ":Year"; }
}
```

CreditCardForm6 exposes four new properties named PaymentMethod, CreditCardNo, CardholderName, and ExpirationDate. As shown in Listing 4-6, the LoadPostData method assigns the retrieved values to these properties only if the new values are different from the old values of these properties. This is only possible if these properties can maintain their values across page postbacks, which means that they must use the ViewState collection of the CreditCardForm6 as their backing stores, as shown in Listing 4-9.

Listing 4-9: The new properties of the CreditCardForm6 control

```
public PaymentMethod PaymentMethod
{
  get { return ViewState["PaymentMethod"] != null ?
               (PaymentMethod)ViewState["PaymentMethod"] : PaymentMethod.Visa; }
  set { ViewState["PaymentMethod"] = value; }
}
public string CreditCardNo
{
  get { return ViewState["CreditCardNo"] != null ?
                  (string)ViewState["CreditCardNo"] : string.Empty; }
  set { ViewState["CreditCardNo"] = value; }
}
public string CardholderName
{
  get { return ViewState["CardholderName"] != null ?
                  (string)ViewState["CardholderName"] : string.Empty; }
  set { ViewState["CardholderName"] = value; }
}
public DateTime ExpirationDate
{
  get { return ViewState["ExpirationDate"] != null ?
                  (DateTime)ViewState["ExpirationDate"] : DateTime.Now; }
  set { ViewState["ExpirationDate"] = value; }
}
```

CreditCardForm6 exposes four Boolean fields named hasPaymentMethodChanged, hasCreditCardNoChanged, hasCardholderNameChanged, and hasExpirationDateChanged to indicate whether the values of the PaymentMethod, CreditCardNo, CardholderName, and ExpirationDate properties of CreditCardForm6 have changed.

As shown in Listing 4-6, the LoadPostData method sets the values of these Boolean fields if the values of their associated properties have changed. Notice that the method returns true if the value of at least one of these properties has changed. Otherwise it returns false.

RaisePostDataChangedEvent

In Listing 4-6, the LoadPostData method returns a Boolean value. The containing page calls the RaisePostDataChangedEvent method if and only if the LoadPostData method returns true, that is, if the value of at least one of the following properties of the CreditCardForm6 control has changed. Listing 4-10 contains the implementation of the RaisePostDataChangedEvent method.

Listing 4-10: The RaisePostDataChangedEvent method

```
protected virtual void RaisePostDataChangedEvent()
{
  if (hasPaymentMethodChanged)
    OnPaymentMethodChanged(EventArgs.Empty);

  if (hasCreditCardNoChanged)
    OnCreditCardNoChanged(EventArgs.Empty);

  if (hasCardholderNameChanged)
    OnCardholderNameChanged(EventArgs.Empty);

  if (hasExpirationDateChanged)
    OnExpirationDateChanged(EventArgs.Empty);
}
```

The `RaisePostDataChangedEvent` method checks the values of the `hasPaymentMethodChanged`, `hasCreditCardNoChanged`, `hasCardholderNameChanged`, and `hasExpirationDateChanged` Boolean fields. If a value is true, the method raises its associated event. The following table describes these events:

`PaymentMethodChanged`	This event is raised if the user has made a new selection in the payment method `select` HTML element.
`ExpirationDateChanged`	This event is raised if the user has made a new selection in the year and/or month `select` HTML element.
`CreditCardNoChanged`	This event is raised if the user has entered a new value in the credit card number text field.
`CardholderNameChanged`	This event is raised if the user has entered a new value in the card holder name text field.

`CreditCardForm6` uses the C# event implementation pattern to implement these four events, as shown in Listing 4-11.

Listing 4-11: The new events that CreditCardForm6 raises

```
namespace CustomComponents
{
  public class CreditCardForm6 : CreditCardForm5, IPostBackEventHandler,
                                 IPostBackDataHandler
  {
    private static readonly object PaymentMethodChangedEventKey = new object();
    public event EventHandler PaymentMethodChanged
    {
      add { Events.AddHandler(PaymentMethodChangedEventKey, value); }
      remove { Events.RemoveHandler(PaymentMethodChangedEventKey, value); }
    }

    protected virtual void OnPaymentMethodChanged(EventArgs e)
```

```
  {
    EventHandler handler = Events[PaymentMethodChangedEventKey] as EventHandler;

    if (handler != null)
      handler(this, e);
  }

  private static readonly object CreditCardNoChangedEventKey = new object();
  public event EventHandler CreditCardNoChanged
  {
    add { Events.AddHandler(CreditCardNoChangedEventKey, value); }
    remove { Events.RemoveHandler(CreditCardNoChangedEventKey, value); }
  }

  protected virtual void OnCreditCardNoChanged(EventArgs e)
  {
    EventHandler handler = Events[CreditCardNoChangedEventKey] as EventHandler;

    if (handler != null)
      handler(this, e);
  }

  private static readonly object CardholderNameChangedEventKey = new object();
  public event EventHandler CardholderNameChanged
  {
    add { Events.AddHandler(CardholderNameChangedEventKey, value); }
    remove { Events.RemoveHandler(CardholderNameChangedEventKey, value); }
  }

  protected virtual void OnCardholderNameChanged(EventArgs e)
  {
    EventHandler handler = Events[CardholderNameChangedEventKey] as EventHandler;

    if (handler != null)
      handler(this, e);
  }

  private static readonly object ExpirationDateChangedEventKey = new object();
  public event EventHandler ExpirationDateChanged
  {
    add { Events.AddHandler(ExpirationDateChangedEventKey, value); }
    remove { Events.RemoveHandler(ExpirationDateChangedEventKey, value); }
  }

  protected virtual void OnExpirationDateChanged(EventArgs e)
  {
    EventHandler handler = Events[ExpirationDateChangedEventKey] as EventHandler;

    if (handler != null)
      handler(this, e);
  }
  }
}
```

As an example, take a look at the implementation of the `ExpirationDateChanged` event:

1. Define a private static read-only field of type object:

```
private static readonly object ExpirationDateChangedEventKey = new object();
```

2. Define the event property where you must use the preceding event key as an index into the `Events` collection to access the respective event delegate:

```
public event EventHandler ExpirationDateChanged
{
    add { Events.AddHandler(ExpirationDateChangedEventKey, value); }
    remove { Events.RemoveHandler(ExpirationDateChangedEventKey, value); }
}
```

3. Implement the protected virtual method that raises the event:

```
protected virtual void OnExpirationDateChanged(EventArgs e)
{
    EventHandler handler = Events[ExpirationDateChangedEventKey] as EventHandler;

    if (handler != null)
        handler(this, e);
}
```

In summary, the `RaisePostDataChangedEvent` method checks whether the values of the `PaymentMethod`, `CreditCardNo`, `CardholderName`, and `ExpirationDate` properties have changed. If so, the method raises the appropriate event. Page developers can register callbacks to handle these events.

Listing 4-12 contains a Web page that uses the `CreditCardForm6` control. Notice that this page assigns the `PaymentMethodChangedCallback`, `CreditCardNoChangedCallback`, `CardholderName ChangedCallback`, and `ExpirationDateChangedCallback` methods (see Listing 4-13) to the `OnPaymentMethodChanged`, `OnCreditCardNoChanged`, `OnCardholderNameChanged`, and `OnExpirationDateChanged` attributes of the `<custom:CreditCardForm6>` tag to register these methods as callbacks for the `PaymentMethodChanged`, `CreditCardNoChanged`, `CardholderNameChanged`, and `ExpirationDateChanged` events.

Listing 4-12: A Web page that uses the CreditCardForm6 control

```
<%@ Page Language="C#" AutoEventWireup="true" CodeFile="CreditCardForm6.aspx.cs"
  Inherits="Default5" %>

<%@ Register TagPrefix="custom" Namespace="CustomComponents" %>
<!DOCTYPE html PUBLIC "-//W3C//DTD XHTML 1.1//EN"
"http://www.w3.org/TR/xhtml11/DTD/xhtml11.dtd">
<html xmlns="http://www.w3.org/1999/xhtml">
<head runat="server">
  <title>Untitled Page</title>
</head>
<body>
  <form id="form1" runat="server">
    <custom:CreditCardForm6 runat="server" ID="ccf" Font-Bold="true"
```

```
        OnValidatingCreditCard="ValidatingCreditCard" PaymentMethodText="Payment Method"
        CreditCardNoText="Credit Card No." CardholderNameText="Cardholder's Name"
        ExpirationDateText="Expiration Date" SubmitButtonText="Submit"
        OnPaymentMethodChanged="PaymentMethodChangedCallback"
        OnCreditCardNoChanged="CreditCardNoChangedCallback"
        OnCardholderNameChanged="CardholderNameChangedCallback"
        OnExpirationDateChanged="ExpirationDateChangedCallback" />

        <asp:Label runat="server" ID="info" />
    </form>
 </body>
</html>
```

Listing 4-13: The callback methods

```csharp
protected void PaymentMethodChangedCallback(object sender, EventArgs e)
{
  . . .
}

protected void CreditCardNoChangedCallback(object sender, EventArgs e)
{
  . . .
}

protected void CardholderNameChangedCallback(object sender, EventArgs e)

{
  . . .
}

protected void ExpirationDateChangedCallback(object sender, EventArgs e)
{
  . . .
}

protected void ValidatingCreditCard(object sender, ValidatingCreditCardEventArgs e)
{
  info.Text = "Payment Method: ";
  info.Text += (e.PaymentMethod == PaymentMethod.Visa ? "Visa" : "MasterCard");
  info.Text += "<br/>";
  info.Text += "Credit Card No.: ";
  info.Text += e.CreditCardNo;
  info.Text += "<br/>";
  info.Text += "Cardholder's Name: ";
  info.Text += e.CardholderName;
  info.Text += "<br/>";
  info.Text += "Expiration Date: ";
  info.Text += e.ExpirationDate.Month;
  info.Text += "/";
  info.Text += e.ExpirationDate.Year;
}
```

When the user clicks the Submit button of the CreditCardForm6 control, the control raises the ValidatingCreditCard event and consequently calls the ValidatingCreditCard method that the preceding page has registered for the ValidatingCreditCard event. This method simply displays the credit card information as shown in Figure 4-1.

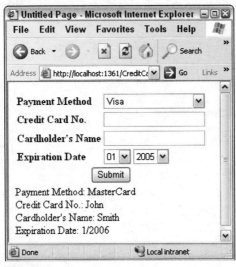

Figure 4-1

Page Life Cycle

As discussed in Chapter 1, the page framework takes the following actions to handle a request for an .aspx file:

1. Parses the .aspx file and creates a tree of control builders.

2. Uses the tree to dynamically implement a class or control that derives from the Page class.

3. Dynamically compiles the class.

4. Caches the compiled class for later use.

5. Dynamically creates an instance of the compiled class. In other words, the page springs to life and starts its life cycle where the page goes through different phases of its life cycle.

As a control developer, you must gain a solid understanding of the page life cycle and its phases, which are shown in Figure 4-2.

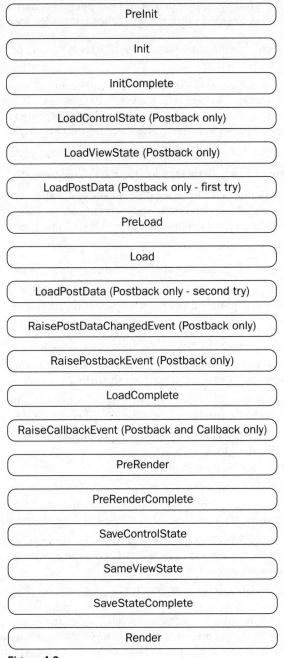

PreInit

Init

InitComplete

LoadControlState (Postback only)

LoadViewState (Postback only)

LoadPostData (Postback only - first try)

PreLoad

Load

LoadPostData (Postback only - second try)

RaisePostDataChangedEvent (Postback only)

RaisePostbackEvent (Postback only)

LoadComplete

RaiseCallbackEvent (Postback and Callback only)

PreRender

PreRenderComplete

SaveControlState

SameViewState

SaveStateComplete

Render

Figure 4-2

The page goes through the following phases (notice some phases are marked as postback only because these are the phases that the page goes through only when it is posted back to the server):

1. The page first retrieves the posted data from the `QueryString` or `Form` collection of the `Request` object.

2. The page then checks whether the posted `Data` collection (the `NameValueCollection Form` or `QueryString`) contains an item with the key `__CALLBACKID`. If it does, it sets its `IsCallback` Boolean property to `true` to signal that the page has been posted back to the server through the ASP.NET client callback mechanism. This mechanism is thoroughly discussed in Chapter 26.

3. **PreInit:** The page takes the following actions in the `PreInit` phase of its life cycle:

   a. Calls its `OnPreInit` method to raise the `PreInit` event.

   b. Initializes the theme by using the contents of the `App_Themes` directory to dynamically implement a class of type `PageTheme`, compiles the class, creates an instance of the compiled class, and assigns the instance to its `PageTheme` property.

   c. Applies the master page.

4. **Init:** The page takes the following actions in the `Init` phase of its life cycle:

   a. Recursively initializes the controls in its `Controls` collection. This initialization includes setting the properties of these controls such as `Page`, `ID`, `NamingContainer`, and so on.

   b. Recursively applies these controls' skins.

   c. Calls its own `OnInit` method to raise its own `Init` event and then recursively calls the child control's `OnInit` methods to raise their `Init` events.

   d. Calls its own `TrackViewState` to start its own view state tracking and then recursively calls the child controls' `TrackViewState` methods to start their view state tracking.

5. **InitComplete:** The page calls its `OnInitComplete` method to raise the `InitComplete` event. This event signals the end of the initialization phase. By this time all controls in the `Controls` collection of the page are initialized.

6. **Load Control State (postback only):** The page recursively calls the `LoadControlState` method of those controls in its `Controls` collection that have called the `RegisterRequiresControlState` method of the page class to express interest in using their control states.

7. **Load View State (postback only):** The page first calls its own `LoadViewState` method and then recursively calls the `LoadViewState` method of the controls in its `Controls` collection to allow them to load their saved view states.

8. **Load Post Data (postback only - first try):** The page calls the `LoadPostData` method of the controls that implement the `IPostBackDataHandler` interface and passes the posted data into it. The `LoadPostData` method of each control must access the posted data and update the respective property of the control accordingly. For example, the `LoadPostData` method of the `TextBox` control assigns the new value of the text box to the `Text` property of the `TextBox` control.

9. **PreLoad:** The page calls its `OnPreLoad` method to raise the `PreLoad` event. This event signals the beginning of the load phase of the page life cycle.

10. **Load:** The page first calls its own `OnLoad` method to raise its own `Load` event and then recursively calls the `OnLoad` methods of the controls in its `Controls` collection to raise their `Load` events. Page developers may register callbacks for the `Load` event, where they may programmatically add child controls to the `Controls` collection of the page.

11. **Load Post Data (postback only second try):** The page calls the `LoadPostData` method of those controls that were programmatically added to its `Controls` collection in the `Load` phase if they implement the `IPostBackDataHandler` interface.

12. **Raise Post Data Changed Event (postback only):** The page calls the `RaisePostData ChangedEvent` method of those controls whose `LoadPostData` method returned true. The `RaisePostDataChangedEvent` method raises post data changed event. For example, the `TextBox` control raises this event when the new value of the text box is different from the old value.

13. **Raise Postback Event (postback only):** The page calls the `RaisePostBackEvent` method of the control whose associated HTML element submitted the form. For example, the `Button` control's associated HTML element posts the page back to the server. The `RaisePostBackEvent` method of a control must map the postback event to one or more server-side events. For example, the `RaisePostBackEvent` method of the `Button` control maps the postback event to the `Command` and `Click` server-side events.

14. **Load Complete:** The page calls its `OnLoadComplete` method to raise the `LoadComplete` event to signal the completion of all loading activities including loading post data and raising post data changed event to allow interested controls to update themselves accordingly.

15. **Raise Callback Event (postback and callback only):** The page calls the `RaiseCallbackEvent` method of the control that uses the ASP.NET client callback mechanism to allow a client-side method (such as a JavaScript function) to call a server-side method without having to post the entire page back to the server. The `RaiseCallbackEvent` method must call the respective server-side methods. If the page is posted back through the client callback mechanism, the page will not go through the rest of its life cycle phases. The ASP.NET client callback mechanism is discussed thoroughly in Chapter 26.

16. **PreRender:** The page takes the following actions in this phase of its life cycle:

    a. Calls its `EnsureChildControls` method to ensure its child controls are created before the page enters its rendering phase.

    b. Calls its own `OnPreRender` method to raise its own `PreRender` event.

    c. Recursively calls the `OnPreRender` methods of the controls in its `Controls` collection to raise their `PreRender` events.

17. **PreRender Complete:** The page calls its `OnPreRenderComplete` method to raise the `PreRenderComplete` event to signal the completion of all prerendering activities.

18. **Save Control State:** The page recursively calls the `SaveControlState` method of those controls in its `Controls` collection that have called the `RegisterRequiresControlState` method of the page class to express interest in saving their control states.

19. **Save View State:** The page first calls its own `SaveViewState` method and then calls the `SaveViewState` method of the controls in its `Controls` collection to allow them to save their view states.

20. **Save State Complete:** The page calls its `OnSaveStateComplete` method to raise the `SaveStateComplete` event to signal the completion of all save state activities.

21. **Rendering:** The page takes the following actions in this phase of its life cycle:

    a.   Creates an instance of the `HtmlTextWriter` class that encapsulates the output stream of the response.

    b.   Calls its `RenderControl` method and passes the `HtmlTextWriter` instance into it.

The `RenderControl` method recursively calls the `RenderControl` methods of the child controls to allow each child control to render its HTML markup text. The HTML markup texts of child controls form the final HTML markup text that is sent to the client browser.

Summary

This chapter showed you how to develop custom controls that raise server-side events such as `ValidatingCreditCard`. It discussed the .NET event implementation pattern, using the `EventHandlerList` class to optimize events, the C# interface implementation pattern, and how to implement the `IPostBackEventHandler` and `IPostBackDataHandler` interfaces to map postback events to server-side events. This chapter also discussed the page life cycle and its phases in detail.

By this point, you should have a good understanding of how simple custom controls work. You've customized your own control that renders its own HTML, and raises its own postback events. This is a good foundation to start from. You're ready to start getting complicated by creating controls that delegate the rendering and event functions to other controls. These are called composite controls, and they are the subject of the next chapter.

5

Developing Custom Composite Controls

The previous chapters showed you how to develop custom controls that derive from the `Control` or `WebControl` base classes and take full responsibility for rendering their HTML markup text. For example, the `CreditCardForm3` custom control (developed in Chapter 2) derives from the `Control` class and overrides its `Render` method to render its own HTML markup text as shown in Listing 2-6. Also, the `CreditCardForm4` and `CreditCardForm5` custom controls (developed in Chapters 3 and 4) derive from the `WebControl` class and override its `RenderContents` method to render their own HTML markup text as shown in Listing 3-16.

You also saw how the custom control classes implement their own postback functionality. For example, the `CreditCardForm6` custom control (developed in Chapter 4) implements the `IPostBackEventHandler` and `IPostBackDataHandler` interfaces to implement its own postback functionality, as shown in Listings 4-5, 4-6, and 4-10.

This chapter shows you how to develop custom controls that delegate these two responsibilities to other standard or custom controls. These controls are known as *composite controls* because you compose other controls to build them. This is based on the well-known object-oriented principle known as Object Composition, where you compose or assemble existing objects to create a new one, allowing you to reuse the existing objects. Object composition simplifies control development because your custom control reuses the features of the existing controls, saving you from having to reimplement these features from scratch.

CreditCardForm6 Revisited

As an example, revisit the `CreditCardForm6` custom control developed in Chapter 4. Because this custom control directly renders its HTML markup text (refer to Listing 3-16) and directly implements its postback functionality (see Listings 4-5, 4-6, and 4-10), you had to write a lot of code to implement this custom control, as discussed in the following two sections.

Rendering HTML

Listing 5-1 shows the code that directly generates the HTML markup text of the `CreditCardForm6` custom control. If you examine this code closely, you'll notice the code can be divided into two groups. The unhighlighted code generates the formatting and layout HTML, and the highlighted code generates the content HTML. This section discusses the highlighted and unhighlighted portions of the boldface code in detail.

Listing 5-1: The RenderContents method of CreditCardForm6

```
protected override void RenderContents(HtmlTextWriter writer)
{
    writer.RenderBeginTag(HtmlTextWriterTag.Tr);
    writer.RenderBeginTag(HtmlTextWriterTag.Td);
    writer.Write(PaymentMethodText);
    writer.RenderEndTag();
    writer.RenderBeginTag(HtmlTextWriterTag.Td);
    writer.AddAttribute(HtmlTextWriterAttribute.Name, PaymentMethodSelectName);
    writer.AddAttribute(HtmlTextWriterAttribute.Id, PaymentMethodSelectId);
    writer.AddStyleAttribute(HtmlTextWriterStyle.Width, "100%");
    writer.RenderBeginTag(HtmlTextWriterTag.Select);
    writer.AddAttribute(HtmlTextWriterAttribute.Value, "0");
    writer.RenderBeginTag(HtmlTextWriterTag.Option);
    writer.Write("Visa");
    writer.RenderEndTag();
    writer.AddAttribute(HtmlTextWriterAttribute.Value, "1");
    writer.RenderBeginTag(HtmlTextWriterTag.Option);
    writer.Write("MasterCard");
    writer.RenderEndTag();
    writer.RenderEndTag();
    writer.RenderEndTag();
    writer.RenderEndTag();
    writer.RenderBeginTag(HtmlTextWriterTag.Tr);
    writer.RenderBeginTag(HtmlTextWriterTag.Td);
    writer.Write(CreditCardNoText);
    writer.RenderEndTag();
    writer.RenderBeginTag(HtmlTextWriterTag.Td);
    writer.AddAttribute(HtmlTextWriterAttribute.Name, CreditCardNoTextInputName);
    writer.AddAttribute(HtmlTextWriterAttribute.Id, CreditCardNoTextInputId);
    writer.AddAttribute(HtmlTextWriterAttribute.Type, "text");
    writer.RenderBeginTag(HtmlTextWriterTag.Input);
    writer.RenderEndTag();
    writer.RenderEndTag();
    writer.RenderEndTag();
    writer.RenderBeginTag(HtmlTextWriterTag.Tr);
    writer.RenderBeginTag(HtmlTextWriterTag.Td);
    writer.Write(CardholderNameText);
    writer.RenderEndTag();
    writer.RenderBeginTag(HtmlTextWriterTag.Td);
    writer.AddAttribute(HtmlTextWriterAttribute.Name, CardholderNameTextInputName);
    writer.AddAttribute(HtmlTextWriterAttribute.Id, CardholderNameTextInputId);
    writer.AddAttribute(HtmlTextWriterAttribute.Type, "text");
    writer.RenderBeginTag(HtmlTextWriterTag.Input);
    writer.RenderEndTag();
```

```
    writer.RenderEndTag();
    writer.RenderEndTag();
    writer.RenderBeginTag(HtmlTextWriterTag.Tr);
    writer.RenderBeginTag(HtmlTextWriterTag.Td);
    writer.Write(ExpirationDateText);
    writer.RenderEndTag();
    writer.RenderBeginTag(HtmlTextWriterTag.Td);
    writer.AddAttribute(HtmlTextWriterAttribute.Name, MonthSelectName);
    writer.AddAttribute(HtmlTextWriterAttribute.Id, MonthSelectId);
    writer.RenderBeginTag(HtmlTextWriterTag.Select);
    for (int day = 1; day < 13; day++)
    {
      writer.AddAttribute(HtmlTextWriterAttribute.Value, day.ToString());
      writer.RenderBeginTag(HtmlTextWriterTag.Option);

      if (day < 10)
        writer.Write("0" + day.ToString());
      else
        writer.Write(day);

      writer.RenderEndTag();
    }
    writer.RenderEndTag();
    writer.Write(" ");
    writer.AddAttribute(HtmlTextWriterAttribute.Name, YearSelectName);
    writer.AddAttribute(HtmlTextWriterAttribute.Id, YearSelectId);
    writer.RenderBeginTag(HtmlTextWriterTag.Select);
    for (int year = 2005; year < 2015; year++)
    {
      writer.AddAttribute(HtmlTextWriterAttribute.Value, year.ToString());
      writer.RenderBeginTag(HtmlTextWriterTag.Option);
      writer.Write(year);
      writer.RenderEndTag();
    }
    writer.RenderEndTag();
    writer.RenderEndTag();
    writer.RenderEndTag();
    writer.RenderBeginTag(HtmlTextWriterTag.Tr);
    writer.AddAttribute(HtmlTextWriterAttribute.Align, "center");
    writer.AddAttribute(HtmlTextWriterAttribute.Colspan, "2");
    writer.RenderBeginTag(HtmlTextWriterTag.Td);
    writer.AddAttribute(HtmlTextWriterAttribute.Type, "submit");
    writer.AddAttribute(HtmlTextWriterAttribute.Value, "Submit");
    writer.AddAttribute(HtmlTextWriterAttribute.Name, SubmitInputName);
    writer.AddAttribute(HtmlTextWriterAttribute.Id, SubmitInputId);
    writer.RenderBeginTag(HtmlTextWriterTag.Input);
    writer.RenderEndTag();
    writer.RenderEndTag();
    writer.RenderEndTag();
}
```

Consider the section marked in boldface in Listing 5-1 as shown again in Listing 5-2.

Listing 5-2: The bold code from Listing 5-1

```
writer.RenderBeginTag(HtmlTextWriterTag.Tr);
writer.RenderBeginTag(HtmlTextWriterTag.Td);
writer.AddAttribute(HtmlTextWriterAttribute.Name, PaymentMethodSelectName);
writer.AddAttribute(HtmlTextWriterAttribute.Id, PaymentMethodSelectId);
writer.AddStyleAttribute(HtmlTextWriterStyle.Width, "100%");
writer.RenderBeginTag(HtmlTextWriterTag.Select);
writer.AddAttribute(HtmlTextWriterAttribute.Value, "0");
writer.RenderBeginTag(HtmlTextWriterTag.Option);
writer.Write("Visa");
writer.RenderEndTag();
writer.AddAttribute(HtmlTextWriterAttribute.Value, "1");
writer.RenderBeginTag(HtmlTextWriterTag.Option);
writer.Write("MasterCard");
writer.RenderEndTag();
writer.RenderEndTag();
writer.RenderEndTag();
writer.RenderEndTag();
```

Listing 5-2 consists of two groups of code. The highlighted code generates the HTML for the payment method list. This is known as *content HTML*. The unhighlighted code generates the HTML for the table row and cell that contain the payment method list. This is known as *formatting* or *layout HTML*. Therefore Listing 5-2 takes responsibility for generating HTML for both the payment method list (content HTML) and the table cell (formatting HTML).

You could've saved yourself time and effort if you had delegated the responsibility of generating the content HTML to an ASP.NET standard `DropDownList` server control, as shown in Listing 5-3. Listing 5-3 calls the `RenderControl` method of the `paymentMethodList` drop-down list and passes the `HtmlTextWriter` object into it. The `RenderControl` method encapsulates the code highlighted in Listing 5-2, saving you from having to write the code yourself. This replaces 13 lines of code — the highlighted code in Listing 5-2 — with a single line of code — the highlighted code in Listing 5-3.

Listing 5-3: Delegating the responsibility for the content HTML list to a DropDownList control

```
writer.RenderBeginTag(HtmlTextWriterTag.Tr);
writer.RenderBeginTag(HtmlTextWriterTag.Td);
paymentMethodList.RenderControl(writer);
writer.RenderEndTag();
writer.RenderEndTag();
```

Therefore you can replace each highlighted section in Listing 5-1 with a single line of code if you delegate the responsibilities of generating the HTML that these highlighted sections generate to the `RenderControl` methods of the appropriate ASP.NET server controls. This will simplify Listing 5-1 and convert it to Listing 5-4. Listing 5-1 contains 109 lines of code, whereas Listing 5-4 contains only 44 lines of code, so you've saved yourself 55 lines of code.

Listing 5-4: The RenderContents method with the content HTML delegated

```
protected override void RenderContents(HtmlTextWriter writer)
{
    writer.RenderBeginTag(HtmlTextWriterTag.Tr);
    writer.RenderBeginTag(HtmlTextWriterTag.Td);
    paymentMethodLabel.RenderControl(writer);
    writer.RenderEndTag();
    writer.RenderBeginTag(HtmlTextWriterTag.Td);
    paymentMethodList.RenderControl(writer);
    writer.RenderEndTag();
    writer.RenderEndTag();
    writer.RenderBeginTag(HtmlTextWriterTag.Tr);
    writer.RenderBeginTag(HtmlTextWriterTag.Td);
    creditCardNoLabel.RenderControl(writer);
    writer.RenderEndTag();
    writer.RenderBeginTag(HtmlTextWriterTag.Td);
    creditCardNoTextBox.RenderControl(writer);
    writer.RenderEndTag();
    writer.RenderEndTag();
    writer.RenderBeginTag(HtmlTextWriterTag.Tr);
    writer.RenderBeginTag(HtmlTextWriterTag.Td);
    cardholderNameLabel.RenderControl(writer);
    writer.RenderEndTag();
    writer.RenderBeginTag(HtmlTextWriterTag.Td);
    cardholderNameTextBox.RenderControl(writer);
    writer.RenderEndTag();
    writer.RenderEndTag();
    writer.RenderBeginTag(HtmlTextWriterTag.Tr);
    writer.RenderBeginTag(HtmlTextWriterTag.Td);
    expirationDateLabel.RenderControl(writer);
    writer.RenderEndTag();
    writer.RenderBeginTag(HtmlTextWriterTag.Td);
    monthList.RenderControl(writer);
    writer.Write(" ");
    yearList.RenderControl(writer);
    writer.RenderEndTag();
    writer.RenderEndTag();
    writer.RenderBeginTag(HtmlTextWriterTag.Tr);
    writer.AddAttribute(HtmlTextWriterAttribute.Align, "center");
    writer.AddAttribute(HtmlTextWriterAttribute.Colspan, "2");
    writer.RenderBeginTag(HtmlTextWriterTag.Td);
    submitButton.RenderControl(writer);
    writer.RenderEndTag();
    writer.RenderEndTag();
}
```

Postback Functionality

As discussed in Chapter 4, the CreditCardForm6 control directly implements the IPostBackEvent Handler and IPostBackDataHandler interfaces to handle its own postback functionality.

Postback Data

Recall from Chapter 4 that `CreditCardForm6` derives from the `IPostBackDataHandler` interface and implements its `LoadPostData` method, where it retrieves the credit card information (payment method, credit card number, cardholder's name, and expiration date) from the posted form data and assigns them to its properties: `PaymentMethod`, `CreditCardNo`, `CardholderName`, and `ExpirationDate`, as shown in Listing 5-5.

Listing 5-5: LoadPostData retrieves the credit card information

```
protected virtual bool LoadPostData(string postDataKey, NameValueCollection values)
{
  PaymentMethod paymentMethod = values[PaymentMethodSelectName] == "0" ?
                                PaymentMethod.Visa : PaymentMethod.MasterCard;
  if (paymentMethod != PaymentMethod)
  {
    PaymentMethod = paymentMethod;
    hasPaymentMethodChanged = true;
  }

  string creditCardNo = values[CreditCardNoTextInputName];
  if (creditCardNo != CreditCardNo)
  {
    CreditCardNo = creditCardNo;
    hasCreditCardNoChanged = true;
  }

  string cardholderName = values[CardholderNameTextInputName];
  if (cardholderName != CardholderName)
  {
    CardholderName = cardholderName;
    hasCardholderNameChanged = true;
  }

  int month = int.Parse(values[MonthSelectName]);
  int year = int.Parse(values[YearSelectName]);
  DateTime expirationDate = new DateTime(year, month, 25);
  if (expirationDate != ExpirationDate)
  {
    ExpirationDate = expirationDate;
    hasExpirationDateChanged = true;
  }

  if (!string.IsNullOrEmpty(values[SubmitInputName]))
    Page.RegisterRequiresRaiseEvent(this);

  return hasPaymentMethodChanged ||
         hasCreditCardNoChanged ||
         hasCardholderNameChanged ||
         hasExpirationDateChanged;
}
```

You could've saved yourself from having to implement this code if you had used `DropDownList` and `TextBox` server controls. These two controls derive from the `IPostBackDataHandler` interface and implement its `LoadPostData` method, where they automatically retrieve the required data from the posted form data and assign them to their own properties.

For example, the `DropDownList` control's implementation of the `LoadPostData` method retrieves the selected value — the value that user has selected from the list — from the posted form data and assigns it to its `SelectedValue` property.

The `TextBox` control's implementation of the `LoadPostData` method, on the other hand, retrieves the text — which the user has entered in the text field — from the posted form data and assigns it to its `Text` property.

Therefore, you don't have to write the code that retrieves the selected value and text from the posted form data. They are already retrieved and assigned to the appropriate properties of the respective server controls. All your custom control needs to do is to call these properties.

Postback Event

As discussed in Chapter 4, `CreditCardForm6` derives from the `IPostBackEventHandler` interface and implements its `RaisePostBackEvent` method, where it maps the postback event to the server-side `ValidateCreditCard` event, as shown in Listing 5-6.

Listing 5-6: RaisePostBackEvent maps the postback event

```
protected virtual void RaisePostBackEvent(string args)
{
  ValidateCreditCardEventArgs ve =
        new ValidateCreditCardEventArgs(PaymentMethod, CreditCardNo,
                                        CardholderName, ExpirationDate);
  OnValidateCreditCard(ve);
}
```

You could've saved yourself from having to implement this code to do the mapping from the postback event to the server-side event by using the ASP.NET standard `Button` server control. This control derives from the `IPostBackEventHandler` interface and implements its `RaisePostBackEvent` method, where it maps the postback event to the server-side `Click` and `Command` events, so the mapping is already done for you. All your custom control needs to do is to register the `OnValidateCreditCard` method as callback for the `Click` event. When the user clicks the Submit button and raises the postback event, the `Button` control maps the postback event to its own `Click` event and automatically calls your `OnValidateCreditCard` method.

Creating Composite Controls

As the previous sections show, it's much easier to assemble existing controls to build a custom control than to build it from scratch. This section walks you through the assembly of a new custom control named `CompositeCreditCardForm` to show you how to assemble your own custom controls from existing standard or custom controls.

The controls from which a composite control is assembled are known as *child controls*. Composite controls delegate most of their responsibilities—such as rendering content HTML and handling postback events—to their child controls. Implementing the `CompositeCreditCardForm` control involves the following actions:

1. Deriving from `CompositeControl`

2. Choosing child controls

3. Choosing layout

4. Implementing a custom container control

5. Creating a container control

6. Creating the child controls of a container control

7. Applying style to a container control

8. Adding a container control to the `CompositeCreditCardForm` control

9. Rendering a container control

10. Overriding the `CreateChildControls` method

11. Overriding the `TagKey` property if necessary

12. Overriding the `CreateControlStyle` method if necessary

13. Exposing the `ControlStyle`'s properties as if they were the properties of the composite control itself

14. Overriding the `RenderContents` method

15. Exposing the properties of the child controls as if they were the properties of the composite control itself

16. Exposing the events that child controls raise as if they were the events of the composite control

The following sections discuss these steps in detail.

Deriving from CompositeControl

The ASP.NET 2.0 Framework comes with a new base class named `CompositeControl` that provides the basic features that every composite control must support. These features are discussed later in this chapter. You must derive your custom composite control from the `CompositeControl` base class to save yourself from having to reimplement the features that your control can easily inherit from this base class:

```
public class CompositeCreditCardForm : CompositeControl
```

Choosing the Child Controls

The next order of business in developing a custom composite control is to choose the child controls that you'll need to assemble your custom control. You'll need the following server controls to assemble the `CompositeCreditCardForm` control (each child control is named for ease of reference):

- ❏ A `Label` control to display the label for the payment method list (`paymentMethodLabel`)

- ❏ A `DropDownList` control to display the payment options or methods (`paymentMethodList`)

- ❏ A `Label` control to display the label for the credit card number text field (`creditCardNoLabel`)

- ❏ A `TextBox` control to allow users to enter their credit card numbers (`creditCardNoTextBox`)

- ❏ A `Label` control to display the label for the cardholder's name text field (`cardholderNameLabel`)

- ❏ A `TextBox` control to allow users to enter their names (`cardholderNameTextBox`)

- ❏ A `Label` control to display the label for the expiration date (`expirationDateLabel`)

- ❏ A `DropDownList` control to display the list of months (`monthList`)

- ❏ A `DropDownList` control to display the list of years (`yearList`)

- ❏ A `Button` control to allow users to submit the credit card information to the server (`submitButton`)

Choosing the Layout

Next you need to choose the desired layout for your child controls. As Figure 5-1 shows, the `CompositeCreditCardForm` control uses a tabular layout for its child controls where each table cell contains one or more child controls. The table cells in Figure 5-1 are numbered for ease of reference.

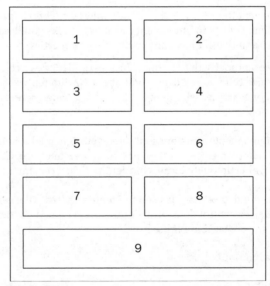

Figure 5-1

The following table shows which numbered cell in Figure 5-1 will contain which child controls:

Containing Cell	Contained Child Controls
Cell number 1	`paymentMethodLabel` child control
Cell number 2	`paymentMethodList` child control
Cell number 3	`creditCardNoLabel` child control
Cell number 4	`creditCardNoTextBox` child control
Cell number 5	`cardholderNameLabel` child control
Cell number 6	`cardholderNameTextBox` child control
Cell number 7	`expirationDateLabel` child control
Cell number 8	`monthList` and `yearList` child controls
Cell number 9	`submitButton` child control

Implementing a Custom Container Control

Because the `CompositeCreditCardForm` control uses a tabular layout for its child controls, where each table cell contains one or more child controls, the appropriate container for the child controls is `TableCell` control. However, the `TableCell` control doesn't meet the following requirements:

❑   It doesn't implement the `INamingContainer` interface. This chapter discusses why it's important for a container control to implement this interface. As you'll see later this interface is a marker interface and doesn't have any methods or properties.

❑   It doesn't expose a property that uniquely locates or identifies a cell among other cells. It's important to know which cell you're dealing with, because different cells contain different types of child controls. For example, cell number 1 contains a `Label` control, and cell number 2 contains a `TextBox` control.

Therefore, this chapter implements a custom container control named `CreditCardFormContainer` that derives from `TableCell`, implements the `INamingContainer` interface, and exposes a property named `ContainerType` whose value uniquely locates or identifies each cell among other cells.

As Figure 5-1 shows, the number of a cell is used to identify or locate the cell among other cells. The `CompositeCreditCardForm` control defines an enumeration named `ContainerType` whose values correspond to the cell numbers used in Figure 5-1:

```
public enum ContainerType
{
  PaymentMethodLabel = 1,
  PaymentMethod = 2,
  CreditCardNoLabel = 3,
  CreditCardNo = 4,
  CardholderNameLabel = 5,
  CardholderName = 6,
  ExpirationDateLabel = 7,
  ExpirationDate = 8,
  SubmitButton = 9
}
```

Listing 5-7 shows the implementation of the `CreditCardFormContainer` container control.

Listing 5-7: The CreditCardFormContainer container control

```
public class CreditCardFormContainer : TableCell, INamingContainer
{
  private ContainerType containerType;

  public CreditCardFormContainer(ContainerType containerType)
  {
    this.containerType = containerType;
  }

  public ContainerType ContainerType
  {
    get { return containerType; }
  }
}
```

Creating a Container Control

The extensibility of a custom control is of paramount importance. As a matter of fact, the extensibility of your custom control is much more important than its feature set. You'd be better off developing an extensible custom control with fewer features than a nonextensible one with more features. An extensible control allows others to extend it to add support for missing features, but the nonextensible one is pretty much it—if it doesn't support the features the clients of your control need, they have no choice but to dump it.

That said, you can't design a custom control that can be extended to support all possible features. This is simply not practical for two reasons. First, you can't see the future, which means you can't plan for all possible extensions. Second, extensibility comes with a price both in terms of time and budget. The more extensible you want your custom control to be, the more time and effort you have to put into it.

This chapter shows you a few examples of how you can make your custom controls more extensible. Here is the first example. As shown in Listing 5-7, the `CreditCardFormContainer` custom container control exposes a single property: `ContainerType`. In the next chapter you'll develop a custom control that extends the `CompositeCreditCardForm` control to add support for templates. As you'll see, such an extension will require some changes in the `CreditCardFormContainer` container control. You can easily add support for this extension if you add a new protected virtual method to your custom control to encapsulate the code that instantiates the container control as shown in Listing 5-8. This will allow others to write new container controls that derive from the `CreditCardFormContainer` control and override this method to return their own container controls.

Listing 5-8: The CreateContainer method encapsulates the code that instantiates the container control

```
protected virtual CreditCardFormContainer CreateContainer(
                                     ContainerType containerType)
{
  return new CreditCardFormContainer(containerType);
}
```

Creating the Child Controls of a Container Control

As discussed, a `CreditCardFormContainer` control is used to represent each numbered cell shown in Figure 5-1. The next order of business is to create the child controls that go into each container control. This is a tricky one because you have to do it in a way that doesn't tie your custom control to a specific set of child controls. The trick is to implement a new protected virtual method (`CreateContainer ChildControls`, shown in Listing 5-9) that encapsulates the code that does the dirty job of creating the child controls. This method must take the container control as its argument, create the child controls, and add them to the container. Therefore the only dependency between your custom control and its child controls is the container control. This dependency is weak considering the fact that others can override the `CreateContainer` method shown in Listing 5-8 to use their own custom container controls.

You can think of the container control as a bucket. Your custom control first calls the `CreateContainer` method to create the bucket. The `CreateContainer` method isolates your custom control from the code that does the dirty job of creating the bucket. Your control then passes the bucket to the `CreateContainerChildControls` method shown in Listing 5-9. `CreateContainerChildControls` creates the child controls and puts them in the bucket. Your custom control doesn't know or care what this method puts into the bucket because your custom control deals with the bucket, not its contents.

Listing 5-9: The CreateContainerChildControls method

```
protected virtual void CreateContainerChildControls(
                                CreditCardFormContainer container)
{
  switch (container.ContainerType)
  {
    case ContainerType.PaymentMethodLabel:
      paymentMethodLabel = new Label();
      paymentMethodLabel.Width = Unit.Percentage(100);
      paymentMethodLabel.ID = "PaymentMethodLabel";
      paymentMethodLabel.Text = PaymentMethodText;
      container.Controls.Add(paymentMethodLabel);
      break;
    case ContainerType.CreditCardNoLabel:
      creditCardNoLabel = new Label();
      creditCardNoLabel.Width = Unit.Percentage(100);
      creditCardNoLabel.ID = "CreditCardNoLabel";
      creditCardNoLabel.Text = CreditCardNoText;
      container.Controls.Add(creditCardNoLabel);
      break;
    case ContainerType.CardholderNameLabel:
      cardholderNameLabel = new Label();
      cardholderNameLabel.Width = Unit.Percentage(100);
      cardholderNameLabel.ID = "CardholderNameLabel";
      cardholderNameLabel.Text = CardholderNameText;
      container.Controls.Add(cardholderNameLabel);
      break;
    case ContainerType.ExpirationDateLabel:
      expirationDateLabel = new Label();
      expirationDateLabel.Width = Unit.Percentage(100);
      expirationDateLabel.ID = "ExpirationDateLabel";
      expirationDateLabel.Text = ExpirationDateText;
```

```
            container.Controls.Add(expirationDateLabel);
            break;
        case ContainerType.SubmitButton:
            submitButton = new Button();
            submitButton.CommandName = "ValidateCreditCard";
            submitButton.Text = SubmitButtonText;
            submitButton.ID = "SubmitButton";
            container.Controls.Add(submitButton);
            break;
        case ContainerType.PaymentMethod:
            paymentMethodList = new DropDownList();
            paymentMethodList.Width = Unit.Percentage(100);
            paymentMethodList.Items.Add(new ListItem("Visa", "Visa"));
            paymentMethodList.Items.Add(new ListItem("MasterCard", "MasterCard"));
            paymentMethodList.ID = "PaymentMethodList";
            container.Controls.Add(paymentMethodList);
            break;
        case ContainerType.CreditCardNo:
            creditCardNoTextBox = new TextBox();
            creditCardNoTextBox.ID = "CreditCardNoTextBox";
            container.Controls.Add(creditCardNoTextBox);
            break;
        case ContainerType.CardholderName:
            cardholderNameTextBox = new TextBox();
            cardholderNameTextBox.ID = "CardholderNameTextBox";
            container.Controls.Add(cardholderNameTextBox);
            break;
        case ContainerType.ExpirationDate:
            monthList = new DropDownList();
            monthList.ID = "MonthList";
            for (int month = 1; month < 13; month++)
            {
                if (month < 10)
                    monthList.Items.Add(new ListItem("0" + month.ToString(),
                                             month.ToString()));

                else
                    monthList.Items.Add(new ListItem(month.ToString(), month.ToString()));
            }

            LiteralControl lc = new LiteralControl(" ");
            yearList = new DropDownList();
            yearList.ID = "YearList";
            for (int year = 2005; year < 2020; year++)
            {
                yearList.Items.Add(new ListItem(year.ToString(), year.ToString()));
            }

            container.Controls.Add(monthList);
            container.Controls.Add(lc);
            container.Controls.Add(yearList);
            break;
    }
}
```

The `CreateContainerChildControls` method first uses the `ContainerType` property of the container control to identify the table cell into which the respective child controls will go. Recall that the values of the `ContainerType` property correspond to the cell numbers shown in Figure 5-1. The containing cell matters because it determines what types of child controls the `CreateContainerChildControls` method must create. For example, the child controls responsible for displaying the label for the payment method list go into cell number 1 in Figure 5-1. The child controls responsible for displaying the payment options, on the other hand, go into cell number 2.

The method then creates the child controls that go into the specified cell or container control. For example, consider the following code fragment that contains the boldface code shown in Listing 5-9. This code fragment creates the `DropDownList` control that goes into cell number 2 in Figure 5-1, initializes the control, and adds the control to the container control passed into the `CreateContainerChildControls` method:

```
case ContainerType.PaymentMethod:
    paymentMethodList = new DropDownList();
    paymentMethodList.Width = Unit.Percentage(100);
    paymentMethodList.Items.Add(new ListItem("Visa", "Visa"));
    paymentMethodList.Items.Add(new ListItem("MasterCard", "MasterCard"));
    paymentMethodList.ID = "PaymentMethodList";
    container.Controls.Add(paymentMethodList);
    break;
```

The `CreateContainerChildControls` method assigns unique values to the ID properties of the child controls, as shown in Listing 5-10.

Listing 5-10: Assigning unique values to the ID properties of the child controls

```
paymentMethodList.ID = "PaymentMethodList";
creditCardNoTextBox.ID = "CreditCardNoTextBox";
cardholderNameTextBox.ID = "CardholderNameTextBox";
yearList.ID = "YearList";
monthList.ID = "MonthList";
paymentMethodLabel.ID = "PaymentMethodLabel";
creditCardNoLabel.ID = "CreditCardNoLabel";
cardholderNameLabel.ID = "CardholderNameLabel";
expirationDateLabel.ID = "ExpirationDateLabel";
submitButton.ID = "SubmitButton";
```

Notice that the `CreateContainerChildControls` method initializes the child controls before they are added to the `Controls` collection.

You must initialize your child controls before you add them to the `Controls` collection of your custom control, because if you initialize them after you add them to the `Controls` collection, these initialized property values will be saved to view state. This will unnecessarily increase the size of your custom control's view state. Recall that the containing page stores the string representation of your control's view state in a hidden field on the page, which means that any increase in the size of your control's view state will increase the size of the page that the requesting browser has to download from the server.

Applying Style to a Container Control

The CompositeCreditCardForm control implements a method named ApplyContainerStyles, shown in Listing 5-11, that encapsulates the code that applies style to a container control. This is yet another example of how you can make your custom control more extensible. Because the ApplyContainerStyles method is marked protected virtual, it allows others to override it to provide their own implementation. You'll see an example of this in the next chapter.

Listing 5-11: The ApplyContainerStyles method

```
protected virtual void ApplyContainerStyles()
{
  ApplyContainerStyle(paymentMethodLabelContainer);
  ApplyContainerStyle(creditCardNoLabelContainer);
  ApplyContainerStyle(cardholderNameLabelContainer);
  ApplyContainerStyle(expirationDateLabelContainer);
  ApplyContainerStyle(submitButtonContainer);
}
```

The ApplyContainerStyles method calls the ApplyContainerStyle method once for each container control. Listing 5-12 shows the implementation of this method.

Listing 5-12: The ApplyContainerStyle method

```
private void ApplyContainerStyle(CreditCardFormContainer container)
{
  container.VerticalAlign = VerticalAlign.Middle;
  container.Wrap = true;
  container.BackColor = Color.FromName("White");
  container.ForeColor = Color.FromName("Black");
  container.Font.Bold = true;

  if (container.ContainerType == ContainerType.SubmitButton)
  {
    container.HorizontalAlign = HorizontalAlign.Center;
    container.ColumnSpan = 2;
  }
  else
    container.HorizontalAlign = HorizontalAlign.Left;
}
```

Adding a Container Control to a Composite Control

The CompositeCreditCardForm control implements a method named AddContainer, shown in Listing 5-13, that encapsulates the code that adds a container control to the Controls collection of the CompositeCreditCardForm control. This method is marked as protected virtual to allow others to override it. For example, others may want to override this method to raise an event before or after the container is added to the Controls collection.

Listing 5-13: The AddContainer method

```
protected virtual void AddContainer(CreditCardFormContainer container)
{
  Controls.Add(container);
}
```

Rendering a Container Control

The `CompositeCreditCardForm` control exposes a method named `RenderContainer`, shown in the following code, that encapsulates the code that renders a container. This method is marked as protected virtual to allow others to override it:

```
protected virtual void RenderContainer(CreditCardFormContainer container,
                                       HtmlTextWriter writer)
{
  container.RenderControl(writer);
}
```

CreateChildControls: One-Stop Shopping for All Your Child Controls

The `Control` class exposes a method named `CreateChildControls` that you must override to create the child controls that you need to assemble your custom control. One important thing to keep in mind about child controls is that they're created on demand. Don't assume that they're created at a particular stage of your custom control's life cycle. They can be created at any time. In other words, the `CreateChildControls` method can be called at any stage of your custom control's life cycle to create the child controls.

This has important consequences. One of these consequences is that you must create the child controls of your custom control in one and only one place — the `CreateChildControls` method. Your custom control mustn't create any of its child controls in any other place. If you create your child controls in any other place, they cannot be created on demand because the on-demand child control creation feature of the ASP.NET Framework is accomplished via calling the `CreateChildControls` method. Think of `CreateChildControls` as your one-stop shopping place for all your child controls. You mustn't shop anywhere else!

Listing 5-14 shows the `CompositeCreditCardForm` control's implementation of the `CreateChildControls` method.

Listing 5-14: The CreateChildControls method

```
protected override void CreateChildControls()
{
  Controls.Clear();

  paymentMethodLabelContainer = CreateContainer(ContainerType.PaymentMethodLabel);
  CreateContainerChildControls(paymentMethodLabelContainer);
```

```
    AddContainer(paymentMethodLabelContainer);

    paymentMethodContainer = CreateContainer(ContainerType.PaymentMethod);
    CreateContainerChildControls(paymentMethodContainer);
    AddContainer(paymentMethodContainer);

    creditCardNoLabelContainer = CreateContainer(ContainerType.CreditCardNoLabel);
    CreateContainerChildControls(creditCardNoLabelContainer);
    AddContainer(creditCardNoLabelContainer);

    creditCardNoContainer = CreateContainer(ContainerType.CreditCardNo);
    CreateContainerChildControls(creditCardNoContainer);
    AddContainer(creditCardNoContainer);

    cardholderNameLabelContainer =
                        CreateContainer(ContainerType.CardholderNameLabel);
    CreateContainerChildControls(cardholderNameLabelContainer);
    AddContainer(cardholderNameLabelContainer);

    cardholderNameContainer = CreateContainer(ContainerType.CardholderName);
    CreateContainerChildControls(cardholderNameContainer);
    AddContainer(cardholderNameContainer);

    expirationDateLabelContainer =
                        CreateContainer(ContainerType.ExpirationDateLabel);
    CreateContainerChildControls(expirationDateLabelContainer);
    AddContainer(expirationDateLabelContainer);

    expirationDateContainer = CreateContainer(ContainerType.ExpirationDate);
    CreateContainerChildControls(expirationDateContainer);
    AddContainer(expirationDateContainer);

    submitButtonContainer = CreateContainer(ContainerType.SubmitButton);
    CreateContainerChildControls(submitButtonContainer);
    AddContainer(submitButtonContainer);

    ChildControlsCreated = true;
}
```

The CreateChildControls method first calls the Clear method of the Controls collection to clear the collection. This ensures that multiple copies of child controls aren't added to the Controls collection when the CreateChildControls method is called multiple times:

```
Controls.Clear();
```

If you examine the implementation of the CompositeCreditCardForm *control, you'll notice this method is never called multiple times. You may be wondering why then bother with clearing the collection. You're right as far as the implementation of the* CompositeCreditCardForm *control goes because you're the author of this control and you can make sure your implementation of this control doesn't call the* CreateChildControls *method multiple times.*

However, you have no control over others when they're deriving from your control to author their own custom controls. There's nothing that would stop them from calling the CreateChildControls *method multiple times. This example shows that when you're writing a custom control you must take the subclasses of your custom control into account.*

Then it takes the following actions for each cell shown in Figure 5-1 to create the child controls that go into the cell:

❑ Calls the `CreateContainer` method to create the container control that represents the cell. For example, the following call to the `CreateContainer` method creates the container control that represents cell number 2 in Figure 5-1:

```
paymentMethodItem = CreateContainer(ContainerType.PaymentMethod);
```

❑ Calls the `CreateContainerChildControls` method and passes the container control into it. As discussed, the `CreateContainerChildControls` method creates the child controls, initializes them, and adds them to the container control. For example, the following call to the `CreateContainerChildControls` method creates the `DropDownList` control that displays the payment options:

```
CreateContainerChildControls(paymentMethodItem);
```

❑ Calls the `AddContainer` method to add the container control to the `CompositeCreditCardForm` control. For example, the following code adds the container control that represents cell number 2 in Figure 5-1 to the `CompositeCreditCardForm` control:

```
AddContainer(paymentMethodItem);
```

After all the child controls are created, the method then sets the `ChildControlsCreated` property to `true`:

```
ChildControlsCreated = true;
```

As discussed, the child controls aren't created at any particular stage of your custom control's life cycle. They're created on demand. This means that the `CreateChildControls` method could be called multiple times. This will waste server resources because this method re-creates the child controls every single time it's called regardless of whether or not the child controls are already created.

To address this problem, the `Control` class exposes a method named `EnsureChildControls` and a Boolean property named `ChildControlsCreated`. The `EnsureChildControls` method checks whether the `ChildControlsCreated` property is set to `false`. If it is, the method first calls the `CreateChildControls` method and then sets the `ChildControlsCreated` property to `true`. The `EnsureChildControls` method uses this property to avoid multiple invocations of the `CreateChildControls` method.

That is why your custom control's implementation of the `CreateChildControls` method must set the `ChildControlsCreated` property to `true` to signal the `EnsureChildControls` method that child controls have been created and the `CreateChildControls` mustn't be called again.

TagKey

As mentioned in Chapter 3, your custom control must use the `TagKey` property to specify the HTML element that will contain the entire contents of your custom control; that is, the containing element of your custom control. Because `CompositeCreditCardForm` displays its contents in a table, the control overrides the `TagKey` property to specify the `table` HTML element as its containing element:

```
protected override HtmlTextWriterTag TagKey
{
  get { return HtmlTextWriterTag.Table; }
}
```

CreateControlStyle

Again, as mentioned in Chapter 3, your custom control must override the CreateControlStyle method to specify the appropriate Style subclass. Recall that the properties of this Style subclass are rendered as CSS style attributes on the containing HTML element. Because CompositeCreditCardForm uses a table HTML element as its containing element, it overrides the CreateControlStyle method to use a TableStyle instance. The TableStyle class exposes properties such as GridLines, CellSpacing, CellPadding, HorizontalAlign, and BackImageUrl that are rendered as CSS table style attributes:

```
protected override Style CreateControlStyle()
{
  return new TableStyle(ViewState);
}
```

Exposing Style Properties

When you override the CreateControlStyle method, you must also define new style properties for your custom control that expose the corresponding properties of the Style subclass. This provides page developers with a convenient mechanism to set the CSS style properties of the containing HTML element.

CompositeCreditCardForm exposes five properties named GridLines, CellSpacing, CellPadding, HorizonalAlign, and BackImageUrl that correspond to the properties of the TableStyle class with the same names, like this:

```
public virtual GridLines GridLines
{
  get { return ((TableStyle)ControlStyle).GridLines; }
  set { ((TableStyle)ControlStyle).GridLines = value; }
}
```

RenderContents

The CreateChildControls method is where you create and initialize the child controls that you need to assemble your custom control. The RenderContents method is where you do the assembly, that is, where you assemble your custom control from the child controls. First you need to understand how the default implementation (the WebControl class's implementation) of the RenderContents method assembles your custom control from the child controls.

The WebControl class's implementation of RenderContents calls the Render method of its base class, the Control class:

```
protected internal virtual void RenderContents(HtmlTextWriter writer)
{
  base.Render(writer);
}
```

Render calls the RenderChildren method of the Control class:

```
protected internal virtual void Render(HtmlTextWriter writer)
{
  RenderChildren(writer);
}
```

RenderChildren calls the RenderControl methods of the child controls in the order in which they are added to the Controls collection:

```
protected internal virtual void RenderChildren(HtmlTextWriter writer)
{
  foreach (Control childControl in Controls)
    childControl.RenderControl(writer);
}
```

In conclusion, the default implementation of the RenderContents method assembles the child controls in the order in which the CreateChildControls method adds them to the Controls collection. This default assembly of the CompositeCreditCardForm custom control will generate the page shown in Figure 5-2. Notice that the default assembly simply lays down the child controls on the page one after another in linear fashion, which is not the layout you want.

Figure 5-2

As Listing 5-15 shows, the CompositeCreditCardForm control overrides the RenderContents method to compose or assemble the child controls in a tabular fashion, as shown in Figure 5-3.

Figure 5-3

Listing 5-15: The RenderContents method of CompositeCreditCardForm

```
protected override void RenderContents(HtmlTextWriter writer)
{
  ApplyContainerStyles();
  writer.RenderBeginTag(HtmlTextWriterTag.Tr);
  RenderContainer(paymentMethodLabelContainer, writer);
  RenderContainer(paymentMethodContainer, writer);
  writer.RenderEndTag();

  writer.RenderBeginTag(HtmlTextWriterTag.Tr);
  RenderContainer(creditCardNoLabelContainer, writer);
  RenderContainer(creditCardNoContainer, writer);
  writer.RenderEndTag();

  writer.RenderBeginTag(HtmlTextWriterTag.Tr);
  RenderContainer(cardholderNameLabelContainer, writer);
  RenderContainer(cardholderNameContainer, writer);
  writer.RenderEndTag();

  writer.RenderBeginTag(HtmlTextWriterTag.Tr);
  RenderContainer(expirationDateLabelContainer, writer);
  RenderContainer(expirationDateContainer, writer);
  writer.RenderEndTag();

  writer.RenderBeginTag(HtmlTextWriterTag.Tr);
  RenderContainer(submitButtonContainer, writer);
  writer.RenderEndTag();
}
```

As Figure 5-1 shows, the `CompositeCreditCardForm` control renders its contents in a table that consists of five rows. The `RenderContents` method in Listing 5-15 first calls the `ApplyContainerStyles` method to apply container styles. Then it performs the following tasks for each table row:

1. Calls the `RenderBeginTag` method of the `HtmlTextWriter` object passed in as its argument to render the opening tag of the `tr` HTML element that represents the row:

```
writer.RenderBeginTag(HtmlTextWriterTag.Tr);
```

2. Calls the `RenderContainer` method once for each cell of the row and passes the container control that represents the cell into it. For example, the following code calls the `RenderContainer` method twice to render the `paymentMethodLabelItem` and `paymentMethodItem` container controls that represent cells number 1 and 2 in Figure 5-1. These two containers contain the `paymentMethodLabel` label and `paymentMethodList DropDownList` child controls.

```
RenderContainer(paymentMethodLabelContainer,writer);
RenderContainer(paymentMethodContainer,writer);
```

3. Calls the `RenderEndTag` method of the `HtmlTextWriter` object to render the closing tag of the `tr` HTML element that represents the row:

```
writer.RenderEndTag();
```

Label Properties

Your composite control must expose the properties of its child controls as if they were its own properties to allow page developers to treat these properties as attributes on the tag that represents your custom control on an ASP.NET page.

`CompositeCreditCardForm` exposes the `Text` properties of its child `Label` and `Button` controls as its own properties, as shown in Listing 5-16.

Listing 5-16: Exposing the Text properties of the child controls

```
public virtual string PaymentMethodText
{
  get
  {
    EnsureChildControls();
    return paymentMethodLabel.Text;
  }
  set
  {
    EnsureChildControls();
    paymentMethodLabel.Text = value;
  }
}

public virtual string CreditCardNoText
{
  get
  {
    EnsureChildControls();
    return creditCardNoLabel.Text;
  }
  set
```

```
    {
      EnsureChildControls();
      creditCardNoLabel.Text = value;
    }
  }

  public virtual string CardholderNameText
  {
    get
    {
      EnsureChildControls();
      return cardholderNameLabel.Text;
    }
    set
    {
      EnsureChildControls();
      cardholderNameLabel.Text = value;
    }
  }

  public virtual string ExpirationDateText
  {
    get
    {
      EnsureChildControls();
      return expirationDateLabel.Text;
    }
    set
    {
      EnsureChildControls();
      expirationDateLabel.Text = value;
    }
  }

  public virtual string SubmitButtonText
  {
    get
    {
      EnsureChildControls();
      return submitButton.Text;
    }
    set
    {
      EnsureChildControls();
      submitButton.Text = value;
    }
  }
```

Because the child controls of your custom composite control are created on demand, there are no guarantees that the child controls are created when the getters and setters of these properties access them. That's why the getters and setters of these properties call `EnsureChildControls` before they access the respective child controls. In general, your custom control must call `EnsureChildControls` before it accesses any of its child controls.

Exposing the properties of child controls as the top-level properties of your composite control provides page developers with the following benefits:

❑ They can set the property values of child controls as attributes on the tag that represents your composite control on an ASP.NET page. The following code shows how page developers can set the values of the Text properties of the Label and Button child controls as attributes on the `<custom:CompositeCreditCardForm>` tag:

```
<custom:CompositeCreditCardForm ID="ccf" runat="server" SubmitButtonText="Submit"
CardholderNameText="Cardholder's name" CreditCardNoText="Credit Card No."
PaymentMethodText="Payment Method" ExpirationDateText="Expiration Date" />
```

If your custom composite control doesn't expose the properties of its child controls as its top-level properties, page developers will have no choice but to use the error-prone approach of indexing the Controls collection of the composite control to access the desired child control and set its properties.

❑ They can treat your custom control as a single entity. In other words, your composite control allows page developers to set the properties of its child controls as if they were setting its own properties.

Event Bubbling

The same argument presented in the previous section to show why your custom composite control must expose the properties of its child controls as its own properties applies to the events that the child controls raise. Your custom composite control must catch the events that its child controls raise and expose them as its own events. This will allow page developers to register callbacks for the events of the child controls as if they were the events of the composite control itself. This saves page developers from having to search in the composite control's Controls collection for the desired child control to register the callback for the child control's event.

This raises the following question: How can a composite control catch the event that one of its child controls raises and raise one of its own events instead? Typically child controls raise events known as Command events. Currently only Button, ImageButton, and LinkButton controls raise the Command event. To help you understand how the Command event works, take a look at how a child control such as Button implements this event.

A child control takes the steps discussed in Chapter 4 to implement the Command event:

1. The control defines an event key that is used to store and retrieve the event delegate from the control's Events collection:

```
private static readonly object CommandEventKey = new object();
```

2. The control defines the event property:

```
public event CommandEventHandler Command
{
   add { Events.AddHandler(CommandEventKey, value); }
   remove { Events.RemoveHandler(CommandEventKey, value); }
}
```

3. The control implements a protected virtual method that raises the event:

```
protected virtual void OnCommand(CommandEventArgs e)
{
  CommandEventHandler handler = Events[CommandEventKey] as CommandEventHandler;

  if (handler != null)
    handler(this, e);

  RaiseBubbleEvent(this, e);
}
```

The CommandEventArgs class is the event data class that holds the event data for the Command event. The event data in this case are the command name and command argument. The CommandEventArgs class exposes two properties named CommandName and CommandArgument to hold these two event data.

The OnCommand method calls the RaiseBubbleEvent method of the child control and passes the CommandEventArgs instance into it. The child control inherits the RaiseBubbleEvent method from the Control class. This method bubbles the Command event that the child control raises up to its parent — the CompositeCreditCardForm composite control.

As this example shows, to bubble an event such as Command you must call the RaiseBubbleEvent method from within the method that raises the event, such as the OnCommand method. Currently only the Command event is bubbled up. However, you can follow the same steps described in this section to bubble up your own custom events.

4. Finally, the control implements the RaisePostBackEvent method of the IPostBackEventHandler interface, where it takes the following two actions:

    a. Creates an instance of the CommandEventArgs class. The child control typically exposes two properties named CommandName and CommandArgument and passes the values of these two properties to the constructor of the CommandEventArgs class when it's creating the instance of the class. The constructor of this class internally assigns these two values to the CommandName and CommandArgument properties of the class.

    b. Calls the OnCommand method and passes the CommandEventArgs instance into it. As just discussed, the OnCommand method calls the RaiseBubbleEvent method to bubble the Command event up to the CompositeCreditCardForm composite control.

```
protected virtual void RaisePostBackEvent(string eventArgument)
{
  ...
  CommandEventArgs e = new CommandEventArgs (CommandName, CommandArgument);
  OnCommand(e);
}
```

Now that you understand how a child control manages to bubble its event up to its parent, the composite control, you can now see how the composite control manages to catch this event.

The Control class exposes a method named OnBubbleEvent that your custom composite control must override to catch the Command event that its child controls raise and bubble up. Listing 5-17 shows the CompositeCreditCardForm control's implementation of the OnBubbleEvent method.

Listing 5-17: The OnBubbleEvent method of CompositeCreditCardForm

```
protected override bool OnBubbleEvent(object source, EventArgs args)
{
  bool handled = false;

  CommandEventArgs ce = args as CommandEventArgs;
  if (ce != null && ce.CommandName == "ValidateCreditCard")
  {
    PaymentMethod paymentMethod = GetPaymentMethod();
    string creditCardNo = GetCreditCardNo();
    string cardholderName = GetCardholderName();
    DateTime expirationDate = GetExpirationDate();
    ValidateCreditCardEventArgs ve = new ValidateCreditCardEventArgs(paymentMethod,
                                 creditCardNo, cardholderName, expirationDate);
    OnValidateCreditCard(ve);
    handled = true;
  }

  return handled;
}
```

The OnBubbleEvent method first checks whether the event that it just caught is a Command event:

```
CommandEventArgs ce = args as CommandEventArgs;
```

It then checks whether the CommandName property of the Command event is set to the string value "ValidateCreditCard". As shown in Listing 5-9, the CompositeCreditCardForm control assigns the string value "ValidateCreditCard" to the CommandName property of its child Button control:

```
if (ce != null && ce.CommandName == "ValidateCreditCard")
```

The method then calls the GetPaymentMethod, GetCreditCardNo, GetCardholderName, and GetExpirationDate methods to retrieve the credit card information from the respective child controls. This is another example of making your custom control extensible. Retrieving the credit card data requires direct access to the child controls. For example, you have to call the SelectedValue of the paymentMethodList DropDownList child control to retrieve the selected payment method:

```
PaymentMethod paymentMethod = GetPaymentMethod();
string creditCardNo = GetCreditCardNo();
string cardholderName = GetCardholderName();
DateTime expirationDate = GetExpirationDate();
```

The GetPaymentMethod, GetCreditCardNo, GetCardholderName, and GetExpirationDateMethods methods encapsulate the code that directly calls the properties and methods of the child controls. Because these methods are marked as protected virtual, others can override them to retrieve the credit card information from other types of child controls, such as RadioBox.

```
protected virtual PaymentMethod GetPaymentMethod()
{
```

```
      return (paymentMethodList.SelectedValue == "Visa") ? PaymentMethod.Visa :
                                                PaymentMethod.MasterCard;
}

protected virtual string GetCreditCardNo()
{
   return creditCardNoTextBox.Text;
}

protected virtual string GetCardholderName()
{
   return cardholderNameTextBox.Text;
}

protected virtual DateTime GetExpirationDate()
{
   return new DateTime(int.Parse(yearList.SelectedValue),
                       int.Parse(monthList.SelectedValue), 25);
}
```

Next, the OnBubbleEvent method passes the retrieved credit card data as arguments to the constructor of the ValidateCreditCardEventArgs class. Recall that this class holds the event data for the ValidateCreditCard event as shown in Listing 4-1. The event data include payment method, credit card number, cardholder's name, and expiration date (for more information about the ValidateCreditCard event, refer to Chapter 4):

```
ValidateCreditCardEventArgs ve = new ValidateCreditCardEventArgs(paymentMethod,
                             creditCardNo, cardholderName, expirationDate);
```

Finally, the method calls the OnValidateCreditCard method and passes the ValidateCreditCardEventArgs instance to raise the ValidateCreditCard event (for more information about the OnValidateCreditCard method, refer to Chapter 4):

```
OnValidateCreditCard(ve);
```

In conclusion, CompositeCreditCardForm overrides the OnBubbleEvent method to catch the Command event that the Submit child control raises and raise its own ValidateCreditCard event instead.

What Your Custom Control Inherits from CompositeControl

The ASP.NET CompositeControl provides the basic features that every composite control must support:

❑   Overriding the Controls collection.

❑   Implementing INamingInterface.

❑   Overriding the DataBind method.

❑   Implementing the `ICompositeControlDesignerAccessor` interface. This interface exposes a single method named `ReCreateChildControls` that allows designer developers to re-create the child controls of a composite control on the designer surface. This is useful if you want to develop a custom designer for your composite control. A designer is a component that allows page developers to work with your custom composite control in a designer such as Visual Studio. This chapter doesn't cover designers.

❑   Overriding the `Render` method to call `EnsureChildControls` when the control is in design mode before the actual rendering begins. This ensures child controls are created before they are rendered.

Overriding the Controls Collection

As discussed, the child controls that you need to assemble your custom control aren't created at any particular phase of your control's life cycle. They're created on demand. Therefore, there are no guarantees that the child controls are created when the `Controls` collection is accessed. That's why `CompositeControl` overrides the `Collection` property to call the `EnsureChildControls` method to ensure the child controls are created before the collection is accessed:

```
public override ControlCollection Controls
{
  get
  {
    EnsureChildControls();
    return base.Controls;
  }
}
```

INamingContainer Interface

As shown in Listing 5-10, the `CompositeCreditCardForm` control assigns unique values to the ID properties of all of its child controls. For example, it assigns the string value `"PaymentMethodLabel"` to the ID property of the `paymentMethodLabel` child control. This string value is unique in that no other child control of the `CompositeCreditCardForm` control has the same ID property.

Now examine what happens when page developers use two instances of the `CompositeCreditCardForm` control on the same ASP.NET Web page. Call the first instance `CompositeCreditCardForm_1` and the second instance `CompositeCreditCardForm_2`. Even though the ID properties of the child controls of each instance are unique within the scope of the instance, they aren't unique within the page scope because the ID property of a given child control of one instance is the same as the ID property of the corresponding child control of the other instance. For example, the ID property of the `paymentMethodLabel` child control of the `CompositeCreditCardForm_1` instance is the same as the ID property of the `paymentMethodLabel` child control of the `CompositeCreditCardForm_2` instance.

So, can the ID property value of a child control of a composite control be used to locate the control? It depends. Any code within the scope of the composite control can use the ID property value of a child control to locate it because the ID property values are unique within the scope of the composite control.

However, if the code isn't within the scope of the composite control, it can't use the ID property to locate the child control on the page if the page contains more than one instance of the composite control. Two very good examples of this case are as follows:

❑ The client-side code uses the id attribute of a given HTML element to locate it on the page. This scenario is very common considering how popular DHTML is.

❑ The page also needs to uniquely identify and locate a server control on the page to delegate postback and postback data events to it.

So what property of the child control should the code that is not within the scope of the composite control use to locate the child control on the page? The Control class exposes two important properties named ClientID and UniqueID. The page is responsible for assigning values to these two properties that are unique on the page. The ClientID and UniqueID properties of a control are rendered as the id and name HTML attributes on the HTML element that contains the control. As you know, client code uses the id attribute to locate the containing HTML element on the page, and the page uses the name attribute to locate the control on the page.

The page doesn't automatically assign unique values to the ClientID and UniqueID properties of the child controls of a composite control. The composite control must implement the INamingContainer interface to request the page to assign unique values to these two properties. The INamingContainer interface is a marker interface and doesn't expose any methods, properties, or events.

You may wonder how the page manages to assign unique values to the ClientID and UniqueID properties of the child controls of a composite control. A child control inherits the NamingContainer property from the Control class. This property refers to the first ascendant control of the child control that implements the INamingContainer interface. If your custom composite control implements this interface, it becomes the NamingContainer of its child controls. The page concatenates the ClientID of the NamingContainer of a child control to its ID with an underscore character as the separator to create a unique string value for the ClientID of the child control. The page does the same thing to create a unique string value for the UnqiueID of the child control with one difference — the separator character is a colon (in ASP.NET 1x) or dollar (in ASP.NET 2.0) rather than an underscore character.

The reason the page doesn't use the colon character as the separator when it is generating the unique string value for the ClientID is that JavaScript doesn't allow its variables to contain colon characters. As a matter of fact, ASP.NET doesn't allow page developers to set the ID property of a control to a string value that contains a colon character because the page uses the ID property value of a control to generate the unique string value for its ClientID property.

You may wonder why the server-side code doesn't use the ClientID instead of the UniqueID considering the fact that the ClientID has a unique value on the page. Why two separate properties? When the page is trying to locate a control on the page, it uses the separator character to recursively split the UniqueID of the control into two strings, where the first string is the UniqueID of one of the ascendants of the control. For example, the first split provides the page with the UniqueID of the root ascendant of the control. The second split provides the page with the UniqueID of the second ascendant control from the root.

Since the ID property of a child control cannot contain a colon or dollar character, this character can be used to extract the UniqueIDs of all the ascendants of the child control, which is then used to locate the child control on the page.

Summary

This chapter showed you how to assemble your custom controls from existing standard and custom controls instead of building them from scratch. These controls, known as composite controls, delegate their responsibilities such as rending HTML and mapping postback events to server-side events to other custom and standard controls.

The chapter provided you with a detailed step-by-step recipe for developing custom composite controls and used the recipe to develop a custom composite control named CompositeCreditCardForm. The recipe included steps such as implementing a custom container control, creating a container control, creating the child controls of a container control, overriding CreateChildControls, RenderContents, TagKey, and CreateControlStyle, and so on.

The assembly of a composite control involves two major methods—CreateChildControls and RenderContents. CreateChildControls is where you create the child controls you need to assemble your composite control. RenderContents is where you assemble your composite control from the child controls. The next chapter shows you how to make the assembly of a composite control more customizable.

6

Developing Custom Templated Controls

As you learned in Chapter 5, the assembly of a composite control such as CompositeCredit CardForm involves two important methods: CreateChildControls and RenderContents. CreateChildControls (see Listing 5-14) creates the child controls that RenderContents (see Listing 5-15) uses to assemble the composite control.

Listing 5-15 shows how RenderContents assembles CompositeCreditCardForm from its child controls. RenderContents uses a table with five rows, where each row contains two cells, except for the last row, which contains a single cell. This chapter shows you how to develop a custom composite credit card form that will allow the page developer to customize the child controls that go into the odd cells, that is, cell numbers 1, 3, 5, 7, and 9, as shown in Figure 6-1.

Customizing the Contents of a Container Control

Listing 6-1 shows the portion of the CreateContainerChildControls method of the CompositeCreditCardForm control (refer to Listing 5-9). As this code listing illustrates, CreateContainerControls hard-codes the child controls that go into the odd cells in Figure 6-1.

Listing 6-1: The child controls portion of the CreateContainerChildControls method

```
protected virtual void CreateContainerChildControls(
                                CreditCardFormContainer container)
{
   switch (container.ContainerType)
```

(continued)

Listing 6-1: *(continued)*

```
{
    case ContainerType.PaymentMethodLabel:
        // Hardcodes the child control that goes into the cell number 1
        paymentMethodLabel = new Label();
        paymentMethodLabel.Width = Unit.Percentage(100);
        paymentMethodLabel.ID = "PaymentMethodLabel";
        paymentMethodLabel.Text = PaymentMethodText;
        container.Controls.Add(paymentMethodLabel);
        break;
    case ContainerType.CreditCardNoLabel:
        // Hardcodes the child control that goes into the cell number 3
        creditCardNoLabel = new Label();
        creditCardNoLabel.Width = Unit.Percentage(100);
        creditCardNoLabel.ID = "CreditCardNoLabel";
        creditCardNoLabel.Text = CreditCardNoText;
        container.Controls.Add(creditCardNoLabel);
        break;
    case ContainerType.CardholderNameLabel:
        // Hardcodes the child control that goes into the cell number 5
        cardholderNameLabel = new Label();
        cardholderNameLabel.Width = Unit.Percentage(100);
        cardholderNameLabel.ID = "CardholderNameLabel";
        cardholderNameLabel.Text = CardholderNameText;
        container.Controls.Add(cardholderNameLabel);
        break;
    case ContainerType.ExpirationDateLabel:
        // Hardcodes the child control that goes into the cell number 7
        expirationDateLabel = new Label();
        expirationDateLabel.Width = Unit.Percentage(100);
        expirationDateLabel.ID = "ExpirationDateLabel";
        expirationDateLabel.Text = ExpirationDateText;
        container.Controls.Add(expirationDateLabel);
        break;
    case ContainerType.SubmitButton:
        // Hardcodes the child control that goes into the cell number 9
        submitButton = new Button();
        submitButton.CommandName = "ValidateCreditCard";
        submitButton.Text = SubmitButtonText;
        submitButton.ID = "SubmitButton";
        container.Controls.Add(submitButton);
        break;
    ...
    }
}
```

Because the child controls are hard-coded, page developers have no say in what child controls are used to assemble `CompositeCreditCardForm`, and consequently `RenderContents` always assembles this control from the same set of child controls.

To tackle this problem, the ASP.NET Framework provides you with a mechanism to write custom composite controls known as *templated controls*, which allow page developers to specify the child controls that are used to assemble the composite control. In this chapter you develop a custom templated control named `TemplatedCreditCardForm` that derives from `CompositeCreditCardForm` and uses this mechanism to allow page developers to specify the child controls that go into the odd cells in Figure 6-1.

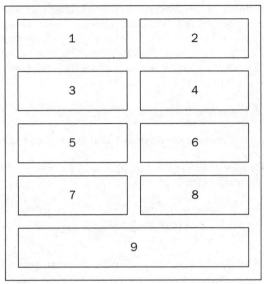

Figure 6-1

Deriving from `CompositeCreditCardForm` saves you from having to write a lot of code to reimplement the features that `CompositeCreditCardForm` already supports. `CompositeCreditCardForm` saves you from having to do the following:

❑ Derive your custom control from the ASP.NET 2.0 `CompositeControl` base class

❑ Implement the `CreditCardFormContainer` custom container control

❑ Override the `CreateChildControls` method

❑ Override the `TagKey` property to use the table HTML element as the element that contains the entire contents of the `TemplatedCreditCardForm` control because this control displays its contents in a table

❑ Override the `ControlStyle` method to use `TableStyle` to style the containing element because the containing element is a table HTML element

❑ Implement the table style properties, that is, `GridLines`, `CellSpacing`, `CellPadding`, `HorizontalAlign`, and `BackImageUrl` to expose the `TableStyle` properties

❑ Override the `RenderContents` method

❑ Implement the `ValidateCreditCard` event

❑ Implement the `OnValidateCreditCard` method to raise the `ValidateCreditCard` event

❑ Override the `OnBubbleEvent` method to catch the `Command` events that the child controls raise and raise the `ValidateCreditCard` event instead

TemplatedCreditCardForm

The `switch` statement used in the `CreateContainerChildControls` method of the `CompositeCredit CardForm` control (see Listing 6-1) consists of one `case` statement for each odd cell in which the `case` statement hard-codes the child controls that go into the cell. The `TemplatedCreditCardForm` control first exposes one read-write property of type `ITemplate` for each `case` statement, as shown in the following table. The properties of type `ITemplate` are known as *template properties*. Each template property uses a private field of type `ITemplate` as its backing store. The `ITemplate` interface exposes a single method named `InstantiateIn`. The syntax for each property is the same. For example, here's the first `case` statement from `CreateContainerChildControls`:

```
case ContainerType.PaymentMethodLabel
```

And here's the corresponding template property in `TemplatedCreditCardForm`:

```
private ITemplate paymentMethodLabelTemplate;
public ITemplate PaymentMethodLabelTemplate
{
   get { return paymentMethodLabelTemplate; }
   set { paymentMethodLabelTemplate = value; }
}
```

The case enumerations and their corresponding template property names are as follows:

Case Enumerations	Associated Property Name
PaymentMethodLabel	paymentMethodLabelTemplate
CreditCardNoLabel	creditCardNoLabelTemplate
CardholderNameLabel	cardholderNameLabelTemplate
ExpirationDateLabel	expirationDateLabelTemplate
SubmitButton	submitButtonTemplate

The `TemplatedCreditCardForm` control then overrides the `CreateContainerChildControls` method of the `CompositeCreditCardForm` control to remove the code that hard-codes the child controls from each `case` statement and replaces it with a call to the `InstantiateIn` method of its associated template property, as shown in Listing 6-2.

Listing 6-2: Using the InstantiateIn methods of the template properties

```
protected override void CreateContainerChildControls(
                                   CreditCardFormContainer container)
{
   switch (container.ContainerType)
   {
     case ContainerType.PaymentMethodLabel:
       if (paymentMethodLabelTemplate != null)
         paymentMethodLabelTemplate.InstantiateIn(container);
```

```
      else
        base.CreateContainerChildControls(container);
      break;
    case ContainerType.CreditCardNoLabel:
      if (creditCardNoLabelTemplate != null)
        creditCardNoLabelTemplate.InstantiateIn(container);
      else
        base.CreateContainerChildControls(container);
      break;
    case ContainerType.CardholderNameLabel:
      if (cardholderNameLabelTemplate != null)
        cardholderNameLabelTemplate.InstantiateIn(container);
      else
        base.CreateContainerChildControls(container);
      break;
    case ContainerType.ExpirationDateLabel:
      if (expirationDateLabelTemplate != null)
        expirationDateLabelTemplate.InstantiateIn(container);
      else
        base.CreateContainerChildControls(container);
      break;
    case ContainerType.SubmitButton:
      if (submitButtonTemplate != null)
        submitButtonTemplate.InstantiateIn(container);
      else
        base.CreateContainerChildControls(container);
      break;
    default:
      base.CreateContainerChildControls(container);
      break;
  }
}
```

As Listing 6-2 shows, each `case` statement checks whether its associated template property is null. If it is, it delegates the responsibility of creating the child controls to the `CreateContainerChildControls` method of its base class, that is, `CompositeCreditCardForm`. Recall that the `CreateContainerChildControls` method of the base class creates the associated hard-coded child controls.

If the template property isn't null, the `case` statement delegates the responsibility of creating the child controls to the `InstantiateIn` method of its associated template property. The `InstantiateIn` method of the template property creates the child controls that the page developer has specified within the opening and closings tags of the template property on the respective `.aspx` file.

Using the Template in an ASP.NET Page

Listing 6-3 shows an ASP.NET page where the page developer has declaratively specified the contents of the `PaymentMethodLabelTemplate`, `CreditCardNoLabelTemplate`, `CardholderNameLabelTemplate`, `ExpirationDateLabelTemplate`, and `SubmitButtonTemplate` template properties of the `TemplatedCreditCardForm` control.

Listing 6-3: Using the template to specify the contents of the ASP page

```
<%@ Page Language="C#" AutoEventWireup="true" CodeFile="Default8.aspx.cs"
Inherits="Default8" %>
<%@ Register TagPrefix="custom" Namespace="CustomComponents" %>

<html xmlns="http://www.w3.org/1999/xhtml" >
<head runat="server"><title>Untitled Page</title></head>
<body>
  <form id="form1" runat="server">
    <custom:TemplatedCreditCardForm ID="ccf" runat="server" Font-Bold="true"
    OnValidateCreditCard="ValidateCreditCard" SubmitButtonText="Submit"
    CardholderNameText="Cardholder's name" CreditCardNoText="Credit Card No."
    PaymentMethodText="Payment Method" ExpirationDateText="Expiration Date">
      <PaymentMethodlabelTemplate>
        <table width="100%" style="font-size:x-large;background-image:url(img.bmp);
        font-style:italic;font-weight:bold;color:White;">
          <tr>
            <td width="100%">Payment Method</td>
          </tr>
        </table>
      </PaymentMethodlabelTemplate>
      <CreditCardNolabelTemplate>
        <table width="100%" style="font-size:x-large;background-image:url(img.bmp);
        font-style:italic;font-weight:bold;color:White;">
          <tr>
            <td width="100%">Credit Card No.</td>
          </tr>
        </table>
      </CreditCardNolabelTemplate>
      <CardholderNamelabelTemplate>
        <table width="100%" style="font-size:x-large;background-image:url(img.bmp);
        font-style:italic;font-weight:bold;color:White;">
          <tr>
            <td width="100%">Cardholder's Name</td>
          </tr>
        </table>
      </CardholderNamelabelTemplate>
      <ExpirationDatelabelTemplate>
        <table width="100%" style="font-size:x-large;background-image:url(img.bmp);
        font-style:italic;font-weight:bold;color:White;">
          <tr>
            <td width="100%">Expiration Date</td>
          </tr>
        </table>
      </ExpirationDatelabelTemplate>
      <SubmitButtonTemplate>
        <table width="100%" style="font-size:x-large;background-image:url(img.bmp);
        font-style:italic;font-weight:bold;color:White;">
          <tr>
            <td width="100%">
              <asp:LinkButton runat="server" CommandName="ValidateCreditCard"
              Text="Submit" Font-Italic="true"
```

```
                  Font-Bold="true" ForeColor="White" Font-Size="X-Large" />
            </td>
          </tr>
        </table>
      </SubmitButtonTemplate>
    </custom:TemplatedCreditCardForm><br /><br />
    <asp:Label runat="server" ID="info" />
  </form>
</body>
</html>
```

Figure 6-2 shows what the users see in their browsers.

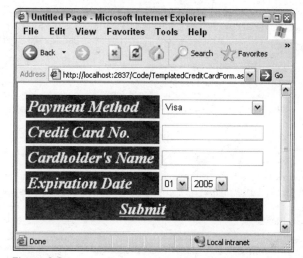

Figure 6-2

Under the Hood of the Template

As you saw in the previous section, it took the following two easy steps to enable the
`TemplatedCreditCardForm` control to support templates:

1. Define read-write properties of type `ITemplate`.

2. Override the `CreateContainerChildControls` method to remove the code that hard-codes
    the child controls from each `case` statement and replace it with a call to the `InstantiateIn`
    method of its associated template property.

This section takes you behind the scenes to show you how the ASP.NET Framework template model
works. As an example, consider the simple page shown in Listing 6-4, where the page developer has
specified a `Label` control within the opening and closing tags of the `PaymentMethodLabelTemplate`
property of the `TemplatedCreditCardForm` control.

Listing 6-4: A simple page where the page developer has specified a Label control within the PaymentMethodLabelTemplate property's tags

```
<%@ Page Language="C#" AutoEventWireup="true" CodeFile="Default8.aspx.cs"
Inherits="Default8" %>
<%@ Register TagPrefix="custom" Namespace="CustomComponents" %>

<html xmlns="http://www.w3.org/1999/xhtml" >
<head runat="server"><title>Untitled Page</title></head>
<body>
  <form id="form1" runat="server">
    <custom:TemplatedCreditCardForm ID="templatedCreditCardForm"
    runat="server" Font-Bold="true"
    OnValidateCreditCard="ValidateCreditCard" SubmitButtonText="Submit"
    CardholderNameText="Cardholder's name" CreditCardNoText="Credit Card No."
    PaymentMethodText="Payment Method" ExpirationDateText="Expiration Date">
      <PaymentMethodlabelTemplate>
        <asp:Label runat="server" ID="PaymentMethodLabel" Text="Payment Method" />
      </PaymentMethodlabelTemplate>
    </custom:TemplatedCreditCardForm><br /><br />
    <asp:Label runat="server" ID="info" />
  </form>
</body>
</html>
```

The ASP.NET Framework parses the content within the opening and closing tags of the `PaymentMethodLabelTemplate` property. It then dynamically implements a component or class that derives from the `ITemplate` interface. Call this class `PaymentMethodLabelCreator`. Listing 6-5 shows the implementation of this class.

Listing 6-5: The PaymentMethodLabelCreator class

```
public class PaymentMethodLabelCreator : ITemplate
{
  void ITemplate.InstantiateIn(Control container)
  {
    Label childControl = new Label();
    childControl.Width = Unit.Percentage(100);
    childControl.ID = "PaymentMethodLabel";
    childControl.Text ="Payment Method";
    container.Controls.Add(childControl);
  }
}
```

The `InstantiateIn` method of the `PaymentMethodLabelCreator` class contains the code that creates the `Label` child control that the page developer has declaratively specified within the opening and closing tags of the `PaymentMethodLabelTemplate` property. `InstantiateIn` assigns the values of the `ID`, `Text`, and `Width` attributes that the page developer has specified on the `<asp:Label>` tag (see Listing 6-4) to the `ID`, `Text`, and `Width` properties of the newly created `Label` child control.

The Framework then dynamically compiles the `PaymentMethodLabelCreator` class, and dynamically creates an instance of the class:

```
PaymentMethodLabelCreator paymentMethodLabelCreator =
                                      new PaymentMethodLabelCreator();
```

Finally, the Framework dynamically assigns this instance to the `PaymentMethodLabelTemplate` property of the `TemplatedCreditCardForm` control declared in Listing 6-4. From this point on, the `TemplatedCreditCardForm` control enters the scene. The following code shows the portion of the `CreateChildControls` method shown in Listing 5-14:

```
protected override void CreateChildControls()
{
  Controls.Clear();
  paymentMethodLabelContainer = CreateContainer(ContainerType.PaymentMethodLabel);
  CreateContainerChildControls(paymentMethodLabelContainer);
  AddContainer(paymentMethodLabelContainer);  ...
  ...
}
```

As the code shows, the `CreateChildControls` method first calls the `CreateContainer` method to create the `paymentMethodLabelContainer` container control:

```
paymentMethodLabelContainer = CreateContainer(ContainerType.PaymentMethodLabel);
```

Then it calls the `CreateContainerChildControls` method and passes the `paymentMethodLabelContainer` container control into it:

```
CreateContainerChildControls(paymentMethodLabelContainer);
```

The following code shows the portion of the `CreateContainerChildControls` method shown in Listing 6-2:

```
protected override void CreateContainerChildControls(CreditCardFormContainer item2)
{
  switch (container.ContainerType)
  {
    case ContainerType.PaymentMethodLabel:
      if (paymentMethodLabelTemplate != null)
        paymentMethodLabelTemplate.InstantiateIn(container);
      else
        base.CreateContainerChildControls(container);
      break;
    ...
  }
}
```

The `CreateContainerChildControls` method calls the `InstantiateIn` method of the `PaymentMethodLabelTemplate` property and passes the `paymentMethodLabelContainer` container control into it. Because the ASP.NET Framework has assigned an instance of the `PaymentMethodLabelCreator` class to the `PaymentMethodLabelTemplate` property, this automatically calls the `InstantiateIn` method shown in Listing 6-5 and passes the `paymentMethodLabelContainer` container control into it. As Listing 6-5 shows, the `InstantiateIn` method creates the `Label` child control, initializes its `Width`, `Text`, and `ID` properties, and adds it to the `Controls` collection of the `paymentMethodLabelContainer` container control.

The `CreateChildControls` method then calls the `AddContainer` method to add the `paymentMethodLabelContainer` container control to the `Controls` collection of the `TemplatedCreditCardForm` control:

```
AddContainer(paymentMethodLabelContainer);
```

Data Binding Expressions

When you're writing a templated custom control, you should allow page developers to use data binding expressions (<%# %>) within the opening and closing tags of your custom control's template property to access the data they need. For example, the `TemplatedCreditCardForm` control exposes five properties named `PaymentMethodText`, `CreditCardNoText`, `CardholderNameText`, `ExpirationDateText`, and `SubmitButtonText` that page developers can use to specify the labels for the payment method list, credit card number text field, cardholder's name text field, expiration date, and Submit button.

`TemplatedCreditCardForm` must allow page developers to use data binding expressions within the opening and closing tags of the `PaymentMethodLabelTemplate`, `CreditCardNoLabelTemplate`, `CardholderNameLabelTemplate`, `ExpirationDateLabelTemplate`, and `SubmitButtonTemplate` template properties to access the values of these properties as shown in Listing 6-6.

Listing 6-6: A Web page that uses data binding expressions

```
<%@ Page Language="C#" AutoEventWireup="true" CodeFile="Default8.aspx.cs"
Inherits="Default8" %>
<%@ Register TagPrefix="custom" Namespace="CustomComponents" %>

<html xmlns="http://www.w3.org/1999/xhtml" >
<head runat="server"><title>Untitled Page</title></head>
<body>
  <form id="form1" runat="server">
    <custom:TemplatedCreditCardForm ID="ccf" runat="server" Font-Bold="true"
    OnValidateCreditCard="ValidateCreditCard" SubmitButtonText="Submit"
    CardholderNameText="Cardholder's name" CreditCardNoText="Credit Card No."
    PaymentMethodText="Payment Method" ExpirationDateText="Expiration Date">
      <PaymentMethodlabelTemplate>
        <table width="100%" style="font-size:x-large;background-image:url(img.bmp);
        font-style:italic;font-weight:bold;color:Yellow;">
          <tr>
            <td width="100%"><%# DataBinder.Eval(Container, "LabelText") %></td>
          </tr>
        </table>
      </PaymentMethodlabelTemplate>
      <CreditCardNolabelTemplate>
        <table width="100%" style="font-size:x-large;background-image:url(img.bmp);
        font-style:italic;font-weight:bold;color:Yellow;">
          <tr>
            <td width="100%"><%# DataBinder.Eval(Container, "LabelText")%></td>
          </tr>
        </table>
      </CreditCardNolabelTemplate>
```

```
        <CardholderNamelabelTemplate>
          <table width="100%" style="font-size:x-large;background-image:url(img.bmp);
          font-style:italic;font-weight:bold;color:Yellow;">
            <tr>
              <td width="100%"><%# DataBinder.Eval(Container, "LabelText")%></td>
            </tr>
          </table>
        </CardholderNamelabelTemplate>
        <ExpirationDatelabelTemplate>
          <table width="100%" style="font-size:x-large;background-image:url(img.bmp);
          font-style:italic;font-weight:bold;color:Yellow;">
            <tr>
              <td width="100%"><%# DataBinder.Eval(Container, "LabelText") %></td>
            </tr>
          </table>
        </ExpirationDatelabelTemplate>
        <SubmitButtonTemplate>
          <table width="100%" style="font-size:x-large;background-image:url(img.bmp);
          font-style:italic;font-weight:bold;color:Yellow;">
            <tr>
              <td width="100%">
                <asp:LinkButton runat="server" CommandName="ValidateCreditCard"
                Text='<%# DataBinder.Eval(Container, "LabelText") %>'
                 Font-Italic="true"
                 Font-Bold="true" ForeColor="Yellow" Font-Size="X-Large" />
              </td>
            </tr>
          </table>
        </SubmitButtonTemplate>
      </custom:TemplatedCreditCardForm><br /><br />
      <asp:Label runat="server" ID="info" />
    </form>
  </body>
</html>
```

As the highlighted portions of Listing 6-6 show, data binding expressions use the `Eval` method of the
`DataBinder` class to access the property values. For example, the data binding expression used in the
content within the `PaymentMethodLabelTemplate` property uses the `Eval` method to access the value
of the `PaymentMethodText` property:

```
        <PaymentMethodlabelTemplate>
          <table width="100%" style="font-size:x-large;background-image:url(img.bmp);
          font-style:italic;font-weight:bold;color:Yellow;">
            <tr>
              <td width="100%"><%# DataBinder.Eval(Container, "LabelText") %></td>
            </tr>
          </table>
        </PaymentMethodlabelTemplate>
```

The `Container` variable used in the `Eval` method refers to the first control up in the control hierarchy
that implements the `INamingContainer` interface — the `CreditCardFormContainer` container control.
The `Eval` method searches the properties of the `CreditCardFormContainer` container control for a
property named `LabelText` and returns its value.

This has the following two implications:

- ❏ The `Eval` method expects the `CreditCardFormContainer` control to expose a property named `LabelText`. As shown in Listing 5-7, the `CreditCardFormContainer` control doesn't expose this property.

- ❏ The `LabelText` property must expose the value of its associated `PaymentMethodText`, `CreditCardNoText`, `CardholderNameText`, `ExpirationDateText`, or `SubmitButtonText` property of the `TemplatedCreditCardForm` control.

To address these two issues and to add support for data binding expressions, you must first implement a new container control named `CreditCardFormContainer2` that extends `CreditCardFormContainer` to add support for the `LabelText` property, as shown in Listing 6-7.

Listing 6-7: The CreditCardFormContainer2

```
public class CreditCardFormContainer2 : CreditCardFormContainer
{
  private string labelText;

  public CreditCardFormContainer2(ContainerType ContainerType) :
                                      base(ContainerType) {}

  public string LabelText
  {
    get { return labelText; }
    set { labelText = value; }
  }
}
```

The `TemplateCreditCardForm` control must override the `CreateContainer` method of the `CompositeCreditCardForm` control to return an instance of the `CreditCardFormContainer2` container control, as shown in Listing 6-8.

Listing 6-8: TemplatedCreditCardForm overrides CreateContainer

```
protected override CreditCardFormContainer CreateContainer(
                                      ContainerType ContainerType)
{
  return new CreditCardFormContainer2(ContainerType);
}
```

The `CreateContainerChildControls` method of the `TemplatedCreditCardForm` control must assign the value of the `PaymentMethodText`, `CreditCardNoText`, `CardholderNameText`, `ExpirationDateText`, or `SubmitButtonText` property of the `TemplatedCreditCardForm` control to the `LabelText` property of the respective `CreditCardFormContainer2` container controls, as shown in Listing 6-9.

Listing 6-9: Assigning the values of the TemplatedCreditCardForm control's properties to the LabelText property

```
protected override void CreateContainerChildControls(
                                    CreditCardFormContainer container2)
{
   CreditCardFormContainer2 container = container2 as CreditCardFormContainer2;
   switch (container.ContainerType)
   {
     case ContainerType.PaymentMethodLabel:
        container.LabelText = PaymentMethodText;
        if (paymentMethodLabelTemplate != null)
           paymentMethodLabelTemplate.InstantiateIn(container);
        else
           base.CreateContainerChildControls(container);
        break;
     case ContainerType.CreditCardNoLabel:
        container.LabelText = CreditCardNoText;
        if (creditCardNoLabelTemplate != null)
           creditCardNoLabelTemplate.InstantiateIn(container);
        else
           base.CreateContainerChildControls(container);
        break;
     case ContainerType.CardholderNameLabel:
        container.LabelText = CardholderNameText;
        if (cardholderNameLabelTemplate != null)
           cardholderNameLabelTemplate.InstantiateIn(container);
        else
           base.CreateContainerChildControls(container);
        break;
     case ContainerType.ExpirationDateLabel:
        container.LabelText = ExpirationDateText;
        if (expirationDateLabelTemplate != null)
           expirationDateLabelTemplate.InstantiateIn(container);
        else
           base.CreateContainerChildControls(container);
        break;
     case ContainerType.SubmitButton:
        container.LabelText = SubmitButtonText;
        if (submitButtonTemplate != null)
           submitButtonTemplate.InstantiateIn(container);
        else
           base.CreateContainerChildControls(container);
        break;
     default:
        base.CreateContainerChildControls(container);
        break;
   }
}
```

As Listing 6-9 shows, the `CreateContainerChildControls` method of the `TemplatedCredit CardForm` sets the value of the `LabelText` property by type casting the container control to `CreditCardFormContainer2`:

```
CreditCardFormContainer2 container = container2 as CreditCardFormContainer2;
```

It then assigns the value of the respective property of the `TemplatedCreditCardForm` control to the `LabelText` property. Which property of the `TemplatedCreditCardForm` control is used depends on which cell the child control will go in. For example, if the child control being created goes into cell number 9 in Figure 6-1, the value of the `SubmitButtonText` property is assigned to the `LabelText` property:

```
container.LabelText = SubmitButtonText;
```

The last thing you need to do to enable data binding is mark all the template properties of the `TemplatedCreditCardForm` control with the `TemplateContainerAttribute` metadata attribute, as shown in Listing 6-10. You must set the argument of the `TemplateContainer` attribute to the type of the first control up in the control hierarchy that implements the `INamingContainer` interface. Because `CreditCardFormContainer2` derives from the `CreditCardFormContainer`, which implements the `INamingContainer` interface, Listing 6-10 passes the type of `CreditCardFormContainer2` as the argument to the attribute. The page parser uses the value of this argument to infer the control that the `Container` variable of the data binding expression refers to.

Listing 6-10: Marking the template properties with the TemplateContainer attribute

```
[TemplateContainer(typeof(CreditCardFormContainer2))]
public ITemplate PaymentMethodLabelTemplate
{
  get { return paymentMethodLabelTemplate; }
  set { paymentMethodLabelTemplate = value; }
}

[TemplateContainer(typeof(CreditCardFormContainer2))]
public ITemplate CreditCardNoLabelTemplate
{
  get { return creditCardNoLabelTemplate; }
  set { creditCardNoLabelTemplate = value; }
}

[TemplateContainer(typeof(CreditCardFormContainer2))]
public ITemplate CardholderNameLabelTemplate
{
  get { return cardholderNameLabelTemplate; }
  set { cardholderNameLabelTemplate = value; }
}

[TemplateContainer(typeof(CreditCardFormContainer2))]
public ITemplate ExpirationDateLabelTemplate
{
  get { return expirationDateLabelTemplate; }
  set { expirationDateLabelTemplate = value; }
}

[TemplateContainer(typeof(CreditCardFormContainer2))]
```

```
public ITemplate SubmitButtonTemplate
{
  get { return submitButtonTemplate; }
  set { submitButtonTemplate = value; }
}
```

Under the Hood of Data Binding Expressions

This section takes you behind the scenes to show you how the ASP.NET Framework template data binding mechanism works. As an example, consider the simple Web page shown in Listing 6-4 but with one difference. This time the page developer uses a data binding expression to access the value of the PaymentMethodText property, as shown in Listing 6-11.

Listing 6-11: Using a data binding expression to access the PaymentMethodText property

```
<%@ Page Language="C#" AutoEventWireup="true" CodeFile="Default8.aspx.cs"
Inherits="Default8" %>
<%@ Register TagPrefix="custom" Namespace="CustomComponents" %>

<html xmlns="http://www.w3.org/1999/xhtml" >
<head runat="server"><title>Untitled Page</title></head>
<body>
  <form id="form1" runat="server">
    <custom:TemplatedCreditCardForm ID="templatedCreditCardForm"
    runat="server" Font-Bold="true"
    OnValidateCreditCard="ValidateCreditCard" SubmitButtonText="Submit"
    CardholderNameText="Cardholder's name" CreditCardNoText="Credit Card No."
    PaymentMethodText="Payment Method" ExpirationDateText="Expiration Date">
      <PaymentMethodlabelTemplate>
        <asp:Label runat="server"
        ID="PaymentMethodLabel"
        Text= '<%# DataBinder.Eval(Container, "LabelText")%>'
        Width="100%"
        />
      </PaymentMethodlabelTemplate>
    </custom:TemplatedCreditCardForm>
  </form>
</body>
</html>
```

As discussed earlier in the chapter, the ASP.NET Framework parses the content within the opening and closing tags of the PaymentMethodLabelTemplate property and dynamically implements the PaymentMethodLabelCreator class shown in Listing 6-5. However, this time around, the content within the opening and closing tags of the template property doesn't hard-code the value of the Text property of the Label control. Instead it uses a data binding expression to dynamically set the value of this property:

```
<PaymentMethodlabelTemplate>
  <asp:Label runat="server"
  ID="PaymentMethodLabel"
  Text= '<%# DataBinder.Eval(Container, "LabelText") %>'
  Width="100%"
  />
</PaymentMethodlabelTemplate>
```

This time around the ASP.NET Framework dynamically implements the `PaymentMethodLabelCreator` class shown in Listing 6-12.

Listing 6-12: ASP.NET dynamically implements the PaymentMethodLabelCreator class

```csharp
public class PaymentMethodLabelCreator : ITemplate
{
  void ITemplate.InstantiateIn(Control container)
  {
    Label childControl = new Label();
    childControl.Width = Unit.Percentage(100);
    childControl.DataBinding +=
                          new EventHandler(ChildControl_DataBinding);
    childControl.ID = "PaymentMethodLabel";
    container.Controls.Add(childControl);
  }

  private static void ChildControl_DataBinding(object sender, EventArgs e)
  {
    Label childControl = sender as Label;
    if (childControl != null)
    {
      CreditCardFormContainer2 container =
                      childControl.NamingContainer as CreditCardFormContainer2;
      if (item != null)
        childLabel.Text = container.LabelText;
    }
  }
}
```

ASP.NET dynamically implements a method named `ChildControl_DataBinding` (the name is immaterial) that uses the `NamingContainer` property of the `Label` control to access its container control, that is, the `CreditCardFormContainer2` control that contains the `Label` control. The `NamingContainer` of a control refers to the first control up in the control hierarchy that implements the `INamingContainer` interface. Because the `CreditCardFormContainer2` implements this interface, it becomes the naming container of its child controls:

```csharp
CreditCardFormContainer2 container =
                    childControl.NamingContainer as CreditCardFormContainer2;
```

The method also assigns the value of the `LabelText` property of the container control to the `Text` property of the `Label` child control:

```csharp
childLabel.Text = container.LabelText;
```

As Listing 6-12 shows, ASP.NET also dynamically implements the code that registers the `ChildControl_DataBinding` method as the callback for the `DataBinding` event of the `Label` control:

```csharp
childControl.DataBinding += new EventHandler(ChildControl_DataBinding);
```

When the page developer calls the `DataBind` method of the `TemplatedCreditCardForm` control, it raises the `DataBinding` event, which automatically calls the `ChildControl_DataBinding` method. As shown in Listing 6-12, this method dynamically assigns the value of the `PaymentMethodText` property of the `TemplatedCreditCardForm` control to the `Text` property of the `Label` child control.

Default Template

As shown in Listing 6-9, each `case` statement of the `CreateContainerChildControls` method of the `TemplatedCreditCardForm` control checks whether its associated template property is null. If it is, the `case` statement delegates the responsibility of creating the child controls to the `CreateContainer ChildControls` method of the base class, that is, the `CompositeCreditCardForm` control. The highlighted section of the following code shows the portion of the `CreateContainerChildControls` method of the `TemplatedCreditCardForm` control that delegates the responsibility of creating the child controls that go into cell number 1 (see Figure 6-1) to the `CreateContainerChildControls` method of the `CompositeCreditCardForm` control:

```
protected override void CreateContainerChildControls(
                                      CreditCardFormContainer container2)
{
  CreditCardFormContainer2 container = container2 as CreditCardFormContainer2;
  switch (container.ContainerType)
  {
    case ContainerType.PaymentMethodLabel:
      container.LabelText = PaymentMethodText;
      if (paymentMethodLabelTemplate != null)
        paymentMethodLabelTemplate.InstantiateIn(container);
      else
        base.CreateContainerChildControls(container);
      break;
    ...
  }
}
```

As shown in Listing 5-9, each `case` statement of the `CreateContainerChildControls` method of the `CompositeCreditCardForm` control hard-codes its associated child controls. The highlighted section of the following code listing shows the portion of the `CreateContainerChildControls` method of the `CompositeCreditCardForm` control that hard-codes the child control that goes into cell number 1:

```
protected virtual void CreateContainerChildControls(
                                      CreditCardFormContainer container)
{
  switch (container.ContainerType)
  {
    case ContainerType.PaymentMethodLabel:
      paymentMethodLabel = new Label();
      paymentMethodLabel.Width = Unit.Percentage(100);
      paymentMethodLabel.ID = "PaymentMethodLabel";
      paymentMethodLabel.Text = PaymentMethodText;
      container.Controls.Add(paymentMethodLabel);
      break;
    ...
  }
}
```

Therefore, the `TemplatedCreditCardForm` control, as is, hard-codes the default child controls — the child controls that are created by default when the page developer doesn't specify any content within a given template property. This section implements a templated custom control named `Templated CreditCardForm2` that derives from the `TemplatedCreditCardForm` and extends its functionality to allow page developers to specify the default child controls for each odd cell shown in Figure 6-1.

The `TemplatedCreditCardForm2` accomplishes this by exposing five string properties named `PaymentMethodLabelTemplateType`, `CreditCardNoLabelTemplateType`, `CardholderName LabelTemplateType`, `ExpirationDateLabelTemplateType`, and `SubmitButtonTemplateType` that page developers must set to register their default templates for displaying the labels for the payment method list, credit card number text field, cardholder's name text field, expiration date, and Submit button, respectively. The string value that page developers assign to each property must contain one or both of the following about the default template being registered:

❑ The fully qualified name of the type of the default template. A fully qualified name of a class includes its namespace. The fully qualified name is required.

❑ The (strong or weak) name of the assembly that contains the default template. The strong name of an assembly consists of the name, version, culture, and public key. The assembly (strong or weak) is not required if the executing assembly contains the default template.

`TemplatedCreditCardForm2` also overrides the `CreateContainerChildControls` method of the `TemplatedCreditCardForm` control to use the registered templates as default templates, as shown in Listing 6-13.

Listing 6-13: TemplatedCreditCardForm2 overrides the CreateContainerChildControls

```
protected override void CreateContainerChildControls(CreditCardFormContainer
                                                     container2)
{
  CreditCardFormContainer2 container = container2 as CreditCardFormContainer2;
  switch (container.ContainerType)
  {
    case ContainerType.PaymentMethodLabel:
      container.LabelText = PaymentMethodText;
      if (PaymentMethodLabelTemplate != null)
        PaymentMethodLabelTemplate.InstantiateIn(container);
      else
        CreateContainerDefaultChildControls(container,
                                DefaultTemplateType.PaymentMethodLabel);
      break;
    case ContainerType.CreditCardNoLabel:
      container.LabelText = CreditCardNoText;
      if (CreditCardNoLabelTemplate != null)
        CreditCardNoLabelTemplate.InstantiateIn(container);
      else
        CreateContainerDefaultChildControls(container,
                                DefaultTemplateType.CreditCardNoLabel);
      break;
    case ContainerType.CardholderNameLabel:
      container.LabelText = CardholderNameText;
      if (CardholderNameLabelTemplate != null)
        CardholderNameLabelTemplate.InstantiateIn(container);
      else
        CreateContainerDefaultChildControls(container,
                                DefaultTemplateType.CardholderNameLabel);
      break;
    case ContainerType.ExpirationDateLabel:
```

```
          container.LabelText = ExpirationDateText;
          if (ExpirationDateLabelTemplate != null)
            ExpirationDateLabelTemplate.InstantiateIn(container);
          else
            CreateContainerDefaultChildControls(container,
                                      DefaultTemplateType.ExpirationDateLabel);
          break;
      case ContainerType.SubmitButton:
          container.LabelText = SubmitButtonText;
          if (SubmitButtonTemplate != null)
            SubmitButtonTemplate.InstantiateIn(container);
          else
            CreateContainerDefaultChildControls(container,
                                      DefaultTemplateType.SubmitButton);
          break;
      default:
          base.CreateContainerChildControls(container);
          break;
    }
  }
```

As the highlighted portions of Listing 6-13 show, each `case` statement of the `CreateContainer ChildControls` method delegates the responsibility of creating the child controls to the `CreateContainerDefaultChildControls` method if its associated template property is null. Listing 6-14 shows the implementation of the `CreateContainerDefaultChildControls` method.

Listing 6-14: The CreateContainerDefaultChildControls method

```
protected virtual void CreateContainerDefaultChildControls(
                 CreditCardFormContainer2 container, DefaultTemplateType type)
{
  ITemplate defaultTemplate = null;
  defaultTemplate = GetDefaultTemplate(type);

  if (defaultTemplate != null)
    defaultTemplate.InstantiateIn(container);
  else
    base.CreateContainerChildControls(container);
}
```

The `CreateContainerDefaultChildControls` method first calls the `GetDefaultTemplate` method to return the default template, if any, that the page developer has registered. If the `GetDefaultTemplate` method doesn't return null, that is, if the page developer has indeed registered a default template, the `CreateContainerDefaultChildControls` method calls the `InstantiateIn` method of the registered default template to create the child controls.

If the `GetDefaultTemplate` method returns null, the `CreateContainerDefaultChildControls` method delegates the responsibility of creating the child controls to the `CreateContainerChildControls` method of the base class — the `CompositeCreditCardForm` control.

Listing 6-15 presents the implementation of the `GetDefaultTemplate` method.

Listing 6-15: The GetDefaultTemplate method

```
protected virtual ITemplate GetDefaultTemplate(DefaultTemplateType type)
{
  ITemplate defaultTemplate = null;
  switch (type)
  {
    case DefaultTemplateType.PaymentMethodLabel:
      defaultTemplate = GetDefaultTemplateFromType(PaymentMethodLabelTemplateType);
      if (defaultTemplate == null)
        defaultTemplate =
            GetDefaultTemplateFromConfigFile("PaymentMethodLabelDefaultTemplate");
      break;
    case DefaultTemplateType.CreditCardNoLabel:
      defaultTemplate = GetDefaultTemplateFromType(CreditCardNoLabelTemplateType);
      if (defaultTemplate == null)
        defaultTemplate =
            GetDefaultTemplateFromConfigFile("CreditCardNoLabelDefaultTemplate");
      break;
    case DefaultTemplateType.CardholderNameLabel:
      defaultTemplate =
            GetDefaultTemplateFromType(CardholderNameLabelTemplateType);
      if (defaultTemplate == null)
        defaultTemplate =
          GetDefaultTemplateFromConfigFile("CardholderNameLabelDefaultTemplate");
      break;
    case DefaultTemplateType.ExpirationDateLabel:
      defaultTemplate =
            GetDefaultTemplateFromType(ExpirationDateLabelTemplateType);
      if (defaultTemplate == null)
        defaultTemplate =
          GetDefaultTemplateFromConfigFile("ExpirationDateLabelDefaultTemplate");
      break;
    case DefaultTemplateType.SubmitButton:
      defaultTemplate = GetDefaultTemplateFromType(SubmitButtonTemplateType);
      if (defaultTemplate == null)
        defaultTemplate =
            GetDefaultTemplateFromConfigFile("SubmitButtonDefaultTemplate");
      break;
  }

  return defaultTemplate;
}
```

Each `case` statement in Listing 6-15 calls the `GetDefaultTemplateFromType` method and passes the respective template type property into it. For example, the following `case` statement passes the value of the `ExpirationDateLabelTemplateType` property into the `GetDefaultTemplateFromType` method:

```
case DefaultTemplateType.ExpirationDateLabel:
  defaultTemplate = GetDefaultTemplateFromType(ExpirationDateLabelTemplateType);
  if (defaultTemplate == null)
    defaultTemplate =
          GetDefaultTemplateFromConfigFile("ExpirationDateLabelDefaultTemplate");
  break;
```

Recall that the page developer sets the value of the ExpirationDateLabelTemplateType property to a string value that contains the fully qualified name of the type of the default template and the (strong or weak) name of the assembly that contains the default template.

If the GetDefaultTemplateFromType method returns null, the case statement calls the GetDefault TemplateFromConfigFile method and passes the string value "ExpirationDateLabelDefault Template" into it.

Listing 6-16 shows the implementation of the GetDefaultTemplateFromType method.

Listing 6-16: The GetDefaultTemplateFromType method

```
protected virtual ITemplate GetDefaultTemplateFromType(string type)
{
  if (string.IsNullOrEmpty(type))
    return null;
  string templateType = type.Trim().Split(new char[] { ',' })[0];

  string assemblyName = type.Trim().Remove(type.IndexOf(templateType),
                                           templateType.Length);
  Assembly myAssembly;
  if (string.IsNullOrEmpty(assemblyName))
    myAssembly = Assembly.GetExecutingAssembly();

  else
  {
    assemblyName = assemblyName.Trim().Remove(0, 1);
    myAssembly = Assembly.Load(assemblyName);
  }

  return (ITemplate)myAssembly.CreateInstance(templateType);
}
```

The GetDefaultTemplateFromType method takes a string value as its argument. As discussed, this string value is a comma-separated list of up to five string values — the fully qualified name of the type of the default template, and the name, version, culture, and public key of the assembly that contains the default template. As Listing 6-16 shows, the GetDefaultTemplateFromType method retrieves the first string value from its input string. This string value is the fully qualified name of the type of the default template:

```
string templateType = type.Trim().Split(new char[] { ',' })[0];
```

It then retrieves a string value that contains the rest of the input string value. This string value is the (strong or weak) name of the assembly that contains the default template:

```
string assemblyName = type.Trim().Remove(type.IndexOf(templateType),
                                         templateType.Length);
```

If the input string doesn't contain the assembly name, the GetDefaultTemplateFromType method assumes the currently executing assembly contains the specified default template and calls the GetExecutingAssembly static method of the Assembly class to access the Assembly object that represents the currently executing assembly:

```
if (string.IsNullOrEmpty(assemblyName))
    myAssembly = Assembly.GetExecutingAssembly();
```

If the input string contains the (strong or weak) assembly name, the GetDefaultTemplateFromType method calls the Load static method of the Assembly class to load the assembly that contains the default template and access the Assembly object that represents this assembly:

```
myAssembly = Assembly.Load(assemblyName);
```

Finally, the GetDefaultTemplateFromType method calls the CreateInstance method of the Assembly object that represents the assembly that contains the default template to dynamically instantiate the default template:

```
return (ITemplate)myAssembly.CreateInstance(templateType);
```

The TemplatedCreditCardForm2 control provides page developers with two different ways to specify the string value that contains the fully qualified name of the type of the default template and (strong or weak) name of the assembly that contains the default template. The previous discussions covered the first approach, where the page developer directly assigns the string value to the PaymentMethod LabelTemplateType, CreditCardNoLabelTemplateType, CardholderNameLabelTemplateType, ExpirationDateLabelTemplateType, and SubmitButtonTemplateType properties.

The problem with this approach is that page developers must set the values of these properties every time they use the TemplatedCreditCardForm2 control. The second approach allows the page developer to specify the string value in the <appSettings> section of the config file. The TemplatedCredit CardForm2 control takes the key that is needed to locate the string value and automatically retrieves the value.

Listing 6-17 shows the implementation of the GetDefaultTemplateFromConfigFile method, which takes the key as its argument, retrieves the string value that contains the complete information about the default assembly from the config file, and passes the value into the GetDefaultTemplateFromType method.

Listing 6-17: The GetDefaultTemplateFromConfigFile method

```
protected virtual ITemplate GetDefaultTemplateFromConfigFile(string key)
{
    string type = ConfigurationManager.AppSettings[key];
    if (string.IsNullOrEmpty(type))
        return null;

    return GetDefaultTemplateFromType(type);
}
```

Page developers can use the same approach discussed earlier in the chapter to implement their own custom default templates. For example, Listing 6-18 shows the implementation of a custom default template component that creates an ImageButton child control.

Listing 6-18: The ImageButtonCreator template component

```
public class ImageButtonCreator : ITemplate
{
  void ITemplate.InstantiateIn(Control container)
  {
    ImageButton button = new ImageButton();
    button.CommandName = "ValidateCreditCard";
    button.DataBinding += new EventHandler(Button_DataBinding);
    container.Controls.Add(button);
  }

  private static void Button_DataBinding(object sender, EventArgs e)
  {
    ImageButton button = sender as ImageButton;
    CreditCardFormContainer2 container =
                        button.NamingContainer as CreditCardFormContainer2;
    button.ImageUrl = container.LabelText;
  }
}
```

The `InstantiateIn` method creates an `ImageButton` control, sets its `CommandName` property to the string value `"ValidateCreditCard"` to raise the `ValidateCreditCard` event when the user clicks the image button, registers the `Button_DataBinding` method as the callback for the `DataBinding` event of the image button, and finally adds the image button to the `Controls` collection of the container control.

The following code shows how page developers can use the `config` file to register the `ImageButtonCreator` template component as the default template for creating the child control that goes into cell number 9 in Figure 6-1:

```
<configuration>
  <appSettings>
    <add key="SubmitButtonTemplateType" value="ImageButtonCreator"/>
  </appSettings>
</configuration>
```

The following code contains a page that uses the `TemplatedCreditCardForm2` control:

```
<%@ Page Language="C#" AutoEventWireup="true"
CodeFile="TemplatedCreditCardForm2.aspx.cs" Inherits="Default10" %>

<%@ Register TagPrefix="custom" Namespace="CustomComponents" %>
<!DOCTYPE html PUBLIC "-//W3C//DTD XHTML 1.1//EN"
"http://www.w3.org/TR/xhtml11/DTD/xhtml11.dtd">
<html xmlns="http://www.w3.org/1999/xhtml">
<head runat="server">
  <title>Untitled Page</title>
</head>
```

```
<body>
  <form id="form1" runat="server">
    <custom:TemplatedCreditCardForm2 ID="ccf" runat="server"
    OnValidateCreditCard="ValidateCreditCard"
    PaymentMethodLabelTemplateType="CustomComponents.PaymentMethodLabelCreator"
    CardholderNameText="Cardholder's Name" CreditCardNoText="Credit Card No."
    PaymentMethodText="Payment Method" ExpirationDateText="Expiration Date"
    SubmitButtonText="go.gif" Font-Italic="true"
    GridLines="None" CellSpacing="5" BackImageUrl="images4.bmp" Font-Size="Larger"
    BorderColor="Yellow" BorderWidth="20px" BorderStyle="Ridge" />
    <br /> <br/>
    <asp:Label runat="server" ID="info" />
  </form>
</body>
</html>
```

Figure 6-3 illustrates what end users see on their browsers when they access this page. Notice that the Submit button has been replaced with the GO ImageButton that the ImageButtonCreator default template renders. The TemplatedCreditCardForm2 control automatically picks up this default template from the Web.config file.

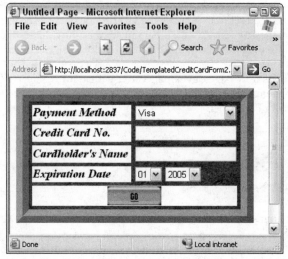

Figure 6-3

The following code contains the same page but with one difference. As the highlighted portion illustrates, the page developer has specified the value of the SubmitButtonTemplateType attribute. End users will still see the same page shown in Figure 6-3.

```
<%@ Page Language="C#" AutoEventWireup="true"
CodeFile="TemplatedCreditCardForm2.aspx.cs" Inherits="Default10" %>
<%@ Register TagPrefix="custom" Namespace="CustomComponents" %>
<html xmlns="http://www.w3.org/1999/xhtml">
```

```
<body>
  <form id="form1" runat="server">
    <custom:TemplatedCreditCardForm2 ID="ccf" runat="server"
    OnValidateCreditCard="ValidateCreditCard"
    CardholderNameText="Cardholder's name" CreditCardNoText="Credit Card No."
    PaymentMethodText="Payment Method" ExpirationDateText="Expiration Date"
    SubmitButtonText="go.gif" BackColor="Blue" ForeColor="Yellow"
    SubmitButtonTemplateType="CustomComponents.ImageButtonCreator"
    Font-Bold="true" Font-Italic="true" GridLines="Both" CellSpacing="5"
    BorderColor="Yellow" BorderWidth="20px" BorderStyle="Outset"/><br/><br/>

    <asp:Label runat="server" ID="info" />
  </form>
</body>
</html>
```

You've seen how page developers can implement their own custom default templates and register them with the `TemplatedCreditCardForm2` control. Another way to go is for you, the author of the `TemplatedCreditCardForm2` control, to provide page developers with a catalog of default templates to choose from. This will save them from having to write these default templates themselves.

Summary

This chapter showed you how to develop custom templated controls to allow page developers to specify the child controls that go into each container control. The chapter provided you with a detailed step-by-step recipe and used the recipe to develop a custom templated control named `TemplatedCreditCardForm`.

This chapter also showed you how to enable your templated controls to support data binding expressions that page developers use within the opening and closing tags of a template property to access data.

Page developers may or may not specify contents within a template property's tags. Your custom control should create default child controls for each container control when page developers don't specify contents within the property's tags. This chapter showed you how to develop a templated control that allows page developers to specify a default template for your control.

Although all the content up until now may have seemed challenging, it wasn't all that difficult once you looked under the hood to see how the code operates. In the next chapter, you see how to develop custom controls with complex properties.

7

Developing Custom Controls with Complex Properties

All the controls developed in previous chapters expose simple properties. This chapter shows you how to develop custom controls that expose complex properties. You'll see how to develop custom composite controls that expose the style properties of their container controls as top-level complex style properties. You'll see two different ways to manage the state of complex properties across page postbacks. First you'll learn how to implement the `IStateManager` interface to allow your custom controls to take full control of their state management where they can participate in the `TrackViewState`, `SaveViewState`, and `LoadViewState` phases of the page life cycle to track, save, and load their view states across page postbacks. This chapter contains concrete examples to show you how to implement the methods and property of the `IStateManager` interface.

Second, you'll learn how to implement a custom type converter that knows how to convert from your custom type to and from other types. You'll see how you can use this custom type converter to manage the state of your custom control's complex properties across page postbacks without having to implement the `IStateManager` interface.

You'll also see how to enable page developers and visual designers to declaratively persist or set the complex properties of your custom controls. This will allow page developers to declaratively set the values of these properties on an ASP.NET page that contains your custom control without writing a single line of code.

Container Control Style Properties

The previous chapter discussed one of the problems with the `CompositeCreditCardForm` control developed in Chapter 5 — the control hard-codes the child controls that go into each container control. Chapter 6 showed you how to develop a custom templated control named

TemplatedCreditCardForm that derives from CompositeCreditCardForm and extends its functionality to allow page developers to specify the child controls that go into each container control.

Both CompositeCreditCardForm and TemplatedCreditCardForm suffer from another problem, however. As shown in Listing 5-12, the ApplyContainerStyle method hard-codes the style properties of each container control and doesn't allow page developers to set these properties. The relevant code is reproduced here:

```
private void ApplyContainerStyle(CreditCardFormContainer container)
{
  container.VerticalAlign = VerticalAlign.Middle;
  container.Wrap = true;
  container.BackColor = Color.FromName("White");
  container.ForeColor = Color.FromName("Black");
  container.Font.Bold = true;

  if (container.ContainerType == ContainerType.SubmitButton)
  {
    container.HorizontalAlign = HorizontalAlign.Center;
    container.ColumnSpan = 2;
  }
  else
    container.HorizontalAlign = HorizontalAlign.Left;
}
```

Page developers who need to style a given cell or container control have no choice but to search the Controls collection of the CompositeCreditCardForm or TemplatedCreditCardForm control for the container control, and then set the style properties of the container control.

This approach has two downsides:

❑   It's error-prone because it's based on indexing a collection.

❑   It doesn't allow page developers to treat the CompositeCreditCardForm or TemplatedCreditCardForm control as a single entity or black box where they can use the control without any knowledge of its internal structure.

Because the CompositeCreditCardForm and TemplatedCreditCardForm controls hard-code the style properties of each container control, the appearance of a container control isn't customizable.

Customizing the Appearance of a Container Control

In this section you develop a custom composite control named StyledCreditCardForm that derives from CompositeCreditCardForm and allows page developers to customize the appearance of its container controls. The following listing contains the code for the StyledCreditCardForm control. The implementation of these methods and properties are discussed later in this section.

```
public class StyledCreditCardForm : CompositeCreditCardForm
{
  public TableStyle PaymentMethodLabelStyle {get;}
  public TableStyle CreditCardNoLabelStyle {get;}
  public TableStyle CardholderNameLabelStyle {get;}
  public TableStyle ExpirationDateLabelStyle {get;}
  public TableStyle SubmitButtonStyle {get;}

  protected override void ApplyContainerStyles();

  protected override void TrackViewState();
  protected override object SaveViewState();
  protected override void LoadViewState(object savedState);
}
```

Recall that container controls are of type `CreditCardFormContainer`. As shown in Listing 5-7, the `CreditCardFormContainer` class derives from the `TableCell` control, which in turn derives from `WebControl`. As discussed in Chapter 3, every control that derives from `WebControl` exposes a property named `ControlStyle`. The real type of this property may vary from one control to another. The `ControlStyle` property of the `TableCell` control is of type `TableItemStyle`.

The `TableItemStyle` class exposes the following 12 style properties: `ForeColor`, `BorderColor`, `BackColor`, `BorderWidth`, `BorderStyle`, `Width`, `Height`, `Font`, `CssClass`, `HorizontalAlign`, `VerticalAlign`, and `Wrap`. This means that the `ControlStyle` of each container control exposes these style properties.

The `StyledCreditCardForm` control exposes five properties of type `TableItemStyle` where each property internally maps to the `ControlStyle` property of its associated container control, as shown in the following table:

Style Property	Associated Container Control
paymentMethodLabelStyle	ContainerType.PaymentMethodLabelContainer
creditCardNoLabelStyle	ContainerType.CreditCardNoLabelContainer
cardholderNameLabelStyle	ContainerType.CardholderNameLabelContainer
expirationDateLabelStyle	ContainerType.ExpirationDateLabelContainer
submitButtonStyle	ContainerType.SubmitButtonLabelContainer

These five properties have similar implementation. The following code presents the implementation of the `PaymentMethodLabelStyle` property:

```
private TableStyle paymentMethodLabelStyle;
public TableStyle PaymentMethodLabelStyle
{
  get
  {
    if (paymentMethodLabelStyle == null)
```

```
      paymentMethodLabelStyle = new TableItemStyle();
    return paymentMethodLabelStyle;
  }
}
```

These five properties allow page developers to set the `ControlStyle` property of a container control
as if they were setting the style properties of the `StyledCreditCardForm` control itself. In other words,
the `StyledCreditCardForm` control hides the `ControlStyle` properties of its container controls and
exposes them as its own properties.

The `StyledCreditCardForm` control also overrides the `ApplyContainerStyles` method of its base
class (`CompositeCreditCardForm`) as shown in Listing 7-1.

Listing 7-1: The ApplyContainerStyles method

```
protected override void ApplyContainerStyles()
{
  foreach (CreditCardFormContainer container in Controls)
  {
    switch (container.ContainerType)
    {
      case ContainerType.PaymentMethodLabel:
        if (paymentMethodLabelStyle != null)
          container.ApplyStyle(paymentMethodLabelStyle);
        break;
      case ContainerType.CreditCardNoLabel:
        if (creditCardNoLabelStyle != null)
          container.ApplyStyle(creditCardNoLabelStyle);
        break;
      case ContainerType.CardholderNameLabel:
        if (cardholderNameLabelStyle != null)
          container.ApplyStyle(cardholderNameLabelStyle);
        break;
      case ContainerType.ExpirationDateLabel:
        if (expirationDateLabelStyle != null)
          container.ApplyStyle(expirationDateLabelStyle);
        break;
      case ContainerType.SubmitButton:
        if (submitButtonStyle != null)
          container.ApplyStyle(submitButtonStyle);
        break;
    }
  }
}
```

The `ApplyContainerStyles` method iterates through the container controls in the `Controls` collection
of the `StyledCreditCardForm` control and calls the `ApplyStyle` method of each enumerated container
control if its associated style property isn't null. Notice that the `ApplyContainerStyles` method uses
the `ContainerType` property of each enumerated container control to determine which container control it's dealing with.

State Management

Object-oriented applications use objects to service their users. Each object normally keeps the information that it needs to function properly in memory. This information includes, but is not limited to, the property and field values of the object. This in-memory information is known as the *state* of the object. Invoking the methods and properties of an object normally changes its state. The state of an object is lost forever when the object is disposed of. This isn't an issue in a desktop application, because the objects are disposed of only when they're no longer needed.

However, this causes a big problem in a Web application where each user session normally consists of more than one request. Due to the nature of HTTP protocol, the objects are disposed of at the end of each request, even though the session that the request belongs to still needs the objects. That is, the states of these objects are lost at the end of each request and new objects of the same types are re-created at the beginning of the next request. These newly created objects have no memory of the previous objects and start off with their default states.

The ASP.NET view state mechanism allows you to save the states of your objects at the end of each request and load them at the beginning of the next request. The next request does the following:

❑ Creates new objects of the same types as the objects that were disposed of at the end of the previous request.

❑ Loads the states of the old objects into the new objects.

Because the newly created objects at the beginning of each request have the same types and states as the objects disposed of at the end of the previous request, it gives the illusion that objects are not disposed of at the end of each request and the same objects are being used all along.

Now you'll see how the ASP.NET view state mechanism works. Every server control inherits three methods named `TrackViewState`, `SaveViewState`, and `LoadViewState` from the `Control` class. At the end of each request, the following sequence of events occurs:

1. The page automatically calls the `SaveViewState` method of the controls in its `Controls` collection. Recall that the `Controls` collection contains all the controls page developers declare in the respective `.aspx` file. Page developers can also programmatically create server controls and manually add them to the `Controls` collection of the page.

2. The `SaveViewState` method of each control must save the state of the control and its child controls into an appropriate object and return the object.

3. The page collects the objects returned from the `SaveViewState` methods of the controls in its `Controls` collection and forms a tree of objects known as an object graph.

4. The page framework then uses the type converter associated with each object to convert the object into a string representation and combines these string representations into a single string that represents the entire object graph.

5. The page framework then stores the string representation of the entire object graph in a hidden field named `__VIEWSTATE`, which looks something like the following:

```
<input type="hidden" name="__VIEWSTATE" id="__VIEWSTATE" value="/wEPDwULLTE3MDU5MjY
4MTkPZBYCAgMPZBYCAgEPFCsAAmRkFgZmD2QWAmYPDxYCHgRUZXh0BQ5QYX1tZW50IE1ldGhvZGRkAgEPZB
YCZg8PDxYCHgtfIURhdGFCb3VuZGdkZGQCBw9kFgRmDw8PFgIfAWdkZGQCAg8PDxYCHwFnZGRkZJDAqbyjC
j4rjagRWSiVYTp7nQfM" />
```

Therefore, the __VIEWSTATE hidden field is sent to the client browser as part of the containing page. When the page is posted back to the server, the following sequence of events occurs:

1. The page framework retrieves the string representation of the object graph from the __VIEWSTATE hidden field.

2. The page framework extracts the string representation of each object.

3. The page framework uses the type converter associated with each object to re-create the object from its string representation.

4. The page framework calls the LoadViewState method of each control in its Controls collection and passes the respective object into it. Recall that this object contains the state of the control and its child controls at the end of the previous request.

5. The LoadViewState method of each control must load the contents (the state of the control at the end of the previous request) of this object into itself. Therefore the control will have the same state as it did in the previous request.

6. The page framework calls the TrackViewState method of each control in its Controls collection.

7. The TrackViewState of each control must set an internal Boolean field to true to specify that it's tracking its state. What this means is that from this point on any changes in the state of the object will be marked as dirty and saved at the end of the request, as discussed earlier.

As mentioned, the state of a control includes, but is not limited to, its property values. In general, there are two types of properties:

❑   **Simple properties:** A simple property is a property whose type doesn't expose any properties. For example, the PaymentMethodText property of the StyledCreditCardForm control is of type string, which doesn't expose any properties.

❑   **Complex properties:** A complex property is a property whose type exposes properties. For example, the PaymentMethodLabelStyle, CreditCardNoLabelStyle, CardholderNameLabelStyle, ExpirationDateLabelStyle, and SubmitButtonStyle properties of the StyledCreditCardForm control are of type TableItemStyle, which exposes properties such as Font, Width, Height, and so on.

As discussed in Chapter 2, simple properties such as PaymentMethodText use the ViewState collection as their backing stores to manage their states across page postbacks. What method you should use to manage the state of a complex property across page postbacks depends on whether or not the type of the property implements the IStateManager interface.

Types That Implement IStateManager

A complex property implements the IStateManager interface to take control of its own state management across page postbacks. IStateManager exposes one Boolean property named IsTrackingViewState and three methods named TrackViewState, SaveViewState, and LoadViewState.

When the `TrackViewState` method of a control is called, the method calls the `TrackViewState` methods of its complex properties. The `TrackViewState` method of a complex property does exactly what the `TrackViewState` of a control does — sets an internal Boolean field to true to specify that any state changes will be marked as dirty and will be saved at the end of the current request.

When the `SaveViewState` method of a control is called, the method does the following:

1. Calls the `SaveViewState` methods of its complex properties. The `SaveViewState` method of a complex property does exactly what the `SaveViewState` of a control does — it saves its state into an appropriate object and returns the object.

2. Collects the objects returned from the `SaveViewState` methods of its complex properties and saves them into the same object where it saves its own state.

3. Returns the object that contains the states of both the control and its complex properties.

When the `LoadViewState` method of a control is called, the method takes the following actions:

1. Retrieves the objects that contain the states of its complex properties.

2. Calls the `LoadViewState` method of each complex property and passes the object that contains the saved state into it. The `LoadViewState` method of a complex property does exactly what the `LoadViewState` of a control does.

To make the discussions more concrete, you'll develop a complex property that implements the `IStateManager` interface. In the previous chapter you developed a custom templated control named `TemplatedCreditCardForm2` that allows page developers to specify a default template for each template property. To accomplish this, `TemplatedCreditCardForm2` exposed five properties of type string named `PaymentMethodLabelTemplateType`, `CreditCardNoLabelTemplateType`, `CardholderNameLabelTemplateType`, `ExpirationDateLabelTemplateType`, and `SubmitButton TemplateType` to allow page developers to specify the information needed to instantiate the respective default templates. Recall that this information includes the fully qualified name of the type of the respective default template and optionally the weak or strong name of the assembly that contains the default template. `TemplatedCreditCardForm2` also exposed three methods named `GetDefaultTemplate`, `GetDefaultTemplateFromType`, and `GetDefaultTemplateFromConfigFile`.

One of the important object-oriented design principles that you should keep in mind when you're designing and implementing a class is its cohesion — that is, all members of the class (methods and properties) must be working together to support a single concept or abstraction. To put it differently, the class must be responsible for a single task. The `TemplatedCreditCardForm2` class contains the logic that manages the default templates in addition to the logic that all controls must contain. In other words, two different responsibilities and tasks are assigned to the same class, the `TemplatedCreditCardForm2` control.

In this section you develop a new version of the templated credit card form control named `Templated CreditCardForm3` that delegates the responsibility of managing the default templates to a new class named `DefaultTemplateManager`. `DefaultTemplateManager` will encapsulate the `PaymentMethod LabelTemplateType`, `CreditCardNoLabelTemplateType`, `CardholderNameLabelTemplateType`, `ExpirationDateLabelTemplateType`, and `SubmitButtonTemplateType` properties and the `GetDefaultTemplate`, `GetDefaultTemplateFromType`, and `GetDefaultTemplateFromConfigFile` methods.

DefaultTemplateManager

Listing 7-2 contains the code for the `DefaultTemplateManager` class. The implementation of the methods and properties of this class are discussed in the following sections.

Listing 7-2: The DefaultTemplateManager class

```
public class DefaultTemplateManager : IStateManager
{
  public virtual string PaymentMethodLabelTemplateType {get; set;}
  public virtual string CreditCardNoLabelTemplateType {get; set;}
  public virtual string CardholderNameLabelTemplateType {get; set;}
  public virtual string ExpirationDateLabelTemplateType {get; set;}
  public virtual string SubmitButtonTemplateType {get; set;}

  protected virtual StateBag ViewState {get;}
  protected virtual bool IsTrackingViewState {get;}
  bool IStateManager.IsTrackingViewState {get;}
  protected virtual void TrackViewState();
  void IStateManager.TrackViewState();;
  protected virtual void LoadViewState(object savedState);
  void IStateManager.LoadViewState(object savedState);
  protected virtual object SaveViewState();
  object IStateManager.SaveViewState();

  protected virtual ITemplate GetDefaultTemplateFromType(string type);
  protected virtual ITemplate GetDefaultTemplateFromConfigFile(string key);
  public virtual ITemplate GetDefaultTemplate(DefaultTemplateType type);
}
```

The `DefaultTemplateManager` class takes the following actions, which are covered in the sections that follow:

1. Implements the `IStateManager` to manage its state across page postbacks.

2. Exposes five public properties of type `string`, named `PaymentMethodLabelTemplateType`, `CreditCardNoLabelTemplateType`, `CardholderNameLabelTemplateType`, `ExpirationDateLabelTemplateType`, and `SubmitButtonTemplateType`

3. Exposes a public virtual method named `GetDefaultTemplate`.

4. Exposes a protected virtual method named `GetDefaultTemplateFromType`.

5. Exposes a protected virtual method named `GetDefaultTemplateFromConfigFile`.

Implementing IStateManager

A type such as `DefaultTemplateManager` implements the `IStateManager` interface to take complete control over its state management. As mentioned, this interface exposes a Boolean property named `IsTrackingViewState` and three methods named `TrackViewState`, `SaveViewState`, and `LoadViewState`.

To implement the `IStateManager` interface, first implement a protected virtual property of type `StateBag` named `ViewState` that uses a private field of type `StateBag` as its backing store. Listing 7-3 shows the typical implementation of the `ViewState` property. As you'll see shortly, this collection property provides the properties of the complex property with a convenient mechanism to manage their states across page postbacks.

Listing 7-3: Typical implementation of the ViewState property

```
private StateBag viewState;
protected virtual StateBag ViewState
{
  get
  {
    if (viewState == null)
    {
      viewState = new StateBag();
      if (IsTrackingViewState)
        ((IStateManager)viewState).TrackViewState();
    }
    return viewState;
  }
}
```

Then follow the C# interface implementation pattern to implement the methods and property of the `IStateManager` interface. As discussed in Chapter 4, the C# interface implementation pattern consists of the following three steps:

1. Implement a protected virtual method for each method of the interface. The method must have the same signature as its respective interface method. Recall that the signature of a method consists of its name, argument types, and return type. This will allow the subclasses of your component to override these protected methods to provide their own implementations.

2. Implement a protected virtual property for each property of the interface. The property must be of the same type as its respective interface property.

3. Explicitly implement each method and property of the interface where you have to take the following actions:

   a. Qualify the name of each method and property with the name of the interface.

   b. Do not use any modifiers such as private, public, and so on.

   c. Call the respective protected virtual method or property from each method or property.

IsTrackingViewState

A class such as `DefaultTemplateManager` uses the `IsTrackingViewState` property to check whether its view state is being tracked. Following the C# interface implementation pattern, `DefaultTemplateManager` exposes a virtual protected property named `IsTrackingViewState`:

```
private bool isTrackingViewState;
protected virtual bool IsTrackingViewState
{
  get { return isTrackingViewState; }
}
```

DefaultTemplateManager also explicitly implements the IsTrackingViewState of the IStateManager interface to call the above IsTrackingViewState property:

```
bool IStateManager.IsTrackingViewState
{
  get { return IsTrackingViewState; }
}
```

TrackViewState

A class such as DefaultTemplateManager uses the TrackViewState method to set a Boolean private field to true to start view state tracking. What this means is that from this point on any changes in the property values of the class are marked as dirty and will be saved to the view state at the end of the current request. In other words, the class will remember these values when the page is posted back to the server. Any property value changes prior to the start of view state tracking will not be saved to the view state — the class will not remember these values when the page is posted back to the server.

Following the C# interface implementation pattern, DefaultTemplateManager implements a virtual protected method with the same signature as the TrackViewState method of the IStateManager interface:

```
protected virtual void TrackViewState()
{
  isTrackingViewState = true;

  if (viewState != null)
    ((IStateManager)ViewState).TrackViewState();
}
```

This method sets the isTrackingViewState field to true, and calls the TrackViewState method of the ViewState collection to allow this collection to start its own view state tracking.

DefaultTemplateManager also explicitly implements the TrackViewState method of the IStateManager interface to call the TrackViewState method:

```
void IStateManager.TrackViewState()
{
  TrackViewState();
}
```

SaveViewState

A class such as DefaultTemplateManager uses the SaveViewState method to save property value changes that occurred after the start of view state tracking. Following the C# interface implementation pattern, DefaultTemplateManager implements a virtual protected method with the same signature as the SaveViewState method of the IStateManager interface:

```
protected virtual object SaveViewState()
{
  if (viewState != null)
    return ((IStateManager)ViewState).SaveViewState();
  return null;
}
```

This method calls the `SaveViewState` method of the `ViewState` collection to allow this collection to save its view state.

`DefaultTemplateManager` then explicitly implements the `SaveViewState` method of the `IStateManager` interface to call the `SaveViewState` method:

```
object IStateManager.SaveViewState()
{
  return SaveViewState();
}
```

LoadViewState

The `LoadViewState` method does just what its name says it does — it loads the view state of the `DefaultTemplateManager` component from the saved view state. Following the C# interface implementation pattern, `DefaultTemplateManager` implements a virtual protected method with the same signature as the `LoadViewState` method of the `IStateManager` interface:

```
protected virtual void LoadViewState(object savedState)
{
  if (savedState != null)
    ((IStateManager)ViewState).LoadViewState(savedState);
}
```

This method calls the `LoadViewState` method of the `ViewState` collection to allow this collection to load its view state.

`DefaultTemplateManager` then explicitly implements the `LoadViewState` method of the `IStateManager` interface to call the `LoadViewState` method:

```
void IStateManager.LoadViewState(object savedState)
{
  LoadViewState(savedState);
}
```

Exposing Properties

`DefaultTemplateManager` exposes one string property associated with each template property of the `TemplatedCreditCardForm` control to allow page developers to specify the information needed to instantiate the default template for the respective template property. This information contains the fully qualified name of the type of the default template and optionally the weak or strong name of the assembly that contains the default template. Listing 7-4 shows the implementation of these properties.

Listing 7-4: The implementation of the properties of the DefaultTemplateManager class

```
public virtual string PaymentMethodLabelTemplateType
{
  get { return ViewState["PaymentMethodLabelTemplateType"] != null ?
          (string)ViewState["PaymentMethodLabelTemplateType"] : string.Empty; }
  set { ViewState["PaymentMethodLabelTemplateType"] = value; }
```

(continued)

Listing 7-4: *(continued)*

```
  }

  public virtual string CreditCardNoLabelTemplateType
  {
    get { return ViewState["CreditCardNoLabelTemplateType"] != null ?
               (string)ViewState["CreditCardNoLabelTemplateType"] : string.Empty; }
    set { ViewState["CreditCardNoLabelTemplateType"] = value; }
  }

  public virtual string CardholderNameLabelTemplateType
  {
    get { return ViewState["CardholderNameLabelTemplateType"] != null ?
               (string)ViewState["CardholderNameLabelTemplateType"] : string.Empty; }
    set { ViewState["CardholderNameLabelTemplateType"] = value; }
  }

  public virtual string ExpirationDateLabelTemplateType
  {
    get { return ViewState["ExpirationDateLabelTemplateType"] != null ?
               (string)ViewState["ExpirationDateLabelTemplateType"] : string.Empty; }
    set { ViewState["ExpirationDateLabelTemplateType"] = value; }
  }

  public virtual string SubmitButtonTemplateType
  {
    get { return ViewState["SubmitButtonTemplateType"] != null ?
                (string)ViewState["SubmitButtonTemplateType"] : string.Empty; }
    set { ViewState["SubmitButtonTemplateType"] = value; }
  }
```

As Listing 7-4 shows, these properties use the `ViewState` collection defined in Listing 7-3 to manage their states across page postbacks. The `ViewState` collection provides a convenient mechanism for the simple properties of `DefaultTemplateManager` to manage their states.

TemplatedCreditCardForm3

This section implements a custom templated control named `TemplatedCreditCardForm3` that extends `TemplatedCreditCardForm` to use `DefaultTemplateManager` as shown in Listing 7-5.

Listing 7-5: The TemplatedCreditCardForm3 control

```
public class TemplatedCreditCardForm3 : TemplatedCreditCardForm
{
  protected override void TrackViewState();
  protected override object SaveViewState();
  protected override void LoadViewState(object savedState);

  protected virtual DefaultTemplateManager CreateDefaultTemplateManager();
  public virtual DefaultTemplateManager DefaultTemplateManager {get;}

  protected virtual void
```

```
    CreateContainerDefaultChildControls(CreditCardFormContainer2 container,
                              DefaultTemplateType type);
    protected override void CreateContainerChildControls(
                                        CreditCardFormContainer container2);
}
```

Because the `TemplatedCreditCardForm3` derives from `TemplatedCreditCardForm`, it saves you from having to implement the features that `TemplatedCreditCardForm` already supports. The next few sections cover the implementation of the methods and properties of `TemplatedCreditCardForm3`.

DefaultTemplateManager

`TemplatedCreditCardForm3` exposes a property of type `DefaultTemplateManager` named `DefaultTemplateManager`, as shown in Listing 7-6.

Listing 7-6: The DefaultTemplateManager property of TemplatedCreditCardForm3

```
    private DefaultTemplateManager defaultTemplateManager;
    public virtual DefaultTemplateManager DefaultTemplateManager
    {
      get
      {
        if (defaultTemplateManager == null)
        {
          defaultTemplateManager = CreateDefaultTemplate();
          if (IsTrackingViewState)
            ((IStateManager)defaultTemplateManager).TrackViewState();
        }
        return defaultTemplateManager;
      }
    }
```

If the view state of the `TemplatedCreditCardForm3` is being tracked, the `TrackViewState` method of `DefaultTemplateManager` is called. Notice that the `DefaultTemplateManager` property doesn't directly contain the code that instantiates the `DefaultTemplateManager` instance. Instead it calls the `CreateDefaultTemplate` method. This method is marked protected virtual to allow the subclasses of `TemplatedCreditCardForm3` to override the method:

```
    protected virtual DefaultTemplateManager CreateDefaultTemplate()
    {
      return new DefaultTemplateManager();
    }
```

CreateContainerDefaultChildControls

`TemplatedCreditCardForm3` exposes a method named `CreateContainerDefaultChildControls` to create the default child controls of a given container control:

```
    protected virtual void CreateContainerDefaultChildControls(
                  CreditCardFormContainer2 container, DefaultTemplateType type)
    {
      ITemplate template = null;
```

```
    template = this.DefaultTemplateManager.GetDefaultTemplate(type);

    if (template != null)
      template.InstantiateIn(container);
    else
      base.CreateContainerChildControls(container);

}
```

The `CreateContainerDefaultChildControls` method calls the `GetDefaultTemplate` method of the `DefaultTemplateManager` property (see Listing 7-2) to return the respective default template. If the `GetDefaultTemplate` method returns null (if the page developer hasn't specified a default template), the `CreateContainerDefaultChildControls` method delegates the responsibility of creating the child controls of the container to the `CreateContainerChildControls` method of its base class, `TemplatedCreditCardForm`. If the page developer has specified a default template, it calls the `InstantiateIn` method of the template to create the child controls of the container control.

CreateContainerChildControls

`TemplatedCreditCardForm3` overrides the `CreateContainerChildControls` method, as shown in Listing 7-7.

Listing 7-7: The overridden CreateContainerChildControls method

```
protected override void CreateContainerChildControls(
                                    CreditCardFormContainer container2)
{
  CreditCardFormContainer2 container = container2 as CreditCardFormContainer2;
  switch (container.ContainerType)
  {
    case ContainerType.PaymentMethodLabel:
      container.LabelText = PaymentMethodText;
      if (PaymentMethodLabelTemplate != null)
        PaymentMethodLabelTemplate.InstantiateIn(container);
      else
        CreateContainerDefaultChildControls(container,
                                    DefaultTemplateType.PaymentMethodLabel);
      break;
    case ContainerType.CreditCardNoLabel:
      container.LabelText = CreditCardNoText;
      if (CreditCardNoLabelTemplate != null)
        CreditCardNoLabelTemplate.InstantiateIn(container);
      else
        CreateContainerDefaultChildControls(container,
                                    DefaultTemplateType.CreditCardNoLabel);
      break;
    case ContainerType.CardholderNameLabel:
      container.LabelText = CardholderNameText;
      if (CardholderNameLabelTemplate != null)
        CardholderNameLabelTemplate.InstantiateIn(container);
      else
        CreateContainerDefaultChildControls(container,
                                    DefaultTemplateType.CardholderNameLabel);
```

```
          break;
        case ContainerType.ExpirationDateLabel:
          container.LabelText = ExpirationDateText;
          if (ExpirationDateLabelTemplate != null)
            ExpirationDateLabelTemplate.InstantiateIn(container);
          else
            CreateContainerDefaultChildControls(container,
                                DefaultTemplateType.ExpirationDateLabel);
          break;
        case ContainerType.SubmitButton:
          container.LabelText = SubmitButtonText;
          if (SubmitButtonTemplate != null)
            SubmitButtonTemplate.InstantiateIn(container);
          else
            CreateContainerDefaultChildControls(container,
                                DefaultTemplateType.SubmitButton);
          break;
        default:
          base.CreateContainerChildControls(container);
          break;
    }
}
```

CreateContainerChildControls first type casts the container control to CreditCardFormContainer2 so it can access the LabelText property:

```
CreditCardFormContainer2 container = container2 as CreditCardFormContainer2;
```

Then, for each type of container control, it assigns the respective property of the TemplatedCreditCardForm3 control to the LabelText property of the container control. For example, if the container type is SubmitButton, it assigns the SubmitButtonText value to the LabelText property:

```
container.LabelText = SubmitButtonText;
```

If the associated template isn't null, it calls the InstantiateIn method of the template to create the child controls of the container control:

```
if (SubmitButtonTemplate != null)
   SubmitButtonTemplate.InstantiateIn(container);
```

If the associated template is null, it calls the CreateContainerDefaultChildControls method to create the default child controls of the container control:

```
else
   CreateContainerDefaultChildControls(container, DefaultTemplateType.SubmitButton);
```

State Management

TemplatedCreditCardForm3 overrides the TrackViewState method to call the TrackViewState method of the DefaultTemplateManager property. Recall that the page calls the TrackViewState method of each control to notify the control that it should start tracking its state changes:

```
protected override void TrackViewState()
{
  base.TrackViewState();
  if (defaultTemplateManager != null)
    ((IStateManager)this.DefaultTemplateManager).TrackViewState();
}
```

TemplatedCreditCardForm3 then overrides the SaveViewState method to call the SaveViewState method of the DefaultTemplateManager property:

```
protected override object SaveViewState()
{
  object[] state = new object[2];
  state[0] = base.SaveViewState();
  if (defaultTemplateManager != null)
    state[1] = ((IStateManager)this.DefaultTemplateManager).SaveViewState();

  return state;
}
```

As this code shows, the SaveViewState method first calls the SaveViewState method of its base class (TemplatedCreditCardForm control) to return the object that contains the base state. It then calls the SaveViewState method of the DefaultTemplateManager property to return the object that contains this property's state, and finally returns the array that contains these two objects.

TemplatedCreditCardForm3 then overrides the LoadViewState method to call the LoadViewState method of the DefaultTemplateManager property:

```
protected override void LoadViewState(object savedState)
{
  if (savedState != null)
  {
    object[] state = savedState as object[];
    if (state != null && state.Length == 2)
    {
      base.LoadViewState(state[0]);
      if (state[1] != null)
        ((IStateManager)this.DefaultTemplateManager).LoadViewState(state[1]);
    }
  }
  else
    base.LoadViewState(savedState);
}
```

LoadViewState checks whether the object passed into it is null. Recall that the page calls the LoadViewState method of each control in its Controls collection and passes the object that contains the saved state of the control into it. If the object is null, it calls the LoadViewState method of its base class (TemplatedCreditCardForm). You should always call the LoadViewState method of the base class even when the object is null:

```
else
  base.LoadViewState(savedState);
```

If the object isn't null, it retrieves the two objects that contain the base state and the state of the `DefaultTemplateManager` property and passes them into the `LoadViewState` methods of the base class and the `DefaultTemplateManager` property, respectively.

Using TemplatedCreditCardForm3

Listing 7-8 contains a page that uses the `TemplatedCreditCardForm3` control. The page developer can use a hyphenated syntax to set the properties of a complex property such as `DefaultTemplateManager`. This syntax is discussed later in this chapter. Figure 7-1 shows what end users see when they access this page. As this figure shows, `DefaultTemplateManager` under the hood dynamically creates and uses an instance of the `ImageButtonCreator` template.

Listing 7-8: A Web page that uses TemplatedCreditCardForm3

```
<%@ Page Language="C#" AutoEventWireup="true"
CodeFile="TemplatedCreditCardForm3.aspx.cs" Inherits="Default12" %>
<%@ Register TagPrefix="custom" Namespace="CustomComponents" %>
<html xmlns="http://www.w3.org/1999/xhtml">
<body>
  <form id="form1" runat="server">
    <custom:TemplatedCreditCardForm3 ID="ccf"
    OnValidateCreditCard="ValidateCreditCard"
    runat="server" CardholderNameText="Cardholder's Name" Font-Bold="true"
    CreditCardNoText="Credit Card No." PaymentMethodText="Payment Method"
    ExpirationDateText="Expiration Date" SubmitButtonText="go.gif"
    DefaultTemplateManager-PaymentMethodLabelTemplateType=
                        "CustomComponents.PaymentMethodLabelCreator"
    DefaultTemplateManager- SubmitButtonTemplateType=
                        "CustomComponents.ImageButtonCreator"/><br/><br/>
    <asp:Label runat="server" ID="info" />
  </form>
</body>
</html>
```

Figure 7-1

Types That Don't Implement IStateManager

As discussed previously, what approach you should take to manage the state of a complex property of your custom controls depends on whether or not the property implements `IStateManager`. The previous section discussed how you should manage the state of a complex property that implemented `IStateManager`. This section discusses how you should manage the state of a complex property that doesn't implement `IStateManager`.

To make the discussions of this section more concrete, you'll implement a version of the `DefaultTemplateManager` class that doesn't implement the `IStateManager` interface. Call this version `DefaultTemplateManager2`.

As discussed, at the end of each request, the page framework calls the `SaveViewState` method of each control in its `Controls` collection. The `SaveViewState` method of a control must store its state into an appropriate object and return the object. The page framework then uses the type converter associated with this object to convert the object to its string representation.

A *type converter* is a class that is designed to convert a specific type to and from other types. For example, `BooleanConverter` knows how to convert a Boolean type to and from other types. When you write a custom class or type such as `DefaultTemplateManager2`, you should also write a type converter for it to allow its clients to convert it to and from other types. This section shows you how to develop a custom type converter named `DefaultTemplateManager2Converter` for the `DefaultTemplateManager2` custom type.

TypeConverter

Every type converter must derive from the `TypeConverter` base class and implement its methods. The `TypeConverter` class exposes the following important methods:

❑ Your custom converter must override the `CanConvertFrom` method to specify whether it can convert from the specified source type:

```
public virtual bool CanConvertFrom(ITypeDescriptorContext context,
                                   Type sourceType)
```

❑ Your custom converter must override the `CanConvertTo` method to specify whether it can convert to the specified destination type:

```
public override bool CanConvertTo(ITypeDescriptorContext context,
                                  Type destinationType)
```

❑ Your custom converter must override the `ConvertFrom` method to convert the specified value to the type your converter is designed for:

```
public override object ConvertFrom(ITypeDescriptorContext context,
                                   CultureInfo culture, object value)
```

❑ Your custom converter must override the `ConvertTo` method to convert the specified value to the specified destination type:

```
public override object ConvertTo(ITypeDescriptorContext context,
            CultureInfo culture, object value, Type destinationType)
```

The `TypeConverter` base class provides the clients of your custom converter with a generic API that allows them to use your custom converter in generic fashion without knowing its real type. As far as the clients of your converter are concerned, your converter, like any other type converter, is of type `TypeConverter`.

DefaultTemplateManager2

The implementation of the `DefaultTemplateManager2` base class is the same as the `DefaultTemplate Manager` base class except for one thing — `DefaultTemplateManager2` doesn't implement the `IStateManager` interface. Therefore, the `PaymentMethodLabelTemplateType`, `CreditCardNoLabel TemplateType`, `CardholderNameLabelTemplateType`, `ExpirationDateLabelTemplateType`, and `SubmitButtonTemplateType` properties of the `DefaultTemplateManager2` class use private fields as their backing stores, as shown in Listing 7-9.

Listing 7-9: The properties of the DefaultTemplateManager2 class

```
string paymentMethodLabelTemplateType;
public virtual string PaymentMethodLabelTemplateType
{
  get { return paymentMethodLabelTemplateType; }
  set { paymentMethodLabelTemplateType = value; }
}

string creditCardNoLabelTemplateType;
public virtual string CreditCardNoLabelTemplateType
{
  get { return creditCardNoLabelTemplateType; }
  set { creditCardNoLabelTemplateType = value; }
}

string cardholderNameLabelTemplateType;
public virtual string CardholderNameLabelTemplateType
{
  get { return cardholderNameLabelTemplateType; }
  set { cardholderNameLabelTemplateType = value; }
}

string expirationDateLabelTemplateType;
public virtual string ExpirationDateLabelTemplateType
{
  get { return expirationDateLabelTemplateType; }
  set { expirationDateLabelTemplateType = value; }
}

string submitButtonTemplateType;
public virtual string SubmitButtonTemplateType
{
  get { return submitButtonTemplateType; }
  set { submitButtonTemplateType = value; }
}
```

DefaultTemplateManager2Converter

The DefaultTemplateManager2Converter derives from the TypeConverter base class and is specifically designed to convert the DefaultTemplateManager2 type to and from its string representation.

CanConvertFrom

DefaultTemplateManager2Converter overrides the CanConvertFrom method of its base class to specify that it can convert from string to DefaultTemplateManager2:

```
public override bool CanConvertFrom(ITypeDescriptorContext context,
                                    Type sourceType)
{
  if (sourceType == typeof(string))
    return true;

  return base.CanConvertFrom(context, sourceType);
}
```

The CanConvertFrom method checks whether the specified source type is string type. If it is, the method returns true because DefaultTemplateManager2Converter can convert from string type to the DefaultTemplateManager2 type. If the specified source type is not a string type, the method calls the CanConvertFrom method of its base class to decide whether it can convert from the specified source type.

CanConvertTo

DefaultTemplateManager2Converter overrides the CanConvertTo method of the TypeConverter base class to specify that it can convert from DefaultTemplateManager2 to string:

```
public override bool CanConvertTo(ITypeDescriptorContext context,
                                  Type destinationType)
{
  if (destinationType == typeof(string))
    return true;
  return base.CanConvertTo(context, destinationType);
}
```

The CanConvertTo method checks whether the specified destination type is string type. If it is, the method returns true because DefaultTemplateManager2Converter can convert from DefaultTemplateManager2 type to string type. If the specified destination type isn't string, the method calls the CanConvertTo method of its base class to ask its base class whether it can convert to the specified destination type.

ConvertTo

DefaultTemplateManager2Converter overrides the ConvertTo method to convert the specified value from the DefaultTemplateManager2 type to string, as shown in Listing 7-10.

Listing 7-10: The ConvertTo method

```
public override object ConvertTo(ITypeDescriptorContext context,
                    CultureInfo culture, object value, Type destinationType)
{
  if (value != null && !(value is DefaultTemplateManager2))
    throw new ArgumentException();

  if (destinationType == typeof(string))
  {
    if (value == null)
      return string.Empty;

    DefaultTemplateManager2 defaultTemplateManager =
                            value as DefaultTemplateManager2;
    string ss = string.Join(",",
      new string[] {
        defaultTemplateManager.PaymentMethodLabelTemplateType,
        defaultTemplateManager.CreditCardNoLabelTemplateType,
        defaultTemplateManager.CardholderNameLabelTemplateType,
        defaultTemplateManager.ExpirationDateLabelTemplateType,
        defaultTemplateManager.SubmitButtonTemplateType
      });
    return ss;
  }

  return base.ConvertTo(context, culture, value, destinationType);
}
```

First you should decide how you want to represent the `DefaultTemplateManager2` type in string format. Recall that `DefaultTemplateManager2` exposes five properties. This example uses a comma-separated list of these five properties as the string representation of `DefaultTemplateManager2` type.

As Listing 7-10 shows, the `ConvertTo` method accesses the five property values of the specified `DefaultTemplateManager2` object and forms a comma-separated list of these values. Notice that if the specified destination type isn't a string, the method calls the `ConvertTo` method of its base class.

ConvertFrom

`DefaultTemplateManager2Converter` overrides the `ConvertFrom` method to convert the specified value from the specified source type to the `DefaultTemplateManager2` type, as shown in Listing 7-11.

Listing 7-11: The ConvertFrom method

```
public override object ConvertFrom(ITypeDescriptorContext context,
                        CultureInfo culture, object value)
{
  if (value == null)
    return new DefaultTemplateManager2();

  string svalue = value as string;
```

(continued)

Listing 7-11: *(continued)*

```
    if (svalue == null)
      return base.ConvertFrom(context, culture, value);

    string[] templateTypes = svalue.Split(new char[] { ',' });
    if (templateTypes.Length != 5)
      throw new ArgumentException();

    DefaultTemplateManager2 defaultTemplateManager =
                              new DefaultTemplateManager2();
    defaultTemplateManager.PaymentMethodLabelTemplateType = templateTypes[0];
    defaultTemplateManager.CreditCardNoLabelTemplateType = templateTypes[1];
    defaultTemplateManager.CardholderNameLabelTemplateType = templateTypes[2];
    defaultTemplateManager.ExpirationDateLabelTemplateType = templateTypes[3];
    defaultTemplateManager.SubmitButtonTemplateType = templateTypes[4];


    return defaultTemplateManager;
  }
```

This method is the opposite of the `ConvertTo` method — it converts the specified string representation to its associated `DefaultTemplateManager2` object. Recall that this string representation is a comma-separated list of property values. As Listing 7-11 shows, the `ConvertFrom` method first extracts the values of the `PaymentMethodLabelTemplateType`, `CreditCardNoLabelTemplateType`, `CardholderNameLabelTemplateType`, `ExpirationDateLabelTemplateType`, and `SubmitButtonTemplateType` properties from the specified string representation:

```
    string[] templateTypes = svalue.Split(new char[] { ',' });
```

It then creates an instance of type `DefaultTemplateProvider2`:

```
    DefaultTemplateManager2 defaultTemplateManager =
                              new DefaultTemplateManager2();
```

Finally, it assigns the extracted property values to the respective properties of the `DefaultTemplateProvider2` instance:

```
    defaultTemplateManager.PaymentMethodLabelTemplateType = templateTypes[0];
    defaultTemplateManager.CreditCardNoLabelTemplateType = templateTypes[1];
    defaultTemplateManager.CardholderNameLabelTemplateType = templateTypes[2];
    defaultTemplateManager.ExpirationDateLabelTemplateType = templateTypes[3];
    defaultTemplateManager.SubmitButtonTemplateType = templateTypes[4];
```

Marking DefaultTemplateManager2 with Its Converter

The previous two sections implemented the `DefaultTemplateManager2` and `DefaultTemplateManager2Converter` classes. You must annotate your custom type with the `TypeConverterAttribute` attribute to specify its associated type converter:

```
    [TypeConverter(typeof(DefaultTemplateManager2Converter))]
    public class DefaultTemplateManager2
```

The .NET Framework comes with a component named `TypeDescriptor` that exposes a method named `GetConverter`. The clients of your custom type can call this method to access the type converter associated with your type. Under the hood, the `GetConverter` method accesses the argument of the `TypeConverterAttribute` that annotates your type. As the code fragment shows, this argument is the `Type` object that represents the type converter associated with your type. The `GetConverter` method dynamically creates an instance of the associated type converter.

Using the Non-IStateManager Class

This section implements a new custom control named `TemplatedCreditCardForm4` that derives from `TemplatedCreditCardForm` and extends its functionality to use `DefaultTemplateManager2`. The implementation of `TemplatedCreditCardForm4` is the same as `TemplatedCarditCardForm3` except for the following differences:

❑ The `DefaultTemplateManager` property of `TemplatedCreditCardForm4` is of type `DefaultTemplateManager2`, as shown in following code, whereas the same property of `TemplatedCreditCardForm3` is of type `DefaultTemplateManager`, as shown in Listing 7-6.

```
private DefaultTemplateManager2 defaultTemplateManager;
public virtual DefaultTemplateManager2 DefaultTemplateManager
{
  get
  {
    if (defaultTemplateManager == null)
      defaultTemplateManager = CreateDefaultTemplate();

    return defaultTemplateManager;
  }
}
```

❑ The `CreateDefaultTemplateManager` method of `TemplatedCreditCardForm4` creates a `DefaultTemplateManager2` object as shown in the following code, whereas the same method of `TemplatedCreditCardForm3` creates a `DefaultTemplateManager` object, as shown in Listing 7-6.

```
protected virtual DefaultTemplateManager2 CreateDefaultTemplateManager()
{
  return new DefaultTemplateManager2();
}
```

❑ Because `DefaultTemplateManager2` doesn't implement the `IStateManager` interface, `TemplatedCreditCardForm4` must take a different approach to managing the state of its `DefaultTemplateManager` property across page postbacks, as shown in the following sections.

TrackViewState

`TemplatedCreditCardForm4` overrides `TrackViewState` as shown here:

```
protected override void TrackViewState()
{
  if (defaultTemplateManager != null)
  {
```

```
        TypeConverter converter = TypeDescriptor.GetConverter(defaultTemplateManager);
        if (converter.CanConvertTo(typeof(string)))
        {
          string svalue = (string)converter.ConvertTo(defaultTemplateManager,
                                              typeof(string));
          ViewState["DefaultTemplateManager"] = svalue;
        }
      }
      base.TrackViewState();
    }
```

TrackViewState calls the GetConverter method of the TypeDescriptor class to access the type converter associated with its DefaultTemplateManager property in generic fashion:

```
    TypeConverter converter = TypeDescriptor.GetConverter(defaultTemplateManager);
```

It then calls the CanCovertTo method of the type converter to check whether the converter can convert the value of the DefaultTemplateManager property to string:

```
    if (converter.CanConvertTo(typeof(string)))
```

It then calls the ConvertTo method of the type converter to convert the value of the DefaultTemplateManager property to its string representation:

```
    string svalue = (string)converter.ConvertTo(defaultTemplateManager,
                                        typeof(string));
```

Finally, it adds this string representation to the ViewState collection:

```
    ViewState["DefaultTemplateManager"] = svalue;
```

SaveViewState

TemplatedCreditCardForm4 overrides SaveViewState to save the string representation of the value of its DefaultTemplateManager property to view state:

```
    protected override object SaveViewState()
    {
      if (defaultTemplateManager != null)
      {
        TypeConverter converter = TypeDescriptor.GetConverter(defaultTemplateManager);
        if (converter.CanConvertTo(typeof(string)))
        {
          string newValue = (string)converter.ConvertTo(defaultTemplateManager,
                                              typeof(string));
          string oldValue = (string)ViewState["DefaultTemplateManager"];
          if (newValue != oldValue)
            ViewState["DefaultTemplateManager"] = newValue;
        }
      }

      return base.SaveViewState();
    }
```

SaveViewState works like TrackViewState to convert the new value of its DefaultTemplateManager property to its string representation. It then compares the string representation of the new value with the string representation of the old value. (Recall that TrackViewState stores the string representation of the old value in the ViewState collection.) If they are different, it means that the state of the property has changed, and therefore the new string representation is stored in the ViewState collection.

LoadViewState

TemplatedCreditCardForm4 overrides LoadViewState as follows:

```
protected override void LoadViewState(object savedState)
{
  string svalue = ViewState["DefaultTemplateManager"] as string;
  if (svalue != null)
  {
    TypeConverter converter =
                TypeDescriptor.GetConverter(typeof(DefaultTemplateManager2));
    if (converter.CanConvertFrom(typeof(string)))
      defaultTemplateManager =
                    (DefaultTemplateManager2)converter.ConvertFrom(svalue);
  }

  else
    base.LoadViewState(savedState);
}
```

LoadViewState retrieves the string representation of the value of its DefaultTemplateManager property from the ViewState collection. Recall that the SaveViewState method stored this value in the view state at the end of the previous request, as discussed in the previous section:

```
string svalue = ViewState["DefaultTemplateManager"] as string;
```

It then calls the GetConverter method to access the type converter associated with the type of its DefaultTemplateManager property:

```
TypeConverter converter =
                TypeDescriptor.GetConverter(typeof(DefaultTemplateManager2));
```

Next it calls the CanConvertFrom method of the type converter to check whether the converter can convert from a string type to the DefaultTemplateManager2 type:

```
if (converter.CanConvertFrom(typeof(string)))
```

Finally, it calls the ConvertFrom method of the type converter to convert the string representation to an object of type DefaultTemplateManager2 and assigns the object to its DefaultTemplateManager property:

```
defaultTemplateManager = (DefaultTemplateManager2)converter.ConvertFrom(svalue);
```

Why You Need to Use TypeDescriptor

As previous sections show, the `TemplatedCreditCardForm4` control's implementation of the `TrackViewState`, `SaveViewState`, and `LoadViewState` methods call the `GetConverter` static method of the `TypeDescriptor` class to access the type converter. You may wonder why these methods don't use the `DefaultTemplateManager2Converter` converter directly, considering the fact that the `GetConverter` method will return an instance of the `DefaultTemplateManager2Converter` converter anyway.

To answer this question, you need to revisit the `CreateDefaultTemplateManager` method of `TemplatedCreditCardForm4` as shown again in the following code:

```
protected virtual DefaultTemplateManager2 CreateDefaultTemplateManager()
{
    return new DefaultTemplateManager2();
}
```

As this code shows, this method creates a `DefaultTemplateManager2` object. As far as this implementation of this method is concerned, there is no difference between using `GetConverter` or using the `DefaultTemplateManager2Converter` directly because the `GetConverter` returns a `DefaultTemplateManager2Converter` object.

However, the `CreateDefaultTemplateManager` method is marked as protected virtual to allow the subclasses of the `TemplatedCreditCardForm4` control to override this method to create a different type of `DefaultTemplateManager2` object that may have a different type converter associated with it.

If the `TrackViewState`, `SaveViewState`, and `LoadViewState` methods of the `TemplatedCredit CardForm4` control were directly using the `DefaultTemplateManager2Converter` converter, these methods would fail because they would use this converter to perform the type conversion as opposed to the new type converter. Recall that each type converter is specifically designed to work with a specific type.

You may wonder how the `GetConverter` method of `TypeDescriptor` class manages to get around this problem. Every type that has an associated type converter is annotated with the `TypeConverterAttribute` attribute that specifies the type of converter that must be used to convert the type to and from other types. Under the hood, the `GetConverter` method of the `TypeDescriptor` class uses the `TypeConverterAttribute` of a type to dynamically discover the type of the converter. In other words, instead of hard-coding what type of converter must be used, the `GetConverter` method dynamically discovers the type of the converter.

State Management of Container Control Styles

At the beginning of this chapter, you developed a custom composite control named `StyledCredit CardForm` that exposes five properties of type `TableItemStyle`. Because the type of these properties (`TableItemStyle`) exposes properties (`Width`, `Height`, and so on), these five style properties are complex properties, which means that the `StyleCreditCardForm` custom control must manage their states across page postbacks.

As discussed, what approach you should take to manage the state of a complex property depends on whether the type of the property implements the `IStateManager` interface. Because `TableItemStyle` implements the `IStateManager` interface, `StyledCreditCardForm` takes the steps discussed in the following sections to manage the states of its five style properties.

Property Declaration

As the highlighted sections in Listing 7-12 show, when one of these five style properties is created and `StyledCreditCardForm` control is tracking its view state, the control calls the `TrackViewState` method of the property to inform the property that it must start tracking its view state.

Listing 7-12: The style properties of the StyledCreditCardForm control

```
private TableStyle paymentMethodLabelStyle;
public TableStyle PaymentMethodLabelStyle
{
  get
  {
    if (paymentMethodLabelStyle == null)
    {
      paymentMethodLabelStyle = new TableStyle();
      if (IsTrackingViewState)
        ((IStateManager)paymentMethodLabelStyle).TrackViewState();
    }

    return paymentMethodLabelStyle;
  }
}

private TableStyle creditCardNoLabelStyle;
public TableStyle CreditCardNoLabelStyle
{
  get
  {
    if (creditCardNoLabelStyle == null)
    {
      creditCardNoLabelStyle = new TableStyle();
      if (IsTrackingViewState)
        ((IStateManager)creditCardNoLabelStyle).TrackViewState();
    }

    return creditCardNoLabelStyle;
  }
}

private TableStyle cardholderNameLabelStyle;
public TableStyle CardholderNameLabelStyle
{
  get
  {
    if (cardholderNameLabelStyle == null)
    {
      cardholderNameLabelStyle = new TableStyle();
```

(continued)

Listing 7-12: *(continued)*

```
        if (IsTrackingViewState)
            ((IStateManager)cardholderNameLabelStyle).TrackViewState();
    }

    return cardholderNameLabelStyle;
  }
}

private TableStyle expirationDateLabelStyle;
public TableStyle ExpirationDateLabelStyle
{
  get
  {
    if (expirationDateLabelStyle == null)
    {
      expirationDateLabelStyle = new TableStyle();
      if (IsTrackingViewState)
        ((IStateManager)expirationDateLabelStyle).TrackViewState();
    }

    return expirationDateLabelStyle;
  }
}

private TableStyle submitButtonStyle;
public TableStyle SubmitButtonStyle
{
  get
  {
    if (submitButtonStyle == null)
    {
      submitButtonStyle = new TableStyle();
      if (IsTrackingViewState)
        ((IStateManager)submitButtonStyle).TrackViewState();
    }

    return submitButtonStyle;
  }
}
```

TrackViewState

StyledCreditCardForm overrides TrackViewState to call the TrackViewState methods of its style properties, as shown in Listing 7-13.

Listing 7-13: The TrackViewState of the StyledCreditCardForm control

```
protected override void TrackViewState()
{
  base.TrackViewState();

  if (paymentMethodLabelStyle != null)
```

```
    ((IStateManager)paymentMethodLabelStyle).TrackViewState();

  if (creditCardNoLabelStyle != null)
    ((IStateManager)creditCardNoLabelStyle).TrackViewState();

  if (cardholderNameLabelStyle != null)
    ((IStateManager)cardholderNameLabelStyle).TrackViewState();

  if (expirationDateLabelStyle != null)
    ((IStateManager)expirationDateLabelStyle).TrackViewState();

  if (submitButtonStyle != null)
    ((IStateManager)submitButtonStyle).TrackViewState();
}
```

TrackViewState calls the TrackViewState method of a style property if and only if the style isn't null, that is, if the page developer has specified the respective style.

SaveViewState

StyledCreditCardForm overrides SaveViewState to call the SaveViewState methods of its style properties, as shown in Listing 7-14.

Listing 7-14: The SaveViewState of the StyledCreditCardForm control

```
protected override object SaveViewState()
{
  object[] state = new object[6];

  state[0] = base.SaveViewState();

  if (paymentMethodLabelStyle != null)
    state[1] = ((IStateManager)paymentMethodLabelStyle).SaveViewState();

  if (creditCardNoLabelStyle != null)
    state[2] = ((IStateManager)creditCardNoLabelStyle).SaveViewState();

  if (cardholderNameLabelStyle != null)
    state[3] = ((IStateManager)cardholderNameLabelStyle).SaveViewState();

  if (expirationDateLabelStyle != null)
    state[4] = ((IStateManager)expirationDateLabelStyle).SaveViewState();

  if (submitButtonStyle != null)
    state[5] = ((IStateManager)submitButtonStyle).SaveViewState();

  foreach (object obj in state)
  {
    if (obj != null)
      return state;
  }

  return null;
}
```

The SaveViewState method of each style property stores its view state in an appropriate object and returns the object to the SaveViewState method of SyledCreditCardForm, which in turn puts all these objects and the object that contains the view state of its base class in an array and returns the array to its caller.

SaveViewState checks whether all the objects that the array contains are null. If they are, it returns null. If they are not, it returns the whole array.

LoadViewState

StyledCreditCardForm overrides LoadViewState to call the LoadViewState methods of its style properties, as shown in Listing 7-15.

Listing 7-15: The LoadViewState of the StyledCreditCardForm control

```
protected override void LoadViewState(object savedState)
{
  if (savedState != null)
  {
    object[] state = savedState as object[];
    if (state != null && state.Length == 6)
    {
      base.LoadViewState(state[0]);

      if (state[1] != null)
        ((IStateManager)PaymentMethodLabelStyle).LoadViewState(state[1]);

      if (state[2] != null)
        ((IStateManager)CreditCardNoLabelStyle).LoadViewState(state[2]);

      if (state[3] != null)
        ((IStateManager)CardholderNameLabelStyle).LoadViewState(state[3]);

      if (state[4] != null)
        ((IStateManager)ExpirationDateLabelStyle).LoadViewState(state[4]);

      if (state[5] != null)
        ((IStateManager)SubmitButtonStyle).LoadViewState(state[5]);
    }
  }

  else
    base.LoadViewState(savedState);
}
```

The LoadViewState method of StyledCreditCardForm retrieves the array of objects that contain the saved view state of its base class and style properties. The method then calls the LoadViewState methods of its base class and properties in the order in which the SaveViewState method of StyledCreditCardForm called their SaveViewState methods. The LoadViewState method of each style property loads its view state with the saved view state.

Declarative Persistence

Declarative persistence is a feature that enables page developers and visual designers such as Visual Studio to declaratively set the properties of your custom control on an ASP.NET page. This feature allows page developers to set these properties without writing a single line of procedural code such as C# and VB.NET.

Simple Properties

The page framework enables page developers and visual designers such as Visual Studio to declaratively persist the simple properties of your custom control as attributes on the tag that represents your control on an ASP.NET page. These attributes have the same names as their associated properties.

For example, page developers can declaratively persist the `PaymentMethodText`, `CreditCardNoText`, `CardholderNameText`, `ExpirationDateText`, and `SubmitButtonText` properties of `StyledCredit CardForm` control as attributes named `PaymentMethodText`, `CreditCardNoText`, `CardholderNameText`, `ExpirationDateText`, and `SubmitButtonText` on the `<custom:StyledCreditCardForm>` tag that represents `StyledCreditCardForm` as shown here:

```
<custom:StyledCreditCardForm ID="ccf" runat="server"
PaymentMethodText="Payment Method"
CardholderNameText="Cardholder's Name"
CreditCardNoText="Credit Card No."
ExpirationDateText="Expiration Date"
SubmitButtonText="Submit" Font-Bold="true" />
```

Therefore the simple properties of your custom controls automatically support declarative persistence without any coding effort on your part.

Complex Properties (Hyphenated Declarative Persistence)

The page framework automatically enables page developers to use syntax known as *hyphenated declarative syntax* to declaratively persist the complex properties of your custom control as attributes on the tag that represents your control on an ASP.NET page. The *hyphenated declarative syntax* consists of the name of the complex property, followed by a hyphen and the name of its subproperty. Here is the hyphenated declarative persistence of the `PaymentMethodLabelStyle` property of `StyledCreditCardForm`:

```
<custom:StyledCreditCardForm ID="ccf" runat="server"
PaymentMethodLabelStyle-BackColor="Black"
PaymentMethodLabelStyle-ForeColor="white" />
```

You can enable visual designers such as Visual Studio to use hyphenated syntax to declaratively persist the complex properties of your custom control as attributes on the tag that represents your control on an ASP.NET page if you annotate each complex property with the `Designer VisualizationVisibilityAttribute(DesignerVisualizationVisibility.Content)` and `NotifyParentProperty(true)` design-time attributes. The `DesignerVisualizationVisibility Attribute(DesignerVisualizationVisibility.Content)` design-time attribute tells the designer that the annotated property is a complex property, meaning it has content or subproperties. The

177

`NotifyParentProperty(true)` design-time attribute tells the designer that every time the page developer changes the value of a subproperty of this property in Visual Studio, a change notification must be sent.

You also need to annotate the properties of the type of the complex property with the `NotifyParentProperty(true)` design-time attribute.

Recall that the `TemplatedCreditCardForm3` and `TemplatedCarditCardForm4` custom controls expose a complex property named `DefaultTemplateManager`. The page framework automatically enables page developers to use hyphenated syntax to declaratively persist the `DefaultTemplateManager` property as attributes on the `<custom:TemplatedCreditCardForm3>` or `<custom:TemplatedCreditCardForm4>` tags that represent the `TemplatedCreditCardForm3` and `TemplatedCarditCardForm4` custom controls:

```
<custom:TemplatedCreditCardForm3 ID="ccf" runat="server"
CardholderNameText="Cardholder's name"
CreditCardNoText="Credit Card No."
PaymentMethodText="Payment Method"
ExpirationDateText="Expiration Date"
SubmitButtonText="Submit" Font-Bold="true"
DefaultTemplateManager-PaymentMethodLabelTemplateType=
                          "CustomComponents.PaymentMethodLabelCreator" />
```

However, the page framework doesn't automatically enable visual designers to use hyphenated syntax to declaratively persist the `DefaultTemplateManager` property as attributes on the `<custom:TemplatedCreditCardForm3>` tag. To instruct the visual designer to accomplish this task, you must annotate the `DefaultTemplateManager` property with the `DesignerVisualizationVisibility Attribute(DesignerVisualizationVisibility.Content)` and `NotifyParentProperty(true)` design-time attributes as shown here:

```
[DesignerSerializationVisibility(DesignerSerializationVisibility.Content)]
[NotifyParentProperty(true)]
public virtual DefaultTemplateManager DefaultTemplateManager
{
  get
  {
    if (defaultTemplateManager == null)
    {
      defaultTemplateManager = CreateDefaultTemplateManager();
      if (IsTrackingViewState)
        ((IStateManager)defaultTemplateManager).TrackViewState();
    }
    return defaultTemplateManager;
  }
}
```

You must also annotate the `PaymentMethodLabelTemplateType`, `CreditCardNoLabelTemplateType`, `CardholderNameLabelTemplateType`, `ExpirationDateLabelTemplateType`, and `SubmitButtonTemplateType` properties of the `DefaultTemplateManager` class with `NotifyParentProperty(true)` design-time attribute:

```csharp
[NotifyParentProperty(true)]
public virtual string PaymentMethodLabelTemplateType
{
  get { return ViewState["PaymentMethodLabelTemplateType"] != null ?
           (string)ViewState["PaymentMethodLabelTemplateType"] : string.Empty; }
  set { ViewState["PaymentMethodLabelTemplateType"] = value; }
}

[NotifyParentProperty(true)]
public virtual string CreditCardNoLabelTemplateType
{
  get { return ViewState["CreditCardNoLabelTemplateType"] != null ?
           (string)ViewState["CreditCardNoLabelTemplateType"] : string.Empty; }
  set { ViewState["CreditCardNoLabelTemplateType"] = value; }
}

[NotifyParentProperty(true)]
public virtual string CardholderNameLabelTemplateType
{
  get { return ViewState["CardholderNameLabelTemplateType"] != null ?
           (string)ViewState["CardholderNameLabelTemplateType"] : string.Empty; }
  set { ViewState["CardholderNameLabelTemplateType"] = value; }
}

[NotifyParentProperty(true)]
public virtual string ExpirationDateLabelTemplateType
{
  get { return ViewState["ExpirationDateLabelTemplateType"] != null ?
         (string)ViewState["ExpirationDateLabelTemplateType"] : string.Empty; }
  set { ViewState["ExpirationDateLabelTemplateType"] = value; }
}

[NotifyParentProperty(true)]
public virtual string SubmitButtonTemplateType
{
  get { return ViewState["SubmitButtonTemplateType"] != null ?
             (string)ViewState["SubmitButtonTemplateType"] : string.Empty; }
  set { ViewState["SubmitButtonTemplateType"] = value; }
}
```

Complex Properties (Inner-Property Declarative Persistence)

You can enable page developers to declaratively persist the complex properties of your custom control as child elements of the tag that represents your control on an ASP.NET page if you mark your custom control with the ParseChildrenAttribute(true) attribute. This is known as *inner-property declarative persistence*. The following code shows the inner-property declarative persistence of the PaymentMethodLabelStyle property of StyledCreditCardForm, where the property is persisted as the child element of the <custom:StyledCreditCardForm> tag:

```
<custom:StyledCreditCardForm ID="ccf" runat="server">
  <PaymentMethodLabelStyle BackColor="Black" ForeColor="white" />
</custom:StyledCreditCardForm>
```

The `ParseChildrenAttribute(true)` attribute tells the page parser to treat the content within the opening and closing tags of the `StyledCreditCardForm` control as the property of the control. The next chapter discusses this in detail. Because `WebControl` is marked with the `ParseChildrenAttribute(true)` attribute, every control that directly or indirectly derives from `WebControl` automatically supports inner-property declarative persistence.

You can instruct visual designers such as Visual Studio to declaratively persist the complex properties of your custom control as child elements of the tag that represents your control on an ASP.NET page if you take the following steps:

1. Mark your custom control with the `PersistChildrenAttribute (false)` attribute. Because `WebControl` is marked with the `PersistChildrenAttribute(false)` attribute, every control that directly or indirectly derives from `WebControl` automatically inherits this attribute.

2. Mark each complex property of your custom control with the `PersistenceModeAttribute(PersistenceMode.InnerProperty)` attribute. This attribute tells the designer that it should persist the complex property as the child element of the tag that represents the respective control, and persist the subproperties of the complex property as attributes on the child element that represents the complex property.

3. Annotate each complex property with the `DesignerVisualizationVisibilityAttribute (DesignerVisualizationVisibility.Content)` and `NotifyParentProperty(true)` design-time attributes as you did before.

4. Mark each property of the type of each complex property of your custom control with the NotifyParentProperty(true) design-time attribute as you did before.

Revisit the `DefaultTemplateManager` complex property of the `TemplatedCreditCardForm3` and `TemplatedCarditCardForm4` custom controls. Because these two controls indirectly derive from `WebControl`, they inherit the `ParseChildrenAttribute(true)` attribute from `WebControl`. This allows page developers to declaratively persist the `DefaultTemplateManager` property as the child element of the `<custom:TemplatedCreditCardForm3>` tag and its sub properties as attributes on this child element:

```
<custom:TemplatedCreditCardForm3 ID="ccf" runat="server"
CardholderNameText="Cardholder's name"
CreditCardNoText="Credit Card No."
PaymentMethodText="Payment Method"
ExpirationDateText="Expiration Date"
SubmitButtonText="Submit" Font-Bold="true">
  <DefaultTemplateManager
  PaymentMethodLabelTemplateType="CustomComponents.PaymentMethodLabelCreator" />
</custom:TemplatedCreditCardForm3>
```

To instruct visual designers to declaratively persist the `DefaultTemplateManager` property as the child element of the `<custom:TemplatedCreditCardForm3>` tag and its subproperties as attributes on this child element, you need to annotate the `DefaultTemplateManager` property with the `DesignerVisualizationVisibilityAttribute(DesignerVisualizationVisibility.Content)`, `NotifyParentProperty(true)`, and `PersistenceMode(PersistenceMode.InnerProperty)` design-time attributes as shown here:

```
[DesignerSerializationVisibility(DesignerSerializationVisibility.Content)]
[NotifyParentProperty(true)]
[PersistenceMode(PersistenceMode.InnerProperty)]
public virtual DefaultTemplateManager DefaultTemplateManager
{
  get
  {
    if (defaultTemplateManager == null)
    {
      defaultTemplateManager = CreateDefaultTemplateManager();
      if (IsTrackingViewState)
        ((IStateManager)defaultTemplateManager).TrackViewState();
    }
    return defaultTemplateManager;
  }
}
```

You also need to annotate the PaymentMethodLabelTemplateType, CreditCardNoLabelTemplate
Type, CardholderNameLabelTemplateType, ExpirationDateLabelTemplateType, and
SubmitButtonTemplateType properties of the DefaultTemplateManager class with
NotifyParentProperty(true) design-time attribute as shown in the previous section.

Summary

This chapter showed you how to develop custom controls that expose complex properties such as Style
properties. You also saw how to develop controls that manage the states of their complex properties
across page postbacks. You learned how to use complex properties whose types implement the
IStateManager interface, and how to create a type converter for those that don't.

Finally, you learned how to allow page developers and visual designers to declaratively persist their
complex properties on an ASP.NET page. This chapter presented two different declarative persistence
options — hyphenated and inter-property declarative persistence. Your custom controls, like all
ASP.NET components, are part of the ASP.NET request processing architecture where they directly or
indirectly contribute to the final markup text that's sent back to the requester as part of the response
message. The next chapter looks at the ASP.NET request processing architecture more closely. You'll
learn how to extend different components of this architecture to add support for new features.

8

ASP.NET Request Processing Architecture

The main goal of the ASP.NET Framework is to process incoming requests. The ASP.NET request processing architecture is a framework that consists of extensible components. These components support what is referred to as "plug-and-play." In other words, you can plug in your own custom components to extend the functionality of these extensible components.

This chapter follows a request for a resource with the extension `.aspx` from the time it arrives at the Web server all the way through the request processing architecture. Along the way, you'll identify some of the extensible components of the framework and learn how to develop your own custom components to extend their functionality.

Following the Request

Once the request is made, Internet Information Services (IIS 5 or 6) picks up the request and examines the extension of the requested resource as shown in Figure 8-1. Because the extension `.aspx` is not included in the list of extensions that IIS can handle (such as `.html`), IIS searches for an ISAPI extension in its metabase that can handle the extension `.aspx`. As Figure 8-1 shows, you can use the Application Configuration dialog to access the IIS metadata. Later in this chapter, you see how to access this dialog. This dialog has two important columns named Extension and Executable Path. Each row registers a particular executable for handling requests for resources with a particular extension. The first column contains the extension of the requested resource and the second column contains the path to the executable file that handles the requests for that extension. When you install the .NET Framework, the `aspnet_isapi.dll` is automatically registered for handling requests for the `.aspx` extension, as illustrated in the highlighted row of the Application Configuration dialog shown in Figure 8-1. You can find the `aspnet_isapi.dll` assembly under the directory where you've installed the .NET Framework. Therefore the path to this assembly looks something like `C:\WINDOWS\Microsoft.NET\Framework\v2.0.50727\aspnet_isapi.dll`.

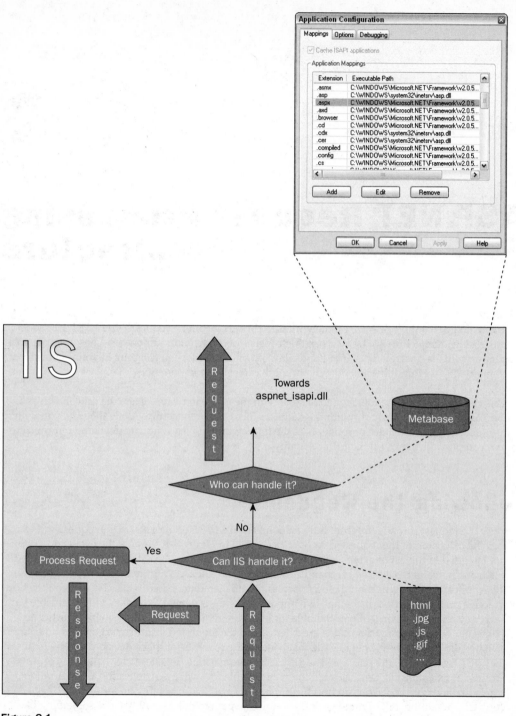

Figure 8-1

What happens next depends on what version of IIS is being used. As Figure 8-2 shows, IIS 5 loads directly, hosts `aspnet_isapi.dll`, and forwards the request to it. The `aspnet_isapi.dll` in turn spawns a new `aspnet_wp.exe` worker process and dispatches the request to it. This worker process loads and hosts the .NET runtime and forwards the request to it. Because the `aspnet_isapi.dll` and .NET runtime are in two separate processes, they use a named pipe to communicate.

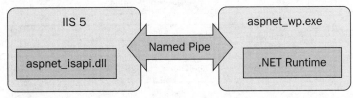

Figure 8-2

As Figure 8-3 shows, IIS 6, on the other hand, doesn't directly host `aspnet_isapi.dll`; instead it spawns a new `w3wp.exe` worker process that hosts both `aspnet_isapi.dll` and the .NET runtime. This improves the performance because both `aspnet_isapi.dll` and the .NET runtime are in the same process and don't have to communicate via a named pipe.

Figure 8-3

Once the runtime is loaded into the appropriate worker process (`aspnet_wp.exe` in IIS 5 and `w3wp.exe` in IIS6) and is up and running, `aspnet_isapi.dll` uses some intermediary COM APIs to dispatch the request to an ASP. NET component named `ISAPIRuntime`, and passes a handle to this component as shown in Figure 8-4. This handle provides access to the complete information about the underlying client request.

As Figure 8-4 illustrates, `ISAPIRuntime` creates an `HttpWorkerRequest` object that acts as a managed wrapper around this unmanaged handle and passes the object to an ASP.NET component named `HostingEnvironment`, which in turn passes the object to another ASP.NET component named `HttpRuntime`.

`HttpRuntime` creates an `HttpContext` object and passes the `HttpWorkerRequest` object into it as shown in Figure 8-4. The `HttpContext` object exposes the information that the `HttpWorkerRequest` object contains in the form of well-known convenient managed objects such as `Request`, `Response`, `Server`, and so on.

`HttpRuntime` then asks an ASP.NET component called `HttpApplicationFactory` to assign the task of handling the request to an `HttpApplication` object from a pool of available `HttpApplication` objects.

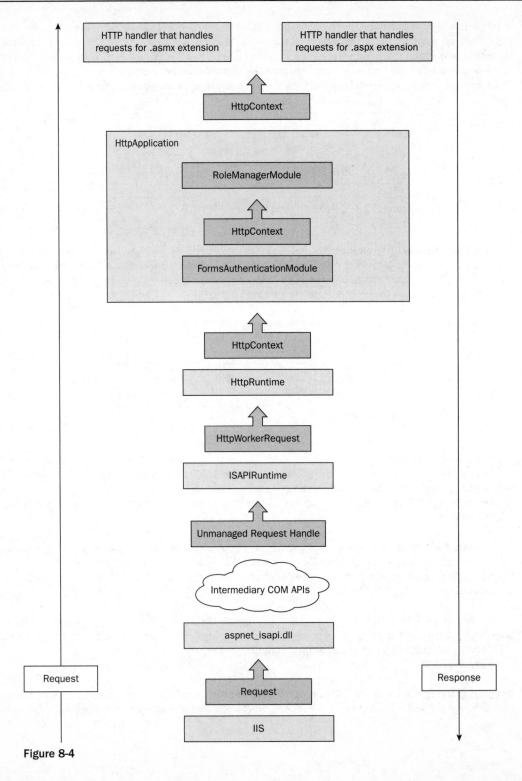

Figure 8-4

HTTP Modules

`HttpApplicationFactory` maintains a pool of `HttpApplication` objects and assigns an `HttpApplication` object from the pool to the task of handling the request. If there is no object in the pool, `HttpApplictionFactory` instantiates and initializes an `HttpApplication` object. As part of its initialization, the `HttpApplication` object reads the contents of the `<httpModules>` section of the `machine.config` and `Web.config` files. The `<httpModules>` section is used to register components, known as *HTTP modules*, as shown in Listing 8-1.

The `<httpModules>` element contains one `<add>` element for each registered HTTP module. The `<add>` element has two important attributes: `name` and `type`. The value of the `name` attribute is the friendly name of the module. The value of the `type` attribute consists of two parts. The first part is the fully qualified name of the module including its namespace. The second part is the weak or strong name of the assembly that contains the module. Recall that the strong name of an assembly consists of its name, version, culture, and public key token. If the type attribute doesn't contain the assembly information, ASP.NET will assume the executing assembly contains the module. Therefore the type attribute of the `<add>` element that registers a module contains all the information needed to instantiate the module.

Listing 8-1: The <httpModules> section is used to register HTTP modules

```
<configuration>
  <system.web>
    <httpModules>
      <httpModules>
        <add name="FormsAuthentication"
        type="System.Web.Security.FormsAuthenticationModule" />
        <add name="RoleManager" type="System.Web.Security.RoleManagerModule" />
        <add name="UrlAuthorization"
        type="System.Web.Security.UrlAuthorizationModule" />
        <add name="ErrorHandlerModule"
        type="System.Web.Mobile.ErrorHandlerModule, System.Web.Mobile,
            Version=2.0.0.0, Culture=neutral, PublicKeyToken=b03f5f7f11d50a3a" />
      </httpModules>
    </httpModules>
  </system.web>
</configuration>
```

The `HttpApplication` object then uses the values of the `type` attributes of the `<add>` elements associated with the registered modules to dynamically create a pipeline of modules as shown in Figure 8-4.

Finally, the `HttpApplication` object calls the `Init` method of all the modules in the pipeline. All HTTP modules implement the `IHttpModule` interface. This interface exposes two methods named `Dispose` and `Init`, as shown in Listing 8-2.

Listing 8-2: Every HTTP module must implement the IHttpModule interface

```
public interface IHttpModule
{
  void Dispose();
  void Init(HttpApplication context);
}
```

The `Dispose` method of a module releases the resources used by the module before the module is removed for the pipeline. `HttpApplication` exposes numerous application-level events, such as `AuthenticateRequest` and `AuthorizeRequest`, to signal important phases of the request handling process. `HttpApplication` calls the `Init` method of each module in the pipeline and passes a reference to itself into it.

The `Init` method of each module must register one or more callbacks for one or more events of the `HttpApplication` object. For example, the `Init` methods of the `FormsAuthenticationModule` and `UrlAuthorizationModule` HTTP modules register callbacks for the `AuthenticateRequest` and `AuthorizeRequest` events of `HttpApplication`, respectively.

The `HttpApplication` object pool provides the following two benefits:

❑ Because each request is handled by a different `HttpApplication` object from the pool, several requests can be processed simultaneously without interfering with each other.

❑ Because all the `HttpApplication` objects in the pool are running in the same application domain, ASP.NET guarantees that all the changes made in the `Web.config` or `.aspx` file are seen by all requests because these changes restart the application domain itself.

The `HttpApplication` object that the `HttpApplicationFactory` assigns to the task of handling the current request raises its events one by one, and consequently calls the callback methods that the modules in the pipeline have registered for these events.

The `HttpContext` object contains the complete information and data about the current request. Each callback method must access the required data from the `HttpContext` object, process the data, and update the information content of the `HttpContext` object accordingly. For example, the callback method that the `FormsAuthenticationModule` has registered for the `AuthenticateRequest` event accesses the information about the requester, authenticates the requester and establishes the requester's identity, and updates the `HttpContext` object accordingly. Therefore, the `HttpContext` object gets updated as it is passed from one module to another.

HTTP Handlers

Notice that HTTP modules don't handle the request themselves. For example, the `FormsAuthentication Module` establishes the identity of the requester, but doesn't process the request. In other words, HTTP modules preprocess and postprocess the request. The components that actually process the request itself are known as *HTTP handlers* (see Figure 8-4). They're called handlers because they handle the request.

ASP.NET Framework comes with several standard HTTP handlers, where each handler is responsible for handling requests for a particular extension. For example, the `Page` class is the HTTP handler that is responsible for handling requests for extension `.aspx`.

All HTTP handlers implement the `IHttpHandler` interface (shown in Listing 8-3), which exposes an important method named `ProcessRequest`. As you may have guessed, this method handles the request.

Listing 8-3: The IHttpHandler interface

```
public interface IHttpHandler
{
  void ProcessRequest(HttpContext context);
  bool IsReusable { get; }
}
```

HTTP Handler Factories

The ASP.NET Framework comes with components collectively known as *HTTP handler factories*, where each HTTP handler factory knows how to create an instance of its associated HTTP handler. For example, PageHandlerFactory knows how to create an instance of the handler that handles the request for the extension .aspx. All HTTP handler factories implement the IHttpHandlerFactory interface (shown in Listing 8-4). This interface exposes an important method named GetHandler that creates an instance of the appropriate HTTP handler and returns the instance.

Listing 8-4: The IHttpHandlerFactory interface

```
public interface IHttpHandlerFactory
{
  IHttpHandler GetHandler(HttpContext context, string requestType, string url,
                          string pathTranslated);
  void ReleaseHandler(IHttpHandler handler);
}
```

Control Builders

This section takes you through the process that creates the HTTP handler that handles the request for the CreditCardForm.aspx page, shown in Listing 8-5.

Listing 8-5: The CreditCardForm.aspx page

```
<%@ Page Language="C#" %>
<%@ Register TagPrefix="custom" Namespace="CustomComponents" %>
<html>
  <body>
    <form id="MyForm" runat="server">
      <custom:CompositeCreditCardForm ID="MyCompositeCreditCardForm"
      CardholderNameText="Cardholder's Name" CreditCardNoText="Credit Card No."
      PaymentMethodText="Payment Method" OnValidateCreditCard="ValidateCreditCard"
      ExpirationDateText="Expiration Date" SubmitButtonText="Submit"
      Font-Bold="true" runat="server" />
    </form>
  </body>
</html>
```

Handling the request in this case means turning the contents of the `CreditCardForm.aspx` file into pure HTML content, as shown in Listing 8-6.

Listing 8-6: The end result of the request handling process

```html
<html>
<body>
  <form method="post" action="CreditCardForm.aspx" id="MyForm">
    <div>
      <input type="hidden" name="__VIEWSTATE" id="__VIEWSTATE"
      value="/wEPDwULLTE4NTcxMjY1MjhkZEz+HG3vA0+Cglg5QGYSJBjeWfZl" />
    </div>
    <table id="MyCompositeCreditCardForm" style="font-weight: bold;">
      <tr>
        <td align="left" valign="middle"
        style="color: Black; background-color: White; font-weight: bold;">
          <span id="MyCompositeCreditCardForm_ctl00_PaymentMethodLabel"
          style="width: 100%;">PaymentMethod</span>
        </td>
        <td>
          <select name="MyCompositeCreditCardForm$ctl01$PaymentMethodList"
          id="MyCompositeCreditCardForm_ctl01_PaymentMethodList"
          style="width:100%;">
            <option value="Visa">Visa</option>
            <option value="MasterCard">MasterCard</option>
          </select>
        </td>
      </tr>
      <tr>
        <td align="left" valign="middle"
        style="color: Black; background-color: White; font-weight: bold;">
          <span id="MyCompositeCreditCardForm_ctl02_CreditCardNoLabel"
          style="width: 100%;">Credit Card No.</span>
        </td>
        <td>
          <input name="MyCompositeCreditCardForm$ctl03$CreditCardNoTextBox"
          type="text" id="MyCompositeCreditCardForm_ctl03_CreditCardNoTextBox" />
        </td>
      </tr>
      <tr>
        <td align="left" valign="middle"
        style="color: Black; background-color: White; font-weight: bold;">
          <span id="MyCompositeCreditCardForm_ctl04_CardholderNameLabel"
          style="width: 100%;">Cardholder's Name</span>
        </td>
        <td>
          <input name="MyCompositeCreditCardForm$ctl05$CardholderNameTextBox"
          type="text" id="MyCompositeCreditCardForm_ctl05_CardholderNameTextBox" />
        </td>
      </tr>
      <tr>
        <td align="left" valign="middle"
        style="color: Black; background-color: White; font-weight: bold;">
          <span id="MyCompositeCreditCardForm_ctl06_ExpirationDateLabel"
```

```
      style="width: 100%;">Expiration Date</span>
    </td>
    <td>
      <select name="MyCompositeCreditCardForm$ct107$MonthList"
      id="MyCompositeCreditCardForm_ct107_MonthList">
        <option value="1">01</option>
        <option value="2">02</option>
        . . .
      </select> 
      <select name="MyCompositeCreditCardForm$ct107$YearList"
      id="MyCompositeCreditCardForm_ct107_YearList">
        <option value="2005">2005</option>
        <option value="2006">2006</option>
        . . .
      </select>
    </td>
  </tr>
  <tr>
    <td align="center" valign="middle" colspan="2"
    style="color: Black; background-color: White; font-weight: bold;">
      <input type="submit" name="MyCompositeCreditCardForm$ct108$SubmitButton"
      value="Submit" id="MyCompositeCreditCardForm_ct108_SubmitButton" />
    </td>
  </tr>
    </table>
  </form>
</body>
</html>
```

The page framework takes the following actions to create the HTTP handler that turns the `CreditCardForm.aspx` file shown in Listing 8-5 to the pure HTML content shown in Listing 8-6:

1. Parses the `CreditCardForm.aspx` file.

2. Uses the parsed information to dynamically implement a class that derives from the `Page` class. Because the `Page` class itself implements the `IHttpHandler` interface, an instance of this class will be assigned to the task of handling the request for the `CreditCardForm.aspx` file.

3. Dynamically compiles the class.

4. Caches the compiled class.

5. Dynamically creates an instance of the compiled class.

6. Assigns the task of handling the request for the `CreditCardForm.aspx` file to this instance. Recall that handling the request for the `CreditCardForm.aspx` file means turning the `CreditCardForm.aspx` file shown in Listing 8-5 into the pure HTML content shown in Listing 8-6.

In other words, the HTTP handler that processes the request for the `CreditCardForm.aspx` file is a class that the page framework dynamically implements from the contents of the `CreditCardForm.aspx` file. As discussed in Chapter 1, by default, ASP.NET concatenates the name of the `.aspx` file with the string `"_aspx"` and uses it as the name of this dynamically generated class. Therefore, the name of this class in the case of the `CreditCardForm.aspx` file is `CreditCardForm_aspx`. You may wonder how the page framework manages to convert an XML-like file such as the `CreditCardForm.aspx` file into a C#

or VB.NET class. Before you attempt to find the answer to this question, you need to understand the following four important things about an ASP.NET page, such as the `CreditCardForm.aspx` file:

❑ Each tag on the page that has `runat="server"` attribute represents a server control. For example, the `CreditCardForm.aspx` file contains two tags with `runat="server"` attributes: `<form id="MyForm" runat="server">` and `<custom:CompositeCreditCardForm runat="server">`. These two tags represent the `HtmlForm` and `CompositeCreditCardForm` controls, respectively.

❑ Any consecutive sequence of tags (without the `runat="server"` attribute) and string characters represents a `LiteralControl` server control. For example, the `CreditCardForm.aspx` file contains four consecutive sequences of characters: `"\r\n<html>\r\n <body>\r\n "`, `"\r\n "`, `"\r\n "`, and `"\r\n </body>\r\n</html>\r\n"`, where `\n` and `\r` represent the new line and carriage return. Each of these four sequences of characters represents a `LiteralControl` server control.

❑ These server controls form a hierarchy of controls, as shown in Figure 8-5. Notice the root of the tree is the `CreditCardForm_aspx` control.

❑ Every server control is associated with a component known as a *control builder*. This component knows how to parse the control and its contents. In other words, the control builder associated with a control knows the following:

  ❑ What child tags are allowed between the opening and closing tags of the control on an ASP.NET page.

  ❑ Whether these child tags represent the properties or child controls of the control. For example, in the case of a templated control, a child tag within the opening and closing tags of the control represents a template property, not a child control.

  ❑ What type of child controls or properties these child tags represent.

  ❑ What type of control builders are associated with these child controls or properties.

  ❑ How to create instances of these child controls or properties and their associated control builders.

All control builders derive from the `ControlBuilder` base class. As a matter of fact, this base class is the default control builder for every ASP.NET control if the control isn't explicitly annotated with the `ControlBuilderAttribute` attribute. This attribute is discussed later in this chapter.

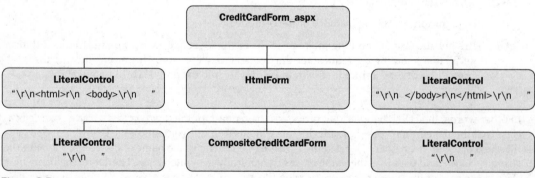

Figure 8-5

The `CreditCardForm_aspx` control, like any other control, is associated with a control builder. This builder is known as *root control builder*. The root control builder derives from the `ControlBuilder` base class.

How does the page framework manage to implement or develop the `CreditCardForm_aspx` control out of the `CreditCardForm.aspx` file? Obviously, the first order of business is to parse the file. This is where the page parser comes into play. The page parser first creates an instance of the root control builder and adds the instance on the top of its internal stack of control builders. At the beginning, the stack contains only one control builder — the root control builder. The page parser then uses its internal regular expression patterns to parse the `CreditCardForm.aspx` file from the top to the bottom. These regular expression patterns pick up the following parsed texts:

- ❑   `"\r\n<html>\r\n <body>\r\n "`
- ❑   `<form>`
- ❑   `"\r\n    "`
- ❑   `<custom:CompositeCreditCardForm>`
- ❑   `"\r\n    "`
- ❑   `"\r\n </body>\r\n</html>\r\n"`
- ❑   `</form>`

As an example, here's what the parser does with the following parsed text:

```
<form id="MyForm" runat="server">
```

The page parser accesses the control builder on top of its internal stack of control builders (the root control builder) and passes the parsed text to it.

The root control builder then calls its `GetChildControlType` method and passes the parsed text into it. The root control builder inherits the `GetChildControlType` method from the `ControlBuilder` base class. This method returns the `System.Type` object that represents the type of the child control server that the parsed text represents. In this case, the parsed text represents an `HtmlForm` control.

The root control builder then calls its `CreateBuilderFromType` method, which it also inherits from `ControlBuilder`, and passes the `System.Type` object into it. The `CreateBuilderFromType` method calls the `GetCustomAttributes` method of the `System.Type` object to check whether this type has been annotated with the `ControlBuilderAttribute` attribute. Recall that the `ControlBuilderAttribute` attribute is used to associate a control builder with a type or control. If the type is associated with a control builder, the `CreateBuilderFromType` method retrieves the type of the control builder from the associated `ControlBuilderAttribute` and uses reflection to dynamically create an instance of the builder. If the type is not annotated with `ControlBuilderAttribute`, this method creates an instance of the `ControlBuilder` base class.

The page parser then calls the `AppendSubBuilder` method of the root control builder (again inherited from `ControlBuilder`) and passes the child control builder into it. Every control builder maintains an internal list of its associated child builders. The `AppendSubBuilder` method adds the child builder associated with the `HtmlForm` control to the internal list of the root builder.

Finally, the page parser adds the control builder associated with the `HtmlForm` control on the top of its internal stack.

Next, look at the sequence of events that occurs to process the following parsed text:

```
<custom:CompositeCreditCardForm ID="MyCompositeCreditCardForm"
CardholderNameText="Cardholder's Name" CreditCardNoText="Credit Card No."
PaymentMethodText="Payment Method" OnValidateCreditCard="ValidateCreditCard"
ExpirationDateText="Expiration Date" SubmitButtonText="Submit"
Font-Bold="true" runat="server" />
```

First, the page parser accesses the control builder on the top of its stack, which is the HtmlForm control's control builder, and passes the parsed text to it.

The HtmlForm control's control builder then calls its GetChildControlType method and passes the parsed text into it. This method returns the System.Type object that represents the type of the child control server that the parsed text represents. In this case, the parsed text represents a CompositeCreditCardForm control.

The HtmlForm control's control builder calls its CreateBuilderFromType method and passes the System.Type object into it. This method calls the GetCustomAttributes method of the System.Type object to check whether this type has specified a control builder. Because the CompositeCreditCardForm control isn't annotated with the ControlBuilder attribute, the CreateBuilderFromType method creates and returns an instance of the ControlBuilder base class.

The page parser then calls the AppendSubBuilder method of the HtmlForm control's control builder and passes the CompositeCreditCardForm control's control builder into it. The AppendSubBuilder method adds the CompositeCreditCardForm control's control builder to the internal list of the HtmlForm control's control builder.

Finally, the page parser removes the HtmlForm control's control builder from its internal stack.

As this discussion shows, the page parser creates a hierarchy of control builders, which is very similar to Figure 8-1. Notice the big difference between the two trees. The tree that the page parser creates is a tree of control builders, whereas the tree shown in Figure 8-1 is a tree of server controls.

This control builder tree contains all the information needed to dynamically implement the CreditCardForm_aspx control. The page framework uses this tree and the System.CodeDom classes to dynamically generate the code for the CreditCardForm_aspx. Listing 8-7 contains a simplified version of this code.

Follow the steps discussed in Chapter 1 if you want to see for yourself that the page framework indeed generates the code shown in Listing 8-7. Keep in mind that the CreditCardForm_aspx control doesn't represent a particular control on the CreditCardForm.aspx page. Instead, this control represents the page as a whole.

Listing 8-7: The dynamically generated CreditCardForm_aspx class

```
public class CreditCardForm_aspx : Page
{
   protected CompositeCreditCardForm MyCompositeCreditCardForm;
   protected HtmlForm MyForm;

   private CompositeCreditCardForm @__BuildControlMyCompositeCreditCardForm()
```

```
  {
    MyCompositeCreditCardForm @__ctrl = new CompositeCreditCardForm();
    @__ctrl.CardholderNameText = "Cardholder\'s Name";
    @__ctrl.CreditCardNoText = "Credit Card No.";
    @__ctrl.ExpirationDateText = "Expiration Date";
    @__ctrl.Font.Bold = true;
    @__ctrl.ID = "MyCompositeCreditCardForm";
    @__ctrl.PaymentMethodText = "Payment Method";
    @__ctrl.SubmitButtonText = "Submit";
    @__ctrl.ValidateCreditCard +=
      new CustomComponents.ValidateCreditCardEventHandler(this.ValidateCreditCard);
    MyCompositeCreditCardForm = @__ctrl;

    return @__ctrl;
  }

  private HtmlForm @__BuildControlMyForm()
  {
    HtmlForm @__ctrl = new HtmlForm();
    @__ctrl.ID = "MyForm";
    MyForm = @__ctrl;
    IParserAccessor @__parser = ((IParserAccessor)(@__ctrl));
    @__parser.AddParsedSubObject(new LiteralControl("\r\n      "));
    CompositeCreditCardForm @__ctrl1;
    @__ctrl1 = @__BuildControlMyCompositeCreditCardForm();
    @__parser.AddParsedSubObject(@__ctrl1);
    @__parser.AddParsedSubObject(new LiteralControl("\r\n    "));
    return @__ctrl;
  }

  private void @__BuildControlTree(CreditCardForm_aspx @__ctrl)
  {
    IParserAccessor @__parser = ((IParserAccessor)(@__ctrl));
    @__parser.AddParsedSubObject(
                        new LiteralControl("\r\n<html>\r\n  <body>\r\n    "));
    HtmlForm @__ctrl1;
    @__ctrl1 = this.@__BuildControlMyForm();
    @__parser.AddParsedSubObject(@__ctrl1);
    @__parser.AddParsedSubObject(
                        new LiteralControl("\r\n  </body>\r\n</html>\r\n"));
  }

  protected override void FrameworkInitialize()
  {
    base.FrameworkInitialize();
    this.@__BuildControlTree(this);
  }
}
```

The page framework then dynamically compiles the CreditCardForm_aspx control, caches the compiled control or class, and uses reflection to dynamically create an instance of the compiled class. Because the CreditCardForm_aspx control derives from the Page class and the Page class implements the IHttpHandler, the CreditCardForm_aspx class inherits the ProcessRequest method from the Page class. The page framework calls the ProcessRequest method of the newly created CreditCardForm_aspx control to start the page life cycle, which was discussed thoroughly in Chapter 4.

So far you've learned a great deal about the parse time. Parsing is done only once, when the page is accessed the first time. There are other things that happen for every single request, however. Every control builder inherits the `BuildObject` method from the `ControlBuilder` base class. This method builds the server control associated with the control builder. When the `BuildObject` method of a control builder is called, the control builder internally takes the following actions:

1. Enumerates its child control builders. Recall that every control builder keeps an internal list of its associated child control builders.

2. Calls the `BuildObject` method of each enumerated child control builder to create the child control associated with that child control builder.

3. Calls the `AddParsedSubObject` method of its associated server control once for each child control and passes the child control into it.

Every server control inherits the `AddParsedSubObject` method from the `Control` class. The default implementation of the `AddParsedSubObject` method adds the child control passed in as the argument of the method to the `Controls` collection of the server control.

Developing Custom HTTP Modules

This section shows you how to implement an HTTP module to add support for what is known as URL rewriting. URL rewriting allows end users to access a page using a URL that isn't the actual URL of the page. In other words, URL rewriting allows you to *virtualize* the URL of your Web application's pages. URL rewriting especially comes to your rescue in the following two situations:

❑   When your Web application goes through restructuring that moves existing pages to different URLs. This causes problems for users who have bookmarked your pages, or are used to the old URLs. URL rewriting allows you to transparently map the old URLs to new ones, giving the users the illusion that they are still accessing the old URLs.

❑   Most Web applications use query strings to transfer data from one page to another. This leads into URLs that are very hard for users to remember and use.

In this section you learn how to implement a custom HTTP module named `ArticlesModule` for a Web application that allows users to access the articles written by a particular author. Typically, these kinds of applications pass the author's name or idas part of the URL to the page that displays the list of the articles written by the author. Call this page `Articles.aspx`. The URL for accessing the articles written by an author named Smith will look something like this:

```
http://localhost/Articles/Articles.aspx?AuthorName=Smith
```

Such an URL is not memorable and causes all kinds of usability issues. You'll make life easier on the visitors of your site if you allow them to use the following URL to access the same page:

```
http://localhost/Articles/Smith.aspx
```

This is a much more memorable and usable URL than the previous one. Behind the scenes, the ArticlesModule HTTP module transparently rewrites the URL that the user uses (http://localhost/ Articles/Smith.aspx) back to the actual URL (http://localhost/Articles/Articles.aspx? AuthorName=Smith). Listing 8-8 shows the implementation of the ArticlesModule HTTP module.

Listing 8-8: The ArticlesModule HTTP module

```
public class ArticlesModule : IHttpModule
{
  void IHttpModule.Init(HttpApplication app)
  {
    app.BeginRequest += new EventHandler(App_BeginRequest);
  }

  void App_BeginRequest(object sender, EventArgs e)
  {
    HttpApplication app = sender as HttpApplication;
    HttpContext context = app.Context;

    Regex regex =
            new Regex(@"Articles/(.*)\.aspx", RegexOptions.IgnoreCase);
    Match match = regex.Match(context.Request.Path);

    if (match.Success)
    {
      string newPath =
              regex.Replace(context.Request.Path, @"Articles.aspx?AuthorName=$1");
      context.RewritePath(newPath);
    }
  }

  void IHttpModule.Dispose() { }
}
```

The ArticlesModule HTTP module implements the IHttpModule interface. As shown in Listing 8-2, this interface exposes two methods named Init and Dispose. The Dispose method is where your custom HTTP module must release the resources it is holding. This method is automatically called before your module is removed from the pipeline of modules. Because ArticlesModule doesn't hold on to any resources, the Dispose method of this module doesn't contain any code.

The Init method of ArticlesModule registers a method named App_BeginRequest as callback for the BeginRequest event of the HttpApplication object to rewrite the URL right at the beginning of the request:

```
app.BeginRequest += new EventHandler(App_BeginRequest);
```

As discussed, the HttpApplication object raises the BeginRequest event and automatically calls the App_BeginRequest method. This method casts its sender argument to HttpApplication. Recall that the sender argument refers to the object that raised the event, which is the HttpApplication object:

```
HttpApplication app = sender as HttpApplication;
```

The method then uses the `Context` property of the `HttpApplication` object to access the `HttpContext` object. Recall that the `HttpContext` object contains the complete information about the request and exposes this information in the form of convenient managed objects such as `Request`, `Response`, and so on.

```
HttpContext context = app.Context;
```

The method then creates an instance of the `Regex` class:

```
Regex regex = new Regex(@"Articles/(.*)\.aspx", RegexOptions.IgnoreCase);
```

The argument passed into the constructor of the `Regex` class is the regular expression pattern to match. In other words, the instance of the `Regex` class represents this regular expression pattern.

The method then calls the `Match` method of the `Regex` instance and passes the URL of the requested resource. This is the memorable URL that the end user uses, which is `http://localhost/Articles/Smith.aspx` in this example. You can use the `Path` property of the `Request` object to access this URL. The `Match` method of the `Regex` instance searches this URL for a substring that matches the `"Articles/(.*)\.aspx"` regular expression pattern. For example, this regular expression pattern will pick the `Articles/Smith.aspx` substring from the `http://localhost/Articles/Smith.aspx` URL:

```
Match match = regex.Match(context.Request.Path);
```

If the `Regex` instance finds a substring of the URL that matches the `"Articles/(.*)\.aspx"` regular expression pattern, it calls the `Replace` method of the `Regex` instance to replace the substring with `"Articles.aspx?AuthorName=$1"`. The dollar sign ($) instructs the `Regex` instance to replace it with the string that the star sign (*) in the pattern matches with. For example, in the case of `http://localhost/Articles/Smith.aspx`, the star sign matches the string `"Smith"`. Therefore, the `Regex` instance will replace the dollar sign with the string `"Smith"`, which is exactly what you need.

```
string newPath =regex.Replace(context.Request.Path,@"Articles.aspx?AuthorName=$1");
```

Finally, the `App_BeginRequest` method calls the `Rewrite` method of the `HttpContext` object to rewrite the URL:

```
context.RewritePath(newPath);
```

Registering Your Custom HTTP Module

As discussed, as part of its initialization, the `HttpApplication` object reads the contents of the `<httpModules>` section of the `Web.config` file to retrieve the type information for all the registered modules. The `HttpApplication` object uses the type information of each registered module to dynamically create an instance of the module.

Therefore, you must add your custom HTTP module to the `<httpModules>` section of the `Web.config` or `machine.config` file so it gets picked by the `HttpApplication` object. The following code adds the `ArticlesModule` to the `<httpModules>` section:

```
<configuration>
  <httpModules>
    <add name="ArticlesModule" type="CustomComponents.ArticlesModule"/>
  </httpModules>
</configuration>
```

The value of the `name` attribute of the `<add>` element is the friendly name of your module. You can pick any friendly name you want. The value of the `type` attribute consists of up to two parts. The first part is the fully qualified name of the type of the module including its namespace, such as `CustomComponents` `.ArticlesModule`. The second argument is the weak or strong name of the assembly that contains the module. You don't need to include this argument if your module belongs to the executing assembly.

Developing Custom HTTP Handler Factories

Recall that each HTTP handler factory is designed to create a specific HTTP handler. This section shows you how to develop a custom HTTP handler factory named `ArticlesHandlerFactory` to learn how to develop your own custom HTTP handler factories and how to register them.

The previous section performed URL rewriting in an HTTP module named `ArticlesModule`. This section shows you that you can perform URL rewriting in a custom HTTP handler factory called `ArticlesHandlerFactory` instead of a custom HTTP module.

Like any HTTP handler factory, `ArticlesHandlerFactory` implements the `IHttpHandlerFactory` interface. As shown in Listing 8-4, this interface exposes two methods named `GetHandler` and `ReleaseHandler`. The `GetHandler` method takes four arguments:

❑ context: The `HttpContext` object

❑ requestType: The HTTP verb such as `POST` or `GET`

❑ url: The virtual path of the requested resource

❑ pathTranslated: The physical path of the requested resource

Listing 8-9 shows the implementation of `ArticlesHandlerFactory`. The implementation of the `GetHandler` method is the same as the `App_BeginRequest` method, except for the last line:

```
PageParser.GetCompiledPageInstance(url,
                         context.Server.MapPath("Articles.aspx"), context);
```

Recall from the previous sections that the page parser parses the ASP.NET page and creates a tree of control builders. The page framework uses this tree to dynamically implement a class that derives from the `Page` class and represents the ASP.NET page. Listing 8-7 shows the dynamically generated class that represents the `CreditCardForm.aspx` file. The page framework then dynamically compiles this class.

The `GetCompiledPageInstance` of the `PageParser` class returns an instance of this compiled page class.

Listing 8-9: The ArticlesHandlerFactory HTTP handler factory

```
public class ArticlesHandlerFactory : IHttpHandlerFactory
{
  IHttpHandler IHttpHandlerFactory.GetHandler(HttpContext context,
                     string requestType, string url, string pathTranslated)
  {
    Regex regex =
             new Regex(@"/CreditCardForm/(.*)\.aspx", RegexOptions.IgnoreCase);
    Match match = regex.Match(url);
    string newPath = string.Empty;

    if (match.Success)
    {
      newPath = regex.Replace(url, @"Articles.aspx?AuthorName=$1");
      context.RewritePath(newPath);
    }

    return PageParser.GetCompiledPageInstance(url,
                     context.Server.MapPath("Articles.aspx"), context);
  }

  void IHttpHandlerFactory.ReleaseHandler(IHttpHandler handler) {}
}
```

The next order of business is to register your custom handler. The `machine.config` and `Web.config` come with a section named `<httpHandlers>`. You must use an `<add>` element to add your custom HTTP handler factory to this section. The following code registers the `ArticlesHandlerFactory`:

```
<httpHandlers>
  <add path="*.aspx" verb="*" type="CustomComponents.ArticlesHandlerFactory"/>
</httpHandlers>
```

The `<add>` element has three important attributes:

❑   `path`: The path for which the handler is being registered

❑   `verb`: The list of HTTP verbs that this handler will support, such as `POST` and `GET`

❑   `type`: The fully qualified name of the handler and the weak or strong name of the assembly that contains the handler

Developing Custom HTTP Handlers

As mentioned, HTTP handlers are components that are responsible for handling client requests. Each handler is designed to handle a specific extension. For example, the page handler discussed in the previous sections is specifically designed to handle requests for the extension `.aspx`. This section develops a custom HTTP handler named `RssHandler` to show you how to implement your own custom HTTP handlers and how to register them.

RSS

Really Simple Syndication (RSS) is a format for syndicating news. This section briefly describes RSS 2.0 in preparation for the next section, where you learn how to develop an HTTP handler named `RssHandler` to dynamically generate RSS for your Web site. Listing 8-10 shows an example of an RSS document.

Listing 8-10: An example of RSS

```xml
<?xml version="1.0" encoding="utf-8"?>
<rss version="2.0">
  <channel>
    <title>New Articles On greatarticles.com</title>
    <link>http://www.articles.com</link>
    <description>List of newly published articles on articles.com</description>
    <item>
      <title>ASP.NET 2.0</title>
      <description>Discusses new ASP.NET 2.0 features</description>
      <link>http://localhost:1507/CreditCardForm/Smith.aspx</link>
    </item>
    <item>
      <title>View State Management</title>
      <description>In-depth coverage of view state management</description>
      <link>http://localhost:1507/CreditCardForm/Murray.aspx</link>
    </item>
    <item>
      <title>XSLT</title>
      <description>Discusses common applications of XSLT</description>
      <link>http://localhost:1507/CreditCardForm/Brown.aspx</link>
    </item>
    <item>
      <title>Introduction to XML</title>
      <description>Provides an introduction to XML</description>
      <link>http://localhost:1507/CreditCardForm/Smith.aspx</link>
    </item>
    <item>
      <title>XML Web Services</title>
      <description>In-depth coverage of XML Web services</description>
      <link>http://localhost:1507/CreditCardForm/Murray.aspx</link>
    </item>
  </channel>
</rss>
```

As Listing 8-10 shows, RSS is an XML document with a root element named `<rss>`. The root element has a mandatory attribute named `version`. This section covers the latest version, 2.0. The `<rss>` element has a single child element named `<channel>`. The `<channel>` element has three required elements named `<title>`, `<link>`, and `<description>`. The `<channel>` element may also contain zero or more `<item>` elements. Listing 8-10 shows three child elements of the `<item>` element: `<title>`, `<description>`, and `<link>`.

RssHandler

Think back to the articles Web application discussed earlier in this chapter. Recall that this application allows users to read articles written by different authors. In this section you learn how to generate an RSS document for this application.

You could use a data-bound control such as Repeater to generate the RSS document. The problem with this approach is that every time the user accesses the document, the request goes through the typical page life cycle even though the RSS document doesn't contain any HTML markup text. To avoid the overhead of normal ASP.NET request processing, this section implements a custom HTTP handler named RssHandler to replace the normal page handler.

RssHandler implements the IHttpHandler interface. As shown in Listing 8-3, this interface exposes a method named ProcessRequest and a property named IsReusable. ProcessRequest does just what its name says it does—it processes the client request. The IsReusable Boolean property specifies whether the same instance of the HTTP handler should be used to process different requests. Your custom HTTP handler's implementation of IsReusable should return false:

```
bool IHttpHandler.IsReusable
{
  get { return false; }
}
```

Listing 8-11 shows the RssHandler HTTP handler's implementation of the ProcessRequest method.

Listing 8-11: The ProcessRequest method

```
void IHttpHandler.ProcessRequest(HttpContext context)
{
  context.Response.ContentType = "text/xml";
  DbDataReader reader = GetDataReader();
  XmlWriterSettings settings = new XmlWriterSettings();
  settings.Indent = true;
  using (XmlWriter writer = XmlWriter.Create(context.Response.OutputStream,
                                             settings))
  {
    writer.WriteStartDocument();
    writer.WriteStartElement("rss");
    writer.WriteAttributeString("version", "2.0");
    writer.WriteStartElement("channel");
    writer.WriteElementString("title", "New Articles On articles.com");
    writer.WriteElementString("link", "http://www.greatarticles.com");
    writer.WriteElementString("description",
              "List of newly published articles on articles.com");
    while (reader.Read())
    {
      writer.WriteStartElement("item");
      writer.WriteElementString("title",(string)reader["Title"]);
      writer.WriteElementString("description",(string)reader["Abstract"]);
      writer.WriteElementString("link", "http://localhost:1507/CreditCardForm/" +
                                (string)reader["AuthorName"] + ".aspx");
```

```
        writer.WriteEndElement();
    }
    writer.WriteEndElement();
    writer.WriteEndElement();
    writer.WriteEndDocument();
  }
}
```

The `ProcessRequest` method first sets the content type to `text/xml` to inform the clients of the application that the RSS document contains XML data:

```
context.Response.ContentType = "text/xml";
```

Then it retrieves all the article data rows from the `Articles` database table. Each data row contains three columns (`Title`, `Abstract`, and `AuthorName`):

```
DbDataReader reader = GetDataReader();
```

Then it creates an instance of the `XmlWriter` class. This instance will be used to dynamically generate the RSS document from the retrieved article data rows:

```
XmlWriterSettings settings = new XmlWriterSettings();
settings.Indent = true;
using (XmlWriter writer = XmlWriter.Create(context.Response.OutputStream,settings))
```

Because the `Create` method takes the output stream as its argument, the XML writer will directly write into the response's output stream.

Keep in mind that you're trying to dynamically generate an RSS document similar to the one shown in Listing 8-10. As Listing 8-11 shows, the `ProcessRequest` generates the RSS document line by line. In Listing 8-10, the first line of the RSS document is the XML declaration:

```
<?xml version="1.0" encoding="utf-8"?>
```

`ProcessRequest` calls the `WriteStartDocument` method of the XML writer to start the document and add the XML declaration on the top of the RSS document.

The second line of the RSS document is the opening tag of the `rss` element and its version attribute:

```
<rss version="2.0">
```

`ProcessRequest` calls the `WriteStartElement` and `WriteAttributeString` methods of the XML writer to render the opening tag of the `rss` element and its version attribute, respectively:

```
writer.WriteStartElement("rss");
writer.WriteAttributeString("version", "2.0");
```

The third line of the RSS document is the opening tag of the `channel` element:

```
<channel>
```

`ProcessRequest` calls the `WriteStartElement` method to render the opening tag of the `channel` element.

The fourth, fifth, and sixth lines of the RSS document are the `title`, `link`, and `description` subelements of the channel element:

```
<title>New Articles On greatarticles.com</title>
<link>http://www.greatarticles.com</link>
<description>List of newly published articles on articles.com</description>
```

`ProcessRequest` calls the `WriteElementString` method three times to generate the `title`, `link`, and `description` child elements of the channel element:

```
writer.WriteElementString("title", "New Articles On articles.com");
writer.WriteElementString("link", "http://www.greatarticles.com");
writer.WriteElementString("description",
                           "List of newly published articles on articles.com");
```

The RSS document can have zero or more item elements, where each item element contains three elements named `title`, `description`, and `link`:

```
<item>
   <title>ASP.NET 2.0</title>
   <description>Discusses new ASP.NET 2.0 features</description>
   <link>http://localhost:1507/CreditCardForm/Smith.aspx</link>
</item>
```

`ProcessRequest` enumerates the retrieved article data rows and renders an item element for each enumerated data row. The first line of each item element is the opening tag of the `item` element:

```
<item>
```

`ProcessRequest` calls the `WriteStartElement` method to render the opening tag of the `item` element:

```
writer.WriteStartElement("item");
```

`ProcessRequest` accesses the `Title` and `Abstract` columns of the enumerated data row and passes the value of each column into the `WriteAttributeString` method to generate the title and description elements and their contents:

```
writer.WriteElementString("title",(string)reader["Title"]);
writer.WriteElementString("description",(string)reader["Abstract"]);
```

`ProcessRequest` accesses the `AuthorName` column of the enumerated data row, which is then used to generate the URL of the document that contains the articles of the specified author:

```
writer.WriteElementString("link", "http://localhost:1507/CreditCardForm/" +
                           (string)reader["AuthorName"] + ".aspx");
```

The last line of each `item` element is the closing tag of the `item` element:

```
</item>
```

`ProcessRequest` calls the `WriteEndElement` method to render the closing tag of the `item` element:

```
writer.WriteEndElement();
```

`ProcessRequest` then calls the `WriteEndElement` method to render the closing tag of the `channel` element.

Finally, `ProcessRequest` calls the `WriteEndElement` method to render the closing tag of the `rss` element.

Registering Your Custom HTTP Handler

After you implement your custom HTTP handler, you need to register it. Add your handler to the `<httpHandlers>` section of the `machine.config` or `Web.config` file. Adding an HTTP handler to the `<httpHandlers>` section is identical to adding an HTTP handler factory to this section, which was discussed earlier:

```
<httpHandlers>
    <add path="*.rss" verb="*" type="CustomComponents.RssHandler"/>
</httpHandlers>
```

Next, tell IIS to dispatch requests for your custom extension (`.rss`) to the `aspnet_isapi.dll` extension. This step is required if your HTTP handler must handle a custom extension. Recall that when IIS picks up a request, it examines the extension of the requested resource and takes one of the following actions:

❑   If the extension is one of the extensions such as `.html` that IIS itself can handle, IIS processes the request.

❑   If the extension is not one that IIS can handle, IIS searches its metabase for an ISAPI extension that can handle this extension. The `aspnet_isapi.dll` extension is the extension that picks up the ASP.NET request. You must register this ISAPI extension with the IIS metadata for handling requests for your own custom extension, which is `.rss` in the case of `RssHandler`.

Because `RssHandler` handles the request for the custom extension `.rss`, follow these steps to tell IIS to dispatch requests for the extension `.rss` to the `aspnet_isapi.dll` extension:

1.   Launch the Internet Information Services dialog.

2.   Right-click your Web application's root directory and select Properties to launch the Properties dialog shown in Figure 8-6.

3.   Click the Configuration button on the Properties dialog to launch the Application Configuration dialog shown in Figure 8-7.

Figure 8-6

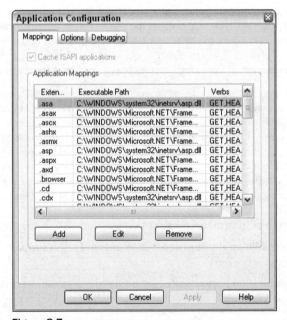

Figure 8-7

4. Click the Add button on the Application Configuration dialog to launch the Add/Edit Application Extension Mapping dialog shown in Figure 8-8.

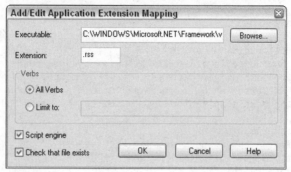

Figure 8-8

5. Enter your custom extension in the Extension text box and click the Browse button. Go to the directory where you've installed the .NET Framework, and select the `aspnet_isapi.dll`.

Developing Custom Control Builders

As discussed, the page parser parses an `.aspx` file such as `CreditCardForm.aspx` shown in Listing 8-5 and creates a tree of control builders, which is subsequently used to dynamically generate the code for a control that derives from the `Page` class, such as the `CreditCardForm_aspx` control shown in Listing 8-7.

A control builder is a component associated with a server control that knows what child elements are allowed within the opening and closing tags of the server control, what server controls these child elements represent, and how to instantiate these child server controls and their associated control builders. In other words, a control builder has complete control over how its associated control is parsed and built.

In this section, you develop a custom control builder named `CompositeCreditCardForm2Builder`. You then develop a custom composite control named `CompositeCreditCardForm2` that derives from the `CompositeCreditCardForm` custom control developed in previous chapters. Finally, you use the `ControlBuilderAttribute` attribute to assign `CompositeCreditCardForm2Builder` as the control builder of the `CompositeCreditCardForm2` control.

Before diving into the details of the implementation of the control builder and composite control, first take a look at how the `CompositeCreditCardForm2` custom control is used in an ASP.NET page. As Listing 8-12 shows, the `CompositeCreditCardForm2` control exposes a property named `Data` that allows the page developer to declaratively specify the payment list within the opening (`<Data>`) and closing (`</Data>`) tags of this property.

Listing 8-12: An ASP.NET page that uses CompositeCreditCardForm2 control

```
<%@ Page Language="C#" %>
<%@ Register TagPrefix="custom" Namespace="CustomComponents" %>
<html>
<body>
  <form id="form1" runat="server">
    <custom:CompositeCreditCardForm2 ID="ccf" runat="server" Font-Bold="true"
    OnValidateCreditCard="ValidateCreditCard" PaymentMethodText="Payment Method"
    CardholderNameText="Cardholder's Name" CreditCardNoText="Credit Card No."
    ExpirationDateText="Expiration Date" SubmitButtonText="Submit">
      <Data>
        <PaymentMethodList>
          <PaymentMethod text="Visa" value="Visa" />
          <PaymentMethod text="MasterCard" value="MasterCard" />
        </PaymentMethodList>
      </Data>
    </custom:CompositeCreditCardForm2>
  </form>
</body>
</html>
```

Notice that Listing 8-12 is the same as Listing 8-5 except for one big difference. The `<custom: CompositeCreditCardForm2>` element in Listing 8-12 has a child element, `<Data>`, whereas the `<custom:CompositeCreditCardForm>` element in Listing 8-5 doesn't have any child elements. Therefore the parsing of Listing 8-12 is similar to the parsing of Listing 8-5 up to a point. Here's a quick review of the sequence of events that occurs when the page parser starts parsing the `<form>` element:

1. The page parser uses its internal regular expression patterns to parse the `<form id="form1" runat="server">` text.

2. The page parser accesses the control builder on top of its internal stack of control builders. When the parser is parsing the `<form id="form1" runat="server">` text, its internal stack only includes the root control builder, as discussed earlier.

3. The page parser passes the parsed text to the root control builder.

4. The root control builder calls its `GetChildControlType` method and passes the parsed text into it.

5. The `GetChildControlType` method returns the `System.Type` object that represents the server control associated with the parsed text (`HtmlForm`).

6. The root control builder calls its `CreateBuilderFromType` method and passes the `System.Type` object that represents the `HtmlForm` control into it.

7. The `CreateBuilderFromType` method creates an instance of the control builder associated with the `HtmlForm` control, which is then returned to the page parser.

8. The page parser calls the `AppendSubBuilder` method of the root control builder to add the `HtmlForm` control's control builder to its internal list of child control builders.

9. The page parser adds the `HtmlForm` control's control builder on the top of its internal stack of control builders. This means that the stack now contains two control builders — the root builder and the `HtmlForm` control's control builder.

10. The page parser then uses its internal regular expression patterns and parses the following text:

```
<custom:CompositeCreditCardForm2 ID="ccf" runat="server" Font-Bold="true"
OnValidateCreditCard="ValidateCreditCard" PaymentMethodText="Payment Method"
CardholderNameText="Cardholder's Name" CreditCardNoText="Credit Card No."
ExpirationDateText="Expiration Date" SubmitButtonText="Submit">
```

11. The page parser accesses the control builder on top of its internal stack — the HtmlForm control's control builder.

12. The page parser passes the parsed text to the HtmlForm control's control builder.

13. The HtmlForm control's control builder calls its GetChildControlType method and passes the parsed text into it.

14. The GetChildControlType method returns the System.Type object that represents the server control associated with the parsed text (the CompositeCreditCardForm2 control).

15. The HtmlForm control's control builder then calls its CreateBuilderFromType method and passes the System.Type object that represents the CompositeCreditCardForm2 control.

16. The CreateBuilderFromType method creates an instance of the control builder associated with the CompositeCreditCardForm2 control (an instance of the CompositeCreditCard Form2Builder builder), which is subsequently returned to the page parser.

17. The page parser calls the AppendSubBuilder method of the HtmlForm control's control builder to add the CompositeCreditCardForm2Builder control builder to its internal list of child control builders.

18. The page parser adds the CompositeCreditCardForm2Builder control builder on the top of its internal stack of control builders. Therefore, the stack now contains three control builders — the root builder, the HtmlForm control's control builder, and CompositeCreditCardForm2Builder.

19. The page parser uses its internal regular expressions and parses the following text:

```
<Data>
  <PaymentMethodList>
    <PaymentMethod text="Visa" value="Visa" />
    <PaymentMethod text="MasterCard" value="MasterCard" />
  </PaymentMethodList>
</Data>
```

20. The page parser accesses the control builder on top of its stack of control builders (CompositeCreditCardForm2Builder).

21. The page parser passes the parsed text to the CompositeCreditCreditCardForm2Builder control builder.

22. CompositeCreditCardForm2Builder calls its GetChildControlType method and passes the parsed text into it.

23. The GetChildControlType method returns the System.Type object that represents the server control associated with the parsed text (CreditCardFormData). This custom control is discussed later.

24. CompositeCreditCardForm2Builder then calls its CreateBuilderFromType method and passes the System.Type object that represents the CreditCardFormData control into it.

25. The CreateBuilderFromType method creates an instance of the control builder associated with the CreditCardFormData control. As you'll see later, the CreditCardFormData control derives from the Literal control. Therefore, the CreateBuilderFromType method returns an instance of the control builder associated with the Literal control, LiteralControlBuilder, which is subsequently returned to the page parser.

26. The page parser calls the AppendSubBuilder method of the CompositeCreditCardForm2 Builder control builder to add the LiteralControlBuilder control builder to its internal list of child control builders.

Developing the CompositeCreditCardForm2Builder Custom Control Builder

As the preceding sequence shows, the type of the control builder that the CreateBuilderFromType creates depends on the System.Type object that the GetChildControlType method returns.

CompositeCreditCardForm2Builder derives from the ControlBuilder base class and overrides its GetChildControlType method, as shown in Listing 8-13.

Listing 8-13: The CompositeCreditCardForm2Builder method

```
public class CompositeCreditCardForm2Builder : ControlBuilder
{
  public override Type GetChildControlType(string tagName, IDictionary attribs)
  {
    if (tagName == "Data")
      return typeof(CreditCardFormData);

    return null;
  }
}
```

The GetChildControlType method checks whether the parsed tag name is "Data". If it is, it return a System.Type object that represents the CreditCardFormData type. The following is the definition of the CreditCardFormData type:

```
public class CreditCardFormData : Literal { }
```

This type simply derives from the Literal control without overriding any of its methods or properties.

Developing the CompositeCreditCardForm2 Custom Control

As Listing 8-14 shows, the CompositeCreditCardForm2 control derives from the CompositeCredit CardForm control developed in Chapter 5. Deriving from CompositeCreditCardForm saves you from having to write a lot of code to reimplement the features that CompositeCreditCardForm already supports.

Listing 8-14: The declaration of the CompositeCreditCardForm2 control

```
public class CompositeCreditCardForm2 : CompositeCreditCardForm
{
  protected override void AddParsedSubObject(object obj);
  protected override PaymentMethod GetPaymentMethod();

  protected override void
  CreateContainerChildControls(CreditCardFormContainer container);
}
```

CompositeCreditCardForm2 overrides the AddParsedSubObject, PaymentMethod, and CreateContainerChildControls methods of its base classes, as described in the following sections.

Overriding AddParsedSubObject

The CompositeCreditCardForm2Builder control builder inherits a method named BuildObject from the ControlBuilder base class. This method instantiates the CompositeCreditCardForm2 custom control, then enumerates its internal list of child control builders. Recall that every control builder maintains an internal list of its child control builders. The internal list of the CompositeCreditCardForm2Builder control builder contains one control builder — LiteralControlBuilder, as discussed earlier.

BuildObject then calls the BuildObject method of the LiteralControlBuilder control builder to instantiate the CreditCardFormData control. Finally, it calls the AddParsedSubObject method of the CompositeCreditCardForm2 custom control and passes the CreditCardFormData control into it.

The default implementation of the AddParsedSubObject method simply adds the child control passed in as its argument to the Controls collection of the parent control, as shown in Listing 8-15.

Listing 8-15: The default implementation of AddParsedSubObject

```
protected virtual void AddParsedSubObject(object obj)
{
  Control control = obj as Control;
  if (control != null)
    Controls.Add(control);
}
```

The CompositeCreditCardForm2 custom control overrides the AddParsedSubObject method to provide the implementation shown in Listing 8-16.

Listing 8-16: The overridden implementation of AddParsedSubObject

```
private XPathDocument document;

protected override void AddParsedSubObject(object obj)
{
  if (obj is CreditCardFormData)
  {
    using (StringReader reader = new StringReader(((CreditCardFormData)obj).Text))
```

(continued)

211

Listing 8-16: *(continued)*

```
        {
           document = new XPathDocument(reader);
        }
     }
  }
```

The `AddParsedSubObject` method checks whether the object passed into it is of type `CreditCard FormData`. If it is, the method accesses the value of the `Text` property of the `CreditCardFormData` control. This control inherits the `Text` property from its base class, the `Literal` control. The `Text` property of the `Literal` control simply returns the text that the `Literal` control represents. This text is shown in Listing 8-17.

Listing 8-17: The text that the Literal control represents

```
<PaymentMethodList>
  <PaymentMethod text="Visa" value="Visa" />
  <PaymentMethod text="MasterCard" value="MasterCard" />
</PaymentMethodList>
```

As Listing 8-16 shows, the `AddParsedSubObject` method instantiates a `StringReader` to encapsulate the text shown in Listing 8-17 and uses the `StringReader` to populate an `XPathDocument` object.

Overriding CreateContainerChildControls

The `CompositeCreditCardForm2` control inherits the `CreateContainerChildControls` method from its base class, `CompositeCreditCardForm`. Listing 8-18 shows the `CompositeCreditCardForm2` control's implementation of the `CreateContainerChildControls` method.

Listing 8-18: The CreateContainerChildControls method

```
protected override void
CreateContainerChildControls(CreditCardFormContainer container)
{
  switch (container.ContainerType)
  {
    case ContainerType.PaymentMethod:
      paymentMethodList = new DropDownList();
      ListItem listItem;
      XPathNavigator nav = document.CreateNavigator();
      nav.MoveToChild(XPathNodeType.Element);
      nav.MoveToFirstChild();
      do
      {
        string text = nav.GetAttribute("text", "");
        string value = nav.GetAttribute("value", "");
        listItem = new ListItem(text, value);
        paymentMethodList.Items.Add(listItem);
```

```
            } while (nav.MoveToFollowing(XPathNodeType.Element));
            container.Controls.Add(paymentMethodList);
            break;
        default:
            base.CreateContainerChildControls(container);
            break;
    }
}
```

As Listing 8-18 shows, the `CreateContainerChildControls` method first instantiates a `DropDownList` control:

```
paymentMethodList = new DropDownList();
```

It then calls the `CreateNavigator` method of the `XPathDocument` object to access its navigator object. Recall that the `XPathDocument` object contains the XML text shown in Listing 8-17:

```
XPathNavigator nav = document.CreateNavigator();
```

Then it calls the `MoveToChild` method of the navigator object:

```
nav.MoveToChild(XPathNodeType.Element);
```

This method moves the navigator to the document element of the XML text shown in Listing 8-17, the `<PaymentMethodList>` element:

```
<PaymentMethodList>
    <PaymentMethod text="Visa" value="Visa" />
    <PaymentMethod text="MasterCard" value="MasterCard" />
</PaymentMethodList>
```

Then `CreateContainerChildControls` calls the `MoveToFirstChild` method of the navigator:

```
nav.MoveToFirstChild();
```

This method moves the navigator to the first child of the `<PaymentMethodList>` element, the first `<PaymentMethod>` child element:

```
<PaymentMethodList>
    <PaymentMethod text="Visa" value="Visa" />
    <PaymentMethod text="MasterCard" value="MasterCard" />
</PaymentMethodList>
```

Next `CreateContainerChildControls` calls the `GetAttribute` method of the navigator:

```
string text = nav.GetAttribute("text", "");
```

This method accesses the value of the `text` attribute of the first `<PaymentMethod>` child element (Visa):

```
<PaymentMethodList>
  <PaymentMethod
  text="Visa"
  value="Visa" />
  <PaymentMethod text="MasterCard" value="MasterCard" />
</PaymentMethodList>
```

`CreateContainerChildControls` then calls the `GetAttribute` method of the navigator once more:

```
string value = nav.GetAttribute("value", "");
```

This method accesses the value of the `value` attribute of the first `<PaymentMethod>` child element (Visa):

```
<PaymentMethodList>
  <PaymentMethod
  text="Visa"
  value="Visa" />
  <PaymentMethod text="MasterCard" value="MasterCard" />
</PaymentMethodList>
```

Then `CreateContainerChildControls` uses the values it just accessed to instantiate a `ListItem` object and adds the object to the `Items` collection of the `DropDownList` control:

```
listItem = new ListItem(text, value);
paymentMethodList.Items.Add(listItem);
```

`CreateContainerChildControls` next calls the `MoveToFollowing` method of the navigator:

```
nav.MoveToFollowing(XPathNodeType.Element)
```

This method moves the navigator to next sibling of the first `<PaymentMethod>` child element, which is the second `<PaymentMethod>` child element:

```
<PaymentMethodList>
  <PaymentMethod text="Visa" value="Visa" />
  <PaymentMethod text="MasterCard" value="MasterCard" />
</PaymentMethodList>
```

`CreateContainerChildControls` then repeats the gathering of the `text` and `value` data for the second `<PaymentMethod>` child element, and adds it to the `DropDownList` control.

Finally, `CreateContainerChildControls` adds the `DropDownList` control to the `Controls` collection of the container control:

```
container.Controls.Add(paymentMethodList);
```

Overriding ParseChildrenAttribute

The CompositeCreditCardForm2 custom control derives from the CompositeCreditCardForm custom control, which in turn derives from the WebControl base class. WebControl is annotated with the ParseChildrenAttribute(true) attribute:

```
[ParseChildrenAttribute(true)]
public class WebControl : Control
```

The ParseChildrenAttribute(true) attribute tells the page parser to treat the content within the opening and closing tags of the CompositeCreditCardForm2 custom control as properties, not child controls. The highlighted section in the following code shows the content within the opening and closing tags of the CompositeCreditCardForm2 control:

```
<custom:CompositeCreditCardForm2 ID="ccf" runat="server" Font-Bold="true"
OnValidateCreditCard="ValidateCreditCard" PaymentMethodText="Payment Method"
CardholderNameText="Cardholder's Name" CreditCardNoText="Credit Card No."
ExpirationDateText="Expiration Date" SubmitButtonText="Submit">
  <Data>
    <PaymentMethodList>
      <PaymentMethod text="Visa" value="Visa" />
      <PaymentMethod text="MasterCard" value="MasterCard" />
    </PaymentMethodList>
  </Data>
</custom:CompositeCreditCardForm2>
```

In other words, the ParseChildrenAttribute(true) attribute tells the page parser that the CompositeCreditCardForm2 control has a property named Data, and the content within the opening and closing tags of the Data child element must be treated as the value of this property. There are two problems with this scenario. First, the CompositeCreditCardForm2 control doesn't expose a property named Data. Second, the AddParsedSubObject method of a control such as CompositeCreditCardForm2 control is called only when the content within the opening and closing tags of the control represents child controls, not properties.

That is why you must override the ParseChildrenAttribute attribute that CompositeCreditCardForm2 inherits from WebControl:

```
[ParseChildrenAttribute(false)]
public class CompositeCreditCardForm2 : CompositeCreditCardForm
```

Annotating Your Custom Control with ControlBuilderAttribute

You must annotate your custom control with ControlBuilderAttribute to tell the page parser to use your custom control builder to parse and build your custom control. If you don't annotate your custom control with this attribute, the page parser will use the default control builder, the ControlBuilder base class, to parse and build your custom control.

The following code annotates the CompositeCreditCardForm2 custom control with the ControlBuilderAttribute(typeof(CompositeCreditCardForm2Builder)) attribute to tell the page parser to use the CompositeCreditCardForm2Builder to parse and build the CompositeCreditCardForm2 custom control:

```
[ControlBuilder(typeof(CompositeCreditCardForm2Builder))]
public class CompositeCreditCardForm2 : CompositeCreditCardForm
```

Summary

This chapter discussed some of the extensible components of the ASP.NET request processing architecture and used a step-by-step approach to show you how to develop your own custom HTTP modules, HTTP handler factories, HTTP handlers, and control builders. This chapter developed four custom components:

- ❏ The `ArticlesModule` custom HTTP module, which you can use to add URL rewriting support to your Web applications.

- ❏ The `ArticlesHandlerFactory` custom HTTP handler factory.

- ❏ The `RssHandler` custom HTTP handler, which you can use to generate RSS documents for your Web applications.

- ❏ The `CompositeCreditCardForm2Builder` custom control builder and `CompositeCredit CardForm2` custom composite control that allow page developers to declaratively specify the payment method list within the opening and closing tags of `Data` child element.

In the two articles examples, you saw some brief use of data binding to retrieve and display information from a database. In Chapter 9, you'll find out more about how to incorporate data binding into your custom controls.

Data Binding

Displaying data records is one of the most common operations in data-driven Web applications. These applications enumerate the data records and generate the appropriate HTML markup text for each enumerated record. ASP.NET standard and custom data-bound controls such as `DataGrid` and `GridView` automate this process, saving page developers from having to write a lot of code to accomplish this task.

This chapter builds on top of the previous chapters and uses a detailed step-by-step approach to show you how to develop your own custom data-bound controls. This chapter also sets the stage for Chapters 17 and 18, where you'll see how the new ASP.NET 2.0 data-bound control model can help you develop data-bound controls that can access any type of data store.

In this chapter you develop a custom data-bound control named `CustomTable` that derives from the `WebControl` base class.

The CustomTable Control

The requirements for the `CustomTable` control are as follows:

❑ Display data records in a table

❑ Enumerate the specified data records and display each enumerated record in a table row

❑ Allow users to delete a row

❑ Allow users to update the data fields of a specified data row

❑ Allow users to sort the data based on a particular column

❑ Allow users to page through data records

You should keep these requirements in mind as you're implementing the CustomTable control. These are the steps you take throughout this chapter to implement the control:

1. Implement the mechanism that allows page developers to specify the data records or source that CustomTable control must enumerate.

2. Override the CreateChildControls method to create the child control hierarchy from the saved view state.

3. Override the DataBind method to create the control hierarchy from the data source.

4. Implement a method named EnumerateDataAndCreateControlHierarchy to enumerate the specified real or dummy data source.

5. Override the CreateControlStyle method.

6. Implement the events that the CustomTable control raises.

7. Override the OnBubbleEvent method.

8. Implement the custom control that displays a data record.

9. Implement the collection class that contains the controls that display the data records.

10. Expose child style properties.

11. Override the Render method.

12. Manage the state of complex properties across page postbacks.

Specifying the Data Source

The second requirement for the control states that the CustomTable control must enumerate the specified data records and display each record in a table row. Therefore the first order of business is to provide page developers with a mechanism to specify the data source or records to be enumerated. This typically involves adding three members to your custom control.

First, you need to expose a private field of type System.Object named dataSource. To keep the discussions focused; this control uses a field of type IEnumerable:

```
private IEnumerable dataSource;
```

Second, you must expose a public property of type System.Object named DataSource that delegates to the private field. For this example you use a property of type IEnumerable:

```
public IEnumerable DataSource
{
  get { return dataSource; }
  set
  {
    ValidateDataSource(value);
    dataSource = value;
  }
}
```

Third, you need to implement a protected virtual method named `ValidateDataSource` to validate the data source that page developers specify. You have to decide what type of data source your custom control will support. The `CustomTable` control only supports `IEnumerable` data sources:

```
protected virtual void ValidateDataSource(object dataSource)
{
  if (!(dataSource is IEnumerable))
    throw new Exception("This data source is not supported");
}
```

Typically, the page developer writes a method that contains the appropriate data access code to retrieve data records from the underlying data store and to populate a collection with the retrieved data records. Listing 9-1 shows an example of such a method, where the ADO.NET classes are used to retrieve data records from a Microsoft SQL Server database and to populate a `DataView` with the retrieved data records.

The type of the data records, the type of the fields of the data records, and the type of the collection that contains the data records all depend on the data access code. For example, the data records, the fields of the data records, and the collection that contains the data records in Listing 9-1 are of type `DataRowView`, `DataColumn`, and `DataView`, respectively.

Listing 9-1: The RetrieveData method uses ADO.NET classes to retrieve the data records

```
IEnumerable RetrieveData()
{
  DataTable dt = new DataTable();
  SqlDataAdapter ad = new SqlDataAdapter("Select * From Books", connectionString);
  ad.Fill(dt);
  return dt.DefaultView;
}
```

The page developer implements the `Page_Load` method (see Listing 9-2). When the page is accessed for the first time, `Page_Load` calls the method that contains the data access code (the method shown in Listing 9-1) to retrieve the data records and to populate the appropriate collection with the retrieved data records. `Page_Load` then assigns the collection that contains the retrieved data records to the `DataSource` property of the `CustomTable` control, and finally calls the `DataBind` method of the `CustomTable` control.

Listing 9-2: The Page_Load method

```
void Page_Load(object sender, EventArgs e)
{
  if (!IsPostback)
  {
    DataView dv = RetrieveData();
    CustomTable1.DataSource = dv;
    CustomTable1.DataBind();
  }
}
```

Overriding CreateChildControls

The child controls of a composite control such as `CustomTable` form a tree where each node of the tree is a child control. As Listing 9-2 shows, when the user accesses the page that contains your custom control for the first time, the `DataBind` method of your custom control is called.

This method must enumerate the specified data source and create the control hierarchy of your custom control from the data source. At the end of the first request, each child control in the control hierarchy saves its view state in an object and passes the object to your control.

Your control populates an array with the objects that it receives from the child controls in its control hierarchy, and passes the array to its parent. When the page is posted back to the server, the parent of your custom control passes the same array back to your control. Your custom control then passes the objects in the array to the controls in its control hierarchy in the same order that it received the objects from these controls in the first request. This assumes that your custom control creates the same control hierarchy in the second request as it did in the first request.

Recall that in the first request, the `DataBind` method of your custom control created the control hierarchy from the data source. You may wonder which method of your custom control is supposed to create the control hierarchy in the second request. The `Control` class exposes a method named `CreateChildControls` that your custom control must override to create the control hierarchy from the saved view state.

In other words, you custom control must override the `DataBind` and `CreateChildControls` methods to create the control hierarchy from the data source and saved view state, respectively. To ensure that the same control hierarchy is created from the saved view state and data source, both `CreateChildControls` and `DataBind` must delegate the responsibility for creating the control hierarchy to the same method. Call this method `EnumerateDataAndCreateControlHierarchy`.

The `EnumerateDataAndCreateControlHierarchy` method must enumerate the specified data source and create the control hierarchy. However, there is no data source when the control hierarchy is created from the saved view state. The remedy is to pass a dummy data source to the `EnumerateDataAndCreateControlHierarchy` method as its first argument and `false` as its second argument. The false value signals the fact that the first argument is a dummy data source and doesn't contain real data records (see Listing 9-3).

Listing 9-3: The CustomTable control overrides the CreateChildControls method

```
protected override void CreateChildControls()
{
  Controls.Clear();

  if (ViewState["RowCount"] != null)
  {
    Int numOfRows = [(int)ViewState["RowCount"];
    Object dummayDataSource = new object[numOfRows];
    ViewState["RowCount"] = EnumerateDataAndCreateControlHierarchy(
                                          dummayDataSource, false);
  }
}
```

As Listing 9-3 shows, the CreateChildControl method needs to know how many rows were created when the control hierarchy was created from the data source. As you'll see in the next section, the DataBind method will store the total row count in the ViewState collection to make this number available to the CreateChildControls method.

The ASP.NET data-bound control model provides standard and custom data-bound controls with the infrastructure they need to automate the creation of the control hierarchy from the saved view state. Now take a look at how the model accomplishes this task. This will also give you important clues that will help with the reverse engineering of the ASP.NET 2.0 BaseDataBoundControl base class in Chapter 17.

The Control class exposes a method named EnsureChildControls. This method first checks whether the value of the ChildControlsCreated property is set to false. If so, it first calls the CreateChildControls method, and then sets the ChildControlsCreated property to true. The ChildControlsCreated property is used to ensure that the CreateChildControls method isn't called multiple times in the same request.

The Control class's implementation of the OnPreRender method calls the EnsureChildControls method to ensure that the CreateChildControls method is called (if ChildControlsCreated is set to false) before the control enters its rendering phase. Because the OnPreRender method is automatically called for every request, the EnsureChildControls method and, consequently, the CreateChildControls method are also called automatically (if the ChildControlsCreated property is set to false).

Overriding the DataBind Method

The CustomTable control overrides the DataBind method to call the EnumerateDataAndCreate ControlHierarchy method with a real data source and a true value as its arguments (see Listing 9-4).

Listing 9-4: The CustomTable control overrides the DataBind method

```
public override void DataBind()
{
  base.DataBind();
  Controls.Clear();
  ClearChildViewState();
  TrackViewState();
  ViewState["RowCount"] =
                  EnumerateDataAndCreateControlHierarchy(_dataSource, true);
  ChildControlsCreated = true;
}
```

The DataBind method first calls the DataBind method of its base class to raise the DataBinding event. Then it calls the Clear method to clear the Controls collection because the method re-creates the control hierarchy from scratch.

Next, DataBind calls the ClearChildViewState method to clear the saved view states associated with the child controls because the DataBind method uses the actual data records to set the states of the child controls.

221

It then calls the TrackViewState method to start the view state tracking to ensure that the new states of the server controls are saved into view state at the end of the current request. This allows the CreateChildControls method to re-create the same control hierarchy from the saved view state when the page is posted back to the server.

Next, it calls the EnumerateDataAndCreateControlHierarchy method to create the control hierarchy from the data source. Then it saves the return value of the EnumerateDataAndCreateControlHierarchy method in the ViewState collection. As you'll see in the next section, this value is nothing but the total table row count. This allows the CreateChildControl method to know how many table rows it must create when the containing page is posted back to the server.

Finally, DataBind sets the value of the ChildControlsCreated property to true. This is necessary because the EnsureChildControls method could be called at any stage of the control's life cycle. Recall that this method checks whether the value of the ChildControlCreated property is set to false. If so, it calls the CreateChildControls method to re-create the control hierarchy from the saved view state.

Creating the Control Hierarchy

Listing 9-5 shows the CustomTable control's implementation of the EnumerateDataAndCreateControlHierarchy method.

Listing 9-5: The EnumerateDataAndCreateControlHierarchy method

```
protected virtual int
EnumerateDataAndCreateControlHierarchy(IEnumerable data, bool useDataSource)
{
  if (useDataSource)
    DataKeyArray.Clear();

  table = new Table();
  Controls.Add(table);
  CreateFields(data, useDataSource);
  CreateHeaderRow(useDataSource);

  ArrayList dataRows = new ArrayList();
  int rowIndex = 0;
  IEnumerator iter = data.GetEnumerator();
  while (iter.MoveNext())
  {
    Object record = iter.Current;
    CreateBodyRow(useDataSource, rowIndex, record, dataRows);
    CachePrimaryKey(useDataSource, iter.Current);
    rowIndex++;
  }

  rows = new CustomTableRowCollection(dataRows);

  CreatePagerRow(useDataSource);
  return rowIndex;
}
```

The `EnumerateDataAndCreateControlHierarchy` method first clears the collection that contains the primary keys of the data records if the method is creating the control hierarchy from the data source. This collection is discussed later in this chapter.

```
if (useDataSource)
  DataKeyArray.Clear();
```

Next, it creates the `Table` child control that displays the data and adds it to the `Controls` collection of the `CustomTable` control:

```
table = new Table();
Controls.Add(table);
```

It then creates an array of `DataControlField` objects, where each object describes a table column. The `DataControlField` class is discussed later in this chapter.

```
Createfields(data, useDataSource);
```

Next it creates the header row:

```
CreateHeaderRow(useDataSource);
```

Then it creates an `ArrayList` collection that will be populated with data rows, table rows that display data records:

```
ArrayList dataRows = new ArrayList();
```

It then enumerates the data records, first creating the data row that displays the record and adding it to the `ArrayList` collection:

```
CreateBodyRow(useDataSource, rowIndex, iter.Current, dataRows);
```

And then caching the primary key of the record:

```
CachePrimaryKey(useDataSource, iter.Current);
```

Next it creates a `CustomTableRowCollection` collection and loads it with data rows, and assigns the collection to the `rows` field:

```
rows = new CustomTableRowCollection(dataRows);
```

`CustomTable` exposes a property of type `CustomTableRowCollection` named `Rows` that uses the `rows` field as its backing store:

```
public CustomTableRowCollection Rows
{
  get
  {
    EnsureChildControls();
    return rows;
  }
}
```

Notice that the `Rows` property calls the `EnsureChildControls` method before it accesses the rows collection. As discussed in Chapter 5, composite controls such as `CustomTable` must call `EnsureChildControl` before they access their child controls to ensure the child controls are created.

After creating the `rows` collection, `EnumerateDataAndCreateControlHierarchy` creates the pager row. This is discussed in the following sections.

```
CreatePagerRow(useDataSource);
```

And finally, it returns the total row count:

```
return rowIndex;
```

As discussed, the `DataBind` method stores the total row count in the `ViewState` collection to make it available to `CreateChildControls` when the page is posted back to the server.

Notice that the `EnumerateDataAndCreateControlHierarchy` method takes a collection of type `IEnumerable` that contains items of type `System.Object`. Here's why: The real type of the collection, the real type of the records that the collection contains, and the real type of the fields that each record contains depend on the data access code. In this example, the collection, records of the collection, and the fields of each record are of type `DataView`, `DataRowView`, and `DataColumn`, respectively, in the case of the data access code shown in Listing 9-1.

Therefore, if the `EnumerateDataAndCreateControlHierarchy` method were to deal with the real type of the collection (`DataView`), the real type of the records of the collection (`DataRowView`), and the real type of the fields of each record (`DataColumn`), your custom control would be tied to a particular data store (Microsoft SQL Server, in this case) and wouldn't be able to work with other types of data stores. That's why the method takes a collection of generic `IEnumerable` type that contains records of generic `System.Object` type.

As Listing 9-5 shows, the `EnumerateDataAndCreateControlHierarchy` method calls the `GetEnumerator` method of the `IEnumerable` collection to access its enumerator, and uses the enumerator to enumerate the records of the collection in generic fashion without having to know the real type of the collection (`DataView`):

```
IEnumerator iter = data.GetEnumerator();
while (iter.MoveNext())
{
  System.Object record = iter.Current;
  ...
}
```

The `EnumerateDataAndCreateControlHierarchy` method uses the `Current` property of the enumerator to access the enumerated record as an item of type `System.Object` without having to know the real type of the record (`DataRowView`):

```
IEnumerator iter = data.GetEnumerator();
while (iter.MoveNext())
{
  System.Object record = iter.Current;
  ...
}
```

DataControlField

CustomTable exposes a method named CreateFields that creates objects of type DataControlField. The DataControlField class contains the complete information about a table column, as shown in Listing 9-6.

Listing 9-6: The DataControlField class

```
public class DataControlField : IStateManager
{
  public string HeaderText {get; set;}
  public string SortExpression {get; set;}
  public bool ReadOnly {get; set;}
  public Type DataType {get; set;}
  . . .
}
```

The following table describes each property:

Property	Description
HeaderText	Gets or sets the header text of the respective column.
SortExpression	Gets or sets the name of the data field associated with the column. The value of this property is used in the Order By section of the respective Select SQL statement to sort the data.
ReadOnly	Specifies whether the data field values that this column displays are editable.
DataType	Gets or sets the System.Type object that represents the type of the data that the column displays.

As mentioned, CustomTable exposes an array field of type DataControlField named fields:

```
private DataControlField[] fields = null;
```

Because the DataControlField class exposes the properties listed in the table, the fields collection of the CustomTable control is a complex property. As discussed in Chapter 7, one common way to manage the state of a custom complex property across page postbacks is to derive the class that represents the property from the IStateManager interface. The DataControlField class follows the same implementation pattern discussed in Chapter 7 to implement the IStateManager interface.

CreateFields

The CreateFields method creates one DataControlField object to represent each data column, as shown in Listing 9-7.

Listing 9-7: The CreateFields method

```
protected virtual void Createfields(IEnumerable dataSource, bool useDataSource)
{
  if (!useDataSource)
    return;

  ArrayList list = new ArrayList();
  IEnumerator iter = dataSource.GetEnumerator();
  iter.MoveNext();
  PropertyDescriptorCollection pds = TypeDescriptor.GetProperties(iter.Current);
  DataControlField field;
  foreach (PropertyDescriptor pd in pds)
  {
    field = new DataControlField();
    if (IsTrackingViewState)
      ((IStateManager)field).TrackViewState();
    field.DataType = pd.PropertyType;
    field.HeaderText = pd.Name;
    field.ReadOnly = pd.IsReadOnly;
    field.SortExpression = pd.Name;
    list.Add(field);
  }

  if (fields == null)
    fields = new DataControlField[list.Count];
  list.CopyTo(fields);
  ViewState["FieldsLength"] = list.Count;
}
```

CreateFields first creates a local ArrayList collection:

```
ArrayList list = new ArrayList();
```

Next it calls the GetEnumerator method of the IEnumerable collection that contains the retrieved data records to access its enumerator:

```
IEnumerator iter = dataSource.GetEnumerator();
```

Then it moves the enumerator to the first data record:

```
iter.MoveNext();
```

Next, the method calls the GetProperties method of the TypeDescriptor class to access the PropertyDescriptorCollection collection, which contains one PropertyDescriptor object for each data field of the first record. Each PropertyDescriptor object fully describes its associated data field in generic fashion:

```
PropertyDescriptorCollection pds = TypeDescriptor.GetProperties(iter.Current);
```

CreateFields then enumerates the PropertyDescriptorCollection collection. For each enumerated PropertyDescriptor object in the collection, CreateFields creates a DataControlField object:

```
field = new DataControlField();
```

It then uses the `PropertyType` and `Name` properties of the enumerated `PropertyDescriptor` object to access the type and name of the respective data field in generic fashion, and uses them to set the respective properties of the `DataControlField` object:

```
field.DataType = pd.PropertyType;
field.HeaderText = pd.Name;
field.SortExpression = pd.Name;
```

Then it adds the `DataControlField` object to the local `ArrayList` collection:

```
list.Add(field);
```

Finally, `CreateFields` instantiates the `fields` collection of `CustomTable` and uses the local `ArrayList` collection to populate it with the `DataControlField` objects that represent the data columns:

```
if (fields == null)
    fields = new DataControlField[list.Count];
list.CopyTo(fields);
```

CreateHeaderRow

The `CreateHeaderRow` method creates the header row as shown in Listing 9-8.

Listing 9-8: The CreateHeaderRow method

```
protected virtual void CreateHeaderRow(bool useDataSource)
{
  CustomTableRow hrow =
      new CustomTableRow(-1, DataControlRowType.Header, DataControlRowState.Normal);
  table.Rows.Add(hrow);

  TableHeaderCell hcell = new TableHeaderCell();
  hrow.Cells.Add(hcell);

  hcell = new TableHeaderCell();
  hrow.Cells.Add(hcell);

  for (int k = 0; k < fields.Length; k++)
  {
    hcell = new TableHeaderCell();
    hrow.Cells.Add(hcell);
    LinkButton lb = new LinkButton();

    hcell.Controls.Add(lb);

    if (useDataSource)
    {
      lb.Text = fields[k].SortExpression;
      lb.CommandName = "Sort";
```

(continued)

Listing 9-8: *(continued)*

```
        lb.CommandArgument = fields[k].SortExpression;

        if (fields[k].SortExpression == DataKeyField)
          DataKeyFieldIndex = k;
      }
    }
  }
```

Notice that the CreateHeaderRow method enumerates the DataControlField objects in the fields collection. For each enumerated DataControlField, CreateHeaderRow first creates a LinkButton control to allow users to sort the displayed data:

```
  LinkButton lb = new LinkButton();
```

Then it assigns the value of the SortExpression property of the enumerated DataControlField object to the Text property of the LinkButton control:

```
  lb.Text = fields[k].SortExpression;
```

Next it assigns the text "Sort" to the CommandName property of the LinkButton control:

```
  lb.CommandName = "Sort";
```

Finally, it assigns the value of the SortExpression property of the enumerated DataControlField object to the CommandArgument property of the LinkButton control. Recall that the SortExpression property contains the name of its associated database field. When the user clicks the LinkButton control to sort the data, page developers will use this value to determine which column was clicked.

```
  lb.CommandArgument = fields[k].SortExpression;
```

CreateBodyRow

Listing 9-9 shows the implementation of the CreateBodyRow method.

Listing 9-9: The CreateBodyRow method

```
protected virtual void CreateBodyRow(bool useDataSource, int rowIndex,
                                  object dataItem, ArrayList dataRows)
{
  DataControlRowState dataRowState = (rowIndex % 2) == 0 ?
                    DataControlRowState.Normal : DataControlRowState.Alternate;
  if (rowIndex == EditRowIndex)
    dataRowState |= DataControlRowState.Edit;

  CustomTableRow brow =
          new CustomTableRow(rowIndex, DataControlRowType.DataRow, dataRowState);

  table.Rows.Add(brow);
```

```
        dataRows.Add(brow);
        brow.DataItem = dataItem;
        CreateDeleteCell(brow, useDataSource);
        CreateEditCell(brow, useDataSource);
        CreateDataCells(brow, useDataSource);
    }
```

Recall that the `EnumerateDataAndCreateControlHierarchy` method enumerates the data records and calls the `CreateBodyRow` method once for each enumerated data record. The `CreateBodyRow` method takes the following four arguments:

❑ `useDataSource`: Specifies whether the enumerated record is a real record.

❑ `rowIndex`: The index of the enumerated record.

❑ `dataItem`: The enumerated record itself.

❑ `dataRows`: The collection that contains the data rows. Recall that data rows are the table rows that display data records.

The `CreateBodyRow` method first determines the state of the data row:

```
DataControlRowState dataRowState = (rowIndex % 2) == 0 ?
                    DataControlRowState.Normal : DataControlRowState.Alternate;
if (rowIndex == EditRowIndex)
  dataRowState |= DataControlRowState.Edit;
```

Then it creates a `CustomTableRow` control to represent the data row:

```
        CustomTableRow brow =
            new CustomTableRow(rowIndex, DataControlRowType.DataRow, dataRowState);
```

The `CreateBodyRow` method calls the `CreateDeleteCell`, `CreateEditCell`, and `CreateDataCells` methods to create three types of cells for the enumerated record: delete, edit, and data cells. The delete and edit cells are used to display the Delete and Edit buttons. The data cells are used to display the fields of the enumerated record.

CreateDeleteCell

The `CustomTable` control renders a `Delete` button for each row to allow users to delete the respective data record from the underlying data store. The `CreateDeleteCell` method looks like Listing 9-10.

Listing 9-10: The CreateDeleteCell method

```
    protected virtual void CreateDeleteCell(CustomTableRow brow, bool useDataSource)
    {
      TableCell deletecell = new TableCell();
      brow.Cells.Add(deletecell);

      LinkButton deletelb = new LinkButton();
      deletecell.Controls.Add(deletelb);

      if (useDataSource)
```

(continued)

Listing 9-10: *(continued)*

```
    {
      deletelb.Text = "Delete";
      deletelb.CommandName = "Delete";
      deletelb.CommandArgument = brow.RowIndex.ToString();
    }
  }
```

This method takes the following arguments:

❑ brow: The CustomTableRow control that will contain the Delete cell

❑ useDataSource: Specifies whether the control hierarchy is being created from the data source or saved view state

CreateDeleteCell first creates a TableCell control and adds it to the Cells collection of the containing CustomTableRow control:

```
TableCell deletecell = new TableCell();
brow.Cells.Add(deletecell);
```

It then creates a LinkButton control to allow users to delete the containing CustomTableRow control and consequently the data record that the table row is bound to:

```
LinkButton deletelb = new LinkButton();
deletecell.Controls.Add(deletelb);
```

Next it sets the CommandName property of the LinkButton control to the string "Delete". As you'll see later, the CustomTable control uses the value of this property to determine the type of the event. In this case the event is a Delete event.

```
deletelb.CommandName = "Delete";
```

Then it sets the CommandArgument property of the LinkButton control to the index of the containing table row. As you'll see later, the CustomTable control uses the value of this argument to determine which row is being deleted.

```
deletelb.CommandArgument = brow.RowIndex.ToString();
```

Notice that the CreateDeleteCell method sets these properties if and only if the value of the useDataSource argument is set to true, that is, when the control hierarchy is being created from the data source. If the hierarchy is being created from saved view state, there'd be no need to set these properties.

CreateEditCell

The CustomTable control renders an Edit button for each table row to allow users to edit the data fields associated with the row. The CreateEditCell method looks like Listing 9-11.

Listing 9-11: The CreateEditCell method

```
protected virtual void CreateEditCell(CustomTableRow brow, bool useDataSource)
{
  TableCell editcell = new TableCell();
  brow.Cells.Add(editcell);

  if ((brow.RowState & DataControlRowState.Edit) != 0)
  {
    LinkButton updatelb = new LinkButton();
    editcell.Controls.Add(updatelb);

    if (useDataSource)
    {
      updatelb.Text = "Update";
      updatelb.CommandName = "Update";
      updatelb.CommandArgument = brow.RowIndex.ToString();
    }

    LiteralControl lc = new LiteralControl("  ");
    editcell.Controls.Add(lc);

    LinkButton cancellb = new LinkButton();
    editcell.Controls.Add(cancellb);

    if (useDataSource)
    {
      cancellb.Text = "Cancel";
      cancellb.CommandName = "Cancel";
      cancellb.CommandArgument = brow.RowIndex.ToString();
    }
  }

  else
  {
    LinkButton editlb = new LinkButton();
    editcell.Controls.Add(editlb);

    if (useDataSource)
    {
      editlb.Text = "Edit";
      editlb.CommandName = "Edit";
      editlb.CommandArgument = brow.RowIndex.ToString();
    }
  }
}
```

Notice that the CreateEditCell method takes the same arguments as the CreateDeleteCell method. Also notice that both methods set the same properties of the LinkButton control. The only difference is that the CreateEditCell method must render two LinkButton controls when the containing row is in edit mode. After making the required data field changes, users have two options. They can click either the first LinkButton to commit the changes to the underlying data store or the second LinkButton to cancel the edit operation.

CreateDataCells

Listing 9-12 shows the implementation of the `CreateDataCells` method.

Listing 9-12: The CreateDataCells method

```
protected virtual void CreateDataCells(CustomTableRow brow, bool useDataSource)
{
  for (int k = 0; k < fields.Length; k++)
  {
    TableCell bcell = new TableCell();
    brow.Cells.Add(bcell);

    if ((brow.RowState & DataControlRowState.Edit) != 0)
    {
      if (useDataSource && fields[k].ReadOnly)
        bcell.Text =
            DataBinder.Eval(brow.DataItem, fields[k].SortExpression).ToString();

      else if (!fields[k].ReadOnly)
      {
        TextBox tb = new TextBox();
        bcell.Controls.Add(tb);

        if (useDataSource)
          tb.Text =
              DataBinder.Eval(brow.DataItem, fields[k].SortExpression).ToString();
      }
    }

    else if (useDataSource)
      bcell.Text =
            DataBinder.Eval(brow.DataItem, fields[k].SortExpression).ToString();
  }
}
```

The `CreateDataCells` method first enumerates the `fields` collection and creates one cell to display the value of each field of the record:

```
TableCell bcell = new TableCell();
brow.Cells.Add(bcell);
```

Then it checks whether the containing table row is in edit mode. If so, it uses a `TextBox` control to display the value of the associated data field to allow users to edit the field value:

```
TextBox tb = new TextBox();
bcell.Controls.Add(tb);

if (useDataSource)
  tb.Text = DataBinder.Eval(brow.DataItem, fields[k].SortExpression).ToString();
```

If not, it displays the field value in a simple text format:

```
  else if (useDataSource)
    bcell.Text = DataBinder.Eval(brow.DataItem, fields[k].SortExpression).ToString();
```

Notice that the CreateDataCells method sets the values of the Text properties of the TextBox and the containing cell if and only if the useDataSource property is set to true, that is, if the EnumerateDataAndCreateControlHierarchy method is creating the control hierarchy from the data source.

Also notice that the CreateDataCells method uses the Eval method of the DataBinder class to access the value of each field in generic fashion without knowing its type. To help you gain a better understanding of the significance of accessing fields in generic fashion, take another look at Listing 9-1. Recall that records in this listing are of type DataRowView. The following code shows how you can access a particular field of a DataRowView object:

```
DataRowView record;
...
DataColumn field = record[fieldname];
```

If the CreateDataCells method were to access the fields of the enumerated record using this approach, it would be tied to relational databases and wouldn't work with non-relational databases such as XML documents.

CachePrimaryKey

Listing 9-13 contains the implementation of the CachePrimaryKey method.

Listing 9-13: The CachePrimaryKey method

```
protected virtual void CachePrimaryKey(bool useDataSource, object dataItem)
{
  if (useDataSource && (DataKeyField.Length != 0))
  {
    object o = DataBinder.GetPropertyValue(dataItem, DataKeyField);
    DataKeyArray.Add(o);
    foreach (DataControlField field in fields)
    {
      if (field.SortExpression == DataKeyField)
      {
        field.ReadOnly = true;
        break;
      }
    }
  }
}
```

This method calls the GetPropertyValue method of the DataBinder class to access the value of the primary key data field in generic fashion and caches the value in the DataKeyArray collection. The method searches the fields collection for the DataControlField object that represents the column associated with the primary key field and sets its ReadOnly property to true. This is necessary because the primary key values are normally autogenerated and can't be edited.

CreatePagerRow

The CreatePagerRow method creates the paging interface of the CustomTable control as shown in Listing 9-14.

Listing 9-14: The CreatePageRow method

```
protected virtual void CreatePagerRow(bool useDataSource)
{
  CustomTableRow pagingrow =
      new CustomTableRow(-1, DataControlRowType.Pager, DataControlRowState.Normal);
  table.Rows.Add(pagingrow);
  TableCell pagingcell = new TableCell();
  pagingcell.ColumnSpan = fields.Length + 2;
  pagingrow.Cells.Add(pagingcell);

  Table pagingtable = new Table();
  pagingcell.Controls.Add(pagingtable);

  TableRow ipagingrow = new TableRow();
  pagingtable.Rows.Add(ipagingrow);

  TableCell ipagingcell;

  int totalNumberOfPages =
            (int)Math.Ceiling((double)TotalNumberOfRecords / (double)PageSize);
  if (totalNumberOfPages == 0) totalNumberOfPages = 1;
  int jj;
  for (int ii = 0; ii < totalNumberOfPages; ii++)
  {
    ipagingcell = new TableCell();
    ipagingrow.Cells.Add(ipagingcell);

    jj = ii + 1;

    if (jj != CurrentPageIndex)
    {
      LinkButton lb = new LinkButton();
      ipagingcell.Controls.Add(lb);

      if (useDataSource)
      {
        lb.Text = jj.ToString();
        lb.CommandName = "Page";
        lb.CommandArgument = jj.ToString();
      }
    }

    else if (useDataSource)
      ipagingcell.Text = jj.ToString();
  }
}
```

There are two important things to notice in this listing. First, the `CreatePagerRow` method uses the `TotalNumberOfRecords` and `PageSize` properties of the `CustomTable` control to evaluate the total page count. Page developers must retrieve the total row count from the underlying data store and assign it to the `TotalNumberOfRecords` property of the `CustomTable` control:

```
int totalNumberOfPages =
            (int)Math.Ceiling((double)TotalNumberOfRecords / (double)PageSize);
if (totalNumberOfPages == 0) totalNumberOfPages = 1;
```

The `CreatePagerRow` method creates one `LinkButton` control for each page and assigns the page number to the `CommandArgument` property of the associated `LinkButton` control. As you'll see later, the `CustomTable` control uses this value to determine the page of records that the user wishes to see.

Overriding CreateControlStyle

As discussed in Chapter 3, every control that derives from `WebControl` inherits a method named `CreateControlStyle` that the control can override to instantiate the appropriate subclass of the `Style` class. Because `CustomTable` displays its data in a table, the most appropriate `Style` subclass is the `TableStyle` class:

```
protected override Style CreateControlStyle()
{
  return new TableStyle();
}
```

Any custom control that overrides the `CreateControlStyle` method must also expose the style properties of the new `Style` subclass as its own top-level style properties, where each top-level style property must use the associated property of the `Style` subclass as its backing store. The `TableStyle` class exposes five new properties: `GridLines`, `CellSpacing`, `CellPadding`, `HorizontalAlign`, and `BackImageUrl`, which the `CustomTable` exposes as top-level style properties with the same names and types.

Implementing the CustomTable Events

The `CustomTable` control exposes six events as shown in the following table:

Event	Raised When
DeleteCommand	The user clicks the Delete button of a table row to delete a data record
EditCommand	The user clicks the Edit button of a table row
UpdateCommand	The user clicks the Update button of a table row to update a data record
CancelCommand	The user clicks the Cancel button of a table row to cancel an update operation
PageCommand	The user clicks a LinkButton control in its paging interface to jump to the respective page of records
SortCommand	The user clicks a LinkButton control in its header row to sort the displayed data

As discussed in Chapter 4, every event has two associated classes: event delegate and event data classes. The event data class does just what its name says it does — it holds the event data. The following table shows the event delegate and event data classes associated with the preceding six events:

Event	Event Delegate Class	Event Data Class
Delete	CustomTableCommandEventHandler	CustomTableCommandEventArgs
Edit	CustomTableCommandEventHandler	CustomTableCommandEventArgs
Update	CustomTableCommandEventHandler	CustomTableCommandEventArgs
Cancel	CustomTableCommandEventHandler	CustomTableCommandEventArgs
Page	CustomTablePageChangedEventHandler	CustomTablePageChangedEventArgs
Sort	CustomTableSortCommandEventHandler	CustomTableSortCommandEventArgs

CustomTable follows the C# event implementation pattern discussed in Chapter 4 to implement these six events. For example, to implement the PageCommand event, CustomTable first implements the event data class:

```
public class CustomTablePageChangedEventArgs : EventArgs
{
  private int newPageIndex;

  public CustomTablePageChangedEventArgs(int newPageIndex)
  {
    this.newPageIndex = newPageIndex;
  }

  public int NewPageIndex
  {
    get { return this.newPageIndex; }
  }
}
```

The CustomTablePageChangedEventArgs event data class holds the new page index event datum.

Then it declares the event delegate class:

```
public delegate void CustomTablePageChangedEventHandler(object sender,
                                        CustomTablePageChangedEventArgs e);
```

Next, CustomTable defines a private static readonly object that will be used as the event key:

```
private static readonly object PageEventKey = new object();
```

Then it defines the event property:

```
public event CustomTablePageChangedEventHandler PageCommand
  {
```

```
   Add { Events.AddHandler(PageEventKey, value); }
   Remove { Events.RemoveHandler(PageEventKey, value); }
}
```

Finally, it implements a virtual protected method to raise the event:

```
protected virtual void OnPageCommand(CustomTablePageChangedEventArgs e)
{
  CustomTablePageChangedEventHandler handler =
                   (CustomTablePageChangedEventHandler)Events[PageEventKey];
  if (handler != null)
    handler(this, e);
}
```

Overriding OnBubbleEvent

As discussed in Chapter 5, every composite control must override the OnBubbleEvent method to catch its child controls' events and expose them as its own top-level events. Listing 9-15 shows the CustomTable control's implementation of OnBubbleEvent.

Listing 9-15: The overridden OnBubbleEvent method

```
protected override bool OnBubbleEvent(object source, EventArgs args)
{
  bool handled = false;

  CustomTableCommandEventArgs ce = args as CustomTableCommandEventArgs;
  if (ce != null)
  {
    switch (ce.CommandName)
    {
      case "Delete":
        OnDeleteCommand(ce);
        break;
      case "Update":
        OnUpdateCommand(ce);
        break;
      case "Edit":
        OnEditCommand(ce);
        break;
      case "Cancel":
        OnCancelCommand(ce);
        break;
      case "Page":
        CustomTablePageChangedEventArgs pe = new CustomTablePageChangedEventArgs(
                                  int.Parse(ce.CommandArgument.ToString()));
        OnPageCommand(pe);
        break;
      case "Sort":
        CustomTableSortCommandEventArgs se = new CustomTableSortCommandEventArgs(
                                        (string)ce.CommandArgument);
```

(continued)

Listing 9-15: *(continued)*

```
        OnSortCommand(se);
        break;
   }

    handled = true;
  }

  return handled;
}
```

OnBubbleEvent uses the value of the CommandName property of the event data class to determine what type of event it must raise. For example, if the CommandName is "Delete", OnBubbleEvent calls the OnDeleteCommand method to raise the DeleteCommand event.

CustomTableRow

Because CustomTable displays each data record in a table row, the most appropriate server control to represent each table row is the TableRow control. However, this control does not contain all the information needed to render a row. The type of the row is one factor that determines how the row is rendered. For example, a header row is rendered differently from a data row. The state of the row also affects how the row is rendered. For example, if a row is in edit mode, it must render a text box in each cell to allow users to update the field values. However, the same row in normal mode must render the value of each data field in simple text format.

Therefore, you must implement a custom control that derives from the TableCell control and supports these features. Listing 9-16 presents the implementation of the CustomTableRow control.

Listing 9-16: The CustomTableRow control

```
public class CustomTableRow : TableRow, INamingContainer
{
  private int rowIndex;
  private DataControlRowType rowType;
  private DataControlRowState rowState;
  private object dataItem;

  public CustomTableRow(int rowIndex, DataControlRowType rowType,
                        DataControlRowState rowState)
  {
    this.rowIndex = rowIndex;
    this.rowType = rowType;
    this.rowState = rowState;
  }

  public int RowIndex
  {
    get { return this.rowIndex; }
```

```
    }

    public DataControlRowType RowType
    {
      get { return this.rowType; }
    }

    public DataControlRowState RowState
    {
      get { return this.rowState; }
    }

    public object DataItem
    {
      get {return this.dataItem;}
      set {this.dataItem = value;}
    }

    protected override bool OnBubbleEvent(object source, EventArgs args)
    {
      bool handled = false;

      CommandEventArgs ce = args as CommandEventArgs;
      if (ce != null)
      {
        CustomTableCommandEventArgs te =
                        new CustomTableCommandEventArgs(this, source, ce);
        RaiseBubbleEvent(this, te);
        handled = true;
      }

      return handled;
    }
  }
}
```

CustomTableRow exposes four properties:

❑　RowType: Gets the type of the row, with possible values Header, DataRow, and Pager.

❑　RowState: Gets the state of the row with possible values Normal, Alternate, Edit, Insert, and Selected. An alternate row is a row with an odd row index. You won't be using the Insert or Selected values in this chapter.

❑　RowIndex: Gets the index of the row in the Rows collection of the CustomTable control.

❑　DataItem: Gets or sets the data record that the CustomTableRow control is bound to.

CustomTableRow also overrides the OnBubbleEvent method where it catches the Command events of its child controls and maps them to the CustomTableCommandEventHandler type of event. Notice that OnBubbleEvent calls the RaiseBubbleEvent method to bubble the CustomTableCommand EventHandler type of event to its parent control, CustomTable.

As discussed before, the OnBubbleEvent method of the CustomTable control catches this bubbled event and maps it to the appropriate event based on the value of the CommandName property.

CustomTableRowCollection

The `CustomTable` control stores its child `CustomTableRow` controls in a collection named `Rows`. This raises the following question: What type of a collection should `CustomTable` use? An obvious choice is the `ArrayList` class. However, this class suffers from two limitations:

❑ When you index an `ArrayList` collection, it returns an item of type `Object`, not `CustomTableRow`.

❑ It lacks a version of the `CopyTo` method that would copy an array of `CustomTableRow` controls.

The `CustomTableRowCollection` class derives from the `ArrayList` class and extends its functionality to address these two shortcomings, as shown in Listing 9-17.

Listing 9-17: The CustomTableRowCollection class

```
public class CustomTableRowCollection : ArrayList
{
  public CustomTableRowCollection(ArrayList rows)
  {
    this.AddRange(rows);
  }

  public new CustomTableRow this[int index]
  {
    get { return (CustomTableRow)base[index]; }
  }

  public void CopyTo(CustomTableRow[] array, int index)
  {
    base.CopyTo(array, index);
  }
}
```

Child Control Styles

As discussed in Chapter 7, every composite control must expose the `ControlStyle` properties of its child controls as its own top-level style properties. Recall that `CustomTable` exposes a collection property of type `CustomTableCollection` named `Rows` that contains its `CustomTableRow` child controls. `CustomTable` exposes one style property of type `TableItemStyle` for each type of `CustomTableRow` control. As mentioned previously, the `Rows` collection contains five different types of `CustomTableRow` controls: header row, alternating row, normal row, edit row, and pager row.

You learned in Chapter 7 how to implement a top-level style property that maps to the `ControlStyle` property of its associated child control. As an example, the following code shows the implementation of the `PagerStyle` property of the `CustomTable` control:

```
private TableItemStyle pagerStyle;
public TableItemStyle PagerStyle
{
  get
```

```
    {
      if (pagerStyle == null)
      {
        pagerStyle = new TableItemStyle();
        if (IsTrackingViewState)
          ((IStateManager)pagerStyle).TrackViewState();
      }
      return pagerStyle;
    }
  }
```

This code shows that the `PagerStyle` property is of type `TableItemStyle` because it has to map to the `ControlStyle` property of the `CustomTableRow` control that represents the pager row. Because the `CustomTableRow` control derives from the `TableRow` control, its `ControlStyle` property is of type `TableItemStyle`.

In addition, the `PagerStyle` property uses a private field as its backing store. You can also see that the `PagerStyle` property is read-only because it's a complex property.

Finally, when the private field is instantiated, its `TrackViewState` is called if `CustomTable` itself is tracking its own view state. This ensures that any changes in the property values of this private field will be stored in the view state at the end of the current request.

Overriding Render

As discussed in the previous section, `CustomTable` exposes five top-level style properties of type `TableItemStyle`, named `HeaderStyle`, `ItemStyle`, `AlternatingItemStyle`, `EditItemStyle`, and `PagerStyle` that map to the `ControlStyle` properties of its `CustomTableRow` child controls.

This raises the following question: When should `CustomTable` control apply these top-level style properties to their respective `CustomTableRow` child controls? As discussed thoroughly in Chapter 7, they must be applied in the render phase to avoid duplicating the same information in the saved view state.

That's why `CustomTable` overrides the `Render` method to call the `PrepareControlHierarchy` method. The main responsibility of the `PrepareControlHierarchy` method is to apply the top-level style properties to their respective `CustomTableRow` child controls. Listing 9-18 contains the code for this method.

Listing 9-18: The PrepareControlHierarchy method

```
protected virtual void PrepareControlHierarchy()
{
  table.CopyBaseAttributes(this);
  if (ControlStyleCreated)
    table.ApplyStyle(ControlStyle);

  if (headerStyle != null)
    table.Rows[0].ApplyStyle(headerStyle);

  for (int i = 0; i < table.Rows.Count - 1; i++)
```

(continued)

Listing 9-18: *(continued)*

```
  {
    bool isAlternatingRow = (i % 2 == 1);

    if (isAlternatingRow && alternatingRowStyle != null)
      table.Rows[i].MergeStyle(alternatingRowStyle);

    else if (rowStyle != null)
      table.Rows[i].MergeStyle(rowStyle);

    if (i == EditRowIndex && editRowStyle != null)
      table.Rows[i].MergeStyle(editRowStyle);
  }

  if (pagerStyle != null)
    table.Rows[table.Rows.Count - 1].MergeStyle(pagerStyle);
}
```

This method first calls the `CopyBaseAttributes` method of the child `Table` control to apply the `CustomTable` control's base attributes to the child `Table` control. This will render the base attributes on the table HTML element that represents the child `Table` control.

```
table.CopyBaseAttributes(this);
```

Next it calls the `ApplyStyle` method of the child `Table` control to apply the `ControlStyle` of the `CustomTable` control to the `ControlStyle` of the child `Table` control. This will render the CSS style attributes associated with `CustomTable` on the table HTML element that represents the child `Table` control.

```
if (ControlStyleCreated)
  table.ApplyStyle(ControlStyle);
```

Then it calls the `ApplyStyle` method of the header `CustomTableRow` control to apply the `HeaderStyle` to the `ControlStyle` of this control:

```
if (headerStyle != null)
    table.Rows[0].ApplyStyle(HeaderStyle);
```

Next, `PrepareControlHierarchy` enumerates the `CustomTableRow` controls that display the data records. For each enumerated control, it calls the `MergeStyle` method of the enumerated `CustomTableRow` control to apply the `AlternatingRowStyle` to the control's `ControlStyle` if it's an alternating row and `RowStyle` if it's not an alternating row:

```
if (isAlternatingRow && alternatingRowStyle != null)
  table.Rows[i].MergeStyle(alternatingRowStyle);

else if (rowStyle != null)
  table.Rows[i].MergeStyle(rowStyle);
```

It also calls the `MergeStyle` method of the enumerated `CustomTableRow` control to apply the `EditRowStyle` to the control's `ControlStyle` if it's in edit mode:

```
if (i == EditRowIndex && editRowStyle != null)
  table.Rows[i].MergeStyle(editRowStyle);
```

Finally, PrepareControlHierarchy calls the MergeStyle method of the pager CustomTableRow control to apply the PagerStyle to the control's ControlStyle:

```
if (pagerStyle != null)
  table.Rows[table.Rows.Count - 1].MergeStyle(pagerStyle);
```

As the following code illustrates, CustomTable overrides the Render method to call the PrepareControlHierarchy method:

```
protected override void Render(HtmlTextWriter writer)
{
  PrepareControlHierarchy();
  base.Render(writer);
}
```

State Management

As discussed, CustomTable exposes an array of DataControlField objects named fields, and HeaderStyle, RowStyle, AlternatingRowStyle, EditRowStyle, and PagerStyle style properties of type TableItemStyle.

As discussed in Chapter 7, if complex properties of your custom control implement the IStateManager interface, your control must override the TrackViewState, SaveViewState, and LoadViewState methods to call the TrackViewState, SaveViewState, and LoadViewState methods of its complex properties. As discussed, the fields collection and the child style properties implement the IStateManager interface.

TrackViewState

CustomTable overrides the TrackViewState method to call the TrackViewState methods of the DataControlField objects in the fields collection and the child style properties, as shown in Listing 9-19.

Listing 9-19: The overridden TrackViewState method

```
protected override void TrackViewState()
{
  base.TrackViewState();
  if (headerStyle != null)
    ((IStateManager)headerStyle).TrackViewState();
  if (rowStyle != null)
    ((IStateManager)rowStyle).TrackViewState();
  if (alternatingRowStyle != null)
    ((IStateManager)alternatingRowStyle).TrackViewState();

  if (editRowStyle != null)
```

(continued)

Listing 9-19: *(continued)*

```
      ((IStateManager)editRowStyle).TrackViewState();

  if (pagerStyle != null)
    ((IStateManager)pagerStyle).TrackViewState();

  if (fields != null)
  {
    foreach (DataControlField field in fields)
    {
      if (field != null)
        ((IStateManager)field).TrackViewState();
    }
  }
}
```

SaveViewState

CustomTable overrides SaveViewState to call the SaveViewState methods of the DataControlField objects in the fields collection and the child style properties as shown in Listing 9-20.

Listing 9-20: The overridden SaveViewState method

```
protected override object SaveViewState()
{
  object[] state = new object[7];
  state[0] = base.SaveViewState();

  if (headerStyle != null)
    state[1] = ((IStateManager)headerStyle).SaveViewState();

  if (rowStyle != null)
    state[2] = ((IStateManager)rowStyle).SaveViewState();

  if (alternatingRowStyle != null)
    state[3] = ((IStateManager)alternatingRowStyle).SaveViewState();

  if (editRowStyle != null)
    state[4] = ((IStateManager)editRowStyle).SaveViewState();

  if (pagerStyle != null)
    state[5] = ((IStateManager)pagerStyle).SaveViewState();

  if (fields != null)
  {
    object[] s = new object[fields.Length];
    for (int i = 0; i < fields.Length; i++)
    {
      s[i] = ((IStateManager)fields[i]).SaveViewState();
    }
    state[6] = s;
```

```
    }

    foreach (object obj in state)
    {
      if (obj != null)
        return state;
    }

    return null;
  }
```

When the `SaveViewState` method of a `DataControlField` object or a child style property is called, the method saves its view state in the appropriate object and returns the object to the caller, which is the `SaveViewState` method of `CustomTable`. The `SaveViewState` method of the `CustomTable` control loads these objects into an array and returns the array to its caller.

LoadViewState

`CustomTable` overrides `LoadViewState` to call the `LoadViewState` methods of the `DataControlField` objects and child style properties as presented in Listing 9-21.

Listing 9-21: The overridden LoadViewState method

```
protected override void LoadViewState(object savedState)
{
  if (savedState == null)
  {
    base.LoadViewState(savedState);
    return;
  }

  object[] state = savedState as object[];
  if (state != null && state.Length == 7)
  {
    base.LoadViewState(state[0]);

    if (state[1] != null)
      ((IStateManager)HeaderStyle).LoadViewState(state[1]);

    if (state[2] != null)
      ((IStateManager)RowStyle).LoadViewState(state[2]);

    if (state[3] != null)
      ((IStateManager)AlternatingRowStyle).LoadViewState(state[3]);

    if (state[4] != null)
      ((IStateManager)EditRowStyle).LoadViewState(state[4]);

    if (state[5] != null)
      ((IStateManager)PagerStyle).LoadViewState(state[5]);

    if (state[6] != null)
```

(continued)

245

Listing 9-21: *(continued)*

```
        {
          object[] s = state[6] as object[];
          if (fields == null)
            fields = new DataControlField[(int)ViewState["FieldsLength"]];
          if (s != null && s.Length == fields.Length)
          {
            for (int i = 0; i < s.Length; i++)
            {
              if (s[i] != null)
              {
                if (fields[i] == null)
                  fields[i] = new DataControlField();
                ((IStateManager)fields[i]).LoadViewState(s[i]);
              }
            }
          }
        }
      }
    }
  }
}
```

The `LoadViewState` method of `CustomTable` receives the same array of objects from its caller that its `SaveViewState` returned to its caller. The method calls the `LoadViewState` methods of the `DataControlField` objects and child style properties in the same order in which the `SaveViewState` method of `CustomTable` called their `SaveViewState` methods. `CustomControl` returns the same object to each `LoadViewState` method that it received when it called the corresponding `SaveViewState`.

Using CustomTable in a Page

Listing 9-22 contains a page that uses the `CustomTable` control. Figure 9-1 shows what end users see on their browsers when they access this page.

Listing 9-22: A page that uses the CustomTable control

```
<html xmlns="http://www.w3.org/1999/xhtml">
<head runat="server">
  <title>Untitled Page</title>
</head>
<body>
  <form id="form1" runat="server">
    <custom:CustomTable runat="server" ID="ct" OnDeleteCommand="DeleteCallback"
    OnSortCommand="SortCallback" OnEditCommand="EditCallback"
    OnUpdateCommand="UpdateCallback" OnCancelCommand="CancelCallback"
    OnPageCommand="PageCallback" CellSpacing="0" DataKeyField="BookID"
    BackColor="LightGoldenrodYellow" BorderColor="Tan" BorderWidth="1px"
    CellPadding="10" ForeColor="Black" GridLines="None">
      <PagerStyle BackColor="PaleGoldenrod" ForeColor="DarkSlateBlue"
      HorizontalAlign="Center" />
      <HeaderStyle BackColor="Tan" Font-Bold="True" />
      <AlternatingRowStyle BackColor="PaleGoldenrod" />
```

```
        </custom:CustomTable>
    </form>
</body>
</html>
```

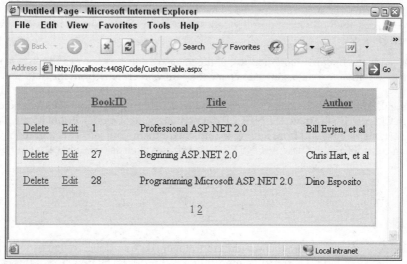

Figure 9-1

Shortcomings of the CustomTable Control

The main goal of this chapter was to familiarize you with the basic concepts of how to develop custom controls that support data binding. Notice that this chapter didn't use any of the new ASP.NET 2.0 features discussed in the next chapters to develop the CustomTable data-bound control. As a matter of fact, you can use the same skills and techniques you learned in this chapter to extend the functionality of the CustomTable data-bound control to support all the features that a complex data-bound control such as DataGrid supports.

This may seem to suggest that the ASP.NET 1.x Framework provides you with all you need to write a complex, feature-rich custom data-bound control. Why then bother with learning the new ASP.NET 2.0 features?

The CustomTable control like all ASP.NET 1.x data-bound controls such as DataGrid suffers from some fundamental shortcomings.

The first shortcoming is discussed thoroughly in Chapter 12, where you'll see that page developers must write a lot of code to take advantage of the rich features of the ASP.NET 1.x data-bound controls. Chapters 12–19 show you how the new ASP.NET 2.0 data source and data-bound control models allow you to develop custom data-bound controls that page developers can use without writing a single line of code.

Chapter 9

Second, you have to take the following three actions to implement an ASP.NET 1.x data-bound control such as CustomTable:

❑ Implement a mechanism consisting of three steps to allow page developers to specify the data records or source that the CustomTable control must enumerate.

❑ Override the CreateChildControls method to call the EnumerateDataAndCreateControl Hierarchy method with a dummy data source to create the control hierarchy from the saved view state.

❑ Override the DataBind method to call the EnumerateDataAndCreateControlHierarchy method with a real data source to create the control hierarchy from the data source.

You have to take these three actions every time you're developing a custom data-bound control. As you'll see in Chapter 17, the new ASP.NET 2.0 data-bound control model automatically takes care of these three actions, saving you from having to implement them yourself. This will require you to derive your custom control from the new ASP.NET 2.0 base classes such as CompositeDataBoundControl instead of the WebControl class.

Summary

This chapter developed a custom data-bound control named CustomTable that extends the functionality of the WebControl base class to add support for data binding. The first goal of this chapter was to help you familiarize yourself with the basic concepts and principles of developing custom controls that support data binding.

The second goal of this chapter was to discuss the shortcomings of an ASP.NET 1.x data-bound control such as CustomTable and DataGrid to set the stage for Chapters 12–19, where the new ASP.NET 2.0 data source and data-bound control models are discussed in detail. The next chapter develops an XML Web service–based custom component that will be used in the discussions of the ASP.NET 2.0 data source control model.

10

XML Web Services

XML Web services are among the fastest growing areas in today's technology market. Many Web applications are expected to provide support for XML Web services. This chapter uses a step-by-step approach to develop a custom component named `XmlWebServiceMethodInvoker` that will allow other components of an application to dynamically invoke the methods of XML Web services. The following chapters use the `XmlWebServiceMethodInvoker` component to develop XML Web service–enabled custom components such as data source controls and parameters.

As you'll see in this chapter, the `InvokeXmlWebServiceMethod` method of the `XmlWebServiceMethodInvoker` component is all you will need to enable your custom components to programmatically invoke the methods of XML Web services. A single method call will do the trick!

Because WSDL documents play such a crucial role in XML Web services, this chapter also helps you gain a solid understanding of these documents.

To provide you with concrete examples of how you can use the `XmlWebServiceMethodInvoker` component to develop your own XML Web service–enabled custom components, the chapter also uses the `XmlWebServiceMethodInvoker` component to develop two real-world XML Web service–enabled custom components that you can use in your own Web applications.

Because several examples in the next chapters of this book use the `XmlWebServiceMethodInvoker` component, you must learn how to use this component. This chapter includes two sections titled "How to Use the XmlWebServiceMethodInvoker" and "Using the Caching Feature." The former teaches you how to use the component, while the latter teaches you how to use the caching feature of the component to improve its performance. Although this chapter discusses the implementation of the `XmlWebServiceMethodInvoker` component in detail, this component is designed in a way that you can use it without having to know how it's implemented.

Developing and Consuming
an XML Web Service

You begin by developing a simple XML Web service named Math that exposes a single Web method named Add, which takes two integer numbers as its arguments, adds them, and returns the result. Listing 10-1 contains the code for the Math XML Web service.

Listing 10-1: The Math XML Web service

```
public class Math : System.Web.Services.WebService
{
  [WebMethod]
  public int Add(int x, int y)
  {
    return x + y;
  }
}
```

Next, you'll develop a client application that consumes the Math XML Web service. First, you need to implement the user interface of the application. As Listing 10-2 and Figure 10-1 illustrate, this user interface consists of the following server controls:

❑   Two TextBox controls where the user enters the integer numbers to be added

❑   A Button control that the user clicks to add the two integer numbers

❑   A Label control where the application displays the sum of the two integer numbers

Listing 10-2: The client application

```
<%@ Page Language="C#" AutoEventWireup="true" CodeFile="Default.aspx.cs"
Inherits="_Default" %>
<html xmlns="http://www.w3.org/1999/xhtml">
<body>
  <form id="form1" runat="server">
    <table border="0">
      <tr>
        <td align="right" width="200px">
          <strong>First Integer Number:</strong></td>
        <td align="left">
          <asp:TextBox runat="Server" ID="FirstIntegerNumber" /></td>
      </tr>
      <tr>
        <td align="right" width="200px">
          <strong>Second Integer Number:</strong></td>
        <td align="left">
          <asp:TextBox runat="Server" ID="SecondIntegerNumber" /></td>
      </tr>
      <tr>
        <td align="right" width="200px">
          <strong>Result:</strong></td>
        <td align="left">
          <asp:Label runat="Server" ID="Result" /></td>
```

```
      </tr>
      <tr>
        <td align="center" colspan="2">
          <asp:Button ID="Button1" runat="Server" Text="Submit"
          OnClick="ClickCallback" /></td>
      </tr>
    </table>
  </form>
</body>
</html>
```

Figure 10-1

Next, you need to right-click the root node of the client application in Visual Studio and select the Add Web References option from the pop-up menu to launch the Add Web Reference dialog shown in Figure 10-2. This dialog allows you to navigate to the Web site where the Math XML Web service resides.

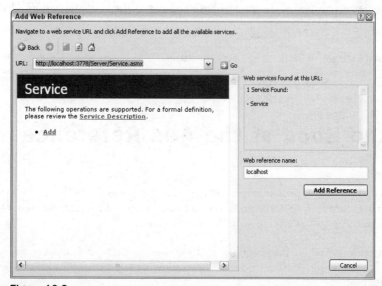

Figure 10-2

Then, you need to click the Add Reference button on this dialog. Under the hood, ASP.NET adds a reference to an assembly that contains a class with the same name and members as the Math XML Web service. In other words, this assembly contains a class named Math that exposes a method with the same signature as the Add method of the Math XML Web service. Recall that the signature of a method includes its name, argument types, and return type. The Math class that the assembly contains is known as the proxy class. As you'll see later, this class acts as proxy for the Math XML Web service, hence the name.

Finally, you need to implement the callback for the Click event of the Submit button as illustrated in Listing 10-3.

Listing 10-3: The callback for the Click event of the Submit button

```
protected void ClickCallback(object sender, EventArgs e)
{
  int x = int.Parse(FirstIntegerNumber.Text);
  int y = int.Parse(SecondIntegerNumber.Text);
  Math math = new Service();
  int result = math.Add(x, y);
  Result.Text = result.ToString();
}
```

Here are the steps that the ClickCallback method implements:

1. Retrieves the integer numbers that the user has entered in the TextBox controls:

```
int x = int.Parse(FirstIntegerNumber.Text);
int y = int.Parse(SecondIntegerNumber.Text);
```

2. Creates an instance of the Math proxy class. Recall that the Add Reference button on the Add Web References dialog has added a reference to an assembly that contains this proxy class:

```
Service service = new Service();
```

3. Calls the Add method of this proxy object and passes the two integer numbers into it:

```
int result = service.Add(x, y);
```

4. Displays the result in the Label server control:

```
Result.Text = result.ToString();
```

Under the Hood of the Add Reference Button

As discussed in the previous section, when you click the Add Reference button of the Add Web References dialog shown in Figure 10-2, ASP.NET adds a reference to an assembly that contains a class with the same name and members as the underlying XML Web service class.

You may be wondering where the assembly that contains the Math proxy class comes from. A look under the hood reveals the secret. ASP.NET performs the following tasks under the hood when you click the Add Reference button:

1. It generates the code for the `Math` proxy class. This code is normally saved in a temp file in a folder named `Temporary ASP.NET Files` under the folder where you've installed the .NET Framework. For example, when I clicked the Add Reference button, the framework automatically added a source file named `App_WebReferences.nkp8cpsv.0.cs` to the following folder:

```
C:\WINDOWS\Microsoft.NET\Framework\v2.0.50727\Temporary ASP.NET Files\client\
4d09cca4\85cc8b14
```

Listing 10-4 illustrates the portion of this source file.

2. It compiles the code for the `Math` proxy class into an assembly, which is normally saved in a file that resides in the same directory as the source file. For example, in my case, the framework compiled the proxy class into an assembly and saved the assembly into a file named `App WebReferences.nkp8cpsv.dll` located in the following directory:

```
C:\WINDOWS\Microsoft.NET\Framework\v2.0.50727\Temporary ASP.NET Files\client\
4d09cca4\85cc8b14
```

Listing 10-4: The client proxy class

```
namespace localhost
{
  [WebServiceBindingAttribute(Name = "ServiceSoap",
  Namespace = "http://MathOperations.com")]
  public class Math : System.Web.Services.Protocols.SoapHttpClientProtocol
  {
    public Math()
    {
      this.Url = "http://localhost:22024/Server/Math.asmx";
    }

    [SoapDocumentMethodAttribute("http://MathOperations.com/Add",
    RequestNamespace = "http://MathOperations.com",
    ResponseNamespace = "http://MathOperations.com",
    Use = SoapBindingUse.Literal,
    ParameterStyle = SoapParameterStyle.Wrapped)]
    public int Add(int x, int y)
    {
      object[] results = this.Invoke("Add", new object[] { x, y });
      return ((int)(results[0]));
    }
  }
}
```

Now, have a closer look at the `Math` proxy class shown in Listing 10-4. As this code listing illustrates, the proxy class has the same name as the XML Web service itself, `Math`. The proxy class derives from the ASP.NET `SoapHttpClientProtocol` base class. Here is the reason for this base class. Because the `Math` XML Web service resides in a remote Web site, the `Math` proxy class must use the .NET infrastructure that allows it to access the Web service and to call its `Add` method remotely. The `SoapHttpClientProtocol` base class provides the `Math` proxy class with a convenient API that encapsulates this .NET infrastructure.

The proxy class exposes a default constructor. Notice that this constructor assigns the URL of the XML Web service to the `Url` property of the `SoapHttpClientProtocol` base class. The .NET infrastructure that the base class encapsulates uses this URL to locate and to connect to the `Math` XML Web service.

The proxy class exposes a method with the same signature as the Add XML Web service method. Recall that the signature of a method consists of its name, argument types, and return type. As Listing 10-4 shows, the Add method of the proxy class uses the Invoke method of the SoapHttpClientProtocol base class to invoke the Add XML Web service method. The Invoke method takes two arguments. The first argument is a string that contains the name of the method being invoked, Add. The second argument is an array of objects, where each object contains the value of an argument of the XML Web service method being invoked. In this case, this array consists of two integer numbers because the Add method of the Math XML Web service takes two integer numbers as its arguments.

The Invoke method of the SoapHttpClientProtocol base class under the hood uses the necessary .NET infrastructure to connect to the XML Web service whose URL is given by the Url property and to invoke the XML Web service method whose name is given by the first argument of the Invoke method, which is Add.

Therefore, ASP.NET needs the following information to generate the code for the proxy class:

- ❑ The name of the XML Web service class (Math), because the proxy class uses the same name

- ❑ The name of the method of the XML Web service class (Add), because the corresponding method of the proxy class uses the same name

- ❑ The names, types, and order of the arguments of the Add method of the XML Web service, because the arguments of the Add method of the proxy class must have the same names, types, and order

- ❑ The type of the return value of the Add method of the XML Web service, because the return value of the Add method of the proxy class must be of the same type

- ❑ The values of the Name and Namespace properties of the WebServiceBindingAttribute metadata attribute that annotates the Math proxy class as shown in Listing 10-4

- ❑ The URL of the site where the Add method of the XML Web service must be accessed from, because the Url property of the SoapHttpClientProtocol class must have the same value

- ❑ The values of the SoapAction, RequestNamespace, ResponseNamespace, Use, and ParameterStyle properties of the SoapDocumentMethodAttribute metadata attribute that annotates the Math proxy class, as shown in Listing 10-4

This raises the following question: Where does ASP.NET get these seven pieces of information that it needs to generate the code for a proxy class?

Every XML Web service exposes an XML document known as the *WSDL document* that provides all the information needed to generate the code for the proxy class. The next few sections of this chapter cover WSDL documents in detail.

When you click the Add Reference button of the Add Web References dialog shown in Figure 10-2, the ASP.NET XML Web service infrastructure under the hood automatically takes care of the following tasks for you:

1. Downloads the WSDL document from the remote site

2. Uses the WSDL document to generate the code for the proxy class

3. Compiles the proxy class into an assembly

You can count on the ASP.NET XML Web service infrastructure to take care of these tasks for you automatically, as long as you do everything statically at compile time as opposed to programmatically or dynamically at runtime. In the static approach you have to use the Add Web References dialog shown in Figure 10-2 to download the WSD document, generate the code for the proxy, and compile the code into an assembly before running the application. In other words, everything should be ready before you run the application.

This chapter implements a custom component named `XmlWebServiceMethodInvoker` that you can use to enable your custom components to *programmatically* or dynamically download the WSDL document from the remote site, generate the code for the proxy class, and compile the code right from within your C# code at runtime.

The implementation of the `XmlWebServiceMethodInvoker` component also takes you under the hood of the ASP.NET XML Web service infrastructure where you can see for yourself how this infrastructure works from the inside out.

WSDL Document

Because the Web Service Description Language (WSDL; pronounced whiz-dull) document of an XML Web service provides all the information that you need to generate the code for the proxy class, the following sections will help you gain a solid understanding of the contents of a WSDL document. The WSDL document of an XML Web service provides you with the following information about the method of the XML Web service that you want to invoke:

- ❑ The names, types, and order of the arguments of the method

- ❑ The types and order of the return values of the method

- ❑ The name of the method

- ❑ The communication protocol through which the method must be accessed

- ❑ The URL of the site the method must be accessed from

- ❑ The name of the class that the method belongs to

The WSDL document uses the XML constructs of the WSDL markup language to provide all this information about a given method of the XML Web service. Listing 10-5 shows the WSDL document that describes the `Math` XML Web service (see Listing 10-1). The following sections discuss different parts of this WSDL document in detail.

Listing 10-5: The WSDL document that describes the Math XML Web service

```xml
<?xml version="1.0" encoding="utf-8"?>
<definitions
xmlns:soap="http://schemas.xmlsoap.org/wsdl/soap/"
xmlns:tns="http://CustomComponents/webservices/"
xmlns:s="http://www.w3.org/2001/XMLSchema"
xmlns:soap12="http://schemas.xmlsoap.org/wsdl/soap12/"
xmlns:http="http://schemas.xmlsoap.org/wsdl/http/"
targetNamespace="http://CustomComponents/webservices/"
```

(continued)

Listing 10-5: *(continued)*

```
xmlns="http://schemas.xmlsoap.org/wsdl/">

  <types>
    <s:schema elementFormDefault="qualified"
    targetNamespace="http://CustomComponents/webservices/">
      <s:element name="Add">
        <s:complexType>
          <s:sequence>
            <s:element minOccurs="1" maxOccurs="1" name="x" type="s:int" />
            <s:element minOccurs="1" maxOccurs="1" name="y" type="s:int" />
          </s:sequence>
        </s:complexType>
      </s:element>
      <s:element name="AddResponse">
        <s:complexType>
          <s:sequence>
            <s:element minOccurs="1" maxOccurs="1" name="AddResult" type="s:int" />
          </s:sequence>
        </s:complexType>
      </s:element>
    </s:schema>
  </types>

  <message name="AddSoapIn">
    <part name="parameters" element="tns:Add" />
  </message>
  <message name="AddSoapOut">
    <part name="parameters" element="tns:AddResponse" />
  </message>

  <portType name="ServiceSoap">
    <operation name="Add">
      <input message="tns:AddSoapIn" />
      <output message="tns:AddSoapOut" />
    </operation>
  </portType>

  <binding name="ServiceSoap12" type="tns:ServiceSoap">
    <soap12:binding transport="http://schemas.xmlsoap.org/soap/http"
     style="document" />
    <operation name="Add">
      <soap12:operation soapAction="http://MathOperations.com/Add"
       style="document" />
      <input>
        <soap12:body use="literal" />
      </input>
      <output>
        <soap12:body use="literal" />
      </output>
    </operation>
  </binding>

  <service name="Service">
```

```
        <port name="ServiceSoap12" binding="tns:ServiceSoap12">
          <soap12:address location="http://localhost:22024/Server/Service.asmx" />
        </port>
      </service>

  </definitions>
```

A WSDL document, like all XML documents, has a single outermost element called the *document element*. As Listing 10-5 shows, the document element of a WSDL document is an element named `<definitions>`. This element contains the following child elements: `<types>`, `<message>`, `<portType>`, `<binding>`, and `<service>`. These child elements are discussed in the following sections.

The complete coverage of WSDL markup language and WSDL documents is beyond the scope of this book. This chapter covers only those aspects of WSDL markup language and WSDL documents that relate to the discussions presented in the chapter.

The Names, Types, and Order of the Arguments

The `<types>` section of the WSDL document shown in Listing 10-5 uses an XML schema `<element>` element with the name attribute value of `Add` to describe the names, types, and order of the arguments of the `Add` method of the XML Web service. The `<element>` element contains a `<sequence>` element, which in turn contains two `<element>` elements. The `<sequence>` element is used to specify the order of the arguments of the method, while the two `<element>` elements are used to specify the names and types of the arguments. The order of the two `<element>` elements within the `<sequence>` element determines the order of the arguments of the method. The name and type attributes of each `<element>` element determine the name and type of the respective argument of the method:

```
<s:element name="Add">
  <s:complexType>
    <s:sequence>
      <s:element minOccurs="1" maxOccurs="1" name="x" type="s:int" />
      <s:element minOccurs="1" maxOccurs="1" name="y" type="s:int" />
    </s:sequence>
  </s:complexType>
</s:element>
```

The Types and Order of the Return Values

The `<types>` section of the WSDL document shown in Listing 10-5 uses an `<element>` element with the name attribute value of `AddResponse` to describe the names, types, and order of the return values of the `Add` method of the XML Web service. The `<element>` element contains a `<sequence>` element, which in turn contains an `<element>` element. The `<sequence>` element specifies the order of the return values of the method. Because the `Add` method returns a single value, the order is not an issue. The type attribute of the `<element>` element specifies the type of the return value of the `Add` method:

```
<s:element name="AddResponse">
  <s:complexType>
    <s:sequence>
      <s:element minOccurs="1" maxOccurs="1" name="AddResult" type="s:int" />
    </s:sequence>
  </s:complexType>
</s:element>
```

Describing the Method

In a non-distributed environment, invoking the Add method is considered a single action where the caller passes two integer numbers as the arguments of the method and receives an integer number as the return value. However, in a distributed environment, invoking the Add method is simulated through the exchange of two messages, a request and a response message. The content of the request message is nothing but the two input integer numbers, and the content of the response message is the return integer value.

The WSDL document shown in Listing 10-5 uses a <message> element with the name attribute value of AddSoapIn to represent the request message, and a <part> element to represent the content of the message. Because the content of the request message is nothing but the two input integer numbers and because the <types> section of the WSDL document uses an <element> element with the name attribute value of Add to describe the names, types, and order of the arguments of the Add method, the <part> element simply references this <element> element of the <types> section. This reference is assigned to the element attribute of the <part> element as shown in the following code:

```
<message name="AddSoapIn">
  <part name="parameters" element="tns:Add" />
</message>
```

The WSDL document uses a <message> element with the name attribute value of AddSoapOut to represent the response message, and a <part> element to represent the content of the message. Because the content of the response message is the return value of the Add method, and because the <types> section uses an <element> element with the name attribute value of AddResponse to describe the type of the return value of the Add method, the <part> element simply references this <element> element of the <types> section:

```
<message name="AddSoapOut">
  <part name="parameters" element="tns:AddResponse" />
</message>
```

These two <message> elements define the two messages that simulate the Add method. The WSDL document show in Listing 10-5 uses an <operation> element with the name attribute value of Add to represent the Add method itself, and the <input> and <output> elements to represent the contents of the Add method. Because the content of the Add method is nothing but the request and response messages that simulate the method, the <input> and <output> elements simply refer to the respective request and response messages:

```
<portType name="ServiceSoap">
  <operation name="Add">
    <input message="tns:AddSoapIn" />
    <output message="tns:AddSoapOut" />
  </operation>
</portType>
```

Notice that the <operation> element is the child element of the <portType> element. The <portType> element is used to group different methods of the XML Web service when the XML Web service exposes numerous methods. This doesn't apply to this example because the XML Web service exposes a single method.

Describing the Communication Protocol for Accessing the Method

The WSDL document uses the `<binding>` element to describe the communication protocol that clients must use to access the `Add` method:

```
<binding name="ServiceSoap12" type="tns:ServiceSoap">
  <soap12:binding transport="http://schemas.xmlsoap.org/soap/http"
   style="document" />
  <operation name="Add">
    <soap12:operation soapAction="http://MathOperations.com/Add"
     style="document" />
    <input>
      <soap12:body use="literal" />
    </input>
    <output>
      <soap12:body use="literal" />
    </output>
  </operation>
</binding>
```

Recall that the WSDL document uses the `<portType>` element to group the related methods of the XML Web service. Grouping is very useful when it comes to defining the communication protocol. It wouldn't make sense to force the clients of the XML Web service to use different communication protocols to access different methods of the same group. That's why the WSDL document defines a single communication protocol to access all methods in the same `portType`. The `type` attribute of the `<binding>` element refers to the `<portType>` element for which the communication protocol is defined.

The WSDL document uses the `<soap12:binding>` element to specify that its clients must use SOAP 1.2 messages to access the methods of the respective `portType`. The `transport` attribute of the `<soap12:binding>` element specifies that SOAP messages must be exchanged via HTTP protocol. The `style` attribute of the `<soap12:binding>` element specifies that SOAP messages must use document style instead of RPC style.

The `<soap12:binding>` element specifies the settings that apply to all methods of the respective `portType`. However, there are some settings that are method-specific. For example, XML Web services assign a unique string id to each method for identification purposes. The `SOAPAction` header of the respective HTTP message is normally set to the unique string id of the respective method.

Recall that the WSDL document uses an `<operation>` element to represent a method. The operation element that represents the `Add` method is reused in the `<binding>` element to set the appropriate parameters of the method.

The `<soap12:operation>` element is used to set the parameters of a given method of the XML Web service. The `soapAction` attribute of the `<soap12:operation>` element is set to the unique string id that uniquely identifies the method among other methods of the XML Web service. The `style` attribute overrides the `style` setting of the `<soap12:binding>` element.

The `<soap12:operation>` element specifies the settings that apply to the entire method. However, the `Add` method consists of two messages. The `<soap12:body>` element allows you to set the parameters that apply to individual messages. Recall that the WSDL document uses a `<part>` element to specify the content of a message. The use attribute of the <soap12:body> element is set to "literal" to signal that the content of the message is literally the content of the <part> element, and there is no need for further encoding.

Specifying the Site for Method Access

The WSDL document uses the <port> element to specify the URL of the site that the method must be accessed from. The binding attribute of the <port> element refers to the <binding> element that describes the communication protocol that clients must use to access the method. Because the <binding> element defines the communication protocol for a portType (a group of methods), the <port> element specifies the URL of the site from which all the methods of a given portType can be accessed. It would not make much sense to force users to access different methods of the same group from different sites. The location attribute of the <soap12:address> element determines the URL of the site where the clients can access the method. The same <port> element may contain more than one <soap12:address> element. This means that the same method can be accessed from different sites.

```
<port name="ServiceSoap12" binding="tns:ServiceSoap12">
  <soap12:address location="http://localhost:22024/Server/Service.asmx" />
</port>
```

Specifying the Class of the Method

The WSDL document uses the name attribute of the <service> element to specify the name of the class that the method belongs to:

```
<service name="Service">
  <port name="ServiceSoap12" binding="tns:ServiceSoap12">
    <soap12:address location="http://localhost:22024/Server/Service.asmx" />
  </port>
</service>
```

The XmlWebServiceMethodInvoker Class

The previous sections explained the contents of the WSDL document that will be used to generate the code for the proxy class. The XmlWebServiceMethodInvoker class exposes the following methods:

❑ The DownloadWSDLDocument method allows you to programmatically download the WSDL document right from within your C# code.

❑ The DeserializeWSDLDocument method deserializes a convenient .NET object from the WSDL document to allow you to programmatically access the contents of the WSDL document right from within your C# code.

❑ The GenerateCodeForProxyClass method allows you to programmatically generate the code for the proxy class right from within your C# code.

❑ The CompileCodeForProxyClass method allows you to programmatically compile the code for the proxy class right from within your C# code.

❑ The CreateProxyClassInstance method dynamically creates an instance of the proxy class.

- ❑ The `InvokeProxyClassInstanceMethod` method dynamically invokes the specified method of the instance.

- ❑ The `InvokeXmlWebServiceMethod` method automatically calls the previous six methods in the proper order and returns the return value of the `InvokeProxyClassInstanceMethod` method to the client of the XML Web service.

The following sections provide you with the implementation of all seven methods of the `XmlWebServiceMethodInvoker` class.

Programmatically Downloading the WSDL Document

The `DownloadWSDLDocument` method programmatically downloads the WSDL document from the remote site. The `XmlWebServiceMethodInvoker` class exposes a property named `WSDLPath` that must be set to the URL of the site from where the WSDL document can be downloaded. .NET network programming comes with a host of classes that you can use to download a file from a remote site. This section examines a few of these classes.

The following version of the `DownloadWSDLDocument` method uses an object of type `XmlReader` to download the WSDL document. .NET comes with three concrete classes that implement the `XmlReader` class: `XmlTextReader`, `XmlNodeReader`, and `XmlValidatingReader`. Each class provides certain capabilities. For instance, the `XmlValidatingReader` class is capable of validating an XML document against its respective schema document. The .NET 2.0 Framework recommends that developers use the `Create` method of the `XmlReader` class to create an instance of the appropriate `XmlReader` subclass. Most overloads of the `Create` method take an argument of type `XmlReaderSettings` that you can use to specify the capabilities you are interested in. Notice the `XmlReader` object is capable of retrieving XML documents from both local and remote sites:

```
public virtual XmlReader DownloadWSDLDocument()
{
  return XmlReader.Create(WSDLPath);
}
```

The following version of the `DownloadWSDLDocument` method uses the `WebRequest` and `WebResponse` classes to download the WSDL document. .NET 2.0 comes with three concrete classes that implement the `WebRequest` class: `FileWebRequest`, `FtpWebRequest`, and `HttpWebRequest`. The `WebRequest` class exposes a static method named `Create` that takes the URL of the resource as its argument and creates an instance of the appropriate subclass.

The `DownloadWSDLDocument` method sets the `Method` property of the `WebRequest` instance to the value `GET` to specify that the instance must use the `GET` HTTP protocol to download the WSDL document. Calling the `Create` method of the `WebRequest` class does not automatically send the request to the server. To send the request to the server and actually download the WSDL document, the `DownloadWSDLDocument` method calls the `GetResponse` method of the `WebRequest` class. The `GetResponse` method returns an object of type `WebResponse`. The `GetResponseStream` method of the `WebResponse` object returns a reference to the `Stream` object that contains the WSDL document.

```
public virtual Stream DownloadWSDLDocument()
{
  WebRequest req = WebRequest.Create(WSDLPath);
  req.Method = "GET";
  req.Credentials = CredentialCache.DefaultCredentials;
```

```
    WebResponse res = req.GetResponse();
    return res.GetResponseStream();
}
```

The following version of the `DownloadWSDLDocument` method uses the `WebClient` class to download the WSDL document. The `WebClient` class exposes a method named `DownloadString` that takes the URL of the resource as its argument and returns a string that contains the WSDL document:

```
public virtual string DownloadWSDLDocument()
{
  WebClient client = new WebClient();
  return client.DownloadString(WSDLPath);
}
```

De-serializing a .NET Object from the WSDL Document

The WSDL document contains all the information you need to generate the code for the proxy class. However, the WSDL document is not written in a procedural programming language such as C# or VB.NET. The typical programmatic approach to access the contents of an XML document such as WSDL is to deserialize an instance of an appropriate class from the contents of the document. The appropriate class in the case of WSDL documents is the `ServiceDescription` class:

```
public virtual ServiceDescription DeserializeWSDLDocument(XmlReader WSDLDocument)
{
  ServiceDescription WSDLDocumentDescription =
                                  ServiceDescription.Read(WSDLDocument);

  bool found = false;
  foreach (Service service in WSDLDocumentDescription.Services)
  {
    if (service.Name == TypeName)
    {
      found = true;
      break;
    }
  }

  if (!found)
     throw new Exception("Invalid class name!");

  return WSDLDocumentDescription;
}
```

One way to deserialize an object from an XML document is to use the `Deserialize` method of the `XmlSerializer` class. The `Read` method of the `ServiceDescription` class uses an instance of the `XmlSerializer` class to deserialize an instance of the `ServiceDescription` class from the WSDL document. As a matter of fact, the `ServiceDescription` class exposes a property of type `XmlSerializer` named `Serializer` that returns the `XmlSerializer` instance that the `Read` method uses to deserialize the `ServiceDescription` instance. This means that you can also directly call the `Deserialize` method of the `Serializer` property to deserialize the instance:

```
ServiceDescription.Serializer.Deserialize (WSDLDocument);
```

The `ServiceDescription` instance fully describes the WSDL document and provides programmatic access to the contents of the document.

The `XmlWebServiceMethodInvoker` class exposes a property named `TypeName` that the client of the class must set to the name of the class that represents the XML Web service. Notice that the `DeserializeWSDLDocument` method ensures that the value of the `TypeName` property represents a valid class name. The method uses the `ServiceDescription` object, `WSDLDocumentDescription`, to programmatically access the values of the `name` attributes of all the `<service>` elements of the WSDL document. Recall that the value of each `name` attribute contains the name of the class that represents an XML Web service. If the method doesn't find a `<service>` element with the same `name` attribute value as the value of the `TypeName` property, it raises an exception because the client is trying to access a non-existent XML Web service.

Generating the Code for the Proxy Class

The `GenerateCodeForProxyClass` method takes the `ServiceDescription` object that contains the WSDL document and programmatically generates the code for the proxy class:

```
public virtual ServiceDescriptionImportWarnings
GenerateCodeForProxyClass (ServiceDescription WSDLDocumentDescription,
                        CodeCompileUnit myCodeCompileUnit)
{
  ServiceDescriptionImporter myServiceDescriptionImporter =
                                        new ServiceDescriptionImporter();

  myServiceDescriptionImporter.ProtocolName = "Soap";
  myServiceDescriptionImporter.AddServiceDescription( WSDLDocumentDescription,
                                        String.Empty, String.Empty);

  CodeNamespace myCodeNamespace = new CodeNamespace();
  myCodeCompileUnit.Namespaces.Add(myCodeNamespace);

  return myServiceDescriptionImporter.Import( myCodeNamespace, myCodeCompileUnit);
}
```

The `GenerateCodeForProxyClass` method creates an instance of the `ServiceDescriptionImporter` class. This class exposes a method named `Import` that uses the `ServiceDescription` object to programmatically access the contents of the WSDL document, and generates the code for the proxy class.

Under the Hood of the Import Method

This section serves the following two important purposes:

❑ It takes you under the hood of the `Import` method so you can see for yourself how this method manages to generate the code for the proxy class.

❑ It introduces you to the .NET classes that allow you to programmatically generate code from within your C# code. This will prepare you for the next chapter, where you'll use these classes to customize the code for the proxy class.

The `Import` method doesn't generate language-specific code such as C# or VB.NET. Instead it generates what is known as Code Document Object Model (CodeDom). If you implement the same code in more than one .NET-compliant language (such as C# and VB.NET), you'll notice the syntax varies from one language to another, but the structure of the code remains the same. As an example, consider the proxy class in Listing 10-4. Regardless of whether you implement this proxy class in C# or some other .NET-compliant language, you still have to take the following steps to implement the same structural components:

1. Annotate the proxy class with the `WebServiceBinding` attribute

2. Set the `Name` and `Namespace` arguments of the attribute

3. Declare the proxy class (`Public Class Service` in VB.NET, and `public class Service` in C#)

4. Derive the proxy class from the `SoapHttpClientProtocol` base class

5. Implement the default constructor of the proxy class, where you have to set the value of the `Url` property of the base class

6. Implement a method named `Add` that takes two integer values and returns an integer value

7. Call the `Invoke` method of the `SoapHttpClientProtocol` class in the body of the `Add` method

8. Annotate the `Add` method with the `SoapDocumentMethod` attribute

9. Set the `RequestNamespace`, `ResponseNamespace`, `Use`, and `ParameterStyle` properties of the attribute

These components constitute the structure of the proxy class, which remains the same no matter which .NET-compliant language you use to implement it. You can think of CodeDom as a meta-language that allows you to transcend the syntax of your C# or VB.NET code to represent its structure. To put it differently, CodeDom provides you with a language-agnostic representation of the structure of your C# or VB.NET code.

The `System.CodeDom` namespace exposes one class to represent each common structural component of your C# or VB.NET code. For example, the `CodeTypeDeclaration` class represents the declaration of a class, interface, or struct. As an example, consider the following C# class declaration:

```
public class Math
```

You can use an instance of the `CodeTypeDeclaration` class to represent the C# class declaration:

```
CodeTypeDeclaration math = new CodeTypeDeclaration();
math.Name = "Math";
math.Attributes = MemberAttributes.Public;
```

Notice that the `MemberAttributes.Public` enumeration value is assigned to the `Attributes` property of the `CodeTypeDeclaration` instance to represent the public access modifier of the `Math` class.

As you can see, you can use instances of the appropriate classes of the `System.CodeDom` namespace to represent common programming constructs such as class declarations, assignments, and so on. These instances form a hierarchy of nodes known as CodeDom object model. The root node of this hierarchy is an object of type `CodeCompileUnit`. You can think of the `CodeCompileUnit` instance as a container that holds all of the CodeDom representation of your C# or VB.NET code.

Because all of the code included in the `CodeCompileUnit` object compiles to a single assembly, the `CodeCompileUnit` object represents an assembly. Because every assembly consists of one or more namespaces, the `CodeCompileUnit` class exposes a collection property named `Namespaces` that contains `CodeNamespace` objects where each object represents a namespace in the respective assembly.

To help you gain a better understanding of how the `Import` method manages to create the CodeDom representation of a proxy class from the contents of a WSDL document, Listing 10-6 shows you the CodeDom representation of the proxy class in Listing 10-4 from its respective WSDL document. Because CodeDom is quite verbose and takes up lot of space, the CodeDom in Listing 10-6 only represents the proxy class itself and doesn't cover its constructor or `Add` method.

Listing 10-6: The CodeDom that describes the proxy class in Listing 10-4

```
CodeTypeDeclaration proxyClass = new CodeTypeDeclaration();
myCodeNamespace.Types.Add(proxyClass);
proxyClass.Name = WSDLDocumentDescription.Services[0].Name;
proxyClass.Attributes = MemberAttributes.Public;
CodeTypeReference soapHttpClientProtocol = new CodeTypeReference();
soapHttpClientProtocol.BaseType =
                        "System.Web.Services.Protocols.SoapHttpClientProtocol";
proxyClass.BaseTypes.Add(soapHttpClientProtocol);

CodePrimitiveExpression bindingName =
            new CodePrimitiveExpression(WSDLDocumentDescription.Bindings[0].Name);

CodeAttributeArgument bindingNameAssignment =
                            new CodeAttributeArgument("Name", bindingName);

CodePrimitiveExpression bindingNamespace =
            new CodePrimitiveExpression(WSDLDocumentDescription.TargetNamespace);
CodeAttributeArgument bindingNamespaceAssignment =
            new CodeAttributeArgument("Namespace", bindingNamespace);

CodeAttributeArgument[] bindingAssignments =
                        { bindingNameAssignment, bindingNamespaceAssignment };
CodeAttributeDeclaration bindingDeclaration =
        new CodeAttributeDeclaration("System.Web.Services.WebServiceBindingAttribute",
                            bindingAssignments);

proxyClass.CustomAttributes.Add(bindingDeclaration);
```

The CodeDom in Listing 10-6 first uses an instance of the `CodeTypeDeclaration` class to represent the proxy class:

```
CodeTypeDeclaration proxyClass = new CodeTypeDeclaration();
proxyClass.Attributes = MemberAttributes.Public;
```

Because every class must belong to a namespace in the respective assembly, the `CodeTypeDeclaration` object is added to the `Types` collection of the respective `CodeNamespace` object to represent the namespace membership of the proxy class:

```
myCodeNamespace.Types.Add(proxyClass);
```

The `Name` property of the `CodeTypeDeclaration` object specifies the name of the proxy class. As mentioned, the name of the proxy class is the same as the name of the XML Web service class. As discussed, the

WSDL document exposes the name of the XML Web service class as the value of the name attribute of the respective `<service>` element. Listing 10-6 uses the `ServiceDescription` object to programmatically access the value of the name attribute of the `<service>` element of the WSDL document, which is then used to set the `Name` property of the `CodeTypeDeclaration` object that represents the proxy class:

```
proxyClass.Name = WSDLDocumentDescription.Services[0].Name;
```

The CodeDom then creates an instance of the `CodeTypeReference` class to refer to the `SoapHttpClientProtocol` class and adds the instance to the `BaseTypes` collection of the `CodeTypeDeclaration` object, which represents the proxy class, to represent the derivation of the proxy class from the `SoapHttpClientProtocol` class:

```
CodeTypeReference soapHttpClientProtocol = new CodeTypeReference();
soapHttpClientProtocol.BaseType =
                        "System.Web.Services.Protocols.SoapHttpClientProtocol";
proxyClass.BaseTypes.Add(soapHttpClientProtocol);
```

It then uses the `ServiceDescription` object to programmatically retrieve the value of the name attribute of the respective `<binding>` element of the WSDL document and creates an instance of the `CodePrimitiveExpression` class to represent the retrieved value:

```
CodePrimitiveExpression bindingName =
            new CodePrimitiveExpression(WSDLDocumentDescription.Bindings[0].Name);
```

Next, the CodeDom creates an instance of the `CodeAttributeArgument` class to represent the `Name` property of the `WebServiceBinding` attribute:

```
CodeAttributeArgument bindingNameAssignment =
            new CodeAttributeArgument("Name", bindingName);
```

Then it uses the `ServiceDescription` object to programmatically retrieve the value of the `targetNamespace` attribute of the `<definitions>` element of the WSDL document and uses an instance of the `CodePrimitiveExpression` class to represent the retrieved value:

```
CodePrimitiveExpression bindingNamespace =
            new CodePrimitiveExpression( WSDLDocumentDescription.TargetNamespace);
```

Next it creates an instance of the `CodeAttributeArgument` class to represent the `Namespace` property of the `WebServiceBinding` attribute:

```
CodeAttributeArgument bindingNamespaceAssignment =
            new CodeAttributeArgument("Namespace", bindingNamespace);
```

The CodeDom then uses the two `CodeAttributeArgument` instances and creates an instance of the `CodeAttributeDeclaration` class to represent the `WebServiceBinding` attribute:

```
CodeAttributeArgument[] bindingAssignments =
                { bindingNameAssignment, bindingNamespaceAssignment };

CodeAttributeDeclaration bindingDeclaration =
    new CodeAttributeDeclaration("System.Web.Services.WebServiceBindingAttribute",
                            bindingAssignments);
```

Finally, it adds the CodeAttributeDeclaration object to the CustomAttributes collection of the CodeTypeDeclaration object to represent the annotation of the proxy class with the WebServiceBinding attribute:

```
proxyClass.CustomAttributes.Add(bindingDeclaration);
```

This example shows how the Import method uses the ServiceDescription object to programmatically access the contents of the WSDL document and retrieve the required information such as the name of the proxy class and the values of the Name and Namespace properties of the WebServiceBindingAttribute attribute.

The Import method also uses the instances of the classes in the System.CodeDom namespace such as CodeTypeDeclaration, CodeTypeReference, and CodeAttributeDeclaration to programmatically generate the code for the proxy class.

Compiling the Code for the Proxy Class

The CompileCodeForProxyClass method programmatically compiles all of the code included in the CodeCompileUnit object to a single in-memory assembly, as shown in Listing 10-7.

Listing 10-7: The CompileCodeForProxyClass method

```
public virtual Assembly CompileCodeForProxyClass(CodeCompileUnit myCodeCompileUnit)
{
  CodeDomProvider myCodeDomProvider = CodeDomProvider.CreateProvider("CSharp");

  CompilerParameters myCompilerParameters = new CompilerParameters();

  myCompilerParameters.GenerateExecutable = false;
  myCompilerParameters.GenerateInMemory = true;
  myCompilerParameters.IncludeDebugInformation = false;
  myCompilerParameters.ReferencedAssemblies.Add("System.dll");

  myCompilerParameters.ReferencedAssemblies.Add("System.Data.dll");
  ICodeCompiler myCodeCompiler = myCodeDomProvider.CreateCompiler();

  CompilerResults myCompilerResults =
    myCodeCompiler.CompileAssemblyFromDom(myCompilerParameters, myCodeCompileUnit);

  return myCompilerResults.CompiledAssembly;
}
```

.NET-compliant languages such as C# and VB.NET implement a class that derives from the CodeDomProvider base class. For instance, C# implements a class named CSharpCodeProvider that derives from the CodeDomProvider class. The CodeDomProvider class exposes a static method named CreateProvider that takes the friendly name of the language and generates an instance of the language-specific code provider class. The CompileCodeForProxyClass passes the string "CSharp" as the argument to the CreateProvider method to access an instance of the CSharpCodeProvider class.

The CodeDomProvider class also exposes a method named CreateCompiler that returns an ICodeCompiler object. The ICodeCompiler interface exposes all the methods and properties that a

.NET-compliant language must implement in order to compile language-specific or language-agnostic code to MSIL (an assembly). One of the methods that the ICodeCompiler interface exposes is a method named CompileAssemblyFromDom. This method compiles all of the code included in the CodeCompileUnit object to a single assembly.

The method also takes an object of type CompilerParameters as an argument. The CompileCodeForProxyClass method uses the CompilerParameters object to specify the compiler options. The method sets the GenerateExecutable property to false to have the compiler generate a DLL. The method also sets the GenerateInMemory property to true to have the compiler compile the code to an in-memory assembly.

Creating an Instance of the Proxy Class

When the compiler is compiling the code for the proxy class, it also emits a fair amount of metadata into the assembly to fully describe the assembly and its contents. The .NET Framework reflection exposes a class named Assembly that can be used to access the metadata of the assembly. The Assembly class exposes a method named CreateInstance that takes the name of the actual type of the proxy class and uses the assembly metadata to dynamically create an instance of the proxy class. The XmlWebServiceMethodInvoker class exposes a property named TypeName that must be set to the fully qualified name of the type of the proxy class. In this case, the name of the type of the proxy class is the same as the name of the type of the actual XML Web service:

```
public virtual object
CreateProxyClassInstance(Assembly assembly)
{
  return assembly.CreateInstance(TypeName);
}
```

Invoking the Specified Method of the Proxy Class Instance

As Listing 10-8 shows, the InvokeProxyClassInstanceMethod takes four arguments. The first argument is the name of the method of the proxy class instance being invoked. The second argument is the argument names and values to be passed to the method. The third argument is the instance of the proxy class being used. The last argument specifies whether the argument names and values must be validated and sorted before they are passed to the method.

The InvokeProxyClassInstanceMethod method first calls the GetType method of the proxy instance to access the Type object that represents the type of the instance. The Type object provides access to the metadata that fully describes the proxy class and its contents. The Type class exposes a method named GetMethods that returns an array of MethodInfo objects, where each object represents a method of the proxy class. The value of the Name property of each object is the name of the method of the proxy class that the object represents. The InvokeProxyClassInstanceMethod method enumerates the Method Info objects to find the MethodInfo object whose Name property has the same value as the methodName argument. If the InvokeProxyClassInstanceMethod method does not find the MethodInfo object, it raises an exception.

Listing 10-8: Invoking the specified method of the proxy class instance

```
public virtual Object InvokeProxyClassInstanceMethod(string methodName,
                                    IOrderedDictionary methodArgumentValues,
                                    object proxyClassInstance,
                                    bool validateAndSortValues)
{
  Type t = proxyClassInstance.GetType();
  MethodInfo[] mis = t.GetMethods();
  MethodInfo mi = null;

  foreach (MethodInfo minfo in mis)
  {
    if (minfo.Name == methodName)
    {
      mi = minfo;
      break;
    }
  }

  if (mi == null)
    throw new Exception("Method not found!");

  if (validateAndSortValues && methodArgumentValues != null &&
      methodArgumentValues.Count > 0)
    ValidateAndSortMethodArgumentNamesAndValues(mi, methodArgumentValues);

  if (methodArgumentValues != null && methodArgumentValues.Count > 0)
  {
    object[] values = new object[methodArgumentValues.Count];
    methodArgumentValues.Values.CopyTo(values, 0);
    return mi.Invoke(proxyClassInstance, values);
  }
  else
    return mi.Invoke(proxyClassInstance, null);
}
```

At the end of the method, `InvokeProxyClassInstanceMethod` calls the `Invoke` method of the `MethodInfo` object to invoke the method that the `MethodInfo` object represents. The `Invoke` method takes two arguments. The first argument is the proxy instance being used. The second argument is an array that contains the values that are being passed as arguments to the method being invoked. The values must meet the following requirements:

❑   The order of the values in the array must be the same as the order of the arguments of the method.

❑   The values in the array must be of the same type as the respective arguments of the method.

❑   The number of the values in the array must be equal to the number of the arguments of the method.

However, the clients of an XML Web service may not be able to meet all three conditions. The `Invoke ProxyClassInstanceMethod` method takes a Boolean argument named `validateAndSortValues`. If the argument is set to true, the method calls the `ValidateAndSortMethodArgumentNamesAndValues` method, shown in Listing 10-9.

Listing 10-9: Validates and sorts the names and values of the arguments being passed to the method

```
protected virtual void
ValidateAndSortMethodArgumentNamesAndValues(MethodInfo mi,
                                            IOrderedDictionary values)
{
  if (values != null && values.Count > 0)
  {
    ParameterInfo[] parameters = mi.GetParameters();
    KeyedList list = new KeyedList();

    foreach (ParameterInfo parameter in parameters)
    {
      bool found = false;
      foreach (DictionaryEntry entry in values)
      {
        if (parameter.Name == entry.Key.ToString())
        {
          found = true;
          TypeConverter converter =
                          TypeDescriptor.GetConverter(parameter.ParameterType);

          if(converter.CanConvertFrom(entry.Value.GetType()))
            list.Add(entry.Key, converter.ConvertFrom(entry.Value));

          else if (converter.CanConvertFrom(Type.GetType("System.String")))
            list.Add(entry.Key, converter.ConvertFrom(entry.Value.ToString()));

          else
            throw new Exception("Cannot convert value");
          break;
        }
      }

      if (!found)
        throw new Exception("Argument not found");
    }

    values.Clear();
    foreach (DictionaryEntry entry in list)
    {
      values.Add(entry.Key, entry.Value);
    }
  }
}
```

The `ValidateAndSortMethodArgumentNamesAndValues` method first calls the `GetParameters` method of the `MethodInfo` object that represents the method being called. The `GetParameters` method provides the `ValidateAndSortMethodArgumentNamesAndValues` method with the following information about the actual order of the arguments of the method, their types, and their values:

- ❏ The GetParameters method returns an array of ParameterInfo objects where each object represents an argument of the method. The order of the ParameterInfo objects in the array is the same as the actual order of the arguments of the method.

- ❏ Each ParameterInfo object exposes a property named ParameterType that represents the actual type of the respective argument of the method.

- ❏ Each ParameterInfo object exposes a property named Name whose value is the name of the respective argument of the method.

This information allows the ValidateAndSortMethodArgumentNamesAndValues method to perform the following tasks:

1. Change the order of the values to make them match the order of the arguments of the method

2. Convert the values to the type that the respective arguments of the method expect

3. Ensure that the number of values is equal to the number of arguments of the method

The second argument of the ValidateAndSortMethodArgumentNamesAndValues method is of type IOrderedDictionary, which contains DictionaryEntry objects. Each DictionaryEntry object represents a value being passed to the method. The DictionaryEntry class exposes two important properties, Key and Value, that represent the name and value of the argument being passed to the method, respectively.

The ValidateAndSortMethodArgumentNamesAndValues method enumerates the ParameterInfo array and for each iteration, it enumerates the IOrderedDictionary collection object to locate the DictionaryEntry object with the same Key value as the name of the argument of the method. Recall that the value of the Name property of the ParameterInfo object is the name of the respective argument of the method. After the DictionaryEntry object is found, it is time to check the type of the value and convert it to the type that the respective argument of the method expects, if necessary.

The TypeDescriptor class in the System.ComponentModel namespace exposes methods that use the .NET Framework reflection to provide access to the metadata of a given type. The GetConverter method of the TypeDescriptor class takes an argument of type Type and returns an instance of type TypeConverter. Most .NET types come with a type converter that derives from the TypeConverter class and implements its methods and properties. For example, the DateTimeConverter class knows how to convert values of certain types to a DateTime object.

Because all type converters derive from the TypeConverter base class, you can use the methods and properties of the TypeConverter class to convert from any type without having to know the actual target type. Two important methods of the TypeConverter class are the CanConvertFrom and ConvertFrom methods. The ValidateAndSortMethodArgumentNamesAndValues method first calls the CanConvertFrom method to ensure that the value can actually be converted to the target type, which is the actual type of the respective argument of the method. If so, the method then calls the ConvertFrom method of the TypeConverter class to convert the value to the type that the respective argument of the method expects.

The ValidateAndSortMethodArgumentNamesAndValues method uses the local variable found to make sure that the IOrderedDictionary object contains the values of all the arguments of the method being invoked. If the object does not contain the value for an argument of the method, the ValidateAndSortMethodArgumentNamesAndValues method raises an exception.

Putting It All Together: The InvokeXmlWebServiceMethod Method

The `InvokeXmlWebServiceMethod` method calls all the other methods of the `XmlWebServiceMethodInvoker` class in the right order, as shown in Listing 10-10.

Listing 10-10: InvokeXmlWebServiceMethod automatically calls all the other methods of the XmlWebServiceMethodInvoker class

```
public virtual object InvokeXmlWebServiceMethod(string methodName,
                            IOrderedDictionary methodArgumentNamesAndValues,
                            bool validateAndSortMethodArgumentNamesAndValues)
{
   XmlReader WSDLDocument = DownloadWSDLDocument();
   ServiceDescription WSDLDocumentDescription =
                            DeserializeWSDLDocument(WSDLDocument);
   CodeCompileUnit myCodeCompileUnit = new CodeCompileUnit();

   ServiceDescriptionImportWarnings warnings =
           GenerateCodeForProxyClass(WSDLDocumentDescription, myCodeCompileUnit);

   if (warnings == 0)
   {
     Assembly myAssembly = CompileCodeForProxyClass( myCodeCompileUnit);
     object proxyInstance =
                   CreateProxyClassInstance(WSDLDocumentDescription, myAssembly);

     return InvokeProxyClassInstanceMethod(methodName, methodArgumentNamesAndValues,
                   proxyInstance, validateAndSortMethodArgumentNamesAndValues);
   }

   return null;
}
```

Now your components can use a single method, `InvokeXmlWebServiceMethod`, to invoke the methods of an XML Web service. A single call does the trick! The `InvokeXmlWebServiceMethod` method takes three important arguments. The first argument is the name of the method being invoked. The second argument is an `IOrderedDictionary` object that contains both the names and values of the arguments being passed to the method. The last argument specifies whether the argument names and values should be validated and sorted.

How to Use XmlWebServiceMethodInvoker

Follow these steps to use the `XmlWebServiceMethodInvoker` component to dynamically invoke the methods of XML Web services:

1. Create an instance of the `XmlWebServiceMethodInvoker` class.

2. Set the value of the `TypeName` property of the instance to the fully qualified name of the class that represents the XML Web service.

3. Set the value of the WSDLPath property of the instance to the URL of the site where the WSDL document can be downloaded.

4. Create an instance of the OrderedDictionary class or any other class that implements the IOrderedDictionary interface.

5. Call the Add method of the OrderedDictionary class once for each argument of the XML Web service method and pass the name and value of the argument as the first and second arguments of the Add method.

6. Call the InvokeXmlWebServiceMethod method and pass the name of the XML Web service method as its first argument and the OrderedDictionary instance as its second argument.

7. Pass false as the third argument value of the InvokeXmlWebServiceMethod method if the argument values are added to the OrderedDictionary instance in the same order as the arguments of the XML Web service method; otherwise pass true.

Next, you'll implement a new version of the client application shown in Figure 10-1. Recall that the old version required you to use the Add Web References dialog shown in Listing 10-2 to statically generate the assembly for the proxy class before running the application.

The new version allows you to do everything programmatically. Listing 10-11 contains the code for the new version of the ClickCallback method. This version uses the XmlWebServiceMethodInvoker component to dynamically invoke the Add method of the XML Web service.

Listing 10-11: Using the XmlWebServiceMethodInvoker method to dynamically call an XML Web service

```
void ClickCallback(object sender, EventArgs e)
{
  XmlWebServiceMethodInvoker methodInvoker = new XmlWebServiceMethodInvoker();
  methodInvoker.TypeName = "Math";
  methodInvoker.WSDLPath = "http://localhost:9746/Server/Math.asmx?wsdl";
  OrderedDictionary list = new OrderedDictionary();
  list.Add("x", int.Parse(FirstIntegerNumber.Text));
  list.Add("y", int.Parse(SecondIntegerNumber.Text));
  int result = (int)methodInvoker.InvokeXmlWebServiceMethod("Add", list, false);
  Result.Text = result.ToString();
}
```

The ClickCallback method invokes the Add method by first creating an instance of the XmlWebServiceMethodInvoker class:

```
XmlWebServiceMethodInvoker methodInvoker = new XmlWebServiceMethodInvoker();
```

Then it sets the value of the TypeName property of the instance to the string value Math, which is the name of the class that represents the XML Web service:

```
methodInvoker.TypeName = "Math";
```

Then it sets the value of the WSDLPath property to the URL of the site from where the WSDL document can be downloaded. This URL normally consists of the URL of the Web site where the XML Web service resides plus the query string parameter named WSDL. For example, if you open the server application in the Visual Studio and run it, you should see something like Figure 10-3.

Figure 10-3

Click the Service Description link to view the WSDL document, as shown in Figure 10-4. Notice that the URL of this page consists of the URL of the Web service plus the query string WSDL:

```
methodInvoker.WSDLPath = "http://localhost:1510/Server/Service.asmx?wsdl";
```

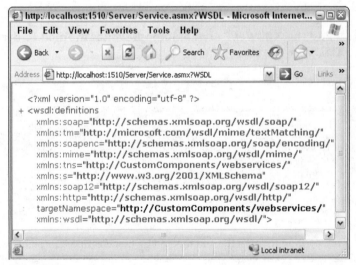

Figure 10-4

The `ClickCallback` method then goes on to create an instance of the `OrderedDictionary` class:

```
OrderedDictionary list = new OrderedDictionary();
```

The method then populates the `OrderedDictionary` instance with the names (`"x"` and `"y"`) and values of the arguments being passed to the `Add` method. The `Text` properties of the two `TextBox` server controls provide the values of the arguments:

```
list.Add("x", int.Parse(FirstIntegerNumber.Text));
list.Add("y", int.Parse(SecondIntegerNumber.Text));
```

Finally, the method calls the `InvokeXmlWebServiceMethod` method and passes it the name of the method being invoked (`Add`) and the `OrderedDictionary` object. Because the arguments being passed have the same names, types, and order of the arguments of the `Add` method, and there is no need for further argument validation and sorting, the `ClickCallback` method passes the Boolean value `false` as the third argument of the `InvokeXmlWebServiceMethod` method. At the end, the `ClickCallback` method displays the return value of the `InvokeXmlWebServiceMethod` method:

```
int result = (int)methodInvoker.InvokeXmlWebServiceMethod("Add", list, false);
Result.Text = result.ToString();
```

Caching the Compiled Proxy Class

As discussed, the `InvokeXmlWebServiceMethod` method of the `XmlWebServiceMethodInvoker` component calls the other methods of this component in the proper order to programmatically:

1. Download the WSDL document

2. Deserialize a `ServiceDescription` object from the downloaded WSDL document

3. Generate the code for the proxy class

4. Compile the proxy class

5. Instantiate an instance of the compiled proxy class

6. Invoke the `Add` method of the proxy instance

Due to the nature of the HTTP protocol, the proxy instance is disposed of at the end of each request. In other words, each request must instantiate a new instance of the proxy class. Therefore, steps 5 and 6 have to be repeated for each request. How about steps 1 through 4?

Steps 1 through 4 are quite expensive and degrade the performance of the client application if they have to be repeated for each request. In this section you modify the implementation of the `XmlWebServiceMethodInvoker` component to cache the result of the steps 1 through 4 in the ASP.NET `Cache` object. The result of these steps is the compiled proxy class. In other words, downloading the WSDL document, de-serializing the `ServiceDescription` object from the downloaded WSDL document, generating the code for the proxy class, and compiling the proxy class will be performed only for the first request. The subsequent requests will instantiate an instance of the cached compiled proxy class. This will improve the performance and usability of the client application as you'll see later in this section.

Cache-Related Properties

The `XmlWebServiceMethodInvoker` component exposes four cache-related properties:

❑ `CacheDuration`: Number of seconds that the `XmlWebServiceMethodInvoker` component keeps the compiled proxy class in cache.

❑ `CacheExpirationPolicy`: Specifies the cache expiration policy. The possible values are `Absolute` and `Sliding`. `Absolute` means the compiled proxy class will remain in the `Cache` object for the amount of time specified by the `CacheDuration` property. `Sliding` means the compiled proxy class will be removed from the cache if no requests are made for the amount of time specified by the `CacheDuration` property. If a request is made within this specified time frame, the time window is reset.

❑ `CacheKeyDependency`: The clients of the `XmlWebServiceMethodInvoker` component can set the `CacheKeyDependency` property to create a dependency between the cache entry that the component creates and the key. They can programmatically expire the cache entry at any time by expiring the key.

❑ `EnableCaching`: The `XmlWebServiceMethodInvoker` component automatically caches the compiled proxy class when the `EnableCaching` property is set to true and the `CacheDuration` property is set to a value greater than 0.

CompileCodeForProxyClass

Listing 10-12 contains the code for the new version of the `CompileCodeForProxyClass` method of the `XmlWebServiceMethodInvoker` component that caches the compiled proxy class in the ASP.NET `Cache` object.

Listing 10-12: The CompileCodeForProxyClass method caches the compiled proxy class

```
public virtual Assembly CompileCodeForProxyClass(CodeCompileUnit myCodeCompileUnit)
{
    CodeDomProvider myCodeDomProvider = CodeDomProvider.CreateProvider("CSharp");

    CompilerParameters myCompilerParameters = new CompilerParameters();
    myCompilerParameters.GenerateExecutable = false;
    myCompilerParameters.GenerateInMemory = true;
    myCompilerParameters.IncludeDebugInformation = false;
    myCompilerParameters.ReferencedAssemblies.Add("System.dll");
    myCompilerParameters.ReferencedAssemblies.Add("System.Data.dll");

    CompilerResults myCompilerResults =
        myCodeDomProvider.CompileAssemblyFromDom(myCompilerParameters,
                                                 myCodeCompileUnit);
    Assembly assembly = myCompilerResults.CompiledAssembly;

    if (!EnableCaching)
      return assembly;

    Cache cache = HttpContext.Current.Cache;
    if (cache[CacheKeyDependency] != null)
      cache.Remove(CacheKeyDependency);

    DateTime absoluteExpiration = Cache.NoAbsoluteExpiration;
    TimeSpan slidingExpiration = Cache.NoSlidingExpiration;

    if (CacheExpirationPolicy ==
            XmlWebServiceMethodInvokerCacheExpirationPolicy.Absolute)
```

```
          absoluteExpiration = DateTime.UtcNow.AddSeconds((CacheDuration == 0) ?
                                ((double)0x7fffffff) : ((double)CacheDuration));
       else
          slidingExpiration = TimeSpan.FromSeconds((double)CacheDuration);

       cache.Insert(CacheKeyDependency, assembly, null, absoluteExpiration,
                    slidingExpiration);
       return assembly;
   }
```

The `CompileCodeForProxyClass` method first checks whether caching is enabled. If so, it uses the `HttpContext` object to access the `Cache` object:

```
   Cache cache = HttpContext.Current.Cache;
```

It then uses the value of the `CacheKeyDependency` property as an index into the `Cache` collection object to access and to remove the old cache entry:

```
   if (cache[CacheKeyDependency] != null)
      cache.Remove(CacheKeyDependency);
```

The method then declares two local variables of type `DateTime` and `TimeSpan` and sets their initial values to the `Cache.NoAbsoluteExpiration` and `Cache.NoSlidingExpiration` values, respectively. As you'll see shortly, these initial values ensure that only the value of one of these variables is set.

```
   DateTime absoluteExpiration = Cache.NoAbsoluteExpiration;
   TimeSpan slidingExpiration = Cache.NoSlidingExpiration;
```

It then checks whether the value of the `CacheDependencyPolicy` property is set to `Absolute`. If so, it sets the value of the `absoluteExpiration` variable:

```
   absoluteExpiration = DateTime.UtcNow.AddSeconds((CacheDuration == 0) ?
                         ((double)0x7fffffff) : ((double)CacheDuration));
```

If the value of the `CacheDependencyPolicy` property is set to `Sliding`, it sets the value of the `slidingExpiration` variable:

```
   slidingExpiration = TimeSpan.FromSeconds((double)CacheDuration);
```

Finally, the method inserts a new cache entry:

```
   cache.Insert(CacheKeyDependency, assembly, null, absoluteExpiration,
                slidingExpiration);
```

InvokeXmlWebServiceMethod

Listing 10-13 contains the code for the new version of the `InvokeXmlWebServiceMethod` of the `XmlWebServiceMethodInvoker` component that uses the cached compiled proxy class.

Listing 10-13: The InvokeXmlWebServiceMethod method uses the cached compiled proxy class

```
public virtual object InvokeXmlWebServiceMethod(string methodName,
                        IOrderedDictionary methodArgumentNamesAndValues,
                        bool validateAndSortMethodArgumentNamesAndValues)
{
  Assembly assembly = null;

  Cache cache = HttpContext.Current.Cache;
  if (EnableCaching && cache[CacheKeyDependency] != null)
    assembly = (Assembly)cache[CacheKeyDependency];

  else
  {
    XmlReader WSDLDocument = DownloadWSDLDocument();
    ServiceDescription WSDLDocumentDescription =
                            DeserializeWSDLDocument(WSDLDocument);
    CodeCompileUnit myCodeCompileUnit = new CodeCompileUnit();

    ServiceDescriptionImportWarnings warnings =
          GenerateCodeForProxyClass(WSDLDocumentDescription, myCodeCompileUnit);

    if (warnings == 0)
      assembly = CompileCodeForProxyClass(myCodeCompileUnit);
  }

  if (assembly != null)
  {
    object proxyInstance = CreateProxyClassInstance(assembly);
    return InvokeProxyClassInstanceMethod(methodName, methodArgumentNamesAndValues,
            proxyInstance, validateAndSortMethodArgumentNamesAndValues);
  }

  return null;
}
```

If caching is enabled, the InvokeXmlWebServiceMethod method uses the value of the CacheKeyDependency property as an index into the Cache collection object to check whether the compiled proxy class has already been cached. If so, it uses the cached compiled proxy class and bypasses the expensive logic that downloads the WSDL document, deserializes the ServiceDescription object, generates the code for the proxy class, and compiles the proxy code.

Using the Caching Feature

Listing 10-14 contains the code for the new version of the ClickCallback method that sets the CacheExpirationPolicy, CacheDuration, and EnableCaching properties of the XmlWebService MethodInvoker component to cache the compiled proxy class in order to improve the performance of the client application.

Listing 10-14: The ClickCallback method

```
void ClickCallback(object sender, EventArgs e)
{
  XmlWebServiceMethodInvoker methodInvoker = new XmlWebServiceMethodInvoker();
  methodInvoker.TypeName = "Service";
  methodInvoker.WSDLPath = "http://localhost:9746/Server/Service.asmx?wsdl";
  methodInvoker.CacheExpirationPolicy =
                      XmlWebServiceMethodInvokerCacheExpirationPolicy.Absolute;
  methodInvoker.CacheDuration = 600;
  methodInvoker.EnableCaching = true;
  OrderedDictionary list = new OrderedDictionary();
  list.Add("x", int.Parse(FirstIntegerNumber.Text));
  list.Add("y", int.Parse(SecondIntegerNumber.Text));
  int result = (int)methodInvoker.InvokeXmlWebServiceMethod("Add", list, false);
  Result.Text = result.ToString();
}
```

Next, implement a new version of the client application that will help you understand the role of the CacheKeyDependency property in the overall caching capability of the XmlWebServiceMethodInvoker component. Listing 10-15 and Figure 10-5 illustrate a new version of the client application that uses a new button named Clear Cache.

Listing 10-15: The version of the client application that allows you to clear the cache

```
<%@ Page Language="C#" AutoEventWireup="true"
CodeFile="XmlWebServiceMethodInvoker2.aspx.cs"
Inherits="XmlWebServiceMethodInvoker2" %>
<html xmlns="http://www.w3.org/1999/xhtml">
<body>
  <form id="form1" runat="server">
    <table width="100%" border="0">
      <tr>
        <td align="right" width="200px">
          <strong>First Integer Number:</strong></td>
        <td align="left">
          <asp:TextBox runat="Server" ID="FirstIntegerNumber" /></td>
      </tr>
      <tr>
        <td align="right" width="200px">
          <strong>Second Integer Number:</strong></td>
        <td align="left">
          <asp:TextBox runat="Server" ID="SecondIntegerNumber" /></td>
      </tr>
      <tr>
        <td align="right" width="200px">
          <strong>Result:</strong></td>
        <td align="left">
          <asp:Label runat="Server" ID="Result" /></td>
      </tr>
      <tr>
        <td align="right">
          <asp:Button ID="Button2" runat="Server" Text="Clear Cache"
```

(continued)

Listing 10-15: *(continued)*

```
            OnClick="ClearCacheCallback" /></td>
        <td align="left">
          <asp:Button ID="Button1" runat="Server" Text="Submit"
          OnClick="ClickCallback" /></td>
      </tr>
    </table>
  </form>
</body>
</html>
```

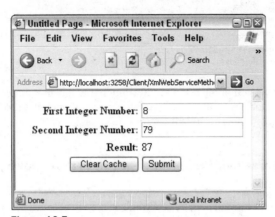

Figure 10-5

As Listing 10-16 shows, the `ClickCallback` method specifies a value for the `CacheKeyDependency` property to instruct the `XmlWebServiceMethodInvoker` component to cache the compiled proxy class under the specified key.

Listing 10-16: The ClickCallback method specifies a value for the CacheKeyDependency property

```
protected void ClickCallback(object sender, EventArgs e)
{
  XmlWebServiceMethodInvoker methodInvoker = new XmlWebServiceMethodInvoker();
  methodInvoker.TypeName = "Service";
  methodInvoker.WSDLPath = "http://localhost:3778/Server/Service.asmx?WSDL";
  methodInvoker.CacheExpirationPolicy =
                    XmlWebServiceMethodInvokerCacheExpirationPolicy.Absolute;
  methodInvoker.CacheDuration = 600;
  methodInvoker.EnableCaching = true;
  methodInvoker.CacheKeyDependency = "CompiledProxyClassKey";
  OrderedDictionary list = new OrderedDictionary();
  list.Add("x", int.Parse(FirstIntegerNumber.Text));
  list.Add("y", int.Parse(SecondIntegerNumber.Text));
  int result = (int)methodInvoker.InvokeXmlWebServiceMethod("Add", list, false);
  Result.Text = result.ToString();
}
```

Listing 10-17 contains the code for the `ClearCacheCallback` method. When you click the Clear Cache button, this method calls the `Remove` method of the `Cache` object and passes the same string value assigned to the `CacheKeyDependency` property of the `XmlWebServiceMethodInvoker` component into it to remove the cached compiled proxy from the `Cache` object.

Listing 10-17: The ClearCacheCallback method

```
protected void ClearCacheCallback(object sender, EventArgs e)
{
  if (EnableCaching && Cache["CompiledProxyClassKey"] != null)
    Cache.Remove("CompiledProxyClassKey");
}
```

Try the following workflow to see the difference in performance when the item is removed from the cache:

1. Enter two numbers in the `TextBox` controls and click the Submit button. Notice the degradation of performance due to the fact that the compiled proxy hasn't been cached yet.

2. Enter two new numbers and click the Submit button. Notice the dramatic improvement in performance due to the fact that the cached compiled proxy is used.

3. Click the Clear Cache button to remove the cached compiled proxy from the `Cache` object.

4. Enter two new numbers and click the `Submit` button. Notice the degradation of performance again.

Developing XML Web Service–Enabled Custom Controls

You've been enhancing the `CreditCardForm` custom control over the course of last few chapters. This section implements a new version of this control named `XmlWebServiceCreditCardForm` that derives from the `CompositeCreditCardForm` control developed in Chapter 5 and extends its functionality to use a specified XML Web service to automatically validate the user's credit card information without a single line of code from the page developer.

The `XmlWebServiceCreditCardForm` control exposes a method named `Validate` (shown in Listing 10-18) that uses the `XmlWebServiceMethodInvoker` component to invoke the method of the underlying XML Web service that validates credit card information.

Listing 10-18: The Validate method

```
protected virtual bool Validate(PaymentMethod paymentMethod,string creditCardNo,
                                string cardholderName, DateTime expirationDate)
{
  XmlWebServiceMethodInvoker methodInvoker = new XmlWebServiceMethodInvoker();
  methodInvoker.TypeName = TypeName;
  methodInvoker.WSDLPath = WSDLPath;
  methodInvoker.EnableCaching = true;
  methodInvoker.CacheExpirationPolicy =
                    XmlWebServiceMethodInvokerCacheExpirationPolicy.Absolute;
```

(continued)

Listing 10-18: *(continued)*

```
    methodInvoker.CacheDuration = 600;
    OrderedDictionary list = new OrderedDictionary();
    list.Add(PaymentMethodParameterName, paymentMethod);
    list.Add(CreditCardNoParameterName, creditCardNo);
    list.Add(CardholderNameParameterName, cardholderName);
    list.Add(ExpirationDateParameterName, expirationDate);
    return (bool)methodInvoker.InvokeXmlWebServiceMethod(MethodName, list, true);
}
```

The `XmlWebServiceCreditCardForm` exposes the following new properties:

❑   `TypeName`: Gets and sets the fully qualified name of the class that represents the XML Web service

❑   `WSDLPath`: Gets and sets the URL of the site where the WSDL document can be downloaded

❑   `MethodName`: Gets and sets the name of the XML Web service method that validates the credit card information

❑   `PaymentMethodParameterName`: Gets and sets the name of the XML Web service method parameter that specifies the payment method

❑   `CreditCardNoParameterName`: Gets and sets the name of the XML Web service method parameter that specifies the credit card number

❑   `CardholderNameParameterName`: Gets and sets the name of the XML Web service method parameter that specifies the cardholder's name

❑   `ExpirationDateParameterName`: Gets and sets the name of the XML Web service parameter method that specifies the expiration date

The `XmlWebServiceCreditCardForm` control's implementation of the `OnBubbleEvent` method calls the `Validate` method before it raises the `ValidateCreditCard` event. That's all there is to it. As you can see it's really easy to use the `XmlWebSerivceMethodInvoker` component to develop XML Web service–enabled custom components:

```
protected override bool OnBubbleEvent(object source, EventArgs args)
{
  bool handled = false;

  CommandEventArgs ce = args as CommandEventArgs;
  if (ce != null && ce.CommandName == "ValidateCreditCard")
  {
    PaymentMethod paymentMethod = GetPaymentMethod();
    string creditCardNo = GetCreditCardNo();
    string cardholderName = GetCardholderName();
    DateTime expirationDate = GetExpirationDate();

    if (Validate())
    {
      ValidateCreditCardEventArgs ve =
          new ValidateCreditCardEventArgs(paymentMethod, creditCardNo,
                                  cardholderName, expirationDate);
```

```
            OnValidateCreditCard(ve);
        }
        handled = true;
    }

    return handled;
}
```

The following code contains a page where the page developer uses the `XmlWebServiceCreditCardForm` control without writing any C# or VB.NET code. It's all done declaratively!

```
<%@ Page Language="C#" AutoEventWireup="true"
CodeFile="XmlWebServiceCreditCardForm.aspx.cs" Inherits="_Default" %>

<%@ Register TagPrefix="custom" Namespace="CustomComponents" %>
<!DOCTYPE html PUBLIC "-//W3C//DTD XHTML 1.1//EN"
"http://www.w3.org/TR/xhtml11/DTD/xhtml11.dtd">
<html xmlns="http://www.w3.org/1999/xhtml">
<head runat="server">
  <title>Untitled Page</title>
</head>
<body>
  <form id="form1" runat="server">
    <custom:XmlWebServiceCreditCardForm ID="ccf" runat="server" Font-Bold="true"
    OnValidateCreditCard="ValidateCreditCard" SubmitButtonText="Submit"
    CardholderNameText="Cardholder's Name" CreditCardNoText="Credit Card No."
    PaymentMethodText="Payment Method" ExpirationDateText="Expiration Date"
    MethodName="ValidateCreditCard" TypeName="Service"
    PaymentMethodParameterName="paymentMethod"
    CreditCardNoParameterName="creditCardNo"
    CardholderNameParameterName="cardholderName"
    ExpirationDateParameterName="expirationDate"
    WSDLPath="http://localhost:1735/Server/Service.asmx?WSDL" />
    <br />
    <br />
    <asp:Label runat="server" ID="info" />
  </form>
</body>
</html>
```

XmlWebServiceResolver

This section uses the `XmlWebServiceMethodInvoker` component to develop a real-world custom `XmlResolver` named `XmlWebServiceResolver` that you can use in your own applications.

XMLResolver

Listing 10-19 contains the definition of the `XmlResolver` base class.

Listing 10-19: The XmlResolver base class

```
public abstract class XmlResolver
{
   public abstract object GetEntity(Uri absoluteUri, string role,
                                    Type TypeOfObjectToReturn);
   public virtual Uri ResolveUri(Uri baseUri, string relativeUri);
   public abstract ICredentials Credentials { set; }
}
```

As this listing illustrates, this base class exposes two methods named ResolveUri and GetEntity and one property named Credentials. The .NET Framework comes with two concrete implementations or subclasses of the XmlResolver abstract base class: XmlUrlResolver and XmlSecureResolver.

You can think of the methods and property of the XmlResovler abstract base class as the API that the clients of its subclasses such as XmlUrlResolver use to interact with them. Each subclass such as XmlUrlResovler provides its own implementation of this API.

To help you understand the methods and property of the XmlResolver base class, that is, the XmlResolver API, consider the example shown in Listing 10-20 where the XmlResovler is used.

Listing 10-20: The code fragment that uses the XmlResovler

```
XmlReaderSettings settings = new XmlReaderSettings();
settings.IgnoreComments = true;
settings.XmlResolver = new XmlUrlResolver();
XmlReader reader1 = XmlReader.Create("rss.xml", settings);
```

As Listing 10-20 illustrates, the XmlReader class exposes a static method named Create that takes the URI of an XML document (such as rss.xml) as an argument, creates an XmlReader instance, and loads the instance with the contents of the XML document that the URI references. Notice that the Create method takes an instance of a .NET class named XmlReaderSettings as its second argument. You can use this instance to specify the features that you'd like the XmlReader instance being created to support. For example, Listing 10-20 sets the IgnoreComments property of the XmlReaderSettings instance to specify that the XmlReader instance being created must ignore the comments that the rss.xml document contains. Notice that Listing 10-20 also assigns an XmlUrlResolver instance to the XmlResolver property of the XmlReaderSettings instance. This property is of type XmlResolver.

Now take a look under the hood of the Create static method of the XmlReader class where all the action is. Listing 10-21 contains the simplified version of the code for the Create method.

Listing 10-21: The simplified version of the Create method

```
public static XmlReader Create(string inputUri, XmlReaderSettings settings)
{
   XmlResolver resolver = settings.GetXmlResolver();
   Uri uri = resolver.ResolveUri(null, inputUri);
   Stream stream = (Stream)resolver.GetEntity(uri, string.Empty, typeof(Stream));
   // the code that creates the XmlReader object goes here
}
```

The `Create` method first Calls the `GetXmlResolver` method of the `XmlReaderSettings` instance to access the `XmlResolver` instance that the `XmlResolver` property of the `XmlReaderSettings` instance references. Recall that Listing 10-20 assigned an `XmlUrlResolver` instance to this property. The `GetXmlResolver` method returns this `XmlUrlResolver` instance as an `XmlResolver` instance, not an `XmlUrlResolver` instance. In other words, the `Create` method treats this `XmlUrlResolver` instance as an `XmlResolver` instance, not an `XmlUrlResolver` instance. This allows the method to work with all subclasses of the `XmlResolver` base class.

```
XmlResolver resolver = GetXmlResolver();
```

The method then calls the `ResolveUri` method of the `XmlResolver` instance that the `GetXmlResolver` method returns. Recall that each subclass of the `XmlResolver` base class provides its own implementation for the `ResolveUri` method. This means that the `XmlUrlResolver`'s implementation is being used under the hood.

```
Uri uri = resolver.ResolveUri(null, inputUri);
```

This step is important because the `rss.xml` URI is relative, not absolute. The absolute URI in this case would be something like the following:

```
file:///D:/Dir1/Dir2/rss.xml
```

The absolute URI begins with what is known as *URI scheme*. In this case, the URI scheme is `file://`. The main responsibility of the `ResolveUri` method is to resolve the relative URI passed into it (such as `rss.xml` URI) and return an `Uri` object that contains the absolute URI. This `Uri` object contains the complete information needed to locate the resource that the `Uri` references.

The `Create` method then calls the `GetEntity` method of the `XmlResolver` instance that the `GetXmlResolver` method returns and passes the `Uri` object into it:

```
Stream stream = (Stream)resolver.GetEntity(uri, string.Empty, typeof(Stream));
```

Recall that each subclass of the `XmlResolver` base class provides its own implementation for the `GetEntity` method. Therefore, what this method does under the hood depends on the particular `XmlResolver` subclass being used. In this case, the `XmlUrlResolver`'s implementation of the `GetEntity` method is used under the hood.

Each `XmlResolver` subclass's implementation of the `GetEntity` method must use the `Uri` object passed into it to locate the specified resource (the `rss.xml` file), load the resource into an appropriate object, and return the object to its caller. This object is normally of type `Stream`.

Therefore, as Figure 10-6 illustrates, the communication between `XmlResolver` and its client such as `XmlReader` involves four steps:

1. The client (`XmlReader`) calls the `ResolveUri` method and passes two argument values — the base URI and relative URI of the resource (`rss.xml`) — into it.

2. `ResolveUri` uses the base URI to resolve the relative URI and returns a `Uri` object that contains the absolute URI.

3. The client calls the `GetEntity` method and passes the preceding `Uri` object into it.

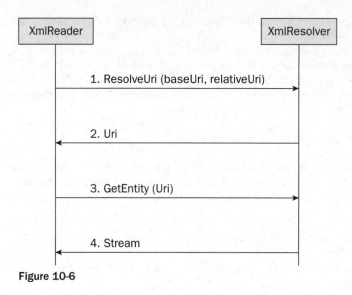

Figure 10-6

4. GetEntity uses the Uri object to locate the resource and returns a Stream object that streams out the resource.

As Figure 10-7 shows, the XmlResolver API shields the clients (XmlReader) from different implementations of the API, allowing them to work with all XmlResolver subclasses. You can think of the ResolveUri and GetEntity methods as the contract between XmlResolver subclasses and their clients. As long as these subclasses honor the contract, that is, as long as they implement these methods, the clients don't care which subclass is being used. In other words, you can switch from one subclass to another without breaking the client code. You may be wondering why you would want to switch from one subclass to another.

Each subclass is specifically designed to resolve URIs with specific schemes. For example, the XmlUrlResolver subclass is specifically designed to resolve URIs with file:// schemes (such as file:///D:/Dir1/rss.xml) and http:// schemes (such as http://msdn.microsoft.com/rss .xml). Later in this chapter you'll implement a new subclass of the XmlResolver named XmlWebServiceResolver that resolves URIs with the webservice:// custom scheme.

Each scheme corresponds to a specific source. For example, URIs with the file:// scheme reference resources that reside in a file system. URIs with the http:// scheme, on the other hand, reference resources that reside on a remote site and can be accessed via HTTP protocol. As you'll see later, the webservice:// custom scheme references resources that reside on a remote site and can be accessed via an XML Web service.

In conclusion, each subclass is specifically designed to locate and to retrieve resources from specific type of source. For example, the XmlUrlResolver subclass is specifically designed to locate and retrieve resources from a file system or remote site via HTTP protocol. As you'll see later, the XmlWebServiceResolver will be designed to locate and to retrieve resources from remote sites via XML Web services.

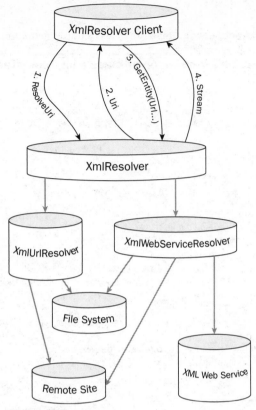

Figure 10-7

Therefore you switch from one subclass to another so you can retrieve resources from a different source. For example, you can switch to XmlWebServiceResolver subclass so you can download a resource from an XML Web service. As Figure 10-7 shows, the XmlResolver shields the clients (for example, XmlReader) from the specific type of the subclass being used. As long as the subclass returns a Uri object when the client calls its ResolveUri method and returns a Stream (that contains the resource) when the client calls its GetEntity method, the client doesn't care which subclass is being used. In other words, the client doesn't care from what source the resource is being retrieved, whether it's retrieved from a file system, from a remote site via HTTP protocol, or from an XML Web service.

Now you get down to the implementation of the XmlWebServiceResolver class, which derives from the XmlUrlResolver class. This will provide you with the following two benefits:

❑ You can use the XmlUrlResolver class's implementation of the ResolveUri method. This saves you from having to implement the method.

❑ The XmlWebServiceResolver will automatically support the schemes that the XmlUrlResolver class supports, such as file:// and http://

GetEntity

Listing 10-22 shows the XmlWebServiceResolver class's implementation of the GetEntity method.

Listing 10-22: The XmlWebSericeResolver class's implementation of the GetEntity method

```
public override object
GetEntity(Uri absoluteUri, string role, Type ofObjectToReturn)
{
  Stream stream = null;

  switch (absoluteUri.Scheme)
  {
    case "webservice":
      XmlWebServiceMethodInvoker methodInvoker = new XmlWebServiceMethodInvoker();
      methodInvoker.TypeName = TypeName;
      methodInvoker.WSDLPath = WSDLPath;
      methodInvoker.CacheDuration = 600;
      methodInvoker.CacheExpirationPolicy =
                      XmlWebServiceMethodInvokerCacheExpirationPolicy.Absolute;
      methodInvoker.EnableCaching = true;

      OrderedDictionary list = new OrderedDictionary();
      string result =
          (string)methodInvoker.InvokeXmlWebServiceMethod(SelectMethod, list, false);
      byte[] bytes = System.Text.Encoding.UTF8.GetBytes(result);
      stream = new MemoryStream(bytes);
      break;
    default:
      stream = (Stream) base.GetEntity(absoluteUri, role, ofObjectToReturn);
      break;
  }

  return stream;
}
```

The GetEntity method takes three arguments. The first argument is an object of type Uri. Recall that the clients of an XmlResolver implementation call the ResolveUri method to access the Uri object and pass the object as an argument to the GetEntity method. The XmlWebServiceResolver doesn't use the second and the third arguments.

The GetEntity method uses the value of the Scheme property of the Uri object to determine what to do next. Notice that the switch statement consists of two parts. The first part handles the custom scheme (webservice), while the second part delegates the responsibility of handling other schemes such as file:// and http:// to the base class, XmlUrlResolver. The XmlWebServiceResolver class supports all the schemes that the XmlUrlResolver supports, which means that you can use the XmlWebServiceResolver to locate and to retrieve resources (such as rss.xml) from file systems, remote sites via HTTP protocol, and XML Web services.

The GetEntity method retrieves the XML data from the underling XML Web service by first creating an instance of the XmlWebServiceMethodInvoker class:

```
XmlWebServiceMethodInvoker methodInvoker = new XmlWebServiceMethodInvoker();
```

Then it sets the value of the `TypeName` property of the instance:

```
methodInvoker.TypeName = TypeName;
```

The method next sets the value of the `WSDLPath` property of the instance:

```
methodInvoker.WSDLPath = WSDLPath;
```

Next it creates an instance of the `OrderedDictionary` class:

```
OrderedDictionary list = new OrderedDictionary();
```

It then calls `InvokeXmlWebServiceMethod`:

```
string result = (string)methodInvoker.InvokeXmlWebServiceMethod(SelectMethod,
                                                    list, false);
```

Finally, it creates and returns a `MemoryStream` object that contains the XML data:

```
byte[] bytes = System.Text.Encoding.UTF8.GetBytes(result);
stream = new MemoryStream(bytes);
```

The `XmlWebServiceResolver` class exposes three properties of its own, as follows:

❑   `TypeName`: The fully qualified name of the class that represents the XML Web service

❑   `SelectMethod`: The method of the XML Web service to be invoked

❑   `WSDLPath`: The URL of the location from where the WSDL document can be downloaded

Consider an example of a simple page that uses the `XmlWebServiceResolver`. The example consists of a client and a server application. The server application is a simple Web service. The client application uses the `XmlWebServiceResolver` class to retrieve XML data from the server, as shown in Listing 10-23.

Listing 10-23: A simple client application that uses the XmlWebServiceResolver class

```
protected void Page_Load(object sender, EventArgs e)
{
  CustomComponents.XmlWebServiceResolver resolver =
                              new CustomComponents.XmlWebServiceResolver();
  resolver.TypeName = "Service";
  resolver.SelectMethod = "Select";
  resolver.WSDLPath = "http://localhost:1591/Server/Service.asmx?WSDL";

  XmlReaderSettings settings = new XmlReaderSettings();
  settings.XmlResolver = resolver;

  using (XmlReader reader = XmlReader.Create("webservice://",settings))
  {
```

(continued)

Listing 10-23: *(continued)*

```
      reader.MoveToContent();
      MySource.Data = reader.ReadOuterXml();
  }
}
```

The client first creates an instance of the `XmlWebServiceResolver` class:

```
CustomComponents.XmlWebServiceResolver resolver =
                            new CustomComponents.XmlWebServiceResolver();
```

Then it sets the `TypeName` property of the instance to the fully qualified name of the class that represents the XML Web service (`Service`, in this case):

```
resolver.TypeName = "Service";
```

Next it sets the `SelectMethod` property of the instance to the name of the method of the XML Web service that retrieves XML data from the underlying data store (`Select`, in this case):

```
resolver.SelectMethod = "Select";
```

The client then sets the `WSDLPath` property of the instance to the URL of the site where the WSDL document can be downloaded:

```
resolver.WSDLPath = "http://localhost:1396/Server/Service.asmx?WSDL";
```

Next it creates an instance of the `XmlReaderSettings` class and assigns the `XmlWebServiceResolver` instance to its `XmlResolver` property:

```
XmlReaderSettings settings = new XmlReaderSettings();
settings.XmlResolver = resolver;
```

Finally, it passes the string value `webservice://` and the `XmlReaderSettings` instance to the `Create` method of the `XmlReader` class to instantiate an `XmlReader` object:

```
XmlReader reader = XmlReader.Create("webservice://", settings)
```

Also notice that Listing 10-23 takes advantage of a new feature of the `XmlReader` class in the .NET 2.0 Framework. The `XmlReader` class in .NET 2.0 implements the `IDisposable` interface. This allows developers to use the class in C# or VB.NET `using` statement. Recall that the `using` statement automatically calls the `Dispose` method of the class when the class instance goes out of scope. The `Dispose` method of the `XmlReader` class calls its `Close` method. The recommended practice in .NET 2.0 Framework is to use the `XmlReader` class in a `using` statement. This way you can avoid the bugs in cases where you may forget to call the `Close` method when the `XmlReader` class goes out of scope.

The client invokes the `Select` method of the underlying XML Web service, shown in Listing 10-24 to retrieve the XML data and display the data as shown in Figure 10-8.

Listing 10-24: The XML Web service

```csharp
public class Service : System.Web.Services.WebService
{
  [WebMethod]
  public string Select()
  {
    string str = string.Empty;

    using (XmlReader reader = XmlReader.Create(Server.MapPath("data.xml")))
    {
      reader.MoveToContent();
      str = reader.ReadOuterXml();
    }

    return str;
  }
}
```

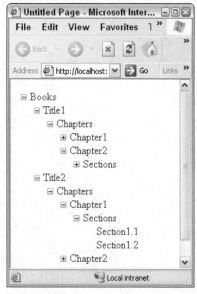

Figure 10-8

Summary

This chapter used a step-by-step approach to implement three XML Web service-based custom components:

1.   A custom component named XmlWebServiceMethodInvoker that exposes an important method named InvokeXmlWebServiceMethod. This method is all you need to enable your custom components to dynamically invoke the methods of XML Web services. The following

chapters use the `XmlWebServiceMethodInvoker` component to implement custom components that use XML Web services as their underlying data stores.

2. A new version of the `CreditCardForm` custom control that uses the `XmlWebServiceMethodInvoker` component to invoke the XML Web service method that validates credit card information.

3. A custom `XmlResolver` named `XmlWebServiceResolver` that uses the `XmlWebServiceMethodInvoker` component to allow other classes in the `System.Xml` namespace to retrieve XML data from XML Web services.

This chapter showed you how the ASP.NET XML Web service infrastructure generates the code for the proxy class. The next chapter shows you how you can intervene in this proxy code generation process to customize the proxy code.

Implementing Schema Importer Extensions and ISerializable Interface

As discussed in the previous chapter, the ASP.NET XML Web service infrastructure uses the content of the WSDL document to generate the code for the proxy class. This infrastructure uses an internal default mapping to determine what .NET types map to the XSD types used in the WSDL document and generates the code for these .NET types.

The ASP.NET 2.0 Framework allows you to bypass this internal default mapping of the ASP.NET XML Web service infrastructure to map your own custom .NET types to these XSD types and generate the code for these .NET types instead. In other words, this allows you to customize the code for the proxy class.

You must take two steps to accomplish this task. First, you'll need to implement the IXmlSerializable interface. Implementing this interface allows your custom components to take full control of their serialization/deserialization process. Next, you'll need to implement a custom schema importer extension to generate the code for the .NET type that you want to map to a specified XSD type.

You can use the skills you learn in this chapter to improve the performance and responsiveness of XML Web services that service huge amount of data by having the server to send the data in chunks and the client to read the data in chunks.

Implementing IXmlSerializable

This section shows you how to develop custom components that take full control of their serialization and deserialization mechanisms. These components must implement the IXmlSerializable interface, which exposes three methods: GetSchema, ReadXml, and WriteXml. The GetSchema method takes no arguments and returns an instance of the XmlSchema class. This method is reserved and shouldn't be used.

Your custom components implement the ReadXml method to take full control of their deserialization mechanism. This method allows these components to deserialize themselves from a given XML representation or document. The ReadXml method takes an XmlReader instance as its argument, which the component uses to access the contents of the XML document and populates its own properties with the appropriate values from the XML document.

Your custom components implement the WriteXml method to take full control of their serialization mechanism. The WriteXml method takes an XmlWriter instance, which these components use to generate the appropriate XML representations.

You must annotate your component with the XmlSchemaProvider metadata attribute. This attribute is used to specify the name of the method that generates the XML schema document that fully describes the structure of the XML document that the WriteXml method generates and the ReadXml method consumes.

To make the discussion in more concrete, this chapter uses an example in which the client side is a discussion forum application that creates one forum for each newly published book. The visitors of the forum application navigate to a given book forum to post their comments about the particular book. The client application retrieves the information about a newly published book from an XML Web service. To keep the discussions focused, the example does not implement the GUI that allows visitors to post their comments.

The client and server applications in this example have different requirements. Because the server side is a repository of information about books, it makes lot of sense to have a server-side component named Book that exposes properties such as Title and Author.

Because the client side is a discussion forum application, it makes lot of sense to have a client-side component named Forum that exposes properties such as Title, Messages, and Moderator. The forum application uses the title and author of a book in the title of the respective forum. In other words, both the Title and Author properties of the server-side Book component are mapped to the Title property of the client-side Forum component.

The server-side Book component implements the IXmlSerializable interface to take full control of its XML representation. The client-side Forum component implements the IXmlSerializable interface to deserialize itself from the XML representation of its respective server-side Book component.

Implementing the Server-Side Component

Listing 11-1 contains the code for the Book class. The implementation of the methods of this class is discussed in the following sections.

Listing 11-1: The Book class

```
public class Book : IXmlSerializable
{
  private string title;
```

```
    private string author;

    public string Title
    {
      get { return title; }
      set { title = value; }
    }

    public string Author
    {
      get { return author; }
      set { author = value; }
    }

    public static XmlQualifiedName BookSchema(XmlSchemaSet xs)
    {
      . . .
    }

    XmlSchema IXmlSerializable.GetSchema()
    {
      return null;
    }

    void IXmlSerializable.ReadXml(XmlReader reader) {}

    void IXmlSerializable.WriteXml(XmlWriter writer)
    {
      . . .
    }
}
```

WriteXml

The Book class implements the WriteXml method, which uses the XmlWriter instance, passed in as input argument, to generate its XML representation (see Listing 11-2). This XML representation like all XML documents contains a single outermost or containing element known as document element. The document element in this case is the <book> element.

The WriteXml method calls the WriteAttributeString method of the XmlWriter instance to serialize its title and author fields into XML attributes. Notice that your custom component's implementation of the WriteXml method mustn't generate the document element of your component's XML representation.

Listing 11-2: The WriteXml method generates the appropriate XML representation

```
void IXmlSerializable.WriteXml(XmlWriter writer)
{
  writer.WriteAttributeString("title", title);
  writer.WriteAttributeString("author", author);
}
```

For example, the implementation of the `WriteXml` method shown in the following code generates the `book` element as the child element of the containing element, which is not what you want:

```
void IXmlSerializable.WriteXml(XmlWriter writer)
{
  writer.WriteStartElement("book", http://books);
  writer.WriteAttributeString("title", title);
  writer.WriteAttributeString("author", author);
  writer.WriteEndElement();
}
```

BookSchema

You must annotate your custom component with the `XmlSchemaProviderAttribute` to specify which method of your component generates the schema document. This schema must describe the structure of the XML document that the `WriteXml` method generates (see Listing 11-2). Any mismatch will result in runtime errors. The method that generates the XML schema (`BookSchema`) must be a static, public method that takes a single argument of type `XmlSchemaSet` and returns an object of type `XmlQualifiedName`. This return value must contain the name and the namespace of the document element, which is the `<book>` element in this case.

There are two approaches to implementing the method that generates the XML schema document, as discussed in the following sections.

Using an External XML Schema File

You can use the W3C XML Schema markup language to externally write the XML schema document and save the document in a file with extension `.xsd`. Listing 11-3 shows the XML schema document for the `Book` class.

Listing 11-3: The XML schema document

```
<schema xmlns="http://www.w3.org/2001/XMLSchema" targetNamespace="http://books"
xmlns:tns="http://books" elementFormDefault="qualified"
attributeFormDefault="unqualified">
  <complexType name="book">
    <sequence />
    <attribute name="title" type="string" />
    <attribute name="author" type="string" />
  </complexType>
</schema>
```

Listing 11-4 contains the code for the `BookSchema` method. Notice that the `Book` class is annotated with the `XmlSchemaProvider` attribute to specify that this method generates the schema document.

Listing 11-4: The BookSchema method generates the appropriate XML schema

```
[XmlSchemaProvider("BookSchema")]
public class Book : IXmlSerializable
{
  public static XmlQualifiedName BookSchema(XmlSchemaSet xs)
  {
    XmlSerializer serializer = new XmlSerializer(typeof(XmlSchema));
    XmlReader reader =
```

```
                        XmlReader.Create(HttpContext.Current.Server.MapPath("Book.xsd"));
        XmlSchema schema = (XmlSchema)serializer.Deserialize(reader);
        xs.Add(schema);
        return new XmlQualifiedName("book", "http://books");
    }
}
```

BookSchema instantiates an XmlSerializer object and calls its Deserialize method to deserialize an XmlSchema object from the contents of the specified schema file. The BookSchema method then adds the XmlSchema object to the XmlSchemaSet collection that is passed into it as its sole argument. Finally, the method returns an XmlQualifiedName object that contains the name and namespace of the document element of the XML representation of the Book component.

This approach to schema generation is very convenient because it's much easier to use the W3C XML schema markup language to write the schema document. However, this convenience comes with a price. You lose the flexibility and extensibility that the second approach to dynamic schema generation provides.

Using the System.Xml.Schema Classes

Listing 11-5 contains the code for the second version of the BookSchema method.

Listing 11-5: The BookSchema method generates the appropriate XML schema

```
[XmlSchemaProvider("BookSchema")]
public class Book : IXmlSerializable
{
    public static XmlQualifiedName BookSchema(XmlSchemaSet xs)
    {
        XmlSchema schema = new XmlSchema();
        schema.TargetNamespace = "http://books";
        schema.ElementFormDefault = XmlSchemaForm.Qualified;
        schema.AttributeFormDefault = XmlSchemaForm.Unqualified;

        XmlSchemaComplexType book = new XmlSchemaComplexType();
        book.Particle = new XmlSchemaSequence();
        book.Name = "book";

        XmlSchemaAttribute title = new XmlSchemaAttribute();
        title.Name = "title";
        title.SchemaTypeName =
                new XmlQualifiedName("string", "http://www.w3.org/2001/XMLSchema");
        book.Attributes.Add(title);

        XmlSchemaAttribute author = new XmlSchemaAttribute();
        author.Name = "author";
        author.SchemaTypeName =
                new XmlQualifiedName("string", "http://www.w3.org/2001/XMLSchema");
        book.Attributes.Add(author);

        schema.Items.Add(book);
        xs.Add(schema);
        return new XmlQualifiedName("book", "http://books");
    }
}
```

This version uses the classes in `System.Xml.Schema` namespace to dynamically generate the appropriate XML schema document. The `System.Xml.Schema` namespace exposes one class for each W3C XML schema construct.

Follow these steps to write a method such as `BookSchema` that uses the classes in `System.Xml.Schema` namespace to dynamically generate an XML schema document at runtime:

1. Use the appropriate W3C XML schema constructs to write the XML schema document (the `.xsd` file) that the method is supposed to generate.

2. Read the XML schema document line by line and identify the appropriate `System.Xml.Schema` namespace class for each W3C XML schema construct used in the document.

Now use these steps to implement the `BookSchema` method. Listing 11-3 shows the XML schema document that uses the W3C XML schema constructs to describe the structure of the XML document that the `WriteXml` method generates. The schema document contains a single XSD complex type named `book` that exposes two attributes and contains no elements. This is because the `WriteXml` method doesn't generate any XML elements.

The next step is to read the XML schema document line by line and identify the appropriate `System.Xml.Schema` namespace classes that represent the W3C XML schema constructs used in the document.

The root element of the schema document in Listing 11-4 is the `<schema targetNamespace="http://books">` element. Create a single instance of the `XmlSchema` class to represent this element, and assign the value of the `targetNamespace` attribute of the element to the `TargetNamespace` property of the instance:

```
XmlSchema schema = new XmlSchema();
schema.TargetNamespace = "http://books";
```

The first child element of the `<schema>` element in Listing 11-4 is the `<complexType name="book">` element. Use an instance of the `XmlSchemaComplexType` class to represent this element and assign the value of the `name` attribute of the element to the `Name` property of the instance:

```
XmlSchemaComplexType book = new XmlSchemaComplexType();
book.Name = "book";
```

The first child element of the `<complexType>` element in Listing 11-4 is an empty `<sequence>` element. Use an instance of the `XmlSchemaSequence` class to represent this empty element and assign the instance to the `Particle` property of the `XmlSchemaComplexType` instance:

```
book.Particle = new XmlSchemaSequence();
```

The second child element of the `<complexType>` element in Listing 11-4 is the `<attribute name="title" type="string">` element. Use an instance of the `XmlSchemaAttribute` class to represent this element and use the values of the `name` and `type` attributes of the element to set the `Name` and `SchemaTypeName` properties of the instance. Notice that the `SchemaTypeName` property is of type

XmlQualifiedName. You also have to add the XmlSchemaAttribute instance to the Attributes collection of the XmlSchemaComplexType instance that represents the book type:

```
XmlSchemaAttribute title = new XmlSchemaAttribute();
title.Name = "title";
title.SchemaTypeName =
            new XmlQualifiedName("string", "http://www.w3.org/2001/XMLSchema");
book.Attributes.Add(title);
```

The third child element of the <complexType> element in Listing 11-4 is the <attribute name="author" type="string"> element. If you treat this element the same as the title element, you arrive at:

```
XmlSchemaAttribute author = new XmlSchemaAttribute();
author.Name = "author";
author.SchemaTypeName =
            new XmlQualifiedName("string", "http://www.w3.org/2001/XMLSchema");
book.Attributes.Add(author);
```

Because the XmlSchemaComplexType instance represents a child element of the <schema> element, you have to add the instance to the Items collection of the XmlSchema instance:

```
schema.Items.Add(book);
```

Recall that the ForumSchema method takes an XmlSchemaSet instance as argument. The XmlSchema instance represents the entire XML schema document. However, this document will not be available until you add the XmlSchema instance to the XmlSchemaSet instance:

```
xs.Add(schema);
```

Finally, use an instance of the XmlQualifiedName class to represent the name and namespace of the <complexType> that defines the schema document:

```
return new XmlQualifiedName("book", "http://books");
```

As mentioned, the GetSchema method of the IXmlSerializable interface is reserved and shouldn't be used to generate the XML schema document. However, you still have to implement the method. This implementation must return null, as shown in the following code:

```
XmlSchema IXmlSerializable.GetSchema()
{
  return null;
}
```

Developing the Client-Side Component

Listing 11-6 contains the code for the Forum class. The implementation of the methods of this class is discussed in the following sections.

Listing 11-6: The Forum class

```
public class Forum : IXmlSerializable
{
  private ArrayList messages;
  private string title;

  public string Title
  {
    get { return title; }
  }

  public ArrayList Messages
  {
    get
    {
      if (messages == null)
        messages = new ArrayList();

      return messages;
    }
  }

  /// <summary>
  /// This method is reserved and must return null
  /// </summary>
  /// <returns></returns>
  XmlSchema IXmlSerializable.GetSchema()
  {
    . . .
  }

  void IXmlSerializable.ReadXml(XmlReader reader)
  {
    . . .
  }

  void IXmlSerializable.WriteXml(XmlWriter writer) {}

  public static XmlQualifiedName ForumSchema(XmlSchemaSet xs)
  {
    . . .
  }
}
```

The Forum class implements the IXmlSerializable interface to deserialize itself from the XML representation of its server-side Book counterpart.

ReadXml

The Forum class implements the ReadXml method where it uses the XmlReader instance, passed in as input argument, to access the title and author property values of its respective Book instance and use them to set its own title field:

```
void IXmlSerializable.ReadXml(XmlReader reader)
{
  this.title = reader.GetAttribute("title")+" by "+reader.GetAttribute("author");
}
```

ForumSchema

The `Forum` class is annotated with the `XmlSchemaProvider` attribute, where the `ForumSchema` method is specified as the method that returns the appropriate XML schema document. As discussed, this XML schema document must describe the structure of the XML document that the `ReadXml` method consumes. However, as Listing 11-7 shows, the `Forum` class's implementation of the `ForumSchema` method returns null. This is because the `XmlSerializer` class doesn't validate XML documents, and there is no need to generate the XML schema document.

Listing 11-7: The Forum class's implementation of the ForumSchema method returns null

```
[XmlSchemaProvider("ForumSchema")]
public class Forum : IXmlSerializable
{
  public static XmlQualifiedName ForumSchema(XmlSchemaSet xs)
  {
    return null;
  }
}
```

Developing Custom Schema Importer Extensions

The previous section showed how the client-side `Forum` component can implement the `IXmlSerializable` interface to deserialize itself from the XML representation of its server-side `Book` component. This allows the client application to receive a `Forum` object when it invokes a server-side method that returns a `Book` object. However, simply having the client-side `Forum` component implement the `IXmlSerializable` will not automatically help the client application achieve this goal.

Recall that the clients of XML Web services only receive XML representations of the respective server-side components. Tools such as `wsdl.exe`, `xsd.exe`, the Add Web References dialog box in Visual Studio, and the `ServiceDescription` class use the `XmlSchemaImporter` class to generate the code for the appropriate client-side components from these XML representations.

For each XSD type used in a given XML representation, the `XmlSchemaImporter` class uses a default XSD to .NET mapping to generate the code for the .NET type that maps to the XSD type. The default XSD to .NET mapping ends up generating the default client-side components, which is a `Book` component in the case of the forum application, rather than the desired `Forum` component.

The `XmlSchemaImporter` class exposes a collection property of type `SchemaImporterExtension Collection` named `Extensions`. If the collection is not empty, the class delegates the responsibility of generating the client-side code to the objects in this collection, bypassing the default XSD to .NET mapping. This section shows you how to develop custom schema importer extensions that will generate code for desired client-side components and how to add these custom extensions to the `Extensions` collection of the respective `XmlSchemaImporter` instance.

All custom schema importer extensions must derive from the `SchemaImporterExtension` abstract base class. Following are the three important methods of the base class. The first method is the `ImportSchemaType` method shown in the following code:

```
public virtual string
ImportSchemaType (string name, string ns, XmlSchemaObject context,
                 XmlSchemas schemas, XmlSchemaImporter importer,
                 CodeCompileUnit compileUnit, CodeNamespace mainNamespace,
                 CodeGenerationOptions options, CodeDomProvider codeProvider);
```

For each XSD type used in a given XML representation, the `XmlSchemaImporter` class calls the `ImportSchemaType` method of a given `SchemaImporterExtension` object in its `Extensions` collection. Your custom schema importer extension can override the `ImportSchemaType` method to generate the code for the .NET type (`Forum`) that you want to map to the specified XSD type. The `XmlSchemaImporter` class passes the following information to the `ImportSchemaType` method:

❑ The name of the XSD type that the method generates the code for

❑ The XML namespace of the XSD type

❑ The XML schema information about the XSD type

❑ The list of all the XML schemas used in the respective XML representation

❑ The `XmlSchemaImporter` instance that calls the method

❑ The `CodeCompileUnit` object that will contain the code that the method generates

❑ The .NET namespace that the client-side component will belong to

❑ The `CodeGenerationOptions` object that the method can use to set the compiler options

❑ The `CodeDomProvider` object that the method can use to generate the language-dependent code from the CodeDom. Recall that the CodeDom is language-agnostic.

The second important method of the `SchemaImporterExtensions` base class is the `ImportAnyElement` method shown in the following code. Your custom schema importer extension can override this method to generate code for the .NET type that you want to map to the `<xs:any>` XSD types used in a given XML representation:

```
public virtual string
ImportAnyElement (XmlSchemaAny any, bool mixed, XmlSchemas schemas,
                 XmlSchemaImporter importer, CodeCompileUnit compileUnit,
                 CodeNamespace mainNamespace, CodeGenerationOptions options,
                 CodeDomProvider codeProvider);
```

The third important method of the `SchemaImporterExtensions` base class is the `ImportDefaultValue` method shown in the following code. Your custom schema importer extension can override this method to generate the code that handles the default values of the XSD types used in a given XML representation:

```
public virtual CodeExpression ImportDefaultValue (string value, string type);
```

The `XmlSchemaImporter` class passes the name of the imported XSD type and its default value as arguments to the `ImportDefaultValue` method. You can override this method to return a different default value for the type.

The forum application implements a custom schema importer extension named `ForumSchema ImporterExtension` that derives from the `SchemaImporterExtension` base class and overrides its `ImportSchemaType` method.

Follow these steps to override the `ImportSchemaType` method of your custom schema importer extension:

1. Recall that for each XSD type found in the respective XML representation, the `XmlSchemaImporter` component calls the `ImportSchemaType` method of your custom schema importer extension to allow you to generate the code for the .NET type that you want to map to the specified XSD type. The method must first examine the values of its two first arguments. Recall that these values are the name of the XSD type and its XML namespace. You have to choose which XSD type you want the `ImportSchemaType` method to handle. In this case, the method handles the XSD type named `book` that belongs to the `http://books` namespace because `book` is the XSD type that represents the `Book` server-side component.

2. Decide on how to generate the code for the .NET type (`Forum`) that you want to map to the specified XSD type.

There are two different approaches to generate the code for the desired .NET type, as discussed in the following sections.

Write the Code in Your Favorite Language

One approach is to write the code externally in your favorite language, such as C# or VB.NET, and compile it to an assembly. Recall that the forum application implements a custom serializable component named `Forum` that implements the `IXmlSerializable` interface as shown in Listing 11-6. This approach requires you to compile the code for the `Forum` class to an assembly, called `Forum.dll`. Listing 11-8 shows how to add this assembly to the CodeDom representation.

Listing 11-8: The ImportSchemaType method using externally written code

```
  public override string
ImportSchemaType(string name, string ns, XmlSchemaObject context,
             XmlSchemas schemas, XmlSchemaImporter importer,
             CodeCompileUnit compileUnit, CodeNamespace mainNamespace,
             CodeGenerationOptions options, CodeDomProvider codeProvider)
{
  if (name.Equals("book") && ns.Equals("http://books"))
  {
    compileUnit.ReferencedAssemblies.Add("Forum.dll");
    CodeNamespaceImport imp = new CodeNamespaceImport("CustomComponents");
    mainNamespace.Imports.Add(imp);

    return "Forum";
  }

  return null;
}
```

Recall that the XmlSchemaImporter class passes an instance of the CodeCompileUnit class to the ImportSchemaType method. As discussed, all of the code included in the CodeCompileUnit instance compiles to a single assembly. This assembly, like any other assembly, may reference other assemblies. The CodeCompileUnit instance exposes a collection property of type StringCollection named ReferencedAssemblies that contains the filenames of all of the assemblies that this assembly (the assembly that the CodeCompileUnit instance represents) references.

Listing 11-8 adds the filename of the Forum.dll library to this collection. The ImportSchemaType method of your custom extension must return the name of the .NET type being mapped to the specified XSD type. In this case, the string value Forum is returned.

This approach to code generation is very convenient because it's much easier to write code in a language such as C# or VB.NET than a verbose language such as CodeDom. However, this convenience comes with a price. You lose the flexibility and extensibility that the CodeDom approach to dynamic code generation provides.

CodeDom Approach

In this approach all of the code for the client-side component (Forum) is written in CodeDom language. This section uses this approach to implement the ImportSchemaType method of the ForumSchema ImporterExtension component. Recall that the ImportSchemaType method generates the CodeDom object model that represents the client-side component or .NET type that maps to a given XSD type.

Follow these steps to implement the CodeDom representation of your custom component or type:

1. Implement the type in your favorite .NET language, C# or VB.NET.

2. Divide the C# or VB.NET code that you wrote in step 1 into code blocks.

3. Write the CodeDom representation of each code block.

These three steps help you modularize the CodeDom representation of your custom component. This modularization is important for the following reasons:

❑ The CodeDom language is verbose. Modularization organizes your code, making it easier for you to write the CodeDom.

❑ Modularization makes your CodeDom more readable considering how verbose CodeDom is.

❑ Modularization allows others to override your modules to provide their own implementation. For example, if your custom schema importer extension uses separate modules to generate the required CodeDom for the methods and properties of your client-side component (Forum), developers who want to add a new property to the component can simply write a new custom extension that derives from yours and overrides only the module responsible for generating the CodeDom for properties. The new custom extension will automatically inherit the module responsible for generating the CodeDom for methods.

Because you've already implemented the Forum class in C# (see Listing 11-6), you can move on to the next step where the code shown in Listing 11-6 is divided into code blocks shown in Listing 11-9.

Listing 11-9: Dividing the code into code blocks

```
// The code block that contains the using statements
using System.Xml.Serialization;
using System.Xml.Schema;
using System.Xml;
using System.Collections;

// The code block that contains the attributes that annotate the Forum
[XmlSchemaProvider("ForumSchema")]


// The code block that contains the declaration of the Forum class
public class Forum


// The code block contains the base classes
                : IXmlSerializable
{


// The code block that contains the private fields
  private ArrayList messages;
  private string title;


// The code block that contains the properties
  public string Title {get;}
  public ArrayList Messages {get;}

// The code block that contains the methods
  XmlSchema IXmlSerializable.GetSchema();
  void IXmlSerializable.ReadXml(XmlReader reader);
  void IXmlSerializable.WriteXml(XmlWriter writer);
  public static XmlQualifiedName ForumSchema(XmlSchemaSet xs);
}
```

You need to delegate the responsibility of generating the CodeDom representation of each code block shown in Listing 11-9 to a separate method:

❑ `GenerateCodeDomForImportNamespaces`: Generates the CodeDom representation of the code block in Listing 11-9 that contains the C# `using` statements

❑ `GenerateCodeDomForComponent`: Generates the CodeDom representation of the code block in Listing 11-9 that contains the declaration of the `Forum` class

❑ `GenerateCodeDomForAttributes`: Generates the CodeDom representation of the code block in Listing 11-9 that contains the metadata attributes that annotate the `Forum` class

❑ `GenerateCodeDomForBaseTypes`: Generates the CodeDom representation of the code block in Listing 11-9 that contains the base classes of the `Forum` class

❑   GenerateCodeDomForFields: Generates the CodeDom representation of the code block in Listing 11-9 that contains the private fields of the Forum class

❑   GenerateCodeDomForProperties: Generates the CodeDom representation of the code block in Listing 11-9 that contains the properties of the Forum class

❑   GenerateCodeDomForMethods: Generates the CodeDom representation of the code block in Listing 11-9 that contains the methods of the Forum class

ForumSchemaImporterExtension overrides the ImportSchemaType method of its base class to call the methods listed, as shown in Listing 11-10. The following sections present the implementation of these methods. Notice that the ImportSchemaType method generates code for the book schema type only and ignores other schema types. Also notice the method returns the string value Forum after it generates the CodeDom representation of the Forum class.

Listing 11-10: The overridden ImportSchemaType method

```
public override string
ImportSchemaType(string name, string ns, XmlSchemaObject context,
                 XmlSchemas schemas, XmlSchemaImporter importer,
                 CodeCompileUnit compileUnit, CodeNamespace mainNamespace,
                 CodeGenerationOptions options, CodeDomProvider codeProvider)
{
  if (name.Equals("book") && ns.Equals("http://books"))
  {
    GenerateCodeDomForImportNamespaces(mainNamespace);
    CodeTypeDeclaration forum = GenerateCodeDomForComponent(mainNamespace);

    GenerateCodeDomForAttributes(forum);
    GenerateCodeDomForBaseTypes(forum);
    GenerateCodeDomForFields(forum);
    GenerateCodeDomForProperties(forum);
    GenerateCodeDomForMethods(forum);

    return "Forum";
  }

  return null;
}
```

The GenerateCodeDomForImportNamespaces Method

The GenerateCodeDomForImportNamespaces method generates the CodeDom representation of the code block in Listing 11-9 that contains the following C# using statements:

```
using System.Xml.Serialization;
using System.Xml.Schema;
using System.Xml;
using System.Collections;
```

The method creates one instance of the CodeNamespaceImport class to represent each C# using statement and adds the instance to the Imports collection of the CodeNamespace object — which represents the

main namespace of the assembly to which the CodeDom representation of the Forum class compiles —
to indicate that the Forum class will be using the types from the respective namespace:

```
protected virtual void
GenerateCodeDomForImportNamespaces(CodeNamespace mainNamespace)
{
  CodeNamespaceImport imp = new CodeNamespaceImport("System.Xml.Schema");
  mainNamespace.Imports.Add(imp);

  imp = new CodeNamespaceImport("System.Xml.Serialization");
  mainNamespace.Imports.Add(imp);

  imp = new CodeNamespaceImport("System.Xml");
  mainNamespace.Imports.Add(imp);

  imp = new CodeNamespaceImport("System.Collections");
  mainNamespace.Imports.Add(imp);
}
```

The GenerateCodeDomForComponent Method

The main responsibility of the GenerateCodeDomForComponent method is to generate the CodeDom
representation of the code block in Listing 11-9 that contains the C# code that declares the Forum class:

```
public class Forum
```

The following is the code for the GenerateCodeDomForComponent method:

```
protected virtual CodeTypeDeclaration
GenerateCodeDomForComponent(CodeNamespace mainNamespace)
{
  CodeTypeDeclaration forum = new CodeTypeDeclaration("Forum");
  mainNamespace.Types.Add(forum);
  forum.Attributes = MemberAttributes.Public;
  return forum;
}
```

This method creates a CodeTypeDeclaration object to represent the Forum class itself:

```
CodeTypeDeclaration forum = new CodeTypeDeclaration("Forum");
```

It then adds the CodeTypeDeclaration object to the Types collection of the CodeNamespace object that
represents the main namespace to specify that Forum class belongs to this namespace:

```
mainNamespace.Types.Add(forum);
```

It then assigns the MemberAttributes.Public enumeration to the Attributes property of the
CodeTypeDeclaration object to specify that Forum is a public class:

```
forum.Attributes = MemberAttributes.Public;
```

The GenerateCodeDomForAttributes Method

The `GenerateCodeDomForAttributes` method generates the `CodeDom` representation of the code block shown in Listing 11-9 that contains the `XmlSchemaProvider` metadata attribute that annotates the `Forum` class:

```
[XmlSchemaProvider("ForumSchema")]
```

The following code is the implementation of the `GenerateCodeDomForAttributes` method:

```
protected virtual void GenerateCodeDomForAttributes(CodeTypeDeclaration forum)
{
   CodePrimitiveExpression forumSchema = new CodePrimitiveExpression("ForumSchema");
   CodeAttributeArgument methodName = new CodeAttributeArgument();
   methodName.Value = forumSchema;
   CodeAttributeDeclaration xmlSchemaProvider =
       new CodeAttributeDeclaration("XmlSchemaProvider",
                          new CodeAttributeArgument[] { methodName });

   forum.CustomAttributes.Add(xmlSchemaProvider);
}
```

This method creates a `CodePrimitiveExpression` object to represent the string value `ForumSchema`:

```
CodePrimitiveExpression forumSchema = new CodePrimitiveExpression("ForumSchema");
```

It then creates a `CodeAttributeArgument` object and assigns the `CodePrimitiveExpression` object to its `Value` property to specify that the string value `ForumSchema` is a metadata attribute argument:

```
CodeAttributeArgument methodName = new CodeAttributeArgument();
methodName.Value = forumSchema;
```

Next, the method creates a `CodeAttributeDeclaration` object and passes the following two arguments into it to represent the `XmlSchemaProvider` metadata attribute:

❑   The name of the attribute, the string value `XmlSchemaProvider`

❑   The `CodeAttributeArgument` object that represents the `ForumSchema` attribute

```
CodeAttributeDeclaration xmlSchemaProvider =
       new CodeAttributeDeclaration("XmlSchemaProvider",
                          new CodeAttributeArgument[] { methodName });
```

Finally, the method adds the `CodeAttributeDeclaration` object to the `CustomAttributes` collection of `CodeTypeDeclaration` object that represents the `Forum` class to specify that the `XmlSchemaProvider` ("ForumSchema") metadata attribute annotates the `Forum` class:

```
forum.CustomAttributes.Add(xmlSchemaProvider);
```

The GenerateCodeDomForBaseTypes Method

The `GenerateCodeDomForBaseTypes` method generates the CodeDom representation of the code block in Listing 11-9 that contains the `IXmlSerializable` interface. The following is the code for this method:

```
protected virtual void GenerateCodeDomForBaseTypes(CodeTypeDeclaration forum)
{
  CodeTypeReference ixmlserializable =
                         new CodeTypeReference(typeof(IXmlSerializable));
  forum.BaseTypes.Add(ixmlserializable);
}
```

This method creates a `CodeTypeReference` object to reference the `IXmlSerializable` interface:

```
CodeTypeReference ixmlserializable =
                         new CodeTypeReference(typeof(IXmlSerializable));
```

It then adds the `CodeTypeReference` object to the `BaseTypes` collections of the `CodeTypeDeclaration` object that represents the `Forum` class to specify that the `Forum` class implements the `IXmlSerializable` interface:

```
forum.BaseTypes.Add(ixmlserializable);
```

The GenerateCodeDomForFields Method

As Listing 11-11 shows, the `GenerateCodeDomForFields` method generates the CodeDom representation of the fields of the Forum class:

```
private ArrayList messages;
private string title;
```

Listing 11-11: The GenerateCodeDomForFields method

```
protected virtual void GenerateCodeDomForFields(CodeTypeDeclaration forum)
{
  CodeTypeReference arrayListType = new CodeTypeReference(typeof(ArrayList));
  CodeMemberField messagesField = new CodeMemberField(arrayListType, "messages");
  forum.Members.Add(messagesField);

  CodeTypeReference stringType = new CodeTypeReference(typeof(string));
  CodeMemberField titleField = new CodeMemberField(stringType,"title");
  forum.Members.Add(titleField);
}
```

This method uses an instance of the `CodeTypeReference` class to represent the type of the `messages` field of the `Forum` class:

```
CodeTypeReference arrayListType = new CodeTypeReference(typeof(ArrayList));
```

It then uses an instance of the `CodeMemberField` class and the `CodeTypeReference` instance to represent the `messages` field of the `Forum` class:

```
CodeMemberField messagesField = new CodeMemberField(arrayListType,"messages");
```

Next it adds the `CodeMemberField` instance to the `Members` collection of the `CodeTypeDeclaration` object — which represents the `Forum` class — to represent the class membership of the `messages` field:

```
forum.Members.Add(messagesField);
```

Finally, the method repeats the preceding steps to generate the CodeDom representation of the `title` field of the class.

The GenerateCodeDomForProperties Method

As Listing 11-12 shows, the `GenerateCodeDomForProperties` method generates the CodeDom representation of the `Messages` and `Title` properties of the `Forum` component:

```
public string Title { get;}
public ArrayList Messages { get;}
```

Listing 11-12: The GenerateCodeDomForProperties method

```
protected virtual void
GenerateCodeDomForProperties(CodeTypeMemberCollection members)
{
  CodeMemberProperty messagesProperty = new CodeMemberProperty();
  messagesProperty.Attributes = MemberAttributes.Public | MemberAttributes.Final;

  messagesProperty.Name = "Messages";
  messagesProperty.Type = new CodeTypeReference(typeof(ArrayList));
  members.Add(messagesProperty);

  CodeThisReferenceExpression thisRef = new CodeThisReferenceExpression();
  CodeFieldReferenceExpression messages =
                        new CodeFieldReferenceExpression(thisRef, "messages");
  CodePrimitiveExpression nullRef = new CodePrimitiveExpression(null);
  CodeBinaryOperatorExpression ifCondition =
        new CodeBinaryOperatorExpression(messages,
                        CodeBinaryOperatorType.IdentityEquality, nullRef);
  CodeConditionStatement ifStatement = new CodeConditionStatement();
  ifStatement.Condition = ifCondition;

  CodeObjectCreateExpression list =
        new CodeObjectCreateExpression(typeof(ArrayList),
                new CodePrimitiveExpression[] { new CodePrimitiveExpression(2) });
  CodeAssignStatement trueStatement = new CodeAssignStatement(messages, list);
  ifStatement.TrueStatements.Add(trueStatement);

  messagesProperty.GetStatements.Add(ifStatement);
  messagesProperty.GetStatements.Add(new CodeMethodReturnStatement(
    new CodeFieldReferenceExpression(new CodeThisReferenceExpression(),
                                "messages")));

  CodeMemberProperty titleProperty = new CodeMemberProperty();
  titleProperty.Attributes = MemberAttributes.Public | MemberAttributes.Final;
  titleProperty.GetStatements.Add(new CodeMethodReturnStatement(
    new CodeFieldReferenceExpression(new CodeThisReferenceExpression(),"title")));
  titleProperty.Name = "Title";
  titleProperty.Type = new CodeTypeReference(typeof(string));
  members.Add(titleProperty);
}
```

This method uses an instance of the `CodeMemberProperty` class and sets its `Name` property to the string value `Messages` to represent the `Messages` property of the `Forum` class:

```
CodeMemberProperty messagesProperty = new CodeMemberProperty();
messagesProperty.Name = "Messages";
```

Next, it assigns the `MemberAttributes.Public` enumeration value to the `Attributes` property of the `CodeMemberProperty` instance to represent the public access modifier of the `Messages` property:

```
messagesProperty.Attributes = MemberAttributes.Public;
```

Then the method uses an instance of the `CodeTypeReference` class and assigns it to the `Type` property of the `CodeMemberProperty` instance to represent the type of the `Message` property:

```
messagesProperty.Type = new CodeTypeReference(typeof(ArrayList));
```

The method then takes a series of actions to generate the CodeDom representation of the various C# statements:

❑   The first statement of the getter of the `Messages` properties:

```
if (this.messages == null) this.messages = new ArrayList();
```

❑   An instance of the `CodeConditionStatement` class to represent the `if` statement as a whole:

```
CodeConditionStatement ifStatement = new CodeConditionStatement();
```

❑   An instance of the `CodeThisReferenceExpression` class to represent the `this` keyword:

```
CodeThisReferenceExpression thisRef = new  CodeThisReferenceExpression();
```

❑   An instance of the `CodeFieldReferenceExpression` class to represent the messages field of the `Forum` class: `this.messages`:

```
CodeFieldReferenceExpression messages =
                    new CodeFieldReferenceExpression(thisRef, "messages");
```

❑   An instance of the `CodePrimitiveExpression` class to represent the C# `null` value:

```
CodePrimitiveExpression nullRef = new CodePrimitiveExpression(null);
```

❑   An instance of the `CodeBinaryOperatorExpression` class to represent the condition statement: `(this.messages == null)`:

```
CodeBinaryOperatorExpression ifCondition =
    new CodeBinaryOperatorExpression(messages,
                CodeBinaryOperatorType.IdentityEquality, nullRef);
```

❑   Assigns the `CodeBinaryOperatorExpression` instance to the `Condition` property of the `CodeConditionStatement` object — which represents the `if` statement as a whole — to indicate that the `(this.message == null)` is the condition statement for the `if` statement:

```
ifStatement.Condition = ifCondition;
```

❑   An instance of the `CodeObjectCreateExpression` class to represent the `new ArrayList()` expression:

311

```
CodeObjectCreateExpression list =
        new CodeObjectCreateExpression(typeof(ArrayList),
                new CodePrimitiveExpression[] { new CodePrimitiveExpression(2) });
```

❑ An instance of the `CodeAssignStatement` class to represent the `this.messages = new ArrayList();` assignment statement:

```
CodeAssignStatement trueStatement = new CodeAssignStatement(messages, list);
```

❑ Adds the `CodeAssignStatement` instance to the `TrueStatements` collection of the `CodeConditionStatement` object — which represents the `if` statement as a whole — to indicate that the `this.messages = new ArrayList();` statement is executed when the `if`-condition (`this.messages == null`) is true:

```
ifStatement.TrueStatements.Add(trueStatement);
```

Once all this translation is done, the method adds the `CodeConditionStatement` object to the `GetStatements` collection of the `CodeMemberProperty` object, which represents the `Messages` property, to represent the fact that the `if` statement belongs to the getter of the `Messages` property:

```
messagesProperty.GetStatements.Add(ifStatement);
```

Next the method uses an instance of the `CodeMethodReturnStatement` class and adds it to the `GetStatements` collection of the `CodeMemberProperty` object to represent the `return` statement of the getter of the `Messages` property (`return this.messages;`):

```
messagesProperty.GetStatements.Add(new CodeMethodReturnStatement(
    new CodeFieldReferenceExpression(new CodeThisReferenceExpression(),"messages")));
```

Then it adds the `CodeMemberProperty` object, which represents the `Messages` property, to the `Members` collection of the `CodeTypeDeclaration` object, which represents the `Forum` class, to represent the (`Forum`) class membership of the `Messages` property:

```
members.Add(messagesProperty);
```

The method then uses a similar procedure to generate the CodeDom representation of the `Title` property of the `Forum` class.

The GenerateCodeDomForMethods Method

The `ForumSchemaImporterExtension` component exposes one virtual method for each method of the `Forum` class. Each virtual method is responsible for generating the CodeDom representation of its respective `Forum` class method. For example, the `GenerateCodeDomForReadXmlMethod` method generates the CodeDom representation of the `ReadXml` method of the `Forum` class. The `GenerateCodeDomForMethods` method calls all the virtual methods:

```
protected virtual void GenerateCodeDomForMethods(CodeTypeMemberCollection members)
{
  members.Add(GenerateCodeDomForGetSchemaMethod());
  members.Add(GenerateCodeDomForReadXmlMethod());
  members.Add(GenerateCodeDomForWriteXmlMethod());
  members.Add(GenerateCodeDomForumSchemaMethod());
}
```

The GenerateCodeDomForGetSchemaMethod Method

The `GenerateCodeDomForGetSchemaMethod` method generates the CodeDom that represents the `GetSchema` method:

```
public XmlSchema GetSchema()
{
  return null;
}
```

The following code presents the code for the `GenerateCodeDomeForGetSchemaMethod` method:

```
protected virtual CodeMemberMethod GenerateCodeDomForGetSchemaMethod()
{
  CodeMemberMethod GetSchema = new CodeMemberMethod();
  GetSchema.Attributes = MemberAttributes.Public;
  CodeTypeReference xmlSchemaType = new CodeTypeReference(typeof(XmlSchema));
  GetSchema.ReturnType = xmlSchemaType;
  GetSchema.Name = "GetSchema";

  CodeMethodReturnStatement GetSchemaReturn = new CodeMethodReturnStatement();
  CodePrimitiveExpression nullRef = new CodePrimitiveExpression(null);
  GetSchemaReturn.Expression = nullRef;
  GetSchema.Statements.Add(GetSchemaReturn);

  return GetSchema;
}
```

This method first instantiates a `CodeMemberMethod` object to represent the `GetSchema` method:

```
CodeMemberMethod GetSchema = new CodeMemberMethod();
```

It sets the value of the `Name` property of the `CodeMemberMethod` object to specify the name of the method:

```
GetSchema.Name = "GetSchema";
```

It then assigns the `MemberAttributes.Public` enumeration to the `Attributes` property of the `CodeMemberMethod` object to specify that `GetSchema` is a public method:

```
GetSchema.Attributes = MemberAttributes.Public;
```

It instantiates a `CodeTypeReference` object to represent the `XmlSchema` type:

```
CodeTypeReference xmlSchemaType = new CodeTypeReference(typeof(XmlSchema));
```

It then assigns the `CodeTypeReference` object to the `ReturnType` property of the `CodeMemberMethod` object to specify that the return value of the `GetSchema` method is of type `XmlSchema`:

```
GetSchema.ReturnType = xmlSchemaType;
```

Next the method instantiates a `CodeMethodReturnStatement` object to represent the return statement of the `GetSchema` method:

```
CodeMethodReturnStatement GetSchemaReturn = new CodeMethodReturnStatement();
```

313

It creates a `CodePrimitiveExpression` object to represent the `null` value:

```
CodePrimitiveExpression nullRef = new CodePrimitiveExpression(null);
```

It also assigns the `CodePrimitiveExpression` object to the `Expression` property of the `CodeMethodReturnStatement` object to specify that the `return` statement returns `null`:

```
GetSchemaReturn.Expression = nullRef;
```

Finally, the method adds the `CodeMethodReturnStatement` object to the `Statements` collection of the `CodeMemberMethod` to specify that the `return null;` statement belongs to the `GetSchema` method:

```
GetSchema.Statements.Add(GetSchemaReturn);
```

The GenerateCodeDomForReadXmlMethod Method

As Listing 11-13 shows, the `GenerateCodeDomForReadXmlMethod` method generates the CodeDom representation of the `ReadXml` method of the `Forum` class:

```
void IXmlSerializable.ReadXml(XmlReader reader)
{
    this.title = reader.GetAttribute("title") + " by " +
                        reader.GetAttribute("author");
}
```

Listing 11-13: The GenerateCodeDomForReadXmlMethod method

```
protected virtual CodeMemberMethod GenerateCodeDomForReadXmlMethod()
{
    CodeMemberMethod ReadXml = new CodeMemberMethod();

    ReadXml.Name = "ReadXml";
    ReadXml.Attributes = MemberAttributes.Public;
    ReadXml.Parameters.Add(
            new CodeParameterDeclarationExpression(typeof(XmlReader), "reader"));

    CodeThisReferenceExpression thisReference = new CodeThisReferenceExpression();
    CodeFieldReferenceExpression title =
                        new CodeFieldReferenceExpression(thisReference, "title");
    CodeArgumentReferenceExpression reader =
                        new CodeArgumentReferenceExpression("reader");
    CodeMethodInvokeExpression getTitle =
        new CodeMethodInvokeExpression(reader, "GetAttribute",
            new CodePrimitiveExpression[] { new CodePrimitiveExpression("title") });
    CodePrimitiveExpression by = new CodePrimitiveExpression(" by ");
    CodeMethodInvokeExpression getAuthor =
        new CodeMethodInvokeExpression(reader, "GetAttribute",
            new CodePrimitiveExpression[] { new CodePrimitiveExpression("author") });
    CodeBinaryOperatorExpression add1 =
        new CodeBinaryOperatorExpression(getTitle, CodeBinaryOperatorType.Add, by);
    CodeBinaryOperatorExpression add2 =
        new CodeBinaryOperatorExpression(add1, CodeBinaryOperatorType.Add, getAuthor);
```

```
    CodeAssignStatement statement = new CodeAssignStatement(title, add2);

    ReadXml.Statements.Add(statement);
    return ReadXml;
}
```

This method uses a `CodeMemberMethod` instance and sets its `Name` property to the string value `ReadXml` to represent the `ReadXml` method:

```
CodeMemberMethod ReadXml = new CodeMemberMethod();
ReadXml.Name = "ReadXml";
```

It then assigns the `MemberAttributes.Public` enumeration value to the `Attributes` property of the `CodeMemberMethod` instance to represent the public access modifier of the `ReadXml` method:

```
ReadXml.Attributes = MemberAttributes.Public;
```

Next, the method uses an instance of the `CodeParameterDeclarationExpression` class and adds it to the `Parameters` collection of the `CodeMemberMethod` instance to represent the parameter name (reader) and type (`XmlReader`) of the `ReadXml` method:

```
ReadXml.Parameters.Add(
        new CodeParameterDeclarationExpression(typeof(XmlReader), "reader"));
```

It then uses the following series of actions to generate the CodeDom representation of the body of the `ReadXml` method:

```
this.title = reader.GetAttribute("title") + " by " + reader.GetAttribute("author");
```

❑ An instance of the `CodeThisReferenceExpression` class to represent the `this` object:

```
CodeThisReferenceExpression thisReference = new CodeThisReferenceExpression();
```

❑ An instance of the `CodeFieldReferenceExpression` class to represent the reference to the `title` field member of the `Forum` class (`this.title`):

```
CodeFieldReferenceExpression title =
                    new CodeFieldReferenceExpression(thisReference, "title");
```

❑ An instance of the `CodeArgumentReferenceExpression` class to represent the reference to the `XmlReader` argument of the `ReadXml` method:

```
CodeArgumentReferenceExpression reader =
                        new CodeArgumentReferenceExpression("reader");
```

❑ An instance of the `CodeMethodInvokeExpression` class to represent the invocation of the `GetAttribute` method of the `XmlReader` argument(`reader.GetAttribute("title")`):

```
CodeMethodInvokeExpression getTitle =
    new CodeMethodInvokeExpression(reader, "GetAttribute",
        new CodePrimitiveExpression[] { new CodePrimitiveExpression("title") });
```

❑ An instance of the `CodePrimitiveExpression` class to represent the string value `" by "`:

```
CodePrimitiveExpression by = new CodePrimitiveExpression(" by ");
```

❑ An instance of the `CodeMethodInvokeExpression` class to represent the invocation of the `GetAttribute` method of the `XmlReader` argument (`reader.GetAttribute("Author")`):

```
CodeMethodInvokeExpression getAuthor =
  new CodeMethodInvokeExpression(reader, "GetAttribute",
    new CodePrimitiveExpression[] { new CodePrimitiveExpression("author") });
```

❑ Uses two instances of the `CodeBinaryOperatorExpression` class to represent the string concatenation `reader.GetAttribute("title") + " by " + reader.GetAttribute("author")`:

```
CodeBinaryOperatorExpression add1 =
  new CodeBinaryOperatorExpression(getTitle, CodeBinaryOperatorType.Add, by);

CodeBinaryOperatorExpression add2 =
  new CodeBinaryOperatorExpression(add1, CodeBinaryOperatorType.Add, getAuthor);
```

❑ An instance of the `CodeAssignStatement` class to represent the assignment statement `this.title = reader.GetAttribute("title") + " by " + reader.GetAttribute("author");`:

```
CodeAssignStatement statement = new CodeAssignStatement(title, add2);
```

Finally, the method adds the `CodeAssignStatement` instance to the `Statements` collection of the `CodeMemberMethod` object, which represents the `ReadXml` method, to represent the fact that the assignment statement is part of the body of the `ReadXml` method:

```
ReadXml.Statements.Add(statement);
```

The GenerateCodeDomForWriteXmlMethod Method

The `GenerateCodeDomForWriteXmlMethod` method is responsible for generating the CodeDom that represents the `WriteXml` method:

```
void IXmlSerializable.WriteXml(XmlWriter writer) { }
```

Notice that this method doesn't contain any code as discussed before. The following code presents the code for the `GenerateCodeDomForWriteXmlMethod` method:

```
protected virtual CodeMemberMethod GenerateCodeDomForWriteXmlMethod()
{
  CodeMemberMethod WriteXml = new CodeMemberMethod();
  WriteXml.Name = "WriteXml";
  WriteXml.Attributes = MemberAttributes.Public;
  CodeParameterDeclarationExpression writer =
          new CodeParameterDeclarationExpression(typeof(XmlWriter), "writer"));
  WriteXml.Parameters.Add(writer);

  return WriteXml;
}
```

This method instantiates a `CodeMemberMethod` to represent the `WriteXml` method:

```
CodeMemberMethod WriteXml = new CodeMemberMethod();
```

It then sets the `Name` property of the `CodeMemberMethod` object to specify the name of the method:

```
WriteXml.Name = "WriteXml";
```

It assigns the `MemberAttributes.Public` enumeration to the `Attributes` property of the `CodeMemberMethod` object to specify that `WriteXml` is a public method:

```
WriteXml.Attributes = MemberAttributes.Public;
```

It next instantiates a `CodeParameterDeclarationExpression` object to specify that the `writer` parameter is a method argument of type `XmlWriter`:

```
CodeParameterDeclarationExpression writer =
            new CodeParameterDeclarationExpression(typeof(XmlWriter), "writer"));
```

Finally, it adds the `CodeParameterDeclarationExpression` object to the `Parameters` collection of the `CodeMemberMethod` object to specify that the `writer` parameter is indeed the argument of the `WriteXml` method:

```
WriteXml.Parameters.Add(writer);
```

Finally, the `ForumSchemaImporterExtension` custom component overrides the second overload of the `ImportSchemaType` method to return null:

```
public override string
ImportSchemaType(XmlSchemaType type, XmlSchemaObject context, XmlSchemas schemas,
                XmlSchemaImporter importer, CodeCompileUnit compileUnit,
                CodeNamespace codeNamespace, CodeGenerationOptions options,
                CodeDomProvider codeGenerator)
{
    return null;
}
```

Registering Your Custom Schema Importer Extension

The previous section showed how to develop your own custom schema importer extension to generate the code for your desired client-side component. For example, the `ForumSchemaImporterExtension` extension generates the code for the `Forum` component.

The next step is to add an instance of your custom schema importer extension to the `Extensions` collection of the respective `XmlSchemaImporter` instance to have the instance automatically call the `SchemaImportType` method of your custom extension for each XSD type found in the respective XML representation. You can't directly add your custom extension to the `Extensions` collection of the `XmlSchemaImporter` instance. However, you can take the following actions to get the ASP.NET 2.0 XML Web service infrastructure to do it for you:

1. Use the following command line to generate a SNK file that contains your digital signature:

```
sn -k mysign.snk
```

2. Modify the `AssemblyInfo.cs` file to specify the assembly culture and version and add a reference to your digital signature. These three elements are necessary to create strongly named assemblies.

```
[assembly: AssemblyTitle("Client")]
[assembly: AssemblyDescription("")]
[assembly: AssemblyConfiguration("")]
[assembly: AssemblyCompany("")]
[assembly: AssemblyProduct("Client")]
[assembly: AssemblyCopyright("")]
[assembly: AssemblyTrademark("")]
[assembly: AssemblyCulture("")]
[assembly: AssemblyVersion("1.0.0.0")]
[assembly: AssemblyFileVersion("1.0.0.0")]
[assembly: AssemblyKeyFile("mysign.snk")]
```

3. Compile your custom extension and the `AssemblyInfo.cs` file to an assembly, such as `ForumSchemaImporterExtension.dll`.

4. Use the Windows Explorer to go to the `C:\WINDOWS\assembly` folder (the location may vary on different operating systems) to access the Global Assembly Cache (GAC).

5. Drag and drop your strongly named assembly into the assembly folder.

6. Modify the `machine.config` file to register your custom extension:

```
<configuration>
  <system.xml.serialization>
    <schemaImporterExtensions>
      <add name="ClientBook type="CustomComponents.BookSchemaImporterExtension,
      mydll, Version=1.0.0.0, Culture=neutral, PublicKeyToken=35ca85b8c419efae"/>
    </schemaImporterExtensions>
  </system.xml.serialization>
</configuration>
```

When the forum application calls the `Select` method of the XML Web service, the method will return a `Forum` instance instead of `Book` instance:

```
protected void Page_Load(object sender, EventArgs e)
{
  localhost.Service s = new localhost.Service();
  s.Credentials = System.Net.CredentialCache.DefaultCredentials;
  localhost.Forum forum = s.Select();
}
```

Sending and Receiving Data in Chunks

The proxy code customization discussed throughout this chapter is only possible in the ASP.NET 2.0 Framework. These customization techniques aren't available in the ASP.NET 1.x Framework. Microsoft decided to add this feature to the ASP.NET 2.0 Framework because there's a lot of demand for it.

One of the main reasons for this demand is the performance degradation of an XML Web service when it has to send huge amounts of data over the wire. By default, the ASP.NET XML Web service infrastructure caches all the data in memory and sends the data in one shot. This introduces the following issues:

❑   Degrades the performance and responsiveness of the XML Web service.

❑   Wastes lot of server memory.

❑   Degrades the user experience of the client applications. Because these applications don't get any feedback from the XML Web service, they can't give any feedback to end users either. The user is sitting there wondering whether the application has crashed or the data is still being downloaded.

This section shows you how you can use what you've learned in this chapter to bypass this default caching mechanism and send and receive the data in chunks instead. This will improve the performance dramatically and consume minimal server resources to process a request. To make the discussions more concrete, you'll add a LinkButton control to the forum application to allow visitors of a book forum to download the electronic version of the associated book from the XML Web service. By default, the XML Web service has to first load the entire book into memory before sending it to the user. The default approach puts a huge burden on the server and degrades the performance and responsiveness of both the XML Web service and the client application.

In this section, you develop a server-side component named BookContent and a client-side component named ForumBook. Both these components implement the IXmlSerializable interface to take control of their serialization or deserialization process.

BookContent

Listing 11-14 contains the code for the BookContent class's implementation of the WriteXml method of the IXmlSerializable interface.

Listing 11-14: The BookContent class's implementation of WriteXml

```
void IXmlSerializable.WriteXml(XmlWriter writer)
{
  using (StreamReader reader =
            new StreamReader(HttpContext.Current.Server.MapPath(this.bookID)))
  {
    writer.WriteAttributeString("bookContentSize",
                               reader.BaseStream.Length.ToString());
    char[] buf = new char[4096];
    int numOfCharsRead = reader.Read(buf, 0, 4096);

    while (numOfCharsRead > 0)
    {
      writer.WriteStartElement("bookContentChunk", "http://books");
      writer.WriteChars(buf, 0, numOfCharsRead);
      writer.WriteEndElement();
      writer.Flush();
      numOfCharsRead = reader.Read(buf, 0, 4096);
    }
  }
}
```

BookContent expose a private string field named `bookID` that uniquely locates the specified book. The `bookID` field could represent the unique identifier of the book in the underlying database, the filename in a file system, and so on. To keep the discussions focused, the `bookID` in this example contains a filename.

As shown in Listing 11-14, `WriteXml` first uses a `StreamReader` to stream out the content of the file with the specified filename. It then writes the stream size as the value of an attribute named `bookContentSize`. Next, `WriteXml` reads the content of the `StreamReader` one chunk at a time and renders each chunk of data within the opening and closing tags of an element named `bookContentChunk`. Notice that `WriteXml` calls the `Flush` method of the `XmlWriter` object at the end of each chunk of data to send the data to the client application. In other words, the `WriteXml` method doesn't cache the data. Instead it sends the data to the client application chunk by chunk. This streaming technique consumes minimal server resources and improves the performance and responsiveness of the server because the client application doesn't have to wait for the whole file to be loaded in the server memory.

BookContent like all classes that implement the `IXmlSerializable` exposes a method that generates the XML schema that describes the structure of the XML document or representation that the `WriteXml` generates. Listing 11-15 contains the implementation of this method.

Listing 11-15: The BookContentSchema method

```
public static XmlQualifiedName BookContentSchema(XmlSchemaSet xs)
{
    XmlSchema schema = new XmlSchema();
    schema.TargetNamespace = "http://books";
    schema.ElementFormDefault = XmlSchemaForm.Qualified;
    schema.AttributeFormDefault = XmlSchemaForm.Unqualified;

    XmlSchemaComplexType bookContent = new XmlSchemaComplexType();
    bookContent.Name = "bookContent";

    XmlSchemaAttribute bookContentSize = new XmlSchemaAttribute();
    bookContentSize.Name = "bookContentSize";
    bookContentSize.SchemaTypeName =
            new XmlQualifiedName("string", "http://www.w3.org/2001/XMLSchema");
    bookContent.Attributes.Add(bookContentSize);

    XmlSchemaSequence seq = new XmlSchemaSequence();
    bookContent.Particle = seq;

    XmlSchemaElement bookContentChunk = new XmlSchemaElement();
    seq.Items.Add(bookContentChunk);
    bookContentChunk.Name = "bookContentChunk";
    bookContentChunk.SchemaTypeName =
            new XmlQualifiedName("string", "http://www.w3.org/2001/XMLSchema");
    bookContentChunk.MinOccurs = 0;
    bookContentChunk.MaxOccurs = Decimal.MaxValue;

    schema.Items.Add(bookContent);
    xs.Add(schema);
    return new XmlQualifiedName("bookContent", "http://books");
}
```

The implementation of the `BookContentSchema` method is very similar to the implementation of the `BookSchema` method shown in Listing 11-5. The main difference is that the XML Schema document the `BookSchema` method generates doesn't contain any child elements, whereas the XML Schema document that the `BookContentSchema` method generates contains one or more `bookContentChunk` child elements.

Listing 11-16 contains the code for the XML Web service. The XML Web service exposes a new method named `GetBookContent` that takes the `bookID` as its argument and returns a `BookContent` object that contains the content of the book.

Listing 11-16: The XML Web service

```
[WebService(Namespace = "http://books")]
public class Service : System.Web.Services.WebService
{
  [WebMethod]
  public Book Select()
  {
    Book book = new Book();
    book.Title = "title1";
    book.Author = "author1";
    book.BookID = "title1.htm";
    return book;
  }

  [WebMethod]
  [System.Web.Services.Protocols.SoapDocumentMethodAttribute
  (ParameterStyle = SoapParameterStyle.Bare)]
  public BookContent GetBookContent(string bookID)
  {
    System.Web.HttpContext.Current.Response.Buffer = false;
    return new BookContent(bookID);
  }
}
```

The client application first calls the `Select` method of the XML Web service as it did before to display the title of the forum. Recall that the forum title uses the title and name of the author of the associated book. As you'll see later, when the user clicks the appropriate `LinkButton` control to download the associated book, the client application calls the `GetBookContent` method of the XML Web service to download the book in streaming fashion.

Notice that the `GetBookContent` method sets the `Buffer` property of the `Response` object to false to turn off the caching. This step is necessary:

```
System.Web.HttpContext.Current.Response.Buffer = false;
```

ForumBook

Listing 11-17 presents the `ForumBook` class's implementation of the `ReadXml` method of the `IXmlSerializable` interface.

Listing 11-17: The ReadXml method

```
void IXmlSerializable.ReadXml(XmlReader reader)
{
  reader.ReadStartElement("GetBookContentResult", "http://books");
  int bookContentSize = Convert.ToInt32(reader.GetAttribute("bookContentSize"));
  string bookID = reader.GetAttribute("bookID");
  XmlWriterSettings settings = new XmlWriterSettings();
  settings.Indent = true;
  settings.OmitXmlDeclaration = true;

  using (XmlWriter xw =
     XmlWriter.Create(HttpContext.Current.Server.MapPath(bookID), settings))
  {
    while (reader.IsStartElement("bookContentChunk", "http://books"))
    {
      xw.WriteRaw(reader.ReadElementString());
      xw.Flush();
    }
  }

  reader.ReadEndElement();
}
```

ReadXml first reads the size of the book:

```
int bookContentSize = Convert.ToInt32(reader.GetAttribute("bookContentSize"));
```

It then uses an XmlWriter object to write out the book in streaming fashion. Notice that ReadXml uses an XmlWriterSettings object to request the writer not to render the XML declaration on the top of the file because the client application saves the book as an HTML file:

```
XmlWriterSettings settings = new XmlWriterSettings();
settings.Indent = true;
settings.OmitXmlDeclaration = true;
```

As Listing 11-17 shows, ReadXml uses the IsStartElement method of the XmlReader object (that is passed into it) to read through the stream to locate the bookContentChunk elements. Notice that ReadXml calls the Flush method of the XmlWriter object to flush the writer after writing out the content of each bookContentChunk element. In other words, the ReadXml method of the client application reads the data chunk by chunk.

```
xw.WriteRaw(reader.ReadElementString());
xw.Flush();
```

Custom Schema Importer Extension

The client application implements a custom schema importer extension named ForumSchemaImporter Extension3 to bypass the default XSD to .NET type mapping. Listing 11-18 presents the implementation of this custom extension.

Listing 11-18: The ForumSchemaImporterExtension3 extension

```
public class ForumSchemaImporterExtension3 : SchemaImporterExtension
{
  public override string ImportSchemaType(XmlSchemaType type,
        XmlSchemaObject context, XmlSchemas schemas, XmlSchemaImporter importer,
        CodeCompileUnit compileUnit, CodeNamespace codeNamespace,
        CodeGenerationOptions options, CodeDomProvider codeGenerator)
  {
    return null;
  }

  public override string ImportSchemaType(string name, string ns,
        XmlSchemaObject context,
        XmlSchemas schemas, XmlSchemaImporter importer,
        CodeCompileUnit compileUnit, CodeNamespace mainNamespace,
        CodeGenerationOptions options, CodeDomProvider codeProvider)
  {
    if (name.Equals("bookContent") && ns.Equals("http://books"))
    {
      compileUnit.ReferencedAssemblies.Add("ForumBook.dll");
      return "ForumBook";
    }

    return null;
  }
}
```

As discussed in the previous sections, you have two options when it comes to implementing the ImportSchemaType method:

❑ You can write the associated code in C# or VB.NET, compile the code to an assembly, and add a reference to this assembly to the ReferencedAssemblies collection of the CodeCompileUnit object passed into the ImportSchemaType method.

❑ You can use CodeDom approach to implement a language-agnostic version of your code as you did in previous sections.

Listing 11-18 shows that the ImportSchemaType method uses the first approach:

```
compileUnit.ReferencedAssemblies.Add("ForumBook.dll");
```

As discussed in the previous sections, you have to compile the ForumSchemaImporterExtension3 into a strongly named assembly, add the assembly to GAC, and register the assembly with the machine.config file.

Extensibility of the XmlWebServiceMethodInvoker

Because the `XmlWebServiceMethodInvoker` component uses the `ServiceDescription` class, it will automatically return a `Forum` object from its `InvokeWebServiceMethod` method. Recall that the `ServiceDescription` class uses the `XmlSchemaImporter` class to generate the code for the client-side component, `Forum`:

```
protected void Page_Load(object sender, EventArgs e)
{
  XmlWebServiceMethodInvoker methodInvoker = new XmlWebServiceMethodInvoker();
  methodInvoker.TypeName = "Service";
  methodInvoker.WSDLPath = "http://localhost:1710/Server/Service.asmx?wsdl";
  OrderedDictionary list = new OrderedDictionary();
  Forum forum = (Forum)methodInvoker.InvokeXmlWebServiceMethod("Select", list,
                                                               false);
}
```

Summary

The default proxy code generation mechanism generates code for client-side components that may not meet the requirements of the client application. For example, the client application may want to generate code for a component that reads the data in streaming fashion to improve performance and responsiveness of the application. You must take the following steps to bypass the default behavior:

1. Develop server and client components that implement the `IXmlSerializable` interface to take full control of their serialization/deserialization.

2. Develop a custom schema importer extension to dynamically generate code for client-side components that meet the requirements of the client application.

The next few chapters discuss the ASP.NET data source control model, where you'll develop a data source control that uses an XML Web service as its underlying data store.

12

Understanding the ASP.NET 2.0 Tabular Data Source Control Model

This chapter serves two important purposes. First, as the following chapters illustrate, many custom server controls must contain data access code to access their underlying data stores. Such data access code must be generic because in data-driven Web applications, data comes from many different types of data stores, such as Microsoft SQL Server, Microsoft Access, Oracle, XML documents, Web services, and flat files, to name a few. This chapter shows you how to use the ASP.NET 2.0 data source control model to write generic data access code.

The second purpose is to drill down to the details of the ASP.NET 2.0 data source control model, because the model is the part of the ASP.NET 2.0 Framework that you must extend in order to write your own custom data source controls.

Why You Need the ASP.NET 2.0 Data Source Control Model

Before you get into to the details of the ASP.NET 2.0 data source control model, you need to understand why you need the model in the first place. Chapter 9 taught you the techniques and skills that you need to develop complex, feature-rich data-bound controls. As an example, Chapter 9 implemented a custom data-bound control named `CustomTable` that allows users to sort, page, delete, and update database records. You can use the skills you learned in Chapter 9 to extend the functionality of `CustomTable` to implement all the features that a complex, feature-rich data-bound control such as `DataGrid` supports. Chapter 9 didn't use any of the new features of the ASP.NET 2.0 to develop the `CustomTable` control. It was all based on the ASP.NET 1.x Framework.

If the ASP.NET 1.x Framework allows you to implement data-bound controls as feature-rich as
`DataGrid`, you may wonder what you need the ASP.NET 2.0 data source control model for.

The answer lies in the answers to the following questions: What does it take for page developers to take
advantage of the rich features of an ASP.NET 1.x control such as `DataGrid`? Can they use these features
out of the box? How much code do they have to write to use each feature? To answer these questions,
this chapter takes a closer look at the amount of code that page developers must write to take advantage
of some of the rich features of the ASP.NET 1.x `DataGrid` control.

Listing 12-1 shows a Web page that uses a `DataGrid` control to display, edit, insert, delete, sort, and page
through database records. As Listing 12-1 shows, it's quite amazing how much page developers can accomplish with a `DataGrid` control by simply setting the values of a few attributes on the `<asp:DataGrid>`
tag in the `.aspx` file. For example, page developers can enable paging and sorting by simply setting the
`AllowPaging` and `AllowSorting` attributes to true.

Listing 12-1: Using a DataGrid control to manipulate database records

```
<%@ Page Language="C#" AutoEventWireup="true" CodeFile="Default.aspx.cs"
  Inherits="_Default" %>

<!DOCTYPE html PUBLIC "-//W3C//DTD XHTML 1.1//EN"
"http://www.w3.org/TR/xhtml11/DTD/xhtml11.dtd">
<html xmlns="http://www.w3.org/1999/xhtml">
<head runat="server">
  <title>Untitled Page</title>
</head>
<body>
  <form id="form1" runat="server">
    <asp:DataGrid runat="server" ID="DataGrid1" AllowPaging="True"
      AllowCustomPaging="True" AllowSorting="True" DataKeyField="BookID"
      OnCancelCommand="CancelCallback" OnDeleteCommand="DeleteCallback"
      OnEditCommand="EditCallback" AutoGenerateColumns="false"
      OnPageIndexChanged="PageCallback" OnSortCommand="SortCallback"
      OnUpdateCommand="UpdateCallback" PageSize="3" PagerStyle-Mode="NumericPages"
      BackColor="LightGoldenrodYellow" BorderColor="Tan"
      BorderWidth="1px" CellPadding="5" ForeColor="Black"
      GridLines="None">
      <FooterStyle BackColor="Tan" />
      <SelectedItemStyle BackColor="DarkSlateBlue" ForeColor="GhostWhite" />
      <PagerStyle BackColor="PaleGoldenrod" ForeColor="DarkSlateBlue"
        HorizontalAlign="Center" />
      <AlternatingItemStyle BackColor="PaleGoldenrod" />
      <HeaderStyle BackColor="Tan" Font-Bold="True" />
      <Columns>
        <asp:ButtonColumn ButtonType="LinkButton" CommandName="Delete"
          Text="Delete" />
        <asp:EditCommandColumn ButtonType="LinkButton" EditText="Edit"
          UpdateText="Update" CancelText="Cancel" />
        <asp:BoundColumn DataField="Title" SortExpression="Title"
          HeaderText="Title" />
        <asp:BoundColumn DataField="Author" SortExpression="Author"
          HeaderText="Author" />
        <asp:BoundColumn DataField="Publisher" SortExpression="Publisher"
```

```
                HeaderText="Publisher" />
            <asp:BoundColumn DataField="Price" SortExpression="Price"
                HeaderText="Price" />
        </Columns>
      </asp:DataGrid>
    </form>
  </body>
</html>
```

The .aspx file shows the beautiful side of the DataGrid server control, where page developers use declarative programming to declare and enable different features of the control. However, things look quite ugly in the code-behind file (.aspx.cs file), where page developers have to write a lot of code to use each feature.

The ASP.NET 1.x standard and custom data-bound controls leave the responsibility of retrieving the data from the underlying data store and handling the Load, Sort, Page, Delete, Edit, Update, and Cancel events to page developers. Page developers must write a lot of code to handle these events and to retrieve the data. This also requires page developers to have a solid understanding of the ADO.NET classes and page life cycle. As an example, take a closer look at the code page developers must write to retrieve the data and to handle the Update event.

> *The source code for this example, available at* www.wrox.com, *contains the complete code for the* PageCallback, SortCallback, DeleteCallback, InsertCallback, EditCallback, UpdateCallback, CancelCallback, *and* Page_Load *methods.*

Retrieving Data

The ASP.NET 1.x standard and custom data-bound controls leave the responsibility of retrieving the data from the underlying data store to page developers. The RetrieveData method in Listing 12-2 retrieves the data from a SQL Server database and returns an IEnumerable object that contains the retrieved data. Notice that the GetOnePageOfData stored procedure takes three arguments: the current page index, page size, and sort expression, which page developers must set to the appropriate values. The stored procedure uses the current page index and page size values to retrieve the appropriate page of records from the database. The stored procedure uses the sort expression value in the Order By section of the relevant Select SQL statement to sort the data.

Listing 12-2: The RetrieveData method

```
IEnumerable RetrieveData()
{
  SqlConnection con = new SqlConnection();
  con.ConnectionString = connectionString;
  SqlCommand com = new SqlCommand();
  com.Connection = con;
  string sortExpression = ViewState["SortExpression"] != null ?
                     (string)ViewState["SortExpression"] : "BookID";
  string sortDirection = ViewState["SortDirection"] != null ?
                     (string)ViewState["SortDirection"] : "Asc";

  com.CommandText = "GetOnePageOfData";
  com.CommandType = System.Data.CommandType.StoredProcedure;
```

(continued)

Listing 12-2: *(continued)*

```
        com.Parameters.AddWithValue("@PageSize", DataGrid1.PageSize);
        com.Parameters.AddWithValue("@CurrentPageIndex", DataGrid1.CurrentPageIndex);

        if (sortExpression != null && sortExpression.Trim() != "")
          com.Parameters.AddWithValue("@SortExpression", sortExpression + " " +
                                      sortDirection);
        DataTable dt = new DataTable();
        SqlDataAdapter ad = new SqlDataAdapter();
        ad.SelectCommand = com;
        con.Open();
        ad.Fill(dt);
        con.Close();
        return dt.DefaultView;
    }
```

Update Event

The ASP.NET 1.x standard and custom data-bound controls leave the responsibility of handling the `Update` event to page developers. The `UpdateCallback` method in Listing 12-3 takes the following actions:

1. Extracts the primary key field value of the record being updated.

2. Extracts the new values of the fields being updated.

3. Uses ADO.NET classes such as `SqlConnection` and `SqlCommand` to update the underlying database record.

4. Sets the value of the `EditItemIndex` of the `DataGrid` control to -1.

5. Calls the `BindGrid` method to retrieve fresh data and to update the display of the `DataGrid` control (see Listing 12-4).

Listing 12-3: The UpdateCallback method

```
protected void UpdateCallback(object sender, DataGridCommandEventArgs e)
{
  int primaryKey = (int)DataGrid1.DataKeys[e.Item.ItemIndex];
  SqlConnection con = new SqlConnection();
  con.ConnectionString = connectionString;
  SqlCommand com = new SqlCommand();
  com.Connection = con;
  com.CommandText = "Update Books Set Title=@Title, Author=@Author,
                    Publisher=@Publisher, Price=@Price Where BookID=@BookID";
  com.Parameters.AddWithValue("@BookID", primaryKey);
  com.Parameters.AddWithValue("@Title",
                              ((TextBox)(e.Item.Cells[2].Controls[0])).Text);
  com.Parameters.AddWithValue("@Author",
                              ((TextBox)(e.Item.Cells[3].Controls[0])).Text);
  com.Parameters.AddWithValue("@Publisher",
                              ((TextBox)(e.Item.Cells[4].Controls[0])).Text);
```

```
    com.Parameters.AddWithValue("@Price",
                    decimal.Parse(((TextBox)(e.Item.Cells[5].Controls[0])).Text));
    con.Open();
    com.ExecuteNonQuery();
    con.Close();
    DataGrid1.EditItemIndex = -1;
    BindGrid();
}
```

Listing 12-4: The BindGrid method

```
void BindGrid()
{
    IEnumerable data = RetrieveData();
    DataGrid1.DataSource = data;
    DataGrid1.DataBind();
}
```

Listings 12-2–12-4 clearly show that page developers must write a lot of code to retrieve the data from the data store and to handle events such as Load, Sort, Delete, Edit, Update, Cancel, and Page. Why don't the ASP.NET 1.x standard and custom data-bound controls directly encapsulate the method that retrieves the data (such as the RetrieveData method) and the methods that handle the events (such as the UpdateCallback method) to save page developers from having to implement these methods themselves?

To answer this question, you need to examine Listings 12-2–12-4 more closely. Notice that the methods that retrieve the data and handle the events use ADO.NET classes such as SqlConnection, SqlCommand, and SqlDataAdapter, which are specifically designed to work with Microsoft SQL Server databases.

If the ASP.NET 1.x standard and custom data-bound controls were to encapsulate these methods, they would be tied to Microsoft SQL Server databases and wouldn't be able to work with other types of data stores such as Oracle.

You can make these methods more generic if you replace the ADO.NET SQL Server–specific classes with new generic ADO.NET 2.0 classes such as DbConnection, DbCommand, and DbDataAdapter. For example, Listing 12-5 shows a new version of the RetrieveData method that uses these new ADO.NET 2.0 classes.

Listing 12-5: The ADO.NET 2.0 version of the RetrieveData method

```
IEnumerable RetrieveData()
{
    string ProviderName = "System.Data.SqlClient";
    DbProviderFactory provider = DbProviderFactories.GetFactory(ProviderName);
    DbConnection con = provider.CreateConnection();
    con.ConnectionString = connectionString;
    DbCommand com = provider.CreateCommand();
    com.Connection = con;
    string sortExpression = ViewState["SortExpression"] != null ?
                    (string)ViewState["SortExpression"] : "BookID";
```

(continued)

Listing 12-5: *(continued)*

```
    string sortDirection = ViewState["SortDirection"] != null ?
                          (string)ViewState["SortDirection"] : "Asc";
    com.CommandText = "GetOnePageOfData";
    com.CommandType = System.Data.CommandType.StoredProcedure;
    DbParameter param = provider.CreateParameter();
    param.ParameterName = "@PageSize";
    param.Value = DataGrid1.PageSize;
    com.Parameters.Add(param);
    param = provider.CreateParameter();
    param.ParameterName = "@CurrentPageIndex";
    param.Value = DataGrid1.CurrentPageIndex;
    com.Parameters.Add(param);
    param = provider.CreateParameter();
    param.ParameterName = "@SortExpression";
    param.Value = sortExpression + " " + sortDirection;
    com.Parameters.Add(param);
    DataTable dt = new DataTable();
    DbDataAdapter ad = provider.CreateDataAdapter();
    ad.SelectCommand = com;
    con.Open();
    ad.Fill(dt);
    con.Close();
    return dt.DefaultView;
}
```

Even with these new changes, the `RetrieveData` method isn't generic because ADO.NET classes (even the new ones) are specifically designed to work with relational databases such as Microsoft SQL Server and Oracle, and can't be used with non-relational data stores such as XML files, Web services, and flat files, to name a few.

In summary, the ASP.NET standard and custom data-bound controls will not be able to encapsulate the methods that retrieve the data and the methods that handle the `Load`, `Sort`, `Delete`, `Edit`, `Update`, `Cancel`, `Insert`, and `Page` events unless the ASP.NET Framework provides the infrastructure that will allow these controls to retrieve, update, insert, and delete data from the underlying data store in generic fashion. Enter the ASP.NET 2.0 data source control model.

The ASP.NET 2.0 Data Source Control Model

This section begins by revisiting the `RetrieveData` method (see Listing 12-5). Because the method retrieves the data for a tabular data-bound control (`DataGrid`), it expects tabular data from its underlying data store. If the method were to retrieve the data for a hierarchical data-bound control such as `TreeView`, it would expect hierarchical data from its underlying data store.

This causes a major problem in data-driven Web applications where data comes from many different types of data stores, such as Microsoft SQL Server, Microsoft Access, Oracle, XML documents, flat files, and Web services. Some of these data stores, such as Microsoft SQL Server and Oracle, return tabular data, whereas some others, such as XML documents, return hierarchical data. Therefore there is no guarantee that the `RetrieveData` method will always receive tabular data from its underlying data store.

What you need is a new set of components that will present tabular and hierarchical data-bound controls with tabular and hierarchical views, respectively, of the underlying data store regardless of whether the data store itself is tabular or hierarchical. These components are collectively known as *data source controls*.

The ASP.NET 2.0 data source control model comes with standard data source controls such as SqlDataSource, AccessDataSource, ObjectDataSource, XmlDataSource, and SiteMapDataSource, where each data source control is specifically designed and implemented to present one or more tabular or hierarchical views of a specific type of data store.

For example, the SqlDataSource and XmlDataSource controls are specifically designed to work with relational databases and XML documents, respectively. The same data source control can present both tabular and hierarchical views of its underlying data store. For example, the XmlDataSource and SiteMapDataSource controls support both types of views.

If the methods that retrieve (the RetrieveData method), delete (the DeleteCallback method), insert (the InsertCallback method), and update (the UpdateCallback method) the data records were to directly use any of the standard ASP.NET 2.0 data source controls (such as SqlDataSource, AccessDataSource, ObjectDataSource, XmlDataSource, and SiteMapDataSource), they would be tied to the data store that the respective data source control is specifically designed to work with, and wouldn't be able to work with all types of data stores.

To address this problem, all tabular and hierarchical data source controls implement the IDataSource and IHierarchicalDataSource interfaces, respectively. Therefore the methods that retrieve, delete, insert, and update data records don't have to directly deal with any specific type of data source control such as SqlDataSource, AccessDataSource, and so on. Instead, they use the methods and properties of the IDataSource and IHierarchicalDataSource interfaces to indirectly deal with these data source controls. In other words, as far as these methods are concerned, all data source controls are of type IDataSource and/or IHierarchicalDataSource. The rest of this chapter discusses the tabular data source control model in detail. Chapter 15 covers the hierarchical data source control model.

ASP.NET 2.0 Tabular Data Source Control Model

Tabular data source controls make the underlying data store, which may or may not be relational, look like a database where the tabular data source views act like database tables. The ASP.NET 2.0 tabular data source control model consists of the following main components:

- ❏   IDataSource
- ❏   DataSourceControl
- ❏   DataSourceView
- ❏   The ASP.NET 2.0 data source control parameter model

This chapter discusses the first three components in detail and leaves the discussions of the ASP.NET 2.0 data source control parameter model to the next chapter. To make the discussions of these two chapters more concrete, you'll also implement a fully functional replica of the SqlDataSource control built into the ASP.NET 2.0 Framework. Each section of these two chapters present the implementation of the part of this control that relates to the discussions presented in that section. By the end of the next chapter, you should have a fully functional replica of the ASP.NET 2.0 SqlDataSource control that you can use in your Web applications.

This replica will support a feature that the actual SqlDataSource control lacks. As you'll see later in this chapter, this feature will allow data-bound controls such as GridView to retrieve data one page at a time from the underlying database. This will improve the performance and responsiveness of these controls, especially in data-driven Web applications.

IDataSource

All tabular data source controls (such as the SqlDataSource, AccessDataSource, ObjectDataSource, SiteMapDataSource, and XmlDataSource controls) implement the IDataSource interface. The interface exposes two methods and a single event (see Listing 12-6).

Listing 12-6: All tabular data source controls implement the IDataSource interface

```
public interface IDataSource
{
    DataSourceView GetView(string viewName);
    ICollection GetViewNames();
    event EventHandler DataSourceChanged;
}
```

As mentioned, because tabular data-bound controls such as GridView only deal with the IDataSource interface, they aren't tied to any specific type of data source and therefore will work with all types of data stores. However, the IDataSource interface has one drawback — the clients (tabular data-bound controls) of an interface can't create an instance of the interface.

The ASP.NET 2.0 data source control model comes with an implementation of the IDataSource interface named DataSourceControl. All ASP.NET 2.0 standard and custom tabular data source controls derive from the DataSourceControl abstract base class. Because the DataSourceControl class derives from the Control class, all ASP.NET 2.0 standard and custom tabular data source controls inherit the following important features from the Control class:

❑ Like all server controls, they can be used declaratively in an .aspx file. Recall that a server control is a component that directly or indirectly derives from the Control base class.

❑ The ASP.NET Framework automatically parses the .aspx file, creates an instance of the declared tabular data source control, and adds the instance to the control tree of the containing page.

❑ The containing page object exposes a method named FindControl that takes the value of the ID property of a tabular data source control, locates the control in the control tree, and returns a reference to it.

A typical workflow is as follows:

1. Page developers decide what type of tabular data source control to use. The type depends on the type of underlying data store. Recall that each type of tabular data source control is designed to expose tabular views of a specific type of data store.

2. Page developers declare the appropriate type of the tabular data source control in the .aspx file and set its ID property to a unique string value.

3. Page developers declare a tabular data-bound control, such as `GridView`, in the `.aspx` file and set its `DataSourceID` property to the value of the `ID` property of the declared tabular data source control.

4. As you'll see in Chapter 17, the tabular data-bound control calls the `FindControl` method of its `Page` property and passes the value of its `DataSourceID` property as the argument. The `FindControl` method locates the tabular data source control in the control tree of the containing page, and returns a reference to it:

```
Control myControl = Page.FindControl(DataSourceID);
```

The tabular data-bound control type casts the return value of the `FindControl` method to `IDataSource`:

```
IDataSource tabularDataSourceControl = (IDataSource) myControl;
```

This means that as far as tabular data-bound controls are concerned, all tabular data source controls are of type `IDataSource`. They don't know or care about the actual type of the data source control; for example, whether it's a `SqlDataSource` or `XmlDataSource` control. The only information that they care about is the value of the `ID` property of the data source control. In other words, the only dependency between them and the data source control (such as `SqlDataSource`) is the `ID` property, which is nothing but a string value.

This allows page developers to switch from an existing data source control to a new one by simply declaring the new one in the .aspx file without any code change. You may wonder why page developers would want to switch from one data source control to another. Recall that each data source control is designed to work with a specific type of data store. Page developers switch from one data source control to another to access a different type of data store. For instance, they may switch from a `SqlDataSource` control to an `XmlDataSource` control to access an XML document.

As Listing 12-6 shows, the `IDataSource` interface exposes an event named `DataSourceChanged`. This event is raised when properties of the respective data source control or the underlying data store changes. As you'll see in Chapter 17, tabular data-bound controls such as `GridView` register callback methods for this event, where they retrieve fresh data from the data store and update their display.

Under the Hood of DataSourceControl

This section takes you under the hood of the main methods, properties, and events of the `DataSourceControl` abstract base class as shown in Listing 12-7. Notice that the `DataSourceControl` class uses the C# interface design pattern discussed in Chapter 4 to implement the `IDataSource` interface. Following the pattern, here's what Listing 12-7 does:

1. It implements two protected methods named `GetView` and `GetViewNames` with the same signatures as the `GetView` and `GetViewNames` methods of the `IDataSource` interface.

2. It explicitly implements the `GetView` and `GetViewNames` methods of the `IDataSource` interface where the names of these two methods are qualified with the name of the interface.

3. The explicit implementations of the `GetView` and `GetViewNames` methods simply delegate to the `GetView` and `GetViewNames` protected methods.

This means that when subclasses of the DataSourceControl override the GetView and GetViewNames protected methods, they automatically override the explicit implementation of the GetView and GetViewNames methods of the IDataSource interface.

In other words, when you are developing a custom data source control, you shouldn't explicitly implement the GetView and GetViewNames methods of the IDataSource interface. Instead you must override the GetView and GetViewNames protected methods of the DataSourceControl base class.

Listing 12-7: The main methods, properties, and events of the DataSourceControl abstract base class

```
public abstract class DataSourceControl : Control, IDataSource
{
  DataSourceView IDataSource.GetView(string viewName)
  {
    return this.GetView(viewName);
  }

  ICollection IDataSource.GetViewNames()
  {
    return this.GetViewNames();
  }

  protected virtual DataSourceView GetView(string viewName)
  {
    return null;
  }

  protected virtual ICollection GetViewNames()
  {
    return null;
  }

  private static readonly object EventKey = new object();
  public event EventHandler DataSourceChanged
  {
    add { Events.AddHandler(EventKey, value); }
    remove { Events.RemoveHandler(EventKey, value); }
  }

  protected virtual void RaiseDataSourceChangedEvent(EventArgs e)
  {
    EventHandler handler = (EventHandler)Events[EventKey];

    if (handler != null)
      handler(this, e);
  }
}
```

Notice that the DataSourceControl class uses the C# event implementation pattern discussed in Chapter 4 to implement the DataSourceChanged event, where an event key is used to access the EventHandler object in the Events collection and the RaiseDataSourceChangedEvent protected virtual method is implemented to raise the event. Your custom data source control must call the RaiseDataSourceChangedEvent method every time it changes.

Deriving from the DataSourceControl Base Class

The previous sections discussed the ASP.NET 2.0 IDataSource interface and took you under the hood of the DataSourceControl abstract base class. As discussed, in this chapter and the next chapter you implement a fully functional replica of the SqlDataSource control built into the ASP.NET 2.0 Framework to make the discussions of these two chapters more concrete.

Like any other tabular data source control, the SqlDataSource control derives from the DataSourceControl base class and overrides its GetView and GetViewNames protected methods. Before getting into the details of the SqlDataSource control's implementation of these methods, take a moment to review the typical workflow where these methods are used.

As mentioned, tabular data-bound controls such as GridView first call the FindControl method of the containing page to access the underlying tabular data source control (SqlDataSource) in generic fashion without knowing its actual type, that is, whether it is a SqlDataSource or XmlDataSource control or something else entirely.

As you'll see in Chapter 17, tabular data-bound controls then call the GetView method of the data source control to access the view object that represents the desired tabular view of the underlying data store. The type of the view object depends on the type of the data source control. For example, the GetView methods of the SqlDataSource and XmlDataSource controls return objects of type SqlDataSourceView and XmlDataSourceView, respectively. All view classes derive from the DataSourceView abstract base class. This base class defines the methods, properties, and events that its subclasses must implement in order to expose tabular views of their underlying data stores. DataSourceView is thoroughly discussed later in this chapter.

Notice that the GetView method takes the view name as its argument because tabular views are named such that each name uniquely identifies its own view among other views. The GetViewNames method returns the names of all tabular views that the data source control exposes.

Tabular data-bound controls such as GridView call the GetViewNames method to access the names of all the available tabular views and then call the GetView method to access the view object that represents the tabular view with a given name.

Now that you know how the GetView and GetViewNames are used, here is the SqlDataSource control's implementation of these two methods. As the following code shows, the SqlDataSource control exposes a single tabular view named DefaultView:

```
protected override ICollection GetViewNames()
{
  return new string[] { "DefaultView" };
}
```

The SqlDataSource control exposes a protected method named CreateDataSourceView that creates the default tabular view of the control. The subclasses of the SqlDataSource control can override the CreateDataSourceView method to provide their own implementations:

```
protected virtual SqlDataSourceView CreateDataSourceView(string viewName)
{
  if (!string.IsNullOrEmpty(viewName) && (viewName.ToLower() != "defaultview"))
```

```
      throw new ArgumentException("Wrong view name!");

  if (view == null)
  {
    view = new SqlDataSourceView(this, viewName, Context);
    if (IsTrackingViewState)
      ((IStateManager)view).TrackViewState();
  }

  return view;
}
```

The `SqlDataSource` control overrides the `GetView` method of its base class to call the `CreateDataSourceView` method:

```
protected override DataSourceView GetView(string viewName)
{
  return CreateDataSourceView(viewName);
}
```

DataSourceView

The previous sections discussed the first two components of the ASP.NET 2.0 data source control model: `IDataSource` and `DataSourceControl`. This section discusses the third component: `DataSourceView`. The following code contains the code for the `DataSourceView` base class. The implementations of the methods, properties, and events of this base class are discussed in the following sections:

```
using System;
using System.Collections;
using System.Web.UI;
using System.Web.UI.WebControls;
using System.ComponentModel;

namespace CustomComponents2
{
  public abstract class DataSourceView
  {
    public event EventHandler DataSourceViewChanged {add; remove;}

    protected virtual void OnDataSourceViewChanged(EventArgs e);
    public string Name {get;}
    protected DataSourceView(IDataSource owner, string viewName);

    protected internal abstract
    IEnumerable ExecuteSelect(DataSourceSelectArguments arguments);

    public virtual void Select(DataSourceSelectArguments arguments,
                            DataSourceViewSelectCallback callback);

    public virtual bool CanDelete {get;}
    protected virtual int ExecuteDelete(IDictionary keys, IDictionary oldValues);
    public virtual void Delete(IDictionary keys, IDictionary oldValues,
                            DataSourceViewOperationCallback callback);
    public virtual bool CanInsert {get;}
```

```
      protected virtual int ExecuteInsert(IDictionary values);
      public virtual void Insert(IDictionary values,
                               DataSourceViewOperationCallback callback);
      public virtual bool CanUpdate {get;}
      protected virtual int ExecuteUpdate(IDictionary keys, IDictionary values,
                                          IDictionary oldValues);

      public virtual void Update(IDictionary keys, IDictionary values,
                 IDictionary oldValues, DataSourceViewOperationCallback callback);

      public virtual bool CanPage {get;}
      public virtual bool CanRetrieveTotalRowCount {get;}
      public virtual bool CanSort {get;}
      protected EventHandlerList Events {get;]

      public virtual void RaiseUnsupportedCapabilityError(
                                        DataSourceCapabilities capability);
    }
  }
```

Select

As you'll see in Chapter 17, tabular data-bound controls such as `GridView` and `DetailsView` call the `Select` method to retrieve tabular data from the underlying data store. Because the `Select` operation is asynchronous, tabular data-bound controls register a callback for this operation. Listing 12-8 contains the `DataSourceView` class's implementation of the `Select` method, where the method calls the `ExecuteSelect` method to retrieve the data records from the underlying data store and passes the `IEnumerable` collection that contains the retrieved data to the client callback method. As you'll see in Chapter 17, the client callback method enumerates the retrieved data and creates the appropriate control hierarchy.

Listing 12-8: The Select Method

```
public virtual void Select(DataSourceSelectArguments arguments,
                           DataSourceViewSelectCallback callback)
{
  if (callback == null)
    throw new ArgumentNullException();

  IEnumerable data = ExecuteSelect(arguments);
  callback(data);
}
```

The `Select` method takes two arguments. The first argument is of type `DataSourceSelectArguments`. As you'll see in Chapter 17, tabular data-bound controls use this argument to request extra operations on the retrieved tabular data. The `DataSourceSelectArguments` class supports the following operations:

❑ **Sorting:** The class exposes a property named `SortExpression` that tabular data-bound controls such as `GridView` must set to the appropriate sort expression value, which normally consists of two parts: the name of the data field to sort on followed by the keyword `Asc` or `Desc`. This value is normally used in the Order By section of the `Select` SQL statement to sort the retrieved data.

Tabular data-bound controls first call the `CanSort` property of the view object to ensure that the view supports sorting before they attempt to set the `SortExpression` property.

❏ **Retrieving the total number of rows:** Paging improves the usability and performance of data-bound controls (such as `GridView`) by allowing them to retrieve data one page at a time. However, most data-bound controls render link buttons in their paging interface to provide random page access. This means that they need to know the total row count up front, even though they are retrieving data one page at a time.

As you'll see in Chapter 19, they set the `RetrieveTotalRowCount` property of the `DataSourceSelectArguments` object to true to request that the view object retrieve the total row count. The view object retrieves the total row count and assigns it to the `TotalRowCount` property of the `DataSourceSelectArguments` object. Data-bound controls subsequently use the `TotalRowCount` property to access the total row count and divide it by the page size to arrive at the total number of pages and consequently the total number of link buttons they need to render in their paging interface.

Tabular data-bound controls call the `CanRetrieveTotalRowCount` property of the view object before setting the `RetrieveTotalRowCount` property to ensure that the view is capable of retrieving the total row count.

❏ **Paging:** As you'll see in Chapter 19, data-bound controls (such as `GridView`) that support paging set the `StartRowIndex` property of the `DataSourceSelectArguments` object to the index of the first data record to be retrieved, and set the `MaximumRows` property to the page size. This will instruct the underlying data source view object to retrieve only those records whose index values are greater than `StartRowIndex` and less than `MaximumRow+StartRowIndex`.

Data-bound controls call the `CanPage` property of the view object before they set these two properties to ensure the view supports paging.

As you can see, the `DataSourceView` base class takes full responsibility for implementing the `Select` method. However, it leaves the responsibility of implementing the `ExecuteSelect` method to its subclasses. This means that your custom tabular data source control is only responsible for implementing the `ExecuteSelect` method, and shouldn't override the `Select` method.

Deriving from the DataSourceView Class

The ASP.NET 2.0 Framework comes with a class named `SqlDataSourceView` that represents the default tabular view of the `SqlDataSource` control and, like any other view class, derives from the `DataSourceView` abstract base class. You'll implement a fully functional replica of this class in this chapter and the next chapter. Begin with the implementation of the `ExecuteSelect` method of this class in this section and leave the implementations of other methods and properties of the class to the upcoming sections of these two chapters. Listing 12-9 contains the code for the `SqlDataSourceView` class's implementation of the `ExecuteSelect` method.

Listing 12-9: The SqlDataSourceView class's implementation of the ExecuteSelect method

```
protected override IEnumerable ExecuteSelect(DataSourceSelectArguments arguments)
{
    if (CanPage)
        arguments.AddSupportedCapabilities(DataSourceCapabilities.Page);

    if (CanSort)
        arguments.AddSupportedCapabilities(DataSourceCapabilities.Sort);

    if (CanRetrieveTotalRowCount)
```

```
                    arguments.AddSupportedCapabilities(
                                    DataSourceCapabilities.RetrieveTotalRowCount);

       arguments.RaiseUnsupportedCapabilitiesError(this);
       DbProviderFactory provider = owner.GetDbProviderFactory();
       DbConnection con = provider.CreateConnection();
       con.ConnectionString = owner.ConnectionString;
       DbCommand com = provider.CreateCommand();
       com.Connection = con;
       if (arguments.RetrieveTotalRowCount)
         arguments.TotalRowCount = RetrieveTotalRowCount(com, provider);
       com.Parameters.Clear();
       return RetrieveRows(arguments, com, provider);
    }
```

The `DataSourceSelectArguments` class exposes two methods named `AddSupportedCapabilities` and `RaiseUnsupportedCapabilitiesError`. The first method is used to specify the capabilities that the view object supports, such as paging. The second method is used to check whether the view object supports the requested capabilities. As you'll see in Chapter 19, data-bound controls use the `DataSourceSelectArguments` to request these capabilities. If the view object doesn't support the requested capabilities, the `RaiseUnsupportedCapabilitiesError` method raises an exception.

As Listing 12-9 shows, the `ExecuteSelect` method checks the values of the `CanPage`, `CanSort`, and `CanRetrieveTotalRowCount` properties to determine whether it should call the `AddSupportedCapabilities` method to add the respective capability.

The `ExecuteSelect` method first calls the `GetDbProviderFactory` method of the `SqlDataSource` control (the `owner` variable references the `SqlDataSource` control that owns the view) to return an instance of the `DbProviderFactory` class:

```
DbProviderFactory provider = owner.GetDbProviderFactory();
```

Each subclass of the `DbProviderFactory` class is designed to work with a specific type of relational database. For example, the `SqlClientFactory` and `OleDbFactory` subclasses are specifically designed to work with Microsoft SQL Server databases and OLE DB data sources, respectively. If the `ExecuteSelect` method were to use one of the subclasses of the `DbProviderFactory` class directly, it would be tied to the relational database that the subclass is specifically designed to work with.

The `DbProviderFactory` class defines the API that the `ExecuteSelect` method can use to access the underlying relational database in generic fashion. The API isolates this method from the actual type of the underlying `DbProviderFactory` subclass. This allows the page developers to use the same `SqlDataSource` control to display records from different types of relational databases, such as Microsoft SQL Server and OLE DB.

Because the `GetDbProviderFactory` method has no way of knowing what the real type of the underlying `DbProviderFactory` subclass is, it can't use the `new` operator to create an instance of the subclass. ADO.NET 2.0 comes with a new class named `DbProviderFactories` that the `GetDbProviderFactory` method uses to create an instance of the subclass in generic fashion:

```
public virtual DbProviderFactory GetDbProviderFactory()
{
   return DbProviderFactories.GetFactory(ProviderName);
}
```

The `GetFactory` method takes the value of the `ProviderName` property of the `SqlDataSource` control as its argument. This value is the friendly name of the desired provider factory, which is normally the namespace that the provider factory belongs to.

For example, the friendly names `System.Data.SqlClient` and `System.Data.OleDb` instruct the `GetFactory` method to create an instance of the `SqlClientFactory` and `OleDbFactory` classes, respectively. The default value of the `ProviderName` property is `System.Data.SqlClient`.

The `ExecuteSelect` method (see Listing 12-9) then calls the `CreateConnection` and `CreateCommand` methods of the `DbProviderFactory` instance to create the appropriate connection and command objects in generic fashion:

```
DbConnection con = provider.CreateConnection();
con.ConnectionString = owner.ConnectionString;
DbCommand com = provider.CreateCommand();
com.Connection = con;
```

Notice that the `ExecuteSelect` method performs two different queries (see Listing 12-9). The first query retrieves the total row count and the second query retrieves the actual data records. The first query is performed only if the `RetrieveTotalRowCount` property of the `DataSourceSelectArguments` is set to true. As you'll see in Chapter 19, tabular data-bound controls such as `GridView` set this property to true to request the `ExecuteSelect` method to retrieve the total row count. As mentioned before, the `SqlDataSource` control built into the ASP.NET 2.0 Framework doesn't support this first query. In other words, it doesn't retrieve the total row count from the underlying data store. The `SqlDataSource` replica developed in this chapter and the next chapter, on the other hand, provides full support for this feature to improve the performance and responsiveness of the control.

The `ExecuteSelect` method calls the `RetrieveTotalRowCount` method to retrieve the total row count and assigns it to the `TotalRowCount` property of the `DataSourceSelectArguments` instance. As you'll see in Chapter 19, tabular data-bound controls such as `GridView` use the value of this property to determine the number of link buttons they need to render in their paging interface to support random page access.

```
arguments.TotalRowCount = RetrieveTotalRowCount(com);
```

The `ExecuteSelect` method then calls the `RetrieveRecords` method to retrieve the actual data records from the underlying relational database:

```
return RetrieveRows(arguments, com, provider);
```

Retrieving Total Row Count

Listing 12-10 contains the implementation of the `RetrieveTotalRowCount` method.

Listing 12-10: The RetrieveTotalRowCount method

```
protected virtual int RetrieveTotalRowCount( DbCommand com,
                                              DbProviderFactory provider)
{
  com.CommandText = SelectCountCommand;
  if (SelectCountCommandType == SqlDataSourceCommandType.StoredProcedure)
    com.CommandType = System.Data.CommandType.StoredProcedure;
```

```
        int totalRowCount = -1;
        com.Connection.Open();
        totalRowCount = (int)com.ExecuteScalar();
        com.Connection.Close();
        return totalRowCount;
    }
```

The `SqlDataSource` control exposes a property named `SelectCountCommand` that page developers must set to a string value that contains the appropriate `Select` SQL statement or stored procedure name, for example:

```
<SqlDataSource ID="MySource" runat="server" SelectCountCommand="Select Count(*)
From Products" .../>
```

The `SqlDataSource` control also exposes a property of type `SqlDataSourceCommandType` named `SelectCountCommandType` that page developers must set to one of its possible values, either `StoredProcedure` or `Text`, to specify whether the `SelectCountCommand` property contains a `Select` SQL statement or a stored procedure name:

```
if (SelectCountCommandType == SqlDataSourceCommandType.StoredProcedure)
    com.CommandType = CommandType.StoredProcedure;
```

Retrieving Data Rows

Listing 12-11 presents the implementation of the `RetrieveRows` method.

Listing 12-11: The RetrieveRows method

```
protected virtual IEnumerable RetrieveRows(DataSourceSelectArguments arguments,
                                 DbCommand com, DbProviderFactory provider)
{
    com.CommandText = SelectCommand;
    if (SelectCommandType == SqlDataSourceCommandType.StoredProcedure)
        com.CommandType = System.Data.CommandType.StoredProcedure;
    SetDbParameters(arguments, com, provider);
    IEnumerable result = null;
    SqlDataSourceSelectingEventArgs e =
                        new SqlDataSourceSelectingEventArgs(com, arguments, false);
    OnSelecting(e);
    if (!e.Cancel)
    {
        com.Connection.Open();
        if (this.owner.DataSourceMode == SqlDataSourceMode.DataSet)
        {
            DataSet ds = new DataSet();
            DbDataAdapter ad = provider.CreateDataAdapter();
            ad.SelectCommand = com;
            ad.Fill(ds);
            com.Connection.Close();
            result = ds.Tables[0].DefaultView;
        }
```

(continued)

Listing 12-11: *(continued)*

```
      else
        result = com.ExecuteReader(CommandBehavior.CloseConnection);
      SqlDataSourceStatusEventArgs ee =
                              new SqlDataSourceStatusEventArgs(com, -1, null);
      OnSelected(ee);
    }
    return result;
  }
```

The `RetrieveRows` method sets the `CommandText` property of the `DbCommand` object to the value of the `SelectCommand` property of the `SqlDataSource` control. Page developers must set the value of this property to a string value that contains the appropriate `Select` SQL statement or stored procedure name. This stored procedure normally takes up to three parameters. The `RetrieveRows` method delegates the responsibility of setting these parameters to the `SetDbParameters` method. This method is discussed shortly.

The `RetrieveRows` method raises two events named `Selecting` and `Selected`. These events are raised right before and right after the method retrieves the data from the underlying database. These two events are discussed later in this chapter.

The `SqlDataSource` control exposes a property of type `SqlDataSourceMode` named `DataSourceMode`, with the possible values of `SqlDataSourceMode.DataSet` and `SqlDataSourceMode.DataReader`. Page developers set the value of this property to specify whether the `RetrieveRows` method should use a `DataSet` or a `DbDataReader` to retrieve the data from the underlying data store.

The Selecting Event

The `SqlDataSourceView` class uses the steps outlined in Chapter 4 to implement the `Selecting` event. First, it defines the class whose instance holds the event data (`SqlDataSourceSelectingEventArgs`). The event data includes the following:

❑   The `DbCommand` object being used to retrieve the data

❑   The `DataSourceSelectArguments` instance passed to the `ExecuteSelect` method

❑   The Boolean flag that specifies whether or not the total row count will be retrieved as well:

```
public class SqlDataSourceSelectingEventArgs : SqlDataSourceCommandEventArgs
{
  private DataSourceSelectArguments arguments;
  private bool executingSelectCount;

  public SqlDataSourceSelectingEventArgs(DbCommand command,
                  DataSourceSelectArguments arguments,
                  bool executingSelectCount)
    : base(command)
  {
    this.arguments = arguments;
    this.executingSelectCount = executingSelectCount;
  }

  public DataSourceSelectArguments Arguments
```

```
  {
    get { return arguments; }
  }

  public bool ExecutingSelectCount
  {
    get { return executingSelectCount; }
  }
}
```

Next, the class defines the event delegate:

```
public delegate void SqlDataSourceSelectingEventHandler(object sender,
                                          SqlDataSourceSelectingEventArgs e);
```

Then it creates an event key:

```
private static readonly object SelectingKey = new object();
```

Next it defines the `Selecting` event where the event key is used to add and remove events:

```
public event SqlDataSourceSelectingEventHandler Selecting
{
  add { Events.AddHandler(SelectingKey, value); }
  remove { Events.RemoveHandler(SelectingKey, value); }
}
```

Finally, the class defines a protected method that raises the event:

```
protected virtual void OnSelecting(SqlDataSourceSelectingEventArgs e)
{
  SqlDataSourceSelectingEventHandler handler =
                      Events[SelectingKey] as SqlDataSourceSelectingEventHandler;
  if (handler != null)
    handler(this, e);
}
```

Notice that the `SqlDataSourceSelectingEventArgs` class derives from the `SqlDataSource CommandEventArgs` class. As you will see later, the `SqlDataSourceCommandEventArgs` instances are also used to hold event data for the `Updating`, `Deleting`, and `Inserting` events.

```
public class SqlDataSourceCommandEventArgs : CancelEventArgs
{
  private DbCommand command;
  public SqlDataSourceCommandEventArgs(DbCommand command)
  {
    this.command = command;
  }

  public DbCommand Command
  {
    get { return this.command; }
  }
}
```

The instances of the CancelEventArgs class are used to hold event data for cancelable events such as Selecting, Updating, Deleting, and Inserting. This class exposes a single Boolean property named Cancel that the clients of the SqlDataSource control can use to cancel these events. As Listing 12-11 shows, the RetrieveRows method proceeds with the Select operation only if the Cancel property isn't set to false:

```
SqlDataSourceSelectingEventArgs e =
        new SqlDataSourceSelectingEventArgs(com, arguments, false);
OnSelecting(e);
if (!e.Cancel)
{
   com.Connection.Open();
```

Selected Event

The SqlDataSourceView class uses the same steps from Chapter 4 to implement the Selected event. First, it defines the class that holds the event data (SqlDataSourceStatusEventArgs). The event data includes the following:

- ❏ The DbCommand object used to retrieve the data

- ❏ The number of database rows affected by the Select operation

- ❏ The Exception object, if any

- ❏ The Boolean flag that specifies whether or not the exception (if any) has been handled. The clients of the SqlDataSource control that want to use a custom exception handling schema must set the value of this flag to true to stop the SqlDataSource control from handling the exception:

```
public class SqlDataSourceStatusEventArgs : EventArgs
{
   private DbCommand command;
   private int affectedRows;
   private Exception exception;
   private bool exceptionHandled;

   public SqlDataSourceStatusEventArgs(DbCommand command,
           int affectedRows, Exception exception)
   {
     this.command = command;
     this.affectedRows = affectedRows;
     this.exception = exception;
     this.exceptionHandled = false;
   }

   public int AffectedRows
   {
     get { return this.affectedRows; }
   }

   public DbCommand Command
```

```
{
  get { return this.command; }
}

public Exception Exception
{
  get { return this.exception; }
}

public bool ExceptionHandled
{
  get { return this.exceptionHandled; }
  set { this.exceptionHandled = value; }
}
}
```

The class then defines the event delegate:

```
public delegate void SqlDataSourceStatusEventHandler(object sender,
                                        SqlDataSourceStatusEventArgs e);
```

Then it creates an event key:

```
private static readonly object SelectedKey = new object();
```

Next, it defines the Selected event where the event key is used to add and remove events:

```
public event SqlDataSourceStatusEventHandler Selected
{
  add { Events.AddHandler(SelectedKey, value); }
  remove { Events.RemoveHandler(SelectedKey, value); }
}
```

Finally, it defines a protected method that raises the event:

```
protected virtual void OnSelected(SqlDataSourceStatusEventArgs e)
{
  SqlDataSourceStatusEventHandler handler =
              Events[SelectingKey] as SqlDataSourceStatusEventHandler;
  if (handler != null)
    handler(this, e);
}
```

Setting the Parameters

To set a parameter, you need to set both the name and value of the parameter. Because the underlying stored procedure takes up to three parameters, the SqlDataSource control exposes three properties that page developers must set to the names of the three parameters of the stored procedure. The DataSourceSelectArguments class, on the other hand, exposes three properties that data-bound controls must set to the values of the three parameters of the stored procedure. This is discussed in detail in Chapter 19.

The following code shows how the SetDbParameters method uses these properties of the SqlDataSource and DataSourceSelectArguments to set the names and values of the parameters of the stored procedure:

```
protected virtual void SetDbParameters(DataSourceSelectArguments arguments,
                                       DbCommand com, DbProviderFactory provider)
{
  DbParameter p;
  if (SelectCommandType == SqlDataSourceCommandType.StoredProcedure)
  {
    if (!string.IsNullOrEmpty(SortParameterName))
    {
      p = provider.CreateParameter();
      p.ParameterName = ParameterPrefix + SortParameterName;
      p.Value = arguments.SortExpression;
      com.Parameters.Add(p);
    }
    if (!string.IsNullOrEmpty(StartRecordParameterName))
    {
      p = provider.CreateParameter();
      p.ParameterName = ParameterPrefix + StartRecordParameterName;
      p.Value = arguments.StartRowIndex;
      com.Parameters.Add(p);
    }
    if (!string.IsNullOrEmpty(MaxRecordsParameterName))
    {
      p = provider.CreateParameter();
      p.ParameterName = ParameterPrefix + MaxRecordsParameterName;
      p.Value = arguments.MaximumRows;
      com.Parameters.Add(p);
    }
  }
  else
  {
    if (!string.IsNullOrEmpty(arguments.SortExpression))
      com.CommandText += (" Order By " + arguments.SortExpression);
  }
}
```

To set the name and value of the parameter that the stored procedure uses to sort the data, the SqlDataSource control exposes a property named SortParameterName that page developers must set to the name of the argument of the stored procedure that is used for sorting. The SetDbParameters method uses the value of this property to set the name of the parameter:

```
p.ParameterName = ParameterPrefix + SortParameterName;
```

The DataSourceSelectArguments class also exposes a property named SortExpression that data-bound controls set to the appropriate sort expression value. This value normally consists of the name of the desired database field followed by the string value Asc or Desc. The stored procedure normally uses the sort expression value in the Order By section of the appropriate Select SQL statement to sort the data:

```
p.Value = arguments.SortExpression;
```

The other two arguments of the stored procedure are the index of the first record and the total number of the records being retrieved. The stored procedure uses these two values to retrieve a single page of data.

The `SetDbParameters` method needs to set the name and value of the parameter that the procedure uses to specify the index of the first record to be retrieved. The `SqlDataSource` control exposes a property named `StartRecordParameterName` that page developers must set to the name of the argument of the stored procedure that specifies the index of the first record. The `SetDbParameters` method uses the value of this property to set the name of the parameter:

```
p.ParameterName = ParameterPrefix + StartRecordParameterName;
```

The `DataSourceSelectArguments` class exposes a property named `StartRowIndex` that data-bound controls must set to the index of the first record being retrieved. The `SetDbParameters` method uses the value of this property to set the value of the parameter:

```
p.Value = arguments.StartRowIndex;
```

The `SetDbParameters` method then sets the name and value of the parameter that the procedure uses to specify the maximum number of records to be retrieved. The `SqlDataSource` control exposes a property named `MaxRecordsParameterName` that page developers must set to the name of the argument of the stored procedure that specifies the maximum records to be retrieved. The `SetDbParameters` method uses the value of this property to set the name of the parameter:

```
p.ParameterName = ParameterPrefix + MaxRecordsParameterName;
```

The `DataSourceSelectArguments` class exposes a property named `MaximumRows` that data-bound controls must set to the maximum number of rows to be retrieved. The `SetDbParameters` method uses the value of this property to set the value of the parameter:

```
p.Value = arguments.MaximumRows;
```

Delete

The clients of a data source view object call the `Delete` method of the view object to delete records from a data store. Listing 12-12 shows the `DataSourceView` class's implementation of the `Delete` method. The method first calls the `ExecuteDelete` method to delete the record from the database:

```
affectedRows = ExecuteDelete(keys, oldValues);
```

Then it calls the client's delete callback method. Because the `Delete` method is asynchronous, the clients of the `DataSourceView` object register a callback method:

```
callback(affectedRows, ex);
```

Listing 12-12: The DataSourceView class's implementation of the Delete method

```
public virtual void Delete(IDictionary keys, IDictionary oldValues,
                           DataSourceViewOperationCallback callback)
{
  Exception ex = null;
  int affectedRows = 0;
  try
  {
    affectedRows = ExecuteDelete(keys, oldValues);
  }
  catch (Exception e)
  {
    ex = e;
  }
  callback(affectedRows, ex);

}
```

The `Delete` method takes three arguments. The first argument is an `IDictionary` object that contains the names and values of the database fields that constitute the primary key of the record being deleted. This means that the `Delete` method supports multiple-field primary keys.

The second argument is an `IDictionary` object that contains the names and old values of the database fields of the record being deleted. The replica `SqlDataSource` control will not use this argument. Because the `Delete` operation is asynchronous, the clients must wrap a callback method in an instance of the `DataSourceViewOperationCallback` delegate and pass it as the third argument to the `Delete` method:

```
public delegate bool DataSourceViewOperationCallback( int affectedRows,
                                                      Exception ex);
```

The clients of a view object must first call the `CanDelete` property of the view object to make sure the view can delete records from its underlying data store before they attempt to call the `Delete` method.

Because the `Delete`, `Insert`, and `Update` operations change the underlying data store, the `DataSourceView` base class provides the `ExecuteDelete`, `ExecuteInsert`, and `ExecuteUpdate` methods with the following mechanism to send change notifications to their clients. The `DataSourceView` abstract base class exposes an event of type `EventHandler` named `DataSourceViewChanged` that is raised when one or more properties of the view object changes value, or the underlying data store changes due to the data operations such as `Delete`, `Update`, and `Insert`.

The `DataSourceView` class, like any other component, follows the steps outlined in Chapter 4 to implement the `DataSourceViewChanged` event. This class exposes a method named `OnDataSourceViewChanged` that raises this event.

As you'll see shortly, the `ExecuteDelete` method (see Listing 12-13) calls the `OnDataSourceViewChanged` method to raise the `DataSourceViewChanged` event because the `Delete` operation changes the underlying data store. As you'll see in Chapter 17, data-bound controls register a callback method for this event where they retrieve fresh data from the data store and update their display.

As this discussion shows, the `DataSourceView` base class takes full responsibility for implementing the `Delete` method (see Listing 12-12). However, it leaves the responsibility of implementing the

ExecuteDelete method to its subclasses. This means that your custom tabular data source control is only responsible for implementing the ExecuteDelete method, and shouldn't override the Delete method itself.

Next, continue with the implementation of the SqlDataSourceView class. Recall that the previous sections implemented the ExectueSelect method of this class. This section presents the implementation of the ExecuteDelete method, as shown in Listing 12-13.

Listing 12-13: The SqlDataSourceView class overrides the ExecuteDelete method

```
protected override int ExecuteDelete(IDictionary keys, IDictionary oldValues)
{
  if (!CanDelete)
    throw new NotSupportedException("Delete is not supported!");
  DbProviderFactory provider = owner.GetDbProviderFactory();
  DbConnection con = provider.CreateConnection();
  con.ConnectionString = owner.ConnectionString;
  DbCommand com = provider.CreateCommand();
  com.Connection = con;
  DbParameter p;
  com.CommandText = DeleteCommand;
  if (DeleteCommandType == SqlDataSourceCommandType.StoredProcedure)
    com.CommandType = System.Data.CommandType.StoredProcedure;
  foreach (DictionaryEntry entry in keys)
  {
    p = provider.CreateParameter();
    p.ParameterName = ParameterPrefix + entry.Key.ToString();
    p.Value = entry.Value;
    com.Parameters.Add(p);
  }
  int affectedRows = 0;
  Exception exception = null;
  SqlDataSourceCommandEventArgs e = new SqlDataSourceCommandEventArgs(com);
  OnDeleting(e);
  if (!e.Cancel)
  {
    con.Open();
    try
    {
      affectedRows = com.ExecuteNonQuery();
    }
    catch (Exception ex)
    {
      exception = ex;
    }
    con.Close();
    OnDataSourceViewChanged(EventArgs.Empty);
    SqlDataSourceStatusEventArgs ee =
            new SqlDataSourceStatusEventArgs(com, rowsAffected, exception);
    OnDeleted(ee);
    if (ee.Exception != null && !ee.ExceptionHandled)
      throw ee.Exception;
  }
  return affectedRows;
}
```

The `ExecuteDelete` method first calls the `CanDelete` property to ensure that the view is capable of deleting database records.

The `SqlDataSource` control exposes a property named `DeleteCommand` that page developers must set to a string value that contains the appropriate `Delete` SQL statement or stored procedure name, such as:

```
<custom:SqlDataSource ID="MySource" runat="server" DeleteCommand="Delete From
Products Where ProductID=@ProductID" .../>
```

The `ExecuteDelete` method assigns the value of this `DeleteCommand` parameter to the `CommandText` property of the `DbCommand` object:

```
com.CommandText = DeleteCommand;
```

Notice that the `Delete` SQL statement contains a parameter named `@ProductID`, which is the primary key field value of the record being deleted. As you'll see in Chapter 19, data-bound controls create an `IDictionary` object that contains the names (such as `ProductID`) and values of the primary key fields of the record being deleted and pass the object to the `Delete` method of the `SqlDataSourceView` object, which is subsequently passed to the `ExecuteDelete` method.

The `ExecuteDelete` method enumerates the `IDictionary` object and creates one `DbParameter` object for each enumerated `DictionaryEntry` object. The method uses the values of the `Key` and `Value` properties of each enumerated `DictionaryEntry` object to set the values of the `ParameterName` and `Value` properties of the each `DbParameter` object:

```
foreach (DictionaryEntry entry in keys)
{
  p = provider.CreateParameter();
  p.ParameterName = ParameterPrefix + entry.Key.ToString();
  p.Value = entry.Value;
  com.Parameters.Add(p);
}
```

Notice that the `ExecuteDelete` method raises the `Deleting` event before it attempts to delete the record from the database:

```
SqlDataSourceCommandEventArgs e = new SqlDataSourceCommandEventArgs(com);
OnDeleting(e);
if (!e.Cancel)
{
  con.Open();
```

If a client of the `SqlDataSource` control registers a callback for the `Deleting` event, the `OnDeleting` method will automatically call this callback and pass an instance of the `SqlDataSourceCommand EventArgs` to it. This allows the client callback to apply application-specific business rules to determine whether or not the `Delete` operation is permitted. If not, the callback can simply set the `Cancel` property of the `SqlDataSourceCommandEventArgs` instance to instruct the `ExecuteDelete` method to abort the `Delete` operation. Notice that the `ExecuteDelete` method checks the value of the `Cancel` property before it proceeds with the `Delete` operation:

```
SqlDataSourceCommandEventArgs e = new SqlDataSourceCommandEventArgs(com);
OnDeleting(e);
if (!e.Cancel)
```

```
{
  con.Open();
  try
  {
    affectedRows = com.ExecuteNonQuery();
  }
```

The `ExecuteDelete` method raises the `Deleted` event after it deletes the record from the database:

```
if (!e.Cancel)
{
  ...
  OnDataSourceViewChanged(EventArgs.Empty);
  SqlDataSourceStatusEventArgs ee =
              new SqlDataSourceStatusEventArgs(com, rowsAffected, null);
  OnDeleted(ee);
}
```

If a client of the `SqlDataSource` control registers a callback for the `Deleted` event, the `OnDeleted` method will automatically call this callback and pass an instance of the `SqlDataSourceStatusEventArgs` to it. If the client chooses to use a custom exception handling mechanism to handle the exception (if any), the client callback must set the `ExceptionHandled` property of the `SqlDataSourceStatusEventArgs` instance to true to bypass the default exception handling mechanism:

```
if (ee.Exception != null && !ee.ExceptionHandled)
    throw ee.Exception;
```

Update

The clients of a data source view object use the `Update` method of the view object to update database records. Listing 12-14 shows the `DataSourceView` class's implementation of the `Update` method. The method first calls the `ExecuteUpdate` method to update the record:

```
affectedRows = ExecuteUpdate(keys, values, oldValues);
```

It calls the client's update callback method. Because the `Update` method is asynchronous, the clients of the `DataSourceView` object register a callback method:

```
callback(affectedRows, ex);
```

Listing 12-14: The DataSourceView class's implementation of the Update method

```
public virtual void Update(IDictionary keys, IDictionary values,
                IDictionary oldValues, DataSourceViewOperationCallback callback)
{
  Exception ex = null;
  int affectedRows = 0;
  try
  {
    affectedRows = ExecuteUpdate(keys, values, oldValues);
  }
```

(continued)

Listing 12-14: *(continued)*

```
    catch (Exception e)
    {
      ex = e;
    }
    callback(affectedRows, ex);
  }
```

The `Update` method takes four arguments. The first argument is an `IDictionary` object that contains the names and values of the data fields that constitute the primary key of the record being updated. This means that the `Update` method supports multiple-field primary keys. The second argument is an `IDictionary` object that contains the names and new values of the data fields being updated.

As you'll see in Chapter 19, data-bound controls such as `GridView` extract the new values from their editing interface (such as text boxes), create an `IDictionary` object, populate the object with the names and new values of the respective data fields, and pass the object as the third argument to the `Update` method.

Because the `Update` method is asynchronous, the clients of a view object must wrap a callback method in an instance of the `DataSourceViewOperationCallback` delegate and pass the instance as the last argument of the `Update` method. The clients must first call the `CanUpdate` property to make sure the view can update the records of its underlying data store.

As this discussion shows, the `DataSourceView` base class takes full responsibility for implementing the `Update` method (see Listing 12-14). However, it leaves the responsibility of implementing the `ExecuteUpdate` method to its subclasses. This means that your custom tabular data source control is only responsible for implementing the `ExecuteUpdate` method and shouldn't override the `Update` method.

Next, you continue with the implementation of the `SqlDataSourceView` class. Recall that the previous sections implemented the `ExecuteSelect` and `ExecuteDelete` methods of this class. This section presents the implementation of the `ExecuteUpdate` method, as shown in Listing 12-15.

Listing 12-15: The ExecuteUpdate method of the SqlDataSourceView class

```
protected override int ExecuteUpdate(IDictionary keys, IDictionary values,
                                     IDictionary oldValues)
{
  if (!CanUpdate)
    throw new NotSupportedException("Update is not supported!");
  DbProviderFactory provider = owner.GetDbProviderFactory();
  DbConnection con = provider.CreateConnection();
  con.ConnectionString = owner.ConnectionString;
  DbCommand com = provider.CreateCommand();
  com.Connection = con;
  DbParameter p;
  com.CommandText = UpdateCommand;
  if (UpdateCommandType == SqlDataSourceCommandType.StoredProcedure)
    com.CommandType = System.Data.CommandType.StoredProcedure;
  foreach (DictionaryEntry entry in keys)
  {
    p = provider.CreateParameter();
    p.ParameterName = ParameterPrefix + entry.Key.ToString();
```

```
      p.Value = entry.Value;
      com.Parameters.Add(p);
    }
    foreach (DictionaryEntry entry in values)
    {
      p = provider.CreateParameter();
      p.ParameterName = ParameterPrefix + entry.Key.ToString();
      p.Value = entry.Value;
      com.Parameters.Add(p);
    }
    int affectedRows = 0;
    SqlDataSourceCommandEventArgs e = new SqlDataSourceCommandEventArgs(com);
    OnUpdating(e);
    if (!e.Cancel)
    {
      con.Open();
      Exception exception = null;
      try
      {
        affectedRows = com.ExecuteNonQuery();
      }
      catch (Exception ex)
      {
        exception = ex;
      }
      finally
      {
        con.Close();
        SqlDataSourceStatusEventArgs ee =
                new SqlDataSourceStatusEventArgs(com, rowsAffected, exception);
        OnDataSourceViewChanged(EventArgs.Empty);
        OnUpdated(ee);
        if (ee.Exception != null && !ee.ExceptionHandled)
          throw ee.Exception;
      }
    }
    return affectedRows;
}
```

The `ExecuteUpdate` method first calls the `CanUpdate` property to ensure that the view is capable of updating database records.

The `SqlDataSource` control exposes a property named `UpdateCommand` that page developers must set to a string value that contains the appropriate `Update` SQL statement or stored procedure name. For example:

```
<custom:SqlDataSource ID="MySource" runat="server" UpdateCommand="Update Products
Set Price=@Price, CategoryName=@CategoryName Where ProductID=@ProductID" .../>
```

The `ExecuteUpdate` method assigns the value of the `UpdateCommand` parameter to the `CommandText` property of the `DbCommand` object:

```
com.CommandText = UpdateCommand;
```

Notice that the `UpdateCommand` attribute contains two sets of parameters. The first set consists of one parameter named `@ProductID` whose value is the primary key value of the record being updated. The second set consists of two parameters named `@Price` and `@CategoryName`.

As you'll see in Chapter 19, data-bound controls take the following actions to set the values of these parameters:

1. Extract the names and values of the data fields (such as the `ProductID` field) of the primary key of the record being updated.

2. Create and populate an `IDictionary` object with the names and values of the data fields.

3. Extract the names and new values of the data fields (such as the `Price` and `CategoryName`) being updated from their editing interface.

4. Create and populate an `IDictionary` object with the names and values of the data fields.

5. Extract the names and old values of the data fields being updated from their cache.

6. Create and populate an `IDictionary` object with the names and old values of the fields.

7. Pass the three `IDictionary` objects as arguments to the `Update` method of the view object. The view object automatically passes the objects as arguments to the `ExecuteUpdate` method.

The `ExecuteUpdate` method (see Listing 12-15) enumerates the `IDictionary` objects that contain the names and values of the primary key fields and the names and new values of the fields of the record being updated, creates one `DbParameter` object for each enumerated `DictionaryEntry` object, and uses the values of the `Key` and `Value` properties of the enumerated `DictionaryEntry` object to set the `ParameterName` and `Value` properties of the `DbParameter` object:

```
foreach (DictionaryEntry entry in keys)
{
  p = provider.CreateParameter();
  p.ParameterName = ParameterPrefix + entry.Key.ToString();
  p.Value = entry.Value;
  com.Parameters.Add(p);
}
foreach (DictionaryEntry entry in values)
{
  p = provider.CreateParameter();
  p.ParameterName = ParameterPrefix + entry.Key.ToString();
  p.Value = entry.Value;
  com.Parameters.Add(p);
}
```

The `ExecuteUpdate` method raises the `Updating` event before it attempts to update the underlying database record:

```
SqlDataSourceCommandEventArgs e = new SqlDataSourceCommandEventArgs(com);
OnUpdating(e);
if (!e.Cancel)
{
  con.Open();
```

If a client of the `SqlDataSource` control registers a callback for the `Updating` event, the `OnUpdating` method will automatically call this callback and pass an instance of the `SqlDataSourceCommand`

EventArgs to it. This allows the client callback to apply application-specific business rules to determine whether or not the Update operation is permitted. If not, the callback can simply set the Cancel property of the SqlDataSourceCommandEventArgs instance to instruct the ExecuteUpdate method to abort the Update operation. Notice that the ExecuteUpdate method checks the value of the Cancel property before it proceeds with the Update operation:

```
int rowsAffected = 0;
SqlDataSourceCommandEventArgs e = new SqlDataSourceCommandEventArgs(com);
OnUpdating(e);
if (!e.Cancel)
{
  con.Open();
  Exception exception = null;
    try
    {
      affectedRows = com.ExecuteNonQuery();
    }
```

The ExecuteUpdate method raises the Updated event after it updates the underlying database record:

```
if (!e.Cancel)
{
  ...
  con.Close();
  SqlDataSourceStatusEventArgs ee =
                    new SqlDataSourceStatusEventArgs(com, rowsAffected, null);
      OnUpdated(ee);
  OnDataSourceViewChanged(EventArgs.Empty);
}
```

Insert

As you'll see in Chapter 19, data-bound controls use the Insert method of a view object to insert a new record into the underlying data store. Listing 12-16 presents the implementation of the Insert method of the DataSourceView class.

Listing 12-16: The DataSourceView class's implementation of the Insert method

```
public virtual void Insert(IDictionary values,
                        DataSourceViewOperationCallback callback)
{
  if (callback == null)
    throw new ArgumentNullException("You must register a callback!");

  Exception ex = null;
  int affectedRows = 0;
  try
  {
    affectedRows = ExecuteInsert(values);
  }
  catch (Exception e)
  {
```

(continued)

Listing 12-16: *(continued)*

```
    ex = e;
    }

    callback(affectedRows, ex);
}
```

First, `Insert` calls `ExecuteInsert` to insert the record in the underlying data store. It then calls the callback method that its client has registered for the insert data operation.

As Listing 12-16 shows, the `Insert` method takes two arguments. The first argument is an `IDictionary` collection that contains the names and values of the data fields of the record being inserted.

As you'll see in Chapter 19, data-bound controls extract these values from their inserting interface, create an `IDictionary` collection, populate the collection with the names and values of the associated data fields, and pass the collection as the first argument to the `Insert` method.

Because the `Insert` method is asynchronous, the clients of a view object must wrap a callback method in an instance of the `DataSourceViewOperationCallback` delegate and pass the instance as the second argument of the `Insert` method. The clients must first call the `CanInsert` property to ensure the view is capable of inserting records into the underlying data store.

Notice that the `DataSourceView` base class leaves the responsibility of implementing the `ExecuteInsert` method to its subclasses. This means that your custom tabular data source control is only responsible for implementing the `ExecuteInsert` method and shouldn't override the `Insert` method.

Now back to the implementation of the `SqlDataSourceView` class. So far, you've implemented the `ExecuteSelect`, `ExecuteDelete`, and `ExecuteUpdate` methods of this class. This section presents and discusses the implementation of the `ExecuteInsert` method, as shown in Listing 12-17.

Listing 12-17: The ExecuteInsert method of the SqlDataSourceView class

```
protected override int ExecuteInsert(IDictionary values)
{
  if (!CanInsert)
    throw new NotSupportedException("Insert is not supported!");

  DbProviderFactory provider = owner.GetDbProviderFactory();
  DbConnection con = provider.CreateConnection();
  con.ConnectionString = owner.ConnectionString;
  DbCommand com = provider.CreateCommand();
  com.Connection = con;
  DbParameter p;
  com.CommandText = InsertCommand;
  if (InsertCommandType == SqlDataSourceCommandType.StoredProcedure)
    com.CommandType = System.Data.CommandType.StoredProcedure;

  foreach (DictionaryEntry entry in values)
  {
    p = provider.CreateParameter();
    p.ParameterName = ParameterPrefix + entry.Key.ToString();
```

```
      p.Value = entry.Value;
      com.Parameters.Add(p);
   }

   int affectedRows = 0;
   SqlDataSourceCommandEventArgs e = new SqlDataSourceCommandEventArgs(com);
   OnInserting(e);
   if (!e.Cancel)
   {
     con.Open();
     Exception exception = null;
     try
     {
       affectedRows = com.ExecuteNonQuery();
     }
     catch (Exception ex)
     {
       exception = ex;
     }
     Finally
     {
       con.Close();
       OnDataSourceViewChanged(EventArgs.Empty);
       SqlDataSourceStatusEventArgs ee =
               new SqlDataSourceStatusEventArgs(com, affectedRows, exception);
       OnInserted(ee);
       if (ee.Exception != null && !ee.ExceptionHandled)
         throw ee.Exception;
     }
   }

   return affectedRows;
}
```

The `SqlDataSource` control exposes a string property named `InsertCommand` that page developers must set to a string value that contains the appropriate `Insert` SQL statement or stored procedure name. For example:

```
<custom:SqlDataSource ID="MySource" runat="server"
InsertCommand="Insert Into Products
Values(Price=@Price, CategoryName=@CategoryName)" .../>
```

As Listing 12-17 shows, the `ExecuteMethod` method assigns the value of the `InsertCommand` property to the `CommandText` property of the `DbCommand` object:

```
com.CommandText = UpdateCommand;
```

Notice that the `InsertCommand` attribute of the `<custom:SqlDataSource>` tag in the previous code fragment contains two parameters named `@Price` and `@CategoryName`. As you'll see in Chapter 19, data-bound controls set the values of these two parameters by extracting the names and values of the data fields (such as the `Price` and `CategoryName`) of the record being inserted from their inserting interface. They then create and populate an `IDictionary` collection with the names and values of the preceding data fields. Then they pass the `IDictionary` collection as argument to the `Insert` method of the view object. The view object automatically passes this collection as an argument to the `ExecuteInsert` method.

As Listing 12-17 illustrates, the `ExecuteInsert` method enumerates this `IDictionary` collection, creates one `DbParameter` object for each enumerated `DictionaryEntry` object, and uses the values of the `Key` and `Value` properties of the enumerated `DictionaryEntry` object to set the `ParameterName` and `Value` properties of the `DbParameter` object:

```
foreach (DictionaryEntry entry in values)
{
  p = provider.CreateParameter();
  p.ParameterName = ParameterPrefix + entry.Key.ToString();
  p.Value = entry.Value;
  com.Parameters.Add(p);
}
```

The `ExecuteInsert` method then raises the `Inserting` event before inserting the specified record in the underlying database:

```
SqlDataSourceCommandEventArgs e = new SqlDataSourceCommandEventArgs(com);
OnInserting(e);
if (!e.Cancel)
{
  con.Open();
```

Clients of the `SqlDataSource` control can register callbacks for the `Inserting` event to apply application-specific business rules to determine whether the `Insert` operation should be allowed. If not, the callback can simply set the `Cancel` property of the `SqlDataSourceCommandEventArgs` instance to ask the `ExecuteInsert` method to abort the `Insert` operation. As Listing 12-17 shows, the `ExecuteInsert` method checks the value of the `Cancel` property to determine whether it should insert the record in the database:

```
int rowsAffected = 0;
SqlDataSourceCommandEventArgs e = new SqlDataSourceCommandEventArgs(com);
OnUpdating(e);
if (!e.Cancel)
{
  con.Open();
  Exception exception = null;
    try
    {
      affectedRows = com.ExecuteNonQuery();
    }
```

The `ExecuteInsert` method raises the `Inserted` event after inserting the specified database record:

```
if (!e.Cancel)
{
  ...
  con.Close();
  SqlDataSourceStatusEventArgs ee =
                  new SqlDataSourceStatusEventArgs(com, rowsAffected, null);
  OnInserted(ee);
  if (ee.Exception != null && !ee.ExceptionHandled)
    throw ee.Exception;
  OnDataSourceViewChanged(EventArgs.Empty);
}
```

State Management

As mentioned, the SqlDataSourceView class exposes numerous properties such as SelectCommand, SelectCountCommand, DeleteCommand, UpdateCommand, and so on. Because this class isn't a server control, it doesn't inherit the built-in ViewState StateBag property that every server control inherits from the Control base class to save and load its property values across page postbacks. This means that the class must manage its own state.

The SqlDataSourceView class implements the IStateManager interface and follows these steps to manage its state across page postbacks (as discussed in Chapter 5):

1. Because it doesn't inherit a ViewState StateBag property, it defines its own ViewState StateBag property to allow its simple properties such as SelectCommand to manage their states across page postbacks by simply saving and loading their values from the ViewState collection:

```
private StateBag viewState = null;
protected StateBag ViewState
{
  get
  {
    if (viewState == null)
    {
      viewState = new StateBag();
      if (isTrackingViewState)
        ((IStateManager)viewState).TrackViewState();
    }

    return viewState;
  }
}
```

2. It also exposes three protected virtual methods named TrackViewState, SaveViewState, and LoadViewState, and one protected virtual property named IsTrackingViewState. The TrackViewState, SaveViewStae, and LoadViewState methods simply delegate to the TrackViewState, SaveViewState, and LoadViewState methods of the ViewState property. For example:

```
protected virtual object SaveViewState()
{
  if (ViewState != null)
    return ((IStateManager)ViewState).SaveViewState();

  return null;
}
```

3. It also explicitly implements the TrackViewState, SaveViewState, and LoadViewState methods and IsTrackingViewState property of the IStateManager, where they simply delegate to their respective protected member. For example:

```
object IStateManager.SaveViewState()
{
  return this.SaveViewState();
}
```

Subclasses of the Control class don't have to worry about calling the TrackViewState, SaveViewState, and LoadViewState methods because the ASP.NET runtime automatically calls these methods. Because the SqlDataSourceView class isn't a subclass of the Control class, the runtime doesn't automatically call its TrackViewState, SaveViewState, and LoadViewState methods.

Because the SqlDataSource control is a subclass of the Control class, it overrides these three methods, where it calls the respective methods of its associated SqlDataSourceView object:

```csharp
protected override void LoadViewState(object savedState)
{
  if (savedState != null)
  {
    object[] state = savedState as object[];
    if (state != null && state.Length == 2)
    {
      base.LoadViewState(state[0]);

      if (state[1] != null)
        ((IStateManager)View).LoadViewState(state[1]);
    }
  }

  else
    base.LoadViewState(savedState);
}
```

Summary

This chapter covered three of the four main components of the ASP.NET 2.0 tabular data source control model: IDataSource, DataSourceControl, and DataSourceView. The chapter took you under the hood of these three components to help you gain a solid understanding of how these components work from the inside out.

This chapter also implemented a functional replica of the ASP.NET 2.0 SqlDataSource control to show you how a real-world data source control is implemented. The next chapter discusses the last component of the ASP.NET 2.0 tabular data source control: the ASP.NET 2.0 data source control parameter model. The next chapter also implements the rest of the methods and properties of the SqlDataSourceView control.

13

The ASP.NET 2.0 Data Source Control Parameter Model

This chapter continues the discussions of the previous chapter and presents the last component of the ASP.NET data source control model: the ASP.NET data source control parameter model. This chapter takes you under the hood of this model, where you can see for yourself how the model works from the inside out and how you can extend it. The chapter then delves into the implementation of a few real-world custom parameters to show you how to develop your own custom parameters to add support for new parameter sources.

Parameters

Closer examination of the `SqlDataSourceView` class's implementation of the `ExecuteSelect` (see Listing 12-9), `ExecuteDelete` (see Listing 12-13), `ExecuteUpdate` (see Listing 12-15), and `ExecuteInsert` (see Listing 12-17) methods shows that these methods don't provide page developers with an extensible infrastructure to specify the `Select`, `Delete`, `Update`, and `Insert` parameters. This raises the following four questions:

❑ What is meant by the `Select`, `Delete`, `Update`, and `Insert` parameters?

❑ What kind of information do you have to specify for each parameter?

❑ What is meant by an infrastructure to specify these parameters? What are the main components of this infrastructure?

❑ Why does the infrastructure have to be extensible?

To answer these questions, consider the declaration of the `SqlDataSource` control in Listing 13-1. This control is used to retrieve, delete, and update the records of a database that consists of two tables named `Books` and `Authors`, whose primary key fields are `BookID` and `AuthorID`, respectively. The `AuthorID` field in the `Books` table is a foreign key referring to the `AuthorID` field in the `Authors` table.

Listing 13-1: The declaration of a SqlDataSource control

```
<asp:SqlDataSource ID="MySource" runat="Server"
SelectCommand="Select * From Books Where AuthorID=@AuthorID"
DeleteCommand="Delete From Books Where Publisher=@Publisher"
UpdateCommand="Update Books Set Title=@Title, Publisher=@Publisher, Price=@Price
Where BookID=@BookID"/>
```

As Listing 13-1 shows, the `SelectCommand`, `DeleteCommand`, and `UpdateCommand` properties of the `SqlDataSource` control contain parameters such as `@AuthorID`, `@Publisher`, `@Title`, and `@Price`. You need a mechanism that will allow you to specify the following three types of information about each parameter:

❑ The name of the parameter (such as `@AuthorID` and `@Publisher`)

❑ The value of the parameter (such as the values of the `@AuthorID` and `@Publisher` parameters)

❑ The type of the parameter (the type of the values of the `@AuthorID` and `@Publisher` parameters, which are `System.Int32` and `System.String`, respectively)

As you'll see in Chapter 19, data-bound controls, such as `GridView`, automatically provide these three types of information about some of these parameters. For example, Figure 13-1 shows a `GridView` that displays the records of the `Books` table. The `GridView` caches the names and values of the primary key fields of its rows (the value of the `BookID` field) in a collection property named `DataKeys` that contains one `DataKey` object for the primary key value of each row.

Notice that the second row of the `GridView` control in Figure 13-1 is in edit mode to allow the user to edit its fields. When the user is done with editing and clicks the `Update` button, the containing page is posted back to the server, where the `GridView` control extracts the names and new values of the fields of the row being updated (Title, AuthorID, Publisher, and Price) and passes them to the `SqlDataSource` control.

	BookID	Title	AuthorID	Publisher	Price
Edit Delete	35	Title13	3	Publisher13	130
Update Cancel	36	Title14	3	Publisher14	140
Edit Delete	37	Title15	3	Publisher15	150
			1 2		

Figure 13-1

Page developers don't have to worry about the parameters discussed so far, because they're automatically handled by data-bound controls. The only exception to this rule is the cases where data-bound controls may not be able to perform the right type conversion. In these cases, page developers may have to specify the types of these parameters.

Now take a look at the parameters that data-bound controls don't handle. The @AuthorID and @Publisher parameters in the Select and Delete SQL statements of the SqlDataSource control are examples of such parameters:

```
<asp:SqlDataSource ID="MySource" runat="Server"
SelectCommand="Select * From Books Where AuthorID=@AuthorID"
DeleteCommand="Delete From Books Where Publisher=@Publisher"
UpdateCommand="Update Books Set Title=@Title, Publisher=@Publisher, Price=@Price
Where BookID=@BookID"/>
```

One of the requirements of most data-driven Web applications is to allow users to dynamically specify the values of these parameters. For example, the DropDownList control in Figure 13-2 displays the names of all the available authors (the values of the AuthorName field of the Authors table) to allow users to dynamically set the value of the @AuthorID parameter in the Select SQL statement to display the book records for the selected author.

	BookID	Title	AuthorID	Publisher	Price
Edit Delete	35	Title13	3	Publisher13	130
Edit Delete	36	Title14	3	Publisher14	140
Edit Delete	37	Title15	3	Publisher15	150

Select an Author: Author3

1 2

Figure 13-2

In this case what you need is a component that will allow you to specify the SelectedValue property of the DropDownList control as the source for the value of the @AuthorID parameter of the Select SQL statement. This is an example of an application that uses the property (SelectedValue) of a control (DropDownList) as the source for the dynamic evaluation of a parameter used in a SQL statement or stored procedure of a tabular data source control. The properties of server controls aren't the only available sources for parameter values. There are many other possible sources such as the following:

❑ Properties of the Profile object

❑ Objects stored in the Session object

❑ Values stored in the QueryString collection of the Request object

❑ Values stored in HTTP cookies

The list goes on and on. You are pretty much limited only by your imagination. This answers the question: Why does the infrastructure have to be extensible? The extensibility of the infrastructure allows you to add support for new sources.

In short, what you need is a set of components that will dynamically evaluate the values of the parameters used in the properties of a tabular data source control (such as the SelectCommand and DeleteCommand of a SqlDataSource control). These components are collectively known as *parameters*. Each parameter component is specifically designed to evaluate the value of a parameter from a specific source. For example, the ControlParameter and SessionParameter components are specifically designed to evaluate the value of a parameter from the specified property of a specified control and from a specified object in the Session collection, respectively.

If a tabular data source control (such as the SqlDataSource in Listing 13-1) were to directly use a particular parameter component to set the value of a parameter in any of its properties (such as the SelectCommand and DeleteCommand properties of a SqlDataSource control), the control would be tied to the source that the parameter component is specifically designed to work with and would not be able to work with other sources.

The ASP.NET 2.0 parameter model provides you with an extensible infrastructure that allows you to isolate tabular data source controls from the types of the parameter components used to evaluate parameters. This infrastructure consists of two important components known as Parameter and ParameterCollection. Before you look under the hood of these components to find out how they work, you need to see how they're used.

As an example, revisit the application shown in Figure 13-2. Recall that the user selects an author's name from the DropDownList control to display the list of author's books in the GridView control. The GridView control is bound to the SqlDataSource control declared in Listing 13-1. Listing 13-2 shows how the SqlDataSource control can dynamically evaluate the value of the @AuthorID parameter used in its Select SQL statement.

Listing 13-2: Declaration of the SqlDataSource control

```
<asp:SqlDataSource ID="MySource" Runat="Server"
SelectCommand="Select * From Books Where AuthorID=@AuthorID"
ConnectionString="<%$ ConnectionStrings:MyConnectionString %>">
  <SelectParameters>
    <asp:ControlParameter ControlID="ddl" PropertyName="SelectedValue"
    Name="AuthorID" />
  </SelectParameters>
</asp:SqlDataSource>
```

This listing shows the following:

❑ As you'll see later, the SqlDataSource control exposes a property of type ParameterCollection named SelectParameters that contains all of the parameter objects used to evaluate the values of the parameters used in the Select SQL statement or stored procedure. Listing 13-2 adds an instance of the ControlParameter component to the SelectParameters collection.

❑ The PropertyName property of the ControlParameter component in Listing 13-2 is set to the name of the SelectedValue property of the DropDownList control that is used as the source for the value of the @AuthorID parameter.

❑ The value of the ID property of the DropDownList control is assigned to the ControlID property of the ControlParameter component. As you'll see later, the ControlParameter uses this value to locate the control in the control tree of the containing page.

❑ The Name property of the component is set to the name of the parameter, in this case, AuthorID.

The ASP.NET 2.0 infrastructure that allows you to specify the names and values of parameters consists of the following three important components:

❑ The Parameter class

❑ ParameterCollection

❑   Built-in support of tabular data source controls such as SqlDataSource for automatic invocation of the GetValues and UpdateValues methods of the ParameterCollection component

The following sections look under the hood of these three components to help you understand how they work and how you can extend them to implement your own custom components.

The Parameter Class

The ASP.NET 2.0 Parameter class is the base class for all parameter classes such as ProfileParameter, SessionParameter, CookieParameter, QueryStringParameter, ControlParameter, and FormParameter. This section discusses some of the important methods of the Parameter class to help you understand how this class interacts with the ParameterCollection class to isolate data source controls from the underlying source of the parameter. This base class exposes six important properties, as follows:

❑   DefaultValue: Gets and sets the default value of the parameter.

❑   Direction: Gets and sets the direction of the parameter. The possible values are Input, Output, InputOutput, and ReturnValue.

❑   Name: Gets and sets the name of the parameter.

❑   Size: Gets and sets the size of the parameter. For example, a parameter of type System.Int32 will be of size 4 bytes.

❑   Type: Gets and sets the type code of the parameter.

❑   Container: Gets and sets the ParameterCollection instance that contains the parameter. This property (the name of the property is not important) is marked as internal to hide the interaction between the Parameter and ParameterCollection classes from the subclasses of the Parameter class.

The Parameter class exposes three important methods:

❑   Evaluate: Evaluates the current value of the parameter from the source. This method is protected.

❑   SaveCurrentValue: Calls the Evaluate method to retrieve the current value of the parameter and saves this value in the ViewState collection and calls the OnParameterChanged method if the current value is different from the saved one. The SaveCurrentValue method (the name of the method is not important) is marked as internal to hide the interaction between the Parameter and ParameterCollection classes from the subclasses of the Parameter class.

❑   OnParameterChanged: Calls the RaiseParametersChangedEvent method of its container.

The OnParameterChanged Method

OnParameterChanged is called when the value of the parameter changes. As mentioned, the SaveCurrentValue method calls the Evaluate method to access the current value of the parameter. If the current value is different from the saved one, the SaveCurrentValue method calls the OnParameterChanged method to signal the change in parameter value.

Listing 13-3 shows the implementation of the OnParameterChanged method.

Listing 13-3: The OnParameterChanged method

```
protected void OnParameterChanged()
{
  if (container != null)
    container.RaiseParametersChangedEvent();
}
```

As mentioned, the Parameter class exposes a property of type ParameterCollection named Container that references the ParameterCollection instance that contains it. The OnParameterChanged method calls the RaiseParametersChangedEvent method of the container to notify the container that the parameter has changed. This method is discussed in detail later in the chapter.

SaveCurrentValue Method

Listing 13-4 shows the implementation of the SaveCurrentValue method of the Parameter class.

Listing 13-4: The SaveCurrentValue method

```
internal object SaveCurrentValue(HttpContext context, Control control)
{
  object savedValue = ViewState["savedValue"];
  object currentValue = Evaluate(context, control);
  if (savedValue != null && !savedValue.Equals(currentValue))
  {
    ViewState["SavedValue"] = currentValue;
    OnParameterChanged();
  }
  return currentValue;
}
```

The SaveCurrentValue method first retrieves the saved value of the parameter from the ViewState collection:

```
object savedValue = ViewState["SavedValue"];
```

It then calls the Evaluate method of the Parameter class to access the current value of the parameter:

```
object currentValue = Evaluate(context, control);
```

Finally, it saves the current value to the ViewState collection and calls the OnParameterChanged method if the current value is different from the saved one:

```
viewState["SavedValue"] = currentValue;
OnParameterChanged();
```

Evaluate Method

Listing 13-5 shows the implementation of the Evaluate method of the Parameter class.

Listing 13-5: The Evaluate method

```
protected virtual object Evaluate(HttpContext context, Control control)
{
  return DefaultValue;
}
```

The `Evaluate` method simply returns the value of the `DefaultValue` property. Recall that each subclass of the `Parameter` class is specifically designed to evaluate the value of its associated parameter from a specific source. For example, the `SessionParameter` component evaluates the value from a specified object in the `Session` collection. It's the responsibility of the subclasses of the `Parameter` class to override the `Evaluate` method, where they must access the specified source to evaluate the value of the parameter.

The ASP.NET 2.0 data source control model comes with the following parameter classes:

❑ `SessionParameter`: Retrieves the value of its associated parameter from the `Session` object

❑ `QueryStringParameter`: Retrieves the value of its associated parameter from the `QueryString` collection of the `Request` object

❑ `ControlParameter`: Retrieves the value of its associated parameter from a server control

❑ `FormParameter`: Retrieves the value of its associated parameter from a `Form` element

❑ `ProfileParameter`: Retrieves the value of its associated parameter from the `Profile` object

❑ `CookieParameter`: Retrieves the value of its respective parameter from a cookie

In the following sections you implement fully functional replicas of the `CookieParameter` and `ControlParameter` components built into ASP.NET 2.0 to help you understand how these standard parameter components are implemented and how you can follow their implementations to implement your own custom parameter components.

CookieParameter

The ASP.NET 2.0 `CookieParameter` class uses an HTTP cookie as the source for the value of its associated parameter. This parameter class, like any other parameter class, derives from the `Parameter` base class and overrides its `Evaluate` method. This class exposes a property named `CookieName` that page developers must set to the name of the appropriate HTTP cookie:

```
public class CookieParameter : Parameter
{
  public string CookieName
  {
    get { return ViewState["CookieName"] != null ?
          (string)ViewState["CookieName"] : string.Empty; }
    set { ViewState["CookieName"] = value; }
  }

  protected override object Evaluate(HttpContext context, Control control)
  {
    return context.Request.Cookies[CookieName].Value;
  }
}
```

The `Request` object exposes a collection property of type `HttpCookieCollection` named `Cookies` that contains one `HttpCookie` object for each HTTP cookie in the request. The `Evaluate` method uses the value of the `CookieName` property to locate the `HttpCookie` object that represents the respective cookie. The method then calls the `Value` property of the `HttpCookie` object to access the current value of its associated parameter.

ControlParameter

The ASP.NET 2.0 `ControlParameter` component allows page developers to use a server control as the source for the value of a parameter. Listing 13-6 shows the implementation of this component.

Listing 13-6: The ControlParameter component

```
public class ControlParameter : Parameter
{
  public string ControlID
  {
    get { return ViewState["ControlID"] != null ?
                      (string)ViewState["ControlID"] : string.Empty; }
    set { ViewState["ControlID"] = value;  }
  }

  public string PropertyName
  {
    get { return ViewState["PropertyName"] != null ?
                  (string)ViewState["PropertyName"] : string.Empty; }
    set { ViewState["PropertyName"] = value; }
  }

  protected override object Evaluate(HttpContext context, Control control)
  {
    object val = null;
    Control c = control.Page.FindControl(ControlID);
    if (c != null)
    {
      PropertyDescriptorCollection pds = TypeDescriptor.GetProperties(c);
      foreach (PropertyDescriptor pd in pds)
      {
        if (pd.Name == PropertyName)
        {
          val = pd.GetValue(c);
          break;
        }
      }

      // Or you could use DataBinder.Eval(c, PropertyName)
    }
    return val;
  }
}
```

Page developers must set the values of the ControlID and PropertyName properties of the ControlParameter class to the value of the ID property of the desired server control and the name of desired property of the control, respectively. For example, Listing 13-2 sets the value of the ControlID property to the value of the ID property of the DropDownList server control (see Figure 13-2) and the value of the PropertyName property to the string value SelectedValue, which is the name of the appropriate property of the DropDownList control.

The Evaluate method takes an argument of type Control that refers to the tabular data source control that owns the parameter. For example, in the case of Listing 13-2, the SqlDataSource control is the owner. The Control class exposes a property named Page that refers to the containing page. The Evaluate method calls the FindControl method of the containing page and passes the value of the ControlID property as its argument. The FindControl method uses this value to locate the desired control in the control tree of the containing page and returns a reference to it. For example, in the case of Listing 13-2, this control is the DropDownList control:

```
Control c = control.Page.FindControl(ControlID);
```

The Evaluate method then calls the GetProperties method of the TypeDescriptor class to return a PropertyDescriptorCollection object that contains one PropertyDescriptor object for each property of the server control. For example, in the case of the Listing 13-2, the collection will contain one PropertyDescriptor object for each property of the DropDownList control shown in Figure 13-2. Recall that the DropDownList control exposes numerous properties such as Width, SelectedValue, and so on.

```
PropertyDescriptorCollection pds = TypeDescriptor.GetProperties(c);
```

The Evaluate method then enumerates the PropertyDescriptorCollection object and locates the PropertyDescriptor object whose Name property has the same value as the PropertyName property of the ControlParameter class. The method then calls the GetValue method of this PropertyDescriptor object to access the new value of the parameter.

For example, in the case of Listing 13-2, the method will call the GetValue method of the PropertyDescriptor object associated with the SelectedValue property of the DropDownList control.

```
foreach (PropertyDescriptor pd in pds)
{
  if (pd.Name == PropertyName)
  {
    val = pd.GetValue(c);
    break;
  }
}
```

The .NET Framework comes with a class named DataBinder that exposes a method named Eval that encapsulates the logic that evaluates the value of a given property. This method takes two arguments. The first argument is the object whose property value is being evaluated. The second argument is the name of the property whose value is being evaluated. If you use this class, you can save yourself from having the write all the previous code. The following code presents the version of the Evaluate method that uses the DataBinder class:

```
protected override object Evaluate(HttpContext context, Control control)
{
  object val = null;
  Control c = control.Page.FindControl(ControlID);
  if (c != null)
  {
    Val = DataBinder.Eval(c, PropertyName)
  }
  return val;
}
```

ParameterCollection

The ASP.NET 2.0 data source parameter model provides you with the infrastructure you need to specify the names and values of parameters. As mentioned, this infrastructure consists of three main components: Parameter, ParameterCollection, and built-in support of tabular data source controls for automatic invocation of the GetValues and UpdateValues methods of the ParameterCollection class.

The previous sections discussed the Parameter class and its subclasses. This section looks under the hood of some of the important members of the ASP.NET 2.0 ParameterCollection class built into the ASP.NET 2.0 Framework to show you how this class interacts with the Parameter class to isolate data source controls from the underlying parameter source.

ParametersChanged Event

The ParameterCollection component raises an event of type EventHandler named ParametersChanged when any of the parameter components that it contains changes. As described in Chapter 4, the ParameterCollection component takes the following steps to implement this event:

1. It exposes a private field of type EventHandler named parametersChanged:

```
private event EventHandler parametersChanged;
```

2. It exposes a public property of type EventHandler named ParametersChanged that delegates to the parametersChanged field:

```
public event EventHandler ParametersChanged
{
  add { parametersChanged += value;}
  remove {parametersChanged -= value;}
}
```

3. It exposes a protected method named OnParametersChanged that raises the ParametersChanged event (see Listing 13-7).

Listing 13-7: The OnParametersChanged method

```
protected virtual void OnParametersChanged(EventArgs e)
{
  if (parametersChanged != null)
    parametersChanged(this, e);
}
```

4. It exposes an internal method named `RaiseParametersChangedEvent` that calls the `OnParametersChanged` method to raise the `ParametersChanged` event (see Listing 13-8).

Listing 13-8: The RaiseParametersChangedEvent method

```
internal void RaiseParametersChangedEvent()
{
  OnParametersChanged(EventArgs.Empty);
}
```

Recall that the `OnParameterChanged` method of the `Parameter` class calls the `RaiseParameters ChangedEvent` method to raise the `ParametersChanged` event when the value of the parameter changes (see Listing 13-3). That is exactly the reason the `RaiseParameterChangedEvent` method (the name of this method is not important) is marked as internal.

OnInsert Method

The `OnInsert` method is called before a new parameter is added to the `ParameterCollection` collection. This method delegates to the `OnInsert` method of its base class and assigns itself to the `Container` property of the parameter object being inserted. Recall that the `Parameter` class exposes a collection property of type `ParameterCollection` named `Container` that references the `ParameterCollection` that contains the `Parameter`:

```
protected override void OnInsert(int index, object value)
{
  base.OnInsert(index, value);
  ((Parameter)value).Container = this;
}
```

GetValues Method

The `GetValues` method takes two arguments. The first argument is the current context object. The second argument is the data source control that owns the `ParameterCollection` collection. Later in this chapter, you'll see an example of a data source control that owns this collection. Listing 13-9 presents the implementation of the `GetValues` method.

Listing 13-9: The GetValues method

```
public IOrderedDictionary GetValues(HttpContext context, Control control)
{
  OrderedDictionary parameterValues = new OrderedDictionary();
  string parameterName = string.Empty;
  object parameterValue = null;
  foreach (Parameter p in this)
  {
    parameterValue = p.SaveCurrentValue(context, control);
    parameterName = p.Name;
    int id = 1;
    while (parameterValues.Contains(parameterName))
    {
      parameterName = p.Name + id.ToString();
```

(continued)

Listing 13-9: *(continued)*

```
        id++;
    }

    parameterValues.Add(parameterName, parameterValue);
  }
  return parameterValues;
}
```

As you'll see later in this chapter, data source controls call the `GetValues` method to return the values of the parameters that the `ParameterCollection` contains. The `GetValues` method first creates an instance of the `OrderedDictionary` class and uses it as a container to hold the parameter names and values:

```
OrderedDictionary parameterValues = new OrderedDictionary();
```

Then it enumerates the parameter objects in the `ParameterCollection` collection. For each enumerated parameter object, `GetValues` uses the `Name` property and `SaveCurrentValue` method of the parameter object to access the name and current value of the parameter:

```
parameterValue = p.SaveCurrentValue(context, control);
parameterName = p.Name;
```

Because the `ParameterCollection` class doesn't guarantee that the names of its parameters will be unique, the `GetValues` method appends a number to the name of each parameter object to ensure the uniqueness of the name:

```
int id = 1;
while (parameterValues.Contains(parameterName))
{
  parameterName = p.Name + id.ToString();
  id++;
}
```

`GetValues` then adds the name and value of each parameter object to the `OrderedDictionary` collection and returns the collection to its caller, which is a data source control:

```
parameterValues.Add(parameterName, parameterValue);
```

UpdateValues Method

Listing 13-10 shows the implementation of the `UpdateValues` method. Notice that this method takes the same arguments as the `GetValues` method. As Listing 13-10 shows, the `UpdateValues` method simply enumerates the parameter objects and calls the `SaveCurrentValue` method of each enumerated object.

Listing 13-10: The UpdateValues Method

```
public void UpdateValues(HttpContext context, Control control)
{
  foreach (Parameter p in this)
```

```
    {
      p.SaveCurrentValue(context, control);
    }
  }
}
```

Automatic Invocation of GetValues and UpdateValues Methods

The previous sections discussed the first two of the three main components of the ASP.NET 2.0 data source control parameter model: the `Parameter` and `ParameterCollection` classes. This section discusses the third component of the model in the context of the ASP.NET 2.0 `SqlDataSource` control. It presents the implementation of the remaining parts of the replica `SqlDataSource` control discussed in the previous chapter. By the end of this chapter, you should have a fully functional replica of the `SqlDataSource` control built into the ASP.NET Framework.

The remaining parts of the replica `SqlDataSource` control provide built-in support for automatic invocation of the `UpdateValues` and `GetValues` methods:

❑   Four properties of type `ParameterCollection`

❑   The `OnInit` and `Page_LoadComplete` methods

❑   The `ExecuteSelect` method's support for `ParameterCollection`

❑   The `ExecuteDelete` method's support for `ParameterCollection`

❑   The `ExecuteUpdate` method's support for `ParameterCollection`

❑   The `ExecuteInsert` method's support for `ParameterCollection`

Properties of Type ParameterCollection

The `SqlDataSource` control exposes four properties of type `ParameterCollection` named `SelectParameters`, `DeleteParameters`, `UpdateParameters`, and `InsertParameters`. Listing 13-11 shows the implementation of the `SelectParameters`.

Listing 13-11: The SelectParameters property of the SqlDataSource control

```
[PersistenceModeAttribute(PersistenceMode.InnerProperty)]
public ParameterCollection SelectParameters
{
  get { return View.SelectParameters; }
}
```

All of these four properties are annotated with `[PersistenceModeAttribute(PersistenceMode. InnerProperty)]`. Recall that .NET components expose two types of properties: simple and complex. The `SelectParameters`, `DeleteParameters`, `InsertParameters`, and `UpdateParameters` properties of the `SqlDataSource` control are complex properties. Visual designers such as Visual Studio serialize the simple properties of a component as attributes on the tag that represents the component.

By default, visual designers serialize complex properties the same way, as attributes. However, you can annotate the complex properties of your custom component with the [PersistenceModeAttribute (PersistenceMode.InnerProperty)] attribute to instruct Visual Studio to serialize them as the child elements of the element that represents your custom component.

As Listing 13-11 shows, the SelectParameters, DeleteParameters, UpdateParameters, and InsertParameters properties of the SqlDataSource control delegate to the respective properties of the View object. This means that the SqlDataSourceView class also exposes four properties of type ParameterCollection named SelectParameters, DeleteParameters, UpdateParameters, and InsertParameters. For example, Listing 13-12 shows the implementation of the SelectParameters property of the SqlDataSourceView class.

Listing 13-12: The SelectParameters property of the SqlDataSourceView class

```
private ParameterCollection selectParameters = null;
public ParameterCollection SelectParameters
{
  get
  {
    if (selectParameters == null)
    {
      selectParameters = new ParameterCollection();
      if (isTrackingViewState)
        ((IStateManager)selectParameters).TrackViewState();
      selectParameters.ParametersChanged +=
              new EventHandler(ParameterCollectionChangedCallback);
    }
    return selectParameters;
  }
}
```

The SqlDataSourceView class registers the ParameterCollectionChangedCallback method as the callback for the ParametersChanged event of the SelectParameters property. As Listing 13-13 shows, the ParameterCollectionChangedCallback method calls the OnDataSourceViewChanged method of the SqlDataSourceView class. The SqlDataSourceView class inherits the OnDataSourceViewChanged method from its base class, DataSourceView. Recall that the DataSourceView class's implementation of the OnDataSourceViewChanged method raises the DataSourceViewChanged event, as shown in Listing 13-14.

Listing 13-13: The ParameterCollectionChangedCallback method

```
protected virtual void
ParameterCollectionChangedCallback(object sender, EventArgs e)
{
    this.OnDataSourceViewChanged(e);
}
```

Listing 13-14: The OnDataSourceViewChanged method of the DataSourceView base class

```
protected virtual void OnDataSourceViewChanged(EventArgs e)
{
```

```
EventHandler handler = Events[DataSourceViewChangedKey] as EventHandler;

if (handler != null)
  handler(this, e);
}
```

OnInit and Page_LoadComplete Methods

The `SqlDataSource` control overrides the `OnInit` method to register the `Page_LoadComplete` method as the callback for the `LoadComplete` page event:

```
protected override void OnInit(EventArgs e)
{
  Page.LoadComplete += new EventHandler(Page_LoadComplete);
  base.OnInit(e);
}
```

The containing page raises the `LoadComplete` event at the end of the loading stage of its life cycle. In other words, this event marks the end of all loading activities, including loading postback data and view state data. This is a perfect stage for the `SqlDataSource` control to call the `UpdateValues` methods of the `SelectParameters` collection. Listing 13-15 shows the `Page_LoadComplete` method.

Listing 13-15: The Page_LoadComplete Method

```
void Page_LoadComplete(object sender, EventArgs e)
{
  SelectParameters.UpdateValues (Context, this);
}
```

ExecuteSelect

As Listing 13-16 shows, the `ExecuteSelect` method of the `SqlDataSourceView` class calls the `GetValues` method of the `SelectParameters` property. The `GetValues` method returns an `IOrderedDictionary` object that contains the names and values of the parameters used in the `SelectCommand` property of the `SqlDataSource` control.

The `ExecuteSelect` method enumerates the `IOrderedDictionary` object, creates one `DbParameter` object for each enumerated `DictionaryEntry` object, and assigns the values of the `Key` and `Value` properties of the enumerated `DictionaryEntry` object to the `ParameterName` and `Value` properties of the respective `DbParameter` object.

Listing 13-16: The ExecuteSelect method that calls the GetValues method of SelectParameters

```
protected override IEnumerable ExecuteSelect(DataSourceSelectArguments arguments)
{
  DbProviderFactory provider = owner.GetDbProviderFactory();
  DbConnection con = provider.CreateConnection();
  con.ConnectionString = owner.ConnectionString;
  DbCommand com = provider.CreateCommand();
```

(continued)

Listing 13-16: *(continued)*

```
        com.Connection = con;

        IOrderedDictionary parameters = SelectParameters.GetValues(context, owner);

        IOrderedDictionary parametersDirection =
                        RetrieveParametersDirection(SelectParameters, parameters);
        if (arguments.RetrieveTotalRowCount)
                    arguments.TotalRowCount = RetrieveTotalRowCount(com,provider,
                                                 parameters, parametersDirection);

        com.Parameters.Clear();
        return RetrieveRows(arguments, com,provider, parameters, parametersDirection);
    }
```

ExecuteDelete

One of the main responsibilities of the `ExecuteDelete` method is to create and initialize one `DbParameter` object for each parameter used in the `Delete` SQL statement or `Delete` stored procedure. There are two sets of parameters. The first set includes parameters that represent the data fields that constitute the primary key of the record being deleted. The `IDictionary` object that is passed as the first argument of the `ExecuteDelete` method contains the names and values of the first set of parameters.

The `DeleteParameters` property of the `SqlDataSource` control contains the names, values, and types of the second set of parameters. The `ExecuteDelete` method calls the `GetValues` method of the `ParameterCollection` class to access the `IOrderedDictionary` object that contains the names and values of the second set of parameters (see Listing 13-17).

Listing 13-17: The ExecuteDelete method that calls the GetValues method of DeleteParameters

```
    protected override int ExecuteDelete(IDictionary keys, IDictionary oldValues)
    {
      if (!CanDelete)
        throw new NotSupportedException("Delete is not supported!");

      DbProviderFactory provider = owner.GetDbProviderFactory();

      DbConnection con = provider.CreateConnection();
      con.ConnectionString = owner.ConnectionString;

      DbCommand com = provider.CreateCommand();
      com.Connection = con;

      IOrderedDictionary odic = DeleteParameters.GetValues(context, owner);
      OrderedDictionary dic = new OrderedDictionary();
      foreach (DictionaryEntry entry in odic)
      {
        foreach (Parameter p2 in DeleteParameters)
```

```csharp
    {
      if (p2.Name == entry.Key.ToString())
      {
        dic.Add(p2.Name, p2.Direction);
        break;
      }
    }
  }
}

DbParameter p;
com.CommandText = DeleteCommand;
if (DeleteCommandType == SqlDataSourceCommandType.StoredProcedure)
  com.CommandType = System.Data.CommandType.StoredProcedure;

foreach (DictionaryEntry entry in odic)
{
  p = provider.CreateParameter();
  p.ParameterName = ParameterPrefix + entry.Key.ToString();
  p.Value = entry.Value;
  p.Direction = (ParameterDirection)dic[entry.Key];
  com.Parameters.Add(p);
}

foreach (DictionaryEntry entry in keys)
{
  p = provider.CreateParameter();
  p.ParameterName = ParameterPrefix + entry.Key.ToString();
  p.Value = entry.Value;
  com.Parameters.Add(p);
}
int affectedRows = 0;
SqlDataSourceCommandEventArgs e = new SqlDataSourceCommandEventArgs(com);
OnDeleting(e);
if (!e.Cancel)
{
  con.Open();
  Exception exception = null;
  try
  {
    affectedRows = com.ExecuteNonQuery();
  }
  catch (Exception ex)
  {
    exception = ex;
  }
  con.Close();
  OnDataSourceViewChanged(EventArgs.Empty);
  SqlDataSourceStatusEventArgs ee =
            new SqlDataSourceStatusEventArgs(com, affectedRows, exception);
  OnDeleted(ee);
}
  return affectedRows;
}
```

ExecuteUpdate

The ExecuteUpdate method must create and initialize one DbParameter object for each parameter used in the Update SQL statement or stored procedure. The update operation has three sets of parameters. The first set includes those parameters that represent data fields that constitute the primary key of the record being updated. The IDictionary object that is passed in as the first argument of the ExecuteUpdate method contains the names and values of these parameters.

The second set includes those parameters that represent data fields that are being updated. The IDictionary object that is passed in as the second argument of the ExecuteUpdate method contains the names and values of these parameters. The third set includes the rest of the parameters. The UpdateParameters property of the SqlDataSource control contains the names, values, and types of these parameters.

The ExecuteUpdate method calls the GetValues method of the UpdateParameters property to access the IOrderedDictionary object that contains the names and values of the parameters in the third set of parameters. The method then enumerates the IOrderedDictionary object, creates one DbParameter object for each enumerated DictionaryEntry object, and sets the ParameterName and Value properties of the DbParameter object to the values of the Key and Value properties of the respective DictionaryEntry object (see Listing 13-18).

Listing 13-18: The ExecuteUpdate method that uses UpdateParameters

```
protected override int ExecuteUpdate(IDictionary keys, IDictionary values,
IDictionary oldValues)
{
  if (!CanUpdate)
    throw new NotSupportedException("Update is not supported!");
  DbProviderFactory provider = owner.GetDbProviderFactory();
  DbConnection con = provider.CreateConnection();
  con.ConnectionString = owner.ConnectionString;
  DbCommand com = provider.CreateCommand();
  com.Connection = con;

  IOrderedDictionary odic = UpdateParameters.GetValues(context, owner);
  OrderedDictionary dic = new OrderedDictionary();
  foreach (DictionaryEntry entry in odic)
  {
    foreach (Parameter p2 in UpdateParameters)
    {
      if (p2.Name == entry.Key.ToString())
      {
        dic.Add(p2.Name, p2.Direction);
        break;
      }
    }
  }

  DbParameter p;
  com.CommandText = UpdateCommand;
  if (UpdateCommandType == SqlDataSourceCommandType.StoredProcedure)
    com.CommandType = System.Data.CommandType.StoredProcedure;

  foreach (DictionaryEntry entry in odic)
```

```
{
    p = provider.CreateParameter();
    p.ParameterName = ParameterPrefix + entry.Key.ToString();
    p.Value = entry.Value;
    p.Direction = (ParameterDirection)dic[entry.Key];
    com.Parameters.Add(p);
}

foreach (DictionaryEntry entry in keys)
{
    p = provider.CreateParameter();
    p.ParameterName = ParameterPrefix + entry.Key.ToString();
    p.Value = entry.Value;
    com.Parameters.Add(p);
}
foreach (DictionaryEntry entry in values)
{
    p = provider.CreateParameter();
    p.ParameterName = ParameterPrefix + entry.Key.ToString();
    p.Value = entry.Value;
    com.Parameters.Add(p);
}
int affectedRows = 0;
SqlDataSourceCommandEventArgs e = new SqlDataSourceCommandEventArgs(com);
OnUpdating(e);
if (!e.Cancel)
{
    con.Open();
    Exception exception = null;
    try
    {
        affectedRows = com.ExecuteNonQuery();
    }
    catch (Exception ex)
    {
        exception = ex;
    }
    con.Close();
    SqlDataSourceStatusEventArgs ee =
            new SqlDataSourceStatusEventArgs(com, affectedRows, exception);
    OnDataSourceViewChanged(EventArgs.Empty);
    OnUpdated(ee);
}
return affectedRows;
}
```

ExecuteInsert

The ExecuteInsert method must create and initialize one DbParameter object for each parameter used in the Insert SQL statement or stored procedure. The insert data operation has two sets of parameters. The first set includes those parameters that represent data fields of the record being inserted. The IDictionary object that is passed in as the argument of the ExecuteInsert method contains the names and values of these parameters. The second set includes the rest of the parameters. The InsertParameters property of the SqlDataSource control contains the names, values, and types of these parameters.

As Listing 13-19 shows, the `ExecuteInsert` method calls the `GetValues` method of the `Insert Parameters` property to access the `IOrderedDictionary` object that contains the names and values of the parameters in the second set of parameters.

Listing 13-19: The ExecuteInsert method that uses InsertParameters

```
protected override int ExecuteInsert(IDictionary values)
{
  if (!CanInsert)
    throw new NotSupportedException("Insert is not supported!");

  DbProviderFactory provider = owner.GetDbProviderFactory();
  DbConnection con = provider.CreateConnection();
  con.ConnectionString = owner.ConnectionString;
  DbCommand com = provider.CreateCommand();
  com.Connection = con;

  IOrderedDictionary odic = InsertParameters.GetValues(context, owner);
  OrderedDictionary dic = new OrderedDictionary();
  foreach (DictionaryEntry entry in odic)
  {
    foreach (Parameter p2 in InsertParameters)
    {
      if (p2.Name == entry.Key.ToString())
      {
        dic.Add(p2.Name, p2.Direction);
        break;
      }
    }
  }

  DbParameter p;
  com.CommandText = InsertCommand;
  if (InsertCommandType == SqlDataSourceCommandType.StoredProcedure)
    com.CommandType = System.Data.CommandType.StoredProcedure;

  foreach (DictionaryEntry entry in odic)
  {
    p = provider.CreateParameter();
    p.ParameterName = ParameterPrefix + entry.Key.ToString();
    p.Value = entry.Value;
    p.Direction = (ParameterDirection)dic[entry.Key];
    com.Parameters.Add(p);
  }

  foreach (DictionaryEntry entry in values)
  {
    p = provider.CreateParameter();
    p.ParameterName = ParameterPrefix + entry.Key.ToString();
    p.Value = entry.Value;
    com.Parameters.Add(p);
  }

  int affectedRows = 0;
  SqlDataSourceCommandEventArgs e = new SqlDataSourceCommandEventArgs(com);
```

```
OnInserting(e);
if (!e.Cancel)
{
  con.Open();
  Exception exception = null;
  try
  {
    affectedRows = com.ExecuteNonQuery();
  }
  catch (Exception ex)
  {
    exception = ex;
  }
  con.Close();
  OnDataSourceViewChanged(EventArgs.Empty);
  SqlDataSourceStatusEventArgs ee =
              new SqlDataSourceStatusEventArgs(com, affectedRows, exception);
  OnInserted(ee);
}

  return affectedRows;
}
```

Putting It All Together

The previous sections discussed the three main components of the ASP.NET 2.0 infrastructure that allows you to specify the names and values of parameters: Parameter, ParameterCollection, and built-in support of tabular data source controls and their views for automatic invocation of the GetValues and UpdateValues methods of the ParameterCollection class.

This section revisits the application shown in Figure 13-2 to help you understand how these three components of the infrastructure work together to enable you to specify parameter names and values. When the users of this application select an author name from the DropDownList control to display the author's books in the GridView control, the following sequence is triggered:

1. The containing page is posted back to the server.

2. The Page object springs into life and starts its life cycle.

3. The Page object goes through the stages of its life cycle as usual until it reaches the end of the loading stage, where it raises the LoadComplete event and consequently calls the Page_LoadComplete method of the SqlDataSource control.

4. The Page_LoadComplete method calls the UpdateValues method of the SelectParameters property (see Listing 13-15).

5. The UpdateValues method of the SelectParameters collection calls the SaveCurrentValue method of the ControlParameter component (see Listing 13-10).

6. The SaveCurrentValue method calls the Evaluate method of the ControlParameter component to retrieve the current value of the parameter (see Listing 13-4).

7. The Evaluate method retrieves the value of the SelectedValue property of the DropDownList control (see Listing 13-6).

8. The `SaveCurrentValue` method checks whether this value is different from the saved value. Because the user has selected a new author name from the `DropDownList` control, the new value will be different from the saved one. Therefore, the `SaveCurrentValue` method calls the `OnParameterChanged` method (see Listing 13-4).

9. The `OnParameterChanged` method calls the `RaiseParametersChangedEvent` method of the `SelectParameters` collection to notify the collection that the parameter value has changed (see Listing 13-3).

10. The `RaiseParametersChangedEvent` method calls the `OnParametersChanged` method of the `SelectParameters` collection (see Listing 13-8).

11. The `OnParametersChanged` method raises the `ParametersChanged` event, which subsequently calls the callback method that the `SqlDataSourceView` has registered for the `ParametersChanged` event, `ParameterCollectionChangedCallback` (see Listing 13-12).

12. The `ParameterCollectionChangedCallback` method calls the `OnDataSourceViewChanged` method of the `SqlDataSourceView` (see Listing 13-13).

13. The `OnDataSourceViewChanged` method raises the `DataSourceViewChanged` event, which subsequently calls the callback method that the `GridView` has registered for the `DataSourceViewChanged` event (see Listing 13-14).

14. As you will see in Chapter 19, the `GridView` control's callback method takes the following actions:

   a. Creates an instance of the `DataSourceSelectArguments` class.

   b. Sets the `SortExpression` property of the instance to the appropriate value. This value consists of the name of the database field associated with the column of the `GridView` control whose header link was clicked previously, and the keyword `Asc` or `Desc`.

   c. Uses the value of the `PageIndex` property of the `GridView` control to evaluate the index of the first record to be retrieved and assigns this index to the `StartRowIndex` property of the `DataSourceSelectArguments` instance. Recall that the underlying stored procedure uses this value to identify the first record to be retrieved.

   d. Assigns the value of the `PageSize` property of the `GridView` control to the `MaximumRows` property of the `DataSourceSelectArguments` instance. Recall that the underlying stored procedure uses this value to identify the last record to be retrieved.

   e. Wraps a callback method in an instance of the `DataSourceViewSelectCallback` delegate.

   f. Calls the `Select` method of the `DataSourceView` class and passes the `DataSource SelectArguments` and `DataSourceViewSelectCallback` instances as its arguments.

15. The `Select` method of the `DataSourceView` class calls the `ExecuteSelect` method of the `SqlDataSourceView` class (see Listing 12-9 in Chapter 12).

16. The `ExecuteSelect` method calls the `GetValues` method of the `SelectParameters` collection (see Listing 13-16).

17. The `GetValues` method calls the `SaveCurrentValue` method of the `ControlParameter` (see Listing 13-9).

18. The `SaveCurrentValue` method calls the `Evaluate` method of the `ControlParameter` class (see Listing 13-4).

19. The `Evaluate` method retrieves the value of the `SelectedValue` property of the `DropDownList` control (see Listing 13-6). Recall that the value of this property is nothing but the value of the `AuthorID` database field.

20. The `ExecuteSelect` method of the `SqlDataSourceView` class calls the `RetrieveTotal RowCount` method to retrieve the total row count and assigns this value to the `TotalRowCount` property of the `DataSourceSelectArguments` instance (see Listing 13-16).

21. The `ExecuteSelect` method calls the `RetrieveRows` method to retrieve the book records for the selected author (see Listing 13-16).

22. The `RetrieveRows` method calls the `SetDbParameters` method (see Chapter 12).

23. The `SetDbParameters` method takes the following actions (see Chapter 12):

   a. Uses the values of the `SortParameterName` property of the `SqlDataSource` control and the `SortExpression` property of the `DataSourceSelectArguments` instance to set the name and value of the stored procedure parameter that is used to sort the data.

   b. Uses the values of the `StartRecordParameterName` property of the `SqlDataSource` control and the `StartRowIndex` property of the `DataSourceSelectArguments` instance to set the name and value of the stored procedure parameter that is used to identify the first record to be retrieved.

   c. Uses the values of the `MaxRecordsParameterName` property of the `SqlDataSource` control and the `MaximumRows` property of the `DataSourceSelectArguments` instance to set the name and value of the stored procedure parameter that is used to identify the last record to be retrieved.

24. The `Select` method calls the `DataSourceViewSelectCallback` delegate instance that encapsulates the `GridView` control's callback for the `Select` operation and passes it the `IEnumerable` object that contains the retrieved book records for the selected author.

25. The `GridView` control's callback displays the book records of the selected author.

Developing Custom Parameters

This section uses a step-by-step approach to develop three real-world custom parameters that you can use in your own Web applications. This section not only presents the code for these new custom parameters, but it also provides you with an in-depth coverage of the techniques used to write the code to help you gain the skills you need to write your own custom parameters.

XmlWebServiceParameter

This section implements a new custom parameter named `XmlWebServiceParameter` that will use an XML Web service as the source for the value of its associated parameter. The `XmlWebServiceParameter` uses the `XmlWebServiceMethodInvoker` component to dynamically retrieve the value of its associated parameter from its underlying XML Web service. Recall from Chapter 10 that the `XmlWebService MethodInvoker` component allows other components to dynamically invoke XML Web service methods. This component exposes two properties named `TypeName` and `WSDLPath` that you must set to the fully qualified name of the class that represents the XML Web service and the URL of the site from where the WSDL document can be downloaded, respectively.

The `XmlWebServiceParameter` also exposes two properties named `TypeName` and `WSDLPath` that are used to set the values of these two properties of the `XmlWebServiceMethodInvoker`. The `XmlWebServiceParameter` also exposes a property named `MethodName` that page developers must set to the name of the XML Web service method that returns the value of its associated parameter.

XML Web service methods can have arguments. The `XmlWebServiceParameter` component only supports XML Web service methods that take a single argument. However, it doesn't put any restriction on the type of the argument. The component exposes the following properties to allow page developers to specify the name and value of the argument of the XML Web service method to be invoked:

❑ `ArgumentName`: Gets and sets the name of the argument.

❑ `ArgumentValueSource`: Get and sets the source for the value of the argument. The possible values are `Session`, `QueryString`, `Profile`, `Cookie`, and `Control`. This allows page developers to specify the `Session` object, `QueryString` collection of the `Request` object, `Profile` object, HTTP cookie, or a server control as the source for the value of the argument. Page developers must also set one of the following properties of the `XmlWebServiceParameter` component. What property is set depends on what source has been specified for the parameter value:

   ❑ `SessionField`: Gets and sets the key that identifies the object in the `Session` collection

   ❑ `QueryStringField`: Gets and sets the key that identifies the value in the `QueryString` collection

   ❑ `ProfilePropertyName`: Gets and sets the name of the property of the `Profile` object

   ❑ `CookieName`: Gets and sets the name of the HTTP cookie object

   ❑ `ControlID`: Gets and sets the value of the `ControlID` property of the server control

   ❑ `ControlPropertyName`: Gets and sets the name of the property of the control server

The `XmlWebServiceParameter` derives from the `Parameter` base class and overrides its `Evaluate` method. The method takes the following actions:

1. Calls the `GetArgumentValue` method to retrieve the value of the argument of the XML Web service method from the specified source.

2. Creates an instance of the `OrderedDictionary` collection to hold the name and value of the argument of the XML Web service method.

3. Creates an instance of the `XmlWebServiceMethodInvoker` component and sets its `TypeName` and `WSDLPath` properties.

4. Calls the `InvokeXmlWebServiceMethod` to invoke the XML Web service method whose name is the value of the `MethodName` property and passes the `OrderedDictionary` collection as its argument:

```
protected override object Evaluate(HttpContext context, Control control)
{
    object ArgumentValue = GetArgumentValue(context, control);
    OrderedDictionary arguments = new OrderedDictionary();
    arguments.Add(ArgumentName, ArgumentValue);

    XmlWebServiceMethodInvoker invoker = new XmlWebServiceMethodInvoker();
    invoker.TypeName = TypeName;
    invoker.WSDLPath = WSDLPath;
    return invoker.InvokeXmlWebServiceMethod(MethodName, arguments, true);
}
```

The GetArgumentValue method retrieves the value of the argument of the XML Web service method from the specified source, which, as discussed earlier, can be a Session object, QueryString collection, Profile object, HTTP cookie, or server control:

```
protected virtual object GetArgumentValue(HttpContext context, Control control)
{
  object ArgumentValue = null;
  switch (ArgumentValueSource)
  {
    case ArgumentValueSource.Session:
      ArgumentValue = context.Session[SessionField];
      break;
    case ArgumentValueSource.Control:
      Control c = control.Page.FindControl(ControlID);
      if (c == null)
        throw new Exception();

      PropertyDescriptorCollection pds = TypeDescriptor.GetProperties(c);
      foreach (PropertyDescriptor pd in pds)
      {
        if (pd.Name == ControlPropertyName)
        {
          ArgumentValue = pd.GetValue(c);
          break;
        }
      }
      break;
    case ArgumentValueSource.Cookie:
      ArgumentValue = context.Request.Cookies[CookieName].Value;
      break;
    case ArgumentValueSource.Profile:
      ArgumentValue = context.Profile.GetPropertyValue(ProfilePropertyName);
      break;
    case ArgumentValueSource.QueryString:
      ArgumentValue = context.Request.QueryString[QueryStringField];
      break;
    default:
      throw new ArgumentOutOfRangeException();
  }

  return ArgumentValue;
}
```

The GetArgumentValue method branches off based on the type of the specified source. Each branch uses the value of the appropriate property of the XmlWebServiceParameter component to retrieve the value of the argument of the XML Web service method from the appropriate source. For example, if an HTTP cookie is specified as the source, the branch uses the value of the CookieName property as the key to retrieve the value of the argument from the Cookies collection of the Request object.

Listing 13-20 contains a page that uses the XmlWebServiceParameter. Figure 13-2 shows what end users see when they access this page. Notice that this page uses the replica SqlDataSource control that you've been implementing in the previous chapter and this chapter.

Listing 13-20: A page that uses XmlWebServiceParameter

```
<%@ Page Language="C#" %>
<%@ Register TagPrefix="custom" Namespace="CustomComponents" %>
<html xmlns="http://www.w3.org/1999/xhtml">
<body>
  <form id="form2" runat="server">
    <strong>Select an Author: </strong>
    <asp:DropDownList runat="server" ID="DropDownList1" AutoPostBack="true"
    DataSourceID="DropDownListSource"
    DataTextField="Author" DataValueField="Author" />

    <asp:GridView runat="server" ID="GridView1" DataSourceID="MySource"
    DataKeyNames="BookID" AllowSorting="True" AllowPaging="True" PageSize="3"
    AutoGenerateColumns="false" AutoGenerateEditButton="True"
    AutoGenerateDeleteButton="True" BackColor="LightGoldenrodYellow"
    BorderColor="Tan" BorderWidth="1px" CellPadding="7" ForeColor="Black"
    GridLines="None">
      <FooterStyle BackColor="Tan" />
      <PagerStyle BackColor="PaleGoldenrod" ForeColor="DarkSlateBlue"
      HorizontalAlign="Center" />
      <SelectedRowStyle BackColor="DarkSlateBlue" ForeColor="GhostWhite" />
      <HeaderStyle BackColor="Tan" Font-Bold="True" />
      <AlternatingRowStyle BackColor="PaleGoldenrod" />
      <Columns>
        <asp:BoundField DataField="Title" HeaderText="Title"
        SortExpression="Title" />
        <asp:BoundField DataField="Author" HeaderText="Author"
        SortExpression="Author" />
        <asp:BoundField DataField="Publisher" HeaderText="Publisher"
        SortExpression="Publisher" />
        <asp:BoundField DataField="Price" HeaderText="Price" SortExpression="Price"
        ItemStyle-HorizontalAlign="Center" />
      </Columns>
    </asp:GridView>

    <custom:SqlDataSource ID="SqlDataSource1" runat="Server"
    SortParameterName="SortExpression" StartRecordParameterName="StartRowIndex"
    MaxRecordsParameterName="MaximumRows"
    SelectCommand="GetOnePageOfAuthorBooks"
    SelectCommandType="StoredProcedure"
    DeleteCommand="Delete From Books Where BookID=@BookID"
    SelectCountCommand="Select Count(*) From Books Where Author=@Author"
    ConnectionString="<%$ ConnectionStrings:MyConnectionString %>"
    UpdateCommand="Update Books Set Title=@Title,Author=@Author,
                   Publisher=@Publisher,Price=@Price Where BookID=@BookID"
    InsertCommand="InsertBook">
      <selectparameters>
        <custom:XmlWebServiceParameter DefaultValue="1" TypeName="Service"
        MethodName="GetAuthor" ControlID="ddl" ArgumentName="Author"
        WSDLPath="http://localhost:4749/Code2/Service.asmx?WSDL" Name="Author"
        ArgumentValueSource="Control" ControlPropertyName="SelectedValue" />
```

```
      </selectparameters>
    </custom:SqlDataSource>

    <custom:SqlDataSource ID="DropDownListSource" runat="Server"
    SelectCommand="Select Distinct Author From Books"
    ConnectionString="<%$ ConnectionStrings:MyConnectionString %>" />
  </form>
</body>
</html>
```

ObjectParameter

Both the `ObjectParameter` and `XmlWebServiceParameter` components invoke the specified method of a specified object to retrieve the value of their associated parameter. The main difference is the object location. The object is local in the case of the `ObjectParameter` and remote in the case of the `XmlWebServiceParameter`.

This means that the `ObjectParameter` exposes all the properties of the `XmlWebServiceParameter` except for the `ArgumentName` and `WSDLPath` because local objects don't need these two properties. This also means that the `ObjectParameter` allows the page developer to specify any of the various sources for the value of the argument of the specified method: `Session` object, `QueryString` collection of the `Request` object, `Profile` object, HTTP cookie, or server control.

The `ObjectParameter` component derives from the `Parameter` base class and overrides its `Evaluate` method:

```
protected override object Evaluate(HttpContext context, Control control)
{
  object ArgumentValue = GetArgumentValue(context, control);

  string className = TypeName.Trim().Split(new char[] { ',' })[0];
  string assemblyName =
          TypeName.Trim().Remove(TypeName.IndexOf(className), className.Length);
  Assembly assembly = null;
  if (string.IsNullOrEmpty(assemblyName))
    assembly = Assembly.GetExecutingAssembly();
  else
  {
    assemblyName = assemblyName.Trim().Remove(0, 1);
    assembly = Assembly.Load(assemblyName);
  }

  object obj = assembly.CreateInstance(className);
  MethodInfo mi = obj.GetType().GetMethod(MethodName);
  ParameterInfo[] pis = mi.GetParameters();
  TypeConverter converter = TypeDescriptor.GetConverter(pis[0].ParameterType);
  if (converter.CanConvertFrom(ArgumentValue.GetType()))
    ArgumentValue = converter.ConvertFrom(ArgumentValue);
  return mi.Invoke(obj, new object[] { ArgumentValue });
}
```

The Evaluate method first calls the GetArgumentValue method to retrieve the value of the argument of the method from the specified source. The implementation of the GetArgumentValue method is the same as the implementation of the GetArgumentValue method of the XmlWebServiceParameter:

```
object ArgumentValue = GetArgumentValue(context, control);
```

The Evaluate method then uses .NET reflection to load the assembly that contains the type that the TypeName property specifies. The value of this property consists of up to two parts: the fully qualified name of the specified class and the strong name of the assembly that contains the class. Recall that the strong name of an assembly consists of four parts: the assembly name, assembly version, assembly culture, and the public key that can be used to identify the source of the assembly.

```
string className = TypeName.Trim().Split(new char[] { ',' })[0];
string assemblyName =
        TypeName.Trim().Remove(TypeName.IndexOf(className), className.Length);
Assembly assembly = null;
if (string.IsNullOrEmpty(assemblyName))
  assembly = Assembly.GetExecutingAssembly();
else
{
  assemblyName = assemblyName.Trim().Remove(0, 1);
  assembly = Assembly.Load(assemblyName);
}
```

Notice that if the TypeName property doesn't contain the strong name of the containing assembly, the Evaluate method assumes that the executing assembly contains the specified type.

The Evaluate method then calls the CreateInstance method of the Assembly object to dynamically create an instance of the appropriate type:

```
object obj = assembly.CreateInstance(className);
```

Next, it calls the GetMethod method of the appropriate type to access the MethodInfo instance that describes the method to be invoked:

```
MethodInfo mi = obj.GetType().GetMethod(MethodName);
```

It then calls the GetParameters method of the MethodInfo instance to access the ParameterInfo instances that describe the arguments of the method:

```
ParameterInfo[] pis = mi.GetParameters();
```

The Evaluate method then calls the GetConverter method of the TypeDescriptor class to access the TypeConverter instance that knows how to convert other types to the type of the argument of the method to be invoked. Notice that the ObjectParameter component only supports methods that have a single argument:

```
TypeConverter converter = TypeDescriptor.GetConverter(pis[0].ParameterType);
```

The Evaluate method then uses the TypeConverter instance to convert the value. The TypeConverter class exposes two important methods: CanCovertFrom and ConvertFrom. The Evaluate method first calls the `CanConvertFrom` method to check whether the converter can convert from the given type. The method then calls the `ConvertFrom` method to convert from the given type to the type of the associated argument of the method being invoked:

```
if (converter.CanConvertFrom(ArgumentValue.GetType()))
    ArgumentValue = converter.ConvertFrom(ArgumentValue);
```

Finally, `Evaluate` calls the `Invoke` method of the `MethodInfo` instance to invoke the method. The `Invoke` method takes two arguments. The first argument is the object whose method is being invoked. The second argument is the value of the argument of the method being invoked:

```
return mi.Invoke(obj, new object[] { ArgumentValue });
```

Listing 13-21 contains a page that uses the `ObjectParameter`. Notice that this page is the same as the page shown in Listing 13-20 with one difference: this page uses an `ObjectParameter` to set the value of the parameter.

Listing 13-21: A page that uses the ObjectParameter

```
<%@ Page Language="C#" %>
<%@ Register TagPrefix="custom" Namespace="CustomComponents" %>
<html xmlns="http://www.w3.org/1999/xhtml">
<body>
  <form id="form2" runat="server">
    <strong>Select an Author: </strong>
    <asp:DropDownList runat="server" ID="DropDownList1" . . ./>

    <asp:GridView runat="server" DataSourceID="MySource" . . .>
     . . .
    </asp:GridView>

    <custom:SqlDataSource ID="SqlDataSource1" runat="Server"
    SortParameterName="SortExpression" StartRecordParameterName="StartRowIndex"
    MaxRecordsParameterName="MaximumRows"
    SelectCommand="GetOnePageOfAuthorBooks"
    SelectCommandType="StoredProcedure"
    DeleteCommand="Delete From Books Where BookID=@BookID"
    SelectCountCommand="Select Count(*) From Books Where Author=@Author"
    ConnectionString="<%$ ConnectionStrings:MyConnectionString %>"
    UpdateCommand="Update Books Set Title=@Title,Author=@Author,
                   Publisher=@Publisher,Price=@Price Where BookID=@BookID"
    InsertCommand="InsertBook">
      <selectparameters>
        <custom:ObjectParameter DefaultValue="1" TypeName="Class1"
        MethodName="GetAuthor" ArgumentValueSource="Control" ControlID="ddl"
        ControlPropertyName="SelectedValue" Name="Author" />
      </selectparameters>
    </custom:SqlDataSource>
    . . .
  </form>
</body>
</html>
```

ClientParameter

The `XmlWebServiceParameter` component uses server-side code to invoke the specified XML Web service method. You can think of the `ClientParameter` component as the client-side version of the `XmlWebServiceParameter`, where client-side rather than server-side code is used to invoke the XML Web service method.

> The `ClientParameter` *component uses* `WebService` *behavior to invoke the specified XML Web service method. If you are interested, go to* `http://msdn.microsoft.com/library/default .asp?url=/workshop/author/webservice/overview.asp` *for more information.*

This section uses the Web application shown in Figure 13-2. Listing 13-22 shows the `.aspx` file for this Web application. Keep the shaded areas in mind as you read this section.

Listing 13-22: The Web page that uses the ClientParameter component

```
<html xmlns="http://www.w3.org/1999/xhtml">
<body>
  <form id="form1" runat="server">
    <div id="attach" runat="server" />

    <strong>Select an Author: </strong>
    <asp:DropDownList runat="server" ID="ddl">
      <asp:ListItem Text="Author1" Value="1" />
      <asp:ListItem Text="Author2" Value="2" />
      <asp:ListItem Text="Author3" Value="3" />
    </asp:DropDownList>

    <asp:GridView runat="server" ID="gv" DataSourceID="MySource"
    DataKeyNames="BookID" AllowSorting="True" AllowPaging="True" PageSize="3"
    AutoGenerateEditButton="True" AutoGenerateDeleteButton="True" />

    <asp:SqlDataSource ID="MySource" runat="Server"
    SelectCommand="GetOnePageOfData" SelectCommandType="StoredProcedure"
    ConnectionString="<%$ ConnectionStrings:MyConnectionString %>">
      <SelectParameters>
        <custom:ClientParameter TypeName="Service" MethodName="GetAuthor"
        ArgumentName="AuthorID" InvokerControlID="ddl"
        WSDLPath="http://localhost:1821/Server/Service.asmx?WSDL" Name="AuthorID"
        InvokerAttribute="onchange" InvokerName="invoker" AttachControlID="attach"
        ArgumentValue="invoker.options[invoker.selectedIndex].value" />
      </SelectParameters>
    </asp:SqlDataSource>
  </form>
</body>
</html>
```

The `ClientParameter` component derives from the `Parameter` class and overrides its `Evaluate` method:

```
protected override object Evaluate(HttpContext context, Control control)
{
  control.Page.PreRender += new EventHandler(Page_PreRender);
  string val = context.Request.Form["__XML_WEBSERVICE_METHOD_RETURNVALUE"];
```

```
    if (val == "__INVALID_VALUE")
      val = Value;
    else
      Value = val;

    return val;
  }
```

The `Evaluate` method registers the `Page_PreRender` method as the callback for the `PreRender` event of the containing page. It then uses `__XML_WEBSERVICE_METHOD_RETURNVALUE` as the key to retrieve the new value of the associated parameter from the `Form` collection of the `Request` object. This key is the name of a hidden field that is discussed shortly.

The following code shows the implementation of the `Page_PreRender` method:

```
void Page_PreRender(object sender, EventArgs e)
{
  Page page = (Page)sender;
  string script = GetScript();

  page.RegisterClientScriptBlock(Type.GetType().ToString(), script);
  page.RegisterHiddenField("__XML_WEBSERVICE_METHOD_RETURNVALUE",
                           "__INVALID_VALUE");
  WebControl c = (WebControl)page.FindControl(InvokerControlID);
  c.Attributes[InvokerAttribute] = "javascript:InvokeXmlWebServiceMethod(this)";
  HtmlControl c2 = (HtmlControl)page.FindControl(AttachControlID);
  c2.Attributes["style"] = "behavior:url(webservice.htc)";
  c2.Attributes["id"] = AttachControlID;
}
```

The method first calls the `GetScript` method to return the client-side script that must be added to the containing page:

```
string script = GetScript();
```

It then calls the `RegisterClientScriptBlock` method to add the script to the containing page:

```
page.RegisterClientScriptBlock(Type.GetType().ToString(), script);
```

Next, the `Page_PreRender` method calls the `RegisterHiddenField` method to add a hidden field named `__XML_WEBSERVICE_METHOD_RETURNVALUE` with the default value `__INVALID_VALUE` to the containing page:

```
page.RegisterHiddenField("__XML_WEBSERVICE_METHOD_RETURNVALUE","__INVALID_VALUE");
```

`Page_PreRender` next calls the `FindControl` method of the containing page to return a reference to the `WebControl` that will invoke the XML Web service method. In the case of the application shown in Figure 13-2, page developers must set the value of the `InvokerControlID` property to the value of the `ID` property of the `DropDownList` control because, as you'll see shortly, the callback for the `onchange` event of this control will invoke the XML Web service method:

```
WebControl c = (WebControl)page.FindControl(InvokerControlID);
```

`Page_PreRender` then assigns the client-side code `InvokeXmlWebServiceMethod(this)` to the appropriate attribute of the `WebControl`. As you'll see shortly, the `InvokeXmlWebServiceMethod` JavaScript method invokes the specified XML Web service method. In the case of the application shown in Figure 13-2, page developers must set the value of the `InvokerAttribute` property to the `OnChange` attribute of the `DropDownList` control because the callback for the `onchange` event of this control must invoke the XML Web service method. This way, when the user selects an author name from the `DropDownList` control, the `onchange` client-side event will be raised and consequently the `InvokeXmlWebServiceMethod` JavaScript function will be called:

```
c.Attributes[InvokerAttribute] = "javascript:InvokeXmlWebServiceMethod(this)";
```

`Page_PreRender` then calls the `FindControl` method of the containing page to return a reference to the `HtmlControl` control to which the `WebService` behavior will be attached:

```
HtmlControl c2 = (HtmlControl)page.FindControl(AttachControlID);
```

In the case of the application in Figure 13-2, page developers must set the value of the `AttachControlID` property to the value of the `ID` property of the following `Div` HTML element:

```
<div id="attach" runat="server"/>
```

You must attach the `WebService` behavior to an HTML element before you can use it. Refer to the Microsoft Web site for more information.

Finally, `Page_PreRender` assigns the `WebService` behavior to the style attribute of the preceding HTML control:

```
c2.Attributes["style"] = "behavior:url(webservice.htc)";
```

The following code shows the implementation of the `GetScript` method:

```
protected virtual string GetScript()
{
  return
  "<SCRIPT language='JavaScript'>\n" +
    "function InvokeXmlWebServiceMethod(" + InvokerName + ")\n" +
    "{\n" +
      "var " + ArgumentName + " = " + ArgumentValue + ";\n" +
      AttachControlID + ".useService('" + WSDLPath + "','" + TypeName + "');\n" +
      AttachControlID + "." + TypeName +
          ".callService(XmlWebServiceMethodReturnValue,'" + MethodName + "'," +
                      ArgumentName + ");\n" +
    "}\n" +
    "function XmlWebServiceMethodReturnValue(returnValue)\n" +
    "{\n" +
      "if(returnValue.error)\n" +
      "{\n" +
        "var xfaultcode    = returnValue.errorDetail.code;\n" +
        "var xfaultstring  = returnValue.errorDetail.string;\n" +
        "var xfaultsoap    = returnValue.errorDetail.raw;\n" +
      "}\n" +
      "else\n" +
      "{\n" +
```

```
        "document.all['__XML_WEBSERVICE_METHOD_RETURNVALUE'].value =
        returnValue.value;\n" + "document.forms[0].submit();\n" +
    "}\n" +
  "}\n" +
"</SCRIPT>\n";
}
```

The `GetScript` method generates two JavaScript functions: the `InvokeXmlWebServiceMethod` and `XmlWebServiceMethodReturnValue` methods. The `InvokeXmlWebServiceMethod` function takes the value of the `InvokeName` property as its argument. This value refers to the HTML element that calls the method. For example, in the case of the application shown in Figure 13-2, this value refers to the `DropDownList` control. The following code shows the `InvokeXmlWebServiceMethod` function that the `GetScript` method generates for the Web page in Listing 13-22:

```
function InvokeXmlWebServiceMethod(invoker)
{
  var AuthorID = invoker.options[invoker.selectedIndex].value;
  attach.useService('http://localhost:1821/Server/Service.asmx?WSDL','Service');
  attach.Service.callService(XmlWebServiceMethodReturnValue,'GetAuthor',
                                  AuthorID);
}
```

Because invoking the XML Web service method is asynchronous, the `InvokeXmlWebServiceMethod` registers the `XmlWebServiceMethodReturnValue` JavaScript function as the callback. The following code shows the `XmlWebServiceMethodReturnValue` function that the `GetScript` method generates for the Web page shown in Listing 13-22:

```
function XmlWebServiceMethodReturnValue(returnValue)
{
  if(!returnValue.error)
  {
    document.all['__XML_WEBSERVICE_METHOD_RETURNVALUE'].value = returnValue.value;
    document.forms[0].submit();
  }
}
```

Notice that the `XmlWebServiceMethodReturnValue` assigns the return value of the XML Web service method to the value attribute of the hidden field named `__XML_WEBSERVICE_METHOD_RETURNVALUE` and calls the `submit` function to post the page back to the server.

Listing 13-23 contains a page that uses the `ClientParameter`. This page is also the same as the page shown in Listing 13-22 with one difference: this page uses a `ClientParameter` to set the value of the parameter.

Listing 13-23: A page that uses the ClientParameter

```
<%@ Page Language="C#" %>
<%@ Register TagPrefix="custom" Namespace="CustomComponents" %>
<html xmlns="http://www.w3.org/1999/xhtml">
<body>
  <form id="form2" runat="server">
    <strong>Select an Author: </strong>
```

(continued)

393

Listing 13-23: *(continued)*

```
<asp:DropDownList runat="server" ID="DropDownList1" . . ./>

<asp:GridView runat="server" DataSourceID="MySource" . . .>
 . . .
</asp:GridView>

<custom:SqlDataSource ID="SqlDataSource1" runat="Server"
SortParameterName="SortExpression" StartRecordParameterName="StartRowIndex"
MaxRecordsParameterName="MaximumRows"
SelectCommand="GetOnePageOfAuthorBooks"
SelectCommandType="StoredProcedure"
DeleteCommand="Delete From Books Where BookID=@BookID"
SelectCountCommand="Select Count(*) From Books Where Author=@Author"
ConnectionString="<%$ ConnectionStrings:MyConnectionString %>"
UpdateCommand="Update Books Set Title=@Title,Author=@Author,
                Publisher=@Publisher,Price=@Price Where BookID=@BookID"
InsertCommand="InsertBook">
   <selectparameters>
      <custom:ClientParameter DefaultValue="3" TypeName="Service"
      MethodName="GetAuthor"
      WSDLPath="http://localhost:3137/Server/Service.asmx?WSDL"
      ArgumentName="Author" InvokerControlID="ddl" InvokerAttribute="onchange"
      InvokerName="invoker" AttachControlID="attach" Name="Author"
      ArgumentValue="invoker.options[invoker.selectedIndex].value" />
   </selectparameters>
</custom:SqlDataSource>
 . . .
</form>
</body>
</html>
```

Summary

The ASP.NET 2.0 data source control model provides you with an infrastructure that allows you to specify the names and values of the parameters used in a tabular data source control. This infrastructure consists of three important components:

❑ `Parameter`

❑ `ParameterCollection`

❑ The built-in support of tabular data source controls for automatic invocation of the `GetValues` and `UpdateValues` methods of the `ParameterCollection` collection

This chapter looked under the hood of these components to help you understand how they work from the inside out and how you can extend them. You then developed three real-world custom parameter components named `XmlWebServiceParameter`, `ObjectParameter`, and `ClientParameter` to help you gain the skills you need to write your own custom parameters. In the next chapter you'll use the skills that you have learned in the previous chapter and this chapter to develop a real-world custom tabular data source control that you can use in your own Web applications.

14

Developing ASP.NET 2.0 Custom Tabular Data Source Controls

In data-driven Web applications, data comes from many different types of data stores, such as Microsoft SQL Server, Oracle, Microsoft Access, XML files, flat files, Web services, and so on. Each type of data store has its own data access API. This means that applications that use the data access API of a specific type of data store will not be able to access other types of data stores. The ASP.NET 2.0 data source control model defines a generic data access API that can be used to access all types of data stores. The model delegates the responsibility of mapping the generic data access API to the data access API of a given type of data store such as SQL Server to a particular implementation of the generic API.

For example, the `SqlDataSource` control provides a specific implementation of the generic API that maps the generic data access API to the data access API of a relational database, such as Microsoft SQL Server or OLE DB. The separation of the generic API from its implementations presents an extensible framework that allows you to provide your own implementations of the API to access new types of data stores. Because all implementations honor the API contract, switching from one implementation to another will have no impact on the applications that use the API. Chapters 12 and 13 discussed the ASP.NET 2.0 data source control model and its generic API in detail.

The ASP.NET 2.0 Framework comes with several data source controls that implement the generic API to provide access to their underlying data stores. However, because there are numerous types of data stores, the ASP.NET 2.0 Framework doesn't come with standard data source controls for all types of data stores. For example, none of the existing data source controls directly stores data in and retrieves data from XML Web services.

Chapters 12 and 13 implemented a fully functional replica of the ASP.NET 2.0 `SqlDataSource` control and provided you with an in-depth coverage of the techniques, tools, and technologies used to implement the control. This chapter builds on the experience and knowledge you gained in those chapters and uses a detailed step-by-step approach to implement a real-world custom data source control named `XmlWebServiceDataSource` that uses an XML Web service as its underlying data store.

The XmlWebServiceMethodInvoker Component

The `XmlWebServiceDataSource` control dynamically invokes the appropriate methods of its underlying XML Web service to update, select, delete, and insert data. Chapter 10 implemented a new custom component named `XmlWebServiceMethodInvoker` that allows other ASP.NET 2.0 components such as `XmlWebServiceDataSource` to dynamically invoke the methods of their underlying XML Web services. As discussed in Chapter 10, this component exposes an important method named `InvokeXmlWebServiceMethod` as follows:

```
public virtual object InvokeXmlWebServiceMethod(string methodName,
                        IOrderedDictionary methodArgumentNamesAndValues,
                bool validateAndSortMethodArgumentNamesAndValues)
```

This method is all you need to enable your .NET custom components to dynamically invoke the methods of XML Web services. The method takes three arguments. The first argument is the name of the XML Web service method being invoked. The second argument is an `IOrderedDictionary` object that contains the names and values of the arguments of the method. The `IOrderedDictionary` object is a collection of `DictionaryEntry` objects where each object represents an argument of the XML Web service method. The `DictionaryEntry` class exposes two properties named `Key` and `Value`, whose values are the name and value of the method argument, respectively. The last argument of the `InvokeXmlWebServiceMethod` method determines whether the argument names and values contained in the `IOrderedDictionary` object must be validated and sorted before they're passed to the respective XML Web service method. The `XmlWebServiceDataSource` control will use the `InvokeXmlWebServiceMethod` method to invoke the methods of the underlying XML Web service that insert, delete, select, and update data.

As discussed in Chapter 12, there are two types of ASP.NET 2.0 data source controls: tabular and hierarchical. Tabular and hierarchical data source controls present tabular and hierarchical views of their underlying data stores, respectively. The same data source control may expose both hierarchical and tabular views. For example, the `XmlDataSource` control presents both views of its underlying XML document. The first step in designing a new custom data source control is to decide on its type: tabular, hierarchical, or both. Type matters because the clients of the data source control expect a specific type of view. For example, ASP.NET 2.0 tabular data-bound controls (such as `GridView` and `DetailsView`) expect tabular data, and hierarchical controls (such as `TreeView` and `Menu`) expect hierarchical data. The `XmlWebServiceDataSource` control is both a tabular and hierarchical data source control, meaning it provides its clients with both tabular and hierarchical views of its underlying XML Web service.

However, the implementation of the `XmlWebServiceDataSource` control as a hierarchical data source control is presented in Chapter 16 after the ASP.NET 2.0 hierarchical data source control model is discussed in detail in Chapter 15. This chapter presents the implementation of the `XmlWebServiceDataSource` control as a tabular data source control.

Chapter 13 presented a sample Web application (see Figure 13-2) that used the `SqlDataSource` control to retrieve data from a Microsoft SQL Server database. To make the discussions more concrete, this chapter uses the same Web application (see Figure 14-1) but this time the application uses the XmlWebServiceDataSource control to retrieve data from an XML Web service.

As you will see, thanks to the ASP.NET 2.0 tabular data source control model, switching from the SqlDataSource control to the new XmlWebServiceDataSource control will have no impact on the functioning of the GridView control. This allows the same GridView control work with both Microsoft SQL Server databases and XML Web services. This is because the GridView control has no knowledge of the type of the underlying tabular data source control, that is, whether it's a SqlDataSource or an XmlWebServiceDataSource control. As far as the GridView control is concerned, both SqlDataSource and XmlWebServiceDataSource controls are of the same type — IDataSource.

Select an Author: Author3 ∨					
	BookID	**Title**	**AuthorID**	**Publisher**	**Price**
Edit Delete	35	Title13	3	Publisher13	130
Edit Delete	36	Title14	3	Publisher14	140
Edit Delete	37	Title15	3	Publisher15	150
		1 <u>2</u>			

Figure 14-1

The following code fragment shows the declaration of the XML Web service methods that the application shown in Figure 14-1 invokes to select, delete, insert, and update data records:

```
public class Service : System.Web.Services.WebService
{
  [WebMethod]
  public int SelectCount(string Author);

  [WebMethod]
  public string Select(string SortParameter, int StartRowIndex, int MaximumRows,
                   string Author);

  [WebMethod]
  public int Delete(int BookID);

  [WebMethod]
  public int Insert(string Title, string Author, string Publisher, decimal Price);

  [WebMethod]
  public int Update(int BookID, string Title, string Author, string Publisher,
                   decimal Price);
}
```

The XML Web service exposes five methods as follows:

❑ SelectCount: Retrieves the total row count of the book records of the author with the specified name.

❑ Select: Retrieves the book records of the author with the specified name whose indices are greater than the value of the StartRowIndex argument and less than the value of the StartRowIndex argument plus the value of the MaximumRows argument. In other words, the Select method retrieves the book records of the author with the specified name one page at a time.

❑   `Delete`: Deletes the book record with the specified `BookID`.

❑   `Insert`: Inserts a new book record with the specified title, author name, publisher, and price.

❑   `Update`: Updates the title, author name, publisher, and price of the book record with the specified `BookID`.

The following sections present the implementation of these XML Web service methods.

DataSourceControl

The `XmlWebServiceDataSource` control presents its clients with tabular views of its underlying XML Web service. The control makes the XML Web service look like a database where the tabular views act like the tables of this virtual database. These virtual tables, like any other table, are named entities where the name of a table uniquely locates the table among others.

The `XmlWebServiceDataSource` control derives from the `DataSourceControl` base class and overrides its methods. The base class exposes two important methods: `GetViewNames` and `GetView`. The `GetViewNames` method returns an `ICollection` object that contains the names of all available tabular views:

```
protected override ICollection GetViewNames()
{
  return new string[] { "DefaultView" };
}
```

Notice that the `XmlWebServiceDataSource` control exposes a single tabular view named `DefaultView`. In other words, the control makes the underlying XML Web service look like a database that contains a single table.

The `XmlWebServiceDataSource` control exposes a protected virtual method named `CreateData SourceView` that creates an instance of the `XmlWebServiceDataSourceView` class. You can implement your own custom data source view classes that derive from the `XmlWebServiceDataSourceView` class and override the `CreateDataSourceView` method to return an instance of your own custom data source views.

```
private XmlWebServiceDataSourceView view = null;

protected virtual XmlWebServiceDataSourceView CreateDataSourceView(string viewName)
{
  if (!string.IsNullOrEmpty(viewName) && (viewName.ToLower() != "defaultview"))
    throw new ArgumentException("Wrong view name!");

  if (view == null)
  {
    view = new XmlWebServiceDataSourceView(this, viewName, Context);
    if (IsTrackingViewState)
      ((IStateManager)view).TrackViewState();
  }

  return view;
}
```

The GetView method simply calls the CreateDataSourceView method:

```
protected override DataSourceView GetView(string viewName)
{
  return CreateDataSourceView(viewName);
}
```

DataSourceView

The XmlWebServiceDataSource control delegates the responsibility of invoking the underlying XML Web service methods to its associated XmlWebServiceDataSourceView object. The XmlWeb ServiceDataSourceView class derives from the DataSourceView abstract base class. The base class exposes all the properties and methods that the XmlWebServiceDataSourceView class needs to implement in order to provide its clients with the tabular views of its underlying XML Web service. The class exposes seven public properties: CanUpdate, CanDelete, CanInsert, CanPage, CanSort, CanRetrieveTotalRowCount, and Name. The class also exposes four important protected virtual methods: ExecuteUpdate, ExecuteDelete, ExecuteInsert, and ExecuteSelect.

The following sections present the XmlWebServiceDataSourceView class's implementations of the properties and methods of the DataSourceView abstract base class.

ExecuteSelect

The XmlWebServiceDataSourceView class overrides the ExecuteSelect method of its base class to retrieve tabular data from its underlying XML Web service as shown in Listing 14-1. Notice that the ExecuteSelect method consists of two queries. The first query retrieves the total row count, and the second query retrieves the actual data records. You may wonder why you need to retrieve the total row count.

To answer this question, take another look at the Web application shown in Figure 14-1. The GridView control used in this application retrieves book records one page at a time to improve the performance and responsiveness of the application. However, the paging interface of the GridView control still needs to render one link button for each page of data to provide random page access. Therefore, the GridView control needs to know the total page count and consequently the total row count up front.

This means that the GridView control needs a way to signal the ExecuteSelect method to retrieve the total row count and the ExecuteSelect method, in turn, needs a way to pass the total row count back to the GridView control. This is where the DataSourceSelectArguments class comes into play.

The following sequence shows how the ExecuteSelect method and GridView control exchange information:

1. As you'll see in Chapter 19, the GridView control creates an instance of the DataSource SelectArguments class, sets the value of its RetrieveTotalRowCount property to true, and passes the instance to the Select method of the relevant XmlWebServiceDataSourceView object. The Select method subsequently passes the DataSourceSelectArguments instance to the ExecuteSelect method.

2. As Listing 14-1 shows, the ExecuteSelect method checks whether the RetrieveTotalRowCount property of the DataSourceSelectArguments instance is set to true. If so, the method retrieves the total row count and assigns it to the TotalRowCount property of the instance:

```
if (arguments.RetrieveTotalRowCount &&
    !string.IsNullOrEmpty(SelectCountMethod))
  arguments.TotalRowCount = GetTotalRowCount();
```

3. As you'll see in Chapter 19, the `GridView` control, subsequently, accesses the value of the `TotalRowCount` property of the instance and uses the value to find out how many link buttons it needs to render in its paging interface.

Listing 14-1: The ExecuteSelect method

```csharp
protected override IEnumerable ExecuteSelect(DataSourceSelectArguments arguments)
{
  DetermineCapabilities(arguments);
  if (arguments.RetrieveTotalRowCount &&
      !string.IsNullOrEmpty(SelectCountMethod))
    arguments.TotalRowCount = GetTotalRowCount();

  IEnumerable result = null;
  IOrderedDictionary methodArgumentNamesAndValues =
        RetrieveMethodArgumentNamesAndValues(SelectParameters, null, arguments);

  XmlWebServiceDataSourceSelectingEventArgs e =
    new XmlWebServiceDataSourceSelectingEventArgs(MethodInvoker, SelectMethod,
                        methodArgumentNamesAndValues, true, false);
  OnSelecting(e);
  if (!e.Cancel)
  {
    Exception ex = null;
    try
    {
      object returnValue = methodInvoker.InvokeXmlWebServiceMethod(SelectMethod,
                                methodArgumentNamesAndValues, true);
      StringReader reader = new StringReader((string)returnValue);
      DataSet myDataSet = new DataSet();
      myDataSet.ReadXml(reader, XmlReadMode);

      if (DataMember != null && DataMember.Length > 0)
        result = myDataSet.Tables[DataMember].DefaultView;
      else
        result = myDataSet.Tables[0].DefaultView;
    }
    catch (Exception ex1)
    {
      ex = ex1;
    }
    finally
    {
      XmlWebServiceDataSourceStatusEventArgs ee =
        new XmlWebServiceDataSourceStatusEventArgs(MethodInvoker, SelectMethod,
                          methodArgumentNamesAndValues, true, -1, ex);
      OnSelected(ee);
      if (ex != null && !ee.ExceptionHandled)
        throw ex;
```

```
      }
    }

    return result;
  }
```

Retrieving the Total Row Count

The `XmlWebServiceDataSource` control exposes a property named `SelectCountMethod` that page developers must set to the name of the XML Web service method that returns the total row count. The XML Web service in this example exposes a method named `SelectCount` that retrieves the total row count from its underlying Microsoft SQL server database, as shown in Listing 14-2.

Listing 14-2: The SelectCount method of the XML Web service

```
[WebMethod]
public int SelectCount(string Author)
{
  SqlConnection con = new SqlConnection(GetConnectionString());
  SqlCommand com = new SqlCommand("Select Count(*) From Books Where
                             Author=@Author", con);
  com.Parameters.AddWithValue("@Author", Author);
  con.Open();
  object result = com.ExecuteScalar();
  con.Close();
  return (int)result;
}
```

The `XmlWebServiceDataSourceView` class exposes a method named `GetTotalRowCount` whose main responsibility is to use the `XmlWebServiceMethodInvoker` component to invoke the specified XML Web service method:

```
protected virtual int GetTotalRowCount()
{
  IOrderedDictionary methodArgumentNamesAndValues =
          RetrieveMethodArgumentNamesAndValues(SelectParameters, null, null);
  return (int)MethodInvoker.InvokeXmlWebServiceMethod(SelectCountMethod,
                                    methodArgumentNamesAndValues, true);
}
```

The `ExecuteSelect` method uses the `GetTotalRowCount` method to invoke the XML Web service method whose name is the value of the `SelectCountMethod` property (see Listing 14-1). In this example this XML Web service method is the `SelectCount` method shown in Listing 14-2. The `XmlWebServiceDataSourceView` class exposes a method named `RetrieveMethodArgument` `NamesAndValues` that returns an `IOrderedDictionary` collection that contains the names and values of a specified method, which is the `SelectCount` method shown in Listing 14-2. The `RetrieveMethod` `ArgumentNamesAndValues` method is discussed later in this chapter. Notice that the `GetTotalRowCount` method passes the `SelectParameters` property of the `XmlWebServiceDataSource` as the first argument to the `RetrieveMethodArgumentNamesAndValues` method. This property is discussed in the following section.

SelectParameters

The `SelectParameters` property of the `XmlWebServiceDataSource` control allows page developers to use the `Parameter` class and its subclasses to specify the names, values, and types of the arguments of the following two XML Web service methods:

❑ The method that retrieves the total row count, such as the `SelectCount` method shown in Listing 14-2

❑ The method that retrieves the actual data records, such as the `Select` method discussed later in this chapter in Listing 14-8

For example, in the case of this example Web application, both the `SelectCount` and `Select` methods of the XML Web service expect an argument of type `string` named `Author`. Page developers can use a subclass of the `Parameter` class to specify a source for the value of this argument. Listing 14-3 uses a `ControlParameter` instance to specify the `SelectedValue` property of a `DropDownList` control as the source for the value of the `Author` argument of the `SelectCount` and `Select` methods of the XML Web service.

Listing 14-3: The declaration of the XmlWebServiceDataSource control

```
<asp:DropDownList ID="ddl" runat="server" AutoPostBack="true">
  <asp:ListItem Text="Author1" Value="Author1" Selected="True" />
  <asp:ListItem Text="Author2" Value="Author2" />
  <asp:ListItem Text="Author3" Value="Author3" />
</asp:DropDownList>

<custom:XmlWebServiceDataSource ID="MySource" runat="Server" TypeName="Service"
SelectMethod="Select" XmlReadMode="Auto" SortParameterName="SortParameter"
UpdateMethod="Update" DeleteMethod="Delete" SelectCountMethod="SelectCount"
StartRecordParameterName="StartRowIndex" MaxRecordsParameterName="MaximumRows"
WSDLPath="http://localhost:1252/Server/Service.asmx?WSDL">
  <SelectParameters>
    <asp:ControlParameter Name="Author" PropertyName="SelectedValue"
    ControlID="ddl" DefaultValue="Author2" />
  </SelectParameters>
</custom:XmlWebServiceDataSource>
```

Listing 14-4 shows the implementation of the `SelectParameters` property.

Listing 14-4: The SelectParameters property

```
private ParameterCollection selectParameters = null;
public ParameterCollection SelectParameters
{
  get
  {
    if (selectParameters == null)
    {
      selectParameters = new ParameterCollection();
      if (isTrackingViewState)
        ((IStateManager)selectParameters).TrackViewState();

      selectParameters.ParametersChanged +=
```

```
                              new EventHandler(ParameterCollectionChangedCallback);
    }
    return selectParameters;
  }
}
```

The `SelectParameters` property calls the `TrackViewState` method to start view state tracking. This is done only if the view state of the `XmlWebServiceDataSourceView` class is being tracked. It also registers the `ParameterCollectionChangedCallback` method (see Listing 14-5) of the `XmlWebServiceDataSourceView` class as the callback for the `ParametersChanged` event of the `ParameterCollection`.

Listing 14-5: The ParameterCollectionChangedCallback method

```
protected virtual void
ParameterCollectionChangedCallback(object sender, EventArgs e)
{
   this.OnDataSourceViewChanged(e);
}
```

The `ParameterCollectionChangedCallback` method calls the `OnDataSourceViewChanged` method of the `DataSourceView` base class. As discussed in Chapter 12, the `OnDataSourceViewChanged` method raises the `DataSourceViewChanged` event. As you'll see in Chapter 17, tabular data-bound controls such as the `GridView` in Figure 14-1 register a callback for this event where they retrieve fresh data and update their display.

You may wonder what triggers the `ParametersChanged` event. As discussed in Chapter 13, the `ParameterCollection` class exposes two methods named `GetValues` and `UpdateValues`. Both methods enumerate the parameter objects in the `ParameterCollection` and call the `SaveCurrentValue` method of each enumerated parameter object. For example, the `ParameterCollection` in Listing 14-3 contains a single parameter object of type `ControlParameter`. As mentioned, this parameter object is used to set the value of the `Author` argument of the `SelectCount` and `Select` methods of the XML Web service.

The `GetValues` and `UpdateValues` methods, in this case, call the `SaveCurrentValue` method (see Listing 13-4 in Chapter 13) of the `ControlParameter` object, which, in turn, calls the `Evaluate` method. The `Evaluate` method (see Listing 13-5) retrieves the value of the `SelectedValue` property of the `DropDownList` control shown in Figure 14-1 and returns this value to its caller, the `SaveCurrentValue` method. If the new value of the parameter is different from the old value, the `SaveCurrentValue` method sends a change notification to its containing `SelectParameters` collection (see Listing 13-11), which, in turn, raises the `ParametersChanged` event.

Now that you know the `GetValues` and `UpdateValues` methods trigger the `ParametersChanged` event, you may wonder who calls these two methods. The `XmlWebServiceDataSource` control uses the following two mechanisms to call the `GetValues` and `UpdateValues` methods of the `SelectParameters` collection, respectively:

❑   The `XmlWebServiceDataSource` control overrides the `OnInit` method that it inherits from the `Control` class to register the `Page_LoadComplete` method as the callback for the `LoadComplete` event of the containing page (see Listing 14-6). When the containing page raises the `LoadComplete` event and automatically calls the `Page_LoadComplete` method, the method automatically calls the `UpdateValues` method of the `SelectParameters` object (see Listing 14-7).

❑ As you'll see in the next section, the `ExecuteSelect` method of the `XmlWebServiceDataSource View` class passes the `SelectParameters` collection to the `RetrieveMethodArgumentNames AndValues` method of the `XmlWebServiceDataSourceView` class. This method calls the `GetValues` method of the `SelectParameters` object.

Listing 14-6: The OnInit method

```
protected override void OnInit(EventArgs e)
{
  Page.LoadComplete += new EventHandler(Page_LoadComplete);
  base.OnInit(e);
}
```

Listing 14-7: The Page_Load method

```
void Page_LoadComplete(object sender, EventArgs e)
{
  SelectParameters.UpdateValues(Context, this);
}
```

Retrieving the Data Records

As discussed, the `ExcuteSelect` method consists of two queries (see Listing 14-1). The first query invokes the method of the underlying XML Web service that retrieves the total row count, and the second query invokes the method of the XML Web service that retrieves the actual data records.

In the example application, the `SelectCount` and `Select` methods of the XML Web service are responsible for retrieving the total row count and the data records, respectively. The previous sections discussed the first query in detail. This section focuses on the second query.

As Listing 14-8 shows, the `Select` method of the XML Web service takes four arguments. The first argument is used in the Order By section of the `Select` SQL statement to sort the retrieved data. This argument normally consists of a database field name followed by the string `"ASC"` or `"DESC"`. The second and third arguments instruct the underlying stored procedure to retrieve only those records whose indexes are greater than `StartRowIndex` and less than the `StartRowIndex+MaximumRows`. The last argument is the name of the author whose books are being retrieved.

Listing 14-8: The Select method of the XML Web service

```
[WebMethod]
public string Select(string SortParameter, int StartRowIndex,
                     int MaximumRows, string Author)
{
  SqlConnection con = new SqlConnection(GetConnectionString());
  string commandText = "GetOnePageOfData";

  SqlCommand com = new SqlCommand(commandText, con);
  com.CommandType = CommandType.StoredProcedure;
  com.Parameters.AddWithValue("@MaximumRows", MaximumRows);
  com.Parameters.AddWithValue("@StartRowIndex", StartRowIndex);
  if (SortParameter == null || SortParameter.Trim() == "")
    SortParameter = "BookID ASC";
```

```
    if (!SortParameter.Contains("ASC") && !SortParameter.Contains("DESC"))
      SortParameter = SortParameter.Insert(SortParameter.Length, " ASC");

    com.Parameters.AddWithValue("@SortParameter", SortParameter);
    com.Parameters.AddWithValue("@Author", Author);
    DataTable dt = new DataTable("Books");
    SqlDataAdapter ad = new SqlDataAdapter();
    ad.SelectCommand = com;
    con.Open();
    ad.Fill(dt);
    StringWriter writer = new StringWriter();
    dt.WriteXml(writer, XmlWriteMode.WriteSchema);
    string res = writer.ToString();
    writer.Close();
    con.Close();
    return res;
}
```

The `XmlWebServiceDataSource` control exposes the following three properties:

❑   `SortParameterName`: Page developers must set the value of this property to the name of the argument of the XML Web service method that is used for sorting. In this case, page developers must set the value of this property to `SortParameter`, which is the name of the first argument of the `Select` method of the XML Web service.

❑   `StartRecordParameterName`: Page developers must set the value of this property to the name of the argument of the XML Web service method whose value specifies the index of the first record to be retrieved. In this case, this property must be set to `StartRowIndex`, which is the name of the second argument of the `Select` method of the XML Web service.

❑   `MaxRecordsParameterName`: The value of this property must be set to the name of the argument of the XML Web service method whose value specifies the maximum records to be retrieved. In this case, this property must be set to `MaximumRows`, which is the name of the third argument of the `Select` method of the XML Web service.

The following code shows how page developers can set the values of these properties.

```
<custom:XmlWebServiceDataSource ID="MySource" Runat="Server"
  SortParameterName="SortParameter" StartRecordParameterName="StartRowIndex"
  MaxRecordsParameterName="MaximumRows"
</custom:XmlWebServiceDataSource>
```

This declaration only specifies the names of the arguments of the `Select` method of the XML Web service — `SortParameter`, `StartRowIndex`, and `MaximumRows`. However, it doesn't specify the values of these arguments. Page developers are only responsible for specifying the names of the arguments of the `Select` method of the XML Web service, not their values. The responsibility of specifying the values of these arguments lies with the `GridView`.

This means that the `GridView` control needs a way to pass these values to the `ExecuteSelect` method. This is where the `DataSourceSelectArguments` class comes into play again. As you'll see in Chapter 19, the `GridView` control takes the following actions:

1.   Creates an instance of the `DataSourceSelectArguments` class, as discussed earlier.

2. Sets the values of the `SortExpression`, `StartRowIndex`, and `MaximumRows` properties of the instance. This means that the `GridView` control, like any other tabular data source control, must keep track of the following:

❑ Sort expression and sort order values

❑ Index of the last retrieved data record

❑ Maximum number of records to be retrieved (page size)

3. Passes the instance as an argument to the `Select` method of the `XmlWebServiceDataSourceView` class, which is subsequently passed to the `ExecuteSelect` method.

As shown in Listing 14-1, the `ExecuteSelect` invokes the method of the XML Web service that retrieves the actual data records by first calling the `RetrieveMethodArgumentNamesAndValues` method and passing the `SelectParameters` collection and the `DataSourceSelectArguments` as its arguments. As discussed shortly, the `RetrieveMethodArgumentNamesAndValues` method uses the `SelectParameters` collection and the `DataSourceSelectArguments` object to populate an `IOrderedDictionary` collection that contains one `DictionaryEntry` object for each argument of the underlying XML Web service method. In this case, the XML Web service method is the `Select` method shown in Listing 14-8.

```
IOrderedDictionary methodArgumentNamesAndValues =
        RetrieveMethodArgumentNamesAndValues(SelectParameters, null, arguments);
```

The `ExecuteSelect` method then raises the `Selecting` event before it attempts to invoke the respective XML Web service method. Page developers can register a callback for this event where they can use application-specific business rules to determine whether or not the specified query is permitted. The `Selecting` event is discussed in detail later in this chapter.

```
XmlWebServiceDataSourceSelectingEventArgs e =
   new XmlWebServiceDataSourceSelectingEventArgs(MethodInvoker, SelectMethod,
                        methodArgumentNamesAndValues, true, false);
OnSelecting(e);
```

If the query is permitted, the `ExecuteSelect` method then calls the `InvokeXmlWebServiceMethod` of the `MethodInvoker` property to invoke the XML Web service method. This property is discussed in the next section. As mentioned, page developers must set the value of the `SelectMethod` property of the `XmlWebServiceDataSource` control to the name of the XML Web service that retrieves the actual data records. In this case, the `Select` method shown in Listing 14-8 is the XML Web service method that retrieve the data records:

```
object returnValue = MethodInvoker.InvokeXmlWebServiceMethod(SelectMethod,
                            methodArgumentNamesAndValues, true);
```

The underlying XML Web service method (the `Select` method in this case) returns a string that contains an XML document. However, the `ExecuteSelect` method must return the data as an object of type `IEnumerable`. As you saw in Chapter 13, this allows the `GridView` control to call the `GetEnumerator` method of the object to access the `IEnumerator` object and use the enumerator to enumerate the data records and generate the appropriate HTML markup text for each enumerated record. The `ExecuteSelect` method converts the data into an object of type `IEnumerable` by loading the data into an instance of the `StringReader` class, creating an instance of the `DataSet` class and calling its `ReadXml` method to load and convert the contents of the `StringReader` instance, and then using the `DefaultView` property of the `DataTable` object to return an `IEnumerable` object.

Finally, the `EventSelect` method raises the `Selected` event to mark the end of the `Select` data operation. This event is discussed in detail shortly.

```
XmlWebServiceDataSourceStatusEventArgs ee =
        new XmlWebServiceDataSourceStatusEventArgs(MethodInvoker, SelectMethod,
                                methodArgumentNamesAndValues, true, -1, ex);
OnSelected(ee);
```

The MethodInvoker Property

The `XmlWebServiceDataSourceView` class exposes a property of type `XmlWebServiceMethod Invoker` named `MethodInvoker` that uses a private field of the same type named `methodInvoker` as its backing store:

```
private XmlWebServiceMethodInvoker methodInvoker;
protected virtual XmlWebServiceMethodInvoker MethodInvoker
{
  get
  {
    if (methodInvoker == null)
    {
      methodInvoker = new XmlWebServiceMethodInvoker();
      methodInvoker.WSDLPath = owner.WSDLPath;
      methodInvoker.TypeName = owner.TypeName;
      methodInvoker.CacheDuration = owner.CacheDuration;
      methodInvoker.CacheExpirationPolicy = owner.CacheExpirationPolicy;
      methodInvoker.CacheKeyDependency = owner.CacheKeyDependency;
      methodInvoker.EnableCaching = owner.EnableCaching;
    }
    return methodInvoker;
  }
}
```

The `MethodInvoker` property checks whether the `methodInvoker` private field is initialized. If not, the property creates an instance of the `XmlWebServiceMethodInvoker` class and assigns it to the `methodInvoker` private field:

```
methodInvoker = new XmlWebServiceMethodInvoker();
```

It then assigns the value of the `WSDLPath` property of the `XmlWebServiceDataSource` control to the `WSDLPath` property of the `XmlWebServiceMethodInvoker` instance. Page developers must set the value of the `WSDLPath` property of the `XmlWebServiceDataSource` control to the URL of the site from where the WSDL document can be downloaded:

```
methodInvoker.WSDLPath = owner.WSDLPath;
```

The `MethodInvoker` property next assigns the value of the `TypeName` property of the `XmlWebService DataSource` control to the `TypeName` property of the `XmlWebServiceMethodInvoker` instance. Page developers must set the value of the `TypeName` property of the `XmlWebServiceDataSource` control to the fully qualified name of the class that represents the XML Web service:

```
methodInvoker.TypeName = owner.TypeName;
```

MethodInvoker then assigns the value of the CacheDuration property of the XmlWebServiceData Source control to the CacheDuration property of the XmlWebSeriveMethodInvoker instance. Page developers must set the value of the CacheDuration property of the XmlWebServiceDataSource control to the length of time, in seconds, that they want the complied proxy class to remain in cache:

```
methodInvoker.CacheDuration = owner.CacheDuration;
```

The XmlWebServiceDataSource control exposes a property of type XmlWebServiceMethodInvoker CacheExpirationPolicy named CacheExpirationPolicy that the page developers must set to specify the cache expiration policy. The possible values are Absolute and Sliding. Page developers use the Absolute value to specify that the compiled proxy class should remain in the cache for the duration specified by the CacheDuration property. Page developers use the Sliding value to specify that the compiled proxy class should remain in the cache as long as the time interval between consecutive requests is not longer than the value specified by the CacheDuration property. The MethodInvoker property assigns the value of the CacheExpirationPolicy of the XmlWebServiceDataSource control to the CacheExpirationPolicy property of the XmlWebServiceMethodInvoker instance:

```
methodInvoker.CacheExpirationPolicy = owner.CacheExpirationPolicy;
```

Finally, the MethodInvoker property assigns the EnableCaching property of the XmlWebServiceData Source control to the EnableCaching property of the XmlWebServiceMethodInvoker instance. Page developers must set the value of the EnableCaching property of the XmlWebServiceDataSource control to specify whether the compiled proxy class should be cached at all:

```
methodInvoker.EnableCaching = owner.EnableCaching;
```

Selecting Event

As Listing 14-1 shows the ExecuteSelect method raises the Selecting event before it attempts to call the InvokeXmlWebServiceMethod of the XmlWebServicMethodInvoker object. To implement this event, you first need to implement a subclass of the CancelEventArgs class named XmlWebServiceDataSourceCommandEventArgs that holds the event data common to the Selecting, Deleting, Updating, and Inserting events. These event data include the following:

❑ The XmlWebServiceMethodInvoker instance that will be used to invoke the XML Web service method.

❑ The name of the XML Web service method to be invoked.

❑ The IOrderedDictionary object that contains one DictionaryEntry object for each argument of the XML Web service method. Each DictionaryEntry object holds the name and value of its associated argument.

❑ The flag that specifies whether the argument names and values in IOrderedDictionary collection need to be validated and sorted:

```
public class XmlWebServiceDataSourceCommandEventArgs : CancelEventArgs
{
    private XmlWebServiceMethodInvoker methodInvoker;
    private string methodName;
    private IOrderedDictionary methodArgumentNamesAndValues;
```

```
    private bool validateAndSortMethodArguments;

    public XmlWebServiceDataSourceCommandEventArgs(
            XmlWebServiceMethodInvoker methodInvoker, string methodName,
            IOrderedDictionary methodArgumentNamesAndValues,
            bool validateAndSortMethodArguments)
    {
      this.methodInvoker = methodInvoker;
      this.methodName = methodName;
      this.methodArgumentNamesAndValues = methodArgumentNamesAndValues;
      this.validateAndSortMethodArguments = validateAndSortMethodArguments;
    }

    // Properties are not shown
}
```

Then, you need to implement a subclass of the `XmlWebServiceDataSourceCommandEventArgs` named `XmlWebServiceDataSourceSelectingEventArgs` to hold the event datum specific to the `Select` data operation. This event datum is a flag that specifies whether the total row count is being retrieved:

```
public class XmlWebServiceDataSourceSelectingEventArgs :
XmlWebServiceDataSourceCommandEventArgs
{
  private DataSourceSelectArguments arguments;
  private bool executingSelectCount;

  public XmlWebServiceDataSourceSelectingEventArgs(
            XmlWebServiceMethodInvoker methodInvoker, string methodName,
            IOrderedDictionary methodArgumentNamesAndValues,
            bool validateAndSortMethodArguments,
            bool executingSelectCount)
    :
      base(methodInvoker, methodName, methodArgumentNamesAndValues,
          validateAndSortMethodArguments)
  {
    this.executingSelectCount = executingSelectCount;
  }

  // Properties are not shown
}
```

Next, you need to declare the following event delegate:

```
public delegate void XmlWebServiceDataSourceSelectingEventHandler(object sender,
                                  XmlWebServiceDataSourceSelectingEventArgs e);
```

`XmlWebServiceDataSourceView` exposes the `Selecting` event as follows:

```
private static readonly object SelectingKey = new object();
public event XmlWebServiceDataSourceSelectingEventHandler Selecting
{
  add { Events.AddHandler(SelectingKey, value); }
  remove { Events.RemoveHandler(SelectingKey, value); }
}
```

XmlWebServiceDataSourceView then exposes the following method to raise the Selecting event:

```
protected virtual void OnSelecting(XmlWebServiceDataSourceSelectingEventArgs e)
{
  XmlWebServiceDataSourceSelectingEventHandler handler =
          Events[SelectingKey] as XmlWebServiceDataSourceSelectingEventHandler;
  if (handler != null)
    handler(this, e);
}
```

Selected Event

As shown in Listing 14-1, the ExecuteSelect method raises the Selected event to signal the end of the Select data operation. You need to implement a subclass of the EventArgs base class named XmlWebServiceDataSourceStatusEventArgs to hold the event data common to the Selected, Deleted, Updated, and Inserted events. These data include all of the four event data that the XmlWebServiceDataSourceCommandEventArgs holds, plus three more as follows:

❑ An integer number that represents the number of data records affected by the data operation.

❑ The Exception object, if any is raised.

❑ The flag that specifies whether the default exception handling mechanism should be used to handle the exception. Page developers can register a callback for the relevant event (Selected, Deleted, Updated, or Inserted) where they can use their own custom exception handling mechanism to handle the exception and set the value of this flag to true to signal the ExecuteSelect, ExecuteDelete, ExecuteUpdate, or ExecuteInsert that the exception has been handled:

```
public class XmlWebServiceDataSourceStatusEventArgs : EventArgs
{
  private XmlWebServiceMethodInvoker methodInvoker;
  private string methodName;
  private IOrderedDictionary methodArgumentNamesAndValues;
  private bool validateAndSortMethodArguments;
  private int affectedRows;
  private Exception exception;
  private bool exceptionHandled;

  public XmlWebServiceDataSourceStatusEventArgs(
      XmlWebServiceMethodInvoker methodInvoker, string methodName,
      IOrderedDictionary methodArgumentNamesAndValues,
      bool validateAndSortMethodArguments, int affectedRows, Exception exception)
  {
    this.methodInvoker = methodInvoker;
    this.methodName = methodName;
    this.methodArgumentNamesAndValues = methodArgumentNamesAndValues;
    this.validateAndSortMethodArguments = validateAndSortMethodArguments;
    this.affectedRows = affectedRows;
    this.exception = exception;
    this.exceptionHandled = false;
  }
  // Properties are not shown
}
```

ExecuteUpdate

When the user clicks the Edit button of a row in the GridView control of the Web application, the row enters its Edit mode where it renders its editing interface, including the Update and Cancel buttons. After making the desired changes, the user clicks the Update button and posts the containing page back to the server, where the Update event is raised and consequently the internal callback of the GridView—that is registered for the Update event—is automatically invoked.

The UpdateCallback method in Listing 14-9 simulates this internal callback of the GridView control. Don't worry about the details of the implementation of this method because it is discussed thoroughly in Chapter 19. The main idea here is to help you understand the arguments that are passed to the ExecuteUpdate method.

The UpdateCallback method calls the GetData method to access the underlying data source view object. In this case, the underlying data source view object is of type XmlWebServiceDataSourceView:

```
DataSourceView dv = GetData();
```

It then extracts the value of the primary key field of the record being updated from the DataKeys collection of the GridView control. Recall from Chapter 13 that every tabular data-bound control normally caches the primary key field values of all its records.

```
int primaryKey = (int)DataKeys[index];
```

The UpdateCallback method then extracts the name of the primary key field of the record being updated from the DataKeyNames property of the GridView control. Page developers must set the value of this property to the name of the primary key field.

It then Creates a Hashtable collection and populates it with the name and value of the primary key field of the record being updated:

```
Hashtable keys = new Hashtable();
keys.Add(primaryKeyField, primaryKeyValue);
```

Next it creates another Hashtable collection:

```
Hashtable values = new Hashtable();
```

It then enumerates the cells of the row being updated, retrieves the name and value of the data field corresponding to each enumerated cell, and adds the name and value of the data field to the second Hashtable collection:

```
foreach (TableCell cell in this[index].Cells)
{
  if (cell.Controls.Count > 0)
  {
    TextBox tb = cell.Controls[0] as TextBox;
    if (tb != null)
    {
      values.Add(tb.Attributes["FieldName"], tb.Text);
    }
  }
}
```

The `UpdateCallback` method then instantiates a `DataSourceViewOperationCallback` object to register a callback method for the `Update` operation. This is necessary because the `Update` data operation is asynchronous.

Finally, it calls the `Update` method of the `XmlWebServiceDataSourceView` object and passes the two hashtables and `DataSourceViewOperationCallback` object to the method. The `Update` method subsequently calls the `ExecuteUpdate` method and passes the two `Hashtable` objects as its arguments:

```
dv.Update(keys, values, oldValues,
        new DataSourceViewOperationCallback(UpdateOperationCallback));
```

Listing 14-9: The UpdateCallback method

```
void UpdateCallback(CustomTableCommandEventArgs e)
{
  DataSourceView dv = GetData();
  if (dv.CanUpdate)
  {
    int index = int.Parse(e.CommandArgument);
    int primaryKeyValue = (int)DataKeys[index];

    Hashtable keys = new Hashtable();
    keys.Add(primaryKeyName, primaryKeyValue);

    Hashtable values = new Hashtable();
    Hashtable oldValues = new Hashtable();

    foreach (TableCell cell in this[index].Cells)
    {
      if (cell.Controls.Count > 0)
      {
        TextBox tb = cell.Controls[0] as TextBox;
        if (tb != null)
        {
          values.Add(tb.Attributes["FieldName"], tb.Text);
          oldValues.Add(tb.Attributes["FieldName"], tb.Text);
        }
      }
    }

    dv.Update(keys, values, oldValues,
            new DataSourceViewOperationCallback(UpdateOperationCallback));

    EditRowIndex = -1;
    RequiresDataBinding = true;
  }
}
```

The `ExecuteUpdate` method (see Listing 14-10) takes steps similar to the `ExecuteSelect` method to invoke the XML Web service method that updates the record. Listing 14-11 shows the implementation of this XML Web service method for the XML Web service used by the example application.

Listing 14-10: The ExecuteUpdate method

```
protected override int ExecuteUpdate(IDictionary keys, IDictionary values,
                                     IDictionary oldValues)
{
  if (!CanUpdate)
    throw new NotSupportedException("Update is not supported!");

  int rowsAffected = 0;
  ArrayList list = null;
  if (keys != null && keys.Count > 0)
  {
    list = new ArrayList();
    list.Add(keys);
  }

  if (values != null && values.Count > 0)
  {
    if (list == null)
      list = new ArrayList();

    list.Add(values);
  }

  IOrderedDictionary methodArgumentNamesAndValues =
            RetrieveMethodArgumentNamesAndValues(UpdateParameters, list, null);

  XmlWebServiceDataSourceCommandEventArgs e =
    new XmlWebServiceDataSourceCommandEventArgs(MethodInvoker, UpdateMethod,
                        methodArgumentNamesAndValues, true);
  OnUpdating(e);
  if (!e.Cancel)
  {
    Exception ex = null;
    try
    {
      rowsAffected = (int)MethodInvoker.InvokeXmlWebServiceMethod(UpdateMethod,
                        methodArgumentNamesAndValues, true);
      OnDataSourceViewChanged(EventArgs.Empty);
    }
    catch (Exception ex1)
    {
      ex = ex1;
    }
    finally
    {
      XmlWebServiceDataSourceStatusEventArgs ee =
        new XmlWebServiceDataSourceStatusEventArgs(MethodInvoker, UpdateMethod,
                    methodArgumentNamesAndValues, true, rowsAffected, ex);
      OnUpdated(ee);
```

(continued)

Listing 14-10: *(continued)*

```
        if (ex != null && !ee.ExceptionHandled)
          throw ex;
      }
    }

  return rowsAffected;
}
```

The `ExecuteUpdate` method creates an instance of the `XmlWebServiceDataSourceCommandEvent Args` class and sets its appropriate properties. Recall that this class is used to hold event data common to the `Updating`, `Selecting`, `Deleting`, and `Inserting` events:

```
XmlWebServiceDataSourceCommandEventArgs e =
    new XmlWebServiceDataSourceCommandEventArgs(MethodInvoker, UpdateMethod,
                        methodArgumentNamesAndValues, true);
```

The `ExecuteUpdate` method raises the `Updating` event. Page developers can register a callback for this event where they can check whether the `Update` operation would break any of the application-specific business rules. If so, they must set the `Cancel` property of the `XmlWebServiceDataSourceCommandEventArgs` object to true.

```
  OnUpdating(e);
```

The method then checks whether the value of the `Cancel` property of the `XmlWebServiceData SourceCommandEventArgs` object is set to true. If not, it invokes the XML Web service method that updates the record:

```
  rowsAffected = (int)MethodInvoker.InvokeXmlWebServiceMethod(UpdateMethod,
                        methodArgumentNamesAndValues, true);
```

The `XmlWebServiceDataSource` control exposes a property named `UpdateMethod` that page developers must set to the name of the XML Web service method that updates the record. Listing 14-11 shows the implementation of this XML Web service method for the example XML Web service.

The method then calls the `OnDataSourceViewChanged` method to raise the `DataSourceViewChanged` event. This is necessary because the `Update` data operation changes the underlying data store. Tabular data-bound controls such as the `GridView` control shown in Figure 14-1 register a callback for this event where they retrieve fresh data and update their display:

```
  OnDataSourceViewChanged(EventArgs.Empty);
```

The method then creates an instance of the `XmlWebServiceDataSourceStatusEventArgs` class and sets its properties. Recall that this class is used to hold event data common to `Selected`, `Updated`, `Deleted`, and `Inserted` events.

```
  XmlWebServiceDataSourceStatusEventArgs ee =
      new XmlWebServiceDataSourceStatusEventArgs(MethodInvoker, UpdateMethod,
                        methodArgumentNamesAndValues, true, rowsAffected, ex);
```

Finally, the ExecuteUpdate method raises the Updated event to signal the end of the Update data operation. Page developers can register a callback for this event where they can use their own custom exception handling mechanism to handle the exception, if any. They must set the value of the ExceptionHandled property of the XmlWebServiceDataSourceStatusEventArgs object to true to specify that the exception has already been handled. This will bypass the default exception handling mechanism:

```
OnUpdated(ee);
```

Listing 14-11: The Update method of the XML Web service

```
[WebMethod]
public int Update(int BookID, string Title, string Author, string Publisher,
                  decimal Price)
{
  SqlConnection con = new SqlConnection(GetConnectionString());
  string commandString = "Update Books " + "Set Title=@Title, Author=@Author,
                     Publisher=@Publisher, Price=@Price" + " Where BookID=@BookID";

  SqlCommand com = new SqlCommand(commandString, con);
  com.Parameters.AddWithValue("@Title", Title);
  com.Parameters.AddWithValue("@Author", Author);
  com.Parameters.AddWithValue("@Publisher", Publisher);
  com.Parameters.AddWithValue("@Price", Price);
  com.Parameters.AddWithValue("@BookID", BookID);
  con.Open();
  int rowsAffected = com.ExecuteNonQuery();
  con.Close();
  return rowsAffected;
}
```

The XML Web service method that updates the data record normally takes three sets of arguments:

❑ The values of the data fields being updated. As shown in Listing 14-9, tabular data-bound controls enumerate the cells of the row being updated and retrieve the values of the data fields. Therefore, this is all done automatically and page developers don't need to worry about these arguments except for those cases where tabular data-bound controls may have a problem with type conversion.

❑ The values of the primary key fields of the record being updated. As shown in Listing 14-9, tabular data-bound controls normally cache the primary key field values of all records. Therefore this is also done automatically without any work on the part of page developers.

❑ Values other than those two. For example, you can have a version of the Update XML Web service method that also takes the name of the person (operator) that updates the record (see Listing 14-12). Obviously, the GridView control of the example application doesn't know the identity of the person who updates the record. The Page class in the ASP.NET 2.0 Framework exposes a new property named Profile that contains information about the user. The great thing about the Profile object is that the Framework automatically populates it when the user logs in to the system. The UpdateParameters property of the XmlWebServiceDataSource control allows page developers to use a ProfileParameter object to specify the Profile object as the source for the value of the OperatorName argument of the Update method of the XML Web service (see Listing 14-13).

Listing 14-12: The Update method that takes the operator name

```
[WebMethod]
public int Update(int BookID, string Title, string Author, string Publisher,
                  decimal Price, string OperatorName)
{
  SqlConnection con = new SqlConnection(GetConnectionString());
  string commandString = "Update Books Set Title=@Title, Author=@Author,
                          Publisher=@Publisher, Price=@Price,
                          OperatorName=@OperatorName Where BookID=@BookID";

  SqlCommand com = new SqlCommand(commandString, con);

  com.Parameters.AddWithValue("@Title", Title);
  com.Parameters.AddWithValue("@Author", Author);
  com.Parameters.AddWithValue("@Publisher", Publisher);
  com.Parameters.AddWithValue("@Price", Price);
  com.Parameters.AddWithValue("@BookID", BookID);
  com.Parameters.AddWithValue("@OperatorName", OperatorName);

  con.Open();
  int rowsAffected = com.ExecuteNonQuery();
  con.Close();
  return rowsAffected;
}
```

Listing 14-13: The declaration of the XmlWebServiceDataSource

```
<custom:XmlWebServiceDataSource ID="XmlWebServiceDataSource1" Runat="Server"
 UpdateMethod="Update">
  <UpdateParameters>
    <asp:ProfileParameter Name="OperatorName" PropertyName="UserName" />
  </UpdateParameters>
</custom:XmlWebServiceDataSource>
```

ExecuteInsert

When the user clicks the Insert button of a tabular data-bound control such as DetailsView, the Insert event is raised and the control's internal callback registered for this event is called. The InsertCallback method shown in Listing 14-14 simulates this internal callback. Don't worry about the implementation details of this method because this is thoroughly discussed in Chapters 17–19. The main idea here is to help you understand the arguments of the ExecuteInsert method.

Listing 14-14: The InsertCallback method

```
void InsertCallback(CustomTableCommandEventArgs e)
{
  DataSourceView dv = GetData();
  if (dv.CanInsert)
  {
    Hashtable values = new Hashtable();
    foreach (TableCell cell in this[index].Cells)
```

```
    {
      if (cell.Controls.Count > 0)
      {
        TextBox tb = cell.Controls[0] as TextBox;
        if (tb != null)
          values.Add(tb.Attributes["FieldName"], tb.Text);
      }
    }
    dv.Insert(values,new DataSourceViewOperationCallback(InsertOperationCallback));
  }
}
```

The `InsertCallback` method calls the `GetData` method to access the underlying tabular data source view object. In this case, this object is of type `XmlWebServiceDataSourceView`:

```
DataSourceView dv = GetData();
```

The method then creates a `Hashtable` collection:

```
Hashtable values = new Hashtable();
```

It then enumerates the cells of the row being added, retrieves the name and value of the data field associated with each enumerated cell, and adds the name and value of the data field to the `Hashtable` collection:

```
foreach (TableCell cell in this[index].Cells)
{
  if (cell.Controls.Count > 0)
  {
    TextBox tb = cell.Controls[0] as TextBox;
    if (tb != null)
    values.Add(tb.Attributes["FieldName"], tb.Text);
  }
}
```

Finally, it calls the `Insert` method and passes the `Hashtable` as its argument. The `Insert` method subsequently calls the `ExecuteInsert` method (see Listing 14-15) and passes the `Hashtable` as its argument:

```
dv.Insert(values,new DataSourceViewOperationCallback(InsertOperationCallback));
```

Listing 14-15: The ExecuteInsert method

```
protected override int ExecuteInsert(IDictionary values)
{
  if (!CanInsert)
    throw new NotSupportedException("Insert is not supported!");

  int rowsAffected = 0;
  ArrayList list = null;
  if (values != null && values.Count > 0)
```

(continued)

417

Listing 14-15: *(continued)*

```
  {
    list = new ArrayList();
    list.Add(values);
  }

  IOrderedDictionary methodArgumentNamesAndValues =
              RetrieveMethodArgumentNamesAndValues(InsertParameters, list, null);

  XmlWebServiceDataSourceCommandEventArgs e =
    new XmlWebServiceDataSourceCommandEventArgs(MethodInvoker, InsertMethod,
                        methodArgumentNamesAndValues, true);
  OnInserting(e);
  if (!e.Cancel)
  {
    Exception ex = null;
    try
    {
      rowsAffected = (int)methodInvoker.InvokeXmlWebServiceMethod(InsertMethod,
                              methodArgumentNamesAndValues, true);
      OnDataSourceViewChanged(EventArgs.Empty);
    }
    catch (Exception ex1)
    {
      ex = ex1;
    }
    finally
    {
      XmlWebServiceDataSourceStatusEventArgs ee =
        new XmlWebServiceDataSourceStatusEventArgs(methodInvoker, InsertMethod,
                        methodArgumentNamesAndValues, true, rowsAffected, null);
      OnInserted(ee);
      if (ex != null && !ee.ExceptionHandled)
        throw ex;
    }
  }

  return rowsAffected;
}
```

The ExecuteInsert method behaves much like the ExecuteUpdate method, and invokes the XML Web service method that inserts the new record. Listing 14-16 shows the implementation of this XML Web service method for the example XML Web service.

Listing 14-16: The Insert method of the XML Web service

```
public int Insert(string Title, string Author, string Publisher, decimal Price)
{
  SqlConnection con = new SqlConnection(GetConnectionString());
  SqlCommand com = new SqlCommand("Insert Into Books (Title,Author,Publisher,Price)
                        Values (@Title,@Author,@Publisher,@Price)", con);

  com.Parameters.AddWithValue("@Title", Title);
```

```
    com.Parameters.AddWithValue("@Author", Author);
    com.Parameters.AddWithValue("@Publisher", Publisher);
    com.Parameters.AddWithValue("@Price", Price);
    con.Open();
    int rowsAffected = com.ExecuteNonQuery();
    con.Close();
    return rowsAffected;
}
```

The XML Web service method that inserts records in the underlying data store, Insert, takes two sets of parameters:

❑   The values of the data fields being inserted. In the example Web application, these values are the values of the Title, Author, Publisher, and Price parameters (see Listing 14-16). As shown in Listing 14-14, tabular data-bound controls automatically retrieve these values from their editing interface without any work on the part of page developers.

❑   Any other values. For example, Listing 14-17 shows a version of the Insert XML Web service method that takes one more argument named OperatorName, which is the name of the user that inserts the record. Obviously, you can't expect the GridView control to provide the value for this field. The InsertParameters property of the XmlWebServiceDataSource control allows page developers to use a ProfileParameter instance to specify the value of the OperatorName field (see Listing 14-18).

Listing 14-17: The Insert method that uses the operator name

```
public int Insert(string Title, string Author, string Publisher,
                  decimal Price, string OperatorName)
{
  SqlConnection con = new SqlConnection(GetConnectionString());

  SqlCommand com = new SqlCommand("Insert Into Books (Title,Author,Publisher,Price)
                    Values (@Title,@Author,@Publisher,@Price,@OperatorName)", con);

  com.Parameters.AddWithValue("@Title", Title);
  com.Parameters.AddWithValue("@Author", Author);
  com.Parameters.AddWithValue("@Publisher", Publisher);
  com.Parameters.AddWithValue("@Price", Price);
  com.Parameters.AddWithValue("@OperatorName", OperatorName);

  con.Open();
  int rowsAffected = com.ExecuteNonQuery();
  con.Close();
  return rowsAffected;
}
```

Listing 14-18: The XmlWebServiceDataSource control with InsertParameters

```
<custom:XmlWebServiceDataSource ID="MySource" Runat="Server" InsertMethod="Insert">
  <InsertParameters>
    <asp:ProfileParameter Name="OperatorName" PropertyName="UserName" />
  </InsertParameters>
</custom:XmlWebServiceDataSource>
```

Listing 14-19 shows the `XmlWebServiceDataSource` control's implementation of the `InsertParameters` property. This property takes the same two actions as the `SelectParameters` property.

Listing 14-19: The UpdateParameters property

```
private ParameterCollection insertParameters = null;
public ParameterCollection InsertParameters
{
  get
  {
    if (insertParameters == null)
    {
      insertParameters = new ParameterCollection();
      if (isTrackingViewState)
        ((IStateManager)insertParameters).TrackViewState();

      insertParameters.ParametersChanged +=
                      new EventHandler(ParameterCollectionChangedCallback);
    }
    return insertParameters;
  }
}
```

Recall that the `GetValues` method of the `ParameterCollection` class triggers the `ParametersChanged` event. The `ExecuteInsert` method (see Listing 14-15) passes the `InsertParameters` collection to the `RetrieveMethodArgumentNamesAndValues` method. This method calls the `GetValues` method, as discussed later.

ExecuteDelete

When the user clicks the Delete button of a row in a tabular data-bound control such as `GridView`, the `Delete` event is raised and the control's internal callback method is automatically called. The `DeleteCallback` method in Listing 14-20 simulates this internal callback method. Chapters 17–19 discuss this method in detail. The idea here is to help you understand the arguments of the `ExecuteDelete` method.

Listing 14-20: The DeleteCallback method

```
void DeleteCallback(CustomTableCommandEventArgs e)
{
  DataSourceView dv = GetData();
  if (dv.CanDelete)
  {
    int index = int.Parse(e.CommandArgument);
    int primaryKeyValue = (int)DataKeys[index];

    Hashtable keys = new Hashtable();
    keys.Add(primaryKeyName, primaryKeyValue);

    dv.Delete(keys, null,
```

```
                         new DataSourceViewOperationCallback(DeleteOperationCallback));

      EditRowIndex = -1;
      RequiresDataBinding = true;
   }
}
```

The `DeleteCallback` method calls the `GetData` method to access the underlying tabular data source view. In this case, this view is an instance of the `XmlWebServiceDataSourceView` class:

```
DataSourceView dv = GetData();
```

The method then retrieves the primary key field names and values from the `DataKeyNames` property and `DataKeys` collection of the control. It then creates a `Hashtable` collection and populates it with the primary key field name and value:

```
Hashtable keys = new Hashtable();
keys.Add(DataKeyField, primaryKey);
```

Finally, the method calls the `Delete` method and passes the `Hashtable` as its argument The `Delete` method, in turn, calls the `ExecuteDelete` method and passes the `Hashtable` as its argument.

As Listing 14-21 shows, the `ExecuteDelete` method takes steps similar to the `ExecuteSelect`, `ExecuteUpdate`, and `ExecuteInsert` methods to invoke the XML Web service method that deletes the record. Listing 14-22 shows the XML Web service method that deletes records for this application.

Listing 14-21: The ExecuteDelete method

```
protected override int ExecuteDelete(IDictionary keys, IDictionary oldValues)
{
   if (!CanDelete)
      throw new NotSupportedException("Delete is not supported!");

   int rowsAffected = 0;
   ArrayList list = null;
   if (keys != null && keys.Count > 0)
   {
      list = new ArrayList();
      list.Add(keys);
   }

   IOrderedDictionary methodArgumentNamesAndValues =
              RetrieveMethodArgumentNamesAndValues(DeleteParameters, list, null);

   XmlWebServiceDataSourceCommandEventArgs e =
      new XmlWebServiceDataSourceCommandEventArgs(MethodInvoker, DeleteMethod,
                        methodArgumentNamesAndValues, true);
   OnDeleting(e);
   if (!e.Cancel)
```

(continued)

Listing 14-21: *(continued)*

```
  {
    Exception ex = null;
    try
    {
      rowsAffected = (int)methodInvoker.InvokeXmlWebServiceMethod(DeleteMethod,
                            methodArgumentNamesAndValues, true);
      OnDataSourceViewChanged(EventArgs.Empty);
    }
    catch (Exception ex1)
    {
      ex = ex1;
    }
    finally
    {
      XmlWebServiceDataSourceStatusEventArgs ee =
        new XmlWebServiceDataSourceStatusEventArgs(methodInvoker, DeleteMethod,
                        methodArgumentNamesAndValues, true, rowsAffected, null);
      OnDeleted(ee);
      if (ex != null && !ee.ExceptionHandled)
        throw ex;
    }
  }

  return rowsAffected;
}
```

Listing 14-22: The Delete method of the XML Web service

```
public int Delete(int BookID)
{
  SqlConnection con = new SqlConnection(GetConnectionString());

  SqlCommand com = new SqlCommand("Delete From Books Where BookID=@BookID", con);
  com.Parameters.AddWithValue("@BookID", BookID);

  con.Open();
  int rowsAffected = com.ExecuteNonQuery();
  con.Close();
  return rowsAffected;
}
```

The XML Web service method that deletes records takes two different sets of arguments:

❑   The values of the primary key fields of the record being deleted. For example, the `Delete` XML Web service method in Listing 14-22 takes the `BookID` as its parameter. Listing 14-20 shows that tabular data-bound controls automatically retrieve these values without any work on the part of page developers.

❑   Values other than the primary key field values. For example, Listing 14-23 shows a version of the `Delete` XML Web service method that takes an extra parameter named `OperatorName`. The `DeleteBook` stored procedure first validates the user name against `Users` table to make sure the user has permission to delete the given record. You can't expect the `GridView` control to provide the value for the `OperatorName` parameter. The `DeleteParameters` property of the `XmlWebServiceDataSource` control allows page developers to use a `ProfileParameter` to set the value (see Listing 14-24).

Listing 14-23: The second version of the Delete method of the XML Web service

```
public int Delete(int BookID, string OperatorName)
{
  if (!Validate(OperatorName))
    throw new Exception(OperatorName + " is not permitted to delete this record");

  SqlConnection con = new SqlConnection(GetConnectionString());
  SqlCommand com = new SqlCommand("Delete From Books Where BookID=@BookID", con);
  com.Parameters.AddWithValue("@BookID", BookID);

  con.Open();
  int rowsAffected = com.ExecuteNonQuery();
  con.Close();
  return rowsAffected;
}
```

Listing 14-24: The XmlWebServiceDataSource control with DeleteParameters

```
<custom:XmlWebServiceDataSource ID="XmlWebServiceDataSource1" Runat="Server"
 DeleteMethod="Delete">
  <DeleteParameters>
    <asp:ProfileParameter Name="OperatorName" PropertyName="UserName" />
  </DeleteParameters>
</custom:XmlWebServiceDataSource>
```

RetrieveMethodArgumentNamesAndValues

As discussed in the previous sections, all the execute methods (`ExecuteSelect`, `ExecuteUpdate`, `ExecuteDelete`, and `ExecuteInsert`) call the `RetrieveMethodArgumentNamesAndValues` method (see Listing 14-25), which takes three arguments. These arguments specify the names, values, and types of the parameters that are passed to the XML Web service method being invoked. This means that there are three ways to specify the names, values, and types of the parameters of an XML Web service method:

1. As discussed, tabular data-bound controls such as the `GridView` in the application shown in Figure 14-1 use an instance of the `DataSourceSelectArguments` class to specify the values of the following parameters of an XML Web service method:

   ❑ **Sorting parameter:** This parameter normally consists of the name of a data field followed by "Asc" or "Desc" and is used in the Order By section of the respective `Select` SQL statement.

   ❑ **Paging parameters:** These two parameters are used to specify the indexes of the first and last records to be retrieved.

2. As discussed, tabular data-bound controls automatically specify the following parameters of an XML Web service method:

❑ Names and new values of the data fields being updated (see Listing 14-9)

❑ Names and values of the data fields being inserted (see Listing 14-14)

❑ Names and values of the primary key fields of the record being updated (see Listing 14-9)

❑ Names and values of the primary key fields of the record being deleted (see Listing 14-16)

As Listings 14-9, 14-14, and 14-16 show, tabular data-bound controls create one `IDictionary` collection for each of the four groups of parameters, populate each collection with the names and values of the respective parameters, and pass each collection to the respective execute method — `ExecuteUpdate`, `ExecuteInsert`, or `ExecuteDelete`.

As discussed, each execute method adds its respective `IDictionary` collections to the `ArrayList` collection and passes the `ArrayList` to the `RetrieveMethodArgumentNamesAndValues` method.

3. Page developers can use the `SelectParameters`, `DeleteParameters`, `UpdateParameters`, and `InsertParameters` methods of the `XmlWebServiceDataSource` control to specify the names, values, and types of those parameters that tabular data-bound controls don't handle.

The `RetrieveMethodArgumentNamesAndValues` method exposes one argument for each of these three approaches. These three arguments are of type `ParameterCollection`, `ArrayList`, and `DataSourceSelectArguments` (see Listing 14-25).

Listing 14-25: The RetrieveMethodArgumentNamesAndValues method

```
protected virtual IOrderedDictionary RetrieveMethodArgumentNamesAndValues
(ParameterCollection parameters,
                 ArrayList list, DataSourceSelectArguments arguments)
{
  string sortParameter = string.Empty;
  OrderedDictionary methodArgumentValues = new OrderedDictionary();

  if (parameters != null && parameters.Count > 0)
  {
    IOrderedDictionary dic = parameters.GetValues(HttpContext.Current, owner);
    foreach (DictionaryEntry entry in dic)
    {
      methodArgumentValues.Add(entry.Key, entry.Value);
    }
  }

  if (list != null && list.Count > 0)
  {
    foreach (IDictionary dic in list)
    {
      if (dic != null && dic.Count > 0)
```

```
          {
            IEnumerator iterk = dic.Keys.GetEnumerator();
            IEnumerator iterv = dic.Values.GetEnumerator();
            while (iterk.MoveNext() && iterv.MoveNext())
            {
              methodArgumentValues.Add(iterk.Current, iterv.Current);
            }
          }
        }
      }
    }

    if (arguments != null)
    {
      if (MaxRecordsParameterName.Length > 0)
        methodArgumentValues.Add(MaxRecordsParameterName, arguments.MaximumRows);
      if (SortParameterName.Length > 0)
        methodArgumentValues.Add(SortParameterName, arguments.SortExpression);
      if (StartRecordParameterName.Length > 0)
        methodArgumentValues.Add(StartRecordParameterName, arguments.StartRowIndex);
    }

    if (methodArgumentValues.Count > 0)
      return methodArgumentValues;
    else
      return null;
  }
```

The `RetrieveMethodArgumentNamesAndValues` method creates an `OrderedDictionary` collection:

```
OrderedDictionary methodArgumentValues = new OrderedDictionary();
```

It then calls the `GetValues` method of its first argument, the `ParameterCollection` object. The method returns an `IOrderedDictionary` collection that contains the names and values of the parameters of the XML Web service being invoked:

```
IOrderedDictionary dic = parameters.GetValues(HttpContext.Current, owner);
```

The method then enumerates the `IOrderedDictionary` collection and adds each enumerated `DictionaryEntry` object to the `OrderedDictionary` collection:

```
foreach (DictionaryEntry entry in dic)
{
  methodArgumentValues.Add(entry.Key, entry.Value);
}
```

Next it enumerates each `IDictionary` collection in its second argument (the `ArrayList` collection) and adds each enumerated `DictionaryEntry` object to the `OrderedDictionary` collection.

Finally, the method retrieves the values of the sorting and paging parameters from its third argument, the `DataSourceSelectArguments` object, and adds them to the `OrderedDictionary` collection.

State Management

The `XmlWebServiceDataSource` control exposes a private field of type `XmlWebServiceDataSourceView` named `view` that represents its default tabular view. The `XmlWebServiceDataSourceView` object exposes all the properties that the respective `XmlWebServiceDataSource` control exposes. This is because the properties of the `XmlWebServiceDataSource` control simply delegate to the corresponding properties of the `XmlWebServiceDataSourceView` object. This means that the `XmlWebServiceDataSourceView` object must have a way to save and restore its property values across page postbacks to function properly. Because the view object is a complex property, it can't use the `ViewState` property of its `XmlWebServiceDataSource` control as the storage mechanism.

Instead the `XmlWebServiceDataSourceView` class implements the `IStateManager` interface to save and restore its property values across page postbacks. The `XmlWebServiceDataSourceView` class exposes a property of type `StateBag` named `ViewState` to provide its simple properties with a convenient storage to save and restore their values across page postbacks:

```
private StateBag viewState = null;
protected StateBag ViewState
{
  get
  {
    if (viewState == null)
    {
      viewState = new StateBag();
      if (isTrackingViewState)
        ((IStateManager)viewState).TrackViewState();
    }
    return viewState;
  }
}
```

The `XmlWebServiceDataSourceView` class takes the same steps as the `SqlDataSourceView` class (see Chapter 12) to implement the `SaveViewState`, `LoadViewState`, and `TrackViewState` methods and the `IsTrackingViewState` property.

The following code contains a page that uses the `XmlWebServiceDataSource` control. Figure 14-1 shows what end users see when they access this page.

```
<%@ Page Language="C#" %>
<%@ Register TagPrefix="custom" Namespace="CustomComponents" %>
<html xmlns="http://www.w3.org/1999/xhtml">
<body>
  <form id="form1" runat="server">
    <asp:DropDownList ID="ddl" runat="server" AutoPostBack="true">
      <asp:ListItem Text="Author1" Value="Author1" Selected="True" />
      <asp:ListItem Text="Author2" Value="Author2" />
      <asp:ListItem Text="Author3" Value="Author3" />
    </asp:DropDownList>

    <asp:GridView ID="gv" runat="Server" AllowSorting="True"
```

```
    DataSourceID="MySource1" AutoGenerateDeleteButton="True"
    AutoGenerateEditButton="True" DataKeyNames="BookID"
    AllowPaging="true" PageSize="3" BorderWidth="1px"
    BackColor="LightGoldenrodYellow"
    GridLines="None" CellPadding="2" BorderColor="Tan" ForeColor="Black">
      <FooterStyle BackColor="Tan"></FooterStyle>
      <PagerStyle ForeColor="DarkSlateBlue" HorizontalAlign="Center"
      BackColor="PaleGoldenrod"/>
      <HeaderStyle Font-Bold="True" BackColor="Tan"/>
      <AlternatingRowStyle BackColor="PaleGoldenrod" />
      <SelectedRowStyle ForeColor="GhostWhite" BackColor="DarkSlateBlue"/>
    </asp:GridView>

    <custom:XmlWebServiceDataSource ID="MySource1" runat="Server"
    SelectMethod="Select" XmlReadMode="Auto" SortParameterName="SortParameter"
    UpdateMethod="Update" DeleteMethod="Delete" TypeName="Service"
    StartRecordParameterName="StartRowIndex" MaxRecordsParameterName="MaximumRows"
    SelectCountMethod="SelectCount"
    WSDLPath="http://localhost:1634/Server/Service.asmx?WSDL"
    CacheDuration="600" CacheExpirationPolicy="Absolute" EnableCaching="true">
      <SelectParameters>
        <asp:ControlParameter Name="Author" PropertyName="SelectedValue"
        ControlID="ddl" DefaultValue="Author2" />
      </SelectParameters>
    </custom:XmlWebServiceDataSource>

    <custom:SqlDataSource ID="MySource2" runat="Server"
    StartRecordParameterName="StartRowIndex" MaxRecordsParameterName="MaximumRows"
    SelectCommand="GetOnePageOfBooks" SelectCommandType="StoredProcedure"
    DeleteCommand="Delete From Books Where BookID=@BookID"
    SelectCountCommand="Select Count(*) From Books"
    ConnectionString="<%$ ConnectionStrings:MyConnectionString %>"
    UpdateCommand="Update Books Set Title=@Title,
        Author=@Author,Publisher=@Publisher,Price=@Price Where BookID=@BookID"
    InsertCommand="InsertBook" SortParameterName="SortExpression" />

  </form>
</body>
</html>
```

Notice that this page contains two tabular data source controls: XmlWebServiceDataSource and SqlDataSource. As the boldface portion of the code shows, the page developer has assigned the value of the ID property of the XmlWebServiceDataSource control (MySource1) to the DataSourceID property of the GridView control. This means that if you run the application, the GridView control will automatically use the XmlWebServiceDataSource control to perform data operations such as select, delete, and update.

The page developer switches from the XmlWebServiceDataSource control to the SqlDataSource control by simply assigning the value of the ID property of the SqlDataSource control to the DataSourceID property of the GridView control. That's it! A simple assignment allows the page developer to switch from one data source control to another without having to write a single line of code!

Summary

This chapter used a detailed step-by-step approach to develop a real-world custom data source control named `XmlWebServiceDataSource` that uses an XML Web service as its underlying data store. The `XmlWebServiceDataSource` control uses the `XmlWebServiceMethodInvoker` component to invoke the XML Web service methods that select, insert, delete, and update data. This chapter discussed in detail the important parts of the `XmlWebServiceDataSource` control's code and provided an in-depth coverage of the tools, techniques, and technologies used in the code. You can easily extend the functionality of the `XmlWebServiceDataSource` control to add support for the features that it currently doesn't support. For example, you can use the caching infrastructure of the control to cache the total row count so the control doesn't have to retrieve this value for every request. The current implementation raises the `Selecting` and `Selected` events only when the actual data records are being retrieved. You can extend this implementation to raise these events when the control is retrieving the total row count as well.

In the next several chapters, as promised, you'll switch from the tabular data source controls to the hierarchical ones. You'll start in Chapter 15 by taking a good look at the hierarchical model.

Understanding the ASP.NET 2.0 Hierarchical Data Source Control Model

Hierarchical data source controls provide hierarchical data-bound controls, such as `TreeView`, with hierarchical views of the underlying data store, whether or not the data store itself is hierarchical. You may wonder what a hierarchical view is and what constitutes a hierarchical view.

Recall that tabular data source controls such as `SqlDataSource` make their underlying data store look like a database where tabular data source views act as virtual tables. These virtual tables are named entities where the name of a virtual table uniquely locates the table in the virtual database. The clients (normally tabular data-bound controls, such as `GridView`) of a tabular data source control pass the name of a view to the `GetView` method of the tabular data source control to locate and access the view.

Hierarchical data source controls, on the other hand, make the underlying data store look like a tree of nodes, where each node and its children also form a tree. For example, the `Title1` node and its child nodes in Figure 15-1 form a subtree. Therefore, the tree consists of one or more subtrees. In other words, hierarchical data source controls make the underlying data store look like a collection of subtrees rather than a collection of tables. Each hierarchical view represents a subtree. For example, the `Title1` node and all its child nodes in Figure 15-1 form a subtree that defines a hierarchical view.

You may wonder how a subtree is located and accessed in a hierarchy of subtrees. Because every subtree has a single root node, the question then becomes: How is a node located and accessed in a tree of nodes?

To answer this question, consider an imaginary journey from the root node of the tree to the desired node. The journey consists of one or more steps, where each step takes you from the current node to the next one. Therefore the path from the root node of the tree to a given node uniquely locates and identifies the node. The node path consists of one or more location steps, where each location step is the path from one node to the next. Because the location path of the root node of a subtree also locates the subtree itself and because each subtree represents a hierarchical view, the location path is also known as *view path*.

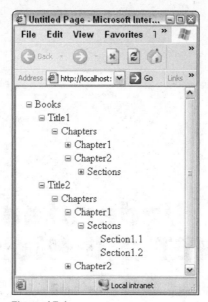

Figure 15-1

The ASP.NET 2.0 hierarchical data source control model consists of the following main components:

- ❑ IHierarchicalDataSource
- ❑ HierarchicalDataSourceControl
- ❑ IHierarchyData
- ❑ IHierarchicalEnumerable
- ❑ HierarchicalDataSourceView

This chapter implements replicas of the main components of the ASP.NET 2.0 hierarchical data source control model to help you understand the model from the inside out. Following each section that implements a replica of a component, this chapter also implements the replica of the corresponding component of the ASP.NET 2.0 XmlDataSource control to provide you with a concrete example for the discussions presented in the section.

IHierarchicalDataSource

Each hierarchical data source control is specifically designed to present its clients (normally hierarchical data-bound controls such as TreeView) with hierarchical views of a specific type of data store. For example, the XmlDataSource control is specifically designed to present its clients with hierarchical views of XML documents. Therefore, if the clients were to use a specific type of hierarchical data source control (such as XmlDataSource) directly, they would be tied to a specific type of data store and wouldn't be able to work with other types of data stores. For example, if the clients were to use the XmlDataSource control directly, they wouldn't be able to work with relational databases. This is where the .NET 2.0 Provider Pattern comes to the rescue.

Following the Provider Pattern, all hierarchical data source controls implement the `IHierarchical DataSource` interface. This allows hierarchical data-bound controls such as `TreeView` to treat all hierarchical data source controls the same with no regard to their types. As far as hierarchical data-bound controls are concerned, all hierarchical data source controls are of type `IHierarchicalDataSource`.

The `IHierarchicalDataSource` interface exposes a single method named `GetHierarchicalView` and a single event of type `EventHandler` named `DataSourceChanged`, as shown in Listing 15-1.

Listing 15-1: The IHierarchicalDataSource interface

```
public interface IHierarchicalDataSource
{
  HierarchicalDataSourceView GetHierarchicalView(string viewPath);
  event EventHandler DataSourceChanged;
}
```

The `GetHierarchicalView` method takes the view path as its argument and returns a `HierarchicalDataSourceView` object that represents the hierarchical view with the specified view path. The actual type of the view object depends on the type of the hierarchical data source control. For instance, the `GetHierarchicalView` method of the `XmlDataSource` control returns a view object of type `XmlHierarchicalDataSourceView`. All view classes such as `XmlHierarchicalDataSourceView` derive from the `HierarchicalDataSourceView` abstract base class.

The `DataSourceChanged` event is raised when the data source or its view object changes in a way that affects the clients of the data source control. The clients of a hierarchical data source control are normally hierarchical data-bound controls such as `TreeView`. These controls normally register a callback for the `DataSourceChanged` event where they retrieve fresh data and update their display.

HierarchicalDataSourceControl

The `IHierarchicalDataSource` interface allows the clients of a hierarchical data source control (such as `XmlDataSource`) to work with the data source control without knowing its real type. This allows page developers to switch from one hierarchical data source control to another without any code change. Why would page developers want to switch from one hierarchical data source control to another?

Recall that each hierarchical data source control is specifically designed to present its clients with one or more hierarchical views of a specific type of data store. Page developers switch from one hierarchical data source control to another to access a different type of data store. For example, they may switch to an `XmlDataSource` control to access XML documents.

The ASP.NET 2.0 hierarchical data source control model contains a class named `HierarchicalData SourceControl` that implements the `IHierarchicalDataSource` interface. As the name implies, `HierarchicalDataSourceControl` is a server control. This makes all hierarchical data source controls, including the ones that you implement yourself, server controls because they all derive from the `HierarchicalDataSourceControl` base class. This provides two benefits. First, the page developer can use them declaratively in an `.aspx` file. Second, hierarchical data-bound controls can use the `FindControl` method of the page to access them in generic fashion.

Here is the typical workflow. First the page developer declares the desired hierarchical data source control in the .aspx file and assigns a unique string value to its ID property, just like any other server control. Which type of hierarchical data source control page developers use depend on which type of data store they're trying to access. Next, the page developer declares the desired hierarchical data-bound control (such as TreeView) in the .aspx file and assigns the ID property value of the data source control to its DataSourceID property. Every hierarchical data-bound control exposes this property. At runtime, the hierarchical data-bound control calls the FindControl method of the page and passes its DataSourceID property value into it to access the hierarchical data-source control in generic fashion without knowing its real type. In other words, the only dependency between the hierarchical data source control and the hierarchical data-bound control that uses it is its ID, which is nothing but a string value.

This section implements replicas of the main members of the HierarchicalDataSourceControl abstract base class.

The following code shows the HierarchicalDataSourceControl class's implementation of the GetHierarchicalView method of the IHierarchicalDataSource interface:

```
protected abstract HierarchicalDataSourceView GetHierarchicalView(string viewPath);
HierarchicalDataSourceView IHierarchicalDataSource.GetHierarchicalView(
                                                                string viewPath)
  {
    return GetHierarchicalView(viewPath);
  }
```

Notice that this implementation follows the typical C# interface implementation pattern where the GetHierarchicalView method of the interface is explicitly implemented, and a new protected GetHierarchicalView method is introduced. This means that when you're writing your own custom hierarchical data source control, you only need to override the protected method and you mustn't implement the interface directly.

The HierarchicalDataSourceControl class also follows the typical C# event implementation pattern (see Chapter 4) to implement the DataSourceChanged event where a key is used to add and remove events from the Events collection that the HierarchicalDataSourceControl inherits from the Control class and the protected OnDataSourceViewChanged method is introduced to raise the event:

```
event EventHandler IHierarchicalDataSource.DataSourceChanged
{
  add { DataSourceChanged += value; }
  remove { DataSourceChanged -= value; }
}

private static readonly object EventKey = new object();
public event EventHandler DataSourceChanged
{
  Add { Events.AddHandler(EventKey, value);}
  Remove { Events.RemoveHandler(EventKey, value);}
}

protected virtual void OnDataSourceChanged(EventArgs e)
{
  EventHandler handler = (EventHandler)Events[EventKey];
  if (handler != null)
      handler(this, e);
}
```

The `HierarchicalDataSourceControl` saves you from having to implement the `DataSourceChanged` event of the `IHierarchicalDataSource` interface. As mentioned, your custom hierarchical data source control is only responsible for implementing the `GetHierarchicalView` abstract method.

This section implements a replica of the ASP.NET 2.0 `XmlDataSource` control to provide you with a concrete example for the discussions just presented. The `XmlDataSource` control derives from the `HierarchicalDataSourceControl` base class and implements its `GetHierarchicalView` method as follows:

```
protected override HierarchicalDataSourceView GetHierarchicalView(string viewPath)
{
  if (null == this.view)
    this.view = new XmlHierarchicalDataSourceView(this, XPath);

  return this.view;
}
```

The `XmlDataSource` control exposes a property named `XPath` that page developers must set to the appropriate `XPath` expression. The `GetHierarchicalView` method passes the `XPath` expression as an argument to the constructor of the `XmlHierarchicalDataSourceView` class. This means that the value of the `XPath` property is nothing but the view path that locates the specified hierarchical view or subtree in the tree structure that represents the underlying data store, that is, an XML document. The `XmlDataSource` control exposes a property named `DataFile` that page developers must set to the path of the appropriate XML file.

HierarchicalDataSourceView

The ASP.NET 2.0 `HierarchicalDataSourceView` abstract base class exposes a single method called `Select` that returns an `IHierarchicalEnumerable` collection of `IHierarchyData` objects:

```
public abstract class HierarchicalDataSourceView
{
  public abstract IHierarchicalEnumerable Select();
}
```

Here you take a little detour from hierarchical data source controls to see a similar situation in tabular data source controls to set the stage for the discussions of the `IHierarchicalEnumerable` and `IHierarchyData` interfaces later in this section. Start by revisiting the `ExecuteSelect` method of the `DataSourceView` class (see Chapter 12). Recall that this method returns a collection object whose type depends on the type of the tabular data source view. For example, the `ExecuteSelect` method of the `SqlDataSourceView` class (see Listing 12-8) returns a collection of type `DataView` that contains items of type `DataRowView`. If the clients of a tabular data source control knew about the real type of the collection object and the real type of the items that the collection contains, they would be tied to that tabular data source control and consequently to the data store that the tabular data source control is specifically designed to work with.

For example, if the clients of the `SqlDataSource` control knew that the collection that the `ExecuteSelect` method returns is of type `DataView` and the items that the collection contains are of type `DataRowView`, they would be tied to relational databases and wouldn't be able to work with non-relational data stores such as XML documents.

The `ExecuteSelect` method of the `DataSourceView` class returns a collection of type `IEnumerable` that contains items of type `System.Object` to hide the real type of the collection and the real type of the items that the collection contains. The `CreateControlHierarchy` method in the following code simulates how tabular data-bound controls such as `GridView` access the collection items in generic fashion without having to know the real type of the collection and its items. Don't worry about the details of the implementation of this method because it is discussed in Chapters 17 and 19 in detail. The main idea here is to help you understand how tabular data-bound controls generically access the retrieved data. These controls enumerate the collection items and generate the appropriate HTML markup text for each enumerated item:

```
protected virtual void CreateControlHierarchy(IEnumerable data)
{
  _table = new Table();
  Controls.Add(_table);
  TableRow brow;
  TableCell bcell;
  TableHeaderCell hcell;

  bool renderHeader = true;
  int colcnt = 0;
  PropertyDescriptorCollection pds = null;

  IEnumerator iter = data.GetEnumerator();
  while (iter.MoveNext())
  {
    if (renderHeader)
    {
      TableRow hrow = new TableRow();
      _table.Rows.Add(hrow);

      hcell = new TableHeaderCell();
      hrow.Cells.Add(hcell);

      hcell = new TableHeaderCell();
      hrow.Cells.Add(hcell);

      pds = TypeDescriptor.GetProperties(iter.Current);
      colcnt = pds.Count;

      for (int k = 0; k < colcnt; k++)
      {
        hcell = new TableHeaderCell();
        hrow.Cells.Add(hcell);
        hcell.Text = pds[k].Name;
      }

      renderHeader = false;
    }

    brow = new TableRow();
    _table.Rows.Add(brow);

    for (int k = 0; k < colcnt; k++)
```

```
        {
            bcell = new TableCell();
            brow.Cells.Add(bcell);
            bcell.Text = pds[k].GetValue(iter.Current).ToString();
        }
    }
}
```

Notice that the argument of the `CreateControlHierarchy` method is the `IEnumerable` collection that the `ExecuteSelect` method returns. The `CreateControlHierarchy` method accesses the retrieved data by first calling the `GetEnumerator` method of the `IEnumerable` collection to access the `IEnumerator` object and using the object to enumerate the collection items in generic fashion:

```
IEnumerator iter = data.GetEnumerator();
```

The method then calls the `GetProperties` method of the `TypeDescriptor` class for each enumerated item. This method returns a `PropertyDescriptorCollection` collection:

```
int colcnt = 0;
PropertyDescriptorCollection pds = null;
while (iter.MoveNext())
{
    // code not shown

    pds = TypeDescriptor.GetProperties(iter.Current);
    colcnt = pds.Count;
```

The `PropertyDescriptorCollection` collection contains one `PropertyDescriptor` object for each property of the enumerated item. The `Name` property and `GetValue` method of a given `PropertyDescriptor` object return the name and value of its associated property:

```
for (int k = 0; k < colcnt; k++)
{
    hcell = new TableHeaderCell();
    hrow.Cells.Add(hcell);
    hcell.Text = pds[k].Name;
}

// Code not shown

for (int k = 0; k < colcnt; k++)
{
    bcell = new TableCell();
    brow.Cells.Add(bcell);
    bcell.Text = pds[k].GetValue(iter.Current).ToString();
}
```

Now back to hierarchical data source controls. You can use the same line of arguments for the `Select` data operation that the `Select` method of the `HierarchicalDataSourceView` class performs as you just did for the `Select` data operation that the `ExecuteSelect` method of the `DataSourceView` class performs. The result of this data operation is a collection whose type depends on the type of the underlying hierarchical data source view. For example, in the case of the `XmlDataSource` control, this data operation returns a collection of type `XmlNodeList` that contains items or nodes of type `XmlNode`.

If the clients of a hierarchical data source control knew about the real type of the collection object and the real type of the items or nodes that the collection contains, they would be tied to that hierarchical data source control and consequently to the data store that the hierarchical data source control is specifically designed to work with.

For example, if the clients of the XmlDataSource control knew that the collection is of type XmlNodeList and the nodes that the collection contains are of type XmlNode, they would be tied to XML documents and wouldn't be able to work with relational databases. Following the same line of argument as just discussed for tabular data source controls, this may seem to suggest that the Select method of the HierarchicalDataSourceView class must return a collection of type IEnumerable that contains nodes of type System.Object to hide the types of the collection and its items or nodes.

This solution won't work for hierarchical data source controls because each node that the collection contains may have child and parent nodes. When a hierarchical data-bound control such as TreeView is enumerating the nodes in the collection, the control is interested not only in the enumerated node itself but also in its child and parent nodes.

Here is an example. The TreeView control in Figure 15-1 displays information about two books titled "Title1" and "Title2." Notice that each Title node has a child node named Chapters. When the TreeView control is displaying a Title node, it also needs to display its child node.

The control can't treat a Title node as just an instance of the System.Object class because this class doesn't expose any methods or properties that would provide access to the child node of the Title node. In other words, the System.Object type is too general, and doesn't adequately describe the nodes that the collection contains. What you need is a new generic type that adequately describes a node and exposes properties and methods that provide access to its parent and child nodes. Enter the IHierarchyData interface.

IHierarchyData

As mentioned, in the case of tabular data source controls, the System.Object class provides a generic mechanism for tabular data-bound controls to access row objects without knowing their real type. The IHierarchyData interface shown in Listing 15-2 does the same thing for hierarchical data-bound controls such as TreeView; that is, it provides a generic mechanism for them to access node objects and their child nodes without knowing their real types.

Listing 15-2: The methods and properties of the IHierarchyData interface

```
public interface IHierarchyData
{
  bool HasChildren { get;}
  object Item { get;}
  string Path { get;}
  string Type { get;}
  IHierarchicalEnumerable GetChildren();
  IHierarchyData GetParent();
}
```

The `IHierarchyData` interface exposes a property of type `System.Object` named `Item` that refers to the node object that the interface represents. The actual type of the `Item` property depends on the type of the hierarchical data source control. For example, in the case of the `XmlDataSource` control, the `item` property is of type `XmlElement`. You can think of the `IHierarchyData` interface as the generic representation of the node that it encapsulates.

Because the `IHierarchyData` interface exposes the `node` object as an item of type `System.Object` and hides its real type (such as `XmlElement`), there's no way for hierarchical data-bound controls to access its parent and child nodes. That's why the `IHierarchyData` interface exposes two methods named `GetChildren` and `GetParent`. `GetParent` returns an `IHierarchyData` object, which is a generic representation of the parent node.

The `GetChildren` method returns a collection object that contains the child nodes of the node that the `IHierarchyData` interface encapsulates and represents. This raises the following question: What type should this collection object be? The desired type must satisfy the following requirements:

- ❑ It must be of type `IEnumerable` to allow hierarchical data-bound controls such as `TreeView` to enumerate the child nodes that it contains in generic fashion.

- ❑ It must contain the generic representations of the child nodes to hide their real type from the hierarchical data-bound controls. In other words, it must contain the child nodes as objects of type `IHierarchyData`, not `System.Object`.

The `IEnumerable` interface isn't adequate because it doesn't meet the second requirement. What you need is a new type that extends the functionality of the `IEnumerable` type. Enter the `IHierarchicalEnumerable` interface.

IHierarchicalEnumerable

The `IHierarchicalEnumerable` interface derives from the `IEnumerable` interface and exposes a single method named `GetHierarchyData` that takes an enumerated object as its argument and returns the associated `IHierarchyData` object. The subclasses of the `IHierarchicalEnumerable` interface must implement the methods and properties of the `IEnumerable` interface in addition to the `GetHierarchyData` method:

```
public interface IHierarchicalEnumerable : IEnumerable
{
  IHierarchyData GetHierarchyData(object enumeratedObject);
}
```

Next, you implement replicas of the ASP.NET 2.0 `XmlHierarchyData` and `XmlHierarchicalEnumerable` classes to provide you with concrete examples for the discussions presented in the previous two sections. In order to understand the implementation of these two classes, first you need a solid understanding of the interaction between a hierarchical data-bound control such as `TreeView` and a hierarchical data source control such as `XmlDataSource`. This section uses a simple example to simulate the interaction between the `TreeView` and `XmlDataSource` controls. Listing 15-3 shows a Web page (`.asxp` file) that declares a `TreeView` server control and an `XmlDataSource` control.

Listing 15-3: The .aspx file declares a TreeView server control and an XmlDataSource control

```
<%@ Page Language="C#" AutoEventWireup="true" CodeFile="Default4.aspx.cs"
Inherits="Default4" %>

<!DOCTYPE html PUBLIC "-//W3C//DTD XHTML 1.1//EN"
"http://www.w3.org/TR/xhtml11/DTD/xhtml11.dtd">
<html xmlns="http://www.w3.org/1999/xhtml">
<head runat="server">
  <title>Untitled Page</title>
</head>
<body>
  <form id="form1" runat="server">
    <asp:TreeView ID="tv" runat="server">
      <DataBindings>
        <asp:TreeNodeBinding DataMember="Books" Text="Books" />
        <asp:TreeNodeBinding DataMember="Book" TextField="Title" />
        <asp:TreeNodeBinding DataMember="Chapters" Text="Chapters" />
        <asp:TreeNodeBinding DataMember="Chapter" TextField="Title" />
        <asp:TreeNodeBinding DataMember="Sections" Text="Sections" />
        <asp:TreeNodeBinding DataMember="Section" TextField="Title" />
      </DataBindings>
    </asp:TreeView>
    <asp:XmlDataSource ID="MySource" runat="server" DataFile="data.xml"
        XPath="//Books" />
  </form>
</body>
</html>
```

Notice that the `DataSourceID` property of the `TreeView` control isn't set to the value of the `ID` property of the `XmlDataSource` control as you would expect because you want to take over the data-binding process and simulate what the `TreeView` control does behind the scenes to generate the nodes that it displays. Listing 15-4 shows this simulation in the `Page_Load` method.

Listing 15-4: The Page_Load method

```
protected void Page_Load(object sender, EventArgs e)
{
  if (!IsPostBack)
  {
    IHierarchicalDataSource ds = (IHierarchicalDataSource)MySource;
    HierarchicalDataSourceView dv = ds.GetHierarchicalView(String.Empty);
    IHierarchicalEnumerable data = dv.Select();
    IEnumerator iter = data.GetEnumerator();

    TreeNodeBinding tnb;

    while (iter.MoveNext())
    {
      TreeNode node = new TreeNode();
      tv.Nodes.Add(node);

      IHierarchyData hd = data.GetHierarchyData(iter.Current);
```

```
      PropertyDescriptorCollection pds = TypeDescriptor.GetProperties(hd);

      tnb = null;
      foreach (TreeNodeBinding b in tv.DataBindings)
      {
        if (b.DataMember == hd.Type)
        {
          tnb = b;
          break;
        }
      }

      if (tnb != null)
      {
        if (tnb.TextField.Length == 0)
          node.Text = tnb.Text;

        else
        {
          foreach (PropertyDescriptor pd in pds)
          {
            if (tnb.TextField == pd.Name)
              node.Text = pd.GetValue(hd).ToString();
          }
        }
      }

      if (hd.HasChildren)
        AddChildren(node, hd);
    }
  }
}
```

The `Page_Load` method first accesses the declared hierarchical data source control (the `XmlDataSource`) in generic fashion. Notice that the method type casts the data source control to the `IHierarchicalDataSource` type. In other words, as far as this method is concerned, the declared hierarchical data source control is of type `IHierarchicalDataSource`, not `XmlDataSource`:

```
IHierarchicalDataSource ds = (IHierarchicalDataSource)MySource;
```

The method then calls the `GetHierarchicalView` method of the `IHierarchicalDataSource` interface to access the underlying hierarchical data source view object (`XmlDataSourceView`) in generic fashion. Notice that the `GetHierarchicalView` method returns this view object as an object of type `HierarchicalDataSourceView`, not `XmlDataSourceView`:

```
HierarchicalDataSourceView dv = ds.GetHierarchicalView(String.Empty);
```

Next, the method calls the `Select` method of the view object to access the underlying node collection (`XmlHierarchicalEnumerable`) in generic fashion. Notice that the `Select` method returns this node collection as a collection of type `IHierarchicalEnumerable`, not `XmlHierarchicalEnumerable`:

```
IHierarchicalEnumerable data = dv.Select();
```

It then calls the `GetEnumerator` method of the `IHierarchicalEnumerable` collection to access its enumerator and uses it to enumerate the nodes in the collection in generic fashion:

```
IEnumerator iter = data.GetEnumerator();
```

Because this enumerator, like any other enumerator, returns the enumerated `IHierarchyData` object as an object of type `System.Object`, not `IHierarchyData`, the `Page_Load` method calls the `GetHierarchyData` method of the `IHierarchicalEnumerable` collection to convert the enumerated object to the `IHierarchyData` type:

```
IHierarchyData hd = data.GetHierarchyData(iter.Current);
```

Finally, the `Page_Load` method calls the `GetProperties` method of the `TypeDescriptor` class to access the properties of the enumerated `IHierarchyData` object:

```
PropertyDescriptorCollection pds = TypeDescriptor.GetProperties(hd);
```

The default implementation of the `GetProperties` method of the `TypeDescriptor` class uses .NET reflection and returns a `PropertyDescriptorCollection` that contains one `PropertyDescriptor` object to describe each property of the enumerated `IHierarchyData` object. As shown in Listing 15-2, the properties of this object are `HasChildren`, `Item`, `Path`, and `Type`.

Obviously, you're not trying to display the values of the properties of the `IHierarchyData` object itself. For example, in the case of `XmlDataSource` control, you're not trying to display the values of the properties of the `XmlHierarchyData` class itself. Rather you want to display the values of the attributes of the `XmlElement` node that the `XmlHierarchyData` encapsulates and represents.

This is where the `ICustomTypeDescriptor` interface comes to the rescue. This interface exposes a method named `GetProperties` that takes an argument of type `System.Object` and returns a `PropertyDescriptorCollection` collection that contains one `PropertyDescriptor` object for each property.

The `XmlHierarchyData` class implements the `GetProperties` method of the `ICustomTypeDescriptor` interface to expose the attributes of the encapsulated `XmlElement` object as its own properties. When the `TreeView` control calls the `GetProperties` method of the `TypeDescriptor` class and passes the `XmlHierarchyData` object as its argument, the `TypeDescriptor` class notices that the `XmlHierarchyData` object provides its own implementation of the `GetProperties` method. Therefore the class bypasses its own implementation of the `GetProperties` method and calls the `GetProperties` method of `XmlHierarchyData`.

In other words, you're tricking the `TreeView` control into thinking that the attributes of the encapsulated `XmlElement` object are the properties of the `XmlHierarchyData` class itself. The `TreeView` control thinks it's displaying the values of the properties of the `IHierarchyData` interface, but in reality it's displaying the values of the attributes of the `XmlElement` object that the interface encapsulates.

XmlHierarchyData

Listing 15-5 shows the declaration of the `XmlHierarchyData` class. The class implements both the `IHierarchyData` and `ICustomTypeDescriptor` interfaces. This means that the class must implement the methods and properties of both interfaces. You begin with the methods and properties of the `IHierarchyData` interface.

Listing 15-5: The XmlHierarchyData class

```
public class XmlHierarchyData : IHierarchyData, ICustomTypeDescriptor
{
  public XmlHierarchyData(XmlElement item);
  public override string ToString();

  // IHierarchical Members
  private XmlElement item;
  bool IHierarchyData.HasChildren {get;}
  object IHierarchyData.Item {get;}
  string IHierarchyData.Path {get;}
  string IHierarchyData.Type {get;}
  IHierarchicalEnumerable IHierarchyData.GetChildren();
  IHierarchyData IHierarchyData.GetParent();

  // ICustomTypeDescriptor Members
  System.ComponentModel.AttributeCollection ICustomTypeDescriptor.GetAttributes();
  string ICustomTypeDescriptor.GetClassName();
  string ICustomTypeDescriptor.GetComponentName();
  TypeConverter ICustomTypeDescriptor.GetConverter();
  EventDescriptor ICustomTypeDescriptor.GetDefaultEvent();
  PropertyDescriptor ICustomTypeDescriptor.GetDefaultProperty();
  object ICustomTypeDescriptor.GetEditor(Type editorBaseType);
  EventDescriptorCollection ICustomTypeDescriptor.GetEvents(
                                              Attribute[] attributes);
  EventDescriptorCollection ICustomTypeDescriptor.GetEvents();
  PropertyDescriptorCollection ICustomTypeDescriptor.GetProperties(
                                              Attribute[] attributes);
  PropertyDescriptorCollection ICustomTypeDescriptor.GetProperties();
  object ICustomTypeDescriptor.GetPropertyOwner(PropertyDescriptor pd);
}
```

Listing 15-6 shows the XmlHierarchyData class's implementation of the HasChildren and Item properties of the IHierarchyData interface. Notice that the XmlHierarchyData class exposes a private field of type XmlElement that refers to the node that the XmlHierarchyData class represents.

Listing 15-6: The XmlHierarchyData class's implementation of the HasChildren and Item properites of the IHierarchyData interface

```
bool IHierarchyData.HasChildren
{
  get { return item.HasChildNodes;}
}

private XmlElement item;
object IHierarchyData.Item
{
  get { return item; }
}
```

To understand the significance of the `Type` property and to understand why the `XmlHierarchyData` class implements this property the way it does, take another look at Listing 15-4. Recall that the `CreateControlHierarchy` method in this listing simulates what the `TreeView` control does behind the scenes to create the nodes that it displays. Notice that the `TreeView` control exposes a collection property of type `TreeNodeBindingCollection` named `DataBindings`. Page developers declaratively create and add `TreeNodeBinding` instances to this collection (see Listing 15-3). The `TreeNodeBinding` class exposes three important properties: `DataMember`, `TextField`, and `Text`.

To understand the significance of these properties, take a look at the XML file that the `XmlDataSource` control in Listing 15-3 uses (see Listing 15-7).

Listing 15-7: The XML file used in Listing 15-3

```xml
<?xml version="1.0" encoding="utf-8"?>
<Books>
  <Book Title="Title1" Price="50" author="author1">
    <Chapters>
      <Chapter Title="Chapter1" NumOfPages="20">
        <Sections>
          <Section Title="Section1.1" />
          <Section Title="Section1.2" />
        </Sections>
      </Chapter>
      <Chapter Title="Chapter2" NumOfPages="30">
        <Sections>
          <Section Title="Section2.1" />
          <Section Title="Section2.2" />
        </Sections>
      </Chapter>
    </Chapters>
  </Book>

  <Book Title="Title2" Price="100" author="author2">
    <Chapters>
      <Chapter Title="Chapter1" NumOfPages="35">
        <Sections>
          <Section Title="Section1.1" />
          <Section Title="Section1.2" />
        </Sections>
      </Chapter>
      <Chapter Title="Chapter2" NumOfPages="23">
        <Sections>
          <Section Title="Section2.1" />
          <Section Title="Section2.2" />
        </Sections>
      </Chapter>
    </Chapters>
  </Book>
</Books>
```

The `TreeView` control creates one `TreeNode` object for each node in the XML document. The control uses the `Text` property of each `TreeNode` object to display the appropriate information about its respective node. Page developers declare one `TreeNodeBinding` instance for each node where they specify what information the respective `TreeNode` object should display.

They set the `DataMember` property of a `TreeNodeBinding` instance to the name of its respective node. The possible values of the `DataMember` property in the case of Listing 15-7 are `Books`, `Book`, `Chapters`, `Chapter`, `Sections`, and `Section`.

Page developers set the `TextField` property of a `TreeNodeBinding` instance to the name of one of the attributes of the respective node. For example, the possible values for the `TextField` property in the case of the `Book` node are `Title`, `Price`, and `Author`.

Some nodes, such as `Books`, `Chapters`, and `Sections`, don't expose any attributes. In these cases, page developers don't set the value of the respective `TextField` property. Instead they set the value of the `Text` property of the appropriate `TreeNodeBinding`.

The `CreateControlHierarchy` method in Listing 15-4 enumerates the `DataBindings` collection and compares the value of the `DataMember` property with the value of the `Type` property of the relevant `IHierarchyData` object:

```
IHierarchyData hd = data.GetHierarchyData(iter.Current);
TreeNodeBinding tnb = null;
foreach (TreeNodeBinding b in tv.DataBindings)
{
  if (b.DataMember == hd.Type)
  {
    tnb = b;
    break;
  }
}
```

This means that the `Type` property of the `XmlHierarchyData` class is the name of the XML element that it represents. Recall that the `item` field of the `XmlHierarchyData` class refers to this XML element:

```
string IHierarchyData.Type
{
  get { return item.Name; }
}
```

The `XmlHierarchyData` class's implementation of the `IHierarchyData` interface's `Path` property uses the concept of the *location path* in the XPath technology. XPath and SQL model the same data very differently. SQL models the data as a database of named tables where each table consists of rows. The primary key of each row in a table uniquely locates the row in the table.

XPath models the same data as a tree of nodes where the location path of a node uniquely locates the node. The location path of a node is based on an imaginary journey from the root node of the tree to the node itself. The location path consists of one or more location steps where each location step takes you from one node to the next one. A location step consists of three parts. The first part is known as the *axis* — you can think of the axis as the direction of the journey from one node to the next. The second part is known as the *node test*. The node test selects those nodes along the axis that meet the test criterion. This criterion could be as simple as a node name where all the nodes along the axis with the given name are selected. The third part is known as the *predicate*. The predicate filters the node set that meet the test criterion and returns a subset of nodes that meet the predicate condition.

To make the discussion more concrete, take a look at the following example. Figure 15-2 shows the hierarchical diagram for part of the XML file shown in Listing 15-7. The goal is to determine the location path of the gray node in the diagram. Start your imaginary journey from the document element, the Books element. You need to take the following actions to determine each location step:

1. Choose the axis along which to travel. Obviously you should travel along the child axis of the current node. XPath uses the / notation to represent the child axis.

2. Define a node test to select those nodes along the child axis that meet the test criterion. XPath uses the * notation to represent any child element. Use this notation to specify the node test.

3. Define a predicate to select a subset of nodes that the node test returns. XPath uses the position() function to determine the position of a node in a node set. Use the [position()=1] predicate to specify that you're only interested in the first node of the node set that the node test returns.

Therefore, each location step is /*[position()=1]. Because your journey from the root element to the gray node takes five steps, the hierarchical or location path of the gray node is as follows:

```
/*[position()=1]/*[position()=1]/*[position()=1]/*[position()=1]/*[position()=1]
```

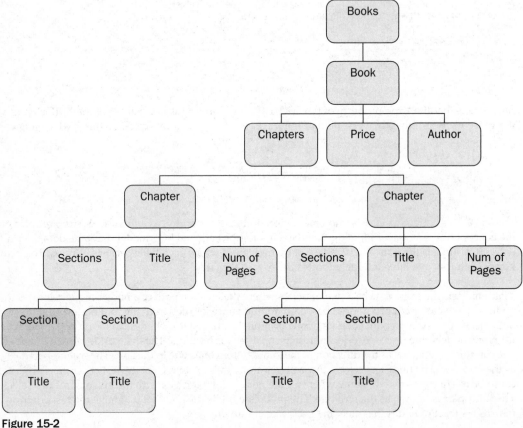

Figure 15-2

This location path uniquely identifies and locates the gray node in the tree. This means that the location path plays the same role in XPath data model that primary key plays in SQL data model. It also means that nodes in the XPath data model play the same role as rows in the SQL data model. Because each row in the SQL data model belongs to a table, each node in the XPath data model belongs to a subtree or hierarchical view. Therefore, hierarchical views in the XPath data model play the same role as tables in the SQL data model and consequently the view path of a hierarchical view plays the same role as the name of a table.

Following the earlier discussions, this section implements the replica of the XmlHierarchyData class's implementation of the Path property as shown in Listing 15-8.

Listing 15-8: The XmlHierarchyData class's implementation of the Path property

```
string IHierarchyData.Path
{
  get
  {
    string path = string.Empty;
    XmlElement parent = item.ParentNode as XmlElement;
    while (parent != null)
    {
      path = "/*[position()=1]" + path;
      parent = parent.ParentNode as XmlElement;
    }
    return path;
  }
}
```

You may wonder what happens if page developers don't declare the appropriate TreeNodeBinding for a particular node. For example, what happens if you remove the following TreeNodeBinding declaration from Listing 15-3?

```
<asp:TreeNodeBinding DataMember="Chapter" TextField="Title" />
```

To answer this question, take another look at the following section of Listing 15-4:

```
foreach (TreeNodeBinding b in tv.DataBindings)
{
  if (b.DataMember == hd.Type)
  {
    tnb = b;
    break;
  }
}
```

This section enumerates the TreeNodeBinding objects in the DataBindings collection to locate the TreeNodeBinding object whose DataMember property has the same value as the Type property of the respective IHierarchyData object. However, because you have removed the TreeNodeBinding associated with the Chapter element, the foreach loop in the earlier code will fail. In cases like this, the TreeView control simply displays the value returned by the ToString() method of the associated IHierarchyData object.

The XmlHierarchyData class overrides the ToString() method to return the name of the node:

```
public override string ToString()
{
  return item.Name;
}
```

For example, the ToString() method will return the value "Chapter" in the case of the Chapter element.

Listing 15-9 shows the XmlHierarchyData class's implementation of the GetParent method of the IHierarchyData interface. Recall that the item field of the XmlHierarchyData class refers to the XML element that the class represents. This means that the ParentNode property of the item field refers to the parent element of the field. Notice that the GetParent method doesn't return the parent element as an object of type XmlElement or XmlNode. Instead it returns the generic representation of the parent element — the XmlHierarchyData instance that encapsulates it.

Listing 15-9: The XmlHierarchyData class's implementation of the GetParent method

```
IHierarchyData IHierarchyData.GetParent()
{
  if (item.ParentNode != null)
    return new XmlHierarchyData((XmlElement)item.ParentNode);

  else
    return null;
}
```

So far you've seen the XmlHierarchyData class's implementation of all of the methods of the IHierarchyData interface except for the GetChildren method. Because this method returns an XmlHierarchicalEnumerable object, you first need to understand the XmlHierarchicalEnumerable class.

XmlHierarchicalEnumerable

The XmlHierarchicalEnumerable class derives from the ArrayList class and implements the IHierarchicalEnumerable interface. The GetHierarchyData method simply type casts the enumerated object to the XmlHierarchyData type (see Listing 15-10).

Listing 15-10: The XmlHierarchicalEnumerable class

```
public class XmlHierarchicalEnumerable : ArrayList, IHierarchicalEnumerable
{
    IHierarchyData IHierarchicalEnumerable.GetHierarchyData(object enumeratedItem)
    {
        return (XmlHierarchyData)enumeratedItem;
    }
}
```

Now implement the replica of the GetChildren method of the XmlHierarchyData class (see Listing 15-11). Recall that the XmlHierarchyData class is a generic representation of the XmlElement node that its item field references. Therefore the ChildNodes property of the item field refers to the child nodes of the node. The GetChildren method doesn't directly return the child nodes as objects of type XmlElement or XmlNode. Instead, it creates one XmlHierarchyData object for each child node, where each object is a generic representation of the child node that its item field references. The GetChildren method creates an XmlHierarchicalEnumerable collection, adds the preceding XmlHierarchyData objects to this collection, and returns the collection to its clients, such as TreeView.

Listing 15-11: The XmlHierarchyData class's implementation of the GetChildren method

```
IHierarchicalEnumerable IHierarchyData.GetChildren()
{
  XmlHierarchicalEnumerable children = new XmlHierarchicalEnumerable();
  if (item.HasChildNodes)
  {
    foreach (XmlElement child in item.ChildNodes)
    {
      children.Add(new XmlHierarchyData(child));
    }
  }
  return children;
}
```

So far you've implemented the replicas of the XmlHierarchyData class's implementation of the IHierarchyData interface's methods and properties. Recall that the XmlHierarchyData class also implements the ICustomTypeDescriptor interface. This interface exposes numerous methods. However, you don't have to implement all of them because the TypeDescriptor class comes with a default implementation for each method. You only have to implement those methods whose default implementations don't meet your requirements. The rest of the methods can simply delegate to the respective methods of the TypeDescriptor class.

Therefore the first order of business is to decide which methods of the TypeDescriptor class don't meet your requirements. As discussed before, you need to override the GetProperties method. This method returns a PropertyDescriptorCollection collection of XmlHierarchyDataProperyDescriptor objects, where each object is a generic representation of an attribute of the element node that the respective XmlHierarchyData object represents.

Before getting into the implementation of the GetProperties method, though, you need to implement the replica the XmlHierarchyDataPropertyDescriptor class.

XmlHierarchyDataPropertyDescriptor

The XmlHierarchyDataPropertyDescriptor class derives from the PropertyDescriptor base class and overrides its methods and properties. The following is the constructor of the class:

```
private string name;
public XmlHierarchyDataPropertyDescriptor(string name) : base(name, null)
{
  this.name = name;
}
```

The argument of the constructor is the name of the attribute that the `XmlHierarchyDataProperty` `Descriptor` represents. The `XmlHierarchyDataPropertyDescriptor` class's implementation of the `Name` property of the `PropertyDescriptor` base class returns the name of the attribute that the class represents:

```
public override string Name
{
  get { return name; }
}
```

The class's implementation of the `IsReadOnly` property of the `PropertyDescriptor` class returns true because the class doesn't allow its clients to set the value of the attribute that it represents. The value of the attribute can only be specified when the `XmlHierarchyDataPropertyDescriptor` object is being created:

```
public override bool IsReadOnly
{
  get { return true; }
}
```

Therefore the `SetValue` method raises an exception if it's called. The clients of the class must call the `IsReadOnly` property to ensure that the class supports writing before they call the `SetValue` method to change the value of the attribute:

```
public override void SetValue(object o, object value)
{
  throw new NotSupportedException();
}
```

This also means that the `CanResetValue` method must return false and the `ResetValue` method must raise an exception. The clients of the `XmlHierarchyDataPropertyDescriptor` class must first call the `CanResetValue` property to make sure the class allows its clients to reset the value of the specified attribute before they attempt to call the `ResetValue` method:

```
public override bool CanResetValue(object o)
{
  return false;
}

public override void ResetValue(object o)
{
  throw new NotSupportedException();
}
```

Because the `XmlHierarchyDataPropertyDescriptor` class represents an attribute, its implementation of the `PropertyType` property of the `PropertyDescriptor` base class returns `typeof(string)`:

```
public override Type PropertyType
{
  get { return typeof(string); }
}
```

Therefore, the `Coverter` property returns a string converter:

```
public override TypeConverter Converter
{
  get { return TypeDescriptor.GetConverter(Type.GetType("System.String")); }
}
```

The `GetValue` method allows the clients of the class to get the value of the attribute that the class represents:

```
public override object GetValue(object o)
{
  XmlHierarchyData xhd = o as XmlHierarchyData;
  if (xhd != null)
  {
    IHierarchyData hd = (IHierarchyData)xhd;
    return ((XmlElement)(hd.Item)).GetAttribute(name);
  }

  return String.Empty;
}
```

This method first ensures that the object passed in as its argument is of type `XmlHierarchyData`:

```
XmlHierarchyData xhd = o as XmlHierarchyData;
if (xhd != null)
```

The method then casts the object to an `IHierarchyData` type so it can access the `Item` property of the `IHierarchyData` interface:

```
IHierarchyData hd = (IHierarchyData)xhd;
```

Recall that the `Item` property of the `XmlHierarchyData` class refers to the `XmlElement` object that the class encapsulates or represents. The `GetValue` method type casts the `Item` property to its real type (`XmlElement`) so it can call its `GetAttribute` method to access the value of the attribute that the `XmlHierarchyDataPropertyDescriptor` class represents:

```
((XmlElement)(hd.Item)).GetAttribute(name);
```

The `ComponentType` property returns `typeof(XmlHierarchyData)`:

```
public override Type ComponentType
{
  get {return typeof(XmlHierarchyData); }
}
```

The clients of the `XmlHierarchyDataPropertyDescriptor` class call the `ComponentType` property to determine what type of object they need to pass to the `GetValue` method.

ICustomTypeDescriptor

Recall that the XmlHierarchyData class implements the ICustomTypeDescriptor interface to provide its own implementation of the GetProperties method. This method returns a PropertyDescriptorCollection of XmlHierarchyDataPropertyDescriptor objects, where each object represents an attribute of the element node that the XmlHierarchyData represents, as shown in Listing 15-12.

Listing 15-12: The XmlHierarchyData class's implementation of the GetProperties method

```
PropertyDescriptorCollection ICustomTypeDescriptor.GetProperties(
                                             Attribute[] attributes)
{
  if (item.HasAttributes)
  {
    List<XmlHierarchyDataPropertyDescriptor> list =
                       new List<XmlHierarchyDataPropertyDescriptor>();

    foreach (XmlAttribute attr in item.Attributes)
    {
      list.Add(new XmlHierarchyDataPropertyDescriptor(attr.Name));
    }
    return new PropertyDescriptorCollection(list.ToArray());
  }
  return PropertyDescriptorCollection.Empty;
}
```

The GetProperties method checks whether the XmlElement that the XmlHierarchyData represents has any attributes. It creates an instance of the List<XmlHierarchyDataPropertyDescriptor> generic class. Then it enumerates the attributes of the element node that the XmlHierarchyData class represents. It creates one XmlHierarchyDataPropertyDescriptor object for each enumerated attribute. Finally, it creates an instance of the PropertyDescriptorCollection object and populates the collection.

The following code shows the XmlHierarchyData class's implementation of the second overload of the GetProperties method of the ICustomTypeDescriptor interface. Notice that the method simply calls the first overload of the GetProperties method (see Listing 15-12) with the null value as its argument:

```
PropertyDescriptorCollection ICustomTypeDescriptor.GetProperties()
{
  return ((ICustomTypeDescriptor)this).GetProperties(null);
}
```

The clients of the XmlHierarchyData class call the GetPropertyOwner method to determine whether the class supports a given PropertyDescriptor type. As the following code shows, the class only supports the XmlHierarchyDataPropertyDescriptor type:

```
object ICustomTypeDescriptor.GetPropertyOwner(PropertyDescriptor pd)
{
  Return (pd is XmlHierarchyDataPropertyDescriptor) ? this : null;
}
```

Because the `XmlHierarchyData` class implements the `ICustomTypeDescriptor` interface, it must implement all of the methods and properties of the interface. So far this section has presented the `XmlHierarchyData` class's implementation of some of these methods and properties. The class's implementation of the rest of the methods and properties of the `ICustomTypeDescriptor` interface simply delegate to the respective methods and properties of the `TypeDescriptor` class. For example, the implementation of the `GetAttributes` method is as follows:

```
System.ComponentModel.AttributeCollection ICustomTypeDescriptor.GetAttributes()
{
    return TypeDescriptor.GetAttributes(this, true);
}
```

XmlHierarchicalDataSourceView

This section implements the replica of the `XmlHierarchicalDataSourceView` class. This class, like any other hierarchical data source view, derives from the `HierarchicalDataSourceView` abstract base class and overrides its methods. The following code shows the constructor of the class:

```
public XmlHierarchicalDataSourceView(XmlDataSource owner, string viewPath)
{
    this.viewPath = viewPath;
    this.owner = owner;
}
```

The constructor takes two arguments. The first argument refers to the `XmlDataSource` control that owns the view. The second argument is the location path of the subtree that the view represents.

The following code shows the `XmlDataSourceView` class's implementation of the `Select` method of the `HierarchicalDataSourceView` base class. Hierarchical data-bound controls such as `TreeView` call the `Select` method to access the `IHierarchicalEnumerable` collection that contains the respective `IHierarchyData` (in this case, `XmlHierarchyData`) objects:

```
public override IHierarchicalEnumerable Select()
{
    XmlHierarchicalEnumerable data = new XmlHierarchicalEnumerable();
    XmlDocument doc = new XmlDocument();
    doc.Load(HttpContext.Current.Server.MapPath(owner.DataFile));
    XmlElement node = (XmlElement)doc.SelectSingleNode(viewPath);
    if (node.HasChildNodes)
    {
        foreach (XmlNode cnode in node.ChildNodes)
        {
            if (cnode.NodeType == XmlNodeType.Element)
                data.Add(new XmlHierarchyData((XmlElement)cnode));
        }
    }
    return data;
}
```

The `Select` method first creates an `XmlHierarchicalEnumerable` collection:

```
XmlHierarchicalEnumerable data = new XmlHierarchicalEnumerable();
```

451

It then loads the XML file into an instance of the `XmlDocument` class:

```
XmlDocument doc = new XmlDocument();
doc.Load(HttpContext.Current.Server.MapPath(owner.DataFile));
```

Next, the `Select` method calls the `SelectSingleNode` method of the `XmlDocument` instance and passes the view path as its argument. This method locates the subtree that the view object represents and returns a reference to the root node of the subtree:

```
XmlElement node = (XmlElement)doc.SelectSingleNode(viewPath);
```

Finally, the method enumerates the child nodes of the root node, creates one `XmlHierarchyData` object for each enumerated node, and adds the object to the `XmlHierarchicalEnumerable` collection:

```
data.Add(new XmlHierarchyData((XmlElement)cnode));
```

Summary

This chapter discussed and implemented the following main components of the ASP.NET 2.0 hierarchical data source control model:

- ❑ `IHierarchicalDataSource`
- ❑ `HierarchicalDataSourceControl`
- ❑ `IHierarchyData`
- ❑ `IHierarchicalEnumerable`
- ❑ `HierarchicalDataSourceView`

The chapter also implemented and discussed the ASP.NET 2.0 `XmlDataSource` control to provide you with concrete examples for the discussions presented in the chapter. The implementation of this standard control showed you everything you need to know to develop your own custom hierarchical data source control.

The next chapter builds on what you've learned in this chapter to develop a real-world custom hierarchical data source control that you can use in your own applications.

Developing ASP.NET 2.0 Custom Hierarchical Data Source Controls

This chapter builds on the previous chapter to show you how to develop your own custom hierarchical data source controls. The chapter extends the functionality of the ASP.NET `SqlDataSource` control and implements a new data source control named `CustomSqlDataSource` that provides its clients with both tabular and hierarchical views of its underlying SQL Server database.

CustomSqlDataSource

The ASP.NET `SqlDataSource` control can be used with tabular data-bound controls such as `GridView` because it's a tabular data source control, meaning it exposes tabular views of its underlying relational database. However, it can't be used with hierarchical data-bound controls such as `TreeView` because it's not a hierarchical data source control, meaning it doesn't expose hierarchical views of its underlying relational database.

The `CustomSqlDataSource` control derives from the `SqlDataSource` control and extends its functionality to provide hierarchical data-bound controls such as `TreeView` with hierarchical views of the underlying relational database.

Because the `CustomSqlDataSource` control derives from `SqlDataSource`, it inherits all its base class's functionality, meaning that `CustomSqlDataSource` also provides tabular data-bound controls such as `GridView` with tabular views of its underlying relational database. Listing 16-1 contains the code for the `CustomSqlDataSource` control.

Listing 16-1: The CustomSqlDataSource control

```
public class CustomSqlDataSource : SqlDataSource, IHierarchicalDataSource
{
  private SqlHierarchicalDataSourceView view = null;
  HierarchicalDataSourceView
  IHierarchicalDataSource.GetHierarchicalView(string viewPath)
  {
    if (null == this.view)
      this.view = new SqlHierarchicalDataSourceView(this, viewPath);
    return this.view;
  }

  private static readonly object EventKey = new object();
  event EventHandler IHierarchicalDataSource.DataSourceChanged
  {
    add { Events.AddHandler(EventKey, value);}
    remove { Events.RemoveHandler(EventKey, value);}
  }

  public string DataParentIdField
  {
    get { return ViewState["DataParentIdField"] != null ?
                    (string)ViewState["DataParentIdField"] : string.Empty; }
    set { ViewState["DataParentIdField"] = value; }
  }

  public string DataIdField
  {
    get { return ViewState["DataIdField"] != null ?
                      (string)ViewState["DataIdField"] : string.Empty; }
    set { ViewState["DataIdField"] = value; }
  }
}
```

The CustomSqlDataSource control implements the DataSourceChanged event and
GetHierarchicalView method of the IHierarchicalDataSource interface. GetHierarchicalView
also creates an instance of a class named SqlHierarchicalDataSourceView if it hasn't been already
been created. This class is discussed shortly.

Notice that the CustomSqlDataSource control exposes two properties named DataIdField and
DataParentIdField. To help you understand the significance of these two properties, take a look at an
example of a typical database table that CustomSqlDataSource supports. This example table is named
Messages, and contains the messages that users post on a discussion forum where each record of the
table represents a posted message. The Messages table is a simple table that consists of three columns:

❏   MessageID: Contains the values of the primary key database field of data records

❏   ParentID: Contains the MessageID values of the parent records

❏   Subject: Contains the contents of posted messages

In the case of this example, the DataIdField and DataParentIdField properties of the
CustomSqlDataSource control contains the strings MessageID and ParentID, respectively.

As mentioned, `CustomSqlDataSource` can be used with hierarchical data-bound controls such as `TreeView`. To help you understand the discussions presented in the following sections, this section simulates how a `TreeView` control interacts with a hierarchical data source control such as `Custom SqlDataSource`. Listing 16-2 contains a Web page that uses a `TreeView` and a `CustomSqlDataSource` control. Notice that this page doesn't assign the ID of the `CustomSqlDataSource` control to the `DataSourceID` property of the `TreeView` control because you would like to take over the data binding to simulate the interaction between the `TreeView` and `CustomSqlDataSource` controls.

The `Page_Load` method contains the simulation code as shown in Listing 16-3. Notice that this code listing is the same as Listing 15-4 because `TreeView` doesn't know or care about the real type of the hierarchical data source control it's interacting with, whether it's an `XmlDataSource` or a `CustomSqlDataSource` control.

Listing 16-2: A Web page that uses the CustomSqlDataSource control

```
<%@ Page Language="C#" AutoEventWireup="true" CodeFile="Default.aspx.cs"
Inherits="_Default" %>
<%@ Register TagPrefix="custom" Namespace="CustomComponents" %>
<html xmlns="http://www.w3.org/1999/xhtml">
<body>
  <form id="form1" runat="server">

    <asp:TreeView runat="Server" ID="tv">
      <DataBindings>
        <asp:TreeNodeBinding DataMember="MessageID" TextField="Subject"
        ValueField="MessageID" />
      </DataBindings>
    </asp:TreeView>

    <custom:CustomSqlDataSource
    ConnectionString="<%$ connectionsStrings:MyConnectionString%>"
    SelectCommand="Select * From Messages Where ParentID=@ParentID Or
                MessageID=@ParentID"
    DataIdField="MessageID" DataParentIdField="ParentID"
    DataSourceMode="DataSet" ID="MySource" runat="server">
      <SelectParameters>
        <asp:Parameter Name="ParentID" DefaultValue="1" />
      </SelectParameters>
    </custom:CustomSqlDataSource>
  </form>
</body>
</html>
```

The interesting part of Listing 16-2 is how the page developer declares the `TreeView` control. Notice that the page developer adds an `<asp:TreeNodeBinding>` element as the subelement of the `<DataBindings>` element:

```
<asp:TreeView runat="Server" ID="tv">
  <DataBindings>
    <asp:TreeNodeBinding DataMember="MessageID" TextField="Subject"
    ValueField="MessageID" />
  </DataBindings>
</asp:TreeView>
```

The page developer sets the attributes on the `<asp:TreeNodeBinding>` element as follows:

1. The developer assigns the name of the database field or column that contains the primary keys of data records to the `DataMember` attribute. In the case of the `Messages` table, this attribute is set to the `MessageID` string.

2. The developer assigns the name of the database field or column that contains the primary keys of data records to the `ValueField` attribute. In the case of the `Messages` table, the name of this database field or column is `MessageID`.

3. The developer assigns the name of the database field or column whose values the `TreeView` control displays to the `TextField` attribute. In the case of the `Messages` table, the `TreeView` control will display the subject of each message.

Listing 16-3: The Page_Load method simulates the interaction between the TreeView control and CustomSqlDataSource control

```
protected void Page_Load(object sender, EventArgs e)
{
  if (!IsPostBack)
  {
    IHierarchicalDataSource ds = (IHierarchicalDataSource)MySource;
    HierarchicalDataSourceView dv = ds.GetHierarchicalView(String.Empty);
    IHierarchicalEnumerable data = dv.Select();
    IEnumerator iter = data.GetEnumerator();

    TreeNodeBinding tnb;

    while (iter.MoveNext())
    {
      TreeNode node = new TreeNode();
      tv.Nodes.Add(node);

      IHierarchyData hd = data.GetHierarchyData(iter.Current);
      PropertyDescriptorCollection pds = TypeDescriptor.GetProperties(hd);

      tnb = null;
      foreach (TreeNodeBinding b in tv.DataBindings)
      {
        if (b.DataMember == hd.Type)
        {
          tnb = b;
          break;
        }
      }

      if (tnb != null)
      {
        if (tnb.TextField.Length == 0)
          node.Text = tnb.Text;

        else
        {
          foreach (PropertyDescriptor pd in pds)
          {
```

```
                    if (tnb.TextField == pd.Name)
                        node.Text = pd.GetValue(hd).ToString();
                }
            }
        }

        if (hd.HasChildren)
            AddChildren(node, hd);
    }
  }
}

void AddChildren(TreeNode pnode, IHierarchyData phd)
{
  IHierarchicalEnumerable data = phd.GetChildren();
  IEnumerator iter = data.GetEnumerator();

  TreeNodeBinding tnb;

  while (iter.MoveNext())
  {
    TreeNode node = new TreeNode();
    pnode.ChildNodes.Add(node);

    IHierarchyData hd = data.GetHierarchyData(iter.Current);
    PropertyDescriptorCollection pds = TypeDescriptor.GetProperties(hd);

    tnb = null;
    foreach (TreeNodeBinding b in tv.DataBindings)
    {
      if (b.DataMember == hd.Type)
      {
        tnb = b;
        break;
      }
    }

    if (tnb != null)
    {
      if (tnb.TextField.Length == 0)
        node.Text = tnb.Text;

      else
      {
        foreach (PropertyDescriptor pd in pds)
        {
          if (tnb.TextField == pd.Name)
            node.Text = pd.GetValue(hd).ToString();
        }
      }
    }

    if (hd.HasChildren)
      AddChildren(node, hd);
  }
}
```

Here are the main steps that the `TreeView` control takes in Listing 16-3 to find out what the control expects from a hierarchical data source control such as `CustomSqlDataSource`.

First, the `TreeView` control casts the data source control to the `IHierarchicalDataSource` interface:

```
IHierarchicalDataSource ds = (IHierarchicalDataSource)MySource;
```

This means that it expects the `CustomSqlDataSource` control to implement `IHierarchicalDataSource` (see Listing 16-1).

The `TreeView` then calls the `GetHierarchicalView` method of the data source control to return a `HierarchicalDataSourceView` object:

```
HierarchicalDataSourceView dv = ds.GetHierarchicalView(String.Empty);
```

This means that it expects the `CustomSqlDataSource` control's implementation of the `GetHierarchicalView` method to return an instance of a class that derives from the `HierarchicalDataSourceView` base class. Later you'll implement a class named `CustomSqlDataSourceView` that derives from this base class. You can think of the `CustomSqlDataSourceView` as the hierarchical representation of the underlying database table, the `Messages` table.

`TreeView` then calls the `Select` method of the `HierarchicalDataSourceView` object to return an `IHierarchicalEnumerable` collection of `IHierarchyData` objects, where each object represents a data record:

```
IHierarchicalEnumerable data = dv.Select();
```

This means that `TreeView` expects the `CustomSqlDataSource` control's implementation of the `Select` method to return a collection that implements the `IHierarchicalEnumerable` interface. Later in this chapter you'll write a custom collection named `SqlHierarchicalEnumerable` that implements this interface. You can think of `SqlHierarchicalEnumerable` as the hierarchical representation of the collection of database records that a database query returns.

`TreeView` then calls the `GetEnumerator` method of the `IHierarchicalEnumerable` collection to access its enumerator, and uses the enumerator to iterate through the objects that the `IHierarchicalEnumerable` collection contains and performs the following tasks for each enumerated object:

1. It calls the `GetHierarchyData` method of the collection to return the `IHierarchyData` associated with the enumerated object:

```
IHierarchyData hd = data.GetHierarchyData(iter.Current);
```

This means that `TreeView` expects the `SqlHierarchicalEnumerable` method's implementation of the `GetHierarchyData` method to return an instance of a class that implements the `IHierarchyData` interface. Later you'll write a custom class named `SqlHierarchyData` that implements this interface. You can think of `SqlHierarchyData` as the hierarchical representation of a database record.

2. Then it calls the `GetProperties` method of the `TypeDescriptor` class and passes the `IHierarchyData` object into it to return a `PropertyDescriptorCollection` collection of `PropertyDescriptor` objects, where each object represents a property of the `IHierarchyData` object:

```
PropertyDescriptorCollection pds = TypeDescriptor.GetProperties(hd);
```

This means that `TreeView` expects two things from the `SqlHierarchyData` method. First, it expects `SqlHierarchyData` to expose the database fields of its associated database record as its own properties. As you'll see later, `SqlHierarchyData` implements the `GetProperties` method of the `ICustomTypeDescriptor` interface to accomplish this. Second, it expects the `GetProperties` method of `SqlHierarchyData` to return a collection of `PropertyDescriptor` objects. This means that it expects `SqlHierarchyData` to wrap each database field of its associated database record in an instance of a class that derives from the `PropertyDescriptor` base class. You'll implement a class named `SqlHierarchyDataPropertyDescriptor` that derives from this base class. You can think of `SqlHierarchyDataPropertyDescriptor` as the hierarchical representation of a database field.

In summary, you need to implement the following four classes:

❑ `SqlHierarchyDataPropertyDescriptor`, to represent the database fields of the database records that a database query returns. As far as `TreeView` is concerned, it's dealing with `PropertyDescriptors`, *not* a database field.

❑ `SqlHierarchyData`, to represent the database records that the database query returns. As far as `TreeView` is concerned, it's retrieving `IHierarchyData` objects from the underlying data store, *not* database records.

❑ `SqlHierarchicalEnumerable`, to represent the collection that contains database records that a database query returns. As far as `TreeView` is concerned, it's retrieving an `IHierarchicalEnumerable` collection of `IHierarchyData` objects from the underlying data store, *not* a database record collection.

❑ `SqlHierarchicalDataSourceView`, to represent the database table whose records a database query returns. As far as `TreeView` is concerned, it's retrieving data from a `SqlHierarchicalDataSourceView`, *not* a database table.

SqlHierarchyDataPropertyDescriptor

As discussed, `SqlHierarchyDataPropertyDescriptor` represents the database fields of the data records that a database query returns. This class derives from the `PropertyDescriptor` base class and implements the methods and properties of its base class, as described in this section.

First, take a look at the constructor of this class. The argument of the constructor is the name of the database field that the `SqlHierarchyDataPropertyDescriptor` represents:

```
private string name;
public SqlHierarchyDataPropertyDescriptor(string name) : base(name, null)
{
  this.name = name;
}
```

The `SqlHierarchyDataPropertyDescriptor` class's implementation of the `Name` property of the `PropertyDescriptor` base class returns the name of the database field that the class represents:

```
public override string Name
{
   get { return name; }
}
```

The class's implementation of the `IsReadOnly` property of the `PropertyDescriptor` class returns true because the class doesn't allow its clients to set the value of the database field that it represents, because these values come from the underlying database:

```
public override bool IsReadOnly
{
   get { return true; }
}
```

Therefore the class's implementation of `SetValue` method of the `PropertyDescriptor` class raises an exception if it's called:

```
public override void SetValue(object o, object value)
{
   throw new NotSupportedException();
}
```

This also means that the `CanResetValue` method must return false and the `ResetValue` method must raise an exception:

```
public override bool CanResetValue(object o)
{
   return false;
}

public override void ResetValue(object o)
{
   throw new NotSupportedException();
}
```

Because the `SqlHierarchyDataPropertyDescriptor` class only supports database fields whose values can be coverted to strings, its implementation of the `PropertyType` property of the `PropertyDescriptor` base class returns `typeof(string)`:

```
public override Type PropertyType
{
   get { return typeof(string); }
}
```

Therefore the `Coverter` property returns a string converter:

```
public override TypeConverter Converter
{
  get { return TypeDescriptor.GetConverter(Type.GetType("System.String")); }
}
```

The `GetValue` method allows the clients of the class to get the value of the database field that the class represents. This method takes the `SqlHierarchyData` object that represents a database record and extracts the value of the database field that the `SqlHierarchyDataPropertyDescriptor` represents:

```
public override object GetValue(object o)
{
  SqlHierarchyData shd = o as SqlHierarchyData;

  if (shd != null)
  {
    IHierarchyData hd = (IHierarchyData)shd;
    string subject = ((DataRowView)(hd.Item))[name].ToString();
    return subject;
  }

  return null;
}
```

This method first ensures that the object passed in as its argument is of type `SqlHierarchyData`:

```
SqlHierarchyData shd = o as SqlHierarchyData;
if (shd != null)
```

The method then casts the object to `IHierarchyData` type so it can access the `Item` property of the `IHierarchyData` interface. As you'll see later, `SqlHierarchyData` implements the `IHierarchyData` interface:

```
IHierarchyData hd = (IHierarchyData)shd;
```

The `Item` property of the `SqlHierarchyData` class references the `DataViewRow` object associated with the database record that the class represents or encapsulates. The `GetValue` method type casts the `Item` property to its real type (`DataRowView`) so it can access the value of the database field that the `SqlHierarchyDataPropertyDescriptor` class represents:

```
string subject = ((DataRowView)(hd.Item))[name].ToString();
```

The `ComponentType` property of `SqlHierarchyDataPropertyDescriptor` returns `typeof(SqlHierarchyData)`:

```
public override Type ComponentType
{
  get {return typeof(SqlHierarchyData); }
}
```

The clients of the `SqlHierarchyDataPropertyDescriptor` class call the `ComponentType` property to determine what type of object they need to pass to the `GetValue` method:

SqlHierarchyData

As discussed, the SqlHierarchyData class represents a database record. Listing 16-4 shows the declaration of this class. The class implements both the IHierarchyData and ICustomTypeDescriptor interfaces. This means that the class must implement the methods and properties of both interfaces. The following sections discuss and present the code for these methods and properties.

Listing 16-4: The SqlHierarchyData class

```
public class SqlHierarchyData : IHierarchyData, ICustomTypeDescriptor
{
  public override string ToString();

  // IHierarchical Members
  bool IHierarchyData.HasChildren {get;}
  object IHierarchyData.Item {get;}
  string IHierarchyData.Path {get;}
  string IHierarchyData.Type {get;}
  IHierarchicalEnumerable IHierarchyData.GetChildren();
  IHierarchyData IHierarchyData.GetParent();

  // ICustomTypeDescriptor Members
  System.ComponentModel.AttributeCollection ICustomTypeDescriptor.GetAttributes();
  string ICustomTypeDescriptor.GetClassName();
  string ICustomTypeDescriptor.GetComponentName();
  TypeConverter ICustomTypeDescriptor.GetConverter();
  EventDescriptor ICustomTypeDescriptor.GetDefaultEvent();
  PropertyDescriptor ICustomTypeDescriptor.GetDefaultProperty();
  object ICustomTypeDescriptor.GetEditor(Type editorBaseType);
  EventDescriptorCollection ICustomTypeDescriptor.GetEvents(
                                          Attribute[] attributes);
  EventDescriptorCollection ICustomTypeDescriptor.GetEvents();
  PropertyDescriptorCollection ICustomTypeDescriptor.GetProperties(
                                          Attribute[] attributes);
  PropertyDescriptorCollection ICustomTypeDescriptor.GetProperties();
  object ICustomTypeDescriptor.GetPropertyOwner(PropertyDescriptor pd);
}
```

Constructor

Listing 16-5 presents the implementation of the constructor of the SqlHierarchyData class. This class contains the following private fields:

❑   item: References the DataRowView object or database record that the SqlHierarchyData represents

❑   dataIdField: The name of the primary key database field of the record that the SqlHierarchyData represents

❑   dataParentIdField: The name of the database field that references the parent record of the record that the SqlHierarchyData represents

Listing 16-5: The constructor of SqlHierarchyData class

```
public SqlHierarchyData(string dataParentIdField, string dataIdField,
                        DataRowView item)
{
  this.item = item;
  this.dataParentIdField = dataParentIdField;
  this.dataIdField = dataIdField;
}
```

Implementing HasChildren

Listing 16-6 shows the SqlHierarchyData class's implementation of the HasChildren property of the IHierarchyData interface. As mentioned, the SqlHierarchyData class exposes a private field of type DataRowView that references the database record or DataRowView object that the SqlHierarchyData class represents.

Listing 16-6: The SqlHierarchyData class's implementation of the HasChildren property

```
bool IHierarchyData.HasChildren
  {
    get
    {
      foreach (DataRowView row in item.DataView)
      {
        if (row[dataParentIdField].ToString() == item[dataIdField].ToString())
          return true;
      }

      return false;
    }
  }
```

HasChildren searches through data records for a record whose dataParentIdField references the record that the SqlHierarchyData represents. If the search fails, it indicates that the record has no child records.

Implementing the Type Property

To understand the significance of the Type property and why the SqlHierarchyData class implements this property the way it does, take another look at Listing 16-3. As the highlighted portion of the following code fragment shows, TreeView searches through the TreeNodeBinding objects in its DataBindings collection for the TreeNodeBinding object whose DataMember property has the same value as the Type property of the IHierarchyData (in this case, SqlHierarchyData) object that represents the current database record:

```
protected void Page_Load(object sender, EventArgs e)
{
  if (!IsPostBack)
```

```
{
    IHierarchicalDataSource ds = (IHierarchicalDataSource)MySource;
    HierarchicalDataSourceView dv = ds.GetHierarchicalView(String.Empty);
    IHierarchicalEnumerable data = dv.Select();
    IEnumerator iter = data.GetEnumerator();
    TreeNodeBinding tnb;
    while (iter.MoveNext())
    {
        . . .
        foreach (TreeNodeBinding b in tv.DataBindings)
        {
            if (b.DataMember == hd.Type)
            {
                tnb = b;
                break;
            }
        }
        . . .
    }
}
}
```

For example, in the case of Listing 16-2, the `DataBindings` collection contains a single `TreeNodeBinding` object as shown here:

```
<asp:TreeView runat="Server" ID="tv">
  <DataBindings>
    <asp:TreeNodeBinding DataMember="MessageID" TextField="Subject"
    ValueField="MessageID" />
  </DataBindings>
</asp:TreeView>
```

As discussed, the page developer sets the `DataMember` property of `TreeNodeBinding` to the name of the primary key database field, which means that the `Type` property of `SqlHierarchyData` must return the value of `dataIdField`:

```
string IHierarchyData.Type
{
    get {return dataIdField;}
```

For the reasons discussed in the previous chapter, your custom `IHierarchyData` class must override the `ToString` method to return a default value. The following code shows the `SqlHierarchyData` class's implementation of the `ToString()` method:

```
public override string ToString()
{
    return dataIdField;
}
```

Listing 16-7 shows the `SqlHierarchyData` class's implementation of the `GetParent` method of the `IHierarchyData` interface. Recall that the `item` field of the `SqlHierarchyData` class refers to the `DataViewRow` object that the class represents. `GetParent` searches through the `DataRowView` objects contained in the `item.DataView` collection for a parent `DataRowView` object of the `DataRowView` object that `SqlHierarchyData` represents.

Notice that the GetParent method doesn't return the parent DataRowView object as an object of type DataRowView. Instead it returns the generic representation of the parent object, the SqlHierarchyData object that encapsulates the parent object.

Listing 16-7: The SqlHierarchyData class's implementation of the GetParent method

```
IHierarchyData IHierarchyData.GetParent()
{
  foreach (DataRowView row in item.DataView)
  {
    if (item[dataParentIdField].ToString() == row[dataIdField].ToString())
      return new SqlHierarchyData(dataParentIdField, dataIdField, row);
  }

  return null;
}
```

So far you've seen the SqlHierarchyData class's implementation of all of the methods of the IHierarchyData interface except for the GetChildren method. This is similar to the XmlHierarchyData class discussed in the previous chapter, in that you need to understand the enumerable class before discussing the GetChildren method.

SqlHierarchicalEnumerable

As discussed, a SqlHierarchicalEnumerable collection represents the collection that contains the database records that a database query returns. The SqlHierarchicalEnumerable class derives from the ArrayList class and implements the IHierarchicalEnumerable interface. The GetHierarchyData method simply casts the enumerated object to the SqlHierarchyData type (see Listing 16-8).

Listing 16-8: The SqlHierarchicalEnumerable class

```
public class SqlHierarchicalEnumerable : ArrayList, IHierarchicalEnumerable
{
    IHierarchyData IHierarchicalEnumerable.GetHierarchyData(object enumeratedItem)
    {
        return (SqlHierarchyData)enumeratedItem;
    }
}
```

Now you can implement the GetChildren method of the SqlHierarchyData class (see Listing 16-9). Recall that the SqlHierarchyData class is a generic representation of the DataRowView object or the database record that its item field references. The GetChildren method searches through the DataRowView objects contained in the item.DataView collection for DataRowView objects whose parent DataRowView is the DataRowView object that SqlHierarchyData represents.

Notice that the GetChildren method doesn't directly return the child DataRowView objects as objects of type DataRowView. Instead it creates a SqlHierarchyData object to represent each child DataRowView, creates a SqlHierarchicalEnumerable collection, adds the SqlHierarchyData objects to this collection, and returns the collection to its clients.

Listing 16-9: The SqlHierarchyData class's implementation of the GetChildren method

```
IHierarchicalEnumerable IHierarchyData.GetChildren()
{
  SqlHierarchicalEnumerable children = new SqlHierarchicalEnumerable();

  foreach (DataRowView row in item.DataRow)
  {
    if (row[dataParentIdField].ToString() == item[dataIdField].ToString())
      children.Add(new SqlHierarchyData(dataParentIdField, dataIdField, row));
  }

  return children;
}
```

So far you've implemented the `SqlHierarchyData` class's implementation of the `IHierarchyData` interface's methods and properties. Recall that the `SqlHierarchyData` class also implements the `ICustomTypeDescriptor` interface. For the same reasons discussed in the previous chapter, the `SqlHierarchyData` class only implements the `GetProperties` method and delegates the responsibility of other methods of the interface to the `TypeDescriptor` class.

Listing 16-10 contains the code for the `GetProperties` method.

Listing 16-10: The GetProperties method

```
PropertyDescriptorCollection
ICustomTypeDescriptor.GetProperties(Attribute[] attributes)
{
  PropertyDescriptorCollection pds = TypeDescriptor.GetProperties(item);

  if (pds.Count > 0)
  {
    List<SqlHierarchyDataPropertyDescriptor> list =
                      new List<SqlHierarchyDataPropertyDescriptor>();

    foreach (PropertyDescriptor pd in pds)
    {
      list.Add(new SqlHierarchyDataPropertyDescriptor(pd.Name));
    }

    SqlHierarchyDataPropertyDescriptor[] arr =
                      new SqlHierarchyDataPropertyDescriptor[list.Count];
    list.CopyTo(arr);

    return new PropertyDescriptorCollection(arr);
  }
  return PropertyDescriptorCollection.Empty;
}
```

The `item` field of the `SqlHierarchyData` class references the `DataRowView` object that the `SqlHierarchyData` represents. The ASP.NET `DataRowView` class derives from the `ICustomTypeDescriptor` interface and implements its `GetProperties` method to expose its data fields as its own properties. In other words, if you call the `GetProperties` method and pass a `DataRowView` object into it, you'll get back a collection of `PropertyDescriptor` objects, where each object represents a data field.

```
PropertyDescriptorCollection pds = TypeDescriptor.GetProperties(item);
```

The `GetProperties` method then creates an instance of the `List<SqlHierarchyDataProperty Descriptor>` generic class:

```
List<SqlHierarchyDataPropertyDescriptor> list =
                    new List<SqlHierarchyDataPropertyDescriptor>();
```

It then enumerates the `PropertyDescriptor` objects that represent the database fields of the `DataRowView` object or database record that the `SqlHierarchyData` class represents.

Next, it creates a `SqlHierarchyDataPropertyDescriptor` object to represent each enumerated database field.

Finally, the method creates an instance of the `PropertyDescriptorCollection` object and populates the collection.

The following code shows the `SqlHierarchyData` class's implementation of the second overload of the `GetProperties` method of the `ICustomTypeDescriptor` interface. This overload delegates to the first one.

```
PropertyDescriptorCollection ICustomTypeDescriptor.GetProperties()
{
   return ((ICustomTypeDescriptor)this).GetProperties(null);
}
```

For the same reasons discussed in the previous chapter, you must also implement the `GetPropertyOwner` method:

```
object ICustomTypeDescriptor.GetPropertyOwner(PropertyDescriptor pd)
{
   Return (pd is SqlHierarchyDataPropertyDescriptor) ? this : null;
}
```

SqlHierarchicalDataSourceView

The `SqlHierarchicalDataSourceView` class derives from the `HierarchicalDataSourceView` abstract base class. The following code presents the implementation of the constructor of the class. As discussed in the previous chapter, the `viewPath` argument contains the location path of the subtree that the view represents:

```
public SqlHierarchicalDataSourceView(XmlDataSource owner, string viewPath)
{
   this.viewPath = viewPath;
   this.owner = owner;
}
```

The following code contains the code for the `SqlHierarchicalDataSourceView` class's implementation of the `Select` method of the `HierarchicalDataSourceView` base class:

```
public override IHierarchicalEnumerable Select()
{
  DataView dv = (DataView)this.owner.Select(DataSourceSelectArguments.Empty);
  SqlHierarchicalEnumerable data = new SqlHierarchicalEnumerable();

  bool hasParent = false;
  foreach (DataRowView crow in dv)
  {
    hasParent = false;

    foreach (DataRowView prow in dv)
    {
      if (crow[owner.DataParentIdField].ToString() ==
                            prow[owner.DataIdField].ToString())
      {
        hasParent = true;
        break;
      }
    }

    if (!hasParent)
      data.Add(
          new SqlHierarchyData(owner.DataParentIdField, owner.DataIdField, crow));
  }

  return data;
}
```

The `Select` method calls the `Select` method of its owner, `CustomSqlDataSource`. `CustomSqlDataSource` inherits the `Select` method from its base class, `SqlDataSource` control. The `Select` method of the `SqlDataSource` control returns a `DataView` object that contains the retrieved data records. The `Select` method of `SqlHierarchicalDataSourceView` iterates through the retrieved data records and creates a `SqlHierarchyData` object for each top-level parent data record. A top-level parent data record is a data record that has no parent data record. For example, in the case of a discussion forum, top-level data records are the messages that start discussion threads.

Summary

This chapter developed a custom hierarchical data source control named `CustomSqlDataSource` that extends the functionality of the ASP.NET `SqlDataSource` to provide hierarchical data-bound controls such as `TreeView` with the hierarchical views of the underlying database table.

The next chapters show you how data-bound controls use data source controls to isolate themselves from the underlying data store so they can work with any type of data store. You start out with a good look at the ASP.NET 2.0 tabular data-bound control model, which has changed substantially from ASP.NET 1.1.

17

Understanding the ASP.NET 2.0 Tabular Data-Bound Control Model

In Chapter 9 you used the ASP.NET 1.x data-bound control model to develop a custom data-bound control named `CustomTable` that allows end users to edit and to display database records. You can use what you learned in Chapter 9 to extend the functionality of the `CustomTable` control to add support for all the features that a complex ASP.NET 1.x data-bound control such as `DataGrid` supports. This chapter examines one of the main shortcomings of the ASP.NET 1.x data-bound controls, such as `CustomTable` and `DataGrid`, and shows how the ASP.NET 2.0 tabular data-bound control model uses the ASP.NET 2.0 data source control model discussed in Chapters 12–16 to address this shortcoming.

In this chapter you implement fully functional replicas of the base classes built into the ASP.NET 2.0 data-bound control model. These replicas will serve the following important purposes:

❑ They'll help you understand the new ASP.NET 2.0 data-bound control model from the inside out.

❑ They'll help you understand how you can extend the base classes of the new ASP.NET 2.0 data-bound control model to develop your own custom data-bound controls.

❑ They'll help you look under the hood of the new ASP.NET 2.0 data-bound control model to address important questions such as the following: How does the new ASP.NET 2.0 data-bound control model relate to what you already know — the ASP.NET 1.x data-bound control model? How did the old model turn into the new one? Whatever happened to the old ways of developing custom data-bound controls in ASP.NET 1.x? What was wrong with them? What does this new model provide that you wouldn't be able to accomplish in ASP.NET 1.x?

❑ In Chapter 31, you'll use the source code of these replicas to implement a set of base Web Parts controls that you can use to develop data-bound Web Parts controls that automate all data operations such as select, delete, update, insert, page, and sort, can access any type of data store, can be developed with minimal effort, and can be used declaratively.

The Big Picture

The ASP.NET 2.0 data-bound control model consists of five base classes: BaseDataBoundControl, DataBoundControl, HierarchicalDataBoundControl, ListControl, and CompositeData BoundControl. This chapter implements fully functional replicas of the BaseDataBoundControl, DataBoundControl, and CompositeDataBoundControl base classes built into ASP.NET to help you delve into the ASP.NET 2.0 implementation of these classes. Because the implementation of these base classes is fully functional, you have the option of using the ASP.NET 2.0 implementation or this chapter's implementation.

To make the discussions more concrete, this chapter provides different implementations of a custom data-bound control that displays data records in a table and allows users to delete, update, sort, and page through the records. For ease of reference, each implementation uses a different name for the custom data-bound control. The discussions begin by revisiting the custom data-bound control developed in Chapter 9. Recall that you used the ASP.NET 1.x data-bound control model to implement a custom data-bound control named CustomTable. You can think of this implementation as the first implementation of the series of different implementations of the same data-bound control presented in this chapter.

This chapter then discusses the shortcomings of the ASP.NET 1.x data-bound control model and demonstrates that these shortcomings are due to the fact that the model doesn't include a rich base class such as the ASP.NET 2.0 BaseDataBoundControl that would provide its subclasses (data-bound controls) with the infrastructure they need to automate the data-binding process. Such automation would allow page developers to use data-bound controls declaratively without writing a single line of code.

Then you'll implement a fully functional replica of the BaseDataBoundControl base class built into ASP.NET and see how this base class manages to provide its subclasses with the infrastructure they need to automate data-binding process.

Next, the chapter presents the second implementation of the custom data-bound control to replace the first implementation, CustomTable. In the second implementation the control is named CustomTable2. Because the CustomTable2 control derives from the ASP.NET 2.0 BaseDataBoundControl base class, it allows page developers to use it declaratively without writing any code.

Then you'll implement a fully functional replica of the ASP.NET 2.0 DataBoundControl base class and see how this base class manages to retrieve data from any type of data store. This is extremely important in data-driven Web applications where data comes from different types of data stores such as Microsoft SQL Server, Microsoft Access, Oracle, XML documents, flat files, and Web services, to name a few.

Next is the third implementation of the custom data-bound control to replace CustomTable2. In the third implementation the control is named CustomTable3. Because the CustomTable3 control derives from the DataBoundControl base class it allows page developers to access any type of data store.

You'll implement a fully functional replica of the ASP.NET 2.0 CompositeDataBoundControl base class and see that you can develop ASP.NET 2.0 custom data-bound controls with minimal effort if you derive your custom controls from the ASP.NET 2.0 CompositeDataBoundControl base class.

The fourth implementation of the custom data-bound control to replaces CustomTable3. In the fourth implementation the control is named CustomTable4. Because the CustomTable4 control derives from the CompositeDataBoundControl base class, you can implement the control with a minimum amount of code.

The ASP.NET 2.0 data-bound control model has a number of goals to achieve. One of these goals is to provide custom data-bound controls with the infrastructure they need to automate the following three data-binding tasks without any code from page developers:

❑ *Retrieve the data from the underlying data store.* Normally, a particular method of some class is responsible for this task. For ease of reference, the method is named `RetrieveData`. It retrieves the data from the underlying data store and returns an object of type `IEnumerable` that contains the retrieved data.

❑ *Enumerate the retrieved data and create the appropriate control hierarchy.* Normally a particular method of some class is responsible for this task. For ease of reference, the method is named `EnumerateDataAndCreateControlHierarchy`. It takes the `IEnumerable` object that contains the retrieved data as its argument, enumerates the retrieved data, and creates the appropriate control hierarchy.

❑ *Take the preceding two actions in response to the events that require fresh data from the data store, such as* `Load`, `Delete`, `Update`, `Sort`, *and* `Page` *events.* For each event, there's normally a particular method or function that takes the two actions in response to the event. For ease of reference, these methods are named `SortCallback`, `DeleteCallback`, `EditCallback`, `UpdateCallback`, `CancelCallback`, and `PageCallback`. When the user clicks the Edit, Update, or Cancel button of a particular row in a data-bound control, the `EditCallback`, `UpdateCallback`, or `CancelCallback` is called. The `PageCallback` method is called when the user clicks an element of the paging interface of a data-bound control.

Why is it so important to automate these three data-binding tasks? What are the shortcomings of the ASP.NET 1.x data-bound control model when it comes to data-binding process? The next section provides the answers to these and other similar questions.

ASP.NET 1.x Data-Bound Control Model

The discussion begins by revisiting the first implementation of the custom data-bound control presented in Chapter 9, where the ASP.NET 1.x data-bound control model was used to implement the control. In Chapter 9 this implementation was named `CustomTable`.

The `CustomTable` control and page developers together take the following actions to handle the three data-binding tasks:

❑ Implement and invoke the `RetrieveData` method to handle the first data-binding task

❑ Implement and invoke the `EnumerateDataAndCreateConrolHierarchy` method to handle the second data-binding task

❑ Implement and invoke the `SortCallback`, `DeleteCallback`, `EditCallback`, `UpdateCallback`, `CancelCallback`, and `PageCallback` methods to handle the third data-binding task

The following sections briefly discuss these methods.

> You can download the complete code for the `CustomTable` control, `RetrieveData`, `Enumerate DataAndCreateConrolHierarchy`, `SortCallback`, `DeleteCallback`, `EditCallback`, `UpdateCallback`, `CancelCallback`, and `PageCallback` methods, and the sample Web application that uses them from the Wrox Web site at www.wrox.com.

The RetrieveData Method

The ASP.NET 1.x data-bound control model leaves the responsibility of implementing the RetrieveData method to page developers. Chapter 12 (see Listing 12-2) presented a typical implementation of the RetrieveData method where the page developer uses ADO.NET objects such as SqlConnection, SqlCommand, and SqlDataAdapter to retrieve the data from the underlying Microsoft SQL Server database. As shown in Listing 12-2, writing the RetrieveData method requires page developers to have a solid understanding of ADO.NET.

The ASP.NET 1.x data-bound control model also leaves the responsibility of invoking the RetrieveData method to page developers. Chapter 12 presented an example of the situation where the page developer has to call the RetrieveData method.

Because the ASP.NET 1.x data-bound control model leaves the responsibilities of implementing and invoking the RetrieveData method to page developers, the model doesn't provide the ASP.NET 1.x data-bound controls such as CustomTable and DataGrid with the necessary infrastructure to automate the first data-binding task.

Overriding the DataBind Method

As discussed in Chapter 9, the ASP.NET 1.x custom data-bound controls override the CreateChildControls method to call the EnumerateDataAndCreateControlHierarchy with a dummy data source and a false value as its arguments (see Listing 9-3). Recall that the CreateChildControls method creates the control hierarchy from the saved view state. Because the ASP.NET 1.x data-bound control model automates the invocation of the CreateChildControls method as discussed in Chapter 9, the ASP.NET 1.x custom data-bound controls are able to automate the creation of the control hierarchy from the saved view state.

Recall from Chapter 9 that the ASP.NET 1.x custom data-bound controls must also override the DataBind method to call the EnumerateDataAndCreateControlHierarchy method with a real data source and a true value as its arguments (see Listing 9-4) to create the control hierarchy from the data source.

The ASP.NET 1.x custom data-bound controls can't automate the creation of the control hierarchy from actual data records because the ASP.NET 1.x data-bound control model doesn't automate the invocation of the DataBind method. This means that the ASP.NET 1.x data-bound control model doesn't provide standard and custom data-bound controls with the infrastructure they need to automate the second data-binding task.

Handling the Third Data-Binding Task

Recall that the SortCallback, DeleteCallback, EditCallback, UpdateCallback, CancelCallback, and PageCallback methods handle the third data-binding task. The ASP.NET 1.x data-bound control model leaves the responsibility of implementing these methods to page developers. Chapter 12 (see Listing 12-3) shows an example of the code that page developers must write to implement these methods. Therefore, the ASP.NET 1.x custom data-bound controls can't automate the third data-binding task either.

In short, the main problem with the ASP.NET 1.x data-bound control model is that it doesn't include a base class such as the ASP.NET 2.0 `BaseDataBoundControl` class that would provide its subclasses with the infrastructure they need to automate the three data-binding tasks. This means that the ASP.NET 1.x custom data-bound controls don't support codeless scenarios where page developers would be able to use them declaratively.

The next section implements a replica of the `BaseDataBoundControl` class built into ASP.NET 2.0 and shows how this base class provides its subclasses with the infrastructure they need to automate the three data-binding tasks, allowing page developers to use ASP.NET 2.0 custom data-bound controls declaratively without writing a single line of code.

Before proceeding with the discussions, first examine the following common themes in the ASP.NET 2.0 data-bound control model. When it comes to a given method of a base class, you must separate the following two responsibilities:

- ❑ Implementing the method
- ❑ Automating its invocation

These are two different responsibilities that should be assigned to two different classes.

BaseDataBoundControl

As mentioned, the main goal of the `BaseDataBoundControl` class is to provide its subclasses with the infrastructure they need to automate the three data-binding tasks. Start with the second data-binding task. Recall that the main reason the ASP.NET 1.x custom data-bound controls don't automate the second data-binding task is the fact that the ASP.NET 1.x data-bound control model doesn't automate the invocation of the `DataBind` method.

Automating the Invocation of the DataBind Method

The first goal of the `BaseDataBoundControl` class is to automate the invocation of the `DataBind` method. The class uses a mechanism very similar to the mechanism that the `Control` class uses to automate the invocation of the `CreateChildControls` method as discussed in Chapter 9.

The `BaseDataBoundControl` class introduces a new Boolean field named `requiresDataBinding`, which operates similarly to the `ChildControlsCreated` property. The field is used to make sure that the `DataBind` method isn't called more than once for each request. The class also introduces a new method named `EnsureDataBound`, which operates similarly to the `EnsureChildControls` method. The method first checks whether the value of the `requiresDataBinding` field is set to true. If so, it first calls the `DataBind` method and then sets the `requiresDataBinding` field to false:

```
protected void EnsureDataBound()
{
  if (requiresDataBinding)
    DataBind();

  requiresDataBinding = false;
}
```

The BaseDataBoundControl class then overrides the OnPreRender method to do exactly what the Control class did to automate the invocation of the EnsureChildControls method — it calls the EnsureDataBound method:

```
protected override void OnPreRender(EventArgs e)
{
  EnsureDataBound();
  base.OnPreRender(e);
}
```

Because the OnPreRender method is automatically called for every single request, the EnsureDataBound method and, consequently, the DataBind method (if the requiresDataBinding field is true) are automatically called as well.

The First and Second Data-Binding Tasks

The BaseDataBoundControl class inherits the DataBind method from the WebControl class, which in turn inherits the method from the Control class. The Control class's implementation of the DataBind method doesn't do much; it simply raises the OnDataBinding event. Therefore, automating the invocation of the DataBind method would do nothing to help automate the second data-binding task unless the subclasses of the BaseDataBoundControl class override the DataBind method to call the EnumerateDataAndCreateControlHierarchy method.

Because the DataBind method isn't an abstract method, the BaseDataBoundControl class can't enforce the requirement that its base classes must implement the method. That's why the BaseDataBoundControl class exposes a new abstract method, as follows:

```
protected abstract void PerformSelect();
```

The class overrides the DataBind method and calls the PerformSelect method:

```
public override void DataBind()
{
  PerformSelect();
  base.DataBind();
}
```

This forces the subclasses of the BaseDataBoundControl class to implement the PerformSelect method. The subclasses must take the following actions:

❑   Implement the RetrieveData method

❑   Implement the EnumerateDataAndCreateControlHierarchy method

❑   Override the PerformSelect method to call the other two methods

This will allow subclasses to automate both the first and the second data-binding tasks because of the following sequence:

1.   The BaseDataBoundControl class automatically calls the DataBind method as discussed before.

2.   The DataBind method automatically calls the PerformSelect method of the subclass as discussed before.

3. The `PerformSelect` method automatically calls the `RetrieveData` method of the subclass. This automates the first data-binding task.

4. The `PerformSelect` method also automatically calls the `EnumerateDataAndCreateControlHierarchy` method of the subclass. This automates the second data-binding task.

The Third Data-Binding Task

Now you'll see how the `BaseDataBoundControl` class provides its subclasses with the infrastructure they need to automate the third data-binding task. The class exposes a Boolean property named `RequiresDataBinding` whose getter and setter delegate to the `requiresDataBinding` field. Recall that the `BaseDataBoundControl` class uses the `requiresDataBinding` field to ensure the `DataBind` method (and consequently the `PerformSelect` method) isn't called more than once for each request.

```
private bool requiresDataBinding;
protected bool RequiresDataBinding
{
  get {return requiresDataBinding; }
  set
  {
    requiresDataBinding = value;
    EnsureDataBound();
  }
}
```

Notice that the setter of the `RequiresDataBinding` property calls the `EnsureDataBound` method. Therefore setting the `RequiresDataBinding` property of the subclass of the `BaseDataBoundControl` class to true automatically triggers the following sequence:

1. The `RequiresDataBinding` property sets the `requiresDataBinding` field to true.

2. The `RequiresDataBinding` property automatically calls the `EnsureDataBound` method of the `BaseDataBoundControl` base class.

3. The `EnsureDataBound` method automatically calls the `DataBind` method of the `BaseDataBoundControl` base class.

4. The `DataBind` method automatically calls the `PerformSelect` method of the subclass.

5. The `PerformSelect` method automatically calls the `RetrieveData` method of the subclass. Recall that the subclasses of the `BaseDataBoundControl` class must implement the `RetrieveData` method and override the `PerformSelect` method to call the method.

6. The `RetrieveData` method retrieves the data from the underlying data store and returns an object of type `IEnumerable` that contains the retrieved data.

7. The `PerformSelect` method automatically calls the `EnumerateDataAndCreateControlHierarchy` method of the subclass and passes the `IEnumerable` object as its argument. Recall that the subclasses of the `BaseDataBoundControl` class must implement the `EnumerateDataAndCreateControlHierarchy` method and override the `PerformSelect` method to call the method.

8. The `EnumerateAndCreateControlHierarchy` method enumerates the `IEnumerable` object and creates the control hierarchy.

This means that a single line of code (setting the `RequiresDataBinding` property to true) automatically triggers the entire data-binding process. This allows custom data-bound controls to implement methods such as `SortCallback`, `DeleteCallback`, `EditCallback`, `UpdateCallback`, `CancelCallback`, and `PageCallback` that handle the third data-binding task. These methods simply set the `RequiresDataBinding` property to true to trigger the whole data-binding process where fresh data is automatically retrieved and enumerated to update the display of the respective custom data-bound control.

Therefore the `RequiresDataBinding` property helps to automate the third data-binding task. The next section implements a new custom data-bound control that shows how this process works. However, first this section finishes the discussion of the `BaseDataBoundControl` class before getting into the implementation of this custom control.

There are two approaches for retrieving data from the underlying data store. One approach is the traditional ASP.NET 1.x approach where page developers do all the work. The `BaseDataBoundControl` class exposes a property named `DataSource` to support this approach:

```
private object dataSource;
public virtual object DataSource
{
  get { return dataSource; }
  set
  {
    ValidateDataSource(value);
    dataSource = value;
  }
}
```

The `BaseDataBoundControl` class exposes a method named `ValidateDataSource` that is used to validate a data source before it's assigned to the `dataSource` field:

```
protected abstract void ValidateDataSource(object dataSource);
```

The `BaseDataBoundControl` class automatically calls the `ValidateDataSource` method every time the `DataSource` property is set. However, it's not its responsibility to implement the method. The descendants of the `BaseDataBoundControl` class are responsible for implementing the method where they decide what types of data sources they support. You'll see an example of this later in this chapter.

The second approach for retrieving data from the data store is the new ASP.NET 2.0 approach. The `BaseDataBoundControl` class exposes a new property named `DataSourceID` to support this approach, as well. This approach is discussed in detail in the following sections.

Developing Custom Data-Bound Controls That Derive from BaseDataBoundControl

Take another look at your sample custom data-bound control. The first section used the ASP.NET 1.x data-bound control model to implement the custom control and named the control `CustomTable`. This section replaces the `CustomTable` control with a new custom control named `CustomTable2` that derives from the `BaseDataBoundControl` class, which allows the control to automate all three data-binding tasks where page developers can use it without writing any code. In other words, the `CustomTable2` control implements the `RetrieveData`, `SortCallback`, `DeleteCallback`, `EditCallback`, `UpdateCallback`, `CancelCallback`, and `PageCallback` methods, saving page developers from having to implement these methods themselves. The following sections discuss only a few of the methods of the `CustomTable2` control.

> *You can download the complete code for the `CustomTable2` control and the sample Web application that uses the control from the Wrox Web site at* www.wrox.com. *Feel free to tweak and play with the code to get the hang of how it works.*

Handling the Load Event

The `CustomTable2` control overrides the `OnLoad` method (see Listing 17-1) to automate the third data-binding task in response to the `Load` event. This saves page developers from having to implement the `Page_Load` method.

Listing 17-1: The CustomTable2 control overrides the OnLoad method

```
protected override void OnLoad(EventArgs e)
{
  if (!Page.IsPostBack)
    RequiresDataBinding = true;

  base.OnLoad(e);
}
```

Notice that the `CustomTable2` control's implementation of the `OnLoad` method simply sets the `RequiresDataBinding` property to true. That's it. As discussed, this automatically triggers the entire data-binding process where data is retrieved from the database and displayed to end users.

Overriding the PerformSelect Method

The `CustomTable2` control implements the `PerformSelect` method of the `BaseDataBoundControl` class, as shown in Listing 17-2.

Listing 17-2: The CustomTable2 control implements the PerformSelect method

```
protected override void PerformSelect()
{
  IEnumerable data = RetrieveData();
  Controls.Clear();
  ClearChildViewState();
  TrackViewState();
  ViewState["RowCount"] = EnumerateDataAndGenerateHtmlMarkupText(data, true);
  RequiresDataBinding = false;
}
```

Notice that the `CustomTable2` control's implementation of the `PerformSelect` method is the same as the `CustomTable` control's implementation of the `DataBind` method (see Listing 9-4) except for one big difference: the `CustomTable2` control's implementation automatically calls the `RetrieveData` method. Because the `PerformSelect` method calls both the `RetrieveData` and `EnumerateData AndCreateControlHierarchy` methods, the `CustomTable2` control automates both the first and second data-binding tasks.

Listing 17-3 shows the CustomTable2 control's implementation of the RetrieveData method. The control exposes few data access-related properties that are used in this method:

- ❑ SelectCountCommand: Gets and sets the Select SQL statement or the name of the stored procedure that retrieves the total row count.

- ❑ SelectCountCommandType: Has the possible values of StoredProcedure and Text.

- ❑ TotalNumberOfRecords: The CustomTable2 control uses the value of this property to decide how many LinkButton controls to render in its paging interface.

- ❑ StartIndexParameterName: Gets and sets the name of the parameter of the SQL statement or stored procedure that is used to specify the index of the first record being retrieved.

- ❑ MaximumRowsParameterName: Gets and sets the name of the parameter of the SQL statement or stored procedure that is used to specify the page size, that is, the maximum number of records being retrieved.

- ❑ SortParameterName: Gets and sets the name of the parameter of the SQL statement or stored procedure that is used to specify the name of the database field used to sort the data.

Listing 17-3: The RetrieveData method

```
IEnumerable RetrieveData()
{
  SqlConnection con;
  SqlCommand com;

  if (!Page.IsPostBack)
  {
      con = new SqlConnection();
      con.ConnectionString = ConnectionString;
      com = new SqlCommand();
      com.Connection = con;

      com.CommandText = SelectCountCommand;

      if (SelectCountCommandType == CommandType.StoredProcedure)
          com.CommandType = System.Data.CommandType.StoredProcedure;

      con.Open();
      TotalNumberOfRecords = (int)com.ExecuteScalar();
      con.Close();
  }

  con = new SqlConnection();
  con.ConnectionString = ConnectionString;
  com = new SqlCommand();
  com.Connection = con;

  string sortExpression = ViewState["SortExpression"] != null ?
                          (string)ViewState["SortExpression"] : DataKeyField;
  string sortDirection = ViewState["SortDirection"] != null ?
```

```
                            (string)ViewState["SortDirection"] : "Asc";

    com.CommandText = SelectCommand;

    if (SelectCommandType == CommandType.StoredProcedure)
        com.CommandType = System.Data.CommandType.StoredProcedure;

    com.Parameters.AddWithValue("@"+StartIndexParameterName, CurrentPageIndex - 1);
    com.Parameters.AddWithValue("@"+MaximumRowsParameterName, PageSize );

    if (sortExpression != null && sortExpression.Trim() != "")
        com.Parameters.AddWithValue("@"+SortParameterName, sortExpression + " " +
                                sortDirection);

    DataTable dt = new DataTable();
    SqlDataAdapter ad = new SqlDataAdapter();
    ad.SelectCommand = com;

    con.Open();
    ad.Fill(dt);
    con.Close();

    return dt.DefaultView;
}
```

Declarative Programming Without Writing Code

As Listing 17-4 shows, page developers can use the `CustomTable2` control declaratively without writing a single line of code.

Listing 17-4: Using the CustomTable2 control declaratively

```
<%@ Page Language="C#" %>
<%@ Register TagPrefix="custom" Namespace="CustomComponents" %>
<!DOCTYPE html PUBLIC "-//W3C//DTD XHTML 1.1//EN"
"http://www.w3.org/TR/xhtml11/DTD/xhtml11.dtd">
<html xmlns="http://www.w3.org/1999/xhtml">
<head runat="server">
  <title>Untitled Page</title>
</head>
<body>
  <form id="form1" runat="server">
    <custom:CustomTable2 runat="server" ID="ct" DataKeyField="BookID"
    ConnectionString="<% $ConnectionStrings:MySqlConnectionString %>"
    SelectCommand="GetOnePageOfData" StartIndexParameterName="CurrentPageIndex"
    MaximumRowsParameterName="PageSize" SortParameterName="SortExpression"
    SelectCommandType="StoredProcedure"
    SelectCountCommand="Select Count(*) From Books"
    UpdateCommand="Update Books Set Title=@Title, AuthorID=@AuthorID,
                Publisher=@Publisher, Price=@Price Where BookID=@BookID"
    DeleteCommand="Delete From Books Where BookID=@BookID" />
  </form>
</body>
</html>
```

Shortcomings of the CustomTable2 Control

It may seem that the BaseDataBoundControl class provides everything you need; in fact, you may wonder what you need the DataBoundControl base class for. To answer this question you need to take a closer look at the CustomTable2 control's implementation of the methods such as RetrieveData (see Listing 17-3), DeleteCallback, and so on.

As the implementation of these methods show, these methods use the ADO.NET classes such as SqlConnection, SqlCommand, and SqlDataAdapter, which are specifically designed to work with Microsoft SQL Server databases. This means that the CustomTable2 control can only work with Microsoft SQL Server databases and can't be used with other types of data stores such as Oracle.

As discussed in Chapter 12, you can make the CustomTable2 control's implementation of the RetrieveData, DeleteCallback, and so on more generic if you replace the SQL Server–specific ADO.NET objects with the new ADO.NET 2.0 objects such as DbConnection, DbCommand, and DbDataAdapter.

Even with these new changes, the RetrieveData method still will not be generic because it suffers from a more fundamental limitation — it directly uses the data store–specific data access APIs, which are ADO.NET objects. Because data access APIs vary from one type of data store to another, the RetrieveData method and consequently the CustomTable2 control would not be able to work with all types of data stores.

Another problem with the CustomControl2 control is the fact that the control itself exposes data access–related properties such as ConnectionString, SelectCommand, UpdateCommand, DeleteCommand, SelectCommandType, and so on. This goes against the best object-oriented programming practices where each component must handle a single task. The data access–related properties shouldn't be part of the control itself. They should be moved to a different component. As you saw in Chapters 12–16, the ASP.NET 2.0 Framework comes with dedicated controls known as data source controls that expose and handle the data access-store properties.

In summary, the main problem with the BaseDataBoundControl base class is the fact that it doesn't provide its subclasses with a generic data access mechanism to retrieve data from all types of data stores. Enter the DataBoundControl class.

DataBoundControl

In general, there are two types of data-bound controls: tabular and hierarchical. Tabular and hierarchical data-bound controls are those data-bound controls that expect tabular and hierarchical data, respectively, from their underlying data stores. For instance, the CustomTable2 control is a tabular data-bound control as can be clearly seen from the fact that the RetrieveData method returns a DataView object.

As discussed in Chapter 12, this causes a major problem in data-driven Web applications where data comes from many different types of data stores and some of them return tabular data while some others return hierarchical data. Therefore there's no way to guarantee that tabular and hierarchical data-bound controls will always receive tabular and hierarchical data, respectively, from their underlying data stores.

As discussed in Chapters 12–16, the ASP.NET 2.0 data source control model comes with two types of data source controls known as tabular and hierarchical data source controls. Tabular data source controls such as SqlDataSource provide tabular data-bound controls such as GridView with tabular views of their underlying data store whether or not the data store itself is tabular. Hierarchical data source controls such as XmlDataSource, on the other hand, provide hierarchical data-bound controls such as TreeView with hierarchical views of their underlying data store whether or not the data store itself is hierarchical.

As mentioned, this chapter only focuses on the tabular data-bound controls. As discussed in previous chapters, the ASP.NET 2.0 tabular data source control model comes with several standard tabular data source controls such as SqlDataSource, XmlDataSource, and so on.

Each type of tabular data source control and its associated view class are designed to work with a specific type of data store. For instance, the SqlDataSource control and its associated SqlDataSourceView class know how to update and query data from relational data stores such as Microsoft SQL Server databases, whereas the XmlDataSource control and its associated XmlDataSourceView class know how to query data from an XML document.

However, because all tabular data source controls and their associated view classes implement the IDataSource interface and DataSourceView abstract base class, respectively, the DataBoundControl class doesn't have to deal with the particular features of each data source control and its associated view class and can treat all of them as objects of type IDataSource and DataSourceView, respectively.

In other words, the DataBoundControl uses the methods and properties of the IDataSource interface and DataSourceView abstract base class to deal with the underlying tabular data source control and its associated view class and doesn't use any methods and properties that are specific to a particular type of data source control and data source view such as SqlDataSource and SqlDataSourceView.

This section implements a fully functional replica of the ASP.NET 2.0 DataBoundControl class to show you how this class takes advantage of the ASP.NET 2.0 data source control model to access any type of data store.

Because the DataBoundControl class derives from the BaseDataBoundControl class, it provides its subclasses with the infrastructure they need to automate all three data-binding tasks as discussed earlier. This means that all custom controls that derive from the DataBoundControl class can be used declaratively without writing any C# code.

The DataBoundControl class takes the following actions:

1. Implements a method named GetDataSource to access the data source control that provides tabular views of the underlying data store.

2. Implements a method named GetData to access the default tabular view of the data source control.

3. Overrides the methods of its base class, specifically the PerformSelect, ValidateDataSource, and On_Load methods.

The GetDataSource Method

The first challenge that the DataBoundControl base class must face is how to access the underlying ASP.NET 2.0 tabular data source control in generic fashion. In other words, the DataBoundControl class mustn't directly access any particular type of data source control such as SqlDataSource, or else the class would be tied to a particular type of data store and wouldn't be able to work with other types of data stores.

Because the declared data source controls are automatically added to the control tree of the containing page, the GetDataSource method calls the FindControl method of the Page class to access the underlying data source control. The FindControl method takes the value of the ID property of the data source control, locates the data source control in the control tree, and returns a reference to it:

```
protected IDataSource GetDataSource()
{
    return (IDataSource)Page.FindControl(DataSourceID);
}
```

Notice that the GetDataSource control returns an object of type IDataSource. As far as the DataBoundControl class is concerned, all data source controls are of type IDataSource. This allows page developers to switch from one type of tabular data source control to another without breaking the application. Recall that page developers switch from one type of tabular data source control to another to access a different type of data store.

The GetData Method

The IDataSource interface exposes a method named GetView that takes the view name as its argument and returns a view object. The type of the view object depends on the type of the data source control. For instance, the SqlDataSource and XmlDataSource controls expose view objects of type SqlDataSourceView and XmlDataSourceView, respectively.

Because all view classes derive from the DataSourceView abstract class, the DataBoundControl class uses the methods and properties of this class to access the underlying data source view object in generic fashion without knowing its real type:

```
protected DataSourceView GetData()
{
  IDataSource ds = GetDataSource();
  DataSourceView dv = ds.GetView("DefaultView");
  return dv;
}
```

The GetData method first calls the GetDataSource method to access the data source control, then calls the GetView method of the data source control with an empty string as its argument to access the default tabular DataSourceView object.

To keep things simple, this chapter provides a straightforward implementation for the GetData method. Another approach is to encapsulate the DataSource value in a DataSourceView object. This chapter's implementation can easily be extended to use a DataSourceView object instead.

For data access, the GetData method is the most important method of the DataBoundControl class because the method returns the DataSourceView object that represents the default tabular view of the underlying data store. As you'll see later, the DataSourceView object is all you need to update, delete, insert, and retrieve data from the underlying data store.

Overriding the Abstract Methods of the BaseDataBoundControl

Because the DataBoundControl class derives from the BaseDataBoundControl class, it must implement the PerformSelect and ValidateDataSource methods. The DataBoundControl class's implementation of the ValidateDataSource method is kept very simple to keep the focus on the main theme of this chapter. However, you can easily extend it to support any data source of type IListSource:

```
protected override void ValidateDataSource(object dataSource)
{
  if (!dataSource is IEnumerable
    throw new Exception("This data source is not supported");
}
```

Now for the DataBoundControl class's implementation of the PerformSelect method. Recall that all subclasses of the BaseDataBoundControl class must take the following actions:

1. Implement the RetrieveData method.

2. Implement the EnumerateDataAndCreateControlHierarchy method.

3. Override the PerformSelect method to call the other two methods.

The DataBoundControl class is no exception, and takes these three steps as detailed here:

1. Because the DataBoundControl class is a base class, it doesn't expose or implement the EnumerateDataAndCreateControlHierarchy method. However, it defines a new abstract method named PerformDataBinding. The subclasses of the DataBoundControl class must implement the EnumerateDataAndCreateControlHierarchy method and call the method from their implementation of the PerformDataBinding method. You'll see an example of this later in this chapter:

```
protected abstract void PerformDataBinding(IEnumerable data);
```

2. The DataBoundControl class's implementation of the PerformSelect method automatically calls the RetrieveData and PerformDataBinding methods (see Listing 17-5).

3. Thanks to the ASP.NET 2.0 data source control model, the DataBoundControl class is able to implement the RetrieveData method in generic fashion where the method is capable of retrieving tabular data from any type of data store (see Listing 17-6).

The PerformSelect Method

The DataBoundControl class, like all other classes that derive from the BaseDataBoundControl class, implements the PerformSelect method of its base class, as shown in Listing 17-5.

Listing 17-5: The PerformSelect method

```
protected override void PerformSelect()
{
  if (IsBoundUsingDataSourceID && DataSource != null)
    throw new Exception("Both DataSourceID and DataSource properties cannot be set
                         at the same time!");

  OnDataBinding(EventArgs.Empty);
  if (IsBoundUsingDataSourceID)
    RetrieveData();
  else
    PerformDataBinding(GetEnumerableDataSource());
}
```

The `PerformSelect` method first checks whether the value of the `IsBoundUsingDataSourceID` property is set to true. If so, the `PerformSelect` method takes control of data query, and calls the `RetrieveData` method. As discussed, there are two different approaches for retrieving data records from the underlying data store. The first approach is the traditional ASP.NET 1.x approach where the page developer must retrieve the data, populate an `IEnumerable` collection with the retrieved data, and assign the collection to the `DataSource` property. The second approach is the new ASP.NET 2.0 approach where the page developer sets the `DataSourceID` property to the value of the `ID` property of a data source control such as `SqlDataSource` and leaves the task of retrieving the data to the ASP.NET 2.0 Framework.

`DataBoundControl` inherits the `IsBoundUsingDataSourceID` property from the `BaseDataBound Control` class. `BaseDataBoundControl` sets the value of this property to true if the second approach is being used to retrieve the data from the underlying data store and false otherwise.

The RetrieveData Method

Listing 17-6 contains the code for the `DataBoundControl` class's implementation of the `RetrieveData` method.

Listing 17-6: The RetrieveData method

```
void RetrieveData()
{
  DataSourceView dv = GetData();
  dv.Select(CreateDataSourceSelectArguments(),
            new DataSourceViewSelectCallback(PerformDataBinding));
}
```

If you compare Listing 17-6 with Listing 17-3, you can see that the ASP.NET 2.0 data source control model dramatically simplifies the `RetrieveData` method. This shows how much easier it is to write generic data access code in the ASP.NET 2.0 Framework.

As Listing 17-6 shows, the `RetrieveData` method first calls the `GetData` method to access the `DataSourceView` object that represents the default tabular view of the underlying data store, and then calls the `Select` method of the view object to retrieve tabular data from the underlying data store. The `Select` method takes two arguments. The first argument takes an object of type `DataSourceSelectArguments`. As discussed in previous chapters, this object is used to request extra operations such as sorting and paging on the retrieved data.

Different subclasses of the DataBoundControl class might be interested in different operations of the DataSourceSelectArguments class. For example, those custom controls that support sorting but not paging are only interested in the sorting capability of the DataSourceSelectArguments class, not its paging capability. Therefore the DataBoundControl class must provide its subclasses with a mechanism that will allow them to choose the desired capabilities of the DataSourceSelectArguments object. But how?

The DataBoundControl class exposes a method named CreateDataSourceSelectArguments that its subclasses can override to set the desired properties of the DataSourceSelectArguments class:

```
protected virtual DataSourceSelectArguments CreateDataSourceSelectArguments()
{
  return new DataSourceSelectArguments();
}
```

The DataBoundControl class's implementation of the CreateDataSourceSelectArguments method simply creates an instance of the DataSourceSelectArguments class without setting any of its properties. In other words, the DataBoundControl class doesn't request any extra operations such as sorting and paging on the retrieved data.

As Listing 17-6 shows, the RetrieveData method calls the CreateDataSourceSelectArguments method and passes the appropriate DataSourceSelectArguments object as the first argument of the Select method of the view object. Because the Select method is asynchronous, the RetrieveData method registers the PerformDataBinding abstract method as the callback.

The Select method first retrieves the tabular data from the underlying data store, stores the retrieved data in an object of type IEnumerable, and then automatically calls the PerformDataBinding method and passes the IEnumerable object as its argument. The subclasses of the DataBoundControl class must implement the PerformDataBinding method, where they must enumerate the IEnumerable object and create the appropriate control hierarchy.

Overriding the OnLoad Method

The DataBoundControl class also overrides the OnLoad method, where it sets the RequiresDataBinding property to true to trigger the data-binding process (see Listing 17-7). Therefore when the containing page is accessed for the first time, the DataBoundControl class automatically retrieves the required data from the data store and calls the PerformDataBinding method of its respective subclass to create the appropriate control hierarchy.

Listing 17-7: The DataBoundControl class overrides the OnLoad method

```
protected override void OnLoad(EventArgs e)
{
  if (!Page.IsPostBack)
  {
    if (IsBoundUsingDataSourceID)
    {
      Control c = Page.FindControl(DataSourceID);
      if (c == null)
        throw new Exception("The data source " + DataSourceID + "does not exist!");
      IDataSource ds = c as IDataSource;
      if (ds == null)
```

(continued)

Listing 17-7: *(continued)*

```
        throw new Exception("The data source " + DataSourceID + " is not of type
                          IDataSource!");
    }
    RequiresDataBinding = true;
  }
  base.OnLoad(e);
}
```

In summary, the `DataBoundControl` base class provides its subclasses with the following features:

❑   Because the `DataBoundControl` base class derives from the `BaseDataBoundControl` base class, it provides its subclasses with the infrastructure they need to automate all three data-binding tasks. This means that the custom data-bound controls that derive from the `DataBoundControl` class can be used declaratively without writing C# code.

❑   Chapters 12, 13, and 14 showed you how to develop tabular custom data source controls for any desired data store whether or not the data store itself is tabular. This means that the `DataBoundControl` class is capable of automatically retrieving tabular data from any type of data store. As you'll see in the next several chapters, this allows you to implement data store–agnostic tabular custom data-bound controls that can display data from any type of data store.

Developing Custom Data-Bound Controls That Derive from DataBoundControl

Now revisit the example custom data-bound control. So far this chapter has presented two different approaches to implement the custom control. The second approach derived the custom control from the `BaseDataBoundControl` class. Recall that the second approach named the control `CustomTable2`. The great thing about the `CustomTable2` control is that page developers can use the control declaratively.

The main problem with the `CustomTable2` control is the fact that it's tied to specific types of data stores, that is, those that expose tabular data. This means that the `CustomTable2` control wouldn't work with data stores such as XML files that don't expose tabular data.

This section replaces the `CustomTable2` control with a new custom data-bound control named `CustomTable3` that derives from the `DataBoundControl` class.

Overriding the CreateDataSourceSelectArguments Method

Because the `CustomTable3` control supports sorting and paging, it overrides the `CreateDataSource SelectArguments` method of the `DataBoundControl` class to set the appropriate properties of the `DataSourceSelectArguments` object (see Listing 17-8).

Listing 17-8: The Overridden CreateDataSourceSelectArguments method

```
DataSourceSelectArguments dataSourceSelectArguments = null;
protected override DataSourceSelectArguments CreateDataSourceSelectArguments()
{
  dataSourceSelectArguments = new DataSourceSelectArguments();

  DataSourceView dv = GetData();
  if (dv.CanSort)
  {
    string sortExpression = (string)ViewState["SortExpression"] + " " +
                            (string)ViewState["SortDirection"];
    if (sortExpression != null && sortExpression.Trim() != "")
      dataSourceSelectArguments.SortExpression = sortExpression;

    else
      dataSourceSelectArguments.SortExpression = DataKeyField + " " + "Asc";
  }

  if (dv.CanPage)
  {
    dataSourceSelectArguments.StartRowIndex = CurrentPageIndex - 1;
    dataSourceSelectArguments.MaximumRows = PageSize;
  }

  if (dv.CanRetrieveTotalRowCount)
    dataSourceSelectArguments.RetrieveTotalRowCount = true;

  return dataSourceSelectArguments;
}
```

The `CreateDataSourceSelectArguments` method first creates an instance of the `DataSourceSelectArguments` class:

```
dataSourceSelectArguments = new DataSourceSelectArguments();
```

Next it calls the `GetData` method of the `DataBoundControl` class to access the view object that represents the default tabular view of the underlying data store:

```
DataSourceView dv = GetData();
```

The method then calls the `CanSort` property of the view object to check whether the view supports sorting. If so, it retrieves the required information from the `ViewState` collection, evaluates the sort expression value, and assigns the value to the `SortExpression` property of the `DataSourceSelectArguments` instance. The underlying stored procedure uses the value of the `SortExpression` property to sort the retrieved data:

```
if (dv.CanSort)
{
  string sortExpression = (string)ViewState["SortExpression"] + " " +
                          (string)ViewState["SortDirection"];
```

```
    if (sortExpression != null && sortExpression.Trim() != "")
      dataSourceSelectArguments.SortExpression = sortExpression;

    else
      dataSourceSelectArguments.SortExpression = DataKeyField + " " + "Asc";
}
```

Next, the method calls the CanPage property of the view object to check whether the view supports paging. If so, it assigns the current page index and page size to the StartRowIndex and MaximumRows properties of the DataSourceSelectArguments object. The underlying stored procedure uses these two values to retrieve the appropriate page of records:

```
if (dv.CanPage)
{
  dataSourceSelectArguments.StartRowIndex = CurrentPageIndex - 1;
  dataSourceSelectArguments.MaximumRows = PageSize;
}
```

Finally, the method calls the CanRetrieveTotalRowCount property of the view object to check whether the view is capable of retrieving the total row count. If so, it sets the RetrieveToalRowCount property of the DataSourceSelectArguments object to true to request the view object to retrieve the total row count from the data store. The EnumerateDataAndCreateControlHierarchy method of the CustomTable3 control uses the total row count to determine how many LinkButton controls it needs to render in its paging interface:

```
if (dv.CanRetrieveTotalRowCount)
    dataSourceSelectArguments.RetrieveTotalRowCount = true;
```

Overriding the PerformDataBinding Method

The CustomTable3 control implements the PerformDataBinding abstract method of the DataBoundControl class, as shown in Listing 17-9. Notice that the PerformDataBinding method first assigns the value of the TotalRowCount property of the DataSourceSelectArguments object to the TotalNumberOfRecords property of the CustomTable3 control.

Listing 17-9: The PerformDataBinding method

```
protected override void PerformDataBinding(IEnumerable data)
{
  TotalNumberOfRecords = dataSourceSelectArguments.TotalRowCount;
  Controls.Clear();
  ClearChildViewState();
  TrackViewState();
  ViewState["RowCount"] = EnumerateDataAndCreateControlHierarchy(data, true);
  RequiresDataBinding = false;
}
```

Recall that the main reason for replacing the CustomTable2 control with the CustomTable3 control is the fact that the CustomTable2 control's implementations of the RetrieveData, UpdateCallback, DeleteCallback, and so on aren't data store–agnostic.

Listing 17-18 shows how the DataBoundControl base class provides a data store–agnostic version of the RetrieveData method. Because the CustomTable3 control derives from the DataBoundControl base class, it automatically inherits the DataBoundControl class's data store–agnostic implementation of the RetrieveData method. Next you'll see how the CustomTable3 control implements the data store–agnostic versions of the UpdateCallback and DeleteCallback methods.

The UpdateCallback Method

Listing 17-10 presents the CustomTable3 control's implementation of the UpdateCallback method.

Listing 17-10: The UpdateCallback method

```
void UpdateCallback(CustomTableCommandEventArgs e)
{
  DataSourceView dv = GetData();
  if (dv.CanUpdate)
  {
    int index = int.Parse(e.CommandArgument);
    int primaryKey = (int)DataKeys[index];

    Hashtable keys = new Hashtable();
    keys.Add(DataKeyField, primaryKey);

    Hashtable values = new Hashtable();
    Hashtable oldValues = new Hashtable();

    foreach (TableCell cell in this[index].Cells)
    {
      if (cell.Controls.Count > 0)
      {
        TextBox tb = cell.Controls[0] as TextBox;
        if (tb != null)
        {
          values.Add(tb.Attributes["FieldName"], tb.Text);
          oldValues.Add(tb.Attributes["FieldName"], tb.Text);
        }
      }
    }

    dv.Update(keys, values, oldValues,
            new DataSourceViewOperationCallback(UpdateOperationCallback));

    EditRowIndex = -1;
    RequiresDataBinding = true;
  }
}
```

This method first calls the GetData method to access the view object that represents the default tabular view of the data store:

```
DataSourceView dv = GetData();
```

It then checks whether the CanUpdate property of the view object is set to true to ensure that the view is capable of updating the data store. The Update method of the view object takes three important arguments. The first argument is an IDictionary object that contains the primary key field names and values. This means that the Update method supports multiple field primary keys. The CustomTable3 control extracts the primary key value from the DataKeys collection and stores the primary key field name and value into a Hashtable object:

```
int index = int.Parse(e.CommandArgument);
int primaryKey = (int)DataKeys[index];

Hashtable keys = new Hashtable();
keys.Add(DataKeyField, primaryKey);
```

The second argument is an IDictionary object that contains the names and new values of the database fields being updated. The CustomTable3 control enumerates the cells of the specified row to locate those cells that contain a text box. It then extracts the name and value of the respective database field from the Attributes and Text properties of the respective text box. The UpdateCallback method then stores these field names and values into a Hashtable object:

```
foreach (TableCell cell in this[index].Cells)
{
  if (cell.Controls.Count > 0)
  {
    TextBox tb = cell.Controls[0] as TextBox;
    if (tb != null)
    {
      values.Add(tb.Attributes["FieldName"], tb.Text);
      oldValues.Add(tb.Attributes["FieldName"], tb.Text);
    }
  }
}
```

The last argument of the Update method is a DataSourceViewOperationCallback delegate object that encapsulates the callback for the Update method. This is necessary because the Update method is asynchronous:

```
dv.Update(keys, values, oldValues,
            new DataSourceViewOperationCallback(UpdateOperationCallback));
```

Notice that the UpdateCallback method finally sets the RequiresDataBinding property to true to trigger the data-binding process where fresh data is retrieved and enumerated to update the display of the control.

The DeleteCallback Method

Listing 17-11 shows the CustomTable3 control's implementation of the DeleteCallback method.

Listing 17-11: The DeleteCallback method

```
void DeleteCallback(CustomTableCommandEventArgs e)
{
  DataSourceView dv = GetData();
  if (dv.CanDelete)
```

```
    {
        int index = int.Parse(e.CommandArgument);
        int primaryKey = (int)DataKeys[index];

        Hashtable keys = new Hashtable();
        keys.Add(DataKeyField, primaryKey);

        Hashtable oldValues = new Hashtable();

        dv.Delete(keys, oldValues,
                new DataSourceViewOperationCallback(DeleteOperationCallback));

        EditRowIndex = -1;
        RequiresDataBinding = true;
    }
}
```

The method first calls the GetData method to access the default tabular view object. It then calls the
CanDelete property to check whether the view object is capable of deleting data records from the data
store.

The Delete method of the view object takes two important arguments. The first argument is an
IDictionary object that contains the primary key field names and values. The DeleteCallback
method extracts the primary key value from the DataKeys collection and stores the primary key name
and value into a Hashtable object. The last argument is a DataSourceViewOperationCallback delegate object that encapsulates the callback for the Delete operation. This is necessary because the Delete
method is asynchronous:

```
dv.Delete(keys, oldValues,
        new DataSourceViewOperationCallback(DeleteOperationCallback));
```

Codeless Data-Agnostic Declarative Programming

As Listing 17-12 shows, page developers can use the CustomTable3 control declaratively without writing a single line of code.

Listing 17-12: Use the CustomTable3 control declaratively

```
<%@ Page Language="C#" %>
<%@ Register TagPrefix="custom" Namespace="CustomComponents" %>
<!DOCTYPE html PUBLIC "-//W3C//DTD XHTML 1.1//EN"
"http://www.w3.org/TR/xhtml11/DTD/xhtml11.dtd">
<html xmlns="http://www.w3.org/1999/xhtml">
<head runat="server">
  <title>Untitled Page</title>
</head>
<body>
  <form id="form1" runat="server">
    <custom:CustomTable3 runat="server" ID="ct" DataSourceID="MySource"
    DataKeyField="BookID" />

    <asp:ObjectDataSource ID="MySource" runat="Server" EnablePaging="true"
```

(continued)

Listing 17-12: *(continued)*

```
        SortParameterName="SortExpression" SelectMethod="GetOnePageOfData"
        StartRowIndexParameterName="CurrentPageIndex" TypeName="Books"
        MaximumRowsParameterName="PageSize" DeleteMethod="DeleteBook"
        SelectCountMethod="GetTotalCount" UpdateMethod="UpdateBook"
        InsertMethod="InsertBook">
        <SelectParameters>
          <asp:Parameter Name="PageSize" Type="Int32" />
          <asp:Parameter Name="CurrentPageIndex" Type="Int32" />
          <asp:Parameter Name="SortExpression" Type="String" />
        </SelectParameters>
        <UpdateParameters>
          <asp:Parameter Name="BookID" Type="Int32" />
          <asp:Parameter Name="Price" Type="Decimal" />
        </UpdateParameters>
        <DeleteParameters>
          <asp:Parameter Name="original_BookID" Type="Int32" />
        </DeleteParameters>
        <InsertParameters>
          <asp:Parameter Name="Price" Type="Decimal" />
        </InsertParameters>
      </asp:ObjectDataSource>
    </form>
  </body>
</html>
```

Notice that the `DataSourceID` property of the `CustomTable3` control is set to the value of the `ID` property of the `ObjectDataSource` control. In other words, the only thing that ties the `CustomTable3` control to the data source control is the `ID` property value, which is a string value.

This means that page developers can easily switch from the `ObjectDataSource` control to another tabular data source control such as `XmlDataSource` without breaking the application. The `CustomTable3` control doesn't care what type of tabular data source control is used as long as the data source control is tabular, that is, it implements the `IDataSource` interface.

It doesn't matter whether the underlying data store is tabular. For example, the underlying data store of the `XmlDataSource` control is an XML document, which isn't tabular. This doesn't cause any problems because the `XmlDataSource` control exposes tabular views of its underlying XML document.

CompositeDataBoundControl

It may seem that you should derive all of your custom controls from the `DataSourceControl` base class because it provides everything a custom data-bound control needs, specifically:

❑ Page developers can use the custom controls declaratively.

❑ The custom controls can access any type of data store.

Then why do you need the `CompositeDataBoundControl` base class? To find the answer to this question, take another look at the `CustomTable3` control. Many custom data-bound controls follow the same implementation pattern as the `CustomTable3` control:

1. They all expose a method such as `EnumerateDataAndCreateControlHierarchy` that takes two arguments. The first argument takes an `IEnumerable` object whose contents depend on the value of the second argument. If the second argument is set to true, the `IEnumerable` object contains the actual data records. Otherwise, the `IEnumerable` object is a dummy data source for enumeration purposes.

2. They all override the `CreateChildControls` method to create the control hierarchy from the saved view state and take the following actions if the view state contains the required information:

a.   Call the `Clear` method of the `Controls` collection to clear the collection:

```
Controls.Clear();
```

b.   Create a dummy data source of type `IEnumerable`:

```
object[] dummyDataSource = new object[(int)ViewState["RowCount"];
```

c.   Call the `EnumerateDataAndCreateControlHierarchy` method and pass the method the `IEnumerable` object as its first argument and false as its second argument:

```
EnumerateDataAndCreateControlHierarchy(dummyDataSource, false);
```

The false value signals the fact that the `IEnumerable` object doesn't contain real data records.

3. They all override the `PerformDataBinding` method, where they take the following actions:

a.   Call the `Clear` method of the `Controls` collection to clear the collection.

b.   Call the `ClearChildViewState` method to delete the view state information for all child controls.

c.   Call the `TrackViewState` method to start view state tracking.

d.   Call the `EnumerateDataAndCreateControlHierarchy` method and pass the method the `IEnumerable` object as its first argument and `true` as its second argument, and store the return value in the `ViewState` collection:

```
ViewState["RowCount"] = EnumerateDataAndCreateControlHierarchy(data, true);
```

e.   Set the `RequiresDataBinding` property to false.

4. They all override the `Collections` property to call the `EnsureChildControls` method:

```
public override ControlCollection Controls
{
  get
  {
    EnsureChildControls();
    return base.Controls;
  }
}
```

The `CompositeDataBoundControl` base class encapsulates the code for all four of these steps, saving you from having to implement them each time you develop a custom tabular data-bound control.

Because the `CompositeDataBoundControl` base class derives from the `DataBoundControl` class, custom data-bound controls that derive from the `CompositeDataBoundControl` base class can be used declaratively, and can access any type of data store.

Overriding the PerformDataBinding Method

The `CompositeDataBoundControl` base class provides the following implementation for the `PerformDataBinding` abstract method that it inherits from the `DataBoundControl` base class:

```
private IEnumerable dataSource;
protected override void PerformDataBinding(IEnumerable data)
{
    dataSource = data;
    DataBind(false);
}
```

The method assigns the `IEnumerable` object that contains the retrieved data to the `dataSource` field and calls the `DataBind` method with the `false` argument.

Overriding the DataBind Method

The `CompositeDataBoundControl` class inherits the overload of the `DataBind` method from the `Control` class and implements it as follows:

```
protected override void DataBind(bool raiseOnDataBinding)
{
  if (raiseOnDataBinding)
    base.OnDataBinding(System.EventArgs.Empty);
  Controls.Clear();
  ClearChildViewState();
  TrackViewState();
  ViewState["RowCount"] = CreateChildControls(dataSource, true);
  ChildControlsCreated = true;
}
```

The method first clears the `Controls` collection, deletes the view state information of the child controls, and calls the `TrackViewState` method to start the view state tracking. It then calls the following overload of the `CreateChildControls` method:

```
protected abstract int CreateChildControls(IEnumerable dataSource,
                                           bool useDataSource);
```

Notice that the overload of the `CreateChildControls` method is nothing but what the text has been referring to as the `EnumeratDataAndCreateControlHierarchy` method.

Because the `DataBoundControl` class guarantees to automatically call the `PerformDataBinding` method every time the `RequiresDataBinding` property is set to true, the `CompositeDataBoundControl` guarantees to automatically call the `CreateChildControls` method every time the `RequiresDataBinding` property is set to true. In other words, the `CompositeDataBoundControl` class automates the invocation of the `CreateChildControls` method, but leaves the responsibility of implementing the method to its subclasses.

The method takes two arguments. The second argument specifies whether the first argument contains real data or dummy data for enumeration purposes. The subclasses must override the `CreateChildControls` method, where they must enumerate the data and create the control hierarchy from the saved view state if `useDataSource` is false, and from the data source otherwise.

Overriding the CreateChildControls Method

As discussed in Chapter 9, the following overload of the `CreateChildControls` method creates the control hierarchy from the saved view state:

```
protected override void CreateChildControls();
```

The `CompositeDataBoundControl` overrides this method to delegate the responsibility of creating the control hierarchy to the previous overload of the `CreateChildControls` method:

```
protected override void CreateChildControls()
{
  Controls.Clear();

  if (ViewState["RowCount"] != null)
    ViewState["RowCount"] = CreateChildControls(
                                    new object[(int)ViewState["RowCount"]], false);
}
```

The method creates an array of objects and passes it as the first argument of the `CreateChildControls` method. The subclasses of the `CompositeDataBoundControl` must enumerate this dummy data source to create the control hierarchy from the saved view state.

Overriding the Controls Collection

The `CompositeDataBoundControl` class also overrides the `Controls` collection to call the `EnsureChildControls` method:

```
public override ControlCollection Controls
{
  get
  {
      EnsureChildControls();
      return base.Controls;
  }
}
```

This ensures that the `Controls` collection is populated before it is accessed.

Implementing a custom data-bound control that derives from the `CompositeDataBoundControl` base class is pretty easy. The only method that the custom data-bound control must implement is the `CreateChildControls` abstract method. The ASP.NET 2.0 data-bound control model automatically takes care of everything else.

Developing Controls That Derive from CompositeDataBoundControl

Now revisit the custom data-bound control for the last time. So far this chapter has presented three different approaches to implement the control. The third approach derives the control from the `DataBoundControl` base class, and is named `CustomTable3`.

This section replaces the `CustomTable3` control with a new custom data-bound control named `CustomTable4` that derives from the `CompositeDataBoundControl` base class. Deriving from the `CompositeDataBoundControl` base class will save you from having to implement and override the following methods:

```
protected override void CreateChildControls();
protected override void PerformDataBinding(IEnumerable data);
public override ControlCollection Controls { get;}
```

The `CustomTable4` control implements the `CreateChildControls` abstract method of the `CompositeDataBoundControl` class. The implementation of this method is the same as the `EnumerateDataAndCreateControlHierarchy` method discussed before. The following section implements another custom data-bound control that derives from the `CompositeDataBoundBase` base class.

MasterDetailForm

In this section you develop a new custom data-bound control named `MasterDetailForm` that renders two tables. The top table displays the desired database records in table rows where each row comes with a link button that allows the user to select the row. The bottom table allows the user to select a record from the top table to view its details, update its fields, or delete it. The bottom table also allows the user to add a new record.

The top and bottom tables are referred to as the master and detail tables, respectively. The `MasterDetailForm` control exposes a property named `MasterFields` that allows page developers to specify which database fields should be displayed in the top table.

The `MasterDetailForm` data-bound control derives from the `CompositeDataBoundControl` base class and implements its `CreateChildControls` method as shown in Listing 17-13.

Listing 17-13: The CreateChildControls method for MasterDetailForm

```
protected override int CreateChildControls(IEnumerable dataSource,
                                           bool useDataSource)
{
  this.useDataSource = useDataSource;

  if (dataSource != null)
  {
    CreateMasterDetailsTables();
    renderHeader = true;
```

```
        currentRowIndex = 0;
        IEnumerator iter = dataSource.GetEnumerator();
        while (iter.MoveNext())
        {
          this.currentDataItem = iter.Current;
          currentMasterBodyRow = new TableRow();

          if (currentRowIndex % 2 == 1)
            currentMasterBodyRow.SkinID = MasterAlternatingRowSkinID;
          else
            currentMasterBodyRow.SkinID = MasterRowSkinID;

          masterTable.Rows.Add(currentMasterBodyRow);
          SetParameters();

          for (int i = 0; i < columnCount; i++)
          {
            currentFieldIndex = i;
            AddDetailRow();
            AddMasterCell();
          }

          AddMasterSelectButton();
          renderHeader = false;
          currentRowIndex++;
        }

        AddDetailsCommandBar();
        AddErrorMessageLabel();

        if (useDataSource)
          ViewState["ColumnCount"] = columnCount;
      }

    return currentRowIndex;
  }
```

The method enumerates the records in the IEnumerable collection (dataSource argument) to create the control hierarchy from the data source if useDataSource is true (if the records are real database records) and from the saved view state otherwise (if the records are dummy records for enumeration purposes). The for loop enumerates the fields or columns of each enumerated record and calls the AddDetailsRow and AddMasterCell methods to render each enumerated field in the master and detail tables, respectively. The master table displays each enumerated field as a cell; the detail table displays it as a row.

As Listing 17-13 illustrates, the CreateChildControls method first creates the master and detail tables:

```
CreateMasterDetailTables();
```

Listing 17-14 contains the implementation of the CreateMasterDetailTables method.

Listing 17-14: The CreateMasterDetailTables method

```
private void CreateMasterDetailTables()
{
  masterTable = new Table();
  masterTable.SkinID = MasterTableSkinID;
  masterTable.EnableTheming = MasterTableEnableTheming;
  Controls.Add(masterTable);

  LiteralControl c = new LiteralControl("<br/>");
  Controls.Add(c);

  detailTable = new Table();
  detailTable.SkinID = DetailsTableSkinID;
  detailTable.EnableTheming = DetailsTableEnableTheming;
  Controls.Add(detailTable);

  masterHeaderRow = new TableHeaderRow();
  masterHeaderRow.SkinID = MasterHeaderRowSkinID;
  masterTable.Rows.Add(masterHeaderRow);
}
```

The `CreateChildControls` method next calls the `GetEnumerator` method of the `IEnumerable` collection that contains the (real or dummy) data records to access its enumerator and uses the enumerator to iterate through the data records in generic fashion:

```
IEnumerator iter = dataSource.GetEnumerator();
while (iter.MoveNext())
{
  . . .
}
```

The method then stores the reference to the current enumerated data record in a private field named `currentDataItem` for future reference:

```
this.currentDataItem = iter.Current;
```

Then it creates the table row that will be used to display the enumerated record in the master table, stores the reference to this table row in a private field named `currentMasterBodyRow` for future reference, and adds this table row to the master table:

```
currentMasterBodyRow = new TableRow();
masterTable.Rows.Add(currentMasterBodyRow);
```

Next, the method sets the parameters of the `MasterDetailForm` control:

```
SetParameters();
```

Listing 17-15 contains the code for the `SetParameters` method.

Listing 17-15: The SetParameters method initializes the MasterDetailForm control

```
private void SetParameters()
{
  if (!renderHeader)
    return;

  if (useDataSource)
  {
    PropertyDescriptorCollection tempDataItemFields =
                              TypeDescriptor.GetProperties(currentDataItem);
    ArrayList list = new ArrayList();
    foreach (PropertyDescriptor pd in tempDataItemFields)
    {
      if (pd.Converter.CanConvertTo(Type.GetType("System.String")))
      {
        list.Add(pd);
        if (pd.Name == DataKeyField)
          DataKeyFieldIndex = list.IndexOf(pd);
      }
    }
    currentDataItemFieldsPropertyDescriptors = new PropertyDescriptor[list.Count];
    list.CopyTo(currentDataItemFieldsPropertyDescriptors);

    columnCount = currentDataItemFieldsPropertyDescriptors.Length;
    string[] strs = MasterFields.Split(new char[] { ',' }, 20);
    foreach (string str in strs)
    {
      for (int i = 0; i < columnCount; i++)
      {
        if (currentDataItemFieldsPropertyDescriptors[i].Name == str)
          MasterFieldIndices.Add(i);
      }
    }
  }

  else
    columnCount = (int)ViewState["ColumnCount"];
}
```

The SetParameters method sets the following parameters before the CreateChildControls method begins iterating through the fields or columns of the current data record:

❑ currentDataItemFieldsPropertyDescriptors: The SetParameters method populates this array with the PropertyDescriptor objects that represent the fields or columns of the database records in generic fashion. The method calls the GetProperties of the TypeDescriptor class and passes the current data record into it to return the collection that contains the PropertyDescriptor objects:

```
PropertyDescriptorCollection tempDataItemFields =
                            TypeDescriptor.GetProperties(currentDataItem);
```

MasterDetailForm only supports those fields whose values can be converted to strings. That is why SetParameters iterates through the PropertyDescriptor objects and uses the TypeConverter object associated with each enumerated PropertyDescriptor object to determine whether the value of the data field or column that the PropertyDescriptor object represents can be converted to string. In other words, the currentDataItemFieldProperty Descriptors collection only contains those PropertyDescriptor objects whose associated data field values can be converted to strings:

```
foreach (PropertyDescriptor pd in tempDataItemFields)
{
  if (pd.Converter.CanConvertTo(Type.GetType("System.String")))
  {
    list.Add(pd);
    if (pd.Name == DataKeyField)
      DataKeyFieldIndex = list.IndexOf(pd);
  }
}
```

❑ DataKeyFieldIndex: As the code fragment illustrates, SetParameters stores the index of the PropertyDescriptor object that represents the primary key field or column in the DataKeyFieldIndex property of the MasterDetailForm for future reference.

❑ MasterFieldIndices: SetParameters iterates through the PropertyDescriptor objects and stores the indices of those objects that represent the database fields whose names are included in the MasterFields property:

```
string[] strs = MasterFields.Split(new char[] { ',' }, 20);
foreach (string str in strs)
{
  for (int i = 0; i < columnCount; i++)
  {
    if (currentDataItemFieldsPropertyDescriptors[i].Name == str)
      MasterFieldIndices.Add(i);
  }
}
```

❑ columnCount: SetParameters retrieves the column count from the saved view state if the control hierarchy is being created from the saved view state:

```
columnCount = (int)ViewState["ColumnCount"];
```

If the control hierarchy is being created from the data source, the total count of the PropertyDescriptor objects represents the column count:

```
columnCount = currentDataItemFieldsPropertyDescriptors.Length;
```

After SetParameters is finished, the CreateChildControls method iterates through the columns or fields of the enumerated data record and calls the AddDetailRow and AddMasterCell methods for each enumerated column or field. These calls display the field in the detail and master tables, respectively. The AddDetailRow and AddMasterCell are discussed in the following sections.

```
for (int i = 0; i < columnCount; i++)
{
  currentFieldIndex = i;
```

```
        AddDetailRow();
        AddMasterCell();
    }
```

The `CreateChildControls` method then calls the `AddMasterSelectButton` method to add a Select button to the table row that displays the enumerated data record. This method is discussed in the following sections.

```
        AddMasterSelectButton();
```

Next it calls the `AddDetailsCommandBar` method to display the command bar of the detail table. This method is discussed later in this chapter:

```
        AddDetailsCommandBar();
```

The method then stores the total column count in the saved view state if the control hierarchy is being created from the data source. This allows the page framework to re-create the same control hierarchy when the page is posted back to the server:

```
    if (useDataSource)
        ViewState["ColumnCount"] = columnCount;
```

Finally, the `CreateChildControls` method returns the total row count. Recall that the `CompositeDataBoundControl` automatically stores this value in the saved view state so the page framework can re-create the same control hierarchy from the saved view state when the page is posted back to the server:

```
    return currentRowIndex;
```

AddDetailRow

Listing 17-16 contains the code for the `AddDetailRow` method.

Listing 17-16: The AddDetailRow method

```
private void AddDetailRow()
{
    if (currentRowIndex != SelectedIndex ||
        (MasterDetailFormMode == MasterDetailFormMode.Insert &&
         DataKeyFieldIndex == currentFieldIndex))
        return;

    TableRow drow = new TableRow();

    if (currentFieldIndex % 2 == 1)
drow.SkinID = DetailsAlternatingRowSkinID;
    else
        drow.SkinID = DetailsRowSkinID;

    detailTable.Rows.Add(drow);
    TableCell dhcell = new TableCell();
```

(continued)

Listing 17-16: *(continued)*

```csharp
    drow.Cells.Add(dhcell);

    TableCell dcell = new TableCell();
    drow.Cells.Add(dcell);

    if (MasterDetailFormMode == MasterDetailFormMode.ReadOnly && useDataSource)
    {
      PropertyDescriptor pd =
                  currentDataItemFieldsPropertyDescriptors[currentFieldIndex];
      dcell.Text = pd.Converter.ConvertTo(pd.GetValue(currentDataItem),
                                    Type.GetType("System.String")).ToString();
    }

    else if (MasterDetailFormMode != MasterDetailFormMode.ReadOnly)
    {
      if (DataKeyFieldIndex != currentFieldIndex)
      {
        TextBox tbx = new TextBox();
        dcell.Controls.Add(tbx);

        if (useDataSource)
        {
          PropertyDescriptor pd =
                  currentDataItemFieldsPropertyDescriptors[currentFieldIndex];
          tbx.Attributes["FieldName"] = pd.Name;
          if (MasterDetailFormMode == MasterDetailFormMode.Edit)
            tbx.Text = pd.Converter.ConvertTo(pd.GetValue(currentDataItem),
                                    Type.GetType("System.String")).ToString();
        }
      }

      else if (useDataSource)
      {
        PropertyDescriptor pd =
                  currentDataItemFieldsPropertyDescriptors[currentFieldIndex];
        dcell.Text = pd.Converter.ConvertTo(pd.GetValue(currentDataItem),
                                    Type.GetType("System.String")).ToString();
      }
    }

    if (useDataSource)
    {
      PropertyDescriptor pd =
                  currentDataItemFieldsPropertyDescriptors[currentFieldIndex];
      dhcell.Text = pd.Name;

      if (pd.Name == DataKeyField)
        DataKeyFieldValue = dcell.Text;
    }
  }
```

The `AddDetailRow` method renders an instance of the `TextBox` control for each enumerated field when the detail table is in the Insert or Edit state. The method then stores the name of the enumerated field in the `Attributes` collection of the `TextBox` instance for future references:

```
TextBox tbx = new TextBox();
PropertyDescriptor pd =
                currentDataItemFieldsPropertyDescriptors[currentFieldIndex];
tbx.Attributes["FieldName"] = pd.Name;
```

The preceding code uses the value of the `Name` property of the respective `PropertyDescriptor` object to access the name of the field in generic fashion. The `AddDetailRow` method also displays the actual value of the enumerated field in the `TextBox` instance when the detail table is in the Edit state:

```
tbx.Text = pd.Converter.ConvertTo(pd.GetValue(currentDataItem),
                        Type.GetType("System.String")).ToString();
```

This code uses the `GetValue` method of the appropriate `PropertyDescriptor` object to access the value of the enumerated field, and uses the `ConvertTo` method of the `Converter` property of the `PropertyDescriptor` object to convert the value to a string. Recall that the current implementation of the `MasterDetailForm` control only displays fields whose values can be converted to string. Also notice that the method sets the value of the `DataKeyFieldValue` property to the primary key field value of the selected record. This property will be used in data operations such as `Delete`, `Update`, `Insert`, and `Sort` (discussed later).

AddMasterCell

The `AddMasterCell` method first calls the `AddMasterHeaderCell` method to add the header cell and then adds the data cell. Notice that the method uses the `currentFieldIndex` as an index into the `currentDataItemFieldsPropertyDescriptors` collection to access the `PropertyDescriptor` object that represents the current column or field. The method then uses the `GetValue` method to access the value of the field and displays the value in a table cell:

```
private void AddMasterCell()
{
  if (!MasterFieldIndices.Contains(currentFieldIndex))
    return;

  AddMasterHeaderCell();

  TableCell cell = new TableCell();
  currentMasterBodyRow.Cells.Add(cell);

  if (useDataSource)
  {
    PropertyDescriptor pd =
                currentDataItemFieldsPropertyDescriptors[currentFieldIndex];
    cell.Text = pd.Converter.ConvertTo(pd.GetValue(currentDataItem),
                        Type.GetType("System.String")).ToString();
  }
}
```

AddMasterHeaderCell

AddMasterHeaderCell renders a LinkButton if sorting is enabled, as shown in Listing 17-17. Notice that the CommandName of the LinkButton specifies the type of the event, such as sort.

Listing 17-17: The AddMasterHeaderCell method

```
private void AddMasterHeaderCell()
{
  if (renderHeader)
  {
    TableHeaderCell hcell = new TableHeaderCell();
    masterHeaderRow.Cells.Add(hcell);

    if (AllowSorting)
    {
      LinkButton hbtn = new LinkButton();
      hbtn.CommandName = "Sort";
      hbtn.Command += new CommandEventHandler(CommandCallback);
      hcell.Controls.Add(hbtn);

      if (useDataSource)
      {
        hbtn.CommandArgument =
               currentDataItemFieldsPropertyDescriptors[currentFieldIndex].Name;
        hbtn.Text =
               currentDataItemFieldsPropertyDescriptors[currentFieldIndex].Name;
      }
    }

    else if (useDataSource)
      hcell.Text =
             currentDataItemFieldsPropertyDescriptors[currentFieldIndex].Name;
  }
}
```

AddMasterSelectButton

Listing 17-18 presents the implementation of the AddMasterSelectButton method.

Listing 17-18: The AddMasterSelectButton method

```
private void AddMasterSelectButton()
{
  TableCell scell = new TableCell();
  currentMasterBodyRow.Cells.Add(scell);

  if (renderHeader)
  {
    TableCell cell = new TableCell();
    masterHeaderRow.Cells.Add(cell);
```

```
            }

            LinkButton lbtn = new LinkButton();
            scell.Controls.Add(lbtn);
            lbtn.Text = "Select";
            lbtn.CommandName = "Select";
            lbtn.CommandArgument = currentRowIndex.ToString();
            lbtn.Command += new CommandEventHandler(CommandCallback);
        }
```

After displaying all the fields of the enumerated record, the `CreateChildControls` method calls the `AddMasterSelectButton` method to display a select link button for the record and registers the `CommandCallback` method as the callback for the `Command` event of the button. The `AddMasterSelect Button` method sets the `CommandArgument` of the link button to the index of the enumerated record:

```
LinkButton lbtn = new LinkButton();
Lbtn.CommandName = "Select";
lbtn.CommandArgument = currentRowIndex.ToString();
```

The `CommandCallback` method calls the `SelectCallback` method:

```
protected void SelectCallback(int index)
{
    SelectedIndex = index;
    MasterDetailFormMode = MasterDetailFormMode.ReadOnly;
    RequiresDataBinding = true;
}
```

The `SelectCallback` method switches the detail table back to the ReadOnly mode and sets the `RequiresDataBinding` property to true to trigger the entire data-binding process where fresh data is automatically retrieved from the underlying data store and the display of the `MasterDetailForm` control is updated.

AddDetailCommandBar

Listing 17-19 illustrates the code for the `AddDetailCommandBar` method.

Listing 17-19: The AddDetailCommandBar method

```
private void AddDetailCommandBar()
{
    TableRow ddrow = new TableRow();
    detailTable.Rows.Add(ddrow);
    TableCell ddcell = new TableCell();
    ddrow.Cells.Add(ddcell);
    LinkButton firstbtn = new LinkButton();
    ddcell.Controls.Add(firstbtn);
    firstbtn.Command += new CommandEventHandler(CommandCallback);

    LiteralControl c = new LiteralControl("   ");
```

(continued)

Listing 17-19: *(continued)*

```
      ddcell.Controls.Add(c);

      LinkButton secondbtn = new LinkButton();
      ddcell.Controls.Add(secondbtn);
      secondbtn.Command += new CommandEventHandler(CommandCallback);

      switch (MasterDetailFormMode)
      {
        case MasterDetailFormMode.ReadOnly:
          firstbtn.CommandName = "New";
          firstbtn.Text = "New";

          secondbtn.CommandName = "Edit";
          secondbtn.Text = "Edit";

          c = new LiteralControl("   ");
          ddcell.Controls.Add(c);

          LinkButton deletebtn = new LinkButton();
          ddcell.Controls.Add(deletebtn);
          deletebtn.CommandName = "Delete";
          deletebtn.Command += new CommandEventHandler(CommandCallback);
          deletebtn.Text = "Delete";
          break;
        case MasterDetailFormMode.Edit:
          firstbtn.CommandName = "Update";
          firstbtn.Text = "Update";

          secondbtn.CommandName = "Cancel";
          secondbtn.Text = "Cancel";
          break;
        case MasterDetailFormMode.Insert:
          firstbtn.CommandName = "Insert";
          firstbtn.Text = "Insert";

          secondbtn.CommandName = "Cancel";
          secondbtn.Text = "Cancel";
          break;
      }
  }
```

The `CreateChildControls` method of the `MasterDetailForm` calls the `AddDetailCommandBar` to add the standard New, Edit, Update, Cancel, Delete, and Insert command buttons to the detail table. The type of command buttons depends on the mode the detail table is in:

1. The three New, Edit, and Delete standard command buttons are used when the detail table is in the ReadOnly mode. When the user clicks the New button, the detail table switches to Insert mode, allowing the user to add a new record. When the user clicks the Edit button, the detail table switches to Edit mode, allowing the user to edit the existing record.

2. The two Update and Cancel command buttons are used when the detail table is in Edit mode.

3. The two Insert and Cancel command buttons are used when the detail table is in Insert mode.

The following sections show you how to use the methods and properties of the `BaseDataBoundControl`, `DataBoundControl`, and `CompositeDataBoundControl` to automate the `Delete`, `Update`, `Insert`, and `Sort` data operations so that page developers will be able to use the `MasterDetailForm` control without writing a single line of code.

The `Delete`, `Update`, and `Insert` operations change the underlying data store. Therefore, the `MasterDetailForm` control must extract fresh data from the underlying data store and refresh its display after these operations. However, thanks to the `DataBoundControl` class, that is no longer necessary. As discussed earlier, the `DataBoundControl` class takes the following two actions:

❑ Exposes a new method named `OnDataSourceViewChanged` that sets the `RequiresDataBinding` property to true.

❑ Its `GetData` method registers the `OnDataSourceViewChanged` as the callback for the `DataSourceViewChanged` event of the default view object.

Therefore, the view object automatically calls the `OnDataSourceViewChanged` method right after deleting, updating, or inserting a record. Because the `OnDataSourceViewChanged` method sets the `RequiresDataBinding` property to true, everything else automatically falls through.

However, it's important that the detail table switches back to its ReadOnly mode after deleting, updating, or inserting a record. That is why the `MasterDetailForm` class overrides the `OnDataSourceViewChanged` method:

```
protected override void OnDataSourceViewChanged(object sender, EventArgs e)
{
  MasterDetailFormMode = MasterDetailFormMode.ReadOnly;
  base.OnDataSourceViewChanged(sender, e);
}
```

Delete Data Operation

The `CommandCallback` calls the `Delete` method to handle the `Delete` event:

```
private void Delete()
{
  DataSourceView dv = GetData();
  if (dv.CanDelete)
  {
    Hashtable keys = new Hashtable();
    keys.Add(DataKeyField, DataKeyFieldValue);
    Hashtable oldValues = new Hashtable();
    oldValues.Add(DataKeyField, DataKeyFieldValue);
    dv.Delete(keys, oldValues,
            new DataSourceViewOperationCallback(DeleteCallback));
  }
}
```

As the Delete method shows, you must take the following steps to automate the delete data operation:

1. Call the GetData method of the DataBoundControl class to access the default tabular view object.

2. Check the value of the CanDelete property of the view object to make sure it supports the delete data operation.

3. Create an instance of the Hashtable class and populate it with the primary key field values. The MasterDetailForm control exposes two properties, DataKeyField and DataKeyFieldValue, whose values are the name of the primary key field and its value.

4. Create another instance of the Hashtable class and populate it with the old field values.

5. Call the Delete method of the view object.

6. Pass the two instances of the Hashtable class as the first two arguments of the Delete method.

7. Because the delete operation is asynchronous, register a callback.

8. The first two arguments of the Delete method take objects of type IDictionary. Therefore, you can use objects of any class that implements IDictionary, such as Hashtable or SortedList.

Update Data Operation

The CommandCallback method calls the Update method to handle the Update event, as shown in the following listing:

```
private void Update()
{
  DataSourceView dv = GetData();

  if (dv.CanUpdate)
  {
    Hashtable keys = new Hashtable();
    keys.Add(DataKeyField, DataKeyFieldValue);
    Hashtable values = new Hashtable();
    Hashtable oldValues = new Hashtable();
    foreach (TableRow row in detailTable.Rows)
    {
      foreach (TableCell cell in row.Cells)
      {
        if (cell.Controls.Count > 0)
        {
          TextBox tbx = cell.Controls[0] as TextBox;
          if (tbx != null)
          {
            values.Add(tbx.Attributes["FieldName"], tbx.Text);
            oldValues.Add(tbx.Attributes["FieldName"], tbx.Text);
          }
        }
      }
    }

    dv.Update(keys, values, oldValues,
                new DataSourceViewOperationCallback(UpdateInsertCallback));
  }
}
```

As the Update method shows, you must take the following steps to automate the update data operation:

1. Call the GetData method of the DataBoundControl class to access the default tabular view object.

2. Check the value of the CanUpdate property of the view object to make sure it supports the update data operation.

3. Create an instance of the Hashtable class and populate it with the primary key field values.

4. Create two more instances of the Hashtable class.

5. Enumerate all the cells that contain text boxes and extract the names of the fields and their values. Recall that the AddDetailsRow method added the name of the respective field to the Attributes property of the corresponding TextBox instance.

6. Populate the two Hashtable instances with the field values you just obtained.

7. Call the Delete method of the view object.

8. Pass the three Hashtable instances as the first three arguments of the Update method.

9. Because the update operation is asynchronous, register a callback.

In step 5, custom controls that use server controls other than text boxes must extract the names and values of the fields from whatever server control is being used.

The insert operation is very similar to the update operation. The only difference is that the Insert method only takes a single instance of the Hashtable class, because inserting a record doesn't involve primary key field values and old values.

Sort Data Operation

The MasterDetailForm control exposes a property named AllowSorting that allows page developers to turn sorting on or off. When the value of this property is true, the AddMasterHeaderCell method (see Listing 17-17) renders the header text as a link button, allowing users to sort the records. The method sets the CommandArgument of the link button to the name of the field and registers the CommandCallback as the callback for the Command event of the link button as shown in Listing 17-17. When the user clicks the header text of a column, the CommandCallback method calls the Sort method (see Listing 17-20).

Listing 17-20: The Sort method handles the Sort event

```
private void Sort(string sortExpression)
{
  if (SortExpression == sortExpression)
  {
    if (SortDirection == "Asc")
      SortDirection = "Desc";
    else
      SortDirection = "Asc";
  }
  else
  {
    SortExpression = sortExpression;
    SortDirection = "Asc";
  }
  RequiresDataBinding = true;
}
```

The Sort method sets the values of the SortExpression and SortDirection properties and sets the RequiresDataBinding property to true.

Recall that the GetData method of the DataBoundControl class calls the Select method of the underlying default view object. The first argument of the Select method calls the CreateDataSourceSelectArguments method to access the DataSourceSelectArguments object. The MasterDetailForm control overrides the CreateDataSourceSelectArguments method as follows:

```
protected override DataSourceSelectArguments CreateDataSourceSelectArguments()
{
  DataSourceView dv = GetData();
  DataSourceSelectArguments args = new DataSourceSelectArguments();

  if (dv.CanSort)
    args.SortExpression = this.SortExpression + " " + this.SortDirection;

  return args;
}
```

The method first calls the GetData method of the DataBoundControl class to access the default tabular view object. It then creates an instance of the DataSourceSelectArguments class and checks the value of the CanSort property of the view object to make sure it supports sorting. The method then sets the SortExpression property of the DataSourceSelectArguments object to the combination of the values of the SortExpression and SortDirection properties of the MasterDetailForm control.

Control State

Many ASP.NET 1.x server controls provide features that rely on view state to function properly across page postbacks. For instance, the pagination feature of a DataGrid relies on view state to recover the current page index when the user clicks the Next button and posts the page back to the server. Without recovering the current page index, the control would not know what the next page is. The problem with view state is that the page developer can turn it off. Obviously, those features of server controls that rely on view state will not function properly when the view state is turned off.

ASP.NET 2.0 provides server controls with their own private storage named *control state*. Technically, both the control and view states are stored in the same hidden field named __VIEWSTATE. However, the control state is private to the control and page developers can't turn it off. Therefore, custom controls must use their control states as storage for those properties that are essential to their main features.

The MasterDetailForm control uses its control state to store those properties that are essential to its functionality and features. The control overrides the SaveControlState method of the Control class to save its essential properties. The following shows a portion of the method:

```
protected override object SaveControlState()
{
  object[] state = new object[20];
  state[0] = base.SaveControlState();
  state[1] = _sortExpression;
  state[2] = _masterFieldIndices;
  . . .
  return state;
}
```

The `MasterDetailForm` control also overrides the `LoadControlState` method of the `Control` class to recover its essential properties. The following shows a portion of the method:

```
protected override void LoadControlState(object savedState)
{
  if (savedState != null)
  {
    object[] state = savedState as object[];
    if (state != null && state.Length == 20)
    {
      base.LoadControlState(state[0]);
      if (state[1] != null)
        sortExpression = (string)state[1];
      if (state[2] != null)
        masterFieldIndices = (ArrayList)state[2];
      . . .
    }
  }
  else
    base.LoadControlState(savedState);
}
```

The `MasterDetailForm` control overrides the `OnInit` method to notify the containing page that it needs to use its control state:

```
protected override void OnInit(EventArgs e)
{
  Page.RegisterRequiresControlState(this);
  base.OnInit(e);
}
```

Appearance Properties

Composite data-bound controls normally expose style properties that apply to their child controls, as discussed in Chapter 7. For instance, the `GridView` control exposes a property named `SelectedItemStyle` that applies to the selected row of the control. To get a better understanding of the problems associated with style properties, consider the following similar client-side situation.

There are two ways to apply appearance parameters to HTML tags. One way is to do it inline, where the appearance attributes are directly applied to each tag. This mixes content (HTML tags) with presentation (appearance) properties. Cascading Style Sheets were introduced to separate content from presentation. Notice that Cascading Style Sheets are client-side technology.

The style properties of composite data-bound controls also mix content with presentation, but on the server side. ASP.NET 2.0 comes with what are known as *themes* to separate content from presentation on the server side. Therefore, the ASP.NET 2.0 themes are the preferred way to apply appearance properties to the child controls of composite data-bound controls.

The `MasterDetailForm` control exposes `SkinID` and `EnableTheming` properties that apply to its child controls. For instance, the `MasterDetailForm` control sets the `SkinID` property of the master table to the value of the `MasterTableSkinID` property.

The `MasterDetailForm` control exposes seven `SkinID` properties:

- ❏ `MasterTableSkinID`: The `SkinID` property of the master table.

- ❏ `MasterHeaderRowSkinID`: The `SkinID` property of the header row of the master table.

- ❏ `MasterRowSkinID`: The `SkinID` property of a row in the master table.

- ❏ `MasterAlternatingRowSkinID`: The `SkinID` property of an alternating row in the master table.

- ❏ `DetailsTableSkinID`: The `SkinID` property of the detail table.

- ❏ `DetailsRowSkinID`: The `SkinID` property of a row in the detail table.

- ❏ `DetailsAlternatingRowSkinID`: The `SkinID` property of an alternating row in the detail table.

Codeless Master/Detail Form

As Listing 17-21 shows, page developers can declaratively use the `MasterDetailForm` custom data-bound control without writing a single line of code. Figure 17-1 shows what end users see on their browsers when they access this page.

Listing 17-21: Using the MasterDetailForm declaratively

```
<%@ Page Language="C#" Theme="SandAndSky" %>
<%@ Register TagPrefix="custom" Namespace="CustomControls" %>
<html xmlns="http://www.w3.org/1999/xhtml">
<body>
  <form id="form1" runat="server">
    <custom:MasterDetailForm DataKeyField="BookID" AllowSorting="true"
    ID="MyControl" runat="Server" DataSourceID="MySource"
    MasterAlternatingRowSkinID="AlternatingRow"
    MasterTableSkinID="Table" DetailsAlternatingRowSkinID="AlternatingRow"
    DetailsTableSkinID="Table" MasterHeaderRowSkinID="HeaderRow"
    MasterFields="BookID,Title" />

    <asp:ObjectDataSource ID="MySource" runat="Server"
    SortParameterName="sortParameterName" TypeName="Books"
    SelectMethod="SelectBooks" DeleteMethod="DeleteBook" UpdateMethod="UpdateBook"
    InsertMethod="InsertBook">
      <UpdateParameters>
        <asp:Parameter Name="BookID" Type="Int32" />
        <asp:Parameter Name="Price" Type="Decimal" />
      </UpdateParameters>
      <DeleteParameters>
        <asp:Parameter Name="original_BookID" Type="Int32" />
      </DeleteParameters>
      <InsertParameters>
        <asp:Parameter Name="Price" Type="Decimal" />
      </InsertParameters>
    </asp:ObjectDataSource>
  </form>
</body>
</html>
```

The example page in Listing 17-21 uses the `ObjectDataSource` control to access the underlying data source. The `Books` class is a custom class that exposes the `SelectBooks`, `DeleteBook`, `UpdateBook`, and `InsertBook` methods. Page developers can use any type of data source control that implements `IDataSource`, such as `ObjectDataSource`, `SqlDataSource`, and `AccessDataSource`.

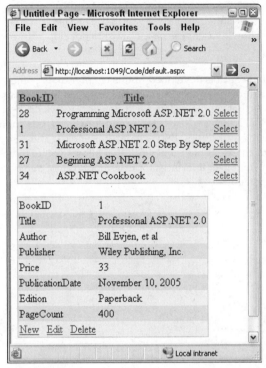

Figure 17-1

Summary

This chapter used a detailed step-by-step approach to implement and reverse-engineer the important methods and properties of the base classes of the ASP.NET 2.0 data source control model, `BaseDataBoundControl`, `DataBoundControl`, and `CompositeDataBoundControl`.

The `BaseDataBoundControl` base class provides its subclasses, including custom data-bound controls, with the infrastructure they need to automate all three data-binding tasks. This means that custom data-bound controls that derive from the `BaseDataBoundControl` base class can be used declaratively.

The `DataBoundControl` base class is capable of retrieving tabular data from any type of data store. This means that custom data-bound controls that derive from the `DataBoundControl` base class will work with any type of data store.

The CompositeDataBoundControl class encapsulates and implements the boilerplate code that ASP.NET 1.x control developers have to write every time they develop a custom data-bound control. In other words, the CompositeDataBoundControl base class allows you to write custom data-bound controls with minimal effort.

This chapter also developed three custom tabular data-bound controls that derive from the BaseDataBoundControl, DataBoundControl, and CompositeDataBoundControl base classes, respectively, to show you how to use these base classes to develop your own custom tabular data-bound controls.

All the custom data-bound controls developed in this chapter display the value of a database field in simple text if its associated row is in normal mode and in a text box if its associated row is in edit or insert mode. This assumes that simple text and text box are always the best user interface for displaying and editing database fields, which isn't true. For example, a check box control is a more user-friendly user interface for displaying and editing Boolean database fields. The ASP.NET 2.0 data control field model provides you with an extensible framework that allows you to develop custom data-bound controls that can display different user interfaces for different types of database fields. The next chapter discusses this model in detail.

The ASP.NET 2.0 Data Control Field Model

This chapter builds on top of Chapter 9 to help you gain a solid understanding of the ASP.NET 2.0 data control field model from the inside out and develops several custom data control fields to show you how to develop your own custom data control fields. As you'll see in the next chapter, the ASP.NET 2.0 data control field model provides data-bound controls such as GridView with a generic API to isolate them from the code that displays the data values of each column.

Why You Need the ASP.NET 2.0 Data Control Field Model

Begin by revisiting the CustomTable control developed in Chapter 9. Recall that this control displays data records in a table and allows users to update, sort, and page through the records.

As discussed in Chapter 9, this control exposes a method named CreateDataCells that creates one cell for each data field of the respective data row, as shown in Listing 18-1. The method uses a TextBox control to display the value of a data field if the containing row is in edit mode and a simple text format if the containing row is in normal mode.

Listing 18-1: The CreateDataCells method

```
protected virtual void CreateDataCells(CustomTableRow brow, bool
useDataSource)
{
  for (int k = 0; k < fields.Length; k++)
  {
    TableCell bcell = new TableCell();
```

(continued)

Listing 18-1: *(continued)*

```
      brow.Cells.Add(bcell);

      if ((brow.RowState & DataControlRowState.Edit) != 0)
      {
        if (useDataSource && fields[k].ReadOnly)
          bcell.Text =
              DataBinder.Eval(brow.DataItem, fields[k].SortExpression).ToString();

        else if (!fields[k].ReadOnly)
        {
          TextBox tb = new TextBox();
          bcell.Controls.Add(tb);

          if (useDataSource)
            tb.Text =
                DataBinder.Eval(brow.DataItem, fields[k].SortExpression).ToString();
        }
      }

      else if (useDataSource)
        bcell.Text =
                DataBinder.Eval(brow.DataItem, fields[k].SortExpression).ToString();
    }
  }
```

Because the CreateDataCells method uses a TextBox control to display data fields in edit mode and
a simple text format in normal mode, it can't be used to display all types of data fields. For example, a
CheckBox control is a more appropriate way to display the value of a Boolean data field than a TextBox
or simple text format.

Because the CreateDataCells method directly includes the code that displays data fields, the method
is tied to a particular type of data field and will not be able to display other types such as Boolean. The
remedy is to move the code from the CustomTable control to a different component. In other words, the
CustomTable control must delegate the responsibility of displaying the data field values to another
component, but which component?

Recall from Chapter 9 that the CustomTable control uses instances of a component or class named
DataControlField to represent its columns, where each DataControlField instance contains the
complete information about its associated column, such as its header text, the type of the data that the
column displays, and the name of the database field whose values the column displays (see Listing 9-6).

The following code shows the declaration of the properties of the DataControlField component
shown in Listing 9-6:

```
public class DataControlField : IStateManager
{
  public string HeaderText {get; set;}
  public string SortExpression {get; set;}
  public bool ReadOnly {get; set;}
  public Type DataType {get; set;}

  . . .

}
```

You're looking for a component to take responsibility for displaying the values of a column. Because the `DataControlField` component holds the complete information about its associated column, it makes sense to have this component to take responsibility for displaying the values of its associated column as well. This is exactly what the ASP.NET 2.0 `DataControlField` base class does. This chapter takes a look under the hood of this base class to help you understand this class from the inside out.

Moving the code that displays the values of a column from a data-bound control such as `CustomTable` to the `DataControlField` is not enough to isolate the data-bound control from this code, because every time you made changes in the implementation of `DataControlField`, you would have to recompile the data-bound control as well. Therefore, `DataControlField` mustn't contain the code that displays the values of a column. In other words, `DataControlField` must only define the appropriate APIs and must delegate the responsibility of implementing these APIs and displaying the values of the associated column to its subclasses.

This is exactly what the ASP.NET 2.0 `DataControlField` base class does. The ASP.NET Framework comes with several data control fields that implement the `DataControlField` API, such as `BoundField` and `CheckBoxField`.

Each data control field is designed to display the values of a specific type of data field. For example, the `CheckBoxField` data control field is specifically designed to display the values of data fields of type `System.Boolean`.

The ASP.NET 2.0 data control field model provides you with an extensible infrastructure that allows you to isolate tabular data-bound controls from the types of the data control fields used to display its data fields. Before you look under the hood of this infrastructure to find out how it works, you need to see how it's used.

The following code shows an example:

```
<custom:GridView runat="server" ID="gv" AutoGenerateColumns="false" >
  <Columns>
    <custom:BoundField DataField="Title" />
    <custom:BoundField DataField="Author" />
  </Columns>
</custom:GridView>
```

As you'll see in Chapter 19, the `GridView` control exposes a property of type `DataControlField Collection` named `Columns` that contains all of the data control fields used to display data fields. This code adds two instances of the `BoundField` component to the `Columns` collection. In addition, the `DataField` property of each `BoundField` component in the code is set to the name of the database field that the component displays.

The ASP.NET 2.0 infrastructure that allows the same tabular data-bound control such as `GridView` to display different types of data fields consists of the following three important components:

❑   `DataControlField`

❑   `DataControlFieldCollection`

❑   Built-in support of tabular data-bound controls such as `GridView` to automatically invoke the `ExtractValuesFromCell` method of the `DataControlField` component

The following sections implement replicas of the first two components. The third component is discussed in the next chapter in the context of the implementation of the GridView control.

DataControlField

The ASP.NET 2.0 DataControlField class is the base class for all data control field classes such as BoundField, CheckBoxField, HyperLinkField, ImageField, TemplateField, ButtonField, and CommandField. This section implements the main methods and properties of this base class.

Listing 18-2 shows the declaration of these methods and properties. Notice that the DataControlField class implements the IStateManager interface to manage its state across page postbacks. The class exposes seven important properties:

- ❑ Control: Gets the data-bound control that contains the data control field.

- ❑ HeaderText: Gets and sets the header text of the data control field.

- ❑ FooterText: Gets and sets the footer text of the field.

- ❑ ShowHeader: Specifies whether the header of the field should be rendered.

- ❑ SortExpression: Gets and sets the name of the data field that will be used to sort the displayed data.

- ❑ Visible: Gets and sets the visibility of the field.

- ❑ Container: Gets and sets the DataControlFieldCollection collection that contains the data control field. This property (the name of the property isn't important) is marked as internal to hide the interaction between the DataControlField and DataControlFieldCollection from the subclasses of the DataControlField base class.

The DataControlField class also exposes the following style properties:

- ❑ ControlStyle: Gets the Style instance that specifies the style properties of the control that the data control field uses to display its associated data field. For example, this control is a CheckBox control in the case of a CheckBoxField data control field.

- ❑ HeaderStyle: Gets the TableItemStyle instance that specifies the style properties of the header cell of the data control field.

- ❑ ItemStyle: Gets the TableItemStyle instance that specifies the style properties of the data cells of the data control field.

- ❑ FooterStyle: Gets the TableItemStyle instance that specifies the style properties of the footer of the column.

The DataControlField class exposes five important methods as follows:

- ❑ CreateField: Creates an instance of the data control field.

- ❑ ExtractValuesFromCell: Extracts the data field value from the containing cell.

- ❑ Initialize: Performs general initialization.

❑   `InitializeCell`: Renders the containing cell.

❑   `OnFieldChanged`: Calls the `RaiseFieldsChangedEvent` method of the `DataControlField Collection` container.

Listing 18-2: The DataControlField base class

```
public abstract class DataControlField : IStateManager,
                                         IDataSourceViewSchemaAccessor
{
  protected Control Control {get;}
  public virtual string HeaderText {get; set;}
  public virtual string FooterText {get; set;}
  public virtual bool ShowHeader {get; set;}
  public virtual string SortExpression {get; set;}
  public bool Visible {get; set;}
  internal DataControlFieldCollection Container {get; set; }

  public Style ControlStyle {get; }
  public TableItemStyle FooterStyle {get; }
  public TableItemStyle HeaderStyle {get;}
  public TableItemStyle ItemStyle {get; }

  protected abstract DataControlField CreateField();
  public virtual void ExtractValuesFromCell(IOrderedDictionary dictionary,
              DataControlFieldCell cell, DataControlRowState rowState,
              bool includeReadOnly);
  public virtual bool Initialize(bool sortingEnabled, Control control);
  public virtual void InitializeCell(DataControlFieldCell cell, DataControlCellType
                      cellType, DataControlRowState rowState, int rowIndex);
  protected virtual void OnFieldChanged();
}
```

The OnFieldChanged Method

The `OnFieldChanged` method is called when the data control field changes. For example, the setter of the `SortExpression` property calls the `OnFieldChanged` method when its value changes:

```
public string SortExpression
{
  get
  {
    return ViewState["SortExpression "] != null ?
                    (string)ViewState["SortExpression "] : string.Empty;
  }

  set
  {
    if (SortExpression != value)
    {
      ViewState["SortExpression "] = value;
      OnFieldChanged();
    }
  }
}
```

Listing 18-3 shows the implementation of the OnFieldChanged method.

Listing 18-3: The OnFieldChanged method

```
protected virtual void OnFieldChanged()
{
  if (container != null)
    container.RaiseFieldsChangedEvent();
}
```

As mentioned, the DataControlField class exposes a property of type DataControlFieldCollection named Container that refers to its containing DataControlFieldCollection instance. The OnFieldChanged method calls the RaiseFieldsChangedEvent method of the container to notify the container that the data control field has changed. This method is discussed in detail later in this chapter.

Initialize Method

Listing 18-4 shows the implementation of the Initialize method of the DataControlField class.

Listing 18-4: The Initialize method

```
public virtual bool Initialize(bool sortingEnabled, Control control)
{
  this.sortingEnabled = sortingEnabled;
  this.control = control;
  return false;
}
```

The method takes two arguments. The first argument specifies whether the sorting feature of the data source control is enabled. The second argument refers to the data-bound control that contains the data source control. As you'll see later, your custom data control field must override this method to perform general initialization.

InitializeCell Method

Listing 18-5 shows the implementation of the InitializeCell method of the DataControlField class.

Listing 18-5: The InitializeCell method

```
public virtual void InitializeCell(DataControlFieldCell cell,
      DataControlCellType cellType, DataControlRowState rowState, int rowIndex)
{
  switch (cellType)
  {
    case DataControlCellType.Header:

      if (this.sortingEnabled && SortExpression.Length > 0)
      {
        LinkButton btn = new LinkButton();
```

```
        btn.Text = HeaderText;
        btn.CommandName = "Sort";
        btn.CommandArgument = SortExpression;
        cell.Controls.Add(btn);
      }
      else
        cell.Text = HeaderText;

    break;
  case DataControlCellType.Footer:
    cell.Text = FooterText;
    break;
  }
}
```

Your custom data control field must override this method to generate the HTML markup text that displays the specified data field on the client browser. The arguments of the method provide the method with all the information it needs to decide what HTML markup text to generate. The method takes four arguments. The first argument is the table cell that acts as the container for the HTML markup text that the method generates. The second argument is used to specify the type of the cell. There are in general three cell types: header, data, and footer. As Listing 18-5 shows, the DataControlField base class's implementation of the InitializeCell method generates the HTML markup text for the header and footer cells only, and leaves the responsibility of generating the HTML markup text for data cells to its subclasses, where each subclass is specifically designed to generate the appropriate HTML markup text to display a specific type of data field. For example, the CheckBoxField class generates a CheckBox control to display the value of a Boolean data field.

The third argument specifies the state of the containing row. The possible values are Alternate, Edit, Insert, Normal, and Selected. This allows the subclasses to generate different HTML markup text for different row states. For example, the subclass could generate a TextBox control when the containing row is in edit mode to allow users to edit the field value. The last argument is the index of the containing row. As you'll see later, your custom data control field must override this method, and must use the provided information to generate the appropriate HTML markup text.

ExtractValuesFromCell Method

Listing 18-6 shows the implementation of the ExtractValuesFromCell method of the DataControlField class.

Listing 18-6: The ExtractValuesFromCell method

```
public virtual void ExtractValuesFromCell(IOrderedDictionary dictionary,
    DataControlFieldCell cell, DataControlRowState rowState, bool includeReadOnly)
{
}
```

Notice that the DataControlField base class leaves the responsibility of implementing this method to its subclasses. As you'll see later, your custom data control fields must override this method where you must implement the logic that retrieves the respective data field value from the cell that displays it.

The ASP.NET 2.0 data control field model comes with the following standard data control fields:

❑ BoundField: Displays the value of its associated data field in a TextBox if the containing row is in edit mode and in simple text if the containing row is in normal mode.

❑ HyperLinkField: Uses a HyperLink control to display the value of its associated data field.

❑ ImageField: Uses an Image control to display the value of its associated image data field.

❑ CheckBoxField: Uses a CheckBox control to display the value of its associated Boolean data field.

❑ TemplateField: Allows page developers to specify the HTML markup text that will be used to display the value of its associated data field.

❑ ButtonField: Allows page developers to add a button to each displayed data row to trigger application-specific events. For example, an e-commerce application may add an Add To Shopping Cart button to each row to allow users to add the item to their shopping carts.

❑ CommandField: Allows page developers to add standard command buttons (Select, Edit, Delete, and so on) to each displayed data row to allow users to perform the relevant operation (such as deleting a row) on the row.

The following sections implement a fully functional replica of the standard BoundField component built into ASP.NET to help you gain a solid understanding of how these standard data control fields are implemented and how you can follow the implementation of these components to implement your own custom data control field.

BoundField

Listing 18-7 shows the declaration of the important methods and properties of the BoundField data control field.

Listing 18-7: The BoundField data control field

```
public class BoundField : DataControlField
{
  public virtual string DataField {get; set;}
  public virtual string NullDisplayText {get; set;}
  public override string HeaderText {get; set;}
  public virtual bool ReadOnly {get; set;}
  protected override DataControlField CreateField();
  public override bool Initialize(bool enableSorting, Control control);
  public override void InitializeCell(DataControlFieldCell cell,
                                      DataControlCellType cellType,
                                      DataControlRowState rowState, int rowIndex);
  protected virtual void InitializeDataCell(DataControlFieldCell cell,
                                            DataControlRowState rowState);
  protected virtual void OnDataBindField(object sender, EventArgs e);
  public override void ExtractValuesFromCell(IOrderedDictionary dictionary,
    DataControlFieldCell cell, DataControlRowState rowState, bool includeReadOnly);
  protected virtual object GetValue(Control controlContainer);
}
```

The following sections present the implementation of some of these members.

InitializeCell

As mentioned, there are three different types of cells: header, data, and footer. Recall that the `DataControlField` base class's implementation of the `InitializeCell` method generates HTML markup text for the header and footer cells only and leaves the responsibility of generating the HTML markup text for data cells to its subclasses, and each subclass is specifically designed to generate the appropriate HTML markup text to display a specific type of data field. For example, the `CheckBoxField` class generates a `CheckBox` control to display the value of a Boolean data field.

The `BoundField` class overrides the `InitializeCell` method of its base class, and delegates the responsibility of generating the HTML markup text for data cells to the `InitializeDataCell` method (discussed shortly) and delegates the responsibility of generating the HTML markup text for other two types of cells (header and footer) to its base class:

```
public override void InitializeCell(DataControlFieldCell cell,
        DataControlCellType cellType,DataControlRowState rowState, int rowIndex)
{
  if (cellType == DataControlCellType.DataCell)
    InitializeDataCell(cell, rowState);

  base.InitializeCell(cell, cellType, rowState, rowIndex);
}
```

InitializeDataCell

Listing 18-8 shows the `BoundField` data control field's implementation of the `InitializeDataCell` method.

Listing 18-8: The InitializeDataCell method of the BoundField data control field

```
protected virtual void InitializeDataCell(DataControlFieldCell cell,
                                  DataControlRowState rowState)
{
  if (((rowState & DataControlRowState.Edit) != 0 && !ReadOnly) ||
      (rowState & DataControlRowState.Insert) != 0)
  {
    TextBox tbx = new TextBox();
    cell.Controls.Add(tbx);
  }

  if (!string.IsNullOrEmpty(DataField))
    cell.DataBinding += new EventHandler(OnDataBindField);
}
```

As Listing 18-8 shows, if the containing row is in insert mode or in edit mode but it's not read-only, the `InitializeDataCell` method creates a `TextBox` control and adds it to the `Controls` collection of the cell that displays the associated data field:

```
TextBox tbx = new TextBox();
cell.Controls.Add(tbx);
```

The method also registers the OnDataBindField method as the callback for the DataBinding event of the cell. As you'll see shortly, this method retrieves and displays the value of the respective data field.

OnDataBindField

Listing 18-9 shows the implementation of the OnDataBindField method.

Listing 18-9: The OnDataBindField method of the BoundField data control field

```
protected virtual void OnDataBindField(object sender, EventArgs e)
{
  DataControlFieldCell cell = sender as DataControlFieldCell;
  if (cell != null)
  {
    object dataValue = GetValue(cell.Parent);
    if (dataValue == null)
      throw new Exception("No value found");

    if (cell.Controls.Count > 0)
    {
      TextBox tbx = cell.Controls[0] as TextBox;
      if (tbx != null)
        tbx.Text = dataValue.ToString();
    }

    else
      cell.Text = dataValue.ToString();
  }
}
```

This method calls the GetValue method (discussed shortly) to access the value of its associated data field. Notice that the OnDataBindField method passes the parent control of the cell to the GetValue method. The parent control is a GridViewRow control in the case of the GridView control and a DetailsViewRow control in the case of the DetailsView control:

```
object dataValue = GetValue(cell.Parent);
```

The method then checks whether the cell contains any controls. If so, the containing row is in edit or insert mode, so the method displays the value in the TextBox control:

```
TextBox tbx = cell.Controls[0] as TextBox;
if (tbx != null)
  tbx.Text = dataValue.ToString();
```

If not, the containing row must be in normal mode, so the method displays the value in simple text format:

```
cell.Text = dataValue.ToString();
```

GetValue

As discussed in Chapter 9, each table row of a data-bound control is bound to a specific data record or data row. Obviously, the GetValue method must retrieve the value of its associated data field from the data row that its containing table row is bound to. The method faces two challenges:

❑ The type of the containing table row depends on the type of the data-bound control. For example, as you'll see in the next chapter, the GridView and DetailsView rows are of type GridViewRow and DetailsViewRow, respectively.

❑ The type of the data row that the containing table row is bound to depends on the type of the data store. For example, if you're using ADO.NET classes to access a relational database, the data row is typically of type DataRowView.

If the GetValue method were to know the types of the containing table row and its associated data row, the BoundField data control field would be tied to particular data-bound control and data store and would not work with other types of data-bound controls and data stores.

That is why the GetValue method takes the containing table row as an object of generic Control type as its argument. This allows the GetValue method to deal with the containing table row in generic fashion. What about the data row that the containing row is bound to? This is where the IDataItemContainer interface comes to the rescue.

The containing table row implements the IDataItemContainer interface to allow the GetValue method to access its associated data row in generic fashion without knowing its real type. The interface exposes a property named DataItem that refers to the associated data row.

Recall from Chapter 9 that the associated data row exposes its data fields as its own properties. This allows the GetValue method to call the GetProperties method of the TypeDescriptor class to access the data field as if it were the property of the data row.

The GetProperties method returns a collection of type PropertyDescriptorCollection that contains one PropertyDescriptor object for each property (data field) of the data row. The Name property and GetValue method of each PropertyDescriptor object returns the name and value of the associated property.

The BoundField component exposes a property named DataField that page developers must set to the name of the data field that the BoundField is bound to. As Listing 18-10 shows, the GetValue method uses the value of this property to locate the PropertyDescriptor object that describes the associated data field.

> As discussed in Chapter 13, the .NET Framework comes with a class named DataBinder that exposes a method named Eval that encapsulates the logic that evaluates the value of a given property. This method takes two arguments. The first argument is the object whose property value is being evaluated. The second argument is the name of the property whose value is being evaluated. If you use this class, you can save yourself from having to write the code that evaluates the value of a property and consequently simplify Listing 18-7.

Listing 18-10: The GetValue method of the BoundField data control field

```
protected virtual object GetValue(Control controlContainer)
{
  object dataValue = null;

  IDataItemContainer container = controlContainer as IDataItemContainer;
  if (container != null)
  {
    object dataItem = container.DataItem;
    bool found = false;
    PropertyDescriptorCollection properties =
                                      TypeDescriptor.GetProperties(dataItem);
    foreach (PropertyDescriptor property in properties)
    {
      if (property.Name == DataField)
      {
        found = true;
        dataValue = property.GetValue(dataItem);
        break;
      }
    }

    if (!found)
      throw new Exception("The record does not contain the " +
                          DataField + " data field");
  }

  else
    throw new Exception("No data record is bound to the containing row");

  return dataValue;
}
```

ExtractValuesFromCell

As you'll see in the next chapter, data-bound controls call the ExtractValuesFromCell method to access the value of the data field that the cell displays. The method adds the value to an IOrderedDictionary collection passed in as its first argument, as shown in Listing 18-11.

The method checks whether the containing table row is in edit or insert mode. If so, it retrieves the value of the TextBox control. Otherwise it retrieves the value from the Text property of the cell itself if the read-only fields should be included.

Listing 18-11: The ExtractValuesFromCell method of the BoundField data control field

```
public override void ExtractValuesFromCell(IOrderedDictionary dictionary,
    DataControlFieldCell cell, DataControlRowState rowState, bool includeReadOnly)
{
  string dataValue = null;

  if (((rowState & DataControlRowState.Edit) != 0) ||
```

```
            ((rowState & DataControlRowState.Insert) !=0))
    {
      if (cell.Controls.Count > 0)
      {
        TextBox tbx = cell.Controls[0] as TextBox;
        if (tbx == null)
          throw new InvalidOperationException("BoundField could not extract
                                        control.");
        dataValue = tbx.Text;
      }
      else if (includeReadOnly)
        dataValue = cell.Text;

      if (dataValue != null)
      {
        if (dictionary.Contains(DataField))
          dictionary[DataField] = dataValue;

        else
          dictionary.Add(DataField, dataValue);
      }
    }
}
```

DataControlFieldCollection

As discussed, the ASP.NET 2.0 data-bound control model provides you with the infrastructure you need to isolate your custom data-bound controls from the real types of the data control fields used to display data fields. This infrastructure consists of three main components: DataControlField, DataControlFieldCollection, and tabular data-bound controls' built-in support for automatically invoking the ExtractValuesFromCell method of the DataControlField class.

The previous sections implemented replicas of the ASP.NET 2.0 DataControlField class and its BoundField subclass. This section helps you look under the hood of the ASP.NET 2.0 DataControlFieldCollection class. Listing 18-12 shows the declaration of the main members of this class.

Listing 18-12: The DataControlFieldCollection class

```
public sealed class DataControlFieldCollection : StateManagedCollection
{
  public event EventHandler FieldsChanged {add; remove;}
  void OnFieldsChanged(EventArgs e);
  internal void RaiseFieldsChangedEvent();

  protected override void OnClearComplete();
  protected override void OnInsert(int index, object value);
  protected override void OnInsertComplete(int index, object value);
  protected override void OnRemoveComplete(int index, object value);
}
```

FieldsChanged Event

The `DataControlFieldCollection` collection raises an event of type `EventHandler` named `FieldsChanged` when any of the data control fields that it contains changes. The collection takes the steps discussed in Chapter 4 to implement this event:

1. It exposes a private field of type `EventHandler` named `fieldsChanged`:

```
private event EventHandler fieldsChanged;
```

2. It exposes a public property of type `EventHandler` named `FieldsChanged` that delegates to the `fieldsChanged` field:

```
public event EventHandler FieldsChanged
{
  add { fieldsChanged += value;}
  remove { fieldsChanged -= value;}
}
```

3. It exposes a protected method named `OnFieldsChanged` that raises the `FieldsChanged` event:

```
void OnFieldsChanged(EventArgs e)
{
  if (fieldsChanged != null)
    fieldsChanged(this, e);
}
```

4. It exposes an internal method named `RaiseFieldsChangedEvent` that calls the `OnFieldsChanged` method to raise the `FieldsChanged` event:

```
internal void RaiseFieldsChangedEvent()
{
  OnFieldsChanged(EventArgs.Empty);
}
```

Recall that the `OnFieldChanged` method of a `DataControlField` instance (such as the `BoundField` instance) calls the `RaiseFieldsChangedEvent` method to raise the `FieldsChanged` event when the instance changes (see Listing 18-3). That is exactly the reason why the `RaiseFieldsChangedEvent` method is marked as internal.

OnInsert Method

This method is called before a new data control field is added to the `DataControlFieldCollection` collection. The method delegates to the `OnInsert` method of its base class and assigns itself to the `Container` property of the data control field being inserted. Recall that the `DataControlField` class exposes a collection property of type `DataControlFieldCollection` named `Container` that refers to the `DataControlFieldCollection` that contains it:

```
protected override void OnInsert(int index, object value)
{
  base.OnInsert(index, value);
  ((DataControlField)value).Container = this;
}
```

Developing Custom Data Control Fields

The previous sections implemented replicas of the `DataControlField` and `BoundField` data control fields built into ASP.NET. This section builds on what you learned in those sections to implement two custom data control fields.

DropDownListField

The foreign and primary key pairs establish relationships among database tables. The value of a foreign key field in a given record is one of the existing values of its corresponding primary key field. ASP.NET page developers must take extra steps to allow users to display and edit the foreign key fields of a row in data-bound controls such as `GridView` and `DetailsView`.

The state of the row that contains a foreign key field determines what steps must be taken.

As mentioned, the current foreign key value is one of the values of its corresponding primary key field. Most database tables automatically generate the primary key value of a record when the record is added to its table. Therefore the actual foreign key value is an auto-generated integer that doesn't mean anything to users. However, the table that contains the primary key field normally exposes another field with more meaningful values to users.

For instance, consider a database that contains tables named `Products` and `Categories`. The `Products` table has a foreign key field named `CategoryID`. The `Categories` table contains the corresponding primary key field, `CategoryID`. The `Categories` table also exposes a field named `CategoryName`, which is more meaningful to users. In other words, the table containing the primary key field normally exposes a user-friendly field. When the containing row is not in the Edit or Insert state, page developers can retrieve the current value of the user-friendly field, in this case, `CategoryName`. They can then display the current value of the user-friendly field as simple text.

When the containing row is in the Edit or Insert state, developers can take the following steps to allow users to edit the current value of the foreign key field:

1. Write the appropriate data access code to retrieve the legal values of both the foreign key field (`CategoryID`) and its associated user-friendly field (`CategoryName`).

2. Instantiate a `DropDownList` server control and bind it to the retrieved data.

3. Set the `DataValueField` property of the `DropDownList` control to the name of the corresponding primary key field, such as `CategoryID`.

4. Set the `DataTextField` property of the `DropDownList` control to the name of the user-friendly field, such as `CategoryName`.

5. Retrieve the current value of the foreign key field.

6. Set the `SelectedIndex` of the `DropDownList` control to the index of the current value of the user-friendly field.

7. Allow users to select a null value for the foreign key field because most database tables allow null values for their foreign key fields.

Because none of the existing data control fields (BoundField, HyperLinkField, ImageField, CheckBoxField, CommandField, ButtonField, and TemplateField) provide built-in support for all of these steps, page developers have no choice but to take care of all the steps themselves. In this section you design and implement a custom data control field named DropDownListField that will automatically take care of all the steps. Page developers will then be able to use the DropDownListField declaratively.

Extending BoundField

Most of the standard data control fields internally use server controls to display the values of their respective database fields. For example, the ImageField and CheckBoxField data control fields internally use Image and CheckBox server controls, respectively, to display their field values. The data type of the field and the state of its containing row determine the type of server control used to display the value of the field. For instance, an ImageField data control field uses an Image server control to display its field value when its containing row is in normal state, and a TextBox server control when its containing row is in the Edit or Insert state.

The DropDownListField custom data control field will use a DropDownList server control to display all the legal values of its field when its containing row is in the Edit or Insert state. The DropDownListField data control field will display the current value of its field as simple text when its containing row isn't in the Edit or Insert state. The DropDownListField data control field derives from the BoundField data control field because BoundField provides all the necessary base functionality when the containing row isn't in the Edit or Insert state, such as:

❑ Extracting the current value of the field whose name is the value of the DataField property. The DropDownListField overrides this property and defines a new property named DataTextField to replace it because DataTextField is a more appropriate name than DataField.

❑ Displaying the current value as simple text if the current value isn't null.

❑ Displaying the value of the NullDisplayText property if the current value is null.

❑ Displaying the value of the HeaderText property as simple text if sorting is disabled and as a hyperlink if sorting is enabled.

❑ Raising the sort event when sorting is enabled and the header hyperlink is clicked.

The main shortcoming of the BoundField data control field is that it displays the current value of the field in a TextBox control when the containing row is in the Edit or Insert state. The TextBox control is not the appropriate server control for editing foreign key fields because it allows users to enter any value and doesn't restrict the values to the legal ones. The DropDownListField data control field overrides the InitializeDataCell, OnDataBindField, and ExtractValuesFromCell methods of the BoundField data control field to add the support needed when the containing row is in the Edit or Insert state. Listing 18-13 shows all the properties and methods of the DropDownListField data control field. The following sections present the implementation of these properties and methods.

Listing 18-13: The DropDownListField data control field

```
public class DropDownListField : BoundField
{
    public override string DataField { get; set; }
    public virtual string DataTextField { get; set; }
    public virtual string SkinID { get; set;}
```

```
    public virtual bool EnableTheming { get; set;}
    public virtual string DataValueField { get; set;}
    public virtual string DataSourceID { get; set;}

    protected override void OnDataBindField(Object sender, EventArgs e);
    protected override void InitializeDataCell(DataControlFieldCell cell,
                                    DataControlRowState rowState);
    public override void ExtractValuesFromCell(IOrderedDictionary dictionary,
                        DataControlFieldCell cell, DataControlRowState rowState,
                        bool includeReadOnly);
}
```

Overriding InitializeDataCell

As shown in Listing 18-7, the `BoundField` data control field exposes a method named `InitializeDataCell` that contains the code that generates the appropriate HTML markup text for the data cell. The `InitializeDataCell` method takes two arguments. The first argument is the `DataControlFieldCell` cell being initialized. The second argument is the state of the containing row.

What HTML markup text the `BoundField` class's implementation of the `InitializeDataCell` method emits depends on the state of its containing row. If the containing row is not in the Edit or Insert state, the method simply registers the `OnDataBindField` method as the callback for the `DataBinding` event of the respective `DataControlFieldCell` instance as shown in Listing 18-7. When the `DataBinding` event of the cell is raised, the `OnDataBindField` method extracts the current value of the respective field (the name of the field is the value of the `DataField` property). If the current value is null, the value of the `NullDisplayText` property is displayed. Otherwise the current value is displayed as simple text.

The `BoundField` class's implementation of the `InitializeDataCell` method in normal state is exactly what you need. However, the `BoundField` class's implementation of the method when the containing row is in the Edit or Insert state is not acceptable, because the method instantiates an instance of the `TextBox` control. You need an implementation that instantiates an instance of the `DropDownList` control. That is why the `DropDownListField` data control field overrides the `InitializeDataCell` method. The `DropDownListField` data control field calls the base version of the `InitializeDataCell` method when the containing row is in the normal state because the behavior of the base version is exactly what you need. However, the `DropDownListField` data control field provides its own implementation when the containing row is in the Edit or Insert state.

The `DropDownListField` data control field's implementation of `InitializeDataCell` method instantiates an instance of the `DropDownList` control and sets its `DataSourceID` property to the value of the `DataSourceID` property of the `DropDownListField` data control field. It is the responsibility of page developers to set the `DataSourceID` property of the `DropDownListField` data control field to the value of the `ID` property of the appropriate data source control in the containing page. Page developers must also set the `DataTextField` and `DataValueField` properties of the `DropDownListField` data control field to the names of the appropriate database fields. This allows the `DropDownListField` data control field to automatically populate its `DropDownList` control with the valid values of the foreign key field:

```
DropDownList ddl = new DropDownList();
ddl.DataSourceID = DataSourceID;
ddl.DataTextField = DataTextField;
ddl.DataValueField = DataValueField;
```

As discussed, one of the requirements for the `DropDownListField` data control field is that it has to set the selected value of the `DropDownList` control to the current value of the respective foreign key field. This is done in a callback registered for the `DataBound` event of the `DropDownList` control. The `DropDownList` control inherits the `DataBound` event from the `BaseDataBoundControl` class. There is a difference between the `DataBound` event that the `BaseDataBoundControl` class exposes and the `DataBinding` event that the `Control` class exposes.

The `DataBinding` event is raised before the data is actually bound, whereas the `DataBound` event is raised after the data binding process finishes. Because the selected value of the `DropDownList` control must be set after the control is bound to its data source, it is set within the callback for the `DataBound` event. The `InitializeDataCell` method registers the `OnDataBindField` method as the callback for the `DataBound` event of the `DropDownList` control:

```
if (DataTextField.Length != 0 && DataValueField.Length != 0)
    ddl.DataBound += new EventHandler(OnDataBindField);
```

Listing 18-14 shows the code for the `InitializeDataCell` method.

Listing 18-14: The InitializeDataCell method of DropDownListField data control field

```
protected override void
InitializeDataCell(DataControlFieldCell cell,DataControlRowState rowState)
{
  if ((rowState & DataControlRowState.Edit) != 0 ||
      (rowState & DataControlRowState.Insert) != 0)
  {
    DropDownList ddl = new DropDownList();
    ddl.SkinID = SkinID;
    ddl.EnableTheming = EnableTheming;
    ddl.DataSourceID = DataSourceID;
    ddl.DataTextField = DataTextField;
    ddl.DataValueField = DataValueField;
    if (DataTextField.Length != 0 && DataValueField.Length != 0)
       ddl.DataBound += new EventHandler(OnDataBindField);
    cell.Controls.Add(ddl);
  }
  else
    base.InitializeDataCell(cell, rowState);
}
```

Handling the DataBound Event

When the `DataBinding` event of the cell is raised, the `OnDataBindField` method is called to display the current value in display mode, that is, as simple text. When the `DataBound` event of the `DropDownList` control is raised, the `OnDataBindField` method is called to display the current value in edit mode, that is, as the selected item of the `DropDownList` control.

Before the `OnDataBindField` method can display the current value in the edit or insert mode, it has to extract the value. The `OnDataBindField` method uses the parent control of the cell to access the value:

```
IDataItemContainer container = (IDataItemContainer)cell.Parent;
object dataItem = container.DataItem;
```

The parent of the cell is a row of type GridViewRow in GridView controls and of type DetailsViewRow in DetailsView controls. Both these types implement the IDataItemContainer interface. IDataItemContainer exposes a property named DataItem of type Object. The DataItem object represents the record of the database that the row is bound to. After you access the dataItem object, you can use the DataBinder class to extract the current value of the field whose name is the value of the DataValueField property:

```
object dataValueField = DataBinder.Eval(dataItem, DataValueField);
```

The value of the DataValueField property is the name of the foreign key field. After the OnDataBindField method extracts the dataValueField value, it takes two additional actions. Because most database tables allow null values for foreign key fields, the OnDataBindField method inserts a new item into the DropDownList control and sets its Text property to the value of the NullDisplayText property:

```
if (NullDisplayText.Length > 0)
   ddl.Items.Insert(0, new ListItem(NullDisplayText, "-1"));
```

The next section delves into the details of the ExtractValuesFromCell method. This method extracts the SelectedValue of the DropDownList control and inserts it into an IDictionary container that is passed in as its first argument. The OnDataBindField method sets the value of the Value property of the newly added item to the string "-1" to signal the ExtractValuesFromCell method to insert a null value in the IDictionary container.

The OnDataBindField method then sets the SelectedIndex of the DropDownList control to the index of dataValueField if dataValueField is not equal to DBNull. Otherwise it configures the DropDownList control to display the newly added item as its selected item:

```
if (dataValueField.Equals(DBNull.Value))
   ddl.SelectedIndex = 0;
else
   ddl.SelectedIndex = ddl.Items.IndexOf(
                              ddl.Items.FindByValue(dataValueField.ToString()));
```

Listing 18-15 shows the code for the OnDataBindField method.

Listing 18-15: The OnDataBindField method

```
protected override void OnDataBindField(Object sender, EventArgs e)
{
  DropDownList ddl = sender as DropDownList;
  if (ddl == null)
  {
    base.OnDataBindField(sender, e);
    return;
  }

  DataControlFieldCell cell = (DataControlFieldCell)ddl.Parent;

  IDataItemContainer container = (IDataItemContainer)cell.Parent;
```

(continued)

Listing 18-15: *(continued)*

```
    object dataItem = container.DataItem;
    object dataValueField = DataBinder.Eval(dataItem, DataValueField);

    if (NullDisplayText.Length > 0)
      ddl.Items.Insert(0, new ListItem(NullDisplayText, "-1"));

    if (dataValueField.Equals(DBNull.Value))
      ddl.SelectedIndex = 0;
    else
      ddl.SelectedIndex = ddl.Items.IndexOf(
                            ddl.Items.FindByValue(dataValueField.ToString()));
}
```

Extracting Values from Cells

As you'll see in the next chapter, data-bound controls such as GridView and DetailsView allow users to edit database fields. Users click the Update button after they make the desired changes. GridView and DetailsView controls are equipped with internal handlers to handle the Update event. The handlers call the ExtractRowValues method of the GridView or DetailsView control, which in turn calls the ExtractValuesFromCell methods of its cells. The ExtractRowValues method provides each ExtractValuesFromCell method with a container of type IOrderedDictionary. Each ExtractValuesFromCell method extracts the value of its cell and inserts the value into the container. The internal handler for the Update event then uses these values in its internal data access code to update the underlying database fields.

The ExtractValuesFromCell method of the DropDownListField data control field extracts the selected value of the DropDownList control and inserts it into the IOrderedDictionary container passed in as its first input argument. Recall that the OnDataBindField method inserted a new item with the Value property of "-1" into the DropDownList control. This item allows users to select a null value for the foreign key field. The ExtractValuesFromCell method checks the SelectedValue property of the DropDownList control before it inserts the item into the IOrderedDictionary container. If the value is "-1", the method inserts a null value instead.

Listing 18-16 shows the code for the ExtractValuesFromCell method.

Listing 18-16: The ExtractValuesFromCell method

```
public override void ExtractValuesFromCell(IOrderedDictionary dictionary,
      DataControlFieldCell cell,DataControlRowState rowState,bool includeReadOnly)
{
  if (cell.Controls.Count > 0)
  {
    DropDownList ddl = cell.Controls[0] as DropDownList;
    if (ddl == null)
      throw new InvalidOperationException("DropDownListField could not extract
                                    control.");

    string dataValueField = ddl.SelectedValue;

    if (dictionary.Contains(DataValueField))
```

```
  {
    if (dataValueField == "-1")
      dictionary[DataValueField] = DBNull.Value;
    else
      dictionary[DataValueField] = int.Parse(dataValueField);
  }

  else
  {
    if (dataValueField == "-1")
      dictionary.Add(DataValueField, DBNull.Value);

    else
      dictionary.Add(DataValueField, int.Parse(dataValueField));
  }
 }
}
```

Appearance Properties

The `DataControlField` class exposes a property of type `Style` named `ControlStyle`. The `DataControlField` class internally uses the value of the `ControlStyle` property to set the style properties of the server control that the `DataControlField` instance renders. In the case of the `DropDownListField` data control field, the `ControlStyle` property is applied to the `DropDownList` control that the class contains.

The `ControlStyle` property is not the only styling option available. ASP.NET 2.0 comes with a new feature named *Themes*. A theme is implemented as a subfolder under the `App_Themes` folder. The subfolder must have the same name as the theme. A theme subfolder consists of one or more skin files and their respective image and Cascading Style Sheet files. Because ASP.NET 2.0 merges all the skin files of a theme into a single skin file, page developers can use as many skin files as necessary to organize the theme folder. Themes are assigned to the containing page, not the individual controls.

The `@Page` directive in ASP.NET 2.0 exposes a new attribute named `Theme`, which is set to the name of the desired theme. Because all themes are subfolders of the `App_Themes` folder, the ASP.NET framework knows where to find the assigned theme. A skin file includes one or more control skins. A control skin defines the appearance properties of a class of server controls. The definition of a control skin is very similar to the declaration of an instance of the control on an ASP.NET page. This doesn't mean that all properties of a server control can be set in its skin. In general, only the appearance properties can be included and set in a control skin.

If the `SkinID` property of a control skin isn't set, the control skin is treated as the default skin. A default skin is automatically applied to the control instances whose `SkinID` properties aren't set. If the `SkinID` property of a control skin is set, it will be applied only to the control instances whose `SkinID` property is set to the same value.

The `DropDownListField` class exposes two new properties named `SkinID` and `EnableTheming`. It's the responsibility of page developers to set the `SkinID` property of the `DropDownListField` data control field to the value of the `SkinID` property of the desired `DropDownList` control skin. The `EnableTheming` property of the `DropDownListField` object allows page developers to enable or disable theming for the `DropDownList` control server.

The `InitializeDataCell` method sets the `SkinID` and `EnableTheming` properties of the `DropDownList` control to the values of the `SkinID` and `EnableTheming` properties of the `DropDownListField` object. Themes give page developers full control over the appearance properties of the `DropDownList` control that the `DropDownListField` object renders.

Declarative Programming with DropDownListField

Page developers can use the `DropDownListField` data control field declaratively. Listing 18-17 shows a page that uses an instance of the `DropDownListField` declaratively. As Figure 18-1 shows, when the user clicks the Edit button `DropDownListField` automatically retrieves the legal values of the `CategoryID` foreign key field from the underlying Microsoft SQL server database and uses a `DropDownList` control to display them.

Listing 18-17: Using the DropDownListField data control field declaratively

```
<%@ Page Language="C#" Theme="YellowTheme" %>
<%@ Register TagPrefix="custom" Namespace="CustomFields" %>
<html xmlns="http://www.w3.org/1999/xhtml">
<body>
  <form id="form1" runat="server">
    <asp:GridView BorderWidth="1px" BackColor="#DEBA84" CellPadding="3"
    BorderColor="#DEBA84" CellSpacing="2" BorderStyle="None" ID="gv2"
    runat="Server" AutoGenerateColumns="false" AllowSorting="true"
    DataSourceID="GridViewSource" AutoGenerateEditButton="true"
    DataKeyNames="ProductID">
      <FooterStyle ForeColor="#8C4510" BackColor="#F7DFB5"/>
      <PagerStyle ForeColor="#8C4510" HorizontalAlign="Center"/>
      <HeaderStyle ForeColor="White" Font-Bold="True" BackColor="#A55129"/>
      <SelectedRowStyle ForeColor="White" Font-Bold="True" BackColor="#738A9C"/>
      <RowStyle ForeColor="#8C4510" BackColor="#FFF7E7"/>
      <Columns>
        <asp:BoundField DataField="ProductName" HeaderText="Product Name"
        SortExpression="ProductName"/>
        <custom:DropDownListField SkinID="SkinID1" EnableTheming="true"
        DataValueField="CategoryID" DataTextField="CategoryName"
        DataSourceID="DropDownListSource" SortExpression="CategoryName"
        HeaderText="Category Name" NullDisplayText="Unknown" />
      </Columns>
    </asp:GridView>
    <asp:ObjectDataSource ID="GridViewSource" runat="Server"
    SortParameterName="sortExpression" TypeName="Product" SelectMethod="Select"
    UpdateMethod="Update" />
    <asp:SqlDataSource ID="DropDownListSource" runat="Server"
    ConnectionString="<%$ ConnectionStrings:MyConnectionString %>"
    SelectCommand="Select * From Categories" />
  </form>
</body>
</html>
```

Notice that the page doesn't include a single line of C# or VB.NET code. It's all done declaratively. Theming is enabled for the internal `DropDownList` control by setting its `SkinID` property to the `SkinID` of the control skin defined in the theme named `YellowTheme`. The `YellowTheme` is very simple. It sets the background and foreground colors of the internal `DropDownList` control to blue and yellow, respectively. However, page developers can apply their own complex themes to the `DropDownList` control.

Any type of data source control that presents tabular views of its underlying data store can be bound to the internal `DropDownList` control. Page developers do not have to bind both the `GridView` and the internal `DropDownList` controls to the same type of data source control. Listing 18-17 binds the `GridView` control to an `ObjectDataSource` control and the internal `DropDownList` control to a `SqlDataSource` control. The `Product` class used in the `ObjectDataSource` control is a custom class that provides basic database operations such as `Select` and `Update`.

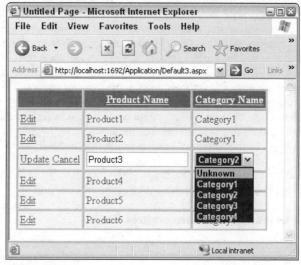

Figure 18-1

CalendarField

ASP.NET page developers must take extra steps to allow users to display and edit date fields of a row in data-bound controls such as `GridView` and `DetailsView`. The state of the row that contains a date field determines what steps must be taken. The control normally does the following when the containing row is not in the Edit or Insert state:

1. Retrieve the current value of the date field.

2. Display the current value of the date field as simple text.

The following are the steps when the containing row is in the Edit or Insert state to allow users to edit the current value of the date field:

1. Instantiate a `Calendar` server control.

2. Retrieve the current value of the date field.

3. Set the `SelectedDate` and `VisibleDate` properties of the `Calendar` control to the current value of the date field.

537

Because none of the existing data control fields provide built-in support for these five steps, page developers must take care of all the steps themselves. In this section you design and implement a custom data control field named `CalendarField` that will automatically take care of all the steps. Page developers will be able to use the `CalendarField` declaratively.

Extending BoundField

The `CalendarField` custom data control field will render a `Calendar` server control when its containing row is in the Edit or Insert state. `CalendarField` will display the current value of its field as simple text when its containing row is not in the Edit or Insert state. `CalendarField` derives from `BoundField` because `BoundField` provides all the necessary base functionality when the containing row is not in the Edit or Insert state, just as it did for the `DropDownListField` earlier in the chapter.

The main shortcoming of `BoundField` is that it displays the current value of the field in a `TextBox` control when the containing row is in the Edit or Insert state. The `TextBox` control isn't the appropriate server control for editing date fields. The `CalendarField` data control field overrides the `InitializeDataCell`, `OnDataBindField`, and `ExtractValuesFromCell` methods of the `BoundField` data control field to add the support needed when the containing row is in the Edit or Insert state.

Listing 18-18 shows all the properties and methods of the `CalendarField` data control field. The following sections present the implementation of these properties and methods.

Listing 18-18: The CalendarField data control field

```
public class CalendarField : BoundField
{
  protected override DataControlField CreateField();
  protected override void OnDataBindField(Object sender, EventArgs e);
  protected override void InitializeDataCell(DataControlFieldCell cell,
                                             DataControlRowState rowState);
  public override void ExtractValuesFromCell(IOrderedDictionary dictionary,
                       DataControlFieldCell cell, DataControlRowState rowState,
                       bool includeReadOnly);
}
```

Overriding InitializeDataCell

As shown in Listing 18-7, the `InitializeDataCell` method of `BoundField` generates the appropriate HTML markup text for the data cell. This method takes two arguments. The first argument is the `DataControlFieldCell` cell being initialized, and the second argument is the state of the containing row.

As discussed, what HTML markup text the `BoundField` class's implementation of the `InitializeDataCell` method emits depends on the state of its containing row. If the containing row is not in the Edit or Insert state, the method simply registers the `OnDataBindField` method as the callback for the `DataBinding` event of the respective `DataControlFieldCell` instance as shown in Listing 18-7. As discussed, when the `DataBinding` event of the cell is raised, the `OnDataBindField` method extracts the current value of the respective field (the name of the field is the value of the `DataField` property). If the current value is null, the value of the `NullDisplayText` property is displayed. Otherwise the current value is displayed as simple text.

As with the `DropDownListField`, the `BoundField` class's implementation of the `InitializeDataCell` method in normal state is exactly what you need, but it is not acceptable in the Edit or Insert state.

You need an implementation that instantiates a Calendar control, so CalendarField overrides the InitializeDataCell method.

The CalendarField data control field's implementation of InitializeDataCell instantiates a Calendar control. As discussed, one of the requirements for CalendarField is that it has to set the SelectedDate and VisibleDate properties of the Calendar control to the current value of the date field. This is done in a callback registered for the DataBinding event of the containing cell control:

```
if (DataField.Length > 0)
  cell.DataBinding += new EventHandler(OnDataBindField);
```

Listing 18-19 shows the implementation of the InitializeDataCell method.

Listing 18-19: The InitializeDataCell method of the Calendar data control field

```
protected override void InitializeDataCell(DataControlFieldCell cell,
                                           DataControlRowState rowState)
{
  if (((rowState & DataControlRowState.Edit) != 0) ||
      ((rowState & DataControlRowState.Insert) != 0))
  {
    Calendar cal = new Calendar();
    cell.Controls.Add(cal);
    if (DataField.Length > 0)
      cell.DataBinding += new EventHandler(OnDataBindField);
  }

  else
    base.InitializeDataCell(cell, rowState);

}
```

Handling the DataBinding Event

When the DataBinding event of the cell is raised the OnDataBindField method is called to display the current value in display mode, that is, as simple text if the cell does not contain any child controls and as the selected date of the Calendar control if the cell does contain child controls.

Before the OnDataBindField method can display the current value in the edit or insert mode, it has to extract the value. The OnDataBindField method uses the parent control of the cell to access the value:

```
IDataItemContainer container = (IDataItemContainer)cell.Parent;
object dataItem = container.DataItem;
```

As you'll see in the next chapter, the parent of the cell is a row of type GridViewRow in GridView controls and of type DetailsViewRow in DetailsView controls. As mentioned, both these types implement the IDataItemContainer interface. IDataItemContainer exposes a property named DataItem of type Object, which represents the record of the database that the row is bound to. After you access the dataItem object, you can use the DataBinder class to extract the current value of the field whose name is the value of the DataField property:

```
object dataFieldValue = DataBinder.Eval(dataItem, DataField);
```

The value of the `DataField` property is the name of the `datetime` database field. `OnDataBindField` then assigns the retrieved date field value to the `SelectedDate` and `VisibleDate` properties of the `Calendar` control:

```
Calendar cal = (Calendar)cell.Controls[0];
DateTime dateTime = Convert.ToDateTime(dataFieldValue);
cal.SelectedDate = dateTime;
cal.VisibleDate = dateTime;
```

Listing 18-20 shows the `OnDataBindField` method.

Listing 18-20: The OnDataBindField method

```
protected override void OnDataBindField(Object sender, EventArgs e)
{
  DataControlFieldCell cell = sender as DataControlFieldCell;
  IDataItemContainer container = (IDataItemContainer)cell.Parent;
  object dataItem = container.DataItem;
  object dataFieldValue = DataBinder.Eval(dataItem, DataField);

  if (cell.Controls.Count > 0)
  {
    if (!(dataFieldValue.Equals(DBNull.Value)))
    {
      Calendar cal = (Calendar)cell.Controls[0];
      DateTime dateTime = Convert.ToDateTime(dataFieldValue);
      cal.SelectedDate = dateTime;
      cal.VisibleDate = dateTime;
    }
  }

  else
    base.OnDataBindField(sender, e);
}
```

Extracting Values from Cells

The `ExtractValuesFromCell` method of the `CalendarField` data control field extracts the selected date of the `Calendar` control and inserts it into the `IOrderedDictionary` container passed in as its first input argument as shown in Listing 18-21.

Listing 18-21: The ExtractValuesFromCell method

```
public override void ExtractValuesFromCell(IOrderedDictionary dictionary,
                      DataControlFieldCell cell, DataControlRowState rowState,
                      bool includeReadOnly)
{
  if (cell.Controls.Count > 0)
  {
    object dataFieldValue = null;

    Calendar cal = cell.Controls[0] as Calendar;
    if (cal == null)
      throw new InvalidOperationException("CalendarField could not extract
                                          control.");
```

```
      else
        dataFieldValue = cal.SelectedDate;

    if (dictionary.Contains(DataField))
        dictionary[DataField] = Convert.ToDateTime(dataFieldValue);

    else
        dictionary.Add(DataField, Convert.ToDateTime(dataFieldValue));
  }
}
```

Appearance Properties

Like the `DropDownListField`, the `CalendarField` class exposes two properties named `SkinID` and `EnableTheming`. It is the responsibility of page developers to set the `SkinID` property of the `Calendar` data control field to the value of the `SkinID` property of the desired `Calendar` control skin. The `EnableTheming` property of the `CalendarField` data control field allows page developers to enable or disable theming for the `Calendar` control server.

The `InitializeDataCell` method sets the `SkinID` and `EnableTheming` properties of the `Calendar` control to the values of the `SkinID` and `EnableTheming` properties of the `CalendarField` data control field. Themes give page developers full control over the appearance properties of the `Calendar` control that the `CalendarField` data control field renders.

Declarative Programming with CalendarField

Page developers can use the `CalendarField` data control field declaratively. Listing 18-22 shows a page that declaratively uses an instance of the `CalendarField`. As Figure 18-2 shows, when the user clicks the Edit button of a row, `CalendarField` automatically renders a `Calendar` server control.

Listing 18-22: Using the CalendarField data control field declaratively

```
<%@ Page Language="C#" Theme="Theme1" %>
<html xmlns="http://www.w3.org/1999/xhtml">
<body>
  <form id="form1" runat="server">
    <asp:GridView ID="GridView1" runat="Server" AutoGenerateEditButton="true"
    AllowSorting="true" AutoGenerateColumns="false" DataSourceID="GridViewSource"
    DataKeyNames="NewsID">
      <Columns>
        <asp:BoundField DataField="Title" HeaderText="Title"
        SortExpression="Title" />
        <asp:BoundField DataField="Body" HeaderText="Body" SortExpression="Body" />
        <custom:CalendarField DataField="ReleaseDate" HeaderText="Release Date"
        NullDisplayText="Unknown" SortExpression="ReleaseDate"
        SkinID="Prefessional2" />
      </Columns>
    </asp:GridView>
    <asp:ObjectDataSource ID="GridViewSource" runat="Server" TypeName="News"
    SelectMethod="Select" UpdateMethod="Update"
    SortParameterName="sortExpression" />
  </form>
</body>
</html>
```

As before, the page doesn't include any C# or VB.NET code; it is all done declaratively. Theming is enabled for the internal `Calendar` control by setting its `SkinID` property to the `SkinID` of the control skin defined in the skin file named `Professional2.skin`. The `News` class used in the `ObjectDataSource` control is a custom class that provides basic database operations such as `Select` and `Update`.

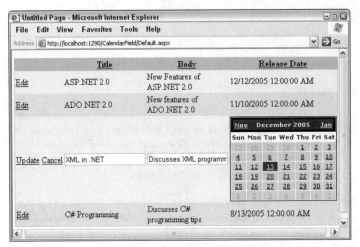

Figure 18-2

Summary

The ASP.NET 2.0 data control field model consists of three important components:

- ❑   `DataControlField`
- ❑   `DataControlFieldCollection`
- ❑   Built-in support of data-bound controls for the `DataControlField` API

This chapter discussed the first two components in detail and designed and implemented two new custom data field controls named `DropDownListField` and `CalendarField` that both inherit from `BoundField`. The next chapter discusses the third component in the context of the implementation of the `GridView` control where you'll see how these three components work together to isolate a data-bound control from the real types of the data control fields that the control uses to display its data columns.

Developing ASP.NET 2.0 Custom Tabular Data-Bound Controls

This chapter builds on Chapters 17 and 18 to show you how to develop ASP.NET 2.0 custom tabular data-bound controls. The ASP.NET 2.0 GridView control is the most complex tabular data-bound control in the ASP.NET 2.0 Framework, and has an amazing feature set. One of the great things about this control is that you can use this feature set declaratively without writing a single line of code.

This chapter implements a fully functional replica of the GridView control from scratch. This replica will serve the following two important purposes:

❑ It will help you gain the knowledge, experience, and skills you need to develop a custom tabular data-bound control as complex and feature-rich as the GridView control.

❑ In Chapter 33 you will use the source code of this replica to implement a custom data-bound WebPart control that you can use in your own Web Parts pages.

When you're writing a feature-rich data-bound control such as GridView, you're embarking on a complex task. You'll save yourself a lot of headache and confusion if you divide the task of writing your custom control into more manageable steps.

These are the steps you follow in this chapter to develop a complex tabular data-bound control such as GridView and DetailsView:

1. Derive your custom control from the CompositeDataBoundControl base class.
2. Override the CreateChildControls method.
3. Override the CreateDataSourceSelectArguments method.

Chapter 19

4. Override the `CreateControlStyle` method.

5. Override the `OnBubbleEvent` method.

6. Override the `Render` method.

7. Manage the states of the simple and complex properties of your custom control across page postbacks.

8. Override the `OnInit` method.

9. Implement the events that your custom control raises.

10. Implement the methods and properties that handle Sort, Page, Delete, Edit, Update, Cancel, and Insert data operations.

11. Implement the custom control that represents each table row.

12. Implement the custom collection class that holds the instances of the custom control.

This chapter consists of different sections, each dedicated to a particular step.

Deriving from the CompositeDataBoundControl

As discussed in Chapter 17, if you derive your custom tabular data-bound control from the `CompositeDataBoundControl` base class, you can save yourself a lot of coding because your control will automatically inherit the following features from base classes of the ASP.NET 2.0 tabular data-bound control model for free:

❑ Thanks to the `BaseDataBoundControl` base class, page developers can use your custom control declaratively without writing any C# or VB.NET code.

❑ Thanks to the `DataBoundControl` base class, your custom control can access any type of data store.

❑ Thanks to the `CompositeDataBoundControl` base class, you can write your custom control without having to implement the following methods:

```
protected override void CreateChildControls();
protected override void PerformDataBinding(IEnumerable data);
public override ControlCollection Controls { get;}
```

The `CompositeDataBoundControl` base class requires you to implement only one method:

```
protected abstract int CreateChildControls(IEnumerable data, bool dataBinding);
```

Your custom control's implementation of this method must enumerate the records contained in the `IEnumerable` object passed in as its argument and create the control hierarchy from the data source if the second argument is set to true and from the saved view state if the second argument is set to false.

Overriding the CreateChildControls Method

This section walks you through the GridView class's implementation of the CreateChildControls method to show you how to override this method in your own custom data-bound controls. Follow these steps to implement the CreateChildControls method of the GridView control:

1. Initialize the parameters that this method uses.

2. Create a collection of type PropertyDescriptorCollection and populate it with PropertyDescriptor objects, where each object fully describes a specified primary key data field. This means that the GridView control supports multi-field primary keys.

3. Create the table that displays data records.

4. Create an instance of the PagedDataSource class and set its properties.

5. Create an array of type DataControlField and populate it with DataControlField objects, where each object fully describes a specified column of the table that displays data records.

6. Create the top pager row.

7. Create the header row.

8. Enumerate the data records and take the following two actions for each enumerated record:

   a. Create a control of type GridViewRow to display the record.

   b. Cache the primary key field values of the record.

9. Create an empty data row if the data source contains no records.

10. Create a collection of type GridViewCollection and populate it with GridView controls, where each control displays a data record.

11. Create the footer row.

12. Create the bottom pager row.

Listing 19-1 shows how the CreateChildControls method uses these 12 steps.

Listing 19-1: The CreateChildControls method

```
protected override int CreateChildControls(IEnumerable dataSource,
                                           bool dataBinding)
{
  InitializeParameters(dataSource, dataBinding);

  if (dataBinding)
    CreatePrimaryKeyPropertyDescriptors();

  table = CreateChildTable();
  Controls.Add(table);

  CreatePagedDataSource();
  CreateDataControlFields();

  if (ShowTopPager)
```

(continued)

Listing 19-1: *(continued)*

```
      CreateTopPagerRow();

   if (ShowHeader)
     CreateHeaderRow();

   foreach (object dataItem2 in pagedDataSource)
   {
     dataItem = dataItem2;
     CreateDataRow();
     CacheDataRowPrimaryKey();
     rowIndex++;
   }

   if (dataRows.Count == 0)
     CreateEmptyDataRow();

   dataKeys = new DataKeyArray(dataKeyArrayList);
   if (IsTrackingViewState)
     ((IStateManager)dataKeys).TrackViewState();

   rows = new GridViewRowCollection(dataRows);

   if (ShowFooter)
     CreateFooterRow();

   if (ShowBottomPager)
     CreateBottomPagerRow();

   return pagedDataSource.DataSourceCount;
}
```

Initializing the Parameters

The following parameters are declared as private fields of the GridView control to simplify the implementation of the CreateChildControls method:

- ❑ table: The Table control used to display data records. This control is the only child control of the GridView control.

- ❑ pagedDataSource: The PagedDataSource object that encapsulates the paging-related properties of the GridView control.

- ❑ fields: The DataControlField array that contains one DataControlField object to represent each column of the Table control that displays data records.

- ❑ rowIndex: The index of the GridViewRow control that displays the current data row.

- ❑ dataItem: The current data row being displayed.

- ❑ primaryKeyPropertyDescriptors: The PropertyDescriptorCollection that contains one PropertyDescriptor to describe each data field of the multi-field primary key.

- ❑ dataRows: The ArrayList object that contains the GridViewRow controls used to display data records.

- ❑ dataKeyArrayList: The ArrayList object that contains one DataKey object for each data record to hold its primary key field names and values.

- ❑ dataSource: The IEnumerable object that contains real or dummy data records. The CreateChildControls method must enumerate this object to create the control hierarchy from the actual data records or saved view state.

- ❑ dataBinding: The flag that specifies whether the IEnumerable object contains real data records.

The CreateChildControls method calls the InitializeParameters method to initialize these parameters:

```
private void InitializeParameters(IEnumerable dataSource, bool dataBinding)
{
  this.table = null;
  this.pagedDataSource = null;
  this.fields = null;
  this.rowIndex = 0;
  this.dataItem = null;
  this.primaryKeyPropertyDescriptors = null;
  this.dataRows.Clear();
  this.dataKeyArrayList.Clear();
  this.dataSource = dataSource;
  this.dataBinding = dataBinding;
}
```

Describing the Primary Key Fields

The GridView control supports multi-field primary keys. As discussed in the previous chapters, the type of the data record and the type of its fields depends on the type of the underlying data source control. For example, the data records and their fields are of type DataRowView and DataColumn, respectively, in the case of the SqlDataSource control.

If the GridView control knew about the real type of the primary key fields (DataColumn), it would be tied to a specific data source control (SqlDataSource) and would not be able to work with all types of data stores. The CreatePrimaryKeyPropertyDescriptors method shown in Listing 19-2 uses the TypeDescriptor class to access the primary key fields in generic fashion without knowing the real field type.

Listing 19-2: The CreatePrimaryKeyPropertyDescriptors method

```
private void CreatePrimaryKeyPropertyDescriptors()
{
  IEnumerator iter = dataSource.GetEnumerator();
  iter.MoveNext();
  PropertyDescriptorCollection pds = TypeDescriptor.GetProperties(iter.Current);
  ArrayList list = new ArrayList();
  foreach (string dataKeyName in DataKeyNames)
  {
```

(continued)

Listing 19-2: *(continued)*

```
      if (pds[dataKeyName] == null)
        throw new NullReferenceException(iter.Current.GetType() +
                               " does not expose the " + dataKeyName + " field");

      list.Add(pds[dataKeyName]);
  }

  primaryKeyPropertyDescriptors = new PropertyDescriptor[list.Count];
  list.CopyTo(primaryKeyPropertyDescriptors);
}
```

The `CreatePrimaryKeyPropertyDescriptors` method first calls the `GetEnumerator` method of the `IEnumerable` object that contains the data records to access its enumerator, and moves the enumerator to the first data record:

```
IEnumerator iter = dataSource.GetEnumerator();
iter.MoveNext();
```

The method then calls the `GetProperties` method of the `TypeDescriptor` class to return a collection of type `PropertyDescriptorCollection` that contains `PropertyDescriptor` objects, where each object provides generic access to a given data field of the data record:

```
PropertyDescriptorCollection pds = TypeDescriptor.GetProperties(iter.Current);
```

Next, the method creates an `ArrayList` object and populates it with the `PropertyDescriptor` objects that describe the primary key fields:

```
ArrayList list = new ArrayList();
foreach (string dataKeyName in DataKeyNames)
{
  if (pds[dataKeyName] == null)
    throw new NullReferenceException(iter.Current.GetType() +
                         " does not expose the " + dataKeyName + " field");
  list.Add(pds[dataKeyName]);
}
```

Finally, the method instantiates the `primaryKeyPropertyDescriptors` array and populates it with the content of the `ArrayList` object:

```
primaryKeyPropertyDescriptors = new PropertyDescriptor[list.Count];
list.CopyTo(primaryKeyPropertyDescriptors);
```

Creating the Child Table Control

The `CreateChildTable` method creates the `Table` control that displays the data records. Notice that this method is marked protected virtual to allow its subclasses to override the method to provide their own implementation:

```
protected virtual Table CreateChildTable()
{
  return new Table();
}
```

You may wonder whether this method is really necessary because you could use its content directly instead: new Table(). The trouble with using the new operator directly in the CreateChildControls method of your custom control is that you tie your control to a particular type of table, specifically the ASP.NET standard Table control. This will not allow your custom control to use other types of table to display the data records. As a matter of fact, Chapter 26 implements a custom tabular data-bound control named CustomGridView that overrides the CreateChildTable method to use a custom table control to display data records.

Creating the PagedDataSource Object

The ASP.NET Framework comes with a standard class named PagedDataSource that encapsulates the paging-related properties of tabular data-bound controls such as GridView. Listing 19-3 shows the GridView control's implementation of the CreatePagedDataSource method.

Listing 19-3: The CreatePagedDataSource method

```
private void CreatePagedDataSource()
{
  pagedDataSource = new PagedDataSource();
  pagedDataSource.DataSource = dataSource;
  if (AllowPaging)
  {
    pagedDataSource.AllowPaging = true;
    pagedDataSource.PageSize = PageSize;
    pagedDataSource.CurrentPageIndex = PageIndex;
  }

  if (dataBinding)
  {
    DataSourceView dv = GetData();
    if (dv.CanPage)
    {
      pagedDataSource.AllowServerPaging = true;
      if (dv.CanRetrieveTotalRowCount)
        pagedDataSource.VirtualCount = SelectArguments.TotalRowCount;
    }

    pageCount = pagedDataSource.PageCount;
  }
}
```

The PagedDataSource class supports two types of paging: custom and server-side. The custom paging feature is specifically designed to support custom paging of the DataGrid control and doesn't apply to the GridView, DetailsView, or FormView controls. These controls only support server-side paging.

The `CreatePagedDataSource` method first instantiates the `pagedDataSource` field and sets its `DataSource` property to the `IEnumerable` object that contains real or dummy records. Recall that this object is passed as the first argument of the `CreateChildControls` method:

```
pagedDataSource = new PagedDataSource();
pagedDataSource.DataSource = dataSource;
```

If the `AllowPaging` property of the `GridView` control is set to true, the method sets the following properties of the `pagedDataSource` field:

```
pagedDataSource.AllowPaging = true;
pagedDataSource.PageSize = PageSize;
pagedDataSource.CurrentPageIndex = PageIndex;
```

The `DataSource`, `AllowPaging`, `PageSize`, and `CurrentPageIndex` properties of the `pagedDataSource` field are set whether or not the `IEnumerable` object contains dummy records, that is, whether the `CreateChildControls` method is creating the control hierarchy from actual or dummy data records. This is because the `CreateChildControls` method needs the values of these properties even when it's creating the control hierarchy from the saved view state.

The `CreatePagedDataSource` method next needs to set those properties of the `pagedDataSource` field that are only applicable when the `CreateChildControls` method is creating the control hierarchy from the actual data records. First it calls the `GetData` method to access the data source view object that represents the default tabular view of the underlying data source control:

```
DataSourceView dv = GetData();
```

Then it checks whether the data source view supports paging. If so, its sets the `AllowServerPaging` property of the `pagedDataSource` field to true:

```
pagedDataSource.AllowServerPaging = true;
```

Recall that the `GridView` control only supports server-side paging, where the underlying data source view is used to page through data records.

To improve performance, the `GridView` control uses the server-side paging to retrieve data one page at a time. Therefore the `GridView` control doesn't know the total row count, which is a problem, as discussed in previous chapters.

As shown in Listing 12-9 of Chapter 12 and Listing 14-1 of Chapter 14, the `ExecuteSelect` method of the view object checks whether the `RetrieveTotalRowCount` property of the `DataSourceSelectArguments` object is set to true. If so, it retrieves the total row count from the underlying data store and assigns it to the `TotalRowCount` property of the `DataSourceSelectArguments` object.

The `CreatePagedDataSource` method assigns the value of the `TotalRowCount` property of this `DataSourceSelectArguments` object to the `VirtualCount` property of the `pagedDataSource` field. As you'll see later, the `GridView` control uses the value of the `VirtualCount` property to evaluate the total page count and consequently the total number of `LinkButtons` it needs to render in its paging interface:

```
if (dv.CanRetrieveTotalRowCount)
   pagedDataSource.VirtualCount = SelectArguments.TotalRowCount;
```

The `CreatePagedDataSource` method first checks whether the underlying data source view is capable of retrieving the total row count before it attempts to access the `TotalRowCount` property of the `DataSourceSelectArgument` object.

Creating the Data Control Fields

The `CreateDataControlFields` method creates and initializes the `DataControlField` objects that represent the columns of the table that displays the data records:

```
private void CreateDataControlFields()
{
  ICollection col = CreateColumns(pagedDataSource, dataBinding);
  fields = new DataControlField[col.Count];
  col.CopyTo(fields, 0);
  foreach (DataControlField field in fields)
    field.Initialize(AllowSorting, this);
}
```

The method calls the `CreateColumns` method to create the `DataControlField` objects, as discussed later:

```
ICollection col = CreateColumns(pagedDataSource, dataBinding);
```

The method then instantiates the `fields` member and populates it with the `DataControlField` objects:

```
fields = new DataControlField[col.Count];
col.CopyTo(fields, 0);
```

Then it enumerates the `fields` collection and initializes each enumerated `DataControlField` object:

```
foreach (DataControlField field in fields)
  field.Initialize(AllowSorting, this);
```

The CreateColumns Method

The `CreateColumns` method uses the `pagedDataSource` and `dataBinding` fields to create the `DataControlField` objects that represent the columns of the table that displays the data records, as shown in Listing 19-4.

Listing 19-4: The CreateColumns method

```
protected virtual ICollection CreateColumns(PagedDataSource dataSource,
                                            bool useDataSource)
{
  ArrayList fieldList = new ArrayList();
  if (AutoGenerateDeleteButton || AutoGenerateEditButton ||
      AutoGenerateSelectButton)
  {
    CommandField field = new CommandField();
    field.ShowDeleteButton = AutoGenerateDeleteButton;
    field.ShowEditButton = AutoGenerateEditButton;
    field.ShowSelectButton = AutoGenerateSelectButton;
    fieldList.Add(field);
```

(continued)

Listing 19-4: *(continued)*

```
  }

  if (AutoGenerateColumns)
  {
    if (useDataSource)
    {
      ArrayList list = new ArrayList();
      AutoGeneratedFieldProperties properties;
      PropertyDescriptorCollection pds =
                       dataSource.GetItemProperties(new PropertyDescriptor[0]);
      foreach (PropertyDescriptor pd in pds)
      {
        if (IsBindableType(pd.PropertyType))
        {
          properties = new AutoGeneratedFieldProperties();
          ((IStateManager)properties).TrackViewState();
          properties.DataField = pd.Name;
          properties.IsReadOnly = pd.IsReadOnly;
          properties.Name = pd.Name;
          properties.Type = pd.PropertyType;
          list.Add(properties);
        }
      }

      autoGeneratedFieldProperties = new AutoGeneratedFieldProperties[list.Count];
      list.CopyTo(autoGeneratedFieldProperties);
    }

    if (autoGeneratedFieldProperties != null && Columns.Count == 0)
    {
      foreach (AutoGeneratedFieldProperties properties in
                                              autoGeneratedFieldProperties)
      {
        AutoGeneratedField field = CreateAutoGeneratedColumn(properties);
        fieldList.Add(field);
      }
    }
  }

  fieldList.AddRange(Columns);
  return fieldList;
}
```

This method first creates the `ArrayList` that will be populated with the data control fields and then takes three actions. The first action creates an instance of the `CommandField` data control field that will render the Edit, Delete, and Select buttons for each table row and adds the instance to the `ArrayList`:

```
CommandField field = new CommandField();
field.ShowDeleteButton = AutoGenerateDeleteButton;
field.ShowEditButton = AutoGenerateEditButton;
field.ShowSelectButton = AutoGenerateSelectButton;
fieldList.Add(field);
```

The `GridView` control exposes three Boolean properties named `AutoGenerateDeleteButton`, `AutoGenerateEditButton`, and `AutoGenerateSelectButton` that allows page developers to specify the desired command buttons.

The second and third actions are performed only if the `AutoGeneratedColumns` property of the `GridView` control is set to true. The main goal of the second action is to create an `AutoGeneratedFieldProperties` collection and populate it with `AutoGeneratedFieldProperties` objects. Each object holds enough information about a data field to create an `AutoGeneratedField` data control field to represent the data field.

The second action is taken only if the control hierarchy is being created from the data source, not the saved view state. The second action creates the `ArrayList` that will be populated with the `AutoGeneratedFieldProperties` objects.

It then calls the `GetItemProperties` of the `pagedDataSource` field to access the `Property DescriptorCollection` that contains one `PropertyDescriptor` object for each data field:

```
PropertyDescriptorCollection pds =
                        dataSource.GetItemProperties(new PropertyDescriptor[0]);
```

Next, it enumerates the `PropertyDescriptorCollection`, creates one `AutoGeneratedField Properties` object for each column, sets the properties of the object, and adds the object to the `ArrayList`:

```
properties = new AutoGeneratedFieldProperties();
((IStateManager)properties).TrackViewState();
properties.DataField = pd.Name;
properties.IsReadOnly = pd.IsReadOnly;
properties.Name = pd.Name;
properties.Type = pd.PropertyType;
list.Add(properties);
```

As mentioned, the `AutoGeneratedFieldProperties` class holds all the information that is required to instantiate an `AutoGeneratedField` data control field. The information includes the following:

- ❑ `DataField`: The name of the data field that the `AutoGeneratedField` represents.
- ❑ `IsReadOnly`: Specifies whether the data field is read-only.
- ❑ `Type`: The `System.Type` object that represents the data type of the data field.

The `TrackViewState` method of the `AutoGeneratedFieldProperties` object is called to track the view state of the object before its properties are set. This ensures that the new property values will be saved to the view state at the end of the current request processing.

Finally, this action instantiates the `autoGeneratedFieldProperties` field and populates it with the `AutoGeneratedFieldProperties` objects:

```
autoGeneratedFieldProperties = new AutoGeneratedFieldProperties[list.Count];
list.CopyTo(autoGeneratedFieldProperties);
```

If the `autoGeneratedFieldProperties` collection isn't empty, the `CreateColumns` method takes the third action, regardless of whether the control hierarchy is being created from the data source or the saved view state. The method simply enumerates the autoGeneratedFieldProperties collection, calls the CreateAutoGeneratedField method to create an AutoGeneratedField data control field for each enumerated autoGeneratedFieldProperties object, and adds the AutoGeneratedField data control fields to the ArrayList:

```
foreach (AutoGeneratedFieldProperties properties in autoGeneratedFieldProperties)
{
  AutoGeneratedField field = CreateAutoGeneratedColumn(properties);
  fieldList.Add(field);
}
```

At the end, the CreateColumns method adds the AutoGeneratedField data control fields to the Columns collection of the GridView control:

```
fieldList.AddRange(Columns);
```

The CreateAutoGeneratedColumn Method

As discussed, one AutoGeneratedFieldProperties object is used to describe each column of the table that displays the data records. This description includes the name and data type of the data field whose values the column displays. The CreateAutoGeneratedColumn method takes an AutoGeneratedFieldProperties object as its argument and uses it to create the AutoGeneratedField data control field that represents the respective column:

```
protected virtual AutoGeneratedField
CreateAutoGeneratedColumn(AutoGeneratedFieldProperties fieldProperties)
{
  AutoGeneratedField field = new AutoGeneratedField(fieldProperties.DataField);

  ((IStateManager)field).TrackViewState();
  field.HeaderText = fieldProperties.Name;
  field.SortExpression = fieldProperties.Name;
  field.ReadOnly = fieldProperties.IsReadOnly;
  field.DataType = fieldProperties.Type;

  return field;
}
```

The AutoGeneratedField class exposes the following properties:

❑   HeaderText: Gets and sets the header text of the column.

❑   SortExpression: Gets and sets the name of the data field whose values the column displays. As you'll see later, when the user clicks the header text of the column, the GridView control uses the SortExpression and SortDirection values to evaluate the expression that will be used in the Order By section of the underlying SQL Select statement to sort the retrieved data records.

❑   ReadOnly: Gets and sets the flag that specifies whether the user will be able to edit the values of this column.

❑   DataType: Gets and sets the System.Type object that represents the data type of the data field values that the column represents.

The `CreateAutoGeneratedColumn` method uses the `Name`, `IsReadOnly`, and `Type` properties of the `AutoGeneratedProperties` to set the properties of the `AutoGeneratedField` class.

Creating the Top Pager Row

The `CreateTopPagerRow` method creates the `GridViewRow` control that displays the top pager of the `GridView` control:

```
private void CreateTopPagerRow()
{
  topPagerRow = CreateRow(-1, -1, DataControlRowType.Pager,
                      DataControlRowState.Normal);
  InitializePager(topPagerRow, fields.Length, pagedDataSource);
  GridViewRowEventArgs tpe = new GridViewRowEventArgs(topPagerRow);
  OnRowCreated(tpe);
  table.Rows.Add(topPagerRow);
}
```

This method calls the `CreateRow` method to create the `GridViewRow` control, then calls the `InitializePager` method to create the contents of the `GridViewRow` control, and finally raises the `RowCreated` event before the `GridViewRow` control is added to the control tree.

The `CreateRow` method and `RowCreated` event are discussed later in this chapter.

The InitializePager Method

The main responsibility of the `InitializePager` method is to create the paging interface of the `GridView` control:

```
protected virtual void InitializePager(GridViewRow row, int columnSpan,
                                   PagedDataSource pagedDataSource)
{
  TableCell cell = new TableCell();
  cell.ColumnSpan = columnSpan;
  row.Cells.Add(cell);

  if (PagerTemplate != null)
    PagerTemplate.InstantiateIn(cell);

  else
    CreateDefaultPager(cell, pagedDataSource);
}
```

The method first creates a `TableCell` control that will contain the paging interface, and adds it to the `Cells` collection of the containing `GridViewRow` control. The method then checks whether the `PagerTemplate` property of the `GridView` control is null. If not, the method calls the `InstantiateIn` method of the property to load the specified paging interface into the `TableCell` control. If so, the method calls the `CreateDefaultPager` method to load the default paging interface into the `TableCell` control.

Notice that the `GridView` control exposes a property of type `ITemplate` named `PagerTemplate` to allow page developers to customize the paging interface of the control.

The CreateDefaultPager Method

The `CreateDefaultPager` method displays the paging interface in a table that has a single row:

```
private void CreateDefaultPager(TableCell pcell, PagedDataSource pagedDataSource)
{
    Table table = new Table();
    pcell.Controls.Add(table);
    TableRow row = new TableRow();
    table.Rows.Add(row);
```

The `GridView` control exposes a property named `PagerSettings` that page developers use to set the paging-related parameters. The `Mode` property of the `PagerSettings` specifies the type of paging interface. There are in general two types. The first type renders one `LinkButton` for each page to provide random page access. The second type doesn't support random page access. The current implementation of the `CreateDefaultPager` method only supports the first type:

```
    TableCell cell;
    LinkButton lb;

    if (this.PagerSettings.Mode == PagerButtons.Numeric ||
        this.PagerSettings.Mode == PagerButtons.NumericFirstLast)
    {
```

The `CreateDefaultPager` method then checks whether the user has requested the last page. If so, the method checks whether the pager settings is set to `NumericFirstLast`. If so, the method creates a `LinkButton` that displays the text "<<" to represent the first page. The method then renders a `LinkButton` that displays the text " . . . ". End users click this link button to see the next page list:

```
        if (pagedDataSource.CurrentPageIndex >= this.PagerSettings.PageButtonCount)
        {
            if (this.PagerSettings.Mode == PagerButtons.NumericFirstLast)
            {
                cell = new TableCell();
                row.Cells.Add(cell);

                lb = new LinkButton();
                cell.Controls.Add(lb);

                lb.Text = "<<";
                lb.CommandName = "First";
            }

            cell = new TableCell();
            row.Cells.Add(cell);

            lb = new LinkButton();
            cell.Controls.Add(lb);

            lb.Text = "...";
            lb.CommandName = "Page";
            lb.CommandArgument = "-2";
        }
```

The `CreateDefaultPager` method then renders one `LinkButton` for each available page where each link button displays its associated page number:

```
if (pagedDataSource.CurrentPageIndex < pagedDataSource.PageCount - 2)
{
  startIndex = pagedDataSource.CurrentPageIndex;
  endIndex = pagedDataSource.CurrentPageIndex + PagerSettings.PageButtonCount;
}
else
{
  startIndex = pagedDataSource.CurrentPageIndex - 1;
  endIndex = pagedDataSource.CurrentPageIndex +
             PagerSettings.PageButtonCount - 1;
}
for (int i = startIndex; i < endIndex; i++)
{
  cell = new TableCell();
  row.Cells.Add(cell);

  if (i != pagedDataSource.CurrentPageIndex)
  {
    lb = new LinkButton();
    cell.Controls.Add(lb);

    lb.Text = (i + 1).ToString();
    lb.CommandName = "Page";
    lb.CommandArgument = i.ToString();
  }

  else
    cell.Text = (i + 1).ToString();
}
```

The `CreateDefaultPager` method then renders the `LinkButton` that displays the text "...". End users click this link button to view the previous page list. The method finally renders the link button that displays the text ">>" to represent the last page:

```
if (pagedDataSource.PageCount >= pagedDataSource.CurrentPageIndex +
    this.PagerSettings.PageButtonCount)
{
  cell = new TableCell();
  row.Cells.Add(cell);

  lb = new LinkButton();
  cell.Controls.Add(lb);

  lb.Text = "...";
  lb.CommandName = "Page";
  lb.CommandArgument = "-1";

  if (this.PagerSettings.Mode == PagerButtons.NumericFirstLast)
  {
    cell = new TableCell();
```

```
            row.Cells.Add(cell);

        lb = new LinkButton();
        cell.Controls.Add(lb);

        lb.Text = ">>";
        lb.CommandName = "Last";
      }
    }
  }
}
```

Creating the Header Row

The CreateHeaderRow method instantiates and initializes the GridViewRow control that renders the header of the GridView control:

```
private void CreateHeaderRow()
{
  headerRow = CreateRow(0, 0, DataControlRowType.Header,
                    DataControlRowState.Normal);
  InitializeRow(headerRow, fields);
  GridViewRowEventArgs he = new GridViewRowEventArgs(headerRow);
  OnRowCreated(he);
  table.Rows.Add(headerRow);
}
```

This method calls the CreateRow method to create the GridViewRow control, then calls the InitializeRow method to create the contents of the control, and finally raises the RowCreated event. The CreateRow and InitializeRow methods and the RowCreated event are discussed shortly.

Enumerating the Data Records

The CreateChildControls method enumerates the data records. For each record, the method calls the CreateDataRow method to create the GridViewRow control that displays the data record, and then calls the CacheDataRowPrimaryKey method to create the DataKey object that caches the names and values of the primary key fields of the enumerated data record:

```
protected override int CreateChildControls(IEnumerable dataSource,
                                          bool dataBinding)
{
  ...
  foreach (object dataItem2 in pagedDataSource)
  {
    dataItem = dataItem2;
    CreateDataRow();
    CacheDataRowPrimaryKey();
    rowIndex++;
  }
  ...
}
```

The CreateDataRow Method

The CreateDataRow method uses the index of the table row being created to determine its state. Notice that the same row can be in more than one state. The ASP.NET Framework exposes an enumeration type named DataControlRowState with possible values of Normal, Alternate, Edit, Selected, and Insert. Tabular data-bound controls such as GridView and DetailsView use these enumeration values to specify row states. You must use the bitwise OR (|) operation to add a new state to the same row, and the bitwise AND (&) operation to determine if a row is in a given state:

```
private void CreateDataRow()
{
  DataControlRowState dataRowState;

  dataRowState = (rowIndex % 2) == 0 ? DataControlRowState.Normal :
                                DataControlRowState.Alternate;
  if (rowIndex == EditIndex)
    dataRowState |= DataControlRowState.Edit;
  if (rowIndex == SelectedIndex)
    dataRowState |= DataControlRowState.Selected;
```

The CreateDataRow method then calls the CreateRow method to create the GridViewRow control that displays the current data record, and the InitializeRow method to create the contents of the control. These two methods are discussed later in the chapter.

```
GridViewRow dataRow = CreateRow(rowIndex, rowIndex, DataControlRowType.DataRow,
                                dataRowState);
InitializeRow(dataRow, fields);
```

The CreateDataRow method then raises the RowCreated event before the GridViewRow control is added to the control tree. Page developers can register a callback for this event where they can customize the GridViewRow control before it's added to the control tree:

```
GridViewRowEventArgs be = new GridViewRowEventArgs(dataRow);
OnRowCreated(be);
dataRows.Add(dataRow);
table.Rows.Add(dataRow);
```

The method then checks whether the current enumerated data record is a dummy record. If not, the method assigns the current data record (the dataItem field) to the DataItem property of the GridViewRow control, calls its DataBind method, and raises the RowDataBound method to signal the end of the data-binding process:

```
if (dataBinding)
{
  dataRow.DataItem = dataItem;
  dataRow.DataBind();
  OnRowDataBound(be);
}
}
```

Page developers can register a callback for the RowDataBound event where they can access the data record to which the GridViewRow control is bound to customize the data binding of the control.

The CacheDataRowPrimaryKey Method

The CacheDataRowPrimaryKey method shown in Listing 19-5 caches the names and values of the primary key fields of the current data record.

Listing 19-5: The CacheDataRowPrimaryKey method

```
private void CacheDataRowPrimaryKey()
{
  DataKey dataKey;
  if (dataBinding)
  {
    OrderedDictionary dic = new OrderedDictionary();
    foreach (PropertyDescriptor pd in primaryKeyPropertyDescriptors)
    {
      dic.Add(pd.Name, pd.GetValue(dataItem));
    }

    dataKey = new DataKey(dic, DataKeyNames);
    dataKeyArrayList.Add(dataKey);
  }

  else
  {
    dataKey = new DataKey(new OrderedDictionary(), DataKeyNames);
    dataKeyArrayList.Add(dataKey);
  }
}
```

The method first checks whether the dataBinding field is set to true, that is, whether the current table row is being created from the data source. If so, the method first creates an OrderedDictionary collection, and then enumerates the primaryKeyPropertyDescriptors collection. Recall that this collection contains the PropertyDescriptor objects that represent the data fields of a multi-field primary key.

The CacheDataRowPrimaryKey method calls the Name property and GetValue method of each propertyDescriptor object to access the name and value of the respective primary key data field of the current data record and adds them to the OrderedDictionary collection.

The method then creates a DataKey object, populates it with the contents of the OrderedDictionary collection, and adds it to the dataKeyArrayList field. Recall that this collection field holds the names and values of the primary key fields of the records being displayed.

Creating the Empty Data Row

There are times when a database query returns no records. The CreateEmptyDataRow method creates an empty data row for these times, as shown in Listing 19-6.

Listing 19-6: The CreateEmptyDataRow method

```
private void CreateEmptyDataRow()
{
  GridViewRow emptyDataRow = CreateRow(-1, -1, DataControlRowType.EmptyDataRow,
                                    DataControlRowState.Normal);
  TableCell cell = new TableCell();
  cell.ColumnSpan = fields.Length;

  if (emptyDataTemplate != null)
    emptyDataTemplate.InstantiateIn(cell);
  else
    cell.Text = EmptyDataText;

  emptyDataRow.Cells.Add(cell);
  GridViewRowEventArgs ee = new GridViewRowEventArgs(emptyDataRow);
  OnRowCreated(ee);
  table.Rows.Add(emptyDataRow);
}
```

The method calls the `CreateRow` method to create the `GridViewRow` control that represents the empty row:

```
GridViewRow emptyDataRow = CreateRow(-1, -1, DataControlRowType.EmptyDataRow,
                                    DataControlRowState.Normal);
```

The method then checks whether the `EmptyDataTemplate` property of the `GridView` control is set. If so, it calls the `InstantiateIn` method of the template property to load a `TableCell` control with the HTML markup text that page developers have specified in the respective `.aspx` file. If not, it simply displays the value of the `EmptyDataText` property of the `GridView` control:

```
if (emptyDataTemplate != null)
  emptyDataTemplate.InstantiateIn(cell);
```

Finally, the method raises the `RowCreated` event before the `GridViewRow` control is added to the control tree. Page developers can register a callback for this event where they can customize the control:

```
GridViewRowEventArgs ee = new GridViewRowEventArgs(emptyDataRow);
OnRowCreated(ee);
table.Rows.Add(emptyDataRow);
```

Creating and Populating the GridViewRowCollection

The `GridView` control exposes a collection property of type `GridViewRowCollection` named `Rows` that contains the `GridViewRow` controls that display the data records:

```
private GridViewRowCollection rows;
public virtual GridViewRowCollection Rows
{
  get
```

```
    {
        EnsureChildControls();
        return rows;
    }
}
```

The getter of this property calls the `EnsureChildControls` method before it attempts to access the rows field. Recall that the `EnsureChildControls` method creates the control hierarchy if it hasn't been created yet. The `CreateChildControls` method instantiates and populates this collection with the appropriate `GridViewRow` controls:

```
protected override int CreateChildControls(IEnumerable dataSource,
                                           bool dataBinding)
{
    ...
    foreach (object dataItem2 in pagedDataSource)
    {
        dataItem = dataItem2;
        CreateDataRow();
        CacheDataRowPrimaryKey();
        rowIndex++;
    }
    ...
    rows = new GridViewRowCollection(dataRows);
    ...
}
```

The CreateRow Method

As you saw in previous sections, the `CreateTopPagerRow`, `CreateHeaderRow`, `CreateDataRow`, `CreateEmptyDataRow`, `CreateFooterRow`, and `CreateBottomPagerRow` methods all call the `CreateRow` method to create the `GridViewRow` control that displays the row:

```
protected virtual GridViewRow CreateRow(int rowIndex, int dataSourceIndex,
                        DataControlRowType rowType, DataControlRowState rowState)
{
    return new GridViewRow(rowIndex, dataSourceIndex, rowType, rowState);
}
```

You may wonder if there is really a need for exposing a new method if it only consists of one line of code. The answer lies in extensibility. If the `CreateChildControls` method of your custom data-bound control were to use the new `GridViewRow(rowIndex, dataSourceIndex, rowType, rowState)` statement directly, it would be tied to a particular type of row, and wouldn't be able to use a different type of row control to display the respective row.

The InitializeRow Method

As mentioned, the `CreateTopPagerRow`, `CreateHeaderRow`, `CreateDataRow`, `CreateEmptyDataRow`, `CreateFooterRow`, and `CreateBottomPagerRow` methods all call the `InitializeRow` method (shown in Listing 19-7) after the `CreateRow` method to create the contents of the `GridViewRow` control that the `CreateRow` method creates:

Listing 19-7: The InitializeRow method

```
protected virtual void InitializeRow(GridViewRow row, DataControlField[] fields)
{
  DataControlCellType cellType;
  DataControlFieldCell cell;

  switch (row.RowType)
  {
    case DataControlRowType.Header:
      cellType = DataControlCellType.Header;
      break;
    case DataControlRowType.Footer:
      cellType = DataControlCellType.Footer;
      break;
    default:
      cellType = DataControlCellType.DataCell;
      break;
  }

  foreach (DataControlField field in fields)
  {
    cell = new DataControlFieldCell(field);
    row.Cells.Add(cell);
    field.InitializeCell(cell, cellType, row.RowState, row.RowIndex);
  }
}
```

If the `InitializeRow` method of the `GridView` control were to render the HTML contents of the cells of the respective `GridViewRow` control directly, the `GridView` control would be tied to particular HTML contents and would not be able to use other HTML contents to display data fields.

As discussed in Chapter 18, the method must delegate the responsibility of rendering the HTML contents of each cell to its associated data control field. The `InitializeRow` method does this by enumerating the data control fields in the `fields` collection, creating a `DataControlFieldCell` control for each enumerated data control field, and adding the control to the `Cells` collection of the relevant `GridViewRow` control:

```
cell = new DataControlFieldCell(field);
row.Cells.Add(cell);
```

The method then calls the `InitializeCell` method of each enumerated data control field:

```
field.InitializeCell(cell, cellType, row.RowState, row.RowIndex);
```

Recall from Chapter 18 that the `InitializeCell` method uses the cell type, row state, and row index to create the appropriate HTML contents for the respective cell.

Overriding the CreateDataSourceSelectArguments Method

The `GridView` control inherits the `CreateDataSourceSelectArguments` method from the `DataBoundControl` base class. As discussed in Chapter 17, this method creates and initializes the `DataSourceSelectArguments` object that is passed to the `Select` method of the underlying data source view. Tabular data-bound controls set the properties of this object to request extra operations such as sorting and paging on the retrieved data. Listing 19-8 shows the `CreateDataSourceSelectArguments` method for the `GridView` class.

Listing 19-8: The CreateDataSourceSelectArguments method

```
protected override DataSourceSelectArguments CreateDataSourceSelectArguments()
{
  DataSourceSelectArguments dataSourceSelectArguments =
                                        new DataSourceSelectArguments();
  DataSourceView dv = GetData();
  if (dv.CanSort)
  {
    string sortExpression = SortExpression + ((sortDirection ==
                                  SortDirection.Ascending) ? " ASC" : " DESC");
    if (sortExpression != null && sortExpression.Trim() != "" &&
        sortExpression != " ASC" && sortExpression != " DESC")
      dataSourceSelectArguments.SortExpression = sortExpression;
  }

  if (dv.CanPage)
  {
    dataSourceSelectArguments.StartRowIndex = PageIndex - 1;
    dataSourceSelectArguments.MaximumRows = PageSize;
  }

  if (dv.CanRetrieveTotalRowCount)
    dataSourceSelectArguments.RetrieveTotalRowCount = true;

  return dataSourceSelectArguments;
}
```

The `CreateDataSourceSelectArguments` method first creates a `DataSourceSelectArguments` object. Then it calls the `GetData` method that it inherits from the `DataBoundControl` base class to access the underlying data source view object.

The method then checks whether the view supports sorting. If so, it uses the `SortExpression` and `SortDirection` properties of the `GridView` control to evaluate the sort expression value:

```
string sortExpression = SortExpression + ((sortDirection ==
                                  SortDirection.Ascending) ? " ASC" : " DESC");
```

Then it assigns this sort expression value to the `SortExpression` property of the `DataSourceSelectArguments` object:

```
dataSourceSelectArguments.SortExpression = sortExpression;
```

The `CreateDataSourceSelectArguments` method then checks whether the view supports paging. If so, it assigns the values of the `PageIndex` and `PageSize` properties of the `GridView` control to the `StartRowIndex` and `MaximumRow` properties of the `DataSourceSelectArguments` object:

```
dataSourceSelectArguments.StartRowIndex = PageIndex - 1;
dataSourceSelectArguments.MaximumRows = PageSize;
```

The underlying data source view uses these two values to instruct the respective stored procedure to retrieve the appropriate page of records from the underlying data store.

The `CreateDataSourceSelectArguments` method then checks whether the view is capable of retrieving the total row count. If so, it sets the `RetrieveTotalRowCount` property of the `DataSourceSelectArguments` object to true:

```
dataSourceSelectArguments.RetrieveTotalRowCount = true;
```

As shown in Listing 12-9 of Chapter 12 and Listing 14-1 of Chapter 14, the `ExecuteSelect` method of the underlying data source view retrieves the total row count if the value of this property is set to true.

Overriding the CreateControlStyle Method

The `GridView` control inherits the `CreateControlStyle` method from the `WebControl` base class. As discussed in Chapter 3, this method creates the `Style` object that will be applied to the HTML element that contains the entire control (in this case the entire `GridView` control). Because the containing HTML element in the case of the `GridView` control is an HTML table element, the control overrides the `CreateControlStyle` method to create a `TableStyle` object:

```
protected override Style CreateControlStyle()
{
  return new TableStyle();
}
```

The `GridView` control exposes five properties named `GridLines`, `CellSpacing`, `CellPadding`, `BackImageUrl`, and `HorizontalAlign` that simply delegate to the respective properties of the `TableStyle` object. For example:

```
public virtual HorizontalAlign HorizontalAlign
{
  get { return ((TableStyle)ControlStyle).HorizontalAlign; }
  set { ((TableStyle)ControlStyle).HorizontalAlign = value; }
}
```

Overriding the OnBubbleEvent Method

As discussed in Chapter 5, composite controls such as `GridView` must override the `OnBubbleEvent` method to expose the events that their child controls raise as their own events. This gives the illusion that the `GridView` control itself raises these events. Listing 19-9 shows the `OnBubbleEvent` for the `GridView` class.

Listing 19-9: The OnBubbleEvent method

```
protected override bool OnBubbleEvent(object source, EventArgs e)
{
  bool handled = false;
  GridViewCommandEventArgs ce = e as GridViewCommandEventArgs;
  if (ce != null)
  {
    OnRowCommand(ce);
    this.EventHandler(ce.CommandName, ce.CommandArgument.ToString());
    handled = true;
  }

  return handled;
}
```

The OnBubbleEvent method first checks whether the event is of type GridViewCommandEventHandler because this is the only type of event that the GridView control handles. If so, the method raises the RowCommand event and calls the EventHandler method to handle the event.

The EventHandler Method

The EventHandler method uses the name of the command to determine which method must handle the event, as shown in Listing 19-10. The ASP.NET Framework exposes an enumeration named DataControlCommands that tabular data-bound controls such as GridView use to identify different events. For example, the CancelCommandName value is equivalent to the Cancel string value.

Listing 19-10: The EventHandler method

```
void EventHandler(string commandName, string commandArgument)
{
  switch (commandName)
  {
    case DataControlCommands.CancelCommandName:
      CancelEdit(int.Parse(commandArgument));
      break;
    case DataControlCommands.DeleteCommandName:
      DeleteRow(int.Parse(commandArgument));
      break;
    case DataControlCommands.EditCommandName:
      EditRow(int.Parse(commandArgument));
      break;
    case DataControlCommands.FirstPageCommandArgument:
      PageRows(0);
      break;
    case DataControlCommands.InsertCommandName:
      break;
    case DataControlCommands.LastPageCommandArgument:
      PageRows(PageCount - 1);
```

```
        break;
    case DataControlCommands.NewCommandName:
      break;
    case DataControlCommands.NextPageCommandArgument:
      if (PageIndex < PageCount - 1)
        PageRows(PageIndex + 1);
      break;
    case DataControlCommands.PageCommandName:
      int arg = int.Parse(commandArgument);
      if (arg == -2)
        arg = PageIndex - this.PagerSettings.PageButtonCount;
      else if (arg == -1)
        arg = PageIndex + this.PagerSettings.PageButtonCount;

      if (arg < 0) arg = 0;
      if (arg > PageCount - 1) arg = PageCount - 1;

      PageRows(arg);
      break;
    case DataControlCommands.PreviousPageCommandArgument:
      if (PageIndex > 0)
        PageRows(PageIndex - 1);
      break;
    case DataControlCommands.SelectCommandName:
      SelectRow(int.Parse(commandArgument));
      break;
    case DataControlCommands.SortCommandName:
      if (SortExpression == commandArgument)
      {
        if (sortDirection == SortDirection.Ascending)
          sortDirection = SortDirection.Descending;
        else
          sortDirection = SortDirection.Ascending;
      }
      else
      {
        sortExpression = commandArgument;
        sortDirection = SortDirection.Ascending;
      }
      Sort(sortExpression, sortDirection);
      break;
    case DataControlCommands.UpdateCommandName:
      UpdateRow(int.Parse(commandArgument), true);
      break;
  }
}
```

The UpdateRow Method

After making the desired changes, the user clicks the Update button and posts the page back to the server, where the UpdateRow method shown in Listing 19-11 is automatically called to handle the event.

Listing 19-11: The UpdateRow method

```
public virtual void UpdateRow(int rowIndex, bool causesValidation)
{
  if (causesValidation)
    Page.Validate();

  DataSourceView dv = GetData();
  if (dv.CanUpdate)
  {
    updateEventsKeys = DataKeys[rowIndex].Values;
    updateEventsNewValues = new OrderedDictionary();
    ExtractRowValues(updateEventsNewValues, Rows[rowIndex], false, false);

    GridViewUpdateEventArgs e = new GridViewUpdateEventArgs(rowIndex,
                            updateEventsKeys, updateEventsNewValues, null);
    OnRowUpdating(e);
    if (!e.Cancel)
      dv.Update(updateEventsKeys, updateEventsNewValues, null,
                new DataSourceViewOperationCallback(UpdateOperationCallback));
  }
}
```

The method first checks whether the causesValidation field is set to true. If so, it calls the Validate method of the containing Page object to validate the new data field values. The method then calls the GetData method of the DataBoundControl base class to access the underlying default tabular view.

The method then checks whether the view can update the underlying data store. If so, it begins the update process. Recall that the GridView control uses one DataKey object for each data record to cache the names and values of the primary key fields of the record, and adds the object to the DataKeys collection. The UpdateRow method uses the index of the row being updated to access its associated DataKey object. The DataKey class exposes a collection property of type OrderedDictionary named Values that contains one DictionaryEntry object for each primary key data field, where the Key and Value properties of the object are set to the name and value of the data field. The UpdateRow method assigns the Values collections to the updateEventsKeys collection field of the GridView control:

```
updateEventsKeys = DataKeys[rowIndex].Values;
```

The UpdateRow method then creates an OrderedDictionary collection, calls the ExtractRowValues method of the GridView control to populate the collection with the names and new values of the data fields being updated, and assigns the collection to the updateEventNewValues collection field of the GridView control:

```
updateEventsNewValues = new OrderedDictionary();
ExtractRowValues(updateEventsNewValues, Rows[rowIndex], false, false);
```

Next, the method raises the RowUpdating event. Page developers can register a callback for this event where they can use application-specific business rules to determine whether the update operation is permitted. If not, they can set the Cancel property to false to signal the UpdateRow method to abort the update operation.

```
GridViewUpdateEventArgs e = new GridViewUpdateEventArgs(rowIndex,
                            updateEventsKeys, updateEventsNewValues, null);
OnRowUpdating(e);
```

Finally, the method checks whether the Cancel property is set to true. If not, it calls the Update method of the view object and passes the updateEventsKeys and updateEventsNewValues collections as its arguments. Because the update operation is asynchronous, the UpdateRow method registers the UpdateOperationCallback method as the callback:

```
if (!e.Cancel)
   dv.Update(updateEventsKeys, updateEventsNewValues, null,
               new DataSourceViewOperationCallback(UpdateOperationCallback));
```

The UpdateOperationCallback Method

The Update method of the view object calls the UpdateOperationCallback method after updating the underlying data store record:

```
protected virtual bool UpdateOperationCallback(int affectedRows, Exception ex)
{
   GridViewUpdatedEventArgs e = new GridViewUpdatedEventArgs(affectedRows, ex,
                            updateEventsKeys, updateEventsNewValues,null);
   OnRowUpdated(e);
    if (ex != null && !e.ExceptionHandled)
       throw ex;
   if (!e.KeepInEditMode)
     EditIndex = -1;
   RequiresDataBinding = true;
   return true;
}
```

This method first raises the RowUpdated event. Page developers can register a callback for this event where they can set the KeepInEditMode Boolean property to true to signal the UpdateOperationCallback method to keep the row in edit mode. Developers can also use a custom exception handling scheme to handle the exception, if any is raised, and set the ExceptionHandled property to true to bypass the default exception handling mechanism.

The UpdateOperationCallback method sets the RequiresDataBinding property of the BaseDataBoundControl base class to true to trigger the entire data-binding process.

The ExtractRowValues Method

Recall that the UpdateRow method calls the ExtractRowValues method to extract the names and values of the data fields being updated:

```
protected virtual void ExtractRowValues(IOrderedDictionary fieldValues,
           GridViewRow row, bool includeReadOnlyFields, bool includePrimaryKey)
{
  Columns.FieldsChanged += new EventHandler(Columns_FieldsChanged);
  foreach (DataControlFieldCell cell in row.Cells)
```

```
                cell.ContainingField.ExtractValuesFromCell(fieldValues, cell, row.RowState,
                                                includeReadOnlyFields);

    if (!includePrimaryKey && DataKeyNames != null)
    {
      foreach (string dataKeyName in DataKeyNames)
       fieldValues.Remove(dataKeyName);
    }
  }
}
```

This method takes the following four arguments:

❑   fieldValues: The OrderedDictionary collection that the UpdateRow method passes to the
    ExtractRowValues method. The ExtractRowValue method will populate this collection with
    the names and values of the data fields being updated.

❑   row: The GridViewRow control whose associated data record is being updated.

❑   includeReadOnlyFields: The Boolean flag that specifies whether the ExtractRowValues
    method must include the names and values of the readonly fields in the fieldValues collection.

❑   includePrimaryKey: The Boolean flag that specifies whether the ExtractRowValues method
    must include the names and values of the primary key fields in the fieldValues collection.

The ExtractRowValues method first registers the Columns_FieldsChanged method as the callback for
the FieldsChanged event of the Columns collection of the GridView control. As discussed in Chapter
18, this event is raised when one of the data control fields in the collection changes:

```
  Columns.FieldsChanged += new EventHandler(Columns_FieldsChanged);
```

The ExtractRowValues method then enumerates the DataControlFieldCells in the Cells collection of the current GridViewRow control and calls the ExtractValuesFromCell method of the
ContainingField of each enumerated DataControlFieldCell. The ContainingField property of
the DataControlFieldCell is of type DataControlField, and refers to the containing data control
field of the class. As discussed in Chapter 18, the DataControlField class exposes a method named
ExtractValuesFromCell that retrieves the data field value from the cell and adds the value to the
IOrderedDictionary collection passed in as its argument:

```
  foreach (DataControlFieldCell cell in row.Cells)
      cell.ContainingField.ExtractValuesFromCell(fieldValues, cell, row.RowState,
                                      includeReadOnlyFields);
```

The DeleteRow Method

The DeleteRow method deletes the row with the specified index:

```
  public virtual void DeleteRow(int rowIndex)
  {
    DataSourceView dv = GetData();
    if (dv.CanDelete)
    {
```

```
      deleteEventsKeys = DataKeys[rowIndex].Values;
      GridViewDeleteEventArgs e =
          new GridViewDeleteEventArgs(rowIndex, deleteEventsKeys, deleteEventsValues);
      OnRowDeleting(e);
      if (!e.Cancel)
      {
        dv.Delete(deleteEventsKeys, null,
                      new DataSourceViewOperationCallback(DeleteOperationCallback));
      }
    }
  }
```

The method first calls the `GetData` method to access the underlying view and checks whether the view can delete records from its underlying data store. If so, it assigns the `Values` collection of the respective `DataKey` object to the `deleteEventsKeys` collection field as discussed before. The `Values` collection contains the names and values of the primary key fields of the record being deleted:

```
      deleteEventsKeys = DataKeys[rowIndex].Values;
```

Then the method raises the `RowDeleting` event to allow page developers to decide whether the delete operation is permitted:

```
  GridViewDeleteEventArgs e =
          new GridViewDeleteEventArgs(rowIndex, deleteEventsKeys, deleteEventsValues);
  OnRowDeleting(e);
```

Finally, the method checks whether page developers have set the `Cancel` property to true to abort the delete operation. If not, it calls the `Delete` method of the view object and passes the `deleteEventsKeys` collection field as its argument. Because the delete operation is asynchronous, it registers the `DeleteOperationCallback` method as the callback:

```
  dv.Delete(deleteEventsKeys, null,
                new DataSourceViewOperationCallback(DeleteOperationCallback));
```

The following code fragment shows the `DeleteOperationCallback` method:

```
  private bool DeleteOperationCallback(int rowsAffected, Exception ex)
  {
    GridViewDeletedEventArgs e =
          new GridViewDeletedEventArgs(rowsAffected, ex,deleteEventsKeys,null);
    OnRowDeleted(e);
     if (ex != null && !e.ExceptionHandled)
         throw ex;
    return true;
  }
```

The `Delete` method of the view object calls the `DeleteOperationCallback` method after deleting the record from the underlying data store. The `DeleteOperationCallback` method first raises the `RowDeleted` event. Page developers can register a callback for this event, where they can use their own custom exception handling mechanism to handle the exception if any exception is raised and set the `ExceptionHandled` property to true to bypass the default exception handling mechanism.

PageRows

The `PageRows` method handles the paging event as shown in the following code:

```
void PageRows(int newPageIndex)
{
  GridViewPageEventArgs e = new GridViewPageEventArgs(newPageIndex);
  OnPageIndexChanging(e);
  if (!e.Cancel)
  {
    PageIndex = newPageIndex;
    OnPageIndexChanged(EventArgs.Empty);
    EditIndex = -1;
    RequiresDataBinding = true;
  }
}
```

This method handles the event by first raising the `PageIndexChanging` event. Page developers can register a callback with this event where they can use application-specific business rules to decide whether the paging operation is permitted. Page developers must set the `Cancel` property to true to signal the `PageRows` method to abort the paging operation.

If the `Cancel` property isn't set to true, `PageRows` assigns the new page index to the `PageIndex` property of the `GridView` control, raises the `PageIndexChanged` event to signal the completion of the paging operation, and calls the `RequiresDataBinding` property to trigger the entire data-binding process.

Sort

The `Sort` method takes the sort expression and sort direction as its arguments and uses them to handle the sort event as shown in the following code:

```
public virtual void Sort(string sortExpression, SortDirection sortDirection)
{
  GridViewSortEventArgs e =
                new GridViewSortEventArgs(sortExpression, sortDirection);
  OnSorting(e);
  if (!e.Cancel)
  {
    this.sortExpression = e.SortExpression;
    this.sortDirection = e.SortDirection;
    EditIndex = -1;
    RequiresDataBinding = true;
    OnSorted(EventArgs.Empty);
  }
}
```

This method first raises the `Sorting` event. Page developers can register a callback for this event where they can set the `Cancel` property to specify whether the sorting operation is permitted, change the value of the `SortExpression` property to the desired value, or change the value of the `SortDirection` property to the desired value.

If the sorting operation is allowed and doesn't violate application-specific business rules, the `Sort` method assigns the values of the `SortExpression` and `SortDirection` properties to the `sortExpression` and `sortDirection` fields of the `GridView` control.

The `Sort` method then sets the `RequiresDataBinding` property to true to trigger the data-binding process. As discussed in Chapter 17, as part of data-binding process, the `CreateDataSourceSelectArguments` method is automatically called. As shown in Listing 19-8, this method uses the values of the `sortExpression` and `sortDirection` fields of the `GridView` control to set the value of the `SortExpression` property of the `DataSourceSelectArguments` object.

As discussed in Chapter 17, as part of data-binding process, the `DataSourceSelectArguments` object is automatically passed to the `Select` method of the view object where the value of the `SortExpression` property of the `DataSourceSelectArguments` object is passed to the Order By section of the underlying SQL `Select` statement.

Finally, the `Sort` method raises the `Sorted` event to signal the completion of the sort operation.

Overriding the Render Method

Recall from Chapter 3 that every control that directly or indirectly derives from `WebControl` exposes a property named `ControlStyle`. The type of this property depends on the type of the control. For example, the `ControlStyle` property of controls of type `TableRow` is of type `TableItemStyle`. Because the `GridViewRow` control derives from `TableRow`, its `ControlStyle` property is also of type `TableItemStyle`.

The `GridView` control exposes eight top-level properties of type `TableItemStyle` named `AlternatingRowStyle`, `EditRowStyle`, `EmptyDataRowStyle`, `FooterStyle`, `HeaderStyle`, `PagerStyle`, `RowStyle`, and `SelectedRowStyle` that map to the `ControlStyle` properties of the alternating, edit, empty data, footer, header, pager, normal, and selected `GridViewRow` controls, respectively. As an example, the following code fragment shows the implementation of the `AlternatingRowStyle` property:

```
private TableItemStyle alternatingRowStyle;

[NotifyParentPropertyAttribute(true)]
[PersistenceModeAttribute(PersistenceMode.InnerProperty)]
[DesignerSerializationVisibilityAttribute(DesignerSerializationVisibility.Content)]
public TableItemStyle AlternatingRowStyle
{
  get
  {
    if (alternatingRowStyle == null)
    {
      alternatingRowStyle = new TableItemStyle();
      if (IsTrackingViewState)
        ((IStateManager)alternatingRowStyle).TrackViewState();
    }
    return alternatingRowStyle;
  }
}
```

As this code shows, you must take the following actions to implement a top-level style property:

1. Expose a private field as the backing store for the top-level style property:

```
private TableItemStyle alternatingRowStyle;
```

2. Check whether the private field is null. If so, create an instance of the appropriate style class, and assign the instance to the private field. Then check whether your custom control (`GridView` in this case) is tracking its view state. If so, call the `TrackViewState` method of the private field:

```
if (IsTrackingViewState)
  ((IStateManager)alternatingRowStyle).TrackViewState();
```

3. Annotate the top-level style property with the following attribute to tell the design-time serializer that the property has subproperties and the serializer must serialize these subproperties as well:

```
[DesignerSerializationVisibilityAttribute(DesignerSerializationVisibility.Content)]
```

4. Annotate the property with the following attribute:

```
[NotifyParentPropertyAttribute(true)]
```

5. Annotate the property with the following attribute to tell the visual designer to serialize the property as the child element of the tag that represents your custom control (`GridView` in this case) on the ASP.NET page:

```
[PersistenceModeAttribute(PersistenceMode.InnerProperty)]
```

`GridView` exposes a method named `PrepareControlHierarchy` that applies the `AlternatingRowStyle`, `EditRowStyle`, `EmptyDataRowStyle`, `FooterStyle`, `HeaderStyle`, `PagerStyle`, `RowStyle`, and `SelectedRowStyle` top-level `TableItemStyle` properties to the appropriate `GridViewRow` controls, as shown in Listing 19-12.

Listing 19-12: The PrepareControlHierarchy method

```
protected virtual void PrepareControlHierarchy()
{
  table.CopyBaseAttributes(this);
  if (ControlStyleCreated)
    table.ApplyStyle(ControlStyle);

  if (ShowTopPager && pagerStyle != null)
    topPagerRow.MergeStyle(pagerStyle);

  if (ShowHeader && headerStyle != null)
    headerRow.MergeStyle(headerStyle);

  if (Rows.Count == 0 && emptyDataRow != null && emptyDataRowStyle != null)
    emptyDataRow.MergeStyle(emptyDataRowStyle);

  TableItemStyle dataRowStyle;
  TableItemStyle mergedDataRowStyle;

  foreach (GridViewRow row in Rows)
  {
```

```
      dataRowStyle = (row.RowState & DataControlRowState.Alternate) != 0 ?
                       alternatingRowStyle : rowStyle;
    mergedDataRowStyle = null;

    if ((row.RowState & DataControlRowState.Edit) != 0 && editRowStyle != null)
    {
      if (dataRowStyle == null)
        dataRowStyle = editRowStyle;
      else
      {
        mergedDataRowStyle = new TableItemStyle();
        mergedDataRowStyle.CopyFrom(dataRowStyle);
        mergedDataRowStyle.CopyFrom(editRowStyle);
      }
    }

    if ((row.RowState & DataControlRowState.Selected) != 0 &&
        selectedRowStyle != null)
    {
      if (dataRowStyle != null)
      {
        mergedDataRowStyle = new TableItemStyle();
        mergedDataRowStyle.CopyFrom(dataRowStyle);
        mergedDataRowStyle.CopyFrom(selectedRowStyle);
      }

      else if (mergedDataRowStyle != null)
        mergedDataRowStyle.CopyFrom(selectedRowStyle);

      else
        dataRowStyle = selectedRowStyle;
    }

    if (mergedDataRowStyle != null)
      row.MergeStyle(mergedDataRowStyle);

    else if (dataRowStyle != null)
      row.MergeStyle(dataRowStyle);
  }

  if (ShowFooter && footerStyle != null)
    footerRow.MergeStyle(footerStyle);

  if (ShowBottomPager && pagerStyle != null)
    bottomPagerRow.MergeStyle(PagerStyle);
}
```

Because the `GridView` control has only one child control (the `Table` control), the `PrepareControlHierarchy` method applies the HTML attributes of the containing HTML element of the `GridView` control to the `Table` child control by calling the `CopyBaseAttributes` method of the `Table` child control to copy the base attributes of the `GridView` control to the `Table` child control:

```
table.CopyBaseAttributes(this);
```

The method then calls the `ApplyStyle` method of the `Table` child control to apply the `ControlStyle` property of the `GridView` control to the `ControlStyle` property of the `Table` child control:

```
if (ControlStyleCreated)
  table.ApplyStyle(ControlStyle);
```

The method then calls the `MergeStyle` methods of the top pager and header `GridViewRow` child controls to apply the `PagerStyle` and `HeaderStyle` properties of the `GridView` control to these child controls' `ControlStyle` properties:

```
if (ShowTopPager && pagerStyle != null)
  topPagerRow.MergeStyle(pagerStyle);

if (ShowHeader && headerStyle != null)
  headerRow.MergeStyle(headerStyle);
```

Next, the method enumerates the `GridViewRow` controls in the `Rows` collection of the `GridView` control and applies the `AlternatingRowStyle`, `EditRowStyle`, `RowStyle`, and `SelectedRowStyle` top-level properties to the `ControlStyle` property of the appropriate `GridViewRow` controls.

Finally, the `PrepareControlHierarchy` method calls the `MergeStyle` methods of the footer and bottom pager `GridViewRow` child controls to apply the `FooterStyle` and the `PagerStyle` properties of the `GridView` control to these child controls' `ControlStyle` properties.

The `GridView` control overrides the `Render` method to call the `PrepareControlHierarchy` method as shown here:

```
protected override void Render(HtmlTextWriter writer)
{
    PrepareControlHierarchy();
    RenderContents(writer);
}
```

In other words, the `GridView` control applies the style properties of its `GridViewRow` child controls in the render phase of its life cycle. Recall that the save view state phase comes before the render phase. Applying the style properties in the render phase ensures that the changes to the properties of the `GridViewRow` child controls aren't saved in the view state. This is important because the top-level style properties of the `GridView` control manage their own view state across page postbacks and you wouldn't want to save the same information twice in the saved view state.

State Management

You must divide the properties and fields of your custom control into two major groups:

❑ **Essential Properties and Fields:** These are properties and fields that are essential to the very functioning of your custom control. For example, the `SelectedIndex`, `EditIndex`, `PageIndex`, `pageCount`, `sortExpression`, and `sortDirection` members of the `GridView` control are essential to the editing, paging, and sorting features of the control. For example, when the user clicks the Next button of the paging interface of the control, the control must remember its old page index to find out what the next page is.

❑ **Nonessential Properties and Fields:** These are properties and fields that aren't essential to the functioning of your custom control. For example, the top-level style properties such as AlternatingStyle, RowStyle, and so on aren't essential. The GridView control can still function properly even when it doesn't remember its top-level styles across page postbacks.

Prior to ASP.NET 2.0, you had to use the same mechanism to store both the essential and nonessential properties across page postbacks—view state. The main problem with view state is that page developers can turn it off. It's all or nothing. The ASP.NET 2.0 Framework introduces the concept of control state. You can think of the control state as the private state of your custom control. The great thing about the control state is that page developers can't turn it off. Behind the scenes both the control state and view state are stored in the _VIEWSTATE hidden field.

Override the SaveControlState method to save the control state of your custom control across page postbacks as shown in the following code:

```
protected override object SaveControlState()
{
  object baseControlState = base.SaveControlState();

  return new object[] {
          baseControlState, SelectedIndex, EditIndex, PageIndex, pageCount,
          sortExpression, sortDirection
       };
}
```

The SaveControlState method saves the essential properties into an array object and returns the object to its caller.

Override the LoadControlState method to load the control state of your custom control as shown in the following code:

```
protected override void LoadControlState(object savedState)
{
  object[] state = savedState as object[];
  if (state != null && state.Length == 7)
  {
    base.LoadControlState(state[0]);
    if (state[1] != null)
      SelectedIndex = (int)state[1];
    if (state[2] != null)
      EditIndex = (int)state[2];
    if (state[3] != null)
      PageIndex = (int)state[3];
    if (state[4] != null)
      pageCount = (int)state[4];
    if (state[5] != null)
      sortExpression = (string)state[5];
    if (state[6] != null)
      this.sortDirection = (SortDirection)state[6];
  }

  else
    base.LoadControlState(savedState);
}
```

The caller of the `LoadControlState` method passes an array object into the method. This array object is the same array object that the `SaveControlState` method returns. The `LoadControlState` method must access the members of the array object in the same order the `SaveControlState` method saves the values of the respective properties and fields.

The `GridView` control overrides the `TrackViewState`, `SaveViewState`, and `LoadViewState` methods to manage the states of its nonessential properties and fields such as `AlternatingStyle`, `RowStyle`, and so on.

Overriding the OnInit Method

The `GridView` control overrides the `OnInit` method to call the `RegisterRequiresControlState` method of the `Page` class to notify the page that it needs to use its control state:

```
protected override void OnInit(EventArgs e)
{
    Page.RegisterRequiresControlState(this);
    base.OnInit(e);
}
```

Events

Your custom control performs different operations during its life cycle. Some of these operations are performed in response to user interactions, such as deleting a record. Others are performed for other reasons, such as your control rendering itself in the rendering phase of its life cycle.

When you're writing a custom control, you should divide these operations into three different groups, as follows:

❑   Operations that may require the page developer's intervention before they're performed. For example, when the user clicks the Delete button of a table row to delete the underlying data record, the page developer may want to intervene before the data record is deleted to determine whether the operation would violate application-specific business rules. Your custom control must raise an event before these operations are performed.

❑   Operations that may require the page developer's intervention after they're performed. For example, when a delete operation raises an exception, the page developer may want to intervene to use a custom exception handler to handle the exception bypassing the default exception handling mechanism. Your custom control must raise an event after these operations.

❑   Operations that may require the page developer's intervention both before and after they're performed. Your custom control must raise one event before and one event after these operations.

The following table shows the operations for which the `GridView` control raises events before, after, or both before and after the operations to allow the page developer to intervene before, after, or both before and after the operations.

Operation	Event Raised Before Operation	Event Raised After Operation
Clicking a pager link button	`PageIndexChanging`	`PageIndexChanged`
Clicking a Cancel button	`RowCancelingEdit`	
Creating a row		`RowCreated`
Data binding a row		`RowDataBound`
Deleting a row	`RowDeleting`	`RowDeleted`
Clicking an Edit button	`RowEditing`	
Updating a row	`RowUpdating`	`RowUpdated`
Selecting a row	`SelectedIndexChanging`	`SelectedIndexChanged`
Sorting the data	`Sorting`	`Sorted`

As discussed in Chapter 4, two classes are associated with each event: delegate and event data classes. The delegate class determines the type of the event, while the event data class holds the event data. Recall from Chapter 4 that each event data class exposes one property for each event datum to hold its value. The following table shows the delegate and event data classes associated with the events shown in the preceding table:

Event	Event Delegate Class	Event Data Class
`PageIndexChanging`	`GridViewPageEventHandler`	`GridViewPageEventArgs`
`PageIndexChanged`	`EventHandler`	`EventArgs`
`RowCancelingEdit`	`GridViewCancelEdit EventHandler`	`GridViewCancelEdit EventArgs`
`RowCreated`	`GridViewRowEventHandler`	`GridViewRowEventArgs`
`RowDataBound`	`GridViewRowEventHandler`	`GridViewRowEventArgs`
`RowDeleting`	`GridViewDeleteEventHandler`	`GridViewDeleteEventArgs`
`RowDeleted`	`GridViewDeletedEventHandler`	`GridViewDeletedEventArgs`
`RowEditing`	`GridViewEditEventHandler`	`GridViewEditEventArgs`
`RowUpdating`	`GridViewUpdateEventHandler`	`GridViewUpdateEventArgs`
`RowUpdated`	`GridViewUpdatedEventHandler`	`GridViewUpdatedEventArgs`
`SelectedIndexChanging`	`GridViewSelectEventHandler`	`GridViewSelectEventArgs`
`SelectedIndexChanged`	`EventHandler`	`EventArgs`
`Sorting`	`GridViewSortEventHandler`	`GridViewSortEventArgs`
`Sorted`	`EventHandler`	`EventArgs`

As discussed in Chapter 4, the `EventHandler` and `EventArgs` classes are the event delegate and event data classes for those events that don't have any event data, such as the `PageIndexChanged`, `SelectedIndexChanged`, and `Sorted` events. The implementation of each event shown in the table follows the .NET event implementation pattern discussed in Chapter 4. As an example, take a look at the implementation of the `RowUpdating` event. The `GridView` control raises this event before a data record is updated. Follow these steps to implement this event:

1. Implement an event data class to hold the event data:

```
public class GridViewUpdateEventArgs : CancelEventArgs
{
  private int rowIndex;
  private IOrderedDictionary keys;
  private IOrderedDictionary newValues;
  private IOrderedDictionary oldValues;

  internal GridViewUpdateEventArgs(int rowIndex, IOrderedDictionary keys,
              IOrderedDictionary newValues, IOrderedDictionary oldValues)
  {
    this.rowIndex = rowIndex;
    this.keys = keys;
    this.newValues = newValues;
    this.oldValues = oldValues;
  }

  public IOrderedDictionary Keys
  {
    get { return this.keys; }
  }

  public IOrderedDictionary NewValues
  {
    get { return this.newValues; }
  }

  public IOrderedDictionary OldValues
  {
    get { return this.oldValues; }
  }

  public int RowIndex
  {
    get { return this.rowIndex; }
  }
}
```

As this code shows, the `RowUpdating` event provides the page developers with the following three important bits of information about the row being updated:

❏ `RowIndex`: The index of the row.

❏ `Keys`: The `IOrderedDictionary` collection that contains one `DictionaryEntry` object for each data field of the primary key of the row. The `Key` and `Value` of each `DictionaryEntry` object holds the name and value of its associated data field.

❑ NewValues: The IOrderedDictionary collection that contains one DictionaryEntry object for each data field of the record. The Key and Value of each DictionaryEntry object holds the name and value of its associated data field.

2. Declare the event delegate class:

```
public delegate void
GridViewUpdateEventHandler(object sender, GridViewUpdateEventArgs e);
```

3. Define a private static read-only object as the event key:

```
private static readonly object RowUpdatingKey = new object();
```

4. Define the event property:

```
public event GridViewUpdateEventHandler RowUpdating
{
  add { Events.AddHandler(RowUpdatingKey, value); }

  remove { Events.RemoveHandler(RowUpdatingKey, value); }
}
```

5. Define a protected virtual method to raise the event:

```
protected virtual void OnRowUpdating(GridViewUpdateEventArgs e)
{
  GridViewUpdateEventHandler h =
                      Events[RowUpdatingKey] as GridViewUpdateEventHandler;
  if (h != null)
    h(this, e);
}
```

GridViewRow

As discussed, GridView displays each data record in a table row. The ASP.NET Framework already comes with a standard control named TableRow to display a table row. However, the TableRow control is missing a few features.

The TableRow control doesn't distinguish between different types of table row, as defined in the following enumeration:

```
public enum DataControlRowType
{
  Header = 0,
  Footer = 1,
  DataRow = 2,
  Separator = 3,
  Pager = 4,
  EmptyDataRow = 5,
}
```

The row type matters because it determines the HTML markup text that the row must render. For instance, a header row may render one link button for each cell to allow users to sort the data, whereas a data row may render a check box to display its Boolean data fields.

The `TableRow` control doesn't distinguish between different states of a table row, as defined in the following enumeration:

```
public enum DataControlRowState
{
  Normal = 0,
  Alternate = 1,
  Selected = 2,
  Edit = 4,
  Insert = 8,
}
```

The row state matters because it determines the HTML markup text that the row must render. For example, a data row may render one text box for each cell when it's in edit mode to allow the user to edit the contents of its cells. The same data row may render the contents of its cell in simple text format when it's in its normal mode.

As shown in Listing 19-9, the `OnBubbleEvent` method of the `GridView` control only catches `RowCommand` events, which means that the control that represents the table row must catch the `Command` event of its child controls and convert them to the `RowCommand` event. The `TableRow` control doesn't support this.

The `TableRow` control doesn't know about the data record it's bound to. The data record matters because data rows are there to display data records.

Therefore, you must implement a new custom control named `GridViewRow` that derives from the `TableRow` control and extends its functionality to provide support for the features that `TableRow` doesn't address, as shown in Listing 19-13.

Listing 19-13: The GridViewRow custom control

```
public class GridViewRow : TableRow, IDataItemContainer
{
  public GridViewRow(int rowIndex, int dataItemIndex, DataControlRowType rowType,
                     DataControlRowState rowState);
  object IDataItemContainer.DataItem {get; }
  public virtual object DataItem {get; set;}
  int IDataItemContainer.DataItemIndex {get; }
  public virtual int DataItemIndex {get; }
  int IDataItemContainer.DisplayIndex {get; }
  public virtual int RowIndex {get; }
  public virtual DataControlRowState RowState {get; set; }
  public virtual DataControlRowType RowType {get; set; }
  protected override bool OnBubbleEvent(object source, EventArgs e);
}
```

As discussed, the `GridViewRow` control must expose a property that refers to the data record that the control is bound to. The `GridViewRow` control isn't the only control that is bound to a data record. There are many others, such as the `DetailsViewRow` control. Now imagine a program that needs to access the data record that a control is bound to. If each control were to use different names or types for the property that refers to the data record, this program would have to be modified each time it needs to use a new type of control.

The ASP.NET Framework has designed an interface named IDataItemContainer that provides a standard API to access the data record associated with any type of control. This interface exposes three properties, as shown in Listing 19-14.

Listing 19-14: The IDataItemContainer interface

```
public interface IDataItemContainer : INamingContainer
{
  object DataItem { get; }
  int DataItemIndex { get; }
  int DisplayIndex { get; }
}
```

The following list describes what each property is for:

❑   DataItem: Gets the data record that the control that implements the IDataItemContainer interface is bound to.

❑   DataItemIndex: Gets the index of the data record that the control that implements the IDataItemContainer interface is bound to.

❑   DisplayIndex: Gets the index of the control that implements the IDataItemContainer.

The GridViewRow control uses the C# interface implementation pattern discussed in Chapter 4 to implement each property of the IDataItemContainer interface. For example, to implement the DataItem property, the GridViewRow control first implements a virtual property with the same name and type as the DataItem property of the IDataItemContainer interface:

```
private object dataItem;

public virtual object DataItem
{
  get { return this.dataItem; }
  set { this.dataItem = value; }
}
```

It then explicitly implements the DataItem property of the IDataItemContainer interface, and calls the virtual DataItem property:

```
object IDataItemContainer.DataItem
{
  get { return this.DataItem; }
}
```

GridViewRow takes the same approach to implement the DataItemIndex and DisplayIndex of the IDataItemContainer interface.

GridViewRow exposes two properties named RowType and RowState of types DataControlRowType and DataControlRowState to represent the type and state of a table row:

```
private DataControlRowState rowState;
public virtual DataControlRowState RowState
{
```

```
   get { return this.rowState; }
   set { this.rowState = value; }
}

private DataControlRowType rowType;
public virtual DataControlRowType RowType
{
   get { return this.rowType; }
   set { this.rowType = value; }
}
```

`GridViewRow` also overrides the `OnBubbleEvent` method to catch the `Command` events of its child controls and expose them as `RowCommand` events:

```
protected override bool OnBubbleEvent(object source, EventArgs e)
{
  bool handled = false;

  CommandEventArgs ce = e as CommandEventArgs;
  if (ce != null)
  {
    GridViewCommandEventArgs ge = new GridViewCommandEventArgs(source, ce);
    RaiseBubbleEvent(this, ge);
    handled = true;
  }

  return handled;
}
```

The `OnBubbleEvent` method first checks whether the event is a `Command` event:

```
CommandEventArgs ce = e as CommandEventArgs;
```

If it is, `OnBubbleEvent` then maps the event to the `RowCommand` event:

```
if (ce != null)
{
  GridViewCommandEventArgs ge = new GridViewCommandEventArgs(source, ce);
```

The method then calls the `RaiseBubbleEvent` method to bubble the `RowCommand` event upward to the `GridView` control. `GridViewRow`, like any other control, inherits `RaiseBubbleEvent` from the `Control` base class:

```
RaiseBubbleEvent(this, ge);
```

Finally, the method returns true to tell the page framework that the child event has been handled:

```
    Handled = true;
  }
  return handled;
}
```

GridViewRowCollection

Recall that the `GridView` control exposes a collection property of type `GridViewRowCollection` that contains the `GridViewRow` controls that represent the `GridView` control's table rows. You may wonder why you need to implement a new collection class when you could use one of the existing ones such as `ArrayList`. `ArrayList` is a good choice except for two problems:

❏ When you index an `ArrayList`, you get an item of type `Object`, not `GridViewRow`.

❏ You also need a new `CopyTo` method to load an array of `GridViewRow` controls to the `GridViewRowCollection` collection.

The `GridViewRowCollection` class derives from `ArrayList` and extends its functionality to handle these two problems, as shown in the following code:

```
public class GridViewRowCollection : ArrayList
{
  public GridViewRowCollection(ArrayList rows)
  {
    this.AddRange(rows);
  }

  public new GridViewRow this[int index]
  {
    get { return (GridViewRow)base[index]; }
  }

  public void CopyTo(GridViewRow[] array, int index)
  {
    base.CopyTo(array, index);
  }
}
```

Summary

This chapter used a detailed, step-by-step recipe to help you gain the skills that you need to develop a custom tabular data-bound control as complex and feature-rich as the `GridView` control. As discussed in Chapters 1 and 8, the ASP.NET Framework is a request processing architecture. Every component of the Framework is there for one reason only: to contribute one way or another to the process of handling requests for Web resources. Some components such as data-bound controls directly contribute to the final markup text, whereas some others such as membership and role components contribute differently. The next few chapters provide an in-depth coverage of the ASP.NET 2.0 membership and role models.

Why You Need the ASP.NET 2.0 Membership/ Role Model

When a request for a protected resource arrives, your Web application must take the following actions:

1. Authenticate and establish the requester's identity.

2. Authorize the authenticated requester to determine whether the requester has the permission to access the protected resource.

3. Secure all the communications between the client and server to protect the integrity and privacy of data in transit.

The SSL and IPSec technologies are normally used to secure the communications. This chapter reviews the ASP.NET 1.x security model. This review will provide you with the following benefits:

❑ Because the ASP.NET 2.0 security model is based on the same security concepts, principles, and workflows as the ASP.NET 1.x security model, the next few chapters build on the discussions presented in this chapter to provide you with an in-depth coverage of the ASP.NET 2.0 security model.

❑ Many of the new features of the ASP.NET 2.0 security model are introduced to address the shortcomings of the ASP.NET 1.x security model. Understanding these shortcomings will help you understand these new features better.

❑ If you've used the ASP.NET 1.x security model over the last few years, you may be wondering why you need the ASP.NET 2.0 security model. What is wrong with the ASP.NET 1.x security model? What new features and capabilities does the new model provide that are lacking in the old one? How does the new model relate to the old one? Is the new model the enhanced version of the old one? If so, what are these enhancements for? What is their significance? The review of the ASP.NET 1.x security model as presented in this chapter will help you address these and many other similar questions.

ASP.NET 1.x Security Model

The discussions of this section are presented in the context of an example to make the discussions more concrete and easy to follow. The example consists of a sample Web application that includes two Web pages, `Default.aspx` and `Login.aspx`, and a local SQL Server database.

The procedure ASP.NET 1.x developers normally take to control access to protected resources goes something like this. First, they set up the appropriate data storage for storing membership information. The sample Web application uses a local SQL Server database table named `Users` that has three columns named `UserID`, `Username`, and `Password`.

Then they set up the appropriate data storage for storing role information. The sample Web application uses two local SQL Server database tables named `Roles` and `UserRoles`. The `Roles` table has three columns named `RoleID`, `Rolename`, and `RoleDescription`. The `UserRoles` table has two columns named `UserID` and `RoleID`. Each record in the `UserRoles` table relates a record in the `Users` table to a record in the `Roles` table.

Next, they implement a class whose methods handle membership operations, such as validating a user against the data store, adding a new user to the data store, deleting an existing user from the data store, and so on. The sample Web application implements a class named `Membership` that exposes a static method named `ValidateUser`, where ADO.NET objects such as `SqlConnection`, `SqlCommand`, and `SqlParameter` are used to validate user credentials (username and password) against the `Users` table, as shown in Listing 20-1.

Listing 20-1: The Membership class exposes a method named ValidateUser

```
public static bool ValidateUser(string username, string password)
{
  SqlConnection con = new SqlConnection();
  con.ConnectionString =
    ConfigurationManager.ConnectionStrings["MyConnectionString"].ConnectionString;

  SqlCommand com = new SqlCommand();
  com.Connection = con;
  com.CommandText = "Select Count(*) From Users Where Username=@Username and
                     Password=@Password";

  com.Parameters.AddWithValue("@Username", username);
  com.Parameters.AddWithValue("@Password", password);

  con.Open();
  int cnt = (int)com.ExecuteScalar();
  con.Close();

  return (cnt > 0);
}
```

Then they implement a class whose methods handle role operations such as adding a new role to the data store, deleting an exiting role from the data store, retrieving the list of roles for a user from the data store, and so on. The sample Web application implements a class named `Roles` that exposes the following static methods, where ADO.NET objects such as `SqlConnection`, `SqlCommand`, and `SqlParameter` are used to perform the respective data operations:

❑   CreateRole: Adds a new role (record) to the Roles table.

❑   AddUserToRole: Adds the specified user to the specified role, as shown in Listing 20-2.

❑   GetRolesForUser: Retrieves the list of the roles that the specified user is in.

Listing 20-2: The AddUserToRole method adds the specified user to the specified role

```
public static void AddUserToRole(string username, string roleName)
{
  SqlConnection con = new SqlConnection();
  con.ConnectionString =
    ConfigurationManager.ConnectionStrings["MyConnectionString"].ConnectionString;

  SqlCommand com = new SqlCommand();
  com.Connection = con;
  com.CommandText = "AddUserToRole";
  com.CommandType = CommandType.StoredProcedure;

  com.Parameters.AddWithValue("@Username", username);
  com.Parameters.AddWithValue("@Rolename", roleName);

  con.Open();
  com.ExecuteNonQuery();
  con.Close();
}
```

Next, developers have to configure IIS for anonymous authentication. IIS will assign the user to the anonymous Internet user account, create the appropriate Windows access token, and pass the token to ASP.NET.

Then they need to configure the ASP.NET Web application for Forms authentication:

```
<authentication mode="Forms">
  <forms name=".mycookie" path="/" loginUrl="Login.aspx" protection="All"
  timeout="40" />
</authentication>
```

Next they disable anonymous access in the Web.config file:

```
<authorization>
    <deny users="?"/>
</authorization>
```

Then they implement a logon Web page that collects user credentials. The sample application uses Listing 20-3 to collect user's username and password.

Listing 20-3: The Logon page collects user credentials

```
<%@ Page Language="C#" AutoEventWireup="true" CodeFile="Login.aspx.cs"
Inherits="Login" %>
<html xmlns="http://www.w3.org/1999/xhtml">
<body>
  <form id="form1" runat="server">
```

(continued)

Listing 20-3: *(continued)*

```
    <table cellpadding="4" style="color:#333333;font-family:Verdana;
    font-size:0.8em;background-color:#F7F6F3;border-color:#E6E2D8;
    border-width:1px;border-style:Solid;">
      <tr>
        <td align="center" colspan="2" style="color:White;background-color:#5D7B9D;
        font-size:0.9em;font-weight: bold;">Log In</td>
      </tr>
      <tr>
        <td align="right"><strong>User Name:</strong></td>
        <td><asp:TextBox runat="server" ID="UserName" /></td>
      </tr>
      <tr>
        <td align="right"><strong>Password:</strong></td>
        <td><asp:TextBox ID="Password" runat="server" /></td>
      </tr>
      <tr>
        <td>
          <asp:Button runat="server" Text="Log In" OnClick="LoginCallback" /></td>
      </tr>
    </table>
  </form>
</body>
</html>
```

The login Web page must take several actions when the user posts the page back to the server, as shown in Listing 20-4.

Listing 20-4: The callback method for the Click event

```
protected void LoginCallback(object sender, EventArgs e)
{
  if (CustomComponents.Membership.ValidateUser(UserName.Text, Password.Text))
  {
    string[] rolenames = CustomComponents.Roles.GetRolesForUser(UserName.Text);
    string roles = string.Empty;
    foreach (string rolename in rolenames)
      roles += (rolename + ',');
    roles = roles.Remove(roles.LastIndexOf(','));
    FormsAuthenticationTicket ticket = new FormsAuthenticationTicket(1,
            UserName.Text, DateTime.Now, DateTime.Now.AddSeconds(40), false, roles);

    string encryptedTicket = FormsAuthentication.Encrypt(ticket);
    HttpCookie cookie = new HttpCookie(FormsAuthentication.FormsCookieName);
    cookie.Value = encryptedTicket;
    Response.Cookies.Add(cookie);
    Response.Redirect(FormsAuthentication.GetRedirectUrl(UserName.Text,false),
                                                true);

  }
}
```

First, the page must validate the user credentials. The sample Web application calls the `ValidateUser` method of the `Membership` class to validate the user:

```
CustomComponents.Membership.ValidateUser(UserName.Text, Password.Text)
```

Next, it must retrieve the list of roles the authenticated user is in. The sample Web application calls the `GetRolesForUser` method of the `Roles` class to retrieve the role list:

```
string[] rolenames = CustomComponents.Roles.GetRolesForUser(UserName.Text);
```

Then it creates a string that contains a comma-separated list of the role names. The sample Web application uses the following logic to accomplish this:

```
string roles = string.Empty;
foreach (string rolename in rolenames)
  roles += (rolename + ',');
roles = roles.Remove(roles.LastIndexOf(','));
```

Next it creates a `FormsAuthenticationTicket` and stores the string value of the comma-separated list in its `UserData` property:

```
FormsAuthenticationTicket ticket = new FormsAuthenticationTicket(1, UserName.Text,
                        DateTime.Now, DateTime.Now.AddSeconds(40),false, roles);
```

The page then calls the `Encrypt` method of the `FormsAuthentication` class to encrypt the `FormsAuthenticationTicket`:

```
string encryptedTicket = FormsAuthentication.Encrypt(ticket);
```

Then it creates a new cookie:

```
HttpCookie cookie = new HttpCookie(FormsAuthentication.FormsCookieName);
```

It stores the encrypted ticket in the cookie:

```
cookie.Value = encryptedTicket;
```

It attaches the cookie to the response message:

```
Response.Cookies.Add(cookie);
```

Then it redirects the user to the originally requested page:

```
Response.Redirect(FormsAuthentication.GetRedirectUrl(UserName.Text, false), true);
```

Developers must also implement the `Application_AuthenticateRequest` method in the `Global.asax` file (see Listing 20-5), which also has several tasks.

Listing 20-5: The Application_AuthenticateRequest method

```
void Application_AuthenticateRequest(object sender, EventArgs e)
{
  HttpApplication app = (HttpApplication)sender;

  HttpCookie cookie = Request.Cookies[FormsAuthentication.FormsCookieName];
  if (cookie != null)
  {
    string encryptedTicket = cookie.Value;
    FormsAuthenticationTicket ticket =
                        FormsAuthentication.Decrypt(encryptedTicket);

    string[] roles = ticket.UserData.Split(new char[] { ',' });

    FormsIdentity identity = new FormsIdentity(ticket);
    System.Security.Principal.GenericPrincipal user =
            new System.Security.Principal.GenericPrincipal(identity, roles);

    app.Context.User = user;
  }
}
```

First the method retrieves the cookie that contains the encrypted ticket from the request message:

```
HttpCookie cookie = Request.Cookies[FormsAuthentication.FormsCookieName];
```

It retrieves the encrypted ticket from the cookie:

```
string encryptedTicket = cookie.Value;
```

Then it decrypts the encrypted ticket:

```
FormsAuthentication.Decrypt(encryptedTicket);
```

It extracts the roles from the ticket:

```
string[] roles = ticket.UserData.Split(new char[] { ',' });
```

It uses the ticket to create a FormsIdentity object that represents the identity of the user:

```
FormsIdentity identity = new FormsIdentity(ticket);
```

Next, the method creates a GenericPrincipal object that references the FormsIdentity object and populates it with the list of roles that the user is in:

```
GenericPrincipal user = new GenericPrincipal(identity, roles);
```

Then the method attaches the GenericPrincipal object to the current context:

```
app.Context.User = user;
```

Now consider the following scenerio in the sample Web application to examine how the clients of the application are authenticated and authorized in the ASP.NET 1.x security model. Suppose an anonymous user attempts to access the protected `Default.aspx` page. Because IIS is configured for anonymous authentication, it delegates the responsibility of authenticating the user to ASP.NET, which in turn redirects the user to the `Login.aspx` page, where the user's credentials (username and password) are collected (see Listing 20-3).

When the user finally posts the Login page back to the server, the `LoginCallback` method is called (see Listing 20-4). As discussed, the method calls the `ValidateUser` method of the `Membership` class to validate the user, retrieves the list of roles that the current user is in, creates a ticket, populates the ticket with the list of roles, encrypts the ticket, creates a cookie, stores the encrypted ticket in the cookie, adds the cookie to the response, and finally redirects the user to the originally requested page, `Default.aspx`.

The redirection starts a new request on behalf of the user, where the `Application_AuthenticateRequest` method is called. The method retrieves the cookie from the request, extracts the encrypted ticket, decrypts the ticket, extracts the list of roles from the ticket, uses the ticket to create a `FormsIdentity` object, creates a `GenericPrincipal` object that references the `FormsIdentity` object, populates the `GenericPrincipal` object with the list of roles, and finally attaches the `GenericPrincipal` object to the current context.

Authorization Mechanisms

The ASP.NET 1.x security model provides page developers with four different mechanisms to authorize an authenticated user. All four mechanisms use the `HttpContext.User` object to authorize the user. The ASP.NET 2.0 security model supports all of these four mechanisms. Recall that the `HttpContext.User` object refers to the `GenericPrincipal` object that contains the list of roles the current user is in, and also references the `FormsIdentity` object that contains the user's identification data.

The first method is to use the `<authorization>` section of the `Web.config` file to control access to files and folders:

```
<authorization>
  <allow roles="Members"/>
  <deny users="?"/>
</authorization>
```

This configuration only allows the users in the `Members` role access the files and subfolders of the folder where the `Web.config` file is located. The `UrlAuthorizationModule` automatically uses the contents of the `<authorization>` section to authorize the user without any work on the part of page developers. Page developers are only responsible for using the `<allow>` and `<deny>` elements to define the access rules.

The second method is to use the `PrinciplePermissionAttribute` to control access to classes and methods:

```
[System.Security.Permissions.PrincipalPermission(System.Security.Permissions.
SecurityAction.Demand,Role="Members")]
public static bool MyMethod()
{
  ...
}
```

The `PrinciplePermission` demand shown here will only allow members of the `Members` role to call the `MyMethod` method. This means that the `PrinciplePermissionAttribute` attribute allows you to create more fine-grained access rules than the `<authorization>` tag in the `Web.config` file. The `<authorization>` tags can be used to control access to a file, not the classes and methods in the file.

The third method is to use the `PrinciplePermission` class programmatically to control access to a block of code:

```
public static bool MyMethod()
{
  System.Security.Permissions.PrincipalPermission perm =
        new System.Security.Permissions.PrincipalPermission(null, "Members");
  perm.Demand();
  ...
}
```

Only members of the `Members` role will be allowed to run the code that comes after the call to the `Demand` method.

The fourth method, using the `IPrincipal.IsInRole` method, allows you to set up even more fine-grained access rules:

```
public static bool MyMethod()
{
  ...
  if (HttpContext.Current.User.IsInRole("Members"))
  {
    //some code
  }
}
```

Only the members of the `Members` role will be allowed to run the code inside the `if` block.

Shortcomings of the ASP.NET 1.x Security Model

The ASP.NET 2.0 security model uses many of the same security concepts, principles, precedures, and workflows discussed in the previous chapters. That said, the ASP.NET 1.x security model has lots of holes. The classes such as the `Membership` and `Roles` classes in the sample Web application that developers implement to handle the membership and role operations contain data store–specific APIs such as ADO.NET classes. The downside of this approach is discussed shortly.

Developers have to implement the login Web page that collects the user credentials, as shown in Listing 20-3, because the ASP.NET 1.x security model doesn't come with standard security controls that the page developers could use out of the box.

Developers have to implement the `Application_AuthenticateRequest` method, which has to take a complex series of actions as discussed earlier: to load the roles the current user is in to the principal object that represents the user because the ASP.NET 1.x security model doesn't come with a component that would automatically do this for page developers.

Developers have to implement the method that handles the `Submit` button in the Login page, as shown in Listing 20-4, which also has a number of complex tasks discussed earlier because the ASP.NET 1.x security model doesn't come with standard security controls that would automatically take care of this behind the scenes.

Now for the shortcomings of the `Membership` and `Roles` classes, which use data store–specific APIs, as noted. Why describe these as shortcomings? Take another look at the `ValidateUser` method of the `Membership` class (in Listing 20-1) and the `AddUserToRole` method of the `Roles` class (in Listing 20-2).

As these code listings clearly show, the methods of the `Membership` and `Roles` classes use SQL Server-specific ADO.NET classes such as `SqlConnection`, `SqlCommand`, `SqlDataAdapter`, and `SqlParameter` to perform their data operations. This means that the `Membership` and `Roles` classes are tied to the relational databases and wouldn't work with non-relational data stores such as XML documents, flat files, XML Web services, and so on.

The .NET 2.0 Provider Pattern

Here is a questions for you: How would you make the `Membership` and `Roles` classes generic so they can access any type of data store? One solution that comes to mind is to make the data access code used in these classes more generic. Different data access–generic APIs exist that you can use to make your data access more generic. The problems with this solution are as follows:

❑   It ties the `Membership` and `Roles` classes to a specific API and consequently doesn't allow these classes to work with all APIs.

❑   Making the data access code generic comes with a price. For example, you can't use data store–specific techniques to optimize the data access code.

You're looking for a solution that doesn't require you to make the data access code generic. This is where the .NET 2.0 Provider Pattern comes to the rescue. The .NET 2.0 Provider Pattern takes a completely different approach to make the `Membership` and `Roles` classes generic. Instead of trying to make the data access code used in the `Membership` and `Roles` classes more generic, the pattern moves the data access code or API out of these two classes into new classes. For ease of reference, this chapter refers to these new classes as data access code or API providers, data access providers, data providers, or simply providers.

To understand the significance of the Provider Pattern in this regard, examine the methods of the `Membership` and `Roles` classes more closely. Each method, like any other method, consists of two main parts, a signature and body. The signature of each method consists of the following three parts:

❑   The name of the method

❑   The type of the return value of the method

❑   The types of the arguments of the method

The signature of a method defines the contract between the method and its callers. As long as a method honors the contract, its callers don't care or know what goes into the body of the method. The set of the signatures of the methods of the Membership and Roles classes defines the contract between these classes and their clients. You can think of this set of signatures or contract as the business API that the Membership and Roles classes expose to their clients.

According to the Provider Pattern, the main responsibility of the Membership and Roles classes is to provide their clients with the appropriate business API. These classes shouldn't be held responsible for finding the appropriate data access API to access the underlying data store. The Membership and Roles classes must delegate this responsibility to the appropriate data access providers.

In other words, the responsibilities of providing business and data access APIs mustn't be assigned to the same classes, that is, the Membership and Roles classes. This separation of responsibilities will allow data access APIs to evolve over time without affecting the clients of the Membership and Roles classes.

However, simply moving the data access code out of the Membership and Roles classes into data access code providers wouldn't automatically isolate the Membership and Roles classes from the data access changes. If the Membership and Roles classes were to call the data access providers directly, they would be tied to these providers and wouldn't work with new data access providers that use new data access APIs.

Following the .NET 2.0 Provider Pattern, the ASP.NET 2.0 security model presents the following solution:

❑ All membership data access providers derive from the same abstract base class named MembershipProvider. The base class defines the contract between the Membership class and the membership providers. This allows the Membership class to treat all membership providers the same. The Membership class doesn't know or care what the real type of the membership provider is. As far as the class is concerned, all membership providers are of type MembershipProvider.

❑ All role data access providers derive from the same abstract base class named RoleProvider. The base class defines the contract between the Roles class and the role providers.

This raises a new problem. If the Membership and Roles classes don't know the real type of the membership and role providers they're supposed to use, how can they instantiate and initialize these providers? Because the issue of provider initialization applies equally to both the MembershipProvider and RoleProvider classes, both classes derive from the same abstract base class named ProviderBase (see Listing 20-6). This base class exposes the following members:

❑ Name: The value of this property is a string idthat uniquely identifies the respective provider class. This unique string id is used as the friendly name of the provider. This is discussed later.

❑ Initialize: This method takes two arguments. The first argument is the friendly name of the provider. The second argument is a NameValueCollection that contains the names and initial values of the properties of the provider. These values are used to initialize the provider. This is discussed later.

Listing 20-6: The base class for all ASP.NET 2.0 provider classes

```
public abstract class ProviderBase
{
  public abstract string Description { get;}
  public abstract string Name { get;}

  public abstract void Initialize(string name, NameValueCollection config);
}
```

The next two chapters show how the ASP.NET 2.0 security model manages to address the previously mentioned instantiation/initialization issue.

Summary

This chapter reviewed the ASP.NET 1.x security model and examined its shortcomings to set the stage for the next chapters, where the ASP.NET 2.0 security model is thoroughly discussed. Because the ASP.NET 2.0 security model uses many of the same security concepts, principles, and techniques as the ASP.NET 1.x security model, the review of the 1.x model also provided you with what you need to follow the discussions of the next few chapters.

21

Understanding the ASP.NET 2.0 Membership Model

The ASP.NET 2.0 security model provides you with an extensible data store–agnostic membership model. This chapter implements fully functional replicas of the main components of the ASP.NET membership model to help you understand the model from the inside out. Such understanding will put you in a much better position to extend the model to meet your application's requirements.

This chapter implements fully functional replicas of the following main classes of the ASP.NET 2.0 membership model:

❑ `Membership`

❑ `MembershipValidatePasswordEventHandler` and `ValidatePasswordEventArgs`

❑ `MembershipUser`

This chapter also shows you how to implement your own custom security controls to use these components to authenticate users.

Membership

The ASP.NET 2.0 `Membership` class provides its clients with the appropriate business API for membership operations, such as adding a new user to the data store, removing a user from the data store, validating user credentials against the data store, and so on. Following the .NET 2.0 Provider Pattern, the `Membership` class delegates the responsibility of providing the appropriate data access API for accessing the underlying data store to the appropriate membership provider, as discussed in the previous chapter.

Membership Provider Instantiation and Initialization

All membership providers derive from the `MembershipProvider` abstract base class, which in turn derives from the `ProviderBase` abstract base class. The `MembershipProvider` base class isolates the `Membership` class from the real type of the underlying membership provider. Such isolation is crucial because each membership provider is designed to work with specific type of data store. For example, the `SqlMembershipProvider` is designed to work with a specific SQL Server database schema. If the `Membership` class were aware of the real type of the underlying membership provider (such as `SqlMembershipProvider`), it would be tied to a specific type of data store and wouldn't work with other types of data stores.

As discussed in the previous chapter, such isolation raises a new problem. If the `Membership` class doesn't know the real type of the membership provider that it's supposed to use, how could it then instantiate and initialize the membership provider? Following the .NET 2.0 Provider Pattern, the ASP.NET 2.0 membership model presents a solution that consists of adding a new section named `<membership>` to the `Web.config` and `Machine.config` files, and two new properties to the `Membeship` class, as discussed in the following sections.

Support for the <membership> Section

The `Web.config` and `Machine.config` files in ASP.NET 2.0 support a new section named `<membership>` (see Listing 21-1). This section contains a subelement named `<providers>`, which in turn contains one or more `<add>` elements. The `<add>` elements are used to register membership providers. Each `<add>` element exposes two important attributes named `name` and `type`.

The `name` attribute is set to the friendly name of the provider being registered. The friendly name of a provider uniquely identifies the provider among other registered providers. The `type` attribute is set to the fully qualified name of the type of the provider being registered. For example, the `<add>` element in Listing 21-1 registers a membership provider with the friendly name `AspNetSqlMembershipProvider`. The fully qualified name of the type of the membership provider contains the following information:

❑ The fully qualified name of the membership provider class including its namespace, in this case, `System.Web.Security.SqlMembershipProvider`.

❑ The name of the assembly that contains the membership provider class. The name consists of one or more of the following parts:

   ❑ The name of the assembly, such as `System.Web`.

   ❑ The version of the assembly, such as 2.0.0.0.

   ❑ The culture of the assembly, such as `neutral`.

   ❑ The public key token of the assembly, such as `b03f5f7f11d50a3a`. This token is used to authenticate and protect the integrity and privacy of the assembly.

Listing 21-1: The <membership> element is used to register membership providers

```
<membership defaultProvider="AspNetSqlMembershipProvider"
userIsOnlineTimeWindow="15" >
  <providers>
    <add name="AspNetSqlMembershipProvider"
```

```
        type="System.Web.Security.SqlMembershipProvider,System.Web, Version=2.0.0.0,
        Culture=neutral, PublicKeyToken=b03f5f7f11d50a3a"
        connectionStringName="LocalSqlServer" enablePasswordRetrieval="false"
        enablePasswordReset="true" requiresQuestionAndAnswer="true"
        applicationName="/" requiresUniqueEmail="false" passwordFormat="Hashed"
        maxInvalidPasswordAttempts="5" passwordAttemptWindow="10"
        passwordStrengthRegularExpression="" />
    </providers>
</membership>
```

The `<membership>` element exposes an attribute named `defaultProvider`, which is set to the friendly name of the default provider. The default provider is used if no other provider is explicitly specified.

The `<add>` element exposes two sets of attributes. The first set consists of attributes that all membership providers have in common:

- ❑ `name`: The friendly name of the membership provider.

- ❑ `type`: The fully qualified type of the membership provider, as discussed before.

- ❑ `enablePasswordRetrieval`: Specifies whether passwords can be retrieved from the data store.

- ❑ `enablePasswordReset`: Specifies whether passwords can be reset in the data store.

- ❑ `requiresQuestionAndAnswer`: Specifies whether users must answer specific questions before they're allowed to retrieve or change their passwords.

- ❑ `applicationName`: A unique string id that identifies a Web application from other applications. This allows more than one application to use the same data store to store membership information. Because user membership data is stored under the name of the application, two different users in two different applications can use the same username. The other benefit is that two or more applications can use the same application name to access the same membership data. This allows two or more applications to use the same membership data for authentication purposes.

- ❑ `requiresUniqueEmail`: Specifies whether users must provide unique e-mails.

- ❑ `passwordFormat`: The possible values are as follows:

  - ❑ `Clear`: Stores passwords in clear text format. This option introduces a security hole.

  - ❑ `Encrypted`: Encrypts passwords and stores encrypted passwords in the data store. This option is more secure than the `Clear` option. However, because the actual passwords are stored in the data store, it's still not as secure as it should be.

  - ❑ `Hashed`: Hashes passwords, encrypts the hash values, and stores the encryped hash values in the data store. This is the most secure way to store passwords. However, because the passwords themselves aren't stored in the data store, they can't be retrieved.

- ❑ `maxInvalidPasswordAttempts`: The maximum number of failed logon attempts. This secures the application against hackers.

The second set of attributes that each `<add>` element exposes is the provider-specific attributes whose values are used to initialize the provider being registered. For example, the `<add>` element in Listing 21-1 exposes an attribute named `connectionStringName`, which is specific to the `SqlMembershipProvider`. The provider uses the value of this attribute to connect to the underlying SQL Server database.

Provider and Providers Properties

The Membership class exposes two properties named Provider and Providers that call the Initialize method of the Membership class to instantiate and initialize the configured membership provider in generic fashion without knowing its real type. Listing 21-2 contains the code for the Initialize method.

Listing 21-2: The Initialize method of the Membership class

```
private static bool IsInitialized = false;
private static void Initialize()
{
  string providerType;
  string assemblyName;
  MembershipProvider tprovider;
  Assembly myAssembly;

  if (IsInitialized)
    return;

  providers = new MembershipProviderCollection();
  Configuration config = WebConfigurationManager.OpenWebConfiguration("/");
  MembershipSection sec =
                (MembershipSection)config.GetSection("system.web/membership");

  foreach (ProviderSettings settings in sec.Providers)
  {
    providerType = settings.Type.Trim().Split(new char[] { ',' })[0];
    assemblyName = settings.Type.Trim().Remove(
                        settings.Type.IndexOf(providerType), providerType.Length);
    if (string.IsNullOrEmpty(assemblyName))
      myAssembly = Assembly.GetExecutingAssembly();

    else
    {
      assemblyName = assemblyName.Trim().Remove(0, 1);
      myAssembly = Assembly.Load(assemblyName);
    }
    tprovider = (MembershipProvider)myAssembly.CreateInstance(providerType);
    tprovider.Initialize(settings.Name, settings.Parameters);
    providers.Add(tprovider);
  }

  userIsOnlineTimeWindow = (int)sec.UserIsOnlineTimeWindow.TotalMinutes;
  if (!string.IsNullOrEmpty(sec.DefaultProvider))
    provider = providers[sec.DefaultProvider];
  else
    provider = providers[sec.Providers[0].Name];

  IsInitialized = true;
}
```

The Initialize method first checks whether the Membership class has already been initialized. If not, the method initializes the Membership class and its properties.

The method must programmatically access the contents of the membership section of the `Web.config` file, which is an XML document. Programmatic access to the contents of an XML document is normally achieved by loading the entire document into the instance of an appropriate class. The `OpenWebConfiguration` method of the `WebConfigurationManager` class loads the entire `Web.config` file into an instance of the `Configuration` class:

```
Configuration config = WebConfigurationManager.OpenWebConfiguration("/");
```

The .NET Framework comes with one class for each main section of the `Web.config` and `Machine.config` files that represents the contents of the section. The name of each class consists of the name of the section followed by the keyword `Section`. All of these classes derive from the `ConfigurationSection` base class.

The `Configuration` class exposes a method named `GetSection` that takes the fully qualified name of a section and returns an instance of the class that represents the section. The `Initialize` method calls the `GetSection` method to access the `MembershipSection` object that represents the contents of the membership section of the `Web.config` file.

```
MembershipSection sec =
                    (MembershipSection)config.GetSection("system.web/membership");
```

The `MembershipSection` class exposes a collection property of type `ProviderSettingsCollection` named `Providers` that contains one `ProviderSettings` object for each registered membership provider. Each `ProviderSettings` object provides programmatic access to the attributes of its membership provider.

The `ProviderSettings` class exposes a property named `Type` that returns the value of the `type` attribute of the respective membership provider. Recall that the `type` attribute consists of two parts. The first part is the fully qualified name of the type of the membership provider. The second part is the (partial or strong) name of the assembly that contains the membership provider. The `Initialize` method first extracts the first part:

```
providerType = settings.Type.Trim().Split(new char[] { ',' })[0];
```

The `Initialize` method then extracts the second part, which is the (partial or strong) name of the assembly that contains the membership provider:

```
assemblyName = settings.Type.Trim().Remove(settings.Type.IndexOf(providerType),
                    providerType.Length);
```

If the assembly name isn't null or empty, the `Initialize` method calls the `Load` method of the `Assembly` class to load the assembly into memory:

```
myAssembly = Assembly.Load(assemblyName);
```

If the `type` attribute doesn't contain the assembly name, the `Initialize` method assumes that the executing assembly contains the provider:

```
myAssembly = Assembly.GetExecutingAssembly();
```

When a .NET-compliant compiler is compiling managed code into an assembly, it also emits metadata into the assembly. The metadata fully describes the contents of the assembly, including its types. The `Load` method returns an `Assembly` object that provides access to the metadata of the assembly that contains the respective membership provider.

The `Assembly` object (`myAssembly`) exposes a method named `CreateInstance` that takes the fully qualified name of a type and dynamically creates an instance of the type. This is possible because the `Assembly` object has access to the information about all the types that the assembly contains. The `Initialize` method calls the `CreateInstance` method to dynamically create an instance of the membership provider:

```
provider = (MembershipProvider)myAssembly.CreateInstance(providerType);
```

The `CreateInstance` method of the `Assembly` class doesn't initialize the membership provider object that it instantiates. Obviously, the instantiated membership provider can't be used until its properties are initialized to the appropriate values. For example, an instantiated `SqlMembershipProvider` can't be used until its `ConnectionStringName` property is initialized to the appropriate value. The `SqlMembershipProvider` instance wouldn't be able to connect to the appropriate database without knowing the connection string. This is where the `Initialize` method of the `ProviderBase` class comes into play. Recall that every ASP.NET provider, including membership providers, inherits the `Initialize` method from the `ProviderBase` class.

As you'll see later, the `Initialize` method takes a `NameValueCollection` that contains the names and values of the provider attributes (such as `connectionStringName`) as its argument and uses the collection to initialize the properties of the respective provider.

The `ProviderSettings` class exposes a property of type `NameValueCollection` named `Parameters` that contains the names and values of these attributes. The `Initialize` method of the `Membership` class calls the `Initialize` method of the instantiated membership provider and passes the `Parameters` `NameValueCollection` as its argument:

```
provider.Initialize(settings.Name, settings.Parameters);
```

The `Initialize` method then sets the `userIsOnlineTimeWindow` property of the `Membership` class:

```
userIsOnlineTimeWindow = (int)sec.UserIsOnlineTimeWindow.TotalMinutes;
```

If the `defaultProvider` attribute of the `<membership>` element has been set, the `Initialize` method uses its value as index to the `Providers` collection to access the default provider and to assign it to the `Provider` property of the `Membership` class. If the `defaultProvider` attribute hasn't been set, the method assigns the first `MembershipProvider` provider in the `Providers` collection to the `Provider` property of the `Membership` class:

```
if (!string.IsNullOrEmpty(sec.DefaultProvider))
    provider = providers[sec.DefaultProvider];
else
    provider = providers[sec.Providers[0].Name];
```

As Listing 21-3 shows, the `Provider` and `Providers` properties of the `Membership` class call the `Initialize` method to ensure the values of the provider and providers fields are set before they're accessed.

Listing 21-3: The Provider and Providers properties call the Initialize method

```
public static MembershipProvider Provider
{
  get
  {
    Initialize();
    return provider;
  }
}

public static MembershipProviderCollection Providers
{
  get
  {
    Initialize();
    return providers;
  }
}
```

Membership API

As the previous chapter demonstrated, the Membership class is only responsible for defining the business API for its clients. The class delegates the responsibility of deciding which data access API to use to the membership provider that the class's Initialize method instantiates and initializes in generic fashion (see Listing 21-2).

The events, methods, and properties of the Membership class define the Membership API. The API allows its clients to perform the following operations:

❑   Add a new user to the data store

❑   Remove a user from the data store

❑   Update user membership information in the data store

❑   Validate user credentials against the data store

❑   Search users in the data store

❑   Retrieve user membership information from the data store

❑   Enforce application-specific password validation rules before passwords are committed to the underlying data store

❑   Access the user online time window

Adding a New User to the Data Store

The clients of the Membership class call the CreateUser method to add a new user to the data store. The method delegates the responsibility for inserting the new user membership information to the data store to the configured membership provider. As Listing 21-4 shows, the method calls the Provider property to access the configured membership provider in generic fashion without knowing its real type.

Listing 21-4: The CreateUser method

```
public static MembershipUser
CreateUser(string username, string password, string email, string passwordQuestion,
           string passwordAnswer, bool isApproved, object providerUserKey,
           out MembershipCreateStatus status)
{
   return Provider.CreateUser(username, password, email, passwordQuestion,
                        passwordAnswer, isApproved, providerUserKey, out status);
}
```

The clients of the Membership class are normally different from the clients of the MembershipProvider class. Recall that the main clients of the Membership and MembershipProvider classes are the ASP.NET 2.0 Login controls and the Membership class, respectively. Because the Membership and MembershipProvider classes define their APIs for different clients, their APIs don't have to mirror each other. For example, the MembershipProvider class exposes a single CreateUser method that takes all the possible arguments. The Membership class, on the other hand, exposes four overloads of the same CreateUser method, where all of them delegate to the same CreateUser method of the MembershipProvider class (see Listings 21-5 through 21-7).

Listing 21-5: The CreateUser overload that takes the new user's username and password

```
public static MembershipUser CreateUser(string username, string password)
{
   MembershipCreateStatus status;
   return Provider.CreateUser(username, password, string.Empty , "question",
                        "answer", false, null, out status);
}
```

Listing 21-6: The CreateUser overload that takes the new user's username, password, and e-mail address

```
public static MembershipUser CreateUser(string username, string password,
                                        string email)
{
   MembershipCreateStatus status;
   return Provider.CreateUser(username, password, email, "question", "answer", true,
                        null, out status);
}
```

Listing 21-7: The CreateUser overload that takes everything but the provider user key

```
public static MembershipUser CreateUser(string username, string password,
           string email, string passwordQuestion, string passwordAnswer,
           bool isApproved, out MembershipCreateStatus status)
{
   return Provider.CreateUser(username, password, email, passwordQuestion,
                        passwordAnswer, isApproved, null, out status);
}
```

Removing a User from the Data Store

The clients (normally ASP.NET 2.0 Login controls) of the Membership class call the DeleteUser method to delete a user from the data store. The DeleteUser method is another example that shows the Membership API doesn't have to mirror the MembershipProvider API. Whereas the MembershipProvider class exposes a single DeleteUser method, the Membership class exposes two overloads of the DeleteUser method (see Listings 21-8 and 21-9). Notice that both overloads delegate the responsibility of deleting the user membership information from the data store to the same DeleteUser method of the MembershipProvider class.

Listing 21-8: The DeleteUser overload that takes two arguments

```
public static bool DeleteUser(string username, bool deleteAllRelatedData)
{
  return Provider.DeleteUser(username, deleteAllRelatedData);
}
```

Listing 21-9: The DeleteUser overload that takes only one argument

```
public static bool DeleteUser(string username)
{
  return Provider.DeleteUser(username, false);
}
```

Updating Specified User Membership Information in the Data Store

The UpdateUser method (see Listing 21-10) updates the specified user membership information in the data store. The method delegates the responsibility of updating the user record to the configured membership provider.

Listing 21-10: The UpdateUser method

```
public static void UpdateUser(MembershipUser user)
{
  Provider.UpdateUser(user);
}
```

Validating User Credentials Against the Data Store

The clients of the Membership class call the ValidateUser method to validate the credentials of the specified user against the data store. This method, like the others, delegates the responsibility of interacting with the data store to the configured membership provider (see Listing 21-11).

Listing 21-11: The ValidateUser method validates user credentials

```
public static bool ValidateUser(string username, string password)
{
  return Provider.ValidateUser(username, password);
}
```

Searching Users in the Data Store

The `Membership` class provides its clients with the following search options:

- ❏ Search users by e-mail
- ❏ Search users by name
- ❏ Get all users
- ❏ Get the number of users online

Each search option (except for the last one) allows clients to return the search result in one shot or one page at a time. Retrieving records one page at a time improves the performance, usability, and responsiveness of the application.

The `Membership` class comes with two overloads of the `FindUsersByEmail` method that allow clients to search users by e-mail. The first overload retrieves the records one page at a time, and the second overload retrieves all the records in one shot (see Listing 21-12). Notice that both overloads delegate to the same method of the configured membership provider.

Listing 21-12: The two overloads of the FindUsersByEmail method

```
public static MembershipUserCollection FindUsersByEmail(string emailToMatch,
                         int pageIndex, int pageSize, out int totalRecords)
{
   return Provider.FindUsersByEmail(emailToMatch, pageIndex, pageSize,
                              out totalRecords);
}

public static MembershipUserCollection FindUsersByEmail(string emailToMatch)
{
   int totalRecords;

   return Provider.FindUsersByEmail(emailToMatch, 0, int.MaxValue,
                              out totalRecords);
}
```

The two overloads of the `FindUsersByName` method class allow clients to search users by name where the records can be retrieved all at once or one page at a time (see Listing 21-13). Both overloads delegate the responsibility of the actual searching the underlying data store to the same method of the configured membership provider.

Listing 21-13: The two overloads of the FindUsersByName method

```
public static MembershipUserCollection FindUsersByName(string usernameToMatch,
                          int pageIndex, int pageSize, out int totalRecords)
{
   return Provider.FindUsersByName(usernameToMatch, pageIndex, pageSize,
                              out totalRecords);
}

public static MembershipUserCollection FindUsersByName(string usernameToMatch)
{
```

```
        int totalRecords;

        return Provider.FindUsersByName(usernameToMatch, 0, int.MaxValue,
                                        out totalRecords);
    }
```

The `Membership` class comes with two overloads of the `GetAllUsers` method that allows its clients to retrieve all users from the data store all at once or one page at a time (see Listing 21-14).

Listing 21-14: The two overloads of the GetAllUsers method

```
    public static MembershipUserCollection GetAllUsers(int pageIndex, int pageSize,
                                                       out int totalRecords)
    {
      return Provider.GetAllUsers(pageIndex, pageSize, out totalRecords);
    }

    public static MembershipUserCollection GetAllUsers()
    {
      int totalRecords;

      return Provider.GetAllUsers(0, int.MaxValue, out totalRecords);
    }
```

The last searching facility of the `Membership` class, `GetNumberOfUsersOnline`, allows clients to retrieve the total number of online users (see Listing 21-15).

Listing 21-15: The GetNumberOfUsersOnline method

```
    public static int GetNumberOfUsersOnline()
    {
      return Provider.GetNumberOfUsersOnline();
    }
```

Retrieving User Membership Information from the Data Store

The `Membership` class provides its clients with the `GetUserNameByEmail` method and six overloads of the `GetUser` method to retrieve the membership information of the specified user (Listing 21-16). The two overloads of the `GetUser` method that don't take the username or an object as their argument retrieve the membership information for the currently logged-on user, that is, `HttpContext.Current.User.Identity.Name`.

Listing 21-16: The methods that retrieve the membership information of the specified user

```
    public static MembershipUser GetUser(object providerUserKey, bool userIsOnline)
    {
      return Provider.GetUser(providerUserKey, userIsOnline);
    }
```

(continued)

Listing 21-16: *(continued)*

```
public static MembershipUser GetUser()
{
  return Provider.GetUser(HttpContext.Current.User.Identity.Name, true);
}

public static MembershipUser GetUser(bool userIsOnline)
{
  return Provider.GetUser(HttpContext.Current.User.Identity.Name, userIsOnline);
}

public static MembershipUser GetUser(object providerUserKey)
{
  return Provider.GetUser(providerUserKey, true);
}

public static MembershipUser GetUser(string username)
{
  return Provider.GetUser(username, true);
}

public static MembershipUser GetUser(string username, bool userIsOnline)
{
  return Provider.GetUser(username, userIsOnline);
}
```

Enforcing Application-Specific Password Validation Rules

Isolating applications from the configured membership provider has its own pros and cons. You've already seen the pros in detail. Now here's one of the cons. The CreateUser method of the Membership class delegates the responsibility of committing the new user membership information to the underlying data store to the configured membership provider. Such an application-agnostic generic mechanism has the following downsides:

❑ It doesn't allow the application to enforce its own application-specific password validation rules before the new user membership information is committed to the data store.

❑ It doesn't allow the application to cancel the new user registration when the application-specific password validation of the new user password fails.

The Membership and MembershipProvider base classes work together to provide the application with the following mechanism to enforce application-specific password validation rules and cancel new user registration when the validation fails. The Membership and MembershipProvider classes both expose an event of type MembershipValidatePasswordEventHandler named ValidatingPassword. The definition of the MembershipValidatePasswordEventHandler delegate is as follows:

```
public delegate void MembershipValidatePasswordEventHandler(object sender,
                                       ValidatePasswordEventArgs e);
```

The clients of the `Membership` class use an instance of the `MembershipValidatePasswordEventHandler` delegate to register a callback method for this event:

```
Membership.ValidatingPassword +=
            new MembershipValidatePasswordEventHandler(ValidatingPasswordCallback);
```

As Listing 21-17 shows, the `ValidatingPassword` event of the `Membership` class adds the clients' `MembershipValidatePasswordEventHandler` instances to the `ValidatingPassword` event of the relevant membership provider. In other words, as far as the `ValidatingPassword` event goes, the `Membership` class acts as a middle man. As you'll see later, the `MembershipProvider` class raises the `ValidatingPassword` event when its `CreateUser`, `ChangePassword`, and `ResetPassword` methods are called.

Listing 21-17: The ValidatingPassword event of the Membership class

```
public event MembershipValidatePasswordEventHandler ValidatingPassword
{
   add { Provider.ValidatingPassword += value; }
   remove { Provider.ValidatingPassword -= value; }
}
```

The client callback method must have the following signature:

```
protected void ValidatingPasswordCallback(object sender,
                                ValidatePasswordEventArgs e);
```

Notice that the client callback method takes an instance of the `ValidatePasswordEventArgs` as its argument. The `ValidatePasswordEventArgs` class stores event data associated with the `ValidatingPassword` event. Listing 21-18 shows the reverse-engineered implementation of the `ValidatePasswordEventArgs` class.

Listing 21-18: The ValidatePasswordEventArgs class

```
public class ValidatePasswordEventArgs : EventArgs
{
   string userName;
   string password;
   bool isNewUser;
   bool cancel;
   Exception failureInformation;

   public ValidatePasswordEventArgs(string userName,
                          string password, bool isNewUser)
   {
      this.userName = userName;
      this.password = password;
      this.isNewUser = isNewUser;
   }

   public bool Cancel
   {
      get { return cancel; }
```

(continued)

Listing 21-18: *(continued)*

```
    set { cancel = value; }
  }
  public Exception FailureInformation
  {
    get { return failureInformation; }
    set { failureInformation = value; }
  }
  public bool IsNewUser
  {
    get { return isNewUser; }
  }
  public string Password
  {
    get { return password; }
  }
  public string UserName
  {
    get { return userName; }
  }
}
```

The client callback uses the `UserName`, `Password`, and `IsNewUser` properties of the `ValidatePasswordEventArgs` instance (the instance passed in as its argument) to access the user membership information. Then it uses the application-specific password validation rules to validate the password of the user. If the validation fails, the callback sets the `Cancel` property of the `ValidatePasswordEventArgs` instance to true to cancel the user registration and creates an instance of the appropriate subclass of the `Exception` class and assigns the instance to the `FailureInformation` property of the `ValidatePasswordEventArgs` instance.

Accessing the User Online Time Window

The `<membership>` element of the `Web.config` or `Machine.config` file has an attribute named `userIsOnlineTimeWindow` that page developers must set to the desired value. The value of this attribute specifies the time interval (since the last user activity) within which the user is considered online. The `Membership` class exposes a static read-only property named `UserIsOnlineTimeWindow` as shown in Listing 21-19. The getter of this property calls the `Initialize` method to ensure that the value of the `userIsOnlineTimeWindow` private field has been set.

Listing 21-19: The UserIsOnlineTimeWindow property

```
private static int userIsOnlineTimeWindow = -1;
public static int UserIsOnlineTimeWindow
{
  get
  {
    Initialize();
    return userIsOnlineTimeWindow;
  }
}
```

Developing Custom Security Controls

The section implements two custom security controls named Login and Register that reverse-engineer the main components of the ASP.NET LoginControl and CreateUserWizard to help you understand how security controls validate user credentials against any type of data store, and how you can write your own custom security controls. These custom composite controls encapsulate the logic that validates the user credentials and the logic that creates new users, allowing the page developer to use the controls without writing any code.

Login

Because the Login control is a composite control, you should follow the composite control pattern discussed in Chapters 5 and 7 to implement the control. First, derive the control from the CompositeControl base class. Recall that this base class provides the basic functionality that every composite control must support:

❑ It overrides the Controls collection to call the EnsureChildControls method.

❑ It implements the INamingContainer interface to request that the page create a new naming scope for its child controls.

❑ It overrides the DataBind method.

❑ It implements the ICompositeControlDesignerAccessor interface.

❑ It overrides the Render method to call EnsureChildControls when the control is in design mode before the actual rendering begins. This ensures that child controls are created before they are rendered.

Next, you need to override the CreateChildControls method to instantiate and initialize the child controls from which you'll assemble the Login control, as shown in Listing 21-20.

Listing 21-20: The CreateChildControls method

```
protected override void CreateChildControls()
{
  Controls.Clear();

  headerLabel = new Label();
  userNameLabel = new Label();
  userNameTextBox = new TextBox();
  passwordLabel = new Label();
  passwordTextBox = new TextBox();
  loginButton = new Button();
  loginButton.Text = "Login";
  loginButton.Click += new EventHandler(OnLogin);
  registerHyperLink = new HyperLink();
  registerHyperLink.Text = "Register";

  Controls.Add(headerLabel);
  Controls.Add(userNameLabel);
  Controls.Add(userNameTextBox);
```

(continued)

Listing 21-20: *(continued)*

```
    Controls.Add(passwordLabel);
    Controls.Add(passwordTextBox);
    Controls.Add(loginButton);
    Controls.Add(registerHyperLink);

    ChildControlsCreated = true;
}
```

As Listing 21-20 shows, the CreateChildControls method registers the OnLogin method as a callback for the Click event of the login Button control. Listing 21-21 shows the implementation of the OnLogin method.

Listing 21-21: The OnLogin method

```
void OnLogin(object sender, EventArgs e)
{
  if (CustomComponents.Membership.ValidateUser(userNameTextBox.Text,
                                        passwordTextBox.Text))
  {
    FormsAuthenticationTicket ticket = new FormsAuthenticationTicket( 1,
                            userNameTextBox.Text, DateTime.Now,
                            DateTime.Now.AddSeconds(40),false, string.Empty);

    string encryptedTicket = FormsAuthentication.Encrypt(ticket);

    HttpCookie cookie = new HttpCookie(FormsAuthentication.FormsCookieName);
    cookie.Value = encryptedTicket;

    Page.Response.Cookies.Add(cookie);
    EnsureChildControls();
    Page.Response.Redirect(
          FormsAuthentication.GetRedirectUrl(userNameTextBox.Text, false), true);
  }
}
```

The OnLogin method first calls the ValidateUser method of the Membership class to validate the user credentials (username and password):

```
if (CustomComponents.Membership.ValidateUser(userNameTextBox.Text,
                                        passwordTextBox.Text))
```

It then creates a FormsAuthenticationTicket:

```
FormsAuthenticationTicket ticket = new FormsAuthenticationTicket( 1,
                        userNameTextBox.Text, DateTime.Now,
                        DateTime.Now.AddSeconds(40),false, string.Empty);
```

It encrypts the ticket to protect its integrity and privacy in transit:

```
string encryptedTicket = FormsAuthentication.Encrypt(ticket);
```

It creates a cookie with the specified name:

```
HttpCookie cookie = new HttpCookie(FormsAuthentication.FormsCookieName);
```

It stores the encrypted ticket in the cookie:

```
cookie.Value = encryptedTicket;
```

It adds the cookie to the response:

```
Page.Response.Cookies.Add(cookie);
```

Finally, the method redirects the user to the originally requested page. The `OnLogin` method calls the `EnsureChildControls` method before the call into the `Redirect` method because it passes the value of the `Text` property of the username `TextBox` into the `Redirect` method. Recall that every composite control must call the `EnsureChildControls` method before it attempts to access its child controls:

```
EnsureChildControls();
Page.Response.Redirect(
        FormsAuthentication.GetRedirectUrl(userNameTextBox.Text, false), true);
```

As the preceding listing shows, thanks to the ASP.NET membership model, the `Login` control encapsulates all the code that the ASP.NET 1.x page developers have to write every time they need to authenticate users.

The next thing you need to do is override the `RenderContents` method to assemble the `Login` composite control from its child controls as shown in Listing 21-22. The main responsibility of the `CreateChildControls` method is to instantiate and initialize the child controls that the `RenderContents` method uses to assemble the composite control. In other words, the `RenderContents` method is where the actual assembly of the composite control is done, as discussed in Chapter 5.

Listing 21-22: The RenderContents method

```
protected override void RenderContents(HtmlTextWriter writer)
{
  PrepareControlHierarchy();

  if (headerStyle != null)
    headerStyle.AddAttributesToRender(writer);

  writer.RenderBeginTag(HtmlTextWriterTag.Tr);
  writer.AddAttribute(HtmlTextWriterAttribute.Colspan, "2");
  writer.RenderBeginTag(HtmlTextWriterTag.Th);
  headerLabel.RenderControl(writer);
  writer.RenderEndTag();
  writer.RenderEndTag();

  writer.RenderBeginTag(HtmlTextWriterTag.Tr);
  writer.AddAttribute(HtmlTextWriterAttribute.Align, "right");
  writer.RenderBeginTag(HtmlTextWriterTag.Td);
  userNameLabel.RenderControl(writer);
  writer.RenderEndTag();
```

(continued)

Listing 21-22: *(continued)*

```
    writer.RenderBeginTag(HtmlTextWriterTag.Td);
    userNameTextBox.RenderControl(writer);
    writer.RenderEndTag();
    writer.RenderEndTag();

    writer.RenderBeginTag(HtmlTextWriterTag.Tr);
    writer.AddAttribute(HtmlTextWriterAttribute.Align, "right");
    writer.RenderBeginTag(HtmlTextWriterTag.Td);
    passwordLabel.RenderControl(writer);
    writer.RenderEndTag();
    writer.RenderBeginTag(HtmlTextWriterTag.Td);
    passwordTextBox.RenderControl(writer);
    writer.RenderEndTag();
    writer.RenderEndTag();

    writer.RenderBeginTag(HtmlTextWriterTag.Tr);
    writer.RenderBeginTag(HtmlTextWriterTag.Td);
    loginButton.RenderControl(writer);
    writer.RenderEndTag();
    writer.RenderEndTag();

    writer.RenderBeginTag(HtmlTextWriterTag.Tr);
    writer.RenderBeginTag(HtmlTextWriterTag.Td);
    registerHyperLink.RenderControl(writer);
    writer.RenderEndTag();
    writer.RenderEndTag();
}
```

The `RenderContents` method renders the formatting or layout HTML directly, that is, the table, table rows, and table cells that contain the child controls. The alternative would be to create `LiteralControls` that encapsulate these layout HTML elements and add these `LiteralControls` to the `Controls` collection of the `Login` control. Obviously this would be done in the `CreateChildControls` method.

You should avoid this alternative, however, because it increases the sizes of both the page's control tree and the saved view state and consequently degrades the performance and usability of the application.

Next, you need to expose the style properties of the `Login` control's child controls as top-level style properties to allow the page developer to set the style properties of its child controls as attributes on the tag that represents the `Login` control on an ASP.NET page. The `Login` control exposes three top-level style properties: `HeaderStyle`, `UserNameLabelStyle`, and `PasswordLabelStyle`. As an example, the following code shows the implementation of the `HeaderStyle` property:

```
private TableItemStyle headerStyle;
[PersistenceMode(PersistenceMode.InnerProperty)]
public virtual TableItemStyle HeaderStyle
{
  get
  {
    if (headerStyle == null)
    {
      headerStyle = new TableItemStyle();
```

```
        if (IsTrackingViewState)
          ((IStateManager)headerStyle).TrackViewState();
      }
    return headerStyle;
  }
}
```

Next, annotate the `HeaderStyle`, `UserNameLabelStyle`, and `PasswordLabelStyle` top-level style properties with the following metadata attribute:

```
[PersistenceMode(PersistenceMode.InnerProperty)]
```

The `PersistenceMode.InnerProperty` instructs Visual Studio to serialize these top-level style properties as child elements of the `Login` control.

Next you need to override the `TrackViewState`, `LoadViewState`, and `SaveViewState` methods to respectively call the `TrackViewState`, `LoadViewState`, and `SaveViewState` methods of the `HeaderStyle`, `UserNameLabelStyle`, and `PasswordLabelStyle` top-level style properties. As an example, the following code shows the implementation of the `TrackViewState` method:

```
protected override void TrackViewState()
{
  base.TrackViewState();

  if (headerStyle != null)
    ((IStateManager)headerStyle).TrackViewState();
  if (userNameLabelStyle != null)
    ((IStateManager)userNameLabelStyle).TrackViewState();
  if (passwordLabelStyle != null)
    ((IStateManager)passwordLabelStyle).TrackViewState();
}
```

Next, override the `TagKey` property to specify the `<table>` HTML element as the containing HTML element:

```
protected override HtmlTextWriterTag TagKey
{
  get { return HtmlTextWriterTag.Table; }
}
```

Then override the `CreateControlStyle` method to specify a `TableStyle` instance as the `ControlStyle` property of the `Login` control. This is necessary because a `<table>` HTML element is used as the containing HTML element:

```
protected override Style CreateControlStyle()
{
  return new TableStyle(ViewState);
}
```

Next you need to expose the `GridLines`, `CellPadding`, `CellSpacing`, `HorizontalAlign`, and `BackImageUrl` style properties of the `TableStyle` instance as top-level style properties. As an example, the following code shows the implementation of the `GridLines` property:

```
public virtual GridLines GridLines
{
  get { return ((TableStyle)ControlStyle).GridLines; }
  set { ((TableStyle)ControlStyle).GridLines = value; }
}
```

These top-level style properties delegate to the respective properties of the `TableStyle` instance.

Finally, you need to expose the properties of the `Login` control's child controls as top-level properties to allow the page developer to set these child control properties as attributes on the tag that represents the `Login` control on an ASP.NET page. The following shows the implementation of the `HeaderLabelText` property as an example:

```
public virtual string HeaderLabelText
{
  get { EnsureChildControls(); return headerLabel.Text; }
  set { EnsureChildControls(); headerLabel.Text = value; }
}
```

As the code shows, these top-level properties delegate to the respective properties of the child controls. Also notice that both the getters and setters of these delegated properties call the `EnsureChildControls` method to ensure the child controls are created before they attempt to access their properties.

Register

The `Register` control is a composite security control that allows a new user to register with your site. The implementation of the `Register` control is very similar to the implementation of the `Login` control. The main difference is the callbacks that these two controls register with their `Button` controls. The `Register` control registers the `OnRegister` method as the callback for the `Click` event of its `Button` control, as shown in Listing 21-23.

Listing 21-23: The OnRegister method

```
void OnRegister(object sender, EventArgs e)
{
  if (!CustomComponents.Membership.CreateUser(userNameTextBox.Text,
                                passwordTextBox.Text, emailTextBox.Text))
    return;

  FormsAuthenticationTicket ticket = new FormsAuthenticationTicket(1,
                          userNameTextBox.Text, DateTime.Now,
                          DateTime.Now.AddSeconds(40),false, string.Empty);

  string encryptedTicket = FormsAuthentication.Encrypt(ticket);

  HttpCookie cookie = new HttpCookie(FormsAuthentication.FormsCookieName);
  cookie.Value = encryptedTicket;

  Page.Response.Cookies.Add(cookie);
  EnsureChildControls();
```

```
    Page.Response.Redirect(
            FormsAuthentication.GetRedirectUrl(userNameTextBox.Text, false), true);
}
```

The `OnRegister` method first calls the `CreateUser` method of the `Membership` class to add the new user's membership information to the underlying data store:

```
CustomComponents.Membership.CreateUser(userNameTextBox.Text, passwordTextBox.Text,
                                       emailTextBox.Text);
```

It then creates a `FormsAuthenticationTicket`:

```
FormsAuthenticationTicket ticket = new FormsAuthenticationTicket(1,
                                userNameTextBox.Text, DateTime.Now,
                                DateTime.Now.AddSeconds(40),false, string.Empty);
```

It encrypts the ticket to protect its integrity and privacy in transit:

```
string encryptedTicket = FormsAuthentication.Encrypt(ticket);
```

Next it creates a cookie with the specified name:

```
    HttpCookie cookie = new HttpCookie(FormsAuthentication.FormsCookieName);
```

It then stores the encrypted ticket in the cookie:

```
cookie.Value = encryptedTicket;
```

Next, the method adds the cookie to the outgoing response message:

```
Page.Response.Cookies.Add(cookie);
```

It then calls the `EnsureChildControls` method and redirects the user to the originally requested page as discussed before:

```
EnsureChildControls();
Page.Response.Redirect(
        FormsAuthentication.GetRedirectUrl(userNameTextBox.Text, false), true);
```

As Listing 21-23 shows, thanks to the ASP.NET 2.0 membership model, the `OnRegister` method encapsulates the logic that the ASP.NET 1.x page developer has to write to register new users. This allows the page developer to use the `Register` control declaratively without writing a single line of code.

Using the Login and Register Controls

This section implements a Web application that uses the `Login` and `Register` controls. The application consists of the following three ASP.NET pages.

The first page is the protected page `Default.aspx`. Only authenticated users should be allowed to access this protected resource. This page simply displays the text "This is a protected resource."

```
<%@ Page Language="C#" %>
<html xmlns="http://www.w3.org/1999/xhtml">
<body>
  <form id="form1" runat="server">
    <strong>This is a protected resource</strong>
  </form>
</body>
</html>
```

The second page is the `Login.aspx` page, which uses the `Login` control to authenticate the user:

```
<%@ Page Language="C#" %>
<%@ Register TagPrefix="custom" Namespace="CustomComponents" %>
<html xmlns="http://www.w3.org/1999/xhtml">
<body>
  <form id="form1" runat="server">
    <custom:Login runat="server" HeaderLabelText="Log In"
    RegisterNavigateUrl="Register.aspx" UserNameLabelText="User Name:"
    PasswordLabelText="Password:" CellPadding="4" BackColor="#F7F6F3"
    BorderColor="#E6E2D8" BorderWidth="1px" BorderStyle="Solid" ForeColor="#333333"
    Font-Names="Verdana" Font-Size="0.8em">
      <HeaderStyle ForeColor="White" BackColor="#5D7B9D" Font-Size="0.9em"
      Font-Bold="true" HorizontalAlign="center" />
    </custom:Login>
  </form>
</body>
</html>
```

The third page is the `Register.aspx` page, which uses the `Register` control to allow a new user to register:

```
<%@ Page Language="C#" %>
<%@ Register TagPrefix="custom" Namespace="CustomComponents" %>
<html xmlns="http://www.w3.org/1999/xhtml">
<body>
  <form id="form1" runat="server">
    <custom:Register runat="server" HeaderLabelText="Sign Up for Your New Account"
    UserNameLabelText="User Name:" PasswordLabelText="Password:"
    ConfirmPasswordLabelText="Confirm Password:" EmailLabelText="E-mail"
    CellPadding="4" BackColor="#F7F6F3" BorderColor="#E6E2D8" BorderWidth="1px"
    BorderStyle="Solid" ForeColor="#333333" Font-Names="Verdana" Font-Size="0.8em">
      <HeaderStyle ForeColor="White" BackColor="#5D7B9D" Font-Size="0.9em"
      Font-Bold="true" HorizontalAlign="center" />
      <ConfirmPasswordLabelStyle Font-Bold="true" />
      <EmailLabelStyle Font-Bold="true" />
      <PasswordLabelStyle Font-Bold="true" />
      <UserNameLabelStyle Font-Bold="true" />
    </custom:Register>
  </form>
</body>
</html>
```

You need to configure the Web application to use the ASP.NET 2.0 `SqlMembershipProvider`. This provider is specifically designed to work with a SQL Server database named `aspnetdb`. The `aspnetdb` database contains all the necessary tables, views, and stored procedures for both authentication and authorization. First, you'll need to run the `aspnet_regsql` command-line tool to set up the `aspnetdb` database. Make sure that the `<connectionStrings>` section of the `Web.config` or `Machine.config` file includes an entry for the required connection string. Here is an example:

```
<connectionStrings>
  <remove name="LocalSqlServer"/>
  <add name="LocalSqlServer"
  connectionString=
   "data source=.\SQLEXPRESS;AttachDbFilename=|DataDirectory|aspnetdb.mdf;
   integrated security=true" />
</connectionStrings>
```

Visual Studio 2005 comes with an administration tool named Web Site Administration Tool (WSAT) (see Figure 21-1) that allows you to specify the membership provider that you want the ASP.NET membership model to use to access the underlying data store. You can launch this tool by selecting Web Site⇨ASP.NET Configuration.

From the Provider tab of the Web Site Administration Tool, select the "Select a single provider for all site management data" option and accept the `AspNetSqlProvider`.

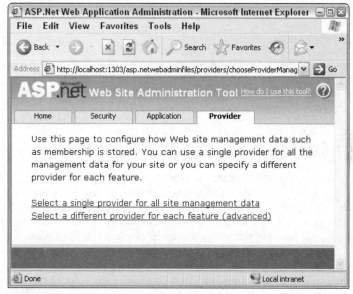

Figure 21-1

Registering the SqlMembershipProvider

Because the `Provider` and `Providers` properties of the reverse-engineered `Membership` class read the configured membership provider from the local `Web.config` file, you need to add the `<membership>` section shown in the following code fragment to the `<system.web>` section of the `Web.config` file:

```
<membership defaultProvider="AspNetSqlMembershipProvider" >
  <providers>
    <clear/>
    <add name="AspNetSqlMembershipProvider"
     type="System.Web.Security.SqlMembershipProvider, System.Web, Version=2.0.0.0,
     Culture=neutral, PublicKeyToken=b03f5f7f11d50a3a"
     connectionStringName="LocalSqlServer" enablePasswordRetrieval="false"
     enablePasswordReset="true" requiresQuestionAndAnswer="false"
     applicationName="/" requiresUniqueEmail="false" passwordFormat="Hashed"
     maxInvalidPasswordAttempts="5" passwordAttemptWindow="10"
     passwordStrengthRegularExpression="" />
    </providers>
  </membership>
```

You also need to enable the Forms authentication and deny anonymous access to your site by making the changes shown in the following code in the Web.config file:

```
<authentication mode="Forms">
  <forms loginUrl="Login.aspx" name=".AUTHCOOKIE" path="/" protection="All"
   timeout="40" />
</authentication>

<authorization>
  <deny users="?"/>
</authorization>
```

When users access your Web site for the first time, they are considered anonymous and are automatically redirected to the Login.aspx Web page. The Login control has a link named Register that directs new users to the Register.aspx page to register.

MembershipUser

This section implements a replica of another important component of the ASP.NET 2.0 membership model named MembershipUser. A given user is represented by an instance of the MembershipUser class that is loaded with the membership information of the user. The MembershipUser class exposes two constructors: the default constructor, and the one shown in Listing 21-24. The arguments that the latter constructor takes are used to set the following properties of the MembershipUser instance:

❑ ProviderName: The friendly name of the membership provider, such as AspNetSqlProvider. The MembershipUser class uses this friendly name as an index to the Membership.Providers collection to access the appropriate membership provider, such as SqlMembershipProvider.

❑ UserName: Username of the user that the MembershipUser instance represents.

❑ ProviderUserKey: Identifier that the membership provider uses to uniquely identify the user that the MembershipUser instance represents. The type of the identifier depends on the type of membership provider. For example, the SqlMembershipProvider uses an identifier of type GUID.

❑ Email: E-mail address of the user that the MembershipUser instance represents.

❑ PasswordQuestion: Question that users must answer before they're allowed to reset their password.

❑ Comment: Comment associated with the user that provides more information.

❑ IsApproved: Boolean flag that specifies whether the user is approved.

❑ IsLockedOut: Boolean flag that specifies whether the user is locked out. After a preset number of failed login attempts within a preset time interval, the user gets locked out and won't be allowed to log on to the application until the UnlockUser method of the MembershipUser instance is explicitly called to unlock the user, as discussed later in this section.

❑ CreationDate: Date and time when the user was added to the membership data store.

❑ LastLoginDate: Date and time when the user was last authenticated.

❑ LastActivityDate: Date and time of the last activity on the membership data of the user. Some methods of the membership provider such as CreateUser, UpdateUser, and ValidateUser update the value of the LastActivityData property to the current date and time.

❑ LastPasswordChangedDate: Date and time when the user's password was last updated.

❑ LastLockoutDate: Date and time when the user was last locked out.

Listing 21-24: The constructor of the MembershipUser class

```
public MembershipUser(string providerName, string name, object providerUserKey,
            string email, string passwordQuestion, string comment,
            bool isApproved, bool isLockedOut, DateTime creationDate,
            DateTime lastLoginDate, DateTime lastActivityDate,
            DateTime lastPasswordChangedDate, DateTime lastLockoutDate)
{
  this.providerName = providerName;
  this.name = name;
  this.providerUserKey = providerUserKey;
  this.email = email;
  this.passwordQuestion = passwordQuestion;
  this.comment = comment;
  this.isApproved = isApproved;
  this.isLockedOut = isLockedOut;
  this.creationDate = creationDate;
  this.lastLoginDate = lastLoginDate;
  this.lastActivityDate = lastActivityDate;
  this.lastPasswordChangedDate = lastPasswordChangedDate;
  this.lastLockoutDate = lastLockoutDate;
}
```

The MembershipUser class exposes a read-only property named IsOnline that is not set in the constructor. Listing 21-25 shows the implementation of this property. Recall that the UserIsOnlineTimeWindow property of the Membership class represents the time interval in minutes (since the last user activity) within which the user is considered online. The IsOnline property subtracts this time interval from the current time and compares the result with the value of the LastActivityDate property to determine whether the user is online.

Listing 21-25: The IsOnline property

```
public bool IsOnline
{
  get
  {
    DateTime authorizedTimeWindow =
               DateTime.Now.AddMinutes(-Membership.UserIsOnlineTimeWindow);
    return LastActivityDate > authorizedTimeWindow;
  }
}
```

Accessing the Membership Provider

As mentioned, the value of the `ProviderName` property of the `MembershipUser` class is set to the friendly name of the membership provider that the `MembershipUser` instance must use to perform data operations on the underlying data store. For example, if the `ProviderName` property is set to `AspNetSqlProvider`, the respective `MembershipUser` instance will use the ASP.NET 2.0 `SqlMembershipProvider` to access the underlying data store, in this case, the `aspnetdb` database.

The `MembershipUser` class exposes a private method named `GetProvider` that uses the value of the `ProviderName` property as an index to the `Providers` collection of the `Membership` class to access the respective membership provider (see Listing 21-26).

Listing 21-26: The GetProvider method

```
private MembershipProvider GetProvider()
{
  if (Membership.Providers[ProviderName] == null)
    throw new Exception(ProviderName + " not found!");

  return Membership.Providers[ProviderName];
}
```

Resetting and Retrieving Passwords

When a Web application needs to store passwords in a membership data store, it can directly store the passwords themselves. This approach allows the application to retrieve the password of a user from the data store and e-mail it to a user who has forgotten the password. The `MembershipUser` class exposes two overloads of a method named `ResetPassword` that support this approach, as shown here:

```
public virtual string ResetPassword()
{
  ResetPassword(null);
}

public virtual string ResetPassword(string passwordAnswer)
{
  bool result = GetProvider().ResetPassword(UserName, passwordAnswer);
  if (result)
    lastPasswordChangedDate = DateTime.Now;
```

```
    return result;
}
```

This approach introduces a security hole because a hacker who somehow manages to break into the data store would be able to access the passwords.

Most Web applications, however, store the hash values of passwords instead of the passwords themselves. This means that these applications wouldn't be able to retrieve the password of a user who has forgotten the password. Instead, they simply reset the password of the user to a randomly generated value and store the hash of the new password in the data store. The `MembershipUser` class exposes two overloads of a method named `GetPassword` that support this approach, as shown here:

```
public virtual string GetPassword()
{
  GetPassword(string.Empty);
}

public virtual string GetPassword(string passwordAnswer)
{
  return GetProvider().GetPassword(UserName, passwordAnswer);
}
```

Both the `ResetPassword` and `GetPassword` methods delegate the responsibility of resetting and retrieving the user to the membership provider instance that the `GetProvider` method returns. The `ResetPassword` method sets the `LastPasswordChangedDate` property to the current date and time if the provider succeeds in resetting the user password in the data store.

Changing Passwords

Every Web application must allow its users to change their passwords. The `MembershipUser` class exposes a method named `ChangePassword` that can be used to change the password of the user that the `MembershipUser` instance represents:

```
public virtual bool ChangePassword(string oldPassword, string newPassword)
{
  bool result = GetProvider().ChangePassword(UserName, oldPassword, newPassword);
  if (result)
    this.lastPasswordChangedDate = DateTime.Now;

  return result;
}
```

The method uses the membership provider instance that the `GetProvider` method returns to change the user's password in the data store. The `ChangePassword` method sets the `LastPasswordChangedDate` property to the current date and time if the membership provider instance succeeds in changing the user's password in the data store.

Changing Password Question and Answer

Most Web applications require users to provide right answers to specified questions before they're allowed to change or reset their passwords. These Web applications should allow their users to change their password questions and answers. The `MembershipUser` class exposes a method named `ChangePasswordQuestionAndAnswer` that can be used to change the password question and answer of the user that the respective `MembershipUser` instance represents:

```
public virtual bool ChangePasswordQuestionAndAnswer(string password,
                            string newPasswordQuestion, string newPasswordAnswer)
{
  bool result = GetProvider().ChangePasswordQuestionAndAnswer(UserName, password,
                                newPasswordQuestion, newPasswordAnswer);

  if (result)
    this.passwordQuestion = newPasswordQuestion;

  return result;
}
```

This method delegates the responsibility of making the actual changes in the data store to the membership provider instance that the `GetProvider` method returns. The `ChangePasswordQuestionAndAnswer` method of the membership provider takes four arguments. The method uses the first two arguments to authenticate the user before the new password question and answer are committed to the data store. The `ChangePasswordQuestionAndAnswer` method of the `MembershipUser` class then assigns the new password question to the `PasswordQuestion` property if the membership provider succeeds in committing the changes to the data store.

Unlocking a User

Most Web applications lock a user after preset number of failed login attempts within a preset time window to stop hackers from guessing passwords. These applications need a way to unlock a locked user. The `MembershipUser` class exposes a method named `UnlockUser` that can be used to unlock a user:

```
public virtual bool UnlockUser()
{
  bool success = false;

  if (GetProvider().UnlockUser(UserName))
  {
    isLockedOut = false;
    success = true;
  }

  return success;
}
```

Summary

This chapter examined the main components of the ASP.NET membership model to help you gain a solid understanding of this model so that you could see for yourself how `Membership`, `MembershipUser`, and membership providers work together to provide you with an extensible framework.

The next chapter builds on this chapter to show you how to develop your own custom membership providers and how to plug them into the ASP.NET membership framework. It also shows you how to write your own custom `MembershipUser` and custom `MembershipProvider` classes to extend the ASP.NET membership API to add support for new methods and properties.

Developing Custom MembershipProvider and MembershipUser Components

In the previous chapter, you learned about the ASP.NET membership model, and saw for yourself how membership providers isolate the other components of the model from the data store data-access–specific APIs, allowing them to work with any type of data store.

The ASP.NET membership model comes with a standard membership provider named `SqlMembershipProvider` that retrieves user membership from and stores user membership in a SQL Server database named `aspnetdb`. Many Web applications store their membership information in SQL Server databases with different schemas than `aspnetdb`. This could be for a number of reasons. For example, they could be ASP.NET 1.x applications that are moving to ASP.NET 2.0. Or they could be brand new ASP.NET 2.0 applications that have a specific requirement to store their membership information in a SQL Server database with different schemas than `aspnetdb`. This means that these Web applications won't be able to use the `SqlMembershipProvider` membership provider, even though they use the SQL Server as their underlying data store.

This chapter implements a fully functional replica of the `SqlMembershipProvider` to show you how you can develop a similar membership provider to store membership information in and retrieve membership information from your own SQL Server database.

This chapter also shows you how to develop custom `MembershipUser` and custom `MembershipProvider` to extend the ASP.NET membership API to add support for new methods and properties. You then learn how to develop a custom `SqlMembershipProvider` that supports these new method and properties.

MembershipProvider

All membership providers derive from the `MembershipProvider` abstract base class. The base class defines the contract between the membership providers and their clients, such as the `Membership` class and `Login` controls. This isolates the clients from the real type of the membership provider class being used. Chapter 20 discussed the significance of this isolation in detail.

The `MembershipProvider` base class exposes all the properties, events, and methods that the clients expect from a membership provider regardless of its real type. This means that all membership providers must implement all of these properties, events, and methods to honor the contract. Listing 22-1 shows the properties and methods of the `MembershipProvider` base class. This class, like all provider base classes, derives from the `ProviderBase` abstract class.

Listing 22-1: The MembershipProvider base class

```
public abstract class MembershipProvider : ProviderBase
{
  public virtual string ApplicationName { get; set;}
  public virtual bool ChangePassword(string username, string oldPassword,
                                     string newPassword);
  public virtual bool ChangePasswordQuestionAndAnswer(string username,
         string password, string newPasswordQuestion, string newPasswordAnswer);
  public virtual MembershipUser CreateUser(string username, string password,
     string email, string passwordQuestion, string passwordAnswer, bool isApproved,
     object providerUserKey, out MembershipCreateStatus status);
  protected virtual byte[] DecryptPassword(byte[] encodedPassword);
  public virtual bool DeleteUser(string username, bool deleteAllRelatedData);
  public override string Description { get;}
  public virtual bool EnablePasswordReset { get;}
  public virtual bool EnablePasswordRetrieval { get;}
  protected virtual byte[] EncryptPassword(byte[] password);
  public virtual MembershipUserCollection FindUsersByEmail(string emailToMatch,
                       int pageIndex, int pageSize, out int totalRecords);
  public virtual MembershipUserCollection FindUsersByName(string usernameToMatch,
                       int pageIndex, int pageSize, out int totalRecords);
  public virtual MembershipUserCollection GetAllUsers(int pageIndex, int pageSize,
                                                   out int totalRecords);
  public virtual int GetNumberOfUsersOnline();
  public virtual string GetPassword(string username, string answer);
  public virtual MembershipUser GetUser(object providerUserKey, bool userIsOnline);
  public virtual MembershipUser GetUser(string username, bool userIsOnline);
  public virtual string GetUserNameByEmail(string email);
  public virtual int MaxInvalidPasswordAttempts { get;}
  public virtual int MinRequiredNonAlphanumericCharacters { get;}
  public virtual int MinRequiredPasswordLength { get;}
  protected virtual void OnValidatingPassword(ValidatePasswordEventArgs e);
  public virtual int PasswordAttemptWindow { get;}
  public virtual MembershipPasswordFormat PasswordFormat { get;}
  public virtual string PasswordStrengthRegularExpression { get;}
  public virtual bool RequiresQuestionAndAnswer { get;}
  public virtual bool RequiresUniqueEmail { get;}
  public virtual string ResetPassword(string username, string answer);
  public virtual bool UnlockUser(string userName);
```

```
    public virtual void UpdateUser(MembershipUser user);
    public virtual bool ValidateUser(string username, string password);
}
```

SqlMembershipProvider

As mentioned, this chapter implements a fully functional replica of the ASP.NET 2.0
SqlMembershipProvider. As discussed, the SqlMembershipProvider is specifically designed to work
with a SQL Server database named aspnetdb. You'll learn more about this database as you implement
SqlMembershipProvider.

SqlMembershipProvider derives from the MembershipProvider base class. Because
MembershipProvider derives from ProviderBase, SqlMembershipProvider must implement the
required methods and properties of both ProviderBase and MembershipProvider classes, as discussed in the following sections.

ProviderBase

The ProviderBase class provides the base functionality that every ASP.NET provider must support.
Listing 22-2 contains the definition of the ProviderBase class. The only method here that
SqlMembershipProvider needs to override is the Initialize method.

Listing 22-2: The definition of the ProviderBase class

```
public abstract class ProviderBase
{
    public virtual string Description { get; }
    public virtual string Name { get; }
    public virtual void Initialize(string name, NameValueCollection config);
}
```

The <membership> section of the Web.config and Machine.config files has a subsection named
<providers> that contains the registered membership providers. Listing 22-3 illustrates an example.

Listing 22-3: An example of a <membership> section

```
<configuration>
  <membership defaultProvider="AspNetSqlMembershipProvider" >
    <providers>
      <clear />
      <add name="AspNetSqlMembershipProvider"
       type="System.Web.Security.SqlMembershipProvider, System.Web,
       Version=2.0.0.0, Culture=neutral, PublicKeyToken=b03f5f7f11d50a3a"
       connectionStringName="LocalSqlServer" enablePasswordRetrieval="false"
       enablePasswordReset="true" requiresQuestionAndAnswer="false"
       applicationName="/" requiresUniqueEmail="false" passwordFormat="Hashed"
       maxInvalidPasswordAttempts="5" passwordAttemptWindow="10"
       passwordStrengthRegularExpression="" />
```

(continued)

Listing 22-3: *(continued)*

```
      </providers>
    </membership>
  </configuration>
```

As Listing 22-3 shows, you must use an <add> element to register a membership provider. The attributes of the <add> element are used to initialize the associated membership provider. As discussed in Chapter 21, the <add> element exposes two sets of attributes. The first set contains those attributes that all membership providers have in common: name, type, enablePasswordReset, requiresPasswordRetrieval, applicationName, requiresUniqueEmail, passwordFormat, maxInvalidPasswordAttempts, passwordAttemptWindow, and passwordStrengthRegularExpression. Chapter 21 discussed these attributes in detail.

The second set contains those attributes that are related to a specific type of membership provider. For example, the connectionStringName attribute used in Listing 22-3 is specific to the SqlMembershipProvider.

Listing 22-4 illustrates the code for the Initialize method of the Membership class, previously shown in Listing 21-2. As discussed in Chapter 21, the Initialize method uses the contents of the <providers> subsection of the <membership> section to instantiate and initialize the appropriate membership providers.

Listing 22-4: The Initialize method of the Membership class

```
private static bool IsInitialized = false;
private static void Initialize()
{
  string providerType;
  string assemblyName;
  MembershipProvider tprovider;
  Assembly myAssembly;

  if (IsInitialized)
    return;

  providers = new MembershipProviderCollection();
  Configuration config = WebConfigurationManager.OpenWebConfiguration("/");
  MembershipSection sec =
                (MembershipSection)config.GetSection("system.web/membership");

  foreach (ProviderSettings settings in sec.Providers)
  {
    providerType = settings.Type.Trim().Split(new char[] { ',' })[0];
    assemblyName = settings.Type.Trim().Remove(
                        settings.Type.IndexOf(providerType), providerType.Length);
    if (string.IsNullOrEmpty(assemblyName))
      myAssembly = Assembly.GetExecutingAssembly();

    else
    {
      assemblyName = assemblyName.Trim().Remove(0, 1);
```

```
      myAssembly = Assembly.Load(assemblyName);
    }
    tprovider = (MembershipProvider)myAssembly.CreateInstance(providerType);
    tprovider.Initialize(settings.Name, settings.Parameters);
    providers.Add(tprovider);
  }

  userIsOnlineTimeWindow = (int)sec.UserIsOnlineTimeWindow.TotalMinutes;
  if (!string.IsNullOrEmpty(sec.DefaultProvider))
    provider = providers[sec.DefaultProvider];
  else
    provider = providers[sec.Providers[0].Name];

  IsInitialized = true;
}
```

As the highlighted section of Listing 22-4 shows, the `Initialize` method first calls the `CreateInstance` method of the `Assembly` object once for each registered membership provider to create an instance of the provider. It then calls the `Initialize` method of the newly created membership provider and passes the following two parameters into it:

❑ The friendly name of the membership provider

❑ The `NameValueCollection` that contains all the information needed to initialize the newly created membership provider

The main responsibility of the `Initialize` method of the newly instantiated membership provider is to iterate through the `NameValueCollection` and initialize the respective membership provider's properties. Listing 22-5 shows the code for the `Initialize` method of the `SqlMembershipProvider`.

Listing 22-5: The Initialize method

```
public override void Initialize(string name, NameValueCollection config)
{
  if (config == null)
    throw new ArgumentNullException("config");

  if (string.IsNullOrEmpty(name))
    name = "SqlMembershipProvider";

  if (string.IsNullOrEmpty(config["description"]))
  {
    config.Remove("description");
    config.Add("description",
            "Stores membership information in SQL Server database");
  }
  base.Initialize(name, config);

  enablePasswordRetrieval = (config["enablePasswordRetrieval"] != null) ?
                      bool.Parse(config["enablePasswordRetrieval"]) : false;
  config.Remove("enablePasswordRetrieval");

  enablePasswordReset = (config["enablePasswordReset"] != null) ?
```

(continued)

Listing 22-5: *(continued)*

```
                                 bool.Parse(config["enablePasswordReset"]) : true;
config.Remove("enablePasswordReset");

requiresQuestionAndAnswer = (config["requiresQuestionAndAnswer"] != null) ?
                 bool.Parse(config["requiresQuestionAndAnswer"]) : true;
config.Remove("requiresQuestionAndAnswer");

requiresUniqueEmail = (config["requiresUniqueEmail"] != null) ?
                         bool.Parse(config["requiresUniqueEmail"]) : true;
config.Remove("requiresUniqueEmail");

maxInvalidPasswordAttempts = config["passwordAttemptWindow"] != null ?
                             int.Parse(config["passwordAttemptWindow"]) : 5;
config.Remove("maxInvalidPasswordAttempts");

passwordAttemptWindow = config["passwordAttemptWindow"] != null ?
                         int.Parse(config["passwordAttemptWindow"]) : 10;
config.Remove("passwordAttemptWindow");

minRequiredPasswordLength = config["minRequiredPasswordLength"] != null ?
                             int.Parse(config["minRequiredPasswordLength"]) : 7;
config.Remove("minRequiredPasswordLength");

minRequiredNonAlphanumericCharacters =
         config["minRequiredNonalphanumericCharacters"] != null ?
          int.Parse(config["minRequiredNonalphanumericCharacters"]) : 1;
config.Remove("minRequiredNonalphanumericCharacters");

passwordStrengthRegularExpression = config["passwordStrengthRegularExpression"];
config.Remove("passwordStrengthRegularExpression");

if (minRequiredNonAlphanumericCharacters > minRequiredPasswordLength)
  throw new HttpException();

applicationName = config["applicationName"];
if (string.IsNullOrEmpty(applicationName))
  applicationName = "/";
config.Remove("applicationName");

string strTemp = config["passwordFormat"];
if (string.IsNullOrEmpty(strTemp))
  strTemp = "Hashed";

switch (strTemp)
{
  case "Clear":
    passwordFormat = MembershipPasswordFormat.Clear;
    break;
  case "Encrypted":
    passwordFormat = MembershipPasswordFormat.Encrypted;
    break;
  case "Hashed":
    passwordFormat = MembershipPasswordFormat.Hashed;
```

```
      break;
    default:
      throw new ProviderException("Bad password format");
  }

  if ((PasswordFormat == MembershipPasswordFormat.Hashed) &&
      EnablePasswordRetrieval)
    throw new ProviderException();
config.Remove("passwordFormat");

  ConnectionStringSettings settings =
         ConfigurationManager.ConnectionStrings[config["connectionStringName"]];
  connectionString = settings.ConnectionString;
  if (string.IsNullOrEmpty(connectionString))
    throw new ProviderException("Invalid connection string name");
  config.Remove("connectionStringName");

  if (config.Count > 0)
  {
    string key = config.GetKey(0);
    if (!string.IsNullOrEmpty(key))
      throw new ProviderException("Unrecognized attribute");
  }
}
```

Here are the main steps you must take to implement the `Initialize` method of any provider regardless of its type, whether it is a role or membership provider:

1. Throw an exception if the `NameValueCollection` is null because you need this collection to initialize your provider:

```
if (config == null)
  throw new ArgumentNullException("config");
```

2. Give your provider a friendly name because the clients of your provider will use this name to locate your provider among other providers. The friendly name of your provider doesn't have to be the same as the name of its type:

```
if (string.IsNullOrEmpty(name))
  name = "SqlMembershipProvider";
```

Keep in mind that you should assign a value to the `name` parameter only if the page developer hasn't set the `name` attribute in `Web.config` or `Machine.config` file. You shouldn't override the page developer's setting because the page developer might be using the specified friendly name to access the membership provider.

3. Provide the clients of your provider with a short description of what your provider does. Again keep in mind that you should do this only if the page developer hasn't already specified a value for the `description` field:

```
if (string.IsNullOrEmpty(config["description"]))
{
  config.Remove("description");
  config.Add("description",
          "Stores membership information in SQL Server database");
}
```

4. Invoke the `Initialize` method of your provider's base class because the base class performs some basic initialization, such as initializing the `Name` and `Description` properties:

```
base.Initialize(name, config);
```

5. Iterate through the rest of the items in the `NameValueCollection` and take the following actions for each enumerated item:

  a. Use the item to initialize the appropriate field or property of your provider:

```
applicationName = config["applicationName"];
```

Notice how the method sets the value of the `connectionString` private field. The `NameValueCollection` contains an item with the `connectionStringName` key. As the name implies, the value of this item is the friendly name of the connection string, not the connection string itself.

The `Web.config` file supports a new section named `<connectionStrings>`. You can think of this section as the repository of connection strings. The page developer must use an `<add>` element to add a connection string to the `<connectionStrings>` repository. The `<add>` element takes two important attributes: `name` and `connectionString`. The page developer must set the value of the `name` attribute to the desired friendly name. This name is used to refer to the connection string. The page developer must assign the actual connection string to the `connectionString` attribute.

The `ConfigurationManager` exposes a collection property named `ConnectionStrings` that contains a `ConnectionStringSettings` object for each `<add>` element in the `<connectionStrings>` section of the `Web.config` file:

```
ConnectionStringSettings settings =
        ConfigurationManager.ConnectionStrings[config["connectionStringName"]];
```

The `ConnectionStringSettings` class exposes a property named `ConnectionString` that contains the value of the `connectionString` attribute on the related `<add>` element. Recall that the value of this attribute is nothing but the actual connection string. The `Initialize` method assigns this value to the `connectionString` private field:

```
connectionString = settings.ConnectionString;
if (string.IsNullOrEmpty(connectionString))
  throw new ProviderException("Invalid connection string name");
config.Remove("connectionStringName");
```

  b. If the `NameValueCollection` doesn't contain an item needed to initialize the relevant field, either assign a default value to the field (if possible) or throw an exception. The `Initialize` method of your custom provider must always raise an exception if a parameter essential to its functioning isn't set. The `Initialize` method of the `SqlMembershipProvider` raises an exception if the page developer hasn't specified a connection string because this provider needs the connection string to perform the required data operations:

```
if (string.IsNullOrEmpty(applicationName))
  applicationName = "/";

if (string.IsNullOrEmpty(connectionString))
    throw new ProviderException("Invalid connection string name");
```

   c.   Remove the item from the `NameValueCollection`:

```
config.Remove("applicationName");
config.Remove("connectionStringName");
```

6.   If the `NameValueCollection` contains an unrecognizable item, you must raise an exception:

```
if (config.Count > 0)
{
  string key = config.GetKey(0);
  if (!string.IsNullOrEmpty(key))
    throw new ProviderException("Unrecognized attribute");
}
```

7.   At the end, you can perform other initializations deemed appropriate. The `Initialize` method of `SqlMembershipProvider` doesn't perform any other initializations.

MembershipProvider

`SqlMembershipProvider` implements all the required methods and properties of the `MembershipProvider` base class, as discussed in the following sections.

ChangePassword

Listing 22-6 contains the code for the `ChangePassword` method. Before changing the password, you have to validate the user information. The `ValidateUserInfo` method is discussed shortly. New user passwords must meet conditions specified by the properties of the `MembershipProvider` class.

The `MinRequiredPasswordLength` property specifies the minimum number of characters that the new password must contain:

```
if (newPassword.Length < this.MinRequiredPasswordLength)
  throw new ArgumentException("Password is too short!");
```

The `MinRequiredNonAlphanumericCharacters` property specifies the minimum number of non-alphanumeric characters that the new password must contain. `ChangePassword` searches through the characters that the new password contains for non-alphanumeric characters to arrive at the total non-alphanumeric character count:

```
int nonAlphanumericCharactersCount = 0;
for (int cnt = 0; cnt < newPassword.Length; cnt++)
{
  if (!char.IsLetterOrDigit(newPassword, cnt))
    nonAlphanumericCharactersCount++;
}

if (nonAlphanumericCharactersCount < MinRequiredNonAlphanumericCharacters)
  throw
    new ArgumentException("Password requires more non aplphanumeric characters");
```

The `PasswordStrengthRegularExpression` specifies the regular expression pattern that new passwords must match to be acceptable. The .NET Framework comes with a class name `Regex` that exposes a static method named `IsMatch` that takes two arguments. The first argument is the string that contains the new password, and the second argument is the string that contains the regular expression pattern. The `IsMatch` method returns true if the specified string (the new password) matches the specified regular expression pattern:

```
if ((PasswordStrengthRegularExpression.Length > 0) &&
    !Regex.IsMatch(newPassword, PasswordStrengthRegularExpression))
  throw new ArgumentException("Password does not match regular expression");
```

You can think of these three validations plus the call into the `ValidateUserInfo` method as part of a standard validation that `SqlMembershipProvider` performs for all Web applications. The problem with standard validation is that it doesn't cover application-specified validation rules. This is where the `ValidatingPassword` event comes into play.

As Listing 22-6 shows, `ChangePassword` raises this event right after it's done with standard validation process. This allows the page developers to register a callback for this event where they can perform application-specific password validation:

```
ValidatePasswordEventArgs args =
                new ValidatePasswordEventArgs(username, newPassword, false);
this.OnValidatingPassword(args);
```

The `ValidatingPassword` event has an associated event data class named `ValidatePasswordEventArgs` that holds the data associated with the event. This class exposes a Boolean property named `Cancel` that the page developer can set to true if the new password doesn't pass the application-specific password validation rules. Your custom membership provider's implementation of `ChangePassword` mustn't change the password if the `Cancel` property is set to true.

The `ValidatePasswordEventArgs` event data class also exposes a property of type `Exception` named `FailureInformation` that the page developer's callback method can set to the appropriate `Exception` object when the new password fails the application-specific validation procedure. Your custom membership provider's implementation of `ChangePassword` must raise this application-specific exception:

```
if (args.Cancel)
{
  if (args.FailureInformation != null)
    throw args.FailureInformation;

  throw new ArgumentException("Application-specific password validation failed!");
}
```

If the new password passes both the standard and application-specific validation rules, `ChangePassword` calls the `Update` method to update the user's record with the new password.

Listing 22-6: The ChangePassword method

```
public override
bool ChangePassword(string username, string oldPassword, string newPassword)
{
  int passwordFormat;
  string passwordSalt = null;
```

```
if (!this.ValidateUserInfo(username, oldPassword, false, false,
                         out passwordSalt, out passwordFormat))
    return false;

if (newPassword.Length < this.MinRequiredPasswordLength)
    throw new ArgumentException("Password is too short!");

int nonAlphanumericCharactersCount = 0;
for (int cnt = 0; cnt < newPassword.Length; cnt++)
{
    if (!char.IsLetterOrDigit(newPassword, cnt))
        nonAlphanumericCharactersCount++;
}

if (nonAlphanumericCharactersCount < MinRequiredNonAlphanumericCharacters)
    throw
        new ArgumentException("Password requires more non aplphanumeric characters");

if ((PasswordStrengthRegularExpression.Length > 0) &&
     !Regex.IsMatch(newPassword, PasswordStrengthRegularExpression))
    throw new ArgumentException("Password does not match regular expression");

string encodedPassword =
                GetEncodedPassword(newPassword, passwordFormat, passwordSalt);

ValidatePasswordEventArgs args =
                new ValidatePasswordEventArgs(username, newPassword, false);
this.OnValidatingPassword(args);
if (args.Cancel)
{
    if (args.FailureInformation != null)
        throw args.FailureInformation;

    throw new ArgumentException(
                        "Application-specific password validation failed!");
}

SqlParameter[] parameters = new SqlParameter[6];
parameters[0] = CreateSqlParameter("@ApplicationName",
                                SqlDbType.NVarChar, ApplicationName);
parameters[1] = CreateSqlParameter("@UserName", SqlDbType.NVarChar, username);
parameters[2] = CreateSqlParameter("@NewPassword",
                                SqlDbType.NVarChar, encodedPassword);
parameters[3] = CreateSqlParameter("@PasswordSalt",
                                SqlDbType.NVarChar, passwordSalt);
parameters[4] = CreateSqlParameter("@PasswordFormat",
                                SqlDbType.Int, passwordFormat);
parameters[5] = CreateSqlParameter("@CurrentTimeUtc",
                                SqlDbType.DateTime, DateTime.UtcNow);
return Update("aspnet_Membership_SetPassword", parameters);
}
```

ValidateUserInfo

Listing 22-7 contains the code for the `ValidateUserInfo` method. The main responsibility of this method is to validate the username and password that the user has entered.

Listing 22-7: The ValidateUserInfo method

```
private bool ValidateUserInfo(string username, string password,
               bool updateLastLoginActivityDate, bool failIfNotApproved,
               out string passwordSalt, out int passwordFormat)
{
  string dbEncodedPassword = null;
  passwordFormat = 0;
  passwordSalt = null;
  int failedPasswordAttemptCount = 0;
  int failedPasswordAnswerAttemptCount = 0;
  bool isApproved = false;
  DateTime lastLoginDate = DateTime.UtcNow;
  DateTime lastActivityDate = DateTime.UtcNow;

  SqlParameter[] parameters = new SqlParameter[4];
  parameters[0] = CreateSqlParameter("@ApplicationName", SqlDbType.NVarChar,
                                   this.ApplicationName);
  parameters[1] = CreateSqlParameter("@UserName", SqlDbType.NVarChar, username);
  parameters[2] = CreateSqlParameter("@UpdateLastLoginActivityDate",
                                   SqlDbType.Bit, updateLastLoginActivityDate);
  parameters[3] = CreateSqlParameter("@CurrentTimeUtc", SqlDbType.DateTime,
                                   DateTime.UtcNow);
  SqlDataReader reader = Select("aspnet_Membership_GetPasswordWithFormat",
                               parameters);

  if (reader.Read())
  {
    dbEncodedPassword = reader.GetString(0);
    passwordFormat = reader.GetInt32(1);
    passwordSalt = reader.GetString(2);
    failedPasswordAttemptCount = reader.GetInt32(3);
    failedPasswordAnswerAttemptCount = reader.GetInt32(4);
    isApproved = reader.GetBoolean(5);
    lastLoginDate = reader.GetDateTime(6);
    lastActivityDate = reader.GetDateTime(7);
  }

  reader.Close();

  if (!isApproved && failIfNotApproved)
    return false;

  string encodedPassword = GetEncodedPassword(password, passwordFormat,
                                            passwordSalt);
  bool isPasswordCorrect = dbEncodedPassword.Equals(encodedPassword);
  UpdateUserInfo(username, isPasswordCorrect, updateLastLoginActivityDate,
                  lastLoginDate, lastActivityDate);
  if (isPasswordCorrect)
    return true;

  return false
}
```

As Listing 22-7 illustrates, this method checks whether a user record with the specified username exists in the database. If it does, the method retrieves the user information:

- ❑ Password
- ❑ Password salt
- ❑ Password format

The password format specifies the format in which the passwords are stored in the underlying data store. There are in general three formats: Clear, Encrypted, and Hashed. The Clear format stores the actual password in clear text in the data store. This introduces a big security hole, as discussed previously. The Encrypted format option encrypts the passwords before it stores them in the database. This option is more secure than the Clear option. The Hashed format option adds a string known as *password salt* to the password, hashes the salted password, and stores the salted hash in the database. This is the most secure way to store passwords because even if the hackers manage to break into the database, they won't be able to use the passwords.

The method then calls the GetEncodedPassword method and passes the password salt and format values and the password that the user has entered into it. The main responsibility of this method is to encode the password that the user has entered based on the same encoding scheme as the passwords stored in the underlying data store, as shown in Listing 22-8.

Listing 22-8: The GetEncodedPassword method

```
private string GetEncodedPassword(string password, int passwordFormat,
                                  string passwordSalt)
{
  string encodedPassword;
  byte[] buff;
  byte[] saltedPassword;

  switch (passwordFormat)
  {
    case 0:
      encodedPassword = password;
      break;
    case 1:
      saltedPassword = GetSaltedPassword(password, passwordSalt);
      HashAlgorithm hashAlgorithm =
                        HashAlgorithm.Create(Membership.HashAlgorithmType);
      buff = hashAlgorithm.ComputeHash(saltedPassword);
      encodedPassword = Convert.ToBase64String(buff);
      break;
    default:
      saltedPassword = GetSaltedPassword(password, passwordSalt);
      buff = EncryptPassword(saltedPassword);
      encodedPassword = Convert.ToBase64String(buff);
      break;
  }

  return encodedPassword;
}
```

The `GetEncodedPassword` method uses the value of the password format parameter to determine in which format the passwords are stored in the database. If the passwords are stored in clear format, no encoding is performed.

If the passwords are stored in encrypted format, `GetEncodedPassword` calls the `GetSaltedPassword` method and passes the salt value and the password that the user has entered into it. This method adds the salt value to the specified password and returns the salted password, as shown in Listing 22-9.

Listing 22-9: The GetSaltedPassword method

```
private byte[] GetSaltedPassword(string password, string salt)
{
  byte[] passwordBuff = Encoding.Unicode.GetBytes(password);
  byte[] saltBuff = Convert.FromBase64String(salt);
  byte[] saltedPassword = new byte[saltBuff.Length + passwordBuff.Length];
  Buffer.BlockCopy(saltBuff, 0, saltedPassword, 0, saltBuff.Length);
  Buffer.BlockCopy(passwordBuff, 0, saltedPassword, saltBuff.Length,
                   passwordBuff.Length);
  return saltedPassword;
}
```

The `GetEncodedPassword` method then calls the `EncryptPassword` method of the `MembershipProvider` base class and passes the salted password into it to encrypt the salted password:

```
buff = EncryptPassword(saltedPassword);
```

The `GetEncodedPassword` then converts the encrypted salted password to Base64 format:

```
encodedPassword = Convert.ToBase64String(buff);
```

If passwords are stored in hashed format, `GetEncodedPassword` calls the `GetSaltedPassword` method to add the salt value to the password that the user has entered:

```
saltedPassword = GetSaltedPassword(password, passwordSalt);
```

The `GetEncodedPassword` method then calls the `Create` static method of the `HashAlgorithm` class and passes the value of the `HashAlgorithmType` property of the `Membership` class into it. This property specifies the type of hashing algorithm that should be used to hash the password. The `Create` method creates an instance of the specified hash algorithm:

```
HashAlgorithm hashAlgorithm = HashAlgorithm.Create(Membership.HashAlgorithmType);
```

The `GetEncodedPassword` method next calls the `ComputeHash` method of the specified hash algorithm and passes the salted password into it to hash the salted password:

```
buff = hashAlgorithm.ComputeHash(saltedPassword);
```

Finally, the `GetEncodedPassword` method converts the hashed salted password to Base64 format:

```
encodedPassword = Convert.ToBase64String(buff);
```

The next thing the `ValidateUserInfo` method does is compare the encoded password that the `GetEncodedPassword` method returns with the password retrieved from the database:

```
bool isPasswordCorrect = dbEncodedPassword.Equals(encodedPassword);
```

The `ValidateUserInfo` method then calls the `UpdateUserInfo` method to update the `LastLoginDate` and `LastActivityDate` of the user record:

```
return UpdateUserInfo(username, isPasswordCorrect, updateLastLoginActivityDate,
                      lastLoginDate, lastActivityDate);
```

If the password that the user has entered is correct, the `ValidateUserInfo` method return true. If not, it returns false:

```
if (isPasswordCorrect)
  return true;

return false
```

UpdateUserInfo

Listing 22-10 contains the code for the `UpdateUserInfo` method. The implementation of this method is pretty simple. It creates an array of `SqlParameter` objects, where each object represents a parameter of the underlying stored procedure, that is, `aspnet_Membership_UpdateUserInfo`. As the name implies, this stored procedure updates the specified user record with the new information.

Listing 22-10: The UpdateUserInfo method

```
private bool UpdateUserInfo(string username, bool isPasswordCorrect, bool
                           updateLastLoginActivityDate, DateTime lastLoginDate,
                           DateTime lastActivityDate)
{
  SqlParameter[] parameters = new SqlParameter[9];
  parameters[0] = CreateSqlParameter("@ApplicationName", SqlDbType.NVarChar,
                                     this.ApplicationName);
  parameters[1] = CreateSqlParameter("@UserName", SqlDbType.NVarChar, username);
  parameters[2] = CreateSqlParameter("@IsPasswordCorrect", SqlDbType.Bit,
                                     isPasswordCorrect);
  parameters[3] = CreateSqlParameter("@UpdateLastLoginActivityDate", SqlDbType.Bit,
                                     updateLastLoginActivityDate);
  parameters[4] = CreateSqlParameter("@MaxInvalidPasswordAttempts", SqlDbType.Int,
                                     this.MaxInvalidPasswordAttempts);
  parameters[5] = CreateSqlParameter("@PasswordAttemptWindow", SqlDbType.Int,
                                     this.PasswordAttemptWindow);
  parameters[6] = CreateSqlParameter("@CurrentTimeUtc", SqlDbType.DateTime,
                                     DateTime.UtcNow);
  parameters[7] = CreateSqlParameter("@LastLoginDate", SqlDbType.DateTime,
                                     isPasswordCorrect ? DateTime.UtcNow : lastLoginDate);
  parameters[8] = CreateSqlParameter("@LastActivityDate", SqlDbType.DateTime,
                                     isPasswordCorrect ? DateTime.UtcNow : lastActivityDate);

  return Update("aspnet_Membership_UpdateUserInfo", parameters);
}
```

Update

The Update method is a helper method that's used to update the user record. Listing 22-11 presents the implementation of the Update method. This method takes two arguments. The first argument is the name of the underlying stored procedure, and the second argument is an array of SqlParameter objects, where each object represents a parameter of the specified stored procedure. The Update method uses ADO.NET classes to call the specified stored procedure.

Listing 22-11: The Update method

```
private bool Update(string storedProcedureName, SqlParameter[] parameters)
{
  SqlConnection con = new SqlConnection(connectionString);
  SqlCommand com = new SqlCommand(storedProcedureName, con);
  com.CommandType = CommandType.StoredProcedure;
  com.Parameters.AddRange(parameters);
  bool success = true;
  int rowsAffected = -1;
  con.Open();

  try
  {
    rowsAffected = com.ExecuteNonQuery();
    success = (rowsAffected > 0);
  }
  catch (Exception ex)
  {
    success = false;
  }

  finally
  {
    con.Close();
  }
  return success;
}
```

ChangePasswordQuestionAndAnswer

Listing 22-12 illustrates the implementation of the ChangePasswordQuestionAndAnswer method. This method takes the user credentials (username and password) and the new question and answer and updates the respective user record with the new information.

First, the method calls the ValidateUserInfo method to validate the user credentials before any changes are made in the user record. Recall that as part of the validation process, the ValidateUserInfo retrieves the user password salt and format from the data store and returns these values:

```
if (!this.ValidateUserInfo(username, password, false, false, out passwordSalt,
                 out passwordFormat))
  return false;
```

The method then calls the GetEncodedPassword method and passes the retrieved password format and salt and the new password answer into it. Recall that this method encodes the password answer based on the value of the password format and returns the encoded password answer. This step is necessary because password answers may be stored in encoded format:

```
encodedNewPasswordAnswer =
    GetEncodedPassword(newPasswordAnswer.ToLower(), passwordFormat, passwordSalt);
```

The method then calls the `Update` method to update the specified user record with the new password question and answer.

Listing 22-12: The ChangePasswordQuestionAndAnswer method

```
public override bool
ChangePasswordQuestionAndAnswer(string username, string password, string
                                newPasswordQuestion, string newPasswordAnswer)
{
  string encodedNewPasswordAnswer;

  int passwordFormat;
  string passwordSalt = null;
  if (!this.ValidateUserInfo(username, password, false, false, out passwordSalt,
                        out passwordFormat))
    return false;

  if (newPasswordAnswer != null)
    newPasswordAnswer = newPasswordAnswer.Trim();

  if (!string.IsNullOrEmpty(newPasswordAnswer))
    encodedNewPasswordAnswer =
      GetEncodedPassword(newPasswordAnswer.ToLower(), passwordFormat, passwordSalt);

  else
    encodedNewPasswordAnswer = newPasswordAnswer;

  SqlParameter[] parameters = new SqlParameter[4];
  parameters[0] = CreateSqlParameter("@ApplicationName", SqlDbType.NVarChar,
                                this.ApplicationName);
  parameters[1] = CreateSqlParameter("@UserName", SqlDbType.NVarChar, username);
  parameters[2] = CreateSqlParameter("@NewPasswordQuestion", SqlDbType.NVarChar,
                                newPasswordQuestion);
  parameters[3] = CreateSqlParameter("@NewPasswordAnswer", SqlDbType.NVarChar,
                                encodedNewPasswordAnswer);
  return Update("aspnet_Membership_ChangePasswordQuestionAndAnswer", parameters);
}
```

CreateUser

Listing 22-13 contains the implementation of the `CreateUser` method. As the name implies, this method adds a new user record to the underlying database.

The `CreateUser` method first performs two types of data validation. The first validation is a set of standard validations that are performed for all Web applications. It uses the value of the `MinRequiredPasswordLength` property to ensure that the specified password is longer than this value:

```
   if (password.Length < MinRequiredPasswordLength)
   {
     status = MembershipCreateStatus.InvalidPassword;
     return null;
   }
```

It iterates through the characters of the specified password and counts the number of non-alphanumeric characters:

```
   int nonAlphanumericCharactersCount = 0;
   for (int cnt = 0; cnt < password.Length; cnt++)
   {
     if (!char.IsLetterOrDigit(password, cnt))
       nonAlphanumericCharactersCount++;
   }
```

It ensures the count is larger than the value of the `MinRequiredNonAlphanumericCharacter` property:

```
   if (nonAlphanumericCharactersCount < MinRequiredNonAlphanumericCharacters)
   {
     status = MembershipCreateStatus.InvalidPassword;
     return null;
   }
```

Then it calls the `IsMatch` static method of the `Regex` class to ensure that the specified password matches the regular expression pattern that `PasswordStrengthRegularExpression` contains:

```
   if ((PasswordStrengthRegularExpression.Length > 0) &&
       !Regex.IsMatch(password, PasswordStrengthRegularExpression))
   {
     status = MembershipCreateStatus.InvalidPassword;
     return null;
   }
```

These standard validations don't enforce application-specific validation or business rules. This is where the `ValidatingPassword` method comes into play. Your custom membership provider's implementation of the `CreateUser` method must always raise the `ValidatingPassword` event before committing the changes to the underlying database. This allows page developers to register callbacks for this event where they can enforce application-specific business rules, as discussed before.

```
   ValidatePasswordEventArgs args =
                   new ValidatePasswordEventArgs(username, password, true);
   this.OnValidatingPassword(args);
   if (args.Cancel)
   {
     status = MembershipCreateStatus.InvalidPassword;
     return null;
   }
```

Next, the `CreateUser` method needs to generate a password salt. It creates an instance of a .NET class named `RNGCryptoServiceProvider`:

```
   RNGCryptoServiceProvider gen = new RNGCryptoServiceProvider();
```

Then it creates a `byte` array:

```
byte[] randomNumber = new byte[1];
```

Next it calls the `GetBytes` method of the `RNGCryptoServiceProvider` to populate the byte array with a cryptographic random byte:

```
gen.GetBytes(randomNumber);
```

Finally, it converts the `byte` array to Base64 format:

```
string passwordSalt = Convert.ToBase64String(randomNumber);
```

This value will be used as the password salt.

Next the `CreateUser` method calls the `GetEncodedPassword` method and passes the new password salt, password format, and the user password into it. This method encodes the password based on the encoding format specified by the password format parameter as discussed earlier. This step is necessary because only encoded passwords are stored in the database.

```
string encodedPassword =
            GetEncodedPassword(password, (int)passwordFormat, passwordSalt);
```

The `CreateUser` method then calls the `GetEncodedPassword` once more and passes the specified password answer, password format, and password salt into it. This method encodes the password answer based on the encoding format specified by the password format parameter, as discussed before. This step is necessary because only encoded password answers can be stored in the database.

```
GetEncodedPassword(passwordAnswer.ToLower(),(int)this.passwordFormat,passwordSalt);
```

Next, the `CreateUser` method creates an array of `SqlParameter` objects where each object represents a parameter of the `aspnet_Membership_CreateUser` stored procedure. As the name implies, this stored procedure creates a new user record in the database. Notice that the array includes a `SqlParameter` that represents the return value of this stored procedure. This return value is the user `ID` associated with the new user record. When the `CreateUser` method finally calls the `Update` method, the method adds the new record, and returns the user `ID`:

```
parameters[12] = CreateSqlParameter("@UserId", SqlDbType.UniqueIdentifier,
                                    providerUserKey);
parameters[12].Direction = ParameterDirection.Output;
```

The `CreateUser` method then uses the new user ID and creates a GUID object known as the provider user key. The provider uses this object or key to identify the user record:

```
providerUserKey = new Guid(parameters[12].Value.ToString());
```

Finally, the `CreateUser` method creates an instance of the `MembershipUser` class and populates it with the user information:

```
return new MembershipUser(Name, username, providerUserKey, email,
                    passwordQuestion, null, isApproved, false, localTime,
                    localTime, localTime, localTime, localTime);
```

Listing 22-13: The CreateUser method

```
public override MembershipUser CreateUser(string username, string password,
               string email, string passwordQuestion, string passwordAnswer,
               bool isApproved, object providerUserKey,
               out MembershipCreateStatus status)
{
  if ((providerUserKey != null) && !(providerUserKey is Guid))
  {
    status = MembershipCreateStatus.InvalidProviderUserKey;
    return null;
  }

  if (password.Length < MinRequiredPasswordLength)
  {
    status = MembershipCreateStatus.InvalidPassword;
    return null;
  }

  int nonAlphanumericCharactersCount = 0;
  for (int cnt = 0; cnt < password.Length; cnt++)
  {
    if (!char.IsLetterOrDigit(password, cnt))
      nonAlphanumericCharactersCount++;
  }

  if (nonAlphanumericCharactersCount < MinRequiredNonAlphanumericCharacters)
  {
    status = MembershipCreateStatus.InvalidPassword;
    return null;
  }

  if ((PasswordStrengthRegularExpression.Length > 0) &&
      !Regex.IsMatch(password, PasswordStrengthRegularExpression))
  {
    status = MembershipCreateStatus.InvalidPassword;
    return null;
  }

  ValidatePasswordEventArgs args =
               new ValidatePasswordEventArgs(username, password, true);
  this.OnValidatingPassword(args);
  if (args.Cancel)
  {
    status = MembershipCreateStatus.InvalidPassword;
    return null;
  }

  string encodedPasswordAnswer;

  byte[] randomNumber = new byte[1];
  RNGCryptoServiceProvider gen = new RNGCryptoServiceProvider();
  gen.GetBytes(randomNumber);
  string passwordSalt = Convert.ToBase64String(randomNumber);
```

```
          string encodedPassword =
                    GetEncodedPassword(password, (int)passwordFormat, passwordSalt);

      if (passwordAnswer != null)
        passwordAnswer = passwordAnswer.Trim();

      if (!string.IsNullOrEmpty(passwordAnswer))
        encodedPasswordAnswer =
            GetEncodedPassword(passwordAnswer.ToLower(), (int)this.passwordFormat,
                            passwordSalt);

      else
        encodedPasswordAnswer = passwordAnswer;

      SqlParameter[] parameters = new SqlParameter[13];
      parameters[0] = CreateSqlParameter("@ApplicationName", SqlDbType.NVarChar,
                                    ApplicationName);
      parameters[1] = CreateSqlParameter("@UserName", SqlDbType.NVarChar, username);
      parameters[2] = CreateSqlParameter("@Password", SqlDbType.NVarChar,
                                    encodedPassword);
      parameters[3] = CreateSqlParameter("@PasswordSalt", SqlDbType.NVarChar,
                                    passwordSalt);
      parameters[4] = CreateSqlParameter("@Email", SqlDbType.NVarChar, email);
      parameters[5] = CreateSqlParameter("@PasswordQuestion", SqlDbType.NVarChar,
                                    passwordQuestion);
      parameters[6] = CreateSqlParameter("@PasswordAnswer", SqlDbType.NVarChar,
                                    encodedPasswordAnswer);
      parameters[7] = CreateSqlParameter("@IsApproved", SqlDbType.Bit, isApproved);
      parameters[8] = CreateSqlParameter("@UniqueEmail", SqlDbType.Int,
                                    RequiresUniqueEmail ? 1 : 0);
      parameters[9] = CreateSqlParameter("@PasswordFormat", SqlDbType.Int,
                                    (int)PasswordFormat);
      parameters[10] = CreateSqlParameter("@CurrentTimeUtc", SqlDbType.DateTime,
                                        DateTime.UtcNow);
      parameters[11] = CreateSqlParameter("@CreateDate", SqlDbType.DateTime,
                                        DateTime.Now);
      parameters[12] = CreateSqlParameter("@UserId", SqlDbType.UniqueIdentifier,
                                        providerUserKey);
      parameters[12].Direction = ParameterDirection.Output;

      if (!Update("aspnet_Membership_CreateUser", parameters))
      {
        status = MembershipCreateStatus.UserRejected;
        return null;
      }

      status = MembershipCreateStatus.Success;
      providerUserKey = new Guid(parameters[12].Value.ToString());
      DateTime localTime = DateTime.UtcNow.ToLocalTime();
      return new MembershipUser(Name, username, providerUserKey, email,
                            passwordQuestion, null, isApproved, false, localTime,
                            localTime, localTime, localTime, localTime);
    }
```

DeleteUser

Listing 22-14 contains the code for the `DeleteUser` method. This method deletes the specified user's records from the underlying data store. The second argument of the method is a Boolean flag that specifies whether the method should delete all the records associated with the specified user. The `aspnet_Users_DeleteUser` stored procedure takes an integer flag named `@ TablesToDeleteFrom` that specifies which tables the specified user's records must be deleted from. The following table describes the possible values of this flag and their meanings: You can use the OR bitwise operator to delete records from more than one table.

Value	Description
1	Deletes the user record from the `aspnet_Membership` database table
2	Deletes the user record from the `aspnet_UsersInRoles` table
4	Deletes the user record from the `aspnet_Profile` table
8	Deletes the user record from the `aspnet_PersonalizationPerUser` table
15	Deletes the user record from the `aspnet_Membership`, `aspnet_UsersIn-Roles`, `aspnet_Profile`, and `aspnet_PersonalizationPerUser` tables

Listing 22-14: The DeleteUser method

```
public override bool DeleteUser(string username, bool deleteAllRelatedData)
{
    SqlParameter[] parameters = new SqlParameter[4];
    parameters[0] = CreateSqlParameter("@ApplicationName", SqlDbType.NVarChar,
                                       ApplicationName);
    parameters[1] = CreateSqlParameter("@UserName", SqlDbType.NVarChar, username);

    if (deleteAllRelatedData)
        parameters[2] = CreateSqlParameter("@TablesToDeleteFrom", SqlDbType.Int, 15);
    else
        parameters[2] = CreateSqlParameter("@TablesToDeleteFrom", SqlDbType.Int, 1);

    parameters[3] = new SqlParameter("@NumTablesDeletedFrom", SqlDbType.Int);
    parameters[3].Direction = ParameterDirection.Output;

    return Update("aspnet_Users_DeleteUser", parameters);
}
```

FindUsersByEmail

Listing 22-15 illustrates the implementation of the `FindUsersByEmail` method. As discussed in Chapter 21, this method returns user information page by page, where the `pageSize` parameter specifies the number of records in each page and the `pageIndex` parameter specifies the index of the current data page.

This method creates an array of `SqlParameter` objects where each object represents a parameter of the `aspnet_Membership_FindUsersByEmail` stored procedure. The stored procedure returns the new page of user records whose e-mail matches the specified `emailToMatch` parameter. Because the stored procedure uses a `LIKE` clause to select the user records, the caller of the `FindUsersByEmail` method can include wildcard characters in the `emailToMatch` argument. For example, if the `emailToMatch` argument contains the string `%@yahoo.com`, the stored procedure will return all the user records whose e-mail address ends with string `@yahoo.com`. If the `emailToMatch` doesn't include any wildcard characters, the stored procedure will return the user whose e-mail address matches the string specified in the `emailToMatch` argument, if any.

The `FindUsersByEmail` method uses the `SqlDataReader` reader that the `Select` method returns to iterate through the retrieved user records, creates a `MembershipUser` object for each enumerated user record, and populates it with the database field values of the record.

Listing 22-15: The FindUsersByEmail method

```
public override MembershipUserCollection
FindUsersByEmail(string emailToMatch, int pageIndex, int pageSize,
                out int totalRecords)
{
  if (pageIndex < 0)
    throw new ArgumentException("Page index cannot be negative!");

  if (pageSize < 1)
    throw new ArgumentException("Page size cannot be less than one!");

  SqlParameter[] parameters = new SqlParameter[5];
  MembershipUserCollection collection = null;
  totalRecords = 0;

  parameters[0] = CreateSqlParameter("@ApplicationName", SqlDbType.NVarChar,
                                     ApplicationName);
  parameters[1] = CreateSqlParameter("@EmailToMatch", SqlDbType.NVarChar,
                                     emailToMatch);
  parameters[2] = CreateSqlParameter("@PageIndex", SqlDbType.Int, pageIndex);
  parameters[3] = CreateSqlParameter("@PageSize", SqlDbType.Int, pageSize);
  parameters[4] = new SqlParameter("@ReturnValue", SqlDbType.Int);
  parameters[4].Direction = ParameterDirection.ReturnValue;
  SqlDataReader reader = Select("aspnet_Membership_FindUsersByEmail", parameters);
  collection = new MembershipUserCollection();

  while (reader.Read())
  {
    string text1 = !reader.IsDBNull(0) ? reader.GetString(0) : null;
    string text2 = !reader.IsDBNull(1) ? reader.GetString(1) : null;
    string text3 = !reader.IsDBNull(2) ? reader.GetString(2) : null;
    string text4 = !reader.IsDBNull(3) ? reader.GetString(3) : null;
    bool flag1 = reader.GetBoolean(4);
    DateTime time6 = reader.GetDateTime(5);
    DateTime time1 = time6.ToLocalTime();
    DateTime time7 = reader.GetDateTime(6);
    DateTime time2 = time7.ToLocalTime();
    DateTime time8 = reader.GetDateTime(7);
    DateTime time3 = time8.ToLocalTime();
    DateTime time9 = reader.GetDateTime(8);
    DateTime time4 = time9.ToLocalTime();
    Guid guid1 = reader.GetGuid(9);
```

(continued)

Listing 22-15: *(continued)*

```
    bool flag2 = reader.GetBoolean(10);
    DateTime time10 = reader.GetDateTime(11);
    DateTime time5 = time10.ToLocalTime();
    collection.Add(new MembershipUser(Name, text1, guid1, text2, text3,
                        text4, flag1, flag2, time1, time2, time3, time4, time5));
  }
  reader.Close();

  if ((parameters[4].Value != null) && (parameters[4].Value is int))
    totalRecords = (int)parameters[5].Value;

  return collection;
}
```

FindUsersByName

Listing 22-16 contains the code for the `FindUsersByName` method. As discussed in Chapter 21, this method retrieves the user records whose username matches the specified string, one page at a time. As usual, this method creates an array of `SqlParameter` objects where each object represents a parameter of the `aspnet_Membership_FindUsersByName` stored procedure. The method uses a `SqlParameter` to represent the return value of this stored procedure. This return value specifies the total number of the retrieved user records, that is, the total number of user records with the specified username:

```
parameters[4] = new SqlParameter("@ReturnValue", SqlDbType.Int);
parameters[4].Direction = ParameterDirection.ReturnValue;
```

Listing 22-16: The FindUsersByName method

```
public override MembershipUserCollection
FindUsersByName(string usernameToMatch, int pageIndex,int pageSize,
                out int totalRecords)
{
  if (pageIndex < 0)
    throw new ArgumentException("Page index cannot be negative!");

  if (pageSize < 1)
    throw new ArgumentException("Page size cannot be less than one!");

  SqlParameter[] parameters = new SqlParameter[5];
  MembershipUserCollection collection = null;
  totalRecords = 0;

  parameters[0] = CreateSqlParameter("@ApplicationName", SqlDbType.NVarChar,
                                     ApplicationName);
  parameters[1] = CreateSqlParameter("@UserNameToMatch", SqlDbType.NVarChar,
                                     usernameToMatch);
  parameters[2] = CreateSqlParameter("@PageIndex", SqlDbType.Int, pageIndex);
  parameters[3] = CreateSqlParameter("@PageSize", SqlDbType.Int, pageSize);
  parameters[4] = new SqlParameter("@ReturnValue", SqlDbType.Int);
  parameters[4].Direction = ParameterDirection.ReturnValue;
```

```
         SqlDataReader reader = Select("aspnet_Membership_FindUsersByName", parameters);
         collection = new MembershipUserCollection();

         while (reader.Read())
         {
           string text1 = !reader.IsDBNull(0) ? reader.GetString(0) : null;
           string text2 = !reader.IsDBNull(1) ? reader.GetString(1) : null;
           string text3 = !reader.IsDBNull(2) ? reader.GetString(2) : null;
           string text4 = !reader.IsDBNull(3) ? reader.GetString(3) : null;
           bool flag1 = reader.GetBoolean(4);
           DateTime time6 = reader.GetDateTime(5);
           DateTime time1 = time6.ToLocalTime();
           DateTime time7 = reader.GetDateTime(6);
           DateTime time2 = time7.ToLocalTime();
           DateTime time8 = reader.GetDateTime(7);
           DateTime time3 = time8.ToLocalTime();
           DateTime time9 = reader.GetDateTime(8);
           DateTime time4 = time9.ToLocalTime();
           Guid guid1 = reader.GetGuid(9);
           bool flag2 = reader.GetBoolean(10);
           DateTime time10 = reader.GetDateTime(11);
           DateTime time5 = time10.ToLocalTime();
           collection.Add(new MembershipUser(Name, text1, guid1, text2, text3, text4,
                                 flag1, flag2, time1, time2, time3, time4, time5));
         }

         reader.Close();

         if ((parameters[4].Value != null) && (parameters[4].Value is int))
           totalRecords = (int)parameters[4].Value;

         return collection;
       }
```

GetAllUsers

Listing 22-17 shows the implementation of the GetAllUsers method. This method retrieves all user records page by page where the pageSize parameter specifies the number of records in each page and the pageIndex parameter specifies the index of the data page to be retrieved. This method creates a SqlParameter object for each parameter of the aspnet_Membership_GetAllUsers stored procedure and calls the Select method to execute the stored procedure. Also notice that the method uses a SqlParameter object to represent the return value of the stored procedure. This return value specifies the total number of retrieved records.

GetAllUsers then iterates through the retrieved user records, creates a MembershipUser to represent each record, adds these MembershipUser objects to its local MembershipUserCollection collection, and returns the collection to its caller:

```
         collection.Add(new MembershipUser(this.Name, text1, guid1, text2, text3, text4,
                                 flag1, flag2, time1, time2, time3, time4, time5));
```

Listing 22-17: The GetAllUsers method

```
public override MembershipUserCollection
GetAllUsers(int pageIndex, int pageSize, out int totalRecords)
{
  if (pageIndex < 0)
    throw new ArgumentException("Page index cannot be negative!");

  if (pageSize < 1)
    throw new ArgumentException("Page size cannot be less than one!");

  SqlParameter[] parameters = new SqlParameter[4];
  MembershipUserCollection collection = null;
  totalRecords = 0;

  parameters[0] = CreateSqlParameter("@ApplicationName", SqlDbType.NVarChar,
                                     ApplicationName);
  parameters[1] = CreateSqlParameter("@PageIndex", SqlDbType.Int, pageIndex);
  parameters[2] = CreateSqlParameter("@PageSize", SqlDbType.Int, pageSize);
  parameters[3] = new SqlParameter("@ReturnValue", SqlDbType.Int);
  parameters[3].Direction = ParameterDirection.ReturnValue;
  SqlDataReader reader = Select("aspnet_Membership_GetAllUsers", parameters);
  collection = new MembershipUserCollection();

  while (reader.Read())
  {
    string text1 = !reader.IsDBNull(0) ? reader.GetString(0) : null;
    string text2 = !reader.IsDBNull(1) ? reader.GetString(1) : null;
    string text3 = !reader.IsDBNull(2) ? reader.GetString(2) : null;
    string text4 = !reader.IsDBNull(3) ? reader.GetString(3) : null;
    bool flag1 = reader.GetBoolean(4);
    DateTime time6 = reader.GetDateTime(5);
    DateTime time1 = time6.ToLocalTime();
    DateTime time7 = reader.GetDateTime(6);
    DateTime time2 = time7.ToLocalTime();
    DateTime time8 = reader.GetDateTime(7);
    DateTime time3 = time8.ToLocalTime();
    DateTime time9 = reader.GetDateTime(8);
    DateTime time4 = time9.ToLocalTime();
    Guid guid1 = reader.GetGuid(9);
    bool flag2 = reader.GetBoolean(10);
    DateTime time10 = reader.GetDateTime(11);
    DateTime time5 = time10.ToLocalTime();
    collection.Add(new MembershipUser(this.Name, text1, guid1, text2, text3, text4,
                          flag1, flag2, time1, time2, time3, time4, time5));
  }
  reader.Close();

  if ((parameters[3].Value != null) && (parameters[3].Value is int))
    totalRecords = (int)parameters[3].Value;

  return collection;
}
```

Select

The Select method is a helper method that's used to execute the specified stored procedure with the specified parameters and to return a SqlDataReader that streams out the retrieved user records, as shown in Listing 22-18.

Listing 22-18: The Select method

```
private SqlDataReader Select(string storedProcedureName, SqlParameter[] parameters)
{
  SqlConnection con = new SqlConnection(connectionString);
  SqlCommand com = new SqlCommand(storedProcedureName, con);
  com.CommandType = CommandType.StoredProcedure;
  com.Parameters.AddRange(parameters);
  con.Open();
  return com.ExecuteReader(CommandBehavior.CloseConnection);
}
```

GetNumberOfUsersOnline

The GetNumberOfUsersOnline method returns the number of users that are currently online, as shown in Listing 22-19. This method uses the Select method to execute the aspnet_Membership_GetNumberOfUsersOnline stored procedure. This stored procedure takes two important arguments named @MinutesSinceLastInActive and @CurrentTimeUtc and uses them to determine how many users are currently online.

Listing 22-19: The GetNumberOfUsersOnline method

```
public override int GetNumberOfUsersOnline()
{
  SqlParameter[] parameters = new SqlParameter[4];
  parameters[0] = CreateSqlParameter("@ApplicationName", SqlDbType.NVarChar,
                                     ApplicationName);
  parameters[1] = CreateSqlParameter("@MinutesSinceLastInActive", SqlDbType.Int,
                                     Membership.UserIsOnlineTimeWindow);
  parameters[2] = CreateSqlParameter("@CurrentTimeUtc", SqlDbType.DateTime,
                                     DateTime.UtcNow);
  parameters[3] = new SqlParameter("@ReturnValue", SqlDbType.Int);
  parameters[3].Direction = ParameterDirection.ReturnValue;
  Select("aspnet_Membership_GetNumberOfUsersOnline", parameters);

  return ((parameters[3].Value != null) ? ((int)parameters[3].Value) : -1);
}
```

GetPassword

The GetPassword method takes the user's username and password answer and returns the user's password as illustrated in Listing 22-20. The method first checks whether the password retrieval feature is enabled:

```
if (!EnablePasswordRetrieval)
  throw new NotSupportedException("Password cannot be retrieved!");
```

It then checks whether the user must answer a specified question before the user is allowed to change the password. The method needs to retrieve the right answer from the database so it can compare it with the answer that the user has provided. First, the method creates an array of `SqlParameter` objects where each object represents a parameter of the `aspnet_Membership_GetPasswordWithFormat` stored procedure. This stored procedure returns the password format and salt. Then it calls the `Select` method to execute the stored procedure with the specified parameters and to return a `SqlDataReader` that contains the user record of the user with the specified username. Next, it retrieves the password format and salt from the reader:

```
if (reader.Read())
{
   format = reader.GetInt32(1);
   salt = reader.GetString(2);
}
```

Finally, the method calls the `GetEncodedPassword` method and passes the user's answer and the password format and salt into it. Recall that this method encodes the user's answer based on the encoding scheme specified by the password format parameter. This step is necessary because the underlying database stores the password answer in encoded format:

```
encodedPasswordAnswer = GetEncodedPassword(passwordAnswer.ToLower(), format, salt);
```

Next, the `GetPassword` method calls the `Select` method to execute the `aspnet_Membership_GetPassword` stored procedure with the specified parameters. One of these parameters is the encoded password answer the method just retrieved if the `RequiresQuestionAndAnswer` property is set to true.

The method then uses the `SqlDataReader` that the `Select` method returns to access the user password:

```
if (reader.Read())
{
   password = reader.GetString(0);
   format = reader.GetInt32(1);
}
```

The user password that the `Select` method returns is in encoded format, just like the password answer. Therefore `GetPassword` must decode the password before it returns it. How the password should be decoded depends on how it was encoded in the first place, which is determined by the password format parameter. The `GetPassword` method examines the value of this parameter to determine the encoding scheme used to encode the password. If the value is two, the password was originally encrypted and therefore the method converts the password from its Base64 representation to the original encrypted byte array:

```
byte[] decodedPassword = Convert.FromBase64String(password);
```

It then calls the `DecryptPassword` method of the `MembershipProvider` base class to decrypt the password:

```
byte[] decryptedPassword = this.DecryptPassword(decodedPassword);
```

Then it converts the decrypted password from its byte representation to its Unicode string representation:

```
password = password = Encoding.Unicode.GetString(decryptedPassword);
```

Listing 22-20: The GetPassword method

```
public override string GetPassword(string username, string passwordAnswer)
{
  if (!EnablePasswordRetrieval)
    throw new NotSupportedException("Password cannot be retrieved!");

  if (string.IsNullOrEmpty(passwordAnswer))
    return passwordAnswer;

  int format = 0;
  string salt = null;

  SqlParameter[] parameters;
  SqlDataReader reader;
  string encodedPasswordAnswer = null;

  if (RequiresQuestionAndAnswer)
  {
    parameters = new SqlParameter[4];
    parameters[0] = CreateSqlParameter("@ApplicationName", SqlDbType.NVarChar,
                                  this.ApplicationName);
    parameters[1] = CreateSqlParameter("@UserName", SqlDbType.NVarChar, username);
    parameters[2] = CreateSqlParameter("@UpdateLastLoginActivityDate",
                                  SqlDbType.Bit, false);
    parameters[3] = CreateSqlParameter("@CurrentTimeUtc", SqlDbType.DateTime,
                                  DateTime.UtcNow);
    reader = Select("aspnet_Membership_GetPasswordWithFormat", parameters);

    if (reader.Read())
    {
      format = reader.GetInt32(1);
      salt = reader.GetString(2);
    }
    reader.Close();
    encodedPasswordAnswer =
                  GetEncodedPassword(passwordAnswer.ToLower(), format, salt);
  }

  if (RequiresQuestionAndAnswer)
    parameters = new SqlParameter[6];
  else
    parameters = new SqlParameter[5];
  parameters[0] = CreateSqlParameter("@ApplicationName", SqlDbType.NVarChar,
                                ApplicationName);
  parameters[1] = CreateSqlParameter("@UserName", SqlDbType.NVarChar, username);
  parameters[2] = CreateSqlParameter("@MaxInvalidPasswordAttempts", SqlDbType.Int,
                                MaxInvalidPasswordAttempts);
  parameters[3] = CreateSqlParameter("@PasswordAttemptWindow", SqlDbType.Int,
                                PasswordAttemptWindow);
  parameters[4] = CreateSqlParameter("@CurrentTimeUtc", SqlDbType.DateTime,
                                DateTime.UtcNow);

  if (requiresQuestionAndAnswer)
```

(continued)

Listing 22-20: *(continued)*

```
      parameters[5] = CreateSqlParameter("@PasswordAnswer", SqlDbType.NVarChar,
                                encodedPasswordAnswer);

  reader = Select("aspnet_Membership_GetPassword", parameters);
  string password = null;

  if (reader.Read())
  {
    password = reader.GetString(0);
    format = reader.GetInt32(1);
  }
  reader.Close();

  if (password != null && format == 2)
  {
    byte[] decodedPassword = Convert.FromBase64String(password);
    byte[] decryptedPassword = this.DecryptPassword(decodedPassword);
    if (decryptedPassword == null)
      password = null;
    else
      password = Encoding.Unicode.GetString(decryptedPassword);
  }
  return password;
}
```

GetUser

As discussed, MembershipProvider exposes two overloads for the GetUser method. Listing 22-21 contains the code for the first overload. This overload returns the user record with the specified provider user key. As illustrated in Listing 22-13, the CreateUser method wraps the userId that it receives from the database in a Guid object known as provider user key. As Listing 22-21 shows, the GetUser method raises as exception if the provider user key is not a Guid object.

The GetUser method calls the Select method to execute the aspnet_Membership_GetUserByUserId stored procedure with the specified provider user key parameter and uses the SqlDataReader that the Select method returns to populate a MembershipUser that represents the specified user.

Listing 22-21: The first overload of the GetUser method

```
public override MembershipUser GetUser(object providerUserKey, bool userIsOnline)
{
  MembershipUser user = null;
  if (providerUserKey == null)
    throw new ArgumentNullException("providerUserKey cannot be null!");

  if (!(providerUserKey is Guid))
    throw new ArgumentException("providerUserKey is not of type Guid!");

  SqlParameter[] parameters = new SqlParameter[3];
  parameters[0] = CreateSqlParameter("@UserId", SqlDbType.UniqueIdentifier,
                              providerUserKey);
  parameters[1] = CreateSqlParameter("@UpdateLastActivity", SqlDbType.Bit,
```

```
                                           userIsOnline);
    parameters[2] = CreateSqlParameter("@CurrentTimeUtc", SqlDbType.DateTime,
                                       DateTime.UtcNow);
    SqlDataReader reader = Select("aspnet_Membership_GetUserByUserId", parameters);

    if (reader.Read())
    {
      string text1 = !reader.IsDBNull(0) ? reader.GetString(0) : null;
      string text2 = !reader.IsDBNull(1) ? reader.GetString(1) : null;
      string text3 = !reader.IsDBNull(2) ? reader.GetString(2) : null;
      bool flag1 = reader.GetBoolean(3);
      DateTime time6 = reader.GetDateTime(4);
      DateTime time1 = time6.ToLocalTime();
      DateTime time7 = reader.GetDateTime(5);
      DateTime time2 = time7.ToLocalTime();
      DateTime time8 = reader.GetDateTime(6);
      DateTime time3 = time8.ToLocalTime();
      DateTime time9 = reader.GetDateTime(7);
      DateTime time4 = time9.ToLocalTime();
      string text4 = !reader.IsDBNull(8) ? reader.GetString(8) : null;
      bool flag2 = reader.GetBoolean(9);
      DateTime time10 = reader.GetDateTime(10);
      DateTime time5 = time10.ToLocalTime();
      user = new MembershipUser(this.Name, text4, providerUserKey, text1, text2,
                          text3, flag1, flag2, time1, time2, time3, time4, time5);
    }
    reader.Close();

    return user;
}
```

Listing 22-22 contains the code for the second overload of the GetUser method. This overload calls the Select method to execute a stored procedure named aspnet_Membership_GetUserByName that returns the user record with the specified username. As Listing 22-22 illustrates, this overloads takes similar steps to the first overload to retrieve the associated user record.

Listing 22-22: The second overload of the GetUser method

```
public override MembershipUser GetUser(string username, bool userIsOnline)
{
  MembershipUser user = null;
  SqlParameter[] parameters = new SqlParameter[4];
  parameters[0] = CreateSqlParameter("@ApplicationName", SqlDbType.NVarChar,
                                     ApplicationName);
  parameters[1] = CreateSqlParameter("@UserName", SqlDbType.NVarChar, username);
  parameters[2] = CreateSqlParameter("@UpdateLastActivity", SqlDbType.Bit,
                                     userIsOnline);
  parameters[3] = CreateSqlParameter("@CurrentTimeUtc", SqlDbType.DateTime,
                                     DateTime.UtcNow);
  SqlDataReader reader = Select("aspnet_Membership_GetUserByName", parameters);

  if (reader.Read())
  {
```

(continued)

Listing 22-22: *(continued)*

```
        string text1 = !reader.IsDBNull(0) ? reader.GetString(0) : null;
        string text2 = !reader.IsDBNull(1) ? reader.GetString(1) : null;
        string text3 = !reader.IsDBNull(2) ? reader.GetString(2) : null;
        bool flag1 = reader.GetBoolean(3);
        DateTime time6 = reader.GetDateTime(4);
        DateTime time1 = time6.ToLocalTime();
        DateTime time7 = reader.GetDateTime(5);
        DateTime time2 = time7.ToLocalTime();
        DateTime time8 = reader.GetDateTime(6);
        DateTime time3 = time8.ToLocalTime();
        DateTime time9 = reader.GetDateTime(7);
        DateTime time4 = time9.ToLocalTime();
        Guid guid1 = reader.GetGuid(8);
        bool flag2 = reader.GetBoolean(9);
        DateTime time10 = reader.GetDateTime(10);
        DateTime time5 = time10.ToLocalTime();
        user = new MembershipUser(Name, username, guid1, text1, text2, text3, flag1,
                            flag2, time1, time2, time3, time4, time5);
    }
    reader.Close();

    return user;
}
```

GetUserNameByEmail

As the name implies, this method returns the username of the user with the specified e-mail address, as illustrated in Listing 22-23. This method executes the `aspnet_Membership_GetUserByEmail` stored procedure and passes the application name and e-mail address into it. Notice the difference between the `FindUsersByEmail` and `GetUserNameByEmail` methods. As discussed, the `FindUsersByEmail` method executes the `aspnet_Membership_FindUsersByEmail` stored procedure. Because this stored procedure uses a `LIKE` clause, the callers of the `FindUsersByEmail` method can include wildcard characters in the `emailToMatch` argument of this method. The `aspnet_Membership_GetUserByEmail` stored procedure, on the other hand, doesn't use a `LIKE` clause, which means that it looks for the user with the specified e-mail.

Recall that every membership query performs the query for a particular application. This allows users of different applications to store the same user information in the same database without conflicts because the information is stored under the name of the application.

Listing 22-23: The GetUserNameByEmail method

```
public override string GetUserNameByEmail(string email)
{
    SqlParameter[] parameters = new SqlParameter[2];
    parameters[0] = CreateSqlParameter("@ApplicationName", SqlDbType.NVarChar,
                                    ApplicationName);
    parameters[1] = CreateSqlParameter("@Email", SqlDbType.NVarChar, email);
    SqlDataReader reader = Select("aspnet_Membership_GetUserByEmail", parameters);
    string text = null;
```

```
    if (reader.Read())
      text = !reader.IsDBNull(0) ? reader.GetString(0) : null;
    reader.Close();

    return text;
}
```

ResetPassword

`ResetPassword` resets the user's password as shown in Listing 22-24. This method takes two arguments. The first argument is the username of the user whose password is being reset. The second argument is the password answer that the user provides for a specified question so the system can authenticate the user.

`ResetPassword` first checks whether the password can indeed be reset. The method then calls the `Select` method to execute the `aspnet_Membership_GetPasswordWithFormat` stored procedure to return the password format and salt for the specified user:

```
format = reader.GetInt32(1);
salt = reader.GetString(2);
```

The method then calls the `GetEncodedPassword` method and passes the user's password answer and the password format and salt into it. As discussed, this method encodes the user's password answer based on the encoding scheme specified by the password format parameter. For instance, if the password format is `Hashed`, this method adds the salt value to the password answer, calculates the hash of the salted password answer, and converts this salted hash to its Base64 string representation.

```
encodedPasswordAnswer = GetEncodedPassword(passwordAnswer.ToLower(), format, salt);
```

The method then calls the `GeneratePassword` method of the `Membership` class to generate a random password for the user:

```
string generatedPassword = Membership.GeneratePassword(MinRequiredPasswordLength,
                                        MinRequiredNonAlphanumericCharacters);
```

Your custom membership provider's implementation of the `ResetPassword` method should raise the `ValidatingPassword` event before it attempts to store the preceding randomly generated password in the database. This allows the page developers to register callbacks for this event where they can validate the newly generated password against application-specific business rules:

```
ValidatePasswordEventArgs args =
            new ValidatePasswordEventArgs(username, generatedPassword, false);
this.OnValidatingPassword(args);
```

Recall that the `ValidatePasswordEventArgs` event data class exposes a property named `Cancel` that the page developers can set to true if the randomly generated password fails the application-specific password validation. Your custom membership provider's implementation of the `ResetPassword` method should use the value of this property to determine whether the page developer has canceled the reset password process. If so, the method should raise the exception that the page developer has assigned to the `FailureInformation` property:

```
  if (args.Cancel)
  {
    if (args.FailureInformation != null)
      throw args.FailureInformation;

    throw new ProviderException();
  }
```

Finally, the `ResetPassword` method calls the `Update` method to execute the
`aspnet_Membership_ResetPassword` stored procedure with the specified parameters
to reset the password for the specified user.

Listing 22-24: The ResetPassword method

```
public override string ResetPassword(string username, string passwordAnswer)
{
  if (!this.EnablePasswordReset)
    throw new NotSupportedException();

  int format = 0;
  string salt = null;

  SqlParameter[] parameters;
  SqlDataReader reader;
  string encodedPasswordAnswer = null;

  parameters = new SqlParameter[4];
  parameters[0] = CreateSqlParameter("@ApplicationName", SqlDbType.NVarChar,
                                     this.ApplicationName);
  parameters[1] = CreateSqlParameter("@UserName", SqlDbType.NVarChar, username);
  parameters[2] = CreateSqlParameter("@UpdateLastLoginActivityDate", SqlDbType.Bit,
                                     false);
  parameters[3] = CreateSqlParameter("@CurrentTimeUtc", SqlDbType.DateTime,
                                     DateTime.UtcNow);
  reader = Select("aspnet_Membership_GetPasswordWithFormat", parameters);

  if (reader.Read())
  {
    format = reader.GetInt32(1);
    salt = reader.GetString(2);
  }
  reader.Close();

  if (!string.IsNullOrEmpty(passwordAnswer))
    encodedPasswordAnswer =
                 GetEncodedPassword(passwordAnswer.ToLower(), format, salt);

  else
    encodedPasswordAnswer = passwordAnswer;

  string generatedPassword = Membership.GeneratePassword(MinRequiredPasswordLength,
                                       MinRequiredNonAlphanumericCharacters);
  ValidatePasswordEventArgs args =
```

```
                new ValidatePasswordEventArgs(username, generatedPassword, false);
this.OnValidatingPassword(args);
if (args.Cancel)
{
  if (args.FailureInformation != null)
    throw args.FailureInformation;

  throw new ProviderException();
}

if (this.RequiresQuestionAndAnswer)
  parameters = new SqlParameter[9];
else
  parameters = new SqlParameter[8];

parameters[0] = CreateSqlParameter("@ApplicationName", SqlDbType.NVarChar,
                            ApplicationName);
parameters[1] = CreateSqlParameter("@UserName", SqlDbType.NVarChar, username);
parameters[2] = CreateSqlParameter("@NewPassword", SqlDbType.NVarChar,
                        GetEncodedPassword(generatedPassword, format, salt));
parameters[3] = CreateSqlParameter("@MaxInvalidPasswordAttempts", SqlDbType.Int,
                            MaxInvalidPasswordAttempts);
parameters[4] = CreateSqlParameter("@PasswordAttemptWindow", SqlDbType.Int,
                            PasswordAttemptWindow);
parameters[5] = CreateSqlParameter("@PasswordSalt", SqlDbType.NVarChar, salt);
parameters[6] = CreateSqlParameter("@PasswordFormat", SqlDbType.Int, format);
parameters[7] = CreateSqlParameter("@CurrentTimeUtc", SqlDbType.DateTime,
                            DateTime.UtcNow);
if (this.RequiresQuestionAndAnswer)
  parameters[8] = CreateSqlParameter("@PasswordAnswer", SqlDbType.NVarChar,
                            encodedPasswordAnswer);
Update("aspnet_Membership_ResetPassword", parameters);

return generatedPassword;
}
```

UnlockUser

The UnlockUser method clears the lock on the specified username, as illustrated in Listing 22-25. This method simply calls the Update method to execute the aspnet_Membership_UnlockUser stored procedure and passes the application name and username into it.

Listing 22-25: The UnlockUser method

```
public override bool UnlockUser(string username)
{
  SqlParameter[] parameters = new SqlParameter[2];
  parameters[0] = CreateSqlParameter("@ApplicationName", SqlDbType.NVarChar,
                            ApplicationName);
  parameters[1] = CreateSqlParameter("@UserName", SqlDbType.NVarChar, username);
  return Update("aspnet_Membership_UnlockUser", parameters);
}
```

UpdateUser

The UpdateUser method takes a MembershipUser as its argument and updates the record of the user that the MembershipUser represents (see Listing 22-26). This method uses the properties of the MembershipUser object to set the parameters of the underlying stored procedure, aspnet_Membership_UpdateUser. This stored procedure, in turn, updates the user record with the new information.

Listing 22-26: The UpdateUser method

```
public override void UpdateUser(MembershipUser user)
{
  if (user == null)
    throw new ArgumentNullException();

  SqlParameter[] parameters = new SqlParameter[9];
  parameters[0] = CreateSqlParameter("@ApplicationName", SqlDbType.NVarChar,
                                     ApplicationName);
  parameters[1] = CreateSqlParameter("@UserName", SqlDbType.NVarChar,
                                     user.UserName);
  parameters[2] = CreateSqlParameter("@Email", SqlDbType.NVarChar, user.Email);
  parameters[3] = CreateSqlParameter("@Comment", SqlDbType.NText, user.Comment);
  parameters[4] = CreateSqlParameter("@IsApproved", SqlDbType.Bit,
                                     user.IsApproved ? 1 : 0);
  parameters[5] = CreateSqlParameter("@LastLoginDate", SqlDbType.DateTime,
                                     user.LastLoginDate.ToUniversalTime());
  parameters[6] = CreateSqlParameter("@LastActivityDate", SqlDbType.DateTime,
                                     user.LastActivityDate.ToUniversalTime());
  parameters[7] = CreateSqlParameter("@UniqueEmail", SqlDbType.Int,
                                     this.RequiresUniqueEmail ? 1 : 0);
  parameters[8] = CreateSqlParameter("@CurrentTimeUtc", SqlDbType.DateTime,
                                     DateTime.UtcNow);
  Update("aspnet_Membership_UpdateUser", parameters);
}
```

ValidateUser

The ValidateUser method is used to validate the user credentials against the database. This method simply calls the ValidateUserInfo method that was discussed in previous sections:

```
public override bool ValidateUser(string username, string password)
{
  return ValidateUserInfo(username, password, true, true);
}
```

Registering SqlMembershipProvider

To register your reversed-engineered or replica SqlMembershipProvider, you need to use an <add> element to add the reversed-engineered SqlMembershipProvider to the <providers> section of the <membership> section of the Web.config file. Recall that the <add> method exposes two sets of attributes. The first set includes the following:

❏ name: You need to choose a friendly name for your custom membership provider. You can choose any name you want as long as no other membership provider in the `<providers>` section has the same name.

❏ type: This attribute contains the complete information needed to instantiate the specified membership provider. The information consists of up to two parts. The first part is the fully qualified name of the membership provider including its namespace, such as `CustomComponents.SqlMembershipProvider`. The second part is the strong name of the assembly, which consists of up to four parts: the assembly name, version, culture, and public key token. If the second part isn't specified, it's assumed that the executing assembly contains the membership provider.

❏ applicationName: A string that uniquely identifies the application from other applications.

❏ description: A short description of what the membership provider does.

The second set of attributes the `<add>` element exposes were thoroughly discussed in the previous chapter.

Adding your membership provider to the `<providers>` section doesn't automatically tell the membership system to use your provider. You must also assign the friendly name of your provider to the `defaultProvider` attribute of the `<membership>` element:

```
<membership defaultProvider="MySqlMembershipProvider" userIsOnlineTimeWindow ="2">
  <providers>

    <clear />

    <add name="MySqlMembershipProvider"
    type="CustomComponents.SqlMembershipProvider"
    connectionStringName="LocalSqlServer"
    enablePasswordRetrieval="false"
    enablePasswordReset="true"
    requiresQuestionAndAnswer="false"
    applicationName="/"
    requiresUniqueEmail="false"
    passwordFormat="Hashed"
    maxInvalidPasswordAttempts="5"
    passwordAttemptWindow="10"
    passwordStrengthRegularExpression=""/>
  </providers>
</membership>
```

Using the Custom Membership Provider

This section develops a simple Web application that uses the reverse-engineered or replica `SqlMembershipProvider` to store user membership to and retrieve user membership from the underlying database. The Web application consists of three Web pages.

The first page is `Login.aspx`, which is used to collect and validate user credentials against the database as shown in the following code:

```
<%@ Page Language="C#" %>
<html xmlns="http://www.w3.org/1999/xhtml">
<body>
  <form id="form1" runat="server">
    <asp:Login runat="server" CreateUserText="Register"
    CreateUserUrl="Register.aspx" />
  </form>
</body>
</html>
```

The second page is Register.aspx. Login.aspx contains a link named Register that new users can click to navigate to the Register.aspx Web page, where they can register with the application, as shown in the following code fragment:

```
<%@ Page Language="C#" %>
<html xmlns="http://www.w3.org/1999/xhtml">
<body>
  <form id="form1" runat="server">
    <asp:CreateUserWizard runat="server" />
  </form>
</body>
</html>
```

The third page is Default.aspx. This extremely simple Web page represents a protected resource, as shown in the following code:

```
<%@ Page Language="C#" %>
<html xmlns="http://www.w3.org/1999/xhtml">
<body>
  <form id="form1" runat="server">
    <strong>This is a protected resource</strong>
  </form>
</body>
</html>
```

When an anonymous user tries to access this protected page, ASP.NET automatically redirects users to the Login.aspx page, where they can log in to the system.

You also need to make the following changes to the Web.config file:

1. Change the authentication mode from Windows to Forms authentication:

```
<authentication mode="Forms">
  <forms loginUrl="Login.aspx" name=".AUTHCOOKIE" path="/" protection="All"
  timeout="40" />
</authentication>
```

2. Deny access to anonymous users:

```
<authorization>
  <deny users="?"/>
</authorization>
```

3. This setting will not allow unregistered users to access the `Register.aspx` page to register with your application. Add the following section to the `Web.config` file to give permission to all users to access the `Register.aspx` page:

```
<location path="Register.aspx">
  <system.web>
    <authorization>
      <allow users="*"/>
    </authorization>
  </system.web>
</location>
```

Try the following workflow:

1. Try to access the `Default.aspx` page, which is a protected page. The application automatically redirects you to the `Login.aspx` page.

2. Enter your username and password to log in to the application. If you put a break point in the `ValidateUser` method of your reverse-engineered `SqlMembershipProvider`, you'll notice that the debugger will stop at the method when you click the Login button on the `Login.aspx` page, which means that your custom provider is being used to validate your credentials.

3. Click the `Register` link on the `Login.aspx` page to navigate to the `Register.aspx` page. Put a break point on the `CreateUser` method of your reverse-engineered `SqlMembershipProvider`. Enter the required registration information and click the Create User button. Notice that the debugger stops at the `CreateUser` method of your custom provider, which means that your custom provider is being used to create new user record.

Extending the ASP.NET 2.0 Membership API

The methods and properties of the standard components of the ASP.NET 2.0 membership model form an API that you can use to interact with any type of data store. In other words, this API isolates your application from data store–specific data access APIs and allows you to use the same API to interact with all types of data stores.

Because the ASP.NET 2.0 Membership API contains a limited set of methods and properties, it may not meet all the requirements of your application. This section shows how to extend the ASP.NET 2.0 Membership API to add support for new methods and properties.

To make the discussions more concrete, this section extends the API to add support for a new method named `GetFailedAttemptCounts` that retrieves the number of failed password attempts and the number of failed password answer attempts of a specified user from any type of data store.

You'll develop the following custom components to extend the API:

❑ `CustomMembershipUser`
❑ `CustomMembershipProvider`

CustomMembershipUser

Chapter 21 implemented a replica of the ASP.NET 2.0 MembershipUser class. This section builds on what you learned in Chapter 21 to implement a custom MembershipUser named CustomMembershipUser that derives from MembershipUser and extends its functionality to add support for a new method named GetFailedAttemptCounts, as shown in Listing 22-27.

Listing 22-27: The CustomMembershipUser class

```csharp
namespace CustomComponents
{
  public class CustomMembershipUser : MembershipUser
  {
    public CustomMembershipUser() : base() { }
    public CustomMembershipUser(string providerName, string name,
                               object providerUserKey, string email,
                               string passwordQuestion, string comment,
                               bool isApproved, bool isLockedOut,
                               DateTime creationDate, DateTime lastLoginDate,
                               DateTime lastActivityDate,
                               DateTime lastPasswordChangedDate,
                               DateTime lastLockoutDate)
      : base(providerName, name, providerUserKey, email, passwordQuestion, comment,
             isApproved, isLockedOut, creationDate, lastLoginDate,
             lastActivityDate, lastPasswordChangedDate, lastLockoutDate) { }

    public CustomMembershipUser(MembershipUser user)
      : base (user.ProviderName,user.UserName,user.ProviderUserKey,user.Email,
              user.PasswordQuestion,user.Comment,user.IsApproved,user.IsLockedOut,
              user.CreationDate,user.LastLoginDate,user.LastActivityDate,
              user.LastPasswordChangedDate,user.LastLockoutDate) {}

    public virtual void GetFailedAttemptCounts(string password,
                                       bool updateLastLoginActivityDate,
                                       out int failedPasswordAttemptCount,
                                       out int failedPasswordAnswerAttemptCount)
    {
      failedPasswordAttemptCount = -1;
      failedPasswordAnswerAttemptCount = -1;

      CustomMembershipProvider provider =
                Membership.Providers[ProviderName] as CustomMembershipProvider;

      if (provider != null)
        provider.GetFailedAttemptCounts(UserName, password,
                                        updateLastLoginActivityDate,
                                        out failedPasswordAttemptCount,
                                        out failedPasswordAnswerAttemptCount);
    }
  }
}
```

As Listing 22-27 shows, `CustomMembershipUser` exposes three constructors. Notice that the third constructor takes an argument of type `MembershipUser`. As this listing illustrates, `GetFailedAttemptCounts` takes the following four arguments:

❑ `password`: The password of the user that the `CustomMembershipUser` represents

❑ `updateLastLoginActivityDate`: Specifies whether the last login activity date of the user record should be updated

❑ `failedPasswordAttemptCount`: The number of failed password attempts

❑ `failedPasswordAnswerAttemptCount`: The number of failed password answer attempts

The `GetFailedAttemptCounts` method uses the value of the `ProviderName` property of the `CustomMembershipUser` as an index into the `Providers` collection of the `Membership` class to access the associated `MembershipProvider` instance and casts the instance to the `CustomMembershipProvider` type. The `CustomMembershipProvider` class is discussed in the following section.

As Listing 22-27 shows, the `GetFailedAttemptCounts` method of the `CustomMembershipUser` class delegates the responsibility of retrieving the number of failed password attempts and the number of failed password answer attempts to the `GetFailedAttemptCounts` method of the `CustomMembershipProvider` instance. It's the responsibility of the membership provider to implement this method where it must use the appropriate data access code to retrieve the preceding two numbers from the underlying data store.

CustomMembershipProvider

Listing 22-28 shows the implementation of the `CustomMembershipProvider` class. This class derives from the `MembershipProvider` base class and extends its functionality to add support for the `GetFailedAttemptCounts` method.

Listing 22-28: The CustomMembershipProvider class

```
namespace CustomComponents
{
  public abstract class CustomMembershipProvider : MembershipProvider
  {
    public abstract void
    GetFailedAttemptCounts(string username, string password,
                           bool updateLastLoginActivityDate,
                           out int failedPasswordAttemptCount,
                           out int failedPasswordAnswerAttemptCount);
  }
}
```

CustomSqlMembershipProvider

The ASP.NET 2.0 `SqlMembershipProvider` derives from the `MembershipProvider` base class, not the `CustomMembershipProvider` class developed in the previous section. This section develops a version of `SqlMembershipProvider` named `CustomSqlMembershipProvider` that derives from the `CustomMembershipProvider` class to support the `GetFailedAttemptCounts` method. Thanks to the Object Composition technique, you don't have to re-implement the methods and properties that the

`SqlMembershipProvider` class already supports. As you'll see in the following sections, `CustomSqlMembershipProvider` delegates the responsibility of handling all of its methods and properties (except for the `GeFailedAttemptCounts` method) to the respective methods and properties of the `SqlMembershipProvider`.

Because `CustomSqlMembershipProvider` derives from `CustomMembershipProvider`, which in turn derives from `MembershipProvider`, which in turn derives from `ProviderBase` class, it must implement the methods and properties of the `CustomMembershipProvider`, `MembershipProvider`, and `ProviderBase` classes.

ProviderBase

`CustomSqlMembershipProvider` implements the `Initialize` method of the `ProviderBase` class, as shown in Listing 22-29.

Listing 22-29: The Initialize method of CustomSqlMembershipProvider

```
public override void Initialize(string name, NameValueCollection config)
{
  if (config == null)
    throw new ArgumentNullException("config");

  if (string.IsNullOrEmpty(name))
    name = "CustomSqlMembershipProvider";

  if (string.IsNullOrEmpty(config["description"]))
  {
    config.Remove("description");
    config.Add("description", "Stores membership information in SQL Server
            database");
  }

  ConnectionStringSettings settings =
          ConfigurationManager.ConnectionStrings[config["connectionStringName"]];
  connectionString = settings.ConnectionString;
  if (string.IsNullOrEmpty(connectionString))
    throw new ProviderException("Invalid connection string name");

  provider = new SqlMembershipProvider();
  provider.Initialize(name, config);

  if (config.Count > 0)
  {
    string key = config.GetKey(0);
    if (!string.IsNullOrEmpty(key))
      throw new ProviderException("Unrecognized attribute");
  }
}
```

The `Initialize` method follows the steps discussed before to retrieve the connection string, and assigns it to the `connectionString` private field. As you'll see later, the `GetFailedAttemptCounts` method of `CustomSqlMembershipProvider` uses this connection string to connect to the underlying SQL Server database to retrieve the number of failed password attempts and the number of failed password answer attempts:

```
ConnectionStringSettings settings =
        ConfigurationManager.ConnectionStrings[config["connectionStringName"]];
connectionString = settings.ConnectionString;
```

Notice that the `Initialize` method raises an exception if the page developer hasn't specified the connection string because `GetFailedAttemptCounts` will fail without the connection string. As mentioned, your custom provider must always raise an exception if the value of a parameter essential to the functioning of your provider hasn't been set:

```
if (string.IsNullOrEmpty(connectionString))
    throw new ProviderException("Invalid connection string name");
```

The `Initialize` method then creates an instance of the `SqlMembershipProvider` and assigns it to the `provider` private field for future reference. As you'll see later, all methods and properties of `CustomSqlMembershipProvider` (except for `GetFailedAttemptCounts` method) delegate to the respective methods and properties of this `SqlMembershipProvider` instance:

```
provider = new SqlMembershipProvider();
```

The `Initialize` method then calls the `Initialize` method of the `SqlMembershipProvider` instance to initialize it:

```
provider.Initialize(name, config);
```

MembershipProvider

The members of the `CustomSqlMembershipProvider` class can be divided into two groups. The first group includes those members that use the `MembershipUser` or `MembershipUserCollection` class. This group includes the `CreateUser`, `GetUser`, `GetAllUsers`, `FindUsersByName`, and `FindUsersByEmail` methods. The second group includes the rest of the members of the `CustomSqlMembershipProvider` class.

The members in both groups delegate to the respective methods and properties of the `SqlMembershipProvider` instance discussed in the previous section. You'll need to take one more step to implement the methods in the second group. That is, you'll need to convert the respective `MembershipUser` objects to `CustomMembershipUser` type.

Here is an example of how you should implement the methods in the first group:

```
public override bool
ChangePassword(string username, string oldPassword, string newPassword)
{
    return provider.ChangePassword(username, oldPassword, newPassword);
}
```

Notice that the `ChangePassword` method simply calls the `ChangePassword` method of the `SqlMembershipProvider` to change the password in the underlying data store.

The following sections show you how to implement the methods in the second group. Because the implementation of these methods will use the `CreateCustomMembershipUser` and `CreateCustomMembershipUsers` methods, the implementations of these two methods are discussed first.

CreateCustomMembershipUser

Listing 22-30 contains the code for the CreateCustomMembershipUser method. This method contains the logic that creates a CustomMembershipUser object out of a specified MembershipUser object. In this case, the implementation of this method is quite simple because the CustomMembershipUser doesn't expose new properties. It only exposes a new method named GetFailedAttemptCounts. However, if your custom MembershipUser exposes new properties, this method is where you should retrieve the appropriate values from the underlying data store and assign them to these new properties.

Listing 22-30: The CreateCustomMembershipUser method

```
protected virtual CustomMembershipUser
CreateCustomMembershipUser(MembershipUser user)
{
  return new CustomMembershipUser(user);
}
```

CreateCustomMembershipUsers

Listing 22-31 presents the implementation of the CreateCustomMembershipUsers method.

Listing 22-31: The CreateCustomMembershipUsers method

```
protected virtual MembershipUserCollection
CreateCustomMembershipUsers(MembershipUserCollection users)
{
  MembershipUserCollection users2 = new MembershipUserCollection();
  CustomMembershipUser cuser;
  foreach (MembershipUser user in users)
  {
    cuser = CreateCustomMembershipUser(user);
    users2.Add(cuser);
  }
  return users2;
}
```

CreateCustomMembershipUsers first creates a new MembershipUserCollection collection:

```
MembershipUserCollection users2 = new MembershipUserCollection();
```

Then, it enumerates the MembershipUser objects in the MembershipUserCollection collection passed into it as its argument and takes the following actions for each enumerated object:

1. It calls the CreateCustomMembershipUser method to convert the enumerated object to the CustomMembershipUser type:

```
CustomMembershipUser cuser = CreateCustomMembershipUser(user);
```

2. It adds the CustomMembershipUser object to the newly created MembershipUserCollection collection:

```
users2.Add(cuser);
```

CreateUser

Listing 22-32 presents the implementation of the CreateUser method. The method first calls the CreateUser method of the SqlMembershipProvider instance discussed earlier to return the MembershipUser object that represents the newly added user:

```
MembershipUser user =
      provider.CreateUser(username, password, email, passwordQuestion,
                          passwordAnswer, isApproved, providerUserKey, out status);
```

The method then calls the CreateCustomMembershipUser method and passes the new MembershipUser object into it to convert the object to CustomMembershipUser type.

Listing 22-32: The CreateUser method

```
public override CustomMembershipUser
CreateUser(string username, string password, string email,
           string passwordQuestion, string passwordAnswer, bool isApproved,
           object providerUserKey, out MembershipCreateStatus status)
{
  MembershipUser user =
      provider.CreateUser(username, password, email, passwordQuestion,
                          passwordAnswer, isApproved, providerUserKey, out status);

  return CreateCustomMembershipUser(user);
}
```

The implementations of the two overloads of the GetUser method of CustomSqlMembershipProvider are very similar to the implementation of the CreateUser method.

FindUsersByEmail

Listing 22-33 contains the CustomSqlMembershipProvider's implementation of the FindUsersByEmail method of the MembershipProvider base class.

Listing 22-33: The FindUsersByEmail method

```
public override MembershipUserCollection
FindUsersByEmail(string emailToMatch, int pageIndex, int pageSize,
                 out int totalRecords)
{
  MembershipUserCollection users =
      provider.FindUsersByEmail(emailToMatch, pageIndex, pageSize, out totalRecords);

  return CreateCustomMembershipUsers(users);
}
```

FindUsersByEmail delegates the responsibility of finding users whose e-mail matches the specified e-mail to the FindUsersByEmail method of the SqlMembershipProvider instance. FindUsersByEmail then calls the CreateCustomMembershipUsers method and passes the MembershipUserCollection collection that contains the retrieved data records into it.

The implementations of the GetAllUsers and GetUsersByEmail methods of CustomSqlMembershipProvider are very similar to the implementation of the FindUsersByEmail method.

671

CustomMembershipProvider

Listing 22-34 presents the `CustomSqlMembershipProvider`'s implementation of the `GetFailedAttemptCounts` method of the `CustomMembershipProvider` base class.

Listing 22-34: The GetFailedAttemptCounts method

```
public override void
GetFailedAttemptCounts(string username, string password,
                       bool updateLastLoginActivityDate,
                       out int failedPasswordAttemptCount,
                       out int failedPasswordAnswerAttemptCount)
{
  failedPasswordAnswerAttemptCount = -1;
  failedPasswordAttemptCount = -1;
  if (!ValidateUser(username, password))
    return;

  SqlParameter[] parameters = new SqlParameter[4];
  parameters[0] = CreateSqlParameter("@ApplicationName", SqlDbType.NVarChar,
                                     this.ApplicationName);
  parameters[1] = CreateSqlParameter("@UserName", SqlDbType.NVarChar, username);
  parameters[2] = CreateSqlParameter("@UpdateLastLoginActivityDate", SqlDbType.Bit,
                                     updateLastLoginActivityDate);
  parameters[3] = CreateSqlParameter("@CurrentTimeUtc", SqlDbType.DateTime,
                                     DateTime.UtcNow);
  SqlDataReader reader = Select("aspnet_Membership_GetPasswordWithFormat",
                                parameters);

  if (reader.Read())
  {
    failedPasswordAttemptCount = reader.GetInt32(3);
    failedPasswordAnswerAttemptCount = reader.GetInt32(4);
  }

  reader.Close();
}
```

The `GetFailedAttemptCounts` method first calls the `ValidateUser` method to authenticate the user:

```
    if (!ValidateUser(username, password))
      return;
```

The method then calls the `CreateSqlParameter` method to create one `SqlParameter` object for each parameter of the `aspnet_Membership_GetPasswordWithFormat` stored procedure. The implementation of the `CreateSqlParameter` method is the same as the `CreateSqlParameter` method discussed in the previous sections.

```
    SqlParameter[] parameters = new SqlParameter[4];
    parameters[0] = CreateSqlParameter("@ApplicationName", SqlDbType.NVarChar,
                                       this.ApplicationName);
    parameters[1] = CreateSqlParameter("@UserName", SqlDbType.NVarChar,
                                       username);
    parameters[2] = CreateSqlParameter("@UpdateLastLoginActivityDate",
```

```
                                        SqlDbType.Bit, updateLastLoginActivityDate);
            parameters[3] = CreateSqlParameter("@CurrentTimeUtc", SqlDbType.DateTime,
                                        DateTime.UtcNow);
```

The `GetFailedAttemptCounts` method then calls the `Select` method to execute the stored procedure and access the `SqlDataReader` object that contains the retrieved data records. The implementation of the `Select` method is the same as the `Select` method discussed in the previous sections.

```
SqlDataReader reader = Select("aspnet_Membership_GetPasswordWithFormat",
                                        parameters);
```

The method then uses the `SqlDataReader` object to access the number of failed password attempts and number of failed password answer attempts:

```
if (reader.Read())
{
   failedPasswordAttemptCount = reader.GetInt32(3);
   failedPasswordAnswerAttemptCount = reader.GetInt32(4);
}
```

Using CustomMembershipUser, CustomMembershipProvider, and CustomSqlMembershipProvider

This section develops a Web application that uses the `CustomMembershipUser`, `CustomMembershipProvider`, and `CustomSqlMembershipProvider` components developed in the previous sections. First, follow the steps discussed previously in this chapter to add the `CustomSqlMembershipProvider` provider to the `<providers>` section of the `<membership>` section of the `Web.config` or `Machine.config` file. Don't forget to assign the friendly name of the `CustomSqlMembershipProvider` to the `defaultProvider` attribute of the `<membership>` element. Pick any friendly name you like. Just make sure it's unique in that no other provider in the `<providers>` section of the `<membership>` section has that friendly name. Listing 22-35 contains the code to register the `CustomSqlMembershipProvider` provider.

Listing 22-35: Registering the CustomSqlMembershipProvider provider

```
<membership defaultProvider="CustomSqlMembershipProvider"
userIsOnlineTimeWindow ="2">
  <providers>
    <clear/>
    <add name="CustomSqlMembershipProvider"
    type="CustomComponents.CustomSqlMembershipProvider"
    connectionStringName="LocalSqlServer"
    enablePasswordRetrieval="false"
    enablePasswordReset="true"
    requiresQuestionAndAnswer="false"
    applicationName="/"
    requiresUniqueEmail="false"
    passwordFormat="Hashed"
```

(continued)

673

Listing 22-35: *(continued)*

```
        maxInvalidPasswordAttempts="5"
        passwordAttemptWindow="10"
        passwordStrengthRegularExpression="" />
    </providers>
</membership>
```

Listing 22-36 contains a page that uses the `CustomMembershipUser` component.

Listing 22-36: A page that uses the CustomMembershipUser component

```
<%@ Page Language="C#" %>

<script runat="server">
  protected void Page_Load(object sender, EventArgs e)
  {
    int failedPasswordAttemptCount;
    int failedPasswordAnswerAttemptCount;

    CustomMembershipUser user =
                    Membership.GetUser() as CustomMembershipUser;
    user.GetFailedAttemptCounts("aB23Rt56#", true, out failedPasswordAttemptCount,
                            out failedPasswordAnswerAttemptCount);

    info.Text = "Failed Password Attempt Count: " +
                failedPasswordAttemptCount.ToString();
    info.Text += ("<br/>Failed Password Answer Attempt Count: " +
                failedPasswordAnswerAttemptCount.ToString());
  }
</script>
<html xmlns="http://www.w3.org/1999/xhtml">
<body>
  <form id="form1" runat="server">
    <div>
      <strong>Welcome</strong>
    </div>
    <br />
    <asp:Label runat="server" ID="info" />
  </form>
</body>
</html>
```

As Listing 22-36 shows, the `Page_Load` method calls the `GetUser` method of the `Membership` class to access the `MembershipUser` object that represents the current user. Notice that the `Page_Load` method type casts the return value of the `GetUser` method to `CustomMembershipUser` type. This is possible because the `GetUser` method of the `CustomSqlMembershipUser` class returns an object of type `CustomMembershipUser`. The `Page_Load` method then invokes the `GetFailedAttemptCounts` method of the `CustomMembershipUser` object to retrieve the number of failed password attempts and the number of failed password answer attempts.

Here are the pros and cons of writing your own custom `MembershipUser` and custom `MembershipProvider` classes. The main benefit is that you can extend the ASP.NET 2.0 membership API to add support for new methods and properties. For example, the `CustomMembershipUser` and `CustomMembershipProvider` classes add support for the `GetFailedAttemptCounts` method.

The main downsides of writing your own custom `MembershipUser` and custom `MembershipProvider` classes are as follows:

❑   The `GetUser` and `CreateUser` methods return a `MembershipUser` object. The clients of your custom `MembershipUser` class must type cast this `MembershipUser` object before they can benefit from the new methods and properties of your custom class. For example, the `Page_Load` method shown in Listing 22-36 must type cast the return value of the `GetUser` method to `CustomMembershipUser` type before it can invoke the `GetFailedAttemptCounts` method.

❑   The `GetAllUsers`, `FindUsersByEmail`, and `FindUsersByName` methods return a `MembershipUserCollection` collection that contains `MembershipUser` objects. The clients of your custom `MembershipUser` class must enumerate these `MembershipUser` objects and cast each enumerated object to `CustomMembershipUser` type before they can invoke the new methods and properties of your custom class.

❑   The `Provider` property of the `Membership` class returns a `MembershipProvider` provider. The clients of your custom `MembershipProvider` class must type cast this `MembershipProvider` provider before they can benefit from the new methods and properties of your custom class.

In other words, you custom `MembershipUser` and custom `MembershipProvider` classes don't seamlessly integrate into the client applications. As a matter of fact, the ASP.NET 2.0 Framework itself comes with a class named `ActiveDirectoryMembershipUser` that derives from `MembershipUser`. The clients of this class must perform the previously mentioned type casts before they can benefit from this class.

Summary

This chapter implemented a fully functional replica of the `SqlMembershipProvider` built into ASP.NET to show you how you can develop a similar membership provider to access a SQL database with a different schema than the `aspnetdb` database. This chapter also showed you how to implement your own custom `MembershipUser` and custom `MembershipProvider` classes.

When an ASP.NET Web application receives a request for a protected resource, the application takes two steps before it allows the requester to access the resource. First, the application uses the ASP.NET 2.0 membership model to authenticate the requester's credentials. Second, the application uses the ASP.NET 2.0 role model to authorize the requester, that is, to determine whether the requester is allowed to access the requested resource.

This chapter and the previous chapter covered the ASP.NET 2.0 membership model. The next two chapters provide you with an in-depth coverage of the ASP.NET 2.0 role model.

23

Understanding the ASP.NET Role Management Model

The .NET Framework uses an `IPrincipal` object to represent the security context under which code is running. The Framework uses an `IIdentity` object to represent the identity of an `IPrincipal` object. A *role* is a group of `IPrincipal` objects with the same privileges. An `IPrincipal` object can be a member of one or more roles.

Here is an example. When you're running .NET code on your machine, the .NET Framework uses an object of type `WindowsPrincipal` to represent the security context under which you're running the code. The `WindowsPrincipal` class implements the `IPrincipal` interface. Your user account on your machine defines the identity of this `WindowsPrincipal` object. The .NET Framework uses a `WindowsIdentity` object to represent this identity. The `WindowsIdentity` class implements the `IIdentity` interface. Your user group accounts on your machine define the roles the `WindowsPrincipal` object is in. Your user account can be a member of one or more group accounts. All user accounts in a given group or role enjoy the same set of privileges.

In this chapter you learn about the main components of the ASP.NET role management model:

❑   Roles
❑   RolePrincipal
❑   RoleManagerModule

This understanding will put you in a position where you can decide for yourself which components don't meet your application's requirements and how you can extend these components to add support for the features that your application needs. The next chapter builds on this chapter to show you how to implement your own custom role providers, role principals, and role manager modules.

Roles API

As Chapter 20 demonstrated, the `Roles` class is only responsible for defining the business API for its clients. The class delegates the responsibility of deciding which data access API to use to the configured role provider.

The `Roles` class exposes two properties named `Provider` and `Providers`, where the former is of type `RoleProvider` and the latter is of type `RoleProviderCollection`. The `Roles` class also exposes a method named `Initialize`. This method does exactly what the `Initialize` method of the `Membership` class does; it populates the `Providers` collection with the registered providers and assigns the default provider to the `Provider` property. The implementation of the `Initialize` method of the `Roles` class is very similar to the implementation of the `Membership` class discussed in Chapter 21.

The methods and properties of the `Roles` class define the `Roles` API. The API allows its clients to perform the following operations:

- ❑ Managing roles, specifically:
    - ❑ Adding a new role to the data store
    - ❑ Deleting a role from the data store
    - ❑ Retrieving all available roles from the data store
    - ❑ Checking whether the specified role exists in the data store
- ❑ Managing users, specifically:
    - ❑ Adding users to roles
    - ❑ Removing users from roles
    - ❑ Retrieving users in roles

Managing Roles

The `Roles` API contains methods that allow you to perform several role management operations. The `CreateRole` method calls the `CreateRole` method of the configured role provider to add the specified role to the underlying data store:

```
public static void CreateRole(string roleName)
{
  Provider.CreateRole(roleName);
}
```

The `DeleteRole` method calls the `DeleteRole` method of the configured role provider to delete the specified role from the data store. As the following code shows, this method has two overloads. The second overload takes a second Boolean argument that specifies whether the provider should raise an exception if the role being deleted contains users:

```
public static bool DeleteRole(string roleName)
{
  return Provider.DeleteRole(roleName, true);
}
```

```
public static bool DeleteRole(string roleName, bool throwOnPopulatedRole)
{
  return Provider.DeleteRole(roleName, throwOnPopulatedRole);
}
```

The `RoleExists` method calls the `RoleExists` method of the configured role provider to check whether the specified role exists in the data store:

```
public static bool RoleExists(string roleName)
{
  return Provider.RoleExists(roleName);
}
```

The `GetAllRoles` method calls the `GetAllRoles` method of the configured role provider to retrieve all the available roles from the data store:

```
public static string[] GetAllRoles()
{
  return Provider.GetAllRoles();
}
```

As these code fragments show, all role management methods of the `Roles` class delegate to the configured role provider. In other words, the `Roles` class doesn't directly talk to the underlying data store. The `Roles` class has no idea what type of data access API the role provider uses to access the data store. The role providers shield the `Roles` class and therefore its clients from the diversity of the data access APIs, allowing them to work with all types of data stores.

Managing Users

The following sections discuss those methods of the `Roles` API that allow you to perform user management operations such as adding specified users to specified roles, removing specified users from specified roles, and retrieving users in specified roles.

Adding Specified Users to Specified Roles

The `Roles` API provides you with four different methods to add users to specified roles, as shown in the following code. Notice that all four methods delegate to the same `AddUsersToRoles` method of the `RoleProvider` base class. As this example shows, the `Roles` API doesn't have to mirror the `RoleProvider` API. The `RoleProvider` API is discussed later in this chapter.

```
public static void AddUsersToRole(string[] usernames, string roleName)
{
  Provider.AddUsersToRoles(usernames, new string[] { roleName });
}

public static void AddUsersToRoles(string[] usernames, string[] roleNames)
{
  Provider.AddUsersToRoles(usernames, roleNames);
}

public static void AddUserToRole(string username, string roleName)
{
  Provider.AddUsersToRoles(new string[] { username }, new string[] { roleName });
```

```
    }

    public static void AddUserToRoles(string username, string[] roleNames)
    {
        Provider.AddUsersToRoles(new string[] { username }, roleNames);
    }
```

Retrieving Users in Specified Roles

The Roles API exposes five methods to allow you inspect and search for users in specified roles. The FindUsersInRole method calls the FindUsersInRole method of the configured role provider to retrieve all users in the specified role whose username contains the specified string:

```
    public static string[] FindUsersInRole(string roleName, string usernameToMatch)
    {
        return Provider.FindUsersInRole(roleName, usernameToMatch);
    }
```

The GetRolesForUser method calls the GetRolesForUser method of the configured role provider to retrieve the roles that the specified user is in:

```
    public static string[] GetRolesForUser(string username)
    {
        return Provider.GetRolesForUser(username);
    }
```

This overload of the GetRolesForUser method retrieves the roles that the current user is in. Recall that the Identity property of the current principal exposes a property named Name that contains the user-name of the current user:

```
    public static string[] GetRolesForUser()
    {
        return Provider.GetRolesForUser(HttpContext.Current.User.Identity.Name);
    }
```

The IsUserInRole method calls the IsUserInRole method of the configured role provider to check whether the specified user is in the specified role:

```
    public static bool IsUserInRole(string username, string roleName)
    {
        return Provider.IsUserInRole(username, roleName);
    }
```

This overload of the IsUserInRole method checks whether the current user is in the specified role:

```
    public static bool IsUserInRole(string roleName)
    {
        return Provider.IsUserInRole(HttpContext.Current.User.Identity.Name, roleName);
    }
```

Notice that the preceding five methods of the Roles class, like other methods of this class, delegate the responsibility of interacting with the underlying data store to the configured role provider. As discussed, this allows the Roles class to work with all types of data stores.

Removing Specified Users from Specified Roles

The `Roles` API contains four methods to remove users from roles, as shown in the following code:

```
public static void RemoveUserFromRole(string username, string roleName)
{
    Provider.RemoveUsersFromRoles(
                new string[] { username }, new string[] { roleName });
}

public static void RemoveUserFromRoles(string username, string[] roleNames)
{
    Provider.RemoveUsersFromRoles(new string[] { username }, roleNames);
}

public static void RemoveUsersFromRole(string[] usernames, string roleName)
{
    Provider.RemoveUsersFromRoles(usernames, new string[] { roleName });
}

public static void RemoveUsersFromRoles(string[] usernames, string[] roleNames)
{
    Provider.RemoveUsersFromRoles(usernames, roleNames);
}
```

Notice that all four methods delegate to the same `RemoveUsersFromRoles` method of the configured role provider. This is yet another example of the fact that the `Roles` API doesn't have to mirror the `RoleProvider` API.

RolePrincipal

The security context of the entity on whose behalf .NET code is running is made up of two components:

❑ Identity

❑ Role membership

The entity could be a user, a program, and so on. The following two sections discuss these two components in detail.

Identity

There are different types of identities, and each type is established through a specific mechanism. For example, the identity of type `FormsIdentity` is established through Forms authentication, whereas the identity of type `WindowsIdentity` is established through Windows authentication. If those applications that need to access the identity were to deal with the underlying identity object directly, they would be tied to a particular type of identity and therefore a particular mechanism to establish the user identity.

For example, if the application were to use the `FormsIdentity` object directly, it would be tied to the Forms authentication mechanism and wouldn't work with other types of authentication mechanisms such as Windows authentication. The `IIdentity` interface isolates the application from the real type of the identity and provides it with a generic API to interact with the underlying identity. All types of identities such as `FormsIdentity` and `WindowsIdentity` implement the `IIdentity` interface.

Listing 23-1 illustrates the definition of the `IIdentity` interface.

Listing 23-1: The IIdentity interface

```
public interface IIdentity
{
  string AuthenticationType { get; }
  bool IsAuthenticated { get; }
  string Name { get; }
}
```

The `IIdentity` interface exposes the following properties:

- ❑ `AuthenticationType`: Specifies the authentication mechanism through which the identity is established. For example, if the identity is established through Forms authentication, the `AuthenticationType` returns the string `Forms`.

- ❑ `IsAuthenticated`: Specifies whether the identity has been established, that is, whether the user, program, and so forth on whose behalf the .NET code is running is authenticated.

- ❑ `Name`: Specifies the name associated with the identity. For example, if the identity is established through Forms authentication, the `Name` property returns the username. If the identity is established through Windows authentication, on the other hand, the `Name` property returns the Windows account name.

You can develop your own custom identity by writing a class that implements the three properties of the `IIdentity` interface.

Role Membership

Recall that the security context of the entity on whose behalf the code is running consists of two components: identity and role membership. There are different ways to establish role membership. As a matter of fact, different ASP.NET 1.x applications use different APIs to manage role membership. As you'll see later, the ASP.NET 2.0 presents its own way of handling role membership.

IPrincipal

The .NET Framework uses an object known as *principal* to represent the security context of the entity on whose behalf the code is running. There are different types of principal objects because there are different types of identities and role membership mechanisms. If an application were to use a particular type of principal object, it would be tied to that particular type and wouldn't be able to work with other types of principals or security contexts. The .NET Framework contains an interface named `IPrincipal` to isolate applications from the type of the underlying principal object. All principal types implement the `IPrincipal` interface. Listing 23-2 shows the definition of this interface.

Listing 23-2: The IPrincipal interface

```
public interface IPrincipal
{
```

```
    IIdentity Identity { get; }
    bool IsInRole(string role);
}
```

The interface contains the following members:

- ❑   `Identity`: Specifies the identity of the entity on whose behalf the code is running
- ❑   `IsInRole`: Determines whether the entity is in the specified role

The ASP.NET 2.0 Framework comes with a specific type of principal known as `RolePrincipal`. This section helps you look under the hood of the `RolePrincipal` where you can see for yourself how this principal is implemented so you learn what steps you must take to implement your own custom principal. Like all principals, `RolePrincipal` implements the `IPrincipal` interface. Listing 23-3 looks under the hood of the `IsInRole` method of the `RolePrincipal` class.

Listing 23-3: The IsInRole method

```
public bool IsInRole(string role)
{
  if (!IsRoleListCached)
  {
    roles.Clear();
    string[] rolesList =
                Roles.Providers[providerName].GetRolesForUser(Identity.Name);
    foreach (string role in roleList)
    {
      if (this.roles[role] == null)
        this.roles.Add(role, string.Empty);
    }
    this.isRoleListCached = true;
    this.cachedListChanged = true;
  }
  return (this.roles[role] != null);
}
```

`RolePrincipal` exposes a collection field of type `HybridDictionary` named `roles` that contains the roles the user is in. `RolePrincipal` also defines a Boolean property named `IsRoleListCached` that specifies whether the content of the `roles` collection is up to date. If it is, the `IsInRole` method uses the specified role name to index into the `roles` collection to check whether the collection contains the role.

If roles aren't already cached, the `IsInRole` method first needs to retrieve and cache the roles the user is in. The method clears the `roles` collection because the collection will be populated with fresh roles retrieved from the data store:

```
roles.Clear();
```

Next it calls the `GetRolesForUser` method of the configured role provider to retrieve the roles the user is in. `RolePrincipal` defines a private field named `providerName` that contains the friendly name of the role provider. The `IsInRole` method uses this friendly name to index into the `Providers` collection of the `Roles` class to access the role provider:

```
string[] rolesList = Roles.Providers[providerName].GetRolesForUser(Identity.Name);
```

The method then iterates through the roles that the GetRolesForUser method returns and adds each one to the roles collection:

```
foreach (string role in roleList)
{
  if (this.roles[role] == null)
    this.roles.Add(role, string.Empty);
}
```

Next the method sets the IsRoleListCached property to true to signal that the roles have already been retrieved from data store and cached. This ensures that the same roles aren't retrieved multiple times from the data store.

```
this.isRoleListCached = true;
```

Finally, the IsInRole method sets the CachedListChanged property to true to signal that the cache has been modified. As you'll see later, at the end of each request, the roles are stored in a cookie to improve the performance of the application. The logic that stores the roles in the cookie uses the CachedListChanged property to determine whether the content of the existing cookie is out of date:

```
this.cachedListChanged = true;
```

RolePrincipal implements a method named GetRoles that returns the list of roles the user is in, as shown in Listing 23-4. Notice that this method performs the same tasks as the IsInRole method if the roles aren't cached. At the end the method loads the content of the roles collection into an array and returns the array.

Listing 23-4: The GetRoles method returns the list of roles the user is in

```
public string[] GetRoles()
{
  if (!isRoleListCached)
  {
    roles.Clear();
    string[] roleList =
            Roles.Providers[providerName].GetRolesForUser(Identity.Name);
    foreach (string role in roleList)
    {
      if (this.roles[role] == null)
        this.roles.Add(role, string.Empty);
    }

    this.isRoleListCached = true;
    this.cachedListChanged = true;
    return roleList;
  }
  string[] roleList = new string[this.roles.Count];
  int num1 = 0;
  foreach (string role in this.roles.Keys)
  {
    roleList[num1++] = role;
  }
  return roleList;
}
```

`RolePrincipal` implements a method named `ToEncryptedTicket`. To keep the discussions focused, this section skips the details of the implementation of this method and presents a pseudocode instead. Listing 23-5 shows this pseudocode. As you'll see later, the return value of this method will be stored in a cookie.

Listing 23-5: The pseudocode for the ToEncryptedTicket method

```
public string ToEncryptedTicket()
{
  byte[] combinedBuffer;
  byte[] serializedRolePrincipal = SerializeRolePrincipal(this);
  AddToBuffer(serializedRolePrincipal, combinedBuffer);

  if ((cookieProtection == CookieProtection.All) ||
      (cookieProtection == CookieProtection.Validation))
  {
    byte[] hash = ComputeBufferHash(combinedBuffer);
    AddToBuffer(hash, combinedBuffer);
  }

  if ((cookieProtection == CookieProtection.All) ||
      (cookieProtection == CookieProtection.Encryption))
    EncryptBuffer(combinedBuffer);

  return EncodeBuffer(combinedBuffer);
}
```

As Listing 23-5 illustrates, the `ToEncryptedTicket` method first serializes the `RolePrincipal` object. Under the hood, `ToEncryptedTicket` uses a `BinaryFormatter` to serialize `RolePrincipal` into its binary format:

```
byte[] serializedRolePrincipal = SerializeRolePrincipal(this);
```

The method then adds the content of the buffer that contains the serialized `RolePrincipal` into a local buffer named `combinedBuffer`:

```
AddToBuffer(serializedRolePrincipal, combinedBuffer);
```

Next, the method checks whether the content of the cookie should be validated. If so, it computes the hash of the content of the `combinedBuffer` (recall that this content is nothing but the `serializedRolePrincipal`) and adds the hash to the `combinedBuffer`. In other words, the `combinedBuffer` now contains both the `serializedRolePrincipal` and its hash. The hash is used in subsequent requests to validate the cookie to ensure it hasn't been tampered with. In other words, the hash is used to ensure the integrity of the cookie.

```
if ((cookieProtection == CookieProtection.All) ||
    (cookieProtection == CookieProtection.Validation))
{
  byte[] hash = ComputeBufferHash(combinedBuffer);
  AddToBuffer(hash, combinedBuffer);
}
```

The method then checks whether the content of the cookie should be encrypted. If so, it encrypts the content of the `combinedBuffer`. The `combinedBuffer` now contains an encrypted content:

```
if ((cookieProtection == CookieProtection.All) ||
    (cookieProtection == CookieProtection.Encryption))
  EncryptBuffer(combinedBuffer);
```

Finally, the method encodes the content of `combinedBuffer` into its Base64 representation, which is suitable for storing in a cookie. As you'll see later, at the end of the request, the return value of the `ToEncryptedTicket` method will be stored in a cookie.

```
return EncodeBuffer(combinedBuffer);
```

`RolePrincipal` implements a method named `InitFromEncryptedTicket` that does the opposite of the `ToEncryptedTicket` method — it rebuilds the original `RolePrincipal` object from the return value of the `ToEncryptedTicket` method.

`RolePrincipal` defines a constructor that takes the following two arguments:

❑ The `IIdentity` object that represents the identity of the user.

❑ The string that contains the `RolePrincipal` object in its encrypted serialized format. This string is nothing but the return value of the `ToEncryptedTicket` method. As you'll see later, at the beginning of the request, the content of the cookie is retrieved and passed into this constructor.

As Listing 23-6 shows, this constructor calls the `InitFromEncryptedTicket` method to rebuild the original `RolePrincipal` object.

Listing 23-6: The RolePrincipal constructor

```
public RolePrincipal(IIdentity identity, string encryptedTicket)
{
  this.identity = identity;
  this.providerName = Roles.Provider.Name;
  InitFromEncryptedTicket(encryptedTicket);
}
```

Another method of `RolePrincipal` of interest is the `SetDirty` method. As Listing 23-7 illustrates, this method sets the `IsRoleListCached` property to false to signal that roles aren't cached and should be retrieved from the underlying data store:

```
this.isRoleListCached = false;
```

It then sets the `CachedListChanged` property to true to signal that content of the role cookie should be updated at the end of the request.

Listing 23-7: The SetDirty method

```
public void SetDirty()
{
    this.isRoleListCached = false;
    this.cachedListChanged = true;
}
```

RoleManagerModule

Chapter 8 followed a request for a resource with extension .aspx from the time it arrived in the Web server all the way through the request processing architecture to help you identify and understand different components of the ASP.NET request processing architecture. One of the components that was discussed in Chapter 8 is a .NET component named HttpApplicationFactory. This component maintains a pool of HttpApplication objects.

HttpApplicationFactory assigns the task of handling the current request to an HttpApplication object from the pool. If the pool is empty, HttpApplicationFactory instantiates and initializes an HttpApplication object. As part of its initialization, the HttpApplication object instantiates all the registered HTTP modules and calls their Init method.

The Init method of each module registers one or more callbacks for one or more events of the HttpApplication object. Recall that the HttpApplication object exposes numerous application-level events such as AuthenticateRequest, PostAuthenticateRequest, and EndRequest.

One of the HTTP modules that the HttpApplication object instantiates is a module named RoleManagerModule. This section looks under the hood of this module so you can see for yourself how the module works from the inside out.

The Init method of this module registers two callbacks named PostAuthenticateRequestCallback and EndRequestCallback for the PostAuthenticateRequest and EndRequest events of the HttpApplication object as shown in Listing 23-8.

Listing 23-8: The Init method of the RoleManagerModule

```
public void Init(HttpApplication application)
{
  application.PostAuthenticateRequest +=
                          new EventHandler(PostAuthenticateRequestCallback);
  application.EndRequest += new EventHandler(EndRequestCallback);
}
```

The HttpApplication object raises its PostAuthenticateRequest event after the AuthenticateRequest event. Recall that this object raises the AuthenticateRequest event after it authenticates the request.

PostAuthenticateRequestCallback

Listing 23-9 reverse-engineers the PostAuthenticateRequestCallback method.

Listing 23-9: The PostAuthenticateRequestCallback method

```
private void PostAuthenticateRequestCallback(object sender, EventArgs e)
{
  if (Roles.Enabled)
  {
    HttpApplication application = sender as HttpApplication;
    HttpContext context = application.Context;
```

(continued)

Listing 23-9: *(continued)*

```
    if (getRoles != null)
    {
      RoleManagerEventArgs args = new RoleManagerEventArgs(context);
      getRoles(this, args);
      if (args.RolesPopulated)
        return;
    }

    string roles = null;
    if (context.User.Identity.IsAuthenticated && Roles.CacheRolesInCookie)
    {
      HttpCookie cookie = context.Request.Cookies[Roles.CookieName];
      if (cookie != null)
        roles = cookie.Value;
    }

    RolePrincipal user = null;

    if (roles != null)
      user = new RolePrincipal(context.User.Identity, roles);

    else
      user = new RolePrincipal(context.User.Identity);

    context.User = user;
  }
}
```

The `PostAuthenticateRequestCallback` method first checks whether the page developer has enabled role management for the current application. The page developer sets the enabled attribute on the `<roleManager>` element of the `Web.config` or `Machine.config` file to enable role management.

As Listing 23-9 illustrates, if role management is enabled, the `PostAuthenticateRequestCallback` method accesses the `HttpContext` object:

```
HttpApplication application = sender as HttpApplication;
HttpContext context = application.Context;
```

The method next raises an event of type `RoleManagerEventHandler` named `GetRoles`. The event data for this event is held in an instance of the `RoleManagerEventArgs` class. This class exposes a Boolean property named `RolesPopulated`. The `RoleManagerEventHandler` and `RoleManagerEventArgs` classes are discussed later in this chapter. Page developers can register a callback for this event where they can set the `RolesPopulated` property to true to bypass the rest of the code in the `PostAuthenticateRequestCallback`.

```
if (getRoles != null)
{
  RoleManagerEventArgs args = new RoleManagerEventArgs(context);
  getRoles(this, args);
```

```
      if (args.RolesPopulated)
        return;
    }
```

If the page developer hasn't set the RolesPopulated property to true,
PostAuthenticateRequestCallback searches the Cookies collection of the Request for a cookie
whose name is given by Roles.CookieName property. If it finds the cookie, it retrieves its content. As
you'll see later, the content of the role cookie is nothing but the return value of the ToEncryptedTicket
method of the RolePrincipal class.

```
    HttpCookie cookie = context.Request.Cookies[Roles.CookieName];
    if (cookie != null)
      roles = cookie.Value;
```

Next, the method calls the RolePrincipal constructor and passes the cookie content into it:

```
    user = new RolePrincipal(context.User.Identity, roles);
```

As shown in Listing 23-6, the RolePrincipal constructor rebuilds the original RolePrincipal object
from the cookie content.

Finally, the method assigns the RolePrincipal object to the User property of the current HttpContext
object:

```
    context.User = user;
```

GetRoles Event

RoleManagerModule exposes an event of type RoleManagerEventHandler named GetRoles. As
shown in Listing 23-9, the PostAuthenticateRequestCallback method raises this event before it
instantiates an instance of the RolePrincipal class and populates it with the roles the user is in. Page
developers can register a callback for this event where they can instantiate and populate their own custom IPrincipal object.

Listing 23-10 contains the code for the RoleManagerEventArgs event data class. This class exposes two
properties: Context, which refers to the current HttpContext object, and RolesPopulated, which
specifies whether the PostAuthenticateRequestCallback method should go ahead and instantiate
an instance of the RolePrincipal class and populate it with the roles that the user is in.

Listing 23-10: The RoleManagerEventArgs event data class

```
    public sealed class RoleManagerEventArgs : EventArgs
    {
      public RoleManagerEventArgs(HttpContext context)
      {
        this.context = context;
      }

      private HttpContext context;
      public HttpContext Context
```

(continued)

Listing 23-10: *(continued)*

```
  {
    get {return context;}
  }

  private bool rolsePopulated;
  public bool RolesPopulated
  {
    get {return rolesPopulated;}
    set {rolesPopulated=value; }
  }
}
```

The following code illustrates the declaration of the `RoleManagerEventHandler` event delegate:

```
public delegate void
RoleManagerEventHandler(object sender, RoleManagerEventArgs e);
```

The following code contains the definition of the `GetRoles` event:

```
Private RoleManagerEventHandler getRoles;
public event RoleManagerEventHandler GetRoles
{
  add
  {
    getRoles = Delegate.Combine(getRoles, value) as RoleManagerEventHandler;
  }
  remove
  {
    getRoles = Delegate.Remove(getRoles, value) as RoleManagerEventHandler;
  }
}
```

EndRequestCallback

Recall that the `RoleManagerModule` registers the `EndRequestCallback` method for the `EndRequest` event of the `HttpApplication` object (see Listing 23-8). Listing 23-11 shows the `EndRequestCallback` method.

Listing 23-11: The EndRequestCallback method

```
private void EndRequestCallback(object sender, EventArgs e)
{
  if (Roles.Enabled && Roles.CacheRolesInCookie)
  {
    HttpApplication application = sender as HttpApplication;
    HttpContext context = application.Context;
    RolePrincipal principal = context.User as RolePrincipal;

    if (principal != null && principal.Identity.IsAuthenticated &&
        principal.CachedListChanged && context.Request.Browser.Cookies)
    {
```

```
        string encryptedTicket = principal.ToEncryptedTicket();
        HttpCookie cookie = new HttpCookie(Roles.CookieName, encryptedTicket);
        cookie.HttpOnly = true;
        cookie.Path = Roles.CookiePath;
        cookie.Domain = Roles.Domain;
        if (Roles.CreatePersistentCookie)
          cookie.Expires = principal.ExpireDate;

        cookie.Secure = Roles.CookieRequireSSL;
        context.Response.Cookies.Add(cookie);
      }
    }
  }
```

The main responsibility of the `EndRequestCallback` method is to store the list of roles that the `RolePrincipal` object contains in a cookie, and add the cookie to the outgoing response. This will improve the performance because it saves the application from having to retrieve the same role information from the data store in the next request.

To store the role information in a cookie, the `EndRequestCallback` method accesses the `RolePrincipal` object that represents the security context of the current user. Recall that this object contains the roles the current user is in:

```
HttpApplication application = sender as HttpApplication;
HttpContext context = application.Context;
RolePrincipal principal = context.User as RolePrincipal;
```

Next, the method checks whether all the following conditions are met:

❑   The user is authenticated:

```
principal.Identity.IsAuthenticated == true
```

❑   The role information has changed:

```
principal.CachedListChanged == true
```

❑   The requesting browser supports cookies:

```
context.Request.Browser.Cookies == true
```

If all these conditions are met, the method calls the `ToEncryptedTicket` method of the `RolePrincipal` object. As shown in Listing 23-5, this method serializes the `RolePrincipal` object into its serialized representation, encrypts this serialized representation, and encodes this encrypted serialized representation into its Base64 string representation, which is suitable for storing in a cookie.

```
        string encryptedTicket = principal.ToEncryptedTicket();
```

The method then creates a cookie to contain the Base64-encoded encrypted serialized string representation of the `RolePrincipal` object:

```
HttpCookie cookie = new HttpCookie(Roles.CookieName, encryptedTicket);
```

The method checks whether the cookie should be persisted on the client machine. If so, it assigns the value of the `ExpireDate` property of the `RolePrincipal` object to the `Expires` property of the cookie to specify how long the cookie should be kept on the client machine before it's no longer valid:

```
if (Roles.CreatePersistentCookie)
  cookie.Expires = principal.ExpireDate;
```

The method then specifies whether the requesting browser should use SSL to send the cookie back to the server to ensure the integrity and privacy of the content of the cookie:

```
cookie.Secure = Roles.CookieRequireSSL;
```

Finally, the method adds the cookie to the outgoing response:

```
context.Response.Cookies.Add(cookie);
```

Summary

This chapter helped you gain a solid understanding of the components of the ASP.NET role management model.

This chapter also helped you understand the following important facts about a role provider:

❑   What role each method or property of the role provider plays in the ASP.NET role management model

❑   How each method or property of the role provider isolates the rest of the model from the diversity of the data access APIs

The next chapter builds on this chapter to show you how to develop your own custom role provider, role principal, and role manager module.

24

Developing Custom Role Providers, Modules, and Principals

In the previous chapter, you learned about the main components of the ASP.NET role model: `Roles`, `RoleManagerModule`, and `RolePrincipal`. You could also see for yourself how role providers isolate the other components of the model from the data store data access-specific APIs, allowing them to work with any type of data store.

This chapter implements the following custom components to show you how to develop your own custom role providers, role manager modules, and role principals:

❑   XmlRoleProvider

❑   CustomRolePrincipal

❑   CustomRoleManagerModule

RoleProvider

All role providers derive from the `RoleProvider` abstract base class. The base class defines the contract between the role providers and their clients, such as the `Roles` class. This isolates the clients from the real type of the role provider class being used.

The `RoleProvider` base class exposes all the properties and methods that the clients expect from a role provider regardless of its type. This means that all role providers must implement all of these properties and methods to honor the contract. Listing 24-1 shows the properties and methods of the `RoleProvider` base class. The `RoleProvider` class, like all provider base classes, derives from the `ProviderBase` abstract class.

Listing 24-1: The RoleProvider base class

```
public abstract class RoleProvider : ProviderBase
{
  public abstract string ApplicationName { get; set; }

  public abstract void AddUsersToRoles(string[] usernames, string[] roleNames);
  public abstract void CreateRole(string roleName);
  public abstract bool DeleteRole(string roleName, bool throwOnPopulatedRole);
  public abstract string[] FindUsersInRole(string roleName,
                                           string usernameToMatch);
  public abstract string[] GetAllRoles();
  public abstract string[] GetRolesForUser(string username);
  public abstract string[] GetUsersInRole(string roleName);
  public abstract bool IsUserInRole(string username, string roleName);
  public abstract void RemoveUsersFromRoles(string[] usernames,
                                            string[] roleNames);
  public abstract bool RoleExists(string roleName);
}
```

XmlRoleProvider

This section develops a custom role provider named XmlRoleProvider that retrieves role information from and stores role information in an XML file. XmlRoleProvider derives from the RoleProvider base class, as mentioned. Because RoleProvider derives from ProviderBase, XmlRoleProvider must implement the methods and properties of both the ProviderBase and RoleProvider classes, as discussed in the following sections.

When you're developing an XML-based component such as XmlRoleProvider, the first order of business is to decide on the XML format or schema that your component will support. Listing 24-2 shows an example of the XML document that XmlRoleProvider supports. As you'll see later, the methods of XmlRoleProvider will retrieve role information from and store role information in this XML document.

Listing 24-2: An example of the XML format the XmlRoleProvider supports

```
<?xml version="1.0" encoding="utf-8"?>
<roles>
  <role roleName="Admin" applicationName="/">
    <user userName="John" />
    <user userName="George" />
    <user userName="Steve" />
  </role>
  <role roleName="Moderator" applicationName="/">
    <user userName="Smith" />
  </role>
</roles>
```

This XML document has a single document element, <roles>. This element contains zero or more <role> elements, where each <role> element, in turn, contains zero or more <user> elements. Each <role> element has two required attributes named roleName and applicationName, and each <user> element has a required attribute named userName.

ProviderBase

Just as you saw with the membership providers in Chapter 22, the `ProviderBase` class provides the base functionality that all ASP.NET providers including role and membership providers must support. As discussed, `ProviderBase` exposes an important method named `Initialize` that all providers must implement.

The main responsibility of the `Initialize` method of a role provider is to iterate through the `NameValueCollection` and initialize the provider's properties. Listing 24-3 shows the code for the `Initialize` method of the `XmlRoleProvider`.

Listing 24-3: The Initialize method of the XmlRoleProvider

```
public override void Initialize(string name, NameValueCollection config)
{
  if (config == null)
    throw new ArgumentNullException("config");

  if (string.IsNullOrEmpty(name))
    name = "XmlRoleProvider";

  if (string.IsNullOrEmpty(config["description"]))
  {
    config.Remove("description");
    config.Add("description", "Stores role information in an XML document");
  }
  base.Initialize(name, config);

  applicationName = config["applicationName"];
  if (string.IsNullOrEmpty(applicationName))
    applicationName = "/";
  config.Remove("applicationName");

  dataFile = config["dataFile"];
  if (string.IsNullOrEmpty(dataFile))
    dataFile = "roles.xml";
  config.Remove("dataFile");

  if (config.Count > 0)
  {
    string key = config.GetKey(0);
    if (!string.IsNullOrEmpty(key))
      throw new ProviderException("Unrecognized attribute");
  }

  CreateXmlFile();
}
```

The `Initialize` method of the `XmlRoleProvider` class follows the same steps described in Chapter 22 to initialize the `XmlRoleProvider`. The `Initialize` method calls the `CreateXmlFile` method to create the XML file where the role information will be stored if the file doesn't already exist. Listing 24-4 contains the code for the `CreateXmlFile` method.

Listing 24-4: The CreateXmlFile method

```
private void CreateXmlFile()
{
  if (!File.Exists(HttpContext.Current.Server.MapPath(dataFile)))
  {
    XmlWriterSettings settings = new XmlWriterSettings();
    settings.Indent = true;

    using (XmlWriter writer = XmlWriter.Create(
                        HttpContext.Current.Server.MapPath(dataFile), settings))
    {
      writer.WriteStartDocument();
      writer.WriteStartElement("roles");
      writer.WriteEndElement();
      writer.WriteEndDocument();
    }
  }
}
```

The CreateXmlFile method first checks whether the file path specified by the dataFile field exists. If it doesn't, the method creates a new XML file as a backing store for role information. As Listing 24-4 shows, CreateXmlFile uses an XmlWriter to generate the <roles> document element of the XML document that will store the role information.

The CreateXmlFile method is one of the many methods of XmlRoleProvider that makes use of XML APIs such as XmlWriter. Developing an XML-based component such as XmlRoleProvider requires a solid understanding of the available XML APIs and their pros and cons, because as you'll see later in this chapter, your choice of XML API will have significant impact on the performance, memory usage, usability, and standard compliance level of your component.

The following sections discuss the available XML APIs and their pros and cons to show you the factors that you should consider when you're choosing an XML API to implement an XML-based custom component such as XmlRoleProvider.

XML APIs

In general, there are two groups of XML APIs: streaming XML APIs and random-access XML APIs. The following sections discuss these two groups in detail.

Streaming XML APIs

As the name implies, streaming XML APIs stream the XML content, as opposed to caching it in memory. As an example, consider loading an XML file in memory. As you'll see later, almost all methods of XmlRoleProvider need to load the underlying XML file in memory before they can perform their tasks. For example, the DeleteRole method needs to load the file in memory so it can locate the role that it needs to delete. To load an XML file in memory, you have two options.

As you'll see later, you can use a random-access XML API to load the entire file, that is, all its XML nodes in memory. This means that when a method such as DeleteRole is invoked, the following two tasks are performed in order:

1. All the nodes are first loaded in memory.

2. The method uses a technology such as XPath to locate the specified node among other nodes in memory to perform its task. For example, the DeleteRole method uses XPath to locate the specified role node among other nodes and deletes it.

Alternatively, you can use a streaming XML API to load the XML file in streaming fashion, where only the currently loaded node is kept in memory. This means that when a method such as DeleteRole is invoked, the following two tasks are performed in order:

1. The next node is loaded in memory.

2. The method checks whether the currently loaded node is the node it's looking for. If so, it performs its task on the node. For example, the DeleteRole method checks whether the currently loaded node is the role that it's supposed to delete. If it is, it deletes the node.

The streaming XML APIs have their own pluses and minuses. On the plus side, they improve performance because they don't cache the XML in memory. As an example, consider the performance of the DeleteRole method when the underlying data store is a large XML file. Loading the entire content of a huge file in memory just to delete a single role would dramatically degrade the performance of the DeleteRole method. Besides, there is really no need to cache all the nodes in memory to delete a role. It's much more efficient if you load the file in streaming fashion, where you load the next node in memory and check whether it's the role that you need to delete. If it is, you can just delete the node and stop loading the rest of the nodes. If it isn't, you can load the next node and repeat the process until you find the role node you're looking for.

The streaming XML APIs also consume far less memory because they don't cache the XML. For example, in the case of loading the XML file that contains the role information, it allows you to load any size XML file no matter how large it is because you only keep the currently loaded node in memory.

On the minus side, the streaming XML APIs don't allow you to access XML nodes in random fashion because only the currently loaded node is kept in memory. As you'll see later, this is really not an issue because in most cases you don't really need to access the XML nodes randomly. For example, when you think about it, the DeleteRole method doesn't really need random access to the nodes of its underlying XML file because the method can easily use a streaming XML API to scan through the document in streaming fashion and locate the specified role.

That said, there are cases where you need to access the nodes in random fashion. For example, if you need to use XSLT, you have no choice but to the load the entire document in memory because XSLT uses XPath queries to access the nodes in random fashion.

The streaming XML APIs also don't let you cache the XML document in memory. In some cases you can actually improve the performance of your application if you cache the frequently used information in memory. For example, if the XML file that contains the role information isn't too large and your application needs to access the file on frequent basis, it makes more sense to use a random-access XML API to load and to cache the entire file in memory.

The .NET Framework provides you with two streaming XML APIs: XmlReader streaming XML API and XmlWriter streaming XML API, as discussed in the following sections.

XmlReader Streaming XML API

The methods, properties, and events of the XmlReader abstract base class define the XmlReader streaming XML API. This API allows you to read and to navigate XML content in streaming fashion. In other words, this API provides you with read-only, forward-only access to the XML content. The .NET Framework comes with three concrete implementations of the XmlReader streaming XML API as follows:

❑ XmlTextReader: Allows you to read XML content serialized as XML 1.0 in streaming fashion. For example, XmlRoleProvider can use an XmlTextReader to read the XML file that contains the role information.

❑ XmlValidatingReader: Allows you to validate the XML content that XmlTextReader reads in streaming fashion. For example, XmlRoleProvider can use an XmlValidatingReader to validate the XML stream that the XmlTextReader reads from the XML file that contains the role information.

❑ XmlNodeReader: Allows you to read a node and its child nodes in streaming fashion. For example, you can use XmlNodeReader to stream the contents of an XmlDocument.

You can also provide your own implementation for the XmlReader API to retrieve data in XML format from data stores where the data isn't serialized as XML 1.0. For example, you can provide an implementation that makes a SQL Server database that holds the role information look like an XML document. This will allow XML-based Web applications to read role information from this SQL Server database as if it were an XML document.

As discussed, there are at least three different implementations of the XmlReader streaming API. If XmlRoleProvider were to use one of these implementations, it would be tied to that implementation and wouldn't work with other implementations. This is where the XmlReader abstract base class comes to the rescue.

As mentioned, the methods, properties, and events of this base class define the XmlReader streaming API. The XmlReader base class isolates components such as XmlRoleProvider from the underlying implementation of this base class, allowing these components to work with all implementations of the base class.

You may be wondering how components such as XmlRoleProvider instantiate the underlying XmlReader subclass if these components have no clue what the type of the subclass is. This is where the Create static method of the XmlReader abstract class comes into play. This method allows components such as XmlRoleProvider to instantiate the underlying XmlReader subclass in generic fashion without knowing its real type, as shown in the following fragment:

```
XmlReader reader = XmlReader.Create("persons.xml")
```

However, this raises another issue. How do you specify the features that you want the XmlReader subclass to support? First you'll see how you would accomplish this in .NET 1.x Framework. If you wanted to instantiate an XmlReader subclass that supports the features you need, such as validating the XML document that contains the role information against one or more schemas, you'd have to take the following steps to accomplish this task in .NET 1.x Framework:

1. Search the existing XmlReader subclasses for a subclass that supports these features. For example, the XmlValidatingReader subclass of XmlReader allows you to validate the XML document that contains the role information before you commit your changes to the underlying XML file.

2. Use the new operator to directly instantiate the preceding subclass. For example, the following fragment instantiates the XmlValidatingReader:

```
XmlValidatingReader vreader = new XmlValidatingReader(
                                    new XmlTextReader("persons.xml"));
```

There are a couple of problems with the .NET 1.x approach. It expects you to search the existing XmlReader subclasses for a subclass that supports the features you need. This requires you to have a solid understanding of these subclasses and their differences. Also, it leads to the proliferation of XmlReader subclasses because the only way to add a new feature is to add a new subclass. This in turn makes your life harder because you have to learn more subclasses.

To avoid these problems, the .NET 2.0 Framework has taken a completely different approach. It provides you with a new class named XmlReaderSettings that you can use to specify the features that you'd like the underlying XmlReader subclass to support. You simply pass this XmlReaderSettings object into the Create method and leave the responsibility of creating the XmlReader subclass that supports your desired features to this method. For example, the XmlReaderSettings shown in the following fragment instructs the Create method to create an XmlReader subclass that allows you to validate the XML document that contains the role information:

```
XmlReaderSettings settings = new XmlReaderSettings();
settings.ValidationType = ValidationType.Schema;
settings.Schemas.Add("http://myschemas.com/roles", "roles.xsd");

using (XmlReader reader = XmlReader.Create("roles.xml", settings))
{
   while (reader.Read())
   {
   }
}
```

The following are the methods and properties of the XmlReader streaming XML API that you'll use to implement XmlRoleProvider. The complete coverage of the XmlReader API is beyond the scope of this book.

❑ NamespaceUri: Gets the namespace that the current node belongs to.

❑ Prefix: Gets the namespace prefix of the current node.

❑ LocalName: Gets the name of the current node without its namespace prefix.

❑ IsEmptyElement: Specifies whether the current element node contains child elements. For example, as you'll see later, the <user> elements are empty elements.

❑ NodeType: Gets the type of the current node. Some of the possible values are XmlNodeType.Element and XmlNodeType.CDATA.

❑ Read(): Loads the next node in memory.

❑ MoveToContent(): Moves to the next content node if the current node isn't a content node. A content node is a node of one of the following types: non-white space text, CDATA, Element, EndElement, EntityReference, or EndEntity. XmlRoleProvider uses this method to locate the <roles> element.

❑ ReadToDescendant(elementName): Locates the first descendant element of the current node with the specified name. XmlRoleProvider uses this method to locate the first <role> element.

699

❑ ReadToNextSibling(elementName): Locates the first sibling element of the current node with the specified name. XmlRoleProvider uses this method to locate the next <role> element.

❑ GetAttribute(attributeName): Gets the value of the attribute with the specified name. XmlRoleProvider uses this method to retrieve the attribute values of the <role> and <user> elements.

❑ ReadSubtree(): Returns an XmlReader that contains the current node and all its descendants. XmlRoleProvider uses this method to access the XmlReader that contains a <role> element and its <user> child elements.

XmlWriter Streaming XML API

The methods, properties, and events of the XmlWriter abstract base class define the XmlWriter streaming XML API. This API allows you to generate XML content in streaming fashion. The .NET Framework comes with a concrete implementation of the XmlWriter API named XmlTextWriter that allows you to generate XML text that complies with the XML 1.0 specification.

You can also provide your own implementation for the XmlWriter API to write XML content in streaming fashion to data stores where the data isn't serialized as XML 1.0. For example, you can provide an implementation that makes a SQL Server database that holds the role information look like an XML document. This will allow XML-based Web applications to write role information to this SQL Server database as if it were an XML document.

As mentioned, the methods, properties, and events of the XmlWriter base class define the XmlWriter streaming API. The XmlWriter base class isolates components such as XmlRoleProvider from the underlying implementation of this base class, allowing these components to work with all implementations of the base class.

Following the same line of argument that showed why the .NET 2.0 Framework introduces the Create method of the XmlReader class and the XmlReaderSettings class, the XmlWriter class exposes a Create method that takes an argument of type XmlWriterSettings. The Create method together with the XmlWriterSettings class provide the same benefits as the Create method and XmlReaderSettings class, as discussed in the previous section.

For example, the XmlWriterSettings shown in the following code fragment instructs the Create method to create an XmlWriter subclass that supports indentation:

```
XmlWriterSettings settings = new XmlWriterSettings();
settings.Indent = true;

using (XmlWriter writer = XmlWriter.Create("persons.xml", settings))
{
    . . .
}
```

The following are some of the methods and properties of the XmlWriter streaming XML API that you'll use to implement XmlRoleProvider. The complete coverage of the XmlWriter API is beyond the scope of this book.

❑ WriteStartElement(elementName): Renders the opening tag of the element with the specified name. XmlRoleProvider uses this method to render the opening tags of the roles, role, and user elements.

❑ WriteEndElement(): Renders the closing tag of the last element whose opening tag was rendered. XmlRoleProvider uses this method to render the closing tags of the roles and role elements.

❑ WriteAttributeString(name,value): Renders the name and value of the specified attribute. XmlRoleProvider uses this method to render the roleName and applicationName attributes of the <role> elements and the userName attribute of the <user> elements.

❑ WriteNode: Renders the specified node and all its descendant nodes. XmlRoleProvider uses this method to save the changes back to the underlying XML file.

❑ WriteAttributes(XmlReader reader, Boolean): Writes out all the attributes of the node that the XmlReader currently points to.

The discussion of the XmlReader and XmlWriter streaming XML APIs wraps up with the following two handy rules of thumb:

❑ Stream your XML unless you have a good reason not to.

❑ Use XmlReader and XmlWriter in using statements. Recall that only instances of classes that implement IDisposable can be used in using statements. IDisposable exposes a method named Dispose that the using statement guarantees to automatically call when the instance goes out of scope. XmlWriter and XmlReader both implement IDisposable, where their implementation of the Dispose method calls their Close methods. It's highly recommended that you use XmlWriter and XmlReader in using statements to ensure their Close methods are called when they go out of scope.

Random-Access XML APIs

As the name implies, random-access XML APIs allow you to access the XML nodes in random fashion. To accomplish this task, these APIs have no choice but to cache all the nodes in memory, as opposed to the streaming XML APIs where only the current node is kept in memory.

The random-access XML APIs have their own pluses and minuses. On the plus side, there are cases where you need to access the nodes in random fashion. As mentioned before, if you need to use XSLT, you have to use a random-access XML API.

In addition, these APIs allow you to cache the XML document in memory. There are cases where you can improve the performance of your application if you cache the frequently used information in memory, as mentioned before.

On the minus side, the random-access XML APIs degrade performance because they cache all the XML nodes in memory. For example, loading the entire content of a huge file in memory just to delete a single role would dramatically degrade the performance of the DeleteRole method. They also consume far more memory because they cache the XML. This puts an upper limit on the size of XML documents that these APIs can handle.

The .NET Framework provides you with two random-access XML APIs: DOM random-access XML API and XPathNavigator random-access XML API, as discussed in the following sections.

DOM Random-Access XML API

The W3C Document Object Model (DOM) API is a huge API that requires the DOM processor to form an in-memory hierarchy or tree of nodes to represent the content of the underlying XML document. Later in this chapter you'll see a version of `XmlRoleProvider` that uses this API. For now, here are the pros and cons of the API.

One of the main advantages of DOM API is that it's intuitive and easy to use. For example, consider how this API adds a new branch to an existing node tree. You first build the branch and then attach it to the tree.

One of the few shortcomings of the DOM API is that it consumes server resources to form the tree structure. This factor plays a significant role when the XML document that contains the role information is too large. The larger the document is, the more resources are consumed. However, this is not an issue when you're loading a small document.

In addition, forming the tree structure is yet another duplication of data, which is a major problem if the XML document that contains the role information is too large. However, this is not an issue with small documents.

Also, because the DOM data model closely mirrors the XML 1.0 specification, it contains types such as `CDATA` that only provide lexical information, which has nothing to do with the information content of the XML document. This is a problem in that it complicates the DOM API because the API has to support lexical types in addition to the types that represent the information content of the XML document. It also doesn't support what is known as XML virtualization. Because the DOM data model is so tied to the XML 1.0 specification, it can't be used to virtualize non-XML document data stores as XML documents.

`XmlDocument` is the .NET Framework's implementation of the W3C DOM API Level 2. `XmlDocument` is also one of the three classes that are known as *XML data stores*. The other two classes are `XPathDocument` and `XmlDataDocument`. These three classes are called XML data stores because they are used to store or cache XML in memory as opposed to the streaming model, where only the current node is cached.

XPathNavigator Random-Access XML API

One of the great things about the `XmlReader` and `XmlWriter` streaming APIs is their cursor-style capability. As an example, look at the cursor-style capability of the `XmlReader`. This capability allows you to use the following two steps to retrieve information about a node of interest:

1. Use a method such as `Read` to position the `XmlReader` on the node of interest.

2. Use the properties and methods of the `XmlReader` itself to retrieve information about the node on which the reader is positioned.

For example, the following fragment uses the `Read` method to position the `XmlReader` on the specified node and uses the `NodeType`, `LocalName`, and `GetAttribute` members of the `XmlReader` to access the node type, local name, and the value of the `roleName` attribute of the element node on which the reader is positioned:

```
using (XmlReader reader = XmlReader.Create("roles.xml"))
{
  while (reader.Read())
  {
    if (reader.NodeType == XmlNodeType.Element)
    {
      if (reader.LocalName == "role" &&
          reader.GetAttribute("roleName") == rolename)
      {
```

```
            . . .
        }
      }
    }
  }
```

The main problem with the cursor-style capability of the XmlReader is that you can't move the cursor backward. Once you position the XmlReader on a node, you can't position the reader on the previous nodes. The reader can only move forward.

The XPathNavigator random-access API offers the same cursor-style capability as the XmlReader without the preceding limitation. The XPathNavigator random-access XML API uses an XML data store such as XmlDocument and XPathDocument as its backing store. Because XML data stores cache the entire XML document in memory, the cursor of the XPathNavigator API can be randomly positioned on any node.

All XML data stores implement the IXPathNavigable interface. This interface exposes a single method named CreateNavigator that returns an object of type XPathNavigator. The methods and properties of the XPathNavigator class define the XPathNavigator random-access API.

You have to follow steps similar to the XmlReader to use an XPathNavigator to access information about a given node:

1. Use one of the methods of the XPathNavigator to position the navigator or cursor on the node.

2. Use the properties and methods of the XPathNavigator to access information about the node.

The following are the methods and properties of the XPathNavigator random-access API that you'll use to implement XmlRoleProvider. The complete coverage of this API is beyond the scope of this book.

❑ bool MoveToChild(XmlNodeType): Positions the cursor on the first node of the specified type. XmlRoleProvider uses this method to position the navigator on the document element.

❑ XmlWriter AppendChild(): Returns an XmlWriter that you can use to create and to append a child node to the list of child nodes of the node on which the navigator is positioned. XmlRoleProvider uses this method to create a new role.

❑ XPathNavigator SelectSingleNode(string xpath): Locates the node specified by the XPath expression and returns an XPathNavigator that is positioned on the node.

❑ void DeleteSelf(): Deletes the node on which the navigator is positioned.

❑ XPathNodeIterator Select (string xpath): Locates all the nodes that satisfy the XPath expression and returns an XPathNodeIterator that contains one XPathNavigator for each located node, where each XPathNavigator is positioned on its associated node.

Implementing RoleProvider's Methods

Listing 24-1 illustrates the methods and properties of the RoleProvider base class that every role provider must implement. The following sections present the XmlRoleProvider class's implementation of these methods and properties. Because all these methods and properties must access the role information from the underlying XML document, XmlRoleProvider exposes two methods named LoadData and SaveData to respectively load XML from and save XML to the XML file.

LoadData

As mentioned, you have two API options for loading XML data: streaming and random-access XML APIs. Following the rule of thumb "Stream your XML unless you have a good reason not to," the LoadData method uses the XmlReader streaming XML API to load the underlying XML file, as shown in Listing 24-5.

Listing 24-5: The LoadData method

```
protected virtual XmlReader LoadData()
{
    return XmlReader.Create(HttpContext.Current.Server.MapPath(dataFile));
}
```

The LoadData method encapsulates the loading logic of XmlRoleProvider, allowing the subclasses of the provider to override the method to provide a different loading logic. The LoadData method doesn't return a concrete class such as XmlTextReader, XmlNodeReader, XmlValidatingReader, XmlDocument, XmlDataDocument, or XPathDocument.

If the LoadData method were to return one of these concrete classes, it would tie the subclasses of XmlRoleProvider to that concrete class and wouldn't allow them to use other classes to override and to implement the LoadData method.

It's highly recommended that those methods and properties of your class or component that expose XML expose the XML via one or more of the following APIs as opposed to a particular implementation of these APIs:

- ❑ XmlReader: Your class's methods and properties should expose XML through an XmlReader if their callers need to read the XML in streaming fashion.

- ❑ XmlWriter: Your class's methods and properties should expose XML through an XmlWriter if their callers need to write XML in streaming fashion.

- ❑ XPathNavigator: Your class's methods and properties should expose XML through an XPathNavigator if their callers need to read or write XML in random fashion.

- ❑ IXPathNavigable: The IXPathNavigable API performs the same task as XPathNavigator API with one difference: it provides direct access to the XML data store itself.

- ❑ System.String: Your class's methods and properties should expose XML via string to allow their callers to write XML to or read XML from a string. In some cases this can improve performance. However, this approach tends to be more error-prone; you lose the benefit of Visual Studio IntelliSense support, and compilers can't catch the problems in compile time.

SaveData

The SaveData method encapsulates the saving logic of XmlRoleProvider, allowing the subclasses of the provider to override the method to provide their own saving logic. XmlRoleProvider comes with two overloads of the SaveData method. Listing 24-6 contains the code for the first overload.

Listing 24-6: The first overload of the SaveData method

```
protected virtual void SaveData(IXPathNavigable nav)
{
  XmlDocument doc = nav as XmlDocument;
  doc.Save(HttpContext.Current.Server.MapPath(dataFile));
}
```

Notice that this overload takes an `IXPathNavigable` object as its input parameter as opposed to one of the concrete implementations of the `IXPathNavigable` interface. This allows the subclasses of `XmlRoleProvider` to use any concrete implementation they want to.

Listing 24-7 contains the implementation of the second overload of the `SaveData` method.

Listing 24-7: The second overload of the SaveData method

```
protected virtual void SaveData(Stream stream)
{
  XmlReaderSettings rsettings = new XmlReaderSettings();
  rsettings.CloseInput = true;

  XmlWriterSettings wsettings = new XmlWriterSettings();
  wsettings.Indent = true;

  using (XmlWriter writer =
                 XmlWriter.Create(HttpContext.Current.Server.MapPath(dataFile)))
  {
    using (XmlReader reader = XmlReader.Create(stream))
    {
      writer.WriteNode(reader, true);
    }
  }
}
```

This overload allows you to save role information as stream of XML content.

Role Management

The following sections show the implementations of the role management methods of the `RoleProvider` base class, which are listed here:

```
public override void CreateRole(string rolename);
public override bool DeleteRole(string rolename, bool throwOnPopulatedRole);
public override string[] GetAllRoles();
public override bool RoleExists(string rolename);
```

CreateRole

Listing 24-8 contains the code for the `CreateRole` method.

Listing 24-8: The CreateRole method

```
public override void CreateRole(string rolename)
{
  if (string.IsNullOrEmpty(rolename))
    throw new Exception("role name cannot be empty or null.");

  if (RoleExists(rolename))
    throw new Exception("role name already exists.");

  if (useStreams)
    CreateRoleStream(rolename);

  else
    CreateRoleRandomAccess(rolename);
}
```

The main responsibility of the `CreateRole` method is to generate the XML that represents the new role and save it to the underlying XML file. As discussed, you can use either streaming or random-access APIs. `XmlRoleProvider` has a private Boolean field named `useStream` that allows you to switch between the `CreateRoleStream` and `CreateRoleRandomAccess` methods. These two methods respectively use the streaming and random-access APIs to generate the XML that represents the new role, as discussed in the next sections. The `useStream` Boolean flag is introduced for educational purposes to allow you to easily switch between the streaming and random-access XML APIs so you can study their differences and their effects on the performance of the `XmlRoleProvider`.

CreateRoleStream

Listing 24-9 contains the code for the `CreateRoleStream` method. This method uses the streaming model to generate the XML that represents the new role.

Listing 24-9: The CreateRoleStream method

```
protected virtual void CreateRoleStream(string rolename)
{
  MemoryStream stream = new MemoryStream();
  using (XmlReader reader = LoadData())
  {
    XmlWriterSettings settings = new XmlWriterSettings();
    settings.Indent = true;
    using (XmlWriter writer = XmlWriter.Create(stream, settings))
    {
      while (reader.Read())
      {
        if (reader.NodeType == XmlNodeType.Element)
        {
          writer.WriteStartElement(reader.Prefix, reader.LocalName,
                                   reader.NamespaceURI);
          writer.WriteAttributes(reader, true);

          if (reader.LocalName == "roles")
          {
            writer.WriteWhitespace("\n\t");
            writer.WriteStartElement("role");
```

```
            writer.WriteAttributeString("roleName", rolename);
            writer.WriteAttributeString("applicationName", applicationName);
            writer.WriteEndElement();
        }

        if (reader.IsEmptyElement)
          writer.WriteEndElement();
      }

      else
        RenderNonElementType(reader, writer);
    }
  }
}

  stream.Position = 0;
  SaveData(stream);
}
```

`CreateRoleStream` uses an `XmlReader` to input nodes in streaming fashion:

```
using (XmlReader reader = LoadData())
{
  . . .
}
```

It then uses an `XmlWriter` to output nodes in streaming fashion:

```
MemoryStream stream = new MemoryStream();
XmlWriterSettings settings = new XmlWriterSettings();
settings.Indent = true;
using (XmlWriter writer = XmlWriter.Create(stream, settings))
{
  . . .
}
```

It calls the `Read` method to position the `XmlReader` on the next input node:

```
reader.Read()
```

Next, it uses the `XmlWriter` to write the next output node where the node has the same type and property values as its associated input node. For example, if the input node is of type `XmlElement`, the `XmlWriter` outputs a node of type `XmlElement` with the same prefix, local name, namespace, and attributes as the input node, as shown in the following code fragment:

```
writer.WriteStartElement(reader.Prefix, reader.LocalName, reader.NamespaceURI);
writer.WriteAttributes(reader, true);
```

If the input node is the `<roles>` element, that is, the document element, the `XmlWriter` first outputs a `<roles>` element as discussed before, and then outputs the `<role>` element that represents the new role as the child element of the `<roles>` element (see Listing 24-2):

```
if (reader.LocalName == "roles")
{
  writer.WriteWhitespace("\n\t");
  writer.WriteStartElement("role");
  writer.WriteAttributeString("roleName", rolename);
  writer.WriteAttributeString("applicationName", applicationName);
  writer.WriteEndElement();
}
```

Finally, `CreateRoleStream` calls the `SaveData` method and passes the stream that contains the XML document into it:

```
SaveData(stream);
```

CreateRoleRandomAccess

Listing 24-10 contains the code for the `CreateRoleRandomAccess` method. This method uses the random-access API to generate the XML that represents the new role.

Listing 24-10: The CreateRoleRandomAccess method

```
protected virtual void CreateRoleRandomAccess(string rolename)
{
  XmlDocument doc = new XmlDocument();
  using (XmlReader reader = LoadData())
  {
    doc.Load(reader);
  }

  if (useNavigator)
  {
    XPathNavigator nav = doc.CreateNavigator();
    nav.MoveToChild(XPathNodeType.Element);
    using (XmlWriter writer = nav.AppendChild())
    {
      writer.WriteStartElement("role");
      writer.WriteAttributeString("roleName", rolename);
      writer.WriteAttributeString("applicationName", applicationName);
      writer.WriteEndElement();
    }
  }

  else
  {
    XmlElement role = doc.CreateElement("role");
    role.SetAttribute("roleName", rolename);
    role.SetAttribute("applicationName", applicationName);
    doc.DocumentElement.AppendChild(role);
  }

  SaveData(doc);
}
```

As discussed, there are two random-access XML APIs: DOM and XPathNavigator. Both APIs cache their XML in an XML data store. To help you see the code for DOM and XPathNavigator APIs side by side, XmlRoleProvider defines a private Boolean field named useNavigator to allow you to switch between these two APIs. The following two sections discuss how you can use these two APIs to generate the XML that represents the new role.

XPathNavigator API

Here are the main steps you must implement to use the XPathNavigator API to generate and add XML that represents the new role to the underlying XML file:

1. Load the XML content of the file into an XmlDocument. Recall that the XPathNavigator API uses an XML data store such as XmlDocument and XPathDocument as its backing store. You can't use XPathDocument because it's read-only and doesn't allow you to add the XML for the new role.

2. Invoke the CreateNavigator method of the XmlDocument to access its XPathNavigator. Recall that all XML data stores in the .NET Framework implement the IXPathNavigable interface. This interface exposes a method named CreateNavigator that returns the XPathNavigator.

The returned XPathNavigator is positioned on the root node of the XmlDocument. The root node of an XML document is different from its document element. For example, the document element of the XML document shown in Listing 24-2 is the <roles> element. The root node of an XML document isn't a real node in the document. Instead it's a node that encapsulates the entire XML document, including the XML declaration and the document element. In other words, the document element is the child element of the root node:

```
XPathNavigator nav = doc.CreateNavigator();
```

3. Call the MoveToChild method of the XPathNavigator. When you're working with a cursor-style API, such as XPathNavigator or XmlReader, you have to be very conscious of the following two important facts:

❏ The navigator is positioned on some node at all times.

❏ The current position of the navigator matters a lot.

The MoveToChild(XPathNodeType.Element) call moves the navigator from the node on which it's currently positioned (the root node), to the first child element of the root node (the <roles> document element):

```
nav.MoveToChild(XPathNodeType.Element);
```

4. Call the AppendChild method of the navigator to access the XmlWriter that you can use to generate and add the XML for the new role. Notice that the XmlWriter is used in a using statement as discussed before:

```
using (XmlWriter writer = nav.AppendChild())
{
    . . .
}
```

Now compare Listings 24-10 and 24-9. As the highlighted sections of these two listings show, the XPathNavigator random-access API uses the XmlWriter streaming XML API to generate the XML for the new role.

In other words, the XPathNavigator random-access API provides you with the best of both random-access and streaming worlds. On the one hand, like all other random-access APIs, it allows you to randomly position the navigator where you want to add the new role node. On the other hand, like all other streaming APIs, it gives you an XmlWriter that you can use to generate the XML for the new role in streaming fashion.

DOM API

Here are the main steps you must implement to use DOM API to generate and to add the XML for the new role:

1. Load the XML file that contains the role information into an XmlDocument. Recall that XmlDocument is the .NET implementation of the DOM API.

2. Call the CreateElement method of the XmlDocument to create a new <role> element:

```
XmlElement role = doc.CreateElement("role");
```

3. Call the SetAttribute method of the newly created XmlElement twice to create and to add the roleName and applicationName attributes of the new <role> element:

```
role.SetAttribute("roleName", rolename);
role.SetAttribute("applicationName", applicationName);
```

4. Call the AppendChild method of the document element (the <roles> element) to append the new <role> element to the list of the child elements of the <roles> element (see Listing 24-2):

```
doc.DocumentElement.AppendChild(role);
```

DeleteRole

The DeleteRole method deletes the specified role from the underlying XML file as shown in Listing 24-11. The method first calls the RolesExists method to ensure the specified role exists in the XML document before it attempts to delete it:

```
if (!RoleExists(rolename))
  throw new Exception("role does not exist.");
```

If the second argument of the method is set to true, the method calls the GetUsersInRole method to ensure no users are in the specified role before it attempts to delete it from the XML file:

```
if (throwOnPopulatedRole && GetUsersInRole(rolename).Length > 0)
  throw new Exception("Cannot delete a populated role.");
```

Listing 24-11: The DeleteRole method

```
public override bool DeleteRole(string rolename, bool throwOnPopulatedRole)
{
  if (!RoleExists(rolename))
    throw new Exception("role does not exist.");

  if (throwOnPopulatedRole && GetUsersInRole(rolename).Length > 0)
    throw new Exception("Cannot delete a populated role.");

  if (useStreams)
```

```
      DeleteRoleStream(rolename);

   else
      DeleteRoleRandomAccess(rolename);

   return true;
}
```

The DeleteRole method then checks whether it should delete the specified role in streaming or random-access fashion. Recall that XmlRoleProvider exposes a private field named useStreams for your convenience to allow you to switch between the streaming and random-access APIs so you can compare them.

DeleteRoleStream

Listing 24-12 illustrates the implementation of the DeleteRoleStream method where the streaming XML API is used to delete the specified role.

Listing 24-12: The DeleteRoleStream method

```
protected virtual void DeleteRoleStream(string rolename)
{
  MemoryStream stream = new MemoryStream();
  using (XmlReader reader = LoadData())
  {
    XmlWriterSettings settings = new XmlWriterSettings();
    settings.Indent = true;
    using (XmlWriter writer = XmlWriter.Create(stream, settings))
    {
      while (reader.Read())
      {
        if (reader.NodeType == XmlNodeType.Element)
        {
          if (!(reader.LocalName == "role" &&
                reader.GetAttribute("roleName") == rolename))
          {
            writer.WriteStartElement(reader.Prefix, reader.LocalName,
                                     reader.NamespaceURI);
            writer.WriteAttributes(reader, true);

            if (reader.IsEmptyElement)
              writer.WriteEndElement();
          }
        }

        else
          RenderNonElementType(reader, writer);
      }
    }
  }

  stream.Position = 0;
  SaveData(stream);
}
```

The `DeleteRoleStream` method performs the following tasks. First it uses an `XmlReader` to read the XML file that contains the role information in a streaming fashion. It then calls the `Read` method of the `XmlReader` to position the reader on the next input node.

Next, it calls the `LocalName` property and `GetAttribute` method of the `XmlReader` to check whether the input node on which the `XmlReader` is positioned is the role to be deleted. If it is, the `XmlWriter` doesn't output any node associated with this input node. If it isn't, the `XmlWriter` outputs a node with the same prefix, local name, namespace, and attributes as the input node.

Notice that the `DeleteRoleStream` method passes the `XmlReader` to the `WriteAttributes` method of the `XmlWriter`. The `WriteAttributes` method writes out all the attributes of the input node on which the `XmlReader` is positioned:

```
writer.WriteAttributes(reader, true);
```

DeleteRoleRandomAccess

The `DeleteRoleRandomAccess` method uses a random-access XML API to load the entire contents of the XML file that contains the role information in memory, as shown in Listing 24-13.

Listing 24-13: The DeleteRoleRandomAccess method

```
protected virtual void DeleteRoleRandomAccess(string rolename)
{
  XmlDocument doc = new XmlDocument();
  using (XmlReader reader = LoadData())
  {
    doc.Load(reader);
  }

  string roleXPath = "//role[@roleName='" + rolename +
                     "' and @applicationName='" + applicationName + "']";

  if (useNavigator)
  {
    XPathNavigator nav = doc.CreateNavigator();
    nav.MoveToChild(XPathNodeType.Element);
    XPathNavigator roleNavigator = nav.SelectSingleNode(roleXPath);
    roleNavigator.DeleteSelf();
  }

  else
  {
    XmlNode roleNode = doc.SelectSingleNode(roleXPath);
    roleNode.ParentNode.RemoveChild(roleNode);
  }

  SaveData(doc);
}
```

As discussed, you have two random-access API options: DOM and `XPathNavigator`.

XPathNavigator API

Here are the steps you must take to use `XPathNavigator` API to delete a node:

1. Load the XML content of the XML file that contains the role information into an XML data store. You have two main XML data store options: `XmlDocument` and `XPathDocument`. Because `XPathDocument` is read-only, it wouldn't allow you to delete the specified role from the document. Therefore you have to load the XML file into an `XmlDocument`.

2. Call the `CreateNavigator` method of the `XmlDocument` to access its `XPathNavigator`. As discussed, the `XPathNavigator` is originally positioned on the root node of the XML document:

   ```
   XPathNavigator nav = doc.CreateNavigator();
   ```

3. Call the `MoveToChild` method of the `XPathNavigator` to move the navigator from the node on which it's currently positioned to the first child element of the root node, the `<roles>` document element (see Listing 24-2):

   ```
   nav.MoveToChild(XPathNodeType.Element);
   ```

4. Call the `SelectSingleNode` method of the `XPathNavigator` to locate the `<role>` node to be deleted. This method returns an `XPathNavigator` that is positioned on the `<role>` node to be deleted. Notice that the `SelectSingleNode` method doesn't move and position the main `XPathNavigator` on the specified `<role>` node. Instead it returns a new `XPathNavigator` already positioned on the specified `<role>` node:

   ```
   XPathNavigator roleNavigator = nav.SelectSingleNode(roleXPath);
   ```

5. Call the `DeleteSelf` method of the new `XPathNavigator` to delete the `<role>` node on which the navigator is positioned:

   ```
   roleNavigator.DeleteSelf();
   ```

DOM API

Here are the main steps you must implement to use DOM API to delete a node:

1. Load the content of the XML file that contains the role information into an XML data store. The only XML data store that supports the DOM API is `XmlDocument`.

2. Call the `SelectSingleNode` method of the `XmlDocument` to locate the `<role>` node to be deleted. This method returns an `XmlNode` that references the `<role>` node to be deleted:

   ```
   XmlNode roleNode = doc.SelectSingleNode(roleXPath);
   ```

3. Call the `RemoveChild` method of the parent node of the `<role>` node to be deleted to delete the `<role>` node. Every node exposes a property of type `XmlNode` named `ParentNode` that references the parent node of the node:

   ```
   roleNode.ParentNode.RemoveChild(roleNode);
   ```

Notice that both the `XPathNavigator` and DOM APIs call the `SelectSingleNode` method. This method in both cases takes a string that contains the following XPath expression and performs an XPath query to locate the `<role>` node to be deleted:

```
string roleXPath = "//role[@roleName='" + rolename +
                   "' and @applicationName='" + applicationName + "']";
```

The XPathNavigator data model mirrors the XPath data model, which is based on W3C XML Information Set (XML InfoSet) specification, whereas the DOM data model mirrors the W3C XML 1.0 specification. The W3C XML 1.0 specification specifies how to serialize or store XML data in XML 1.0 text format where angle brackets are used. The W3C XML InfoSet specification, on the other hand, specifies the XML data model regardless of how it's serialized or stored.

In other words, the W3C XML InfoSet specification specifies the information content of an XML document regardless of how this information content is serialized. Because the DOM data model mirrors the W3C XML 1.0 specification, it also supports data types that only convey lexical information such as CDATA.

Now back to the SelectSingleNode method. Recall that this method performs an XPath query under the hood to locate the <role> node to be deleted. The mismatch between the DOM and XPath data models degrades the performance of the XPath queries that the methods such as SelectSingleNode perform. The performance of XPath queries is great in the case of the XPathNavigator API because the XPathNavigator data model mirrors the XPath data model. Therefore if you need to perform a lot of XPath queries you'd better use the XPathNavigator API, otherwise you'll end up paying a heavy performance price.

Now let me amend the previous rule of thumb: Stream your XML unless you have to perform XPath queries. If you have to perform XPath queries, use the XPathNavigator API unless you have a good reason not to.

GetAllRoles

The GetAllRoles method retrieves all the roles for the specified application. Recall that you have three options for reading XML. It's very tempting to use the following XPath expression to query the XML document for the roles that belong to the specified application:

```
string xpath = "//role[@applicationName='"+applicationName+"']";
```

The handy rule of thumb doesn't say "Stream your XML unless you *want to* perform XPath queries." Instead it says "Stream your XML unless you *have to* perform XPath queries." When you think about it, you don't really have to perform an XPath query to retrieve all the roles for the specified application. Listing 24-14 shows how you can use the XmlReader streaming XML API to retrieve the roles for the specified application much more efficiently.

Listing 24-14: The GetAllRoles method

```
public override string[] GetAllRoles()
{
    ArrayList roleList = new ArrayList();
    using (XmlReader reader = LoadData())
    {
        reader.MoveToContent();
        reader.ReadToDescendant("role");

        do
        {
```

```
        if (applicationName == reader.GetAttribute("applicationName"))
          roleList.Add(reader.GetAttribute("roleName"));
      } while (reader.ReadToNextSibling("role"));
    }
  if (roleList.Count == 0)
    return new string[0];

  string[] roleArray = new string[roleList.Count];
  roleList.CopyTo(roleArray);
  return roleArray;
}
```

The `GetAllRoles` method first instantiates an `ArrayList` that will be used to hold the role names for the specified application:

```
ArrayList roleList = new ArrayList();
```

Next, it uses an `XmlReader` to stream out the content of the XML file that contains the role information. The `XmlReader` is used in a `using` statement as discussed before. The `XmlReader` is originally positioned on the root node of the document:

```
using (XmlReader reader = LoadData())
```

Next, the method calls the `MoveToContent` method of the `XmlReader` to move the reader from the root node to the first content node. A content node is a node of one of the following types: non-white space text, `CDATA`, `Element`, `EndElement`, `EntityReference`, or `EndEntity`. As shown in Listing 24-2, the first content node of the document is the `<roles>` document element:

```
    reader.MoveToContent();
```

The method then calls the `ReadToDescendant` method of the `XmlReader` to move the reader from the `<roles>` document element to the first descendant element node with the specified name, which is the first `<role>` element, as shown in Listing 24-2:

```
    reader.ReadToDescendant("role");
```

The method then enters a `do-while` loop where it takes the following actions for each iteration of the loop:

1. Calls the `GetAttribute` method of the `XmlReader` to check whether the `<role>` node on which the reader is currently positioned belongs to the specified application. If it does, it adds the rolename to the `ArrayList`.

2. Calls the `ReadToNextSibling` method of the `XmlReader` to move the reader from the `<role>` element to the next `<role>` sibling element of the current `<role>` element:

```
do
{
  if (applicationName == reader.GetAttribute("applicationName"))
    roleList.Add(reader.GetAttribute("roleName"));
} while (reader.ReadToNextSibling("role"));
```

715

As you can see, the `ReadToDescendant` and `ReadToNextSibling` methods together simulate the XPath query that uses the following XPath expression:

```
string xpath = "//role[@applicationName='"+applicationName+"']";
```

RoleExists

As its name implies, the `RoleExists` method checks whether the specified role exists in the list of roles of the specified application. Again, it's very tempting to use a random-access XML API such as `XPathNavigator` to perform the following XPath query to check whether the specified role exits:

```
string xpath = "//Role[@roleName='"+rolename+
               "' and @applicationName='"+applicationName+"']";
```

Following your handy rule of thumb, Listing 24-15 shows how you can use a combination of `ReadToDescendant` and `ReadToNextSibling` to simulate this XPath query in much more efficient manner.

Listing 24-15: The RoleExists method

```
public override bool RoleExists(string rolename)
{
  if (string.IsNullOrEmpty(rolename))
    throw new HttpException("role name cannot be empty or null.");

  using (XmlReader reader = LoadData())
  {
    reader.MoveToContent();
    reader.ReadToDescendant("role");
    do
    {
      if (reader.GetAttribute("roleName") == rolename &&
          applicationName == reader.GetAttribute("applicationName"))
        return true;
    } while (reader.ReadToNextSibling("role"));
  }

  return false;
}
```

User Management

The following sections show the implementation of the user management methods of the `RoleProvider` base class, which are listed here:

```
public virtual void AddUsersToRoles(string[] usernames, string[] rolenames);
public virtual void RemoveUsersFromRoles(string[] usernames, string[] rolenames);
public virtual string[] GetRolesForUser(string username);
public virtual string[] GetUsersInRole(string rolename);
public virtual string[] FindUsersInRole(string rolename, string usernameToMatch);
public virtual bool IsUserInRole(string username, string rolename);
```

AddUsersToRoles

As its name implies, the `AddUsersToRoles` method adds the specified users to the specified roles as shown in Listing 24-16.

Listing 24-16: The AddUsersToRoles method

```
public override void AddUsersToRoles(string[] usernames, string[] rolenames)
{
  foreach (string rolename in rolenames)
  {
    if (string.IsNullOrEmpty(rolename))
      throw new HttpException("role name cannot be empty or null.");
    if (!RoleExists(rolename))
      throw new HttpException("role name not found.");
  }

  foreach (string username in usernames)
  {
    if (string.IsNullOrEmpty(username))
      throw new HttpException("User name cannot be empty or null.");

    foreach (string rolename in rolenames)
    {
      if (IsUserInRole(username, rolename))
        throw new HttpException("User is already in role.");
    }
  }

  if (useStreams)
    AddUsersToRolesStream(usernames, rolenames);

  else
    AddUsersToRolesRandomAccess(usernames, rolenames);
}
```

As discussed, `XmlRoleProvider` comes with a private Boolean field named `useStreams` that allows you to switch between the streaming and random-access XML APIs to gain a better understanding of their differences.

AddUsersToRolesStream

The `AddUsersToRolesStream` method uses a combination of the `XmlReader` and `XmlWriter` streaming XML APIs to generate and add the XML that represents the new users, as shown in Listing 24-17.

Listing 24-17: The AddUsersToRolesStream

```
protected virtual void AddUsersToRolesStream(string[] usernames, string[]
rolenames)
{
  MemoryStream stream = new MemoryStream();
  ArrayList usernameList = new ArrayList(usernames);
  ArrayList rolenameList = new ArrayList(rolenames);
```

(continued)

Listing 24-17: *(continued)*

```
using (XmlReader reader = LoadData())
{
  XmlWriterSettings settings = new XmlWriterSettings();
  settings.Indent = true;
  using (XmlWriter writer = XmlWriter.Create(stream, settings))
  {
    while (reader.Read())
    {
      if (reader.NodeType == XmlNodeType.Element)
      {
        writer.WriteStartElement(reader.Prefix, reader.LocalName,
                                 reader.NamespaceURI);
        writer.WriteAttributes(reader, true);

        if (reader.LocalName == "role" &&
            rolenameList.Contains(reader.GetAttribute("roleName")))
        {
          writer.WriteWhitespace("\n\t\t");

          foreach (string username in usernames)
          {
            writer.WriteStartElement("user");
            writer.WriteAttributeString("userName", username);
            writer.WriteEndElement();
          }
        }

        if (reader.IsEmptyElement)
          writer.WriteEndElement();
      }

      else
        RenderNonElementType(reader, writer);
    }
  }
}

stream.Position = 0;
SaveData(stream);
}
```

The implementation of the `AddUsersToRolesStream` method is similar to the implementation of the `CreateRoleStream` method shown in Listing 24-9. First, the `XmlReader` reads in the next input node:

```
while (reader.Read()
```

The `XmlWriter`, in turn, writes out the next output node with the same type and properties as the input node. For example, if the input node is an element node, the `XmlWriter` writes out an element node with the same prefix, local name, namespace, and attributes as the input element node:

```
writer.WriteStartElement(reader.Prefix, reader.LocalName, reader.NamespaceURI);
writer.WriteAttributes(reader, true);
```

If the input node represents one of the specified roles, XmlWriter takes the following actions in order:

1. Writes out the opening tag of a `<role>` element with the same attributes, that is, the same role and application names as the input `<role>` element.

2. Writes out one `<user>` node for each specified usernames:

```
foreach (string username in usernames)
{
  writer.WriteStartElement("user");
  writer.WriteAttributeString("userName", username);
  writer.WriteEndElement();
}
```

AddUsersToRolesRandomAccess

As discussed, to help you compare the differences between the two random-access XML APIs, XmlRoleProvider comes with a Boolean field named useNavigator that you can use to switch between the two, as shown in Listing 24-18.

Listing 24-18: The AddUsersToRolesRandomAccess method

```
protected virtual void AddUsersToRolesRandomAccess(string[] usernames,
                                                   string[] rolenames)
{
  XmlDocument doc = new XmlDocument();
  using (XmlReader reader = LoadData())
  {
    doc.Load(reader);
  }

  string roleXPath = "descendant::role[(";
  foreach (string rolename in rolenames)
    roleXPath += ("@roleName='" + rolename + "' or ");

  roleXPath = roleXPath.Remove(roleXPath.LastIndexOf("or"), 3);
  roleXPath += (") and @applicationName='" + applicationName + "']");

  if (useNavigator)
  {
    XPathNavigator nav = doc.CreateNavigator();
    nav.MoveToChild(XPathNodeType.Element);

    XPathNodeIterator roleNavigators = nav.Select(roleXPath);
    foreach (XPathNavigator roleNavigator in roleNavigators)
    {
      using (XmlWriter writer = roleNavigator.AppendChild())
      {
        foreach (string username in usernames)
        {
          writer.WriteStartElement("user");
          writer.WriteAttributeString("userName", username);
          writer.WriteEndElement();
        }
```

(continued)

Listing 24-18: *(continued)*

```
      }
    }
  }

  else
  {
    XmlNodeList roleNodes = doc.SelectNodes(roleXPath);
    foreach (XmlNode roleNode in roleNodes)
    {
      foreach (string username in usernames)
      {
        XmlElement user = doc.CreateElement("user");
        user.SetAttribute("userName", username);
        roleNode.AppendChild(user);
      }
    }
  }

  SaveData(doc);
}
```

XPathNavigator API

The `AddUsersToRolesRandomAccess` method uses the `XPathNavigator` API to add the specified users to the specified roles by first loading the XML file that contains the role information into an `XmlDocument` because the `XmlDocument` is the only editable XML data store as discussed earlier. It then calls the `CreateNavigator` method of the `XmlDocument` to return an `XPathNavigator` originally positioned on the root node of the XML document:

```
XPathNavigator nav = doc.CreateNavigator();
```

It then calls the `MoveToChild` method of the `XPathNavigator` to move the navigator from the root node to the `<roles>` document element as discussed before:

```
nav.MoveToChild(XPathNodeType.Element);
```

Next, it calls the `Select` method of the `XPathNavigator` to locate nodes that satisfy the specified `XPath` expression:

```
string roleXPath = "descendant::role[(";
foreach (string rolename in rolenames)
  roleXPath += ("@roleName='" + rolename + "' or ");

roleXPath = roleXPath.Remove(roleXPath.LastIndexOf("or"), 3);
roleXPath += (") and @applicationName='" + applicationName + "']");

. . .
XPathNodeIterator roleNavigators = nav.Select(roleXPath);
```

The `XPath` expression starts with `descendant::role`. As mentioned, when you're using a cursor-style API such as `XPathNavigator` or `XmlReader` you must be very conscious of where the navigator is currently positioned. The result of the `XPath` query entirely depends on the current location of the navigator.

In this case, the navigator is currently positioned on the `<roles>` document element, so the `XPath` query will return all the `<role>` nodes that satisfy the `XPath` expression. However, if the navigator were positioned on, say, the first `<role>` node, the result of the `XPath` query would be null. That's why you called the `MoveToChild` method to position the navigator on the `<roles>` element before performing the `XPath` query.

The `Select` method returns an `XPathNodeIterator` that contains one `XPathNavigator` for each selected `<role>` node, where each `XPathNavigator` is originally positioned on its associated `<role>` node.

Finally, the `AddUsersToRolesRandomAccess` method iterates through the `XPathNavigators` and calls the `AppendChild` method of each navigator to return an `XmlWriter` that you can use to generate the XML that represents the new users:

```
using (XmlWriter writer = roleNavigator.AppendChild())
{
  foreach (string username in usernames)
  {
    writer.WriteStartElement("user");
    writer.WriteAttributeString("userName", username);
    writer.WriteEndElement();
  }
}
```

DOM API

The `AddUsersToRolesRandomAccess` method uses the DOM API to add the specified users to the specified roles by first loading the XML file that contains the role information into an `XmlDocument` data store because the `XmlDocument` is the .NET implementation of the DOM API. It then calls the `SelectNodes` method of the `XmlDocument`. This method performs the specified `XPath` query and returns an `XmlNodeList` that contains one `XmlNode` for each node that satisfies the specified `XPath` expression. As the following code fragment shows, this `XPath` expression selects the role nodes with the specified name that belong to the specified application:

```
string roleXPath = "descendant::role[(";
foreach (string rolename in rolenames)
  roleXPath += ("@roleName='" + rolename + "' or ");

roleXPath = roleXPath.Remove(roleXPath.LastIndexOf("or"), 3);
roleXPath += (") and @applicationName='" + applicationName + "']");

. . .

XmlNodeList roleNodes = doc.SelectNodes(roleXPath);
```

It iterates through the role nodes and takes the following steps for each enumerated `<role>` node to generate and render the XML that represents each specified user:

1. Calls the `CreateElement` method of the `XmlDocument` to generate the `<user>` element that will represent the specified user:

```
XmlElement user = doc.CreateElement("user");
```

2. Calls the `SetAttribute` method of the newly created `<user>` node to render its `userName` attribute:

```
              user.SetAttribute("userName", username);
```

3. Calls the `AppendChild` method of the enumerated role node to append the newly created user node to its list of child nodes:

```
roleNode.AppendChild(user);
```

Notice that both the `Select` method of the `XPathNavigator` and the `SelectNodes` method of the `XmlDocument` perform the same `XPath` query. As discussed, the mismatch between the `XmlDocument` (DOM) and `XPath` data model degrades the performance of the `SelectNodes` method compared to the `Select` method. Therefore if you need to call the `AddUsersToRoles` method frequently and you use the DOM API, you'll end up paying a heavy performance price.

RemoveUsersFromRoles

As the name implies, this method removes the specified users from the specified roles, as shown in Listing 24-19.

Listing 24-19: The RemoveUsersFromRoles method

```
public override void RemoveUsersFromRoles(string[] usernames, string[] rolenames)
{
  foreach (string rolename in rolenames)
  {
    if (string.IsNullOrEmpty(rolename))
      throw new HttpException("role name cannot be empty or null.");

    if (!RoleExists(rolename))
      throw new HttpException("role name not found.");
  }

  foreach (string username in usernames)
  {
    if (string.IsNullOrEmpty(username))
      throw new HttpException("User name cannot be empty or null.");

    foreach (string rolename in rolenames)
    {
      if (!IsUserInRole(username, rolename))
        throw new HttpException("User is not in role.");
    }
  }

  if (useStreams)
    RemoveUsersFromRolesStream(usernames, rolenames);

  else
    RemoveUsersFromRolesRandomAccess(usernames, rolenames);
}
```

RemoveUsersFromRolesStream

This method uses a combination of the `XmlReader` and `XmlWriter` streaming XML APIs to remove the specified users from the specified roles, as shown in Listing 24-20.

Listing 24-20: The RemoveUsersFromRolesStream method

```csharp
protected virtual void RemoveUsersFromRolesStream(string[] usernames, string[]
rolenames)
{
  MemoryStream stream = new MemoryStream();
  ArrayList usernameList = new ArrayList(usernames);
  ArrayList rolenameList = new ArrayList(rolenames);

  using (XmlReader reader = LoadData())
  {
    XmlWriterSettings settings = new XmlWriterSettings();
    settings.Indent = true;
    using (XmlWriter writer = XmlWriter.Create(stream, settings))
    {
      while (reader.Read())
      {
        if (reader.NodeType == XmlNodeType.Element)
        {
          writer.WriteStartElement(reader.Prefix, reader.LocalName,
                                   reader.NamespaceURI);
          writer.WriteAttributes(reader, true);

          if (reader.LocalName == "role" &&
              rolenameList.Contains(reader.GetAttribute("roleName")))
          {
            using (XmlReader userReader = reader.ReadSubtree())
            {
              while (userReader.Read())
              {
                if (userReader.LocalName == "user" &&
                    !usernameList.Contains(userReader.GetAttribute("userName")))
                {
                  writer.WriteWhitespace("\n\t\t");
                  writer.WriteStartElement("user");
                  writer.WriteAttributeString("userName",
                                              userReader.GetAttribute("userName"));
                  writer.WriteEndElement();
                }
              }
              writer.WriteWhitespace("\n\t");
            }
          }

          if (reader.IsEmptyElement)
            writer.WriteEndElement();
        }

        else
          RenderNonElementType(reader, writer);
      }
    }
  }
  stream.Position = 0;
  SaveData(stream);
}
```

Here is how it works. The XmlWriter writes out an output node for each input node that the XmlReader reads in from the XML document that contains the role information. Each output node is of the same type as its associated input node and has the same property values. If the input node is one of the specified role nodes, XmlWriter writes out an output role node with the same attributes as the input role node as it did with other nodes, and then calls the ReadSubtree method of the XmlReader. As discussed, you must always be aware of the current position of a cursor-style API such as XmlReader. In this case, the XmlReader is positioned on one of the specified role nodes. The ReadSubtree method of the XmlReader returns a new XmlReader positioned on the same node on which the original XmlReader is positioned. In other words, after calling the ReadSubtree method you have two independent XmlReaders positioned on the same role node.

You may be wondering why you can't use the original XmlReader. The second XmlReader has two very important characteristics. First, it's independent from the original XmlReader. That is, you can move the second XmlReader without affecting the first one. Second, the second XmlReader can only be positioned on the node on which the original XmlReader is positioned and on the child nodes of that node.

These two characteristics allow you to keep calling the Read method on the second XmlReader to traverse the child nodes of the node on which the original XmlReader is positioned. In this case, the ReadSubtree method returns an XmlReader that you can use to traverse the user nodes of the specified role node. You may be wondering why you need to traverse the user nodes of the specified role node. The answer lies in what the XmlWriter is doing. Recall that the XmlWriter writes out an output node for each input node that the XmlReader reads in from the XML document. You have to traverse the user nodes of the specified role node to locate the specified user nodes and to stop XmlWriter from emitting output nodes for these user nodes. This is how you remove the specified user nodes from the specified role nodes in streaming fashion.

The combination of the XmlWriter and XmlReader APIs provides you with a powerful tool to accomplish most tasks that may seem to require a random-access API such as XPathNavigator or DOM.

RemoveUsersFromRolesRandomAccess

The RemoveUsersFromRolesRandomAccess method uses a random-access API to remove users from roles as shown in Listing 24-21.

Listing 24-21: The RemoveUsersFromRolesRandomAccess method

```
protected virtual void RemoveUsersFromRolesRandomAccess(string[] usernames,
string[] rolenames)
{
  XmlDocument doc = new XmlDocument();
  using (XmlReader reader = LoadData())
  {
    doc.Load(reader);
  }

  string roleXPath = "descendant::role[(";
  foreach (string rolename in rolenames)
    roleXPath += ("@roleName='" + rolename + "' or ");

  roleXPath = roleXPath.Remove(roleXPath.LastIndexOf("or"), 2);
  roleXPath += (") and @applicationName='" + applicationName + "']");

  string userXPath = "user[";
```

```
      foreach (string username in usernames)
        userXPath += ("@userName='" + username + "' or ");

  userXPath = userXPath.Remove(userXPath.LastIndexOf("or"), 2);
  userXPath += "]";

  if (useNavigator)
  {
    XPathNavigator nav = doc.CreateNavigator();
    nav.MoveToChild(XPathNodeType.Element);

    XPathNodeIterator roleNavigators = nav.Select(roleXPath);
    XPathNodeIterator userNavigators;
    foreach (XPathNavigator roleNavigator in roleNavigators)
    {
      userNavigators = roleNavigator.Select(userXPath);
      foreach (XPathNavigator userNavigator in userNavigators)
      {
        userNavigator.DeleteSelf();
      }
    }
  }

  else
  {
    XmlNodeList roleNodes = doc.SelectNodes(roleXPath);
    XmlNodeList userNodes;
    foreach (XmlNode roleNode in roleNodes)
    {
      userNodes = roleNode.SelectNodes(userXPath);
      foreach (XmlNode userNode in userNodes)
      {
        userNode.ParentNode.RemoveChild(userNode);
      }
    }
  }

  SaveData(doc);
}
```

XPathNavigator API

The implementation of this method is similar to the implementation of the DeleteRole method. This section covers those parts that are different from the DeleteRole method.

The Select method of the XPathNavigator performs an XPath query to locate the role nodes that satisfy the specified XPath expression:

```
XPathNodeIterator roleNavigators = nav.Select(roleXPath);
```

As discussed, the Select method returns an XPathNodeIterator that contains one XPathNavigator for each selected role node, where each navigator is positioned on its associated role node. The method iterates through these navigators and calls the Select method of each enumerated navigator. The method performs an XPath query to locate those user nodes that satisfy the following XPath expression:

```
string userXPath = "user[";
foreach (string username in usernames)
  userXPath += ("@userName='" + username + "' or ");

userXPath = userXPath.Remove(userXPath.LastIndexOf("or"), 2);
userXPath += "]";
```

Notice that the XPath expression starts with `"user["`. As discussed, XPath expressions are always evaluated with respect to the current node. In this case, the navigator is currently positioned on one of the specified role nodes. If the navigator were positioned on a different node, the preceding XPath query would return null. In this case the Select method returns an XPathNodeIterator that contains one XPathNavigator for each selected user node where each navigator is positioned on its associated user node.

The method then iterates through the user node navigators and calls the DeleteSelf method of each user node navigator to delete the user node on which the navigator is positioned:

```
foreach (XPathNavigator roleNavigator in roleNavigators)
{
  userNavigators = roleNavigator.Select(userXPath);
  foreach (XPathNavigator userNavigator in userNavigators)
  {
    userNavigator.DeleteSelf();
  }
}
```

GetRolesForUser

The GetRolesForUser method is yet another example that may tempt you to use a random-access API such as XPathNavigator or DOM. As Listing 24-22 shows, you can easily use the ReadToDescendant and ReadToNextSibling methods to simulate the XPath query that a random-access API would perform to accomplish the same task.

Listing 24-22: The GetRolesForUser method

```
public override string[] GetRolesForUser(string username)
{
  if (string.IsNullOrEmpty(username))
    throw new HttpException("User name cannot be empty or null.");

  ArrayList roleList = new ArrayList();
  using (XmlReader reader = LoadData())
  {
    reader.MoveToContent();
    reader.ReadToDescendant("role");

    do
    {
      if (applicationName == reader.GetAttribute("applicationName"))
      {
        using (XmlReader userReader = reader.ReadSubtree())
        {
          if (IsUserInRole(userReader, username))
            roleList.Add(reader.GetAttribute("roleName"));
```

```
            }
          break;
        }
    } while (reader.ReadToNextSibling("role"));
  }

  if (roleList.Count == 0)
    return new string[0];

  string[] roleArray = new string[roleList.Count];
  roleList.CopyTo(roleArray);
  return roleArray;
}
```

The interesting part of Listing 24-22 is the part that uses the `ReadSubtree` method. The `GetRolesForUser` calls the `ReadSubtree` method of the `XmlReader` positioned on the specified role node to return a new `XmlReader` positioned on the same role node and passes it to the `IsUserInRole` method shown in the following code:

```
private bool IsUserInRole(XmlReader userReader, string username)
{
  userReader.ReadToDescendant("user");
  do
  {
    if (username == userReader.GetAttribute("userName"))
      return true;
  }
  while (userReader.ReadToNextSibling("user"));

  return false;
}
```

The main responsibility of the `IsUserInRole` method is to determine whether the specified user is in the specified role. The method first calls the `ReadToDescendant` method of the `XmlReader` to move the reader from the role node on which it is currently positioned to its first child user node. It then enters a `do-while` loop where it performs the following tasks for each iteration of the loop:

1. Uses the `GetAttribute` method of the `XmlReader` to determine whether the user node on which the reader is positioned is the specified user node. If it is, it returns true.

2. If it isn't, the method calls the `ReadToNextSibling` method of the reader to move the reader from the user node on which it's currently positioned to its next sibling user node.

Developing Custom Role Principals

As discussed in Chapter 23, the ASP.NET `RolePrincipal` exposes two methods named `ToEncryptedTicket` and `InitFromEncryptedTicket`. The `RoleManagerModule` calls the first method to return the string representation of the `RolePrincipal` object and caches the string in a cookie. This improves the overall performance of the application because the next requests load the role information from the cookie instead of the underlying data store.

Caching role information in a cookie works only for clients that support and accept cookies. This section and the following section build on what you learned in Chapter 23 to develop a custom role principal named `CustomRolePrincipal` and a custom role manager module named `CustomRoleManagerModule` that will allow you to cache role information in the ASP.NET `Cache` object.

The following code fragment shows the members of the `CustomRolePrincipal` component. The next sections present and discuss the implementation of these members in detail.

```
public class CustomRolePrincipal : IPrincipal
{
  public CustomRolePrincipal(IIdentity identity);
  public CustomRolePrincipal(IIdentity identity, string[] roles);
  public string[] GetRoles();
  public bool IsInRole(string role);
  public void SetDirty();
  public bool CachedListChanged {get;}
  public IIdentity Identity {get;}
  public bool IsRoleListCached {get;}
}
```

Constructors

`CustomRolePrincipal` exposes two public constructors. Listing 24-23 contains the code for the first constructor. This constructor takes an `IIdentity` object as its only input parameter and initializes the properties of the `CustomRolePrincipal`.

Listing 24-23: The first constructor of the CustomRolePrincipal

```
public CustomRolePrincipal(IIdentity identity)
{
  if (identity == null)
    throw new ArgumentNullException("identity");

  this.identity = identity;
  isRoleListCached = false;
  cachedListChanged = false;

  if (roles == null)
    roles = new ArrayList();

  if (identity != null)
    username = identity.Name;
}
```

Here are the descriptions of the properties of the `CustomRolePrincipal`:

❑   `isRoleListCached`: Specifies whether the `CustomRolePrincipal` has cached the role information

❑   `cachedListChanged`: Specifies whether the role information cached in the `CustomRolePrincipal` has been modified

❑ roles: The ArrayList that caches the role information for the user that the CustomRolePrincipal represents

❑ username: Specifies the username of the user that the CustomRolePrincipal represents

Listing 24-24 illustrates the code for the second constructor of the CustomRolePrincipal. This constructor takes an array that contains the roles that the user is in.

Listing 24-24: The second constructor of the CustomRolePrincipal

```
public CustomRolePrincipal(IIdentity identity, string[] roles)
{
  if (identity == null)
    throw new ArgumentNullException("identity");

  if (roles == null)
    throw new ArgumentNullException("roles");

  this.identity = identity;
  isRoleListCached = false;
  cachedListChanged = false;
  if (identity != null)
    username = identity.Name;

  if (this.roles == null)
    this.roles = new ArrayList();

  if (roles != null && roles.Length > 0)
  {
    this.roles.Clear();
    this.roles.AddRange(roles);
    isRoleListCached = true;
    cachedListChanged = true;
  }
}
```

This constructor first initializes the same parameters as the first constructor and then clears the ArrayList that caches the roles for the user that the CustomRolePrincipal represents:

```
this.roles.Clear();
```

Then it caches the roles passed into it:

```
this.roles.AddRange(roles);
```

Next, the constructor sets the isRoleListCached field to true to signal other methods of the CustomRolePrincipal, such as IsInRole and GetRoles, that the roles have already been cached. As you'll see later, the IsInRole and GetRoles methods retrieve the roles for the user from the underlying data store if the roles haven't been cached yet:

```
isRoleListCached = true;
```

Finally, this constructor sets the cachedListChanged field to true to signal the CustomRoleManagerModule that the cache has changed. As you'll see later, at the end of each request, the `CustomRoleManagerModule` retrieves the roles from the cache and stores them in the `Cache` object if the cached roles have changed:

```
cachedListChanged = true;
```

GetRoles

The `CustomRoleManagerModule` calls the `GetRoles` method (see Listing 24-25) at the end of each request to retrieve the roles cached in the `CustomRolePrinicipal` and stores them in the `Cache` object.

Listing 24-25: The GetRoles method

```
public string[] GetRoles()
{
  if (identity == null)
    throw new ProviderException("identity is null");

  if (!identity.IsAuthenticated)
    return new string[0];

  if (!isRoleListCached)
  {
    roles.Clear();
    string[] rolesArray = Roles.GetRolesForUser(identity.Name);
    roles.AddRange(rolesArray);
    isRoleListCached = true;
    cachedListChanged = true;
    return rolesArray;
  }
  string[] rolesArray2 = new string[roles.Count];
  roles.CopyTo(rolesArray2);
  return rolesArray2;
}
```

The `GetRoles` method first checks whether the user's identity has been established, because roles are only applicable to authenticated users:

```
if (!identity.IsAuthenticated)
  return new string[0];
```

It then checks whether the roles have been cached. If so, it retrieves the roles from the cache and returns them to the caller:

```
string[] rolesArray2 = new string[roles.Count];
roles.CopyTo(rolesArray2);
return rolesArray2;
```

If the roles haven't been cached, the `GetRoles` method clears the cache:

```
roles.Clear();
```

Then it calls the GetRolesForUser method of the Roles class to retrieve the roles from the underlying data store:

```
string[] rolesArray = Roles.GetRolesForUser(identity.Name);
```

Next, it caches the retrieved roles:

```
roles.AddRange(rolesArray);
```

The method sets the isRolesListCached flag to true to inform other methods of the CustomRolePrincipal that the roles have already been retrieved from the data store and cached. This ensures that roles aren't retrieved multiple times from the data store:

```
isRoleListCached = true;
```

Finally, it sets the cachedListChanged flag to true to inform the CustomRoleManagerModule that the cache has been modified. As you'll see later, the module stores the cached roles in the Cache object at the end of each request if the cache has been modified.

```
cachedListChanged = true;
```

Implementing the IPrincipal Interface

CustomRolePrincipal, like all principals, implements the IPrincipal interface. The following code shows the definition of this interface:

```
public interface IPrincipal
{
  IIdentity Identity { get; }
  bool IsInRole(string role);
}
```

Listing 24-26 shows the CustomRolePrincipal class's implementation of the Identity property of the IPrincipal interface.

Listing 24-26: The Identity property

```
private IIdentity identity;
public IIdentity Identity
{
  get { return identity; }
}
```

As Listing 24-26 shows, the CustomRolePrincipal supports all types of identities, such as FormsIdentity and WindowsIdentity. In other words, the CustomRolePrincipal works with all types of authentication mechanisms such as Form Authentication and Windows Authentication.

Listing 24-27 shows the CustomRolePrincipal class's implementation of the IsInRole method of the IPrincipal interface.

Listing 24-27: The IsInRole method

```
public bool IsInRole(string role)
{
  GetRoles();
  return roles.Contains(role.Trim());
}
```

To determine whether the user is in the specified role, the `IsInRole` method calls the `GetRoles` method to ensure that the cache is populated. Recall that `GetRoles` retrieves the roles for the current user from the underlying data store and caches them if they haven't been already retrieved and cached:

```
GetRoles();
```

Then it uses the cache to determine whether the user is in the specified role:

```
return roles.Contains(role.Trim());
```

Developing Custom Role Manager Modules

This section develops a custom role manager HTTP module named `CustomRoleManagerModule` that caches the roles for the current user in the ASP.NET `Cache` object. `CustomRoleManagerModule`, like all HTTP modules, implements the `IHttpModule` interface. The following code shows the definition of this interface:

```
public interface IHttpModule
{
  void Dispose();
  void Init(HttpApplication application);
}
```

As discussed in Chapter 8, the `Dispose` method is where an HTTP module releases the resources it's holding before the module is disposed of. Because `CustomRoleManagerModule` doesn't hold any resources, its implementation of the `Dispose` method is pretty simple:

```
public void Dispose() { }
```

Your custom HTTP module must implement the `Dispose` method even if it doesn't hold any resources because a class must implement all the members of an interface that it derives from.

Listing 24-28 contains the code for the `Init` method of the `CustomRoleManagerModule`.

Listing 24-28: The Init method

```
public void Init(HttpApplication application)
{
  application.PostAuthenticateRequest +=
                        new EventHandler(PostAuthenticateRequestCallback);
  application.EndRequest += new EventHandler(EndRequestCallback);
}
```

As discussed in Chapter 8, the `HttpApplication` class calls the `Init` method of each registered HTTP module such as `CustomRoleManagerModule` to allow the module to register callbacks for one or more of the numerous events that the `HttpApplication` raises. Therefore, when it comes to writing a custom HTTP module such as `CustomRoleManagerModule`, the first order of business is to decide which `HttpApplication` events the module must handle. This in turn depends on what the module is supposed to be doing.

The main responsibilities of the `CustomRoleManagerModule` are as follows:

❑ Retrieve the roles for the current user from the ASP.NET `Cache` object and cache them in the `CustomRolePrincipal` that represents the user.

❑ Retrieve the roles cached in the `CustomRolePrincipal` that represents the current user and cache them in the ASP.NET `Cache` object. This allows the subsequent requests to retrieve the roles from the ASP.NET `Cache` object as opposed to the data store, to improve the overall performance of the application.

Now that you know what the `CustomRoleManagerModule` is supposed to do, you have to decide when in the request's life cycle the `CustomRoleManagerModule` must perform its two tasks. The first task must be performed after the user has been authenticated because roles are only applicable to authenticated users. The `HttpApplication` raises an event named `PostAuthenticateRequest` after the `AuthenticateRequest` event, that is, after the user has been authenticated.

Therefore, the `Init` method of the `CustomRoleManagerModule` registers a callback named `PostAuthenticateRequestCallback` for the `HttpApplication` class's `PostAuthenticateRequest` event as shown in Listing 24-28. As you'll see shortly, this callback retrieves the roles from the ASP.NET `Cache` object and caches them in the `CustomRolePrincipal` that represents the current user.

What about the second responsibility of the `CustomRoleManagerModule`? When in the request's life cycle should the `CustomRoleManagerModule` perform this task? Obviously the `CustomRoleManagerModule` must perform this task at the end of the request, when the response is about to be sent to the requesting browser.

Therefore, the `Init` method of the `CustomRoleManagerModule` registers a callback named `EndRequestCallback` for the `HttpApplication` class's `EndRequest` event as shown in Listing 24-28. As you'll see shortly, this callback retrieves the roles cached in the `CustomRolePrincipal` that represents the current user and caches them in the ASP.NET `Cache` object.

PostAuthenticateRequestCallback

Listing 24-29 contains the code for the `PostAuthenticateRequestCallback` method.

Listing 24-29: The PostAuthenticateRequestCallback method

```
private void PostAuthenticateRequestCallback(object source, EventArgs e)
{
  if (Roles.Enabled)
  {
    HttpApplication application = (HttpApplication)source;
    HttpContext context = application.Context;
```

(continued)

Listing 24-29: *(continued)*

```
      if (getRoles != null)
      {
        RoleManagerEventArgs args = new RoleManagerEventArgs(context);
        getRoles(this, args);
        if (args.RolesPopulated)
          return;
      }

      if (Roles.CacheRolesInCookie &&
        context.User.Identity.IsAuthenticated &&
        context.Cache[context.User.Identity.Name] != null)
      {
        string[] roles = (string[])context.Cache[context.User.Identity.Name];
        context.User = new CustomRolePrincipal(context.User.Identity, roles);
      }

      if (!(context.User is CustomRolePrincipal))
        context.User = new CustomRolePrincipal(context.User.Identity);
    }
}
```

`PostAuthenticateRequestCallback` first checks whether the role management feature is enabled. If it is, it accesses the `HttpContext` object:

```
      HttpApplication application = (HttpApplication)source;
      HttpContext context = application.Context;
```

It then raises the `GetRoles` event. As you'll see shortly, this event allows the page developer to bypass the rest of the code in the `PostAuthenticateRequestCallback`. In other words, the page developer takes complete control over the process of retrieving the roles and caching them in the principal that represents the current user.

The callback then ensures that the current user is authenticated because the roles are only applicable to authenticated users:

```
    context.User.Identity.IsAuthenticated
```

It next ensures that the page developer has enabled the caching feature:

```
    Roles.CacheRolesInCookie
```

Notice that even though the roles are cached in the ASP.NET `Cache` object as opposed to a cookie, the same `CacheRolesInCookie` property of the `Roles` class is used to specify whether the caching feature is enabled. Otherwise you would have to write your own custom `Roles` class that exposes a Boolean property with a more appropriate name such as `CacheRolesInAspNetCacheObject`.

The callback then ensures that the current user's roles are cached in the ASP.NET `Cache` object:

```
    context.Cache[context.User.Identity.Name] != null
```

If none of the three tests fails, PostAutenticateRequestCallback retrieves the current user's roles from the ASP.NET Cache object:

```
string[] roles = (string[])context.Cache[context.User.Identity.Name];
```

It then instantiates a CustomRolePrincipal to represent the current user, caches the retrieved roles in the internal cache of the CustomRolePrincipal, and assigns the principal to the User property of the HttpContext.

```
context.User = new CustomRolePrincipal(context.User.Identity, roles);
```

If any of the three tests fails, PostAuthenticateRequestCallback instantiates a CustomRolePrincipal to represent the current user without caching any roles in the internal cache of the CustomRolePrincipal because there are no roles to cache and assigns the principal to the User property of the HttpContext:

```
if (!(context.User is CustomRolePrincipal))
    context.User = new CustomRolePrincipal(context.User.Identity)
```

GetRoles Event

As Listing 24-29 shows, PostAuthenticateRequestCallback raises the GetRoles event to allow the page developer to take complete control over the process that retrieves the roles for the current user and caches them in the principal that represents the current user. The GetRoles event is of type RoleManagerEventHandler event delegate and is defined in the following code fragment:

```
private RoleManagerEventHandler getRoles;
public event RoleManagerEventHandler GetRoles
{
  add { getRoles = (RoleManagerEventHandler)Delegate.Combine(getRoles, value); }
  remove { getRoles = (RoleManagerEventHandler)Delegate.Remove(getRoles, value); }
}
```

Notice that GetRoles calls the Combine and Remove static methods of the Delegate class to add and remove delegates. The RoleManagerEventArgs class acts as the event data class for the GetRoles event. As the following code shows, this event data class exposes two properties. The first property is read-only and returns the current HttpContext. The second property, RolesPopulated, is a read-write Boolean property:

```
public sealed class RoleManagerEventArgs : EventArgs
{
  public RoleManagerEventArgs(HttpContext context);

  public HttpContext Context { get; }
  public bool RolesPopulated { get; set; }
}
```

Here is how the GetRoles event works:

1. The page developer registers a callback for the GetRoles event. The callback must have the following signature:

```
void MyCallback (object sender, RoleManagerEventArgs e);
```

735

2. The `HttpApplication` raises the `PostAuthenticateRequest` event and consequently calls the `PostAuthenticateRequestCallback` method of the `CustomRoleManagerModule`.

3. As the boldface code in Listing 24-29 shows, the `PostAuthenticateRequestCallback` method creates an instance of the `RoleManagerEventArgs` event data class and passes the `HttpContext` object into it:

```
RoleManagerEventArgs args = new RoleManagerEventArgs(context);
```

4. The method then raises the `GetRoles` event, which subsequently calls the callback method (the `MyCallback` method mentioned earlier) that the page developer has registered for this event and passes the preceding `RoleManagerEventArgs` object into it:

```
MyCallback(this, args);
```

5. The page developer's callback method can then take over the entire process of retrieving the roles and caching them in the principal that represents the current user. That is, the method can retrieve the roles from sources other than the ASP.NET `Cache` object, instantiate a principal of different type than `CustomRolePrincipal`, and cache the roles in the principal. The method then must set the `RolesPopulated` property of the `RoleManagerEventArgs` event data object passed into it to true to bypass the logic in the `PostAuthenticateRequestCallback` method.

6. The `PostAuthenticateRequestCallback` method then checks whether the page developer has set the `RolesPopulated` property to true. If so, the method returns:

```
if (args.RolesPopulated)
  return;
```

EndRequestCallback

Listing 24-30 illustrates the implementation of the `EndRequestCallback` method.

Listing 24-30: The EndRequestCallback method

```
private void EndRequestCallback(object source, EventArgs e)
{
  if (Roles.Enabled && Roles.CacheRolesInCookie)
  {
    HttpApplication application = (HttpApplication)source;
    HttpContext context = application.Context;
    if ((context.User != null) && (context.User is CustomRolePrincipal) &&
        context.User.Identity.IsAuthenticated)
    {
      CustomRolePrincipal principal = (CustomRolePrincipal)context.User;
      if (principal.CachedListChanged)
      {
        string key = Roles.CookieName;
        string[] roles = principal.GetRoles();
        CacheDependency cacheDependency =
                       (CacheDependency)context.Items["CacheDependencyObject"];

        context.Cache.Add(key, roles, cacheDependency, DateTime.Now.AddDays(2.0),
                   Cache.NoSlidingExpiration, CacheItemPriority.Normal, null);
      }
    }
```

```
        }
    }
```

The main responsibility of the `EndRequestCallback` method is to retrieve the roles cached in the `CustomRolePrincipal` that represents the current user and cache them in the ASP.NET `Cache` object. As Listing 24-30 shows, the method first ensures that the page developer has enabled both the role and role caching features. The page developer must set the `enabled` and `cacheRolesInCookie` attributes on the `<roleManager>` element in the `Web.config` or `Machine.config` file to enable these two features.

If both of these two features are enabled, the `EndRequestCallback` method accesses the current `HttpContext` as follows:

```
HttpApplication application = (HttpApplication)source;
HttpContext context = application.Context;
```

The method then ensures the current user is authenticated because roles are only applicable to authenticated users:

```
context.User.Identity.IsAuthenticated
```

The `EndRequestCallback` method then checks whether the roles cached in the `CustomRolePrincipal` that represents the current user have been modified. If they have, `EndRequestCallback` retrieves the roles cached in the `CustomRolePrincipal`:

```
string[] roles = principal.GetRoles();
```

The ASP.NET Framework comes with a class named `CacheDependency` that you can use to establish dependency between the item you cache in the ASP.NET `Cache` object and a file, a cache key, and so on. The `CacheDependency` automatically removes the item from the `Cache` object when the file or cache key that the cached item depends upon changes.

It's the responsibility of the underlying role provider to perform the following tasks:

❑ Create a `CacheDependency` that establishes dependency between the roles cached in the ASP.NET `Cache` object and a file, cache key, and so on.

❑ Store the `CacheDependency` object in the `Items` collection property of the current `HttpContext`.

Later in this chapter, you'll extend the functionality of the `XmlRoleProvider` to have it perform these two tasks. For now, assume the underlying role provider has added the required `CacheDependency` object to the `Items` collection of the `HttpContext` object. As Listing 24-30 shows, the `EndRequestCallback` method retrieves the `CacheDependency` object from the `Items` collection of the `HttpContext`:

```
CacheDependency cacheDependency =
                (CacheDependency)context.Items["CacheDependencyObject"];
```

It then adds the roles the current user is in to the ASP.NET `Cache` object and registers the retrieved `CacheDependency` object:

```
context.Cache.Add(key, roles, cacheDependency, DateTime.Now.AddDays(2.0),
            Cache.NoSlidingExpiration, CacheItemPriority.Normal, null);
```

XmlRoleProvider and CacheDependency

Listing 24-31 shows a new version of the `Initialize` method of the `XmlRoleProvider` that instantiates a `CacheDependency` object that establishes dependency between the roles that the `CustomRoleManagerModule` caches in the ASP.NET `Cache` object and the underlying XML file. The `XmlRoleProvider` adds this `CacheDependency` object to the `Items` collection of the `HttpContext` object:

```
HttpContext.Current.Items["CacheDependencyObject"] =
                new CacheDependency(HttpContext.Current.Server.MapPath(dataFile));
```

Listing 24-31: The Initialize method

```
public override void Initialize(string name, NameValueCollection config)
{
  if (config == null)
    throw new ArgumentNullException("config");

  if (string.IsNullOrEmpty(name))
    name = "XmlRoleProvider";

  if (string.IsNullOrEmpty(config["description"]))
  {
    config.Remove("description");
    config.Add("description", "Stores role information in an XML document");
  }
  base.Initialize(name, config);

  applicationName = config["applicationName"];
  if (string.IsNullOrEmpty(applicationName))
    applicationName = "/";
  config.Remove("applicationName");

  dataFile = config["dataFile"];
  if (string.IsNullOrEmpty(dataFile))
    dataFile = "roles.xml";
  config.Remove("dataFile");

  HttpContext.Current.Items["CacheDependencyObject"] =
    new CacheDependency(HttpContext.Current.Server.MapPath(dataFile));

  if (config.Count > 0)
  {
    string key = config.GetKey(0);
    if (!string.IsNullOrEmpty(key))
      throw new ProviderException("Unrecognized attribute");
  }
  CreateXmlFile();
}
```

Using the XmlRoleProvider

This section develops a Web application that uses the components developed in this chapter: `XmlRoleProvider`, `CustomRolePrincipal`, and `CustomRoleManagerModule`. Here are the steps you must implement to develop the application:

1. Perform these tasks to register the `XmlRoleProvider` provider with the application as shown in the following code:

    a. Use an `<add>` element to add the `XmlRoleProvider` to the `<providers>` section of the `<roleManager>` section of the `Web.config` or `Machine.config` file.

    b. Assign the friendly name of the `XmlRoleProvider` to the `defaultProvider` attribute of the `<roleManager>` element.

    c. Set the `enabled` attribute of the `<roleManager>` element to true to enable the role management feature.

    d. Set the `cacheRolesInCookie` attribute of the `<roleManager>` element to true to enable the role caching feature.

```
<roleManager defaultProvider="XmlRoleProvider" enabled="true"
cacheRolesInCookie="false">
  <providers>
    <add name="XmlRoleProvider" type="CustomComponents.XmlRoleProvider"
    applicationName="/" dataFile="roles.xml"/>
  </providers>
</roleManager>
```

2. Register the `CustomRoleManagerModule` with the application. To accomplish this, you need to use an `<add>` element to add the `CustomRoleManagerModule` to the `<httpModules>` section of the `Web.config` or `Machine.config` file.

```
<httpModules>
  <add name="CustomRoleManagerModule"
  type="CustomComponents.CustomRoleManagerModule"/>
</httpModules>
```

3. Perform one of the following tasks:

    a. Add the `XmlRoleProvider.cs`, `CustomRoleManagerModule.cs`, and `CustomRolePrincipal.cs` files to the `App_Code` directory of the application.

    b. Create a class library project, add the preceding files to this project, and compile the project into an assembly. If the assembly has a strong name, you can add the assembly to the GAC. Otherwise, you should add the assembly to the bin directory of the application directly.

4. Develop an ASP.NET page that renders the user interface that allows you to do the following:

    a. Add roles

    b. Remove roles

    c. Add users to roles

    d. Remove users from roles

> e. Retrieve all roles
>
> f. Retrieve all users in a specified role

Listing 24-32 contains this ASP.NET page.

Listing 24-32: A Web page that renders the user interface that allows you to manage roles and users

```csharp
<%@ Page Language="C#" %>
<%@ Import Namespace="System.Xml" %>
<script runat="server">
  void Page_Load(object sender, EventArgs arg)
  {
    if (!IsPostBack)
    {
      LoadRoles();
      LoadUsers();
    }
  }

  protected void RolesDropDownListSelectCallback(object sender, EventArgs e)
  {
    RoleTextBox.Text = RolesDropDownList.SelectedItem.Text;
    LoadUsers();
  }

  protected void UsersDropDownListSelectCallback(object sender, EventArgs e)
  {
    UserTextBox.Text = UsersDropDownList.SelectedItem.Text;
  }

  private void LoadRoles()
  {
    RolesDropDownList.Items.Clear();
    UserTextBox.Text = "";
    string[] roles = Roles.GetAllRoles();
    foreach (string role in roles)
    {
      RolesDropDownList.Items.Add(new ListItem(role, role));
    }
    RolesDropDownList.SelectedIndex = 0;
  }

  private void LoadUsers()
  {
    UsersDropDownList.Items.Clear();
    UserTextBox.Text = "";
    if (string.IsNullOrEmpty(RolesDropDownList.SelectedValue))
      return;

    string[] users = Roles.GetUsersInRole(RolesDropDownList.SelectedValue);
    if (users.Length < 1)
      return;
    foreach (string user in users)
    {
```

```
        UsersDropDownList.Items.Add(new ListItem(user, user));
    }
    UsersDropDownList.SelectedIndex = 0;
    UserTextBox.Text = UsersDropDownList.SelectedValue;
}

protected void AddRoleCallback(object sender, EventArgs e)
{
    Roles.CreateRole(RoleTextBox.Text);
    LoadRoles();
    LoadUsers();
}

protected void AddUserCallback(object sender, EventArgs e)
{
    Roles.AddUserToRole(UserTextBox.Text, RolesDropDownList.SelectedValue);
    LoadUsers();
}

protected void DeleteRoleCallback(object sender, EventArgs e)
{
    Roles.DeleteRole(RoleTextBox.Text);
    LoadRoles();
    LoadUsers();
}

protected void DeleteUserCallback(object sender, EventArgs e)
{
    Roles.RemoveUserFromRole(UserTextBox.Text, RolesDropDownList.SelectedValue);
    LoadUsers();
}
</script>

<html xmlns="http://www.w3.org/1999/xhtml">
<body>
  <form id="form1" runat="server">
    <table>
      <tr>
        <td>
          <table>
            <tr>
              <td align="center">
                <strong>Roles:</strong>
                <asp:DropDownList runat="server" ID="RolesDropDownList"
                AutoPostBack="true"
                OnSelectedIndexChanged="RolesDropDownListSelectCallback" />
              </td>
            </tr>
            <tr>
              <td align="left">
                <asp:TextBox runat="server" ID="RoleTextBox" />
                <asp:Button runat="server" Text="Add Role"
                OnClick="AddRoleCallback" />
                <asp:Button runat="server" Text="Delete Role"
```

(continued)

Listing 24-32: *(continued)*

```
                      OnClick="DeleteRoleCallback" />
                  </td>
              </tr>
          </table>
        </td>
    </tr>
    <tr>
      <td>
        <table>
          <tr>
            <td align="center">
              <strong>Users:</strong>
              <asp:DropDownList runat="server" ID="UsersDropDownList"
              AutoPostBack="true"
              OnSelectedIndexChanged="UsersDropDownListSelectCallback" />
            </td>
          </tr>
          <tr>
            <td align="right">
              <asp:TextBox runat="server" ID="UserTextBox" />
              <asp:Button runat="server" Text="Add User"
              OnClick="AddUserCallback" />
              <asp:Button runat="server" Text="Delete User"
              OnClick="DeleteUserCallback" />
            </td>
          </tr>
        </table>
      </td>
    </tr>
  </table>
</form>
</body>
</html>
```

Figure 24-1 illustrates the user interface that you'll see on your browser when you access the page shown in Listing 24-32. This user interface allows you to perform the following role/user management tasks:

❑ **View all the available roles.** When the page is accessed the first time, the Page_Load method automatically retrieves all the available roles for the current application and populates the top DropDownList control with the retrieved roles.

❑ **Add a new role.** Enter the new rolename in the top TextBox control, and then click the top Add Role button.

❑ **Delete a role.** Select the role from the top DropDownList control. This automatically enters the rolename in the top TextBox control. Then click the Delete Role button.

❑ **View all the users in a specified role.** Simply select the role from the top DropDownList control. This will automatically populate the bottom DropDownList control with the list of users in the specified role.

❑ **Add a specified user to a specified role.** Select the role from the top DropDownList control, enter the new username in the bottom TextBox control, and click the Add User button.

❑ **Remove a specified user from the specified role.** Select the role from the top `DropDownList` control, select the user from the bottom `DropDownList` control, and click the Delete User button.

As the boldface portions of Listing 24-32 illustrate, this application uses the static methods of the `Roles` class such as `GetAllRoles`, `CreateRole`, and others to perform the role and user management tasks when you interact with the `DropDownList` and `Button` controls shown in Figure 24-1.

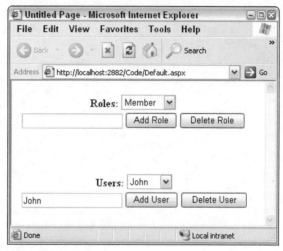

Figure 24-1

Summary

This chapter showed you how to implement the following custom components:

❑ `XmlRoleProvider` custom role provider that retrieves role information from and stores role information in an XML file

❑ `CustomRolePrincipal` custom principal

❑ `CustomRoleManagerModule` HTTP module

The `CustomRolePrincipal` and `CustomRoleManagerModule` work together to allow you to cache role information for the current user in the ASP.NET `Cache` object and to establish a dependency between the cached roles and the underlying XML file.

In the next chapter, you see how to write custom controls that contain client-side code to take full advantage of the DHTML capabilities of the requesting browser to dramatically reduce your application's response time and to enhance the user experience.

25

Developing Custom Provider-Based Services

The previous chapters discussed the following standard ASP.NET 2.0 provider-based services:

❑ Tabular data source control model that services tabular data from any type of data store, whether or not the data store itself is tabular (see Chapters 12, 13, and 14)

❑ Hierarchical data source control model that services hierarchical data from any type of data store, whether or not the data store itself is hierarchical (see Chapters 15 and 16)

❑ Membership model that services membership data from any type of data store (see Chapters 21 and 22)

❑ Role model that services role data from any type of data store (see Chapters 23 and 24)

This chapter provides you with a step-by-step recipe that you can use to develop your own custom provider-based services that can service data from any type of data store. The chapter then uses the recipe to develop a custom provider-based RSS service that can service RSS data from any type of data store.

Recipe for Developing Custom Provider-Based Services

Here are the main steps that you must implement to develop a provider-based service:

1. Implement a custom provider base class that defines the API for providers.

2. Implement a custom provider collection class to contain providers.

3. Configure the `Web.config` or `Machine.config` file to support a custom configuration section for the service.

4. Implement a service class that performs the following tasks:

    a.   Instantiates and initializes the registered providers

    b.   Defines the API for the service

The following sections use this recipe to develop a custom provider-based RSS service.

Provider-Based RSS Service

Chapter 8 developed an HTTP handler named RssHandler that services requests for extension .rss. Listing 25-1 shows the definition of RssHandler, where it generates an RSS document from a SQL Server database. As the highlighted portions of this listing illustrate, RssHandler uses ADO.NET classes to retrieve the required data to generate the RSS document. Because ADO.NET classes are the data access API for relational databases, they can't be used to retrieve data from non-relational data stores such as XML documents, Web services, flat files, and so on. In other words, the implementation of the RssHandler shown in Listing 25-1 is tied to relational databases and can't generate RSS documents from non-relational databases.

Listing 25-1: The ProcessRequest method of RssHandler

```
public class RssHandler : IHttpHandler
{
  bool IHttpHandler.IsReusable
  {
    get { return false; }
  }

  DbDataReader GetDataReader()
  {
    ConnectionStringSettings cssettings =
            ConfigurationManager.ConnectionStrings["MyConnectionString"];
    DbProviderFactory provider =
            DbProviderFactories.GetFactory(cssettings.ProviderName);
    DbConnection con = provider.CreateConnection();
    con.ConnectionString = cssettings.ConnectionString;
    DbCommand com = provider.CreateCommand();
    com.Connection = con;
    com.CommandText = "Select * From Articles";
    con.Open();
    return com.ExecuteReader(CommandBehavior.CloseConnection);
  }

  void IHttpHandler.ProcessRequest(HttpContext context)
  {
    DbDataReader reader = GetDataReader();
    XmlWriterSettings settings = new XmlWriterSettings();
    settings.Indent = true;
    context.Response.ContentType = "text/xml";
    using (XmlWriter writer =
                XmlWriter.Create(context.Response.OutputStream, settings))
    {
      writer.WriteStartDocument();
      writer.WriteStartElement("rss");
```

```
        writer.WriteAttributeString("version", "2.0");
        writer.WriteStartElement("channel");
        writer.WriteElementString("title", "New Articles On greatarticles.com");
        writer.WriteElementString("link", "http://www.greatarticles.com");
        writer.WriteElementString("description",
                    "The list of newly published articles on greatarticles.com");
        while (reader.Read())
        {
          writer.WriteStartElement("item");
          writer.WriteElementString("title", (string)reader["Title"]);
          writer.WriteElementString("description", (string)reader["Abstract"]);
          writer.WriteElementString("link",
                          "http://localhost:1507/CreditCardForm/" +
                                (string)reader["AuthorName"] + ".aspx");
          writer.WriteEndElement();
        }
        writer.WriteEndElement();
        writer.WriteEndElement();
        writer.WriteEndDocument();
      }
    }
  }
```

The following sections use the recipe presented in the previous section to implement a custom provider-based RSS service that will allow components such as RssHandler to retrieve RSS data from any type of data store. Following the recipe, the next sections perform the following tasks:

1. Implement a custom provider base named RssProvider that defines the API for RSS providers.

2. Implement a custom provider collection named RssProviderCollection to contain RSS providers.

3. Take the following steps to configure the Web.config and Machine.config configuration files to add support for a new section named <rssService>:

    a. Implement a custom configuration section named RssSection

    b. Register RssSection

4. Implement a service class named RssService that performs the following tasks:

    a. Instantiate and initialize the registered RSS providers

    b. Define the API for the RSS service

Custom Provider Base

Following the recipe, this section develops a custom provider base named RssProvider that derives from the ProviderBase class and defines the API for RSS providers. The following listing contains the code for the RssProvider base class.

```
public abstract class RssProvider : ProviderBase
{
  public abstract void LoadRss(Stream stream);
}
```

As this listing shows, the API that `RssProvider` defines consists of a single method named `LoadRss` that takes a `Stream` as its input and loads the `Stream` with the RSS document.

Custom Provider Collection

The next order of business is to develop a custom provider collection named `RssProviderCollection` that derives from the `ProviderCollection` base class, as shown in Listing 25-2.

Listing 25-2: The RssProviderCollection class

```
public class RssProviderCollection : ProviderCollection
{
  public new RssProvider this[string name]
  {
    get { return (RssProvider) base[name]; }
  }

  public override void Add(ProviderBase provider)
  {
    if (provider == null)
      throw new ArgumentNullException("provider");

    if (!(provider is RssProvider))
      throw new ArgumentException ("Invalid provider type", "provider");

    base.Add(provider);
  }
}
```

`RssProviderCollection` implements an indexer that returns an `RssProvider` type from the collection, and overrides the `Add` method to ensure that only providers of type `RssProvider` are added to the collection.

Configuring the Web.config and Machine.config Files

The page developer must be allowed to perform the following tasks in `Web.config` or `Machine.config` without writing a single line of code:

❑   Register new RSS providers

❑   Configure the provider-based RSS service to use a specified RSS provider

To make that possible you need to configure the `Web.config` or `Machine.config` file to support a custom section named `<rssService>` (see Listing 25-3) that contains a child element named `<providers>` to allow the page developer to use an `<add>` element to register an RSS provider with the provider-based RSS service. As you'll see later, each RSS provider will be specifically designed to generate RSS data from a specific data store. For example, the `SqlRssProvider` RSS provider will be specifically designed to generate RSS data from a SQL Server database.

The `<rssService>` section also needs to expose an attribute named `defaultProvider` to allow the page developer to configure the RSS service to use the specified RSS provider from the list of registered RSS providers.

Here are the steps you must implement to configure the configuration files:

1. Implement a custom configuration section named `RssServiceSection` that derives from the `ConfigurationSection` base class.

2. Register the `<rssService>` section with the `Web.config` or `Machine.config` file and designate the `RssServiceSection` as its handler.

Listing 25-3: The custom section for RSS providers

```
<configuration>
  <system.web>
    <rssService defaultProvider="FriendlyNameOfRSSProvider">
      <providers>
        <add name="FriendlyNameOfRSSProvider"
        type="FullyQualifiedNameOfRSSProvider, AssemblyThatContainsRSSProvider" />
      </providers>
    </rssService>
  </system.web>
</configuration>
```

Custom Configuration Section

Listing 25-4 contains the code for the `RssServiceSection` custom configuration section.

Listing 25-4: The RssServiceSection custom configuration section

```
using System;
using System.Configuration;

public class RssServiceSection : ConfigurationSection
{
  [ConfigurationProperty("providers")]
  public ProviderSettingsCollection Providers
  {
    get { return (ProviderSettingsCollection) base["providers"]; }
  }

  [StringValidator(MinLength = 1)]
  [ConfigurationProperty("defaultProvider", DefaultValue = "SqlRssProvider")]
  public string DefaultProvider
  {
    get { return (string) base["defaultProvider"]; }
    set { base["defaultProvider"] = value; }
  }
}
```

RssServiceSection defines the following two properties:

❑ Providers: This property is annotated with the [ConfigurationProperty("providers")] metadata attribute to map the property to the <providers> subelement of the <rssService> element.

❑ DefaultProvider: This property is annotated with the [ConfigurationProperty ("defaultProvider")] metadata attribute to map the property to the defaultProvider attribute of the <rssService> element.

Registering the <rssService> Section

Listing 25-5 registers the <rssService> section and designates the RssServiceSection custom configuration section as its handler.

Listing 25-5: Registering the <rssService> section

```
<configuration >
  <configSections>
    <sectionGroup name="system.web">
      <section name="rssService" type="CustomComponents.RssServiceSection"
      allowDefinition="MachineToApplication" restartOnExternalChanges="true" />
    </sectionGroup>
  </configSections>
</configuration>
```

Here are the main steps you must implement to register the <rssService> section:

1. Add a new <sectionGroup> element as the subelement of the <configSections> element and set the value of its name attribute to the name of the section group to which the <rssService> section belongs, that is, <system.web>.

2. Add a <section> element as the subelement of the <sectionGroup> element you just added, and set the values of its attributes as follows:

   a. Set the value of the name attribute to the name of the new section, <rssSection>.

   b. Set the value of the type attribute to a string that consists of two main parts, the fully qualified name of the custom configuration section that handles the new section (CustomComponents.RssServiceSection) and the (weak or strong) name of the assembly that contains the custom configuration section. If you don't include the name of the assembly, ASP.NET will assume that the currently executing assembly contains the RssServiceSection custom configuration section.

Implementing the Service Class

Listing 25-6 illustrates the implementation of the RssService class.

Listing 25-6: The RssService class

```
using System;
using System.Configuration;
using System.Configuration.Provider;
```

```
using System.Web.Configuration;
using System.Web;

public class RssService
{
  private static RssProvider provider = null;
  private static RssProviderCollection providers = null;
  private static bool IsInitialized = false;

  public RssProvider Provider
  {
    get { Initialize(); return provider; }
  }

  public RssProviderCollection Providers
  {
    get { Initialize(); return providers; }
  }

  public static void LoadRss(Stream stream)
  {
    Initialize();
    provider.LoadRss(stream);
  }

  private static void Initialize()
  {
    if (!IsInitialized)
    {
      RssServiceSection section = (RssServiceSection)
                WebConfigurationManager.GetSection("system.web/rssService");

      providers = new RssProviderCollection();
      ProvidersHelper.InstantiateProviders
                  (section.Providers, providers, typeof(RssProvider));
      provider = providers[section.DefaultProvider];

      if (provider == null)
        throw new ProviderException ("Unable to load default RssProvider");
      IsInitialized = true;
    }
  }
}
```

The main responsibilities of the RssService class are as follows.

First, the class must instantiate and initialize the providers registered in the <providers> subelement of the <rssService> section. To do this, the Initialize method of the RssService calls the GetSection method of the WebConfigurationManager class to access the RssServiceSection:

```
RssServiceSection section = (RssServiceSection)
              WebConfigurationManager.GetSection("system.web/rssService");
```

It then instantiates the `Providers` collection:

```
providers = new RssProviderCollection();
```

Next, it calls the `InstantiateProviders` method of the `ProvidersHelper` class. This method instantiates and initializes the providers registered in the <providers> subelement of the <rssService> section and loads them into the `Providers` collection:

```
ProvidersHelper.InstantiateProviders
                    (section.Providers, providers, typeof(RssProvider));
```

The method then uses the value of the `DefaultProvider` property of the `RssServiceSection` object to index into the `Providers` collection to access the default provider and to assign it to the `Provider` property:

```
provider = providers[section.DefaultProvider];
```

Notice that the `Initialize` method expects the page developer to set the value of the `defaultProvider` attribute of the <rssService> element.

The next thing the `RssService` class needs to do is call the `Initialize` method from the `Provider` and `Providers` properties to ensure that the `provider` and `providers` private fields have been initialized before they are accessed:

```
public RssProvider Provider
{
  get
  {
    Initialize();
    return provider;
  }
}

public RssProviderCollection Providers
{
  get
  {
    Initialize();
    return providers;
  }
}
```

Then the class needs to define the API for servicing RSS data. This API consists of a single method named `LoadRss` as shown in the following code fragment:

```
public static void LoadRss(Stream stream)
{
  Initialize();
  provider.LoadRss(stream);
}
```

The `LoadRss` method calls the `Initialize` method to ensure the `RssService` has been initialized:

```
Initialize();
```

It then delegates the responsibility of loading RSS data from the underlying data store to the configured RSS provider:

```
provider.LoadRss(stream);
```

Using the RSS Service

The provider-based RSS service developed in the previous section allows components such as the RssHandler HTTP handler to retrieve RSS data from any type of data store. This section provides a new implementation of RssHandler that delegates the responsibility of generating the RSS document from the underlying data store to the RssService component.

Listing 25-7 contains the code for the new version of the RssHandler HTTP handler.

Listing 25-7: The new version of RssHandler HTTP handler that uses RssService

```
public class RssHandler : IHttpHandler
{
  bool IHttpHandler.IsReusable
  {
    get { return false; }
  }

  void IHttpHandler.ProcessRequest(HttpContext context)
  {
    context.Response.ContentType = "text/xml";
    RssService.LoadRss(context.Response.OutputStream);
  }
}
```

The ProcessRequest method of RssHandler sets the value of the ContentType property of the Response to the string value text/xml to indicate to the requesting browser that the response contains an XML document:

```
context.Response.ContentType = "text/xml";
```

The method then calls the LoadRss static method of RssService and passes the OutputStream of the Response into it. As discussed before, LoadRss uses the configured RSS provider to generate the RSS document from the data retrieved from the data store and to load the document into the OutputStream:

```
RssService.LoadRss(context.Response.OutputStream);
```

SqlRssProvider

The previous sections implemented the new provider-based RSS service that is capable of generating RSS data from any type of data store. This section implements an RSS provider named SqlRssProvider that derives from the RssProvider base class and retrieves RSS data from a SQL Server database. Because the RssProvider base class derives from the ProviderBase class, SqlRssProvider must implement both the `LoadRss` method of `RssProvider` and the `Initialize` method of `ProviderBase`, as discussed in the following sections.

Initialize

Listing 25-8 presents the implementation of the `Initialize` method.

Listing 25-8: The Initialize method

```
public override void Initialize(string name, NameValueCollection config)
{
  if (config == null)
    throw new ArgumentNullException("config");

  if (string.IsNullOrEmpty(name))
    name = "SqlRssProvider";

  if (string.IsNullOrEmpty(config["description"]))
  {
    config.Remove("description");
    config.Add("description", "Retrieve RSS data from the SQL Server database");
  }
  base.Initialize(name, config);

  string connectionStringName = config["connectionStringName"];
  if (string.IsNullOrEmpty(connectionStringName))
    throw new ProviderException("Invalid connection string name");

  connectionString =
     ConfigurationManager.ConnectionStrings[connectionStringName].ConnectionString;
  if (string.IsNullOrEmpty(connectionString))
    throw new ProviderException("Connection string not found");
  config.Remove("connectionStringName");

  channelTitle = config["channelTitle"];
  if (string.IsNullOrEmpty(channelTitle))
    channelTitle = "Unknown";
  config.Remove("channelTitle");

  channelDescription = config["channelDescription"];
  if (string.IsNullOrEmpty(channelDescription))
    channelDescription = "Unknown";
  config.Remove("channelDescription");

  channelLink = config["channelLink"];
  if (string.IsNullOrEmpty(channelLink))
    channelLink = "Unknown";
  config.Remove("channelLink");

  itemTitleField = config["itemTitleField"];
  if (string.IsNullOrEmpty(itemTitleField))
    throw new ProviderException("Title field not found");
  config.Remove("itemTitleField");
```

```
      itemDescriptionField = config["itemDescriptionField"];
      if (string.IsNullOrEmpty(itemDescriptionField))
        throw new ProviderException("Description field not found");
      config.Remove("itemDescriptionField");

      itemLinkField = config["itemLinkField"];
      if (string.IsNullOrEmpty(itemLinkField))
        throw new ProviderException("Link field not found");
      config.Remove("itemLinkField");

      itemLinkFormatString = config["itemLinkFormatString"];
      config.Remove("itemLinkFormatString");

      commandText = config["commandText"];
      if (string.IsNullOrEmpty(commandText))
        throw new ProviderException("Command text not found");
      config.Remove("commandText");

      string commandTypeText = config["commandType"];
      if (string.IsNullOrEmpty(commandTypeText))
        commandType = CommandType.Text;
      else if (commandTypeText.ToLower() == "storedprocedure")
        commandType = CommandType.StoredProcedure;
      else
        commandType = CommandType.Text;
      config.Remove("commandType");

      if (config.Count > 0)
      {
        string key = config.GetKey(0);
        if (!string.IsNullOrEmpty(key))
          throw new ProviderException("Unrecognized attribute");
      }
    }
```

As Listing 25-8 shows, the `Initialize` method first performs the four tasks that the `Initialize` method of all providers must perform:

1. It raises an exception if the `NameValueCollection` is null:

```
if (config == null)
  throw new ArgumentNullException("config");
```

2. It sets the friendly name of the provider if it hasn't already been set:

```
if (string.IsNullOrEmpty(name))
  name = "SqlRssProvider";
```

3. It sets the value of the `description` field if it hasn't already been set:

```
if (string.IsNullOrEmpty(config["description"]))
{
  config.Remove("description");
  config.Add("description", "Retrieve RSS data from the SQL Server database");
}
```

4. It calls the `Initialize` method of the base class to allow the base class to initialize the name and description properties. In other words, the provider must delegate the responsibility of setting these two properties to its base class as opposed to overriding the `Name` and `Description` properties.

```
base.Initialize(name, config);
```

Like the `Initialize` method of all providers, the `Initialize` method then iterates through each name/value pair in the `NameValueCollection` and performs the following tasks for each pair:

1. Uses the `name` part of the pair to index into the `NameValueCollection` to access the value part of the pair.

2. Uses the value to set the respective property of the provider.

3. Calls the `Remove` method of the `NameValueCollection` to remove the name/value pair from the collection.

The `Initialize` method follows this three-step pattern to set the values of the `connectionString`, `commandText`, `commandType`, `channelTitle`, `channelDescription`, `channelLink`, `itemTitleField`, `itemDescriptionField`, `itemLinkField`, and `itemLinkFormatString` private fields of the `SqlRssProvider`. These fields are discussed in the following sections.

Connection String

The `Initialize` method needs to set the `connectionString` private field of the `SqlRssProvider`. First it uses the `connectionStringName` string to index into the `NameValueCollection` to access the associated value. If the value is null or an empty string, the method raises a `ProviderException` exception because `SqlRssProvider` needs this value to access the underlying data store:

```
string connectionStringName = config["connectionStringName"];
if (string.IsNullOrEmpty(connectionStringName))
  throw new ProviderException("Invalid connection string name");
```

Next, it uses the value it just obtained to index into the `ConnectionStrings` collection of the `ConfigurationManager` class to access the connection string and assign it to the `connectionString` private field of the `SqlRssProvider` for future reference. The `ConnectionStrings` collection represents the `<connectionStrings>` section of the configuration file. The page developer must do the following:

❏ Use the `<add>` element to register the required connection string with the configuration file.

❏ Set the `name` attribute of the `<add>` element to the friendly name of the connection string.

❏ Assign the connection string to the `connectionString` attribute of the `<add>` element.

You'll see an example of these three steps later in this chapter.

```
connectionString =
    ConfigurationManager.ConnectionStrings[connectionStringName].ConnectionString;
if (string.IsNullOrEmpty(connectionString))
  throw new ProviderException("Connection string not found");
```

Finally, the `Initialize` method removes the name/value pair associated with the connection string from the `NameValueCollection`:

```
config.Remove("connectionStringName");
```

Command Text

The `SqlRssProvider` uses the connection string to connect to the underlying data store. The command text, on the other hand, specifies the SQL `Select` statement or stored procedure that the `SqlRssProvider` must use to retrieve the required data from the data store. To set the `commandText` private field of the `SqlRssProvider`, the `Initialize` method uses the `commandText` string to index into the `NameValueCollection` to access the value of the `commandText` attribute and assign the value to the `commandText` private field. If the value is null or an empty string, it raises a `ProviderException` exception because the `SqlRssProvider` can't operate without this value:

```
commandText = config["commandText"];
if (string.IsNullOrEmpty(commandText))
  throw new ProviderException("Command text not found");
```

The method then removes the associated name/value pair from the `NameValueCollection`:

```
config.Remove("commandText");
```

Command Type

Because the `commandText` field can contain a SQL `Select` statement or stored procedure, the page developer must set the value of the `commandType` attribute of the `<add>` element that registers the `SqlRssProvider` to one of the following values:

- ❑ `"Text"` (case insensitive) to specify that the `commandText` attribute contains a SQL `Select` statement

- ❑ `"StoredProcedure"` (case insensitive) to specify that the `commandText` attribute contains a stored procedure

The `Initialize` method then follows the same steps as for the `commandText` private field to set the value of the `commandType` private field. The only difference is that the method must map the string value that it retrieves from the `NameValueCollection` to its associated `CommandType` enumeration value as follows:

```
string commandTypeText = config["commandType"];
if (string.IsNullOrEmpty(commandTypeText))
  commandType = CommandType.Text;
else if (commandTypeText.ToLower() == "storedprocedure")
  commandType = CommandType.StoredProcedure;
else
  commandType = CommandType.Text;
config.Remove("commandType");
```

RSS-Related Fields

The `SqlRssProvider` supports RSS version 2.0. Listing 25-9 shows an example of an RSS document that the `SqlRssProvider` generates.

Listing 25-9: A sample RSS document generated by SqlRssProvider

```xml
<?xml version="1.0" encoding="utf-8"?>
<rss version="2.0">
  <channel>
    <title>New Articles On greatarticles.com</title>
    <link>http://www.articles.com</link>
    <description>List of newly published articles on articles.com</description>
    <item>
      <title>ASP.NET 2.0</title>
      <description>Discusses new ASP.NET 2.0 features</description>
      <link>http://localhost:1507/CreditCardForm/Smith.aspx</link>
    </item>
    <item>
      <title>View State Management</title>
      <description>In-depth coverage of view state management</description>
      <link>http://localhost:1507/CreditCardForm/Murray.aspx</link>
    </item>
    <item>
      <title>XSLT</title>
      <description>Discusses common applications of XSLT</description>
      <link>http://localhost:1507/CreditCardForm/Brown.aspx</link>
    </item>
    <item>
      <title>Introduction to XML</title>
      <description>Provides an introduction to XML</description>
      <link>http://localhost:1507/CreditCardForm/Smith.aspx</link>
    </item>
    <item>
      <title>XML Web Services</title>
      <description>In-depth coverage of XML Web services</description>
      <link>http://localhost:1507/CreditCardForm/Murray.aspx</link>
    </item>
  </channel>
</rss>
```

As Listing 25-9 illustrates, and as discussed in Chapter 8, the RSS document, like all other XML documents, has a single root element named `<rss>` with a mandatory attribute named `version` that the `SqlRssProvider` sets to 2.0, as you'll see later. The `<rss>` element contains a single child element named `<channel>`, which in turn contains the following child elements:

❑ A single `<title>` child element

❑ A single `<description>` child element

❑ A single `<link>` child element

❑ Zero or more `<item>` child element(s)

As you'll see later, `SqlRssProvider` renders the values of its `channelTitle`, `channelDescription`, and `channelLink` private fields within the opening and closing tags of the `<title>`, `<description>`, and `<link>` child elements, respectively.

As Listing 25-9 shows, each `<item>` element contains a single instance of `<title>`, `<description>`, and `<link>` child elements. `SqlRssProvider` exposes the following four private fields:

❑ itemTitleField: The name of the database field whose values are rendered within the opening and closing tags of the <title> child elements of the <item> elements.

❑ itemDescriptionField: The name of the database field whose values are rendered within the opening and closing tags of the <description> child elements of the <item> elements.

❑ itemLinkField: The name of the database field whose values are rendered within the opening and closing tags of the <link> child elements of the <item> elements.

❑ itemLinkFormatString: Formats the values of the database field whose name is given by itemLinkField before they are rendered within the opening and closing tags of the <link> child elements of the <item> elements.

LoadRss

Listing 25-10 presents the code for the LoadRss method of the SqlRssProvider.

Listing 25-10: The LoadRss method of SqlRssProvider

```
public override void LoadRss(Stream stream)
{
   SqlDataReader reader = GetDataReader();

   Channel channel = new Channel();
   channel.Title = channelTitle;
   channel.Link = channelLink;
   channel.Description = channelDescription;

   ArrayList items = new ArrayList();
   Item item;
   while (reader.Read())
   {
      item = new Item();
      item.Title = (string)reader[itemTitleField];
      item.Link = (string)reader[itemLinkField];
      item.Description = (string)reader[itemDescriptionField];
      item.LinkFormatString = itemLinkFormatString;
      items.Add(item);
   }
   reader.Close();
   RssHelper.GenerateRss(channel, (Item[])items.ToArray(typeof(Item)), stream);
}
```

The LoadRss method calls the GetDataReader method to access the SqlDataReader object that contains the required data:

```
SqlDataReader reader = GetDataReader();
```

It then instantiates an instance of the Channel struct:

```
Channel channel = new Channel();
```

Listing 25-11 illustrates the definition of the Channel struct.

Listing 25-11: The definition of Channel

```
public struct Channel
{
  public string Title;
  public string Description;
  public string Link;
}
```

The `LoadRss` method then assigns the values of the `channelTitle`, `channelDescription`, and `channelLink` fields to the `Title`, `Description`, and `Link` fields of the `Channel` object:

```
channel.Title = channelTitle;
channel.Link = channelLink;
channel.Description = channelDescription;
```

Next, it instantiates an `ArrayList`:

```
ArrayList items = new ArrayList();
```

The method then iterates through the database records and instantiates an instance of the `Item` struct for each enumerated data record:

```
    item = new Item();
```

Listing 25-12 illustrates the definition of the `Item` struct.

Listing 25-12: The definition of Item

```
public struct Item
{
  public string Title;
  public string Description;
  public string Link;
  public string LinkFormatString;
}
```

For each database record, the `LoadRss` method assigns the values of the database fields whose names are given by the `itemTitleField`, `itemDescriptionField`, and `itemLinkField` private fields to the `Title`, `Description`, and `Link` public fields of the new `Item` object:

```
item.Title = (string)reader[itemTitleField];
item.Link = (string)reader[itemLinkField];
item.Description = (string)reader[itemDescriptionField];
```

The `LoadRss` method then adds each new `Item` object to the `ArrayList`:

```
items.Add(item);
```

The `LoadRss` method then calls the `GenerateRss` static method of the `RssHelper` class and passes the `Channel` and `ArrayList` objects into it. As you'll see shortly, the `GenerateRss` method generates the RSS document and loads the document into the `Stream` object that is passed into the `LoadRss` method as its input parameter:

```
RssHelper.GenerateRss(channel, (Item[])items.ToArray(typeof(Item)), stream);
```

GetDataReader

Listing 25-13 contains the code for the `GetDataReader` method. This method uses ADO.NET to retrieve the data from the underlying SQL Server database.

Listing 25-13: The GetDataReader method

```
SqlDataReader GetDataReader()
{
  SqlConnection con = new SqlConnection();
  con.ConnectionString = connectionString;
  SqlCommand com = new SqlCommand();
  com.Connection = con;
  com.CommandText = commandText;
  com.CommandType = commandType;
  con.Open();
  return com.ExecuteReader(CommandBehavior.CloseConnection);
}
```

Registering SqlRssProvider

Listing 25-14 shows how the page developer can declaratively register `SqlRssProvider` with the RSS service without writing a single line of code.

Listing 25-14: Registering SqlRssProvider

```
<rssService defaultProvider="SqlRssProvider">
  <providers>
    <add name="SqlRssProvider" type="CustomComponents.SqlRssProvider"
      channelTitle="New Articles On greatarticles.com"
      channelLink="http://www.greatarticles.com"
      channelDescription="The list of published articles on greatarticles.com"
      itemTitleField="Title"
      itemDescriptionField="Abstract"
      itemLinkField="AuthorName"
      itemLinkFormatString="http://localhost:1507/CreditCardForm/{0}.aspx"
      connectionStringName="MyConnectionString"
      commandText="Select * From Articles"
      commandType="Text"/>
  </providers>
</rssService>
```

The page developer must add a new `<add>` child element within the opening and closing tags of the `<providers>` element and set its attribute values as follows:

❑ name: The page developer has the freedom of choosing any friendly name for the provider as long as it is different from the friendly names of other registered providers. Listing 25-14 uses the string value `SqlRssProvider` as the friendly name:

```
name="SqlRssProvider"
```

❑   `type`: The value of this attribute consists of two main parts. The first part is the fully qualified name of the type of the provider, including its namespace, `CustomComponents.` `SqlRssProvider`. The second part is the (weak or strong) name of the assembly that contains the provider. If the name of the assembly is not specified, it is assumed that the executing assembly contains the provider.

```
type="CustomComponents.SqlRssProvider"
```

❑   `connectionStringName`: The value of this attribute must be set to the value of the name attribute of the `<add>` element that the page developer adds to the `<connectionStrings>` section of the configuration file as shown in the following:

```
<configuration>
  <connectionStrings>
    <add name="FriendlyName"
    connectionString="Data Source=ServerName;Initial Catalog=DatabaseName;pwd;uid"
  </connectionStrings>
</configuration>
```

❑   `commandText`: The page developer must set the value of this attribute to a string that contains a SQL `Select` statement or stored procedure name:

```
commandText="Select * From Articles"
```

❑   Item-related attributes: The page developer must set the values of the `itemTitleField`, `itemDescriptionField`, and `itemLinkField` attributes to the names of the appropriate database fields:

```
itemTitleField="Title" itemDescriptionField="Abstract" itemLinkField="AuthorName"
```

Registering a provider doesn't automatically tell the RSS service to use the provider, because more than one RSS provider can be registered with the RSS service. The page developer must set the value of the `defaultProvider` attribute of the `<rssService>` element to the friendly name of the desired provider to instruct the RSS service to use the specified provider:

```
<rssService defaultProvider="SqlRssProvider">
```

RssHelper

The `RssHelper` class is a helper class that RSS providers such as `SqlRssProvider` can use to perform typical RSS operations such as generating RSS documents. The current implementation of `RssHelper` class contains a single method named `GenerateRss`, as shown in Listing 25-15.

Listing 25-15: The GenerateRss method of the RssHelper class

```
public static void GenerateRss(Channel channel, Item[] items, Stream stream)
{
  XmlWriterSettings settings = new XmlWriterSettings();
  settings.Indent = true;

  using (XmlWriter writer = XmlWriter.Create(stream,settings))
  {
```

```
        writer.WriteStartDocument();
        writer.WriteStartElement("rss");
        writer.WriteAttributeString("version", "2.0");
        writer.WriteStartElement("channel");
        writer.WriteElementString("title", channel.Title);
        writer.WriteElementString("link", channel.Link);
        writer.WriteElementString("description", channel.Description);
        foreach (Item item in items)
        {
          writer.WriteStartElement("item");
          writer.WriteElementString("title", item.Title);
          writer.WriteElementString("description", item.Description);
          string formattedValue = string.Format(item.LinkFormatString, item.Link);
          writer.WriteElementString("link", formattedValue);
          writer.WriteEndElement();
        }
        writer.WriteEndElement();
        writer.WriteEndElement();
        writer.WriteEndDocument();
    }
}
```

The GenerateRss method takes three arguments:

❏ The Channel object that contains the strings that GenerateRss will render within the opening and closing tags of the <title>, <description>, and <link> child elements of the <channel> element of the RSS document (see Listing 25-11).

❏ An array that contains one Item object for each <item> element of the RSS document. Each Item object contains the strings that GenerateRss will render within the opening and closing tags of the <title>, <description>, and <link> child elements of the associated <item> element (see Listing 25-12).

❏ The Stream object into which GenerateRss will load the RSS document.

As Listing 25-15 shows, the GenerateRss method instantiates an XmlWriter. The XmlWriter class can be used in the using statement because the class implements the IDisposable interface where its Dispose method automatically calls the Close method of the XmlWriter class. Therefore, if you use the XmlWriter in the using statement, .NET will automatically call its Dispose, and consequently its Close method when it goes out of scope.

```
    using (XmlWriter writer = XmlWriter.Create(stream, settings))
```

The method then renders the values of the Title, Description, and Link properties of the Channel object within the opening and closing tags of the <title>, <description>, and <link> child elements of the <channel> element, respectively:

```
    writer.WriteElementString("title", channel.Title);
    writer.WriteElementString("link", channel.Link);
    writer.WriteElementString("description", channel.Description);
```

As you'll see later, the page developer declaratively sets the values of these properties in the <rssService> section of the configuration file.

The method then iterates through the database records. For each enumerated record, the method renders the opening and closing tag of the `<item>` element:

```
writer.WriteStartElement("item");
. . .
writer.WriteEndElement();
```

It then renders the values of the `Title` and `Description` properties of the `Item` object within the opening and closing tags of the `<title>` and `<description>` child elements of the each `<item>` element:

```
writer.WriteElementString("title", item.Title);
writer.WriteElementString("description", item.Description);
```

The method uses the formatting string specified in the `LinkFormatString` property of the `Item` object to format the value of the `Link` property of each `Item` object:

```
string formattedValue = string.Format(item.LinkFormatString, item.Link);
```

Finally, the method renders the formatted value within the opening and closing tags of the `<link>` child element of each `<item>` element:

```
writer.WriteElementString("link", formattedValue);
```

XmlRssProvider

As shown in Listing 25-14, the page developer declaratively plugs the `SqlRssProvider` into the RSS service to have the service generate the RSS document from the specified SQL Server database. This section develops an RSS provider named `XmlRssProvider` that the page developer can declaratively plug into the RSS service to have the service generate the RSS document from the specified XML file.

`XmlRssProvider`, like all other RSS providers, must implement the `Initialize` method of the `ProviderBase` class and the `LoadRss` method of the `RssProvider` class as discussed in the following sections.

Initialize

Listing 25-16 presents the implementation of the `Initialize` method for `XmlRssProvider`.

Listing 25-16: The Initialize method of XmlRssProvider

```
public override void Initialize(string name, NameValueCollection config)
{
  if (config == null)
    throw new ArgumentNullException("config");

  if (string.IsNullOrEmpty(name))
    name = "XmlRssProvider";

  if (string.IsNullOrEmpty(config["description"]))
  {
```

```csharp
        config.Remove("description");
        config.Add("description", "Retrieve RSS data from an XML document");
    }
    base.Initialize(name, config);

    dataFile = config["dataFile"];
    if (string.IsNullOrEmpty(dataFile))
      throw new ProviderException("Data file not found");
    config.Remove("dataFile");

    channelTitle = config["channelTitle"];
    if (string.IsNullOrEmpty(channelTitle))
      channelTitle = "Unknown";
    config.Remove("channelTitle");

    channelDescription = config["channelDescription"];
    if (string.IsNullOrEmpty(channelDescription))
      channelDescription = "Unknown";
    config.Remove("channelDescription");

    channelLink = config["channelLink"];
    if (string.IsNullOrEmpty(channelLink))
      channelLink = "Unknown";
    config.Remove("channelLink");

    itemTitleXPath = config["itemTitleXPath"];
    if (string.IsNullOrEmpty(itemTitleXPath))
      throw new ProviderException("Title XPath not found");
    config.Remove("itemTitleXPath");

    itemDescriptionXPath = config["itemDescriptionXPath"];
    if (string.IsNullOrEmpty(itemDescriptionXPath))
      throw new ProviderException("Description XPath not found");
    config.Remove("itemDescriptionXPath");

    itemLinkXPath = config["itemLinkXPath"];
    if (string.IsNullOrEmpty(itemLinkXPath))
      throw new ProviderException("Link XPath not found");
    config.Remove("itemLinkXPath");

    itemLinkFormatString = config["itemLinkFormatString"];
    config.Remove("itemLinkFormatString");

    itemXPath = config["itemXPath"];
    if (string.IsNullOrEmpty(itemXPath))
      throw new ProviderException("Item XPath not found");
    config.Remove("itemXPath");

    if (config.Count > 0)
    {
      string key = config.GetKey(0);
      if (!string.IsNullOrEmpty(key))
        throw new ProviderException("Unrecognized attribute");
    }
}
```

The following table compares the member fields of the `XmlRssProvider` and `SqlRssProvider`.

SqlRssProvider	XmlRssProvider
`connectionString`: Contains the information needed to locate and to connect to the database.	`dataFile`: Contains the information needed to locate the XML file.
`commandText`: The SQL `Select` statement or stored procedure that selects database records, where each record corresponds to an `<item>` element. Each database record contains the strings that `SqlRssProvider` renders within the opening and closing tags of the `<title>`, `<description>`, and `<link>` subelements of its associated `<item>` element.	`itemXPath`: The `XPath` expression that selects XML nodes, where each node corresponds to an `<item>` element. Each XML node contains the strings that `XmlRssProvider` renders within the opening and closing tags of the `<title>`, `<description>`, and `<link>` subelements of its associated `<item>` element.
`itemTitleField`: Used to select the database field associated with the `<title>` subelement of the `<item>` element.	`itemTitleXPath`: The `XPath` expression that is used to select the child XML node associated with the `<title>` subelement of the `<item>` element.
`itemDescriptionField`: Used to select the database field associated with the `<description>` subelement of the `<item>` element.	`itemDescriptionXPath`: The `XPath` expression that is used to select the child XML node associated with the `<description>` subelement of the `<item>` element.
`itemLinkField`: Used to select the database field associated with the `<link>` subelement of the `<item>` element.	`itemLinkXPath`: The `XPath` expression that is used to select the child XML node associated with the `<link>` subelement of the `<item>` element.

Here is an example to help you understand the `dataFile`, `itemTitleXPath`, `itemDescriptionXPath`, and `itemLinkXPath` fields of the `XmlRssProvider` RSS provider. Listing 25-17 shows an example of an XML file that `XmlRssProvider` uses to generate the RSS document.

Listing 25-17: A sample XML document that XmlRssProvider uses

```xml
<?xml version="1.0" encoding="utf-8" ?>
<Articles>
  <Article title="What's new in ASP.NET 2.0?" authorName="Smith">
    <Abstract>Describes the new ASP.NET 2.0 features</Abstract>
  </Article>
  <Article title="XSLT in ASP.NET Applications" authorName="Carey">
    <Abstract>Shows to use XSLT in your ASP.NET applications</Abstract>
  </Article>
  <Article title="XML programming" authorName="Smith">
    <Abstract>Reviews .NET 2.0 XML programming features</Abstract>
  </Article>
</Articles>
```

The following table shows examples of `XPath` expressions that the `itemTitleXPath`, `itemDescriptionXPath`, and `itemLinkXPath` fields can contain. Notice that the third column of the table shows the current XML node. This is very important because `XPath` expressions are always evaluated with respect to the current node.

Field Name	Field Value XPath Expression	Current XML Node
itemXPath	//Article	<Articles>
itemTitleXPath	@title	<Article>
itemDescriptionXPath	Abstract/text()	<Article>
itemLinkXPath	@link	<Article>

Here are the XML nodes that each XPath expression shown in the preceding table selects from the XML document shown in Listing 25-17. The XPath expression //Article shown in the first row of the table where the current node is <Articles> selects the following XML nodes:

```
<Article title="ASP.NET 2.0" author="Smith">
  <Abstract>
    Reviews ASP.NET 2.0
  </Abstract>
</Article>

<Article title="XSLT in ASP.NET" author="Carey">
  <Abstract>
    Overview of XSLT in ASP.NET
  </Abstract>
</Article>

<Article title="XML programming" author="Smith">
  <Abstract>
    Reviews .NET XML programming
  </Abstract>
</Article>
```

The XPath expression @title shown in the second row of the table selects the attribute node [title="ASP.NET 2.0"] if the current node is the first <Article> element, the attribute node [title="XSLT in ASP.NET"] if the current node is the second <Article> element, and the attribute node [title="XML programming"] if the current node is the third <Article> element.

The XPath expression Abstract/text() shown in the third row of the table selects the text node ["Reviews ASP.NET 2.0"] if the current node is the first <Article> element, the text node ["Overview of XSLT in ASP.NET"] if the current node is the second <Article> element, and the text node ["Reviews .NET XML programming"] if the current node is the third <Article> element.

The XPath expression @link shown in the fourth row of the table selects the attribute node [author="Smith"] if the current node is the first <Article> element, the attribute node [author="Carey"] if the current node is the second <Article> element, and the attribute node [author="Smith"] if the current node is the third <Article> element.

LoadRss

Listing 25-18 contains the code for the LoadRss method.

Listing 25-18: The LoadRss method of XmlRssProvider

```
public override void LoadRss(Stream stream)
{
  XPathNodeIterator iter = RetrieveData();

  Channel channel = new Channel();
  channel.Title = channelTitle;
  channel.Link = channelLink;
  channel.Description = channelDescription;

  ArrayList items = new ArrayList();
  Item item;
  while (iter.MoveNext())
  {
    item = new Item();
    item.Title = iter.Current.SelectSingleNode(itemTitleXPath).Value;
    item.Link = iter.Current.SelectSingleNode(itemLinkXPath).Value;
    item.Description = iter.Current.SelectSingleNode(itemDescriptionXPath).Value;
    item.LinkFormatString = itemLinkFormatString;
    items.Add(item);
  }

  RssHelper.GenerateRss(channel, (Item[])items.ToArray(typeof(Item)), stream);
}
```

The LoadRss method calls the RetrieveData method to access the XPathNodeIterator that contains the retrieved XML nodes. This method is discussed in the next section. XPathNodeIterator allows you to iterate through the retrieved XML nodes:

```
XPathNodeIterator iter = RetrieveData();
```

The method then iterates through the retrieved XML nodes. For each enumerated XML node, LoadRss creates an Item object:

```
item = new Item();
```

The LoadRss method then calls the SelectSingleNode method for each node and passes the XPath expression specified in the itemTitleXPath field into it. This method locates the XML node that the XPath expression represents. LoadRss then assigns the value of this XML node to the Title property of the Item object:

```
item.Title = iter.Current.SelectSingleNode(itemTitleXPath).Value;
```

LoadRss then calls the SelectSingleNode method for each node and passes the XPath expression specified in the itemLinkXPath field into it. This method locates the XML node that the XPath expression represents. LoadRss then assigns the value of this XML node to the Link property of the Item object:

```
item.Link = iter.Current.SelectSingleNode(itemLinkXPath).Value;
```

LoadRss also calls the SelectSingleNode method for each node and passes the XPath expression specified in the itemDescriptionXPath field into it. This method locates the XML node that this XPath expression represents. LoadRss then assigns the value of this XML node to the Description property of the Item object:

Developing Custom Provider-Based Services

```
        item.Description = iter.Current.SelectSingleNode(itemDescriptionXPath).Value;
```

RetrieveData

Listing 25-19 illustrates the implementation of the RetrieveData method.

Listing 25-19: The RetrieveData method

```
protected virtual XPathNodeIterator RetrieveData()
{
  IXPathNavigable document =
                  new XPathDocument(HttpContext.Current.Server.MapPath(dataFile));
  XPathNavigator nav = document.CreateNavigator();
  nav.MoveToChild(XPathNodeType.Element);
  return nav.Select(itemXPath);
}
```

The RetrieveData method loads the XML file into an XPathDocument:

```
IXPathNavigable document =
                new XPathDocument(HttpContext.Current.Server.MapPath(dataFile));
```

The method then calls the CreateNavigator method of the XPathDocument object to access its XPathNavigator. The XPathNavigator contains an XPath engine and has been optimized for XPath queries. If you need to do a lot of XPath queries, the XPathNavigator is the way to go. However, only classes that implement IXPathNavigable interface expose XPathNavigator. Currently .NET contains three concrete implementations of this interface: XmlDocument, XPathDocument, and XmlDataDocument.

All three classes have one thing in common; they all load the entire XML document in memory to make random node access possible. This is not a problem if your XML document is not too large. However, it takes up lot of memory if your XML document is too big. In these cases, you should use the XmlReader and XmlWriter classes instead.

If you need random read access, you should use XPathDocument because it is optimized for XPath queries. You shouldn't use XmlDocument because it uses DOM data model which is different from XPath data model. This data model mismatch degrades the XPath query performance of the XmlDocument. If you need random read/write access, you should use XmlDocument. Because the XmlRssProvider doesn't change the XML document it doesn't need write access. That is why it uses XPathDocument.

```
XPathNavigator nav = document.CreateNavigator();
```

The RetrieveData method moves the navigator to the document (root) element of the XML document. For example, in the case of the XML document shown in Listing 25-17, it moves to the <Articles> element.

```
nav.MoveToChild(XPathNodeType.Element);
```

The method then calls the Select method of the navigator (keep in mind the navigator is located at the root element, such as the <Articles> element) and passes the XPath expression specified in the itemXPath field into it. As mentioned, XPath expressions are always evaluated with respect to the cur-

769

rent node. Because the current node is the document or root element, the `Select` method evaluates the `XPath` expression specified in the `itemXPath` field with respect to the document element.

```
return nav.Select(itemXPath);
```

To help you understand how this works, take another look at the XML document shown in Listing 25-17. The call into the `MoveToNext` method takes the navigator to the `<Articles>` element of this XML document. Suppose the page developer has set the value of the `itemXPath` field to the `XPath` expression `//Article`. The call into the `Select("//Article")` method will select and return all the `<Article>` nodes in the XML document:

```
<Article title="ASP.NET 2.0" author="Smith">
  <Abstract>
    Reviews ASP.NET 2.0
  </Abstract>
</Article>

<Article title="XSLT in ASP.NET" author="Carey">
  <Abstract>
    Overview of XSLT in ASP.NET
  </Abstract>
</Article>

<Article title="XML programming" author="Smith">
  <Abstract>
    Reviews .NET XML programming
  </Abstract>
</Article>
```

Registering XmlRssProvider

The highlighted portion of Listing 25-20 shows how the page developer must register `XmlRssProvider` with the provider-based RSS service.

Listing 25-20: Registering XmlRssProvider

```
<rssService defaultProvider="XmlRssProvider">
  <providers>
    <add name="SqlRssProvider" type="CustomComponents.SqlRssProvider"
      channelTitle="New Articles On greatarticles.com"
      channelLink="http://www.greatarticles.com"
      channelDescription="The list of newly published articles on greatarticles.com"
      itemTitleField="Title"
      itemDescriptionField="Abstract"
      itemLinkField="AuthorName"
      itemLinkFormatString="http://localhost:1507/CreditCardForm/{0}.aspx"
      connectionStringName="MyConnectionString"
      commandText="Select * From Articles"
      commandType="Text"/>

    <add name="XmlRssProvider" type="CustomComponents.XmlRssProvider"
      channelTitle="New Articles On greatarticles.com"
      channelLink="http://www.greatarticles.com"
```

```
            channelDescription="The list of newly published articles on greatarticles.com"
            itemTitleXPath="@title"
            itemDescriptionXPath="Abstract/text()"
            itemLinkXPath="@authorName"
            itemLinkFormatString="http://localhost:1507/CreditCardForm/{0}.aspx"
            dataFile="Articles.xml"
            itemXPath="//Article"/>
        </providers>
    </rssService>
```

Summary

This chapter provided you with a detailed step-by-step recipe for developing custom provider-based services that allow the page developer to declaratively add new plug-and-play providers. The chapter used the recipe to develop a provider-based RSS service that allows the page developer to generate RSS documents from any type of data store.

The next chapters build on what you've learned in the previous chapters to show you how to develop Ajax custom controls and components.

26

Developing Ajax-Enabled Controls and Components: Client-Side Functionality

Traditional controls and components use server-side technologies and resources to operate and to deliver their features and services to end users. These server controls and components require end users to perform full page postbacks to the server, where these components can run the required server-side code to deliver the requested service. In other words, these components and controls use the "click-and-wait" user-unfriendly interaction pattern, which is characterized by waiting periods that disrupt the user's workflow and degrade the user experience. This "click-and-wait" user interaction pattern is what makes the traditional controls and components act and feel very different from their desktop counterparts.

Asynchronous Javascript And Xml (Ajax) is a popular Web application development approach that uses client-side technologies such as HTML/XHTML, CSS, DOM, XML, XSLT, JavaScript, and asynchronous client callback techniques such as XMLHttp requests, hidden frame techniques, and iFrames to develop more sophisticated and responsive Web applications that break free from the "click-and-wait" user interaction pattern, and consequently act and feel more like a desktop application. In other words, Ajax is closing the gap between the Web applications and their desktop counterparts.

This chapter and the next three chapters show you how to use Ajax techniques to develop more sophisticated and responsive Ajax-enabled custom controls and components that act and feel more like their desktop counterparts. This chapter begins by providing you with the definition and characteristics of Ajax-enabled custom components. Then, it provides you with a recipe for developing the client-side functionalities of Ajax-enabled custom controls and components.

Ajax-Enabled Controls and Components

Consider the Web page shown in Figure 26-1. This page displays the list of available books on an online bookstore. The page consists of a table of cells where each cell displays the information about a book. Notice that each cell contains a Details button. When the end user clicks the Details button of a cell, a dialog pops up that contains more detailed information about the associated book.

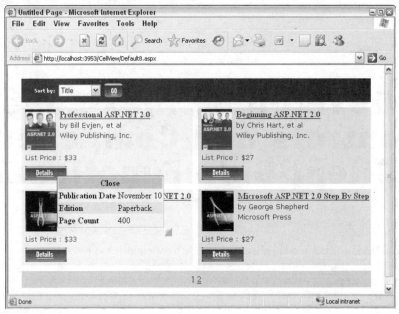

Figure 26-1

The Details button shown in Figure 26-1 is the child control of an Ajax-enabled control named `AjaxDetailsDialog`, which will be implemented and discussed in detail in the next chapter. This section discusses the traditional version of this Ajax-enabled control to help you understand the differences between Ajax-enabled controls and traditional controls. For ease of reference, the traditional version of this control is named `TraditionalDetailsDialog`.

The `TraditionalDetailsDialog` control is a composite control that has two child controls. The first child control is the Details button. The second child control is the dialog that pops up when the user clicks the Details button. You can easily follow the composite control development pattern discussed in Chapter 5 to develop the `TraditionalDetailsDialog` custom composite control.

The `TraditionalDetailsDialog` control uses the "click-and-wait" user interaction pattern, where the user clicks the Details button to perform a full page postback to the server where the `DetailsDialog` control runs the appropriate server-side code to render the pop-up dialog and display the details of the associated book. This "click-and-wait" user interaction pattern is very different from the user interaction pattern that the desktop version of the `DetailsDialog` control would use to pop up the details dialog instantaneously.

Another downside to this "click-and-wait" pattern is that it won't allow you to add sophisticated features to your custom control. For example, you can't allow users to move or resize the pop-up dialog because every single mouse movement has to perform a full page postback to the server to allow the `TraditionalDetailsDialog` to run the server-side code that handles the move or resize event.

As this example shows, traditional controls and components suffer from two fundamental limitations. First, they run server-side code to deliver their services and features to end users. Second, they use full page postback to communicate with the server.

As mentioned, the next chapter develops an Ajax-enabled version of the `TraditionalDetailsDialog` control named `AjaxDetailsDialog` where the control uses the following:

❑ HTML/XHTML, CSS, DOM, XML, and JavaScript client-side technologies to perform tasks such as rendering, moving, resizing, and styling the pop-up dialog

❑ Client callback mechanism to asynchronously retrieve the data from the server

As you'll see in the next chapter, this will allow the `AjaxDetailsDialog` control to act and feel more like its desktop counterpart.

An Ajax-enabled control or component exhibits the following four important characteristics:

❑ It uses HTML/XHTML, CSS, DOM, and JavaScript client-side technologies to implement most of its functionalities. To put it differently, most of its functionalities are client-side functionalities where the code runs locally on the client machine to achieve the same response time as its desktop counterpart. This will allow an Ajax-enabled component to break free from the "click-and-wait" user interaction pattern. This is thoroughly discussed in this chapter. The next section provides you with a step-by-step recipe for implementing the client-side functionality of an Ajax-enabled control.

❑ It uses asynchronous client callback techniques such as `XMLHttpRequest` to communicate with the server. The main goal of this asynchronous communication model is to ensure that the communication with the server doesn't interrupt what the user is doing. In other words, this asynchronous communication model is yet another step to allow an Ajax-enabled component to break free from the "click-and-wait" user interaction pattern. This characteristic of Ajax-enabled components is discussed in detail in the next chapter.

❑ Ajax-enabled components normally send data to and receive data from the server in XML format. This characteristic enables the client-side code to exchange data with any type of server-side code and vice versa because almost all platforms have built-in support for reading, writing, and manipulating XML data. This doesn't mean that every Ajax-enabled component exchanges XML data with the server. Other text data formats are also used. This characteristic of Ajax-enabled components is thoroughly discussed in the next chapter.

❑ The asynchronous communications between the client-side code and the server-side code are normally governed by Ajax communication patterns. These patterns allow Ajax-enabled components to take full advantage of the asynchronous nature of the communication between the client-side code and the server-side code to determine the best time for uploading the data to or downloading the data from the server so the data exchange with the server wouldn't interrupt the user workflow and degrade the user experience. Chapters 28 and 29 discuss Ajax communication patterns in detail.

This chapter and the next three chapters will help you understand Ajax-enabled controls from the inside out. Such solid understanding will put you in a much better position to understand Microsoft's Atlas.

Recipe for Implementing Ajax-Enabled Controls' Client-Side Functionality

Developing the client-side functionality of an Ajax-enabled control involves the following tasks:

1. The page developer will be using your Ajax-enabled control on an ASP.NET page where your control encapsulates the HTML and client script that the page developer would otherwise have to implement. Before starting to write your control, implement a page that contains the HTML and client script that your control is supposed to encapsulate directly.

2. Developing the page that directly contains your Ajax-enabled control's HTML and client script will allow you to determine how to render your control's client script into the containing page. As you'll see in this chapter, there are different ways to render your control's client script. This task involves overriding one or more of the methods that your control inherits from `Control` or `WebControl`. Which method you override depends on how you decide to render your script.

3. As you'll see in this chapter, your control shouldn't always render its client script. In other words, it should contain logic that determines when to render the script.

4. Your control should include the required logic that allows it to fall back on pure server-side code if the Ajax capabilities of the requesting browser don't meet the requirements of its client-side functionality. In other words, the basic functionality of your control should work on all browsers.

The following sections use examples to describe these tasks in detail and to provide you with what you need to implement the client-side functionality of your own Ajax-enabled custom controls.

Rendering Options

In general, you have three options for rendering your control's client script:

❑ Render the script as HTML attribute values

❑ Render the script as script blocks, within the opening and closing tags of `<script>` elements

❑ Package your control's client script into a set of script files known as a *script library*, and render references to these files as the values of the `src` attributes of `<script>` elements

Rendering Client Script as HTML Attribute Values

Consider the following simple example. The page developer wants the font size and background and foreground colors of a link to change when the user moves the mouse pointer over the link. To accomplish this, the page developer adds the client-side code that supports this feature as the values of the `onmouseover` and `onmouseout` HTML attributes of the respective `<a>` HTML element as shown in Listing 26-1. Figures 26-2 and 26-3 show what end users see before and after they move the mouse pointer over the link. Listing 26-1 shows the code for this page.

Listing 26-1: A simple Web page that uses client-side code as attribute values

```
<%@ Page Language="C#" %>
<html xmlns="http://www.w3.org/1999/xhtml">
<head runat="server"><title>Untitled Page</title></head>
<body>
  <form id="form1" runat="server">
    <a href="http://www.wrox.com"
    style="background-color:White;color:Blue;font-size:small;font-weight:normal"
    onmouseover="this.style.backgroundColor='Blue'; this.style.color='Yellow';
                 this.style.fontSize='xx-large';this.style.fontWeight='bold'"
    onmouseout="this.style.backgroundColor='White';this.style.color='Blue';
                this.style.fontSize='small';this.style.fontWeight='normal'">
      Wrox Web Site</a>
  </form>
</body>
</html>
```

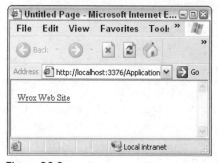

Figure 26-2

Figure 26-3

As Listing 26-1 shows, to add support for the DHTML feature, the page developer had to write the required client script and assign the script to the onmouseover and onmouseout attributes of the <a> element.

Now you'll develop a custom control named CustomHyperLinkAttr that automatically takes care of these two steps, saving the page developer from having to implement them. The CustomHyperLinkAttr control derives from the ASP.NET HyperLink control, which in turn derives from the WebControl base class. As discussed in Chapter 3, the HTML markup text that a `WebControl` control such as `HyperLink` renders consists of two main parts, as follows:

❑ The outer or containing HTML element — the HTML element that encapsulates or contains the rest of the control's rendered HTML content. For example, the containing element of the `HyperLink` control is an `<a>` HTML element.

❑ The content HTML — the HTML markup text that the containing HTML element contains or encapsulates.

As shown in Chapter 3, `WebControl` exposes a method named `AddAttributesToRender` that renders the attributes of the containing HTML element. As Listing 26-2 shows, the `CustomHyperLinkAttr` control overrides this method to render its client script as the values of the `onmouseover` and `onmouseout` attributes of the containing HTML element, the `<a>` element.

Listing 26-2: CustomHyperLinkAttr custom control

```
public class CustomHyperLinkAttr : HyperLink
{
  protected override void AddAttributesToRender(HtmlTextWriter writer)
  {
    base.AddAttributesToRender(writer);
    writer.AddStyleAttribute(HtmlTextWriterStyle.BackgroundColor, "White");
    writer.AddStyleAttribute(HtmlTextWriterStyle.Color, "Blue");
    writer.AddStyleAttribute(HtmlTextWriterStyle.FontSize, "small");
    writer.AddStyleAttribute(HtmlTextWriterStyle.FontWeight, "normal");
    writer.AddAttribute("onmouseover",
                  "this.style.backgroundColor='Blue';this.style.color='Yellow';
                  this.style.fontSize='xx-large';this.style.fontWeight='bold';");
    writer.AddAttribute("onmouseout",
                  "this.style.backgroundColor='White';this.style.color='Blue';
                  this.style.fontSize='small';this.style.fontWeight='normal';");
  }
}
```

Listing 26-3 replaces the boldface portion of Listing 26-1 with an instance of the `CustomHyperLinkAttr` control. As this listing shows, `CustomHyperLinkAttr` has encapsulated the HTML and the client-side script.

Listing 26-3: A page that uses CustomHyperLinkAttr

```
<%@ Page Language="C#" %>
<%@ Register TagPrefix="custom" Namespace="CustomComponents" %>
<html xmlns="http://www.w3.org/1999/xhtml">
<head runat="server"><title>Untitled Page</title></head>
<body>
  <form id="form1" runat="server">
    <custom:CustomHyperLinkAttr runat="server"
    NavigateUrl="http://www.wrox.com" Text="Wrox Web Site" />
  </form>
</body>
</html>
```

Rendering Client Script as Script Blocks

Take another look at Listing 26-1. Recall that the page developer assigned the required client script to the onmouseover and onmouseout attributes. The approach taken in Listing 26-1 is good if the page includes only a few links. However, if the page includes a lot of links, the page developer will end up copying and pasting the same client-side code over and over again. This will clutter the page and unnecessarily increase the page size. To tackle this problem, the page developer defines two JavaScript functions and calls them from the onmouseover and onmouseout attributes of the <a> HTML element as shown in Listing 26-4.

Listing 26-4: A simple Web page that uses client-side code as script blocks

```
<%@ Page Language="C#" %>
<script type="text/javascript">
  function MouseOverCallback(aElement)
  {
    aElement.style.backgroundColor='Blue';
    aElement.style.color='Yellow';
    aElement.style.fontSize='xx-large';
    aElement.style.fontWeight='bold';
  }

  function MouseOutCallback(aElement)
  {
    aElement.style.backgroundColor='White';
    aElement.style.color='Blue';
    aElement.style.fontSize='small';
    aElement.style.fontWeight='normal';
  }
</script>
<html xmlns="http://www.w3.org/1999/xhtml">
<head runat="server"><title>Untitled Page</title></head>
<body>
  <form id="form1" runat="server">
    <a href="http://www.wrox.com"
    style="background-color:White;color:Blue;font-size:small;font-weight:normal"
    onmouseover="MouseOverCallback(this)"
    onmouseout="MouseOutCallback(this)">
      Wrox Web Site</a>
  </form>
</body>
</html>
```

To save the page developer from having to implement all this functionality, you can develop a custom control named CustomHyperLinkBlock that derives from HyperLink. Recall that CustomHyperLinkAttr rendered the client script as the values of the onmouseover and onmouseout attributes. CustomHyperLinkBlock, on the other hand, renders the same client script as a script block, within the opening and closing tags of a <script> element, as shown in Listing 26-5.

Listing 26-5: CustomHyperLinkBlock custom control

```
public class CustomHyperLinkBlock : HyperLink
{
  protected override void AddAttributesToRender(HtmlTextWriter writer)
  {
    base.AddAttributesToRender(writer);
    writer.AddStyleAttribute(HtmlTextWriterStyle.BackgroundColor, "White");
    writer.AddStyleAttribute(HtmlTextWriterStyle.Color, "Blue");
    writer.AddStyleAttribute(HtmlTextWriterStyle.FontSize, "small");
    writer.AddStyleAttribute(HtmlTextWriterStyle.FontWeight, "normal");
    writer.AddAttribute("onmouseover", "MouseOverCallback(this)");
    writer.AddAttribute("onmouseout", "MouseOutCallback(this)");
  }

  protected override void Render(HtmlTextWriter writer)
  {
    writer.Write("<script type='text/javascript'>\n");
    writer.Write("function MouseOverCallback(aElement)\n");
    writer.Write("{\n");
    writer.Write("\taElement.style.backgroundColor='Blue';\n");
    writer.Write("\taElement.style.color='Yellow';\n");
    writer.Write("\taElement.style.fontSize='xx-large';\n");
    writer.Write("\taElement.style.fontWeight='bold';\n");
    writer.Write("}\n\n");

    writer.Write("function MouseOutCallback(aElement)\n");
    writer.Write("{\n");
    writer.Write("\taElement.style.backgroundColor='White';\n");
    writer.Write("\taElement.style.color='Blue';\n");
    writer.Write("\taElement.style.fontSize='small';\n");
    writer.Write("\taElement.style.fontWeight='normal';\n");
    writer.Write("}\n");
    writer.Write("</script>\n");

    base.Render(writer);
  }
}
```

As Listing 26-5 shows, `CustomHyperLinkBlock` overrides the `Render` method to render its client script as a script block and overrides the `AddAttributesToRender` method to render the script that calls the `MouseOverCallback` and `MouseOutCallback` JavaScript functions as values of the `onmouseover` and `onmouseout` HTML attributes of the containing <a> HTML element.

Now take a look at what happens if the page developer uses two instances of the `CustomHyperLinkBlock` control on the same page, as shown in Listing 26-6.

Listing 26-6: A page that uses two instances of CustomHyperLinkBlock control

```
<%@ Page Language="C#" %>
<%@ Register TagPrefix="custom" Namespace="CustomComponents" %>
<html xmlns="http://www.w3.org/1999/xhtml">
<head runat="server"><title>Untitled Page</title></head>
<body>
```

```
        <form id="form1" runat="server">
          <custom:CustomHyperLinkBlock runat="server"
          NavigateUrl="http://www.wrox.com" Text="Wrox Web Site" />
          <br/>
          <custom:CustomHyperLinkBlock runat="server"
          NavigateUrl="http://msdn.microsoft.com" Text="Microsoft MSDN Web Site" />
        </form>
      </body>
    </html>
```

If you access this page from your browser and select the View⇨Source option (if you're using Internet Explorer), you'll see the HTML that the page shown in Listing 26-6 emits and sends to your browser (see Listing 26-7). As the boldface portion of Listing 26-7 shows, this HTML contains two copies of the same script block, which means that each instance of the `CustomHyperLinkBlock` control renders its own copy of the same script block.

Listing 26-7: The HTML that the page shown in Listing 26-6 emits and sends to the requesting browser

```
<html xmlns="http://www.w3.org/1999/xhtml">
<body>
  <form name="form1" method="post" action="CustomHyperLinkBlock.aspx" id="form1">

    <script type='text/javascript'>
      function MouseOverCallback(aElement)
      {
        aElement.style.backgroundColor='Blue';
        aElement.style.color='Yellow';
        aElement.style.fontSize='xx-large';
        aElement.style.fontWeight='bold';
      }

      function MouseOutCallback(aElement)
      {
        aElement.style.backgroundColor='White';
        aElement.style.color='Blue';
        aElement.style.fontSize='small';
        aElement.style.fontWeight='normal';
      }
    </script>

    <a href="http://www.wrox.com" onmouseover="MouseOverCallback(this)"
    onmouseout="MouseOutCallback(this)"
    style="background-color:White;color:Blue;font-size:small;font-weight:normal;">
    Wrox Web Site</a>

    <script type='text/javascript'>
      function MouseOverCallback(aElement)
      {
        aElement.style.backgroundColor='Blue';
        aElement.style.color='Yellow';
        aElement.style.fontSize='xx-large';
        aElement.style.fontWeight='bold';
```

(continued)

781

Listing 26-7: *(continued)*

```
    }

    function MouseOutCallback(aElement)
    {
      aElement.style.backgroundColor='White';
      aElement.style.color='Blue';
      aElement.style.fontSize='small';
      aElement.style.fontWeight='normal';
    }
  </script>

  <a href="http://msdn.microsoft.com" onmouseover="MouseOverCallback(this)"
  onmouseout="MouseOutCallback(this)"
  style="background-color:White;color:Blue;font-size:small;font-weight:normal;">
  Microsoft MSDN Web Site</a>
 </form>
</body>
</html>
```

This means that the `Render` method of your custom control isn't the right place to render your control's script blocks, because this method is called once for each instance of your control on the page. Instead, you should render your control's script blocks in the `Render` method of the containing page because there can only be one instance of the page for each request, which means that the `Render` method of the page can only be called once for each request.

The `Page` class provides you with a mechanism that allows you to render your control's script blocks in the `Render` method of the containing page. The `Page` class has a property of type `ClientScriptManager` named `ClientScript` that exposes methods that your custom control can use to register its script blocks with the containing page for rendering.

As you'll see shortly, your control must pass a `System.Type` object and a string value as the first two arguments of the method that it uses to register a script block. This `System.Type` object and string-value pair together form the key under which the script block is registered.

When your custom control is registering a script block under the specified key, the page checks whether its internal list of registered script blocks contains a script block with the same key. If it does, the page knows another instance of your custom control has already registered the same script block for rendering. As long as all instances of your custom control use the same `System.Type` object and string-value pair to register each client script, the page will not add multiple copies of the same script block to its internal list of registered script blocks. When the page enters its rendering phase where its `Render` method is called, the method iterates through the registered script blocks and renders them.

Your custom control can use a number of methods of the `ClientScriptManager` class to register its script blocks for rendering, as follows:

```
public void RegisterClientScriptBlock (Type type, String key, String script)
```

The first two arguments of this method form a key under which the script block is registered. The third argument is a string that contains the script block being registered. The script block must include the opening and closing tags of the containing `<script>` element. If the HTML that your control renders needs to access a script block, your control must use the preceding `RegisterClientScriptBlock` method to register the script block to tell the page to render the script block at the top of the page. This is necessary because only the HTML that comes after a script block can access the block:

```
public bool IsClientScriptBlockRegistered (Type type, String key)
```

Before your control attempts to register a script block, it can call this method to check whether the script block has already been registered for rendering. Multiple registration of the same client script under the same key is allowed because it doesn't add multiple copies of the same script to the page's internal list of registered scripts. Therefore, your control doesn't really have to call the `IsClientScriptBlockRegistered` method. You may be wondering when you should call this method.

Recall that the `RegisterClientScriptBlock` method requires your control to pass a string value that contains the script into the method. This may degrade the performance of your control if your control has to spend lot of time to generate the script that has already been registered. In these cases, you may want to call the `IsClientScriptBlockRegistered` method first to ensure the script hasn't already been registered before you attempt to generate the script:

```
public bool IsClientScriptBlockRegistered (String key)
```

Under the hood, this method calls the previous overload and passes the `System.Type` object that represents the containing page as its first argument:

```
public void RegisterStartupScript(Type type, string key, string script,
                                  bool addScriptTags)
```

The first two arguments of this method form a key under which the script block is registered. The third argument is a string that contains the script block being registered. The last argument specifies whether the script includes the `<script>` element. If your control's script block needs to access the HTML that your control renders, your control must use this method to register the script block to tell the page to render the script block at the bottom of the page. This is necessary because a script block must come after the HTML it needs to access.

```
public void RegisterStartupScript(Type type, string key, string script)
```

Under the hood, this overload calls the previous method and passes false as its last argument to specify that the script contains the `<script>` element.

```
public bool IsStartupScriptRegistered(Type type, string key)
```

This method checks whether the startup script block with the specified type/key pair has already been registered.

```
public bool IsStartupScriptRegistered(string key)
```

Under the hood this overload calls the previous method and passes the `System.Type` object that represents the containing page as its argument.

Now take another look at Listing 26-5. As this code listing shows, the `Render` method of the `CustomHyperLinkBlock` control directly renders the control's script block. As discussed, the control shouldn't directly render its script block. Instead, it should register its script block with the containing page and have the page render the block on its behalf. Listing 26-8 shows a new version of the `CustomHyperLinkBlock` control that overrides the `OnPreRender` method to register its client script with the containing page.

Listing 26-8: New version of CustomHyperLinkBlock

```
public class CustomHyperLinkBlock : HyperLink
{
  protected override void AddAttributesToRender(HtmlTextWriter writer)
  {
    // The same implementation as Listing 26-5
  }

  protected override void OnPreRender(EventArgs e)
  {
    string script =
    "<script type='text/javascript'>\n" +
    "function MouseOverCallback(aElement)\n" +
    "{\n" +
    "\taElement.style.backgroundColor='Blue';\n" +
    "\taElement.style.color='Yellow';\n" +
    "\taElement.style.fontSize='xx-large';\n" +
    "\taElement.style.fontWeight='bold';\n" +
    "}\n\n" +

    "function MouseOutCallback(aElement)\n" +
    "{\n" +
    "\taElement.style.backgroundColor='White';\n" +
    "\taElement.style.color='Blue';\n" +
    "\taElement.style.fontSize='small';\n" +
    "\taElement.style.fontWeight='normal';\n" +
    "}\n" +
    "</script>\n";

    System.Type type = typeof(CustomHyperLinkBlock);
    if (!Page.ClientScript.IsClientScriptBlockRegistered(type, type.FullName))
      Page.ClientScript.RegisterClientScriptBlock(type, type.FullName, script);

    base.OnPreRender(e);
  }
}
```

As Listing 26-8 shows, the `OnPreRender` method loads the script into a string. It then calls the `IsClientScriptBlockRegistered` method to check whether the script has already been registered.

If the script hasn't been registered, the method calls the `RegisterClientScriptBlock` method to register the script. Recall that this method registers the script under a key that consists of a `System.Type` object and a string value passed in as its first two arguments. All instances of the `CustomHyperLinkBlock` control must use the same `System.Type` object and string value to register the script to ensure that the page adds a single copy of the script to its internal list of registered scripts no matter how many times the script is registered. Because the page adds the script to its internal list of scripts under the key specified by this pair, the pair must be unique across all controls of the page. There is one set of `System.Type` object and string value that meets this requirement, the `System.Type` object that represents the `CustomHyperLinkBlock` control

```
System.Type type = typeof(CustomHyperLinkBlock);
```

and the string value that contains the full name of the `System.Type` object, `type.FullName`:

```
if (!Page.ClientScript.IsClientScriptBlockRegistered(type, type.FullName))
  Page.ClientScript.RegisterClientScriptBlock(type, type.FullName, script);
```

Now if you access the page shown in Listing 26-6 from your browser and select View➪Source, you'll notice this time around the source contains a single copy of the script as shown in Listing 26-9.

Listing 26-9: The HTML that the page shown in Listing 26-6 emits and sends to the requesting browser

```html
<html xmlns="http://www.w3.org/1999/xhtml">
<body>
  <form name="form1" method="post" action="CustomHyperLinkBlock.aspx" id="form1">

    <script type='text/javascript'>
      function MouseOverCallback(aElement)
      {
        aElement.style.backgroundColor='Blue';
        aElement.style.color='Yellow';
        aElement.style.fontSize='xx-large';
        aElement.style.fontWeight='bold';
      }

      function MouseOutCallback(aElement)
      {
        aElement.style.backgroundColor='White';
        aElement.style.color='Blue';
        aElement.style.fontSize='small';
        aElement.style.fontWeight='normal';
      }
    </script>

    <a href="http://www.wrox.com" onmouseover="MouseOverCallback(this)"
    onmouseout="MouseOutCallback(this)"
    style="background-color:White;color:Blue;font-size:small;font-weight:normal;">
    Wrox Web Site</a>

    <a href="http://msdn.microsoft.com" onmouseover="MouseOverCallback(this)"
    onmouseout="MouseOutCallback(this)"
    style="background-color:White;color:Blue;font-size:small;font-weight:normal;">
    Microsoft MSDN Web Site</a>
  </form>
</body>
</html>
```

As shown in Listing 26-9, your control must always register its script blocks in the `PreRender` phase of its life cycle. You shouldn't call the registration methods (`RegisterClientScriptBlock`) of the `ClientScript` property of the containing page in your control's `Render` phase. Here's why.

When the containing page enters the rendering phase of its life cycle, it recursively calls the `RenderControl` method of each control in its control tree to have each control render itself, which means that the page starts its rendering before your control. Therefore if your control were to call the registration methods in its rendering phase, it would end up registering its client script after the page has entered its rendering phase.

Client Script Library

Revisit Listing 26-4, where the page developer directly added the script block to the page. Direct inclusion of client script blocks in a page introduces the following problems:

❑   It clutters the page, making the page difficult to maintain.

❑   Every time you make changes to a script block you have to make sure the change doesn't break anything else because the script and HTML are mixed.

❑   It doesn't allow browsers to cache the script to reuse it across pages that use the same script.

To avoid these problems, page developers normally package their client scripts into a set of external script files known as a *script library* and use references to these files within the containing page. This provides the following important benefits:

❑   Isolates HTML from script, allowing page developers to make changes in the script without breaking the HTML

❑   Allows browsers to cache the script files and use them across different pages

❑   Reduces the page size because the page doesn't include the script

Listing 26-10 shows the version of the page shown in Listing 26-4 that includes a reference to an external .js file that contains the script. The highlighted portion of this listing is known as a *client script include* because it includes the URL of the script file that contains the script.

Listing 26-10: The version of the page shown without the script block

```
<%@ Page Language="C#" %>
<script type="text/javascript" src="CustomHyperLinkBlock.js"></script>
<html xmlns="http://www.w3.org/1999/xhtml">
<head runat="server"><title>Untitled Page</title></head>
<body>
  <form id="form1" runat="server">
    <a href="http://www.wrox.com"
    style="background-color:White;color:Blue;font-size:small;font-weight:normal"
    onmouseover="MouseOverCallback(this)"
    onmouseout="MouseOutCallback(this)">
      Wrox Web Site</a>
  </form>
</body>
</html>
```

Now take another look at Listing 26-8. As this code listing shows, the OnPreRender method of the CustomHyperLinkBlock control calls the RegisterClientScriptBlock method to add its client script to the page's internal list of registered scripts, which means that the page will render the client script directly into the HTML that it sends to the requesting browser. As discussed, this isn't the right thing to do.

That is, the `OnPreRender` method shouldn't add the client script itself to the page's internal list of registered scripts. Instead it should use the URL of the script file that contains the script and generate the client script include that is highlighted in Listing 26-10:

```
<script type="text/javascript" src="CustomHyperLinkBlock.js"></script>
```

It should then call the `RegisterClientScriptBlock` method to add the client script include to the page's internal list of registered scripts, which means that when the page enters its rendering phase, it will render this client script include instead of the script itself.

Listing 26-11 shows a version of the custom hyperlink control named `CustomHyperLinkFile` whose `OnPreRender` method takes these two actions to have the page render the client script include that is highlighted in Listing 26-10.

Listing 26-11: CustomHyperLinkFile custom control

```
public class CustomHyperLinkFile : HyperLink
{
  protected override void AddAttributesToRender(HtmlTextWriter writer)
  {
    // Same implementation as Listing 26-5
  }

  protected override void OnPreRender(EventArgs e)
  {
    string script =
        "<script type='text/javascript' src='CustomHyperLinkFile.js'></script>\n";

    Type type = typeof(CustomHyperLinkBlock);
    if (!Page.ClientScript.IsClientScriptBlockRegistered(type, type.FullName))
      Page.ClientScript.RegisterClientScriptBlock(type, type.FullName, script);

    base.OnPreRender(e);
  }
}
```

The `ClientScript` property of the `Page` class exposes a method named `RegisterClientScriptInclude` that encapsulates the highlighted code shown in Listing 26-11 to help you simplify the `OnPreRender` method of your custom control.

Listing 26-12 shows a new version of the `CustomHyperLinkFile` control whose `OnPreRender` method calls the `RegisterClientScriptInclude` method and passes the URL of the script file as its third argument.

Listing 26-12: CustomHyperLinkFile custom control

```
public class CustomHyperLinkFile : HyperLink
{
  protected override void AddAttributesToRender(HtmlTextWriter writer)
  {
    // Same implementation as Listing 26-5
  }
```

(continued)

Listing 26-12: *(continued)*

```
protected override void OnPreRender(EventArgs e)
{
  . .
  Type type = typeof(CustomHyperLinkBlock);
  if (!Page.ClientScript.IsClientScriptIncludeRegistered(type, type.FullName))
    Page.ClientScript.RegisterClientScriptInclude(type, type.FullName,
                                          "CustomHyperLinkFile.js");
  }
}
```

The following are the methods of the `ClientScriptManager` class that your custom control can use to register its client script includes. The following also includes some other important methods of this class.

```
public voidRegisterClientScriptInclude(Type type, string key, string url)
```

This method works in similar fashion to `RegisterClientScriptBlock` to register a script block include. The last argument is the URL of the `.js` file.

```
public boolIsClientScriptBlockIncludeRegistered(Type type, String key)
```

This method works in similar fashion to `IsClientScriptBlockRegistered` to check whether the script block include with the specified type/key pair has already been registered.

```
public boolIsClientScriptBlockIncludeRegistered(string key)
```

This overload calls the previous method and passes the `System.Type` object that represents the containing page as its first argument.

```
public voidRegisterOnSubmitStatement(Type type, string key, string script)
```

Call this method to register your control's script if you want the script to be executed before the page is submitted.

```
public boolIsOnSubmitStatementRegistered(Type type, string key)
```

This method checks whether the `OnSubmit` script statement with the specified type/key pair has already been registered.

```
public boolIsOnSubmitStatementRegistered(string key)
```

This overload calls the previous method and passes the `System.Type` object that represents the containing page as its first argument.

```
public void RegisterHiddenField (string hiddenFieldName,
                          string hiddenFieldInitialValue)
```

If your control's client-side script and server-side code need to use a hidden field to communicate, your control should call this method to request the containing page to render the hidden field with the specified name and value. If your control were to directly render the hidden field in its `Render` method, you would end up with multiple copies of the hidden field in the page because the Render method of your control is called once for each instance of your control.

```
public void RegisterArrayDeclaration (string arrayName, string arrayValue)
```

If your control's client-side script needs to declare an array that is used by all instances of your control, it must call this method to request the containing page to declare the array, if it hasn't been declared yet, and add the specified value to the array.

Deployment Issues

As discussed, the recommended practice is to package your custom control's client script into a set of script files and render client script includes that reference these files. This approach has its own downside. Because your custom control's client script is no longer included in the page that is sent to the client browser, you must deploy your client script files to the client. This complicates the deployment of your custom control, especially if you want two different versions of your control to run side-by-side on the client machine.

The same problem applies to other resource files of your custom control such as image files, CSS files, and so on. The ASP.NET 2.0 Framework provides you with two deployment options to tackle the deployment problems: you can deploy the resource files to a shared location or you can embed the resource files into an assembly. Both these options are discussed in the following two sections.

Deploying Resource Files to a Shared Location

The installation program of the .NET Framework automatically creates a subdirectory named aspnet_client under the directory where IIS is installed and registers the aspnet_client directory with IIS as virtual root aspnet_client. The installation program also creates a subdirectory under the aspnet_client directory named system_web and a subdirectory named 2_0_50727 under the system_web directory.

Notice the naming convention used to name the directory system_web and its subdirectory 2_0_50727. The names of the directory and its subdirectory respectively correspond to the name (System.Web.dll) and version (2_0_50727) of the assembly whose resource files the subdirectory contains.

The installation program of your custom control should follow this procedure and naming convention. This means that it should create a directory under the aspnet_client directory whose name corresponds to the name of your custom control's assembly and a subdirectory under this directory whose name corresponds to the version of your control's assembly. The installation program should then deploy your control's resource files to this subdirectory.

This deployment option provides the following benefits:

❑ Because you have created a separate directory under the aspnet_client directory for your custom control, your control's resource files will not interfere with other resource files installed in the aspnet_client directory.

❑ Because you have created different subdirectories for different versions of your custom control, different versions of your control's resource files can coexist.

❑ Because the client script files of your control are deployed to a shared location on the client's machine, the page developer can use your control in all applications running on that machine without having to copy the script files to these applications.

This deployment option is especially very useful when you're deploying your custom control to the global assembly cache (GAC) where different versions of your control can run side-by-side. However, this deployment option is still error-prone and could lead into deployment problems. Because your control and its resources are in separate files, every time you deploy your control, you have to make sure its associated resource files are deployed as well. This complicates the deployment of your control.

Embedding Resource Files into an Assembly

The ASP.NET 2.0 Framework offers you a deployment option that makes the deployment of your custom controls a piece of cake. This option allows you to embed your control's resource files directly into your control's assembly. There are no separate resource files to deploy. This also automatically resolves the versioning problems discussed before because each version of your control's assembly contains its own resource files. This section consists of two parts. The first part shows you how to use this deployment option, and the second part takes you behind the scenes where you can see for yourself how this option works.

How to Use This Deployment Option

First you need to take the following two actions to instruct Visual Studio to embed your control's resource files into your control's assembly:

1. Add your control's resource files to your control's project in Visual Studio.

2. Set the Build Action property of each resource file in the Visual Studio Property Browser to Embedded Resource. This tells Visual Studio to embed the resource files into your control's assembly.

Just because a resource is embedded into an assembly doesn't mean that it should be served. For security reasons, you have to add the following assembly-level attribute to the `AssemblyInfo.cs` file to give explicit permission to serve the resource:

```
[assembly: WebResource("Library.CustomHyperLinkFile.js","text/javascript")]
```

The first argument of the `WebResource` attribute is the name of the resource, and the second argument is the resource's MIME type. For example, the MIME types of JavaScript and JPEG image files are `text/javascript` and `image/jpeg`, respectively.

As shown in Listing 26-12, when your control's script is in a separate file, your control must override the `OnPreRender` method to call the `RegisterClientScriptInclude` method where `OnPreRender` must pass the URL of the script file as the third argument of the `RegisterClientScriptInclude` method. Under the hood, the `RegisterClientScriptInclude` method generates the following client script include where the URL of the script file is assigned to the `src` attribute of the `<script>` element:

```
<script type='text/javascript' src='CustomHyperLinkFile.js'></script>
```

This raises the following question: What is the URL of an embedded resource file? Before answering this question, you need to answer the following more fundamental question: Why do you need to use a URL? What is a URL for? As you know, the URL of a resource is used to locate the resource. Therefore the URL of a resource must include all the information needed to locate the resource. The `OnPreRender` method in Listing 26-12 uses the name of the resource file, `CustomHyperLinkFile.js`, as the URL because that's all that's needed to locate the script file.

Therefore the URL of an embedded resource file is a string that contains all the information needed to locate the file. This raises the following question: What information do you need to locate a resource embedded in an assembly?

Locating an embedded resource consists of two tasks. First, you have to locate the assembly that contains the resource. What information do you need to locate an assembly? It depends on where the assembly is installed. If it's installed in global assembly cache (GAC), you need the strong name of the assembly to locate it in GAC. The strong name of an assembly consists of four parts: the assembly name, version, culture, and public key token. If the assembly is installed in the `bin` directory of an application, you just need the assembly name. There's no need for the assembly version, culture, and public key token because two assemblies with the same name aren't allowed in the bin directory. Second, you have to locate the resource in the assembly. The fully qualified name of the resource is all you need to locate the resource in the assembly.

Therefore, the URL of an embedded resource must contain these two pieces of information. For example, if the `CustomHyperLinkFile.js` resource file is embedded into an assembly named `CustomHyperLinkFile` that is installed in GAC, the URL of the resource file must include the following two pieces of information:

❑ `CustomHyperLinkFile,Version=1.0.0.0,Culture=neutral,` `PublicKeyToken=b03f5f7f11d50a3a`

❑ `CustomHyperLinkFile.CustomHyperLinkFile.js`

You may be wondering how you're supposed to build a URL that contains these two pieces of information. The answer is you don't have to. The `ClientScript` property of the `Page` class exposes a method named `GetWebResourceUrl` that automatically builds the URL that contains the two required pieces of information.

Listing 26-13 shows a version of the `CustomHyperLinkFile` control whose `OnPreRender` method calls the `GetWebResourceUrl` method to retrieve the URL of the embedded resource, and then calls the `RegisterClientScriptInclude` method and passes the URL into it.

Listing 26-13: The version of CustomHyperLinkFile control that uses an embedded resource

```
public class CustomHyperLinkFile : HyperLink
{
  protected override void AddAttributesToRender(HtmlTextWriter writer)
  {
    // The same implementation as Listing 26-5
  }

  protected override void OnPreRender(EventArgs e)
  {
    Type type = typeof(CustomHyperLinkFile);
```

(continued)

Listing 26-13: *(continued)*

```
      string url = Page.ClientScript.GetWebResourceUrl(type,
                                     "Library.CustomHyperLinkFile.js");

      if (!Page.ClientScript.IsClientScriptIncludeRegistered(type,type.FullName))
        Page.ClientScript.RegisterClientScriptInclude(type, type.FullName, url);

      base.OnPreRender(e);
    }
  }
```

The ClientScript property of the Page class exposes a method named RegisterClientScriptResource that encapsulates the highlighted code shown in Listing 26-13 to help you simplify the OnPreRender method of your custom control. Listing 26-14 shows a version of the CustomHyperLinkFile control that uses the RegisterClientScriptResource method.

Listing 26-14: The version of CustomHyperLinkFile control that uses RegisterClientScriptResource

```
public class CustomHyperLinkFile : HyperLink
{
  protected override void AddAttributesToRender(HtmlTextWriter writer)
  {
    // The same implementation as Listing 26-5
  }

  protected override void OnPreRender(EventArgs e)
  {
    Type type = typeof(CustomHyperLinkFile);
    Page.ClientScript.RegisterClientScriptResource(type,
                                     "Library.CustomHyperLinkFile.js");

    base.OnPreRender(e);
  }
}
```

How This Deployment Option Works

Before discussing how this deployment option works, take a look at an example that will set the stage for the discussion. Imagine you want to access an HTML file named favoriteLinks.html located at the URL http://somesite/myHomePage/favoriteLinks.html. Listing 26-15 shows the content of the favoriteLinks.html file. Notice that this file contains a script block that references a script file named mouseCallbacks.js located in a directory named scripts.

Listing 26-15: The content of the favoriteLinks.html file

```
<%@ Page Language="C#" %>
<script type="text/javascript" src="scripts/mouseCallbacks.js"></script>
<html xmlns="http://www.w3.org/1999/xhtml">
<head runat="server"><title>Untitled Page</title></head>
<body>
  <form id="form1" runat="server">
```

```
      <a href="http://www.wrox.com"
      style="background-color:White;color:Blue;font-size:small;font-weight:normal"
      onmouseover="MouseOverCallback(this)"
      onmouseout="MouseOutCallback(this)">
        Wrox Web Site</a>
   </form>
 </body>
 </html>
```

Your browser makes two HTTP GET requests to display this page. Your browser sends its first GET request to the http://somesite/myHomePage/favoriteLinks.html URL to download the HTML file, favoriteLinks.html. The second GET request is sent to the http://somesite/myHomePage/scripts/mouseCallbacks.js URL to download the script file, mouseCallback.js.

Now take a look at what happens when your browser's second GET request arrives in IIS. IIS first examines the extension of the requested resource, mouseCallback.js. Because the extension .js is one of the extensions that IIS can handle, IIS takes over processing the request. IIS parses the URL (http://somesite/myHomePage/scripts/mouseCallbacks.js) to retrieve the name of the virtual root of the application that contains the requested resource (myHomePage) and the virtual path of the requested resource (/scripts/mouseCallbacks.js).

IIS then searches its virtual roots for the virtual root with the specified name, myHomePage. It then searches this virtual root for the resource file with the specified virtual path, scripts/mouseCallbacks.js. In other words, IIS uses the virtual path of the requested script file, scripts/mouseCallbacks.js, to locate the file in the application's virtual root, myHomePage.

Now check out what happens if the mouseCallbacks.js script file is embedded in an assembly named MyAssembly.dll that is installed in the GAC and has the following strong name:

```
MyAssembly, Version=1.0.0.0, Culture=neutral, PublicKeyToken=b03f5f7f11d50a3a
```

As discussed, the URL of an embedded script file includes the strong name of the assembly that contains the script file, as opposed to the virtual path of the script file. When your browser's GET request for the mouseCallbacks.js script file arrives in IIS, because the extension of the requested file is in the list of extensions that IIS can handle, IIS takes over processing the request. However, this time around, when IIS is parsing the URL, it runs into the following weird-looking string:

```
MyAssembly, Version=1.0.0.0, Culture=neutral, PublicKeyToken=b03f5f7f11d50a3a
```

Thinking this string is the virtual path of the requested resource, it searches the myHomePage virtual root for the resource file with the preceding virtual path. Because IIS can't find the resource file, it informs your browser that the requested script file doesn't exist on the server.

Obviously, IIS can't process the request for an embedded resource. As discussed in Chapter 8, you can configure IIS to delegate the responsibility of handling a request to the aspnet_isapi.dll extension, which in turn dispatches the request to ASP.NET. Chapter 8 showed you how ASP.NET can be configured to dispatch the request to an HTTP handler. The ASP.NET 2.0 Framework comes with an HTTP handler named AssemblyResourceLoader that knows how to process requests for an embedded resource.

However, this requires you to change the extension of the requested resource to an extension that IIS can't handle, because IIS only delegates requests for those extensions that it can't process. This means that you have to change the extension of a script file from `.js` to something else, or the extension of a JPEG file from `.jpeg` to something else. Obviously, this isn't acceptable.

The ASP.NET 2.0 Framework has come up with a solution for this problem. ASP.NET has made up an imaginary or virtual resource named `WebResource.axd`, which doesn't represent any physical resource on the server. ASP.NET builds a string that consists of two substrings separated by the character `|`. The first substring can contain one of the following string values:

❑ The strong name of the assembly that embeds the specified resource file if the assembly is installed in GAC. The strong name of the assembly must be preceded by the letter f to signify the fact that the substring contains the strong or full name of the assembly:

```
fMyAssembly,1.0.0.0,en,b03f5f7f11d50a3a
```

❑ The simple name of the assembly that embeds the specified resource file if the assembly is a private assembly, that is, if it's installed in the `bin` directory of the application. The simple name of the assembly must be preceded by the letter p to signify the fact that the substring contains the name of a private assembly:

```
pAssemblyName
```

❑ If the specified resource is embedded in the ASP.NET `System.Web.dll` assembly, there's no need to specify the strong name of the assembly because this assembly is already loaded in memory. The letter s is used to signify the fact that the resource is embedded in the `System.Web.dll` assembly:

```
s
```

The second substring contains the name of the embedded resource, for example:

```
MyLibrary.mouseCallback.js
```

The following is an example of a string that consists of these two substrings separated by the | character:

```
fMyAssembly,1.0.0.0,en,b03f5f7f11d50a3a|MyLibrary.mouseCallback.js
```

ASP.NET then encrypts the string, like this:

```
JOL0Mx92geNMSVlJfSrPGXt_ktxyy4uKLVy0_QToHXPl0WIuKtXwtGA9rLPGwWM30
```

ASP.NET then uses the encrypted string as the value of a new `querystring` parameter named `d`, like this:

```
d=JOL0Mx92geNMSVlJfSrPGXt_ktxyy4uKLVy0_QToHXPl0WIuKtXwtGA9rLPGwWM30
```

Therefore, the URL of the embedded `mouseCallbacks.js` script file is as shown in Listing 26-16.

Listing 26-16: The URL of the embedded mouseCallback.js script file

```
/myHomePage/WebResource.axd?
        d=JOL0Mx92geNMSVlJfSrPGXt_ktxyy4uKLVy0_QToHXPl0WIuKtXwtGA9rLPGwWM30
        &t=1234567890048
```

Notice that the URL of an embedded resource also contains a querystring named t whose value specifies the timestamp of the assembly that embeds the resource, that is, the last time the assembly was updated.

Encrypting the assembly and resource information is necessary. The following URL shows the unencrypted version of the URL shown in Listing 26-16:

```
/myHomePage/WebResource.axd?
        d=fMyAssembly,1.0.0.0,en,b03f5f7f11d50a3a|MyLibrary.mouseCallback.js
        &t=1234567890048
```

If the ASP.NET were to allow such URLs for embedded resources, they would introduce a security loophole. Suppose a hacker makes the following request for the someNonExistentResource.js embedded resource:

```
/myHomePage/WebResource.axd?
        d=fSystem.Data,1.0.0.0,neutral,b03f5f7f11d50a3a|someNonExistentResource.js
        &t=1234567890048
```

As you'll see later, the AssemblyResourceLoader HTTP handler has to first load the specified assembly in memory before it can determine whether the assembly contains the requested resource. Therefore, the AssemblyResourceLoader HTTP handler loads the System.Data.dll assembly in memory and searches the assembly for the resource named someNonExistentResource.js. Obviously, the search fails and the AssemblyResourceLoader informs the requesting browser that this resource doesn't exist on the server.

Now imagine what happens if the hacker makes numerous GET requests for nonexistent resources. This will keep AssemblyResourceLoader busy loading assemblies in memory and searching for nonexistent resources.

Now take another look at the favoriteLinks.html file shown in Listing 26-15. Notice that the URL of the mouseCallbacks.js script file — the value of the src attribute of the <script> element — contains the virtual path of the script file. Listing 26-17 shows a new version of the favoriteLinks.html file where the page uses the URL shown in Listing 26-16.

Listing 26-17: The content of the favoriteLinks.html file

```
<%@ Page Language="C#" %>
<script type="text/javascript"
src="/myHomePage/WebResource.axd?
        d=JOLOMx92geNMSVlJfSrPGXt_ktxyy4uKLVy0_QToHXPl0WIuKtXwtGA9rLPGwWM30
        &t=1234567890048"
</script>
<html xmlns="http://www.w3.org/1999/xhtml">
<head runat="server"><title>Untitled Page</title></head>
<body>
   <form id="form1" runat="server">
     <a href="http://www.wrox.com"
     style="background-color:White;color:Blue;font-size:small;font-weight:normal"
     onmouseover="MouseOverCallback(this)"
     onmouseout="MouseOutCallback(this)">
       Wrox Web Site</a>
   </form>
</body>
</html>
```

When your browser is parsing the page shown in Listing 26-17, it runs into the highlighted script block and retrieves the value of the `src` attribute:

```
/myHomePage/WebResource.axd?
        d=JOLOMx92geNMSVlJfSrPGXt_ktxyy4uKLVy0_QToHXP10WIuKtXwtGA9rLPGwWM30
        &t=1234567890048
```

Your browser thinks that there's a resource named `WebResource.axd` that it needs to download, and interprets the rest of the URL as `querystring` parameters. Therefore your browser makes a GET request to download the `WebResource.axd` resource.

When your browser's request arrives in IIS, IIS examines the extension of the requested resource, the extension `.axd`. Because this extension isn't one of the extensions that IIS can handle, IIS searches its metabase for an ISAPI extension that can handle the extension `.axd`. Because ASP.NET has registered the `aspnet_isapi.dll` extension for handling the extension `.axd`, IIS dispatches the request to this extension, which in turn dispatches the request to ASP.NET. Because the `AssemblyResourceLoader` HTTP handler has been registered to handle this extension, the ASP.NET runtime dispatches the request to this handler.

Now take a look at how the `AssemblyResourceLoader` HTTP handler processes a request for an embedded resource. `AssemblyResourceLoader`, like all HTTP handlers, implements the `ProcessRequest` method of the `IHttpHandler` interface. This method contains the code that handles a request for an embedded resource.

The `ProcessRequest` method takes the `HttpContext` object as its argument and processes the request. First it retrieves the value of the `d` `querystring` parameter (recall that this value is in encrypted form):

```
JOLOMx92geNMSVlJfSrPGXt_ktxyy4uKLVy0_QToHXP10WIuKtXwtGA9rLPGwWM30
```

The method then decrypts the encrypted `d` value. As mentioned, this decrypted string consists of two substrings separated by the | character:

```
fMyAssembly,1.0.0.0,en,b03f5f7f11d50a3a|MyLibrary.mouseCallback.js
```

Recall that the first substring contains the assembly information, and the second substring contains the resource name. The method then extracts the resource name from the decrypted `d` value:

```
MyLibrary.mouseCallback.js
```

It also extracts the assembly information from the decrypted `d` value:

```
fMyAssembly,1.0.0.0,en,b03f5f7f11d50a3a
```

The method then extracts the first letter of the decrypted assembly information string:

```
f
```

If the first letter is the letter `f`, the assembly information contains the full name or strong name of the assembly. The `ProcessRequest` method then creates an instance of the `AssemblyName` object and uses the assembly name, version, culture, and public key token to set the properties of this object. It then calls the `Load` static method of the `Assembly` class and passes the `AssemblyName` object into it to load the embedding assembly in memory.

If the first letter of the assembly information is the letter p, the assembly information contains the name of a private assembly. The ProcessRequest method calls the Load static method of the Assembly class and passes the name of the private assembly into it to load the embedding assembly in memory.

If the first letter is the letter s, the embedding assembly is the System.Web.dll assembly, which is already loaded in memory.

Because the embedding assembly is loaded in memory, the ProcessRequest method can access its WebAttribute metadata attribute. Recall that this assembly-level attribute is used to give permission to serve the embedded resource, and specify the MIME type of the resource.

The ProcessRequest method sets the content type of the response to the MIME type of the resource. The client browser uses the content type of the response to determine the type of the information it receives from the server:

```
context.Response.ContentType = contentType;
```

The ProcessRequest method then accesses the Cache property of the Response object to set the caching policy for the response. This step is very important because one of the reasons the client scripts are in separate files is to allow client browsers to cache these files and use them across different pages to improve performance:

```
HttpCachePolicy cachingPolicy = context.Response.Cache;
```

The ProcessRequest method sets the cacheability attribute to Public to specify that both the client and proxy caches can cache the response:

```
cachingPolicy.SetCacheability(HttpCacheability.Public);
```

It then specifies that the client and proxy caches should cache a separate version of the response for each d value:

```
cachingPolicy.VaryByParams["d"] = true;
```

Next, the ProcessRequest method specifies that the client and proxy caches should never invalidate their caches. You may be wondering why the client and proxy caches are allowed to keep their cached responses forever. The reason is that every time the resource changes, you have to recompile the assembly, which means that the assembly will have a different timestamp. Because the URL of the embedded resource includes the assembly's timestamp, every time the assembly's timestamp changes, the URL changes. This means that the client and proxy caches will not find the response for the new URL in their caches and therefore will automatically invalidate the respective cache entry and send a new request:

```
cachingPolicy.SetExpires(DateTime.Now + TimeSpan.FromDays(365));
```

Notice that the SetExpires method sets the expiration date to one year from now, as opposed to 10 or 20 years from now. This is because most browsers don't trust expiration dates longer than one year and default to zero expiration date if the expiration data is longer than one year.

Because the embedding assembly is loaded in memory, the ProcessRequest method can call the GetManifestResourceStream method of the Assembly object that represents the in-memory assembly. This method loads the embedded resource into a Stream object:

```
Stream resourceStream = assembly.GetManifestResourceStream(resourceName);
```

The `ProcessRequest` method then accesses the output stream of the response:

```
Stream responseStream = context.Response.OutputStream;
```

The `ProcessRequest` method then reads from the resource stream and writes to the response stream. Finally, the `ProcessRequest` sends the response that contains the requested embedded resource to the requesting browser.

When to Render Your Control's Client Script

The previous section showed you different ways to render your control's client script. However, your control shouldn't *always* render its client script. The Ajax capabilities of the requesting browser may not meet the requirements of your control's client-side functionality. If your control were to render its client script regardless of the Ajax capabilities of the requesting browser, your control wouldn't operate properly on all browsers.

In addition, the page developer should have the option of turning off your control's client-side behavior regardless of the Ajax capabilities of the requesting browser. This section shows you how to add the required logic to your control to determine when your control should render its client script.

Disabling Your Control's Client-Side Capabilities

Your custom control must expose a Boolean property to allow the page developer to explicitly disable its client-side capabilities regardless of the requesting browser's Ajax capabilities, as shown in Listing 26-18. Your control mustn't render its client script when this property is set to false.

Listing 26-18: Allowing the page developer to disable your control's client-side behavior

```
public bool EnableClientScript
{
  get
  {
    ViewState["EnableClientScript"] != null ?
                    (bool)ViewState["EnableClientScript"] : true;
  }
  set { ViewState["EnableClientScript"] = value; }
}
```

Discovering Ajax Capabilities of the Requesting Browser

Your custom control must include the logic to inspect the Ajax capabilities of the requesting browser to check whether they meet the requirements of your control's client-side functionality. This logic must be run only if the page developer hasn't explicitly disabled your control's client-side functionality. Your control shouldn't render its client script if the capabilities of the requesting browser don't meet the requirements of its client-side behavior.

The `Request` object exposes a property of type `HttpBrowserCapabilities` named `Browser`. The `HttpBrowserCapabilities` class exposes properties that provide information about the Ajax capabilities of the requesting browser. Some of these properties are as follows:

- ❑ `MajorVersion`: The major version of the browser, for example, the major version of IE 5.4 is 5

- ❑ `MinorVersion`: The minor version of the browser, for example, the minor version of IE 5.4 is 4

- ❑ `MSDomVersion`: The DOM version that the browser supports

- ❑ `EcmaScriptVersion`: The JavaScript (also known as EcmaScript) version that the browser supports

To determine when to render its client script, your control must expose a private Boolean field named `renderClientScript` (or any other desired name):

```
private bool renderClientScript;
```

It must also expose a protected virtual method named `DetermineRenderClientScript` (or any other desired name) that uses the `EnableClientScript` property to check whether the page developer wants your control to turn off its client-side behavior regardless of the Ajax capabilities of the requesting browser. If so the method should set the `renderClientScript` field to false and return. In other words, it should bypass the logic that inspects the Ajax capabilities of the requesting browser.

If not, the method should use the `Browser` property of the `Request` object to check whether the Ajax capabilities of the requesting browser meet the requirements of your control's client-side functionality. If they do, it should set the `renderClientScript` field to true and return. If they don't, it should set the `renderClientScript` field to false and return.

Listing 26-19 shows the typical implementation of the `DetermineRenderClientScript` method.

Listing 26-19: The typical implementation of the DetermineRenderClientScript method

```
private bool renderClientScript = false;

protected virtual void DetermineRenderClientScript()
{
  // Checks whether the page developer wants your control to turn of its client
  // side functionality regardless of the Ajax capabilities of the requesting
  // browser
  if (!EnableClientScript)
  {
    renderClientScript = false;
    return;
  }

  HttpBrowserCapabilities browser = Page.Request.Browser;
  // The code that inspects the Ajax capabilities of the requesting browser goes
  // here.
}
```

You should keep in mind that the `DetermineRenderClientScript` method isn't responsible for rendering the client script. Instead, its sole responsibility is to set the value of the `renderClientScript` private field to specify whether the script should be rendered. This means that the rendering methods of your control must first check the value of this private field before they attempt to render the client script.

Because your control's client script is rendered in the rendering phase of the containing page's life cycle, your control must override the OnPreRender method to call the DetermineRenderClientScript method to set the value of the renderClientScript private field before the page enters its rendering phase, as shown in the following listing:

```
protected override void OnPreRender (EventArgs e)
{
  DetermineRenderClientScript();
  . . .
}
```

Where to Render Your Control's Client Script

Based on how you decide to render your control's client script, you should override one or more of the following methods to render the script:

```
void OnPreRender (EventArgs e)
void AddAttributesToRender(HtmlTextWriter writer)
void RenderContents (HtmlTextWriter writer)
void Render (HtmlTextWriter writer)
```

Which method to override depends on which type of client script your control needs to render into the containing page, as discussed in the following sections.

Overriding OnPreRender

If the client script that your control needs to render into the containing page is a script block (that is, it's within the opening and closing tags of a <script> element), your control must override the OnPreRender method to call the appropriate method of the ClientScript property of the containing page to request the page to render the script block on your control's behalf. This was thoroughly covered in the previous sections of this chapter.

Overriding AddAttributesToRender

If the client script that your control needs to render into the containing page should be rendered as attribute values on the containing element of your control, your control must override the AddAttributesToRender method. Recall from Chapter 3 that the containing element of a control is an HTML element that contains the rest of the HTML content that the control renders.

You saw an example of this case in Listing 26-5, where the CustomHyperLinkBlock control overrides the AddAttributesToRender method to render the calls into the MouseOverCallback and MouseOutCallback JavaScript functions as the values of the onmouseover and onmouseout attributes of the control's containing element:

```
public class CustomHyperLinkBlock : HyperLink
{
  protected override void AddAttributesToRender(HtmlTextWriter writer)
  {
    base.AddAttributesToRender(writer);
    if (renderClientScript)
    {
      writer.AddAttribute("onmouseover", "MouseOverCallback(this)");
      writer.AddAttribute("onmouseout", "MouseOutCallback(this)");
    }
  }
}
```

The `AddAttributesToRender` method must first examine the value of the `renderClientScript` field to check whether it should render the client script.

Overriding RenderContents

If the client script that your control needs to render into the containing page should be rendered within the opening and closing tags of the containing element of your control, your control must override the `RenderContents` method. The `RenderContents` method must first examine the value of the `renderClientScript` field to check whether it should render the client script.

You'll see an example of this case later in this chapter.

Overriding Render

Your control should override the `Render` method to render its client script if it doesn't directly or indirectly derive from `WebControl`, or if it derives from `WebControl` but it still needs to override the `Render` method. Typically, if your control derives from `WebControl`, directly or indirectly, your control shouldn't override the `Render` method itself. Instead, it should override the `AddAttributesToRender` or `RenderContents` method as discussed before.

Falling Back on Server-Side Code

As discussed previously, the page developer may sometimes want to disable your control's client-side functionality. In these cases, your control must fall back on its pure server-side code where its basic functionality operates properly.

For example, the basic functionality of the `CustomHyperLinkFile` control shown in Listing 26-14 must operate properly when its client-side behavior is disabled. As Listing 26-20 shows, both the `AddAttributesToRender` and `OnPreRender` methods fall back on the basic functionality of its base class, the `HyperLink` control. In other words, the `CustomHyperLinkFile` control turns into a simple `HyperLink` control when its client-side functionality is disabled. This allows the control to continue to operate properly without its client-side behavior.

Listing 26-20: The version of CustomHyperLinkFile control that uses an embedded resource

```
public class CustomHyperLinkFile : HyperLink
{
  protected override void AddAttributesToRender(HtmlTextWriter writer)
  {
    if (renderClientScript)
    {
      writer.AddAttribute("onmouseover", "MouseOverCallback(this)");
      writer.AddAttribute("onmouseout", "MouseOutCallback(this)");
    }

    base.AddAttributesToRender(writer);
  }

  protected override void OnPreRender(EventArgs e)
  {
    if (renderClientScript)
    {
      Type type = typeof(CustomHyperLinkFile);
      Page.ClientScript.RegisterClientScriptResource(type,
                                  "Library.CustomHyperLinkFile.js");
    }

    base.OnPreRender(e);
  }
}
```

Developing Ajax-Enabled Controls

The rest of this chapter develops several Ajax-enabled controls to show you how to implement the client-side functionality of your own Ajax-enabled controls. First, review the three fundamental tasks involved in implementing the client-side functionality of an Ajax-enabled control:

1. When to render your control's client script. As discussed, your control must expose the following members to accomplish this task:

   a. A public Boolean property named EnableClientScript to allow the page developer to explicitly turn off your control's client-side functionality regardless of the Ajax capabilities of the requesting browser.

   b. A private Boolean field named renderClientScript. Those methods of your control that need to render client script must use the value of this field to determine whether or not to render the client script.

   c. A protected virtual method named DetermineRenderClientScript. The main responsibility of this method is to set the value of the renderClientScript field. The method should set the value of this field to true only if both of the following conditions are met: the page developer hasn't set the value of the EnableClientScript property to false and the Ajax capabilities of the requesting browser meet the requirements of your control's client-side functionality.

Your control's `DetermineRenderClientScript` method must use the `Browser` property of the `Request` object to inspect the Ajax capabilities of the requesting browser.

Your control must override the `OnPreRender` method to call the `DetermineRenderClientScript` method to determine the value of the `renderClientScript` field before the control enters its rendering phase, where the control uses the value of this field to determine whether or not to render its client script.

2. How to render your control's client script. As discussed there are three different ways to render your client script:

a. Render your script as HTML attribute values. This option is normally used to register a call into a JavaScript function for a client-side event such as `onmouseover`, `onmouseout`, and so on. If your control directly or indirectly derives from the `WebControl` base class, it should override the `AddAttributesToRender` and/or `RenderContents` methods to render its client script as HTML attribute values.

Override the `AddAttributesToRender` method if you need to render the script as HTML attribute values on your control's containing element. Override the `RenderContents` method if you need to render the script as HTML attribute values on the child elements of your control's containing element.

If your control does not directly or indirectly derive from the `WebControl` base class, it should override the `Render` method to render its script as HTML attribute values.

b. Render your script as script blocks, that is, within the opening and closing tags of `<script>` elements. Override the `OnPreRender` method to call the `RegisterClientScriptBlock` and/or `RegisterStartupScript` methods of the `ClientScript` property of the containing page to render your script blocks.

Call the `RegisterClientScriptBlock` method to render the script block at the top of the page if the HTML that your control renders needs to access the script blocks. Call the `RegisterStartupScript` method to render the script blocks at the bottom of the page if the script blocks need to access the HTML that your control renders.

c. Package your script into a set of external script files known as script library and render references to these files. Override the `OnPreRender` method to call the `RegisterClientScriptInclude` and/or `RegisterClientScriptResource` methods of the `ClientScript` property of the containing page to render references to your script files.

Call the `RegisterClientScriptInclude` method if the script files are not embedded into your control's assembly. These script files are normally deployed to a designated directory in a shared location. This shared location is a directory named `aspnet_client`, which is registered with IIS as virtual root `aspnet_client`.

Call the `RegisterClientScriptResource` method if the script files are embedded into your control's assembly. It is highly recommended that you embed your control's script files into your control's assembly to avoid deployment and versioning issues.

3. Falling back on server-side code when your control's client-side functionality is disabled.

The following section uses the preceding knowledge and what you have learned so far to develop several Ajax-enabled controls.

CustomImage Ajax-Enabled Control

This section implements a custom Ajax-enabled control named CustomImage that derives from the ASP.NET Image control and extends its functionality to add support for a DHTML feature known as *transition*. CustomImage uses the transition feature to provide an animated effect to display a new image.

CustomImage exposes two new properties named MouseOverImageUrl and MouseOutImageUrl that the page developer must set to the URLs of the images that the CustomImage control will display when the user moves the mouse pointer over and out of the control, respectively. In other words, CustomImage switches from one image to another when the user moves the mouse pointer over or out of the control.

When to Render the Client Script

The first order of business is to decide when to render the control's client script. Following the implementation pattern discussed before, CustomImage exposes a public Boolean property named EnableClientScript, a private Boolean field named renderClientScript, and a protected virtual method named DetermineRenderClientScript.

Listing 26-21 shows the implementation of the DetermineRenderClientScript method. This method contains the logic that determines whether the control should render its client script.

Listing 26-21: The DetermineRenderClientScript method

```
protected virtual void DetermineRenderClientScript()
{
  renderClientScript = false;

  if (!EnableClientScript)
    return;

  HttpBrowserCapabilities browser = Page.Request.Browser;
  if (browser.MajorVersion >= 4)
    renderClientScript = true;
}
```

As Listing 26-21 shows, DetermineRenderClientScript first checks whether the page developer has explicitly turned off the client-side capabilities of the control. If so, the method sets the renderClientScript field to false and bypasses the logic that inspects the Ajax capabilities of the requesting browser.

If the page developer hasn't turned off the client-side functionality of the control, the method uses the Browser property of the Request object to check whether the requesting browser is IE4 or higher, because only these browsers support the transition capabilities of the CustomImage control. If the requesting browser is IE4 or higher, the method sets the renderClientScript field to true to signal other methods of the control that they can go ahead and render the required client script, as you'll see shortly.

As Listing 26-22 shows, CustomImage overrides the OnPreRender method to call the DetermineRenderClientScript method to set the value of the renderClientScript field before it enters its rendering phase, where it'll use the value of this field to determine whether to render the client script.

Listing 26-22: The OnPreRender method

```
protected override void OnPreRender(EventArgs e)
{
  DetermineRenderClientScript();
  . . .
}
```

How to Render the Client Script

Obviously, `CustomImage` must register client-side callbacks (JavaScript functions) for the `onmouseover` and `onmouseout` events to switch from one image to another. As Listing 26-23 shows, `CustomImage` overrides the `AddAttributesToRender` method to render the required JavaScript function calls as the values of the `onmouseover` and `onmouseout` attributes of its containing HTML element, the `<img>` element.

Listing 26-23: The AddAttributesToRender method

```
protected override void AddAttributesToRender(HtmlTextWriter writer)
{
  if (renderClientScript)
  {
    writer.AddStyleAttribute("filter",
                "revealTrans(duration=" + Duration.ToString() + "," +
                          "transition=" + ((int)Transition).ToString() + ")");

    writer.AddAttribute("onmouseover",
                    "MouseOverCallback(this,'" + MouseOverImageUrl + "');");
    writer.AddAttribute("onmouseout",
                    "MouseOutCallback(this,'" + MouseOutImageUrl + "');");
  }

  base.AddAttributesToRender(writer);
}
```

The `AddAttributesToRender` method first checks whether the `renderClientScript` field is set to true. If so, the method knows that the page developer hasn't turned off the control's client-side functionality and the Ajax capabilities of the requesting browser meet the requirements of the control's client-side behavior. Therefore, the method renders the required script.

The method first calls the `AddAttribute` method of the `HtmlTextWriter` object twice to render the calls into the `MouseOverCallback` and `MouseOutCallback` JavaScript functions as the values of the `onmouseover` and `onmouseout` attributes on the control's containing element, `<img>`:

```
writer.AddAttribute("onmouseover",
                "MouseOverCallback(this,'" + MouseOverImageUrl + "');");
writer.AddAttribute("onmouseout",
                "MouseOutCallback(this,'" + MouseOutImageUrl + "');");
```

Then the method calls the `AddStyleAttribute` method to render the call into the `revealTrans` JavaScript function as the value of the `filter` style attribute on the control's containing element, `<img>`:

```
writer.AddStyleAttribute("filter",
                "revealTrans(duration=" + Duration.ToString() + "," +
                    "transition=" + ((int)Transition).ToString() + ")");
```

The `revealTrans` function is a standard IE function that provides an animated effect when the control switches from one image to another. This function takes two arguments. The first argument specifies the duration of the transition or animation. The second argument determines the type of transition or animation.

`CustomImage` exposes an enumeration property of type `Transition` named `Transition`. The following code shows the possible values of this property. Each value introduces a different animation flavor:

```
public enum Transition
{
  BoxIn, BoxOut, CircleIn, CircleOut, WipeUp, WipeDown, WipeRight, WipeLeft,
  VerticalBlinds, HorizontalBlinds, CheckerboardAcross, CheckerboardDown,
  RandomDissolve, SplitVerticalIn, SplitVerticalOut, SplitHorizontalIn,
  SplitHorizontalOut, StripsLeftDown, StripsLeftUp, StripsRightDown,
  StripsRightUp, RandomBarsHorizontal, RandomBarsVertical, RandomTransition
}
```

Interested readers are referred to the MSDN Web site for the complete information about the possible values of the transition parameter of the `revealTrans` method.

`CustomImage` must render two sets of client scripts. The first set includes calls to the `MouseOverCallback` and `MouseOutCallback` methods as discussed before. The second set includes the client script block that contains a reference to the `CustomImage` control's script file, `CustomImage.js`.

Because the control's script file is embedded into the control's assembly, `CustomImage` overrides the `OnPreRender` method to call the `RegisterClientScriptResource` method of the `ClientScript` property of the containing page to render the client script block that contains the reference to the embedded resource file, as shown in Listing 26-24.

Listing 26-24: The OnPreRender method of the CustomImage control

```
protected override void OnPreRender(EventArgs e)
{
  DetermineRenderClientScript();

  if (renderClientScript)
    Page.ClientScript.RegisterClientScriptResource(typeof(DetailsDialog),
                                    "CustomComponents.CustomImage.js");
  base.OnPreRender(e);
}
```

Notice that the `OnPreRender` method first checks whether it should render the client script block.

Listing 26-25 shows the JavaScript functions that are called when the user moves the mouse pointer out of and over the control.

Listing 26-25: The mouse movement JavaScript functions

```
function MouseOverCallback (customImage,mouseOverImageUrl)
{
  customImage.filters[0].apply();
  customImage.src = mouseOverImageUrl;
  customImage.filters[0].play();
}

function MouseOutCallback (customImage,mouseOutImageUrl)
{
  customImage.filters[0].stop();
  customImage.src = mouseOutImageUrl;
}
```

The customImage JavaScript object references the containing element of the CustomImage control, the
<a> HTML element. This object exposes a collection property named filters that contains all the filters
defined in the style attribute of the <img> element. In this case, this collection contains a single item, the
transition filter. The filter JavaScript object exposes three important methods: apply, play, and stop.

As Listing 26-25 shows, the MouseOverCallback calls the apply method of the filter object to take a
snapshot of the current image that the <img> element displays:

```
customImage.filters[0].apply();
```

It switches to the new image:

```
customImage.src = mouseOverImageUrl;
```

It then calls the play method of the filter object to start the animation:

```
customImage.filters[0].play();
```

As Listing 26-25 shows, the MouseOutCallback method calls the stop method of the filter object to
stop the animation:

```
customImage.filters[0].stop();
```

It then switches to the new image:

```
customImage.src = mouseOutImageUrl;
```

Using the CustomImage Ajax-Enabled Control

Listing 26-26 shows an ASP.NET page that uses the CustomImage control. Notice that the page developer sets the transition and duration parameters as the top-level properties of the CustomImage control.

Listing 26-26: An ASP.NET page that uses the CustomImage control

```
<%@ Page Language="C#" %>
<%@ Register TagPrefix="custom" Namespace="CustomComponents"
Assembly="CustomComponents" %>
<html xmlns="http://www.w3.org/1999/xhtml">
<body>
  <form id="form1" runat="server">
    <custom:CustomImage runat="server" Transition="WipeUp" Duration="0.4" />
  </form>
</body>
</html>
```

Substitution

The `PerformSubstitution` property of the `WebResourceAttribute` metadata attribute was intentionally left out of the discussions of this attribute because it's much easier to understand the role of this property in the context of an example that uses it.

As discussed, when the `AssemblyResourceLoader` HTTP handler receives a request for an embedded resource, it services the resource only if you've explicitly called the `WebResourceAttribute` metadata attribute to give permission to `AssemblyResourceLoader` to service the resource. This metadata attribute exposes a Boolean property named `PerformSubstitution`. This section discusses what you can accomplish if you set this property to true. You can set this property within the `AssemblyInfo.cs` file as shown in the following:

```
[assembly: WebResource("CustomComponents.CustomImage.js", "text/javascript",
PerformSubstitution = true)]
```

The `GetWebResourceUrl` method takes two arguments and uses them to build the URL of an embedded resource as follows. The first argument is the `System.Type` object that represents the type of your custom control. The second argument is the name of the embedded resource. The `GetWebResourceUrl` method uses the first argument to retrieve the assembly information and combines it with its second argument value (the resource information) to build the URL of the embedded resource.

Now take a look at what happens if you set the `PerformSubstitution` property to true. Setting this property to true activates the feature that allows one embedded resource file to use the following convenient syntax to retrieve the URL of another embedded resource:

```
<% = WebResource(ReferencedResourceName) %>
```

Notice the difference between the `WebResource` syntax and the `GetWebResourceUrl` method. The `WebResource` syntax takes only one argument, the name of the referenced embedded resource, whereas the `GetWebResourceUrl` method requires both the resource name and the assembly information. The `WebResource` syntax uses its argument value and builds and returns the URL of the referenced embedded resource. In other words, the `WebResource` syntax uses the resource information alone to build the URL of the resource, which includes both assembly and resource information.

You may be wondering how the `WebResource` syntax figures out what the assembly information is if all you're putting into it is the resource information alone. This is made possible by the fact that both referencing and referenced embedded resources must be embedded into the same assembly. In other words, only resources embedded in the same assembly can use the `WebResource` syntax to access each other's

URLs. To help you understand how this works, consider the version of the `CustomImage.js` script file shown in Listing 26-27 where the script uses the `WebResource` syntax to get the URL of the image files embedded into the `CustomImage` control's assembly.

As discussed, it takes two simple steps to embed your image files into your control's assembly. First, add the image files to your control's Visual Studio project. Second, set the Build Action property of each image file to Embedded Resource. When you compile your control's project, Visual Studio will automatically embed the image files into your control's assembly.

Listing 26-27: The CustomImage.js resource file

```
function MouseOverCallback (customImage,mouseOverImageUrl)
{
   customImage.filters[0].apply();

   if (mouseOverImageUrl.length == 0)
      customImage.src = '<% = WebResource("CustomComponents.MouseOver.gif") %>';

   else
      customImage.src = mouseOverImageUrl;

   customImage.filters[0].play();
}

function MouseOutCallback (customImage,mouseOutImageUrl)
{
   customImage.filters[0].stop();

   if (mouseOutImageUrl.length == 0)
      customImage.src = '<% = WebResource("CustomComponents.MouseOut.gif") %>';

   else
      customImage.src = mouseOutImageUrl;
}
```

As this listing shows, the `MouseOverCallback` and `MouseOutCallback` JavaScript functions fall back on default images if no images are provided. Notice that each function uses the `WebResource` syntax to access the URL of the embedded default image file. This syntax takes only one argument, the name of the resource file. Here is how the workflow goes.

First, the client browser makes a request for the page shown in Listing 26-26. Recall that this page contains the `CustomImage` control. The containing page then calls the `OnPreRender` method of the `CustomImage` control. As shown in Listing 23-23, the `OnPreRender` method calls the `RegisterClientScriptResource` method to retrieve and to render the URL of the `CustomImage.js` embedded resource file:

```
Page.ClientScript.RegisterClientScriptResource(typeof(DetailsDialog),
                                        "CustomComponents.CustomImage.js");
```

This call causes the page to render the following script block into the containing page:

```
<script src="/CellView/WebResource.axd?
          d=PGmShSsB08haJPTx2D8RSmFYQAaxPOtEL1lGeGvib2iaff40wEA2&amp;
          t=632712000562244340"
type="text/javascript"></script>
```

The requesting browser finally receives the following HTML content from the server:

```html
<html xmlns="http://www.w3.org/1999/xhtml">
<body>
  <form name="form1" method="post" action="Default10.aspx" id="form2">
    <script src="/CellView/WebResource.axd?
                d=PGmShSsB08haJPTx2D8RSmFYQAaxPOtEL11GeGvib2iaff40wEA2&amp;
                t=632712000562244340"
    type="text/javascript"></script>

    <img onmouseover="MouseOverCallback(this,'');"
    onmouseout="MouseOutCallback(this,'');"
    src="/CellView/WebResource.axd?d=PGmShSsB08ha&amp;t=632712000562244340"
    style="filter:revealTrans(duration=0.4,transition=4);border-width:0px;" />
  </form>
</body>
</html>
```

When the browser is parsing this HTML, it runs into the script block shown in boldface and sends a request to the URL specified in the value of the `src` attribute of the `<script>` element:

```
/CellView/WebResource.axd?
            d=PGmShSsB08haJPTx2D8RSmFYQAaxPOtEL11GeGvib2iaff40wEA2&amp;
            t=632712000562244340
```

Recall that the value of the `d` querystring parameter contains the assembly and resource information of the `CustomImage.js` resource embedded into the `CustomImage` control's assembly.

When the `AssemblyResourceLoader` HTTP handler receives the request, it decrypts the value of the `d` parameter to extract the assembly and resource information. It then uses the assembly information to load the `CustomImage` control's assembly in memory. It uses the resource information to locate the resource in the assembly. In this case, the resource information is nothing but the resource name, `CustomImage.js`.

Next, it parses the `CustomImage.js` resource file shown in Listing 26-27, where it runs into the following two instances of the `WebResource` syntax:

```
customImage.src = '<% = WebResource("CustomComponents.MouseOver.gif") %>';
customImage.src = '<% = WebResource("CustomComponents.MouseOut.gif") %>';
```

Because the `MouseOver.gif` and `MouseOut.gif` image files are embedded into the same assembly as the `CustomImage.js` script file, and because the `AssemblyResourceLoader` HTTP handler already knows the assembly information within which the script file is embedded, the `WebResource` syntax doesn't need to include the assembly information.

The handler then uses the assembly and resource information to build the URL of the `MouseOver.gif` and `MouseOut.gif` embedded image files. It then replaces the two instances of the `WebResource` syntax shown in Listing 26-27 with the two URLs. The following code shows the content of the `CustomImage.js` file after these substitutions:

```
function MouseOverCallback (customImage,mouseOverImageUrl)
{
  customImage.filters[0].apply();
```

```
    if (mouseOverImageUrl.length == 0)
      customImage.src =
          'WebResource.axd?d=PGmShSsB08haJPTx2D8RSmFYQAaxPOtEL&t=632712000562244340';

    else
      customImage.src = mouseOverImageUrl;

    customImage.filters[0].play();
  }

  function MouseOutCallback (customImage,mouseOutImageUrl)
  {
    customImage.filters[0].stop();

    if (mouseOutImageUrl.length == 0)
      customImage.src =
          'WebResource.axd?d=PGmShSsB08haJPTx2D8RSmFYQAaxPO&t=632712000562244340';

    else
      customImage.src = mouseOutImageUrl;
  }
```

Finally, the handler sends this content to the requesting browser.

ImageDialog Ajax-Enabled Composite Control

Web applications that need to display a lot of images on a page often offer thumbnail images for viewers to click on so they can see the larger versions of the images. This section develops a custom composite Ajax-enabled control named `ImageDialog` that not only supports this feature, but also shows the larger version of the image in a dialog box that the user can move around, resize, and close.

You can think of the `ImageDialog` control as a master/detail control where the thumbnail and the larger version images act as the master and detail components. The user clicks the master component (the thumbnail image) to see its details (the larger version of the image).

Because the `ImageDialog` is an Ajax-enabled composite control, it must follow two different implementation patterns. The first implementation pattern is the one that's used to implement the client-side functionality of every Ajax-enabled control. The second implementation pattern is the pattern that's used to implement every composite control.

ImageDialog as a Composite Control

The `ImageDialog` custom control is a composite control that contains an `Image` server control. The `ImageDialog` control, like all other composite controls, follows a specific set of steps. First, it derives from the `CompositeControl` base class. Recall from Chapter 5 that the ASP.NET `CompositeControl` provides the basic features that every composite control must support:

- ❑ Overriding the `Controls` collection
- ❑ Implementing `INamingInterface`
- ❑ Overriding the `DataBind` method

❑ Implementing the `ICompositeControlDesignerAccessor` interface.

❑ Overriding the `Render` method to call `EnsureChildControls` when the control is in design mode

Next, it overrides the `CreateChildControls` method to create its `Image` child control:

```
private Image image;
protected override void CreateChildControls()
{
  Controls.Clear();
  image = new Image();
  Controls.Add(image);
}
```

It then exposes the properties of its `Image` child control as its own properties to allow the page developer to set the properties of the child control as attributes on the tag that represents the control on the ASP.NET page. The getters and setters of these properties must delegate to the corresponding properties of the child control:

```
public virtual string ImageUrl
{
  get
  {
    EnsureChildControls();
    return image.ImageUrl;
  }
  set
  {
    EnsureChildControls();
    image.ImageUrl = value;
  }
}

public virtual ImageAlign ImageAlign
{
  get
  {
    EnsureChildControls();
    return image.ImageAlign;
  }
  set
  {
    EnsureChildControls();
    image.ImageAlign = value;
  }
}
```

Then it calls the `EnsureChildControls` method in the getters and setters of its delegated properties to ensure that its `Image` child control has been created before it is accessed.

The control next exposes the `ControlStyle` property of its `Image` child control as its own top-level style property to provide the page developer with a convenient mechanism to style the `Image` child control:

```
private Style imageStyle;

public virtual Style ImageStyle
{
  get
  {
    if (imageStyle == null)
    {
      imageStyle = new Style();
      if (IsTrackingViewState)
        ((IStateManager)imageStyle).TrackViewState();
    }
    return imageStyle;
  }
}
```

It exposes a protected virtual method named PrepareControlHierarchy that applies the ImageStyle to its Image child control:

```
protected virtual void PrepareControlHierarchy()
{
  if (imageStyle != null)
    image.ApplyStyle(imageStyle);
}
```

The control then overrides the Render method to call the PrepareControlHierarchy method. It is important that your composite control calls the PrepareControlHierarchy method in its rendering phase. The ApplyStyle method applies the ImageStyle to the ControlStyle property of the Image child control (see Chapter 7), which means that the method is bound to make changes in the property values of the child control.

If you call the ApplyStyle method before your control's rendering phase, these property value changes are marked as dirty and consequently will be saved to your control's child view state. However, the ImageStyle, like all other Style classes, manages its own state. This means that the child control style information is saved twice to the saved view state.

If you call the PrepareControlHierarchy method in your control's Render method, the child control will not save its property changes to the view state because the rendering phase comes after the save view state phase.

```
protected override void Render(HtmlTextWriter writer)
{
  PrepareControlHierarchy();
  base.Render(writer);
}
```

Finally, the control overrides the TagKey property to specify its containing HTML element:

```
protected override HtmlTextWriterTag TagKey
{
  get { return HtmlTextWriterTag.Div; }
}
```

ImageDialog as an Ajax-Enabled Control

Because `ImageDialog` is an Ajax-enabled control, in addition to being a composite control, it also needs to follow the pattern discussed in the previous sections of this chapter to implement its client-side functionality. First, it implements the mechanism that determines whether the control should render its client script. As thoroughly discussed in the previous sections, this mechanism consists of the following four elements:

- ❑ A public Boolean property named `EnableClientScript`
- ❑ A private Boolean field named `renderClientScript`
- ❑ A protected virtual method named `DetermineRenderClientScript`
- ❑ Overriding the `OnPreRender` method to call the `DetermineRenderClientScript` method

The control then overrides the `RenderContents` method to render the call into the `InitializeDetailsPopup` and `PopupImage` JavaScript functions as the value of the `onclick` attribute on the containing element of its `Image` child control, as shown in Listing 26-28. As you'll see later, the `InitializeDetailsPopup` function initializes the pop-up dialog. This method ensures that only one copy of the dialog exits. The `PopupImage` function renders the pop-up dialog that displays the larger version of the thumbnail image.

The `ImageDialog` control exposes a property named `PopupImageUrl` that the page developer must set to the URL of the image file that contains the larger version of the thumbnail image. The `RenderContents` method passes the values of the `PopupImageUrl` and `ClientID` properties into these two JavaScript functions. These functions are discussed later. Notice that the `RenderContents` method first checks whether it should render the script.

Listing 26-28: The RenderContents method

```
protected override void RenderContents(HtmlTextWriter writer)
{
  if (renderClientScript)
    image.Attributes.Add("onclick",
                        "InitializeDetailsPopup('" + this.ClientID + "');" +
                        "PopupImage('" + PopupImageUrl + "');");

  image.RenderControl(writer);
}
```

One important thing to notice about Listing 26-28 is that if the client-side functionality of the `ImageDialog` method is turned off, the control still renders its child control. In other words, the `ImageDialog` control will act like a normal ASP.NET `Image` control when its client-side functionality is turned off. Your custom control should always fall back on its pure server-side functionality when its client-side behavior is disabled to allow it function properly on browsers whose Ajax capabilities don't meet the requirements of your control's client-side functionality.

Rendering Client-Side Style Properties

Recall from Chapter 7 that a composite control exposes the style properties of its child controls as top-level style properties such as `ItemStyle`, `AlternatingItemStyle`, and so on, and uses the `ApplyStyle` method of each child control to apply these top-level style properties to its associated child controls. This works very well in composite controls because their children are server controls.

However, this doesn't apply to the dialog that the `ImageDialog` pops up because this dialog isn't a server control. The `ImageDialog` control uses HTML/XHTML, CSS, DOM, and JavaScript client-side technologies to implement all features and functionalities of this dialog. In other words, this dialog is a pure client-side component.

This section shows you how you can use the same concepts used in composite controls to expose the CSS style attributes of a client entity such as the pop-up dialog as top-level style properties. This will provide page developers with the same benefits as normal top-level style properties:

❏　The CSS style attributes of the pop-up dialog are exposed as strongly typed properties. This means that page developers can take advantage of Visual Studio's IntelliSense support to catch the errors as they're writing the code, and they can take advantage of the type-checking capability of compilers to catch the errors as they're compiling the code.

❏　It automatically maps these strongly typed style properties to their respective CSS style attributes.

The pop-up dialog is rendered as a table with a header and a single row (see Figure 26-4). The header contains the Close button to allow the user to close the pop-up dialog. The row contains a single cell where the larger version of the thumbnail image is displayed.

If the pop-up dialog were a server control, the `ImageDialog` *would* perform the following four tasks to add support for top-level style properties. First, it would expose the three top-level style properties shown in Listing 26-29.

Listing 26-29: Top-level style properties

```
private TableStyle dialogStyle;
public virtual TableStyle DialogStyle {get
{
 get
 {
   if (dialogStyle == null)
   {
     dialogStyle = new TableStyle();
     if (IsTrackingViewState)
       ((IStateManager)dialogStyle).TrackViewState();
   }
   return dialogStyle;
 }
}

private TableItemStyle headerStyle;
public virtual TableItemStyle HeaderStyle
{
 get
 {
   if (headerStyle == null)
   {
     headerStyle = new TableItemStyle();
     if (IsTrackingViewState)
       ((IStateManager)headerStyle).TrackViewState();
   }
```

(continued)

Listing 26-29: *(continued)*

```
      return headerStyle;
    }
  }

  private TableItemStyle itemStyle;
  public virtual TableItemStyle ItemStyle
  {
   get
   {
     if (itemStyle == null)
     {
       itemStyle = new TableItemStyle();
       if (IsTrackingViewState)
         ((IStateManager)itemStyle).TrackViewState();
     }
     return itemStyle;
   }
  }
}
```

This *would* allow the page developer to use the `DialogStyle` property to set the CSS style attributes of the `<table>` HTML element that contains the entire content of the pop-up dialog, the `HeaderStyle` property to set the CSS style attributes of the `<th>` HTML element that contains the Close button, and the `ItemStyle` property to set the CSS style attributes of the `<tr>` HTML element that displays the larger version of the thumbnail image (see Figure 26-4).

Second, the `ImageDialog` *would* override the `TrackViewState`, `SaveViewState`, and `LoadViewState` methods to call the respective methods of its top-level style properties as shown in Listing 26-30.

Listing 26-30: Overriding the TrackViewState, SaveViewState, and LoadViewState

```
protected override void TrackViewState()
{
  base.TrackViewState();

  if (headerStyle != null)
    ((IStateManager)headerStyle).TrackViewState();
  if (itemStyle != null)
    ((IStateManager)itemStyle).TrackViewState();
  if (dialogStyle != null)
    ((IStateManager)dialogStyle).TrackViewState();
}

protected override object SaveViewState()
{
  object[] savedState = new object[4];

  savedState[0] = base.SaveViewState();
  if (headerStyle != null)
    savedState[1] = ((IStateManager)headerStyle).SaveViewState();
  if (itemStyle != null)
    savedState[2] = ((IStateManager)itemStyle).SaveViewState();
  if (dialogStyle != null)
```

```
    savedState[3] = ((IStateManager)dialogStyle).SaveViewState();

  foreach (object obj in savedState)
  {
    if (obj != null)
      return savedState;
  }

  return null;
}

protected override void LoadViewState(object savedState)
{
  if (savedState == null)
  {
    base.LoadViewState(savedState);
    return;
  }

  object[] state = savedState as object[];
  if (state == null || state.Length != 4)
    return;

  base.LoadViewState(state[0]);
  if (state[1] != null)
    ((IStateManager)HeaderStyle).LoadViewState(state[1]);
  if (state[2] != null)
    ((IStateManager)ItemStyle).LoadViewState(state[2]);
  if (state[3] != null)
    ((IStateManager)DialogStyle).LoadViewState(state[3]);
}
```

Third, the ImageDialog *would* expose a method named PrepareControlHierarchy where it *would* call the ApplyStyle method of each child server control to apply its top-level style properties to its child control, as shown in Listing 26-31.

Listing 26-31: The PrepareControlHierarchy method

```
protected virtual void PrepareControlHierarchy()
{
  if (dialogStyle != null)
    dialogTable.ApplyStyle(dialogStyle);
  if (headerStyle != null)
    headerRow.ApplyStyle(headerStyle);
  if (itemStyle != null)
    imageRow.ApplyStyle(itemStyle);
}
```

Fourth, the ImageDialog *would* override the Render method to call the PrepareControlHierarchy method, as shown in Listing 26-32.

Listing 26-32: The Render method

```
protected override void Render (HtmlTextWriter writer)
{
  PrepareControlHierarchy();
  base.Render (writer);
}
```

So far, you've seen the four steps that the `ImageDialog` *would* take to add support for top-level properties if the pop-up dialog were a server control. Because the pop-up dialog isn't a server control and
because only server controls expose the `ApplyStyle` method, the third and fourth steps aren't applicable so you need a different approach to map or render the top-level `DialogStyle`, `HeaderStyle`, and
`ItemStyle` properties as the CSS style attributes of the `<table>`, `<th>`, and `<tr>` HTML elements of the
pop-up dialog.

Because the first two steps are still applicable, the `ImageDialog` control contains the same exact code
shown in Listings 26-29 and 26-30. In other words, the `ImageDialog` control exposes the same
`DialogStyle`, `HeaderStyle`, and `ItemStyle` properties and overrides the `SaveViewState`,
`TrackViewState`, and `LoadViewState` methods to manage their states.

The `ImageDialog` control takes a different approach to render these three top-level style properties as
the CSS style attributes of the pop-up dialog. The control overrides the `AddAttributesToRender`
method, as opposed to the `Render` method (see Listing 26-33).

Listing 26-33: The AddAttributesToRender method

```
protected override void AddAttributesToRender(HtmlTextWriter writer)
{
  base.AddAttributesToRender(writer);

  if (renderClientScript)
  {
    CssStyleCollection col;

    if (dialogStyle != null)
    {
      col = dialogStyle.GetStyleAttributes(this);
      writer.AddAttribute("dialogStyle",col.Value);
    }

    if (headerStyle != null)
    {
      col = headerStyle.GetStyleAttributes(this);
      writer.AddAttribute("headerStyle", col.Value);
    }

    if (itemStyle != null)
    {
      col = itemStyle.GetStyleAttributes(this);
      writer.AddAttribute("itemStyle", col.Value);
    }
  }
}
```

Recall that the `AddAttributesToRender` method is used to render the HTML attributes of the containing HTML element. As Listing 26-33 shows, this method calls the `GetStyleAttributes` method of the top-level style property to access the collection that contains all the CSS style attributes that map to the top-level style property:

```
col = itemStyle.GetStyleAttributes(this);
```

It then calls the `Value` property of the collection to load the content of the collection into a string that can be directly assigned to the `style` attribute of an HTML element. The following is an example of such a string:

```
Width:400px;border:1px solid;
```

The method calls the `AddAttribute` method to assign the string to a made-up attribute on the containing HTML element. This attribute isn't a standard HTML attribute. Client browsers normally ignore attributes that they don't recognize. The `ImageDialog` control uses three made-up attributes: `dialogStyle`, `headerStyle`, and `itemStyle`.

```
writer.AddAttribute("itemStyle", col.Value);
```

Now you'll see how you can use HTML/XHTML, CSS, DOM, and JavaScript to assign the values of these made-up attributes to the `style` properties of the JavaScript objects that reference the `<table>`, `<th>`, and `<tr>` HTML elements of the pop-up dialog.

Listing 26-34 shows the `InitializeDetailsPopup` JavaScript function. As shown in Listing 26-27, the `RenderContents` method renders the call into this JavaScript function as the value of the `onclick` attribute on the `ImageDialog` control's containing HTML element. The `RenderContents` method also passes the value of the `ClientID` property of the `ImageDialog` control into this JavaScript function. Recall that ASP.NET renders the value of this property as the value of the `id` HTML attribute of the containing element.

Listing 26-34: The InitializeDetailsPopup JavaScript function

```javascript
function InitializeDetailsPopup(context)
{
  var detailsPopup = document.getElementById("DetailsPopup");
  if (!document.body.contains(detailsPopup))
  {
    detailsPopup = document.createElement("div");
    detailsPopup.id = "DetailsPopup";
    detailsPopup.style.position = "absolute";
    detailsPopup.style.visibility = "visible";

    document.body.insertBefore(detailsPopup, document.forms[0]);
  }

  detailsPopup.style.left = event.clientX;
  detailsPopup.style.top = event.clientY;

  var sender = document.getElementById(context);

  if (sender.dialogStyle)
```

(continued)

Listing 26-34: *(continued)*

```
    detailsPopup.dialogStyle = sender.dialogStyle;

  if (sender.headerStyle)
    detailsPopup.headerStyle = sender.headerStyle;

  if (sender.itemStyle)
    detailsPopup.itemStyle = sender.itemStyle;
}
```

As Listing 26-34 shows, the `InitializeDetailsPopup` JavaScript function uses CSS and DOM API to initialize the (details) pop-up dialog. DOM models an HTML or XHTML page as a tree of nodes, where each node is the root node of a branch. The JavaScript `document` object represents the root node of the entire tree. The DOM API allows you to add new nodes, remove an existing node, and so on.

The `document` object exposes several important methods that you can use to locate a node or to add a new node. One of these methods is a method named `getElementById` that takes the value of the `id` attribute of an HTML element as its argument and locates the element in the tree.

Another important method of the `document` object is a method named `createElement` that takes the name of an HTML element as its argument creates the element. Keep in mind that the `createElement` method doesn't add the newly created element to the tree. It simply creates it. In other words, at this point, the element node is sitting somewhere in memory by itself isolated from the tree.

As Listing 26-34 shows, the `InitializeDetailsPopup` JavaScript function first calls the `getElementById` method of the `document` object to access the JavaScript object that represents the details pop-up dialog:

```
var detailsPopup = document.getElementById("DetailsPopup");
```

It then calls the `contains` method of the `body` object to check whether an instance of the details pop-up dialog has already been created:

```
if (!document.body.contains(detailsPopup))
```

If the details pop-up dialog hasn't been created yet, the method calls the `createElement` method of the `document` object to create a `<div>` HTML element:

```
detailsPopup = document.createElement("div");
```

It sets the `position` property of the `style` object to "absolute" to enable absolute positioning of the `<div>` HTML element on its containing page:

```
detailsPopup.id = "DetailsPopup";
detailsPopup.style.position = "absolute";
detailsPopup.style.visibility = "visible";
```

Then it calls the `insertBefore` method of the `body` object to insert the newly created `<div>` HTML element before the `<form>` element:

```
document.body.insertBefore(detailsPopup, document.forms[0]);
```

Once the dialog is created, the method uses the X and Y coordinates of the mouse pointer to position the details pop-up dialog where the mouse pointer is located:

```
detailsPopup.style.left = event.clientX;
detailsPopup.style.top = event.clientY;
```

It then calls the `getElementById` method of the `document` object to access the containing HTML element of the `ImageDialog` control. You need to access this element because the `dialogStyle`, `headerStyle`, and `itemStyle` made-up attributes of the containing element of the `ImageDialog` control contain the style attributes of the `<table>`, `<th>`, and `<tr>` HTML elements of the details pop-up dialog (see Listing 26-32):

```
var sender = document.getElementById(context);
```

The method assigns the values of the made-up `dialogStyle`, `headerStyle`, and `itemStyle` attributes of the containing HTML element of the `ImageDialog` control to the made-up `dialogStyle`, `headerStyle`, and `itemStyle` attributes of the details pop-up dialog. This allows the same details pop-up dialog to serve all instances of the `ImageDialog` control on the containing page. Each instance loads its own `dialogStyle`, `headerStyle`, and `itemStyle` style properties into the same details pop-up dialog before it displays the dialog. Because the details pop-up dialog is completely isolated from the `ImageDialog` control, the same details pop-up dialog can serve controls other than the `ImageDialog` control. In the next chapter, you'll use the same details pop-up dialog to serve another Ajax-enabled control named `AjaxDetailsDialog`.

```
if (sender.dialogStyle)
  detailsPopup.dialogStyle = sender.dialogStyle;

if (sender.headerStyle)
  detailsPopup.headerStyle = sender.headerStyle;

if (sender.itemStyle)
  detailsPopup.itemStyle = sender.itemStyle;
```

Listing 26-35 shows the implementation of the `PopupImage` JavaScript function. As shown in Listing 26-28, the `RenderContents` method renders the call into this JavaScript function as the value of the `onclick` attribute on the `ImageDialog` control's containing HTML element. The `RenderContents` method also passes the value of the `PopupImageUrl` property of the `ImageDialog` control into this JavaScript function.

Listing 26-35: The PopupImageUrl JavaScript function

```
function PopupImage(popupImageUrl)
{
  var detailsPopup = document.getElementById("DetailsPopup");

  var content =
    "<tr style='" + detailsPopup.itemStyle + "'>" +
      "<td width='100%' height='100%'>" +
        "<img height='100%' width='100%' src='" + popupImageUrl + "'/>" +
      "</td>" +
    "</tr>";

  DisplayDetailsPopup(content);
}
```

The `PopupImage` JavaScript function calls the `getElementById` method of the `document` object to access the details pop-up dialog. You need to access this dialog because the `dialogStyle`, `headerStyle`, and `itemStyle` made-up attributes of the details pop-up dialog contain the `style` attributes of the `<table>`, `<th>`, and `<tr>` HTML elements of the details pop-up dialog (see Listing 26-31):

```
var detailsPopup = document.getElementById("DetailsPopup");
```

The JavaScript function also generates a string that contains the following HTML:

❑ A table row with a single cell. Notice that the function assigns the value of the `itemStyle` attribute of the details pop-up dialog to the `style` attribute of the table row element. Recall that the `itemStyle` attribute contains the style attributes of the row that displays the larger version of the thumbnail image:

```
"<tr style='" + detailsPopup.itemStyle + "'>" +
```

❑ An `<img>` HTML element that displays the larger version of the thumbnail image:

```
"<img height='100%' width='100%' src='" + popupImageUrl + "'/>" +
```

Finally, the function calls the `DisplayDetailsPopup` JavaScript function and passes the string into it.

Listing 26-36 shows the implementation of the `DisplayDetailsPopup` JavaScript function.

Listing 26-36: The DisplayDetailsPopup JavaScript function

```
function DisplayDetailsPopup (content)
{
  var detailsPopup = document.getElementById("DetailsPopup");

  var Details =
    "<div id='tablediv' onmousedown='MouseDownCallback()'" +
    "style='position:absolute;left:1px;top:1px'>" +
      "<table id='detailsTable' style='" + detailsPopup.dialogStyle + "'>" +
        "<tr>" +
          "<th colspan='2' style='" + detailsPopup.headerStyle + "'>" +
            "<span style='cursor:hand;cursor:pointer;'" +
            "id='closetext' onClick='CloseCallback()'>Close</span>" +
          "</th>" +
        "</tr>" +
        content +
      "</table>" +
    "</div>" +
    "<div id='scalediv' style='position:absolute;left:3px;top:3px;'>" +
      "<img src='<% = WebResource("CustomComponents.scale.gif") %>'" +
      "id='scale' onmousedown='MouseDownCallback()' />" +
    "</div>";

  detailsPopup.innerHTML = Details;

  document.getElementById("scalediv").style.left =
                          document.getElementById("tablediv").offsetWidth + 2;

  document.getElementById("scalediv").style.top =
```

```
                       document.getElementById("tablediv").offsetHeight + 2;
   detailsPopup.style.visibility ="visible";
}
```

The main responsibility of the `DisplayDetailsPopup` JavaScript function is to generate the HTML for the details pop-up dialog. In other words, the `ImageDialog` Ajax-enabled control, like all Ajax-enabled controls, uses HTML/XHTML, CSS, DOM, and JavaScript client-side technologies to implement all features of the details pop-up dialog. Notice how the `DisplayDetailsPopup` JavaScript function uses the `dialogStyle` and `headerStyle` attributes of the details pop-up dialog to set the style attributes of the dialog and its header row. Another point of interest in Listing 26-36 is how the `DisplayDetailsPopup` JavaScript function uses the `WebResource` syntax to retrieve the URL of the embedded image.

Using the ImageDialog Ajax-Enabled Control

Listing 26-37 shows an ASP.NET page that uses the `ImageDialog` Ajax-enabled custom control. As Figure 26-4 shows, when the user clicks the first thumbnail image on the top of the list, the dialog that displays the larger version of the image pops up. The user can move the tiny image on the bottom-right corner of the pop-up dialog to resize the dialog.

Listing 26-37: An ASP.NET page that uses the ImageDialog custom control

```
<%@ Page Language="C#" %>
<%@ Register TagPrefix="custom" Namespace="CustomComponents"
  Assembly="CustomComponents" %>

<html xmlns="http://www.w3.org/1999/xhtml">
<body>
  <form id="form1" runat="server">
    <asp:GridView runat="server" ID="cv" DataSourceID="MySource" AllowPaging="True"
    HorizontalAlign="center" AllowSorting="True" PageSize="3"
    AutoGenerateColumns="false" ShowHeader="false" DataKeyNames="BookID"
    CellPadding="0" CellSpacing="10" ForeColor="#333333" GridLines="None">
      <FooterStyle BackColor="#990000" Font-Bold="True" ForeColor="White" />
      <RowStyle BackColor="#FFFBD6" ForeColor="#333333" />
      <PagerStyle BackColor="#FFCC66" ForeColor="#333333" VerticalAlign="Top"
      HorizontalAlign="Center" />
      <SelectedRowStyle BackColor="#FFCC66" ForeColor="Navy" />
      <HeaderStyle BackColor="#990000" Font-Bold="True" ForeColor="White" />
      <AlternatingRowStyle BackColor="PaleGoldenrod" />
      <Columns>
        <asp:TemplateField>
          <ItemTemplate>
            <table border="0" cellpadding="0" cellspacing="0">
              <tr>
                <td valign="top" align="left">
                  <custom:ImageDialog ID="Image1" runat="server"
                  ImageUrl='<%# "Images/"+Eval("Title").ToString()+".jpg" %>'
                  PopupImageUrl='<%# "Images/Popup
                                    "+Eval("Title").ToString()+".jpg"%>'
                  DialogStyle-BackColor="LightGoldenrodYellow"
                  DialogStyle-BorderColor="Tan" DialogStyle-BorderWidth="1px"
                  DialogStyle-CellPadding="2" DialogStyle-CellSpacing="0"
                  DialogStyle-BorderStyle="Groove" DialogStyle-ForeColor="Black"
```

(continued)

Listing 26-37: *(continued)*

```
                DialogStyle-GridLines="None" HeaderStyle-BackColor="Tan"
                HeaderStyle-Font-Bold="True"
                ItemStyle-BackColor="PaleGoldenrod" />
            </td>
            <td valign="top" align="left">
              <table border="0" cellpadding="0" cellspacing="0">
                <tr>
                  <td valign="top" align="left">
                      <strong><a href="">
                       <%# Eval("Title").ToString() %>
                     </a></strong>
                  </td>
                </tr>
                <tr>
                  <td valign="top" align="left">  
                    <font face="verdana,arial,helvetica" size="-1">by
                      <%# Eval("Author").ToString() %>
                    </font>
                  </td>
                </tr>
                <tr>
                  <td valign="top" align="left">  
                    <font face="verdana,arial,helvetica" size="-1">
                      <%# Eval("Publisher").ToString() %></font>
                  </td>
                </tr>
              </table>
            </td>
          </tr>
          <tr>
            <td align="left" colspan="2">
              <font face="verdana,arial,helvetica" size="-1">
              List Price : $<%# Eval("Price").ToString() %></font>
            </td>
          </tr>
        </table>
      </ItemTemplate>
    </asp:TemplateField>
  </Columns>
</asp:GridView>
<asp:SqlDataSource runat="server" ID="MySource"
ConnectionString="<%$ ConnectionStrings:MySqlConnectionString %>"
SelectCommand="Select * From Books" />
  </form>
</body>
</html>
```

As the boldfaced portion of Listing 26-37 shows, the ImageDialog custom control exposes the CSS style attributes of the <table>, <th>, and <tr> HTML elements of the pop-up dialog as top-level properties: DialogStyle, HeaderStyle, and ItemStyle. In other words, the ImageDialog control hides the details of these CSS style attributes behind a convenient set of top-level properties.

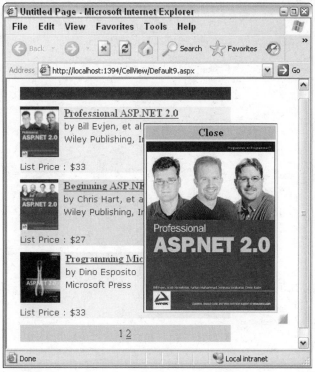

Figure 26-4

Summary

This chapter discussed the first characteristic of Ajax-enabled controls and components; that is, they use HTML/XHTML, CSS, DOM, and JavaScript client-side technologies to implement most of their functionality. This chapter then provided you with a recipe for implementing the client-side functionality of an Ajax-enabled control. You then used the recipe to implement two Ajax-enabled controls named `CustomImage` and `ImageDialog`.

The next chapter discusses the second characteristic of Ajax-enabled controls and components, that is, their asynchronous communications with the server.

27

Developing Ajax-Enabled Controls and Components: Asynchronous Client Callback

The previous chapter showed you how to implement the client-side functionality of an Ajax-enabled control. As you saw, an Ajax-enabled control uses HTML/XHTML, CSS, DOM, and JavaScript to dynamically update itself. Such dynamic updates often involve round-trips to the server to retrieve the required data.

Traditional server controls use the ASP.NET full page postback mechanism to perform these round-trips to the server. This traditional communication model suffers from the following drawbacks:

❑ It performs a full page postback to the server to retrieve the data and to render the entire page all over again. Rendering the entire page just to update a small portion of it is one of the main usability problems with Web applications and one of main factors that makes these applications act and feel very different from their desktop counterparts.

❑ It's synchronous. Synchronous communication models use the "click-and-wait" user interaction pattern, which is characterized by waiting periods that disrupt the user work-flow and degrade the user experience.

As you'll see in this chapter, Ajax-enabled controls use asynchronous client callback techniques such as XMLHttpRequest to communicate with the server. This asynchronous communication model provides the following important benefits:

❑ The users can continue interacting with the application while the data is being down-loaded from the server.

❑   Ajax-enabled controls can contain the logic that allows them to decide when to make the client callback to the server. This logic can use well-known Ajax patterns to determine when is the best time to make the client callback to ensure that the use continues interacting with the component without any interruptions. Ajax patterns are thoroughly discussed in the next two chapters.

The ASP.NET 2.0 client callback mechanism encapsulates the logic that performs the asynchronous client callbacks and provides you with a convenient API that you can use to develop Ajax-enabled controls. The client callback mechanism consists of different components as discussed later in this chapter. The ASP.NET 2.0 Framework comes with built-in implementation for these components.

This chapter consists of four main parts. The first part of this chapter uses a step-by-step approach to show you how to implement replicas of the main components of the ASP.NET 2.0 client callback mechanism. Implementing these replicas will help you look under the hood of the ASP.NET 2.0 implementation of these components where you can see for yourself how the ASP.NET client callback mechanism works from the inside out.

The second part of this chapter uses a step-by-step approach to show you how to take advantage of the ASP.NET 2.0 client callback mechanism to develop Ajax-enabled controls that make asynchronous client callbacks to the server to exchange XML data with the server.

The client callback mechanism allows clients to call server-side methods. These methods normally retrieve the required data from the underlying data store, format the retrieved data (normally XML format), and return the formatted data (normally XML data) to the client. This means that the server-side methods must contain data access code. Such data access code must be generic because in data-driven Web applications, data comes from many different sources, such as Microsoft SQL Server, Oracle, XML documents, flat files, and Web services, just to name a few. The third part of this chapter shows you how to use the ASP.NET 2.0 data source control model to develop data store-agnostic Ajax-enabled controls that can access any type of data store.

The fourth part of this chapter implements several Ajax-enabled components to show you how to use the ASP.NET 2.0 client callback mechanism to implement Ajax-enabled components with minimal effort.

To make the discussions of the first three parts of this chapter more concrete, this chapter implements a new Ajax-enabled control named `AjaxDropDownList` that extends the functionality of the `DropDownList` control.

Motivation for the AjaxDropDownList Control

Data-bound controls such as `GridView` and `DetailsView` are used to display and edit database fields. These controls render different HTML markup text in the display and edit modes. For instance, they may display the value of a field as a simple text when they're in the display mode. However, they may use a text box in the edit mode to allow users to update the field. The type of HTML markup text that they render also depends on the type of the field. For instance, they normally use a checkbox to display a Boolean value because it's more user-friendly.

Some fields in a data-bound control might be foreign key fields. It would make little sense to use a text box to allow users to edit a foreign key field because the user would have to remember the legal values of the field. The more user-friendly control is a `DropDownList` server control. The control displays all the legal values of the respective foreign key field allowing users to select the appropriate value.

Foreign key field values are the values of their corresponding primary key fields. Most database tables automatically generate the primary key field value of a record when the record is being added to the table. This means that the primary key field values and consequently the respective foreign key field values aren't meaningful to users.

The database table that contains the corresponding primary key field normally exposes another field whose values are more meaningful to users. For instance, consider the `Products` and `Categories` tables. The `Products` table exposes a foreign key field named `CategoryID` whose values are nothing but the values of the respective primary key field in the `Categories` table, `CategoryID`. The `Categories` table also exposes another field called `CategoryName` with values that make more sense to users. Page developers normally use a `DropDownList` control to display the values of the field that makes more sense to users, such as `CategoryName`.

Chapter 18 implemented a new custom data control field named `DropDownListField` that allows page developers to add foreign key field editing capability to their `GridView` and `DetailsView` controls without writing a single line of code. The `DropDownListField` data control field automatically loads the legal values of the respective user-friendly field from the underlying data store and uses a `DropDownList` control to display the values.

Even though displaying the values of the user-friendly field such as `CategoryName` makes foreign key editing more user-friendly, it's still not as user-friendly as it should be. For instance, what if the user needs to know more about a category than just the category name in order to make a more intelligent selection? Obviously the `Categories` table exposes more fields than `CategoryName`. However, the `DropDownList` control only allows page developers to display the values of a single field. This chapter implements a new Ajax-enabled control named `AjaxDropDownList` that extends the functionality of the `DropDownList` control to add support for Ajax features. When the user selects an item from the list, a client-side change event is raised. The callback function for the change event automatically uses the client callback mechanism to asynchronously retrieve the detailed information about the selected item from the server and uses DHTML to display the information.

This chapter also shows how to extend the `DropDownListField` custom data control field to add support for the `AjaxDropDownList` control. This will allow page developers to enable their `GridView` and `DetailsView` controls to use the ASP.NET client callback mechanism to display more details of a selected item without having to perform a full page postback to the server.

The `AjaxDropDownList` control can also be used as a master/detail form where the user selects an item from the list to see its details, as you'll see at the end of the chapter.

The Client Callback Mechanism

The client callback mechanism allows client-side code to asynchronously call server-side methods and use the values returned from these methods and the HTML/XHTML, CSS, DOM, and JavaScript client-side technologies to dynamically update the appropriate parts of the page without having to perform a full page postback and consequently render the entire page again. This mechanism involves the following steps:

1. Write a client-side method (such as a JavaScript function) that uses HTML/XHTML, CSS, DOM, and JavaScript client-side technologies to dynamically retrieve the required input data from the Web page. The AjaxDropDownList control uses these client-side technologies to dynamically retrieve the value of the value property of the selected item. This value is usually the primary key field value of the database record that the server-side method must retrieve from the underlying data store.

2. Write a client-side method that uses an asynchronous callback technique such as XMLHttp to make an HTTP request that contains the retrieved input data. The AjaxDropDownList control will include the retrieved value of the value property of the selected item in its asynchronous HTTP request to the server.

3. Write a server-side method that takes the input data as its argument, retrieves the required data from the underlying data store, formats the retrieved data (normally XML format), and returns the formatted data (normally XML data) to the client.

4. Write a client-side method that takes the formatted data as its argument and uses HTML/XHTML, CSS, DOM, and JavaScript to dynamically update the appropriate parts of the Web page.

As mentioned, all the interactions with the server must be done asynchronously in order to allow users to continue interacting with the page as data is being downloaded from the server.

Implementing the ASP.NET 2.0 Client Callback Mechanism

The client callback mechanism consists of different components, as you'll see later in this section. The ASP.NET 2.0 Framework comes with built-in implementation for these components, saving control developers from having to implement them. This part of this chapter uses a step-by-step approach to show you how to implement fully functional replicas of the main parts of the ASP.NET 2.0 client callback mechanism. Implementing these parts will help you to look under the hood of the ASP.NET 2.0 implementation of the client callback mechanism in order to gain an inside perspective of the mechanism.

To make discussions more concrete, the implementation of the client callback mechanism is presented in the context of implementing the AjaxDropDownList Ajax-enabled control. This control derives from the DropDownList control and extends its functionality to add support for Ajax features, as shown in Listing 27-1.

Listing 27-1: The AjaxDropDownList control

```
public class AjaxDropDownList : DropDownList, IMyCallbackEventHandler
{
  string clientMethodArgument;

  public string ServerMethodArgument { get; set;}
  public string ClientCallbackDataSourceID { get; set;}
  public bool EnableClientCallback { get; set;}

  public override bool AutoPostBack { get; set;}

  public void RaiseCallbackEvent(string arg);
```

```
    public string GetCallbackResult();

    private void MyCallback(IEnumerable data);

    protected override void Render(HtmlTextWriter w);
    protected override void OnPreRender(EventArgs e);
}
```

Overriding the OnPreRender Method

The `AjaxDropDownList` control overrides the `OnPreRender` method to write and register the required JavaScript functions with the containing page as shown in Listing 27-2. As discussed in the previous chapter, it's highly recommended that you package your script into a script library and render references to these files. However, to keep this discussion focused and make the script more accessible to these discussions, the replicas of the ASP.NET client callback components will not follow this recommendation.

Listing 27-2: The overridden OnPreRender method

```
protected override void OnPreRender(EventArgs e)
{
  string myScript =

    "<script language='javascript'>" +
    "var xml;\n" +

    "function CreateXmlDocument() {" +
      "var xmlDocumentVersions = " +
        "['MSXML2.DOMDocument.5.0','MSXML2.DOMDocument.4.0'," +
        "'MSXML2.DOMDocument.3.0','MSXML2.DOMDocument','Microsoft.XmlDom'];" +
      "var xmlDocument;" +
      "for (var i=0; i<xmlDocumentVersions.length; i++) {" +
        "try {" +
          "xmlDocument = new ActiveXObject(xmlDocumentVersions[i]);" +
        "}" +
        "catch (ex) {}" +
        "return xmlDocument;" +
      "}" +
    "}" +

    "function MyClientCallback() {" +
      "if (xml.readyState == 4) {" +
        "if (xml.status == 200) {" +
          "var xmlDocument = CreateXmlDocument();" +
          "xmlDocument.loadXML(xml.responseText);" +
          "var dataRow = xmlDocument.documentElement;" +
          "var dataFields = dataRow.childNodes;" +
          "var dataField;" +
          "var dataFieldName;" +
          "var dataFieldValue;" +
          "var detailsDialog = document.all['details'];" +
          "if (detailsDialog.childNodes[0])" +
            "detailsDialog.removeChild(detailsDialog.childNodes[0]);" +
          "table = document.createElement('table');" +
```

(continued)

Listing 27-2: *(continued)*

```
                    "detailsDialog.appendChild(table);" +
                    "var tableRow;" +
                    "var firstTableCell;" +
                    "var secondTableCell;" +
                    "var strongElement;" +
                    "for (var i=0; i<dataFields.length; i++) {" +
                        "dataField = dataFields[i];" +
                        "dataFieldName = dataField.getAttribute('name');" +
                        "dataFieldValue = dataField.getAttribute('value');" +
                        "tableRow = table.insertRow(i);" +
                        "firstTableCell = tableRow.insertCell(0);" +
                        "firstTableCell.innerHTML = '<strong>'+dataFieldName +'</strong>';" +
                        "secondTableCell = tableRow.insertCell(1);" +
                        "secondTableCell.innerHTML = dataFieldValue;" +
                    "}" +
                "}" +
            "}" +
        "}\n" +

        "function CustomWebForm_DoCallbackScript (controlID,controlMethodArg)" +
        "{" +
            "xml = new ActiveXObject('Microsoft.XMLHTTP');" +
            "xml.onreadystatechange = MyClientCallback;" +

            "url = " + "'" + HttpContext.Current.Request.Url +
                    "?__CUSTOMCALLBACKID=' + controlID +" +
                    "'&__CUSTOMCALLBACKPARAM=' + escape(controlMethodArg);" +
            "xml.open('POST', url, true);" +
            "xml.setRequestHeader('Content-Type', " +
            "'application/x-www-form-urlencoded');" +
            "xml.send(null);" +
        "}\n";

        "function CallServerMethod()" +
        "{" +
            "var arg = document.all['" + base.ClientID + "'].value;" +
            "CustomWebForm_DoCallbackScript(" + "'" + this.UniqueID + "', arg);" +
        "}\n" +
    "</script>";


    if (EnableClientCallback)
        Page.ClientScript.RegisterClientScriptBlock(GetType().ToString(), myScript);

    base.OnPreRender(e);
}
```

As discussed, the first step in writing a client callback is to write a client-side method (such as a JavaScript function) that uses HTML/XHTML, CSS, DOM, XML, XSLT and JavaScript client-side technologies to retrieve the required input data from the Web page. The CallServerMethod JavaScript function uses these client-side technologies to retrieve the value of the value property of the selected item (see Listing 27-3). This value is usually the primary key field value of the respective database record.

Listing 27-3: The CallServerMethod JavaScript function

```
"function CallServerMethod()" +
"{" +
  "var arg = document.all['" + base.ClientID + "'].value;" +
        "CustomWebForm_DoCallbackScript(" + "'" + this.UniqueID + "', arg);" +
"}\n" +
```

Notice that `base.ClientID` is used as the index into the `all` array. The containing page automatically sets the value of the `ClientID` property of a control when the control is added to the page. The `CallServerMethod` JavaScript function then calls the `CustomWebForm_DoCallbackScript` JavaScript function and passes the required argument values. These argument values are as follows:

❑ The `UniqueID` property value of the `AjaxDropDownList` control. This value is used to uniquely identify the server control that handles the client callback as discussed later.

❑ As mentioned, the `CallServerMethod` function uses DHTML to retrieve the value of the `value` property of the selected item. The method packs the retrieved data into a variable of type string. This string value will be passed as an argument to the server-side method that handles the client callback as discussed later. Notice that the type of the value is string. However, the content of the string is totally up to the developers. For instance, developers can pass an XML document or JavaScript code as argument to the server-side method. Therefore one important part of the design is to decide on the format of the data being passed from the client to the server. The most common data format is XML. That should explain why XML is part of the Ajax name (Asynchronous Javascript And **XML**). In this case, the `CallServerMethod` function simply passes the value of the `value` property of the selected item.

Listing 27-4 shows the implementation of the `CustomWebForm_DoCallbackScript` JavaScript function. The main responsibility of the function is to establish an asynchronous connection to the server and send an HTTP request. The request also includes the string value that the client needs to pass to the server-side method. In this case, this value is the primary key field value of the item that the user has selected from the `DropDownList` control.

Listing 27-4: The CustomWebForm_DoCallbackScript JavaScript function

```
"function CustomWebForm_DoCallbackScript (controlID,controlMethodArg)" +
"{" +
  "xml = new ActiveXObject('Microsoft.XMLHTTP');" +
  "xml.onreadystatechange = MyClientCallback;" +

  "url = " + "'" + HttpContext.Current.Request.Url +
        "?__CUSTOMCALLBACKID=' + controlID +" +
        "'&__CUSTOMCALLBACKPARAM=' + escape(controlMethodArg);" +
  "xml.open('POST', url, true);" +
  "xml.setRequestHeader('Content-Type', " +
  "'application/x-www-form-urlencoded');" +
  "xml.send(null);" +
"}\n";
```

The `CustomWebForm_DoCallbackScript` function uses an `XmlHttpRequest` object to send the request asynchronously. The object exposes a property named `onreadystatechange` that's set to the name of the appropriate JavaScript function (`MyClientCallback`). The `MyClientCallback` function is called as soon as the response from the server arrives. Therefore the client callback is performed asynchronously where users continue interacting with the page as the data is being downloaded from the server.

Notice how the `CustomWebForm_DoCallbackScript` function evaluates the value of the `url` variable (see Listing 27-4). It first calls the `Url` property of the `Request` object to access the URL of the page being requested. It then adds the following two pieces of information to the URL value:

❑ The value of the `UniqueID` property of the `AjaxDropDownList` control. This value is used to uniquely identify the control that's responsible for handling the client callback. In this case the control is the `AjaxDropDownList` control. Notice that the value `__CUSTOMCALLBACKID` is used as the key for the `UniqueID` property value. The same key will also be used to extract the `UniqueID` property value from the `Request` collection as discussed later.

❑ The string value that the client needs to pass to the server-side method. Notice that the value `__CUSTOMCALLBACKPARAM` is used as the key for the client's string value. The same key will also be used to extract the value that the client needs to pass to the server-side method from the `Request` collection as discussed later.

The `XmlHttpRequest` object exposes a method named `open` that takes three arguments. The first argument is the HTTP verb. The `CustomWebForm_DoCallbackScript` uses the `POST` verb. The second argument is the value of the `url` variable. The object also exposes a method named `setRequestHeader` that's used here to set the content type of the request. The `CustomWebForm_DoCallbackScript` JavaScript function then calls the `send` method of the `XmlHttpRequest` object to send the HTTP request to the server. Because the `CustomWebForm_DoCallbackScript` function adds the required information to the URL itself, the `send` method is called with the `null` argument.

The `XmlHttpRequest` object automatically calls the `MyClientCallback` JavaScript function after the response from the server arrives, as shown in Listing 27-5.

Listing 27-5: The MyClientCallback method uses DHTML to update the appropriate part of the page

```
"function MyClientCallback() {" +
  "if (xml.readyState == 4) {" +
  "if (xml.status == 200) {" +
    "var xmlDocument = CreateXmlDocument();" +
    "xmlDocument.loadXML(xml.responseText);" +
    "var detailsDialog = document.all['details'];" +
    "if (detailsDialog.childNodes[0])" +
      "detailsDialog.removeChild(detailsDialog.childNodes[0]);" +
    "table = document.createElement('table');" +
    "detailsDialog.appendChild(table);" +
    "var tableRow;" +
    "var firstTableCell;" +
    "var secondTableCell;" +
    "var strongElement;" +
    "var dataRow = xmlDocument.documentElement;" +
    "var dataFields = dataRow.childNodes;" +
    "var dataField;" +
    "var dataFieldName;" +
    "var dataFieldValue;" +
    "for (var i=0; i<dataFields.length; i++) {" +
```

```
                "dataField = dataFields[i];" +
                "dataFieldName = dataField.getAttribute('name');" +
                "dataFieldValue = dataField.getAttribute('value');" +
                "tableRow = table.insertRow(i);" +
                "firstTableCell = tableRow.insertCell(0);" +
                "firstTableCell.innerHTML = '<strong>' + dataFieldName + '</strong>';" +
                "secondTableCell = tableRow.insertCell(1);" +
                "secondTableCell.innerHTML = dataFieldValue;" +
            "}" +
          "}" +
        "}" +
      "}\n" +
```

As Listing 27-5 shows, the `MyClientCallback` JavaScript function first calls the `CreateXmlDocument` JavaScript function to create an in-memory XML store. The `CreateXmlDocument` JavaScript function is discussed shortly. As you'll see, the `CreateXmlDocument` JavaScript function creates a JavaScript object that will be used as an in-memory XML store:

```
        "var xmlDocument = CreateXmlDocument();" +
```

The `MyClientCallback` JavaScript function then calls the `loadXML` method of the JavaScript object to load the XML data that it has received from the server into the XML store:

```
        "xmlDocument.loadXML(xml.responseText);"  +
```

The following code shows the type of XML data that the `MyClientCallback` method receives from the server. Later in this chapter you'll see how the server generates this XML data:

```
  <dataRow>
    <dataField name="ProductID" value="1" />
    <dataField name="ProductName" value="Product1" />
    <dataField name="CategoryID" value="2" />
  </dataRow>
```

As this code shows, this XML document has a document element named `<dataRow>`, which has three subelements named `<dataField>`. The document element represents a database record and the subelements represent the database fields. Each `<dataField>` subelement has two attributes named `name` and `value` that contain the name and value of the associated database field. This reveals one aspect of the communication between Ajax-enabled controls such as `AjaxDropDownList` control and the server; that is, the data that Ajax-enabled controls exchange with the server is usually in XML format.

As Listing 27-5 shows, `MyClientCallback` accesses the DOM object that represents the `<div>` HTML element that will contain the detailed information about the selected item:

```
        "var detailsDialog = document.all['details'];" +
```

`MyClientCallback` then calls the `createElement` method of the DOM `document` object to create the table that will contain the information:

```
        "table = document.createElement('table');" +
```

`MyClientCallback` calls the `appendChild` method of the DOM object that represents the `<div>` element to add the `<table>` element as its child element:

```
"detailsDialog.appendChild(table);" +
```

Next, `MyClientCallback` accesses the DOM object that represents the document element of the XML document or data that it has received from the server, that is, the `<dataRow>` element:

```
"var dataRow = xmlDocument.documentElement;" +
```

`MyClientCallback` then uses the `childNodes` collection property of the DOM object to access the DOM objects that represent the `<dataField>` subelements of the `<dataRow>` element:

```
"var dataFields = dataRow.childNodes;" +
```

Next, `MyClientCallback` iterates through the DOM objects and takes the following actions for each enumerated DOM object:

1. Calls the `getAttribute` method the enumerated DOM object twice to retrieve the name and value of the associated database field:

```
"dataFieldName = dataField.getAttribute('name');" +
"dataFieldValue = dataField.getAttribute('value');" +
```

2. Calls the `insertRow` method of the DOM object that represents the containing `<table>` element to add a new row to the table:

```
"tableRow = table.insertRow(i);" +
```

3. Calls the `insertCell` method of the DOM object that represents the newly created table row twice to add two cells to the row:

```
"firstTableCell = tableRow.insertCell(0);" +
"secondTableCell = tableRow.insertCell(1);" +
```

4. Sets the `innerHTML` property of the DOM objects that represent the two cells to name and value of the associated database field, respectively:

```
"firstTableCell.innerHTML = '<strong>' + dataFieldName + '</strong>';" +
"secondTableCell.innerHTML = dataFieldValue;" +
```

As the discussions show, Ajax-enabled controls use DOM and XML APIs to dynamically update their UI on the client side without any involvement from the server.

The following code fragment contains the implementation of the `CreateXmlDocument` JavaScript function:

```
"function CreateXmlDocument() {" +
  "var xmlDocumentVersions = " +
        "['MSXML2.DOMDocument.5.0','MSXML2.DOMDocument.4.0'," +
          "'MSXML2.DOMDocument.3.0','MSXML2.DOMDocument','Microsoft.XmlDom'];" +
  "var xmlDocument;" +
  "for (var i=0; i<xmlDocumentVersions.length; i++) {" +
  "try {" +
    "xmlDocument = new ActiveXObject(xmlDocumentVersions[i]);" +
```

```
    "}" +
    "catch (ex) {}" +
      "return xmlDocument;" +
    "}" +
  "}" +
```

The main responsibility of the `CreateXmlDocument` JavaScript function is to create the DOM object that represents the entire XML document received from the server.

The `OnPreRender` method finally calls the `RegisterClientScriptBlock` method of the `Page` object to register the required JavaScript functions. Notice that the registration is done under the name whose value is evaluated using the `GetType` method of the `AjaxDropDownList` control. This ensures that the containing page emits the required JavaScript functions only once no matter how many instances of the control are used in the same page.

Overriding the Render Method

The `AjaxDropDownList` control overrides the `Render` method of the `DropDownList` control (see Listing 27-6). The `Render` method renders a table HTML element that has single row with two columns. The method calls the `Render` method of the base class, `DropDownList`, to render the `DropDownList` control in the first column. The `AjaxDropDownList` control exposes a public Boolean property named `EnableClientCallback` that page developers can set to turn the client callback feature on or off.

If `EnableClientCallback` is set to true, the `Render` method registers the `CallServerMethod` JavaScript function as callback for the client-side `onchange` event of the `DropDownList` control. The `onchange` event is raised when the user selects a new item from the list. Because `onchange` is a client-side event, the `Render` method uses the `Attributes` collection of the base class to register the callback for this event.

The `Render` method renders a `div` HTML element in the second column. The `div` element doesn't render any content because the content will be rendered dynamically via the client callback mechanism. When the user selects a new item from the list, the client-side `onchange` event is raised, which in turn calls the `CallServerMethod` JavaScript function. The function uses DHTML to retrieve the value of the `value` attribute of the selected item. This value is usually the value of the respective primary key field. The `CallServerMethod` then calls the `CustomWebForm_DoCallbackScript` JavaScript function, which in turn creates the `XmlHttpRequest` object, uses the object to asynchronously call the server-side method, and passes the primary key field value of the selected item as the argument of the server-side method. The server-side method retrieves the database record with the specified primary key field value and returns the value to the client. The `XmlHttpRequest` object then automatically calls the `MyClientCallback` JavaScript function and passes the data as its argument. The `MyClientCallback` function then uses the value of the `responseText` property of the `XmlHttpRequest` object and DOM and XML to dynamically update the contents of the `div` HTML element.

Listing 27-6: The Render method

```
protected override void Render(HtmlTextWriter w)
{
  string js = "javascript:CallServerMethod()";

  w.RenderBeginTag(HtmlTextWriterTag.Table);
```

(continued)

Listing 27-6: *(continued)*

```
    w.RenderBeginTag(HtmlTextWriterTag.Tr);
    w.RenderBeginTag(HtmlTextWriterTag.Td);
    if (EnableClientCallback)
      base.Attributes.Add("onchange", js);
    base.Render(w);
    w.RenderEndTag();
    w.RenderBeginTag(HtmlTextWriterTag.Td);
    w.AddAttribute(HtmlTextWriterAttribute.Id, "details");
    w.RenderBeginTag(HtmlTextWriterTag.Div);
    w.RenderBeginTag(HtmlTextWriterTag.Span);
    w.RenderEndTag();
    w.RenderEndTag();
    w.RenderEndTag();
    w.RenderEndTag();
    w.RenderEndTag();
  }
```

Server Side

The discussions so far have been mostly focused on the client side and how the client uses
XMLHttpRequest to asynchronously send an HTTP request to the server and how it uses
HTML/XHTML, CSS, XML, DOM, and JavaScript to update the appropriate parts of the containing
page with the data it receives from the server. This section discusses what happens on the server side
when the HTTP request from the client arrives. As you know, the Page class implements the
IHttpHandler interface. The interface exposes a method named ProcessRequest. As discussed later,
the ProcessRequest method of the Page object contains the required code that handles the client's
HTTP request. To simplify discussions, this chapter adds the required code to the Page_Load method
(see Listing 27-7) of the Page object instead of the ProcessRequest method.

Listing 27-7: The Page_Load method

```
void Page_Load(object sender, EventArgs e)
{
  if (Request.QueryString["__CUSTOMCALLBACKID"] != null)
  {
    string serverControlID = Request.QueryString["__CUSTOMCALLBACKID"];
    Control serverControl = FindControl(serverControlID);
    IMyCallbackEventHandler handler = serverControl as IMyCallbackEventHandler;
    if (handler != null)
    {
      string serverMethodArgument =
                  Request.QueryString["__CUSTOMCALLBACKPARAM"].ToString();
      handler.RaiseCallbackEvent(serverMethodArgument);
      Response.Write(handler.GetCallbackResult());
      Response.Flush();
      Response.End();
      return;
    }
  }
}
```

The Page_Load method checks to see if the QueryString collection of the Request object contains a value for the key __CUSTOMCALLBACKID. Recall that this value is the value of the UniqueID property of the control that handles the client's request, the AjaxDropDownList control. If the QueryString collection contains the value, the Page_Load method uses it as the sign that the client is making a client callback, not a full postback. The Page_Load method then uses the same key to extract the value of the UniqueID property of the control and passes it as an argument to the FindControl method of the Page class. The FindControl method uses the UniqueID value to locate the AjaxDropDownList control instance in the page's control tree and returns a reference to it.

However, the Page_Load method needs a way to identify which method of the control must be called. One way to standardize the signature of a method is to define an interface that exposes the method:

```
public interface IMyCallbackEventHandler
{
  void RaiseCallbackEvent(string arg);
  string GetCallbackResult();
}
```

The IMyCallbackEventHandler interface exposes a method named RaiseCallbackEvent that takes a string value as its only argument and a method named GetCallbackResult that returns a string value. As shown in Listing 27-1, the AjaxDropDownList control implements the IMyCallbackEventHandler interface. Therefore the Page_Load method first ensures that the control implements the interface and then uses the key __CUSTOMCALLBACKPARAM to extract the string value that the client needs to pass to the server-side method, RaiseCallbackEvent. The Page_Load method then calls the RaiseCallbackEvent method of the AjaxDropDownList control and passes the string value as its argument. The RaiseCallbackEvent method is thoroughly discussed later.

The ASP.NET 2.0 Client Callback Mechanism

The previous sections of this chapter implemented fully functional replicas of the main components of the ASP.NET 2.0 client callback mechanism. As the previous sections showed, you would have to add fair amount of code to add client callback capability to your custom controls if you were to do it yourself. Closer examination of the code shows that most parts of the code are infrastructural and apply to all Web applications. These parts of the code have nothing to do with the specifics of your custom controls, such as:

❑   The CustomWebForm_DoCallbackScript JavaScript function has to be written.

❑   The CustomWebForm_DoCallbackScript function has to be registered and added to the containing page.

❑   The MyClientCallback JavaScript function has to check the values of the readyState and Status properties of the XmlHttpRequest object.

❑   The MyClientCallback function has to retrieve the server's value from the XmlHttpRequest object.

❑   The CallServerMethod JavaScript function has to be written.

- ❑ The `CallServerMethod` function has to be registered and added to the containing page.

- ❑ The required code in the `Page_Load` method has to be written.

- ❑ The `IMyCallbackEventHandler` interface has to be defined.

The ASP.NET 2.0 client callback mechanism has already implemented these eight infrastructural steps. This saves you from having to implement them every time you're adding support for client callbacks to your custom controls. Therefore the ASP.NET 2.0 client callback mechanism allows you to focus on what matters the most to you, that is, the specifics of the custom control you're trying to develop. This part of the chapter discusses the ASP.NET 2.0 client callback mechanism and shows how you can take advantage of the mechanism to add support for client callbacks with minimal efforts.

Overriding the OnPreRender Method

Taking advantage of the ASP.NET 2.0 client callback mechanism simplifies the `OnPreRender` method of the `AjaxDropDownList` control, as shown in Listing 27-8.

Listing 27-8: OnPreRender with the ASP.NET 2.0 client callback mechanism

```
protected override void OnPreRender(EventArgs e)
{
  string myScript =
    "<script language='javascript'>" +
      "function CreateXmlDocument() {" +
        "var xmlDocumentVersions = " +
          "['MSXML2.DOMDocument.5.0','MSXML2.DOMDocument.4.0'," +
          "'MSXML2.DOMDocument.3.0','MSXML2.DOMDocument','Microsoft.XmlDom'];" +
        "var xmlDocument;" +
        "for (var i=0; i<xmlDocumentVersions.length; i++) {" +
          "try {" +
            "xmlDocument = new ActiveXObject(xmlDocumentVersions[i]);" +
          "}" +
          "catch (ex) {}" +
          "return xmlDocument;" +
        "}" +
      "}" +

      "function MyClientCallback(result, context) {" +
        "if (xml.readyState == 4) {" +
          "if (xml.status == 200) {" +
            "var xmlDocument = CreateXmlDocument();" +
            "xmlDocument.loadXML(result);" +
            "var dataRow = xmlDocument.documentElement;" +
            "var dataFields = dataRow.childNodes;" +
            "var dataField;" +
            "var dataFieldName;" +
            "var dataFieldValue;" +
            "var detailsDialog = document.all['details'];" +
            "if (detailsDialog.childNodes[0])" +
              "detailsDialog.removeChild(detailsDialog.childNodes[0]);" +
            "table = document.createElement('table');" +
            "detailsDialog.appendChild(table);" +
```

```
                    "var tableRow;" +
                    "var firstTableCell;" +
                    "var secondTableCell;" +
                    "var strongElement;" +
                    "for (var i=0; i<dataFields.length; i++) {" +
                      "dataField = dataFields[i];" +
                      "dataFieldName = dataField.getAttribute('name');" +
                      "dataFieldValue = dataField.getAttribute('value');" +
                      "tableRow = table.insertRow(i);" +
                      "firstTableCell = tableRow.insertCell(0);" +
                      "firstTableCell.innerHTML = '<strong>'+dataFieldName +'</strong>';" +
                      "secondTableCell = tableRow.insertCell(1);" +
                      "secondTableCell.innerHTML = dataFieldValue;" +
                    "}" +
                  "}" +
                "}" +
              "}\n" +

          "</script>";

      if (EnableClientCallback &&
          !Page.IsClientScriptBlockRegistered(GetType().ToString() + "myScript"))
        Page.RegisterClientScriptBlock(GetType().ToString(), myScript);

      base.OnPreRender(e);
    }
```

The `OnPreRender` method writes and registers the `MyClientCallback` and `CreateXmlDocument` JavaScript functions with the containing page. Notice that `MyClientCallback` takes two arguments. The first argument is a string value that contains the data returned from the server-side method. You have to decide what type of data format makes more sense in your custom controls. In other words, the first argument doesn't put any restriction on the content of the string value returned from the server. As mentioned, XML is the most common data format. The second argument is anything else that the `MyClientCallback` method may need to update the appropriate parts of the page. For instance, it could contain some JavaScript code that will be automatically evaluated on the client side.

Overriding the Render Method

The ASP.NET 2.0 client callback mechanism also saves you from having to implement the `CallServer Method` JavaScript function. Recall that the `CallServerMethod` function uses DHTML to retrieve the input data from the page, and calls the `CustomWebForm_DoClientCallbackScript` JavaScript function and passes the required argument values.

The `ClientScript` property of the `Page` class in ASP.NET 2.0 exposes a method named `GetCallback EventReference` that automatically generates the code for the `CallServerMethod` JavaScript function. The `Render` method calls this method to access the JavaScript code as shown in Listing 27-9. Therefore the `GetCallbackEventReference` method automatically takes care of generating the code for the `Call ServerMethod` JavaScript function, and registering and adding the `CallServerMethod` function to the containing page.

The `GetCallbackEventReference` method takes five arguments, as follows:

❑ The reference to the control that implements the `ICallbackEventHandler`. The `RaiseCallback Event` method of the control handles the client request.

❑ The string value that the client must pass to the server-side method (`RaiseCallbackEvent`). The string contains the JavaScript code that retrieves the respective primary key field value of the selected item.

❑ The name of the JavaScript function (`MyClientCallback`) that will be automatically called when the response from the server arrives.

❑ The string value that is passed to the `MyClientCallback` function.

❑ A Boolean value that specifies whether the callback should be done asynchronously.

Notice that the server and client methods exchange string values. This doesn't place any restriction on the contents of these string values. The contents could be JavaScript code, XML data, or something else.

Listing 27-9: The Render method

```
protected override void Render(HtmlTextWriter w)
{
  string js = Page.ClientScript.GetCallbackEventReference(
                          this,
                          "document.all['" + base.ClientID + "'].value",
                          "MyClientCallback",
                          "null",
                          true);

  w.RenderBeginTag(HtmlTextWriterTag.Table);
  w.RenderBeginTag(HtmlTextWriterTag.Tr);
  w.RenderBeginTag(HtmlTextWriterTag.Td);
  if (EnableClientCallback)
    base.Attributes.Add("onchange", "javascript:" + js);
  base.Render(w);
  w.RenderEndTag();
  w.RenderBeginTag(HtmlTextWriterTag.Td);
  w.AddAttribute(HtmlTextWriterAttribute.Id, "details");
  w.RenderBeginTag(HtmlTextWriterTag.Div);
  w.RenderBeginTag(HtmlTextWriterTag.Span);
  w.RenderEndTag();
  w.RenderEndTag();
  w.RenderEndTag();
  w.RenderEndTag();
  w.RenderEndTag();
}
```

Server Side

As the previous section shows, the ASP.NET 2.0 client callback mechanism simplifies the client-side code dramatically. Now take a look at what happens on the server side. The `ProcessRequest` method of the page contains the code that you had to put into the `Page_Load` method before (see Listing 27-7). The

`ProcessRequest` method also automatically calls the `RaiseCallbackEvent` method of the `AjaxDropDownList` control. Therefore the ASP.NET 2.0 client callback mechanism also simplifies the server-side code.

Both the replica client callback mechanism developed previously in this chapter and the actual ASP.NET 2.0 client callback mechanism require you to attach an appropriate JavaScript function to an HTML element that doesn't submit the page. The appropriate JavaScript function was the `CallServerMethod` function in the case of the replica client callback mechanism and the return value of the `GetCallbackEventReference` method in the case of the actual ASP.NET 2.0 client callback mechanism. If you were to attach the function to an HTML element that submits the page, the following two steps would occur in order every time the user interacts with the element:

1. The respective client-side event would be raised, which in turn would call the attached JavaScript function. As discussed before, this would dynamically update the appropriate parts of the page via the client callback mechanism.

2. The whole page would then be submitted to the server. That would re-render the whole page again, overriding the rendering done via the client callback mechanism.

In other words, when the user interacts with the HTML element that submits the page, both the client callback and full page postback occur. Because the `AjaxDropDownList` control derives from the `DropDownList` control, it also inherits the `AutoPostBack` property. If this property is set to true, every time the user selects a new item from the list, a full page postback will occur. To avoid this, the `AjaxDropDownList` control overrides the `AutoPostBack` property of the `DropDownList` control as shown in Listing 27-10.

Listing 27-10: The overridden AutoPostBack property

```
public override bool AutoPostBack
{
  get
  {
    if (EnableClientCallback)
      base.AutoPostBack = false;

    return base.AutoPostBack;
  }

  set
  {
    if (EnableClientCallback)
      throw new Exception("AutoPostBack cannot be set while client callback is
                           enabled");

    base.AutoPostBack = value;
  }
}
```

If the `EnableClientCallback` property is set to true, the getter of the `AutoPostBack` property sets the `AutoPostBack` property of the base class to false and the setter raises an exception. This won't allow page developers to set the `AutoPostBack` property to true if the `EnableClientCallback` property is set to true. This will ensure that the full page postback won't occur when client callback feature is enabled.

Data Store-Agnostic Ajax-Enabled Controls

The `RaiseCallbackEvent` method is the server-side method that takes the input data it receives from the client, processes the data, and returns the result as a string value. The main responsibility of the `RaiseCallbackEvent` method of the `AjaxDropDownList` control is to retrieve the required data from the underlying data store (see Listing 27-11). This means that the `RaiseCallbackEvent` method must contain data access code. Such data access code must be generic because in data-driven Web applications data comes from different sources. The `RaiseCallbackEvent` method takes advantage of the ASP.NET 2.0 data source control model to generically access the underlying data store.

Listing 27-11: The RaiseCallbackEvent method handles the client's request

```
void ICallbackEventHandler.RaiseCallbackEvent(string arg)
{
  ServerMethodArgument = arg;
  if (EnableSession)
    HttpContext.Current.Session["ServerMethodArgument"] = arg;
  Control c = Page.FindControl(ClientCallbackDataSourceID);
  IDataSource ds = c as IDataSource;
  if (ds != null)
  {
    DataSourceView dv = ds.GetView(String.Empty);
    dv.Select(DataSourceSelectArguments.Empty, MyCallback);
  }
}
```

As you know, different types of data stores such as Microsoft SQL Server and Oracle require different data access code. The ASP.NET 2.0 data source control model isolates the `RaiseCallbackEvent` method from the underlying data store and provides the method with tabular views of the data store.

As discussed in Chapter 12, each tabular data source control is specifically designed to access a specific type of data store. For instance, the `SqlDataSource` and `XmlDataSource` controls are specifically designed to access relational databases and XML documents, respectively. This means that having the `RaiseCallbackEvent` method directly call a tabular data source control would tie the `RaiseCallbackEvent` method to a specific type of data store where the method couldn't be used to access other types of data stores.

To resolve this issue, all tabular data source controls implement the `IDataSource` interface. The interface exposes a method named `GetView` that takes the name of a tabular view and returns a reference to the view object that represents the view. The type of the view object depends on the type of the data source control. For instance, the `SqlDataSource` and `XmlDataSource` controls expose view objects of type `SqlDataSourceView` and `XmlDataSourceView`, respectively.

All view classes derive from the `DataSourceView` abstract class. The `DataSourceView` class exposes all the methods and properties that its subclasses such as `SqlDataSourceView` must implement in order to expose tabular views of their underlying data store. The `RaiseCallbackEvent` method calls the `Select` method of the view object to retrieve the required data from the data store, as discussed shortly.

Obviously, the first thing the `RaiseCallbackEvent` method must do is to access the underlying data source control in generic fashion without knowing its real type. The `AjaxDropDownList` control exposes a property named `ClientCallbackDataSourceID` that page developers must set to the value of the ID property of the desired data source control. Because data source controls are automatically added to the control tree of the containing page, the RaiseCallbackEvent method calls the FindControl method of the Page object to access the underlying data source control:

```
Control c = Page.FindControl (ClientCallbackDataSourceID);
```

This mechanism isolates the AjaxDropDownList control from the type of the tabular data source control being used. This will allow page developers to switch from one tabular data source control to another without any changes in the AjaxDropDownList control.

After the RaiseCallbackEvent method accesses the underlying data source control, it checks whether the control implements the IDataSource interface. Recall that all tabular data source controls implement the IDataSource interface:

```
IDataSource ds = c as IDataSource;
```

The RaiseCallbackEvent method then calls the GetView method of the data source control and passes the empty string as its argument to access its default tabular view (see Listing 27-12). The GetView method returns an object of type DataSourceView. The actual type of the object depends on the type of the data source control being used. For instance, the actual type of the object is SqlDataSourceView in the case of the SqlDataSource control. However, the RaiseCallbackEvent method doesn't care about the actual type of the view object. As far as the method is concerned, all view objects are of type DataSourceView.

The RaiseCallbackEvent method then calls the Select method of the DataSourceView object to retrieve the required data from the underlying data store:

```
dv.Select(DataSourceSelectArguments.Empty, MyCallback);
```

The Select method takes two arguments. The first argument is of type DataSourceSelectArguments. This argument is used to request extra operations such as paging and sorting on the data. Because the Select method operates asynchronously, the RaiseCallbackEvent method registers the MyCallback method as its callback. This method is discussed shortly. The Select method retrieves the data from the underlying data store and automatically calls the MyCallback method, passing the data as its only argument.

The AjaxDropDownList control exposes a property named ServerMethodArgument. To understand the role of this property, consider the declaration of the SqlDataSource control:

```
<custom:AjaxDropDownList Runat="Server" ID="ddl"
DataTextField="ProductName" DataValueField="ProductID"
ClientCallbackDataSourceID="MySource2" EnableClientCallback="true" />

<asp:SqlDataSource Runat="Server" ID="MySource2"
 ConnectionString="<%$ ConnectionStrings:MyConnectionString %>"
 SelectCommand="Select * From Products Where ProductID=@ProductID">
  <SelectParameters>
    <asp:ControlParameter ControlID="ddl"
     PropertyName="ServerMethodArgument" Name="ProductID" />
  </SelectParameters>
</asp:SqlDataSource>
```

The `SqlDataSource` control exposes a property named `SelectCommand` that page developers must set to the appropriate `Select` SQL statement or stored procedure. The stored procedure or `Select` SQL statement normally contains parameters whose values must be evaluated dynamically at runtime. For instance, in this declaration, the `Select` SQL statement contains the `@ProductID` parameter. The `SqlDataSource` control exposes a collection property named `SelectParameters` that page developers use to specify where the values of the parameters come from. For instance, in this declaration, the value of the `@ProductID` parameter comes from the `ServerMethodArgument` property of the `AjaxDropDownList` control. That's why the `AjaxDropDownList` control exposes the `ServerMethodArgument` property.

This raises an obvious question: Who sets the value of the `ServerMethodArgument` property? Recall that the client callback mechanism automatically calls the `RaiseCallbackEvent` method and passes the client value as its argument. Also recall that the client value is nothing but the respective primary key field value of the item that the user selects from the list. The `RaiseCallbackEvent` method then assigns the client value to the `ServerMethodArgument` property (see Listing 27-11).

Listing 27-12 contains the code for the `MyCallback` method.

Listing 27-12: The MyCallback method

```
private void MyCallback(IEnumerable data)
{
  IEnumerator iter = data.GetEnumerator();
  XmlWriterSettings settings = new XmlWriterSettings();
  settings.Indent = true;
  using (StringWriter sw = new StringWriter())
  {
    using (XmlWriter xw = XmlWriter.Create(sw))
    {
      xw.WriteStartDocument();
      xw.WriteStartElement("dataRow");
      while (iter.MoveNext())
      {
        PropertyDescriptorCollection col =
                            TypeDescriptor.GetProperties(iter.Current);
        foreach (PropertyDescriptor pd in col)
        {
          xw.WriteStartElement("dataField");
          xw.WriteAttributeString("name", pd.Name);
          xw.WriteAttributeString("value", pd.GetValue(iter.Current).ToString());
          xw.WriteEndElement();
        }
      }
      xw.WriteEndElement();
      xw.WriteEndDocument();
    }
    clientMethodArgument = sw.ToString();
  }
}
```

As discussed, Ajax-enabled controls usually exchange data with the server in XML format. The main responsibility of the `MyCallback` method is to enumerate the retrieved data and generate the XML document that will be sent to the Ajax-enabled control. As discussed, this XML document looks something like the following:

```
<dataRow>
  <dataField name="ProductID" value="1" />
  <dataField name="ProductName" value="Product1" />
  <dataField name="CategoryID" value="2" />
</dataRow>
```

The method uses the `XmlWriter` API discussed in Chapter 24 to generate the XML data and save the data into an `StringWriter` object. Because the data passed into the `MyCallback` method is of type `IEnumerable`, the method calls the `GetEnumerator` method of the data to access its `IEnumerator` object. The method then uses the `IEnumerator` object to enumerate the data. The `MyCallback` method has no way of knowing what the real type of the enumerated object is because the real type of the enumerated object depends on the type of the data source control being used. This is where the `TypeDescriptor` class comes into play.

The `MyCallback` method calls the `GetProperties` method of the `TypeDescriptor` class and passes the enumerated object as its argument. The `GetProperties` method returns an object of type `Property DescriptorCollection` that contains objects of type `PropertyDescriptor`. The `PropertyDescriptor` objects represent the properties of the enumerated object. The `MyCallback` method enumerates the `PropertyDescriptorCollection` object and generates a `<dataField>` element for each enumerated `PropertyDescriptor` object. Each `<dataField>` element has two attributes. The first attribute contains the name of the property, which is nothing but the value of the `Name` property of the `PropertyDescriptor` object that represents the property. The second attribute contains the value of the property. The `MyCallback` method calls the `GetValue` method of the appropriate `PropertyDescriptor` object to access the value of the property.

The `MyCallback` method finally uses the `StringWriter` object to set the value of the `clientMethod Argument` field. The `GetCallbackResult` method then returns the value of the `clientMethodArgument` field to the client.

The communication between the `AjaxDropDownList` control and the server reveals two important characteristics of the communications between Ajax-enabled controls and the server. First, they communicate asynchronously. Second, they exchange data in XML format.

The following sections discuss two important applications of the `AjaxDropDownList` Ajax-enabled control. The first application uses the control as a master/details form. The second application uses the control in `GridView` and `DetailsView` controls.

Master/Detail Form

The `AjaxDropDownList` control can be used as a master/detail form, where users select an item from the list to see its detailed information without having to perform a full page postback to the server and render the entire page again. Listing 27-13 shows how page developers can declaratively use the `Ajax`

DropDownList control as a master/details form without writing any code. In Figure 27-1 the `AjaxDrop DownList` control displays the details of the selected product.

Figure 27-1

Listing 27-13: Using the AjaxDropDownList control as a master/detail form

```
<%@ Page Language="C#" %>
<%@ Register Namespace="CustomControls" TagPrefix="custom" %>
<html xmlns="http://www.w3.org/1999/xhtml">
<body>
  <form id="form1" runat="server">
    <custom:AjaxDropDownList runat="Server" ID="ddl" DataSourceID="MySource"
    DataTextField="ProductName" DataValueField="ProductID"
    ClientCallbackDataSourceID="MySource2" EnableClientCallback="true" />

    <asp:SqlDataSource runat="Server" ID="MySource"
    ConnectionString="<%$ ConnectionStrings:MyConnectionString %>"
    SelectCommand="Select * From Products" />

    <asp:SqlDataSource runat="Server" ID="MySource2"
    ConnectionString="<%$ ConnectionStrings:MyConnectionString %>"
    SelectCommand="Select * From Products Where ProductID=@ProductID">
      <SelectParameters>
        <asp:ControlParameter ControlID="ddl" PropertyName="ServerMethodArgument"
        Name="ProductID" />
      </SelectParameters>
    </asp:SqlDataSource>
  </form>
</body>
</html>
```

Developing Ajax-Enabled Data Control Fields

Chapter 18 provided the implementation of a custom data control field named `DropDownListField` that allows page developers to add foreign key editing capability to their `GridView` and `DetailsView` controls declaratively! When a `GridView` or `DetailsView` is switched to the edit mode, the `DropDown`

`ListField` component automatically connects to the underlying data store, retrieves the legal values of the respective foreign key field, and uses an ASP.NET `DropDownList` control to display the legal values.

This section implements a new ASP.NET 2.0 custom data control field named `AjaxDropDownListField` that derives from `DropDownListField` and extends its functionality to add support for Ajax features. `AjaxDropDownListField` overrides the `InitializeDataCell` method that it inherits from `DropDownListField` (see Listing 27-14).

The main responsibility of the `InitializeDataCell` method is to render the `AjaxDropDownList` control that will be used to display the legal values of the respective foreign key field and the detailed information about a selected item. The `AjaxDropDownListField` component inherits the `DataSourceID` property from `DropDownListField`. It's the responsibility of page developers to set the value of the `DataSourceID` property to the value of the `ID` property of the appropriate data source control such as `SqlDataSource` or `ObjectDataSource`. The data source control is used to populate the `DropDownList` control that the `AjaxDropDownList` control uses under the hood.

Also notice that the `InitializeDataCell` method renders the `AjaxDropDownList` control if and only if the containing row is in the Edit or Insert mode. Otherwise the `InitializeDataCell` method simply calls the base version of the `InitializeDataCell` method.

Listing 27-14: The Overridden InitializeDataCell method

```
protected override void InitializeDataCell(DataControlFieldCell cell,
                                           DataControlRowState rowState)
{
  if ((rowState & DataControlRowState.Edit) != 0 ||
      (rowState & DataControlRowState.Insert) != 0)
  {
    AjaxDropDownList ddl = new AjaxDropDownList();
    ddl.EnableClientCallback = EnableClientCallback;
    ddl.ClientCallbackDataSourceID = ClientCallbackDataSourceID;
    ddl.SkinID = SkinID;
    ddl.EnableTheming = EnableTheming;
    ddl.EnableSession = EnableSession;
    ddl.DataSourceID = DataSourceID;
    ddl.DataTextField = DataTextField;
    ddl.DataValueField = DataValueField;
    if (DataTextField.Length != 0 && DataValueField.Length != 0)
      ddl.DataBound += new EventHandler(OnDataBindField);
    cell.Controls.Add(ddl);
  }
  else
    base.InitializeDataCell(cell, rowState);
}
```

The `AjaxDropDownListField` component also exposes a new Boolean property named `EnableClient Callback`. Page developers set the `EnableClientCallback` property to turn the client callback feature on or off. The `InitializeDataCell` method sets the `EnableClientCallback` property of the `Ajax DropDownList` control to the value of the `EnableClientCallback` property of the `AjaxDropDown ListField` data control field.

Recall that the `AjaxDropDownList` control exposes a property named `ServerMethodArgument` that data source controls use to access the value that the client passes as an argument to the `RaiseCallback`

Event method. This value is the primary key field value of the selected item. Therefore the Ajax DropDownListField data control field must expose this value to data source controls. There are different ways to achieve this. To simplify the discussions, store the value in the Session object.

The AjaxDropDownList control and AjaxDropDownListField component both expose a property named EnableSession. Page developers set this property to turn the session feature that's used to save the client's value into the Session object on or off.

Listing 27-15 shows a Web page that uses the AjaxDropDownListField data control field declaratively. Figure 27-2 shows the GridView control that uses the AjaxDropDownListField data control field. AjaxDropDownListField displays the details of the item that users select from the respective DropDownList control.

Listing 27-15: Using the AjaxDropDownListField component declaratively

```
<%@ Page Language="C#" %>
<%@ Register TagPrefix="custom" Namespace="CustomFields" %>
<html xmlns="http://www.w3.org/1999/xhtml">
<body>
  <form id="form1" runat="server">
    <asp:GridView BorderWidth="1px" BackColor="#DEBA84" CellPadding="3"
    BorderColor="#DEBA84" CellSpacing="2" BorderStyle="None" ID="gv2"
    runat="Server" AutoGenerateColumns="false" AllowSorting="true"
    DataSourceID="GridViewSource" AutoGenerateEditButton="true"
    DataKeyNames="ProductID">
      <FooterStyle ForeColor="#8C4510" BackColor="#F7DFB5"></FooterStyle>
      <PagerStyle ForeColor="#8C4510" HorizontalAlign="Center" />
      <HeaderStyle ForeColor="White" Font-Bold="True" BackColor="#A55129" />
      <SelectedRowStyle ForeColor="White" Font-Bold="True" BackColor="#738A9C"/>
      <RowStyle ForeColor="#8C4510" BackColor="#FFF7E7"></RowStyle>
      <Columns>
        <asp:BoundField DataField="ProductName" HeaderText="Product Name"
        SortExpression="ProductName"/>
        <custom:AjaxDropDownListField SkinID="SkinID1" EnableTheming="true"
        DataValueField="CategoryID" DataTextField="CategoryName"
        DataSourceID="DropDownListSource" SortExpression="CategoryName"
        HeaderText="Category Name" NullDisplayText="Unknown" EnableSession="true"
        ClientCallbackDataSourceID="MySource2" EnableClientCallback="true" />
      </Columns>
    </asp:GridView>

    <asp:ObjectDataSource ID="GridViewSource" runat="Server" TypeName="Product"
    SortParameterName="sortExpression" SelectMethod="Select"
    UpdateMethod="Update"/>

    <asp:SqlDataSource ID="DropDownListSource" runat="Server"
    ConnectionString="<%$ ConnectionStrings:MyConnectionString %>"
    SelectCommand="Select * From Categories" />

    <asp:SqlDataSource runat="Server" ID="MySource2"
    ConnectionString="<%$ ConnectionStrings:MyConnectionString %>"
    SelectCommand="Select * From Categories Where CategoryID=@CategoryID">
      <SelectParameters>
        <asp:SessionParameter Name="CategoryID"
```

```
                    SessionField="ServerMethodArgument" />
            </SelectParameters>
        </asp:SqlDataSource>
    </form>
</body>
</html>
```

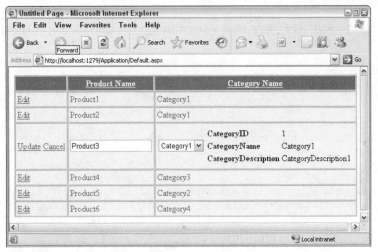

Figure 27-2

AjaxDetailsDialog

This section develops an Ajax-enabled custom composite control named AjaxDetailsDialog that supports the ASP.NET 2.0 client callback mechanism. The AjaxDetailsDialog control consists of two components that form a master/detail control. The master component is the CustomImage server control developed in Chapter 26. This control displays the image of the item that it represents. The details component is a resizable pop-up dialog that contains a table that displays more detailed information about the item. The typical workflow is as follows:

1. The user clicks the master component (the image of an item) to see more detailed information about the item. For example, the CustomImage server control could be displaying the image of a book on an online bookstore. The user clicks on the image to see more detailed information about the book such as its author, publisher, date of publication, and so on.

2. The ASP.NET client callback mechanism is then used to asynchronously call the server method that returns the detailed information about the item.

3. The server method retrieves the detailed information from the underlying data store and returns the result to the client in XML format.

4. The details component uses HTML/XHTML, CSS, DOM, XML, XSLT, and JavaScript to read the XML data and to render the appropriate HTML to display the data.

851

To make the discussions more concrete, revisit the ASP.NET page shown in Listing 26-36 and Figure 26-3. This page displays the list of books available on an online bookstore. Listing 27-16 uses the `AjaxDetailsDialog` control to extend the functionality of this page so that a new image button titled `Details` is added to each table cell. When the user clicks the Details button of a particular cell, the `AjaxDetailsDialog` Ajax-enabled control uses the client callback mechanism to asynchronously retrieve the detailed information about the book from the server and uses DHTML to display the information in a pop-up dialog shown in Figure 27-3.

Listing 27-16: An ASP.NET page that uses the AjaxDetailsDialog control

```
<%@ Page Language="C#" %>
<%@ Register TagPrefix="custom" Namespace="CustomComponents"
Assembly="CustomComponents" %>
<html xmlns="http://www.w3.org/1999/xhtml">
<body>
  <form id="form1" runat="server">
    <custom:CustomGridView runat="server" DataSourceID="MySource" GridLines="None"
    AllowPaging="True" HorizontalAlign="left" AllowSorting="True" PageSize="3"
    AutoGenerateColumns="false" EnableCellView="true" ShowHeader="true"
    DataKeyNames="BookID" CellPadding="0" CellSpacing="10" ForeColor="#333333">
      <FooterStyle BackColor="#990000" Font-Bold="True" ForeColor="White" />
      <RowStyle BackColor="#FFFBD6" ForeColor="#333333" HorizontalAlign="left" />
      <PagerStyle BackColor="#FFCC66" ForeColor="#333333" VerticalAlign="Top"
      HorizontalAlign="Center" />
      <SelectedRowStyle BackColor="#FFCC66" ForeColor="Navy" />
      <HeaderStyle BackColor="#990000" Font-Bold="True" ForeColor="White" />
      <AlternatingRowStyle BackColor="PaleGoldenrod" HorizontalAlign="left" />
      <Columns>
        <asp:TemplateField>
          <itemtemplate>
            <table border="0" cellpadding="0" cellspacing="0">
              <tr>
                <td valign="top" align="left">
                  <table border="0" cellpadding="0" cellspacing="0">
                    <tr>
                      <td valign="top">
                        <custom:ImageDialog ID="Image1" runat="server"
                        ImageUrl='<%# "Images/"+Eval("Title").ToString()+".jpg"%>'
                        PopupImageUrl=
                            '<%#"Images/Popup"+Eval("Title").ToString()+".jpg"%>'
                        DialogStyle-BackColor="LightGoldenrodYellow"
                        DialogStyle-BorderColor="Tan" DialogStyle-BorderWidth="1px"
                        DialogStyle-CellPadding="2" DialogStyle-CellSpacing="0"
                        DialogStyle-BorderStyle="Groove"
                        DialogStyle-ForeColor="Black" DialogStyle-GridLines="None"
                        HeaderStyle-BackColor="Tan" HeaderStyle-Font-Bold="True"/>
                      </td>
                      <td valign="top">
                        <table border="0" cellpadding="0" cellspacing="0">
                          <tr>
                            <td valign="top" align="left">
                              <strong>
                                <a href=""><%# Eval("Title").ToString() %></a>
                              </strong>
                            </td>
```

```
              </tr>
              <tr>
                <td valign="top" align="left">
                  <font face="verdana,arial,helvetica" size="-1">
                    by <%# Eval("Author").ToString() %></font>
                </td>
              </tr>
              <tr>
                <td valign="top" align="left">
                  <font face="verdana,arial,helvetica" size="-1">
                    <%# Eval("Publisher").ToString() %></font>
                </td>
              </tr>
            </table>
            </td>
          </tr>
        </table>
        </td>
      </tr>
      <tr>
        <td align="left">
          <table border="0" cellpadding="0" cellspacing="5">
            <tr>
              <td>
                <font face="verdana,arial,helvetica" size="-1">
                  List Price : $<%# Eval("Price").ToString() %></font>
              </td>
              <td align="left">
                <custom:AjaxDetailsDialog
                DataValue='<%# Eval("BookID").ToString() %>'
                ClientCallbackDataSourceID="MySource2" runat="server"
                DialogStyle-BorderColor="Tan"
                DialogStyle-BackColor="LightGoldenrodYellow"
                DialogStyle-BorderWidth="1px" DialogStyle-CellPadding="2"
                DialogStyle-CellSpacing="0" ID="MyAjaxDetailsDialog"
                DialogStyle-BorderStyle="Groove"
                DialogStyle-ForeColor="Black" DialogStyle-GridLines="None"
                HeaderStyle-BackColor="Tan" HeaderStyle-Font-Bold="True"
                AlternatingItemStyle-BackColor="PaleGoldenrod"/>
              </td>
            </tr>
          </table>
        </td>
      </tr>
    </table>
  </itemtemplate>
  </asp:TemplateField>
  </Columns>
</custom:CustomGridView>

<asp:SqlDataSource runat="server" ID="MySource"
ConnectionString="<%$ ConnectionStrings:MySqlConnectionString %>"
SelectCommand="Select * From Books" />

<asp:SqlDataSource runat="server" ID="MySource2"
```

(continued)

Listing 27-16: *(continued)*

```
      ConnectionString="<%$ ConnectionStrings:MySqlConnectionString %>"
      SelectCommand="Select PublicationDate as 'Publication Date', Edition,
                    PageCount as 'Page Count' From Books Where BookID=@BookID">
       <SelectParameters>
         <asp:FormParameter Name="BookID" FormField="__CALLBACKPARAM" />
       </SelectParameters>
      </asp:SqlDataSource>
    </form>
  </body>
</html>
```

Figure 27-3 shows the page on the client browser. This figure shows the page right after the user clicks the Details button of the top table cell to pop up the dialog that displays more detailed information about the book. The user can move the tiny image on the bottom right of the pop-up dialog to resize the dialog. Resizing the dialog automatically changes the font size. The pop-up dialog uses HTML/XHTML, CSS, DOM, and JavaScript to resize and move the dialog and to make the font size adjustments.

The CustomImage server control, like all other server controls, uses server resources to render its HTML on the server side. The details component isn't a server control and uses client resources to render its HTML. Therefore you need to use the following two patterns to implement AjaxDetailsDialog:

❑ **Composite control pattern:** AjaxDetailsDialog is a composite control because it has a CustomImage child server control.

❑ **Ajax-enabled control development pattern:** AjaxDetailsDialog is an Ajax-enabled control because of the following two reasons. First, its details component is a fully functional client-side component that uses HTML/XHTML, CSS, DOM, XML, and JavaScript to perform all its tasks, including rendering, resizing, moving, and font-size adjustments. Second, it uses client callback mechanism to asynchronously retrieve the required XML data from the server without interrupting the user interactions with the application.

AjaxDetailsDialog as a Composite Control

AjaxDetailsDialog uses the composite control pattern as follows.

First, it derives from the CompositeControl base class.

Then it overrides the CreateChildControls method to instantiate and to initialize its CustomImage child control as shown here:

```
private CustomImage image;
protected override void CreateChildControls()
{
  Controls.Clear();

  image = new CustomImage();
  image.EnableClientScript = EnableClientScript;
  Controls.Add(image);
}
```

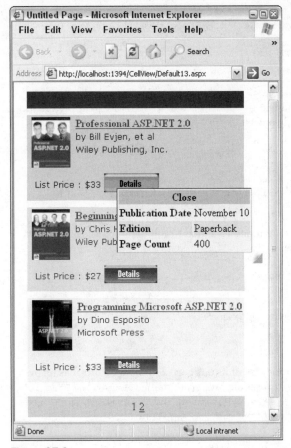

Figure 27-3

Next, it overrides the `TagKey` property to specify the `<div>` HTML element as its containing HTML element:

```
protected override HtmlTextWriterTag TagKey
{
  get { return HtmlTextWriterTag.Div; }
}
```

The control then exposes the `style` property of its `CustomImage` child control as a top-level style property named `ImageStyle`:

```
private Style imageStyle;
public virtual Style ImageStyle
{
  get
  {
    if (imageStyle == null)
    {
      imageStyle = new Style();
```

```
      if (IsTrackingViewState)
        ((IStateManager)imageStyle).TrackViewState();
    }
    return imageStyle;
  }
}
```

It exposes a method named `PrepareControlHierarchy` to apply the top-level `ImageStyle` property to its `CustomImage` child control:

```
protected virtual void PrepareControlHierarchy()
{
  if (imageStyle != null)
    image.ApplyStyle(imageStyle);
}
```

It overrides the `RenderContents` method to call the `PrepareControlHierarchy` method before the actual rendering starts:

```
protected override void RenderContents(HtmlTextWriter writer)
{
  PrepareControlHierarchy();
  image.RenderControl(writer);
  . . .
}
```

Next, it exposes the properties of its `CustomImage` child control as its own top-level properties. `AjaxDetailsDialog` exposes six properties named `MouseOverImageUrl`, `MouseOutImageUrl`, `DescriptionUrl`, `ImageAlign`, `Duration`, and `Transition` whose getters and setters delegate to the corresponding properties of the `CustomImage` control:

```
public virtual string MouseOverImageUrl
{
  get { EnsureChildControls(); return image.MouseOverImageUrl; }
  set { EnsureChildControls(); image.MouseOverImageUrl = value; }
}

public virtual string MouseOutImageUrl
{
  get { EnsureChildControls(); return image.MouseOutImageUrl; }
  set { EnsureChildControls(); image.MouseOutImageUrl = value; }
}

public virtual string DescriptionUrl
{
  get { EnsureChildControls(); return image.DescriptionUrl; }
  set { EnsureChildControls(); image.DescriptionUrl = value; }
}

public virtual ImageAlign ImageAlign
{
  get { EnsureChildControls(); return image.ImageAlign; }
```

```
      set { EnsureChildControls(); image.ImageAlign = value;}
  }

  public double Duration
  {
    get { EnsureChildControls(); return image.Duration; }
    set { EnsureChildControls(); image.Duration = value; ; }
  }

  public Transition Transition
  {
    get { EnsureChildControls(); return image.Transition; }
    set { EnsureChildControls(); image.Transition = value; }
  }
```

Finally, the control calls the `EnsureChildControls` method within the getters and setters of its delegated properties as shown.

AjaxDetailsDialog as an Ajax-Enabled Control

Recall from the previous chapter that an Ajax-enabled control has three important features. First, it uses HTML/XHTML, CSS, DOM, XML, and JavaScript to handle most of the user interactions to improve the response time and to act and feel more like a Windows Forms control. Second, it uses asynchronous client-callbacks to communicate with the server to provide the end users with the same experience and response time that they have come to expect from a desktop application. Third, it exchanges XML data with the server.

This section first presents the implementation of those methods and properties of the `AjaxDetailsDialog` control that handle the first feature. `AjaxDetailsDialog`, like all other Ajax-enabled controls, uses the Ajax-enabled control development pattern discussed in the previous chapter to implement the first feature as follows.

First, it implements the mechanism that determines when to render its client script as follows:

❑ It exposes a public Boolean property named `EnableClientScript` to allow the page developer to explicitly disable its client-side functionality, regardless of the Ajax capabilities of the requesting browser.

❑ It exposes a private Boolean field named `renderClientScript` that specifies whether it should render its client script.

❑ It exposes a protected virtual method named `DetermineRenderClientScript` that contains the logic that determines whether it should render its client script. This method sets the value of the `renderClientScript` field.

❑ It overrides the `OnPreRender` method to call the `DetermineRenderClientScript` method to set the value of the `renderClientScript` field before it enters its rendering phase, where its rendering methods use the `renderClientScript` field to check whether to render the control's client script.

Next, the control overrides the `OnPreRender` method to call the `RegisterClientScriptResource` method of the `ClientScript` property of the containing page to render a reference to the embedded script file `AjaxDetailsDialog.js`:

```
protected override void OnPreRender(EventArgs e)
{
  DetermineRenderClientScript();
  if (renderClientScript)
    Page.ClientScript.RegisterClientScriptResource(typeof(AjaxDetailsDialog),
                                "CustomComponents.AjaxDetailsDialog.js");
  base.OnPreRender(e);
}
```

Then it exposes the CSS style attributes of the details pop-up dialog as top-level style properties. As discussed in the previous chapter, the details pop-up dialog isn't a server control because it uses HTML/XHTML, CSS, DOM, and JavaScript client-side technologies to handle all its tasks including rendering, moving, resizing, and font-size adjustments. The previous chapter showed you how you can expose the CSS style attributes of a purely client-side component, such as the details pop-up dialog, as top-level style properties of your custom control.

```
public virtual TableStyle DialogStyle {get; }
public virtual TableItemStyle HeaderStyle {get;}
public virtual TableItemStyle ItemStyle {get;}
public virtual TableItemStyle AlternatingItemStyle {get;}
```

As shown, `AjaxDetailsDialog` exposes the following four properties:

❑   `DialogStyle`: Maps to the CSS style attributes on the `<table>` HTML element that contains the details pop-up dialog

❑   `HeaderStyle`: Maps to the CSS style attributes on the `<th>` HTML element of the details pop-up dialog

❑   `ItemStyle`: Maps to the CSS style attributes on the `<tr>` HTML elements of the details pop-up dialog that display the detailed information

❑   `AlternatingItemStyle`: Maps to the CSS style attributes on the alternating `<tr>` HTML elements of the details pop-up dialog

The control then overrides the `TrackViewState`, `SaveViewState`, and `LoadViewState` methods to manage the states of the `DialogStyle`, `HeaderStyle`, `ItemStyle`, and `AlternatingItemStyle` properties across page postbacks. This was thoroughly discussed in the previous chapter.

Finally, the control overrides the `AddAttributesToRender` method to render the `DialogStyle`, `HeaderStyle`, `ItemStyle`, and `AlternatingItemStyle` properties as the values of the made-up `dialogStyle`, `headerStyle`, `itemStyle`, and `alternatingItemStyle` attributes of the containing HTML element of the details pop-up dialog. Recall from the previous chapter that these attributes aren't standard HTML attributes. They're made-up and used as temporary storage for the CSS style attributes of the details pop-up dialog.

The `AjaxDetailsDialog` control takes the following steps to add support for the ASP.NET client callback mechanism:

1. Overrides the `RenderContents` method to render the required client script.
2. Uses the C# interface implementation pattern to implement the `ICallbackEventHandler` interface.

These two steps are discussed in the following sections.

Overriding RenderContents

`AjaxDetailsDialog` overrides the `RenderContents` method to render the client script that makes the asynchronous client callback request to the server as shown in Listing 27-17.

First, the method checks whether it should render the client script. Recall that `AjaxDetailsDialog` overrides `OnPreRender` to call the `DetermineRenderClientScript` method to set the value of the `renderClientScript` field before the control enters its rendering phase:

```
if (renderClientScript)
```

Then it calls the `GetCallbackEventReference` method of the `ClientScript` property of its containing page to return the string that contains the client script:

```
string js = Page.ClientScript.GetCallbackEventReference(
                    this, "'" + DataValue + "'", "MyClientCallback", null);
```

Notice that `RenderContents` passes the value of the `DataValue` property of the `AjaxDetailsDialog` control into the `GetCallbackEventReference` method. As Listing 27-16 shows, the page developer sets the value of this property to the primary key field value of the displayed book (`BookID`), as also shown in the highlighted portion of the following listing:

```
<custom:AjaxDetailsDialog ClientCallbackDataSourceID="MySource2" runat="server"
DataValue='<%# Eval("BookID").ToString() %>'
DialogStyle-BorderColor="Tan" DialogStyle-BackColor="LightGoldenrodYellow"
DialogStyle-BorderWidth="1px" DialogStyle-CellPadding="2" ID="MyAjaxDetailsDialog"
DialogStyle-CellSpacing="0" DialogStyle-BorderStyle="Groove"
DialogStyle-ForeColor="Black" DialogStyle-GridLines="None"
HeaderStyle-BackColor="Tan" HeaderStyle-Font-Bold="True"
AlternatingItemStyle-BackColor="PaleGoldenrod"/>
```

When the client script calls the server-side `RaiseCallbackEvent` method, it passes the associated primary key field value into it. As you'll see later, this primary key field value is used in the `WHERE` clause of the respective SQL `Select` statement to retrieve the detailed information about the book with the specified primary key field value.

The method then renders a call into the `InitializeDetailsPopup` JavaScript function as the value of the `onclick` attribute of the containing HTML element of the `CustomImage` server control as shown in the highlighted portion of the following code:

```
image.Attributes.Add("onclick", "InitializeDetailsPopup('" + this.ClientID + "');"
                    + js);
```

As discussed in previous chapter, this JavaScript function creates and initializes the pop-up dialog that displays the detailed information about the selected item.

Finally, the method renders the string that the `GetCallbackEventReference` method returns as the value of the `onclick` attribute of the containing HTML element of the `CustomImage` server control:

```
image.Attributes.Add("onclick",
                        "InitializeDetailsPopup('" + this.ClientID + "');" +
                    js);
```

Listing 27-17: The RenderContents method

```
protected override void RenderContents(HtmlTextWriter writer)
{
  PrepareControlHierarchy();
  if (renderClientScript)
  {
    string js = Page.ClientScript.GetCallbackEventReference(
                        this, "'" + DataValue + "'", "MyClientCallback", null);

    image.Attributes.Add("onclick",
                        "InitializeDetailsPopup('" + this.ClientID + "');" + js);
  }

  image.RenderControl(writer);
}
```

Implementing the ICallbackEventHandler Interface

The `AjaxDetailsDialog` control uses the C# interface implementation pattern to implement the `ICallbackEventHandler` interface as follows:

❑   It exposes two virtual protected methods with the same signature as the `RaiseCallbackEvent` and `GetCallbackResult` methods of the `ICallbackEventHandler` interface.

❑   It explicitly implements the `RaiseCallbackEvent` and `GetCallbackResult` methods of the interface.

The implementation of these four methods are discussed in the following sections.

Protected Virtual Methods

Following the C# interface implementation pattern, `AjaxDetailsDialog` exposes two protected virtual methods with the same signature as the `RaiseCallbackEvent` and `GetCallbackResult` methods of the `ICallbackEventHandler` interface.

Listing 27-18 contains the implementation of the `RaiseCallbackEvent` protected virtual method.

Listing 27-18: The RaiseCallbackEvent protected virtual method

```
protected virtual void RaiseCallbackEvent(string arg)
{
  if (EnableSession)
```

```
        HttpContext.Current.Session["ServerMethodArgument"] = arg;

    Control c = Page.FindControl(ClientCallbackDataSourceID);
    IDataSource ds = c as IDataSource;
    if (ds != null)
    {
      DataSourceView dv = ds.GetView(String.Empty);
      dv.Select(DataSourceSelectArguments.Empty, MyCallback);

    }
  }
```

As Listing 27-18 shows, the `RaiseCallbackEvent` method uses the ASP.NET 2.0 tabular data source control model to access the underlying data source control in generic fashion without knowing its real type. Notice that this method stores its argument value in the `Session` object if the page developer has set the `EnableSession` property of the `AjaxDetailsDialog` control to true.

As discussed, when the client script calls the `RaiseCallbackEvent` method, it passes the primary key field value of the respective item (such as the `BookID` of the selected book in Figure 27-3) into the method. The `RaiseCallbackEvent` method must pass this primary key field value to the underlying tabular data source control so the control knows the detailed information of which book it should retrieve from the underlying data store. To help you understand this, take a look at the SQL `Select` statement of the `SqlDataSource` control used in Listing 27-16:

```
<asp:SqlDataSource runat="server" ID="MySource2"
ConnectionString="<%$ ConnectionStrings:MySqlConnectionString %>"
SelectCommand="Select PublicationDate as 'Publication Date', Edition,
           PageCount as 'Page Count' From Books Where BookID=@BookID">
. . .
</asp:SqlDataSource>
```

As the boldface portion of the code shows, the WHERE clause of the SQL `Select` statement needs to know the primary key field value (`BookID`) of the book whose record is being retrieved from the database. As discussed, the client script passes this primary key field value into the `RaiseCallback Event` method. This method stores this value in the `Session` object to make it available to the tabular data source control, `SqlDataSource`. As the following code shows, the `SqlDataSource` control can use the `SessionParameter` parameter to access this value from the `Session` object:

```
<asp:SqlDataSource runat="server" ID="MySource2"
ConnectionString="<%$ ConnectionStrings:MySqlConnectionString %>"
SelectCommand="Select PublicationDate as 'Publication Date', Edition,
           PageCount as 'Page Count' From Books Where BookID=@BookID">
  <SelectParameters>
    <asp:SessionParameter Name="BookID" SessionField="ServerMethodArgument" />
  </SelectParameters>
</asp:SqlDataSource>
```

The `Session` object isn't the only way to pass the primary key field value to the tabular data source control. The previous discussions mentioned that the client script passes the primary key field value into the `Raise CallbackEvent` method. This doesn't mean that the client script directly passes this value into this method. As discussed, under the hood, the script stores the value in a hidden field named __CALLBACKPARAM and posts the form back to the server. Therefore, the tabular data source control can use __CALLBACK-PARAM as the key to access the primary key field value from the `Form` collection of the `Request` object:

```
<asp:SqlDataSource runat="server" ID="MySource2"
ConnectionString="<%$ ConnectionStrings:MySqlConnectionString %>"
SelectCommand="Select PublicationDate as 'Publication Date', Edition,
               PageCount as 'Page Count' From Books Where BookID=@BookID">
  <SelectParameters>
    <asp:FormParameter Name="BookID" FormField="__CALLBACKPARAM" />
  </SelectParameters>
</asp:SqlDataSource>
```

Here's how the `RaiseCallbackEvent` method retrieves the detailed information about the specified book. As Listing 27-18 shows, the method calls the `FindControl` method of the containing page and passes the value of the `ClientCallbackDataSourceID` property of the `AjaxDetailsDialog` control into it. As shown in Listing 27-16, the page developer must assign the value of the `ID` property of the tabular data source control to the `ClientCallbackDataSourceID` property. The `FindControl` method searches the page's control tree for the data source control with the specified `ID` value and returns a reference to it:

```
Control c = Page.FindControl(ClientCallbackDataSourceID);
```

The method then checks whether the referenced control is indeed a tabular data source control:

```
IDataSource ds = c as IDataSource;
if (ds != null)
```

It then calls the `GetView` method of the tabular data source control to access its default tabular view in generic fashion:

```
    DataSourceView dv = ds.GetView(String.Empty);
```

Next, it calls the `Select` method of the default tabular view to retrieve the record of the specified book. Because the `Select` operation is asynchronous, the method registers the `MyCallback` method as a callback:

```
dv.Select(DataSourceSelectArguments.Empty, MyCallback);
```

The `Select` method of the default tabular view retrieves the book record from the underlying data store, calls the `MyCallback` method, and passes an `IEnumerable` collection that contains the retrieved record into it. Listing 27-19 shows the implementation of the `MyCallback` method.

Listing 27-19: The MyCallback method

```
private void MyCallback(IEnumerable data)
{
  IEnumerator iter = data.GetEnumerator();
  clientMethodArgument = string.Empty;

  while (iter.MoveNext())
  {
    PropertyDescriptorCollection col = TypeDescriptor.GetProperties(iter.Current);
    foreach (PropertyDescriptor pd in col)
    {
      clientMethodArgument +=
```

```
                    (pd.Name + "," + pd.GetValue(iter.Current).ToString() + "|");
        }

    clientMethodArgument =
            clientMethodArgument.Remove(clientMethodArgument.LastIndexOf('|'));
    }
}
```

As Listing 27-19 shows, the `MyCallback` method calls the `GetEnumerator` method of the collection that contains the retrieved data records to access the enumerator object that knows how to iterate through the data records in the collection. In this case, the collection contains a single book record:

```
IEnumerator iter = data.GetEnumerator();
```

The method then uses the enumerator to iterate through the data records in the collection:

```
    while (iter.MoveNext())
```

Next, the method calls the `GetProperties` method of the `TypeDescriptor` class and passes the enumerated data record into it to retrieve the `PropertyDescriptorCollection` that contains one `PropertyDescriptor` for each data column of the enumerated record. As discussed, each `PropertyDescriptor` completely describes its associated data column, including the column name and type, in generic fashion.

```
    PropertyDescriptorCollection col = TypeDescriptor.GetProperties(iter.Current);
```

The method then enumerates the `PropertyDescriptor` objects in the `PropertyDescriptorCollection` and appends the name and value of each column to the `clientMethodArgument` private field of the `AjaxDetailsDialog` control:

```
    clientMethodArgument +=
                    (pd.Name + "," + pd.GetValue(iter.Current).ToString() + "|");
```

Notice that the `clientMethodArgument` string uses the | character as the separator between the name/value pairs and the , character as the separator between the name and value components of each name/value pair. As you'll see later, the `GetCallbackResult` method will send the `clientMethodArgument` string back to the client where the client-side code will retrieve the data field names and values of the book record from this string to use HTML/XHTML, CSS, DOM, and JavaScript to display them in the details pop-up dialog. As this example shows, Ajax-enabled controls and the server don't have to exchange data in XML format, that is, any text format will do, like the one here. That said, it's highly recommended that you use XML data format as you did for the `AjaxDropDownList` control developed in the previous sections.

As mentioned, following the C# interface implementation pattern, the `AjaxDetailsDialog` control exposes two protected virtual methods with the same signature as the `RaiseCallbackEvent` and `GetCallbackResult` methods of the `ICallbackEventHandler` interface. So far, this section has covered the first protected virtual method, `RaiseCallbackEvent`. Now this section discusses the second protected virtual method, `GetCallbackResult`.

As Listing 27-20 shows, the `GetCallbackResult` method simply returns the `clientMethodArgument` string back to the client.

Listing 27-20: The GetCallbackResult protected virtual method

```
protected virtual string GetCallbackResult()
{
  return clientMethodArgument;
}
```

Explicit Implementation of the ICallbackEventHandler Interface

Following the C# interface implementation pattern, the `AjaxDetailsDialog` control explicitly implements the `RaiseCallbackEvent` and `GetCallbackResult` methods of the `ICallbackEventHandler`
interface. Recall that the explicit implementation of the method of an interface requires you to qualify
the name of the method with the name of the interface, and call the associated protected virtual method:

```
string ICallbackEventHandler.GetCallbackResult()
{
  return this.GetCallbackResult();
}

void ICallbackEventHandler.RaiseCallbackEvent(string arg)
{
  this.RaiseCallbackEvent(arg);
}
```

AjaxField Data Control Field

As discussed in Chapter 18, a data control field represents a data field in a data-bound control such as
`GridView` and contains the complete information about its associated data field including field name
and the type of data displayed in the field. A data control field also contains the rendering logic that renders the appropriate HTML to display the field data.

All of the existing data control fields are server components; that is, they use server resources to handle
their tasks such as rendering their HTML. This section develops an Ajax-enabled data control field
named `AjaxField` that uses the ASP.NET client callback mechanism to asynchronously retrieve the data
from the server and uses the HTML/XHTML, CSS, DOM, and JavaScript client-side technologies to display the retrieved data.

You'll need to use the following design patterns to implement the `AjaxField` data control field:

❑ **Data control field design pattern:** Because `AjaxField` is a data control field, you should use
the data control field design pattern discussed in Chapter 18 to implement it.

❑ **Ajax-enabled component development pattern:** Because `AjaxField` is an Ajax-enabled component, you should use the Ajax-enabled component development pattern discussed in the previous chapter and this chapter to implement its Ajax features.

`AjaxField` will take advantage of the object-oriented best practice known as Object Composition to delegate its DHTML and client callback functionality to the `AjaxDetailsDialog` custom control developed in the previous section. Object Composition allows you to use your existing components to

develop a new custom component. In this case, you'll use the existing `AjaxDetailsDialog` custom control to build the `AjaxField` data control field as discussed shortly.

`AjaxField` derives from the `DataControlField` base class and overrides its `InitializeCell`, `ExtractValuesFromCell`, and `CreateField` methods, as discussed in the following sections.

Overriding InitializeCell

As Listing 27-21 shows, the `AjaxField` data control field overrides the `InitializeCell` method to delegate its DHTML and client callback functionality to the `AjaxDetailsDialog` custom control.

Listing 27-21: The InitializeCell method

```
public override void InitializeCell(DataControlFieldCell cell,
        DataControlCellType cellType, DataControlRowState rowState, int rowIndex)
{
  if (cellType != DataControlCellType.DataCell)
    return;

  AjaxDetailsDialog detailsDialog = new AjaxDetailsDialog();
  detailsDialog.ID = "mydialog";
  detailsDialog.MouseOutImageUrl = mouseOutImageUrl;
  detailsDialog.MouseOverImageUrl = mouseOverImageUrl;

  if (dialogStyle != null)
    detailsDialog.DialogStyle.CopyFrom(dialogStyle);

  if (popupHeaderStyle != null)
    detailsDialog.HeaderStyle.CopyFrom(popupHeaderStyle);

  if (popupItemStyle != null)
    detailsDialog.ItemStyle.CopyFrom(popupItemStyle);

  if (alternatingItemStyle != null)
    detailsDialog.AlternatingItemStyle.CopyFrom(alternatingItemStyle);

  detailsDialog.ClientCallbackDataSourceID = DataSourceID;
  detailsDialog.DataBinding += new EventHandler(OnDataBindField);
  cell.Controls.Add(detailsDialog);
}
```

The `InitializeCell` method only handles data cells and ignores other types of cells. The method first instantiates an `AjaxDetailsDialog` control:

```
AjaxDetailsDialog detailsDialog = new AjaxDetailsDialog();
```

Then it initializes the `AjaxDetailsDialog` control:

```
detailsDialog.ID = "mydialog";
detailsDialog.MouseOutImageUrl = MouseOutImageUrl;
detailsDialog.MouseOverImageUrl = MouseOverImageUrl;
```

AjaxField exposes two properties named MouseOutImageUrl and MouseOverImageUrl as follows:

```
private string mouseOverImageUrl;
public virtual string MouseOverImageUrl
{
  get { return mouseOverImageUrl; }
  set { mouseOverImageUrl = value; }
}

private string mouseOutImageUrl;
public virtual string MouseOutImageUrl
{
  get { return mouseOutImageUrl; }
  set { mouseOutImageUrl = value; }
}
```

Notice that both properties use private fields as their backing stores, as opposed to the ViewState collection. AjaxField simply assigns the values of these two properties to the MouseOutImageUrl and MouseOverImageUrl properties of the AjaxDetailsDialog control. In other words, AjaxField delegates the responsibility of managing the values of these properties across page postbacks to the AjaxDetailsDialog control.

Recall from the previous section that the AjaxDetailsDialog control, in turn, delegates this responsibility to the CustomImage control. As discussed in the previous chapter, the MouseOutImageUrl and MouseOverImageUrl properties of the CustomImage control use the ViewState collection as their backing stores.

In short, you should watch out for a pitfall if you're using Object Composition to build your custom component. The properties of your custom component that directly map into the properties of the objects they contain should use private fields as their backing store as opposed to the ViewState collection if these objects manage the values of these properties across page postbacks. If you're not careful, you'll end up saving the same information multiple times into the saved view state, consequently increasing the size of the saved view state, which will have the following adverse effects:

❑ Because the saved view state is stored in a hidden field named __VIEWSTATE on the page that the client browser downloads from the server, the increase in the saved view state size increases the page size, which means it would take much longer for the browser to download the page.

❑ At the end of each request, the page serializes the saved view state into its string representation, which is subsequently stored in the __VIEWSTATE hidden field. Therefore the increase in the saved view state size increases the amount time that it takes to serialize the information. This means that it takes longer for the browser to download the page, and it consumes more server resources to serialize the information.

❑ At the beginning of each request, the page retrieves the string representation of the saved view state from the __VIEWSTATE hidden field and deserializes the original object graph or saved view state from this string representation. Therefore the increase in the saved view state size increases the amount time that it takes to deserialize the saved view state. Again, this means it takes longer for the browser to receive the response back from the server, and it consumes more server resources to deserialize the saved view state.

Next, the `InitializeCell` method initializes the style properties of the `AjaxDetailsDialog` control:

```
if (dialogStyle != null)
  detailsDialog.DialogStyle.CopyFrom(dialogStyle);

if (popupHeaderStyle != null)
  detailsDialog.HeaderStyle.CopyFrom(popupHeaderStyle);

if (popupItemStyle != null)
  detailsDialog.ItemStyle.CopyFrom(popupItemStyle);

if (alternatingItemStyle != null)
  detailsDialog.AlternatingItemStyle.CopyFrom(alternatingItemStyle);
```

`AjaxField` exposes the following four style properties:

- ❑ `DialogStyle`: Gets and sets the CSS table style attributes of the pop-up details dialog

- ❑ `PopupHeaderStyle`: Gets and sets the CSS style attributes of the header row of the pop-up details dialog

- ❑ `PopupItemStyle`: Gets and sets the CSS style attributes of a data row in the pop-up details dialog

- ❑ `AlternatingItemStyle`: Gets and sets the CSS style attributes of an alternating data row in the pop-up dialog

`InitializeCell` calls the `CopyFrom` method of each style property of the `AjaxDetailsDialog` control to copy the properties of its respective style property. The `AjaxField` data control field doesn't override the `SaveViewState`, `LoadViewState`, and `TrackViewState` to call the `SaveViewState`, `LoadViewState`, and `TrackViewState` methods of its `DialogStyle`, `PopupHeaderStyle`, `PopupItemStyle`, and `AlternatingItemStyle` style properties because as discussed in the previous section, the `AjaxDetails Dialog` overrides these methods to manage the state of its style properties across page postbacks. This is yet another example where if you're not careful you'll end up storing the same information multiple times into the saved view state.

Next, the `InitializeCell` method sets the `ClientCallbackDataSourceID` property of the `Ajax DetailsDialog` control. `AjaxField` exposes a property named `DataSourceID` that the page developer must set to the value of the `ID` property of the desired tabular data source control on the page. `AjaxField` assigns the value of its `DataSourceID` property to the `ClientCallbackDataSourceID` property. Recall that the `AjaxDetailsDialog` control uses the `ClientCallbackDataSourceID` property to access the tabular data source control that retrieves the data from the database.

```
detailsDialog.ClientCallbackDataSourceID = DataSourceID;
```

The method then registers the `OnDataBindField` method as the callback for the `DataBinding` event of the `AjaxDetailsDialog` control. This method is discussed in the next section.

```
detailsDialog.DataBinding += new EventHandler(OnDataBindField);
```

Finally, the method adds the `AjaxDetailsDialog` to the `Controls` collection of the containing table cell:

```
cell.Controls.Add(detailsDialog);
```

Overriding OnDataBindField

The OnDataBindField method is invoked when the DataBinding event of the AjaxDetailsDialog control is raised. Listing 27-22 shows the AjaxField field's implementation of the OnDataBindField method.

Listing 27-22: The OnDataBindField method

```
protected virtual void OnDataBindField(Object sender, EventArgs e)
{
  AjaxDetailsDialog dd = sender as AjaxDetailsDialog;
  if (dd == null)
    return;

  DataControlFieldCell cell = (DataControlFieldCell)dd.Parent;
  IDataItemContainer container = (IDataItemContainer)cell.Parent;
  object dataItem = container.DataItem;
  object dataValueField = DataBinder.Eval(dataItem, DataField);
  dd.DataValue = dataValueField.ToString();
}
```

The method first accesses the DataControlFieldCell that contains the AjaxDetailsDialog control:

```
DataControlFieldCell cell = (DataControlFieldCell)dd.Parent;
```

Next, it accesses the table row that contains the DataControlFieldCell. The type of the table row depends on the type of the data-bound control that owns the row. For example, the table rows of GridView and DetailsView controls are of type GridViewRow and DetailsViewRow, respectively. As you'll see shortly, OnDataBindField needs to access the containing row because it contains a reference to the database record or data row that the table row is bound to. If OnDataBindField were to directly use the real type of the table row, AjaxField would be tied to a particular data-bound control.

The table rows of data-bound controls such as GridView and DetailsView implement the IDataItemContainer interface to hide their real types from data control fields such as AjaxField:

```
IDataItemContainer container = (IDataItemContainer)cell.Parent;
```

The method then calls the DataItem property of the IDataItemContainer interface to access the data row or record in generic fashion. Notice that the interface exposes the data row or record as an object of type System.Object to hide the actual type of the data row or record from data control fields such as AjaxField:

```
object dataItem = container.DataItem;
```

Next, the method calls the Eval method of the DataBinder class. AjaxField exposes a property named DataField that the page developer must set to the name of the associated database field. This field is normally the primary key field of the data row or record that the table row is bound to. OnDataBind Field calls the Eval method to access the value of its associated database field or column in generic fashion.

The Eval method of the DataBinder class takes two arguments. The first argument is an object of type System.Object that references the data row or record. The second argument is the name of the database field. The Eval method uses .NET reflection under the hood and retrieves the value of the database field with the specified name from the specified data row or record. In other words, the Eval method allows AjaxField to retrieve the value of the respective database field in generic fashion.

```
object dataValueField = DataBinder.Eval(dataItem, DataField);
```

The method then assigns the database field value to the DataValue property of the AjaxDetails Dialog control. As shown in Listing 27-17, the OnPreRender method of the AjaxDetailsDialog control passes the value of the DataValue property to the client script that makes the asynchronous client callback request to the server:

```
protected override void RenderContents(HtmlTextWriter writer)
{
  PrepareControlHierarchy();
  if (renderClientScript)
  {
    string js = Page.ClientScript.GetCallbackEventReference(
                      this, "'" + DataValue + "'", "MyClientCallback", null);

    image.Attributes.Add("onclick",
                      "InitializeDetailsPopup('" + this.ClientID + "');" + js);
  }

  image.RenderControl(writer);
}
```

As discussed in the previous section, when the client script makes the client callback request to the server, it passes the value of the DataValue property into the RaiseClientCallback method of the server. This method uses this value as the primary key field value of the record that it needs to retrieve from the underlying data store.

Implementing CreateField Method

Recall that AjaxField derives from the DataControlField base class. The base class exposes an abstract method named CreateField that AjaxField must implement:

```
protected override DataControlField CreateField()
{
  return new AjaxField();
}
```

Overriding ExtractValuesFromCell

The DataControlField base class exposes a method named ExtractValuesFromCell. To help you understand how you should implement the ExtractValueFromCell method of AjaxField, consider the following example. When the user clicks the Update button of a table row in a GridView control, the

GridView control's internal callback is called. This callback calls the ExtractRowValues method of the GridView control to retrieve the new datafield values. The callback then uses a tabular data source control to store the new values into the underlying data store.

The ExtractRowValues method, in turn, calls the ExtractValuesFromCell method of each data control field to retrieve its associated datafield value. None of this applies to AjaxField because Ajax Field like all Ajax-enabled components uses the ASP.NET client callback mechanism to interface with the server. Therefore, you should implement the ExtractValuesFromCell method of AjaxField as follows:

```
public override void ExtractValuesFromCell(IOrderedDictionary dictionary,
                    DataControlFieldCell cell, DataControlRowState rowState,
                    bool includeReadOnly)
{

}
```

At the end of this chapter, you'll see an example of a Web page that uses the AjaxField custom data control field.

DropDownListField2

This section develops a custom data control field named DropDownListField2 that derives from the DataControlField base class and overrides its InitializeCell, CreateField, and ExtractValues FromCell methods. Figure 27-4 shows the user interface that the DropDownListField2 data control field renders on a page. As this figure shows, the user interface consists of the following three main parts:

❑ A label with the text "Sort by:"

❑ A DropDownList control

❑ An ImageButton control

The interface of the DropDownListField2 is rendered in the header of a data-bound control such as GridView. All the header texts that normally are rendered as LinkButton controls to allow the user to sort the displayed data are now displayed as list items in the DropDownList control. The user selects an item from the list and clicks the GO ImageButton to sort the displayed data. Listing 27-23 shows how DropDownListField2 is declared on an ASP.NET page.

Figure 27-4

Listing 27-23: Declaration of DropDownListField2 on an ASP.NET page

```
<custom:DropDownListField2 ItemStyle-Width="100%" ItemStyle-HorizontalAlign="Right"
SortExpressionFields="Title,Author,Price,Publisher" />
```

As Listing 27-23 shows, `DropDownListField2` data control field exposes a property named `Sort ExpressionFields` that the page developer must set to a comma-separated list of database field names. These database field names are used to sort the displayed data.

Overriding InitializeCell

Listing 27-24 shows the `DropDownListField2` data control field's implementation of the `InitializeCell` method.

Listing 27-24: The InitializeCell method

```
public override void InitializeCell(DataControlFieldCell cell,
                                    DataControlCellType cellType,
                                    DataControlRowState rowState,
                                    int rowIndex)
{
  if (cellType != DataControlCellType.Header)
    return;

  LiteralControl lc = new LiteralControl(
      "<table width='100%' border='0' cellspacing='5'><tr><td valign='center'>");
  cell.Controls.Add(lc);

  lc = new LiteralControl("<span
     style='font-family:verdana,arial,helvetica,sans-serif; font-size: xx-small;'>
          <b>Sort by: </b></span></td><td valign='center'>");
  cell.Controls.Add(lc);

  DropDownList ddl = new DropDownList();
  ddl.SkinID = SkinID;
  ddl.EnableTheming = EnableTheming;
  ddl.SelectedIndexChanged += new EventHandler(ddl_SelectedIndexChanged);
  string[] strs = SortExpressionFields.Split(new char[] { ',' });
  foreach (string str in strs)
  {
    ddl.Items.Add(new ListItem(str, str));
  }
  ddl.SelectedIndex = SelectedIndex;
  cell.Controls.Add(ddl);

  lc = new LiteralControl("</td><td valign='bottom'>");
  cell.Controls.Add(lc);

  ImageButton btn = new ImageButton();
  btn.Load += new EventHandler(OnLoadField);
  btn.ImageAlign = ImageAlign.Bottom;
  btn.CommandName = DataControlCommands.SortCommandName;
  btn.CommandArgument = ddl.SelectedValue;
  btn.BorderWidth = Unit.Pixel(0);
  btn.BackColor = System.Drawing.Color.FromName("Black");
  cell.Controls.Add(btn);
  lc = new LiteralControl("</td></tr></table>");
  cell.Controls.Add(lc);
}
```

InitializeCell first checks whether the cell being initialized is a header cell. If not, it returns. This ensures that DropDownListField2 renders its user interface in the header of a data-bound control such as GridView.

```
if (cellType != DataControlCellType.Header)
  return;
```

The InitializeCell method instantiates and initializes a DropDownList control and adds it to the Controls collection of the containing table cell. The method retrieves the DropDownList list items from the SortExpressionFields property and adds them to the Items collection of the DropDownList control:

```
string[] strs = SortExpressionFields.Split(new char[] { ',' });
foreach (string str in strs)
  ddl.Items.Add(new ListItem(str, str));
```

The InitializeCell method then instantiates an ImageButton control and adds it to the Controls collection of the containing table cell:

```
ImageButton btn = new ImageButton();
cell.Controls.Add(btn);
```

It sets the value of the CommandName property of the ImageButton to DataControlCommands .SortCommandName to specify that this button raises the sort event:

```
btn.CommandName = DataControlCommands.SortCommandName;
```

Then it registers the OnLoadField method as the callback for the Load event of the ImageButton:

```
btn.Load += new EventHandler(OnLoadField);
```

The following code shows the implementation of the OnLoadField method:

```
void OnLoadField(object sender, EventArgs e)
{
  ImageButton btn = sender as ImageButton;
  if (string.IsNullOrEmpty(ImageUrl))
    btn.ImageUrl =
          btn.Page.ClientScript.GetWebResourceUrl(typeof(DropDownListField2),
                                                  "CustomComponents.go.bmp");
  else
    btn.ImageUrl = ImageUrl;
}
```

The OnLoadField method first checks whether the page developer has specified an image for the ImageButton control. If not, it uses a default image embedded in the DropDownListField2 control's assembly. OnLoadField calls the GetWebResourceUrl method of the ClientScript property of the containing page to retrieve the URL of the embedded image file.

As the code shows, the only use of the OnLoadField method is to call the GetWebResourceUrl method. You may be wondering why you need to call this method in the callback for the Load event, instead of in the InitializeCell method itself.

When the `InitializeCell` method is called, the `Page` property of the `ImageButton`, the containing cell, or the containing table row hasn't been set yet, which means that you can't access the `ClientScript` property of the containing page. However, in the `Load` phase of the page life cycle, the `Page` property of the controls in the control tree of the containing page has already been set.

Overriding CreateField

The `DataControlField` base class exposes an abstract method named `CreateField` that `DropDown ListField2` implements as follows:

```
protected override DataControlField CreateField()
{
  return new DropDownListField2();
}
```

Overriding ExtractValuesFromCell

As discussed in the previous section, you should implement this method as follows:

```
public override void ExtractValuesFromCell(IOrderedDictionary dictionary,
    DataControlFieldCell cell, DataControlRowState rowState,bool includeReadOnly)
{

}
```

At the end of this chapter, you'll see an example of a Web page that uses the `DropDownListField2` custom data control field.

Ajax-Enabled Custom GridView Control

This section implements a custom data-bound control named `CustomGridView` that derives from the ASP.NET `GridView` control and overrides the `CreateChildTable` and `PrepareControlHierarchy` methods of its base class as discussed in the following sections.

Overriding CreateChildTable

Recall from Chapter 19 that the `CreateChildTable` method of the `GridView` control creates the table that contains the entire contents of the control. This method is marked as virtual to allow the subclasses of the control to override its implementation.

The `CustomGridView` control exposes a Boolean property named `EnableCellView` that the page developer can set to specify whether the cell view capability of the control should be enabled. As Listing 27-25 shows, `CustomGridView` overrides `CreateChildTable` to instantiate an instance of a custom control named `CustomizableTable` if its cell view capability is enabled. Notice that `CreateChildTable` falls back on the default implementation of its base class when its cell view capability is disabled. In other words, `CustomGridView` turns into a normal `GridView` when its cell view capability is disabled. The next section discusses what I mean by cell view capability.

Listing 27-25: The CreateChildTable method

```
protected override System.Web.UI.WebControls.Table CreateChildTable()
{
  if (EnableCellView)
  {
    this.PagerSettings.Position = PagerPosition.Bottom;
    CustomizableTable t = new CustomizableTable();

    return t;
  }

    return base.CreateChildTable();
}
```

CustomizableTable (Cell View Capability)

The `CustomizableTable` control is a custom control that derives from the ASP.NET `Table` control and overrides its `RenderContents` method to provide a different rendering logic. `CustomizableTable` exposes an integer property named `Columns` that the page developer can set to specify the number of columns of the `CustomizableTable`.

Listing 27-26 shows the `CustomizableTable` control's implementation of the `RenderContents` method.

Listing 27-26: The RenderContents method

```
protected override void RenderContents(HtmlTextWriter w)
{
  RenderHeaderRow(w);
  RenderDataRows(w);
  RenderPagerRow(w);
}
```

The `RenderContents` method assumes the first and last rows are the header and pager rows, respectively, and the rest of the rows are data rows. However, it can be extended to remove this limitation. As you'll see later, this limitation isn't really a big limitation because in majority of cases tables come with a header and bottom pager.

RenderHeaderRow

Listing 27-27 shows the `RenderHeaderRow` method. Notice that `RenderHeaderRow` assigns the value of the `Columns` property to the `colspan` HTML attribute of the `<td>` HTML element.

Listing 27-27: The RenderHeaderRow method

```
protected virtual void RenderHeaderRow(HtmlTextWriter w)
{
  TableRow row = Rows[0];
  row.ControlStyle.AddAttributesToRender(w);
  RenderRowAttributes(row, w);
  w.RenderBeginTag(HtmlTextWriterTag.Tr);
```

```
      w.AddAttribute(HtmlTextWriterAttribute.Colspan, Columns.ToString());
      w.RenderBeginTag(HtmlTextWriterTag.Td);
      w.RenderBeginTag(HtmlTextWriterTag.Table);
      w.RenderBeginTag(HtmlTextWriterTag.Tr);
      foreach (TableCell cell in row.Cells)
      {
        if (!cell.Visible) continue;

        w.RenderBeginTag(HtmlTextWriterTag.Td);
        cell.RenderControl(w);
        w.RenderEndTag();

      }
      w.RenderEndTag();
      w.RenderEndTag();
      w.RenderEndTag();
      w.RenderEndTag();
    }
```

RenderDataRows

Listing 27-28 illustrates the `RenderDataRows` method.

Listing 27-28: The RenderDataRows method

```
    protected virtual void RenderDataRows(HtmlTextWriter w)
    {
      bool beginNewRow = true;
      for (int rowIndex = 1; rowIndex < Rows.Count - 2; rowIndex++)
      {
        TableRow row = Rows[rowIndex];
        if (beginNewRow)
        {
          w.RenderBeginTag(HtmlTextWriterTag.Tr);
          beginNewRow = false;
        }
        row.ControlStyle.AddAttributesToRender(w);
        RenderRowAttributes(row, w);
        w.RenderBeginTag(HtmlTextWriterTag.Td);
        w.RenderBeginTag(HtmlTextWriterTag.Table);
        foreach (TableCell cell in row.Cells)
        {
          if (!cell.Visible) continue;
          w.RenderBeginTag(HtmlTextWriterTag.Tr);
          w.RenderBeginTag(HtmlTextWriterTag.Td);
          cell.RenderControl(w);
          w.RenderEndTag();
          w.RenderEndTag();
        }
        w.RenderEndTag();
        w.RenderEndTag();

        if ((rowIndex % Columns) == 0)
        {
          w.RenderEndTag();
```

(continued)

Listing 27-28: *(continued)*

```
        beginNewRow = true;
      }
    }
  }
```

As Listing 27-28 shows, the `RenderDataRows` method renders every `Columns` number of `TableRows` in a single `<tr>` HTML element where all `TableCells` of each `TableRow` are rendered in a single `<td>` HTML element.

Overriding PrepareControlHierarchy

As discussed in Chapter 19, the `GridView` control exposes the style properties of its child controls as top-level style properties such as `HeaderStyle`, `ItemStyle`, and so on. The `PrepareControlHierarchy` method of the `GridView` control applies these top-level style properties to their respective child controls.

One of these top-level style properties is the `SelectedItemStyle` property. The `GridView` control's implementation of `PrepareControlHierarchy`, shown in Listing 27-29, uses server resources to apply this style property on the server.

`CustomGridView` control overrides `PrepareControlHierarchy` to take advantage of the DHTML capability of the requesting browser to use client resources to apply the `SelectItemStyle` property on the client side when the user moves the mouse pointer over a cell.

Listing 27-29: The PrepareControlHierarchy method

```
protected override void PrepareControlHierarchy()
{
  base.PrepareControlHierarchy();
  if(!EnableCellView)
    return;

  foreach (GridViewRow row in Rows)
  {
    if (row.RowType == DataControlRowType.DataRow)
    {
      CssStyleCollection col = SelectedRowStyle.GetStyleAttributes(this);
      IEnumerator keys = col.Keys.GetEnumerator();
      string str = string.Empty;
      string key = string.Empty;
      string val = string.Empty;
      string cc = string.Empty;
      string dd = string.Empty;

      while (keys.MoveNext())
      {
        key = (String)keys.Current;
        val = col[key];
        if (key.Contains("-"))
        {
          cc = key.Substring(key.IndexOf('-') + 1, 1);
```

```
            cc = cc.ToUpper();
            dd = key.Substring(key.IndexOf('-'), 2);
            key = key.Replace(dd, cc);
          }
          str += ("this.style."+key+"='" + val + "';");
        }
        row.Attributes.Add("onmouseover", str);

        col = row.ControlStyle.GetStyleAttributes(this);
        keys = col.Keys.GetEnumerator();
        str = string.Empty;
        while (keys.MoveNext())
        {
          key = (String)keys.Current;
          val = col[key];
          if (key.Contains("-"))
          {
            cc = key.Substring(key.IndexOf('-') + 1, 1);
            cc = cc.ToUpper();
            dd = key.Substring(key.IndexOf('-'), 2);
            key = key.Replace(dd, cc);
          }
          str += ("this.style." + key + "='" + val + "';");
        }

        row.Attributes.Add("onmouseout", str);
      }
    }
  }
```

PrepareControlHierarchy first calls the GetStyleAttributes method of the SelectedRowStyle
property to access the CssStyleCollection that contains all the CSS style properties of the selected row:

```
    CssStyleCollection col = SelectedRowStyle.GetStyleAttributes(this);
```

Next it iterates through the Keys collection property of the CssStyleCollection object. The Keys collection contains the names of the CSS style attributes such as background-color, font-size, and so
on. As you know, the style JavaScript object exposes one property for each CSS style attribute.

The CSS style attributes and their respective JavaScript style properties use two different naming conventions when the name consists of two words. The CSS style attributes use the – character as the separator between the two words, whereas their respective JavaScript style properties capitalize the first
letter of the second word.

The PrepareControlHierarchy method iterates through the CSS style attributes and accesses the first
letter after the separator character:

```
    cc = key.Substring(key.IndexOf('-') + 1, 1);
```

It capitalizes this letter:

```
    cc = cc.ToUpper();
```

It then replaces the separator character and the first letter after this character with the capitalized letter. This replacement converts the name of the CSS style attribute to the name of its associated JavaScript style property.

```
dd = key.Substring(key.IndexOf('-'), 2);
key = key.Replace(dd, cc);
```

The method then builds a string that contains the JavaScript code that assigns the value of each CSS style attribute to its respective JavaScript style property:

```
str += ("this.style."+key+"='" + val + "';");
```

Next it assigns the string to the onmouseover attribute of the appropriate table row. When the user moves the mouse pointer over the row, the onmouseover event is raised and the JavaScript code contained in the string is run. This JavaScript code assigns the CSS style attributes associated with the SelectItemStyle property to their respective JavaScript style properties. In other words, the SelectedItemStyle property is applied on the client side, as opposed to the server side.

```
row.Attributes.Add("onmouseover", str);
```

The method then does the same thing with the ControlStyle property of the table row. That is, it builds a string that contains the JavaScript code that assigns the values of the CSS style attributes associated with the ControlStyle property to their respective JavaScript style properties. The PrepareControlHierarchy method assigns this string to the onmouseout attribute of the table row. When the user moves the mouse out of the table row, the JavaScript code contained in the string runs and resets the JavaScript style properties back to their original values.

Listing 27-30 shows an ASP.NET page that uses all the server controls developed in this chapter:

❑ CustomGridView

❑ ImageDialog

❑ DropDownListField2

❑ AjaxField

Listing 27-30: An ASP.NET page that uses the CustomGridView, ImageDialog, DropDownListField, and AjaxField components

```
<%@ Page Language="C#" %>
<%@ Register TagPrefix="custom" Namespace="CustomComponents"
  Assembly="CustomComponents" %>
<html xmlns="http://www.w3.org/1999/xhtml">
<body>
  <form id="form1" runat="server">
    <custom:CustomGridView runat="server" ID="cv" DataSourceID="MySource"
    AllowPaging="True" HorizontalAlign="center" AllowSorting="True" PageSize="3"
    AutoGenerateColumns="false" EnableCellView="true" ShowHeader="true"
    DataKeyNames="BookID" CellPadding="0" CellSpacing="10" ForeColor="#333333"
    GridLines="None" TableColumns="2">
      <FooterStyle BackColor="#990000" Font-Bold="True" ForeColor="White" />
      <RowStyle BackColor="#FFFBD6" ForeColor="#333333" />
```

```
<PagerStyle BackColor="#FFCC66" ForeColor="#333333" VerticalAlign="Top"
HorizontalAlign="Center" />
<SelectedRowStyle BackColor="#FFCC66" ForeColor="Navy" />
<HeaderStyle BackColor="#990000" Font-Bold="True" ForeColor="White" />
<AlternatingRowStyle BackColor="PaleGoldenrod" />
<Columns>
  <asp:TemplateField>
    <itemtemplate>
              <table border="0" cellpadding="0" cellspacing="0">
                <tr>
                  <td valign="top" align="left">
                    <custom:ImageDialog ID="Image1" runat="server"
                    ImageUrl='<%#"Images/"+Eval("Title").ToString()+".jpg"%>'
                    PopupImageUrl=
                      '<%#"Images/Popup "+Eval("Title").ToString()+".jpg" %>'
                    DialogStyle-BackColor="LightGoldenrodYellow"
                    DialogStyle-BorderColor="Tan" DialogStyle-CellSpacing="0"
                    DialogStyle-BorderWidth="1px" DialogStyle-CellPadding="2"
                    DialogStyle-BorderStyle="Groove"
                    DialogStyle-ForeColor="Black"
                    DialogStyle-GridLines="None"
                    HeaderStyle-BackColor="Tan" HeaderStyle-Font-Bold="True"
                    AlternatingItemStyle-BackColor="PaleGoldenrod" />
                  </td>
                  <td valign="top" align="left">
                    <table border="0" cellpadding="0" cellspacing="0">
                      <tr>
                        <td valign="top" align="left">
                           
                          <strong>
                            <a href=""><%# Eval("Title").ToString() %></a>
                          </strong>

                        </td>
                      </tr>
                      <tr>
                        <td valign="top" align="left">
                           <font face="verdana,arial,helvetica" size="-1">
                             by <%# Eval("Author").ToString() %></font>
                        </td>
                      </tr>
                      <tr>
                        <td valign="top" align="left">
                          <font face="verdana,arial,helvetica" size="-1">
                            <%# Eval("Publisher").ToString() %></font>
                        </td>
                      </tr>
                    </table>
                  </td>
                </tr>
                <tr>
                  <td align="left" colspan="2">
                    <font face="verdana,arial,helvetica" size="-1">
                      List Price : $<%# Eval("Price").ToString() %></font>
                  </td>
```

(continued)

Listing 27-30: *(continued)*

```
                         </tr>
                     </table>
                 </itemtemplate>
         </asp:TemplateField>

         <custom:DropDownListField2 ItemStyle-Width="100%"
         ItemStyle-HorizontalAlign="Right"
         SortExpressionFields="Title,Author,Price,Publisher" />

         <custom:AjaxField DataField="BookID" DataSourceID="MySource2"
         DialogStyle-BackColor="LightGoldenrodYellow" DialogStyle-CellPadding="2"
         DialogStyle-BorderColor="Tan" DialogStyle-BorderWidth="1px"
         DialogStyle-CellSpacing="0" DialogStyle-BorderStyle="Groove"
         DialogStyle-ForeColor="Black" DialogStyle-GridLines="None"
         PopupHeaderStyle-BackColor="Tan" PopupHeaderStyle-Font-Bold="True"
         AlternatingItemStyle-BackColor="PaleGoldenrod" />
       </Columns>
   </custom:CustomGridView>

   <asp:SqlDataSource runat="server" ID="MySource"
   ConnectionString="<%$ ConnectionStrings:MySqlConnectionString %>"
   SelectCommand="Select * From Books" />

   <asp:SqlDataSource runat="server" ID="MySource2"
   ConnectionString="<%$ ConnectionStrings:MySqlConnectionString %>"
   SelectCommand="Select PublicationDate as 'Publication Date', Edition,
               PageCount as 'Page Count' From Books Where BookID=@BookID">
     <SelectParameters>
       <asp:FormParameter Name="BookID" FormField="__CALLBACKPARAM" />
     </SelectParameters>
   </asp:SqlDataSource>

   <asp:SqlDataSource runat="server" ID="MySource3"
   ConnectionString="<%$ ConnectionStrings:MySqlConnectionString %>"
   SelectCommand="Select * From Books Where Title=@Title">
     <SelectParameters>
       <asp:SessionParameter Name="Title" SessionField="ServerMethodArgument" />
     </SelectParameters>
   </asp:SqlDataSource>
 </form>
</body>
</html>
```

Figure 27-5 shows the page on the client browser. As this figure shows, this page provides the following features:

❑ The page developer can set the value of the TableColumns property of the CustomGridView control to specify the maximum number of cells in each row. Each row in Figure 27-5 consists of two cells because Listing 27-30 sets the TableColumns property to two.

❑ The header of the table contains a DropDownList and ImageButton control where the DropDownList control displays the database field names that the user can select to sort the displayed data.

❑ When the user clicks a Details button, the following sequence of events is triggered:

    a.   Client-side code makes an asynchronous client callback request to the server via the ASP.NET client callback mechanism without having to perform a full page postback to the server.

    b.   The `AjaxDetailsDialog` control uses the DHTML capabilities of the browser to dynamically render the details pop-up dialog to display the information retrieved from the server.

    c.   The pop-up dialog uses the DHTML capabilities of the browser to allow the user to resize and to move the dialog.

❑ When the user moves the mouse pointer over a Details button, the button takes advantage of the DHTML capabilities of the browser to provide an animated effect to display the new image.

❑ When the user clicks the image of a book, the `ImageDialog` control takes advantage of the DHTML capabilities of the browser to pop up a resizable movable dialog that displays a larger version of the image.

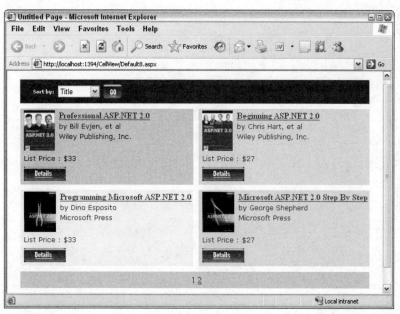

Figure 27-5

Summary

This chapter discussed the second and third important characteristics of Ajax-enabled components, that is, their asynchronous communications with the server and the XML characteristic of the data exchange between Ajax-enabled components and the server. That said, keep in mind that not all Ajax-enabled controls exchange data in XML format.

This chapter consisted of four major parts. The first part implemented replicas of the main components of the ASP.NET 2.0 client callback mechanism to help you look under the hood of the ASP.NET 2.0 implementation of the mechanism. The second part showed you how to use the ASP.NET 2.0 client callback mechanism to implement Ajax-enabled controls with minimal efforts. The third part showed how you can use the ASP.NET 2.0 data source control model to have your Ajax-enabled custom controls access any type of data store in generic fashion. The last part implemented several Ajax-enabled controls to show you how to develop your own Ajax-enabled controls.

The next two chapters discuss the fourth characteristic of Ajax-enabled components, that is, the Ajax patterns.

28

Developing Ajax-Enabled Controls and Components: Ajax Patterns

The previous chapter discussed the asynchronous nature of the communications between the client-side code and server-side code. This chapter and the next discuss the fourth characteristic of Ajax-enabled components: the Ajax patterns. These patterns allow Ajax-enabled components to determine the best time to make a request to the server to ensure that users continue their interactions with the components without interruptions.

This chapter first provides you with in-depth coverage of the Google XML Web service API. It then uses the Predictive Fetch Ajax pattern to implement an Ajax-enabled control named `AjaxGoogle Search` that makes asynchronous client callbacks to the Google XML Web service to fetch and cache the next page of search results to have it ready for the user. This alleviates irritating waiting periods associated with traditional controls.

Patterns

A *pattern* is a proven recurring solution to a recurring problem. For example, the issues regarding Ajax-enabled components communicating with the server are something that every Ajax-enabled component developer has to deal with. A pattern captures the solution to a specific problem in a specific context that has been used again and again and proven to be the most optimized solution to the problem in that context. In other words, a pattern doesn't solve all the problems in the world—it targets a specific problem in a specific context.

Therefore, when you run into a recurring problem such as Ajax communication issues, you shouldn't start from scratch. Instead you should use the solution that others have used and has been proven to be the most optimized solution to the problem. This chapter and the next chapter discuss the following four Ajax patterns and implement Ajax-enabled components that use these patterns to show you how to use them to implement your own Ajax-enabled controls and components:

❑ Predictive Fetch

❑ Periodic Refresh

❑ Submission Throttling

❑ Explicit Submission

Because this chapter and the next chapter implement Ajax-enabled controls that will make asynchronous client callbacks to the Google XML Web service to perform Google search and spell-checking, this chapter begins with an in-depth coverage of the Google XML Web service.

Google XML Web Service API

You need a license key to use this API. To get a license key, you need to create an account with Google at `https:// api.google.com`. After you successfully create the account, you'll get an e-mail from Google that contains your license key. You have to use your license every time you access the Google Web service. The license key currently limits you to 1,000 queries per day.

As discussed in Chapter 10, you should use a proxy class to access a Web service. There are different ways to create the proxy class. If you're working in the Visual Studio 2005 environment, you have two options:

❑ Launch the Add Web References dialog as discussed in Chapter 10, navigate to `http://api .google.com/GoogleSearch.wsdl`, and click the Add Reference button to add the reference. This will automatically download the `GoogleSearch.wsdl` WSDL document from the Google site, create the code for the proxy class, compile the proxy class into an assembly, and add a reference to the assembly as discussed in Chapter 10.

❑ Download the Google Web APIs developer's kit from `http://api.google.com`. This developer's kit contains the following items:

    ❑ Simple examples that show you how to use the API

    ❑ Documentation

    ❑ The `GoogleSearch.wsdl` WSDL document

If you're using the built-in Web server, launch the Add Web References dialog and follow the same steps discussed before, but this time navigate to the directory where the WSDL document is located. The URL should look something like the following:

```
file:///d:/download/googleapi/googleapi/GoogleSearch.WSDL
```

If you're using IIS, you have to copy the `GoogleSearch.wsdl` document to the root directory of your application. The path to this directory should look something like this: `C:\Inetpub\ wwwroot\ApplicationRoot`. Then launch the Add Web References dialog and follow the steps discussed before to navigate to the application root where the WSDL document is located. The URL for the WSDL document should look something like this:

```
http://localhost/(ApplicationRoot)/GoogleSearch.wsdl
```

If you're using the App_Code directory, copy the GoogleSearch.wsdl document to this directory. That's it. The Visual Studio 2005 automatically generates the code for the proxy, compiles the proxy code into an assembly, and adds a reference to the assembly.

If you're not working in the Visual Studio 2005 environment, and you like to do things from the command line, first download the Google Web APIs developer's kit from the Google site as discussed before. Go to the directory where the GoogleSearch.wsdl document is located, and use the following command to generate the code for the proxy class and to save the code to the GoogleSearch.cs file (give it any name you wish):

```
wsdl /out:GoogleSearch.cs GoogleSearch.wsdl
```

The wsdl.exe tool comes with different options. For example, you can use /namespace:GoogleSearch to specify your desired namespace for the proxy class.

Then use the following command to compile the GoogleSearch.cs into the GoogleSearch.dll assembly and use the assembly as you would use any other assembly:

```
csc /t:library /out:GoogleSearch.dll GoogleSearch.cs
```

Next are those parts of the Google XML Web service API that you'll be using in this chapter and the next chapter to develop Ajax-enabled controls. Listing 28-1 shows the portion of the GoogleSearch.wsdl document that describes the API that you'll be using to perform Google search and spell-checking.

Listing 28-1: The GoogleSearch.wsdl document

```xml
<?xml version="1.0"?>
<definitions name="GoogleSearch" targetNamespace="urn:GoogleSearch"
 xmlns:typens="urn:GoogleSearch" xmlns:xsd="http://www.w3.org/2001/XMLSchema"
 xmlns:soap="http://schemas.xmlsoap.org/wsdl/soap/"
 xmlns:soapenc="http://schemas.xmlsoap.org/soap/encoding/"
 xmlns:wsdl="http://schemas.xmlsoap.org/wsdl/"
 xmlns="http://schemas.xmlsoap.org/wsdl/">
  <types>
    <xsd:schema xmlns="http://www.w3.org/2001/XMLSchema"
      targetNamespace="urn:GoogleSearch">

      <xsd:complexType name="GoogleSearchResult">
        <xsd:all>
          <xsd:element name="documentFiltering"          type="xsd:boolean"/>
          <xsd:element name="searchComments"             type="xsd:string"/>
          <xsd:element name="estimatedTotalResultsCount" type="xsd:int"/>
          <xsd:element name="estimateIsExact"            type="xsd:boolean"/>
          <xsd:element name="resultElements"
            type="typens:ResultElementArray"/>
          <xsd:element name="searchQuery"                type="xsd:string"/>
          <xsd:element name="startIndex"                 type="xsd:int"/>
          <xsd:element name="endIndex"                   type="xsd:int"/>
          <xsd:element name="searchTips"                 type="xsd:string"/>
          <xsd:element name="searchTime"                 type="xsd:double"/>
          . . .
```

(continued)

Listing 28-1: *(continued)*

```
          </xsd:all>
      </xsd:complexType>

      <xsd:complexType name="ResultElement">
        <xsd:all>
          <xsd:element name="summary" type="xsd:string"/>
          <xsd:element name="URL" type="xsd:string"/>
          <xsd:element name="snippet" type="xsd:string"/>
          <xsd:element name="title" type="xsd:string"/>
        </xsd:all>
      </xsd:complexType>

      <xsd:complexType name="ResultElementArray">
        <xsd:complexContent>
          <xsd:restriction base="soapenc:Array">
            <xsd:attribute ref="soapenc:arrayType"
               wsdl:arrayType="typens:ResultElement[]"/>
          </xsd:restriction>
        </xsd:complexContent>
      </xsd:complexType>
    </xsd:schema>
</types>

<message name="doGoogleSearch">
  <part name="key"           type="xsd:string"/>
  <part name="q"             type="xsd:string"/>
  <part name="start"         type="xsd:int"/>
  <part name="maxResults"    type="xsd:int"/>
  <part name="filter"        type="xsd:boolean"/>
  <part name="restrict"      type="xsd:string"/>
  <part name="safeSearch"    type="xsd:boolean"/>
  <part name="lr"            type="xsd:string"/>
  <part name="ie"            type="xsd:string"/>
  <part name="oe"            type="xsd:string"/>
</message>

<message name="doGoogleSearchResponse">
  <part name="return" type="typens:GoogleSearchResult"/>
</message>

<message name="doSpellingSuggestion">
  <part name="key" type="xsd:string"/>
  <part name="phrase" type="xsd:string"/>
</message>

<message name="doSpellingSuggestionResponse">
  <part name="return"  type="xsd:string"/>
</message>

<portType name="GoogleSearchPort">

  <operation name="doGoogleSearch">
```

```
    <input message="typens:doGoogleSearch"/>
    <output message="typens:doGoogleSearchResponse"/>
  </operation>

  <operation name="doSpellingSuggestion">
    <input message="typens:doSpellingSuggestion"/>
    <output message="typens:doSpellingSuggestionResponse"/>
  </operation>

</portType>

<binding name="GoogleSearchBinding" type="typens:GoogleSearchPort">
  <soap:binding style="rpc" transport="http://schemas.xmlsoap.org/soap/http"/>

  <operation name="doGoogleSearch">
    <soap:operation soapAction="urn:GoogleSearchAction"/>
    <input>
      <soap:body use="encoded" namespace="urn:GoogleSearch"
        encodingStyle="http://schemas.xmlsoap.org/soap/encoding/"/>
    </input>
    <output>
      <soap:body use="encoded" namespace="urn:GoogleSearch"
        encodingStyle="http://schemas.xmlsoap.org/soap/encoding/"/>
    </output>
  </operation>

  <operation name="doSpellingSuggestion">
    <soap:operation soapAction="urn:GoogleSearchAction"/>
    <input>
      <soap:body use="encoded" namespace="urn:GoogleSearch"
        encodingStyle="http://schemas.xmlsoap.org/soap/encoding/"/>
    </input>
    <output>
      <soap:body use="encoded" namespace="urn:GoogleSearch"
        encodingStyle="http://schemas.xmlsoap.org/soap/encoding/"/>
    </output>
  </operation>

</binding>

<service name="GoogleSearchService">
  <port name="GoogleSearchPort" binding="typens:GoogleSearchBinding">
    <soap:address location="http://api.google.com/search/beta2"/>
  </port>
</service>

</definitions>
```

This document describes everything that a tool such as `wsdl.exe` needs to generate the code for the proxy class. The `name` attribute of the `<service>` element contains the name of the proxy class, that is, `GoogleSearchService`:

```
<service name="GoogleSearchService">
```

The `name` attribute of each `<operation>` element contains the name of a proxy method that you need to invoke. Listing 28-1 contains two `<operation>` elements with `name` attribute values of `doGoogle Search` and `doSpellingSuggestion`. This means that the proxy class contains two methods named `doGoogleSearch` and `doSpellingSuggestion`:

```
<operation name="doGoogleSearch">
  <input message="typens:doGoogleSearch"/>
  <output message="typens:doGoogleSearchResponse"/>
</operation>

<operation name="doSpellingSuggestion">
  <input message="typens:doSpellingSuggestion"/>
  <output message="typens:doSpellingSuggestionResponse"/>
</operation>
```

The `message` attribute of the `<input>` subelement of each `<operation>` element references the `<message>` element that contains the names and types of the arguments of the associated proxy method. As Listing 28-1 shows, the `<input>` child element of the `<operation>` element that represents the `doGoogleSearch` proxy method references the following `<message>` element, which means that this `message` element contains the names and types of the arguments of the `doGoogleSearch` proxy method:

```
<message name="doGoogleSearch">
    <part name="key"        type="xsd:string"/>
    <part name="q"          type="xsd:string"/>
    <part name="start"      type="xsd:int"/>
    <part name="maxResults" type="xsd:int"/>
    <part name="filter"     type="xsd:boolean"/>
    <part name="restrict"   type="xsd:string"/>
    <part name="safeSearch" type="xsd:boolean"/>
    <part name="lr"         type="xsd:string"/>
    <part name="ie"         type="xsd:string"/>
    <part name="oe"         type="xsd:string"/>
</message>
```

Therefore, the declaration of the `doGoogleSearch` method is as follows:

```
doGoogleSearch (string key, string q, int start, int maxResults, boolean filter,
                string restrict, bool safeSearch, string lr, string ie, string oe);
```

As Listing 28-1 illustrates, the `<input>` child element of the `<operation>` element that represents the `doSpellingSuggestion` proxy method references the following `<message>` element, which means that this `message` element contains the names and types of the arguments of the `doSpellingSuggestion` proxy method:

```
<message name="doSpellingSuggestion">
    <part name="key" type="xsd:string"/>
    <part name="phrase" type="xsd:string"/>
</message>
```

Therefore, the declaration of the `doSpellingSuggestion` method is as follows:

```
doSpellingSuggestion (string key, string phrase);
```

The message attribute of the <output> subelement of each <operation> element, on the other hand, references the <message> element that contains information about the return value of the associated method. As Listing 28-1 shows, the <output> subelement of the <operation> element that represents the doGoogleSearch proxy method references the following <message> element, which means that this <message> element contains the type of the return value of the doGoogleSearch proxy method:

```
<message name="doGoogleSearchResponse">
  <part name="return" type="typens:GoogleSearchResult"/>
</message>
```

Therefore, the declaration of the doGoogleSearch method, including its return type, is as follows:

```
GoogleSearchResult doGoogleSearch (string key, string q, int start,
                        int maxResults, boolean filter, string restrict,
                        bool safeSearch, string lr, string ie, string oe);
```

As Listing 28-1 shows, the <output> subelement of the <operation> element that represents the doSpellingSuggestion proxy method references the following <message> element, which means that this <message> element contains the type of the return value of the doSpellingSuggestion method:

```
<message name="doSpellingSuggestionResponse">
  <part name="return"  type="xsd:string"/>
</message>
```

Therefore, the declaration of the doSpellingSuggestion method, including its return type, is as follows:

```
String doSpellingSuggestion (string key, string phrase);
```

As discussed, the return value of the doGoogleSearch method is an instance of a class named Google SearchResult. You can get the definition of this class out of Listing 28-1 as well. The <types> section of this listing contains an <xsd:complexType> element with the same name attribute value as the name of this class. This element contains the names and types of the properties of the GoogleSearchResult class as follows:

```
<xsd:complexType name="GoogleSearchResult">
  <xsd:all>
    <xsd:element name="documentFiltering"          type="xsd:boolean"/>
    <xsd:element name="searchComments"             type="xsd:string"/>
    <xsd:element name="estimatedTotalResultsCount" type="xsd:int"/>
    <xsd:element name="estimateIsExact"            type="xsd:boolean"/>
    <xsd:element name="resultElements"
        type="typens:ResultElementArray"/>
    <xsd:element name="searchQuery"                type="xsd:string"/>
    <xsd:element name="startIndex"                 type="xsd:int"/>
    <xsd:element name="endIndex"                   type="xsd:int"/>
    <xsd:element name="searchTips"                 type="xsd:string"/>
    <xsd:element name="searchTime"                 type="xsd:double"/>
      . . .
  </xsd:all>
</xsd:complexType>
```

Therefore the definition of the `GoogleSearchResult` class is as follows:

```
public class GoogleSearchResult
{
  public bool documentFiltering {get;}
  public string estimatedTotalResultsCount {get;}
  public bool estimateIsExact {get;}
  public ResultElement[] resultElements {get;}
  public string searchQuery {get;}
  public int startIndex {get;}
  public int endIndex {get;}
  public string searchTips {get;}
  public double searchTime {get;}
  . . .
}
```

Notice that the `GoogleSearchResult` class exposes a property named `resultElements`, which is an array of the instances of a class named `ResultElement`. The `<types>` section of the WSDL document shown in Listing 28-1 contains an `<xsd:complexType>` element with the same `name` attribute value as the name of the class. This element contains the names and types of the properties of the `Result Element` class as follows:

```
<xsd:complexType name="ResultElement">
  <xsd:all>
    <xsd:element name="summary" type="xsd:string"/>
    <xsd:element name="URL" type="xsd:string"/>
    <xsd:element name="snippet" type="xsd:string"/>
    <xsd:element name="title" type="xsd:string"/>
  </xsd:all>
</xsd:complexType>
```

Therefore the definition of the `ResultElement` class is as follows:

```
public class ResultElement
{
  public string summary {get;}
  public string URL {get;}
  public string snippet {get;}
  public string title {get;}
  . . .
}
```

In summary, the WSDL document describes the following proxy class:

```
public class GoogleSearchService : . . .
{
  public GoogleSearchResult
  doGoogleSearch (string key, string q, int start, int maxResults, boolean filter,
              string restrict, bool safeSearch, string lr, string ie, string oe);

  pubic string doSpellingSuggestion (string key, string phrase);
  . . .
}
```

In other words, you have to create an instance of the `GoogleSearchService` class and invoke the `doGoogleSearch` method to perform a Google search and the `doSpellingSuggestion` method to perform Google spell-checking. Here are the parameters of these two Google XML Web service methods. The following are the parameters of the `doGoogleSearch` method:

- ❑ `key`: As discussed, you need to create an account with Google to get this key.

- ❑ `q`: Specifies the search query.

- ❑ `start`: Specifies the index of the first search result to be retrieved. You'll use this to specify the next page of search results to be retrieved.

- ❑ `maxResults`: Specifies the maximum number of searh results to be retrieved. You'll use this to specify the maximum number of search results that the Ajax-enabled control should display. Basically, this is nothing but the page size.

- ❑ `filter`: Turns on or off filtering of similar search results or search results coming from the same host. You'll set this to true to improve the performance of the Ajax-enabled controls.

- ❑ `restrict`: Google uses the value of this parameter to filter the search result. You won't be using this filtering in your Ajax-enabled controls. You'll be passing an empty string as the value of this parameter.

- ❑ `safeSearch`: Set this flag to filter adult content. You'll set this flag to true.

- ❑ `lr`: Use this parameter to filter search results based on language. You won't be using any language-based filtering in your Ajax-enabled controls, so you'll pass an empty string as the value of this parameter.

- ❑ `ie`: Don't worry about this parameter because it has been depreciated. You'll pass an empty string as the value of this parameter.

- ❑ `oe`: Don't worry about this parameter either because it has been depreciated. You'll be passing an empty string as the value of this parameter as well.

The following are some of the properties of the `GoogleSearchResult` class. Recall that the `doGoogleSearch` method returns an instance of this class:

- ❑ `resultElements`: This is an array that contains one `ResultElement` object for each search result. You'll be iterating through these objects to extract the information about the search results.

- ❑ `startIndex`: The index of the first `ResultElement` object in the preceding array.

- ❑ `endIndex`: The index of the last `ResultElement` object in the preceding array.

The following are some of the properties of the `ResultElement` class. Recall that the `GoogleSearchResult` class exposes an array property name `resultElements` that contains instances of the `ResultElement` class, where each instance represents a search result. You'll be using these instances to access information about search results:

- ❑ `URL`: The URL of the search result that the `ResultElement` object represents.

- ❑ `snippet`: The HTML markup text that contains summary of the search result. You'll be displaying the value of this property in your Ajax-enabled control.

- ❑ `Title`: The HTML markup text that contains the title of the search result.

Keep the following limitations in mind when you're using Google XML Web service APIs. First, Google limits each query to 10 words or 2048 bytes; if you need to query a phrase that contains more than 10 words, you have to break it into groups of 10 words and perform a separate Google query for each group. Second, Google limits you to 1,000 queries per day. Make sure you don't exceed your daily query quota. Third, Google limits the maximum number of returned search results to 10. If you need to show more than 10 search results in a page, you have to make more requests to Google XML Web service to retrieve the extra records you need.

Predictive Fetch

Traditionally Web applications fetch data from the server on the user's demand. For example, a page may have a link that the user must click to download the data. This fetch-on-demand scenario enforces the click-and-wait user interaction pattern where the user has to click the link and wait for the data to be fetched from the server.

The Predictive Fetch Ajax pattern allows you to fetch the data and have it ready for use before the user clicks the link to alleviate the irritating waiting periods that interrupt the user workflow in a typical traditional Web application. This pattern is especially useful when an Ajax-enabled component has a way to predict the user's next move with a reasonable probability. This section develops a custom Ajax-enabled component named AjaxGoogleSearch that uses the Predictive Fetch pattern.

The AjaxGoogleSearch component is a Google-based search engine that consists of the following GUI elements, as shown in Figure 28-1:

❑   The text box where the user can enter a search query

❑   The button that the user clicks to perform the Google search

❑   The area where the search results are shown one page at time

❑   The command bar with next and previous links that allow the user to page through the search results

AjaxGoogleSearch uses the Google XML Web service API to perform the search. This API was thoroughly discussed in the previous section.

Now that you've learned the Google search XML Web service API, you can develop the AjaxGoogle Search Ajax-enabled control that uses the API to perform Google search. However, before getting into the details of the code, take a look at how the application works. Run the application, access the page shown in Listing 28-1, enter the desired search query, and click the Search button to perform a Google search. Now if you click the Next button, you'll notice AjaxGoogleSearch control displays the next page of search results as fast as a desktop control. This is because the control under the hood uses the Predictive Fetch Ajax pattern where it takes the following actions:

1.   Makes an asynchronous client callback request to the server to download the XML document that contains the next page of search results.

2.   Uses DOM, XML, and JavaScript to dynamically retrieve the search results from the XML document.

3.   Uses DOM and JavaScript to dynamically generate the HTML that displays the search results.

4.   Caches the HTML.

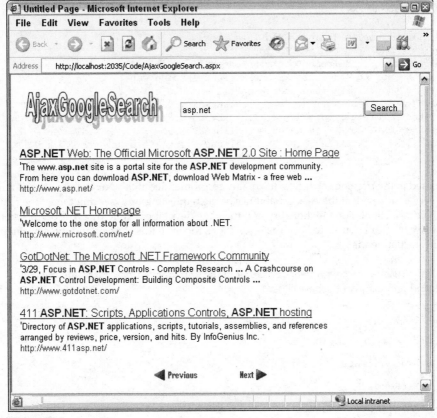

Figure 28-1

When the user clicks the Next button, `AjaxGoogleSearch` simply displays the content of the cache.

Listing 28-2 contains the code for the `AjaxGoogleSearch` control. The implementation of the methods and properties of this control is discussed in the following sections.

Listing 28-2: The AjaxGoogleSearch control

```
public class AjaxGoogleSearch : WebControl, ICallbackEventHandler
{
  public virtual bool EnableClientScript {get; set;}
  public virtual int PageSize {get; set;}
  public virtual string LicenseKey {get; set;}
  protected override void RenderContents(HtmlTextWriter writer);
  protected override void AddAttributesToRender(HtmlTextWriter writer);
  protected override HtmlTextWriterTag TagKey {get;}
  protected override Style CreateControlStyle();
  public virtual int CellPadding {get; set;}
  public virtual int CellSpacing {get; set;}
  public virtual HorizontalAlign HorizontalAlign {get; set;}
  public virtual string BackImageUrl {get; set;}
```

(continued)

Listing 28-2: *(continued)*

```
    public virtual GridLines GridLines {get; set;}
    private bool renderClientScript = false;
    protected virtual void DetermineRenderClientScript();
    private string GetCallbackEventReference(string func);
    protected override void OnPreRender(EventArgs e);
    protected virtual string GetCallbackResult();
    protected virtual void RaiseCallbackEvent(string eventArgument);
    string ICallbackEventHandler.GetCallbackResult();
    void ICallbackEventHandler.RaiseCallbackEvent(string eventArgument);
}
```

As discussed in the previous chapters, it's highly recommended that your custom control fall back on its pure server-side code if the Ajax capabilities of the requesting browser don't meet the requirements of your control's client-side functionality or if the page developer explicitly turns off the client-side functionality of your control. To keep the discussions focused, this chapter and the next chapter do not follow this recommendation.

The AjaxGoogleSearch component derives from the WebControl base class and overrides the following methods and properties of the base class:

❑   TagKey

❑   CreateControlStyle

❑   RenderContents

❑   OnPreRender

❑   AddAttributesToRender

The AjaxGoogleSearch component also implements the following methods of the ICallbackEventHandler interface:

❑   RaiseCallbackEvent

❑   GetCallbackResult

Deriving from WebControl

AjaxGoogleSearch overrides the TagKey property of the WebControl class to specify the table HTML element as its outermost or containing element:

```
protected override HtmlTextWriterTag TagKey
{
    get { return HtmlTextWriterTag.Table; }
}
```

AjaxGoogleSearch overrides the CreateControlStyle method of the WebControl class to use a TableStyle to style its containing table HTML element:

```
protected override Style CreateControlStyle()
{
  return new TableStyle(ViewState);
}
```

As discussed in previous chapters, when you override the CreateControlStyle method to use a new type of Style object you must also expose the properties of the new Style class as top-level properties of the control. Following this pattern AjaxGoogleSearch exposes the following five properties: Gridlines, HorizontalAlign, CellPadding, CellSpacing, and BackImageUrl.

Overriding RenderContents

Listing 28-3 contains the code for the AjaxGoogleSearch control's implementation of the RenderContents method. This method uses the techniques discussed in Chapter 2 to render the HTML markup text of AjaxGoogleSearch control. This control renders a table that includes three rows, where each row has three cells.

The first row contains a logo, the text box where the user enters the search query, and a button that the user clicks to perform the search. The second row contains two div HTML elements. The first div element is used to display the current page of search results. Recall that the AjaxGoogleSearch control displays the search results one page at a time and allows the user to use the Next and Previous buttons to search through the records page by page. The second div element is used to cache the next page of records. As you'll see later in this section, AjaxGoogleSearch uses the client callback behind the scenes to asynchronously retrieve the next page of search results and caches them in the second div HTML element. The third row contains the div HTML element that contains the Previous and Next buttons.

Listing 28-3: The RenderContents method

```
protected override void RenderContents(HtmlTextWriter writer)
{
  writer.RenderBeginTag(HtmlTextWriterTag.Tr);

  writer.AddAttribute(HtmlTextWriterAttribute.Valign, "top");
  writer.RenderBeginTag(HtmlTextWriterTag.Td);
  writer.AddStyleAttribute(HtmlTextWriterStyle.Width, "150");
  writer.AddStyleAttribute(HtmlTextWriterStyle.Height, "55");
  writer.AddStyleAttribute(HtmlTextWriterStyle.BorderWidth, "0");
  writer.AddAttribute(HtmlTextWriterAttribute.Alt, "AjaxGoogleSearch");
  writer.AddAttribute(HtmlTextWriterAttribute.Src, "logo_sm.gif");
  writer.RenderBeginTag(HtmlTextWriterTag.Img);
  writer.RenderEndTag();
  writer.RenderEndTag();

  writer.RenderBeginTag(HtmlTextWriterTag.Td);
  writer.Write("  ");
  writer.RenderEndTag();

  writer.RenderBeginTag(HtmlTextWriterTag.Td);
  writer.AddStyleAttribute(HtmlTextWriterStyle.BorderWidth, "0");
  writer.AddStyleAttribute("cellpadding", "0");
  writer.AddStyleAttribute("cellspacing", "0");
```

(continued)

Listing 28-3: *(continued)*

```
writer.RenderBeginTag(HtmlTextWriterTag.Table);
writer.RenderBeginTag(HtmlTextWriterTag.Tr);
writer.RenderBeginTag(HtmlTextWriterTag.Td);
writer.AddAttribute(HtmlTextWriterAttribute.Type, "text");
writer.AddAttribute(HtmlTextWriterAttribute.Id, ClientID + "_SearchTextBox");
writer.AddAttribute(HtmlTextWriterAttribute.Size, "41");
writer.RenderBeginTag(HtmlTextWriterTag.Input);
writer.RenderEndTag();

writer.AddAttribute(HtmlTextWriterAttribute.Onclick, "javascript:" +
                                        "NewSearch('" + ClientID + "')");
writer.RenderBeginTag(HtmlTextWriterTag.Button);
writer.Write("Search");
writer.RenderEndTag();
writer.RenderEndTag();
writer.RenderEndTag();
writer.RenderEndTag();
writer.RenderEndTag();

writer.RenderEndTag();

writer.RenderBeginTag(HtmlTextWriterTag.Tr);
writer.AddAttribute(HtmlTextWriterAttribute.Colspan, "3");
writer.RenderBeginTag(HtmlTextWriterTag.Td);

writer.AddStyleAttribute(HtmlTextWriterStyle.Display, "none");
writer.AddAttribute(HtmlTextWriterAttribute.Id, ClientID + "_SearchResultArea");
writer.RenderBeginTag(HtmlTextWriterTag.Div);
writer.RenderEndTag();

writer.AddStyleAttribute(HtmlTextWriterStyle.Display, "none");
writer.AddAttribute(HtmlTextWriterAttribute.Id, ClientID + "_Cache");
writer.RenderBeginTag(HtmlTextWriterTag.Div);
writer.RenderEndTag();

writer.RenderEndTag();
writer.RenderEndTag();

writer.RenderBeginTag(HtmlTextWriterTag.Tr);
writer.AddAttribute(HtmlTextWriterAttribute.Align, "center");
writer.AddAttribute(HtmlTextWriterAttribute.Colspan, "3");
writer.RenderBeginTag(HtmlTextWriterTag.Td);
writer.AddStyleAttribute(HtmlTextWriterStyle.Display, "none");
writer.AddAttribute(HtmlTextWriterAttribute.Id, ClientID + "_CommandBarArea");
writer.RenderBeginTag(HtmlTextWriterTag.Div);

writer.AddAttribute(HtmlTextWriterAttribute.Href, "javascript:" +
                                        "GetPreviousPage('" + ClientID + "')");
writer.RenderBeginTag(HtmlTextWriterTag.A);
writer.AddAttribute(HtmlTextWriterAttribute.Border, "0");
writer.AddAttribute(HtmlTextWriterAttribute.Alt, "Previous");
writer.AddAttribute(HtmlTextWriterAttribute.Src, "nav_previous.gif");
writer.RenderBeginTag(HtmlTextWriterTag.Img);
```

```
        writer.RenderEndTag();
        writer.RenderEndTag();


        writer.AddAttribute(HtmlTextWriterAttribute.Href, "javascript:" +
                                            "GetNextPage('"+ClientID+"')");

        writer.RenderBeginTag(HtmlTextWriterTag.A);
        writer.AddAttribute(HtmlTextWriterAttribute.Border, "0");
        writer.AddAttribute(HtmlTextWriterAttribute.Alt, "Next");
        writer.AddAttribute(HtmlTextWriterAttribute.Src, "nav_next.gif");
        writer.RenderBeginTag(HtmlTextWriterTag.Img);
        writer.RenderEndTag();
        writer.RenderEndTag();

        writer.RenderEndTag();
        writer.RenderEndTag();
        writer.RenderEndTag();
    }
```

Here's a review of the important parts of Listing 28-3. This listing sets the value of the id HTML attribute of the following elements to allow the client-side code to use DOM API to access these elements, as you'll see later:

❑   The input text element where the user enters the search query:

```
writer.AddAttribute(HtmlTextWriterAttribute.Type, "text");
writer.AddAttribute(HtmlTextWriterAttribute.Id, ClientID + "_SearchTextBox");
writer.AddAttribute(HtmlTextWriterAttribute.Size, "41");
writer.RenderBeginTag(HtmlTextWriterTag.Input);
```

❑   The div HTML element that displays the current page of search results:

```
writer.AddStyleAttribute(HtmlTextWriterStyle.Display, "none");
writer.AddAttribute(HtmlTextWriterAttribute.Id, ClientID + "_SearchResultArea");
writer.RenderBeginTag(HtmlTextWriterTag.Div);
writer.RenderEndTag();
```

❑   The div HTML element that caches the next page of search results:

```
writer.AddStyleAttribute(HtmlTextWriterStyle.Display, "none");
writer.AddAttribute(HtmlTextWriterAttribute.Id, ClientID + "_Cache");
writer.RenderBeginTag(HtmlTextWriterTag.Div);
writer.RenderEndTag();
```

Notice that the value of the display HTML attribute of this div HTML element is set to none to ensure that the users don't see the contents of the cache.

❑   The div HTML element that contains the Previous and Next buttons:

```
writer.AddStyleAttribute(HtmlTextWriterStyle.Display, "none");
writer.AddAttribute(HtmlTextWriterAttribute.Id, ClientID + "_CommandBarArea");
writer.RenderBeginTag(HtmlTextWriterTag.Div);
. . .
writer.AddAttribute(HtmlTextWriterAttribute.Src, "nav_previous.gif");
writer.RenderBeginTag(HtmlTextWriterTag.Img);
```

```
writer.RenderEndTag();
writer.RenderEndTag();
. . .
writer.AddAttribute(HtmlTextWriterAttribute.Src, "nav_next.gif");
writer.RenderBeginTag(HtmlTextWriterTag.Img);
writer.RenderEndTag();
writer.RenderEndTag();

writer.RenderEndTag();
```

As the highlighted portions of the code listing show, the value of the id HTML attribute of each element consists of two parts: the value of the ClientID property of the AjaxGoogleSearch control and a string value that uniquely identifies the element among other elements of the AjaxGoogleSearch control, such as _SearchTextBox, _SearchResultArea, _Cache, and _CommandBarArea. Recall that the value of the ClientID property is set by the page framework. This means that the combination of the value of this property and its associated string value uniquely identifies the associated element on the page in which the AjaxGoogleSearch has been used. You have to set the value of the id property of each element to a unique value to allow the client-side code to access them via DOM API.

As Listing 28-3 shows, the RenderContents method renders the following JavaScript functions as the values of the specified HTML attributes:

❑ NewSearch: This function uses the ASP.NET 2.0 client callback mechanism to asynchronously perform the specified Google search. RenderContents registers this function as the callback for the onclick client-side event of the Search button:

```
writer.AddAttribute(HtmlTextWriterAttribute.Onclick, "javascript:" +
                                            "NewSearch('" + ClientID + "')");
writer.RenderBeginTag(HtmlTextWriterTag.Button);
writer.Write("Search");
writer.RenderEndTag();
```

❑ GetPreviousPage: This function uses the ASP.NET 2.0 client callback mechanism to asynchronously retrieve the next page of search results. RenderContents renders the call to this function as the value of the href HTML attribute of the <a> HTML element that represents the Previous button:

```
writer.AddAttribute(HtmlTextWriterAttribute.Href, "javascript:" +
                                        "GetPreviousPage('" + ClientID + "')");
writer.RenderBeginTag(HtmlTextWriterTag.A);
writer.AddAttribute(HtmlTextWriterAttribute.Border, "0");
writer.AddAttribute(HtmlTextWriterAttribute.Alt, "Previous");
writer.AddAttribute(HtmlTextWriterAttribute.Src, "nav_previous.gif");
writer.RenderBeginTag(HtmlTextWriterTag.Img);
writer.RenderEndTag();
writer.RenderEndTag();
```

❑ GetNextPage: This function uses the ASP.NET 2.0 client callback mechanism to asynchronously retrieve the next page of search results. RenderContents renders the call to this function as the value of the href HTML attribute of the <a> HTML element that represents the Next button:

```
writer.AddAttribute(HtmlTextWriterAttribute.Href, "javascript:" +
                                        "GetNextPage('"+ClientID+"')");
```

```
writer.RenderBeginTag(HtmlTextWriterTag.A);
writer.AddAttribute(HtmlTextWriterAttribute.Border, "0");
writer.AddAttribute(HtmlTextWriterAttribute.Alt, "Next");
writer.AddAttribute(HtmlTextWriterAttribute.Src, "nav_next.gif");
writer.RenderBeginTag(HtmlTextWriterTag.Img);
writer.RenderEndTag();
writer.RenderEndTag();
```

Overriding OnPreRender

Listing 28-4 contains the code for the OnPreRender method. The main responsibility of this method is to register the required scripts with the page for rendering.

Listing 28-4: The OnPreRender method

```
protected override void OnPreRender(EventArgs e)
{
  DetermineRenderClientScript();
  if (renderClientScript)
  {
    string js =

      "function NewSearch (ajaxGoogleSearchId)
      {" +
        "var ajaxGoogleSearch = document.getElementById(ajaxGoogleSearchId);" +
        "ajaxGoogleSearch.requestedPageIndex = 0;" +
        GetCallbackEventReference("AjaxGoogleSearchNewSearchCallback") +
      ";}";

    js +=

      "function GetNextPage (ajaxGoogleSearchId)" +
      "{" +
        "GetCachedPage(ajaxGoogleSearchId);"+
      "}";

    js +=

      "function GetPreviousPage (ajaxGoogleSearchId)" +
      "{" +
        "var ajaxGoogleSearch = document.getElementById(ajaxGoogleSearchId);" +
        "var pageIndex = parseInt(ajaxGoogleSearch.pageIndex) - "+
                  "parseInt(ajaxGoogleSearch.pageSize);" +
        "ajaxGoogleSearch.requestedPageIndex = pageIndex;" +
        GetCallbackEventReference("AjaxGoogleSearchPreviousPageCallback") +
      ";}";

    js +=

      "function GetNextPageForCache ()" +
      "{" +
        "var ajaxGoogleSearchId = '" + ClientID + "';" +
        "var ajaxGoogleSearch = document.getElementById(ajaxGoogleSearchId);" +
```

(continued)

899

Listing 28-4: *(continued)*

```
                "var pageIndex = parseInt(ajaxGoogleSearch.pageIndex) + " +
                            "parseInt(ajaxGoogleSearch.pageSize);" +
            "ajaxGoogleSearch.requestedPageIndex = pageIndex;" +
            GetCallbackEventReference("AjaxGoogleSearchCacheCallback") + ";" +
           "}";

        Page.ClientScript.RegisterClientScriptBlock(typeof(AjaxGoogleSearch),
                    typeof(AjaxGoogleSearch).FullName + "MakeHttpRequest", js, true);

        Page.ClientScript.RegisterClientScriptResource(typeof(AjaxGoogleSearch),
                                    "CustomComponents.AjaxGoogleSearch.js");

        Page.ClientScript.RegisterStartupScript(typeof(AjaxGoogleSearch),
                    typeof(AjaxGoogleSearch).FullName + "MakeHttpRequest22",
                    "GetNextPageForCache();", true);
    }
    base.OnPreRender(e);
}
```

The following sections discuss the JavaScript functions that the `OnPreRender` method registers with the page for rendering.

Performing a New Google Search

As Listing 28-4 shows, `OnPreRender` registers the `NewSearch` JavaScript function with the containing page for rendering. Listing 28-5 presents the implementation of this function.

Listing 28-5: The NewSearch JavaScript function

```
        "function NewSearch (ajaxGoogleSearchId)
        {" +
          "var ajaxGoogleSearch = document.getElementById(ajaxGoogleSearchId);" +
          "ajaxGoogleSearch.requestedPageIndex = 0;" +
          GetCallbackEventReference("AjaxGoogleSearchNewSearchCallback") +
        ";}";
```

The `NewSearch` function takes the value of the `id` HTML attribute of the containing HTML element of the `AjaxGoogleSearch` control as its argument. `NewSearch` first calls the `getElementById` method of the `document` DOM object to access the containing element of the `AjaxGoogleSearch` control, that is, the `table` HTML element:

```
var ajaxGoogleSearch = document.getElementById(ajaxGoogleSearchId);
```

`NewSearch` then sets the value of the `requestedPageIndex` attribute of the containing `table` HTML element of the `AjaxGoogleSearch` control to zero to specify that the first page of search results should be retrieved. The `requestedPageIndex` attribute is not a standard HTML attribute. It is a custom attribute:

```
ajaxGoogleSearch.requestedPageIndex = 0;
```

NewSearch then runs the JavaScript code that the GetCallbackEventReference method of the AjaxGoogleSearch control returns:

```
GetCallbackEventReference("AjaxGoogleSearchNewSearchCallback")
```

Listing 28-6 contains the implementation of the GetCallbackEventReference method.

Listing 28-6: The GetCallbackEventReference method

```
private string GetCallbackEventReference(string func)
{
  string callbackEventReference = Page.ClientScript.GetCallbackEventReference(
                      this,
                      "GetInputDataForServerMethod('" + ClientID + "')",
                      func,
                      "'" + ClientID + "'", false);
  return callbackEventReference;
}
```

The GetCallbackEventReference method of the AjaxGoogleSearch control calls the GetCallbackEventReference method of the ClientScript property of the page to return the JavaScript function that contains the code that makes the asynchronous callback to the server. Notice that the GetCallbackEventReference method of the AjaxGoogleSearch control passes its argument as the third argument of the GetCallbackEventReference method of the ClientScript property. Recall from the previous chapter that the third argument contains the JavaScript function that will be automatically called when the server response arrives.

As Listing 28-6 shows, the GetCallbackEventReference method of the AjaxGoogleSearch control passes a call to the GetInputDataForServerMethod JavaScript function as the second argument of the GetCallbackEventReference method of the ClientScript property. Recall from the previous chapter that the second argument contains the JavaScript code that uses DHTML to retrieve the data that the client passes to the server-side method that handles the client callback.

Listing 28-7 presents the implementation of the GetInputDataForServerMethod JavaScript function.

Listing 28-7: The GetInputDataForServerMethod JavaScript function

```
function GetInputDataForServerMethod(ajaxGoogleSearchId)
{
  var pageIndex = document.getElementById(ajaxGoogleSearchId).requestedPageIndex;

  if (pageIndex < 0)
     pageIndex = 0;

  var searchText =
          document.getElementById(ajaxGoogleSearchId+"_SearchTextBox").value;

  var xmlDocument = CreateXmlDocument();
  var queryInfo = xmlDocument.createElement("queryInfo");
  xmlDocument.appendChild(queryInfo);

  var pageIndexElement = xmlDocument.createElement("pageIndex");
```

(continued)

Listing 28-7: *(continued)*

```
        pageIndexElement.text = pageIndex;

        queryInfo.appendChild(pageIndexElement);
        var searchQuery = xmlDocument.createElement("searchQuery");

        searchQuery.text = searchText;
        queryInfo.appendChild(searchQuery);

        return xmlDocument.xml;
    }
```

The GetInputDataForServerMethod JavaScript function takes the value of the id HTML attribute of the containing table HTML element of the AjaxGoogleSearch control as its argument. The function then calls the getElementById method of the document DOM object to access the containing table HTML element of the AjaxGoogleSearch control. As shown in Listing 28-5, the NewSearch JavaScript function sets the requestedPageIndex custom HTML attribute to zero to specify that the first page of records should be retrieved.

As Listing 28-7 illustrates, the GetInputDataForServerMethod JavaScript function concatenates the value of the id HTML attribute of the containing table element with the string value _SearchTextBox to evaluate the value of the id HTML attribute of the text box control where the user enters the search query. It then passes this value to the getElementById method of the document DOM object to access the text box and subsequently the search query that the user has entered in the text box:

```
var searchText =
               document.getElementById(ajaxGoogleSearchId+"_SearchTextBox").value;
```

Because the data that AjaxGoogleSearch sends to the server is in XML format, the first order of business is to decide on the structure of the XML document. The following shows an example of the XML document that the AjaxGoogleSearch control sends back to the server:

```
<queryInfo>
   <pageIndex>0</pageIndex>
   <searchQuery>ASP.NET</searchQuery>
</queryInfo>
```

Like all XML documents, this document must have a single document element. The document element in this example is the <queryInfo> element. The document element of this XML document contains two subelements. The first subelement contains the index of the page of search results to be retrieved. The second subelement contains the search query that the user has entered in the search query text box.

As Listing 28-7 illustrates, the GetInputDataForServerMethod function uses DOM and XML to dynamically generate the XML document that will be sent to the server. GetInputDataForServerMethod first calls the CreateXmlDocument JavaScript function discussed in the previous chapter to create the DOM object that will represent the entire XML document. In other words, this DOM object represents the root node of the XML document:

```
var xmlDocument = CreateXmlDocument();
```

GetInputDataForServerMethod then uses the DOM API to generate the <queryInfo>, <pageIndex>, and <searchQuery> elements of the XML document and their contents. The DOM object that represents the root node exposes a method named `createElement` that creates the XML element with the specified name. `GetInputDataForServerMethod` calls the `createElement` method three times to create the three DOM objects that represent the three XML elements of the document:

```
var queryInfo = xmlDocument.createElement("queryInfo");
var pageIndexElement = xmlDocument.createElement("pageIndex");
var searchQuery = xmlDocument.createElement("searchQuery");
```

It then uses the `text` property of the DOM object that represents the `<pageIndex>` and `<searchQuery>` elements to set the contents of these elements:

```
pageIndexElement.text = pageIndex;
searchQuery.text = searchText;
```

The `createElement` method doesn't add the element that it creates to the document. You have to explicitly call the `appendChild` method to append each element to its parent:

```
xmlDocument.appendChild(queryInfo);
queryInfo.appendChild(pageIndexElement);
queryInfo.appendChild(searchQuery);
```

Finally, `GetInputDataForServerMethod` returns the value of the `xml` property of the DOM object that represents the root node. The value of this property contains the entire contents of the XML document:

```
return xmlDocument.xml;
```

Now back to Listing 28-5. As this code listing shows, the `NewSearch` function contains the JavaScript function that the `GetClientCallbackReference` method of the `AjaxGoogleSearch` method returns. Notice that Listing 28-5 passes the string value `AjaxGoogleSearchNewSearchCallback` into the `GetCallbackEventReference` method. This string value is the name of the JavaScript function that will be called when the server response arrives:

```
GetCallbackEventReference("AjaxGoogleSearchNewSearchCallback"
```

Listing 28-8 contains the implementation of the `AjaxGoogleSearchNewSearchCallback` JavaScript function.

Listing 28-8: The AjaxGoogleSearchNewSearchCallback JavaScript function

```
function AjaxGoogleSearchNewSearchCallback(result,context)
{
  var htmlAndPageIndex = GetHtmlAndPageIndex(result);
  var ajaxGoogleSearch = document.getElementById(context);
  var commandBarArea = document.getElementById(context+"_CommandBarArea");
  commandBarArea.style.display = "block";
  var searchResultArea = document.getElementById(context+"_SearchResultArea");
  searchResultArea.style.display = "block";
  ajaxGoogleSearch.pageIndex = htmlAndPageIndex[1];
  searchResultArea.innerHTML = htmlAndPageIndex[0];
  GetNextPageForCache();
}
```

`AjaxGoogleSearchNewSearchCallback` performs the following tasks.

It calls the `GetHtmlAndPageIndex` JavaScript function and passes the return value of the server-side method into it. This function is discussed shortly. This function does exactly what its name says it does — it returns the HTML markup text that displays the search results and the page index of the page of search results being displayed.

```
var htmlAndPageIndex = GetHtmlAndPageIndex(result);
```

Next, the function calls the `getElementById` method of the `document` DOM object and passes its second argument into it to access the containing `table` HTML element of the `AjaxGoogleSearch` control. Recall from Listing 28-6 that the fourth argument of the `GetCallbackEventReference` method of the `ClientScript` property of the page contains the value of the `id` HTML attribute of the containing `table` HTML element of the `AjaxGoogleSearch` control. This value is automatically passed into the `AjaxGoogleSearchNewSearchCallback` function as its second argument:

```
var ajaxGoogleSearch = document.getElementById(context);
```

The function then calls the `getElementById` method to access the `div` HTML element that contains the Previous and Next buttons to display the element. Notice that `AjaxGoogleSearchNewSearchCallback` concatenates the value of the `id` HTML attribute of the containing `table` HTML element of the `AjaxGoogleSearch` control with the string value `_CommandBarArea` to evaluate the value of the `id` HTML attribute of the `div` HTML element that contains the `previous` and `next` buttons:

```
var commandBarArea = document.getElementById(context+"_CommandBarArea");
commandBarArea.style.display = "block";
```

The function then uses the same steps just described to access the `div` HTML element that displays the search results:

```
var searchResultArea = document.getElementById(context+"_SearchResultArea");
searchResultArea.style.display = "block";
```

It then assigns the values that the `GetHtmlAndPageIndex` function returns to the `pageIndex` and `innerHTML` properties of the DOM object that represents the `AjaxGoogleSearch` control. Recall that `pageIndex` isn't a standard HTML attribute. It's a custom attribute.

```
ajaxGoogleSearch.pageIndex = htmlAndPageIndex[1];
searchResultArea.innerHTML = htmlAndPageIndex[0];
```

Next, it calls the `GetNextPageForCache` JavaScript function to retrieve the next page of search results from the server and to cache the results. Because the next page of research results are already cached and ready for use, when the user clicks the Next button, `AjaxGoogleSearch` displays the next page immediately. This allows `AjaxGoogleSearch` to act and feel like its desktop counterpart.

```
GetNextPageForCache();
```

Recall from Listing 28-4 that the `OnPreRender` method registers the `GetNextPageForCache` JavaScript function with the page for rendering. Listing 28-9 presents the implementation of this function.

Listing 28-9: The GetNextPageForCache JavaScript function

```
"function GetNextPageForCache ()" +
"{" +
```

```
"var ajaxGoogleSearchId = '" + ClientID + "';" +
"var ajaxGoogleSearch = document.getElementById(ajaxGoogleSearchId);" +
"var pageIndex = parseInt(ajaxGoogleSearch.pageIndex) + " +
            "parseInt(ajaxGoogleSearch.pageSize);" +
"ajaxGoogleSearch.requestedPageIndex = pageIndex;" +
GetCallbackEventReference("AjaxGoogleSearchCacheCallback") + ";" +
"}";
```

`GetNextPageForCache` passes the value of the `id` HTML attribute of the containing `table` HTML element of the `AjaxGoogleSearch` control to the `getElementbyId` method of the `document` DOM object to access the containing element:

```
"var ajaxGoogleSearchId = '" + ClientID + "';" +
"var ajaxGoogleSearch = document.getElementById(ajaxGoogleSearchId);" +
```

It then adds the page size to the current page index to evaluate the page index for the next page of search results:

```
"var pageIndex = parseInt(ajaxGoogleSearch.pageIndex) + " +
            "parseInt(ajaxGoogleSearch.pageSize);" +
```

Next, it assigns the new page index to the `requestedPageIndex` property of the containing `table` HTML element. As you'll see shortly, the value of this property will be passed to the server so the server knows which page of search results should be retrieved:

```
"ajaxGoogleSearch.requestedPageIndex = pageIndex;" +
```

Finally, `GetNextPageForCache` runs the JavaScript function that contains the code that makes the client request to the server:

```
GetCallbackEventReference("AjaxGoogleSearchCacheCallback") + ";" +
```

Notice that the string value `AjaxGoogleSearchCacheCallback` is passed into the `GetCallbackEventReference` method of the `AjaxGoogleSearch` control. Recall from Listing 28-6 that this string value is the name of the JavaScript function that will be automatically called when the server response arrives.

Listing 28-10 contains the implementation of the `AjaxGoogleSearchCacheCallback` JavaScript function.

Listing 28-10: The AjaxGoogleSearchCacheCallback JavaScript function

```
function AjaxGoogleSearchCacheCallback(result,context)
{
  var htmlAndPageIndex = GetHtmlAndPageIndex(result);
  var ajaxGoogleSearch = document.getElementById(context);
  ajaxGoogleSearch.cachedPageIndex = htmlAndPageIndex[1];
  var cache = document.getElementById(context+"_Cache");
  cache.innerHTML = htmlAndPageIndex[0];
}
```

The implementation of the `AjaxGoogleSearchCacheCallback` function is very similar to the implementation of `AjaxGoogleSearchNewPageCallback` shown in Listing 28-8, with one big difference.

`AjaxGoogleSearchCacheCallback` doesn't assign the HTML to the `innerHTML` property of the `div` HTML element that displays the search results. Instead it assigns the HTML to the `innerHTML` property of the invisible `div` HTML element that is used as the cache:

```
var cache = document.getElementById(context+"_Cache");
cache.innerHTML = htmlAndPageIndex[0];
```

Retrieving and Displaying the Next Page of Search Results

As shown in Listing 28-4, the `OnPreRender` method registers the `GetNextPage` JavaScript function with the page for rendering as shown in Listing 28-11.

Listing 28-11: The GetNextPage JavaScript function

```
"function GetNextPage (ajaxGoogleSearchId)" +
"{" +
  "GetCachedPage(ajaxGoogleSearchId);"+
"}";
```

`GetNextPage` simply calls the `GetCachedPage` JavaScript function to retrieve the next page of search results from the cache. Because the next page is retrieved from the cache as opposed to the server, when the user clicks the Next button, `AjaxGoogleSearch` control displays the next page immediately, allowing the control to act and feel like a desktop component.

Listing 28-12 shows the implementation of the `GetCachedPage` JavaScript function.

Listing 28-12: The GetCachedPage JavaScript function

```
function GetCachedPage(ajaxGoogleSearchId)
{
  var searchResultArea =
              document.getElementById(ajaxGoogleSearchId+"_SearchResultArea");
  var cache = document.getElementById(ajaxGoogleSearchId+"_Cache");

  if (cache.innerHTML != "")
  {
    searchResultArea.innerHTML = cache.innerHTML;
    var ajaxGoogleSearch = document.getElementById(ajaxGoogleSearchId);
    ajaxGoogleSearch.pageIndex = ajaxGoogleSearch.cachedPageIndex;
  }
  GetNextPageForCache();
}
```

`GetCachedPage` first accesses the `div` HTML element that's used as the cache:

```
var searchResultArea =
              document.getElementById(ajaxGoogleSearchId+"_SearchResultArea");
var cache = document.getElementById(ajaxGoogleSearchId+"_Cache");
```

It then checks whether the cache is empty. If not, it loads the content of the cache into the `div` HTML element that displays the search results:

```
searchResultArea.innerHTML = cache.innerHTML;
```

Next, `GetCachedPage` accesses the containing `table` HTML element of the `AjaxGoogleSearch` control and assigns the value of its `cachedPageIndex` property to its `pageIndex` property. Recall that the `pageIndex` attribute of the containing element specifies the index of the currently displayed page of search results:

```
var ajaxGoogleSearch = document.getElementById(ajaxGoogleSearchId);
ajaxGoogleSearch.pageIndex = ajaxGoogleSearch.cachedPageIndex;
```

Finally `GetCachedPage` calls the `GetNextPageForCache` JavaScript function to asynchronously retrieve the next page of search results from the server and to cache the results in the cache. The next time the user clicks the Next button, `AjaxGoogleSearch` control will display the next page of search results immediately, just like a desktop control.

Retrieving and Displaying the Previous Page of Search Results

As shown in Listing 28-4, the `OnPreRender` method registers the `GetPreviousPage` JavaScript function with the page for rendering as shown in Listing 28-13.

Listing 28-13: The GetPreviousPage JavaScript function

```
"function GetPreviousPage (ajaxGoogleSearchId)" +
"{" +
  "var ajaxGoogleSearch = document.getElementById(ajaxGoogleSearchId);" +
  "var pageIndex = parseInt(ajaxGoogleSearch.pageIndex) - "+
              "parseInt(ajaxGoogleSearch.pageSize);" +
  "ajaxGoogleSearch.requestedPageIndex = pageIndex;" +
  GetCallbackEventReference("AjaxGoogleSearchPreviousPageCallback") +
";}";
```

`GetPreviousPage` first accesses the containing `table` HTML element of the `AjaxGoogleSearch` control:

```
"var ajaxGoogleSearch = document.getElementById(ajaxGoogleSearchId);" +
```

It then subtracts the page size from the page index of the currently displayed page to evaluate the index of the previous page:

```
"var pageIndex = parseInt(ajaxGoogleSearch.pageIndex) - "+
              "parseInt(ajaxGoogleSearch.pageSize);" +
```

`GetPreviousPage` then assigns this page index to the `requestedPageIndex` property of the containing element to specify which page of search results should be retrieved. As you'll later, this index will be passed to the server so the server knows which page of search results to retrieve.

```
"ajaxGoogleSearch.requestedPageIndex = pageIndex;" +
```

`GetPreviousPage` then runs the Javascript function that contains the code that makes the asynchronous callback to the server:

```
GetCallbackEventReference("AjaxGoogleSearchPreviousPageCallback") +
```

Notice that the string value `AjaxGoogleSearchPreviousPageCallback` is passed into the `GetCallbackEventReference` method of the `AjaxGoogleSearch` control. Recall from Listing 28-6 that this string value is the name of the JavaScript function that will be automatically called when the server response arrives.

Listing 28-14 shows the implementation of the `AjaxGoogleSearchPreviousPageCallback` JavaScript function.

Listing 28-14: The AjaxGoogleSearchPreviousPageCallback JavaScript function

```
function AjaxGoogleSearchPreviousPageCallback(result,context)
{
  var htmlAndPageIndex = GetHtmlAndPageIndex(result);
  var ajaxGoogleSearch = document.getElementById(context);
  var searchResultArea = document.getElementById(context+"_SearchResultArea");
  ajaxGoogleSearch.pageIndex = htmlAndPageIndex[1];
  searchResultArea.innerHTML = htmlAndPageIndex[0];
  GetNextPageForCache();
}
```

The implementation of `AjaxGoogleSearchPreviousPageCallback` is very similar to the implementation of the `AjaxGoogleSearchNewSearchCallback` JavaScript function.

Using DOM and XML to Generate the HTML

As discussed in the previous sections, `AjaxGoogleSearchNewSearchCallback` (see Listing 28-8), `AjaxGoogleSearchCacheCallback` (see Listing 28-10), and `AjaxGoogleSearchPreviousPage Callback` (see Listing 28-14) first call the `GetHtmlAndPageIndex` JavaScript function to generate the HTML and to access the index of the current page, as shown in Listing 28-15.

Listing 28-15: The GetHtmlAndPageIndex JavaScript function

```
function GetHtmlAndPageIndex(xmlData)
{
  var content = "";
  var title;
  var snippet;
  var url;
  var resultElement;

  var xmlDocument = CreateXmlDocument();
  xmlDocument.loadXML(xmlData);
  var searchResult = xmlDocument.documentElement;

  for (var i=0; i<searchResult.childNodes.length; i++)
  {
    resultElement = searchResult.childNodes[i];
    title = resultElement.childNodes[0].text;
    snippet = resultElement.childNodes[1].text;
    url = resultElement.childNodes[2].text;

    content += "<p class='g'>";
```

```
            content +=   "<a class='l' href='"+url+"'>"+title+"</a><table cellpadding='0'
                         cellspacing='0' border='0'>";
            content +=   "<tr><td class='j'>'<font size='-1'>";
            content += snippet;
            content += "<br><font color='#008000'>"+url+"</font></font></td>
                         </tr></table></p>";
        }

        var pageIndex = searchResult.getAttribute("pageIndex");
        var result = new Array();
        result[0] = content;
        result[1] = pageIndex;
        return result;
    }
```

The main responsibility of the GetHtmlAndPageIndex JavaScript function is to use the XML document or data that it has received from the server to generate the HTML that displays the XML data. Before you get into the details of the implementation of the GetHtmlAndPageIndex JavaScript function, you need to understand the structure of the XML document that the function receives from the server. As an Ajax-enabled component developer, one of your responsibilities is to decide on the structure of the XML document that will contain the data. AjaxGoogleSearch control uses the XML structure shown in Listing 28-16.

Listing 28-16: The XML structure that AjaxGoogleSearch control uses

```
<searchResult pageIndex="1">
  <resultElement>
    <title>ASP.NET 2.0</title>
    <snippet>The msdn site . . .</snippet>
    <url>http://msdn.microsoft.com</url>
  </resultElement>
  . . .
</searchResult>
```

As Listing 28-16 shows, the XML document that the client receives from the server has a document element named <searchResult> that has an attribute named pageIndex whose value specifies the index of the page of search results that the document contains. This document element contains zero or more <resultElement> subelements where each subelement, in turn, contains three child elements: <title>, <snippet>, and <url>.

Now look back at Listing 28-15. As this code listing shows, GetHtmlAndPageIndex first calls the CreateXmlDocument JavaScript function discussed in the previous chapter to create the DOM object that will be used as the data store for the XML document received from the server:

```
var xmlDocument = CreateXmlDocument();
```

It then loads the XML document that it has received from the server into the XML data store:

```
xmlDocument.loadXML(xmlData);
```

Next, it accesses the document element of the XML document; that is, the <searchResult> element shown in Listing 28-16:

```
var searchResult = xmlDocument.documentElement;
```

Next, GetHtmlAndPageIndex iterates through the `<resultElement>` subelements of the `<searchResult>` document element and takes the following actions for each enumerated subelement:

1. It accesses the DOM object that represents the enumerated `<resultElement>` subelement:

```
resultElement = searchResult.childNodes[i];
```

2. It accesses the DOM objects that represent the `<title>`, `<snippet>`, and `<url>` subelements of the enumerated `<resultElement>` element and assigns the values of the text property of these DOM objects to the associated local variables. The text property contains the content within the opening and closing tags of the `<title>`, `<snippet>`, or `<url>` element:

```
title = resultElement.childNodes[0].text;
snippet = resultElement.childNodes[1].text;
url = resultElement.childNodes[2].text;
```

3. It generates the HTML that displays the retrieved title, snippet, and URL values:

```
content += "<p class='g'>";
content += "<a class='l' href='"+url+"'>"+title+"</a><table cellpadding='0'
            cellspacing='0' border='0'>";
content += "<tr><td class='j'><font size='-1'>";
content += snippet;
content += "<br><font color='#008000'>"+url+"</font></font></td>
            </tr></table></p>";
```

GetHtmlAndPageIndex then retrieves the index of the currently displayed page:

```
var pageIndex = searchResult.getAttribute("pageIndex");
```

Finally, it returns both the generated HTML and the page index to its caller.

Overriding AddAttributesToRender

Listing 28-17 contains the code for the AddAttributesToRender method.

Listing 28-17: The AddAttributesToRender method

```
protected override void AddAttributesToRender(HtmlTextWriter writer)
{
  base.AddAttributesToRender(writer);
  writer.AddAttribute("pageIndex", "0");
  writer.AddAttribute("pageSize", PageSize.ToString());
  writer.AddAttribute("requestedPageIndex","0");
  writer.AddAttribute("pageIndexUserIsWaitingFor", "-1");
  writer.AddAttribute("cachedPageIndex", "-1");
}
```

AjaxGoogleSearch overrides the AddAttributesToRender method to initialize the non-standard HTML attributes of its containing table HTML element. Notice that AjaxGoogleSearch exposes a property named PageSize that the page developer can use to specify the maximum number of search results that each page should display.

Implementing ICallbackEventHandler

The `AjaxGoogleSearch` control uses the C# interface implementation pattern to implement the `ICallbackEventHandler`. Following the pattern, the control defines two protected virtual methods with the same signatures as the methods of the `ICallbackEventHandler` interface, as shown in Listing 28-18.

Listing 28-18: The protected virtual methods

```
private string callbackResult = string.Empty;
protected virtual string GetCallbackResult()
{
  return callbackResult;
}

protected virtual void RaiseCallbackEvent(string eventArgument)
{
  int pageIndex = 0;
  string searchQuery = string.Empty;

  using (StringReader sreader = new StringReader(eventArgument))
  {
    using (XmlReader xreader = XmlReader.Create(sreader))
    {
      while (xreader.Read())
      {
        if (xreader.NodeType == XmlNodeType.Element)
        {
          if (xreader.LocalName == "pageIndex")
            pageIndex = xreader.ReadElementContentAsInt();
          if (xreader.LocalName == "searchQuery")
            searchQuery = xreader.ReadElementContentAsString();
        }
      }
    }
  }

  if (pageIndex < 0)
    pageIndex = 0;

  GoogleSearchService service = new GoogleSearchService();

  GoogleSearchResult result = service.doGoogleSearch(LicenseKey, searchQuery,
                              pageIndex, PageSize, true, "", true, "", "", "");

  using (StringWriter sw = new StringWriter())
  {
    using (XmlWriter xw = XmlWriter.Create(sw))
    {
      xw.WriteStartDocument();
      xw.WriteStartElement("searchResult");
      xw.WriteAttributeString("pageIndex", pageIndex.ToString());
      foreach (ResultElement element in result.resultElements)
      {
```

(continued)

911

Listing 28-18: *(continued)*

```
        xw.WriteStartElement("resultElement");
        xw.WriteElementString("title", element.title);
        xw.WriteElementString("snippet", element.snippet);
        xw.WriteElementString("URL", element.URL);
        xw.WriteEndElement();
      }
    xw.WriteEndElement();
    xw.WriteEndDocument();
    }
  callbackResult = sw.ToString();
  }


}
```

As Listing 28-18 shows, the `RaiseCallbackEvent` method takes a string argument. This argument contains the XML document that the `GetInputDataForServerMethod` JavaScript function generates (see Listing 28-7). `RaiseCallbackEvent` first loads the XML document into a `StringReader`, which is then loaded into an `XmlReader`. `RaiseCallbackEvent` uses the `XmlReader` API discussed in Chapter 24 to retrieve the page index and the search query from the XML document:

```
using (StringReader sreader = new StringReader(eventArgument))
{
  using (XmlReader xreader = XmlReader.Create(sreader))
  {
    while (xreader.Read())
    {
      if (xreader.NodeType == XmlNodeType.Element)
      {
        if (xreader.LocalName == "pageIndex")
          pageIndex = xreader.ReadElementContentAsInt();
        if (xreader.LocalName == "searchQuery")
          searchQuery = xreader.ReadElementContentAsString();
      }
    }
  }
}
```

`RaiseCallbackEvent` then creates an instance of the Google proxy class:

```
GoogleSearchService service = new GoogleSearchService();
```

Next, it invokes the `doGoogleSearch` method of the proxy instance to retrieve the search results from the Google XML Web service:

```
GoogleSearchResult result = service.doGoogleSearch(LicenseKey, searchQuery,
                                pageIndex, PageSize, true, "", true, "", "", "");
```

`RaiseCallbackEvent` then uses the `XmlWriter` API discussed in Chapter 24 to generate the XML document shown in Listing 28-16. This XML document will then be sent back to the client.

Listing 28-19 contains a page the uses the `AjaxGoogleSearch` control. Figure 28-1 shows what end users see when they access this page.

Listing 28-19: A page that uses AjaxGoogleSearch control

```
<%@ Page Language="C#" %>
<%@ Register TagPrefix="custom" Namespace="CustomComponents"
Assembly="CustomComponents" %>
<html xmlns="http://www.w3.org/1999/xhtml">
<body>
  <form id="form1" runat="server">
    <custom:AjaxGoogleSearch runat="server" ID="mycontrol" />
  </form>
</body>
</html>
```

Run this page, enter a search query, and click the Search button to perform the Google search. Now if you click the Next button, you'll notice `AjaxGoogleSearch` control displays the next page of search results as fast as a desktop control.

The Predictive Fetch Ajax pattern is applicable in those Web applications or Ajax-enabled components where you can predict the user's next move with a reasonable probability. `AjaxGoogleSearch` is an example of such an Ajax-enabled control. It's reasonable to assume that the user will click the Next button to move to the next page of search results. However, if the command bar of the `AjaxGoogleSearch` control contained number buttons to allow random page access, you wouldn't be able to predict the user's next move because the user could access the pages randomly.

Keep in mind the Predictive Fetch Ajax pattern is just a guessing game. It's all about reasonable probabilities. You should ask yourself what is the most probable thing the user may do next. For example, the current implementation of the `GetNextPage` JavaScript function takes the following two steps, as shown in Listings 28-11 and 28-12:

1. Displays the content of the cache.

2. Makes an asynchronous client callback to the server to download and cache the next page.

If the cache is empty, the current implementation skips the first step and simply downloads and caches the next page. You can go ahead and add more JavaScript code to the `GetNextPage` function to handle this situation. However, before doing this, you should ask yourself under what circumstances the cache could be empty.

As an example, consider the following two circumstances under which the cache could be empty:

❑ The user clicks the Search or Previous button, and then immediately clicks the Next button before the next page is downloaded and cached.

❑ The `GetNextPageForCache` function fails due to network, software, or hardware failure, which means that the next page isn't downloaded and cached.

Keep in mind that the main goal behind the Predictive Pattern is to predict the next move of the user with reasonable probability. What is the most probable thing the user will do after clicking the Search or

Previous buttons? I think it's fair to say most users wouldn't immediately click the Next button. Therefore you can rule out this circumstance with reasonable accuracy. How about the second one? What would the user do in this circumstance? I think it's fair to say the user would click the Next button again, which means you're back to the click-and-wait scenario. Keep in mind that the key thing is probability. How often can you have network, software, or hardware failure? If the answer is very often, then you should go ahead and add more code to the `GetNextPage` to handle the case of a failure. If the answer is very rarely, you may decide that it's OK if the user clicks and waits once in a while. As these discussions show, it can be difficult to implement the Predictive Fetch pattern because it's difficult to predict what will happen next.

Which Ajax pattern you should use depends on the specifics of your applications. In other words, one size doesn't fit all.

Summary

This chapter first provided you with an in-depth coverage of the Google XML Web service API. It then discussed a popular Ajax pattern known as Predictive Fetch and used the pattern to develop an Ajax-enabled control named `AjaxGoogleSearch` that uses Google XML Web service API to perform Google search. The next chapter discusses three more Ajax patterns and uses them to develop three more Ajax-enabled controls.

Developing Ajax-Enabled Controls and Components: More Ajax Patterns

The previous chapter discussed the Predictive Fetch Ajax pattern and used the pattern to develop an Ajax-enabled control named `AjaxGoogleSearch`. This chapter provides you with in-depth coverage of the following three Ajax patterns:

- ❑ Periodic Refresh
- ❑ Submission Throttling
- ❑ Explicit Submission

You then use these patterns to develop three Ajax-enabled controls named `AjaxNotifier`, `Ajax HtmlEditor`, and `AjaxSpellChecker`.

The previous chapter also discussed the Google XML Web service API in detail. This API is used in this chapter as well.

Periodic Refresh

Ajax-enabled components that use the Periodic Refresh pattern periodically poll the server for changes. This section develops an Ajax-enabled custom control named `AjaxNotifier` that will show you how to use the Periodic Refresh pattern to develop your own Ajax-enabled controls.

`AjaxNotifier` is an Ajax-enabled control that periodically polls the server for the latest posted notification and displays the notification in a pop-up dialog, shown in Figure 29-1. As this figure shows, the pop-up dialog exposes two pieces of information about a notification: the source of the notification (notifier) and the content of the notification.

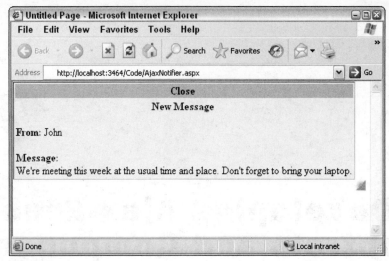

Figure 29-1

Here is how the workflow goes:

1. AjaxNotifier uses DOM and JavaScript to retrieve the latest notification ID that the user has seen. The notification IDs include the complete information needed to determine the order in which the notifications are issued. This could be a timestamp; that is, the creation date of the notification.

2. AjaxNotifier uses the ASP.NET 2.0 client callback mechanism to make an asynchronous callback to the server to download the XML document that contains the information about the latest notification. The client-side code also passes the notification ID of the latest notification that the user has seen to the server so the server can send the next notification back to the client.

3. AjaxNotifier then uses XML, DOM, and JavaScript to dynamically retrieve the required data from the XML document and to display the information in the pop-up dialog.

The AjaxNotifier control derives from the WebControl base class and implements the ICallback EventHandler interface. The control overrides the following methods of the WebControl class:

❑ OnPreRender

❑ AddAttributesToRender

❑ TrackViewState

❑ SaveViewState

❑ LoadViewState

Deriving from WebControl

Listing 29-1 presents the implementation of the OnPreRender method.

Listing 29-1: The OnPreRender method

```
protected override void OnPreRender(EventArgs e)
{
  DetermineRenderClientScript();
  if (renderClientScript)
  {
    string js = Page.ClientScript.GetCallbackEventReference(
                        this,
                        "GetNotificationId('"+ClientID+"')",
                        "AjaxNotifierCallback",
                        "'" + ClientID + "'", true);
    string js2 = "function DoCallback () {" + js + ";}";

    Page.ClientScript.RegisterClientScriptResource(typeof(AjaxNotifier),
                                    "CustomComponents.AjaxNotifier.js");
    Page.ClientScript.RegisterClientScriptBlock(typeof(AjaxNotifier),
                   typeof(AjaxNotifier).FullName + "DoCallback", js2, true);
    Page.ClientScript.RegisterStartupScript(typeof(AjaxNotifier),
                   typeof(AjaxNotifier).FullName + "WebDoCallback", js,true);
  }
  base.OnPreRender(e);
}
```

`OnPreRender` registers three script blocks. The first script block references the `CustomComponents`
`.AjaxNotifier.js` embedded resource:

```
Page.ClientScript.RegisterClientScriptResource(typeof(AjaxNotifier),
                                "CustomComponents.AjaxNotifier.js");
```

Chapter 26 discussed the embedded resources in detail. Later in this chapter, you'll see the content of the
`AjaxNotifier.js` script file.

The second script block contains the code for the `DoCallback` JavaScript function. Notice that this function
runs the JavaScript code that the `GetCallbackEventReference` method of the `ClientScript` property
of the page returns. As discussed in the previous chapter, this JavaScript code includes a call to a
JavaScript function that contains the code that makes the asynchronous client callback to the server:

```
string js = Page.ClientScript.GetCallbackEventReference(
                    this,
                    "GetNotificationId('"+ClientID+"')",
                    "AjaxNotifierCallback",
                    "'" + ClientID + "'", true);
string js2 = "function DoCallback () {" + js + ";}";
```

The third script block includes a call to the JavaScript function that contains the code that makes the
asynchronous client callback to the server. Notice that `OnPreRender` uses the `RegisterStartupScript`
method to register this script to request the page to render the script at the bottom of the page. This
means that the first asynchronous call is made right after the page is loaded. You'll see the significance of
this later in this section.

```
Page.ClientScript.RegisterStartupScript(typeof(AjaxNotifier),
                typeof(AjaxNotifier).FullName + "WebDoCallback", js,true);
```

Listing 29-2 contains the code for the AddAttributesToRender method of the AjaxNotifier control.

Listing 29-2: The AddAttributesToRender method

```
protected override void AddAttributesToRender(HtmlTextWriter writer)
{
  base.AddAttributesToRender(writer);

  if (renderClientScript)
  {
    CssStyleCollection col;
    writer.AddAttribute("notificationId", "0");
    if (dialogStyle != null)
    {
      col = dialogStyle.GetStyleAttributes(this);
      writer.AddAttribute("dialogStyle", col.Value);
    }

    if (headerStyle != null)
    {
      col = headerStyle.GetStyleAttributes(this);
      writer.AddAttribute("headerStyle", col.Value);
    }

    if (itemStyle != null)
    {
      col = itemStyle.GetStyleAttributes(this);
      writer.AddAttribute("itemStyle", col.Value);
    }

    if (alternatingItemStyle != null)
    {
      col = alternatingItemStyle.GetStyleAttributes(this);
      writer.AddAttribute("alternatingItemStyle", col.Value);
    }
  }
}
```

The dialog that the AjaxNotifier pops up handles everything on the client side including rendering, moving, resizing, and font-adjustment when the dialog is resized. Therefore, this pop-up dialog isn't a server control. The previous chapter showed you how you can expose the CSS style attributes of a client-side component such as this pop-up dialog as top-level properties of the Ajax-enabled control itself.

AjaxNotifier exposes the same top-level properties that the AjaxDetailsDialog from the previous chapter exposes. The AjaxNotifier control also overrides the TrackViewState, SaveViewState, and LoadViewState methods to manage the states of these top-level properties across page postbacks. This was thoroughly discussed in Chapter 27.

Implementing ICallbackEventHandler

The AjaxNotifier control implements the ICallbackEventHandler interface to use the ASP.NET 2.0 client callback mechanism to make its asynchronous client callbacks to the server. Listing 29-3 presents the code for the RaiseCallbackEvent and GetCallbackResult methods.

Listing 29-3: Implementing the methods of the ICallbackEventHandler

```csharp
      protected virtual string GetCallbackResult()
      {
        return callbackResult;
      }

      protected virtual void RaiseCallbackEvent(string eventArgument)
      {
        IDataSource ds = (IDataSource)Page.FindControl(DataSourceID);
        int notificationId = int.Parse(eventArgument);
        if (notificationId < 0)
          notificationId = 1;
        Page.Session["NotificationId"] = notificationId;
        if (ds != null)
        {
          DataSourceView dv = ds.GetView(string.Empty);
          dv.Select(DataSourceSelectArguments.Empty, SelectCallback);
        }
      }
    }
```

AjaxNotifier exposes a string property named DataSourceID that the page developer must set to the value of the ID property of the desired tabular data source control. As Listing 29-3 shows, the Raise CallbackEvent method uses the ASP.NET tabular data source control API to retrieve the data from the underlying data store in generic fashion as thoroughly discussed earlier in the book. The argument of the RaiseCallbackEvent method contains the notification ID of the latest notification that the current user has seen. Notice that the RaiseCallbackEvent method stores this notification ID value in the Session object. To help you understand why this is necessary, consider the page shown in Listing 29-4 where the AjaxNotifier control is used. Figure 29-1 shows what the end users see when they access this page.

Listing 29-4: A page that uses the AjaxNotifier control

```
<%@ Page Language="C#" %>
<%@ Register TagPrefix="custom" Namespace="CustomComponents"
Assembly="CustomComponents" %>
<html xmlns="http://www.w3.org/1999/xhtml">
<body>
  <form id="form1" runat="server">
    <custom:AjaxNotifier runat="server" DataSourceID="MySource"
    DialogStyle-BackColor="LightGoldenrodYellow"
    DialogStyle-BorderColor="Tan" DialogStyle-BorderWidth="1px"
    DialogStyle-CellPadding="2" DialogStyle-CellSpacing="0"
    DialogStyle-BorderStyle="Groove" DialogStyle-ForeColor="Black"
    DialogStyle-GridLines="None" HeaderStyle-BackColor="Tan"
    HeaderStyle-Font-Bold="True" AlternatingItemStyle-BackColor="PaleGoldenrod" />

    <asp:SqlDataSource runat="server" ID="MySource"
    ConnectionString="<%$ connectionStrings:MySqlConnectionString %>"
    SelectCommand="Select * From Notifications Where Id > @Id">
      <SelectParameters>
        <asp:SessionParameter Name="Id" SessionField="NotificationId"
        Type="Int32" />
```

```
        </SelectParameters>
      </asp:SqlDataSource>
    </form>
  </body>
</html>
```

As Listing 29-4 shows, this page binds the `AjaxNotifier` control to a `SqlDataSource` control. Notice that the `SelectCommand` attribute of the `<asp:SqlDataSource>` tag contains the following `Select` SQL statement:

```
Select * From Notifications Where Id > @Id
```

This SQL statement contains a parameter named `@Id` whose value is the notification ID of the latest notification that the current user has seen. As Listing 29-4 shows, the `SqlDataSource` control uses a `SessionParameter` to retrieve the notification ID from the `Session` object. That is the reason that Listing 29-4 stores the notification ID in the `Session` object.

```
<asp:SqlDataSource runat="server" ID="MySource"
  ConnectionString="<%$ connectionStrings:MySqlConnectionString %>"
  SelectCommand="Select * From Notifications Where Id > @Id">
    <SelectParameters>
      <asp:SessionParameter Name="Id" SessionField="NotificationId"
        Type="Int32" />
    </SelectParameters>
</asp:SqlDataSource>
```

As Listing 29-3 shows, the `RaiseCallbackEvent` method registers the `SelectCallback` method as the callback for the `Select` data operation. Listing 29-5 presents the implementation of the `SelectCallback` method. The main responsibility of this method is to use the retrieved data record to generate the XML document that will then be sent to the client. In other words, the client and server exchange data in XML format.

Listing 29-5: The SelectCallback method

```
private void SelectCallback(IEnumerable data)
{
  using (StringWriter sw = new StringWriter())
  {
    using (XmlWriter xw = XmlWriter.Create(sw))
    {
      xw.WriteStartDocument();
      xw.WriteStartElement("notification");
      IEnumerator iter = data.GetEnumerator();
      if (iter.MoveNext())
      {
        PropertyDescriptorCollection col =
                            TypeDescriptor.GetProperties(iter.Current);
        foreach (PropertyDescriptor pd in col)
        {
          if (pd.Name == "Source")
            xw.WriteElementString("source", (string)pd.GetValue(iter.Current));
          else if (pd.Name == "Notification")
```

```
            xw.WriteElementString("summary", (string)pd.GetValue(iter.Current));
          else if (pd.Name == "Id")
            xw.WriteElementString("id", pd.GetValue(iter.Current).ToString());
        }
      }

    xw.WriteEndElement();
    xw.WriteEndDocument();
  }
  callbackResult = sw.ToString();
  }
}
```

Therefore, one of your responsibilities as an Ajax-enabled control developer is to decide on the structure or format of the XML document. Listing 29-6 presents an example of an XML document that the `AjaxNotifier` control supports.

Listing 29-6: Example of an XML document that AjaxNotifier supports

```
<notification>
  <id>3</id>
  <source>John</source>
  <summary>We'll meet tomorrow morning</summary>
</notification>
```

This XML document, like all XML documents, has a single document element, that is, `<notification>`, which contains three child elements: `<id>`, `<source>`, and `<summary>`.

As shown in Listing 29-5, the `SelectCallback` method uses the `XmlWriter` streaming API discussed in Chapter 24 to generate the XML document, which is then loaded into a `StringWriter`. The `SelectCallback` method first calls the `WriteStartDocument` method of the `XmlWriter` to signal the beginning of the document and to emit the XML declaration:

```
xw.WriteStartDocument();
```

It then calls the `WriteStartElement` method to write out the opening tag of the `<notification>` document element (see Listing 29-6):

```
xw.WriteStartDocument();
```

Next, it accesses the enumerator object that knows how to enumerate the retrieved data in generic fashion:

```
IEnumerator iter = data.GetEnumerator();
```

It then retrieves the `PropertyDescriptionCollection` collection that contains one `PropertyDescriptor` object for each datafield of the retrieved record:

```
PropertyDescriptorCollection col = TypeDescriptor.GetProperties(iter.Current);
```

Next, it iterates through these `PropertyDescriptor` objects to write out the `<source>`, `<summary>`, and `<id>` elements and their contents:

```
if (pd.Name == "Source")
  xw.WriteElementString("source", (string)pd.GetValue(iter.Current));
else if (pd.Name == "Notification")
  xw.WriteElementString("summary", (string)pd.GetValue(iter.Current));
else if (pd.Name == "Id")
  xw.WriteElementString("id", pd.GetValue(iter.Current).ToString());
```

Now, revisit Listing 29-1 to discuss part of this code listing not yet covered, as highlighted in Listing 29-7.

Listing 29-7: The OnPreRender method revisited

```
protected override void OnPreRender(EventArgs e)
{
  DetermineRenderClientScript();
  if (renderClientScript)
  {
    string js = Page.ClientScript.GetCallbackEventReference(
                        this,
                        "GetNotificationId('"+ClientID+"')",
                        "AjaxNotifierCallback",
                        "'" + ClientID + "'", true);
    string js2 = "function DoCallback () {" + js + ";}";

    Page.ClientScript.RegisterClientScriptResource(typeof(AjaxNotifier),
                                  "CustomComponents.AjaxNotifier.js");
    Page.ClientScript.RegisterClientScriptBlock(typeof(AjaxNotifier),
                      typeof(AjaxNotifier).FullName + "DoCallback", js2, true);
    Page.ClientScript.RegisterStartupScript(typeof(AjaxNotifier),
                      typeof(AjaxNotifier).FullName + "WebDoCallback", js,true);
  }
  base.OnPreRender(e);
}
```

As the highlighted portion of Listing 29-7 shows, the `GetNotificationId` JavaScript function is assigned to the task of determining the notification ID that the client passes to the server. Recall that this notification ID is the ID of the latest notification that the current user has seen. The following code listing presents the implementation of the `GetNotificationId` JavaScript function:

```
function GetNotificationId(ajaxNotifierId)
{
  var ajaxNotifier = document.getElementById(ajaxNotifierId);
  return ajaxNotifier.notificationId;
}
```

As the highlighted code in Listing 29-7 illustrates, `OnPreRender` passes the value of the `ClientID` property of the `AjaxNotifier` control to the `GetNotificationId` JavaScript function. As this code shows, `GetNotificationId` passes this value to the `getElementById` method of the `document` DOM object to access the containing HTML element of the `AjaxNotifier` control. `GetNotificationId` then returns the value of the `notificationId` attribute of the containing element. Notice that this attribute is a custom HTML attribute that holds the notification ID of the latest notification the current user has seen.

As the highlighted code in Listing 29-7 shows, OnPreRender registers the AjaxNotifierCallback JavaScript function as the callback for the client callback requests. This function is automatically called when the server response arrives. Listing 29-8 contains the implementation of the AjaxNotifierCallback JavaScript function.

The AjaxNotifierCallback function first calls the CreateXmlDocument JavaScript function discussed in the previous chapter to create an XML store:

```
var xmlDocument = CreateXmlDocument();
```

It then loads the XML document that it has received from the server to the XML store:

```
xmlDocument.loadXML(result);
```

Next, it accesses the document element of the XML document. As shown in Listing 29-6, the document element is the <notification> element:

```
var notification = xmlDocument.documentElement;
```

It then accesses the first child element of the document element. As shown in Listing 29-6, the first child element is the <id> element:

```
var notificationId = notification.childNodes[0].text;
```

Next, AjaxNotifierCallback accesses the containing HTML element of the AjaxNotifier control:

```
var ajaxNotifier = document.getElementById(context);
```

Recall that the containing HTML element of the AjaxNotifier control has a custom attribute named notificationId that holds the notification ID of the latest notification that the current user has seen. AjaxNotifierCallback checks whether the notification ID of the notification that it has received from the server is different from the notification ID of the latest notification that the user has seen. If so, it assigns the new notification ID to the notificationId attribute of the containing HTML element of the AjaxNotifier control:

```
ajaxNotifier.notificationId = notificationId;
```

AjaxNotifierCallback then calls the InitializeDetailsPopup JavaScript function discussed in Chapter 26 to initialize the pop-up dialog:

```
InitializeDetailsPopup(context);
```

Next, it accesses the text content within the opening and closing tags of the second and third child elements of the <notification> document element. As shown in Listing 29-6, these two child elements are the <source> and <summary> elements:

```
var notificationSource = notification.childNodes[1].text;
var notificationSummary = notification.childNodes[2].text;
```

Next, AjaxNotifierCallback generates the HTML that displays the new notification:

```
        var content = "<r>" +
                "<td colspan='2'>" +
                  "<p><center><b>New Message</b></center></p>" +
                  "<p><b>From: </b>"+notificationSource+"</p>" +
                  "<p><b>Message:</b><br/>"+notificationSummary+"</p>" +
                "</td>" +
              "</r>";
```

It then calls the `DisplayDetailsPopup` function to display the HTML in the details pop-up dialog:

```
        DisplayDetailsPopup (content);
```

Finally, `AjaxNotifierCallback` calls the `setTimeout` JavaScript function:

```
    setTimeout(DoCallback,6000);
```

As shown in Listing 29-1, the `DoCallback` JavaScript function runs the JavaScript code that makes the asynchronous client callback to the server to download the XML document that contains the latest posted notification. The `AjaxNotifierCallback` JavaScript function is automatically called when the page is loaded. This means that when the user downloads the page, the following sequence is automatically triggered:

1. `AjaxNotifierCallback` is called.

2. `AjaxNotifierCallback` pops up the dialog that displays the latest posted notification.

3. AjaxNotifierCallback calls the `setTimeout` function.

The `setTimeout` function *periodically* calls the `DoCallback` function, which in turn runs the JavaScript code that makes a client callback request to the server to download the XML document that contains the latest posted notification. When the server response arrives, this JavaScript code, in turn, calls the `AjaxNotifierCallback` method, which repeats the same steps discussed before.

Listing 29-8: The AjaxNotifierCallback Method

```
function AjaxNotifierCallback(result, context)
{
  var xmlDocument = CreateXmlDocument();
  xmlDocument.loadXML(result);

  var notification = xmlDocument.documentElement;
  if (notification.childNodes.length > 0)
  {
    var notificationId = notification.childNodes[0].text;
    var ajaxNotifier = document.getElementById(context);
    if (notificationId != ajaxNotifier.notificationId)
    {
      ajaxNotifier.notificationId = notificationId;
      InitializeDetailsPopup(context);
      var notificationSource = notification.childNodes[1].text;

      var notificationSummary = notification.childNodes[2].text;

      var content = "<r>" +
```

```
                                 "<td colspan='2'>" +
                                   "<p><center><b>Notification</b></center></p>" +
                                   "<p><b>From: </b>"+notificationSource+"</p>" +
                                   "<p><b>Message:</b><br/>"+notificationSummary+"</p>" +
                                 "</td>" +
                              "</r>";
               DisplayDetailsPopup (content);
         }
      }
   setTimeout(DoCallback,6000);
}
```

Try the following workflow to see for yourself how the `AjaxNotifier` works:

1. Open the application that contains the code files for this chapter in Visual Studio 2005.

2. Run the application to access the `AjaxNotifier.aspx` page. Listing 29-4 shows the contents of this page. Notice that the `AjaxNotifier` automatically makes an asynchronous client callback to the server to retrieve the latest notification and displays the notification in the pop-up dialog as shown in Figure 29-1.

3. Go to the Server Explorer window and access the database table named `Notifications`.

4. Add a new notification record to the table. Notice that the `AjaxNotifier` automatically shows the latest notification.

When you first launch the application, `AjaxNotifier` displays all the notifications one after another because the current implementation of the `AjaxNotifier` doesn't store the notification ID of the latest notification that the user saw in the previous session. That's why `AjaxNotifier` resets this notification ID to zero every time you relaunch the application. You can easily fix this by storing the notification ID of the latest notification in the ASP.NET 2.0 `Profile` object.

Submission Throttling

One of the main problems with traditional controls and components is that every user interaction triggers a callback to the server. This has two drawbacks:

❑   Each callback to the server performs a full page postback to the server, causing the entire page to be rendered all over again.

❑   Making a callback to the server is an expensive operation. This degrades the performance and usability of highly interactive applications where every user interaction triggers an expensive callback to the server.

As discussed before, the ASP.NET 2.0 client callback mechanism resolves the first problem because callbacks to the server aren't done via full page postbacks. The Submission Throttling Ajax pattern resolves the second problem. Instead of making a separate callback to the server for each user interaction, your Ajax-enabled component should cache the data associated with each user interaction and make a single callback to the server to submit the content of the cache. This section uses the Submission Throttling pattern to implement an Ajax-enabled control named `AjaxHtmlEditor`.

As Figure 29-2 shows, `AjaxHtmlEditor` is a WYSIWYG, client-side, feature-rich HTML editor that uses Ajax techniques to asynchronously submit what the user is typing to the server while the user is typing, without interrupting the user. `AjaxHtmlEditor` derives from the `Control` base class and implements the `ICallbackEventHandler` interface.

`AjaxHtmlEditor` overrides the following two methods of the `Control` class:

❑   `OnPreRender`

❑   `Render`

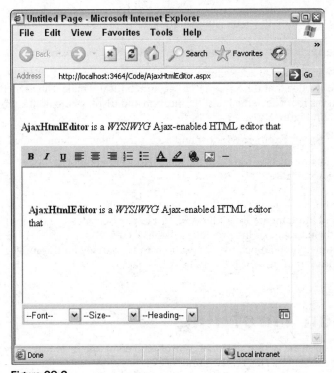

Figure 29-2

Overriding OnPreRender

Listing 29-9 contains the code for the `AjaxHtmlEditor` control's implementation of the `OnPreRender` method. `OnPreRender` first uses the `RegisterArrayDeclaration` method of the `ClientScript` property of the page to request the page to render a global JavaScript array named `idArray` on behalf of the `AjaxHtmlEditor` control. Later you'll see the JavaScript function that uses this array.

`OnPreRender` then registers a call to the `Initialize` JavaScript function. This function is discussed later in this section. Notice that `OnPreRender` uses the `RegisterStartupScript` method to register the call to this function to request the page to render this call at the bottom of the page:

```
string js = "initialize(idArray, '"+ClientID+"_myframe"+"');";
Page.ClientScript.RegisterStartupScript(typeof(AjaxHtmlEditor),
                    typeof(AjaxHtmlEditor).FullName+"Initialize",js,true);
```

OnPreRender then registers the `MakeHttpRequest` JavaScript function with the page for rendering. Notice that this function runs the JavaScript code that makes the asynchronous callback to the server:

```
js = Page.ClientScript.GetCallbackEventReference(this,
                    "GetInputDataForServerMethod('"+ClientID+"_myframe"+"')",
                    "SubmitCallback", "'" + ClientID + "_lbl" + "'", true);
string js2 = "function MakeHttpRequest() {" + js + ";}";
Page.ClientScript.RegisterClientScriptBlock(typeof(AjaxHtmlEditor),
                typeof(AjaxHtmlEditor).FullName + "MakeHttpRequest", js2, true);
```

Finally, `OnPreRender` registers a reference to the `AjaxHtmlEditor.js` script file with the page for rendering. The content of this file is discussed later in this section.

```
Page.ClientScript.RegisterClientScriptInclude(typeof(AjaxHtmlEditor),
                typeof(AjaxHtmlEditor).FullName+"Script","AjaxHtmlEditor.js");
```

Listing 29-9: The OnPreRender method

```
protected override void OnPreRender(EventArgs e)
{
  Page.ClientScript.RegisterArrayDeclaration("idArray", "'bold'");
  Page.ClientScript.RegisterArrayDeclaration("idArray", "'italic'");
  Page.ClientScript.RegisterArrayDeclaration("idArray", "'underline'");
  Page.ClientScript.RegisterArrayDeclaration("idArray", "'left'");
  Page.ClientScript.RegisterArrayDeclaration("idArray", "'center'");
  Page.ClientScript.RegisterArrayDeclaration("idArray", "'right'");
  Page.ClientScript.RegisterArrayDeclaration("idArray", "'ordlist'");
  Page.ClientScript.RegisterArrayDeclaration("idArray", "'bullist'");
  Page.ClientScript.RegisterArrayDeclaration("idArray", "'forecol'");
  Page.ClientScript.RegisterArrayDeclaration("idArray", "'bgcol'");
  Page.ClientScript.RegisterArrayDeclaration("idArray", "'link'");
  Page.ClientScript.RegisterArrayDeclaration("idArray", "'image'");
  Page.ClientScript.RegisterArrayDeclaration("idArray", "'rule'");
  Page.ClientScript.RegisterArrayDeclaration("idArray", "'fontname'");
  Page.ClientScript.RegisterArrayDeclaration("idArray", "'fontsize'");
  Page.ClientScript.RegisterArrayDeclaration("idArray", "'heading'");
  Page.ClientScript.RegisterArrayDeclaration("idArray", "'mode'");

  string js = "initialize(idArray, '"+ClientID+"_myframe"+"');";
  Page.ClientScript.RegisterStartupScript(typeof(AjaxHtmlEditor),
                      typeof(AjaxHtmlEditor).FullName+"Initialize",js,true);
  js = Page.ClientScript.GetCallbackEventReference(this,
                    "GetInputDataForServerMethod('"+ClientID+"_myframe"+"')",
                    "SubmitCallback", "'" + ClientID + "_lbl" + "'", true);
  string js2 = "function MakeHttpRequest() {" + js + ";}";
  Page.ClientScript.RegisterClientScriptBlock(typeof(AjaxHtmlEditor),
                typeof(AjaxHtmlEditor).FullName + "MakeHttpRequest", js2, true);

  Page.ClientScript.RegisterClientScriptInclude(typeof(AjaxHtmlEditor),
```

(continued)

Listing 29-9: *(continued)*

```
                            typeof(AjaxHtmlEditor).FullName+"Script","AjaxHtmlEditor.js");

    base.OnPreRender(e);
}
```

Overriding Render

Listing 29-10 presents the implementation of the Render method.

Listing 29-10: The Render method

```
protected override void Render(HtmlTextWriter w)
{
    w.RenderBeginTag(HtmlTextWriterTag.Span);

    RenderServerResponseArea(w);
    RenderTopToolBar(w);
    RenderEditorArea(w);
    RenderBottomToolBar(w);

    w.RenderEndTag();
}
```

As Figure 29-2 shows, the AjaxHtmlEditor control's user interface consists of the following four components:

❑   The area on the top of the user interface that renders the server response. This is added so you can test the AjaxHtmlEditor control.

❑   The top toolbar.

❑   The editor area.

❑   The bottom toolbar that contains the fontname, fontsize, and heading lists and the mode change button. This button changes the mode from HTML to Text and vice versa. When the AjaxHtmlEditor is in Text mode, the end users can see and edit the HTML tags.

AjaxHtmlEditor exposes one method for rendering each of these components as follows:

❑   RenderServerResponseArea

❑   RenderTopToolBar

❑   RenderEditorArea

❑   RenderBottomToolBar

The following sections discuss the implementation of these four methods.

The RenderServerResponseArea Method

Listing 29-11 presents the implementation of the `RenderServerResponseArea` method. This method renders a `label` HTML element that will display the server response. The server simply returns the text that the user enters in the editor area. However, you can add logic to the server that will do other things such as saving the text to a file, sending the text to other applications, and so on.

Listing 29-11: The RenderServerResponseArea method

```
protected virtual void RenderServerResponseArea(HtmlTextWriter w)
{
  w.AddAttribute(HtmlTextWriterAttribute.Id, ClientID+"_lbl");
  w.RenderBeginTag(HtmlTextWriterTag.Label);
  w.RenderEndTag();
}
```

The RenderTopToolBar Method

Listing 29-12 contains the code for the `RenderTopToolBar` method. This method does exactly what its name says it does — it renders the top toolbar shown in Figure 29-2. `AjaxHtmlEditor` allows users to perform the following operations. As you'll see later, all these operations are client-side operations without any interactions with the server:

- ❏ Make text bold or italic
- ❏ Change the alignment of the text: left, center, or right
- ❏ Add bulleted lists
- ❏ Add ordered lists
- ❏ Underline text
- ❏ Add a link
- ❏ Add an image
- ❏ Change the background and foreground colors
- ❏ Add a horizontal rule

As Listing 29-12 shows, `RenderTopToolBar` renders an `<img>` HTML element for each of these features and takes the following actions for each `<img>` element:

1. Sets the `src` HTML attribute of the element to the path to the appropriate icon. For example:

   ```
   w.AddAttribute("src", "bold.gif");
   ```

2. Registers the `loadCB` JavaScript function as the callback for the `onload` client-side event of the element. Notice the `loadCB` function takes the DOM object that represents the element as its argument:

   ```
   w.AddAttribute("onload", "loadCB(this)");
   ```

3. Registers a JavaScript function as the callback for the `onclick` client-side event of the element. As the following code fragment shows, `AjaxHtmlEditor` contains one JavaScript function for each `<img>` element that handles the `onclick` event for that element:

```
    w.AddAttribute("onclick", "boldCB(this)");
    w.AddAttribute("onclick", "italicCB(this)");
    w.AddAttribute("onclick", "underlineCB(this)");
    w.AddAttribute("onclick", "leftCB(this)");
    w.AddAttribute("onclick", "centerCB(this)");
    w.AddAttribute("onclick", "rightCB(this)");
    w.AddAttribute("onclick", "ordlistCB(this)");
    w.AddAttribute("onclick", "bullistCB(this)");
    w.AddAttribute("onclick", "forecolCB(this)");
    w.AddAttribute("onclick", "bgcolCB(this)");
    w.AddAttribute("onclick", "linkCB(this)");
    w.AddAttribute("onclick", "imageCB(this)");
    w.AddAttribute("onclick", "ruleCB(this)");
```

Listing 29-12: The RenderTopToolBar method

```
protected virtual void RenderTopToolBar(HtmlTextWriter w)
{
    w.AddAttribute("border", "0");
    w.AddAttribute("cellpadding", "0");
    w.AddAttribute("cellspacing", "0");
    w.AddAttribute("width", "415px");
    w.AddAttribute("height", "30px");
    w.AddAttribute("bgcolor", "#D6D3CE");
    w.RenderBeginTag(HtmlTextWriterTag.Table);
    w.RenderBeginTag(HtmlTextWriterTag.Tr);
    w.AddStyleAttribute("padding-left", "3px");
    w.AddStyleAttribute("padding-top", "3px");
    w.RenderBeginTag(HtmlTextWriterTag.Td);

    w.AddAttribute("src", "bold.gif");
    w.AddAttribute("onclick", "boldCB(this)");
    w.AddAttribute("onload", "loadCB(this)");
    w.RenderBeginTag(HtmlTextWriterTag.Img);
    w.RenderEndTag();

    w.AddAttribute("src", "italic.gif");
    w.AddAttribute("onclick", "italicCB(this)");
    w.AddAttribute("onload", "loadCB(this)");
    w.RenderBeginTag(HtmlTextWriterTag.Img);
    w.RenderEndTag();

    w.AddAttribute("src", "underline.gif");
    w.AddAttribute("onclick", "underlineCB(this)");
    w.AddAttribute("onload", "loadCB(this)");
    w.RenderBeginTag(HtmlTextWriterTag.Img);
    w.RenderEndTag();

    w.AddAttribute("src", "left.gif");
    w.AddAttribute("onclick", "leftCB(this)");
    w.AddAttribute("onload", "loadCB(this)");
    w.RenderBeginTag(HtmlTextWriterTag.Img);
    w.RenderEndTag();

    w.AddAttribute("src", "center.gif");
    w.AddAttribute("onclick", "centerCB(this)");
```

```
        w.AddAttribute("onload", "loadCB(this)");
        w.RenderBeginTag(HtmlTextWriterTag.Img);
        w.RenderEndTag();

        w.AddAttribute("src", "right.gif");
        w.AddAttribute("onclick", "rightCB(this)");
        w.AddAttribute("onload", "loadCB(this)");
        w.RenderBeginTag(HtmlTextWriterTag.Img);
        w.RenderEndTag();

        w.AddAttribute("src", "ordlist.gif");
        w.AddAttribute("onclick", "ordlistCB(this)");
        w.AddAttribute("onload", "loadCB(this)");
        w.RenderBeginTag(HtmlTextWriterTag.Img);
        w.RenderEndTag();

        w.AddAttribute("src", "bullist.gif");
        w.AddAttribute("onclick", "bullistCB(this)");
        w.AddAttribute("onload", "loadCB(this)");
        w.RenderBeginTag(HtmlTextWriterTag.Img);
        w.RenderEndTag();

        w.AddAttribute("src", "forecol.gif");
        w.AddAttribute("onclick", "forecolCB(this)");
        w.AddAttribute("onload", "loadCB(this)");
        w.RenderBeginTag(HtmlTextWriterTag.Img);
        w.RenderEndTag();

        w.AddAttribute("src", "bgcol.gif");
        w.AddAttribute("onclick", "bgcolCB(this)");
        w.AddAttribute("onload", "loadCB(this)");
        w.RenderBeginTag(HtmlTextWriterTag.Img);
        w.RenderEndTag();

        w.AddAttribute("src", "link.gif");
        w.AddAttribute("onclick", "linkCB(this)");
        w.AddAttribute("onload", "loadCB(this)");
        w.RenderBeginTag(HtmlTextWriterTag.Img);
        w.RenderEndTag();

        w.AddAttribute("src", "image.gif");
        w.AddAttribute("onclick", "imageCB(this)");
        w.AddAttribute("onload", "loadCB(this)");
        w.RenderBeginTag(HtmlTextWriterTag.Img);
        w.RenderEndTag();

        w.AddAttribute("src", "rule.gif");
        w.AddAttribute("onclick", "ruleCB(this)");
        w.AddAttribute("onload", "loadCB(this)");
        w.RenderBeginTag(HtmlTextWriterTag.Img);
        w.RenderEndTag();

        w.RenderEndTag();

        w.RenderEndTag();
        w.RenderEndTag();
}
```

The RenderEditorArea Method

The `RenderEditorArea` method renders the editor area shown in Figure 29-2. Listing 29-13 presents the code for this method. As this listing shows, `RenderEditorArea` renders an `iframe` HTML element and sets the value of the `id` HTML attribute of this element to a unique string value for future reference. Notice that the method concatenates the value of the `ClientID` property of the `AjaxHtmlEditor` control with the string value `_myframe` to build a unique string value.

Listing 29-13: The RenderEditorArea method

```
protected virtual void RenderEditorArea(HtmlTextWriter w)
{
  w.AddAttribute(HtmlTextWriterAttribute.Id, ClientID+"_myframe");
  w.AddStyleAttribute("width", "415px");
  w.AddStyleAttribute("height", "205px");
  w.RenderBeginTag("iframe");
  w.RenderEndTag();
}
```

The RenderBottomToolBar Method

This method renders the toolbar that contains the following components, as shown in Figure 29-2:

❑ List of available font names

❑ List of available font sizes

❑ List of available headings

❑ A button that allows the user to switch between the HTML and Text modes. Users switch to the Text mode so they can see and edit HTML tags.

`AjaxHtmlEditor` exposes one method for rendering each of these four components. As Listing 29-14 shows, `RenderBottomToolBar` delegates the responsibility of rendering each component to its associated rendering method.

Listing 29-14: The RenderBottomToolBar method

```
protected virtual void RenderBottomToolBar(HtmlTextWriter w)
{
  w.AddAttribute("border", "0");
  w.AddAttribute("cellpadding", "0");
  w.AddAttribute("cellspacing", "0");
  w.AddAttribute("width", "415px");
  w.AddAttribute("height", "30px");
  w.AddAttribute("bgcolor", "#D6D3CE");
  w.RenderBeginTag(HtmlTextWriterTag.Table);
  w.RenderBeginTag(HtmlTextWriterTag.Tr);

  RenderFontNameList(w);
  RenderFontSizeList(w);
  RenderHeadingList(w);
```

```
        RenderModeButton(w);

    w.RenderEndTag();
    w.RenderEndTag();
}
```

The RenderFontNameList Method

This method renders the list of available font names to choose from, as shown in Listing 29-15. This method performs the following tasks:

1. Registers the `fontnameCB` JavaScript function as the callback for the `onchange` client-side event of the `<select>` element:

```
w.AddAttribute(HtmlTextWriterAttribute.Onchange, "fontnameCB(this)");
```

2. Adds one `<option>` element for each font name and sets the value of the `value` HTML attribute of each `<option>` element to the name of the associated font. As you'll see later, the `fontnameCB` JavaScript function will use this value to access the selected font name.

```
w.AddAttribute(HtmlTextWriterAttribute.Value, "Arial");
w.RenderBeginTag(HtmlTextWriterTag.Option);
w.Write("Arial");
w.RenderEndTag();
```

Listing 29-15: The RenderFontNameList method

```
protected virtual void RenderFontNameList(HtmlTextWriter w)
{
    w.AddAttribute("width", "80%");
    w.AddStyleAttribute("padding-left", "3px");
    w.AddStyleAttribute("padding-top", "3px");
    w.RenderBeginTag(HtmlTextWriterTag.Td);
    w.AddAttribute(HtmlTextWriterAttribute.Onchange, "fontnameCB(this)");
    w.RenderBeginTag(HtmlTextWriterTag.Select);
    w.AddAttribute(HtmlTextWriterAttribute.Value, "");
    w.RenderBeginTag(HtmlTextWriterTag.Option);
    w.Write("--Font--");
    w.RenderEndTag();
    w.AddAttribute(HtmlTextWriterAttribute.Value, "Arial");
    w.RenderBeginTag(HtmlTextWriterTag.Option);
    w.Write("Arial");
    w.RenderEndTag();
    w.AddAttribute(HtmlTextWriterAttribute.Value, "Courier");
    w.RenderBeginTag(HtmlTextWriterTag.Option);
    w.Write("Courier");
    w.RenderEndTag();
    w.AddAttribute(HtmlTextWriterAttribute.Value, "Sans Serif");
    w.RenderBeginTag(HtmlTextWriterTag.Option);
    w.Write("Sans Serif");
    w.RenderEndTag();
    w.AddAttribute(HtmlTextWriterAttribute.Value, "Tahoma");
```

```
    w.RenderBeginTag(HtmlTextWriterTag.Option);
    w.Write("Tahoma");
    w.RenderEndTag();
    w.AddAttribute(HtmlTextWriterAttribute.Value, "Verdana");
    w.RenderBeginTag(HtmlTextWriterTag.Option);
    w.Write("Verdana");
    w.RenderEndTag();
    w.AddAttribute(HtmlTextWriterAttribute.Value, "Wingdings");
    w.RenderBeginTag(HtmlTextWriterTag.Option);
    w.Write("Wingdings");
    w.RenderEndTag();
    w.RenderEndTag();
}
```

The RenderFontSizeList Method

This method renders the list of available font sizes to choose from, as shown in Listing 29-16. This method performs the following tasks:

1. Registers the `fontsizeCB` JavaScript function as the callback for the `onchange` client-side event of the `<select>` element:

```
w.AddAttribute(HtmlTextWriterAttribute.Onchange, "fontsizeCB(this)");
```

2. Adds one `<option>` element for each available font size and sets the value of the `value` HTML attribute of the element to the name of the associated font size for future references. For example:

```
w.AddAttribute(HtmlTextWriterAttribute.Value, "Small");
w.RenderBeginTag(HtmlTextWriterTag.Option);
w.Write("Small");
w.RenderEndTag();
```

Listing 29-16: The RenderFontSizeList method

```
protected virtual void RenderFontSizeList(HtmlTextWriter w)
{
    w.AddAttribute(HtmlTextWriterAttribute.Onchange, "fontsizeCB(this)");
    w.RenderBeginTag(HtmlTextWriterTag.Select);
    w.AddAttribute(HtmlTextWriterAttribute.Value, "");
    w.RenderBeginTag(HtmlTextWriterTag.Option);
    w.Write("--Size--");
    w.RenderEndTag();
    w.AddAttribute(HtmlTextWriterAttribute.Value, "Very Small");
    w.RenderBeginTag(HtmlTextWriterTag.Option);
    w.Write("Very Small");
    w.RenderEndTag();
    w.AddAttribute(HtmlTextWriterAttribute.Value, "Small");
    w.RenderBeginTag(HtmlTextWriterTag.Option);
    w.Write("Small");
    w.RenderEndTag();
    w.AddAttribute(HtmlTextWriterAttribute.Value, "Medium");
    w.RenderBeginTag(HtmlTextWriterTag.Option);
    w.Write("Medium");
    w.RenderEndTag();
    w.AddAttribute(HtmlTextWriterAttribute.Value, "Large");
```

```
        w.RenderBeginTag(HtmlTextWriterTag.Option);
        w.Write("Large");
        w.RenderEndTag();
        w.AddAttribute(HtmlTextWriterAttribute.Value, "Larger");
        w.RenderBeginTag(HtmlTextWriterTag.Option);
        w.Write("Larger");
        w.RenderEndTag();
        w.AddAttribute(HtmlTextWriterAttribute.Value, "Very Large");
        w.RenderBeginTag(HtmlTextWriterTag.Option);
        w.Write("Very Large");
        w.RenderEndTag();
        w.RenderEndTag();
    }
```

The RenderHeadingList Method

Listing 29-17 presents the implementation of the `RenderHeadingList` method. The main responsibility of this method is to render the `<select>` HTML element that displays the list of available headings. This method first registers the `headingCB` JavaScript function as the callback for the `onchange` client-side event of the `<select>` element:

```
        w.AddAttribute(HtmlTextWriterAttribute.Onchange, "headingCB(this)");
```

It then renders one `<option>` HTML element for each available heading. Notice that the method sets the `value` HTML attribute of each `<option>` element to the appropriate value. As you'll see later, the `onchange` function will pass this value to the underlying library.

```
        w.AddAttribute(HtmlTextWriterAttribute.Value, "Heading 1");
        w.RenderBeginTag(HtmlTextWriterTag.Option);
        w.Write("Heading 1");
        w.RenderEndTag();
```

Listing 29-17: The RenderHeadingList method

```
    protected virtual void RenderHeadingList(HtmlTextWriter w)
    {
        w.AddAttribute(HtmlTextWriterAttribute.Onchange, "headingCB(this)");
        w.RenderBeginTag(HtmlTextWriterTag.Select);
        w.AddAttribute(HtmlTextWriterAttribute.Value, "");
        w.RenderBeginTag(HtmlTextWriterTag.Option);
        w.Write("--Heading--");
        w.RenderEndTag();
        w.AddAttribute(HtmlTextWriterAttribute.Value, "Heading 1");
        w.RenderBeginTag(HtmlTextWriterTag.Option);
        w.Write("Heading 1");
        w.RenderEndTag();
        w.AddAttribute(HtmlTextWriterAttribute.Value, "Heading 2");
        w.RenderBeginTag(HtmlTextWriterTag.Option);
        w.Write("Heading 2");
        w.RenderEndTag();
        w.AddAttribute(HtmlTextWriterAttribute.Value, "Heading 3");
        w.RenderBeginTag(HtmlTextWriterTag.Option);
        w.Write("Heading 3");
```

(continued)

Listing 29-17: *(continued)*

```
    w.RenderEndTag();
    w.AddAttribute(HtmlTextWriterAttribute.Value, "Heading 4");
    w.RenderBeginTag(HtmlTextWriterTag.Option);
    w.Write("Heading 4");
    w.RenderEndTag();
    w.AddAttribute(HtmlTextWriterAttribute.Value, "Heading 5");
    w.RenderBeginTag(HtmlTextWriterTag.Option);
    w.Write("Heading 5");
    w.RenderEndTag();
    w.AddAttribute(HtmlTextWriterAttribute.Value, "Heading 6");
    w.RenderBeginTag(HtmlTextWriterTag.Option);
    w.Write("Heading 6");
    w.RenderEndTag();
    w.RenderEndTag();
    w.RenderEndTag();
}
```

The RenderModeButton Method

Listing 29-18 contains the code for the `RenderModeButton` method. This method renders the `<img>` HTML element that allows the user to switch between the HTML and Text modes. This method registers the `modeCB` JavaScript function as the callback for the `onclick` client-side event of the `<img>` element and the `loadCB` JavaScript function as the callback for the `onload` event of this element:

```
    w.AddAttribute(HtmlTextWriterAttribute.Onclick, "modeCB(this)");
    w.AddAttribute("onload", "loadCB(this)");
```

Listing 29-18: The RenderModeButton method

```
protected virtual void RenderModeChangeButton(HtmlTextWriter w)
{
    w.AddAttribute("width", "20%");
    w.AddAttribute(HtmlTextWriterAttribute.Align, "right");
    w.AddStyleAttribute("padding-left", "3px");
    w.AddStyleAttribute("padding-top", "3px");
    w.RenderBeginTag(HtmlTextWriterTag.Td);
    w.AddAttribute(HtmlTextWriterAttribute.Src, "mode.gif");
    w.AddAttribute(HtmlTextWriterAttribute.Onclick, "modeCB(this)");
    w.AddAttribute("onload", "loadCB(this)");
    w.RenderBeginTag(HtmlTextWriterTag.Img);
    w.RenderEndTag();
    w.RenderEndTag();
}
```

JavaScript Functions

This section discusses the implementation of the JavaScript functions that the `AjaxHtmlEditor` uses. As shown in Listing 29-9, `OnPreRender` registers a call to the `initialize` JavaScript function with the page for rendering. Notice that `OnPreRender` uses the `RegisterStartupScript` method to request the page to render this call at the bottom of the page. Listing 29-19 contains the code for the `initialize` JavaScript function.

Listing 29-19: The Initialize JavaScript function

```
function initialize(idAr, myfrm)
{
  document.frames[myfrm].document.designMode = "on";
  document.frames[myfrm].mode = 1;

  for (var i=0; i<idAr.length; i++)
    document.getElementById(idAr[i]).frame = document.frames[myfrm];

  Send(myfrm);
}
```

Notice that the `initialize` function calls the `Send` JavaScript function and passes the value of the `id` HTML attribute of the `<iframe>` element as its argument. The `Send` function uses this value to access the DOM object that represents the `<iframe>` element. The `document` property of this DOM object provides access to the DOM object that represents the document associated with the `<iframe>`, which is then used to access its body:

```
var mybody = document.frames[myfrm].document.body;
```

The `innerHTML` property of the DOM object that represents the body contains the text that the user has entered in the editor area of the `AjaxHtmlEditor` control:

```
var newValue = mybody.innerHTML;
```

The `Send` function then uses the value of the `oldValue` attribute to access the previous content of the editor area, that is, the content of the editor area the last time the `Send` function was called:

```
oldValue = mybody.oldValue;
```

Next, the function runs the JavaScript code that performs the following important tasks:

❑ It contains the logic that determines whether it's time to send the text that the user has entered in the editor area back to the server. The current implementation of the `Send` function uses a simple logic. It simply compares the lengths of the old and new values to determine whether it's time to send the text to the server. However, you can easily replace this logic with something more complex. This logic is what makes the `AjaxHtmlEditor` control different from its traditional counterpart. Sending data in a traditional control is based on user demand. There's normally a Submit button somewhere that the user has to click to submit the text. A Submission Throttling-based Ajax-enabled control such as `AjaxHtmlEditor`, on the other hand, takes complete control over when the text is sent to the server.

❑ It uses an asynchronous technique such as the ASP.NET 2.0 client callback mechanism to make an asynchronous client callback request to the server without performing full page postback. The `Send` function calls the `MakeHttpRequest` JavaScript function to accomplish this task. Recall from Listing 29-9 that the `MakeHttpRequest` function contains the JavaScript code that makes the asynchronous client callback request to the server:

```
MakeHttpRequest();
```

It calls the `setTimeout` JavaScript function, which periodically calls the `Send` JavaScript function to allow this function to determine whether it's time to make an asynchronous client callback request to the server to send the text:

```
setTimeout("Send('"+myfrm+"')", 1000);
```

These three tasks are the heart of the Submission Throttling Ajax pattern. Listing 29-20 shows the implementation of the `Send` JavaScript function.

Listing 29-20: The Send JavaScript function

```
function Send(myfrm)
{
  if (document.frames[myfrm].document.body)
  {
    var mybody = document.frames[myfrm].document.body;
    var newValue = mybody.innerHTML;
    var oldValue;
    if (mybody.oldValue)
    {
      oldValue = mybody.oldValue;
    }
    else
    {
      mybody.oldValue = newValue;
      oldValue = newValue;
    }

    if (newValue.length - oldValue.length > 2 ||
        oldValue.length - newValue.length > 2)
    {
      mybody.oldValue = mybody.innerHTML;
      MakeHttpRequest();
    }
  }
  setTimeout("Send('"+myfrm+"')", 1000);
}
```

Listing 29-21 contains the implementation of the `loadCB` JavaScript function. Recall that Listing 29-12 registers this function as callback for the `onload` client-side events of the `<img>` elements that the top toolbar contains. This function registers the `mouseoverCB`, `mouseoutCB`, `mousedownCB`, and `mouseupCB` JavaScript functions as callbacks for the `onmouseover`, `onmouseout`, `onmousedown`, and `onmouseup` events of these `<img>` elements.

Listing 29-21: The loadCB JavaScript function

```
function loadCB(c)
{
  c.onmouseover = mouseoverCB;
  c.onmouseout = mouseoutCB;
  c.onmousedown = mousedownCB;
  c.onmouseup = mouseupCB;
```

```
      c.style.borderWidth = "1px";
      c.style.borderStyle = "solid";
      c.style.borderColor = "#D6D3CE";
    }
```

Listing 29-22 contains the code for the `mouseoverCB`, `mouseoutCB`, `mousedownCB`, and `mouseupCB` JavaScript functions. The net result of these functions is that when you move the mouse pointer over or click the mouse while over an `<img>` HTML element in the top toolbar, the `<img>` element changes color. Notice that each function uses the `srcElement` of the event object to access the `<img>` element that raised the event.

Listing 29-22: The mouseoverCB JavaScript function

```
function mouseoverCB()
{
  var c = window.event.srcElement;
  c.style.borderColor = "#000000";
  c.style.backgroundColor = "#B5BED6";
  c.style.cursor = "hand";
}

function mouseoutCB()
{
  var c = window.event.srcElement;
  c.style.borderColor = "#D6D3CE";
  c.style.backgroundColor = "#D6D3CE";
}

function mousedownCB()
{
  var c = window.event.srcElement;
  c.style.backgroundColor = "#8492B5";
}

function mouseupCB()
{
  var c = window.event.srcElement;
  c.style.backgroundColor = "#B5BED6";
}
```

Recall that Listing 29-12 registers the JavaScript functions shown in the following listing as callbacks for the `onclick` client-side event of the associated `<img>` element. For example, it registers the `boldCB` function as the callback for the `onclick` event of the `<img>` element that the user clicks to make text bold.

As Listing 29-23 shows, each JavaScript function takes a single argument that refers to the `<img>` element that raised the `onclick` event. Each function then uses the `execCommand` method to execute its associated command. For example, the `boldCB` function calls this method to execute the command that makes text bold:

```
c.frame.document.execCommand("bold", false, null);
```

Listing 29-23: The callback functions for the <img> elements of the top toolbar

```
function boldCB(c)
{
  c.frame.document.execCommand("bold", false, null);
}

function italicCB(c)
{
  c.frame.document.execCommand("italic",false,null);
}

function underlineCB(c)
{
  c.frame.document.execCommand("underline", false, null);
}

function leftCB(c)
{
  c.frame.document.execCommand("justifyleft", false, null);
}

function centerCB(c)
{
  c.frame.document.execCommand("justifycenter", false, null);
}

function rightCB(c)
{
  c.frame.document.execCommand("justifyright", false, null);
}

function ordlistCB(c)
{
  c.frame.document.execCommand("insertorderedlist", false, null);
}

function bullistCB(c)
{
  c.frame.document.execCommand("insertunorderedlist", false, null);
}

function linkCB(c)
{
  c.frame.document.execCommand("createlink");
}

function ruleCB(c)
{
  c.frame.document.execCommand("inserthorizontalrule", false, null);
}
```

Listing 29-24 contains the code for the `forecolCB`, `bgcolCB`, and `imageCB` JavaScript functions. Recall that Listing 29-12 registers these three functions as callbacks for the <img> elements that the user clicks to change the foreground and background colors and add a new image, respectively. Each function first calls the `prompt` JavaScript function to allow the user to enter the desired color or path to the desired image. It then calls the `execCommand` method to execute the associated command.

Listing 29-24: The forecolCB, bgcolCB, and imageCB functions

```
function forecolCB(c)
{
  var forecol = prompt("Enter foreground color", "");
  if (forecol != "")
    c.frame.document.execCommand("forecolor", false, forecol);
}

function bgcolCB(c)
{
  var bgcol = prompt("Enter background color", "");
  if (bgcol != "")
    c.frame.document.execCommand("backcolor", false, bgcol);
}

function imageCB(c)
{
  var imgPath = prompt("Enter image path", "");
  if (imgPath != "")
    c.frame.document.execCommand("insertimage", false, imgPath);
}
```

Listing 29-25 presents the implementation of the `fontnameCB` and `fontsizeCB` JavaScript functions. Recall that Listings 29-14 and 29-15 register these two functions as callbacks for the `onchange` client-side events of the `<select>` elements that the user uses to select a `fontname` and `fontsize`, respectively. Each function first accesses the selected value of its associated `<select>` element. It then calls the `exec Command` method and passes the selected font name or font size as its argument to execute the associated command.

Listing 29-25: The fontnameCB and fontsizeCB functions

```
function fontnameCB(c)
{
  var fontname = c.options[c.selectedIndex].value;
  if (fontname != "")
    c.frame.document.execCommand("fontname", false, fontname);
}

function fontsizeCB(c)
{
  var fontsize = c.options[c.selectedIndex].value;
  if (fontsize != "")
    c.frame.document.execCommand("fontsize", false, fontsize);
}
```

Listing 29-26 contains the implementation of the `headingCB` JavaScript function that Listing 29-17 registers as the callback for the `onchange` client-side event of the `<select>` element that the user uses to select a heading. The implementation of this function is the same as the implementation of the previous two functions with one difference. This function needs to call the `fontnameCB` function after it calls the `execCommand` method to change the font name. The `headingCB` function first calls the previous

Sibling property of the DOM object that represents the heading `<select>` element to access the DOM object that represents the font size `<select>` element because, as Figure 29-2 shows, the font size `<select>` element is the previous sibling element of the heading `<select>` element. It then calls the previousSibling property of this DOM object to access the DOM object that represents the font name `<select>` element. Finally, it calls the fontnameCB function and passes this DOM object into it.

Listing 29-26: The headingCB JavaScript function

```
function headingCB(c)
{
  var heading = c.options[c.selectedIndex].value;

  if (heading != "")
  {
    c.frame.document.execCommand("formatblock", false, heading);
    var fontname = c.previousSibling.previousSibling;
    fontnameCB(fontname);
  }
}
```

Listing 29-27 shows the implementation of the modeCB JavaScript function that Listing 29-18 registers as callback for the onclick event of the `<img>` element that the user clicks to switch between the HTML and Text views of the editor area. The modeCB function first checks whether the AjaxHtmlEditor control is in Text mode where the user uses the top toolbar to format the text. If so, it knows that the user wants to switch from Text to HTML where the user can directly use HTML markup text to build the document. The function simply assigns the content of the innerHTML property to the innerText property to switch from HTML to Text mode. Notice that the function also hides the top toolbar.

If the AjaxHtmlEditor is in Text mode where the user can use HTML directly, the function knows that the user wants to switch to the Text mode where he can use the top toolbar to edit the text.

Listing 29-27: The modeCB JavaScript function

```
function modeCB(c)
{
  if (c.frame.mode == 1)
  {
    var html = c.frame.document.body.innerHTML;
    c.frame.document.body.innerText = html;
    toptable.style.visibility = "hidden";
    c.frame.mode = 2;
  }

  else
  {
    var text = c.frame.document.body.innerText;
    c.frame.document.body.innerHTML = text;
    toptable.style.visibility = "visible";
    c.frame.mode = 1;
  }
}
```

Try the following workflow to see for yourself how the `AjaxHtmlEditor` works:

1. Open the application that contains the code files for this chapter in Visual Studio 2005.

2. Run the application to access the `AjaxHtmlEditor.aspx` page.

3. Start typing in the editor area. You'll see the text appear in the server response area as you type.

The following sequence of actions is automatically taken behind the scenes as you're typing, without interrupting you:

1. `AjaxHtmlEditor` makes an asynchronous client callback to the server and passes the content of the editor area to the server.

2. You can add the required logic to the `RaiseCallbackEvent` method to do whatever you want to do with the text that you receive from the client. For example, you can save it or you can pass it to other applications. The current implementation of the `RaiseCallbackEvent` method simply returns the same text back to the client code to display in the server response area.

3. The client-side code renders the text that it has received from the server in the server response area.

Explicit Submission

Ajax-enabled components use the Explicit Submission Ajax pattern to allow users to explicitly trigger the client callback to the server. All the Ajax-enabled controls developed in Chapter 27 use this Ajax pattern. This section implements an Ajax-enabled control named `AjaxSpellChecker` that uses both Submission Throttling and Explicit Submission Ajax patterns so you can compare these two patterns to understand them better.

`AjaxSpellChecker` uses the Google XML Web service API to check the spelling of a specified text. The `AjaxSpellChecker` user interface consists of a text box for the user to type in, a button for the user to explicitly submit the text to the server, and a label that displays the spelling suggestion, as shown in Figure 29-3. `AjaxSpellChecker` derives from the `WebControl` class and implements the `ICallback EventHandler` interface.

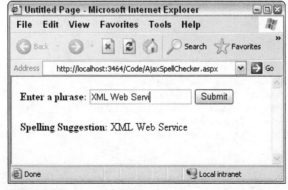

Figure 29-3

Overriding OnPreRender

Listing 29-28 contains the code for the OnPreRender method. OnPreRender first registers the embedded AjaxSpellChecker.js resource. The content of this script file is discussed later in this section.

```
Page.ClientScript.RegisterClientScriptResource(typeof(AjaxSpellChecker),
                                 "CustomComponents.AjaxSpellChecker.js");
```

Next, it registers the MakeHttpRequest JavaScript function with the containing page for rendering. This function contains the JavaScript code that makes the asynchronous callback to the server:

```
string js = Page.ClientScript.GetCallbackEventReference(this,
                             "GetPhrase2('" + ClientID + "_Phrase" + "')",
                             "SubmitCallback",
                             "'" + ClientID + "_Suggestion" + "'", true);
string js2 = "function MakeHttpRequest() {" + js + ";}";
Page.ClientScript.RegisterClientScriptBlock(typeof(AjaxSpellChecker),
             typeof(AjaxSpellChecker).FullName + "MakeHttpRequest", js2, true);
```

Listing 29-28: The OnPreRender method

```
protected override void OnPreRender(EventArgs e)
{
  DetermineRenderClientScript();
  if (renderClientScript)
  {
    Page.ClientScript.RegisterClientScriptResource(typeof(AjaxSpellChecker),
                             "CustomComponents.AjaxSpellChecker.js");
    string js = Page.ClientScript.GetCallbackEventReference(this,
                             "GetPhrase2('" + ClientID + "_Phrase" + "')",
                             "SubmitCallback",
                             "'" + ClientID + "_Suggestion" + "'", true);
    string js2 = "function MakeHttpRequest() {" + js + ";}";
    Page.ClientScript.RegisterClientScriptBlock(typeof(AjaxSpellChecker),
             typeof(AjaxSpellChecker).FullName + "MakeHttpRequest", js2, true);

    string js3 = "function SpellChecker(){" +
        "var phraseTextBox = document.getElementById('"+ClientID+"_Phrase"+"');" +
        "var newValue = phraseTextBox.value;" +
        "var oldValue;" +
        "if (phraseTextBox.phrase) {" +
          "oldValue = phraseTextBox.phrase;}" +
        "else {" +
          "phraseTextBox.phrase = phraseTextBox.value;" +
          "oldValue = phraseTextBox.phrase;}" +
        "if (newValue.length - oldValue.length > 5 ||" +
            "oldValue.length - newValue.length > 5) {" +
          "phraseTextBox.phrase = phraseTextBox.value;" +
          "MakeHttpRequest();}setTimeout(SpellChecker, 100);}";

    Page.ClientScript.RegisterClientScriptBlock(typeof(AjaxSpellChecker),
             typeof(AjaxSpellChecker).FullName + "SpellChecker", js3, true);
    Page.ClientScript.RegisterStartupScript(typeof(AjaxSpellChecker),
                     typeof(AjaxSpellChecker).FullName + "SpellCheckerCall",
                     "SpellChecker();", true);
```

```
        }

    base.OnPreRender(e);
}
```

Next, `OnPreRender` registers the `SpellChecker` JavaScript function with the page for rendering:

```
"function SpellChecker(){" +
  "var phraseTextBox = document.getElementById('"+ClientID+"_Phrase"+"');" +
  "var newValue = phraseTextBox.value;" +
  "var oldValue;" +
  "if (phraseTextBox.phrase) {" +
    "oldValue = phraseTextBox.phrase;}" +
  "else {" +
    "phraseTextBox.phrase = phraseTextBox.value;
    "oldValue = phraseTextBox.phrase;}" +
  "if (newValue.length - oldValue.length > 5 ||
      oldValue.length - newValue.length > 5) {" +
    "phraseTextBox.phrase = phraseTextBox.value;" +
    "MakeHttpRequest();}setTimeout(SpellChecker, 100);}";
```

`SpellChecker` first accesses the text box that contains the phrase to be checked and calls its `value` property to access the phrase:

```
"var phraseTextBox = document.getElementById('"+ClientID+"_Phrase"+"');" +
"var newValue = phraseTextBox.value;" +
```

The implementation of the `SpellChecker` JavaScript function is very similar to the implementation of the `Send` JavaScript function that `AjaxHtmlEditor` uses. This is because `AjaxSpellChecker` uses the Submission Throttling pattern, just like `AjaxHtmlEditor`.

Overriding Render

Listing 29-29 presents the code for the `Render` method. Notice that the `Render` method concatenates the value of the `ClientID` property of the `AjaxSpellChecker` control with the string values `_Phrase` and `_Suggestion` to evaluate unique values for the `id` HTML attributes of the text field and the label that displays spelling suggestion:

```
writer.AddAttribute(HtmlTextWriterAttribute.Id, ClientID + "_Phrase");
writer.AddAttribute(HtmlTextWriterAttribute.Id, ClientID + "_Suggestion");
```

As you'll see later, these `id` values will be used to access the text field and the spelling suggestion label. The `Render` method then registers the JavaScript function that makes the client callback as the callback for the `onclick` client-side event of the button. This will allow the user to asynchronously submit the text for spell-checking without having to perform a full page postback.

In other words, the `AjaxSpellChecker` control provides two different asynchronous mechanisms for submitting the text for checking. The first mechanism is done automatically behind the scenes where the `AjaxSpellChecker` uses Submission Throttling pattern to submit the text. This mechanism doesn't involve the user. What this means is that the `AjaxSpellChecker` dynamically checks the spelling of the text and provides spelling suggestions as the user types, without interrupting the user. The second mechanism is directly triggered by the user where the user explicitly clicks the button to submit the text to the server.

Notice that both mechanisms call the same `SubmitCallback` JavaScript function when the server request arrives. In a production environment, you may want to stick with one of these two mechanisms. I've included both of them so you can compare the Submission Throttling and Explicit Submission Ajax patterns to understand them better.

Listing 29-29: The Render method

```
protected override void RenderContents(HtmlTextWriter writer)
{
  writer.RenderBeginTag(HtmlTextWriterTag.Tr);
  writer.RenderBeginTag(HtmlTextWriterTag.Td);
  writer.RenderBeginTag(HtmlTextWriterTag.Label);
  writer.Write("Enter a phrase");
  writer.RenderEndTag();
  writer.RenderEndTag();
  writer.RenderBeginTag(HtmlTextWriterTag.Td);
  writer.AddAttribute(HtmlTextWriterAttribute.Type, "text");
  writer.AddAttribute(HtmlTextWriterAttribute.Id, ClientID + "_Phrase");
  writer.RenderBeginTag(HtmlTextWriterTag.Input);
  writer.RenderEndTag();
  writer.RenderEndTag();
  writer.RenderBeginTag(HtmlTextWriterTag.Td);
  writer.AddAttribute(HtmlTextWriterAttribute.Id, ClientID + "_SubmitButton");
  string js = Page.ClientScript.GetCallbackEventReference(this,
                                  "GetPhrase('"+ClientID+"_Phrase"+"')",
                                  "SubmitCallback",
                                  "'" + ClientID + "_Suggestion"+"'", true);
  writer.AddAttribute(HtmlTextWriterAttribute.Onclick, js);
  writer.RenderBeginTag(HtmlTextWriterTag.Button);
  writer.Write("Submit");
  writer.RenderEndTag();
  writer.RenderEndTag();
  writer.RenderEndTag();
  writer.RenderBeginTag(HtmlTextWriterTag.Tr);
  writer.RenderBeginTag(HtmlTextWriterTag.Td);
  writer.AddAttribute(HtmlTextWriterAttribute.Id, ClientID + "_Suggestion");
  writer.RenderBeginTag(HtmlTextWriterTag.Div);
  writer.RenderEndTag();
  writer.RenderEndTag();
  writer.RenderEndTag();
}
```

Implementing ICallbackEventHandler

Listing 29-30 contains the code for the `RaiseCallbackEvent` and `GetCallbackResult` methods.

Listing 29-30: The RaiseCallbackEvent and GetCallbackResult methods

```
private string callbackResult;
protected virtual string GetCallbackResult()
{
  return callbackResult;
```

```
    }

    protected virtual void RaiseCallbackEvent(string eventArgument)
    {
      XmlWebServiceMethodInvoker invoker = new XmlWebServiceMethodInvoker();
      invoker.TypeName = TypeName;
      invoker.WSDLPath = WSDLPath;
      invoker.EnableCaching = true;
      invoker.CacheDuration = 600;
      invoker.CacheExpirationPolicy =
                    XmlWebServiceMethodInvokerCacheExpirationPolicy.Absolute;

      OrderedDictionary args = new OrderedDictionary();
      args.Add(LicenseKeyParameterName, LicenseKey);
      args.Add(PhraseParameterName, eventArgument);

      callbackResult = (string)invoker.InvokeXmlWebServiceMethod(MethodName, args,
                                                        false);
    }
```

As Listing 29-30 shows, `RaiseCallbackEvent` uses the `XmlWebServiceMethodInvoker` component developed in Chapter 10 to invoke the method of the underlying XML Web service, such as Google Web service, that performs the spell-checking. `AjaxSpellChecker` exposes the following six properties:

❑ `TypeName`: The name of the class that represents the XML Web service. In the case of the Google API, the page developer must set this to the string value `GoogleSearchService`, which is the name of the Google class discussed in the previous chapter.

❑ `WSDLPath`: The URL of the site where the WSDL document can be downloaded from. In the case of Google XML Web service API, the page developer must set this to `http://api.google .com/GoogleSearch.wsdl`.

❑ `LicenseKey`: The license key for accessing the Web service. In the case of Google XML Web service, you have to create an account with Google to get this license key, as discussed before.

❑ `LicenseKeyParameterName`: The name of the parameter of the XML Web service method that is used to pass the license key. In the case of Google XML Web service, the page developer must set this to the string value `key`.

❑ `PhraseParameterName`: The name of the parameter of the XML Web service method that is used to pass the text to be spell-checked. In the case of Google XML Web service, the page developer must set this to the string value `phrase`.

❑ `MethodName`: The name of the XML Web service method that performs the spell-checking. In the case of Google XML Web service, the page developer must set this to the string value `doSpelling Suggestion`.

JavaScript Functions

As discussed, when the server response arrives, the `SubmitCallback` JavaScript function is automatically called. Listing 29-31 contains the implementation of this function. `SubmitCallback` first checks whether the underlying XML Web service (such as Google XML Web service) has provided a spelling suggestion. If so, it uses the `innerHTML` property of the `label` HTML element on top of the top toolbar to display the spelling suggestion. If not, it uses the same property of the same the `label` element to displays the text "No suggestion". Notice that `SubmitCallback` appends the value of a counter to the text "No suggestion" to provide you with a visual clue that the communication between the client and server keeps going as you're typing without interrupting your typing.

Listing 29-31: The SubmitCallback JavaScript function

```
var cntr = 1;
function SubmitCallback(result,suggestionLabelId)
{
  var content;
  if (result)
  {
    content = "<br/><b>Spelling Suggestion: </b>";
    content += result;
    cntr = 1;
  }
  else
  {
    content = "No suggestion." + cntr;
    cntr++;
  }
  var suggestionLabel = document.getElementById(suggestionLabelId);
  suggestionLabel.innerHTML = content;
}
```

Listing 29-32 presents the implementation of the JavaScript function that retrieves the text to be spell-checked from the text field and passes it to the server.

Listing 29-32: The GetPhrase JavaScript function

```
function GetPhrase(phraseTextBoxId)
{
  var phraseTextBox = document.getElementById(phraseTextBoxId);
  return phraseTextBox.value;
}
```

Listing 29-33 contains a page that uses the `AjaxSpellChecker` control. Figure 29-3 shows what the end users see when they access this page.

Listing 29-33: A page that uses the AjaxSpellChecker control

```
<%@ Page Language="C#" %>
<%@ Register TagPrefix="custom" Namespace="CustomComponents"
Assembly="CustomComponents" %>
<html xmlns="http://www.w3.org/1999/xhtml">
<body>
  <form id="form1" runat="server">
    <custom:AjaxSpellChecker runat="server" ID="spellchecker"
      WSDLPath="http://api.google.com/GoogleSearch.wsdl"
      TypeName="GoogleSearchService" MethodName="doSpellingSuggestion"
      LicenseKeyParameterName="key"
```

```
            PhraseParameterName="phrase" LicenseKey="YourLicenceKeyGoesHere" />
    </form>
</body>
</html>
```

This page uses the Google XML Web service API to perform spell-checking. Notice the page developer has set the values of the `WSDLPath`, `TypeName`, `MethodName`, `LicenseKeyParameterName`, `Phrase ParameterName`, and `LicenseKey` properties of the `AjaxSpellChecker` control to the values of the respective Google parameters. The `AjaxSpellChecker` control isn't tied to the Google API and is able to talk to any XML Web service API that exposes a method that takes two string arguments (license key, query search) and returns a string that contains spelling suggestion.

Summary

This chapter discussed three popular Ajax patterns known as Periodic Refresh, Submission Throttling, and Explicit Submission and used these patterns to develop three Ajax-enabled controls named `AjaxNotifier`, `AjaxHtmlEditor`, and `AjaxSpellChecker` to show you how to use these patterns to implement your own Ajax-enabled controls.

The last four chapters of this book discuss the ASP.NET 2.0 Web Part Framework in detail and show you how to develop your own custom Web Parts controls and components.

Understanding the ASP.NET 2.0 Web Parts Framework

The ASP.NET Web Parts Framework is a component-based architecture that consists of extensible components. This chapter uses examples to discuss the following topics:

❑ Turning a regular server control such as an ASP.NET control, custom control, or user control into a runtime `WebPart` control

❑ Moving, adding, exporting, and importing `WebPart` controls

❑ Personalizing standard and custom properties of `WebPart` controls

❑ In-depth discussions of the `Part` base class

This chapter will also prepare you for the next chapters where you'll learn how to extend the Web Parts control set to write your own custom components.

What Is the ASP.NET Web Parts Framework?

A complex Framework such as the ASP.NET Web Parts Framework can easily overwhelm you if you're new to it. When you're learning a complex Framework, it normally helps if you first get an overview of the main components before diving into their details. This is exactly what this section does. If you don't really follow the components discussed in this section, don't worry because they are covered in depth in the next sections.

The Framework allows you to componentize an ASP.NET page into a set of server controls, where each control occupies a particular region or zone on the page. These server controls are known as *WebZone controls* because they all directly or indirectly derive from the `WebZone` base class.

A `WebZone` server control is a composite control that contains one or more child server controls. These child controls are known as *Part controls* because they all directly or indirectly derive from the `Part` base class. The ASP.NET Web Parts Framework comes with three descendants of the `Part` base class, which means that there are three types of `Part` controls:

❑ **WebPart:** `WebPart` server controls make up the UI of an ASP.NET Web page. You can think of `WebPart` controls as the building blocks of the UI of a Web page.

❑ **EditorPart:** `EditorPart` server controls provide end users with the appropriate UIs to personalize the properties of the `WebPart` controls that make up the UI of a page.

❑ **CatalogPart:** `CatalogPart` server controls provide end users with a catalog or list of `WebPart` controls to choose from.

The ASP.NET Web Parts Framework comes with four descendants of the `WebZone` base class, which means that there are four types of `WebZone` controls:

❑ **WebPartZone:** `WebPartZone` server controls are composite controls that contain the `WebPart` controls that make up the UI of a Web page.

❑ **EditorPartZone:** `EditorPartZone` server controls are composite controls that contain the `EditorPart` controls that provide users with the appropriate UI to personalize the properties of the `WebPart` controls that make up the UI of a Web page

❑ **CatalogPartZone:** `CatalogPartZone` server controls are composite controls that contain the `CatalogPart` controls that provide users with the catalog or list of `WebPart` controls to choose from.

❑ **ConnectionsZone:** A `ConnectionsZone` server control provides users with the appropriate UI to perform the following tasks, as discussed later in this chapter:

    ❑ Establish connections between `WebPart` controls that make up the UI of a page so they can share data

    ❑ Remove existing connections between `WebPart` controls to stop them from sharing data

    ❑ Personalize the connections between `WebPart` controls

The ASP.NET Web Parts Framework comes with four descendants of the `EditorPart` base class, which means that there are four types of `EditorPart` controls: `AppearanceEditorPart`, `LayoutEditorPart`, `BehaviorEditorPart`, and `PropertyGridEditorPart`. These four `EditorPart` controls provide end users with the appropriate UIs to respectively personalize the appearance, layout, behavior, and custom properties of the `WebPart` controls that make up the UI of an ASP.NET Web page.

The ASP.NET Web Parts Framework comes with three subclasses of the `CatalogPart` base class, which means that there are three types of `CatalogPart` controls:

❑ **DeclarativeCatalogPart:** A `DeclarativeCatalogPart` control provides end users with the catalog or list of all available `WebPart` controls that users can add to the `WebPartZone` controls on the page.

❑ **PageCatalogPart:** Users have the option of closing existing `WebPart` controls. The ASP.NET Web Parts Framework automatically adds these `WebPart` controls to the `PageCatalogPart` composite control. In other words, the `PageCatalogPart` control provides the end users with the catalog or list of closed `WebPart` controls that users can add back to the page.

❑ **ImportCatalogPart:** An `ImportCatalogPart` control provides users with the appropriate UI to import `WebPart` controls as XML files.

The ASP.NET Web Parts Framework comes with a server control named `WebPartManager` whose main responsibility is to manage all the zones and parts declared on an ASP.NET page. Every Web Parts page can have one and only one `WebPartManager` control. `WebPartManager` also switches a Web Parts page from one display mode to another.

Every Web Parts page can be in one of the following display modes:

❑ **BrowseDisplayMode:** Renders the `WebPart` controls that make up the UI of the page in their normal mode.

❑ **DesignDisplayMode:** Renders the `WebPartZone` control's UI that enables users to drag `WebPart` controls from one `WebPartZone` to another to change the page layout.

❑ **EditDisplayMode:** Renders the `EditorPart` controls' UIs that enable users to personalize the appearance, layout, behavior, and custom properties of the `WebPart` controls.

❑ **CatalogDisplayMode:** Renders the `CatalogPart` controls' UIs that provide users with a catalog or list of `WebParts` controls to choose from.

❑ **ConnectDisplayMode:** Renders the `ConnectionsZone` control's UI to enable users to connect one `WebPart` control to another so they can share data.

So, what is a `WebPart`? A `WebPart` is a server control that allows users to personalize its following aspects right from their browsers:

❑ Users can dynamically access the `WebPart` control from the catalog or list of `WebPart` controls on the `DeclarativeCatalogPart` control's UI and add the control to a given `WebPartZone` composite control.

❑ Users can use the `WebPartZone` control's UI to dynamically remove, minimize, and restore the `WebPart` control.

❑ Users can close the `WebPart` control and access it again from the catalog or list of closed `WebPart` controls that the `PageCatalogPart` control maintains.

❑ Users can dynamically import the `WebPart` control from the UI that the `ImportCatalogPart` control provides.

❑ Users can dynamically personalize the appearance, layout, behavior, and custom properties of the `WebPart` control from the UIs that the `AppearanceEditorPart`, `LayoutEditorPart`, `BehaviorEditorPart`, and `PropertyGridEditorPart` controls provide.

❑ Users can dynamically move the `WebPart` control from one `WebPartZone` composite control to another.

❑ Users can use the UI that the `ConnectionsZone` control provides to connect the `WebPart` control to another `WebPart` control so they can share data.

Developing WebPart Controls Declaratively

There are different approaches to developing a `WebPart` control. The first approach allows you to turn any of the following server controls into a `WebPart` control without writing a single line of code:

❑ ASP.NET standard server controls, such as `Calendar`

❑ Custom server controls, such as the ones you've been developing in this book

❑ User controls

All you need to do is place any of these server controls within the opening and closing tags of an `<asp:WebPartZone>` element on your ASP.NET Web page. At runtime, the ASP.NET Web Parts Framework automatically wraps your server control in an instance of a control named `GenericWebPart` that derives from the `WebPart` base class. This wrapper allows your server control to act like a normal `WebPart` control at runtime.

Listing 30-1 shows a simple Web page where the `Calendar` control is turned into a `WebPart` control. Here are the steps Listing 30-1 takes to implement the Web page:

1. Declare a single instance of the `WebPartManager` control. Every Web Parts page must contain one and only one instance of the `WebPartManager` control:

```
<asp:WebPartManager runat="server" ID="mgr" />
```

2. Declare an instance of the `WebPartZone` control. Notice that the `WebPartZone` control is a template control with a template property named `ZoneTemplate`:

```
<asp:WebPartZone runat="server" ID="zone1">
```

3. Place the `Calendar` control within the opening and closing tags of the `<ZoneTemplate>` element:

```
<asp:WebPartZone runat="server" ID="zone1">
  <ZoneTemplate>
    <asp:Calendar runat="server" ID="calendar1" Title="Calendar"/>
  </ZoneTemplate>
</asp:WebPartZone>
```

That's all! Three simple steps turn a normal server control such as `Calendar` into a `WebPart` control that supports all the features discussed in the previous section. Figure 30-1 shows what the users see at runtime. Notice that the ASP.NET Web Parts Framework has automatically added a UI known as *chrome* around the `Calendar` control. As Figure 30-1 shows, the chrome consists of elements such as header, footer, border, title, and action buttons. When the user clicks the little arrow on the top right-hand side of the chrome, a menu pops up that consists of two standard action buttons. These action buttons are known as *verbs*. The `Minimize` and `Close` verbs in Figure 30-1 allow the user to minimize or close the `WebPart` control.

Listing 30-1: A Web Parts page where the Calendar control acts as a WebPart control

```
<%@ Page Language="C#" %>
<html xmlns="http://www.w3.org/1999/xhtml">
<body>
```

```
    <form id="form1" runat="server">
      <asp:WebPartManager runat="server" ID="mgr" />

      <asp:WebPartZone runat="server" ID="zone1" . . .>
        <ZoneTemplate>

          . . .
          <asp:Calendar runat="server" ID="calendar1" Title="Calendar"
          BackColor="White" BorderColor="Black" BorderStyle="Solid" CellSpacing="1"
          Font-Names="Verdana" Font-Size="9pt" ForeColor="Black" Height="250px"
          NextPrevFormat="ShortMonth" Width="330px">
            <TodayDayStyle BackColor="#999999" ForeColor="White" />
            <SelectedDayStyle BackColor="#333399" ForeColor="White" />
            <OtherMonthDayStyle ForeColor="#999999" />
            <TitleStyle BackColor="#333399" BorderStyle="Solid" Font-Bold="True"
            Font-Size="12pt" ForeColor="White" Height="12pt" />
            <NextPrevStyle Font-Bold="True" Font-Size="8pt" ForeColor="White" />
            <DayStyle BackColor="#CCCCCC" />
            <DayHeaderStyle Font-Bold="True" Font-Size="8pt" ForeColor="#333333"
            Height="8pt" />
          </asp:Calendar>

        </ZoneTemplate>

      </asp:WebPartZone>
    </form>
  </body>
</html>
```

Figure 30-1

You can also place a user control within the opening and closing tags of an `<asp:WebPartZone>` control to turn it into a `WebPart` control at the runtime. Here is an example. Listing 30-2 contains the implementation of a user control named `RssReaderUserControl` that downloads RSS feeds and displays them in a `DataList` control.

Listing 30-2: The RssReaderUserControl user control

```
<%@ Control Language="C#" ClassName="RssReaderUserControl" %>

<script runat="server">
  private string rssUrl;
  [Personalizable(true)]
  public string RssUrl
  {
    get { return rssUrl; }
    set { rssUrl = value; }
  }

  protected void Page_Load(object sender, EventArgs e)
  {
    MySource.DataFile = RssUrl;
  }
</script>

<div>
  <asp:DataList runat="server" DataSourceID="MySource" ID="dl">
    <ItemTemplate>
      <asp:HyperLink runat="server" ID="title" Font-Bold="true"
      NavigateUrl='<%# XPath("link/text()") %>'
      Text='<%# XPath("title/text()") %>' />
      <br />
      <asp:Label runat="server" ID="description"
      Text='<%# XPath("description/text()") %>' />
    </ItemTemplate>
    <SeparatorTemplate>
      <br />
    </SeparatorTemplate>
  </asp:DataList>
  <asp:XmlDataSource runat="server" ID="MySource" XPath="//item" />
</div>
```

The RssReaderUserControl exposes a property named RssUrl that page developers can set to the URL of the RSS feed that they want to display. Notice that this property is marked with the [Personalizable(true)] metadata attribute to have the ASP.NET Web Parts Framework to store the value of this property in the personalization data store.

As Listing 30-2 shows, the DataList control is bound to an XmlDataSource data source control that downloads the RSS feed. The page uses XPath queries to set the NavigateUrl and Text properties of the HyperLink control and the Text property of the Label control. The Page class exposes a method named XPath that takes the link/text(), title/text(), and description/text() XPath expressions, performs the required XPath queries, and returns the values of the link, title, and description elements of the current item of the RSS feed.

You can easily turn the RssReaderUserControl into a WebPart control by placing the user control within the opening and closing tags of an <asp:WebPartZone>, as shown in Listing 30-3. As Figure 30-2 shows, the ASP.NET Web Parts Framework automatically adds a chrome around the user control just as it did for the Calendar control.

Listing 30-3: A Web page where the RssReaderUserControl acts as a WebPart control

```
<%@ Page Language="C#" %>
<%@ Register TagPrefix="custom" TagName="RssReader"
Src="~/RssReaderUserControl.ascx" %>
<html xmlns="http://www.w3.org/1999/xhtml">
<body>
  <form id="form1" runat="server">
    <asp:WebPartManager runat="server" ID="mgr" />

    <asp:WebPartZone runat="server" ID="zone1" . . ..>
      <ZoneTemplate>

        <custom:RssReader runat="server" ID="rssreader2"
        Title="MSDN Just Published" RssUrl="http://msdn.microsoft.com/rss.xml" />

      </ZoneTemplate>
    </asp:WebPartZone>
  </form>
</body>
</html>
```

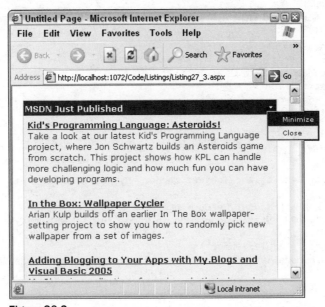

Figure 30-2

Moving WebPart Controls

The previous section showed you how you can turn a normal ASP.NET server control, custom server control, or user control into a WebPart control without writing a single line of code. This section shows you how to enable users to move WebPart controls from one WebPartZone control to another. All you have to do to accomplish this task is add the UI that allows users to switch from the browse mode to the design mode. Recall that when a WebParts page is in design mode, the ASP.NET Web Parts Framework automatically renders the UI that allows the users to move WebPart controls from one WebPartZone control to another.

Listing 30-4 shows an example. As the highlighted portion of this code listing shows, the page has been divided into two columns, where each column is occupied by one WebPartZone control. The first WebPartZone control contains the RssReaderUserControl discussed before, and the second WebPartZone control contains the Calendar control.

The first highlighted portion of Listing 30-4 contains the UI that allows users to switch from the browse mode to the design mode where they can move the RssReaderUserControl and Calendar WebPart controls from one WebPartZone control to another. This UI consists of two main server controls: a DropDownList and a LinkButton control. The DropDownList control displays the list of available display modes, Browse and Design.

Each time the user enters the design mode and moves the RssReaderUserControl and Calendar WebPart controls to change the page layout, the current layout setting of the page are automatically stored in the underlying personalization data store. The LinkButton control allows users to reset the personalization data.

Listing 30-4: A Web page that allows users to move WebPart controls

```
<%@ Page Language="C#" %>
<%@ Register TagPrefix="custom" TagName="RssReader"
Src="~/RssReaderUserControl.ascx" %>
<script runat="server">
  WebPartManager wpmgr;
  void Page_Init(object sender, EventArgs e)
  {
    Page.InitComplete += new EventHandler(InitCompleteCallback);
  }

  void InitCompleteCallback(object sender, System.EventArgs e)
  {
    wpmgr = WebPartManager.GetCurrentWebPartManager(Page);
    foreach (WebPartDisplayMode mode in wpmgr.SupportedDisplayModes)
    {
      if (mode.IsEnabled(wpmgr))
        DisplayModeList.Items.Add(new ListItem(mode.Name, mode.Name));
    }
  }

  void DisplayModeChangedCallback(object sender, EventArgs e)
  {
    wpmgr.DisplayMode = wpmgr.SupportedDisplayModes[DisplayModeList.SelectedValue];
  }

  protected void ResetCallback(object sender, EventArgs e)
  {
    wpmgr.Personalization.ResetPersonalizationState();
  }
```

```
    </script>

<html xmlns="http://www.w3.org/1999/xhtml">
<body>
  <form id="form1" runat="server">
    <asp:WebPartManager runat="server" ID="mgr2" />

    <asp:Label ID="Label1" runat="server" Text="Display Mode: " Font-Bold="true" />
    <asp:DropDownList ID="DisplayModeList" runat="server" AutoPostBack="true"
    OnSelectedIndexChanged="DisplayModeChangedCallback" /> 
    <asp:LinkButton ID="LinkButton1" runat="server" Text="Reset"
    OnClick="ResetCallback" /><br />

    <table>
      <tr>
        <td valign="top">
          <asp:WebPartZone runat="server" ID="zone1" BorderColor="#CCCCCC"
          Font-Names="Verdana" Padding="6">
            <ZoneTemplate>
              <custom:RssReader ScrollBars="Auto" runat="server" ID="rssreader3"
              Title="MSDN Just Published"
              RssUrl="http://msdn.microsoft.com/rss.xml" />
            </ZoneTemplate>
          </asp:WebPartZone>
        </td>
        <td valign="top">
          <asp:WebPartZone runat="server" ID="WebPartZone1" . . .>
            <ZoneTemplate>
              <asp:Calendar runat="server" ID="calendar1" Title="Calendar" . . .>
                . . .
              </asp:Calendar>
            </ZoneTemplate>
          </asp:WebPartZone>
        </td>
      </tr>
    </table>
  </form>
</body>
</html>
```

Here's how the code in Listing 30-4 enables users to switch from Browse to Design mode. First, the code registers the InitCompleteCallback method as the callback for the InitComplete event of the page:

```
void Page_Init(object sender, EventArgs e)
{
    Page.InitComplete += new EventHandler(InitCompleteCallback);
}
```

The InitCompleteCallback method calls the GetCurrentWebPartManager static method of the WebPartManager class to access the WebPartManager control declared on the page. Strictly speaking, you don't really have to call this method in this case to access the declared WebPartManager control because you can directly use the control's ID. This is possible because the page directly contains the HTML and the callback methods for the UI that allows users to switch between modes. Another approach would be to implement a user control or custom control to encapsulate these HTML and call-back methods. Such a user control or custom control should then use the `GetCurrentWebPartManager` static method of the `WebPartManager` class to access the `WebPartManager` instance that the page developer declares on the page.

The `WebPartManager` class exposes a collection property named `SupportedDisplayModes` that contains all the available display modes. The `InitCompleteCallback` method iterates through the list of available display modes and adds those modes that are enabled for the current page to the `DropDownList` control that shows the display modes to the users. In this case, only Browse and Design modes are enabled because enabling other display modes requires you to declare other controls, such as `EditorZone`, on the page, as discussed in the next sections.

```
void InitCompleteCallback(object sender, System.EventArgs e)
{
  wpmgr = WebPartManager.GetCurrentWebPartManager(Page);
  foreach (WebPartDisplayMode mode in wpmgr.SupportedDisplayModes)
  {
    if (mode.IsEnabled(wpmgr))
      DisplayModeList.Items.Add(new ListItem(mode.Name, mode.Name));
  }
}
```

The Web page then registers the `DisplayModeChangedCallback` method as the callback for the `SelectedIndexChanged` event of the `DropDownList` control that displays the list of enabled display modes to users. This method uses the selected value of the `DropDownList` control as an index into the `SupportedDisplayModes` collection property of the `WebPartManager` control to access the associated `WebPartDisplayMode` enumeration value, which is then assigned to the `DisplayMode` property of the `WebPartManager` control.

In other words, setting the `DisplayMode` property of the `WebPartManager` control is all you need to switch the page from one display mode to another:

```
void DisplayModeChangedCallback(object sender, EventArgs e)
{
  wpmgr.DisplayMode = wpmgr.SupportedDisplayModes[DisplayModeList.SelectedValue];
}
```

The page then registers the `ResetCallback` method as the callback for the `Click` event of the `LinkButton` control that allows users to reset their personalization data. The `WebPartManager` class exposes a property of the type `WebPartPersonalization` named `Personalization` that manages low-level personalization operations. The `WebPartPersonalization` class exposes a method named `ResetPersonalizationState` that resets the saved personalization data:

```
protected void ResetCallback(object sender, EventArgs e)
{
  wpmgr.Personalization.ResetPersonalizationState();
}
```

Figure 30-3 shows what users see on the browser after they select the Design option from the `DropDownList` control that displays the enabled display modes for the current page. As this figure shows, the user can drag each `WebPart` control from the `WebPartZone` it is currently in to another `WebPartZone`.

Figure 30-3

Personalizing WebPart Controls' Properties

Here are the steps you must take to enable users to personalize the `WebPart` controls' appearance, layout, behavior, and custom properties:

1. Declare an `EditorZone` control on the page. This declaration automatically enables the page's edit display mode.

2. Add `AppearanceEditorPart`, `LayoutEditorPart`, `BehaviorEditorPart`, and `PropertyGridEditorPart` controls to the `EditorZone` control to provide users with the appropriate UIs to respectively personalize the appearance, layout, behavior, and custom properties of the `WebPart` controls that make up the UI of an ASP.NET Web page.

Listing 30-5 shows an example. As the highlighted section of this code listing shows, the page consists of three columns where the last column is allocated to the `EditorZone` control. This control only shows up when the page switches to the editor display mode. The page shown in Listing 30-5 adds the `AppearanceEditorPart` and `LayoutEditorPart` controls to the `EditorZone` control. These two controls render the appropriate UIs to allow the user to personalize the appearance and layout properties of the `RssReaderUserControl` and `Calendar WebPart` controls.

The user must first select the Edit display mode option from the `DropDownList` control that shows the list of enabled display modes for the page. This selection automatically switches the page to its edit mode. Recall that every `WebPart` control contains a menu in its title bar that consists of action buttons or verbs. When the page is switched to the edit display mode, the ASP.NET Web Parts Framework automatically adds the Edit option to the menu of each `WebPart` control on the page.

Then the user must select the Edit option from the menu of the desired `WebPart` control. This selection automatically renders the `AppearanceEditorPart` and `LayoutEditorPart` controls to provide users with the appropriate UIs to personalize the appearance and layout properties of the control. Figure 30-4 shows the page right after the user selects the Edit option from the menu on the title bar of the `RssReaderUserControl` WebPart.

Listing 30-5: A Web Parts page that allows users to personalize the WebPart controls' properties

```
<%@ Page Language="C#" %>
<%@ Register TagPrefix="custom" TagName="RssReader"
  Src="~/RssReaderUserControl.ascx" %>
<script runat="server">
  WebPartManager wpmgr;
  void Page_Init(object sender, EventArgs e)
  {
    Page.InitComplete += new EventHandler(InitCompleteCallback);
  }

  void InitCompleteCallback(object sender, System.EventArgs e)
  {
    wpmgr = WebPartManager.GetCurrentWebPartManager(Page);
    foreach (WebPartDisplayMode mode in wpmgr.SupportedDisplayModes)
    {
      if (mode.IsEnabled(wpmgr))
        DisplayModeList.Items.Add(new ListItem(mode.Name, mode.Name));
    }
  }
  . . .
</script>
<html xmlns="http://www.w3.org/1999/xhtml">
<body>
  <form id="form1" runat="server">
    <asp:WebPartManager runat="server" ID="mgr2" />
    <table width="700">
      <tr>
        <td colspan="3" align="left">
          . . .
        </td>
      </tr>
      <tr>
        <td valign="top">
          <asp:WebPartZone runat="server" ID="zone1" . . .>
          . . .
            <ZoneTemplate>
              <custom:RssReader runat="server" . . ./>
            </ZoneTemplate>
          </asp:WebPartZone>
        </td>
        <td valign="top">
          <asp:WebPartZone runat="server" ID="WebPartZone1" . . .>
            <ZoneTemplate>
```

```
            <asp:Calendar runat="server" ID="calendar1" Title="Calendar" . . .>
              . . .
            </asp:Calendar>
          </ZoneTemplate>
        </asp:WebPartZone>
      </td>
      <td valign="top" style="width: 150px">
        <asp:EditorZone runat="server" ID="editorzone1" . . .>
          . . .
        <ZoneTemplate>
          <asp:AppearanceEditorPart runat="server" ID="appearance1" />
          <asp:LayoutEditorPart runat="server" ID="layout1" />
        </ZoneTemplate>

        </asp:EditorZone>
      </td>
    </tr>
  </table>
 </form>
</body>
</html>
```

As the boldface section of Listing 30-5 shows, this time around, the IsEnabled property of the EditorDisplayMode option will return true, which means that this option will be added to the list of display modes that the DropDownList control displays to users.

Figure 30-4

Personalizing WebPart Controls' Custom Properties

User controls such as RssReaderUserControl may expose properties of their own. The Property GridEditorPart control automatically renders the appropriate UI to allow users to edit the custom properties of your controls provided that you mark your properties with the [WebBrowsable()] metadata attribute. The PropertyGridEditorPart control uses reflection under the hood to retrieve the type of each property to determine the type of editing interface it needs to render. For example, if the property is a Boolean, the control renders a CheckBox control. If the property is an enumeration, the control renders a DropDownList control that displays the possible values of the enumeration.

As Listing 30-6 shows, the RssReaderUserControl marks its RssUrl custom property with the [WebBrowsable()] attribute to instruct the PropertyGridEditorPart control to render the appropriate UI to allow users to dynamically change the value of this property so they can display the RSS feed from the desired Web site. Listing 30-7 shows a Web page that adds a PropertyGridEditorPart control to an EditorZone composite control. As Figure 30-5 shows, the PropertyGridEditorPart control renders a TextBox control to allow users to specify the URL for the RSS feed.

Listing 30-6: The RssReaderUserControl user control

```
<%@ Control Language="C#" ClassName="RssReaderUserControl" %>
<script runat="server">
  private string rssUrl;

  [WebBrowsable()]
  [Personalizable(true)]
  public string RssUrl
  {
    get { return rssUrl; }
    set { rssUrl = value; }
  }
  . . .
</script>
<div>
  <asp:DataList runat="server" DataSourceID="MySource" ID="dl">
    <ItemTemplate>
      <asp:HyperLink runat="server NavigateUrl='<%# XPath("link/text()") %>'
      Text='<%# XPath("title/text()") %>' />
      <asp:Label runat="server" Text='<%# XPath("description/text()") %>' />
    </ItemTemplate>
    . . .
  </asp:DataList>
  <asp:XmlDataSource runat="server" ID="MySource" XPath="//item" />
</div>
```

Listing 30-7: A Web Parts page that allows users to personalize the WebPart controls' custom properties

```
<%@ Page Language="C#" %>
<%@ Register TagPrefix="custom" TagName="RssReader"
Src="~/RssReaderUserControl.ascx" %>
```

```
<script runat="server">
  . . .
</script>
<html xmlns="http://www.w3.org/1999/xhtml">
<body>
  <form id="form1" runat="server">
    <asp:WebPartManager runat="server" ID="mgr2" />
    <table width="700">
      <tr>
        . . .
      </tr>
      <tr>
        . . .
        <td valign="top" style="width: 150px">
          <asp:EditorZone runat="server" ID="editorzone1" Padding="6" . . .>
            <ZoneTemplate>
              <asp:AppearanceEditorPart runat="server" ID="appearance1" />
              <asp:LayoutEditorPart runat="server" ID="layout1" />
              <asp:PropertyGridEditorPart runat="server" ID="propertygrid1" />
            </ZoneTemplate>
          </asp:EditorZone>
        </td>
      </tr>
    </table>
  </form>
</body>
</html>
```

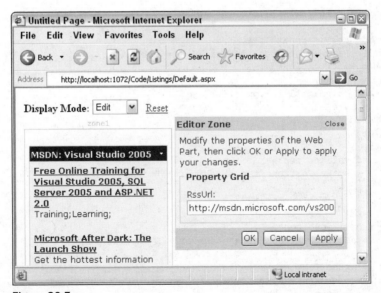

Figure 30-5

Adding Declared WebPart Controls

Declared WebPart controls are controls that are declared within a DeclarativeCatalogPart control. Here are the steps you must implement to allow users to add declared WebPart controls to the page to personalize the page content:

1. Add a CatalogZone control to the page. The presence of this zone control signals the ASP.NET Web Parts Framework to enable the CatalogDisplayMode option for the page, which means that this option will be added to the list of display modes that the DropDownList control displays.

2. Add a DeclarativeCatalogPart control to the CatalogZone control.

3. Add the desired WebPart controls to the DeclarativeCatalogPart control.

Listing 30-8 shows an example. The page shown in this code listing adds the Calendar control to the DeclarativeCatalogPart control to allow users to add Calendar controls on demand.

Listing 30-8: A Web page that uses the DeclarativeCatalogPart control

```
<%@ Page Language="C#" %>
<%@ Register TagPrefix="custom" TagName="RssReader"
  Src="~/RssReaderUserControl.ascx" %>
<script runat="server">
  . . .
</script>

<html xmlns="http://www.w3.org/1999/xhtml">
<body>
  <form id="form1" runat="server">
    <asp:WebPartManager runat="server" ID="mgr2" />
    <table width="700">
      <tr>
        <td colspan="3" align="left">
          . . .
        </td>
      </tr>
      <tr>
        <td valign="top">
          <asp:WebPartZone runat="server" ID="zone1" . . .>
            . . .
          </asp:WebPartZone>
        </td>
        <td valign="top">
          <asp:WebPartZone runat="server" ID="WebPartZone1" . . .>
            . . .
            <ZoneTemplate>
              <custom:RssReader runat="server" ID="rssreader3" . . . />
            </ZoneTemplate>
          </asp:WebPartZone>
        </td>
        <td valign="top" style="width: 150px">
          <asp:EditorZone Width="200px" runat="server" ID="editorzone1" . . . >
```

```
          . . .
         <ZoneTemplate>
           . . .
         </ZoneTemplate>
       </asp:EditorZone>

       <asp:CatalogZone runat="server" ID="catalogzone1" . . .>
         <ZoneTemplate>
           <asp:DeclarativeCatalogPart runat="server" ID="deccatalog1">
             <WebPartsTemplate>
               <asp:Calendar runat="server" Title="Calendar" . . .>
                 . . .
               </asp:Calendar>
             </WebPartsTemplate>
           </asp:DeclarativeCatalogPart>
         </ZoneTemplate>
       </asp:CatalogZone>


       </td>
     </tr>
   </table>
 </form>
</body>
</html>
```

When the user selects the `Catalog` option from the `DropDownList` control that displays the enabled display modes, the ASP.NET Web Parts Framework automatically renders the `CatalogZone` control. This control provides the user with a catalog or list of available `WebParts` to choose from, as shown in Figure 30-6.

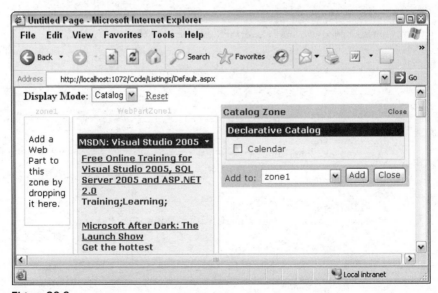

Figure 30-6

Adding Closed WebPart Controls

As discussed, when you add a normal server control such as an ASP.NET standard server control, custom server control, or user control to a `WebPartZone` composite control, the ASP.NET Web Parts Framework automatically wraps the server control in a `GenericWebPart` control to make it act like a `WebPart` control. This means that the server control, like all `WebParts` controls, will have chrome that contains a Close button, which allows the user to close the server control.

If you declare a `CatalogZone` control on the page and add a `PageCatalogPart` control to it, when the user closes a `WebPart` control, the ASP.NET Web Parts Framework will automatically add the closed `WebPart` control to the declared `PageCatalogPart` control so the user can access it later to add it back to the page if necessary.

The highlighted section of Listing 30-9 shows the declaration of a `CatalogZone` control that contains a `PageCatalogPart` control.

Listing 30-9: A Web page that declares a CatalogZone control that contains a PageCatalogPart control

```
<%@ Page Language="C#" %>
<%@ Register TagPrefix="custom" TagName="RssReader"
  Src="~/RssReaderUserControl.ascx" %>
<script runat="server">
  . . .
</script>

<html xmlns="http://www.w3.org/1999/xhtml">
<body>
  <form id="form1" runat="server">
    <asp:WebPartManager runat="server" ID="mgr2" />
    <table width="700">
      <tr>
        <td colspan="3" align="left">
          . . .
        </td>
      </tr>
      <tr>
        <td valign="top">
          <asp:WebPartZone runat="server" ID="zone1" . . .>
            . . .
          </asp:WebPartZone>
        </td>
        <td valign="top">
          <asp:WebPartZone runat="server" ID="WebPartZone1" . . .>
            . . .
            <ZoneTemplate>
              <custom:RssReader runat="server" ID="rssreader3" . . . />
            </ZoneTemplate>
          </asp:WebPartZone>
        </td>
```

```
<td valign="top" style="width: 150px">
   <asp:EditorZone Width="200px" runat="server" ID="editorzone1" . . . >
      . . .
      <ZoneTemplate>
         . . .
      </ZoneTemplate>
   </asp:EditorZone>

   <asp:CatalogZone runat="server" ID="catalogzone1" >
      <ZoneTemplate>
         <asp:DeclarativeCatalogPart runat="server" ID="deccatalog1">
            <WebPartsTemplate>
               <asp:Calendar runat="server" Title="Calendar" . . . />
            </WebPartsTemplate>
         </asp:DeclarativeCatalogPart>

         <asp:PageCatalogPart runat="server" ID="pagepart1" />

      </ZoneTemplate>
      . . .
   </asp:CatalogZone>

</td>
</tr>
</table>
</form>
</body>
</html>
```

When the user selects the Catalog option from the `DropDownList` control, the ASP.NET Web Parts Framework automatically renders the `CatalogZone` control. This control provides the user with a catalog or list of closed `WebParts` to choose from, as shown in Figure 30-7.

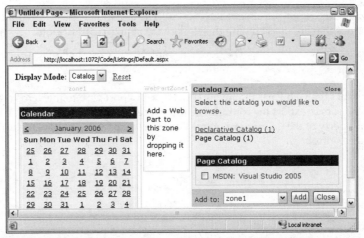

Figure 30-7

Exporting WebPart Controls

You can export the settings of a WebPart control (including runtime WebPart controls such as ASP.NET server controls and custom and user controls that reside in a WebPartZoneBase type zone such as WebPartZone) in XML format and save the XML document in a file with a .WebPart extension. These settings include the following:

❑ The fully qualified name of the type of the WebPart control, including its namespace, such as System.Web.UI.WebControls.Calendar

❑ The weak or strong name of the assembly that contains the WebPart control

❑ The values of the WebPart control's properties

Personalizing complex WebPart controls requires time and effort. The export feature of the Web Parts Framework allows users to share their WebPart controls' settings with others to save them from having to go through the same complex process to personalize the same WebPart controls.

To enable users to export the settings of a WebPart control, you must first set the enableExport attribute on the <webParts> element in the Web.config file to enable your Web application to export its WebPart controls:

```
<configuration>
  <system.web>
    <webParts enableExport="true" />
  </system.web>
</configuration>
```

Then you must set the ExportMode property of a WebPart control to any value other than "None" to enable the control to export its settings. The possible values of this property are as follows:

❑ WebPartExportMode.None: The WebPart control will export none of its properties.

❑ WebPartExportMode.NonSensitiveData: The WebPart control will only export nonsensitive properties that are marked with the [Personalizable()] attribute.

❑ WebPartExportMode.All: The WebPart control will export all of its properties that are marked with the [Personalizable()] attribute.

These steps instruct the Web Parts Framework to add an Export verb to the verbs menu of the WebPart control to allow users to export the control. The following code contains an ASP.NET page where the ExportMode property of the Calendar control has been set to "All" to allow the user to export all of the properties of the control:

```
<%@ Page Language="C#" %>
<html xmlns="http://www.w3.org/1999/xhtml">
<body>
  <form id="form1" runat="server">
    <asp:WebPartManager runat="server" ID="mgr" />
    <asp:WebPartZone runat="server" ID="zone1" . . .>
      <ZoneTemplate>
        <asp:Calendar runat="server" ID="cal" ExportMode="All" />
      </ZoneTemplate>
      . . .
    </asp:WebPartZone>
```

```
    </form>
  </body>
</html>
```

As Figure 30-8 shows, the Web Parts Framework adds an Export verb to the verbs menu of the `Calendar` `WebPart` control.

Figure 30-8

Only those properties of a `WebPart` control that are marked with `[Personalizable(true)]` metadata attribute can be exported. Therefore you must mark the properties of your user control with this metadata attribute if you want to allow users to export these properties. This metadata attribute also takes a second Boolean parameter that allows you to mark a property as sensitive, `[Personalizable(true, true)]`.

You can mark those properties of your user control that contain sensitive information—such as connection strings—as sensitive and set the `ExportMode` property of the user control `WebPart` to `NonSensitiveData` to instruct the Web Parts Framework not to export these properties even though they are marked with the `[Personalizable()]` attribute. For example, if you don't want users to export the `RssUrl` property of the `RssReaderUserControl`, you have to mark the `RssUrl` property with the `[Personalizable(true, true)]` metadata attribute to tell the Web Parts Framework that this property contains sensitive information, as highlighted portion of the following code fragment shows:

```
<%@ Control Language="C#" ClassName="RssReaderUserControl" %>
<script runat="server">
  private string rssUrl;

  [WebBrowsable()]
  [Personalizable(true, true)]
  public string RssUrl
  {
    get { return rssUrl; }
    set { rssUrl = value; }
  }
```

```
  . . .
  </script>
  <div>
    <asp:DataList runat="server" DataSourceID="MySource" ID="dl">
      <ItemTemplate>
        <asp:HyperLink runat="server NavigateUrl='<%# XPath("link/text()") %>'
        Text='<%# XPath("title/text()") %>' />
        <asp:Label runat="server" Text='<%# XPath("description/text()") %>' />
      </ItemTemplate>
      . . .
    </asp:DataList>
    <asp:XmlDataSource runat="server" ID="MySource" XPath="//item" />
  </div>
```

You then have to set the `ExportMode` property of the `RssReaderUserControl` to `NonSensitiveData`, as the highlighted portion of the following code fragment shows:

```
<%@ Page Language="C#" %>
<%@ Register TagPrefix="custom" TagName="RssReader"
Src="~/RssReaderUserControl.ascx" %>
<html xmlns="http://www.w3.org/1999/xhtml">
<body>
  <form id="form1" runat="server">
    <asp:WebPartManager runat="server" ID="mgr2" />
    <asp:WebPartZone runat="server" ID="WebPartZone1" . . .>
      <ZoneTemplate>
        <custom:RssReader ScrollBars="Auto" runat="server" ID="rssreader3"
        Title="MSDN Just Published" RssUrl="http://msdn.microsoft.com/rss.xml"
        ExportMode="NonSensitiveData" />
      </ZoneTemplate>
    </asp:WebPartZone>
  </form>
</body>
</html>
```

Adding Imported WebPart Controls

As discussed in the previous section, you can enable users to export your `WebPart` control to an XML document that can then be saved in a file. The import feature of the Web Parts Framework does the opposite; it uses the exported XML document to add a `WebPart` control of the same type as the originally exported `WebPart` control and with the same property settings.

To enable users to import `WebPart` controls, you should declaratively add an `ImportCatalogPart` control to the `CatalogZone` control on an ASP.NET Web page, as the highlighted portion of the following code fragment shows:

```
<%@ Page Language="C#" %>
<script runat="server">
  . . .
</script>

<html xmlns="http://www.w3.org/1999/xhtml">
<body>
  <form id="form1" runat="server">
```

```
<asp:WebPartManager runat="server" ID="mgr2" />
<table cellspacing="10">
  <tr>
    . . .
  </tr>
  <tr>
    <td colspan="2">
      <asp:CatalogZone runat="server" ID="myzone3" . . .>
        <ZoneTemplate>
          <asp:ImportCatalogPart runat="server" ID="myimport" />
        </ZoneTemplate>
        . . .
      </asp:CatalogZone>
    </td>
  </tr>
</table>
</form>
</body>
</html>
```

Here is how it works:

1. The user selects the Catalog option from the `DropDownList` control that displays the list of enabled display modes to switch the page to Catalog mode.

2. The `ImportCatalogPart` control presents the user with the UI shown in Figure 30-9.

3. The user clicks the Browse button on this UI to navigate to the directory where the XML document that describes the `WebPart` being imported is located.

4. The user clicks the Upload button on the UI to upload the XML file.

5. The `ImportCatalogPart` control uses the XML document as a recipe to add a `WebPart` control with the characteristics described in the document.

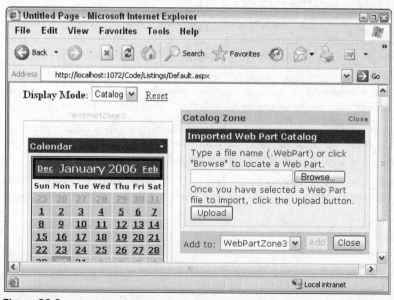

Figure 30-9

973

Main Components of the Web Parts Framework

Figure 30-10 shows the class or control diagram for the main Web Parts controls. The following section and the next three chapters delve into the details of these controls to help you understand what each control does and how you can extend its functionality.

The ASP.NET Web Parts Framework is a component-based architecture that consists of pluggable and replaceable components. In other words, it supports what is known as plug-and-play, where you can plug your own custom components into the Framework.

This is all possible because the components of the Framework talk to one another through well-defined APIs. In other words, the only dependency between these components is the APIs through which they communicate. These APIs shield these components from the specific types of the components they are communicating with. In other words, the components of the Framework have no knowledge of the actual types of the components they are talking to. This means that it doesn't matter what type of component is being used as long as the component complies with the specified API. That is why you can replace an existing component with one of your own without breaking the Framework as long as your component implements the required APIs.

The ASP.NET Web Parts Framework uses base classes such as `WebPart`, `EditorPart`, `CatalogPart`, `WebPartZoneBase`, `EditorZoneBase`, and `CatalogZoneBase` to define the APIs that all components must implement. In other words, the methods and properties of each base class define an API as follows:

❑ `WebPart`: Defines the API for the Web Parts controls that make up the UI of a Web Parts page. You can plug your own custom `WebPart` control into the Framework if your custom control implements the `WebPart` API.

❑ `EditorPart`: Defines the API for the Web Parts controls that are used to edit the `WebPart` controls. You can plug your own custom `EditorPart` control into the Framework if your custom control implements the `EditorPart` API.

❑ `CatalogPart`: Defines the API for the Web Parts controls that provide users with a catalog of `WebPart` controls to choose from. You can plug your own custom `CatalogPart` control into the Framework if your custom control implements the `CatalogPart` API.

❑ `WebPartZoneBase`: Defines the API for the Web Parts controls that act as containers for the `WebPart` controls. You can plug your own custom `WebPartZoneBase` control into the Framework if your custom control implements the `WebPartZoneBase` API.

❑ `EditorZoneBase`: Defines the API for the Web Parts controls that act as containers for the `EditorPart` controls. You can plug your own custom `EditorZoneBase` control into the Framework if your custom control implements the `EditorZoneBase` API.

❑ `CatalogZoneBase`: Defines the API for the Web Parts controls that act as containers for the `CatalogPart` controls.

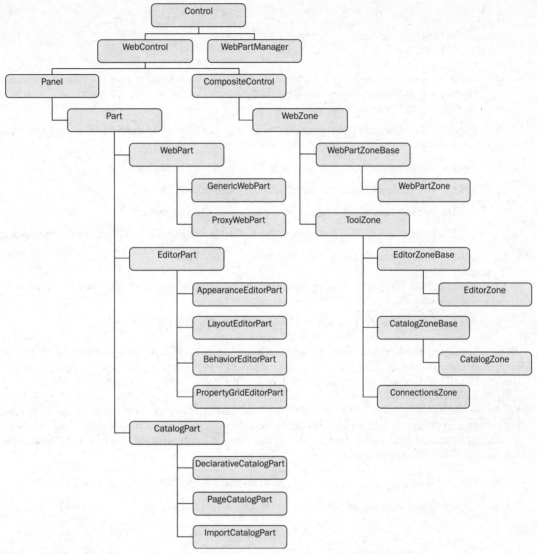

Figure 30-10

Part

As Figure 30-10 shows, the `Part` base class derives from the `Panel` class. `Part` has three subclasses: `WebPart`, `EditorPart`, and `CatalogPart`. The `Part` base class encapsulates those properties that all these subclasses have in common:

```
public virtual PartChromeState ChromeState {get; set;}
public virtual PartChromeType ChromeType {get; set;}
public virtual string Description {get; set;}
public virtual string Title {get; set;}
```

❑ ChromeState: A property of type PartChromeState enumeration that specifies whether a part control is in minimized or normal state. The possible values are PartChromeState.Minimized and PartChromeState.Normal.

❑ ChromeType: A property of type PartChromeType enumeration that specifies the type of border that frames a part control. The possible values are

  ❑ PartChromeType.BorderOnly: Border without a title bar

  ❑ PartChromeType.TitleOnly: A title bar without a border

  ❑ PartChromeType.TitleAndBorder: Both title bar and border

  ❑ PartChromeType.Default: Inherits the containing zone's PartChromeType setting

  ❑ PartChromeType.None: Neither title bar nor border

❑ Description: A short description of what the part control does. ToolTips and CatalogZone controls display this description to end users.

❑ Title: Gets or sets the text that appears in the title bar of a part control.

As you'll see later, another thing that all these three subclasses have in common is that all of them are composite controls, that is, they're all composed of other server controls, which means that these subclasses, like all composite controls, should derive from the CompositeControl base class.

Therefore, these subclasses must derive from two base classes: Part, which contains all their common properties, and CompositeControl. This isn't possible because C# and VB.NET don't support class multiple inheritance. That's why the Part base class literally implements all the functionality that the CompositeControl supports, as discussed in Chapter 5:

❑ Overriding the Controls collection to call the EnsureChildControls:

```
public override ControlCollection Controls
{
  get
  {
    EnsureChildControls();
    return base.Controls;
  }
}
```

❑ Implementing INamingInterface:

```
public abstract class Part : Panel, INamingContainer,
                             ICompositeControlDesignerAccessor
```

❑   Overriding the `DataBind` method:

```
public override void DataBind()
{
  OnDataBinding(EventArgs.Empty);
  EnsureChildControls();
  DataBindChildren();
}
```

❑   Implementing the `ICompositeControlDesignerAccessor` interface. This interface exposes a single method named `ReCreateChildControls` that allows designer developers to re-create the child controls of a composite control on the design surface. This is useful if you want to develop a custom designer for your composite control. A *designer* is a component that allows page developers to work with your custom composite control in a designer such as Visual Studio.

```
public abstract class Part : Panel, INamingContainer,
                           ICompositeControlDesignerAccessor
```

In summary, the `Part` base class is a simple composite control that exposes four simple properties named `ChromeState`, `ChromeType`, `Description`, and `Title`.

Summary

This chapter used examples to help you understand the main components of the ASP.NET Web Parts Framework such as `WebPart`, `EditorPart`, `CatalogPart`, `WebPartZone`, and so on. The next chapters build on what you've learned in this chapter to show you how to develop custom Web Parts controls.

31

Developing Custom WebPart, EditorPart, and CatalogPart Controls

The previous chapter discussed the Part base class and its methods and properties. This chapter discusses the subclasses of this base class, WebPart, EditorPart, and CatalogPart, and shows you how to develop your own custom WebPart, EditorPart, and CatalogPart controls.

This chapter covers the following topics:

❑ The WebPart base class and developing custom WebPart controls

❑ Implementing IWebPart, IWebActionable, IWebEditable, and IPersonalizable interfaces

❑ The WebPartVerb class and developing custom WebPartVerb verbs

❑ The EditorPart class and developing custom EditorPart controls

❑ The CatalogPart class and developing custom CatalogPart controls

WebPart

As you saw in Figure 30-10, the WebPart control derives from the Part control and implements the IWebPart, IWebActionable, and IWebEditable interfaces, as discussed in the following sections. Listing 31-1 contains the definition of the IWebPart interface. As this listing shows, this interface exposes six properties that every WebPart control must support to enhance the user experience.

Listing 31-1: The IWebPart interface

```
public interface IWebPart
{
  string CatalogIconImageUrl { get; set; }
  string Description { get; set; }
  string Subtitle { get; }
  string Title { get; set; }
  string TitleIconImageUrl { get; set; }
  string TitleUrl { get; set; }
}
```

The following list describes these properties:

❏   `CatalogIconImageUrl`: Specifies the URL to an image that the `CatalogZone` control uses to represent the `WebPart` control.

❏   `Description`: A short description of what the `WebPart` control does. ToolTips and `CatalogZone` controls display this description to end users.

❏   `Title`: The text that appears in the title bar of a `WebPart` control.

❏   `Subtitle`: The text that appears in the title bar of a `WebPart` control as subtitle.

❏   `TitleIconImageUrl`: Specifies the URL to an image that the title bar of a WebPart control uses to represent the control.

❏   `TitleUrl`: Specifies the URL to a page that contains more information about the `WebPart` control.

The `WebPart` control implements these properties of the `IWebPart` interface. As you'll see later in this chapter, if you implement a custom control that derives from the `WebPart` base class, your control doesn't have to implement the properties of the `IWebPart` interface because the base class has already implemented all these properties.

As discussed, you can turn any server control such as a standard ASP.NET control, custom server control, and user control into a *runtime* `WebPart` control if you add the control to a `WebPartZone` composite control (or any other custom composite control that derives from the `WebPartZoneBase` control as discussed later). The key word is *runtime*. At runtime, the ASP.NET Web Parts Framework automatically wraps the server control in an instance of the `GenericWebPart` control, allowing it to act like a normal `WebPart` control because the `GenericWebPart` control derives from the `WebPart` base class.

However, this all happens at runtime. Before that, the server control isn't a `WebPart` control, meaning it doesn't implement the properties of the `IWebPart` interface just described. This may seem to suggest that you can't set these properties on the tag that represents the control on an ASP.NET Web page. Yet if you examine Listings 30-1, 30-3, 30-4, 30-5, 30-7, and 30-8, you'll notice you've been setting the `Title` property on the tags that represent the `Calendar` and `RssReaderUserControl` server controls without any problems:

```
<asp:Calendar Title="Calendar" . . . />
```

How's that possible? The answer lies in the fact that the `Calendar` control derives from the `WebControl` base class, which implements an interface named `IAttributeAccessor`. The following code contains the definition of this interface:

```
public interface IAttributeAccessor
{
  string GetAttribute(string attributeName);
  void SetAttribute(string attributeName, string attributeValue);
}
```

The methods of this interface provide programmatic access to the attributes set on the opening tag of a server control such as `Calendar`. At runtime, these two methods are called to set and get the value of the `Title` attribute even though this attribute doesn't correspond to a property of the `Calendar` control.

You may be wondering if the same argument applies to user controls such as `RssReaderUserControl` because they don't seem to implement the `IAttributeAccessor` interface. The answer lies in what the page framework does with the `.ascx` file that contains the user control. Recall from Chapter 2 that the page framework performs the following tasks:

1. Parses the `.ascx` file that contains the user control.

2. Uses the parsed information to dynamically implement a control or class that derives from the `UserControl` base class.

3. Dynamically compiles the control or class.

4. Caches the compiled class.

5. Dynamically creates an instance of the compiled control.

6. Adds the instance to the containing page's control tree.

Because the `UserControl` base class implements the `IAttributeAccessor` interface, the page developer can set the `Title` attribute on the opening tag of a user control such as `RssReaderUserControl` even though this attribute doesn't correspond to a property of the user control.

In summary, you can set all the `WebPart` control's properties on a server control that you add to a `WebPartZoneBase` type zone if the control directly or indirectly implements the `IAttributeAccessor` interface.

The only downside to this approach is that you lose design-time support for these properties. In other words, Visual Studio doesn't recognize these properties as the properties of the server control and therefore you lose design-time features such as IntelliSense. To address this problem, your control should directly implement the `IWebPart` interface. Here is an example.

Listing 31-2 contains the code for a version of the `RssReaderUserControl` control that implements the `IWebPart` interface.

Listing 31-2: The version of RssReaderUserControl that implements IWebPart

```
<%@ Control Language="C#" ClassName="RssReaderUserControl2" %>
<%@ Implements Interface="System.Web.UI.WebControls.WebParts.IWebPart" %>

<script runat="server">
  private string rssUrl;
  [Personalizable(true)]
  [WebBrowsable()]
```

(continued)

Listing 31-2: *(continued)*

```
    public string RssUrl
    {
      get { return rssUrl; }
      set { rssUrl = value; }
    }

    protected void Page_Load(object sender, EventArgs e)
    {
      MySource.DataFile = RssUrl;
    }
```

```
    public string Description
    {
      get { return ViewState["Description"] != null ?
                              (string)ViewState["Description"] : string.Empty; }
      set { ViewState["Description"] = value; }
    }

    public string Title
    {
      get { return ViewState["Title"] != null ?
                                  (string)ViewState["Title"] : string.Empty; }
      set { ViewState["Title"] = value; }
    }

    public string Subtitle
    {
      get { return ViewState["Subtitle"] != null ?
                                  (string)ViewState["Subtitle"] : string.Empty; }
      set { ViewState["Subtitle"] = value; }
    }

    public string TitleIconImageUrl
    {
      get { return ViewState["TitleIconImageUrl"] != null ?
                          (string)ViewState["TitleIconImageUrl"] : string.Empty; }
      set { ViewState["TitleIconImageUrl"] = value; }
    }

    public string TitleUrl
    {
      get { return ViewState["TitleUrl"] != null ?
                                  (string)ViewState["TitleUrl"] : string.Empty; }
      set { ViewState["TitleUrl"] = value; }
    }

    public string CatalogIconImageUrl
    {
      get { return ViewState["CatalogIconImageUrl"] != null ?
                          (string)ViewState["CatalogIconImageUrl"] : string.Empty; }
      set { ViewState["CatalogIconImageUrl"] = value; }
    }
```

```
    </script>

    <div>
      <asp:DataList runat="server" DataSourceID="MySource" ID="dl">
        <ItemTemplate>
          <asp:HyperLink runat="server" ID="title" Font-Bold="true"
          NavigateUrl='<%# XPath("link/text()") %>'
          Text='<%# XPath("title/text()") %>' />
          <br />
          <asp:Label runat="server" ID="description"
          Text='<%# XPath("description/text()") %>' />
        </ItemTemplate>
        <SeparatorTemplate>
          <br />
        </SeparatorTemplate>
      </asp:DataList>
      <asp:XmlDataSource runat="server" ID="MySource" XPath="//item" />
    </div>
```

RssReaderUserControl, like all user controls, uses the <%@ Implements Interface="Interface
Name" %> directive to implement the IWebPart interface. The control then implements the properties of
the IWebPart interface, as shown in the highlighted portion of Listing 31-2.

Because RssReaderUserControl directly implements the IWebPart interface, the page developer can
benefit from the design-time supports such as IntelliSense when setting the Title, Subtitle,
Description, TitleIconImageUrl, TitleUrl, and CatalogIconImageUrl properties of the user
control.

Developing Custom WebPart Controls

So far you've learned one approach to developing custom WebPart controls — you can add any server
control, such as a standard ASP.NET control, custom control, or user control, to a WebPartZoneBase
type zone such as WebPartZone to have the Web Parts Framework turn your server control into a
WebPart control without any code on your part.

The great thing about this approach is that you get the job done with little effort. However, it comes with
a price:

❑   It takes you so far because it's not flexible or extensible.

❑   It limits you to developing custom WebPart controls. As discussed, the WebPart control is just
     one control among the many other Web Parts controls such as WebPartZone, EditorZone,
     CatalogZone, EditorPart, CatalogPart, and WebPartManager.

❑   You lose design-time features such as IntelliSense support unless you implement the required
     interfaces such as IWebPart.

This section implements a custom WebPart control named RssReaderWebPart that derives from the
WebPart base class to show you how to develop your own custom WebPart controls. Listing 31-3 illustrates the declaration of the members of the RssReaderWebPart custom WebPart control. The following
sections discuss the implementation of these members.

Listing 31-3: The declaration of the RssReaderWebPart control

```
public class RssReaderWebPart : WebPart
{
  public string RssUrl {get; set;}
  protected virtual void AddContainer();
  protected virtual void AddItemToContainer(XmlReader reader);
  protected override void CreateChildControls();
}
```

CreateChildControls

Listing 31-4 contains the code for the CreateChildControls method.

Listing 31-4: The CreateChildControls method

```
protected override void CreateChildControls()
{
  Controls.Clear();
  if (string.IsNullOrEmpty(rssUrl))
  {
    ChildControlsCreated = true;
    return;
  }

  using (XmlReader reader = XmlReader.Create(rssUrl))
  {
    AddContainer();
    reader.MoveToContent();
    reader.ReadToDescendant("channel");
    reader.ReadToDescendant("item");
    do
    {
      using (XmlReader itemReader = reader.ReadSubtree())
      {
        AddItemToContainer(itemReader);
      }
    } while (reader.ReadToNextSibling("item"));
  }
  ChildControlsCreated = true;
}
```

The RssReaderWebPart control exposes a property named RssUrl that the page developer must set to the URL to the RSS feed, as shown in Listing 31-5. RssUrl is marked with the [Personalizable(true)] metadata attribute to store the value in the personalization data store.

As Listing 31-4 illustrates, CreateChildControls uses an XmlReader to stream in the RSS document. As discussed in Chapter 24, when reading XML data such as RSS document, you have three options as follows:

❑   You can use the XmlReader streaming XML API to read in the XML document in streaming fashion.

❑ You can use the XPathNavigator random-access XML API to read in the XML document in cursor-style fashion.

❑ You can use the XmlDocument random-access DOM XML API to load the XML document into an XmlDocument.

Recall the handy rule of thumb from Chapter 24: Stream your XML unless you have a good reason not to. When you think about it, you don't really need to access the data in the RSS document in random fashion.

The CreateChildControls method then calls the AddContainer method to create the container control that will contain the entire contents of the RssReaderWebPart control. This method is discussed shortly. Notice that this method is marked as protected virtual to allow subclasses of the RssReaderWebPart control to use a different type of container control. This is an example of how you can make your custom WebPart controls more extensible:

```
AddContainer();
```

The method then calls the MoveToContent method of the XmlReader to position the reader on the document element, the <rss> element:

```
reader.MoveToContent();
```

It then calls the ReadToDescendant method of the XmlReader to move the reader from the <rss> element to the <channel> element. As discussed in Chapter 24, you have to constantly be aware of the node on which the XmlReader is currently positioned because the outcome of the XmlReader's methods, such as ReadToDescendant, depends on where the reader is currently positioned:

```
reader.ReadToDescendant("channel");
```

Next, the method calls the ReadToDescendant method of the XmlReader to move the reader from the <channel> element to the first <item> element:

```
reader.ReadToDescendant("item");
```

The CreateChildControls method then enters a do-while loop. In each iteration of the loop, the method calls the ReadSubtree method of the XmlReader. Recall from Chapter 24 that the ReadSubtree method returns a new XmlReader positioned on the same node as the original XmlReader:

```
using (XmlReader itemReader = reader.ReadSubtree())
```

The method calls the AddItemToContainer method and passes the new XmlReader into it. This method is discussed shortly.

```
AddItemToContainer(itemReader);
```

Then it calls the ReadToNextSibling method of the original XmlReader to move the reader from the current <item> node to the next <item> node:

```
reader.ReadToNextSibling("item")
```

Listing 31-5: The RssUrl property

```
private string rssUrl;
[Personalizable(true)]
[WebBrowsable()]
public string RssUrl
{
  get { return rssUrl; }
  set { rssUrl = value; }
}
```

AddContainer

Listing 31-6 contains the code for the `AddContainer` method. This method uses a `Table` control as the container that contains the entire contents of the `RssReaderWebPart` control. Because this method is marked as protected virtual, you can override it to use a different container.

Listing 31-6: The AddContainer method

```
protected virtual void AddContainer()
{
  table = new Table();
  table.CellSpacing = 5;
  Controls.Add(table);
}
```

AddItemToContainer

Listing 31-7 illustrates the implementation of the `AddItemToContainer` method.

Listing 31-7: The AddItemToContainer method

```
protected virtual void AddItemToContainer(XmlReader reader)
{
  string link = string.Empty; ;
  string title = string.Empty;
  string description = string.Empty;

  while (reader.Read())
  {
    if (reader.NodeType == XmlNodeType.Element)
    {
      if (reader.Name == "link")
        link = reader.ReadElementContentAsString();

      else if (reader.Name == "title")
        title = reader.ReadElementContentAsString();

      else if (reader.Name == "description")
        description = reader.ReadElementContentAsString();
```

```
    }
  }

  TableRow row = new TableRow();
  table.Rows.Add(row);
  TableCell cell = new TableCell();
  row.Cells.Add(cell);

  HyperLink hyperLink = new HyperLink();
  hyperLink.NavigateUrl = link;
  hyperLink.Text = title;
  hyperLink.Font.Bold = true;
  cell.Controls.Add(hyperLink);
  LiteralControl lc = new LiteralControl("<br/>");
  cell.Controls.Add(lc);
  Label label = new Label();
  label.Text = description;
  cell.Controls.Add(label);
}
```

The `AddItemToContainer` method uses the `Name` property of the `XmlReader` to locate the `<link>`, `<title>`, and `<description>` subelements of the current `<item>` element. It then calls the `ReadElementContentAsString` method of the `XmlReader` to read the content within the opening and closing tags of the `<link>`, `<title>`, and `<description>` subelements.

Using the RssReaderWebPart Control

Listing 31-8 contains an ASP.NET page that uses the `RssReaderWebPart` control. Notice that the page assigns the URL of the site where the RSS document should be downloaded from the `RssUrl` property of the `RssReaderWebPart` control.

Listing 31-8: A Web page that uses the RssReaderWebPart control

```
<%@ Page Language="C#" %>
<%@ Register TagPrefix="custom" Namespace="CustomComponents" %>
<html xmlns="http://www.w3.org/1999/xhtml">
<body>
  <form id="form1" runat="server">
    <asp:WebPartManager runat="server" ID="mgr2" />
    <asp:WebPartZone runat="server" ID="zone1" BorderColor="#CCCCCC"
    Font-Names="Verdana" Padding="6">
      <ZoneTemplate>
        <custom:RssReaderWebPart RssUrl="http://msdn.microsoft.com/rss.xml"
        ScrollBars="Auto" runat="server" ID="rssreader3"
        Title="MSDN Just Published" />
      </ZoneTemplate>
    </asp:WebPartZone>
  </form>
</body>
</html>
```

Implementing IWebPart

As discussed, if you implement a custom control that derives from the WebPart control, you don't have to implement the IWebPart interface, because the WebPart base class has already implemented the properties of this interface. However, there are times when a custom control that derives from the WebPart control may still need to implement some of the properties of this interface to provide its own custom implementation.

For example, this section implements a new version of the RssReaderWebPart control named RssReaderWebPart2 that overrides the CatalogIconImageUrl and TitleIconImageUrl properties to provide a default icon if the page developer hasn't specified an icon, as shown in Listing 31-9. Notice that this code listing only contains the implementation of these two properties because the implementation of the rest of the methods and properties of the RssReaderWebPart2 control is the same as RssReaderWebPart control discussed in the previous sections.

Listing 31-9: The CatalogIconImageUrl and TitleIconImageUrl properties

```
public override string CatalogIconImageUrl
{
  get { return ViewState["CatalogIconImageUrl"] != null ?
                       (string)ViewState["CatalogIconImageUrl"] : "news.gif";}
  set { ViewState["CatalogIconImageUrl"] = value; }
}

public override string TitleIconImageUrl
{
  get { return ViewState["TitleIconImageUrl"] != null ?
                       (string)ViewState["TitleIconImageUrl"] : "news.gif"; }
  set { ViewState["TitleIconImageUrl"] = value; }
}
```

IWebActionable

Web Parts controls such as WebPart, EditorPart, CatalogPart, WebPartZone, EditorZone, CatalogZone, and ConnectionsZone contain what are known as *verbs*. A verb is an action UI element such as a button, link, menu option, and so on that the user can click to perform an action. For example, the title bar of a WebPart control by default contains a menu of verbs such as Close and Remove that the user can click to perform the associated action such as closing or removing the WebPart.

The ASP.NET Web Parts Framework represents each verb with an instance of a class named WebPartVerb. Listing 31-10 contains the declaration of the members of the WebPartVerb class.

Listing 31-10: The WebPartVerb class

```
public class WebPartVerb : IStateManager
{
  public WebPartVerb(string id, string clientClickHandler);
  public WebPartVerb(string id, WebPartEventHandler serverClickHandler);
  public WebPartVerb(string id, WebPartEventHandler serverClickHandler,
```

```
                        string clientClickHandler);

    public virtual bool Checked { get; set; }
    public string ClientClickHandler { get; }
    public virtual string Description { get; set; }
    public virtual bool Enabled { get; set; }
    public string ID { get; }
    public virtual string ImageUrl { get; set; }
    public WebPartEventHandler ServerClickHandler { get; }
    public virtual string Text { get; set; }
    protected StateBag ViewState { get; }
    public virtual bool Visible { get; set; }

    protected virtual void LoadViewState(object savedState);
    protected virtual object SaveViewState();
    void IStateManager.LoadViewState(object savedState);
    object IStateManager.SaveViewState();
    void IStateManager.TrackViewState();
    protected virtual void TrackViewState();
    protected virtual bool IsTrackingViewState { get; }
    bool IStateManager.IsTrackingViewState { get; }
}
```

As this code listing shows, the WebPartVerb class is nothing but a bag of properties that manages its property values across page postbacks. These properties contain information about the verb that the class represents:

❑ Checked: Specifies whether the user has already selected the verb. When this property is set to true, the Web Parts Framework displays a check mark next to the verb when the user selects the verb. This gives end users visual cues so they know they've already selected the verb.

❑ ClientClickHandler: Contains the name of the client-side handler (such as a JavaScript function) for the client-side event that the verb raises when the user selects it.

❑ Description: A short description of what the verb does. When the user moves the mouse pointer over the verb, the tooltip displays this description.

❑ Enabled: Specifies whether the verb is enabled. When an application is in a state where certain actions aren't allowed, you can disable the associated verbs to prevent users from selecting them.

❑ ID: Contains a string that uniquely identifies the verb among other verbs.

❑ ImageUrl: Specifies the URL to the image that represents the verb.

❑ ServerClickHandler: The server-side handler that's called when the user selects the verb.

❑ Text: Specifies the text for the verb.

❑ Visible: Specifies whether the verb is visible.

As mentioned, verbs can appear in all Web Parts controls such as WebPart, EditorPart, CatalogPart, WebPartZone, EditorZone, CatalogZone, and ConnectionsZone. This section only focuses on the WebPart controls:

❑ The custom `WebPart` controls that derive from the `WebPart` base class.

❑ Any server control such as an ASP.NET control, custom control, and user control that's added to a zone such as `WebPartZone` that derives from the `WebPartZoneBase` class. Recall that the ASP.NET Web Parts Framework wraps the control in a `GenericWebPart` control at runtime.

In general there are two types of verbs, standard and custom. Standard verbs such as Close and Remove are automatically added without any coding effort on your part. The Web Parts Framework also allows you to add your own custom verbs to a `WebPart` control.

To accomplish this task, you must implement the `IWebActionable` interface to add your custom verb to a `WebPart` control. Listing 31-11 contains the definition of this interface, which exposes a single collection property of type `WebPartVerbCollection` named `Verbs`.

Listing 31-11: The IWebActionable interface

```
public interface IWebActionable
{
  WebPartVerbCollection Verbs { get; }
}
```

`WebPartVerbCollection` is a collection of `WebPartVerb` objects where each object represents a verb on the `WebPart` control.

Developing Custom Web Parts Verbs

This section develops a custom Web Parts verb named `UrlWebPartVerb` that derives from the `WebPartVerb` base class and extends its functionality. Listing 31-12 contains the code for `UrlWebPartVerb` verb.

Listing 31-12: The UrlWebPartVerb verb

```
public class UrlWebPartVerb : WebPartVerb
{
  internal UrlWebPartVerb(string id, WebPartEventHandler serverHandler)
    : base(id, serverHandler) { }

  public override string Description
  {
    get { return string.IsNullOrEmpty(base.Description) ?
                "This verb takes you the specified URL" : base.Description;}
    set { base.Description = value; }
  }

  public virtual string NavigateUrl
  {
    get { return ViewState["NavigateUrl"] != null ?
                    (string)ViewState["NavigateUrl"] : string.Empty; }
    set { ViewState["NavigateUrl"] = value; }
  }

  public override string ImageUrl
```

```
    {
      get { return !string.IsNullOrEmpty(base.ImageUrl) ?
                                      base.ImageUrl : "contact.gif"; }
      set { base.ImageUrl = value;}
    }
  }
```

UrlWebPartVerb overrides the Description and ImageUrl properties of its base class, WebPartVerb, and defines a new property named NavigateUrl. As the name implies, this property specifies a URL. You'll use UrlWebPartVerb in the next section where you'll see what role this new property plays.

Developing WebPart Controls That Support Custom Web Parts Verbs

In this section, you develop a new version of the RSS reader Web Parts control named RssReaderWebPart3 that overrides the Verbs property of its base class to provide support for the UrlWebPartVerb custom verb you created in the previous section. One of the limitations with the RssReaderWebPart and RssReaderWebPart2 controls is that they don't provide the user with the list of available RSS feeds to choose from. The RssReaderWebPart3 control retrieves the list of available RSS feeds from the underlying data store and uses it to populate the Verbs collection.

Listing 31-13 illustrates the declaration of the methods and properties of the RssReaderWebPart3 control.

Listing 31-13: The RssReaderWebPart3 control

```
public class RssReaderWebPart3 : WebPart
{
  public string RssUrl {get; set;}
  public string RssDataSourceID {get; set;}
  public string RssUrlField {get; set;}
  public string RssTextField {get; set;}
  public string RssDescriptionField {get; set;}

  protected virtual void SelectDataOperationCallback(IEnumerable dataSource);
  protected virtual void VerbCallback(object sender, WebPartEventArgs e);
  public override WebPartVerbCollection Verbs {get; }

  public override string CatalogIconImageUrl {get; set;}
  public override string TitleIconImageUrl {get; set;}

  protected virtual void AddContainer();
  protected virtual void AddItemToContainer(XmlReader reader);
  protected override void CreateChildControls();
}
```

As Listing 31-13 shows, RssReaderWebPart3 exposes the following properties:

❑ RssDataSourceID: Contains the ID property value of the tabular data source control that RssReaderWebPart3 uses to retrieve the list of available RSS feeds from the underlying data store.

❑ RssUrlField: Specifies the name of the data store field that contains the URLs of the RSS feeds.

❑ RssTextField: Specifies the name of the data store field that contains the friendly name of the RSS feeds. As you'll see shortly, these friendly names will be assigned to the Text properties of the UrlWebPartVerb verbs.

❑ RssDescriptionField: Specifies the name of the data store field that contains the short descriptions for the available RSS feeds.

Listing 31-14 contains the RssReaderWebPart3 control's implementation of the Verbs property.

Listing 31-14: The Verbs property

```
private List<WebPartVerb> verbs;
public override WebPartVerbCollection Verbs
{
  get
  {
    Control m = Page.FindControl(RssDataSourceID);
    IDataSource ds = m as IDataSource;

    if (ds != null)
    {
      DataSourceView dv = ds.GetView(String.Empty);
      dv.Select(DataSourceSelectArguments.Empty,
                  new DataSourceViewSelectCallback(SelectDataOperationCallback));
      return new WebPartVerbCollection(verbs);
    }

    return null;
  }
}
```

To implement the Verbs property, the RssReaderWebPart3 control calls the FindControl method of the containing page to access the underlying data source control in generic fashion without knowing its real type, such as whether it is a SqlDataSource or XmlDataSource control:

```
Control m = Page.FindControl(RssDataSourceID);
```

The control ensures the specified data source control is a tabular data source control. Recall that all tabular data source controls implement the IDataSource interface:

```
IDataSource ds = m as IDataSource;
if (ds != null)
{
    . . .
}
```

The control then calls the GetView method of the data source control to access its default tabular view in generic fashion without knowing its real type. Recall that all tabular data source views derive from the DataSourceView base class:

```
DataSourceView dv = ds.GetView(String.Empty);
```

It then calls the `Select` method of the default tabular data source view to retrieve the list of available RSS feeds from the underlying data store without knowing its real type. Because the `Select` operation is asynchronous, `RssReaderWebPart3` registers a method named `SelectDataOperationCallback` as the callback:

```
dv.Select(DataSourceSelectArguments.Empty,
                    new DataSourceViewSelectCallback(SelectDataOperationCallback));
```

Under the hood, the `Select` method retrieves the list of RSS feeds from the underlying data store, populates an `IEnumerable` object with the retrieved data, and calls the `SelectDataOperationCallback` method and passes the `IEnumerable` object into it. As you'll see shortly, this method iterates through the data contained in the `IEnumerable` object and populates the local variable of type `List<WebPartVerb>` named `verbs`.

Finally, the control creates a `WebPartVerbCollection` and populates it with the content of the `verbs` local variable.

Listing 31-15 contains the code for the `SelectDataOperationCallback` method.

Listing 31-15: The SelectDataOperationCallback method

```
protected virtual void SelectDataOperationCallback(IEnumerable dataSource)
{
  UrlWebPartVerb verb;
  string text;
  verbs = new List<WebPartVerb>();
  IEnumerator iter = dataSource.GetEnumerator();
  while (iter.MoveNext())
  {
    text = DataBinder.Eval(iter.Current, RssTextField).ToString();
    verb = new UrlWebPartVerb(text,new WebPartEventHandler(VerbCallback));
    verb.Text = text;
    verb.Description = DataBinder.Eval(iter.Current,
                                      RssDescriptionField).ToString();
    verb.NavigateUrl = DataBinder.Eval(iter.Current, RssUrlField).ToString();
    verbs.Add(verb);
  }
}
```

The `SelectDataOperationCallback` method first instantiates the local `verbs` variable of type `List<WebPartVerb>`:

```
verbs = new List<WebPartVerb>();
```

The method then calls the `GetEnumerator` method of the `IEnumerable` object that contains the retrieved data to access its enumerator. The enumerator allows the `SelectDataOperationCallback` method to enumerate the retrieved data records in generic fashion without knowing its real type.

```
IEnumerator iter = dataSource.GetEnumerator();
```

The method then iterates through the data records. For each enumerated record, the method calls the `Eval` method of the `DataBinder` class to access the value of the data field whose name is given by the `RssTextField` in generic fashion without knowing the real type of the data column:

```
text = DataBinder.Eval(iter.Current, RssTextField).ToString();
```

The method then instantiates an `UrlWebPartVerb` verb for each record, uses the `text` value just created as the ID of the newly created verb, and registers the `VerbCallback` method as the server-side callback for the verb:

```
verb = new UrlWebPartVerb(text,new WebPartEventHandler(VerbCallback));
```

The method then calls the `Eval` method two more times to access the values of the data fields whose names are given by the `RssUrlField` and `RssDescriptionField`. The column of data whose name is given by the `RssUrlField` property contains the URLs for the available RSS feeds. The column of data whose name is given by the `RssDescriptionField` property contains the short descriptions for the available RSS feeds.

Notice that the values of the data fields whose names are given by the `RssTextField`, `RssUrlField`, and `RssDescriptionField` properties are assigned to the `Text`, `NavigatorUrl`, and `Description` properties of the `UrlWebPartVerb` verb, respectively:

```
verb.Text = text;
verb.Description = DataBinder.Eval(iter.Current, RssDescriptionField).ToString();
verb.NavigateUrl = DataBinder.Eval(iter.Current, RssUrlField).ToString();
```

The method then adds each newly created `UrlWebPartVerb` to the private `verbs` collection field:

```
verbs.Add(verb);
```

When the user selects an RSS feed from the list of available RSS feeds, the `VerbCallback` method is automatically called. As Listing 31-16 shows, all this method does is assign the value of the `NavigateUrl` property of the verb to the `rssUrl` field. As discussed in the previous sections, the `CreateChildControls` method automatically downloads the RSS document from the URL specified in the `rssUrl` field.

Listing 31-16: The VerbCallback method

```
protected virtual void VerbCallback(object sender, WebPartEventArgs e)
{
  UrlWebPartVerb verb = sender as UrlWebPartVerb;
  rssUrl = verb.NavigateUrl;
  Title = verb.Text;
}
```

Listing 31-17 shows an ASP.NET page that uses the `RssReaderWebPart3` control. Figure 31-1 shows what users see on their browsers when they access this page.

Listing 31-17: An ASP.NET page that uses the RssReaderWebPart3 control

```
<%@ Page Language="C#" %>
<%@ Register TagPrefix="custom" Namespace="CustomComponents" %>
<html xmlns="http://www.w3.org/1999/xhtml">
<body>
  <form id="form1" runat="server">
    <asp:WebPartManager runat="server" ID="mgr" />
    <asp:WebPartZone runat="server" ID="myzone" . . . >
```

```
          . . .
        <ZoneTemplate>
          <custom:RssReaderWebPart3 runat="server" RssDataSourceID="MySource"
          RssUrl="http://msdn.microsoft.com/rss.xml" ID="rss"
          RssDescriptionField="RssDescription" RssTextField="RssText"
          RssUrlField="RssUrl" CatalogIconImageUrl="news.gif"
          TitleIconImageUrl="news.gif" Title="MSDN Just Published" />
        </ZoneTemplate>
      </asp:WebPartZone>

      <asp:SqlDataSource runat="server" ID="MySource"
      ConnectionString="<%$ ConnectionStrings:MySqlConnectionString %>"
      SelectCommand="Select * From Rss" />

    </form>
  </body>
</html>
```

Figure 31-1

EditorPart

The EditorPart control defines the API for Web Parts controls that are used to edit WebPart controls. You can plug your own custom EditorPart control into the ASP.NET Web Parts Framework, provided that your custom control implements the EditorPart API. This section helps you understand this API and shows you how to develop custom EditorPart controls that implement the API.

As shown in Figure 30-10, the EditorPart control derives from the Part class and is the base class for all EditorPart controls such as AppearanceEditorPart, LayoutEditorPart, BehaviorEditor Part, and PropertyGridEditorPart. As discussed, EditorPart controls are used to edit the properties of the WebPart controls that make up the UI of a Web Parts page.

Listing 31-18 illustrates the main properties and methods of the EditorPart base class.

Listing 31-18: The EditorPart base class

```
public abstract class EditorPart : Part
{
  public abstract bool ApplyChanges();
  public abstract void SyncChanges();

  protected WebPartManager WebPartManager { get; }
  protected WebPart WebPartToEdit { get; }
  protected EditorZoneBase Zone { get; }
}
```

The following list describes the main methods and properties of the EditorPart base class:

❏ ApplyChanges(): Applies the changes the user has made in the EditorPart control's UI to the WebPart being edited.

❏ SyncChanges(): Gets the current values of the WebPart being edited and applies them to the EditorPart control to allow the user edit them.

❏ WebPartManager: References the WebPartManager.

❏ WebPartToEdit: References the WebPart control being edited.

❏ Zone: References the EditorZone control that contains the EditorPart control.

Listing 31-18 shows that the EditorPart API consists of two important abstract methods named ApplyChanges and SyncChanges. Your custom EditorPart control must implement these two methods as discussed in the following section.

Developing Custom EditorPart Controls

This section develops a custom EditorPart control named RssReaderEditorPart to show you how to implement the EditorPart API, that is, override the ApplyChanges and SyncChanges methods to write your own custom EditorPart controls.

The RssReaderEditorPart custom EditorPart control will be used to edit the properties of a new version of the RSS reader WebPart control named RssReaderWebPart4, which is discussed later in this chapter. The verbs menu of the RssReaderWebPart4 control, like the verbs menu of RssReaderWebPart3, provides end users with the list of RSS feeds to choose from. The RssReaderEditorPart custom EditorPart control will allow end users to personalize or customize the RSS feeds list. In other words, it allows end users to specify and to populate the verbs menu of the RssReaderWebPart4 control with the list of RSS feeds of their choice.

Listing 31-19 illustrates the declaration of the main methods and properties of the RssReaderEditorPart custom EditorPart control. To help you gain a better understanding of how these methods and properties should be implemented, take a look at a typical workflow where some of these methods and properties are invoked:

1. The user selects the Edit option from the list of enabled display modes as discussed before.

2. The page enters edit mode, where the `EditorZone` control renders its UI and the Edit option is added to the verbs menu of each `WebPart` control, including the `RssReaderWebPart4` control.

3. The user selects the Edit option from the verbs menu of the `RssReaderWebPart4` control.

4. The `OnLoad` method of the `RssReaderEditorPart` control retrieves the RSS feed records from the underlying data store and calls the `DataBind` method of the `RssReaderEditorPart` control.

5. The `DataBind` method of the `RssReaderEditorPart` control calls the `CreateControlHierarchy` method and passes the `IEnumerable` object that contains the retrieved RSS feed records into it.

6. The `CreateControlHierarchy` method iterates through the records and renders each record in a table row, where each row contains a `CheckBox` control.

7. The `SyncChanges` method of the `RssReaderEditorPart` control checks the `CheckBox` controls of those RSS feed records that are already in the user's current list of favorite RSS feeds.

8. The users take one or both of the following actions:

   a. Check the `CheckBox` controls of RSS feed records to add them to their favorite RSS feeds

   b. Uncheck the `CheckBox` controls of RSS feed records to remove them from their favorite RSS feeds

9. The `ApplyChanges` method of the `RssReaderEditorPart` control applies the changes to the `RssReaderWebPart4` control.

Listing 31-19: The RssReaderEditorPart custom EditorPart control

```
public class RssReaderEditorPart : EditorPart
{
  public RssReaderEditorPart();
  public override ControlCollection Controls {get;}
  protected override void OnLoad(EventArgs e);
  protected virtual void RssSelectCallback(IEnumerable dataSource);
  protected virtual void PrepareControlHierarchy();
  protected override void Render(HtmlTextWriter writer);
  public override void DataBind();
  protected override void CreateChildControls();
  protected virtual int CreateControlHierarchy(IEnumerable dataSource,
                                               bool dataBinding);
  // Implementing EditorPart API
  public override bool ApplyChanges();
  public override void SyncChanges();

  // ControlStyle property
  protected override Style CreateControlStyle();
  public virtual int CellPadding {get; set;}
  public virtual int CellSpacing {get; set;}
  public virtual HorizontalAlign HorizontalAlign {get; set;}
  public virtual GridLines GridLines {get; set;}
```

(continued)

Listing 31-19: *(continued)*

```
    public virtual string BackImageUrl {get; set;}

    // Exposing Child Style Properties
    public TableItemStyle HeaderStyle {get;}
    public TableItemStyle ItemStyle {get;}
    public TableItemStyle AlternatingItemStyle {get;}
    protected override void TrackViewState();
    protected override object SaveViewState();
    protected override void LoadViewState(object savedState);
}
```

RssReaderEditorPart as a Composite Control

`RssReaderEditorPart` implements the same steps, which are common to all composite controls, as discussed in the previous chapters. The following sections discuss some of these steps.

Overriding DataBind

Listing 31-20 contains the code for the `DataBind` method.

Listing 31-20: The DataBind method

```
public override void DataBind()
{
  RssReaderWebPart4 rssReaderWebPart = WebPartToEdit as RssReaderWebPart4;
  Control m = Page.FindControl(rssReaderWebPart.RssDataSourceID);
  IDataSource ds = m as IDataSource;

  if (ds != null)
  {
    DataSourceView dv = ds.GetView(String.Empty);
    dv.Select(DataSourceSelectArguments.Empty,
                        new DataSourceViewSelectCallback(RssSelectCallback));
  }
  base.DataBind();
}
```

The `DataBind` method first accesses the `RssReaderWebPart4` control being edited. As mentioned, and as you'll see later in this chapter, this control is a new version of the RSS reader `WebPart` control that exposes several new properties such as `RssDataSourceID`:

```
RssReaderWebPart4 rssReaderWebPart = WebPartToEdit as RssReaderWebPart4;
```

Next, it accesses the `RssDataSourceID` property of the `RssReaderWebPart4` control and passes its value into the `FindControl` method of the containing page. As you'll see later in this chapter, the page developer must declare a tabular data source control such as `SqlDataSource` or `XmlDataSource` on the page and assign its `ID` property value to the `RssDataSourceID` property:

```
Control m = Page.FindControl(rssReaderWebPart.RssDataSourceID);
```

The method then ensures the declared data source control is a tabular data source control:

```
IDataSource ds = m as IDataSource;
if (ds != null)
{
  . . .
}
```

Next, it calls the GetView method of the data source control to access its default tabular view:

```
DataSourceView dv = ds.GetView(String.Empty);
```

Finally, it calls the Select method of the default tabular view to retrieve the RSS feed records from the underlying data store. Because the Select operation is asynchronous, it registers the RssSelectCallback method as the callback for the operation:

```
dv.Select(DataSourceSelectArguments.Empty,
                    new DataSourceViewSelectCallback(RssSelectCallback));
```

RssSelectCallback

Listing 31-21 presents the implementation of the RssSelectCallback method. The Select method of the default tabular view calls the RssSelectCallback method and passes the IEnumerable object that contains the retrieved RSS feed records into it. The RssSelectCallback delegates the responsibility of iterating through the retrieved RSS feed records and creating the control hierarchy to the Create ControlHierarchy method.

Listing 31-21: The RssSelectCallback method

```
protected virtual void RssSelectCallback(IEnumerable dataSource)
{
  Controls.Clear();
  ClearChildViewState();

  TrackViewState();
  ViewState["RowCount"] = CreateControlHierarchy(dataSource, true);
  ChildControlsCreated = true;
}
```

CreateControlHierarchy

Listing 31-22 presents the code for the CreateControlHierarchy method.

Listing 31-22: The CreateControlHierarchy method

```
protected virtual int CreateControlHierarchy(IEnumerable dataSource,
                                             bool dataBinding)
{
  RssReaderWebPart4 rssReader = WebPartToEdit as RssReaderWebPart4;

  Table table = new Table();
  table.CellPadding = 5;
```

(continued)

Listing 31-22: *(continued)*

```
Controls.Add(table);
TableHeaderRow hrow = new TableHeaderRow();
table.Rows.Add(hrow);
TableHeaderCell hcell = new TableHeaderCell();
hrow.Cells.Add(hcell);
hcell = new TableHeaderCell();
hcell.HorizontalAlign = HorizontalAlign.Center;
hcell.Text = "Title";

hrow.Cells.Add(hcell);
hcell = new TableHeaderCell();
hcell.HorizontalAlign = HorizontalAlign.Center;
hcell.Text = "Description";
hrow.Cells.Add(hcell);

hcell = new TableHeaderCell();
hcell.HorizontalAlign = HorizontalAlign.Center;
hcell.Text = "URL";
hrow.Cells.Add(hcell);

TableRow brow;
TableCell checkBoxCell;
TableCell rssTextCell;
TableCell rssDescriptionCell;
TableCell rssUrlCell;

CheckBox checkBox;
ArrayList checkBoxArrayList = new ArrayList();
int rowCount = 0;
IEnumerator iter = dataSource.GetEnumerator();
while (iter.MoveNext())
{
  brow = new TableRow();
  table.Rows.Add(brow);
  checkBoxCell = new TableCell();
  checkBox = new CheckBox();
  checkBoxArrayList.Add(checkBox);
  checkBoxCell.Controls.Add(checkBox);
  rssTextCell = new TableCell();
  rssDescriptionCell = new TableCell();
  rssUrlCell = new TableCell();

  brow.Cells.Add(checkBoxCell);
  brow.Cells.Add(rssTextCell);
  brow.Cells.Add(rssDescriptionCell);
  brow.Cells.Add(rssUrlCell);

  if (dataBinding)
  {
    rssTextCell.Text = DataBinder.Eval(iter.Current,
                                rssReader.RssTextField).ToString();
    rssDescriptionCell.Text = DataBinder.Eval(iter.Current,
                                rssReader.RssDescriptionField).ToString();
    rssUrlCell.Text = DataBinder.Eval(iter.Current,
```

```
            }                                  rssReader.RssUrlField).ToString();

        rowCount++;
    }

    return rowCount;
}
```

As you'll see later, the `RssReaderWebPart4` control exposes three new properties as follows:

- ❏ `RssUrlField`: The page developer must set the value of this property to the name of the data column that contains the URLs to the available RSS feeds.

- ❏ `RssTextField`: The page developer must set the value of this property to the name of the data column that contains the title texts of the RSS feeds. As you'll see later, the `RssReaderWebPart4` control displays these title texts in its verbs menu.

- ❏ `RssDescriptionField`: The page developer must set the value of this property to the name of the data column that contains the short descriptions for the available RSS feeds. As you'll see later, when the user moves the mouse pointer over a verb from the verbs menu of the `RssReaderWebPart4` control, the control will display the associated short description in a tooltip.

As Listing 31-22 illustrates, `CreateControlHierarchy` iterates through the RSS feed records and creates a table row with four table cells to display each enumerated record. First, it adds a `CheckBox` control to the first table cell of each row. Then, it retrieves the values of the required data fields and displays them in the rest of the table cells:

```
rssTextCell.Text = DataBinder.Eval(iter.Current,rssReader.RssTextField).ToString();
rssDescriptionCell.Text = DataBinder.Eval(iter.Current,
                                   rssReader.RssDescriptionField).ToString();
rssUrlCell.Text = DataBinder.Eval(iter.Current, rssReader.RssUrlField).ToString();
```

PrepareControlHierarchy

Listing 31-23 contains the code for the `PrepareControlHierarchy` method. The main responsibility of this method is to apply the child style properties to the respective child controls before the `RssReaderEditorPart` control renders its UI.

Listing 31-23: The PrepareControlHierarchy method

```
protected virtual void PrepareControlHierarchy()
{
    Table table = Controls[0] as Table;
    table.CopyBaseAttributes(this);
    if (ControlStyleCreated)
        table.ApplyStyle(ControlStyle);

    if (headerStyle != null)
        table.Rows[0].ApplyStyle(headerStyle);

    for (int i = 1; i < table.Rows.Count; i++)
```

(continued)

Listing 31-23: *(continued)*

```
  {
    if (i % 2 == 0 && itemStyle != null)
      table.Rows[i].ApplyStyle(itemStyle);

    else if (i % 2 == 1 && alternatingItemStyle != null)
      table.Rows[i].ApplyStyle(alternatingItemStyle);
  }
}
```

Because the `Controls` collection of the `RssReaderEditorPart` contains one and only one child control, the `Table` child control, `PrepareControlHierarchy` applies all of the attributes of the containing HTML element of the `RssReaderEditorPart` control to its `Table` child control.

First, it calls the `CopyBaseAttributes` method of the `Table` child control and passes a reference to the `RssReaderEditorPart` control into it. This method applies all the base attributes of the containing HTML element of the `RssReaderEditorPart` control to the `Table` child control.

```
    table.CopyBaseAttributes(this);
```

Then it applies the `ControlStyle` of the `RssReaderEditorPart` to its `Table` child control. This also explains why the `RssReaderEditorPart` control overrides the `CreateControlStyle` method to return a `TableStyle` object instead of the default implementation that returns a `Style` object.

```
    table.ApplyStyle(ControlStyle);
```

`PrepareControlHierarchy` then iterates through all the table rows and applies the `AlternatingItem Style` to the enumerated table row if the row is an alternating item row, and `ItemStyle` otherwise.

SyncChanges

The `RssReaderEditorPart` control, like all `EditorPart` controls, implements the `SyncChanges` method as shown in Listing 31-24.

Listing 31-24: The SyncChanges method

```
public override void SyncChanges()
{
  RssReaderWebPart4 rssReader = WebPartToEdit as RssReaderWebPart4;
  if (rssReader.RssUrls == null || rssReader.RssTexts == null ||
      rssReader.RssDescriptions == null)
    return;

  EnsureChildControls();

  Table table = Controls[0] as Table;
  CheckBox checkBox;

  for (int i = 1; i < table.Rows.Count; i++)
  {
    checkBox = table.Rows[i].Cells[0].Controls[0] as CheckBox;
```

```
        checkBox.Checked =
                rssReader.RssUrls.Contains(table.Rows[i].Cells[3].ToString());
}
```

As you'll see later, the RssReaderWebPart4 control exposes three ArrayList properties as follows:

❑   RssUrls: Contains the URLs to the current user's favorite RSS feeds.

❑   RssTexts: Contains the title texts that represent the current user's favorite RSS feeds. RssReader WebPart4 displays these title texts in its verbs menu.

❑   RssDescriptions: Contains the short descriptions that briefly describe the current user's favorite RSS feeds. When user moves the mouse pointer over a verb from its verbs menu, RssReader WebPart4 displays the associated short description in the tooltip.

Recall that RssReaderEditorPart renders a table row with four cells for each available RSS feed record. The first cell contains a CheckBox control to allow the user to add the associated RSS feed to or to remove the associated RSS feed from the current user's favorite RSS feeds. The second, third, and fourth cells, respectively, display the associated RSS feed record's title text, short description, and URL.

The main responsibility of the SyncChanges method is to check the CheckBox controls of those table rows that represent the current user's favorite RSS feeds so the users know which ones are already included in their favorite RSS feeds. SyncChanges iterates through all the table rows and accesses the CheckBox control of each enumerated row:

```
checkBox = table.Rows[i].Cells[0].Controls[0] as CheckBox;
```

It then checks the CheckBox control if the row represents one of the current user's favorite RSS feeds. As mentioned, the RssReaderWebPart4 control maintains the list of the URLs of the current user's favorite RSS feeds in its RssUrls property:

```
checkBox.Checked = rssReader.RssUrls.Contains(table.Rows[i].Cells[3].ToString());
```

ApplyChanges

RssReaderEditorPart also implements the ApplyChanges method, as all EditorPart controls must, as illustrated in Listing 31-25.

Listing 31-25: The ApplyChanges method

```
public override bool ApplyChanges()
{
  RssReaderWebPart4 rssReader = WebPartToEdit as RssReaderWebPart4;
  if (rssReader.RssUrls == null)
    rssReader.RssUrls = new ArrayList();
  if (rssReader.RssTexts == null)
    rssReader.RssTexts = new ArrayList();
  if (rssReader.RssDescriptions == null)
    rssReader.RssDescriptions = new ArrayList();

  rssReader.RssUrls.Clear();
```

(continued)

Listing 31-25: *(continued)*

```
rssReader.RssTexts.Clear();
rssReader.RssDescriptions.Clear();

Table table = Controls[0] as Table;
CheckBox checkBox;

for (int i = 1; i < table.Rows.Count; i++)
{
  checkBox = table.Rows[i].Cells[0].Controls[0] as CheckBox;
  if (checkBox.Checked)
  {
    rssReader.RssTexts.Add(table.Rows[i].Cells[1].Text);
    rssReader.RssDescriptions.Add(table.Rows[i].Cells[2].Text);
    rssReader.RssUrls.Add(table.Rows[i].Cells[3].Text);
  }
}

rssReader.IsDirty = true;
return true;
}
```

The main responsibility of `ApplyChanges` is to apply the changes the user has made in the `RssReader EditorPart` control to the `RssReaderWebPart4` control. As discussed, the only changes the user can make is to check or uncheck the `CheckBox` controls of the table rows that display the available RSS feeds.

The `ApplyChanges` method first clears the `RssUrls`, `RssTexts`, and `RssDescriptions` collection properties of the `RssReaderWebPart4` control because it's about to populate them with fresh data. The method then iterates through the `RssReaderEditorPart` control's table rows and accesses the `CheckBox` control of each enumerated row:

```
checkBox = table.Rows[i].Cells[0].Controls[0] as CheckBox;
```

It then checks whether the user has checked the `CheckBox`. If so, it retrieves the title, URL, and short description texts that the second, third, and fourth cells of the row display and respectively adds them to the `RssTexts`, `RssUrls`, and `RssDescriptions` collections of the `RssReaderWebPart4` control:

```
rssReader.RssTexts.Add(table.Rows[i].Cells[1].Text);
rssReader.RssDescriptions.Add(table.Rows[i].Cells[2].Text);
rssReader.RssUrls.Add(table.Rows[i].Cells[3].Text);
```

Next, the method marks the `RssReaderWebPart4` control as dirty. As you'll see later, `RssReaderWebPart4` stores the contents of its `RssTexts`, `RssDescriptions`, and `RssUrls` collections in the underlying personalization data store if it's marked as dirty.

```
rssReader.IsDirty = true;
```

OnLoad

The `RssReaderEditorPart` control overrides the `OnLoad` method to call its `DataBind` method as illustrated in Listing 31-26. This automates the whole data-binding process without any coding effort on the part of the page developer.

Listing 31-26: The OnLoad method

```
protected override void OnLoad(EventArgs e)
{
  if (ViewState["FirstTimeLoad"] == null)
  {
    DataBind();
    ViewState["FirstTimeLoad"] = "Yes";
  }

  base.OnLoad(e);
}
```

RssReaderWebPart4 Control

This section implements the `RssReaderWebPart4` control that the `RssReaderEditorPart` edits. This control, like all other `WebPart` controls, derives from the `WebPart` base class. Listing 31-27 contains the declaration of the main members of the `RssReaderWebPart4` control. Notice that the control implements the `IPersonalizable` interface as discussed in the following sections.

Listing 31-27: The RssReaderWebPart4 control

```
public class RssReaderWebPart4 : WebPart, IPersonalizable
{
  public string RssUrl {get; set;}
  public ArrayList RssUrls {get; set;}
  public ArrayList RssTexts {get; set;}
  public ArrayList RssDescriptions {get; set;}

  public override WebPartVerbCollection Verbs {get;}
  protected virtual void VerbCallback(object sender, WebPartEventArgs e);

  public override EditorPartCollection CreateEditorParts();

  protected internal bool IsDirty {get; set;}

  bool IPersonalizable.IsDirty {get;}
  void IPersonalizable.Load(PersonalizationDictionary state);
  void IPersonalizable.Save(PersonalizationDictionary state);

  public string RssDataSourceID {get; set;}
  public string RssUrlField {get; set;}
  public string RssTextField {get; set;}
```

(continued)

Listing 31-27: *(continued)*

```
    public string RssDescriptionField {get; set;}
    public TableItemStyle EditorHeaderStyle {get;}
    public TableItemStyle EditorItemStyle {get;}
    public TableItemStyle EditorAlternatingItemStyle {get;}
    public TableStyle EditorStyle {get;}

    public override string CatalogIconImageUrl
    public override string TitleIconImageUrl
    protected virtual void AddContainer();
    protected virtual void AddItemToContainer(XmlReader reader);
    protected override void CreateChildControls();
}
```

Implementing IPersonalizable

The Web Parts personalization infrastructure provides Web Parts controls with two different mechanisms to store their personalization data or state in and restore their personalization data or state from the underlying personalization data store.

Web Parts controls can mark their properties with the `[Personalizable(true)]` metadata attribute to instruct the Web Parts personalization infrastructure to store their values in and to restore their values from the personalization data store. The `RssReaderWebPart4` control uses this approach to store the value of its `RssUrl` property in the personalization data store as shown in the following code fragment:

```
    private string rssUrl;
    [Personalizable(true)]
    [WebBrowsable()]
    public string RssUrl
    {
      get { return rssUrl; }
      set { rssUrl = value; }
    }
```

Web Parts controls can directly implement the `IPersonalizable` interface to store their property values in and to restore their property values from the personalization data store. As you'll see in this section, `RssReaderWebPart4` uses this approach to store the contents of its `RssTexts`, `RssDescriptions`, and `RssUrls` collections in the personalization data store.

Listing 31-28 contains the definition of the `IPersonalizable` interface.

Listing 31-28: The IPersonalizable interface

```
public interface IPersonalizable
{
  void Load(PersonalizationDictionary state);
  void Save(PersonalizationDictionary state);

  bool IsDirty { get; }
}
```

The members of this interface are as follows:

❑ Load: The Web Parts personalization infrastructure calls the Load method of a Web Parts control and passes a PersonalizationDictionary collection into it. This collection contains the control's saved personalization data.

❑ Save: The Web Parts personalization infrastructure calls the Save method of a Web Parts control and passes a PersonalizationDictionary collection into it. It's the responsibility of the Save method to store the control's personalization data into this collection.

❑ IsDirty: Specifies whether the personalization data of the Web Parts control is marked dirty. The Web Parts personalization infrastructure calls the Save method of the control to allow the control to save its personalization data if the control has been marked as dirty.

PersonalizationDictionary is a collection of PersonalizationEntry objects where each object contains a piece of personalization data, such as the value of a property. The following code contains the definition of the PersonalizationEntry class:

```
public sealed class PersonalizationEntry
{
    public PersonalizationEntry(object value, PersonalizationScope scope);
    public PersonalizationEntry(object value, PersonalizationScope scope,
                               bool isSensitive);

    public bool IsSensitive { get; set; }
    public PersonalizationScope Scope { get; set; }
    public object Value { get; set; }
}
```

The following are the properties of the PersonalizationEntry class:

❑ Value: The personalization data that the PersonalizationEntry entry contains.

❑ Scope: The personalization scope of the personalization data that the PersonalizationEntry entry contains. The possible values are PersonalizationScope.Shared and PersonalizationScope.User, where the former specifies that the personalization data is shared among all users and the latter specifies that the personalization data only applies to the current user.

❑ IsSensitive: Specifies whether the personalization data that the PersonalizationEntry entry contains includes sensitive information.

As Listing 31-29 illustrates, the RssReaderWebPart4 control implements the Save method to store the contents of the RssUrls, RssTexts, and RssDescriptions collections to the underlying personalization data store. The Save method stores the content of each collection in a PersonalizationEntry entry and adds the entry to the PersonalizationDictionary that the Web Parts personalization infrastructure passes into it.

Listing 31-29: The Save method

```
void IPersonalizable.Save(PersonalizationDictionary state)
{
    if ((rssUrls != null) && (rssUrls.Count != 0))
```

(continued)

Listing 31-29: *(continued)*

```
      state["RssUrls"] = new PersonalizationEntry(rssUrls,
                                                PersonalizationScope.User);

   if ((rssTexts != null) && (rssTexts.Count != 0))
     state["RssTexts"] = new PersonalizationEntry(rssTexts,
                                                PersonalizationScope.User);

   if ((rssDescriptions != null) && (rssDescriptions.Count != 0))
     state["RssDescriptions"] = new PersonalizationEntry(rssTexts,
                                                PersonalizationScope.User);
}
```

Listing 31-30 presents the RssReaderWebPart4 control's implementation of the Load method where the method retrieves the PersonalizationEntry entries that contain the title texts, short descriptions, and URLs of the current user's favorite RSS feeds and respectively adds the contents of these entries to the RssTexts, RssDescriptions, and RssUrls collections of the RssReaderWebPart4 control.

Listing 31-30: The Load method

```
void IPersonalizable.Load(PersonalizationDictionary state)
{
  if (state == null)
    return;

  if (state["RssUrls"] != null)
    rssUrls = state["RssUrls"].Value as ArrayList;

  if (state["RssTexts"] != null)
    rssTexts = state["RssTexts"].Value as ArrayList;

  if (state["RssDescriptions"] != null)
    rssDescriptions = state["RssDescriptions"].Value as ArrayList;
}
```

RssReaderWebPart4 control exposes an internal read-write property named IsDirty (see Listing 31-31). As shown in Listing 31-25, the ApplyChanges method of the RssReaderEditorPart control sets the value of the IsDirty property of the RssReaderWebPart4 control to true to mark the control as dirty. As mentioned, the Web Parts personalization infrastructure calls the Save method of a control to allow the control to save its personalization data if the control is marked dirty.

Listing 31-31: The IsDirty property

```
private bool isDirty;
protected internal bool IsDirty
{
  get { return isDirty; }
  set { isDirty = value; }
}
```

The RssReaderWebPart4 control's implementation of the IsDirty property of the IPersonalization interface calls the preceding IsDirty property as follows:

```
bool IPersonalizable.IsDirty
{
  get { return IsDirty; }
}
```

Overriding Verbs

RssReaderWebPart4 overrides the Verbs collection property as illustrated in Listing 31-32 where the property iterates through the current user's favorite RSS feeds. It instantiates a UrlWebPartVerb for each enumerated RSS feed to display the feed in the verbs menu of the RssReaderWebPart4 control:

```
verb = new UrlWebPartVerb(rssTexts[i].ToString(),
                    new WebPartEventHandler(VerbCallback));
```

It also assigns the title text, short description, and URL of each enumerated RSS feed to the Text, Description, and NavigateUrl properties of the UrlWebPartVerb verb. The verb displays the title text in the verbs menu for the user to select:

```
verb.Text = rssTexts[i].ToString();
verb.Description = rssDescriptions[i].ToString();
verb.NavigateUrl = rssUrls[i].ToString();
```

Listing 31-32: The Verbs property

```
public override WebPartVerbCollection Verbs
{
  get
  {
    if (rssUrls == null || rssUrls.Count < 1)
      return null;
    UrlWebPartVerb verb;
    List<UrlWebPartVerb> verbList = new List<UrlWebPartVerb>();

    for (int i = 0; i < rssUrls.Count; i++)
    {
      verb = new UrlWebPartVerb(rssTexts[i].ToString(),
                        new WebPartEventHandler(VerbCallback));
      verb.Text = rssTexts[i].ToString();
      verb.Description = rssDescriptions[i].ToString();
      verb.NavigateUrl = rssUrls[i].ToString();
      verbList.Add(verb);
    }

    return new WebPartVerbCollection(verbList);
  }
}
```

IWebEditable

The IWebEditable interface allows you to associate your custom EditorPart control with the WebPart control that your custom EditorPart control is designed to edit. Listing 31-33 contains the definition of this interface. Every WebPart control must implement this interface. When you derive from the WebPart base class to implement a custom WebPart control, you shouldn't explicitly implement this interface because the base class has implemented the interface.

Listing 31-33: The IWebEditable interface

```
public interface IWebEditable
{
  EditorPartCollection CreateEditorParts();
  object WebBrowsableObject { get; }
}
```

As Listing 31-33 shows, the interface exposes a property named `WebBrowsableObject`, which references the `WebPart` control being edited. The `WebPart` base class provides the following implementation for this property:

```
public virtual object WebBrowsableObject
{
  get {return this;}
}
```

The `IWebEditable` interface also exposes a method named `CreateEditorParts` whose main responsibility is to instantiate custom `EditorPart` controls associated with the `WebPart` control, and populate an `EditorPartCollection` with the instantiated custom `EditorPart` controls and return the collection.

The following fragment presents the `WebPart` base class's implementation of the `CreateEditorParts` method:

```
public virtual EditorPartCollection CreateEditorParts()
{
  return EditorPartCollection.Empty;
}
```

As this fragment shows, `WebPart` controls by default aren't associated with any custom `EditorPart` controls. In other words, the page developer has to use the standard ASP.NET `EditorPart` controls such as `AppearanceEditorPart`, `LayoutEditorPart`, `BehaviorEditorPart`, and `PropertyGridEditorPart` to edit all `WebPart` controls, including standard and custom `WebPart` controls.

If you want users to use your own custom `EditorPart` controls to edit a `WebPart` control, the `WebPart` control must override the `CreateEditorParts` method to instantiate and to return the specified custom `EditorPart` controls.

The `RssReaderWebPart4` custom `WebPart` control overrides this method to instantiate and to return a `RssReaderEditorPart` custom `EditorPart` control as shown in Listing 31-34.

Listing 31-34: The CreateEditorPart method of RssReaderWebPart control

```
private EditorPartCollection editorParts;
public override EditorPartCollection CreateEditorParts()
{
  if (editorParts == null)
  {
    ArrayList editors = new ArrayList();
    RssReaderEditorPart editorPart = new RssReaderEditorPart();
```

```
                editorPart.ID = ID + "RssReaderWebPart4";
                editors.Add(editorPart);
                editorParts = new EditorPartCollection(editors);
        }
        return editorParts;
    }
```

As you saw in the previous chapter, the page developer declares standard `EditorPart` controls — `AppearanceEditorPart`, `LayoutEditorPart`, `BehaviorEditorPart`, and `PropertyGridEditor Part` — within the opening and closing tags of the `<asp:EditorZone>` element. You may be wondering how custom `EditorPart` controls such as `RssReaderEditorPart` are added to the `EditorZone` zone and how the `CreateEditorParts` method fits in all this.

As you'll see later, the methods and properties of the `EditorZoneBase` base class define the API that all editor zones such as `EditorZone` must honor. This API includes a collection property of type `Editor PartCollection` named `EditorParts` as shown in Listing 31-35.

Listing 31-35: The EditorParts property of the EditorZoneBase base class

```
    private EditorPartCollection editorParts;
    public EditorPartCollection EditorParts
    {
      get
      {
        if (editorParts == null)
        {
          EditorPartCollection myEditorParts = WebPartToEdit.CreateEditorParts();
          editorParts = new EditorPartCollection(myEditorParts, CreateEditorParts());
        }
        return editorParts;
      }
    }
```

The `EditorZoneBase` base class exposes a property of type `WebPart` named `WebPartToEdit` that references the `WebPart` control being edited. As Listing 31-35 shows, the `EditorParts` property calls the `CreateEditorParts` method of the `WebPart` control being edited, such as the `CreateEditorParts` method of the `RssReaderWebPart4` control shown in Listing 31-34, to access the custom `EditorPart` controls associated with the `WebPart` control:

```
        EditorPartCollection myEditorParts = WebPartToEdit.CreateEditorParts();
```

It then calls the `CreateEditorParts` method of the `EditorZoneBase` class to access the standard ASP.NET `EditorPart` controls such as `AppearanceEditorPart`, `LayoutEditorPart`, `BehaviorEditorPart`, and `PropertyGridEditorParts` that the page developer has declaratively added to the `EditorZone` control.

Finally, it combines the custom and standard `EditorPart` controls in a single `EditorPartCollection` and returns the collection:

```
        editorParts = new EditorPartCollection(myEditorParts, CreateEditorParts());
```

EditorPart Style Properties

The `RssReaderWebPart4` custom `WebPart` control exposes style properties, shown in Listing 31-36, that delegate to the respective style properties of the `RssReaderEditorPart` custom `EditorPart` control. Notice that each style property first accesses the `RssReaderEditorPart` control and then returns the associated property of the control.

Listing 31-36: The Style properties

```
public TableItemStyle EditorHeaderStyle
{
  get
  {
    RssReaderEditorPart editorPart = (RssReaderEditorPart)CreateEditorParts()[0];
    return editorPart.HeaderStyle;
  }
}

public TableItemStyle EditorItemStyle
{
  get
  {
    RssReaderEditorPart editorPart = (RssReaderEditorPart)CreateEditorParts()[0];
    return editorPart.ItemStyle;
  }
}

public TableItemStyle EditorAlternatingItemStyle
{
  get
  {
    RssReaderEditorPart editorPart = (RssReaderEditorPart)CreateEditorParts()[0];
    return editorPart.AlternatingItemStyle;
  }
}

public TableStyle EditorStyle
{
  get
  {
    RssReaderEditorPart editorPart = (RssReaderEditorPart)CreateEditorParts()[0];
    return (TableStyle)editorPart.ControlStyle;
  }
}
```

Using the RssReaderWebPart4 Control

Listing 31-37 contains an ASP.NET Web page that uses the `RssReaderWebPart4` control. Figure 31-2 shows what the user sees after performing the following tasks:

1. Select the Edit option from the list of enabled display modes.
2. Select the Edit verb from the verbs menu of the `RssReaderWebPart4` control.

As this figure shows, the `RssReaderEditorPart` custom `EditorPart` control renders the UI that allows the users to add or to remove RSS feeds from the list of their favorite RSS feeds.

Listing 31-37: A Web page that uses RssReaderWebPart4 control

```
<%@ Page Language="C#" %>
<%@ Register TagPrefix="custom" Namespace="CustomComponents" %>
<script runat="server">

    . . .

</script>

<html xmlns="http://www.w3.org/1999/xhtml">
<body>
  <form id="form1" runat="server">
    <asp:WebPartManager runat="server" ID="mgr2" />
    <table cellspacing="10">
      <tr>
        <td colspan="2" align="left">
          . . .
        </td>
      </tr>
      <tr>
        <td valign="top">
          <asp:WebPartZone runat="server" ID="zone1" . . .>
          . . .
          </asp:WebPartZone>
        </td>
        <td valign="top">
          <asp:WebPartZone runat="server" ID="WebPartZone1" . . .>
            . . .
            <ZoneTemplate>
              <custom:RssReaderWebPart4 runat="server" ID="rss"
              RssDataSourceID="MySource" RssDescriptionField="RssDescription"
              RssTextField="RssText" RssUrlField="RssUrl"
              CatalogIconImageUrl="news.gif" TitleIconImageUrl="news.gif">
                <editorheaderstyle backcolor="Tan" font-bold="True" />
                <editoralternatingitemstyle backcolor="PaleGoldenrod" />
                <editorstyle backcolor="LightGoldenrodYellow" bordercolor="Tan"
                borderwidth="1px" cellpadding="2" forecolor="Black"
                gridlines="None" />
              </custom:RssReaderWebPart4>
            </ZoneTemplate>
          </asp:WebPartZone>
        </td>
      </tr>
      <tr>
        <td valign="top" colspan="2" style="width: 100%">
          <asp:EditorZone Width="100%" runat="server" ID="editorzone1" . . . >
            . . .
          </asp:EditorZone>
        </td>
      </tr>
    </table>
    <asp:SqlDataSource runat="server" ID="MySource"
    ConnectionString="<%$ ConnectionStrings:MySqlConnectionString %>"
    SelectCommand="Select * From Rss" />
  </form>
</body>
</html>
```

Figure 31-2

CatalogPart

The methods and properties of the `CatalogPart` base class define the API that all `CatalogPart` controls must honor. This API isolates `CatalogZoneBase`, `CatalogPartChrome`, and `WebPartManager` controls from the real type of the `CatalogPart` control being used, allowing them to work with all types of `CatalogPart` controls such as `DeclarativeCatalogPart`, `PageCatalogPart`, `ImportCatalogPart`, and your own custom `CatalogPart` controls. The `CatalogPart` base class derives from the `Part` class and exposes the main methods and properties presented in Listing 31-38.

Listing 31-38: The CatalogPart control

```
public abstract class CatalogPart : Part
{
   public abstract WebPartDescriptionCollection GetAvailableWebPartDescriptions();
   public abstract WebPart GetWebPart(WebPartDescription description);
   public string DisplayTitle { get; }
   protected WebPartManager WebPartManager { get; }
   protected CatalogZoneBase Zone { get; }
}
```

Notice that `CatalogPart` exposes two abstract methods named `GetAvailableWebPartDescriptions` and `GetWebPart` that you must implement to develop your own custom `CatalogPart` control. To understand what these two methods do, you need to understand the `WebPartDescription` class. As discussed, a `CatalogPart` control presents end users with a catalog of `WebPart` controls that they can add to the page.

Every `CatalogPart` control must reside in a zone of type `CatalogZoneBase`. The ASP.NET Framework comes with a standard zone named `CatalogZone` that derives from the `CatalogZoneBase` base class. You can also derive from `CatalogZoneBase` to implement your own custom catalog zone as discussed later.

The `CatalogZoneBase` zone that contains a `CatalogPart` control uses an instance of a class named `CatalogPartChrome` to display information about each `WebPart` control in the catalog. This information normally contains a title, an icon, and a description. It's the responsibility of a `CatalogPart` control to provide the `CatalogPartChrome` class with this information.

A `CatalogPart` control can create an instance of each `WebPart` control in the catalog to extract the information about the control and to pass the information to the containing `CatalogZoneBase`, `Catalog PartChrome`, or `WebPartManager`.

Because a catalog can contain numerous `WebPart` controls, creating an instance of each `WebPart` control would degrade the performance of the application. That's why the ASP.NET Web Parts Framework comes with a lightweight class named `WebPartDescription` that contains the information such as the title, the URL to an icon, and the description of a given `WebPart` control in a catalog. Listing 31-39 contains the definition of the `WebPartDescription` class.

Listing 31-39: The WebPartDescription class

```
public class WebPartDescription
{
  public WebPartDescription(WebPart part);
  public WebPartDescription(string id, string title, string description,
                            string imageUrl);

  public string CatalogIconImageUrl { get; }
  public string Description { get; }
  public string ID { get; }
  public string Title { get; }
}
```

The `WebPartDescription` class has two constructors. The first constructor takes the `WebPart` control being described as its argument. This constructor is useful in `CatalogPart` controls such as `Declarative CatalogPart` where the `WebPart` control has already been instantiated. The second constructor takes the ID, title, description, and URL to the icon of the `WebPart` being described. In this case, the actual `WebPart` hasn't been instantiated.

Notice that the `WebPartDescription` class's `CatalogIconImageUrl`, `Description`, `ID`, and `Title` properties map to the `CatalogIconImageUrl`, `Description`, `ID`, and `Title` properties of the `WebPart` control that the `WebPartDescription` describes. The `ID` property of a `WebPartDescription` object is used to uniquely identify the object among other `WebPartDescription` objects in a `WebPart DescriptionCollection` collection.

Now look back to Listing 31-38, the `CatalogPart` control. As this code listing shows, `CatalogPart` exposes a method named `GetAvailableWebPartDescriptions` that returns a `WebPartDescription Collection` collection of `WebPartDescription` objects where each object describes a `WebPart` control in the catalog. To help you understand what role this method plays in the Web Parts Framework, imagine the user selects the `Catalog` option from the list of available display modes to switch the page to `Catalog` mode.

The `CatalogZoneBase` zone calls the `RenderCatalogPart` method of its associated `CatalogPartChrome` to display information about each `WebPart` control in each `CatalogPart` control that resides in the zone. This method calls the `GetAvailableWebPartDescription` method of the `CatalogPart` to return a `WebPartDescriptionCollection` collection that contains the `WebPartDescription` objects that describe the `WebPart` controls in the catalog, as shown in Listing 31-40. `RenderCatalogPart` then iterates through these `WebPartDescription` objects. For each `WebPartDescription` object, the `RenderCatalog Part` method renders a checkbox HTML element and assigns the value of the `ID` property of the enumerated `WebPartDescription` object to its `value` HTML attribute. This checkbox allows user to select and to add the `WebPart` control that the `WebPartDescription` object describes. When the user posts the page back to the server, the `CatalogZoneBase` zone will use the value of the `value` HTML attribute of the checkbox control to determine the associated `WebPartDescription` object and consequently identify the type of `WebPart` control that should be added to the page, as discussed later.

```
writer.AddAttribute(HtmlTextWriterAttribute.Value, desc.ID);
writer.AddAttribute(HtmlTextWriterAttribute.Type, "checkbox");
writer.RenderBeginTag(HtmlTextWriterTag.Input);
writer.RenderEndTag();
```

The `RenderCatalogPart` method then renders an `Image` server control and assigns the values of the `Description` and `CatalogIconImageUrl` properties of the enumerated `WebPartDescription` object to its `AlternateText` and `ImageUrl` properties:

```
Image image = new Image();
image.AlternateText = desc.Description;
image.ImageUrl = desc.CatalogIconImageUrl;
image.RenderControl(writer);
```

The `RenderCatalogPart` method then renders the value of the `Title` property of the enumerated `WebPartDescription` object in a `label` HTML element:

```
writer.AddAttribute(HtmlTextWriterAttribute.Title, desc.Description, true);
writer.RenderBeginTag(HtmlTextWriterTag.Label);
writer.WriteEncodedText(desc.Title);
writer.RenderEndTag();
```

Listing 31-40: The RenderCatalogPart method of the CatalogPartChrome

```
public virtual void RenderCatalogPart(HtmlTextWriter writer,
                                      CatalogPart catalogPart)
{
  . . .
  WebPartDescriptionCollection col = catalogPart.GetAvailableWebPartDescriptions();
  if (col != null)
  {
    foreach (WebPartDescription desc in col)
    {
      writer.AddAttribute(HtmlTextWriterAttribute.Value, desc.ID);
      writer.AddAttribute(HtmlTextWriterAttribute.Type, "checkbox");
      writer.RenderBeginTag(HtmlTextWriterTag.Input);
      writer.RenderEndTag();

      Image image1 = new Image();
```

```
            image1.AlternateText = desc.Description;
            image1.ImageUrl = desc.CatalogIconImageUrl;
            image1.RenderControl(writer);

            writer.AddAttribute(HtmlTextWriterAttribute.Title, desc.Description, true);
            writer.RenderBeginTag(HtmlTextWriterTag.Label);
            writer.WriteEncodedText(desc.Title);
            writer.RenderEndTag();
        }
    }
    . . .
}
```

As shown in Listing 31-38, `CatalogPart` also exposes a method named `GetWebPart` that takes a `WebPartDescription` object as input and returns the `WebPart` control that the `WebPartDescription` object describes. To help you understand what this method does, imagine that the user checks the desired checkbox elements on the `CatalogZoneBase` zone and posts the page back to the server.

The ASP.NET Framework automatically calls the `RaisePostBack` method of the `CatalogZoneBase` control because this control implements the `IPostBackEventHandler` method. Listing 31-41 contains the simplified version of the code for the `RaisePostback` method. This method calls the `GetAvailable WebPartDescriptions` method of the `CatalogPart` control to return the `WebPartDescription Collection` collection that contains the `WebPartDescription` objects that describe the `WebPart` controls in the catalog:

```
WebPartDescriptionCollection col = catalogPart.GetAvailableWebPartDescriptions();
```

The method then retrieves the values of the `value` HTML attributes of the checked checkbox element from the posted data. Recall that Listing 31-40 assigns the value of the `ID` property of the associated `WebPartDescription` object to this `value` HTML attribute.

```
String[] checkBoxValues = GetCheckBoxValues();
```

It then iterates through the retrieved values and uses each enumerated value as an index into the `WebPartDescriptionCollection` to access the `WebPartDescription` object whose `ID` property has the same value as the enumerated value:

```
WebPartDescription desc = col[checkBoxValue];
```

Next, the method calls the `GetWebPart` method of the `CatalogPart` control and passes the `WebPartDescription` object into it to return the `WebPart` control that the `WebPartDescription` object describes:

```
WebPart part = catalogPart.GetWebPart(desc);
```

Finally, the method calls the `AddWebPart` method of the `WebPartManager` control to add the `WebPart` control to the page:

```
WebPartManager.AddWebPart(part, part.Zone, 0);
```

Listing 31-41: The RaisePostback method

```
protected override void RaisePostBackEvent(string eventArgument)
{
  WebPartDescriptionCollection col = catalogPart.GetAvailableWebPartDescriptions();
  String[] checkBoxValues = GetCheckBoxValues();
  foreach (string checkBoxValue in checkBoxValues)
  {
    WebPartDescription desc = col[checkBoxValue];
    WebPart part = catalogPart.GetWebPart(desc);
    WebPartManager.AddWebPart(part, part.Zone, 0);
  }
}
```

Developing Custom CatalogPart Controls

As discussed in the previous chapter, users can use the export feature of the Web Parts Framework to export a `WebPart` control to an XML document, which is then saved in an XML file with a `.WebPart` extension known as `WebPart` control description file.

The `ImportCatalogPart` control, on the other hand, imports a description file (a file with a `.WebPart` extension) that describes a `WebPart` control and uses it as a recipe to add a `WebPart` control of the same type and with the same property settings as the original exported `WebPart` control.

One of the shortcomings of the `ImportCatalogPart` control is that it's not capable of importing description files from an XML Web service. This section develops a custom `CatalogPart` control named `XmlWebServiceCatalogPart` that imports `WebPart` control description files from an XML Web service. Listing 31-42 contains the declaration of the members of the `XmlWebServiceCatalogPart` control.

Listing 31-42: The XmlWebServiceCatalogPart control

```
public class XmlWebServiceCatalogPart : CatalogPart
{
  public string TypeName {get; set;}
  public string FileNameParameter {get; set;}
  public string GetWebPartInfoSetMethodName {get; set;}
  public string GetWebPartDescriptionFileMethodName {get; set;}
  public string WSDLPath {get; set;}

  protected virtual string LoadWebPartInfoSet()
  protected virtual string LoadWebPartDescriptionFile(string fileName);

  public override WebPartDescriptionCollection GetAvailableWebPartDescriptions();
  public override WebPart GetWebPart(WebPartDescription description);

  protected override void TrackViewState()
  protected override object SaveViewState();
  protected override void LoadViewState(object savedState);
}
```

Listing 31-43 shows an example of an XML Web service from which `XmlWebServiceCatalogPart` can import `WebPart` control description files. The XML Web service must expose two methods as shown in Listing 31-43. `XmlWebServiceCatalogPart` exposes two properties named `GetWebPartInfoSet MethodName` and `GetWebPartDescriptionFileMethodName` that the page developer must set to the names of the preceding two methods of the XML Web service.

The XML Web service method whose name is given by the `GetWebPartInfoSetMethodName` property must take no arguments and return a string that contains an XML document that includes the following information for each available `WebPart` control:

❑ `ID`: The `ID` property value of the `WebPart` control

❑ `Title`: The title text that will be displayed to users to represent the title or name of the `WebPart` control

❑ `Description`: A short description of what the `WebPart` control does

❑ `Catalog Icon URL`: The URL to the icon that will be displayed to users to represent the `WebPart` control

❑ The path of the `WebPart` control description file (the file with the `.WebPart` extension) that describes the `WebPart` control

Listing 31-44 shows an example of such an XML document. As this code listing shows, this XML document like all XML documents has a single document element named `<webPartInfoSet>`, which contains zero or more `<webPartInfo>` child elements. The attributes on each `<webPartInfo>` element provide information about the `WebPart` control that the element represents. Notice that the `fileName` attribute contains the file path to the description file that describes the `WebPart` control.

The XML Web service method whose name is given by the `GetWebPartDescriptionFileMethodName` property must take the path of a `WebPart` control description file and return a string that contains the contents of the file. `XmlWebServiceCatalogPart` exposes a property named `FileNameParameter` that the page developer must set to the name of the parameter of this XML Web service method. For example, in the case of the XML Web service shown in Listing 31-43, the page developer must set the value of the `FileNameParameter` to the string `fileName`.

Listing 31-43: An XML Web service where you can import WebPart control description files

```
[WebService(Namespace = "http://WebParts.com/")]
[WebServiceBinding(ConformsTo = WsiProfiles.BasicProfile1_1)]
public class Service : System.Web.Services.WebService
{
  [WebMethod]
  public string GetWebPartDescriptionFile(string fileName);

  [WebMethod]
  public string GetWebPartInfoSet();
}
```

`XmlWebServiceCatalogPart` also exposes the following properties:

❑ `TypeName`: The fully qualified name of the class that represents the XML Web service. The fully qualified name of a class must include its namespace, if any. For example, in the case of the XML Web service shown in Listing 31-43, the page developer must set the value of `TypeName` property to string `Service`.

❑ `WSDLPath`: The URL to the WSDL document that describes the XML Web service. This URL normally consists of the URL to the XML Web service itself plus the WSDL querystring parameter, such as `http://localhost/Service.asmx?WSDL`.

Listing 31-44: An XML document that the XML Web service returns

```
<webPartInfoSet>
  <webPartInfo filename="Calendar.WebPart" id="Calendar1" title="Calendar"
  Description="ASP.NET standard Calendar control"
  catalogIconImageUrl="calendar.gif" />
  <webPartInfo filename="RssReaderUserControl.WebPart" id="RssReader1"
  title="RSS Reader" Description="Downloads and displays RSS feeds"
  catalogIconImageUrl="news.gif" />
</webPartInfoSet>
```

The `XmlWebServiceCatalogPart` custom `CatalogPart` control, like all `CatalogPart` controls, derives from the `CatalogPart` base class and implements its `GetAvailableWebPartDescriptions` and `GetWebPart` methods.

GetAvailableWebPartDescriptions

Listing 31-45 contains the code for the `GetAvailableWebPartDescriptions` method. As discussed in the previous sections, the `CatalogPartChrome` and `CatalogZoneBase` controls call this method to return the `WebPartDescriptionCollection` collection that contains the `WebPartDescription` objects that describe the `WebPart` controls in the catalog.

Listing 31-45: The GetAvailableWebPartDescriptions method

```
List<WebPartInfo> list = new List<WebPartInfo>();

public override WebPartDescriptionCollection GetAvailableWebPartDescriptions()
{
  WebPartDescriptionCollection col = null;

  string result = LoadWebPartInfoSet();
  using (StringReader sreader = new StringReader(result))
  {
    XPathDocument doc = new XPathDocument(sreader);
    XPathNavigator nav = doc.CreateNavigator();
    nav.MoveToChild(XPathNodeType.Element);
    XPathNodeIterator webPartInfoSet = nav.Select("//webPartInfo");
    WebPartInfo info;
    WebPartDescription webPartDescription;
    string id = string.Empty ;
    string fileName = string.Empty;
    string description = string.Empty;
    string title = string.Empty;
```

```
            string catalogIconImageUrl = string.Empty;
            ArrayList mylist = new ArrayList();

            foreach (XPathNavigator webPartInfo in webPartInfoSet)
            {
              webPartInfo.MoveToFirstAttribute();

              do
              {
                switch (webPartInfo.LocalName)
                {
                  case "fileName":
                    fileName = webPartInfo.Value;
                    break;
                  case "id":
                    id = webPartInfo.Value;
                    break;
                  case "description":
                    description = webPartInfo.Value;
                    break;
                  case "title":
                    title = webPartInfo.Value;
                    break;
                  case "catalogIconImageUrl":
                    catalogIconImageUrl = webPartInfo.Value;
                    break;
                }
              } while (webPartInfo.MoveToNextAttribute());

              webPartDescription = new WebPartDescription(id, title, description,
                                                     catalogIconImageUrl);
              info = new WebPartInfo();
              info.fileName = fileName;
              info.WebPartDescription = webPartDescription;
              list.Add(info);
              isDirty = true;
              mylist.Add(webPartDescription);
            }

          col = new WebPartDescriptionCollection(mylist);
        }
        return col;
}
```

As Listing 31-45 illustrates, GetAvailableWebPartDescriptions calls the LoadWebPartInfoSet method. As you'll see later, this method downloads the XML document that contains the id, title, description, URL to the catalog icon, and the path of the description file for each available WebPart control. Listing 31-44 shows an example of this XML document.

```
string result = LoadWebPartInfoSet();
```

It then loads the XML document into an XPathDocument. As discussed in Chapter 24, you have three API options for reading an XML document: XmlReader streaming, XmlDocument DOM, and XPathNavigator cursor-style XML APIs. GetAvailableWebPartDescriptions uses the XPathNavigator cursor-style

XML API to read the XML document that the `LoadWebPartInfoSet` method returns. This API requires you to load the XML document into an XML data store such as `XPathDocument` or `XmlDocument`:

```
XPathDocument doc = new XPathDocument(sreader);
```

Next, `GetAvailableWebPartDescriptions` calls the `CreateNavigator` method of the `XPathDocument` to access its `XPathNavigator`. The navigator is originally positioned on the root node of the XML document. Recall from Chapter 24 that the root node of an XML document isn't a physical node present in the document itself. Instead, it's a node that represents the entire document. For example, in the case of the XML document shown in Listing 31-44, the root node contains a single child node, `<webPartInfoSet>`.

```
XPathNavigator nav = doc.CreateNavigator();
```

`GetAvailableWebPartDescriptions` then calls the `MoveToChild` method of the `XPathNavigator` to move the navigator from the node on which it is currently positioned, the `<webPartInfoSet>` node in Listing 31-44.

```
nav.MoveToChild(XPathNodeType.Element);
```

`GetAvailableWebPartDescriptions` next calls the `Select` method of the `XPathNavigator` to select those nodes that satisfy the specified XPath expression. The `"//webPartInfo"` XPath expression selects all `<webPartInfo>` elements in the XML document. For example, in the case of the XML document shown in Listing 31-44, the `Select` method returns an `XPathNodeIterator` object that contains two `XPathNavigator` objects. These navigators are positioned on the first and second `<webPartInfo>` elements.

```
XPathNodeIterator webPartInfoSet = nav.Select("//webPartInfo");
```

`GetAvailableWebPartDescriptions` then iterates through the `XPathNavigator` objects that the `XPathNodeIterator` contains. For each enumerated `XPathNavigator` object, `GetAvailableWebPart Descriptions` calls the `MoveToFirstAttribute` method of the navigator object to move the navigator from the `<webPartInfo>` element on which it is currently positioned to the first attribute of the element.

It then enters a `do-while` loop where it first determines on which attribute the navigator is currently located and assigns the value of the attribute to the specified local variable. Then it calls the `MoveToNext Attribute` method to move the navigator from the attribute node on which the navigator is currently located to the next attribute node. This `do-while` loop allows the navigator to navigate all the id, title, description, catalogIconImageUrl, and fileName attributes of the current `<webPartInfo>` element and store their values in the respective local variables.

For each `XPathNavigator` object, `GetAvailableWebPartDescriptions` creates an instance of the `WebPartDescription` class and passes the id, title, description, catalogIconImageUrl, and fileName attribute values of the current `<webPartInfo>` element into it:

```
webPartDescription = new WebPartDescription(id, title, description,
                                            catalogIconImageUrl);
```

`GetAvailableWebPartDescriptions` next creates an instance of a struct named `WebPartInfo` and sets the values of its two properties:

```
info = new WebPartInfo();
info.FileName = fileName;
info.WebPartDescription = webPartDescription;
list.Add(info);
```

The following code shows the definition of `WebPartInfo` struct:

```
public struct WebPartInfo
{
  public WebPartDescription WebPartDescription;
  public string FileName;
}
```

Finally, `GetAvailableWebPartDescriptions` adds the `WebPartDescription` object that describes the available `WebPart` controls into a `WebPartDescriptionCollection` collection:

```
col = new WebPartDescriptionCollection(mylist);
```

Notice that the `XmlWebServiceCatalogPart` control maintains an internal collection of type `List<WebPartInfo>` that contains a `WebPartInfo` instance for each `WebPart` control in the catalog. Each `WebPartInfo` instance contains two pieces of information: the `WebPartDescription` object and the path of the description file that describe the respective `WebPart` control.

LoadWebPartInfoSet

Listing 31-46 contains the code for the `LoadWebPartInfoSet` method. The main responsibility of this method is to download the XML document that contains the id, title, description, catalog icon path, and the description file path of all available `WebPart` controls. Listing 31-44 shows an example of this XML document.

Listing 31-46: The LoadWebPartInfoSet method

```
protected virtual string LoadWebPartInfoSet()
{
  XmlWebServiceMethodInvoker methodInvoker = new XmlWebServiceMethodInvoker();
  methodInvoker.TypeName = TypeName;
  methodInvoker.WSDLPath = WSDLPath;
  OrderedDictionary list = new OrderedDictionary();
  return
    (string)methodInvoker.InvokeXmlWebServiceMethod(GetWebPartInfoSetMethodName,
                                                    list, true);
}
```

`LoadWebPartInfoSet` uses the `XmlWebServiceMethodInvoker` component that was developed and discussed in Chapter 10 to download the XML document. First it instantiates the `XmlWebServiceMethodInvoker` component:

```
XmlWebServiceMethodInvoker methodInvoker = new XmlWebServiceMethodInvoker();
```

Then it assigns the value of the `TypeName` property of the `XmlWebServiceCatalogPart` control to the `TypeName` property of the `XmlWebServiceMethodInvoker` component. Recall that the `TypeName` property contains the fully qualified name of the class that represents the XML Web service.

```
        methodInvoker.TypeName = TypeName;
```

LoadWebPartInfoSet next assigns the value of the WSDLPath property of the XmlWebServiceCatalog
Part control to the WSDLPath property of the XmlWebServiceMethodInvoker component. Recall that
the WSDLPath property contains the URL to the WSDL document that describes the XML Web service.

```
        methodInvoker.WSDLPath = WSDLPath;
```

Finally, LoadWebPartInfoSet calls the InvokeXmlWebServiceMethod method of the XmlWebService
MethodInvoker component to invoke the XML Web service method whose name is given by the Get
WebPartInfoSetMethodName property. For example, in the case of the XML Web service shown in
Listing 31-43, the GetWebPartInfoSet XML Web service method will be invoked.

```
    (string)methodInvoker.InvokeXmlWebServiceMethod(GetWebPartInfoSetMethodName,
                                        list, true);
```

GetWebPart

The XmlWebServiceCatalogPart custom CatalogPart control, like all CatalogPart controls, implements the GetWebPart method of the CatalogPart base class. As Listing 31-47 shows, the Raise
PostBackEvent method of the CatalogZoneBase control calls the GetWebPart method and passes a
WebPartDescription object into it to return the WebPart control that the WebPartDescription object
describes.

Listing 31-47: The GetWebPart method

```
public override WebPart GetWebPart(WebPartDescription description)
{
  foreach (WebPartInfo info in list)
  {
    if (info.WebPartDescription.Equals(description))
    {
      string result = LoadWebPartDescriptionFile(info.fileName);
      using (StringReader sreader = new StringReader(result))
      {
        using (XmlReader xreader = XmlReader.Create(sreader))
        {
          string error;
          return this.WebPartManager.ImportWebPart(xreader, out error);
        }
      }
    }
  }
  return null;
}
```

As Listing 31-45 shows, XmlWebServiceCatalogPart maintains an internal list of WebPartInfo
objects where each object represents a WebPart control in the catalog. As discussed, each WebPartInfo
object contains two pieces of information, the WebPartDescription object and the name of the
WebPart description file that describes the WebPart control.

As Listing 31-47 illustrates, GetWebPart first searches the internal list of WebPartInfo objects for the object with the specified WebPartDescription and then calls the LoadWebPartDescriptionFile method and passes the name of the WebPart description file into it. As you'll see later, this method invokes the underlying XML Web service method to download the description file with the specified filename. The LoadWebPartDescriptionFile method returns a string that contains the content of the description file:

```
string result = LoadWebPartDescriptionFile(info.fileName);
```

GetWebPart then loads the description file into an XmlReader:

```
XmlReader xreader = XmlReader.Create(sreader)
```

It then calls the ImportWebPart method of the WebPartManager control to import the description file. This method uses the description file as a recipe to create the respective WebPart control.

```
this.WebPartManager.ImportWebPart(xreader, out error);
```

LoadWebPartDescriptionFile

Listing 31-48 contains the code for the LoadWebPartDescriptionFile method. The main responsibility of this method is to invoke the XML Web service method whose name is given by the GetWebPart DescriptionFileMethodName property to download the description file with the specified filename.

Listing 31-48: The LoadWebPartDescriptionFile method

```
protected virtual string LoadWebPartDescriptionFile(string fileName)
{
  XmlWebServiceMethodInvoker methodInvoker = new XmlWebServiceMethodInvoker();
  methodInvoker.TypeName = TypeName;
  methodInvoker.WSDLPath = WSDLPath;
  OrderedDictionary list = new OrderedDictionary();
  list.Add(FileNameParameter, fileName);
  return (string)methodInvoker.InvokeXmlWebServiceMethod(
                        GetWebPartDescriptionFileMethodName, list, true);
}
```

LoadWebPartDescriptionFile follows the same steps as LoadWebPartInfoSet method except for one thing. In the case of LoadWebPartDescriptionFile, the underlying XML Web service method takes an argument, the name of the description file being downloaded. As mentioned, XmlWebService CatalogPart exposes a property named FileNameParameter that the page developer must set to the name of the parameter of the XML Web service method whose name is given by the GetWebPart DescriptionFileMethodName property.

Using the XmlWebServiceCatalogPart Control

This section shows you an example of a Web page that uses the XmlWebServiceCatalogPart custom CatalogPart control to present the users with the catalog of available WebPart controls. Because this custom CatalogPart control uses an XML Web service, first you need to develop a sample XML Web service. As Listing 31-43 shows, the sample XML Web service exposes two webcallable methods named GetWebPartInfoSet and GetWebPartDescriptionFile. The following sections present the implementation of these two methods.

GetWebPartInfoSet

Listing 31-49 presents the implementation of the GetWebPartInfoSet method. The main responsibility of this method is to generate an XML document that contains the id, title, description, catalog icon URL, the description filename of all the available WebPart controls. Listing 31-44 shows an example of such an XML document. As this listing shows, the XML document has a single document element named `<webPartInfoSet>` that contains one or more `<webPartInfo>` child elements, where each child element represents a WebPart control. The id, title, description, catalogIconImageUrl, and fileName attributes of each `<webPartInfo>` child element contains the id, title, description, catalog icon URL, and description filename of the WebPart control.

Listing 31-49: The GetWebPartInfoSet method

```
[WebMethod]
public string GetWebPartInfoSet()
{
  string result = "";
  using (StringWriter sw = new StringWriter())
  {
    XmlWriterSettings settings = new XmlWriterSettings();
    settings.Indent = true;

    using (XmlWriter xw = XmlWriter.Create(sw, settings))
    {
      xw.WriteStartDocument();
      xw.WriteStartElement("webPartInfoSet");
      AddWebPartInfoSet(xw);
      xw.WriteEndElement();
      xw.WriteEndDocument();
    }
    result = sw.ToString();
  }

  return result;
}
```

The GetWebPartInfoSet method uses the XmlWriter streaming API to generate the required XML document. The method first generates the `<webPartInfoSet>` document element and then calls the AddWebPartInfoSet method to generate the `<webPartInfo>` child elements that represent the available WebPart controls, as discussed in the following section.

AddWebPartInfoSet

To understand the implementation of the AddWebPartInfoSet method, you need to understand the structure of a WebPart description file. As discussed in the previous sections, the description file of a WebPart control contains all the information about the control, including the fully qualified name of the type of the control, the weak or strong name of the assembly that contains the type, and the values of properties of the control. You can think of the description file as a recipe that you can use to generate a WebPart control of a specific type with specific settings.

Listing 31-50 shows a description file that describes an ASP.NET `Calendar` control with the specified settings. As this listing shows, every description file has a single document element named `<webParts>` that contains one or more `<webPart>` child elements, where each child element represents a `WebPart` control. The current version of the ASP.NET Framework only supports one `<webPart>` child element for each `<webParts>` document element, which means that each description file describes one and only one `WebPart` control. This could change in future versions of the Framework where the `<webParts>` document element could have more than one `<webPart>` child element.

As Listing 31-50 illustrates, the lone `<webPart>` element has two child elements, `<metaData>` and `<data>`. The `<metaData>` element itself contains two child elements, `<type>` and `<importErrorMessage>`. The `<type>` child element exposes an attribute named `name` that contains the following information:

❑ The fully qualified name of the type of the `WebPart` control, including its namespace, such as `System.Web.UI.WebControls.Calendar`.

❑ The information about the assembly that contains the type. This information normally contains the assembly name, version, culture, and public key token, such as `System.Web, Version=2.0.0.0, Culture=neutral, PublicKeyToken=b03f5f7f11d50a3a`.

The `<importErrorMessage>` child element, on the other hand, contains the error message that will be shown to the user if the import operation fails.

The `<data>` element contains two child elements, `<properties>` and `<genericWebPartProperties>`. The description file only populates one of these two properties. If the control doesn't derive from the `WebPart` control such as an ASP.NET control, custom control, or user control, only the `<genericWebPartProperties>` element is populated and the `<properties>` element is left empty. Listing 31-50 presents an example of this case where the description file describes an ASP.NET `Calendar` control. If the control derives from the `WebPart` control, such as the `RssReaderWebPart` control, only the `<properties>` element is populated and the `<genericWebPartProperties>` element is left empty.

Both the `<properties>` and `<genericWebPartProperties>` elements contain the same type of child element, `<property>`. Each `<property>` element represents a property of the `WebPart` control. The `name` and `type` attributes of a `<property>` element are set to the name and data type of the property that the element represents. The value of the property that the element represents is placed within the opening and closing tags of the `<property>` element.

Listing 31-50: An example of a description file

```xml
<?xml version="1.0" encoding="utf-8"?>
<webParts>
  <webPart xmlns="http://schemas.microsoft.com/WebPart/v3">
    <metaData>
      <type name="System.Web.UI.WebControls.Calendar, System.Web, Version=2.0.0.0,
      Culture=neutral, PublicKeyToken=b03f5f7f11d50a3a" />
      <importErrorMessage>Cannot import this Web Part.</importErrorMessage>
    </metaData>
    <data>
      <properties />
      <genericWebPartProperties>
        <property name="AllowClose" type="bool">True</property>
        <property name="Width" type="unit" />
```

(continued)

Listing 31-50: *(continued)*

```
          <property name="AllowMinimize" type="bool">True</property>
          <property name="AllowConnect" type="bool">True</property>
          <property name="ChromeType" type="chrometype">Default</property>
          <property name="TitleIconImageUrl" type="string" />
          <property name="Description" type="string" />
          <property name="Hidden" type="bool">False</property>
          <property name="TitleUrl" type="string" />
          <property name="AllowEdit" type="bool">True</property>
          <property name="Height" type="unit" />
          <property name="HelpUrl" type="string" />
          <property name="Title" type="string">Calendar</property>
          <property name="CatalogIconImageUrl" type="string" />
          <property name="Direction" type="direction">NotSet</property>
          <property name="ChromeState" type="chromestate">Normal</property>
          <property name="AllowZoneChange" type="bool">True</property>
          <property name="AllowHide" type="bool">True</property>
          <property name="HelpMode" type="helpmode">Navigate</property>
          <property name="ExportMode" type="exportmode">All</property>
        </genericWebPartProperties>
      </data>
    </webPart>
  </webParts>
```

Now that you have a good understanding of the structure of a description file, you can implement the `AddWebPartInfoSet` method. Listing 31-51 presents the code for this method. The method first calls the `GetFileNames` method to get the filenames for all the available description files. The implementation of the `GetFileNames` method is pretty simple. However, you can extend it to retrieve the filenames from other sources, such as a SQL Server database.

The `AddWebPartInfoSet` method then iterates through the filenames. For each enumerated filename, the method loads the description file with the specified filename into an `XmlReader`:

```
XmlReader reader = XmlReader.Create(Server.MapPath(fileName))
```

It then positions the reader on the document element of the description file, the `<webParts>` element:

```
        reader.MoveToContent();
```

Next, it positions the reader on the first `<property>` element in the document:

```
  reader.ReadToDescendant("property");
```

The method then enters a `do-while` loop. For each iteration of the loop, the method reads the value of the name attribute of the current `<property>` element and assigns the value to the appropriate local variable:

```
        switch (reader.GetAttribute("name"))
        {
          case "Title":
            title = reader.ReadElementString();
            break;
          case "Description":
            description = reader.ReadElementString();
```

```
          break;
        case "CatalogIconImageUrl":
          catalogIconImageUrl = reader.ReadElementString();
          break;
      }
```

It then positions the reader on the next `<property>` element and repeats the loop:

```
reader.ReadToNextSibling("property")
```

Finally, the method generates a `<webPart>` element and uses the values of the local variables to set the `title`, `id`, `description`, `catalogIconImageUrl`, and `fileName` attributes of the `<webPart>` element.

Listing 31-51: The AddWebPartInfoSet method

```
private void AddWebPartInfoSet(XmlWriter writer)
{
  string title = string.Empty;
  string description = string.Empty;
  string catalogIconImageUrl = string.Empty;
  string[] fileNames = GetFileNames();

  foreach (string fileName in fileNames)
  {
    using (XmlReader reader = XmlReader.Create(Server.MapPath(fileName)))
    {
      reader.MoveToContent();
      reader.ReadToDescendant("property");

      do
      {
        switch (reader.GetAttribute("name"))
        {
          case "Title":
            title = reader.ReadElementString();
            break;
          case "Description":
            description = reader.ReadElementString();
            break;
          case "CatalogIconImageUrl":
            catalogIconImageUrl = reader.ReadElementString();
            break;
        }
      } while (reader.ReadToNextSibling("property"));

      writer.WriteStartElement("webPartInfo");
      writer.WriteAttributeString("fileName", fileName);
      writer.WriteAttributeString("id", title);
      writer.WriteAttributeString("title", title);
      writer.WriteAttributeString("description", description);
      writer.WriteAttributeString("catalogIconImageUrl", catalogIconImageUrl);
      writer.WriteEndElement();
    }
  }
}
```

GetWebPartDescriptionFile

Listing 31-52 illustrates the implementation of the `GetWebPartDescriptionFile` method. The main responsibility of this method is to load the content of the description file with the specified name into a string. The method loads the content of the description file with the specified name into an `XmlReader`. The `XmlReader` is originally positioned on the root node of the document:

```
XmlReader reader = XmlReader.Create(Server.MapPath(fileName))
```

The method then positions the reader on the document element, the `<webParts>` element:

```
reader.MoveToContent();
```

Then the method calls the `ReadOuterXml` method of the reader to access the document element, `<webParts>`, and its descendant. When you position an `XmlReader` on the document element of an XML document and call its `ReadOuterXml` method, the method will return the content of the entire XML document:

```
result = reader.ReadOuterXml();
```

Listing 31-52: The GetWebPartDescriptionFile method

```
[WebMethod]
public string GetWebPartDescriptionFile(string fileName)
{
  string result;
  using (XmlReader reader = XmlReader.Create(Server.MapPath(fileName)))
  {
    reader.MoveToContent();
    result = reader.ReadOuterXml();
  }
  return result;
}
```

Listing 31-53 contains an ASP.NET page that uses the `XmlWebServiceCatalogPart` control to retrieve `WebPart` controls from the XML Web service whose implementation was presented in these sections.

Listing 31-53: An ASP.NET page that uses the XmlWebServiceCatalogPart control

```
<%@ Page Language="C#" %>
<%@ Register TagPrefix="custom" Namespace="CustomComponents" %>
<script runat="server">
  . . .
</script>

<html xmlns="http://www.w3.org/1999/xhtml">
<body>
  <form id="form1" runat="server">
    <asp:WebPartManager runat="server" ID="mgr2" />
    <table cellspacing="10">
      <tr>
        . . .
```

```
      </tr>
      <tr>
        . . .
        <td>
          <asp:CatalogZone runat="server" ID="myzone3">
            <ZoneTemplate>
              <custom:XmlWebServiceCatalogPart runat="server" ID="mycatalog"
              TypeName="Service" GetWebPartInfoSetMethodName="GetWebPartInfoSet"
              GetWebPartDescriptionFileMethodName="GetWebPartDescriptionFile"
              FileNameParameter="fileName"
              WSDLPath="http://localhost:1064/Server/Service.asmx?WSDL" />
            </ZoneTemplate>
          </asp:CatalogZone>
        </td>
      </tr>
    </table>
  </form>
</body>
</html>
```

Summary

This chapter provided you with an in-depth coverage of the WebPart, EditorPart, CatalogPart, and WebPartVerb base classes and developed several custom component instances of those classes such as RssReaderWebPart, RssReaderEditorPart, XmlWebServiceCatalogPart, and UrlWebPartVerb to show you how to extend the functionality of these base classes. The chapter also discussed the IWebPart, IWebActionable, IWebEditable, and IPersonalizable interfaces in detail and showed you how to implement these interfaces.

In the next chapter, you learn about WebPartZoneBase base class and how to extend it to implement your own custom WebPartZoneBase controls. You also see how to write a custom WebPartChrome chrome to customize the rendering of your WebPart controls.

Developing Custom WebPartZoneBase Controls

A WebPartZoneBase zone defines a region on a Web Parts page that contains WebPart controls. This chapter begins by discussing the base class of all Web Parts zones, WebZone, and then discusses the WebPartZoneBase base zone, which is the base class for all Web Parts zones that contain WebPart controls.

The chapter then discusses the only subclass of WebPartZoneBase, WebPartZone, and shows you how to extend this subclass to develop your own custom WebPartZoneBase zones. The chapter develops several custom WebPartZone controls such as XmlWebServiceWebPartZone and ProviderBasedWebPartZone.

A WebPartZoneBase zone uses a WebPartChrome object to render the WebPart controls that the zone contains. This chapter discusses the WebPartChrome class and develops a custom WebPart Chrome chrome to show you how to develop your own custom WebPartChromes to customize the rendering of WebPart controls contained in a zone.

WebZone

A WebZone control defines a tabular region on a Web page that contains zero or more Part controls. Because a WebZone control contains other controls, it's a composite control and therefore it derives from the CompositeControl base class, as shown in Listing 32-1.

Listing 32-1: The WebZone composite control

```
public abstract class WebZone : CompositeControl
{
  public virtual PartChromeType GetEffectiveChromeType(Part part);
```

(continued)

Listing 32-1: *(continued)*

```
    protected override void OnInit(EventArgs e);
    protected override HtmlTextWriterTag TagKey {get;}
    protected internal override void RenderContents(HtmlTextWriter writer);
    protected virtual void RenderHeader(HtmlTextWriter writer) { }
    protected virtual void RenderBody(HtmlTextWriter writer) { }
    protected virtual void RenderFooter(HtmlTextWriter writer) {}

    public virtual string BackImageUrl  {get; set;}
    public virtual string EmptyZoneText {get;}
    public Style EmptyZoneTextStyle {get;}
    public Style ErrorStyle {get;}
    public TitleStyle FooterStyle {get;}
    protected virtual bool HasFooter {get;}
    protected virtual bool HasHeader {get;}
    public TitleStyle HeaderStyle {get;}
    public virtual string HeaderText {get; set;}
    public virtual int Padding {get; set;}
    public Style PartChromeStyle {get;}
    public virtual PartChromeType PartChromeType {get; set;}
    public TableStyle PartStyle {get;}
    public TitleStyle PartTitleStyle {get;}
    protected internal bool RenderClientScript {get;}
    public virtual ButtonType VerbButtonType {get; set;}
    public Style VerbStyle {get;}
    protected WebPartManager WebPartManager {get;}
}
```

Because a `WebZone` control represents a tabular region on a Web page, it overrides the `TagKey` property to specify a `table` HTML element as its containing element:

```
protected override HtmlTextWriterTag TagKey
{
  get { return HtmlTextWriterTag.Table; }
}
```

It also overrides the `RenderContents` method to render a header, body, and footer as illustrated in Listing 32-2.

Listing 32-2: WebZone overrides RenderContents

```
protected internal override void RenderContents(HtmlTextWriter writer)
{
  if (HasHeader)
  {
    writer.RenderBeginTag(HtmlTextWriterTag.Tr);
    if (headerStyle != null)
      HeaderStyle.AddAttributesToRender(writer, this);
    writer.RenderBeginTag(HtmlTextWriterTag.Td);
    RenderHeader(writer);
    writer.RenderEndTag();
    writer.RenderEndTag();
```

```
    }

    writer.RenderBeginTag(HtmlTextWriterTag.Tr);
    writer.RenderBeginTag(HtmlTextWriterTag.Td);
    RenderBody(writer);
    writer.RenderEndTag();
    writer.RenderEndTag();

    if (HasFooter)
    {
      writer.RenderBeginTag(HtmlTextWriterTag.Tr);
      if (footerStyle != null)
        HooterStyle.AddAttributesToRender(writer, this);
      writer.RenderBeginTag(HtmlTextWriterTag.Td);
      RenderFooter(writer);
      writer.RenderEndTag();
      writer.RenderEndTag();
    }
}
```

As Listing 32-2 shows, because WebZone control renders a table, it exposes table-related methods and properties such as the following:

- ❑ RenderHeader: Subclasses of the WebZone control can override this method to render the header of the table

- ❑ RenderBody: Subclasses of the WebZone control can override this method to render the body of the table

- ❑ RenderFooter: Subclasses of the WebZone control can override this method to render the footer of the table

- ❑ HasHeader: Subclasses of the WebZone control can override this property to specify whether the table has a header

- ❑ HasFooter: Subclasses of the WebZone control can override this property to specify whether the table has a footer

- ❑ HeaderStyle: Specifies the style properties of the header of the table

- ❑ FooterStyle: Specifies the style properties of the footer of the table

- ❑ HeaderText: Specifies the text that the header of the table displays

- ❑ BackImageUrl: Specifies the background image of the table

The WebZone control, like all composite controls, exposes top-level properties that apply to its child controls, that is, the Part controls, such as the following:

- ❑ PartStyle: Specifies a TableStyle that applies to all Part controls that the WebZone contains.

- ❑ PartTitleStyle: Specifies a TitleStyle that applies to the title of all Part controls that the WebZone contains.

- ❑ VerbStyle: Specifies a Style that applies to the verbs of all Part controls that the WebZone contains.

❑ PartChromeStyle: Specifies a Style that applies to the chrome of all Part controls that the WebZone contains.

❑ PartChromeType: Specifies the chrome type of all Part controls that the WebZone contains. The possible values are PartChromeType.None, PartChromType.TitleOnly, PartChromeType.BorderOnly, and PartChromeType.TitleAndBorder.

WebZone has two main subclasses, which means that there are two types of WebZone controls, WebPartZoneBase and ToolZone controls. This chapter only covers the WebPartZoneBase base class.

WebPartZoneBase

WebPartZoneBase is the base class for all zones that contain WebPart controls. Listing 32-3 presents the important methods and properties of this base class. The following sections discuss some of these methods and properties in more detail.

Listing 32-3: The WebPartZoneBase class

```
public abstract class WebPartZoneBase : WebZone, IPostBackEventHandler
{
    protected override void RenderHeader(HtmlTextWriter writer);
    protected override void RenderBody(HtmlTextWriter writer);

    protected internal abstract WebPartCollection GetInitialWebParts();
    protected virtual WebPartChrome CreateWebPartChrome();

    static private readonly object CreateVerbsEventKey = new object();
    public event WebPartVerbsEventHandler CreateVerbs;
    protected virtual void OnCreateVerbs(WebPartVerbsEventArgs e);

    protected virtual void CloseWebPart(WebPart webPart);
    protected virtual void ConnectWebPart(WebPart webPart);
    protected virtual void DeleteWebPart(WebPart webPart);
    protected virtual void EditWebPart(WebPart webPart);
    protected virtual void MinimizeWebPart(WebPart webPart);
    protected virtual void RestoreWebPart(WebPart webPart);

    protected internal override void OnPreRender(EventArgs e);

    void IPostBackEventHandler.RaisePostBackEvent(string eventArgument);
    protected virtual void RaisePostBackEvent(string eventArgument);
    internal WebPartVerbCollection VerbsForWebPart(WebPart webPart);

    public virtual WebPartVerb CloseVerb {get;}
    public virtual WebPartVerb ConnectVerb {get;}
    public virtual WebPartVerb DeleteVerb {get;}
    public virtual WebPartVerb EditVerb {get;}
    public virtual WebPartVerb ExportVerb {get;}
    public virtual WebPartVerb MinimizeVerb {get;}
    public virtual WebPartVerb RestoreVerb {get;}
    public virtual WebPartVerb HelpVerb {get;}

    public virtual bool AllowLayoutChange {get; set;}
```

```
        public virtual Orientation LayoutOrientation {get; set;}
        protected override bool HasFooter {get;}
        protected override bool HasHeader {get;}
        public Style MenuCheckImageStyle {get;}
        public Style MenuLabelHoverStyle {get;}
        public Style MenuVerbHoverStyle {get;}
        public Style MenuVerbStyle {get;}
        public Style MenuLabelStyle {get;}
        public Style TitleBarVerbStyle {get;}
        public WebPartMenuStyle MenuPopupStyle {get;}
        public Style SelectedPartChromeStyle {get;}
        public virtual string MenuCheckImageUrl {get; set;}
        public virtual string MenuLabelText {get; set;}
        public virtual string MenuPopupImageUrl {get; set;}
        public virtual bool ShowTitleIcons {get; set;}
        public virtual ButtonType TitleBarVerbButtonType {get; set;}
        public override ButtonType VerbButtonType {get; set;}
        public virtual WebPartVerbRenderMode WebPartVerbRenderMode {get; set;}

        public WebPartChrome WebPartChrome {get;}
        public WebPartCollection WebParts {get;}

        protected override void TrackViewState();
        protected override void LoadViewState(object savedState);
        protected override object SaveViewState();
    }
```

Deriving from WebZone

WebPartZoneBase class derives from WebZone and overrides its RenderHeader and RenderBody methods. These methods render the header and body of the table that represents a WebZone control on an ASP.NET page. You can derive from WebPartZoneBase and override these two methods to take complete control over rendering the header and body of the table that represents the zone on the page.

Listing 32-4 contains the code for the main parts of the RenderHeader method.

Listing 32-4: The RenderHeader method

```
protected override void RenderHeader(HtmlTextWriter writer)
{
  if (!HeaderStyle.IsEmpty)
    HeaderStyle.AddAttributesToRender(writer, this);

  writer.RenderBeginTag(HtmlTextWriterTag.Td);
  writer.Write(DisplayTitle);
  writer.RenderEndTag();
}
```

RenderHeader renders a <td> HTML element to display the title text, and renders the HeaderStyle as the style attributes on the <td> element.

Listing 32-5 presents the code for the main parts of the RenderBody method.

Listing 32-5: The RenderBody method

```
protected override void RenderBody(HtmlTextWriter writer)
{
  writer.RenderBeginTag(HtmlTextWriterTag.Table);

  foreach (WebPart webPart in WebParts)
  {
    writer.RenderBeginTag(HtmlTextWriterTag.Tr);
    writer.RenderBeginTag(HtmlTextWriterTag.Td);
    WebPartChrome.RenderWebPart(writer, webPart);
    writer.RenderEndTag();
    writer.RenderEndTag();
  }

  writer.RenderEndTag();
}
```

The `RenderBody` method renders a table that contains the content of the entire body of the `WebPartZone Base` zone:

```
writer.RenderBeginTag(HtmlTextWriterTag.Table);
```

It also iterates through the `WebPart` controls that the `WebPartZoneBase` zone contains. For each enumerated `WebPart` control, `RenderBody` renders a table row that contains a single cell:

```
writer.RenderBeginTag(HtmlTextWriterTag.Tr);
writer.RenderBeginTag(HtmlTextWriterTag.Td);
```

`RenderBody` then calls the `RenderWebPart` method of the `WebPartChrome` object to render the enumerated `WebPart` control within the table cell:

```
WebPartChrome.RenderWebPart(writer, webPart);
```

CreateWebPartChrome

As discussed, `RenderBody` delegates the responsibility of rendering all the `WebPart` controls that it contains to a single instance of a class named `WebPartChrome`. The main responsibility of this class is to render the specified `WebPart` control and the visual container or frame around the control. This frame is known as *chrome*. This class is discussed in the next section.

`WebPartZoneBase` exposes a protected virtual method named `CreateWebPartChrome` that creates the `WebPartChrome` object that renders its `WebPart` controls as illustrated in Listing 32-6. As you'll see later, you can derive from `WebPartChrome` to implement your own custom `WebPartChrome` and override the `CreateWebPartChrome` method of `WebPartZoneBase` to have the zone use your custom `WebPartChrome` to render its `WebPart` controls. This will give you complete control over the rendering of the `WebPart` controls that the zone contains.

Listing 32-6: The CreateWebPartChrome method

```
protected virtual WebPartChrome CreateWebPartChrome()
{
  return new WebPartChrome(this, base.WebPartManager);
}
```

CreateInitialWebParts

WebPartZoneBase exposes an abstract method named CreateInitialWebParts as shown in Listing 32-7. When you derive from WebPartZoneBase to implement your own custom WebPartZoneBase, you must implement the CreateInitialWebPart method. The main responsibility of this method is to create the initial WebParts that a WebPartZoneBase zone contains. For example, as you'll see later, WebPartZone derives from WebPartZoneBase and implements this method where it creates the WebPart controls that the page developer has declared within the opening and closing tags of its <ZoneTemplate> element.

Listing 32-7: The CreateInitialWebParts method

```
protected internal abstract WebPartCollection GetInitialWebParts();
```

CreateVerbs Event

WebPartZoneBase exposes an event of type WebPartVerbsEventHandler named CreateVerbs. The WebPartVerbsEventArgs class is the event data class for this event as shown in Listing 32-8. This event data class holds the WebPartVerbCollection collection that contains the verbs for the specified WebPart control. The OnCreateVerbs method of WebPartZoneBase raises the CreateVerbs event.

Listing 32-8: The WebPartVerbsEventArgs event data class

```
public class WebPartVerbsEventArgs : EventArgs
{
  public WebPartVerbsEventArgs() { }
  public WebPartVerbsEventArgs(WebPartVerbCollection verbs)
  {
    this.verbs = verbs;
  }

  private WebPartVerbCollection verbs;
  public WebPartVerbCollection Verbs
  {
    get
    {
      if (verbs == null)
        return WebPartVerbCollection.Empty;

      return this._verbs;
    }
    Set { verbs = value;}
  }
}
```

As you'll see later, you can implement a custom zone that derives from `WebPartZoneBase` and overrides its `OnCreateVerbs` method to add custom verbs to the zone. The zone will automatically add these custom verbs to the verbs menu of all `WebPart` controls that the zone contains.

Implementing IPostBackEventHandler

`WebPartZoneBase` implements the `IPostBackEventHandler` interface to handle its own postback events. As discussed in Chapter 4, this interface exposes a single method named `RaisePostBackEvent`. Listing 32-9 contains the code for the main parts of the `RaisePostBackEvent` method of `WebPartZone Base` class.

Listing 32-9: The RaisePostBackEvent method

```
protected virtual void RaisePostBackEvent(string eventArgument)
{
  WebPartCollection webParts = WebPartManager.WebParts;
  string[] eventArgs = eventArgument.Split(new char[] { ':' });

  if (eventArgs[0] == "drag")
  {
    string webPartID = eventArgs[1].Substring("WebPart_".Length);
    int zoneIndex = int.Parse(eventArgs[2]);
    WebPart webPart = webParts[webPartID];
    base.WebPartManager.MoveWebPart(webPart, this, zoneIndex);
  }
  else if (eventArgs[0] == "partverb")
  {
    string verbID = eventArgs[1];
    string webPartID = eventArgs[2];
    WebPart webPart = webParts[webPartID];
    WebPartVerb verb = webPart.Verbs[verbID];
    verb.ServerClickHandler(verb, new WebPartEventArgs(webPart));
  }
  else if (eventArgs[0] == "zoneverb")
  {
    WebPartVerbsEventArgs e = new WebPartVerbsEventArgs();
    OnCreateVerbs(e);
    verbs = e.Verbs;
    string verbID = eventArgs[1];
    string webPartID = eventArgs[2];
    WebPart webPart = webParts[webPartID];
    WebPartVerb verb = verbs[verbID];
    verb.ServerClickHandler(verb, new WebPartEventArgs(webPart));
  }

  else if (eventArgs[0]== "close")
    CloseWebPart(webParts[eventArgs[1]]);

  else if (eventArgs[0] == "connect")
    ConnectWebPart(webParts[eventArgs[1]]);

  else if (eventArgs[0] == "delete")
```

```
      DeleteWebPart(webParts[eventArgs[1]]);

    else if (eventArgs[0] == "edit")
      EditWebPart(webParts[eventArgs[1]]);

    else if (eventArgs[0] == "minimize")
      MinimizeWebPart(webParts[eventArgs[1]]);

    else if (eventArgs[0] == "restore")
      RestoreWebPart(webParts[eventArgs[1]]);
  }
}
```

The event argument consists of two parts separated by a colon character if the event is a standard event such as close, connect, delete, edit, minimize, and maximize, or three parts separated by a colon character if the event isn't one of the previously mentioned standard events. The following rules apply to these events:

❑ The first part of these two or three parts always specifies the type of the event.

❑ One of these two or three parts always specifies the ID of the WebPart associated with the event.

❑ The remaining part is a helper such as the ID of the verb that raised the event.

WebPartZoneBase supports three types of verbs as follows:

❑ **Standard Verbs:** These verbs include close, connect, delete, edit, minimize, and maximize. The WebPartZoneBase zone automatically adds these standard verbs to the verbs menu of the WebPart controls that the zone contains. WebPartZoneBase exposes the following seven properties to represent these verbs:

```
public virtual WebPartVerb CloseVerb {get;}
public virtual WebPartVerb ConnectVerb {get;}
public virtual WebPartVerb DeleteVerb {get;}
public virtual WebPartVerb EditVerb {get;}
public virtual WebPartVerb ExportVerb {get;}
public virtual WebPartVerb MinimizeVerb {get;}
public virtual WebPartVerb RestoreVerb {get;}
```

Recall that the WebPartVerb class implements the IStateManager interface to handle its own state across page postbacks. WebPartZoneBase overrides the TrackViewState, SaveViewState, and LoadViewState methods to call the respective methods of these standard verbs to allow them to manage their states.

WebPartZoneBase exposes the following methods to handle the events that the standard verbs raise:

```
protected virtual void CloseWebPart(WebPart webPart);
protected virtual void ConnectWebPart(WebPart webPart);
protected virtual void DeleteWebPart(WebPart webPart);
protected virtual void EditWebPart(WebPart webPart);
protected virtual void MinimizeWebPart(WebPart webPart);
protected virtual void RestoreWebPart(WebPart webPart);
```

❑ **Part Verbs:** These verbs include the custom verbs that you want to add to a particular WebPart control that resides in a WebPartZoneBase zone. As discussed in Chapter 30, you should take the following steps to add a custom verb to a WebPart control:

    a.   Implement a custom verb that derives from the WebPartVerb base class. For example, Listing 31-12 shows the implementation of the UrlWebPartVerb custom verb.

    b.   Implement a custom WebPart control that derives from the WebPart base class. For example, Listing 31-27 shows the implementation of the RssReaderWebPart4 custom WebPart control.

    c.   Override the Verbs property to instantiate and to add an instance of your custom verb to your custom WebPart control. For example, Listing 31-32 shows the implementation of the Verbs property of the RssReaderWebPart4 WebPart control that instantiates and adds an instance of the UrlWebPartVerb custom verb to the control.

As Listing 32-9 shows, the RaisePostBackEvent method of WebPartZoneBase zone calls the ServerClickHandler method of your custom WebPartVerb to handle the event raised by your custom verb:

```
verb.ServerClickHandler(verb, new WebPartEventArgs(webPart));
```

❑ **Zone Verbs:** These verbs include the custom verbs that you want the WebPartZoneBase zone to add to all WebPart controls that the zone contains. As you'll see later, you must implement a custom WebPartZoneBase zone that overrides the OnCreateVerbs method to have the zone add a custom verb to all the WebPart controls that the zone contains.

As Listing 32-9 shows, the RaisePostBackEvent method of WebPartZoneBase zone handles the events for zone verbs by raising the CreateVerbs event. As you'll see later, the OnCreateVerbs method of a custom WebPartZoneBase can create custom verbs and add them to the Verbs collection of the WebPartVerbsEventArgs object:

```
WebPartVerbsEventArgs e = new WebPartVerbsEventArgs();
OnCreateVerbs(e);
```

The method also locates the specified verb in the Verbs collection and calls its ServerClickHandler method to handle the event:

```
verbs = e.Verbs;
string verbID = eventArgs[1];
string webPartID = eventArgs[2];
WebPart webPart = webParts[webPartID];
WebPartVerb verb = verbs[verbID];
verb.ServerClickHandler(verb, new WebPartEventArgs(webPart));
```

WebPartZone

The ASP.NET Framework comes with one and only one descendant of the WebPartZoneBase base class named WebPartZone, as shown in Listing 32-10. Recall that WebPartZoneBase exposes an abstract method named GetInitialWebParts. The main responsibility of this method is to retrieve and to add the initial WebPart controls. The initial WebPart controls are WebPart controls that are added to a page when there are no customized WebPart controls associated with the current user.

As Listing 32-10 shows, WebPartZone is a templated WebPartZoneBase control that exposes a template property named ZoneTemplate that allows the page developer to declaratively specify the initial WebPart controls within the opening and closing tags of the <ZoneTemplate> element on an ASP.NET Web page.

Listing 32-10: The WebPartZone control

```
public class WebPartZone : WebPartZoneBase
{
  protected internal override WebPartCollection GetInitialWebParts()
  {
    WebPartCollection webParts = new WebPartCollection();
    if (ZoneTemplate != null)
    {
      Panel panel = new Panel();
      ZoneTemplate.InstantiateIn(panel);
      if (!panel.HasControls())
        return webParts;

      foreach (Control control in panel.Controls)
      {
        if (control is ContentPlaceHolder)
        {
          if (!control.HasControls())
            continue;

          foreach (Control childControl in control.Controls)
          {
            WebPart webPart = childControl as WebPart;
            if (webPart == null)
              webPart = WebPartManager.CreateWebPart(childControl);
            webParts.Add(webPart);
          }
          continue;
        }

        WebPart webPart = control as WebPart;
        if (webPart == null)
          webPart = WebPartManager.CreateWebPart(control);
        webParts.Add(webPart);
      }
    }
    return webParts;
  }

  Private ITemplate zoneTemplate;
  public virtual ITemplate ZoneTemplate
  {
    get { return zoneTemplate; }
    set { zoneTemplate = value;}
  }
}
```

As Listing 32-10 shows, `GetInitialWebParts` first calls the `InstantiateIn` method of the `Zone Template` to load the declared initial controls into a `Panel`:

```
Panel panel = new Panel();
ZoneTemplate.InstantiateIn(panel);
```

The method then iterates through the controls and checks whether each enumerated control is a `Content PlaceHolder` control.

If the control is not a `ContentPlaceHolder`, it checks whether the control is a `WebPart`. If it is, it adds the control to a local `WebPartCollection` collection. If it is not, it calls the `CreateWebPart` method of the `WebPartManager` to wrap the control in a `GenericWebPart` control and adds this control to the local `WebPartCollection` collection:

```
WebPart webPart = control as WebPart;
if (webPart == null)
  webPart = WebPartManager.CreateWebPart(control);
webParts.Add(webPart);
```

If the control is a `ContentPlaceHolder`, it iterates through the child controls of the `ContentPlaceHolder` and performs the same steps just discussed to add each child control to the local `WebPartCollection` collection:

```
foreach (Control childControl in control.Controls)
{
  WebPart webPart = childControl as WebPart;
  if (webPart == null)
    webPart = WebPartManager.CreateWebPart(childControl);
  webParts.Add(webPart);
}
```

Developing Custom WebPartZone Controls

The previous section provided you with in-depth coverage of the internals of the `WebPartZoneBase` and `WebPartZone` controls. This section builds on what you've learned so far to show you to how to extend these base classes to implement your own custom `WebPartZoneBase` zones.

XmlWebServiceWebPartZone

`WebPartZone` adds an `ExportVerb` to the verbs menu of the `WebPart` controls that it contains to allow the user to export the desired `WebPart` control to an XML description document, which is then saved in a file with `.WebPart` extension. This section develops a custom `WebPartZone` zone that derives from `WebPartZone` and extends its functionality to allow users to export a `WebPart` control to an XML description document, which is then sent to the specified XML Web service.

`XmlWebServiceWebPartZone` overrides the `OnCreateVerbs` method of the `WebPartZoneBase` class to add the required verb to all `WebPart` controls that the zone contains. Listing 32-11 illustrates the `Web PartZoneBase` zone's implementation of this method.

Listing 32-11: The WebPartZoneBase zone's implementation of the OnCreateVerbs method

```
static private readonly object CreateVerbsEventKey = new object();
public event WebPartVerbsEventHandler CreateVerbs
{
  add { base.Events.AddHandler(CreateVerbsEventKey, value); }
  remove { base.Events.RemoveHandler(CreateVerbsEventKey, value); }
}

protected virtual void OnCreateVerbs(WebPartVerbsEventArgs e)
{
  WebPartVerbsEventHandler handler =
                  (WebPartVerbsEventHandler)Events[CreateVerbsEventKey];
  if (handler != null)
    handler(this, e);
}
```

As Listing 32-11 illustrates, all the base implementation of the OnCreateVerbs method does is raise the CreateVerbs event. This event is raised to signal that the zone has entered the phase when the verbs are created. However, the base implementation doesn't actually create any verbs. It just raises the event to allow others to create them.

XmlWebServiceWebPartZone overrides the base implementation to create a custom WebPartVerb named XmlWebServiceWebPartVerb. This custom verb is discussed in the next section. Listing 32-12 presents the XmlWebServiceWebPartZone zone's implementation of the OnCreateVerbs method.

Listing 32-12: The XmlWebServiceWebPartZone zone's implementation of the OnCreateVerbs method

```
protected override void OnCreateVerbs(WebPartVerbsEventArgs e)
{
  List<WebPartVerb> verbs = new List<WebPartVerb>();
  XmlWebServiceWebPartVerb verb =
          new XmlWebServiceWebPartVerb("XmlWebServiceVerb",ExportToXmlWebService);
  verbs.Add(verb);

  e.Verbs = new WebPartVerbCollection(e.Verbs, verbs);
  base.OnCreateVerbs(e);
}
```

OnCreateVerbs first creates an instance of the generic List collection to hold the verb:

```
List<WebPartVerb> verbs = new List<WebPartVerb>();
```

Then it creates an instance of the XmlWebServiceWebPartVerb custom verb and registers the Export ToXmlWebService method as a callback:

```
XmlWebServiceWebPartVerb verb =
          new XmlWebServiceWebPartVerb("XmlWebServiceVerb",ExportToXmlWebService);
```

Next, it adds the newly created verb to the generic `List` collection:

```
verbs.Add(verb);
```

Then it adds the `List` collection to the `WebPartVerbCollection` collection of the `WebPartVerbsEventArgs` object passed into it:

```
e.Verbs = new WebPartVerbCollection(e.Verbs, verbs);
```

Finally, it calls the `OnCreateVerbs` method of its base class. This allows others to register callbacks for the `CreateVerbs` event:

```
base.OnCreateVerbs(e);
```

ExportToXmlWebService

As you saw, `OnCreateVerbs` registers the `ExportToXmlWebService` method as callback for the `XmlWebServiceWebPartVerb` custom verb. Listing 32-13 presents the implementation of the `ExportToXmlWebService` method. This method's main responsibilities are to export the selected `WebPart` control to an XML description document and send this document over the wire to the specified XML Web service.

Listing 32-13: The ExportToXmlWebService method

```csharp
void ExportToXmlWebService(object sender, WebPartEventArgs e)
{
  using (StringWriter swriter = new StringWriter())
  {
    WebPartManager mgr = WebPartManager.GetCurrentWebPartManager(Page);
    using (XmlTextWriter writer1 = new XmlTextWriter(swriter))
    {
      writer1.Formatting = Formatting.Indented;
      writer1.WriteStartDocument();
      mgr.ExportWebPart(e.WebPart, writer1);
      writer1.WriteEndDocument();
    }

    SaveXmlDescriptionDocument(swriter.ToString());
  }
}
```

The `ExportToXmlWebService` accesses the current `WebPartManager` control on the page. The `WebPartManager` class exposes a static method named `GetCurrentWebPartManager` that takes a `Page` object as its argument and returns the `WebPartManager` control that the page developer has specified on the page:

```
WebPartManager mgr = WebPartManager.GetCurrentWebPartManager(Page);
```

The method then exports the selected `WebPart` control to an XML description document. The `WebPartManager` class exposes a method named `ExportWebPart` that takes two arguments. The first argument is the reference to the `WebPart` control being exported. The second argument is an `XmlWriter`. The `ExportWebPart` method generates the XML description document that describes the specified `WebPart` control and uses the `XmlWriter` to stream out the document:

```
    mgr.ExportWebPart(e.WebPart, writer1);
```

Finally, the method calls the `SaveXmlDescriptionDocument` method to send the XML description document to the specified XML Web service. This method is discussed in the next section.

```
    SaveXmlDescriptionDocument(swriter.ToString());
```

SaveXmlDescriptionDocument

The `SaveXmlDescriptionDocument` method uses the `XmlWebServiceMethodInvoker` component developed in Chapter 10 to send the XML description document to the specified XML Web service as shown in Listing 32-14. `XmlWebServiceWebPartZone` zone exposes the following XML Web service-related properties:

❑ `TypeName`: Specifies the fully qualified name of the class that represents the XML Web service.

❑ `WSDLPath`: Specifies the URL to the WSDL document that describes the XML Web service.

❑ `SaveXmlDescriptionDocumentMethodName`: Specifies the name of the XML Web service method that must be invoked to send the XML description document to the XML Web service.

❑ `XmlDescriptionDocumentParameterName`: Specifies the name of the parameter of the XML Web service method.

Listing 32-15 shows an example of an XML Web service that the `XmlWebServiceWebPartZone` zone can interact with. Notice that this XML Web service exposes a method named `SaveXmlDescriptionDocument` that takes the XML description document and saves it to a file with a `.WebPart` extension.

Listing 32-14: The SaveXmlDescriptionDocument method

```
protected virtual void SaveDescriptionXmlDocument(string descriptionXmlDocument)
{
   XmlWebServiceMethodInvoker methodInvoker = new XmlWebServiceMethodInvoker();
   methodInvoker.TypeName = TypeName;
   methodInvoker.WSDLPath = WSDLPath;
   OrderedDictionary list = new OrderedDictionary();
   list.Add(XmlDescriptionDocumentParameterName, descriptionXmlDocument);
   methodInvoker.InvokeXmlWebServiceMethod(SaveXmlDescriptionDocumentMethodName,
                                           list, true);
}
```

Listing 32-15: An XML Web service that XmlWebServiceWebPartZone zone interacts with

```
[WebService(Namespace = "http://WebParts.com/")]
public class Service : System.Web.Services.WebService
{
   [WebMethod]
   public void SaveXmlDescriptionDocument(string xmlDescriptionDocument)
   {
      using (StringReader sreader = new StringReader(xmlDescriptionDocument))
```

(continued)

Listing 32-15: *(continued)*

```
    {
      using (XmlReader xreader = XmlReader.Create(sreader))
      {
        XmlWriterSettings settings = new XmlWriterSettings();
        settings.Indent = true;
        using (XmlWriter xwriter =
                        XmlWriter.Create(Server.MapPath("MyDesc.WebPart")))
        {
          xwriter.WriteNode(xreader, true);
        }
      }
    }
  }
}
```

XmlWebServiceWebPartVerb

As discussed, the `OnCreateVerbs` method of the `XmlWebServiceWebPartZone` zone adds an instance of a custom verb named `XmlWebServiceWebPartVerb` to the `Verbs` collection of the respective `WebPartVerbsEventArgs` event data object. `XmlWebServiceWebPartVerb`, like all verbs, derives from the `WebPartVerb` base class and overrides its properties as presented in Listing 32-16.

Listing 32-16: The XmlWebServiceWebPartVerb custom verb

```
public class XmlWebServiceWebPartVerb : WebPartVerb
{
  public XmlWebServiceWebPartVerb(string id,
                              WebPartEventHandler serverClickHandler)
    : base(id, serverClickHandler) {}

  public override bool Checked {get; set;}
  public override string Text {get; set;}
  public override string Description {get; set;}
  public override string ImageUrl {get; set;}
}
```

Recall from Listing 31-10 that the `WebPartVerb` base class exposes a Boolean property named `Checked`. If this property is set to true, a check mark will appear next to the verb in the verbs menu of a `WebPart` control when the user selects the verb to provide users with visual cues that the verb has been selected. The `Checked` property makes sense when the task that the associated verb performs is part of list of tasks where each task relies on the outcome of the previous task. The check mark tells the user that the task has already been performed and the user can move on to the next task. Because the task that the `XmlWebServiceWebPartVerb` performs doesn't really fall in this category of tasks, `XmlWebServic eWebPartVerb` overrides the `Checked` property to ensure this property always returns false and can never be set to true:

```
public override bool Checked
{
  get { return false; }
  set { throw new NotSupportedException("Checked cannot be set!");}
}
```

XmlWebServideWebPartVerb also overrides the Text, Description, and ImageUrl properties to return the default value if the page developer hasn't specified values for these properties:

```
public override string Text
{
  get { return string.IsNullOrEmpty(base.Text) ?
                                  "Export to XML Web Service" : base.Text; }

  set { base.Text = value;}
}

public override string Description
{
  get { return string.IsNullOrEmpty(base.Description) ?
          "This verb will export this Web Parts control to XML Web service" :
                                                     base.Description;}

  set { base.Description = value; }
}

private const String xmlWebServiceWebPartVerbImageUrl = "contact.gif";
public override string ImageUrl
{
  get { return string.IsNullOrEmpty(base.ImageUrl) ?
                              xmlWebServiceWebPartVerbImageUrl : base.ImageUrl; }

  set { base.ImageUrl = value; }
}
```

Using the XmlWebServiceWebPart Zone Custom Zone

Listing 32-17 contains a page that uses the XmlWebServiceWebPartZone custom zone. Notice that a Calendar control has been declared within this custom zone. As Figure 32-1 shows, this custom zone adds the XmlWebServiceWebPartVerb to the verbs menu of the Calendar WebPart control.

Listing 32-17: A Web page that uses the XmlWebServiceWebPartZone custom zone

```
<%@ Page Language="C#" %>
<%@ Register TagPrefix="custom" Namespace="CustomComponents" %>
<html xmlns="http://www.w3.org/1999/xhtml" >
<body>
    <form id="form1" runat="server">
      <asp:WebPartManager runat="server" ID="mgr" />
      <custom:XmlWebServiceWebPartZone runat="server" ID="zone1"
      TypeName="Service"
      SaveDescriptionXmlDocumentMethodName="SaveDescriptionXmlDocument"
      DescriptionXmlDocumentParameterName="descriptionXmlDocument"
      WSDLPath="http://localhost:1064/Server/Service.asmx?WSDL">
       <ZoneTemplate>
         <asp:Calendar runat="server" ID="calendar1" />
       </ZoneTemplate>
      </custom:XmlWebServiceWebPartZone>
    </form>
</body>
</html>
```

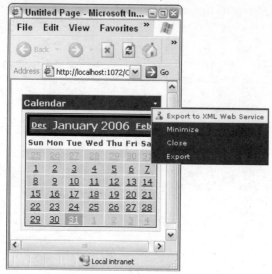

Figure 32-1

ProviderBasedWebPartZone

As discussed, the `WebPartZoneBase` class exposes an abstract method named `GetInitialWebParts` that its subclasses must implement. As mentioned, the main responsibility of this method is to retrieve and to add the initial `WebPart` controls. The initial `WebPart` controls are `WebPart` controls that are added to a page when there are no customized `WebPart` controls associated with the current user.

As Listing 32-10 shows, `WebPartZone` derives from `WebPartZoneBase` and implements the `GetInitial WebParts` method, where it retrieves the controls that the page developer declares within the opening and closing tags of the `<ZoneTemplate>` element. This section uses a provider-based service to implement a custom `WebPartZone` named `ProviderBasedWebPartZone` that can import description files for the initial `WebPart` controls from any type of data source such as relational databases, file system, XML Web services, and so on.

This chapter follows the recipe presented in Chapter 25 to implement a provider-based service that provides `WebPart` description files from any type of data source as follows:

1. It implements a custom provider base named `DescriptionDocumentProvider` that defines the API for all `WebPart` description document providers.

2. It implements a custom provider collection named `DescriptionDocumentProvider Collection` to contain `WebPart` description document providers.

3. It takes the following steps to configure the `Web.config` and `Machine.config` configuration files to add support for a new section named `<descriptionDocumentService>`:

    a. It implements a custom configuration section named `DescriptionDocumentSection`.

    b. It registers `DescriptionDocumentSection`.

4. It implements a service class named `DescriptionDocumentService` that performs the following tasks:

    a. It instantiates and initializes the registered description document providers.

    b. It defines the API for the description document service.

DescriptionDocumentProvider

Following the recipe, this section develops a custom provider base named `DescriptionDocument Provider` that derives from the `ProviderBase` class and defines the API for `WebPart` description document providers. The following is the code for the `DescriptionDocumentProvider` base class:

```
public abstract class DescriptionDocumentProvider : ProviderBase
{
  public abstract XmlReader LoadDescriptionDocument(string descriptionDocumentID);
  public abstract string[] GetDescriptionDocumentIDs();
}
```

As the code shows, the API that `DescriptionDocumentProvider` defines consists of two methods named `LoadDescriptionDocument` and `GetDescriptionDocumentIDs`. Each `WebPart` description document is associated with a unique string ID. The clients of the provider-based `WebPart` description document service first call the `GetDescriptionDocumentIDs` method to retrieve the IDs of all available `WebPart` description documents and then call the `LoadDescriptionDocument` method to load the `WebPart` description document with the specified description document ID.

DescriptionDocumentProviderCollection

The next order of business is to develop a custom provider collection named `DescriptionDocument ProviderCollection` that derives from the `ProviderCollection` base class as shown in Listing 32-18.

Listing 32-18: The DescriptionDocumentProviderCollection class

```
public class DescriptionDocumentProviderCollection : ProviderCollection
{
  public new DescriptionDocumentProvider this[string name]
  {
    get { return (DescriptionDocumentProvider)base[name]; }
  }

  public override void Add(ProviderBase provider)
  {
    if (provider == null)
      throw new ArgumentNullException("provider");

    if (!(provider is DescriptionDocumentProvider))
      throw new ArgumentException("Invalid provider type", "provider");

    base.Add(provider);
  }
}
```

The `DescriptionDocumentProviderCollection` implements an indexer that returns a `Description DocumentProvider` type from the collection, and overrides the `Add` method to ensure only providers of type `DescriptionDocumentProvider` are added to the collection.

Configuring the Web.config and Machine.config Files

The page developer must be allowed to perform the following tasks in `Web.config` or `Machine.config` file without writing any code:

❑ Register new `WebPart` description document providers

❑ Configure the provider-based `WebPart` description document service to use a specified description document provider

To make that possible, you need to configure the `Web.config` and `Machine.config` files to support a custom section named `<descriptionDocumentService>` (see Listing 32-19) that contains a child element named `<providers>` to allow the page developer to use an `<add>` element to register a `WebPart` description document provider with the provider-based `WebPart` description document service. As you'll see later, each `WebPart` description document provider will be specifically designed to retrieve `WebPart` description documents from a specific data store. For example, the `DirectoryDescriptionDocumentProvider` provider will be specifically designed to retrieve description documents from a specified directory.

The `<descriptionDocumentService>` section also needs to expose an attribute named `default Provider` to allow the page developer to configure the `WebPart` description document service to use the specified `WebPart` description document provider from the list of registered description document providers.

To configure the configuration files, you need to implement a custom configuration section named `DescriptionDocumentServiceSection` that derives from the `ConfigurationSection` base class. You also need to register the `<descriptionDocumentService>` section with the `Web.config` and `Machine.config` files and designate the `DescriptionDocumentServiceSection` as its handler.

Listing 32-19: The custom section for WebPart description document providers

```
<configuration>
  <system.web>
    <descriptionDocumentService
     defaultProvider="FriendlyNameOfDescriptionDocumentProvider">
      <providers>
        <add name="FriendlyNameOfDescriptionDocumentProvider"
         type="FullyQualifiedNameOfDescriptionDocumentProvider,
             AssemblyThatContainsDescriptionDocumentProvider" />
      </providers>
    </ descriptionDocumentService>
  </system.web>
</configuration>
```

DescriptionDocumentServiceSection

Listing 32-20 contains the code for the `DescriptionDocumentServiceSection` custom configuration section.

Listing 32-20: The DescriptionDocumentServiceSection custom configuration section

```
public class DescriptionDocumentServiceSection : ConfigurationSection
{
  [ConfigurationProperty("providers")]
  public ProviderSettingsCollection Providers
  {
    get { return (ProviderSettingsCollection)base["providers"]; }
  }

  [StringValidator(MinLength = 1)]
  [ConfigurationProperty("defaultProvider",
                         DefaultValue = "SqlDescriptionDocumentProvider")]
  public string DefaultProvider
  {
    get { return (string)base["defaultProvider"]; }
    set { base["defaultProvider"] = value; }
  }
}
```

DescriptionDocumentServiceSection exposes the following two properties:

❑   Providers: This property is annotated with the [ConfigurationProperty("providers")] metadata attribute to map the property to the <providers> subelement of the <description DocumentService> element.

❑   DefaultProvider: This property is annotated with the [ConfigurationProperty("default Provider")] metadata attribute to map the property to the defaultProvider attribute of the <descriptionDocumentService> element.

Registering the <descriptionDocumentService> Section

Listing 32-21 registers the <descriptionDocumentService> section and designates the Description DocumentServiceSection custom configuration section as its handler.

Listing 32-21: Registering the <descriptionDocumentService> section

```
<configuration >
  <configSections>
    <sectionGroup name="system.web">
      <section name="descriptionDocumentService"
      type="CustomComponents.DescriptionDocumentServiceSection"
      allowDefinition="MachineToApplication" restartOnExternalChanges="true" />
    </sectionGroup>
  </configSections>
</configuration>
```

To register the <descriptionDocumentService> section, you need to add a new <sectionGroup> element as the subelement of the <configSections> element and set the value of its name attribute to the name of the section group to which the <descriptionDocumentService> section belongs, which is <system.web>.

You also need to add a `<section>` element as the subelement of the `<sectionGroup>` element you just created and set the values of its attributes. Set the value of the `name` attribute to the name of the new section, `<descriptionDocumentService>`. Set the value of the `type` attribute to a string that consists of two main parts: the fully qualified name of the custom configuration section that handles the new section (`CustomComponents.DescriptionDocumentServiceSection`) and the information about the assembly that contains the custom configuration section. If you don't include the name of the assembly, ASP.NET will assume that the currently executing assembly contains the `DescriptionDocument ServiceSection` custom configuration section.

DescriptionDocumentService

Listing 32-22 illustrates the implementation of the `DescriptionDocumentService` class.

Listing 32-22: The DescriptionDocumentService class

```
public class DescriptionDocumentService
{
  private static DescriptionDocumentProvider provider = null;
  private static DescriptionDocumentProviderCollection providers = null;
  private static bool IsInitialized = false;

  public DescriptionDocumentProvider Provider
  {
    get { Initialize(); return provider; }
  }

  public DescriptionDocumentProviderCollection Providers
  {
    get { Initialize(); return providers; }
  }

  public static XmlReader LoadDescriptionDocument(string descriptionDocumentID)
  {
    Initialize();
    return provider.LoadDescriptionDocument(descriptionDocumentID);
  }

  public static string[] GetDescriptionDocumentIDs()
  {
    Initialize();
    return provider.GetDescriptionDocumentIDs();
  }

  private static void Initialize()
  {
    if (!IsInitialized)
    {
      DescriptionDocumentServiceSection section =
        (DescriptionDocumentServiceSection)WebConfigurationManager.GetSection(
                                    "system.web/descriptionDocumentService");

      providers = new DescriptionDocumentProviderCollection();
      ProvidersHelper.InstantiateProviders
              (section.Providers, providers, typeof(DescriptionDocumentProvider));
```

```
        provider = providers[section.DefaultProvider];

        if (provider == null)
            throw new ProviderException("Unable to load default provider");
        IsInitialized = true;
    }
  }
}
```

The `DescriptionDocumentService` class instantiates and initializes the providers registered in the `<providers>` subelement of the `<descriptionDocumentService>` section. The `Initialize` method of the `DescriptionDocumentService` calls the `GetSection` method of the `WebConfiguration Manager` class to access the `DescriptionDocumentServiceSection`:

```
DescriptionDocumentServiceSection section =
    (DescriptionDocumentServiceSection)WebConfigurationManager.GetSection(
                            "system.web/descriptionDocumentService");
```

It then instantiates the `Providers` collection:

```
providers = new DescriptionDocumentProviderCollection();
```

Next, it calls the `InstantiateProviders` method of the `ProvidersHelper` class. This method instantiates and initializes the providers registered in the `<providers>` subelement of the `<description DocumentService>` section and loads them into the `Providers` collection:

```
ProvidersHelper.InstantiateProviders
            (section.Providers, providers, typeof(DescriptionDocumentProvider));
```

Next, the `Initialize` method uses the value of the `DefaultProvider` property of the `DescriptionDocumentService` object to index into the `Providers` collection to access the default provider and to assign it to the `Provider` property:

```
provider = providers[section.DefaultProvider];
```

Notice that the `Initialize` method expects the page developer to set the value of the `defaultProvider` attribute of the `<descriptionDocumentService>` element.

The `DescriptionDocumentService` class also calls the `Initialize` method from the `Provider` and `Providers` properties to ensure the provider and providers private fields have been initialized before they're accessed:

```
public DescriptionDocumentProvider Provider
{
  get
  {
    Initialize();
    return provider;
  }
}

public DescriptionDocumentProviderCollection Providers
```

```
  {
    get
    {
      Initialize();
      return providers;
    }
  }
```

The class also defines the API for servicing `WebPart` description documents. This API consists of two methods named `GetDescriptionDocumentIDs` and `LoadDescriptionDocument`:

```
public static string[] GetDescriptionDocumentIDs()
{
  Initialize();
  return provider.GetDescriptionDocumentIDs();
}

public static XmlReader LoadDescriptionDocument(string descriptionDocumentID)
{
  Initialize();
  return provider.LoadDescriptionDocument(descriptionDocumentID);
}
```

These methods call the `Initialize` method to ensure the `DescriptionDocumentService` has been initialized:

```
Initialize();
```

They also delegate the responsibility of retrieving the description document IDs and the actual description documents from the underlying data store to the configured `WebPart` description document provider:

```
provider.GetDescriptionDocumentIDs();
provider.LoadDescriptionDocument(descriptionDocumentID);
```

ProviderBasedWebPartZone

The provider-based `WebPart` description document service developed in the previous section allows components such as `ProviderBasedWebPartZone` custom zone to import `WebPart` description documents from any type of data store. This section presents the implementation of the `ProviderBasedWebPartZone` custom zone where the zone delegates the responsibility of importing `WebPart` description documents from the underlying data store to the `DescriptionDocumentService` component.

Listing 32-23 shows the methods of `ProviderBasedWebPartZone` custom zone.

Listing 32-23: ProviderBasedWebPartZone custom zone

```
public class ProviderBasedWebPartZone : WebPartZone
{
  protected virtual List<WebPart> GetImportedWebParts();
  protected override WebPartCollection GetInitialWebParts();
}
```

`ProviderBasedWebPartZone` derives from `WebPartZone` and overrides its `GetInitialWebParts` method as shown in Listing 32-24. This method calls the `GetImportedWebParts` method to import the `WebPart` description documents from the underlying data store in generic fashion:

```
List<WebPart> importedWebParts = GetImportedWebParts();
```

It also calls the `GetInitialWebParts` method of the base class (`WebPartZone`) to retrieve the controls that the page developer declares within the opening and closing tags of the `<ZoneTemplate>` element on the page:

```
WebPartCollection webParts = base.GetInitialWebParts();
```

Then it loads the contents of these two `WebPart` collections into a single `WebPartCollection` collection and returns the collection:

```
webParts.CopyTo(allWebParts, 0);
importedWebParts.CopyTo(allWebParts, webParts.Count);
return new WebPartCollection(allWebParts);
```

Listing 32-24: The GetInitialWebParts method

```
protected override WebPartCollection GetInitialWebParts()
{
  List<WebPart> importedWebParts = GetImportedWebParts();
  WebPartCollection webParts = base.GetInitialWebParts();
  if (importedWebParts.Count < 1)
    return webParts;

  WebPart[] allWebParts = new WebPart[webParts.Count + importedWebParts.Count];
  webParts.CopyTo(allWebParts, 0);
  importedWebParts.CopyTo(allWebParts, webParts.Count);
  return new WebPartCollection(allWebParts);
}
```

Listing 32-25 contains the code for the `GetImportedWebParts` method. The main responsibility of this method is to use the `DescriptionDocumentService` to import the `WebPart` description documents from the underlying data store. First, it calls the `GetDescriptionDocumentIDs` method of the service to retrieve the IDs of all available description documents:

```
string[] documentIDs = DescriptionDocumentService.GetDescriptionDocumentIDs();
```

It then iterates through the description document IDs. For each enumerated ID, `GetImportedWebParts` calls the `LoadDescriptionDocument` method of the `WebPart` description document service to load the `WebPart` description document with the enumerated ID:

```
XmlReader reader = DescriptionDocumentService.LoadDescriptionDocument(documentID)
```

Then it calls the `ImportWebPart` method of the `WebPartManager` control to create a `WebPart` control with the specifications specified in the description document:

```
webPart = WebPartManager.ImportWebPart(reader, out errorMessage);
```

Finally, it adds the newly created `WebPart` control to a local collection:

```
        importedWebParts.Add(webPart);
```

Listing 32-25: The GetImportedWebParts method

```
protected virtual List<WebPart> GetImportedWebParts()
{
  List<WebPart> importedWebParts = new List<WebPart>();
  string errorMessage;
  WebPart webPart;
  string[] documentIDs = DescriptionDocumentService.GetDescriptionDocumentIDs();
  int i = 1;
  foreach (string documentID in documentIDs)
  {
    using (XmlReader reader =
             DescriptionDocumentService.LoadDescriptionDocument(documentID))
    {
      webPart = WebPartManager.ImportWebPart(reader, out errorMessage);

      if (string.IsNullOrEmpty(errorMessage))
      {
        webPart.ID = "myWebPart" + i.ToString();
        importedWebParts.Add(webPart);
        i++;
      }
    }
  }

  return importedWebParts;
}
```

DirectoryDescriptionDocumentProvider

The previous sections implemented the provider-based `WebPart` description document service that is capable of retrieving `WebPart` description documents from any type of data store. This section implements a `WebPart` description document provider named `DirectoryDescriptionDocumentProvider` that derives from the `DescriptionDocumentProvider` base class and imports `WebPart` description documents from the specified directory. Because the `DescriptionDocumentProvider` base class derives from the `ProviderBase` class, `DirectoryDescriptionDocumentProvider` must implement both the `GetDescriptionDocumentIDs` and `LoadDescriptionDocument` methods of `DescriptionDocument Provider` and the `Initialize` method of `ProviderBase` as discussed in the following sections.

Initialize

Listing 32-26 presents the implementation of the `Initialize` method.

Listing 32-26: The Initialize method

```
public override void Initialize(string name, NameValueCollection config)
{
  if (config == null)
    throw new ArgumentNullException("config");

  if (string.IsNullOrEmpty(name))
```

```
      name = "DirectoryDescriptionDocumentProvider";

  if (string.IsNullOrEmpty(config["description"]))
  {
    config.Remove("description");
    config.Add("description",
              "Retrieves description documents from the specified directory");
  }
  base.Initialize(name, config);

  directoryPath = config["directoryPath"];
  if (string.IsNullOrEmpty(directoryPath))
    throw new ProviderException("Directory not found");
  config.Remove("directoryPath");

  if (config.Count > 0)
  {
    string key = config.GetKey(0);
    if (!string.IsNullOrEmpty(key))
      throw new ProviderException("Unrecognized attribute");
  }
}
```

As Listing 32-26 shows, the `Initialize` method first performs the four tasks that the `Initialize` method of all providers must perform. It raises an exception if the `NameValueCollection` is null:

```
if (config == null)
  throw new ArgumentNullException("config");
```

It sets the friendly name of the provider if it hasn't already been set:

```
if (string.IsNullOrEmpty(name))
  name = "DirectoryDescriptionDocumentProvider";
```

It sets the value of the description field if it hasn't already been set:

```
if (string.IsNullOrEmpty(config["description"]))
{
  config.Remove("description");
  config.Add("description",
            "Retrieves description documents from the specified directory");
}
```

And it calls the `Initialize` method of the base class to allow the base class to initialize the `name` and `description` properties. In other words, the provider must delegate the responsibility of setting these two properties to its base class as opposed to overriding the `Name` and `Description` properties.

```
base.Initialize(name, config);
```

In addition to these required tasks, the `Initialize` method of `DirectoryDescriptionDocument Provider` also uses the `directoryPath` key to index into the `NameValueCollection` to retrieve the path to the directory where the description document files reside and assigns the path to the `directory Path` private field of the `DirectoryDescriptionDocumentProvider` provider:

```
directoryPath = config["directoryPath"];
```

It raises an exception if the page developer hasn't specified the directory path, because this provider can't function without this path:

```
if (string.IsNullOrEmpty(directoryPath))
    throw new ProviderException("Directory not found");
```

It also removes the name/value pair associated with the directory path from the `NameValueCollection`:

```
config.Remove("directoryPath");
```

Finally, it raises an exception if the `NameValueCollection` isn't empty and contains more name/value pairs:

```
if (config.Count > 0)
{
  string key = config.GetKey(0);
  if (!string.IsNullOrEmpty(key))
    throw new ProviderException("Unrecognized attribute");
}
```

GetDescriptionDocumentIDs

Listing 32-27 presents the code for the `GetDescriptionDocumentIDs` method of the `Directory DescriptionDocumentProvider`.

Listing 32-27: The GetDescriptionDocumentIDs method of DirectoryDescription DocumentProvider

```
public override string[] GetDescriptionDocumentIDs()
{
  DirectoryInfo di =
          new DirectoryInfo(HttpContext.Current.Server.MapPath(directoryPath));
  ArrayList list = new ArrayList();
  FileInfo[] fis = di.GetFiles("*.WebPart");
  foreach (FileInfo fi in fis)
  {
    list.Add(fi.Name);
  }
;
  return (string[])list.ToArray(Type.GetType("System.String"));
}
```

The `GetDescriptionDocumentIDs` method instantiates an instance of a .NET class named `Directory Info`. You can think of this `DirectoryInfo` object as the programmatic representation of the directory where the `WebPart` description files reside:

```
DirectoryInfo di =
          new DirectoryInfo(HttpContext.Current.Server.MapPath(directoryPath));
```

The method then calls the `GetFiles` method of the `DirectoryInfo` object to programmatically access the `WebPart` description files that reside in the directory that the `DirectoryInfo` object represents. The

`GetFiles` method returns an array of instances of a .NET class named `FileInfo`. You can think of these `FileInfo` instances as the programmatic representations of the `WebPart` description files that reside in the directory that the `DirectoryInfo` object represents.

```
FileInfo[] fis = di.GetFiles("*.WebPart");
```

Next, the method iterates through the `FileInfo` objects and adds the name of each enumerated `WebPart` description file into a local collection. `DirectoryDescriptionDocumentProvider` uses the name of a `WebPart` description file as the previously mentioned document ID.

```
foreach (FileInfo fi in fis)
  list.Add(fi.Name);
```

LoadDescriptionDocument

Listing 32-28 presents the code for the `LoadDescriptionDocument` method of the `Directory DescriptionDocumentProvider`. This method uses an `XmlReader` to stream out the contents of the specified `WebPart` description file.

Listing 32-28: The LoadDescriptionDocument method of DirectoryDescription DocumentProvider

```
public override XmlReader LoadDescriptionDocument(string documentID)
{
  return XmlReader.Create(
             HttpContext.Current.Server.MapPath(directoryPath+"/"+documentID));
}
```

Registering DirectoryDescriptionDocumentProvider

Listing 32-29 shows how the page developer can declaratively register `DirectoryDescription DocumentProvider` with the `WebPart` description document service without writing any code.

Listing 32-29: Registering DirectoryDescriptionDocumentProvider

```
<descriptionDocumentService defaultProvider="DirectoryDescriptionDocumentProvider">
  <providers>
    <add name="DirectoryDescriptionDocumentProvider"
    type="CustomComponents.DirectoryDescriptionDocumentProvider"
    directoryPath="DescriptionFiles" />
  </providers>
</descriptionDocumentService>
```

The page developer must add a new `<add>` child element within the opening and closing tags of the `<providers>` element and set its attribute values as follows:

❑   name: The page developer has the freedom of choosing any friendly name for the provider as long as it is different from the friendly names of other registered providers. Listing 32-29 uses the string value `DirectoryDescriptionDocumentProvider` as the friendly name:

```
name="DirectoryDescriptionDocumentProvider"
```

❑ type: The value of this attribute consists of two main parts. The first part is the fully qualified name of the type of the provider including its namespace, `CustomComponents.Directory DescriptionDocumentProvider`. The second part is the name of the assembly that contains the provider. If the name of the assembly is not specified, it's assumed that the executing assembly contains the provider.

```
type="CustomComponents.DirectoryDescriptionDocumentProvider"
```

❑ directoryPath: The value of this attribute must be set to the path of the directory where the `WebPart` description files reside.

Registering a provider doesn't automatically tell the `WebPart` description document service to use the provider because more than one `WebPart` description document provider can be registered with the service. The page developer must set the value of the `defaultProvider` attribute of the `<description DocumentService>` element to the friendly name of the desired provider to instruct the `WebPart` description document service to use the specified provider:

```
<descriptionDocumentService defaultProvider="DirectoryDescriptionDocumentProvider">
```

Using the ProviderBasedWebPartZone Custom Zone

Listing 32-30 contains a Web page that uses the `ProviderBasedWebPartZone` custom zone. Notice that the page developers declare and use the `ProviderBasedWebPartZone` as they would the regular ASP.NET `WebPartZone`. In other words, the details of the imported `WebPart` controls are completely hidden from the Web page that uses the `ProviderBasedWebPartZone` control. This allows the page developer to configure the application to import the initial `WebPart` controls from a different source without breaking the application.

Listing 32-30: A Web page that uses the ProviderBasedWebPartZone custom zone

```
<%@ Page Language="C#" %>
<%@ Register TagPrefix="custom" Namespace="CustomComponents" %>
<html xmlns="http://www.w3.org/1999/xhtml">
<body>
  <form id="form1" runat="server">
    <asp:WebPartManager runat="server" ID="mgr" />
    <custom:ProviderBasedWebPartZone runat="server" ID="zone1">
      <ZoneTemplate>
        <asp:DropDownList runat="server" ID="ddl" />
      </ZoneTemplate>
    </custom:ProviderBasedWebPartZone>
  </form>
</body>
</html>
```

SqlDescriptionDocumentProvider

This section implements a `WebPart` description document provider named `SqlDescription DocumentProvider` that derives from the `DescriptionDocumentProvider` base class and imports `WebPart` description documents from a SQL Server 2005 database. This database consists of a table named `DescriptionDocuments` that has two columns as follows:

❑ DescriptionDocumentID: This is the primary key of the table and will be used as the description document ID.

❑ DescriptionDocument: This column is of type XML. SQL Server 2005 supports XML as a native type. WebPart description documents are stored in this column.

Because the DescriptionDocumentProvider base class derives from the ProviderBase class, SqlDescriptionDocumentProvider must implement both the GetDescriptionDocumentIDs and LoadDescriptionDocument methods of SqlDescriptionDocumentProvider and the Initialize method of ProviderBase, as discussed in the following sections.

Initialize

Listing 32-31 presents the implementation of the Initialize method.

Listing 32-31: The Initialize method

```
public override void Initialize(string name, NameValueCollection config)
{
  if (config == null)
    throw new ArgumentNullException("config");

  if (string.IsNullOrEmpty(name))
    name = "SqlDescriptionDocumentProvider";

  if (string.IsNullOrEmpty(config["description"]))
  {
    config.Remove("description");
    config.Add("description",
           "Retrieves WebPart description documents from a SQL Server database");
  }
  base.Initialize(name, config);
  string connectionStringName = config["connectionStringName"];
  if (string.IsNullOrEmpty(connectionStringName))
    throw new ProviderException("Invalid connection string name");

  connectionString =
    ConfigurationManager.ConnectionStrings[connectionStringName].ConnectionString;
  if (string.IsNullOrEmpty(connectionString))
    throw new ProviderException("Connection string not found");

  config.Remove("connectionStringName");

  if (config.Count > 0)
  {
    string key = config.GetKey(0);
    if (!string.IsNullOrEmpty(key))
      throw new ProviderException("Unrecognized attribute");
  }
}
```

As Listing 32-31 illustrates, the Initialize method first performs the four tasks that the Initialize method of all providers must perform as discussed in the previous section. The Initialize method then needs to set the `connectionString` private field of the `SqlDescriptionDocumentProvider`. `Initialize` uses the `connectionStringName` string to index into the `NameValueCollection` to access the associated value. If the value is null or an empty string, it raises a `ProviderException` exception because `SqlDescriptionDocumentProvider` needs this value to access the underlying data store:

```
string connectionStringName = config["connectionStringName"];
if (string.IsNullOrEmpty(connectionStringName))
  throw new ProviderException("Invalid connection string name");
```

The method then uses the value it just obtained to index into the `ConnectionStrings` collection of the `ConfigurationManager` class to access the connection string and assigns it to the `connectionString` private field of the `SqlDescriptionDocumentProvider` for future reference. The `ConnectionStrings` collection represents the `<connectionStrings>` section of the configuration file. The page developer must use the `<add>` element to register the required connection string with the configuration file, set the name attribute of the `<add>` element to the friendly name of the connection string, and assign the connection string to the `connectionString` attribute of the `<add>` element. You'll see an example of these three tasks later in this chapter.

```
connectionString =
    ConfigurationManager.ConnectionStrings[connectionStringName].ConnectionString;
if (string.IsNullOrEmpty(connectionString))
  throw new ProviderException("Connection string not found");
```

Finally, the `Initialize` method removes the name/value pair associated with the connection string from the `NameValueCollection`:

```
config.Remove("connectionStringName");
```

GetDescriptionDocumentIDs

Listing 32-32 presents the code for the `GetDescriptionDocumentIDs` method of the `SqlDescription DocumentProvider`. This method uses ADO.NET objects to retrieve the available description document IDs from the `DescriptionDocuments` table.

Listing 32-32: The GetDescriptionDocumentIDs method of SqlDescription DocumentProvider

```
public override string[] GetDescriptionDocumentIDs()
{
  SqlConnection con = new SqlConnection(connectionString);
  SqlCommand com =
      new SqlCommand("Select DescriptionDocumentID From DescriptionDocuments", con);
  con.Open();
  SqlDataReader dreader = com.ExecuteReader();
  ArrayList documentIDList = new ArrayList();

  while (dreader.Read())
  {
    documentIDList.Add(dreader[0].ToString());
  }

  con.Close();
```

```
        return (string[])documentIDList.ToArray(Type.GetType("System.String"));
    }
```

LoadDescriptionDocument

Listing 32-33 presents the code for the `LoadDescriptionDocument` method of the `SqlDescription DocumentProvider`. This method uses a `SqlDataReader` to retrieve the `WebPart` description document with the specified description document ID. The `SqlDataReader` in ADO.NET 2.0 supports a new method named `GetSqlXml` that returns a `SqlXml` object.

`SqlXml` is a new type added to the `SqlTypes` that exposes a method named `CreateReader` that streams out the XML content of a database field that contains an XML document.

Listing 32-33: The LoadDescriptionDocument method of SqlDescription DocumentProvider

```
public override XmlReader LoadDescriptionDocument(string descriptionDocumentID)
{
    SqlConnection con = new SqlConnection(connectionString);
    SqlCommand com = new SqlCommand();
    com.CommandText = "Select DescriptionDocument From DescriptionDocuments where
                       DescriptionDocumentID=@DescriptionDocumentID";
    com.Connection = con;
    com.Parameters.AddWithValue("@DescriptionDocumentID", descriptionDocumentID);
    con.Open();
    SqlDataReader dreader = com.ExecuteReader(CommandBehavior.CloseConnection);
    dreader.Read();
    SqlXml xml = dreader.GetSqlXml(0);
    return xml.CreateReader();
}
```

Registering SqlDescriptionDocumentProvider

Listing 32-34 shows how the page developer can declaratively register `SqlDescriptionDocument Provider` with the `WebPart` description document service without writing any code.

Listing 32-34: Registering SqlDescriptionDocumentProvider

```
<descriptionDocumentService defaultProvider="SqlDescriptionDocumentProvider">
  <providers>
    <add name="SqlDescriptionDocumentProvider"
    type="CustomComponents.SqlDescriptionDocumentProvider"
    connectionStringName="MyConnectionString" />
  </providers>
</descriptionDocumentService>
```

As you saw previously, registering a provider doesn't automatically tell the `WebPart` description document service to use the provider. The page developer must set the value of the `defaultProvider` attribute of the `<description DocumentService>` element to the friendly name of the desired provider to instruct the `WebPart` description document service to use the specified provider:

```
<descriptionDocumentService defaultProvider="SqlDescriptionDocumentProvider">
```

WebPartChrome

Have another look at Listing 32-5. This listing contains the code for the `RenderBody` method of the `WebPartZoneBase`. As the name implies, this method renders the body of the zone. As Listing 32-5 shows, this method iterates through the `WebPart` controls that the zone contains and calls the `Render WebPart` method of the `WebPartChrome` object to render each enumerated `WebPart` control as also shown in the highlighted portion of the following code fragment:

```
protected override void RenderBody(HtmlTextWriter writer)
{
  writer.RenderBeginTag(HtmlTextWriterTag.Table);

  foreach (WebPart webPart in WebParts)
  {
    writer.RenderBeginTag(HtmlTextWriterTag.Tr);
    writer.RenderBeginTag(HtmlTextWriterTag.Td);
    WebPartChrome.RenderWebPart(writer, webPart);
    writer.RenderEndTag();
    writer.RenderEndTag();
  }

  writer.RenderEndTag();
}
```

In other words, `WebPartZoneBase` delegates the responsibility of rendering its `WebPart` controls to `WebPartChrome`. This section first takes you under the hood to help you gain a solid understanding of the methods and properties of the `WebPartChrome` class. Listing 32-35 shows these methods and properties. The following sections discuss some of these methods and properties in detail.

Listing 32-35: The WebPartChrome class

```
public class WebPartChrome
{
  public WebPartChrome(WebPartZoneBase zone, WebPartManager manager);
  public virtual void RenderWebPart(HtmlTextWriter writer, WebPart webPart);
  protected virtual Style CreateWebPartChromeStyle(WebPart webPart,
                                              PartChromeType chromeType)
  private void RenderTitleBar(HtmlTextWriter writer, WebPart webPart);
  protected virtual WebPartVerbCollection GetWebPartVerbs(WebPart webPart);
  protected virtual WebPartVerbCollection FilterWebPartVerbs(
                          WebPartVerbCollection verbs, WebPart webPart);
  private bool ShouldRenderVerb(WebPartVerb verb, WebPart webPart);
  protected string GetWebPartChromeClientID(WebPart webPart);
  protected string GetWebPartTitleClientID(WebPart webPart);
  protected virtual void RenderPartContents(HtmlTextWriter writer,
                                        WebPart webPart);

  protected WebPartManager WebPartManager {get;}
  protected WebPartZoneBase Zone {get;}
}
```

RenderWebPart

Listing 32-36 contains the implementation of the main parts of the `RenderWebPart` method of the `WebPartChrome` class. The boldface portions of this code listing shows some of the extensible methods of `WebPartChrome` class that you can extend to implement your own custom `WebPartChrome`, as you'll see later in this chapter.

Listing 32-36: The RenderWebPart method

```
public virtual void RenderWebPart(HtmlTextWriter writer, WebPart webPart)
{
  PartChromeType chromeType = this.Zone.GetEffectiveChromeType(webPart);
  Style style = CreateWebPartChromeStyle(webPart, chromeType);
  style.AddAttributesToRender(writer, this.Zone);
  writer.AddAttribute(HtmlTextWriterAttribute.Id,
                      GetWebPartChromeClientID(webPart));
  writer.RenderBeginTag(HtmlTextWriterTag.Table);

  if ((chromeType == PartChromeType.TitleOnly) ||
      (chromeType == PartChromeType.TitleAndBorder))
  {
    writer.RenderBeginTag(HtmlTextWriterTag.Tr);
    writer.RenderBeginTag(HtmlTextWriterTag.Td);
    RenderTitleBar(writer, webPart);
    writer.RenderEndTag();
    writer.RenderEndTag();
  }

  writer.RenderBeginTag(HtmlTextWriterTag.Tr);
  this.Zone.PartStyle.AddAttributesToRender(writer, this.Zone);
  writer.RenderBeginTag(HtmlTextWriterTag.Td);
  RenderPartContents(writer, webPart);
  writer.RenderEndTag();
  writer.RenderEndTag();
  writer.RenderEndTag();
}
```

As mentioned, the main responsibility of the `RenderWebPart` method is to render the `WebPart` control that `WebPartZoneBase` passes into it. A `WebPart` control consists of the following two parts:

❏ **Chrome:** The chrome of a `WebPart` control is a graphical frame on the control that consists of two parts:

  ❏ **Title bar:** The title bar includes a title text, a title icon, and a verbs menu

  ❏ **Border:** The border is the portion of the chrome that frames the `WebPart` control

❏ **Content:** The content of a `WebPart` control constitutes its body, that is, the part that the chrome frames

The Web Parts Framework uses the `PartChromeType` enumeration to specify the type of chrome that the `RenderWebPart` method must render for the specified `WebPart` control. The following are the possible values of this enumeration:

- ❑ PartChromeType.Default: The WebPart control inherits the chrome type from the zone that contains the control. As shown in Listing 32-1, the WebZone base class exposes a property of type PartChromeType named PartChromeType that specifies the chrome type for all the WebPart controls that the zone contains.

- ❑ PartChromeType.BorderOnly: RenderWebPart will not render the title bar of the specified WebPart control. It will only render the border.

- ❑ PartChromeType.TitleOnly: RenderWebPart will not render the border that frames the WebPart control. It will only render the title bar.

- ❑ PartChromeType.TitleAndBorder: RenderWebPart will render both the title bar and border of the specified WebPart control.

- ❑ PartChromeType.None: RenderWebPart will render neither the border nor the title bar of the specified WebPart control.

As Listing 32-36 shows, the RenderWebPart method renders a table that contains two rows where each row contains a single cell. As you'll see shortly, the method renders the title bar within the first row and content or body of the WebPart control within the second row.

Therefore, the first order of business for the RenderWebPart method is to render the table that contains the title bar and body of the specified WebPart control. To render this table, RenderWebPart must render the HTML attributes of the associated <table> HTML element. These HTML attributes mainly consists of the "id" and CSS style attributes. RenderWebPart calls the GetWebPartChromeClientID method of the WebPartChrome to return the client ID value of the specified WebPart control and assigns this value to the id attribute of the <table> HTML element that contains the chrome and body of the WebPart control:

```
writer.AddAttribute(HtmlTextWriterAttribute.Id, GetWebPartChromeClientID(webPart));
```

What does this mean to you as a control developer? You can call the GetWebPartChromeClientID method to access the value of the id attribute of the containing or main <table> HTML element and use this value in your client-side code to take advantage of the DHTML capabilities of the requesting browser as discussed in Chapters 26 and 27.

RenderWebPart also calls the CreateWebPartChromeStyle method of the WebPartChrome to return the Style object that contains the CSS style attributes of the <table> HTML element that contains the chrome and body of the specified WebPart control.

The default implementation of CreateWebPartChromeStyle builds a Style object based on the chrome type of the specified WebPart control. RenderWebPart calls the GetEffectiveChromeType method of its associated zone to return the chrome type of the WebPart control and passes the chrome type to the CreateWebPartChromeStyle method to return the Style object:

```
PartChromeType chromeType = this.Zone.GetEffectiveChromeType(webPart);
Style style = CreateWebPartChromeStyle(webPart, chromeType);
style.AddAttributesToRender(writer, this.Zone);
```

This means two things to you as a developer. First, you can override the CreateWebPartChromeStyle method in your custom WebPartChrome to customize the CSS style attributes of the containing <table> HTML element. Second, you can override the GetEffectiveChromeType method of the WebZone zone to customize the chrome type that is passed into the CreateWebPartChromeType.

Finally, `RenderWebPart` must render the `<table>` HTML element itself:

```
writer.RenderBeginTag(HtmlTextWriterTag.Table);
```

So far, you've learned how the `RenderWebPart` method renders the `<table>` HTML element and its associated HTML attributes. As mentioned, this table contains two rows where each row contains a single cell. `RenderWebPart` renders the title bar within the first row and the body of the `WebPart` control within the second row. Listing 32-37 presents the code that renders the title bar.

Listing 32-37: The code that renders the title bar

```
private void RenderTitleBar(HtmlTextWriter writer, WebPart webPart)
{
  writer.RenderBeginTag(HtmlTextWriterTag.Table);
  writer.RenderBeginTag(HtmlTextWriterTag.Tr);

  writer.RenderBeginTag(HtmlTextWriterTag.Td);
  writer.AddAttribute(HtmlTextWriterAttribute.Src,
                    ResolveClientUrl(webPart.TitleIconImageUrl));
  writer.RenderBeginTag(HtmlTextWriterTag.Img);
  writer.RenderEndTag();

  this.Zone.PartTitleStyle.AddAttributesToRender(writer);
  writer.AddAttribute(HtmlTextWriterAttribute.Id,
                            GetWebPartTitleClientID(webPart));
  writer.RenderBeginTag(HtmlTextWriterTag.Td);
  writer.WriteEncodedText(webPart.DisplayTitle + " - " + webPart.Subtitle);
  writer.RenderEndTag();

  writer.RenderBeginTag(HtmlTextWriterTag.Td);
  WebPartVerbCollection verbs = GetWebPartVerbs(webPart);
  verbs = FilterWebPartVerbs(verbs, webPart);
  RenderVerbs(writer);
  writer.RenderEndTag();

  writer.RenderEndTag();
  writer.RenderEndTag();
}
```

As Listing 32-37 illustrates, the `RenderTitleBar` method renders a table with a single row that contains three cells. The method first renders the title icon within the first cell:

```
writer.RenderBeginTag(HtmlTextWriterTag.Td);
writer.AddAttribute(HtmlTextWriterAttribute.Src,
                  ResolveClientUrl(webPart.TitleIconImageUrl));
writer.RenderBeginTag(HtmlTextWriterTag.Img);
writer.RenderEndTag();
```

The method then renders the title text within the second cell:

```
Zone.PartTitleStyle.AddAttributesToRender(writer);
writer.AddAttribute(HtmlTextWriterAttribute.Id,
                            GetWebPartTitleClientID(webPart));
writer.RenderBeginTag(HtmlTextWriterTag.Td);
```

```
writer.WriteEncodedText(webPart.DisplayTitle + " - " + webPart.Subtitle);
writer.RenderEndTag();
```

Notice that the method calls the `GetWebPartTitleClientID` method of the `WebPartChrome` to return the client ID of the cell that contains the title text. This means you can call the `GetWebPartTitleClientID` method to access the client ID of this cell and use it in your client-side code to add support for the desired DHTML capabilities. You'll see an example of this later in this chapter.

Finally, the method renders the verbs menu within the third cell:

```
writer.RenderBeginTag(HtmlTextWriterTag.Td);
WebPartVerbCollection verbs = GetWebPartVerbs(webPart);
verbs = FilterWebPartVerbs(verbs, webPart);
RenderVerbsMenu(writer, verbs);
writer.RenderEndTag();
```

To render the verbs menu, the `RenderTitleBar` method calls the `GetWebPartVerbs` method of the `WebPartChrome` to return the verbs for the specified `WebPart` control. You can override this method in your custom `WebPartChrome` to filter the verbs that you don't want the current user to see.

Then it calls the `FilterWebPartVerbs` method of the `WebPartChrome` to filter the unwanted verbs. It may seem that `FilterWebPartVerbs` does exactly what `GetWebPartVerbs` does. Why have two different methods doing the same thing? The answer lies in the fact that there are two types of filtering. Sometimes you filter verbs based on some application-specific logic. For example, as you'll see later, you can filter verbs based on the role the current user is in. To accomplish this kind of filtering you should override the `FilterWebPartVerbs` method. There are times when you know in advance what verbs shouldn't be rendered. For example, you may decide your users shouldn't be able to close the `WebPart` controls in your application. To accomplish this kind of filtering you should override the `GetWebPartVerbs` method.

So far you've learned how the `RenderWebPart` method renders the title bar within the first row. Now you'll see how this method renders the body of the `WebPart` control within the second row. As shown in Listing 32-36, the method delegates the responsibility of rendering the body or content of the `WebPart` to the `RenderPartContents` method. Listing 32-38 presents the code for this method.

Listing 32-38: The RenderPartContents method

```
protected virtual void RenderPartContents(HtmlTextWriter writer, WebPart webPart)
{
  if (!string.IsNullOrEmpty(webPart.ConnectErrorMessage))
  {
    if (!this.Zone.ErrorStyle.IsEmpty)
      this.Zone.ErrorStyle.AddAttributesToRender(writer, this.Zone);

    writer.RenderBeginTag(HtmlTextWriterTag.Div);
    writer.WriteEncodedText(webPart.ConnectErrorMessage);
    writer.RenderEndTag();
  }
  else
    webPart.RenderControl(writer);
}
```

`RenderPartContents` first ensures that there're no connection error messages and then calls the `RenderControl` method of the `WebPart` control. The next chapter covers Web Parts connections in detail. You can override `RenderPartContents` in your custom `WebPartChrome` to take control over how the `WebPart` content is rendered.

PerformPreRender

As shown in Listing 32-35, the `WebPartChrome` class doesn't directly or indirectly derive from the `Control` base class, which means that `WebPartChrome` isn't a server control. Recall that every server control exposes methods such as `OnPreRender`, `OnLoad`, and others that are automatically called when the page enters the associated phases of its life cycle. Because `WebPartChrome` isn't a server control, none of its methods or properties is automatically called. `WebPartChrome` relies on its associated `WebPartZoneBase`, which is a server control, to call its methods when the page enters the associated phases of its life cycle.

For example, as Listing 32-2 and 32-5 show, when the page enters its rendering phase, the `Render Contents` method of the `WebPartZoneBase` calls the `RenderWebPart` method of the `WebPartChrome`.

As you learned in Chapters 26 and 27, the prerender phase plays a significant role when it comes to adding support for DHTML capabilities because the client-side scripts must be registered for rendering in this phase. You can't add these scripts to the `RenderWebPart` method because this method is called in the rendering phase, not the prerendering phase.

To address this problem, `WebPartChrome` exposes a method named `PerformPreRender`. However, because `WebPartChrome` isn't a server control, its `PerformPreRender` method will not be automatically called when the page enters its prerender phase. That's why the `OnPreRender` method of the associated `WebPart ZoneBase` calls the `PerformPreRender` method of the `WebPartChrome` as shown in Listing 32-39.

Listing 32-39: The OnPreRender method of the WebPartZoneBase control

```
protected internal override void OnPreRender(EventArgs e)
{
   base.OnPreRender(e);

   WebPartVerbsEventArgs args = new WebPartVerbsEventArgs();
   OnCreateVerbs(args);
   verbs = args1.Verbs;

   WebPartChrome.PerformPreRender();
}
```

Also notice that the `OnPreRender` method raises the `CreateVerbs` event. In other words, this event is raised in two occasions: when the postback event is raised (see Listing 32-9), and when the page enters its prerender phase (see Listing 32-39). You learned in the previous sections how to override the `OnCreateVerbs` method in your own custom zones to customize verbs.

Besides the methods discussed so far, the `WebPartChrome` also exposes two properties named `Zone` and `WebPartManager`, which respectively refer to the `WebPartZoneBase` and `WebPartManager` associated with the `WebPartChrome` object.

The next section builds on what you've learned about WebPartChrome to show you how to develop your own custom WebPartChrome to take control over the rendering of the WebPart controls that the associated zone contains.

Developing a Custom WebPartChrome

This section develops a custom WebPartChrome named CustomWebPartChrome that derives from the WebPartChrome base class and extends its functionality to add support for the following features:

❑ Automatic rendering of a logo in the title bar of every WebPart control that the associated zone contains

❑ Using the DHTML feature known as transition to provide an animated effect when the user moves the mouse pointer over the logo

CustomWebPartChrome exposes two new properties named MouseOverImageUrl and MouseOut ImageUrl that the page developer must set to the URLs of the images that the CustomWebPartChrome control will render when the user moves the mouse pointer over and out of the control, respectively. In other words, CustomWebPartChrome switches from one image to another when the user moves the mouse pointer over or out of the control.

CustomWebPartChrome also exposes two properties named Duration and Transition that are used to set the duration and transition parameters of the DHTML transition feature as discussed in Chapter 26.

As Listing 32-40 shows, CustomWebPartChrome overrides the PerformPreRender method of its base class to render the client script that supports the DHTML transition feature. This method first iterates through the WebPart controls that the associated zone contains to dynamically generate the client script that supports the transition effect. As Listing 32-37 shows, the RenderWebPart method of the Web PartChrome assigns the return value of the GetWebPartTitleClientID method to the id HTML attribute of the table cell that contains the title text for the WebPart control. PerformPreRender passes the return value of this method to the getElementById method of the document object to return a reference to the table cell that contains the title text:

```
js += ("titleBar = document.getElementById('" +
                          GetWebPartTitleClientID(webPart) + "');\n");
```

It then generates the script that returns a reference to the first child element of the table cell:

```
js += "titleBarFirstChild = titleBar.childNodes[0];\n";
```

Next, the method generates the script that creates an <img> HTML element and inserts this element as the first child element of the table cell. This ensures the logo will always appear on the top-left corner of the WebPart control:

```
js += "img = document.createElement('img');\n";
js += "titleBar.insertBefore(img,titleBarFirstChild);\n";
```

It then generates the script that registers the JavaScript functions `MouseOverCallback` and `MouseOutCallback` for the `onmouseover` and `onmouseout` client-side events of the logo:

```
js += "img.onmouseover = MouseOverCallback;\n";
js += "img.onmouseout = MouseOutCallback;\n";
```

Next, the method generates the script that stores the values of the `MouseOutImageUrl` and `Mouse OverImageUrl` properties. As you'll see later, the `MouseOverCallback` and `MouseOutCallback` JavaScript function uses these values to switch between the two versions of the logo:

```
js += ("img.srcOut = '" + MouseOutImageUrl + "';\n");
js += ("img.srcOver = '" + MouseOverImageUrl + "';\n");
```

Then it generates the script that assigns the `revealTrans` filter to the `filter` property of the `style` object and uses the values of the `Duration` and `Transition` properties to set the duration and transition parameters of the filter:

```
js += ("img.style.filter = 'revealTrans(duration=" + Duration.ToString() +
                   ",transition=" + ((int)Transition).ToString() + ")';\n");
```

Once the script is created, `PerformPreRender` calls the `RegisterStartupScript` method to register the script with the containing page. As discussed in Chapter 26, the containing page renders all the registered scripts when it enters its rendering phase.

```
Zone.Page.ClientScript.RegisterStartupScript(typeof(CustomWebPartChrome),
                             typeof(CustomWebPartChrome).FullName, js);
```

Finally, the method calls the `RegisterClientScriptInclude` method to have the containing page render a reference to the `CustomWebPartChrome.js` script file:

```
Zone.Page.ClientScript.RegisterClientScriptInclude(
            typeof(CustomWebPartChrome).FullName, "CustomWebPartChrome.js");
```

Listing 32-40: The PerformPreRender method

```
public override void PerformPreRender()
{
  base.PerformPreRender();

  string js =
    "<script language='javascript'>\n\t" +
      "var titleBar;\n" +
      "var titleBarFirstChild;\n" +
      "var img;\n";

  foreach (WebPart webPart in Zone.WebParts)
  {
    js += ("titleBar = document.getElementById('" +
                            GetWebPartTitleClientID(webPart) + "');\n");
```

(continued)

Listing 32-40: *(continued)*

```
        js += "titleBarFirstChild = titleBar.childNodes[0];\n";
        js += "img = document.createElement('img');\n";
        js += "titleBar.insertBefore(img,titleBarFirstChild);\n";
        js += ("img.src = '" + MouseOutImageUrl + "';\n");
        js += ("img.srcOut = '" + MouseOutImageUrl + "';\n");
        js += ("img.srcOver = '" + MouseOverImageUrl + "';\n");
        js += ("img.style.filter = 'revealTrans(duration=" + Duration.ToString() +
                            ",transition=" + ((int)Transition).ToString() + ")';\n");
        js += "img.onmouseover = MouseOverCallback;\n";
        js += "img.onmouseout = MouseOutCallback;\n";
    }

    js += "</script>";
    Zone.Page.ClientScript.RegisterStartupScript(typeof(CustomWebPartChrome),
                                typeof(CustomWebPartChrome).FullName, js);

    Zone.Page.ClientScript.RegisterClientScriptInclude(
                typeof(CustomWebPartChrome).FullName, "CustomWebPartChrome.js");
}
```

When you develop a custom WebPartChrome, you must also develop a custom WebPartZoneBase that uses your custom WebPartChrome to render its WebPart controls. However, before getting into the implementation of the custom WebPartZoneBase that uses CustomWebPartChrome, you'll need to override one more method of the WebPartChrome base class, RenderWebPart, to ensure that the CustomWebPartChrome is used by your custom WebPartZoneBase.

Listing 32-41 illustrates the implementation of the RenderWebPart method of the CustomWebPart Chrome. As this listing shows, the method ensures the associated zone is of type CustomWebPartZone before it calls the RenderWebPart method of its base class to render the specified WebPart control.

Listing 32-41: The RenderWebPart method of the CustomWebPartChrome

```
public override void RenderWebPart(HtmlTextWriter writer, WebPart webPart)
{
    if (this.Zone.GetType() == typeof(CustomWebPartZone))
        base.RenderWebPart(writer, webPart);
}
```

CustomWebPartZone

CustomWebPartZone is a custom zone that uses CustomWebPartChrome to render its WebPart controls. The CustomWebPartZone custom zone exposes the same four properties that CustomWebPartChrome does: MouseOverImageUrl, MouseOutImageUrl, Duration, and Transition. This custom zone overrides the CreateWebPartChrome method of its base class to instantiate and to return an instance of the CustomWebPartChrome as shown in Listing 32-42.

Listing 32-42: The CreateWebPartChrome method

```
protected override WebPartChrome CreateWebPartChrome()
{
  CustomWebPartChrome webPartChrome =
                        new CustomWebPartChrome(this, this.WebPartManager);
  webPartChrome.MouseOutImageUrl = MouseOutImageUrl;
  webPartChrome.MouseOverImageUrl = MouseOverImageUrl;
  webPartChrome.Duration = Duration;
  webPartChrome.Transition = Transition;
  return webPartChrome;
}
```

CreateWebPartChrome creates a CustomWebPartChrome and assigns the values of the MouseOver ImageUrl, MouseOutImageUrl, Duration, and Transition properties of the CustomWebPartZone control to the respective properties of the newly created CustomWebPartChrome object.

Using the CustomWebPartChrome Control

Listing 32-43 contains a Web page that uses the CustomWebPartZone control and CustomWebPart Chrome chrome. Notice that the page sets the values of the MouseOutImageUrl, MouseOverImageUrl, Duration, and Transition properties of the CustomWebPartZone control. Figure 32-2 shows what the users see on their browsers. Notice that every control added to the CustomWebPartZone automatically contains the logo image in its title bar. When the user moves the mouse pointer over the logo, the WebPart control provides an animated effect.

Listing 32-43: A Web page that uses the CustomWebPartZone control

```
<%@ Page Language="C#" %>
<%@ Register TagPrefix="custom" Namespace="CustomComponents" %>
<html xmlns="http://www.w3.org/1999/xhtml">
<body>
  <form id="form1" runat="server">
    <asp:WebPartManager runat="server" ID="mgr" />
    <custom:CustomWebPartZone runat="server" ID="zone1"
    MouseOutImageUrl="WroxOut.bmp"
    MouseOverImageUrl="WroxOver.bmp" Duration="0.4" Transition="CircleIn">
      <ZoneTemplate>
        <asp:DropDownList runat="server" ID="ddl" />
        <asp:Calendar runat="server" ID="cal" />
      </ZoneTemplate>
    </custom:CustomWebPartZone>
  </form>
</body>
</html>
```

Figure 32-2

Summary

This chapter provided an in-depth coverage of `WebPartZoneBase` type zones and developed several custom `WebPartZoneBase` controls such as `XmlWebServiceWebPartZone` and `ProviderBased WebPartZone`. The chapter then discussed `WebPartChrome` class and showed you how to extend this class to customize the rendering of `WebPart` controls contained in a zone.

The next chapter wraps up the discussion of Web Parts, and in fact the entire book, by showing you how to implement custom data-bound Web Parts controls. This chapter will unite what you've learned about Web Parts in the last three chapters with the data-bound controls techniques you learned earlier in the book.

WebPartManager, Web Parts Connections, and Data-Bound WebPart Controls

`WebPartManager` is one of the most important controls in the Web Parts control set. As the name implies, `WebPartManager` manages Web Part controls that a page contains, such as `WebPart`, `EditorPart`, `CatalogPart`, `WebZone`, and so on. This chapter begins by showing you how to develop your own custom `WebPartManager` control.

The Web Parts connection feature allows you to connect the `WebPart` controls that make up the user interface of a Web Parts page so they can exchange data. This chapter discusses Web Parts connections in detail. It also shows you how to develop custom data-bound `WebPart` controls and provides you with a set of base classes named `BaseDataBoundWebPart`, `DataBoundWebPart`, and `CompositeDataBoundWebPart` that you can derive from to develop data-store agnostic custom data-bound `WebPart` controls that automate all data-binding tasks.

Developing Custom WebPartManager Controls

The `WebPartManager` manager checks whether a `WebPart` control is authorized to be added to the page before it attempts to add the control to the page. `WebPartManager` raises an event named `AuthorizeWebPart` when it's authorizing a `WebPart` control. Listing 33-1 illustrates the event data class associated with the `AuthorizeWebPart` event. As this code listing shows, the `WebPartAuthorizationEventArgs` event data class exposes the following five properties:

❑ `AuthorizationFilter`: Every `WebPart` control exposes a property of type `string` named `AuthorizationFilter` that can be set to any arbitrary value. When the `WebPartManager` raises the `AuthorizeWebPart` event, it assigns the value of the

AuthorizationFilter property of the WebPart control being authorized to the Authorization Filter property of the respective WebPartAuthorizationEventArgs. You'll see later how you can use the AuthorizationFilter property to perform role-based WebPart control authorization.

- ❑ IsAuthorized: Specifies whether the WebPart control can be added to the page.

- ❑ IsShared: Specifies whether all users can see the WebPart control on the page.

- ❑ Path: Specifies the path to the .ascx file if the WebPart control is a user control.

- ❑ Type: Specifies the Systems.Type object that represents the WebPart control.

Listing 33-1: The WebPartAuthorizationEventArgs event data class

```
public class WebPartAuthorizationEventArgs : EventArgs
{
  public WebPartAuthorizationEventArgs(Type type, string path,
                                string authorizationFilter, bool isShared);

  public string AuthorizationFilter { get; }
  public bool IsAuthorized { get; set; }
  public bool IsShared { get; }
  public string Path { get; }
  public Type Type { get; }
}
```

The WebPartManager control exposes a method named OnAuthorizeWebPart that raises the AuthorizeWebPart event as shown in Listing 33-2. Notice that the caller of this method passes a WebPartAuthorizationEventArgs object into the method.

Listing 33-2: The WebPartManager control's OnAuthorizeWebPart method

```
private static readonly object AuthorizeWebPartEventKey = new object();
protected virtual void OnAuthorizeWebPart(WebPartAuthorizationEventArgs e)
{
  WebPartAuthorizationEventHandler handler =
              (WebPartAuthorizationEventHandler)Events[AuthorizeWebPartEventKey];
  if (handler != null)
    handler(this, e);
}
```

As Listing 33-2 shows, all the WebPartManager control's implementation of this method does is to raise the AuthorizeWebPart event. This section implements a custom WebPartManager named RoleBased WebPartManager that derives from the WebPartManager class and overrides the OnAuthorizeWebPart method of its base class. To help you understand the RoleBasedWebPartManager control's implementation of the OnAuthorizeWebPart method, first take a look at a Web page that uses the RoleBased WebPartManager control, as illustrated in Listing 33-3.

Listing 33-3: A Web page that uses the RoleBasedWebPartManager control

```
<%@ Page Language="C#" %>
<%@ Register TagPrefix="custom" Namespace="CustomComponents" %>
<html xmlns="http://www.w3.org/1999/xhtml">
```

```
<body>
  <form id="form1" runat="server">
    <custom:RoleBasedWebPartManager runat="server" ID="mgr" />
    <asp:WebPartZone runat="server" ID="zone1">
      <ZoneTemplate>
        <asp:Calendar runat="server" ID="calendar1"
        AuthorizationFilter="john,george;admin,user" />
        <asp:DropDownList runat="server" ID="ddl" AuthorizationFilter="john;" />
      </ZoneTemplate>
    </asp:WebPartZone>
  </form>
</body>
</html>
```

This Web page sets the values of the `AuthorizationFilter` properties of the `Calendar` and `DropDown List` server controls. The only restriction that the Web Parts Framework sets on the `Authorization Filter` property is its type, `System.String`. However, the Framework doesn't put any restriction on the content of this string.

You can think of the `AuthorizationFilter` property as a string container that is used to transfer data from the `WebPart` control to the `WebPartManager` control. Therefore one of the tasks that you must perform when you're writing a custom `WebPartManager` that makes use of the `AuthorizationFilter` is to decide on the format of the data being transferred.

As Listing 33-3 shows, `RoleBasedWebPartManager` uses a data format that consists of two parts separated by a semicolon character (`;`). The first part is a comma-separated list of usernames, and the second part is a comma-separated list of role names. For example, the `AuthorizationFilter` property of the `Calendar` control in Listing 33-3 is set to the string `john,george;admin,user`. This string specifies that the `Calendar` control should only be shown to users with the usernames `john` or `george`, or to users that are in the roles `admin` or `user`.

Now back to the implementation of the `RoleBasedWebPartManager` control. Listing 33-4 contains the code for the `RoleBasedWebPartManager` control. This control overrides the `OnAuthorizeWebPart` method of its base class, `WebPartManager`, to perform role-based `WebPart` authorization.

The method first calls the `OnAuthorizeWebPart` method of its base class, `WebPartManager`. As shown in Listing 33-2, the base class's implementation of this method raises the `AuthorizeWebPart` event to allow the page developer to perform application-specific `WebPart` authorization. If your custom `WebPartManager` control's implementation of the `OnAuthorizeWebPart` method doesn't call the `OnAuthorizeWebPart` method of the base class, the page developer won't be able to enforce application-specific authorization rules.

```
base.OnAuthorizeWebPart(e);
```

The method then calls the `Split` method on the `AuthorizationFilter` to extract the two strings that contain the comma-separated lists of usernames and role names:

```
string[] usersAndRoles =
        e.AuthorizationFilter.Split(new char[] { ';' }, StringSplitOptions.None);
```

It then calls the `Split` method on the two strings to extract the usernames and role names:

```
string[] users =
            usersAndRoles[0].Split(new char[] { ',' }, StringSplitOptions.None);
string[] roles =
            usersAndRoles[1].Split(new char[] { ',' }, StringSplitOptions.None);
```

Next, the method checks whether the list of usernames contains the username of the current user:

```
        foreach (string user in users)
        {
          if (!string.IsNullOrEmpty(user) && Page.User.Identity.Name == user)
          {
            isAuthorized = true;
            break;
          }
        }
```

If the check fails, it checks whether the current user is in any of the roles specified in the list of role names:

```
        if (!isAuthorized)
        {
          foreach (string role in roles)
          {
            if (!string.IsNullOrEmpty(role) && Roles.IsUserInRole(role))
            {
              isAuthorized = true;
              break;
            }
          }
        }
```

The method then sets the `IsAuthorized` property of the `WebPartAuthorizationEventArgs` object to true if the value of this property was true to begin with, and if one of the checks succeeds. Both conditions are important. You may be wondering why you should care about the original value of the `IsAuthorized` property. Recall that the `RoleBasedWebPartManager` control's implementation of the `OnAuthorize` `WebPart` method calls the `WebPartManager` control's implementation of the same method to raise the `AuthorizeWebPart` event and therefore to allow the page developer to perform application-specific authorization.

The page developer sets the value of the `IsAuthorized` property of the same `WebPartAuthorization` `EventArgs` object to true or false based on whether the application-specific authorization rules authorize the `WebPart` to be rendered. Therefore, if your custom `WebPartManager` control's implementation of the `OnAuthorizeWebPart` method doesn't take the original value of the `IsAuthorized` property of the `WebPartAuthorizationEventArgs` into account, the page developers will not be able to enforce their own authorization rules.

```
        e.IsAuthorized = (e.IsAuthorized && isAuthorized);
```

Listing 33-4: The RoleBasedWebPartManager custom WebPartManager

```
public class RoleBasedWebPartManager : WebPartManager
{
  protected override void OnAuthorizeWebPart(WebPartAuthorizationEventArgs e)
  {
    base.OnAuthorizeWebPart(e);

    if (!String.IsNullOrEmpty(e.AuthorizationFilter))
    {
      string[] usersAndRoles =
          e.AuthorizationFilter.Split(new char[] { ';' }, StringSplitOptions.None);
      string[] users =
              usersAndRoles[0].Split(new char[] { ',' }, StringSplitOptions.None);
      string[] roles =
              usersAndRoles[1].Split(new char[] { ',' }, StringSplitOptions.None);
      bool isAuthorized = false;

      foreach (string user in users)
      {
        if (!string.IsNullOrEmpty(user) && Page.User.Identity.Name == user)
        {
          isAuthorized = true;
          break;
        }
      }

      if (!isAuthorized)
      {
        foreach (string role in roles)
        {
          if (!string.IsNullOrEmpty(role) && Roles.IsUserInRole(role))
          {
            isAuthorized = true;
            break;
          }
        }
      }

      e.IsAuthorized = (e.IsAuthorized && isAuthorized);
    }
  }
}
```

Connecting WebPart Controls

To make the discussions more concrete, this section develops two WebPart controls named RssReader WebPart5 and FavoriteItemsWebPart, both of which are shown in Figure 33-1.

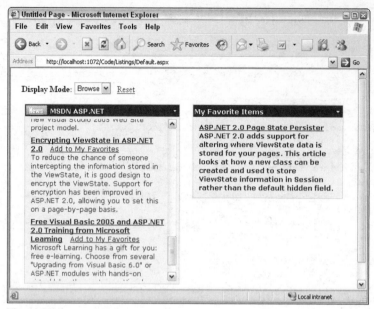

Figure 33-1

The RssReaderWebPart5 control, like its predecessor RssReaderWebPart4, downloads and displays the RSS feed that the user selects from its verbs menu. As discussed, each RSS feed consists of one or more items where each item contains the following information:

- ❑ Title
- ❑ Link
- ❑ Description

Like its predecessor, RssReaderWebPart5 uses a hyperlink to display the title of each item and a label to display its description. As Figure 33-1 shows, RssReaderWebPart5 does one more thing that its predecessor doesn't do — each displayed item in RssReaderWebPart5 includes a LinkButton named "Add to My Favorites." When the user clicks a LinkButton associated with an item, RssReaderWeb Part5 sends the complete information about the selected item (its title, link, and description) to the FavoriteItemsWebPart control. This control adds the selected item to the current user's favorite items.

This raises the following question: How does RssReaderWebPart5 send the selected item's title, link, and description to the FavoriteItemsWebPart control? If you're familiar with the new ASP.NET Web Parts Framework, you know the answer to this question. RssReaderWebPart5 uses the ASP.NET Web Parts connection feature to send the data to FavoriteItemsWebPart control.

However, because the purpose of this section is to help you understand the ASP.NET Web Parts connection feature from the inside out, step back and consider the following question: If you didn't have access to the ASP.NET Web Parts connection feature, how would you implement the feature that allows Rss ReaderWebPart5 to send an item's title, link, and description to FavoriteItemsWebPart control when the user clicks the "Add to My Favorites" LinkButton associated with the item?

One way to do this is to define a new interface named IItem that exposes three properties named Title, Link, and Description as shown in Listing 33-5.

Listing 33-5: The Item class

```
public interface IItem
{
  string Title { get;}
  string Description { get;}
  string Link { get;}
}
```

You could then write a new class named Item that implements the IItem interface:

```
public class Item : IItem
{
  private string title;
  public string Title
  {
    get {return title;}
    set {title = value;}
  }

  private string link;
  public string Link
  {
    get {return link;}
    set { link = value;}
  }

  private string description;
  public string Description
  {
    get {return description;}
    set { description = value;}
  }
}
```

You would then implement and add a new method named AddItemToFavoriteItems to the Favorite ItemsWebPart control. This method takes an instance of the IItem interface and adds it to the internal list of favorite items, as shown in Listing 33-6.

Listing 33-6: The FavoriteItemsWebPart control

```
public class FavoriteItemsWebPart : WebPart
{
  . . .
  List<IItem> favoriteItems;
  public void AddItemToFavoriteItems(IItem item)
  {
    favoriteItems.Add(item);
  }
  . . .
}
```

Next, implement and add a new method named `GetSelectedItem` to the `RssReaderWebPart5` control. This method takes no argument and returns an instance of the `IItem` interface that contains the information about the selected item.

Then, in the callback method for the `Click` event of the "Add to My Favorites" button (shown in Listing 33-7), you would call the `GetSelectedItem` of the `RssReaderWebPart5` control to return the `IItem` instance that contains the title, link, and description of the selected item:

```
IItem item = GetSelectedItem();
```

Then you'd call the `AddItemToFavoriteItems` method of the `FavoriteItemsWebPart` control and pass the `IItem` instance into it:

```
part.AddItemToFavoriteItems(item);
```

Listing 33-7: The RssReaderWebPart5 control

```
public class RssReaderWebPart5 : WebPart
{
  . . .
  private void CallbackMethodForClickEvent(object sender, EventArgs e)
  {
    IItem item = GetSelectedItem();
    FavoriteItemsWebPart part = GetReferenceToFavoriteItemsWebPart();
    part.AddItemToFavoriteItems(item);
  }
}
```

This solution seems to address the question that was raised previously: How does `RssReaderWebPart5` send the selected item's title, link, and description to `FavoriteItemsWebPart` control? If that's the case, why do you need the ASP.NET Web Parts connection feature when you already have a simple solution?

If you examine Listing 33-7 more closely, you'll notice the `CallbackMethodForClickEvent` method of `RssReaderWebPart5` directly uses the `FavoriteItemsWebPart` control, which means that `RssReaderWebPart5` is tied to the `FavoriteItemsWebPart` control. In other words, `RssReaderWebPart5` can service one and only one type of control, `FavoriteItemsWebPart`, and can't service any other types of controls.

Therefore, `RssReaderWebPart5` shouldn't send data directly to the `FavoriteItemsWebPart` control. What you need is a third component that retrieves the data from `RssReaderWebPart5` and passes it along to `FavoriteItemsWebPart`. The ASP.NET Web Parts Framework comes with a class named `WebPartConnection` that acts as this third component. This class includes a method (call it `Exchange Data`) that retrieves the data from `RssReaderWebPart5` and passes it to the `FavoriteItemsWebPart` control.

How would you implement the `ExchangeData` method of the `WebPartConnection` class? Listing 33-8 shows one possible implementation for this method. This implementation calls the `GetSelectedItem` method of the `RssReaderWebPart5` control to return the `IItem` instance that contains the title, link, and description of the selected item:

```
IItem item = provider.GetSelectedItem();
```

Then it calls the `AddItemToFavoriteItems` method of the `FavoriteItemsWebPart` control and passes the `IItem` instance into it:

```
consumer.AddItemToFavoriteItems(item);
```

Listing 33-8: The first version of the WebPartConnection class

```
public class WebPartConnection
{
  RssReaderWebPart5 provider;
  FavoriteItemsWebPart consumer;

  public void ExchangeData()
  {
    IItem item = provider.GetSelectedItem();
    consumer.AddItemToFavoriteItems(item);
  }
}
```

Obviously the implementation that Listing 33-8 presents for `WebPartConnection` class suffers from the same problem as Listing 33-7 — this implementation ties the `WebPartConnection` class to the `RssReaderWebPart5` and `FavoriteItemsWebPart` controls, and doesn't allow it to work with other types of controls.

Later in this section, you'll see an implementation of the `WebPartConnection` class that resolves this problem. Before diving into that implementation, you need to examine a very important concept that the `ExchangeData` method shown in Listing 33-8 promotes. The `ExchangeData` method first calls the `Get SelectedItem` method to get the data from `RssReaderWebPart5` and then calls the `AddItemToFavorite Items` method to pass the data to `FavoriteItemsWebPart` control. In other words, you can think of the `WebPartConnection` as a connection channel between the `GetSelectedItem` and `AddItemToFavorite Items` methods, which means that you can think of the methods themselves as connection points where one connection point (the `GetSelectedItem` method) acts as a data provider and the other connection point (the `AddItemToFavoriteItems` method) acts as a data consumer, as shown in Figure 33-2.

Provider Connection
Point

Consumer Connection
Point

Figure 33-2

The provider connection point is characterized by the following characteristics:

❑ The type of data provider control, in this case, `RssReaderWebPart5`

❑ The method of the data provider control that is called when the connection is established, in this case, `GetSelectedItem`

❑ The type of object that the data provider control provides, in this case, `IItem`

The consumer connection point, on the other hand, is characterized by the following characteristics:

❑ The type of data consumer control, in this case, `FavoriteItemsWebPart`

❑ The method of the data consumer control that is called when the connection is established, in this case, `AddItemToSelectedItems`

❑ The type of object that the data consumer control consumes, in this case, `IItem`

The ASP.NET Web Parts Framework comes with two classes named `ProviderConnectionPoint` and `ConsumerConnectionPoint` that represent the provider and consumer connection points shown in Figure 33-2. Listing 33-9 contains the code for the `ProviderConnectionPoint` class. This class allows you to represent the provider connection point in a generic fashion as follows:

1. The constructor of this class takes a `System.Type` object as its third argument. This object is the generic representation of the data provider control.

2. The constructor takes a `MethodInfo` object as its first argument. This object is the generic representation of the method of the data provider control that is called when the connection is established.

3. The constructor takes a `System.Type` object as its second argument. This object is the generic representation of the type of object that the data provider control provides.

4. The class exposes a method named `GetObject` that allows you to call the data provider method (the method that provides the data) in generic fashion.

Listing 33-9: The ProviderConnectionPoint class

```
public class ProviderConnectionPoint : ConnectionPoint
{
  public ProviderConnectionPoint(MethodInfo callbackMethod, Type interfaceType,
                                 Type controlType, string displayName, string id,
                                 bool allowsMultipleConnections);

  public virtual object GetObject(Control control)
  {
    return base.CallbackMethod.Invoke(control, null);
  }
}
```

Listing 33-10 contains the code for the `ConsumerConnectionPoint` class. This class allows you to represent the consumer connection point shown in Figure 33-2 in a generic fashion as follows:

1. The constructor of this class takes a `System.Type` object as its third argument. This object is the generic representation of the data consumer control.

2. The constructor takes a `MethodInfo` object as its first argument. This object is the generic representation of the method of the data consumer control that is called when the connection is established.

3. The constructor takes a `System.Type` object as its second argument. This object is the generic representation of the type of object that the data consumer control consumes.

4. The class exposes a method named `SetObject` that allows you to call the data consumer method (the method that consumes the data) in generic fashion.

Listing 33-10: The ConsumerConnectionPoint class

```
public class ConsumerConnectionPoint : ConnectionPoint
{
  public ConsumerConnectionPoint(MethodInfo callbackMethod, Type interfaceType,
                                 Type controlType, string displayName, string id,
                                 bool allowsMultipleConnections);

  public virtual void SetObject(Control control, object data)
  {
    CallbackMethod.Invoke(control, new object[] { data });
  }
}
```

Listing 33-11 shows the version of `WebPartConnection` that uses the `ProviderConnectionPoint` and `ConsumerConnectionPoint` classes. As this code listing shows, the new version of `ExchangeData` calls the `GetObject` method of the `ProviderConnectionPoint` to invoke the data provider control's method (the method that provides data) in generic fashion and return the object that contains the data:

```
object obj = this.ProviderConnectionPoint.GetObject(this.Provider.ToControl());
```

It then calls the `SetObject` method of the `ConsumerConnectionPoint` and passes the data object into it to invoke the data consumer control's method (the method that consumer data) in generic fashion.

Listing 33-11: The final version of WebPartConnection class

```
public sealed class WebPartConnection
{
  internal void ExchangeData()
  {
    object obj = this.ProviderConnectionPoint.GetObject(this.Provider.ToControl());
    this.ConsumerConnectionPoint.SetObject(this.Consumer.ToControl(),obj);
  }

  public WebPart Consumer {get;}
  public WebPart Provider {get;}
  public ConsumerConnectionPoint ConsumerConnectionPoint {get;}
  public ProviderConnectionPoint ProviderConnectionPoint {get;}
}
```

As these discussions show, every connection between two `WebPart` controls is represented by an instance of the `WebPartConnection` class. Connecting two `WebPart` controls means creating an instance of the `WebPartConnection` class. As a matter of fact, `WebPartManager` exposes a method named `ConnectWeb Parts` that simply creates and returns an instance of the `WebPartConnection` class. In Web Parts jargon, though, there is a difference between connecting two `WebParts` and activating the connection.

Two `WebParts` are *connected* when the appropriate `WebPartConnection` object has been created and added to the `WebPartManager` control's list of connections. A connection is *activated* when the `Exchange Data` method of the `WebPartConnection` object associated with the connection is called, that is, when the data is exchanged. As you'll see later, there are three different ways to connect two WebPart controls. All three approaches require you as control developer to perform several tasks ahead of time.

You need to define the interface that represents the data being exchanged. In this case, this interface is the IItem interface as defined in Listing 33-5.

You also need to have your data provider WebPart control implement the interface. As Listing 33-12 shows, the RssReaderWebPart5 implements the IItem interface.

Listing 33-12: RssReaderWebPart5 implements IItem

```
public class RssReaderWebPart5 : WebPart, IPersonalizable, IItem
{
  . . .
  private string title;
  string IItem.Title
  {
    get { return title; }
  }

  private string description;
  string IItem.Description
  {
    get { return description; }
  }

  private string link;
  string IItem.Link
  {
    get { return link; }
  }
  . . .
}
```

Next, you need to mark the provider method that provides the data with the ConnectionProviderAttribute metadata attribute. As Listing 33-13 shows, RssReaderWebPart5 marks its GetSelectedItem method with this attribute.

Listing 33-13: RssReaderWebPart5 marks its GetSelectedItem method with ConnectionProviderAttribute

```
public class RssReaderWebPart5 : WebPart, IPersonalizable, IItem
{
  . . .
  [ConnectionProvider("Item")]
  public IItem GetSelectedItem()
  {
    return this;
  }
}
```

This `ConnectionProviderAttribute` metadata attribute serves the following purposes:

❑ Your data provider control, like all controls or classes, may expose numerous methods, which makes it impossible for the `WebPartManager` control to know which method provides the data. The `ConnectionProviderAttribute` metadata attribute tells the `WebPartManager` that the method marked with this attribute is the method that provides the data.

❑ The `ConnectionProviderAttribute` metadata attribute takes two important arguments that the `WebPartManager` must pass to the constructor of the `ProviderConnectionPoint` class when it's creating an instance of the class. These arguments are `displayName` and `id`. As you'll see later, the `displayName` argument provides a friendly name for the connection point that can be displayed to end users. The `id` argument is used to identify the connection point when the data provider supports more than one connection point.

You next need to mark the consumer method that consumes the data with the `ConnectionConsumer Attribute` metadata attribute. As Listing 33-14 shows, `FavoriteItemsWebPart` marks its `AddItem ToFavoriteItems` method with this attribute. As this listing shows, the implementation of a data consumer method normally consists of one line of code, where the method assigns the data object to a private field of the same type as the object.

Listing 33-14: FavoriteItemsWebPart marks its AddItemToFavoriteItems method with ConnectionConsumerAttribute

```
public class FavoriteItemsWebPart : WebPart
{
  private IItem item;
  . . .
  [ConnectionConsumer("Item")]
  public void AddItemToFavoriteItems(IItem item)
  {
    this.item = item;
  }
  . . .
}
```

The `ConnectionConsumerAttribute` metadata attribute serves the same two purposes discussed before, specifically, it tells the `WebPartManager` that the method marked with the attribute is the method that consumes the data, and it provides the `WebPartManager` control with the values of the `displayName` and `id` parameters that the control must pass to the constructor of the `Consumer ConnectionPoint` class when it's creating an instance of the class (see Listing 33-10).

As mentioned, in general, there are three ways to connect two `WebPart` controls. The first approach is known as *Declarative* or *Static Connections*. Recall from Chapter 8 that if a server control is marked with the `[ParseChildren(true)]` metadata attribute, the page parser parses the markup within the opening and closing tags of the server control as the property of the control, as opposed to its child control.

This allows the page developer to declaratively specify the value of the property of a control. Because `WebPartManager` is marked with the `[ParseChildren(true)]` metadata attribute, the page developer can declaratively specify the content of the `StaticConnections` property of the `WebPartManager` control:

```
<asp:WebPartManager runat="server" ID="mgr2">
  <StaticConnections>
    <asp:WebPartConnection ID="wp1" ProviderID="provider1" ConsumerID="consumer1"/>
  </StaticConnections>
</asp:WebPartManager>
```

As this code shows, each `<asp:WebPartConnection>` element represents a connection between the specified `WebPart` controls. At runtime, the page framework automatically creates an instance of the `WebPartConnection` class for each `<asp:WebPartConnection>` element declared within the opening and closing tags of the `StaticConnections` element and adds the instance to the `StaticConnections` collection of the `WebPartManager` control.

Implementing the Provider and Consumer WebPart Controls

This section presents the implementation of the `RssReaderWebPart5` and `FavoriteItemsWebPart` controls and uses the declarative approach to establish a connection between them. First, review what these two controls do. `RssReaderWebPart5` downloads and displays the RSS feed that the user selects from its verbs menu. Each RSS feed consists of one or more items, where each item contains the following information: title, link, and description.

As Figure 33-1 shows, each displayed item in `RssReaderWebPart5` includes a `LinkButton` named "Add to My Favorites." When the user clicks a `LinkButton` associated with an item, the `RssReaderWebPart5` control provides `FavoriteItemsWebPart` with an object of type `IItem` that contains the title, link, and description of the selected item. `FavoriteItemsWebPart`, on its part, adds the selected item to the current user's favorite items.

RssReaderWebPart5

This section discusses only connection-related methods and properties of the `RssReaderWebPart5` control because the implementation of the rest of the methods and properties of the control is the same as its predecessor, `RssReaderWebPart4`, which was covered in Chapter 31.

`RssReaderWebPart5` implements a method named `AddItemToContainer` that adds an item to the `RssReaderWebPart5` control. The implementation of this method is the same as `RssReaderWebPart4` with one main difference. This method also renders the "Add to My Favorites" `LinkButton` and registers a method named `SelectCommandCallback` as callback for the `Click` event of the `LinkButton` as shown in highlighted portion of Listing 33-15.

Listing 33-15: The AddItemToContainer method of RssReaderWebPart5 control

```
protected virtual void AddItemToContainer(XmlReader reader)
{
  string link = string.Empty; ;
  string title = string.Empty;
  string description = string.Empty;

  while (reader.Read())
  {
```

```
        if (reader.NodeType == XmlNodeType.Element)
        {
          if (reader.Name == "link")
            link = reader.ReadElementContentAsString();

          else if (reader.Name == "title")
            title = reader.ReadElementContentAsString();

          else if (reader.Name == "description")
            description = reader.ReadElementContentAsString();
        }
      }

      TableRow row = new TableRow();
      table.Rows.Add(row);
      TableCell cell = new TableCell();
      row.Cells.Add(cell);

      HyperLink hyperLink = new HyperLink();
      hyperLink.NavigateUrl = link;
      hyperLink.Text = title;
      hyperLink.Font.Bold = true;
      cell.Controls.Add(hyperLink);
      LiteralControl lc;

      lc = new LiteralControl("   ");
      cell.Controls.Add(lc);

      LinkButton btn = new LinkButton();
      btn.Text = "Add to My Favorites";
      btn.CommandArgument = table.Rows.GetRowIndex(row).ToString();
      btn.Command += new CommandEventHandler(SelectCommandCallback);
      cell.Controls.Add(btn);

      lc = new LiteralControl("<br/>");
      cell.Controls.Add(lc);
      Label label = new Label();
      label.Text = description;
      cell.Controls.Add(label);
    }
```

Listing 33-16 presents the implementation of the SelectCommandCallback method. This method extracts the title, link, and description values associated with the selected item and assigns them to the title, link, and description private fields of the RssReaderWebPart5 control. Recall that the RssReaderWeb Part5 control implements the IItem interface where its implementation of the Title, Link, and Description properties of this interface return the values of the title, link, and description private fields (see Listing 33-12).

The SelectCommandCallback method doesn't directly send the data to FavoriteItemsWebPart control as Listing 33-7 did. The method leaves the responsibility of sending the values of its Title, Link, and Description properties to the Web Parts Framework.

Listing 33-16: The SelectCommandCallback method

```
void SelectCommandCallback(object sender, CommandEventArgs e)
{
    int rowIndex = int.Parse(e.CommandArgument.ToString());
    TableRow row = table.Rows[rowIndex];
    TableCell cell = row.Cells[0];
    HyperLink hyperLink = cell.Controls[0] as HyperLink;
    title = hyperLink.Text;
    link = hyperLink.NavigateUrl;
    Label label = cell.Controls[4] as Label;
    description = label.Text;
}
```

FavoriteItemsWebPart

Listing 33-17 presents the implementation of FavoriteItemsWebPart. FavoriteItemsWebPart exposes a string property named FavoriteItems that contains the current user's list of favorite items separated by the string ||. Each member of the list contains the title, link, and description of a favorite item separated by the string __.

As discussed, there are two ways to have the Web Parts personalization store the property values of a control. You can either implement the IPersonalizable interface as you did before or you can mark the properties of your control with the [Personalizable(true)] attribute. The FavoriteItems WebPart control takes the second approach and marks its FavoriteItems property with the [Personalizable(true)] metadata attribute:

```
private string favoriteItems;
[Personalizable(true)]
public string FavoriteItems
{
    get { return favoriteItems;}
    set { favoriteItems = value;}
}
```

Also notice that the FavoriteItemsWebPart control marks its AddItemToFavoriteItems method with the [ConnectionConsumerAttribute("Item")] attribute to specify this method as the method that consumes the data that the RssReaderWebPart5 control provides. Notice that this method simply assigns the item that the provider provides to a private field of type IItem named item. The Web Parts Framework automatically calls the AddItemToFavoriteItems method, which means that the value of the item private field is automatically set to the IItem object that the provider provides:

```
private IItem item;
[ConnectionConsumer("Item")]
public void AddItemToFavoriteItems(IItem item)
{
    this.item = item;
}
```

As Listing 33-17 shows, the FavoriteItemsWebPart control overrides the CreateChildControls method, and checks whether the item private field has been set. If it has, it's an indication that the RssReaderWebPart5 provider has provided a new favorite item. FavoriteItemsWebPart adds the new item to the existing list of favorite items:

```
      if (item != null)
      {
        if (!string.IsNullOrEmpty(FavoriteItems))
          FavoriteItems += "||";

        FavoriteItems += item.Title;
        FavoriteItems += "__";
        FavoriteItems += item.Link;
        FavoriteItems += "__";
        FavoriteItems += item.Description;
      }
```

The control then iterates through the favorite items and uses a hyperlink and a label to respectively display the title and description of each enumerated favorite item (see Listing 33-17).

Listing 33-17: The FavoriteItemsWebPart control

```
public class FavoriteItemsWebPart : WebPart
{
  public FavoriteItemsWebPart()
  {
    Title = "My Favorite Items";
    this.Height = Unit.Parse("100%");
    this.Width = Unit.Parse("100%");
    this.ScrollBars = ScrollBars.Auto;
  }

  private IItem item;
  [ConnectionConsumer("Item")]
  public void AddItemToFavoriteItems(IItem item)
  {
    this.item = item;
  }

  private string favoriteItems;
  [Personalizable(true)]
  public string FavoriteItems
  {
    get { return favoriteItems;}
    set { favoriteItems = value;}
  }

  Table table;
  protected override void CreateChildControls()
  {
    Controls.Clear();

    if (item != null)
    {
      if (!string.IsNullOrEmpty(FavoriteItems))
        FavoriteItems += "||";

      FavoriteItems += item.Title;
      FavoriteItems += "__";
```

(continued)

Listing 33-17: *(continued)*

```csharp
      FavoriteItems += item.Link;
      FavoriteItems += "__";
      FavoriteItems += item.Description;
    }

    if (string.IsNullOrEmpty(FavoriteItems))
    {
      ChildControlsCreated = true;
      return;
    }

    table = new Table();
    table.CellSpacing = 5;
    Controls.Add(table);

    string[] items =
            FavoriteItems.Split(new string[] { "||" },StringSplitOptions.None);
    string[] itemElements;
    foreach (string item1 in items)
    {
      itemElements = item1.Split(new string[] { "__" },StringSplitOptions.None);
      if (itemElements == null || itemElements.Length != 3)
        continue;

      string title = itemElements[0];
      string link = itemElements[1];
      string description = itemElements[2];

      if (string.IsNullOrEmpty(title) || string.IsNullOrEmpty(link) ||
          string.IsNullOrEmpty(description))
        continue;

      TableRow row = new TableRow();
      table.Rows.Add(row);
      TableCell cell = new TableCell();
      row.Cells.Add(cell);

      HyperLink hyperLink = new HyperLink();
      hyperLink.NavigateUrl = link;
      hyperLink.Text = title;
      hyperLink.Font.Bold = true;
      cell.Controls.Add(hyperLink);
      LiteralControl lc = new LiteralControl("<br/>");
      cell.Controls.Add(lc);
      Label label = new Label();
      label.Text = description;
      cell.Controls.Add(label);
    }

    ChildControlsCreated = true;
  }
}
```

Listing 33-18 shows a Web page that uses the `RssReaderWebPart5` and `FavoriteItemsWebPart` controls. Notice that the two controls are connected declaratively via the `<asp:WebPartConnection>` element declared within the opening and closing tags of the `<StaticConnections>` element. As the boldface portions of Listing 33-18 show, the values of the `ID` attributes of the `RssReaderWebPart5` and `FavoriteItemsWebPart` controls are respectively assigned to the `ProviderID` and `ConsumerID` attributes of the `<asp:WebPartConnection>` element to specify the `RssReaderWebPart5` control as the data provider and `FavoriteItemsWebPart` control as the data consumer control.

Listing 33-18: A Web page that uses RssReaderWebPart5 and FavoriteItemsWebPart controls

```
<%@ Page Language="C#" %>
<%@ Register TagPrefix="custom" Namespace="CustomComponents" %>
<html xmlns="http://www.w3.org/1999/xhtml">
<body>
  <form id="form1" runat="server">
    <asp:WebPartManager runat="server" ID="mgr2">
      <StaticConnections>
        <asp:WebPartConnection ID="wp1" ProviderID="provider1"
          ConsumerID="consumer1" />
      </StaticConnections>
    </asp:WebPartManager>

    <table cellspacing="10">
      <tr>
        <td valign="top">
          <asp:WebPartZone runat="server" ID="zone1" . . .>
            . . .
            <ZoneTemplate>
              <custom:RssReaderWebPart5 Title="Rss Reader" runat="server"
              ID="provider1" RssDataSourceID="MySource"
              RssDescriptionField="RssDescription" RssTextField="RssText"
              RssUrlField="RssUrl" CatalogIconImageUrl="news.gif"
              TitleIconImageUrl="news.gif">
                <EditorHeaderStyle BackColor="Tan" Font-Bold="True" />
                <EditorAlternatingItemStyle BackColor="PaleGoldenrod" />
                <EditorStyle BackColor="LightGoldenrodYellow" BorderColor="Tan"
                BorderWidth="1px" CellPadding="2" ForeColor="Black"
                GridLines="None" />
              </custom:RssReaderWebPart5>
            </ZoneTemplate>
          </asp:WebPartZone>
        </td>
        <td valign="top">
          <asp:WebPartZone runat="server" ID="WebPartZone1" . . .>
            . . .
            <ZoneTemplate>
              <custom:FavoriteItemsWebPart runat="server" ID="consumer1" />
            </ZoneTemplate>
          </asp:WebPartZone>
        </td>
      </tr>
    </table>
```

(continued)

Listing 33-18: *(continued)*

```
    <asp:SqlDataSource runat="server" ID="MySource"
    ConnectionString="<%$ ConnectionStrings:MySqlConnectionString %>"
    SelectCommand="Select * From Rss" />
  </form>
</body>
</html>
```

Dynamic Connections

The previous section showed you how to establish static connection between two WebPart controls. Because static connections are declared on the ASP.NET page, the respective connection is automatically established every time the user accesses the page. In other words, static connections are permanent.

Static connections don't give end users the option of connecting and disconnecting WebPart controls on demand. Later in this chapter you'll see an example of disconnecting WebPart controls. This is where dynamic connections come into play. The ASP.NET Web Parts Framework comes with a zone control named ConnectionsZone that provides end users with the appropriate user interface to connect and disconnect WebPart controls from their Web browsers. Implementing dynamic connections is pretty simple. All you need to do is add the <asp:ConnectionsZone> element to your page as shown in Listing 33-19. Notice that this listing is the same as Listing 33-18 except for the highlighted portion where the ConnectionsZone has been declared. Also notice this zone doesn't contain any child controls. As the highlighted portion shows, the ConnectionsZone, like all other zones, supports style properties. Figure 33-1 shows what the end users see on their browsers when they access the page that listing 33-19 contains.

Listing 33-19: A Web page that supports dynamic connections

```
<%@ Page Language="C#" %>
<%@ Register TagPrefix="custom" Namespace="CustomComponents" %>
<script runat="server">
 . . .
</script>
<html xmlns="http://www.w3.org/1999/xhtml">
<body>
  <form id="form1" runat="server">
    <asp:WebPartManager runat="server" ID="mgr2">
      <StaticConnections>
        <asp:WebPartConnection ID="wp1" ProviderID="provider1"
        ConsumerID="consumer1" />
      </StaticConnections>
    </asp:WebPartManager>

    <table cellspacing="10">
      <tr>
        . . .
      </tr>
      <tr>
        <td valign="top">
          <asp:WebPartZone runat="server" ID="zone1" . . .>
            . . .
            <ZoneTemplate>
```

```
                    <custom:RssReaderWebPart5 Title="Rss Reader" runat="server"
                    ID="provider1" RssDataSourceID="MySource"
                    RssDescriptionField="RssDescription" RssTextField="RssText"
                    RssUrlField="RssUrl" CatalogIconImageUrl="news.gif"
                    TitleIconImageUrl="news.gif">
                        <EditorHeaderStyle BackColor="Tan" Font-Bold="True" />
                        <EditorAlternatingItemStyle BackColor="PaleGoldenrod" />
                        <EditorStyle BackColor="LightGoldenrodYellow" BorderColor="Tan"
                        BorderWidth="1px" CellPadding="2" ForeColor="Black"
                        GridLines="None" />
                    </custom:RssReaderWebPart5>
                </ZoneTemplate>
            </asp:WebPartZone>
        </td>
        <td valign="top">
            <asp:WebPartZone runat="server" ID="WebPartZone1" . . .>
            . . .
            <ZoneTemplate>
                <custom:FavoriteItemsWebPart runat="server" ID="consumer1" />
            </ZoneTemplate>
            </asp:WebPartZone>
        </td>
    </tr>
    <tr>
        <td>
            <asp:ConnectionsZone runat="server" ID="con" BackColor="#FFFBD6"
            BorderColor="#CCCCCC" BorderWidth="1px" Font-Names="Verdana" Padding="6">
                <LabelStyle Font-Size="0.8em" ForeColor="#333333" />
                <FooterStyle BackColor="#FFCC66" HorizontalAlign="Right" />
                <VerbStyle Font-Names="Verdana" Font-Size="0.8em"
                ForeColor="#333333" />
                <HeaderVerbStyle Font-Bold="False" Font-Size="0.8em"
                Font-Underline="False" ForeColor="#333333" />
                <HeaderStyle BackColor="#FFCC66" Font-Bold="True"
                Font-Size="0.8em" ForeColor="#333333" />
                <InstructionTextStyle Font-Size="0.8em" ForeColor="#333333" />
                <EditUIStyle Font-Names="Verdana" Font-Size="0.8em"
                ForeColor="#333333" />
            </asp:ConnectionsZone>
        </td>
    </tr>
    </table>
    <asp:SqlDataSource runat="server" ID="MySource"
    ConnectionString="<%$ ConnectionStrings:MySqlConnectionString %>"
    SelectCommand="Select * From Rss" />
    </form>
</body>
</html>
```

If the end users want to connect or disconnect the RssReaderWebPart5 and FavoriteItemsWebPart controls, they would need to select the Connect option from the DropDownList on the top of the page shown in Figure 33-1 to switch the page from browse display mode to connect display mode. When the page switches to connect display mode, the Web Parts Framework adds a Connect verb to the verbs menu of the RssReaderWebPart5 and FavoriteItemsWebPart controls, as shown in Figure 33-3.

The user needs to select the `Connect` verb from the verbs menu of either `RssReaderWebPart5` or `FavoriteItemsWebPart` to select the control that the end user wants to connect or disconnect. At this point, the `ConnectionsZone` will display the connection user interface that allows end users to connect or disconnect the selected `WebPart` control as shown in Figure 33-4.

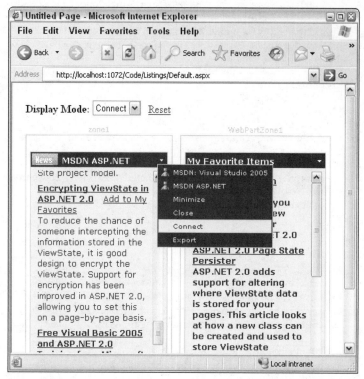

Figure 33-3

The current implementation of the `RssReaderWebPart5` control renders the "Add to My Favorites" `LinkButton` even when `RssReaderWebPart5` is no longer connected. This causes usability problems because end users may still try to click these `LinkButtons` not realizing they're no longer active. This section implements a new version of the control named `RssReaderWebPart6` that fixes this problem.

`RssReaderWebPart6` exposes a new Boolean property named `RenderAddToMyFavoriteLink` as shown in the following code fragment:

```
bool renderAddToMyFavoriteLink;
[Personalizable(true)]
public bool RenderAddToMyFavoriteLink
{
  get { return this.renderAddToMyFavoriteLink; }
  set { renderAddToMyFavoriteLink = value; }
}
```

Figure 33-4

Notice that the code fragment marks the RenderAddToMyFavoriteLink property with the [Personalizable(true)] attribute to instruct the personalization infrastructure to store the value of this property in the underlying personalization data store.

RssReaderWebPart6 then modifies the implementation of the AddItemToContainer method of RssReaderWebPart5 as shown in Listing 33-20. Notice that this implementation is the same as the one shown in Listing 33-15 with one difference, the addition of the if statement that checks the value of RenderAddToMyFavoriteLink property to determine whether the "Add to My Favorites" LinkButton should be rendered.

Listing 33-20: The AddItemToContainer method of RssReaderWebPart6 control

```
protected virtual void AddItemToContainer(XmlReader reader)
{
  . . .
  HyperLink hyperLink = new HyperLink();
  hyperLink.NavigateUrl = link;
  hyperLink.Text = title;
  hyperLink.Font.Bold = true;
  cell.Controls.Add(hyperLink);
  LiteralControl lc;
```

(continued)

Listing 33-20: *(continued)*

```
    if (RenderAddToMyFavoriteLink)
    {
        lc = new LiteralControl("   ");
        cell.Controls.Add(lc);

        LinkButton btn = new LinkButton();
        btn.Text = "Add to My Favorites";
        btn.CommandArgument = table.Rows.GetRowIndex(row).ToString();
        btn.Command += new CommandEventHandler(SelectCommandCallback);
        cell.Controls.Add(btn);
    }
    lc = new LiteralControl("<br/>");
    cell.Controls.Add(lc);
    Label label = new Label();
    label.Text = description;
    cell.Controls.Add(label);
}
```

When the end user connects and disconnects a `WebPart` control, `WebPartManager` raises the `WebParts Connected` and `WebPartsDisconnected` events. `RssReaderWebPart6` overrides the `OnInit` method to respectively register the `WebPartsConnectedCallback` and `WebPartsDisconnectedCallback` methods as callbacks for the `WebPartsConnected` and `WebPartsDisconnected` events, as shown in Listing 33-21.

Listing 33-21: The OnInit method

```
protected override void OnInit(EventArgs e)
{
    base.OnInit(e);
    this.WebPartManager.WebPartsDisconnected +=
                new WebPartConnectionsEventHandler(WebPartsDisconnectedCallback);
    this.WebPartManager.WebPartsConnected +=
                new WebPartConnectionsEventHandler(WebPartsConnectedCallback);
}
```

As the following code fragment illustrates, the `WebPartsConnectedCallback` and `WebParts DisconnectedCallback` methods set the value of the `RenderAddToMyFavoriteLink` property to true and false, respectively:

```
void WebPartsConnectedCallback(object sender, WebPartConnectionsEventArgs e)
{
    if (e.Provider.Equals(this))
        renderAddToMyFavoriteLink = true;
}

void WebPartsDisconnectedCallback(object sender, WebPartConnectionsEventArgs e)
{
    if (e.Provider.Equals(this))
        renderAddToMyFavoriteLink = false;
}
```

Programmatic Connections

The previous sections showed you two different ways to connect `WebPart` controls: static and dynamic connections. Static connections are statically declared on an ASP.NET page, whereas dynamic connections are created at runtime. The previous section showed you how to enable end users to dynamically connect and disconnect `WebPart` controls at runtime. Another dynamic approach is the programmatic approach, where you connect and disconnect `WebPart` controls directly from your code.

Here's a run through the `WebPartManager` control's methods that enable you to programmatically connect or disconnect `WebPart` controls.

```
public virtual ProviderConnectionPointCollection
        GetProviderConnectionPoints(WebPart webPart);
```

The `GetProviderConnectionPoints` method takes a provider `WebPart` control such as `RssReaderWeb Part6` as its argument and creates and returns all the `ProviderConnectionPoints` associated with the `WebPart` control. This method performs two tasks to accomplish this. First, it searches the specified provider `WebPart` control's methods for those methods that meet all of the following requirements because all data provider methods must satisfy all these requirements:

❑   They are marked with the `ConnectionProviderAttribute` metadata attribute

❑   They take no arguments

❑   They return a value

❑   They are public

For example, the `GetSelectedItem` method of the `RssReaderWebPart6` control meets all of these requirements. Second, it creates an instance of the `ProviderConnectionPoint` to represent each method that meets the requirements:

```
public virtual ConsumerConnectionPointCollection
        GetConsumerConnectionPoints(WebPart webPart)
```

The `GetConsumerConnectionPoints` method takes a consumer `WebPart` control such as `Favorite ItemsWebPart` as its argument and creates and returns all the `ConsumerConnectionPoints` associated with the `WebPart` control. This method performs two tasks to accomplish this. First, it searches the specified consumer `WebPart` control's methods for those methods that meet all of the following requirements because all data consumer methods must satisfy all these requirements:

❑   They are marked with the `ConnectionConsumerAttribute` metadata attribute

❑   They take a single argument

❑   They return no value

❑   They are public

For example, the `AddItemToFavoriteItems` method of `FavoriteItemsWebPart` control meets all of the requirements. Second, it creates an instance of the `ConsumerConnectionPoint` to represent each method that meets the requirements:

```
public virtual WebPartConnection
    ConnectWebParts(WebPart provider, ProviderConnectionPoint
                    providerConnectionPoint, WebPart consumer,
                    ConsumerConnectionPoint consumerConnectionPoint);
```

The `ConnectWebParts` method takes references to the following:

❑   The data provider `WebPart` control

❑   The provider connection point

❑   The data consumer `WebPart` control

❑   The consumer connection point

The method creates and returns the `WebPartConnection` object that represents the connection between the specified connection points of the specified data provider and consumer `WebPart` controls:

```
public virtual void DisconnectWebParts(WebPartConnection connection);
```

The `DisconnectWebParts` method takes the `WebPartConnection` object that represents the connection and disconnects the associated data provider and consumer `WebPart` controls:

```
public WebPartConnectionCollection Connections {get; }
```

The `Connections` property returns all the available static and dynamic connections.

This section implements a new version of `RssReaderWebPart6` named `RssReaderWebPart7` to show you how to use the preceding methods and properties of the `WebPartManager` control to programmatically connect or disconnect `WebPart` controls. `RssReaderWebPart7` will add a new verb to its verbs menu to allow end users to connect or disconnect `RssReaderWebPart7` and `FavoriteItemsWebPart` with a single click as opposed to going through the typical ASP.NET Web Parts mechanism.

First you need to develop the custom verb that `RssReaderWebPart7` adds to its verbs menu. This custom verb is named `ProgrammaticConnectVerb`, and like all verbs, it derives from the `WebPartVerb` base class and overrides its `Description` and `Text` properties to assign default values to these properties, as shown in Listing 33-22.

Listing 33-22: The ProgrammaticConnectVerb custom verb

```
public class ProgrammaticConnectVerb : WebPartVerb
{
  public ProgrammaticConnectVerb(string id, WebPartEventHandler serverHandler)
    : base(id, serverHandler) { }

  public override string Description
  {
    get { return string.IsNullOrEmpty(base.Description) ?
              "This verb enables connection" : base.Description;}
    set { base.Description = value; }
  }

  public override string Text
```

```
      {
        get { return string.IsNullOrEmpty(base.Text) ?
                                "Enable Connection" : base.Text;}
        set {base.Text = value;}
      }
    }
```

Now back to the implementation of the RssReaderWebPart7 control. This section discusses only the programmatic connection-related properties and methods of RssReaderWebPart7 because the implementation of the rest of the methods and properties of this control is the same as RssReaderWebPart6 control, which was discussed in previous sections. The RssReaderWebPart7 control first defines a new Boolean property named IsConnected that specifies whether RssReaderWebPart7 is currently connected. As the following code illustrates, this property searches through the connections in the Connection collection of WebPartManager for a connection whose data provider is the RssReaderWebPart7 control:

```
private bool IsConnected
{
  get
  {
    foreach (WebPartConnection connection in this.WebPartManager.Connections)
    {
      if (connection.Provider.Equals(this))
        return true;
    }
    return false;
  }
}
```

RssReaderWebPart7 also exposes a property named ConsumerID that the page developer must set to the ID property value of the data consumer WebPart control. Notice that this property is marked with the [Personalizable(true)] attribute so its value gets saved into the underlying personalization data store:

```
private string consumerID;
[Personalizable(true)]
public string ConsumerID
{
  get { return consumerID; }
  set { consumerID = value; }
}
```

As shown in Listing 33-9, the constructor of the ProviderConnectionPoint class takes a string argument named id, which is assigned to the ProviderConnectionPointID property of the class. When RssReaderWebPart7 is marking the GetSelectedItem method with the ConnectionProviderAttribute metadata attribute, it passes the ItemProvider string as an argument to this attribute as illustrated in the following code fragment. When WebPartManager is creating the ProviderConnectionPoint object that represents the GetSelectedItem method, it passes the ItemProvider string as the id argument to the constructor of the ProviderConnectionPoint class. As you'll see shortly, this id will be used to identify the ProviderConnectionPoint that represents the GetSelectedItem method.

```
[ConnectionProvider("Item","ItemProvider")]
public IItem ProvideSelectedItem()
{
  return this;
}
```

RssReaderWebPart7 overrides the Verbs collection to add the ProgrammaticConnectVerb to the collection. Notice that RssReaderWebPart7 registers a method named ProgrammaticConnectVerbCallback as the callback for the ProgrammaticConncectVerb. Also notice that the Verbs property assigns the value of the IsConnected property to the Checked property of the ProgrammaticConnectVerb verb.

Like all verbs, this verb inherits the Checked property from the WebPartVerb base class. When this property is set to true, a check mark is displayed next to the verb to give visual cues to the end users. In this case, the ProgrammaticConnectVerb is marked as checked when RssReaderWebPart7 is connected:

```
public override WebPartVerbCollection Verbs
{
  get
  {
    List<WebPartVerb> verbList = new List<WebPartVerb>();
    ProgrammaticConnectVerb pverb =
        new ProgrammaticConnectVerb("MyConnect",
                          new WebPartEventHandler(ProgrammaticConnectVerbCallback));
    pverb.Checked = IsConnected;
    verbList.Add(pverb);

    if (rssUrls == null || rssUrls.Count < 1)
      return new WebPartVerbCollection(verbList);

    UrlWebPartVerb verb;

    for (int i = 0; i < rssUrls.Count; i++)
    {
      verb = new UrlWebPartVerb(rssTexts[i].ToString(),
                        new WebPartEventHandler(VerbCallback));
      verb.Text = rssTexts[i].ToString();
      verb.Description = rssDescriptions[i].ToString();
      verb.NavigateUrl = rssUrls[i].ToString();
      verbList.Add(verb);
    }
    return new WebPartVerbCollection(verbList);
  }
}
```

RssReaderWebPart7 implements the callback for the new verb as shown in Listing 33-23. As this code listing illustrates, this callback first checks whether RssReaderWebPart7 control is currently connected. If not, it connects the control programmatically. First it calls the GetProviderConnectionPoints method of the WebPartManager control to return all the ProviderConnectionPoints associated with the RssReader WebPart7 control. Recall that this method searches through RssReaderWebPart7 for methods marked with the ConnectionProviderAttribute metadata attribute and creates a ProviderConnectionPoint object to represent each method. Because the GetSelectedItem method of the RssReaderWebPart7 control is the only method of the control marked with this attribute, GetProviderConnectionPoints will create a single ProviderConnectionPoint to represent this method:

```
ProviderConnectionPointCollection points1 =
                        WebPartManager.GetProviderConnectionPoints(this);
```

The callback then uses the `ItemProvider` string to index into the `ProviderConnectionPoint Collection` collection that `GetProviderConnectionPoints` returns to access the `ProviderConnection Point` that represents the `GetSelectedItem` method. As discussed previously, the `ItemProvider` string is the `ProviderConnectionPointID` of the `ProviderConnectionPoint` that represents the `GetSelectedItem` method:

```
ProviderConnectionPoint point1 = points1["ItemProvider"];
```

Next, the callback uses the value of the `ConsumerID` property to index into the `WebParts` collection of the `WebPartManager` to access the consumer `WebPart` control, `FavoriteItemsWebPart2`. `Favorite ItemsWebPart2` is a new version of `FavoriteItemsWebPart`. The implementation of these two versions is the same except for one difference, as discussed shortly.

```
WebPart consumer = WebPartManager.WebParts[ConsumerID];
```

Then it calls the `GetConsumerConnectionPoints` method of the `WebPartManager` to return all the `ConsumerConnectionPoints` associated with the consumer `WebPart` control, `FavoriteItems WebPart2`. Recall that this method searches through the methods of the `FavoriteItemsWebPart2` control for methods marked with `ConnectionConsumerAttribute` metadata attribute and creates a `Consumer ConnectionPoint` object to represent each method. Because the `AddItemToFavoriteItems` method of `FavoriteItemsWebPart2` control is the only method of the control marked with this attribute, `Get ConsumerConnectionPoints` will create and return a single `ConsumerConnectionPoint` to represent this method:

```
ConsumerConnectionPointCollection points2 =
                        WebPartManager.GetConsumerConnectionPoints(consumer);
```

The callback next uses the `ItemConsumer` string to index into the `ConsumerConnectionPointCollection` collection that `GetConsumerConnectionPoints` returns to access the `ConsumerConnectionPoint` that represents the `AddItemToFavoriteItems` method. This is possible because when the `FavoriteItems WebPart2` control is marking the `AddItemToFavoriteItems` method with the `ConnectionConsumer Attribute` metadata attribute, it passes the `ItemConsumer` string as an argument to this attribute:

```
private IItem item;

[ConnectionConsumer("Item","ItemConsumer")]
public void ConsumeSelectedItem(IItem item)
{
    this.item = item;
}
```

Then the callback calls the `ConnectWebParts` method of the `WebPartManager` and passes the references to the provider control (`RssReaderWebPart7`), the `ProviderConnectionPoint` that represents the `GetSelectedItem` method, the consumer control (`FavoriteItemsWebPart2`), and the `Consumer ConnectionPoint` that represents the `AddItemsToFavoriteItems` method into it to connect the `Rss ReaderWebPart7` and `FavoriteItemsWebPart2` WebPart controls:

```
WebPartConnection connection =
                WebPartManager.ConnectWebParts(this, point1, consumer, point2);
```

Listing 33-23: The ProgrammaticConnectVerbCallback method

```
protected virtual void
ProgrammaticConnectVerbCallback(object sender, WebPartEventArgs e)
{
  WebPartVerb pverb = sender as WebPartVerb;
  if (!IsConnected)
  {
    ProviderConnectionPointCollection points1 =
                             WebPartManager.GetProviderConnectionPoints(this);
    ProviderConnectionPoint point1 = points1["ItemProvider"];
    WebPart consumer = WebPartManager.WebParts[ConsumerID];
    ConsumerConnectionPointCollection points2 =
                             WebPartManager.GetConsumerConnectionPoints(consumer);
    ConsumerConnectionPoint point2 = points2["ItemConsumer"];

    WebPartConnection connection =
                WebPartManager.ConnectWebParts(this, point1, consumer, point2);
  }

  else
  {
    foreach (WebPartConnection connection in this.WebPartManager.Connections)
    {
      if (connection.Provider.Equals(this))
      {
        this.WebPartManager.DisconnectWebParts(connection);
        break;
      }
    }
  }
}
```

As Listing 33-23 illustrates, if the RssReaderWebPart7 control is currently connected, that is, if IsConnected returns true, the ProgrammaticConnectVerbCallback will disconnect the control. The WebPartManager maintains the list of all available WebPartConnection connections in a collection named Connections. The ProgrammaticConnectVerbCallback method searches through these WebPartConnection connections for a WebPartConnection connection whose provider control is RssReaderWebPart7. It then calls the DisconnectWebParts method of the WebPartManager to disconnect the WebPartConnection connection:

```
this.WebPartManager.DisconnectWebParts(connection);
```

Listing 33-24 contains a Web page that uses RssReaderWebPart7 and FavoriteItemsWebPart2 controls. As the boldface portions of the code listing show, the page assigns the value of the ID property of the consumer control, FavoriteItemsWebPart2 to the ConsumerID property of the provider control, RssReaderWebPart7. As Figure 33-5 shows, the verbs menu of RssReaderWebPart7 contains a new verb that allows end users to connect or disconnect RssReaderWebPart7 and FavoriteItemsWeb Part2 without having to go through the normal ASP.NET connection procedure.

Listing 33-24: A Web page that uses RssReaderWebPart7 and FavoriteItemsWebPart2

```
<%@ Page Language="C#" %>

<%@ Register TagPrefix="custom" Namespace="CustomComponents" %>
<script runat="server">
 . . .
</script>

<html xmlns="http://www.w3.org/1999/xhtml">
<body>
  <form id="form1" runat="server">
    <asp:WebPartManager runat="server" ID="mgr2">
    </asp:WebPartManager>
    <table cellspacing="10">
      <tr>
        <td colspan="2" align="left">
         . . .
        </td>
      </tr>
      <tr>
        <td valign="top">
          <asp:WebPartZone runat="server" ID="zone1" . . .>
           . . .
            <ZoneTemplate>
             <custom:RssReaderWebPart7 ConsumerID="consumer1" Title="Rss Reader"
             ExportMode="All" runat="server" ID="provider1"
             RssDataSourceID="MySource" RssDescriptionField="RssDescription"
             RssTextField="RssText" RssUrlField="RssUrl"
             CatalogIconImageUrl="news.gif" TitleIconImageUrl="news.gif">
               <EditorHeaderStyle BackColor="Tan" Font-Bold="True" />
               <EditorAlternatingItemStyle BackColor="PaleGoldenrod" />
               <EditorStyle BackColor="LightGoldenrodYellow"
               BorderColor="Tan" BorderWidth="1px" CellPadding="2"
               ForeColor="Black" GridLines="None" />
             </custom:RssReaderWebPart7>
            </ZoneTemplate>
          </asp:WebPartZone>
        </td>
        <td valign="top">
          <asp:WebPartZone runat="server" ID="WebPartZone1" . . . >
           . . .
            <ZoneTemplate>
              <custom:FavoriteItemsWebPart2 runat="server" ID="consumer1" />
            </ZoneTemplate>
          </asp:WebPartZone>
        </td>
      </tr>
      <tr>
        <td valign="top" colspan="2" style="width: 100%">
          <asp:EditorZone Width="100%" runat="server" . . .>
           . . .
          </asp:EditorZone>
```

(continued)

Listing 33-24: *(continued)*

```
        </td>
        <td>
          <asp:ConnectionsZone runat="server" ID="con" . . .>
            . . .
          </asp:ConnectionsZone>
        </td>
      </tr>
    </table>
    <asp:SqlDataSource runat="server" ID="MySource"
    ConnectionString="<%$ ConnectionStrings:MySqlConnectionString %>"
    SelectCommand="Select * From Rss" />
  </form>
</body>
</html>
```

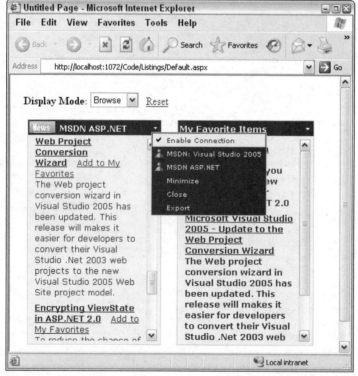

Figure 33-5

Developing Data-Bound WebPart Controls

As discussed in Chapter 17, the ASP.NET tabular data-bound control model consists of three main base classes: `BaseDataBoundControl`, `DataBoundControl`, and `CompositeDataBoundControl`. Here's a quick review of what these base classes provide.

`BaseDataBoundControl` derives from the `WebControl` base class and extends its functionality to provide data-bound controls with the infrastructure that allows them to automate all three data-binding tasks without a single line of code from page developers. Recall from Chapter 17 that the three data-binding tasks are as follows:

❑ Retrieving data records from the underlying data store.

❑ Iterating through the retrieved data records and generating the appropriate HTML markup text to display each enumerated data record.

❑ Taking these two actions in response to events that requires a data-bound control to retrieve fresh data and update its display. These events include the load, page, sort, delete, update, and insert events.

`DataBoundControl` derives from `BaseDataBoundControl` and extends its functionality to provide data-bound controls with the infrastructure that allows them to retrieve data from any type of data source. In other words, it allows you to develop data-store agnostic data-bound controls that automate all three data-binding tasks.

`CompositeDataBoundControl` derives from `DataBoundControl` and extends its functionality to provide you with the infrastructure that allows you to develop data-store agnostic data-bound controls with minimal effort.

Chapter 17 implemented replicas of the main methods, properties, and events of the `BaseDataBoundControl`, `DataBoundControl`, and `CompositeDataBoundControl` base classes. Because these replicas are fully functional, you could derive your custom data-bound controls from these replica base classes instead of the ASP.NET versions.

As discussed in Chapter 17, the replica `BaseDataBoundControl`, `DataBoundControl`, and `CompositeDataBoundControl` base classes served the following two important purposes:

❑ They helped you understand these classes and the ASP.NET tabular data-bound control model from the inside out. Such a solid understanding put you in a much better position to extend the functionality of these base classes to implement your own custom data-bound controls.

❑ They allowed you to learn these base classes by actually implementing them. The best way to learn a component is to implement it yourself.

These two benefits were thoroughly discussed in Chapter 17. Implementing these replica `BaseDataBoundControl`, `DataBoundControl`, and `CompositeDataBoundControl` base classes serves a third purpose, which wasn't discussed in Chapter 17. To help you understand the third purpose, consider the following question: From which base class would you derive to implement a data-store agnostic custom data-bound control that automates all three data-binding tasks?

After all the discussions presented in chapters such as Chapter 17, the answer should be pretty clear; you should derive from the `CompositeDataBoundControl` base class. Now here is the next question for you: From which base class would you derive to implement a data-store agnostic custom data-bound `WebPart` control that automates all three data-binding tasks?

The answer to this question isn't as clear as the answer to the previous question because the ASP.NET 2.0 Web Parts Framework doesn't come with base classes similar to the `BaseDataBoundControl`, `DataBoundControl`, and `CompositeDataBoundControl` base classes to inherit from.

What you need is a set of three base classes that would do for data-bound `WebPart` controls exactly what the `BaseDataBoundControl`, `DataBoundControl`, and `CompositeDataBoundControl` do for regular data-bound controls. I'll call these three new base classes `BaseDataBoundWebPart`, `Data BoundWebPart`, and `CompositeDataBoundWebPart`. You can think of these three classes together as what I'll call the ASP.NET data-bound Web Parts model. This model does for data-bound `WebPart` controls exactly what the ASP.NET data-bound control does for regular data-bound controls.

The implementation of these three new base classes is exactly the same as the implementations of the replica `BaseDataBoundControl`, `DataBoundControl`, and `CompositeDataBoundControl` base classes presented in Chapter 17. The one and only difference is that the `BaseDataBoundControl` derives from `WebControl` and `BaseDataBoundWebPart` derives from the `WebPart` base class.

Therefore, you only have to make the following minor changes to the source code of the replica `Base DataBoundControl`, `DataBoundControl`, and `CompositeDataBoundControl` base classes presented in Chapter 17:

❑ Change the names of the base classes from `BaseDataBoundControl`, `DataBoundControl`, and `CompositeDataBoundControl` to `BaseDataBoundWebPart`, `DataBoundWebPart`, and `CompositeDataBoundWebPart`, respectively.

❑ Replace the base class of `BaseDataBoundControl` (`WebControl`) with `WebPart`.

Now you understand the third benefit you get out of implementing the replica `BaseDataBound Control`, `DataBoundControl`, and `CompositeDataBoundControl` base classes in Chapter 17.

BaseDataBoundWebPart

Listing 33-25 shows the brand new `BaseDataBoundWebPart` base class. The highlighted portion of this code listing is the only difference between the implementation of `BaseDataBoundWebPart` and the implementation of the replica `BaseDataBoundControl` presented in Chapter 17.

Listing 33-25: BaseDataBoundWebPart base class

```
public abstract class BaseDataBoundWebPart : WebPart
{
  public virtual string DataSourceID {get; set;}
  protected override object SaveControlState();
  protected override void LoadControlState(object savedState);
  protected abstract void ValidateDataSource(object dataSource);

  private object myDataSource;
  public virtual object DataSource
  {
    get {return myDataSource;}
    set
    {
      ValidateDataSource(value);
      myDataSource = value;
    }
  }
  protected bool IsBoundUsingDataSourceID
  {
```

```
    get {return (DataSourceID != null && DataSourceID.Length > 0);}
  }

  private bool requiresDataBinding;
  protected bool RequiresDataBinding
  {
    get {return requiresDataBinding;}
    set
    {
      requiresDataBinding = value;
      EnsureDataBound();
    }
  }

  protected void EnsureDataBound()
  {
    if (requiresDataBinding)
      DataBind();

    requiresDataBinding = false;
  }

  public override void DataBind()
  {
    PerformSelect();
    base.DataBind();
  }

  protected override void OnInit(EventArgs e)
  {
    requiresDataBinding = false;
    Page.RegisterRequiresControlState(this);
    base.OnInit(e);
  }

  protected override void OnPreRender(EventArgs e)
  {
    EnsureDataBound();
    base.OnPreRender(e);
  }
}
```

DataBoundWebPart

Listing 33-26 contains the code for the DataBoundWebPart control. The highlighted portion of this code listing is the only difference between the implementation of DataBoundWebPart and the implementation of the replica DataBoundControl presented in Chapter 17.

Listing 33-26: The DataBoundWebPart base class

```
public abstract class DataBoundWebPart : BaseDataBoundWebPart
{
  protected override void ValidateDataSource(object dataSource);
```

(continued)

Listing 33-26: *(continued)*

```
protected IEnumerable GetEnumerableDataSource();
public virtual string DataMember {get; set;}
protected override object SaveControlState();
protected override void LoadControlState(object savedState);
protected IDataSource GetDataSource()
{
  return (IDataSource)Page.FindControl(DataSourceID);
}

protected DataSourceView GetData()
{
  IDataSource ds = GetDataSource();
  DataSourceView dv = ds.GetView("DefaultView");
  return dv;
}

protected virtual void DataSourceControlChangedCallback(object sender,
                                                        EventArgs e)
{
  if (RequiresDataBinding == false)
    RequiresDataBinding = true;
}

void RetrieveData()
{
  DataSourceView dv = GetData();
  SelectArguments = CreateDataSourceSelectArguments();
  dv.Select(SelectArguments,
                    new DataSourceViewSelectCallback(PerformDataBinding));
}

protected override void PerformSelect()
{
  if (IsBoundUsingDataSourceID && DataSource != null)
    throw new Exception("Both DataSourceID and DataSource properties cannot be
                        set at the same time!");

  OnDataBinding(EventArgs.Empty);
  if (IsBoundUsingDataSourceID)
    RetrieveData();
  else
    PerformDataBinding(GetEnumerableDataSource());
}

protected DataSourceSelectArguments SelectArguments;

protected virtual DataSourceSelectArguments CreateDataSourceSelectArguments()
{
  return new DataSourceSelectArguments();
}

protected virtual void OnDataSourceViewChanged(Object sender, EventArgs e)
{
```

```
        RequiresDataBinding = true;
    }

    protected abstract void PerformDataBinding(IEnumerable data);
    protected override void OnLoad(EventArgs e);
    protected override void OnInit(EventArgs e);
}
```

CompositeDataBoundWebPart

Finally, Listing 33-27 contains the code for the CompositeDataBoundWebPart control. The highlighted portion of this code listing is the only difference between the implementation of CompositeDataBoundWebPart and the implementation of the replica CompositeDataBoundControl presented in Chapter 17.

Listing 33-27: The CompositeDataBoundWebPart base class

```
public abstract class CompositeDataBoundWebPart : DataBoundWebPart
{
    private IEnumerable dataSource;
    protected abstract int CreateChildControls(IEnumerable dataSource,
                                               bool useDataSource);

    public override ControlCollection Controls
    {
      get
      {
        EnsureChildControls();
        return base.Controls;
      }
    }

    protected override void PerformDataBinding(IEnumerable data)
    {
      dataSource = data;
      DataBind(false);
    }

    protected override void DataBind(bool raiseOnDataBinding)
    {
      if (raiseOnDataBinding)
        base.OnDataBinding(System.EventArgs.Empty);

      Controls.Clear();
      ViewState["RowCount"] = CreateChildControls(dataSource, true);
      ChildControlsCreated = true;
    }

    protected override void CreateChildControls()
    {
      Controls.Clear();

      if (ViewState["RowCount"] != null)
```

(continued)

Listing 33-27: *(continued)*

```
        ViewState["RowCount"] =
                CreateChildControls(new object[(int)ViewState["RowCount"]], false);
    }
}
```

GridViewWebPart

Chapter 19 implemented a fully functional replica of the `GridView` control built into ASP.NET 2.0. Like the data-bound controls, the implementation in that chapter gave you a better understanding of the control, but it also provided a base to enable you to apply what you've learned to Web Parts.

You can easily turn this replica `GridView` into a new data-bound `WebPart` control named `GridView WebPart`. All you need is a one-line change — replace the base class of the replica `GridView` (`Composite DataBoundControl`) with `CompositeDataBoundWebPart`, as shown in Listing 33-28. The rest of the code for the replica `GridView` stays intact.

Listing 33-28: The GridViewWebPart control

```
public class GridViewWebPart : CompositeDataBoundWebPart, INamingContainer
{
    // The implementation of the methods, properties, and events of the
    // GridViewWebPart is the same as GridView control
}
```

Listing 33-29 contains a Web page that uses the `GridViewWebPart` control. Figure 33-6 show what end users see on their browsers when they access this page. Notice that `GridViewWebPart` is a data-store agnostic data-bound `WebPart` control that automates all three data-binding tasks. It's data-store agnostic because you can replace the `<asp:ObjectDataSource>` control used in Listing 33-29 with `<asp:XmlDataSource>` to switch from SQL Server 2005 to an XML file without breaking `GridViewWebPart`.

Because it automates all three data-binding tasks, `GridViewWebPart` provides automatic data operation features such as paging, sorting, and editing without any code from page developers. Notice that Listing 33-29 doesn't use a single line of C# code. Everything is declarative.

Listing 33-29: A Web page that uses the GridViewWebPart control

```
<%@ Page Language="C#" AutoEventWireup="true" CodeFile="Default.aspx.cs"
    Inherits="_Default" %>
<%@ Register TagPrefix="custom" Namespace="CustomComponents" %>
<html xmlns="http://www.w3.org/1999/xhtml">
<body>
    <form id="form1" runat="server">
        <asp:ObjectDataSource runat="server" ID="MySource"
        SortParameterName="SortExpression"
        TypeName="Books" SelectMethod="GetOnePageOfData"
        SelectCountMethod="GetTotalCount" UpdateMethod="UpdateBook" />

        <asp:WebPartManager runat="server" ID="mgr" />
```

```
    <asp:WebPartZone runat="server" ID="zone" BorderColor="#CCCCCC"
    Font-Names="Verdana" Padding="6">
      <ZoneTemplate>
        <custom:GridViewWebPart runat="server" ID="gv"
        Title="GridView" CellPadding="2"
        AllowSorting="true" DataSourceID="MySource" BorderColor="Tan"
        AllowPaging="true" AutoGenerateColumns="false" DataKeyNames="BookID"
        BackColor="LightGoldenrodYellow" PageSize="3" BorderWidth="1px"
        ForeColor="Black" GridLines="None" AutoGenerateEditButton="true" >
          <HeaderStyle BackColor="Tan" Font-Bold="True" />
          <AlternatingRowStyle BackColor="PaleGoldenrod" />
          <PagerSettings Mode="NumericFirstLast" PageButtonCount="2" />
          <Columns>
            <asp:BoundField DataField="Title" HeaderText="Title"
            SortExpression="Title" />
            <asp:BoundField DataField="Author" HeaderText="Author"
            SortExpression="Author" />
            <asp:BoundField DataField="Publisher" HeaderText="Publisher"
            SortExpression="Publisher" />
            <asp:BoundField DataField="Price" HeaderText="Price"
            SortExpression="Price" />
          </Columns>
        </custom:GridViewWebPart>
      </ZoneTemplate>
      . . .
    </asp:WebPartZone>
  </form>
</body>
</html>
```

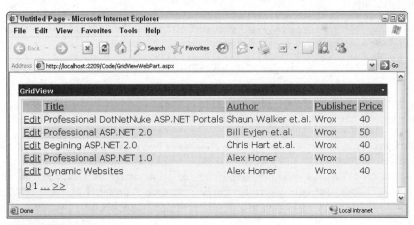

Figure 33-6

With `BaseDataBoundWebPart`, `DataBoundWebPart`, `CompositeDataBoundWebPart`, and `GridView` `WebPart` at your disposal, you can implement many other interesting custom `WebPart` controls. For example, you can use the `GridViewWebPart` control's verbs menu and its content to form a master/detail control where the verbs menu and the control's content act as master and detail components, as discussed in the following section.

MasterDetailGridViewWebPart

This section implements a custom data-bound `WebPart` control named `MasterDetailGridView WebPart` that derives from `GridViewWebPart` as shown in Listing 33-30.

Listing 33-30: MasterDetailGridViewWebPart control

```
public class MasterDetailGridViewWebPart : GridViewWebPart
{
  public virtual string MasterDataSourceID {get; set;}
  public virtual string MasterDataValueField {get; set;}
  public virtual string MasterDataTextField {get; set;}
  public virtual string MasterDataDescriptionField {get; set;}
  public virtual string MasterDataDescription {get; set;}
  public virtual string DetailDataSourceID {get; set;}
  public override string DataSourceID {get; set;}
  public override WebPartVerbCollection Verbs {get;}
  void DataSelectCallback(IEnumerable data);
  private void VerbCallback(object sender, WebPartEventArgs e);
}
```

`MasterDetailGridViewWebPart` exposes the following properties:

❑   `MasterDataSourceID`: Specifies the value of the ID property of the tabular data source control that is used to populate the verbs menu.

❑   `MasterDataValueField`: Specifies the name of the primary key data field.

❑   `MasterDataTextField`: Specifies the name of the data field whose values will be shown in the verbs menu.

❑   `MasterDataDescriptionField`: Specifies the name of the data field whose values will be shown in a tooltip.

❑   `MasterDataDescription`: Specifies the string that will be shown in a tooltip if `MasterData DescriptionField` isn't set.

❑   `DetailDataSourceID`: Specifies the value of the `ID` property of the tabular data source control that is used to populate the content area of the `WebPart` control.

Because the `MasterDetailGridViewWebPart` consists of two major parts, master and detail, it makes more sense to have a property named `DetailDataSourceID` to contain the `ID` property value of the tabular data source control used to populate the content or detail area of the `WebPart` control. That's why `MasterDetailGridViewWebPart` overrides the `DataSourceID` property of the `GridView` control and defines the `DetailDataSourceID` property as shown in the following code fragment:

```
public override string DataSourceID
{
  get {return base.DataSourceID;}
  set {throw new NotSupportedException();}
}

public virtual string DetailDataSourceID
```

```
  {
    get { return base.DataSourceID; }
    set { base.DataSourceID = value; }
  }
```

Overriding Verbs

`MasterDetailGridViewWebPart` overrides the `Verbs` property as illustrated in Listing 33-31. The `Verbs` property first calls the `FindControl` method of the containing page and passes `MasterData SourceID` into it. Recall that `MasterDataSourceID` contains the `ID` of the tabular data source control that retrieves the data that will be used to populate the verbs menu:

```
Control control = Page.FindControl(MasterDataSourceID);
```

`Verbs` raises an exception if the specified data source control isn't tabular because the current implementation of `MasterDetailGridViewWebPart` only supports tabular data source controls. Keep in mind this doesn't mean that `MasterDetailGridView` can't talk to all types of data stores because the ASP.NET tabular data source control model allows you to write a custom tabular data source control for any type of data store, as discussed in Chapters 12, 13, and 14.

```
IDataSource ds = control as IDataSource;
if (ds == null)
  throw new Exception("Data source must be a tabular data source control");
```

The property then calls the `GetView` method of the tabular data source control to access its default view:

```
DataSourceView dv = ds.GetView(string.Empty);
```

Next, it calls the `Select` method of the default view to retrieve the data from the underlying data store:

```
dv.Select(DataSourceSelectArguments.Empty,
                      new DataSourceViewSelectCallback(DataSelectCallback));
```

Because `Select` is an asynchronous operation, the `Verbs` property registers a method named `Data SelectCallback` as the callback. The `Select` method retrieves the data, calls the `DataSelectCallback` method, and passes an `IEnumerable` object that contains the retrieved data, as discussed in Chapters 12, 13, and 14.

Listing 33-31: The Verbs property

```
List<WebPartVerb> verbList;
public override WebPartVerbCollection Verbs
{
  get
  {
    Control control = Page.FindControl(MasterDataSourceID);
    if (control == null)
      return new WebPartVerbCollection(verbList);
    IDataSource ds = control as IDataSource;
    if (ds == null)
      throw new Exception("Data source must be a tabular data source control");
```

(continued)

Listing 33-31: *(continued)*

```
        DataSourceView dv = ds.GetView(string.Empty);
        dv.Select(DataSourceSelectArguments.Empty,
                          new DataSourceViewSelectCallback(DataSelectCallback));
        return new WebPartVerbCollection(verbList);
    }
}
```

DataSelectCallback

Listing 33-32 contains the code for `DataSelectCallback` method. The main responsibility of this method is to iterate through the records that the `IEnumerable` object contains and create a `WebPart` `Verb` for each record. The method first calls the `GetEnumerator` method of the `IEnumerable` object to access the enumerator object that allows the method to iterate through the records in generic fashion without knowing their real types:

```
    IEnumerator iter = data.GetEnumerator();
```

The method then iterates through the records that `IEnumerable` contains. For each enumerated record, the method calls the `Eval` method of the `DataBinder` class to access the value of the data field whose name is given by `MasterDataValueField` property:

```
    string value = (string)DataBinder.Eval(iter.Current,MasterDataValueField);
```

The method next instantiates a `WebPartVerb`, where it assigns the value it just retrieved to the `ID` property of the verb:

```
    verb = new WebPartVerb(value, new WebPartEventHandler(VerbCallback));
```

Notice that `DataSelectCallback` registers a method named `VerbCallback` as the server-side callback for the newly created verb. This method is automatically called when the user selects the verb from the verbs menu and consequently posts the page back to the server.

The method then calls the `Eval` method once more to access the value of the data field whose name is given by `MasterDataTextField` property:

```
        string text = (string)DataBinder.Eval(iter.Current,MasterDataTextField);
```

It assigns the value it just retrieved to the `Text` property of the newly created verb. This is the text that represents the verb in the verbs menu:

```
        verb.Text = text;
```

Next, the method calls the `Eval` method once more to access the value of the data field whose name is given by `MasterDataDescriptionField` property if this property is set. Otherwise, it simply uses the text that the `MasterDataDescription` property contains:

```
    string description = MasterDataDescription;
        if (!string.IsNullOrEmpty(MasterDataDescriptionField))
```

```
description = (string)DataBinder.Eval(iter.Current,
                                      MasterDataDescriptionField);
```

It then assigns the value it just retrieved to the description property of the newly created verb. This is the text that the tooltip displays when the user moves the mouse pointer over the verb:

```
verbList.Add(verb);
```

Listing 33-32: The DataSelectCallback method

```
void DataSelectCallback(IEnumerable data)
{
  WebPartVerb verb;
  verbList = new List<WebPartVerb>();
  IEnumerator iter = data.GetEnumerator();
  while (iter.MoveNext())
  {
    string value = (string)DataBinder.Eval(iter.Current,MasterDataValueField);
    string text = (string)DataBinder.Eval(iter.Current,MasterDataTextField);
    verb = new WebPartVerb(value, new WebPartEventHandler(VerbCallback));
    verb.Text = text;
    string description = MasterDataDescription;
    if (!string.IsNullOrEmpty(MasterDataDescriptionField))
      description = (string)DataBinder.Eval(iter.Current,
                                            MasterDataDescriptionField);
    verb.Description = description;
    verbList.Add(verb);
  }
}
```

VerbCallback

Listing 33-33 illustrates the implementation of VerbCallback method. This method simply stores the value of the ID property of the verb that raised the event in the Session object. As you'll see in Listing 33-34, the underlying tabular data source uses an <asp:SessionParameter> to retrieve this value from the Session object.

Listing 33-33: The VerbCallback method

```
private void VerbCallback(object sender, WebPartEventArgs e)
{
  WebPartVerb verb = sender as WebPartVerb;
  Page.Session["SelectedMasterItem"] = verb.ID;
}
```

Using the MasterDetailGridView WebPart Control

Listing 33-34 contains a Web page that uses MasterDetailGridView WebPart control. Figure 33-7 shows what end users see on their browsers when they access this page. Notice that the Verbs menu includes a verb for each author. When the user selects an author from the verbs menu, the Master DetailGridView WebPart automatically retrieves and displays the list of books written by the selected author in its detail or content area.

Listing 33-34: A Web page that uses MasterDetailGridViewWebPart control

```
<%@ Page Language="C#" %>
<%@ Register TagPrefix="custom" Namespace="CustomComponents" %>
<html xmlns="http://www.w3.org/1999/xhtml">
<body>
  <form id="form1" runat="server">
    <asp:WebPartManager runat="server" ID="mgr" />
    <asp:WebPartZone runat="server" ID="zone" BorderColor="#CCCCCC" . . .>
      <ZoneTemplate>
        <custom:MasterDetailGridViewWebPart DetailDataSourceID="MySource"
        runat="server" ID="MasterDetailGridViewWebPart1" Title="GridView"
        AllowSorting="true" MasterDataSourceID="MasterSource"
        MasterDataDescription="Choose a category" MasterDataTextField="Author"
        MasterDataValueField="Author" AllowPaging="true"
        AutoGenerateColumns="false" DataKeyNames="BookID"
        BackColor="LightGoldenrodYellow" BorderColor="Tan" BorderWidth="1px"
        CellPadding="2" ForeColor="Black" GridLines="None"
        AutoGenerateEditButton="true" PageSize="3">
          <HeaderStyle BackColor="Tan" Font-Bold="True" />
          <AlternatingRowStyle BackColor="PaleGoldenrod" />
          <PagerSettings Mode="NumericFirstLast" PageButtonCount="2" />
          <Columns>
            <asp:BoundField DataField="Title" HeaderText="Title"
            SortExpression="Title" />
            <asp:BoundField DataField="Author" HeaderText="Author"
            SortExpression="Author" />
            <asp:BoundField DataField="Publisher" HeaderText="Publisher"
            SortExpression="Publisher" />
            <asp:BoundField DataField="Price" HeaderText="Price"
            SortExpression="Price" />
          </Columns>
        </custom:MasterDetailGridViewWebPart>
      </ZoneTemplate>
    </asp:WebPartZone>
    <asp:ObjectDataSource runat="server" ID="MySource" TypeName="Books"
    SortParameterName="SortExpression" SelectMethod="GetOnePageOfAuthorBooks"
    UpdateMethod="UpdateBook" SelectCountMethod="GetTotalAuthorBookCount">
      <SelectParameters>
        <asp:SessionParameter Name="Author" SessionField="SelectedMasterItem"
        DefaultValue="Author1" />
      </SelectParameters>
    </asp:ObjectDataSource>
    <asp:SqlDataSource runat="server" ID="MasterSource"
    ConnectionString="<%$ connectionStrings:MySqlConnectionString %>"
    SelectCommand="Select Distinct Author From Books" />
  </form>
</body>
</html>
```

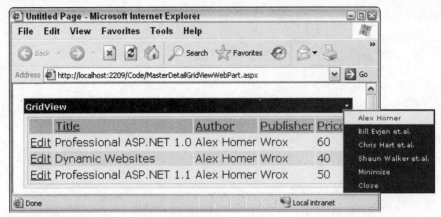

Figure 33-7

Summary

This chapter provided an in-depth coverage of the following three topics:

- Developing custom `WebPartManager` controls
- Web Parts connections
- Developing custom data bound `WebPart` controls

The chapter used real-world examples to help you gain a solid understanding of these topics and to provide you with the skills you need to develop custom `WebPartManager`, data-bound `WebPart` controls, and to extend Web Parts connection features.

Index

M